English-Italian
Italian-English
Dictionary

The Wordsworth
English-Italian
Italian-English
Dictionary

Wordsworth Reference

First published 1968 as *Harrap's Compact Italian and English Dictionary*, and in 1988 as *Harrap's Pocket Italian and English Dictionary*, by Harrap Books Ltd, Edinburgh.

This edition published 1996 by Wordsworth Editions Ltd, Cumberland House, Crib Street, Ware, Hertfordshire SG12 9ET

ISBN 1-85326-367-2

Printed and bound in Great Britain by Mackays of Chatham PLC

NORME, REGOLE E INFORMAZIONI

NORME PER L'USO DEL DIZIONARIO

1. La parte iniziale del presente **Piccolo dizionario** comprende una serie di informazioni che valgono a completare l'opera, a facilitarne la consultazione o ad arricchire le conoscenze del lettore; tali si debbono considerare le **regole di pronuncia**, l'elenco dei **verbi irregolari inglesi**, la **tabella di raffronto fra le unità inglesi o americane e il sistema metrico**, le indicazioni relative al **sistema monetario inglese e americano**, l'elenco dei **numeri ordinali e cardinali** e, infine, l'**elenco delle abbreviazioni** usate nel dizionario stesso.

Inoltre comprende una serie di informazioni in inglese a facilitarne la consultazione per il lettore inglese.

2. La seconda parte comprende il **Compact English-Italian Dictionary** e reca in appendice un ampio elenco di **nomi propri, storici e geografici** (con la relativa traduzione in italiano), nonché l'elenco delle **sigle e abbreviazioni usate nei Paesi di lingua inglese** con l'indicazione dell'equivalente italiano.

3. La terza parte comprende il **Piccolo dizionario italiano-inglese** e reca in appendice un ampio elenco di **nomi propri, storici e geografici** (con la relativa traduzione in inglese), nonché l'elenco delle **sigle e abbreviazioni usate in Italia** con l'indicazione dell'equivalente inglese.

4. Nella parte **italiano-inglese**, i lemmi italiani non recano accento se si tratta di parole piane (es.: *violino, rosa, determinazione*); recano l'accento se si tratta di parole tronche (es.: *così, però, lassù*) o sdrucciole (es.: *richiùdere, rimpròvero, nàutico*) o bisdrucciole o terminanti in *ia, io* con l'accento sulla *i* (es.: *filosofìa, mormorìo*). Tali accenti sono tutti gravi, salvo nelle parole con accento su una *e*, nel qual caso ci si è attenuti a un criterio strettamente ortoepico (es.: *règola, desèrtico, maneggévole, pregévole*): si è, cioè, distinto fra accento grave (pronuncia aperta) e accento acuto (pronuncia chiusa).

5. Nel corpo delle singole voci sono stati ampiamente adottati, secondo la consuetudine generale dei grandi dizionari, i seguenti **segni grafici**:

a) la **doppia barra** (||) che sta a segnalare la peculiarità della fraseologia o una certa differenza di significato nell'ambito del lemma o il passaggio da un senso proprio a uno figurato o il passaggio dal significato corrente a uno più specialistico o, infine, l'inizio dell'elencazione di parole composte e di analoghe associazioni semantiche;

b) i **numeri arabi in neretto** (1., 2., 3. ecc.) che valgono ad attirare l'attenzione sui diversi significati in cui è stato possibile articolare una determinata voce del dizionario;

c) la **losanga nera** (♦) che sta a indicare il cambiamento di natura grammaticale che sopravviene internamente a due omonimi appartenenti a un medesimo gruppo etimologico (es.: passaggio da sostantivo maschile a sostantivo femminile; da sostantivo ad aggettivo; da aggettivo ad avverbio; da verbo transitivo a verbo riflessivo ecc.);

d) gli **esponenti in numeri arabi** (¹, ², ³ ecc.) che servono a distinguere parole omonime appartenenti però a gruppi etimologici diversi:

6. In entrambe le parti, nel caso di sostantivi che abbiano **numero diverso** nelle due lingue, si è data l'indicazione del numero stesso sùbito dopo il lemma. Es.: **fare** *sm.* manners (*pl.*) - **postage** *s.* spese postali (*pl.*) - **embers** *s. pl.* brace (*sing.*).

7. Per i **plurali irregolari inglesi** si sono usati i seguenti criteri:

a) nella parte **inglese-italiano** si è fatta seguire al lemma, fra parentesi, la forma plurale irregolare, per esteso - es.: **child** *s.* (*pl.* children) - nei casi generali o abbreviata - es.: **diagnosis** *s.* (*pl.* -ses) - nei casi di parole derivanti da altre lingue antiche o moderne. Nel primo caso i plurali sono stati elencati anche come voce a sé e con rimando: es.: **children** V. *child*;

b) nella parte **italiano-inglese** si è fatta seguire alla traduzione, fra parentesi, la forma plurale irregolare, per esteso - es.: **bambino** *sm.* child (*pl.* children) - nei casi generali o abbreviata - es.: **diàgnosi** *sf.* diagnosis (*pl.* -ses) - nei casi di parole derivanti da altre lingue antiche o moderne.

8. Per i **verbi irregolari inglesi** si sono usati i seguenti criteri:

a) nella parte **inglese-italiano** si è fatto seguire al lemma, fra parentesi, il paradigma: es.: **to bring (brought, brought).** Le due forme del passato remoto e del participio passato sono state elencate anche come voce a sé e con rimando: es.: **brought** V. *to bring*;

b) nella parte **italiano-inglese** si è fatta seguire alla traduzione, fra parentesi, l'indicazione dell'irregolarità - es.: **costare** *vi.* to cost (*v. irr.*) - a meno che lo stesso verbo inglese ricorra più volte nell'ambito della stessa voce ed escludendo inoltre i due verbi ausiliari *to be* e *to have* (per i quali ultimi si suppone una costante attenzione del lettore circa l'irregolarità).

9. Per i **comparativi** e i **superlativi irregolari inglesi** sono stati seguiti analoghi criteri.

REGOLE DI PRONUNCIA

Alfabeto

L'alfabeto inglese è composto di 26 lettere, 5 in più dell'alfabeto italiano e precisamente: *j, k, w, x, y*. L'elenco completo delle lettere è il seguente:

a	(pron. *ei*)	**n**	(pron. *en*)
b	(pron. *bi*, con la *i* allungata)	**o**	(pron. *ou*)
c	(pron. *si*, con la *i* allungata e la *s* aspra, come in *sordo*)	**p**	(pron. *pi*, con la *i* allungata)
		q	(pron. *chiù*)
d	(pron. *di*, con la *i* allungata)	**r**	(pron. *ar*, con la *a* allungata)
e	(pron. *i*, con la *i* allungata)	**s**	(pron. *es*, con la *s* aspra)
f	(pron. *ef*)	**t**	(pron. *ti*, con la *i* allungata)
g	(pron. *gi*, con la *i* allungata)	**u**	(pron. *iù*)
h	(pron. *eic*, con la *c* dolce)	**v**	(pron. *vi*, con la *i* allungata)
i	(pron. *ai*)	**w**	(pron. *dabliu*)
j	(pron. *gei*)	**x**	(pron. *ecs*)
k	(pron. *kei*)	**y**	(pron. *uai*)
l	(pron. *el*)	**z**	(pron. *sed*, con la *s* dolce, come in *rosa*).
m	(pron. *em*)		

La pronuncia inglese è particolarmente difficile da apprendere ed è altresì difficile dare norme precise per l'apprendimento della stessa. Diamo comunque, qui di seguito, un elenco delle vocali, dei gruppi vocalici, delle consonanti e di alcuni gruppi consonantici con indicazioni approssimative sulla pronuncia.

Vocali

La vocale A ha vari suoni:

1. **ei** in sillaba tonica aperta come nella parola *tale* (racconto); nei gruppi **ange** e **aste** come nelle parole *danger* (pericolo) e *haste* (fretta);

2. **e aperta** in sillaba tonica chiusa come nella parola *cat* (gatto);

3. ha un suono incerto tra **e aperta** e **a** in sillabe atone iniziali o mediane come nelle parole *about* (circa) e *final* (finale);

4. **a allungata** quando è seguita da **r** finale (**r** muta) come nelle parole *car* (automobile) e *far* (lontano);

5. **ea** se è seguita da **re** finale (**e** aperta e **a** appena accennata) come nelle parole *care* (cura) e *dare* (sfida);

6. **o breve** in molti vocaboli che cominciano con il gruppo **qua** come in *quality* (qualità) e in *quantity* (quantità);

7. **o aperta** e prolungata se seguita da **l** o **ll** come in *all* (tutto), *tall* (alto);

nel gruppo **alk** (l muta) come in *talk* (chiacchiera); preceduta da **w** (ma non seguita da **k** o **g**) come in *war* (guerra);

8. a allungata nei gruppi **ance, and, ant, ask, alf** (l muta), **ast, alm** (l muta), **aff, aft, asp** e **ath** quando la a è tonica;

9. i breve e velata nelle desinenze **age** e **ate** non accentate.

La vocale E ha vari suoni:

1. i allungata in sillaba tonica aperta come in *these* (questi) e nei monosillabi, come in *me* (me);

2. e aperta come nella parola italiana *bello*, in sillaba tonica chiusa, come in *let* (lasciare);

3. i come nella parola italiana *vita*, in sillaba atona, come in *repeat* (ripetere);

4. i brevissima quando è preceduta da **s, z, c, ch, sh, g** e seguita da **s** come in *roses* (rose) e quando è tra due dentali come in *rested* (riposato);

5. è muta in fine di parola come in *love* (amore) e nelle desinenze **es, ed,** come in *loves* (amori) e *loved* (amato);

6. eu francese quando è seguita da **r** in sillaba tonica, come in *term* (termine);

7. a gutturale quando è nel gruppo **er** in fine di parola, come in *letter* (lettera);

8. ia con la a appena accennata quando è seguita da **re** in fine di parola come in *severe* (severo) e in *mere* (semplice).

La vocale I ha vari suoni:

1. ai in sillaba tonica aperta, come in *fine* (bello) e in sillaba chiusa quando è seguita dai gruppi **gh** (muto), come in *high* (alto); **ght** (gh muto) come in *night* (notte); **gn** (g muta), come in *sign* (segno); **ld**, come in *child* (bambino) e **nd**, come in *mind* (mente);

2. i breve in sillaba tonica chiusa, come in *tin* (stagno);

3. eu francese, se seguita da **r** come in *fir* (abete);

4. aia, se seguita da **re** come in *fire* (fuoco).

La vocale O ha vari suoni:

1. ou (con la **o** chiusa) in sillaba tonica aperta, come in *home* (casa) e se seguita da **ld** come in *cold* (freddo);

2. o aperta e breve in sillaba tonica chiusa come in *not* (non);

3. o aperta e lunga se seguita da **r** come in *morning* (mattino);

4. oa se seguita da **re** in fine di parola come in *more* (più);

5. eu francese se preceduta da **w** e seguita da **r** come in *work* (lavoro);

6. u allungata nei seguenti vocaboli: *to do* (fare); *to move* (muovere); *to prove* (provare); *to lose* (perdere); *who* (chi); *two* (due); *tomb* (tomba); *womb* (grembo); *shoe* (scarpa); *wolf* (lupo); *woman* (donna);

7. a se preceduta da **w** e seguita da **n** come in *won* (vinto);

8. ua in *one* (uno).

La vocale U ha vari suoni:

1. iù in sillaba tonica aperta, come in *tune* (tono);

2. a in sillaba tonica chiusa, come in *but* (ma);

3. u allungata se preceduta da **l** o **r**, come in *Lucy* (Lucia) e *rule* (regola);

4. u breve, se preceduta da **b**, **f**, **p** e seguita da **l**, **ll**, **sh**, come in *bush* (cespuglio); *to push* (spingere); *bull* (toro); *full* (pieno); *to pull* (tirare);

5. eu francese se seguita da **r** in sillaba aperta, come in *fur* (pelliccia);

6. iua se seguita da **re** in fine di parola, come in *pure* (puro).

Gruppi vocalici

AI si pronuncia **ea** se seguito da **r**, come in *air* (aria).

AU, AW si pronunciano **o** allungata, come in *fraud* (frode) e *law* (legge).

EA si pronuncia **e** in circa 40 parole e loro composti; *bread* (pane); *dead* (morto); *death* (morte); *head* (testa); *heavy* (pesante) ecc.;
    i lunga in moltissime sillabe toniche: *beat* (calore); *meat* (carne);
    ei nelle seguenti parole: *great* (grande); *break* (rompere); *steak* (bistecca);
    eu francese se all'inizio di parola e seguito da **r** come in *earth* (terra);
    ea se in fine di parola seguito da **r**, come in *bear* (sopportare); in molte parole suona però **ia**, come in *tear* (lacrima), o **a** allungata, come in *heart* (cuore).

EE si pronuncia **i** allungata, come in *feeling* (sentimento).

EI si pronuncia **ei** in genere, come in *rein* (briglia);
    i se preceduto da sibilante, come in *ceiling* (soffitto).

EY si pronuncia **ei** in sillaba tonica, come in *prey* (preda);
    i in sillaba atona, come in *money* (denaro). L'eccezione più comune è *key* (chiave) che si pronuncia **ki**.

EU, EW si pronunciano **iù** come in *Europe* (Europa) e in *new* (nuovo).

IE si pronuncia **i** allungata come in *piece* (pezzo).

OI, OY si pronunciano **oi** come in *soil* (suolo) e *royal* (reale).

OA si pronuncia **ou** come in *boat* (barca).

OO si pronuncia **u** allungata come in *moon* (luna);
    u breve se seguita da **k** come in *book* (libro).
    Vi sono alcune eccezioni come *door* (porta) e *floor* (pavimento) dove il gruppo **oo** viene pronunciato **oa** e *blood* (sangue) e *flood* (alluvione) dove il gruppo **oo** viene pronunciato **a**.

OU, OW si pronunciano **au** come in *mouth* (bocca) e *now* (ora).

Consonanti

B è in generale pronunciata come in italiano; è però muta nei gruppi **bt** e **mb** in fine di parola, come in *debt* (debito) e *comb* (pettine).

C suona s aspra come nell'italiano *sordo* davanti a **e, i, y**, come in *cellar* (cantina), *city* (città) e *cyder* (sidro); suona **k** in fine di parola, come in *logic* (logico);
cce, cci, suonano **kse e ksi;**
ch suona c palatale come nell'italiano *città*, se seguito da vocale o in fine di parola; suona **k** in parole di origine greca o orientale. Suona **sc** come in italiano *sciare*, in parole di origine francese, come *machine* (macchina);
ck suona **k;**
tch suona c dolce.

G in fine di parola suona g gutturale come nell'italiano *gomma;*
ge, gi hanno suono palatale come nell'italiano *gesto, gita* in parole di origine latina; hanno suono gutturale in parole di origine germanica;
gh seguito da t o in fine di parola è muto;
gn ha la g muta quando le due lettere fanno parte della stessa sillaba, come in *sign* (segno); si pronunciano separate e la g ha suono gutturale quando le due lettere appartengono a due sillabe diverse, come in *signal* (segnale);
dge suona g palatale.

H è sempre aspirata tranne in *heir* (erede); *honest* (onesto); *honour* (onore) e *hour* (ora) e loro derivati.

J suona g palatale.

K è muta davanti a **n** come in *knee* (ginocchio).

L come in italiano.

M come in italiano.

N è nasale nei gruppi **ng** come in *ring* (anello) (la g è muta).

P suona f nei gruppi **ph**; è muta nel gruppo iniziale **psy**.

Q come in italiano.

R in genere, se mediana, non si pronuncia, ma allunga il suono della vocale che precede, come in *farm* (fattoria). Se è finale non si pronuncia.

S è in genere aspra all'inizio di parola o sillaba; è dolce se è posta tra due vocali;
sc suona s aspra se è seguita da **e, i, y;**
sh suona sc come nell'italiano *sciare*.
La **s** è muta in *aisle* (navata); *isle* e *island* (isola); *viscount* (visconte).

T ha due pronunce caratteristiche nel gruppo **th:**
a) un suono duro pronunciato con la lingua tra i denti, come in *thin* (sottile);
b) un suono dolce pronunciato con la lingua tra i denti, come in *this* (questo).

V come in italiano.

W in principio di parola suona u come in *west*; seguita da **r** è muta, come in *wrong* (sbagliato).

X finale ha il suono sordo **ks**; mediana può avere il suono sordo **ks** o il suono dolce **gs**; in principio di parola suona come la s dolce di *rosa*.

Y è semivocale; all'inizio di parola ha il suono consonantico **i**, come in *yes* (sì); ha tale suono anche in fine di polisillabi, come in *dignity* (dignità), e nel corpo della parola, come in *graveyard* (cimitero); in fine di monosillabi, invece, si pronuncia **ai**, come in *fly* (mosca) e in *cry* (grido).

Z s dolce di *rosa*.

Osservazioni

1. I gruppi finali **ble, cle, kle, gle** hanno la l appena accennata e le due consonanti vengono pronunciate staccate.

2. Nei gruppi **gua, gue, gui, build** e **cuit** finale la **u** è muta, come in *building* (fabbricato).

3. ough seguito da **t** si pronuncia **o** allungato, come in *thought* (pensiero); **ough** suona **of** in: *cough* (tosse) e *trough* (trogolo); suona **af** in: *enough* (abbastanza), *rough* (ruvido) e *tough* (duro); suona **au** in: *plough* (arare) e *bough* (ramo); suona **ou** in *though* (sebbene) e *dough* (pasta); suona **u** allungato in *through* (attraverso).

4. I gruppi **ci, sci, si, ti, xi** seguiti da vocale suonano **sc** come in *scelto*.

5. I gruppi finali **sten** e **stle** suonano rispettivamente **sn** e **sL**.

6. Il gruppo finale **sure** suona **ja** (**j** francese).

7. Il gruppo finale **ture** suona **cia** con la **a** allungata.

I SEGNI D'INTERPUNZIONE
(PUNCTUATION MARKS)

,	*comma*	virgola
;	*semicolon*	punto e virgola
:	*colon*	due punti
.	*full stop*	punto
?	*question mark*	punto di domanda
!	*exclamation mark*	punto esclamativo
'	*apostrophe*	apostrofo
—	*dash*	lineetta
-	*hyphen*	trattino d'unione
« »	*quotation marks*	virgolette basse o quadre
' '	*inverted commas*	virgolette alte o inglesi
( )	*brackets*	parentesi rotonde
[ ]	*square brackets*	parentesi quadre
*	*asterisk*	asterisco
...	*dots*	puntini
	new paragraph	a capo
	full stop and new paragraph	punto e a capo
	capital letter	lettera maiuscola
	small letter	lettera minuscola

VERBI IRREGOLARI INGLESI [1]

Infinito	Passato	Participio passato	
to abide	abode	abode	dimorare
to arise	arose	arisen	sorgere
to awake*	awoke	awoke, awaked	svegliare, svegliarsi
to be	was	been	essere
to bear	bore	born, borne	sopportare, generare
to beat	beat	beaten, beat	battere
to become	became	become	diventare
to befall	befell	befallen	accadere
to beget	begot	begot, begotten	generare
to begin	began	begun	cominciare
to behold	beheld	beheld	mirare
to bend	bent	bent	piegare
to bereave*	bereft	bereft	orbare
to bet	bet	bet	scommettere
to bid	bade, bid	bidden, bid	ordinare
to bind	bound	bound	(ri)legare
to bite	bit	bitten, bit	mordere
to bleed	bled	bled	sanguinare
to blow	blew	blown	soffiare
to break	broke	broken	rompere
to breed	bred	bred	allevare
to bring	brought	brought	portare
to build	built	built	costruire
to burn*	burnt	burnt	bruciare
to burst	burst	burst	scoppiare
to buy	bought	bought	comperare
to cast	cast	cast	gettare, fondere
to catch	caught	caught	prendere, acchiappare
to chide*	chid	chid	sgridare
to choose	chose	chosen	scegliere
to cleave	cleft	cleft	fendere
to cling	clung	clung	attaccarsi
to come	came	come	venire
to cost	cost	cost	costare
to creep	crept	crept	strisciare
to cut	cut	cut	tagliare
to deal	dealt	dealt	trattare, commerciare
to dig*	dug	dug	scavare
to do	did	done	fare
to draw	drew	drawn	tirare, disegnare
to dream*	dreamt	dreamt	sognare
to drink	drank	drunk	bere
to drive	drove	driven	guidare
to dwell*	dwelt	dwelt	dimorare

[1] L'elenco, compilato per comodità del lettore, comprende i verbi di uso più comune. L'asterisco apposto accanto a un verbo indica l'esistenza, per il verbo stesso, di forme anche regolari.

to eat	ate, eat	eaten	mangiare
to fall	fell	fallen	cadere
to feed	fed	fed	nutrire
to feel	felt	felt	sentire, tastare
to fight	fought	fought	combattere
to find	found	found	trovare
to flee	fled	fled	fuggire
to fling	flung	flung	scagliare
to fly	flew	flown	volare
to forbid	forbade	forbidden	proibire
to forecast	forecast	forecast	predire
to forget	forgot	forgotten	dimenticare
to forgive	forgave	forgiven	perdonare
to forsake	forsook	forsaken	abbandonare
to freeze	froze	frozen	gelare
to get	got	got, gotten	ottenere, diventare
to gird	girt	girt	cingere
to give	gave	given	dare
to go	went	gone	andare
to grind	ground	ground	macinare
to grow	grew	grown	crescere, coltivare
to hang	hung	hung, hanged	appendere
to have	had	had	avere
to hear	heard	heard	udire
to hew*	hewed	hewn	recidere
to hide	hid	hidden, hid	nascondere
to hit	hit	hit	colpire
to hold	held	held	tenere, trattenere
to hurt	hurt	hurt	far male, ferire
to keep	kept	kept	tenere, conservare
to kneel*	knelt	knelt	inginocchiarsi
to knit*	knit	knit	lavorare a maglia
to know	knew	known	conoscere, sapere
to lay	laid	laid	deporre, posare
to lead	led	led	condurre, guidare
to lean	leant	leant	appoggiarsi, inclinarsi
to leap	leapt	leapt	saltare
to learn*	learnt	learnt	imparare
to leave	left	left	lasciare, partire
to lend	lent	lent	prestare
to let	let	let	lasciare
to lie	lay	lain	giacere, trovarsi
to light*	lit	lit	accendere
to lose	lost	lost	perdere
to make	made	made	fare
to mean	meant	meant	intendere, significare
to meet	met	met	incontrare
to mislay	mislaid	mislaid	smarrire
to mislead	misled	misled	sviare
to mistake	mistook	mistaken	sbagliare
to mow*	mowed	mown	falciare
to pay	paid	paid	pagare
to put	put	put	mettere

to read	read	read	leggere
to rend	rent	rent	strappare
to ride	rode	ridden	cavalcare
to ring	rang	rung	suonare
to rise	rose	risen	alzarsi, sorgere
to run	ran	run	correre
to saw	sawed	sawn	segare
to say	said	said	dire
to see	saw	seen	vedere
to seek	sought	sought	cercare
to sell	sold	sold	vendere
to send	sent	sent	mandare
to set	set	set	porre
to sew	sewed	sewn	cucire
to shake	shook	shaken	scuotere, tremare
to shear*	sheared	shorn	tosare
to shed	shed	shed	spargere
to shine	shone	shone	brillare, splendere
to shoe	shod	shod	calzare
to shoot	shot	shot	sparare
to show	showed	shown	mostrare
to shred	shred	shred	tagliuzzare
to shrink	shrank, shrunk	shrunk, shrunken	restringersi
to shut	shut	shut	chiudere
to sing	sang	sung	cantare
to sink	sank, sunk	sunk	affondare
to sit	sat	sat	sedere
to slay	slew	slain	trucidare
to sleep	slept	slept	dormire
to slink	slunk	slunk	svignarsela
to smell*	smelt	smelt	fiutare, odorare
to sow*	sowed	sown	seminare
to speak	spoke	spoken	parlare
to spell	spelt	spelt	compitare
to spend	spent	spent	spendere
to spill*	spilt	spilt	spandere, versare
to spin	spun, span	spun	filare
to spit	spat, spit	spat, spit	sputare
to split	split	split	spaccare
to spoil	spoilt	spoilt	guastare, viziare
to spread	spread	spread	diffondere, stendere
to spring	sprang	sprung	saltare
to stand	stood	stood	stare (in piedi)
to steal	stole	stolen	rubare
to stick	stuck	stuck	appiccicare
to sting	stung	stung	pungere
to stink	stank, stunk	stunk	puzzare
to strike	struck	struck	battere, colpire
to strive	strove	striven	sforzarsi
to swear	swore	sworn	giurare
to sweat*	sweat	sweat	sudare
to sweep	swept	swept	spazzare
to swell*	swelled	swollen	gonfiare
to swim	swam	swum	nuotare
to swing	swung	swung	dondolare
to take	took	taken	prendere

to teach	taught	taught	insegnare
to tear	tore	torn	lacerare
to tell	told	told	dire, raccontare
to think	thought	thought	pensare
to thrive	throve	thriven	prosperare
to throw	threw	thrown	gettare
to thrust	thrust	thrust	spingere, gettare
to tread	trode	trod, trodden	calpestare
to understand	understood	understood	capire
to upset	upset	upset	capovolgere
to wake	woke	woke, woken	svegliare, svegliarsi
to wear	wore	worn	indossare, logorare
to weave	wove	woven	intrecciare, tessere
to weep	wept	wept	piangere
to win	won	won	vincere
to wind	wound	wound	serpeggiare
to withdraw	withdrew	withdrawn	ritirare, ritirarsi
to wring	wrung	wrung	torcere
to write	wrote	written	scrivere

TABELLA DI RAFFRONTO
FRA LE UNITÀ INGLESI O AMERICANE
E IL SISTEMA METRICO

	denominazione delle unità inglesi o americane	valore	equivalenza col sistema metrico *	equivalenza del sistema metrico con le unità inglesi **
misure lineari	pollice (inch - in)	—	2,54 cm	0,3937 (cm)
	piede (foot - ft)	12 in	0,304 m	3,28 (m)
	yarda (yard - yd)	3 ft	0,914 m	1,09 (m)
	fathom	6 ft	1,828 m	0,546 (m)
	miglio terrestre (statute mile)	5280 ft	1,609 km	0,621 (km)
	miglio inglese	5000 ft	1,523 km	0,656 (km)
	nodo (nautical mile)	6080 ft	1,853 km	0,539 (km)
superfici	pollice quadr. (square inch - sq.in)	—	6,45 cm²	0,155 (cm²)
	piede quadr. (square foot - sq.ft)	144 sq.in	829 cm²	10,76 (m²)
	yarda quadr. (square yard - sq.yd)	1296 sq.in	0,836 m²	1,196 (m²)
	miglio quadr. (square mile)	—	2,59 km²	0,386 (km²)
volumi e capacità	pollice cubo (cubic inch - cu.in)	—	16,38 cm³	0,061 (cm³)
	piede cubo (cubic foot - cu.ft)	1728 cu.in	28,32 dm³	0,0353 (dm³)
	yarda cubica (cubic yard - cu.yd)	27 cu.ft	0,764 m³	1,308 (m³)
	register ton	100 cu.ft	2,832 m³	0,353 (m³)
	oncia fluida americana (U.S. fl.oz)	1,8 cu.in	29,57 cm³	0,0338 (cm³)
	oncia fluida inglese (imp. fl.oz)	1,73 cu.in	28,4 cm³	0,0353 (cm³)
	bushel	8 gals	28,3 l	0,035 (l)
	gallone americano (U.S. gal)	231 cu.in	3,78 l	0,26 (l)
	gallone inglese (imp. gal)	277 cu.in	4,54 l	0,22 (l)
	pinta (pint)	1/8 gal	0,47 l	2,11 (l)
pesi	oncia avoirdupois (ounce - oz)	—	28,35 g	0,0352 (g)
	oncia troy (ounce troy - oz)	—	31,1 g	0,0321 (g)
	libbra avoirdupois (pound - lb)	16 oz.a.d.p.	453 g	2,204 kg)
	libbra troy (pound - lb)	12 oz.t.	373 g	2,679 (kg)
	tonnellata americana (short ton - ton)	2000 lbs	907 kg	0,102 (t)
	tonnellata ingl. (long ton - ton)	2240 lbs	1016 kg	0,984 (t)

Con la graduale introduzione del sistema metrico, le unità di misura inglesi e americane diventeranno progressivamente meno diffuse.

* Coefficiente per il quale si deve moltiplicare il valore della grandezza per ottenere la misura nel sistema metrico.

** Coefficiente per il quale si deve moltiplicare il valore espresso nell'unità metrica segnato tra parentesi per ottenere la misura nel sistema inglese.

SISTEMA MONETARIO INGLESE
(Denaro circolante)
Unità base = **pound**, sterlina.

Monete *(coins)*

½p piece (half-penny), duecentesima parte della sterlina;
1p piece (one penny), centesima parte sterlina;
2p piece (two pence), cinquantesima parte della sterlina;
5p piece (five pence), ventesima parte della sterlina;
10p piece (ten pence), decima parte della sterlina;
50p piece (fifty pence), metà della sterlina.

Banconote *(banknotes)*

pound note (£1), sterlina carta;
five-pound note (£5), cinque sterline;
ten-pound note (£10), dieci sterline;
twenty-pound note (£20), venti sterline.

Monete nominali *(nominal coins* − usate nelle parcelle dei professionisti, prezzi par articoli di lusso, per libri, ecc.)

guinea (£1.05, 105p), ghinea, centocinque pence;
half (a) guinea (52 ½p), mezza ghinea, cinquantadue pence e mezzo.

SISTEMA MONETARIO AMERICANO
(Denaro circolante)
Unità base = **dollar**, dollaro.

Rame *(copper)*:
cent o *penny (1 c.)*, un centesimo di dollaro.

Lega di rame e nichel *(copper and nickel alloy)*:
nickel o *five cents (5 c.)*, cinque centesimi di dollaro.

Argento *(silver)*:
dime (10 c.), dieci centesimi di dollaro;
quarter (25 c.), un quarto di dollaro;
half-dollar (50 c.), mezzo dollaro, cinquanta centesimi;
dollar ($ 1), dollaro (generalmente in banconota).

Banconote *(bills)*:
si hanno tagli da $ 1, 2, 5, 10, 20, 50, 100, 500.
Esistono inoltre, sebbene non in circolazione normale, banconote da $ 1,000, 5,000 e 10,000.

I NUMERI

CARDINALI

1	one
2	two
3	three
4	four
5	five
6	six
7	seven
8	eight
9	nine
10	ten
11	eleven
12	twelve
13	thirteen
14	fourteen
15	fifteen
16	sixteen
17	seventeen
18	eighteen
19	nineteen
20	twenty
21	twenty-one
22	twenty-two
30	thirty
40	forty
50	fifty
60	sixty
70	seventy
80	eighty
90	ninety
100	one hundred
101	one hundred and one
200	two hundred
1.000	one thousand
1.001	one thousand and one
1.010	one thousand and ten
10.000	ten thousand
100.000	one hundred thousand
200.000	two hundred thousand
1.000.000	one million

ORDINALI

1° -	1st -	the first
2° -	2nd -	the second
3° -	3rd -	the third
4° -	4th -	the fourth
5° -	5th -	the fifth
6° -	6th -	the sixth
7° -	7th -	the seventh
8° -	8th -	the eighth
9° -	9th -	the ninth
10° -	10th -	the tenth
11° -	11th -	the eleventh
12° -	12th -	the twelfth
13° -	13th -	the thirteenth
14° -	14th -	the fourteenth
15° -	15th -	the fifteenth
16° -	16th -	the sixteenth
17° -	17th -	the seventeenth
18° -	18th -	the eighteenth
19° -	19th -	the nineteenth
20° -	20th -	the twentieth
21° -	21st -	the twenty-first
22° -	22nd -	the twenty-second
30° -	30th -	the thirtieth
40° -	40th -	the fortieth
50° -	50th -	the fiftieth
60° -	60th -	the sixtieth
70° -	70th -	the seventieth
80° -	80th -	the eightieth
90° -	90th -	the ninetieth
100° -	100th -	the (one) hundredth
101° -	101st -	the one hundred and first
200° -	200th -	the two hundredth
1.000° -	1,000th -	the (one) thousandth
1.001° -	1,001st -	the one thousand and first
1.010° -	1,010th -	the one thousand and tenth
10.000° -	10,000	the ten thousandth
100.000° -	100,000	the one hundred thousandth
200.000° -	200,000	the two hundred thousandth
1.000.000° -	1,000,000	the one millionth

ELENCO DELLE ABBREVIAZIONI

abbr.	abbreviazione	*gen.*	genitivo
(aer.)	aeronautica	*general.*	generalmente
agg.	aggettivo	*(geogr.)*	geografia
(agr.)	agricoltura	*(geol.)*	geologia
(amer.)	americano, americanismo	*(geom.)*	geometria
		ger.	gerundio
amm.	amministrativo, amministrazione	*(gergo)*	gergo, gergale
		(giorn.)	giornalismo, giornalistico
(anat.)	anatomia		
(ant.)	anticamente, antiquato	*(giur.)*	giuridico
(arch.)	architettura	*(gramm.)*	grammatica
art.	articolo	*i.*	intransitivo
(arte)	arte, artistico	*id.*	idem
assol.	assoluto	*imp.*	impersonale
(astr.)	astronomia	*imperat.*	imperativo
attr.	attributo, attributivo	*ind.*	indicativo
aus.	ausiliare	*indef.*	indefinito
(auto)	automobilismo	*inf.*	infinito
avv.	avverbio	*int.*	interrogativo
(bot.)	botanica	*inter.*	interiezione, interiettivo
(biol.)	biologia	*(iron.)*	ironico
(chim.)	chimica	*irr.*	irregolare
(chir.)	chirurgia	*(itt.)*	ittiologia
(cine)	cinematografia	*(lat.)*	latino, latinismo
coll.	collettivo	*loc. avv.*	locuzione avverbiale
(comm.)	commercio, commerciale	*loc. cong.*	locuzione congiuntiva
comp.	comparativo	*loc. prep.*	locuzione prepositiva
compl.	complemento	*(lett.)*	letteratura, letterario
condiz.	condizionale	*m.*	maschile
cong.	congiunzione	*(mar.)*	marina, marittimo, marinaresco
(costr.)	costruzioni		
(cuc.)	cucina	*(mat.)*	matematica
(dial.)	dialettale	*(mecc.)*	meccanica
dif.	difettivo	*(med.)*	medicina
dim.	diminutivo	*(metal.)*	metallurgia
dimostr.	dimostrativo	*(mil.)*	militare
ecc., etc.	eccetera	*(min.)*	mineralogia, minerario
(eccl.)	ecclesiastico	*(mit.)*	mitologia
(econ.)	economia	*(mus.)*	musica
(edil.)	edilizia	*neg.*	negazione, negativo
(elettr.)	elettricità, elettrotecnica	*(neol.)*	neologismo
escl.	esclamativo, in esclamazione	*ogg.*	oggetto
		(ott.)	ottica
f.	femminile	*p.*	participio
(fam.)	familiare	*pass.*	passato
(farm.)	farmacia, farmaceutico	*pers.*	persona, personale
(ferr.)	ferrovia	*(pitt.)*	pittura
(fig.)	figurato	*pl.*	plurale
(fil.)	filosofia	*(poet.)*	poetico
(fis.)	fisica	*(pol.)*	politica
(foto)	fotografia	*(pop.)*	popolare
fut.	futuro	*poss.*	possessivo

pp.	participio passato	*sost.*	sostantivato
prep.	preposizione	*spec.*	specialmente
pred.	predicato, predicativo	*(sport)*	sport, sportivo
pres.	presente	*(spreg.)*	spregiativo
pron.	pronome, pronominale	*sthg.*	something
prov.	proverbio, proverbiale	*(stor.)*	storia
(psicol.)	psicologia	*superl.*	superlativo
qc.	qualcosa	*t.*	transitivo
qu.	qualcuno	*(teat.)*	teatro
r.	riflessivo	*(tec.)*	tecnica
(radio)	radiofonia	*(tel.)*	telefonia, telefono
rec.	reciproco	*(teol.)*	teologia
reg.	regolare	*(tip.)*	tipografia
rel.	relativo	*(tv.)*	televisione
(relig.)	religione	*(us.)*	uso, usato
s.	(dall'inglese) sostantivo	*v.*	verbo
s.	(dall'italiano) sostantivo	*V.*	vedi
	maschile e femminile	*(vezz.)*	vezzeggiativo
semidif.	semidifettivo	*v. dif.*	verbo difettivo
sf.	sostantivo femminile	*vi.*	verbo intransitivo
sm.	sostantivo maschile	*(v. irr.)*	verbo irregolare
(scherz.)	scherzoso	*(volg.)*	volgare
(scol.)	scolastico	*vr.*	verbo riflessivo
(scult.)	scultura	*v. semidif.*	verbo semidifettivo
sing.	singolare	*vt.*	verbo transitivo
so.	someone	*(zool.)*	zoologia
sogg.	soggetto		

INGLESE-ITALIANO

A

a *art.* **1.** un, uno, una **2.** un certo ‖ *once a week*, una volta alla settimana.
A *s.* (*mus.*) la.
aback *avv.* alla sprovvista.
abacus *s.* **1.** abaco **2.** pallottoliere.
abandon *s.* abbandono.
to **abandon** *vt.* abbandonare.
to **abase** *vt.* abbassare, umiliare.
abasement *s.* umiliazione.
to **abash** *vt.* confondere.
abashment *s.* confusione.
to **abate** *vt.* diminuire. ✦ to **abate** *vi.* placarsi (*di tempo atmosferico*).
abatement *s.* diminuzione.
abbess *s.* badessa.
abbey *s.* abbazia.
abbot *s.* abate.
abbreviation *s.* abbreviazione.
to **abdicate** *vt.* e *vi.* **1.** abdicare a **2.** dimettersi.
abdication *s.* abdicazione.
abdomen *s.* addome.
abdominal *agg.* addominale.
to **abduct** *vt.* rapire.
abduction *s.* rapimento.
abductor *s.* **1.** rapitore **2.** (*anat.*) abduttore.
aberration *s.* aberrazione.
abetter *s.* fautore.
abeyance *s.* sospensione.
to **abhor** *vt.* aborrire.
abhorrence *s.* aborrimento.
to **abide** (**abode, abode**) *vi.* abitare ‖ *to — by*, conformarsi a.
ability *s.* abilità, capacità.
abject *agg.* abietto.
abjection *s.* abiezione.
abjuration *s.* abiura.
to **abjure** *vt.* abiurare.
ablation *s.* ablazione.
ablative *agg.* e *s.* ablativo.
able *agg.* capace ‖ *to be — to*, essere in grado di, potere.
ablution *s.* abluzione.
abnegation *s.* **1.** abnegazione **2.** rinuncia.
abnormal *agg.* anormale.
aboard *avv.* e *prep.* a bordo.
abode V. *to abide*. ✦ **abode** *s.* dimora.
to **abolish** *vt.* abolire.
abolishment, abolition *s.* abolizione.
abolitionism *s.* abolizionismo.
abolitionist *agg.* e *s.* abolizionista.

abominable *agg.* abominevole.
to **abominate** *vt.* detestare.
abomination *s.* abominazione.
aboriginal *agg.* e *s.* aborigeno.
to **abort** *vi.* abortire.
abortion *s.* aborto.
abortive *agg.* abortivo.
to **abound** *vi.* abbondare.
about *avv.* **1.** circa **2.** intorno ‖ *to be —*, stare per. ✦ **about** *prep.* **1.** intorno a **2.** presso di **3.** riguardo a.
above *prep.* **1.** al di sopra di **2.** più di ‖ *— mentioned*, suddetto. ✦ **above** *avv.* in alto, sopra.
abrasion *s.* abrasione.
to **abridge** *vt.* **1.** abbreviare **2.** privare di.
abridg(e)ment *s.* **1.** abbreviazione, sommario **2.** privazione.
abroad *avv.* **1.** all'estero **2.** fuori.
to **abrogate** *vt.* abrogare.
abrogation *s.* abrogazione.
abrupt *agg.* **1.** scosceso **2.** brusco **3.** inaspettato.
abruptness *s.* **1.** ripidezza **2.** rudezza **3.** precipitazione.
abscess *s.* ascesso.
abscissa *s.* ascissa.
absence *s.* assenza.
absent *agg.* assente ‖ *— -minded*, distratto; *— -mindedness*, distrazione.
to **absent** *vt.* *to — oneself*, assentarsi.
absenteeism *s.* assenteismo.
absinth(e) *s.* assenzio.
absolute *agg.* e *s.* assoluto.
absolution *s.* assoluzione.
absolutism *s.* assolutismo.
absolutist *agg.* e *s.* assolutista.
to **absolve** *vt.* assolvere.
to **absorb** *vt.* assorbire.
absorbent *agg.* e *s.* assorbente.
absorption *s.* assorbimento.
to **abstain** *vi.* astenersi.
abstemious *agg.* sobrio.
abstention *s.* astensione.
abstentionist *s.* astensionista.
abstinence *s.* astinenza.
abstract *agg.* astratto. ✦ **abstract** *s.* **1.** astrazione **2.** estratto.
to **abstract** *vt.* **1.** astrarre **2.** estrarre **3.** sottrarre **4.** riassumere.
abstraction *s.* **1.** astrazione **2.** distrazione **3.** furto.
abstractly *avv.* astrattamente.
abstruse *agg.* astruso.
abstruseness *s.* astrusità.

absurd *agg.* assurdo.
absurdity *s.* assurdità.
absurdly *avv.* assurdamente.
abundance *s.* abbondanza.
abundant *agg.* abbondante.
abuse *s.* 1. abuso 2. ingiuria.
to **abuse** *vt.* 1. abusare 2. ingiuriare.
abusive *agg.* 1. abusivo 2. ingiurioso.
abysm, abyss *s.* abisso.
abysmal, abyssal *agg.* abissale.
academic *agg.* e *s.* accademico.
academician *s.* accademico.
academy *s.* accademia: — *of music*, conservatorio.
acanthus *s.* acanto.
acarus *s.* (*pl.* -ri) acaro.
to **accelerate** *vt.* accelerare.
acceleration *s.* accelerazione.
accelerative *agg.* accelerativo.
accelerator *s.* acceleratore.
accent *s.* accento.
to **accent** *vt.* 1. accentare 2. accentuare.
to **accentuate** V. *to accent.*
accentuation *s.* accentuazione.
to **accept** *vt.* accettare, approvare.
acceptable *agg.* accettabile.
acceptance *s.* 1. accettazione 2. consenso.
acceptation *s.* accezione, significato.
access *s.* accesso.
accessible *agg.* accessibile.
accession *s.* 1. assunzione (*al trono*) 2. adesione 3. aggiunta.
accessory *agg.* e *s.* 1. accessorio 2. complice.
accident *s.* 1. caso: *by* —, per caso 2. incidente 3. irregolarità.
accidental *agg.* accidentale.
to **acclaim** *vt.* acclamare.
acclamation *s.* acclamazione.
acclimation, acclimatization *s.* acclimazione, acclimatazione.
to **acclimate**, to **acclimatize** *vt.* acclimatare. ♦ to **acclimate**, to **acclimatize** *vi.* acclimatarsi.
to **accommodate** *vt.* 1. adattare 2. ospitare 3. fornire.
accommodating *agg.* accomodante.
accommodation *s.* 1. accomodamento 2. comodità 3. alloggio 4. (*comm.*) facilitazione.
accompaniment *s.* accompagnamento.
accompanist *s.* (*mus.*) accompagnatore.
to **accompany** *vt.* accompagnare

(*anche mus.*).
accomplice *s.* complice.
to **accomplish** *vt.* compiere, realizzare.
accomplishment *s.* 1. compimento 2. compitezza 3. dote.
accord *s.* accordo.
to **accord** *vt.* accordare. ♦ to **accord** *vi.* accordarsi.
accordance *s.* accordo.
accordant *agg.* concorde, conforme.
according *agg.* 1. concordante, conforme 2. armonioso. ♦ **according** *avv.* — *as*, secondo che; — *to*, secondo.
accordingly *avv.* 1. in conseguenza 2. conformemente.
accordion *s.* fisarmonica.
accordionist *s.* fisarmonicista.
account *s.* 1. (*comm.*) conto 2. (*comm.*) acconto 3. valore 4. resoconto || *to take into* —, prendere in considerazione; *on* — *of*, a causa di.
to **account** *vt.* considerare || *to* — *for*, essere responsabile di.
accountable *agg.* responsabile.
accountancy *s.* ragioneria.
accountant *s.* contabile || *chartered* —, ragioniere.
to **accredit** *vt.* accreditare.
to **accrue** *vi.* 1. derivare 2. accumularsi.
to **accumulate** *vt.* accumulare. ♦ to **accumulate** *vi.* accumularsi.
accumulation *s.* accumulazione.
accumulative *agg.* accumulativo.
accumulator *s.* accumulatore.
accuracy *s.* esattezza.
accurate *agg.* esatto.
accusation *s.* accusa.
accusative *agg.* e *s.* accusativo.
to **accuse** *vt.* accusare.
accused *s.* accusato.
accuser *s.* accusatore.
to **accustom** *vt.* abituare.
accustomed *agg.* 1. abituale 2. abituato.
ace *s.* asso.
acetone *s.* acetone.
acetylene *s.* acetilene.
ache *s.* dolore.
to **ache** *vi.* far male: *my head aches*, mi fa male la testa.
to **achieve** *vt.* 1. compiere 2. ottenere.
achievement *s.* 1. compimento 2. conseguimento 3. gesta.
aching *agg.* 1. doloroso 2. afflitto.

◆ **aching** s. dolore.
acid agg. e s. acido.
acidity s. acidità.
acidulous agg. acidulo.
to **acknowledge** vt. riconoscere ‖ to — receipt of, accusare ricevuta di.
acknowledg(e)ment s. riconoscimento.
acolyte s. accolito.
acorn s. ghianda.
acoustic(al) agg. acustico.
acoustics s. acustica.
to **acquaint** vt. informare ‖ to become acquainted with, fare la conoscenza di.
acquaintance s. conoscenza.
acquiescence s. acquiescenza.
to **acquire** vt. acquisire, acquistare.
acquisition s. acquisto.
to **acquit** vt. 1. pagare 2. liberare 3. assolvere.
acquittal s. (giur.) assoluzione.
acquittance s. 1. saldo 2. quietanza.
acrid agg. acre.
acridity s. asprezza.
acrimony s. acrimonia.
acrobat s. acrobata.
acrobatic(al) agg. acrobatico.
acrobatics s. pl. acrobazia (sing.).
acropolis s. acropoli.
across avv. per traverso. ◆ **across** prep. attraverso ‖ to come —. incontrare.
act s. atto, legge.
to **act** vt. e vi. 1. agire, fare 2. (teat.) recitare.
acting agg. facente funzione di. ◆ **acting** s. 1. azione 2. (teat.) rappresentazione.
action s. 1. azione 2. (giur.) processo 3. (mecc.) funzionamento.
active agg. attivo.
activism s. attivismo.
activist s. attivista.
activity s. attività.
actor s. attore.
actress s. attrice.
actual agg. reale.
actuality s. realtà.
actually avv. realmente.
to **actuate** vt. mettere in moto.
acuminate agg. acuminato.
acute agg. acuto.
ad s. V. advertisement.
adamantine agg. adamantino.
to **adapt** vt. adattare.
adaptable agg. adattabile.
adaptation s. adattamento.

to **add** vt. aggiungere ‖ to — up. fare una somma.
addendum s. (pl. -da) aggiunta.
adder s. vipera.
addict s. tossicomane.
addition s. 1. (mat.) addizione 2. aggiunta.
additional agg. supplementare.
address s. 1. indirizzo 2. abilità. ◆ **addresses** s. pl. omaggi.
to **address** vt. e vi. indirizzare, arringare. ◆ to **address** vi. rivolgersi.
addressee s. destinatario.
addresser s. mittente.
to **adduce** vt. addurre.
adenoids s. pl. adenoidi.
adept agg. e s. perito, esperto.
adequate agg. adeguato.
to **adhere** vi. aderire.
adherence s. aderenza, adesione.
adherent agg. e s. aderente.
adhesion s. V. adherence.
adhesive agg. e s. adesivo.
adipose agg. adiposo.
adjacent agg. adiacente.
adjective agg. 1. aggettivale 2. addizionale. ◆ **adjective** s. aggettivo.
to **adjoin** vt. 1. aggiungere 2. essere contiguo.
adjoining agg. adiacente.
to **adjourn** vt. aggiornare.
adjournment s. aggiornamento.
adjunct s. 1. aggiunta 2. aggiunto 3. (gramm.) complemento.
adjuration s. implorazione.
to **adjust** vt. 1. aggiustare 2. adattare 3. regolare.
adjustment s. 1. adattamento, compromesso 2. (comm.) liquidazione.
adjutant s. aiutante.
to **administer** vt. 1. amministrare 2. fornire. ◆ to **administer** vi. contribuire.
administration s. 1. amministrazione 2. somministrazione.
administrative agg. amministrativo.
administrator s. amministratore.
admirable agg. ammirabile.
admiral s. ammiraglio.
admiralty s. ammiragliato.
admiration s. ammirazione.
to **admire** vt. ammirare.
admirer s. ammiratore.
admiringly avv. con ammirazione.
admissible agg. ammissibile.
admission s. 1. ammissione 2. con-

fessione.

to **admit** vt. **1.** ammettere **2.** contenere.

admittance s. ammissione, ingresso.

to **admonish** vt. ammonire.

admonition s. ammonimento.

ado s. **1.** fatica **2.** confusione.

adolescence s. adolescenza.

adolescent agg. e s. adolescente.

to **adopt** vt. adottare.

adoption s. adozione.

adoptive agg. adottivo.

adorable · agg. adorabile.

adoration s. adorazione.

to **adore** vt. adorare.

to **adorn** vt. adornare.

adornment s. ornamento.

adrenalin s. adrenalina.

adrift avv. alla deriva.

to **adulate** vt. adulare.

adulation s. adulazione.

adulator s. adulatore.

adult agg. e s. adulto.

to **adulterate** vt. adulterare.

adulteration s. adulterazione.

adulterer s. adultero.

adulteress s. adultera.

adulterine agg. adulterino.

adultery s. adulterio.

advance s. **1.** avanzamento **2.** anticipo **3.** approccio.

to **advance** vt. **1.** portar avanti **2.** anticipare (*denaro*) **3.** (*comm.*) aumentare. ♦ to **advance** vi. avanzare.

advancement s. **1.** avanzamento **2.** (*comm.*) rialzo.

advantage s. vantaggio || *to take —
of,* approfittare di.

to **advantage** vt. avvantaggiare.

advantageous agg. vantaggioso.

advent s. avvento.

adventure s. avventura.

to **adventure** vt. rischiare. ♦ to **adventure** vi. avventurarsi.

adventurer s. avventuriero.

adventurous agg. avventuroso.

adverb s. avverbio.

adverbial agg. avverbiale.

adversary s. avversario.

adverse agg. avverso.

adversity s. avversità.

to **advert** vi. alludere, riferirsi.

to **advertise** vt. e vi. fare pubblicità a, divulgare.

advertisement s. **1.** avviso **2.** cartellone pubblicitario **3.** inserzione.

advertiser s. inserzionista.

advertising agg. pubblicitario. ♦
advertising s. pubblicità.

advice s. **1.** consiglio **2.** notizia.

advisability s. opportunità.

advisable agg. consigliabile.

to **advise** vt. **1.** consigliare **2.** avvisare || *to — with so.,* consultarsi con qu.

advised agg. giudizioso.

adviser s. consigliere.

advocacy s. avvocatura.

advocate s. difensore.

aegis s. egida.

Aeolian agg. eolio.

to **aerate** vt. **1.** aerare **2.** gassare.

aeration s. **1.** aerazione **2.** (*chim.*) aggiunta di acido carbonico.

aerial agg. aereo. ♦ **aerial** s. (*radio*) antenna.

aerodrome s. aerodromo.

aerodynamics s. aerodinamica.

aeronaut s. aeronauta.

aeronautics s. aeronautica.

aeroplane s. aeroplano.

aerostat s. aerostato.

aerostatics s. aerostatica.

aesthete s. esteta.

aesthetic(al) agg. estetico.

aestheticism s. estetismo.

aesthetics s. estetica.

aestivation s. letargo estivo.

aether s. etere.

afar avv. lontano.

affability s. affabilità.

affable agg. affabile.

affair s. **1.** affare **2.** tresca.

to **affect**[1] vt. **1.** ostentare **2.** simulare.

to **affect**[2] vt. **1.** concernere **2.** commuovere **3.** (*med.*) intaccare.

affectation s. affettazione.

affected agg. **1.** affettato **2.** affetto **3.** commosso **4.** disposto.

affection s. **1.** affetto **2.** (*med.*) affezione.

affectionate agg. affezionato, affettuoso.

affective agg. affettivo.

to **affiliate** vt. affiliare. ♦ to **affiliate** vi. affiliarsi.

affiliation s. affiliazione.

affinity s. affinità, parentela.

to **affirm** vt. **1.** affermare **2.** ratificare.

affirmation s. **1.** affermazione **2.** ratificazione.

affirmative agg. affermativo || *in
the —,* affermativamente.

to **affix** vt. aggiungere, apporre.

to **afflict** *vt.* affliggere.
affliction *s.* afflizione.
affluence *s.* 1. affluenza 2. abbondanza.
affluent *agg.* ricco. ♦ **affluent** *s.* (*geogr.*) affluente.
afflux *s.* afflusso.
to **afford** *vt.* offrire || *can* —, potersi permettere.
to **afforest** *vt.* imboschire.
afforestation *s.* imboschimento.
affront *s.* affronto || *to take* — *at*, offendersi per.
to **affront** *vt.* 1. affrontare 2. insultare.
afloat *avv.* a galla. ♦ **afloat** *agg.* 1. galleggiante 2. in circolazione.
afore *avv.* precedentemente. ♦ **afore** *prep.* prima di.
aforementioned, aforesaid *agg.* predetto.
afraid *agg.* spaventato || *to be* —, temere.
African *agg.* e *s.* africano.
after *agg.* seguente. ♦ **after** *prep.* 1. dopo, dietro 2. secondo 3. alla maniera di. ♦ **after** *avv.* dopo. ♦ **after** *cong.* dopo che.
afternoon *s.* pomeriggio.
afterthought *s.* riflessione.
afterward(s) *avv.* poi.
again *avv.* ancora, di nuovo.
against *prep.* 1. contro 2. in previsione di.
agape *agg.* e *avv.* a bocca aperta.
age *s.* 1. età 2. secolo || *old* —, vecchiaia; *to be of* —, essere maggiorenne; *to be under* —, essere minorenne; *Middle Ages*, Medioevo.
to **age** *vt.* e *vi.* invecchiare.
aged *agg.* 1. vecchio 2. dell'età di.
agency *s.* 1. causa, azione 2. (*comm.*) agenzia, rappresentanza.
agent *s.* agente.
agglomerate *agg.* e *s.* agglomerato.
to **agglomerate** *vt.* agglomerare. ♦ to **agglomerate** *vi.* agglomerarsi.
agglomeration *s.* agglomerazione.
to **agglutinate** *vt.* agglutinare. ♦ to **agglutinate** *vi.* agglutinarsi.
to **aggravate** *vt.* 1. aggravare 2. irritare.
aggravation *s.* 1. aggravamento 2. esasperazione.
aggregate *agg.* e *s.* aggregato.
to **aggregate** *vt.* 1. aggregare 2. ammontare a. ♦ to **aggregate** *vi.* aggregarsi.

aggregation *s.* aggregazione.
aggression *s.* aggressione.
aggressive *agg.* aggressivo.
aggressiveness *s.* aggressività.
aggressor *s.* aggressore.
aghast *agg.* 1. atterrito 2. stupefatto.
agile *agg.* agile.
agility *s.* agilità.
to **agitate** *vt.* agitare.
agitation *s.* agitazione.
agitator *s.* agitatore.
agnostic *agg.* e *s.* agnostico.
ago *agg.* e *avv.* fa.
agonistic(al) *agg.* agonistico.
to **agonize** *vt.* tormentare. ♦ to **agonize** *vi.* 1. tormentarsi 2. agonizzare.
agony *s.* 1. agonia 2. dolore.
agrarian *agg.* e *s.* agrario.
to **agree** *vt.* e *vi.* 1. accordarsi 2. accettare 3. essere adatto.
agreeable *agg.* 1. gradevole 2. conforme.
agreement *s.* 1. accordo 2. conformità 3. consenso.
agricultural *agg.* agricolo.
agriculture *s.* agricoltura.
agronomist *s.* agronomo.
agronomy *s.* agronomia.
ague *s.* febbre malarica.
ahead *avv.* avanti.
aid *s.* aiuto.
to **aid** *vt.* aiutare, soccorrere.
to **ail** *vt.* affliggere. ♦ to **ail** *vi.* sentirsi male.
aileron *s.* alettone.
aim *s.* 1. mira 2. scopo.
to **aim** *vt.* e *vi.* 1. mirare 2. aspirare a.
aimless *agg.* senza scopo.
air *s.* aria || — *conditioning*, condizionamento d'aria; — *lift*, ponte aereo; —*line*, aviolinea; —*raid*, incursione aerea; — -*mail*, posta aerea.
to **air** *vt.* aerare.
aircraft *s.* aereo, aerei || — -*carrier*, portaerei.
airfield *s.* campo d'aviazione.
airiness *s.* leggerezza, disinvoltura.
airing *s.* 1. ventilazione 2. passeggiata.
to **air-mail** *vt.* trasportare per via aerea.
airman *s.* aviatore.
airport *s.* aeroporto.
airship *s.* aeronave.
airsickness *s.* mal d'aria.

airstrip *s.* pista (*d'areoporto*).
airtight *agg.* a tenuta d'aria.
airway *s.* via aerea.
airy *agg.* **1.** arioso **2.** aereo **3.** gaio.
aisle *s.* navata (*laterale*).
ajar *avv.* socchiuso.
akin *agg.* **1.** consanguineo **2.** simile.
alacrity *s.* alacrità.
alarm *s.* allarme || — -*clock*, sveglia; *to take* —, allarmarsi.
to alarm *vt.* allarmare.
alas *inter.* ahimè.
Albanian *agg.* e *s.* albanese.
albatross *s.* albatro.
albumen *s.* albume.
albumin *s.* albumina.
alchemist *s.* alchimista.
alchemy *s.* alchimia.
alcohol *s.* alcool: *wood* —, alcool metilico.
alcoholic *agg.* alcolico. ♦ **alcoholic** *sm.* alcolizzato.
alcoholism *s.* alcoolismo.
alcove *s.* alcova.
alder *s.* ontano.
alderman *s.* assessore.
ale *s.* birra || —*house*, birreria.
aleatory *agg.* aleatorio.
alembic *s.* alambicco.
alert *agg.* **1.** all'erta **2.** svelto. ♦ **alert** *s.* allarme.
algebraic(al) *agg.* algebrico.
alien *agg.* e *s.* **1.** estraneo **2.** straniero.
to alienate *vt.* alienare.
alienation *s.* alienazione.
alienist *s.* alienista.
alight *agg.* illuminato.
to alight *vi.* **1.** scendere **2.** posarsi, atterrare.
to align *vt.* allineare. ♦ **to align** *vi.* allinearsi.
alignment *s.* allineamento.
alike *agg.* simile. ♦ **alike** *avv.* similmente.
aliment *s.* alimento.
alimentary *agg.* alimentare.
alimentation *s.* alimentazione.
aliquot *agg.* e *s.* aliquota.
alive *agg.* **1.** vivo **2.** vivace **3.** sensibile.
alkaline *agg.* alcalino.
all *agg.* tutto, tutti, ogni || — *the way*, lungo tutto il cammino. ♦ **all** *pron.* tutto, tutti || *not at* —, niente affatto; — *the better*, tanto meglio || — *of us*, noi tutti; *it is* — *up*, tutto è finito. ♦ **all** *avv.* completamente, interamente || —

right, va bene; — *but*, quasi. ♦ **all** *s.* tutto, totalità.
to allege *vt.* addurre.
allegiance *s.* fedeltà.
allegoric(al) *agg.* allegorico.
allegory *s.* allegoria.
allergic *agg.* allergico.
allergy *s.* allergia.
to alleviate *vt.* alleviare.
alleviation *s.* alleviamento.
alley *s.* vialetto, vicolo.
alliance *s.* **1.** alleanza **2.** unione.
allied *agg.* alleato.
alligator *s.* alligatore.
alliteration *s.* allitterazione.
alliterative *agg.* allitterativo.
to allocate *vt.* assegnare, distribuire.
allocution *s.* allocuzione.
to allot *vt.* assegnare.
allotment *s.* **1.** distribuzione **2.** lotto (*di terreno*).
to allow *vt.* **1.** permettere **2.** riconoscere **3.** concedere.
allowance *s.* **1.** permesso **2.** assegno, indennità **3.** razione **4.** riconoscimento **5.** sconto.
alloy *s.* (*metal.*) lega.
to allude *vi.* alludere.
to allure *vt.* attrarre.
allurement *s.* allettamento.
allusion *s.* allusione.
allusive *agg.* allusivo.
alluvion *s.* alluvione.
ally *s.* alleato.
to ally *vt.* **1.** unire **2.** alleare. ♦ **to ally** *vi.* allearsi.
almanac *s.* almanacco.
almighty *agg.* onnipotente: *the Almighty*, l'Onnipotente.
almond *s.* mandorla || — -*tree*, mandorlo.
almost *avv.* quasi.
alms *s.* elemosina || — -*house*, ospizio per i poveri; — -*man*, accattone.
alone *agg.* e *avv.* solo.
along *avv.* e *prep.* **1.** lungo **2.** avanti.
alongside *avv.* (*mar.*) accanto, accosto. ♦ **alongside** *prep.* a fianco di, lungo.
aloof *avv.* a distanza. ♦ **aloof** *agg.* riservato, scontroso.
aloofness *s.* freddezza.
aloud *avv.* ad alta voce.
alp *s.* alpe.
alpha *s.* alfa.
alphabet *s.* alfabeto.
alphabetic(al) *agg.* alfabetico.

alpine *agg.* alpino.
already *avv.* già.
also *avv.* anche, inoltre.
altar *s.* altare || — *-boy,* chierichetto; — *-piece,* pala d'altare.
to alter *vt.* alterare. ♦ **to alter** *vi.* alterarsi, trasformarsi.
alteration *s.* alterazione.
altercation *s.* alterco.
alternacy *s.* alternanza.
alternate *agg.* alterno, alternato.
to alternate *vt.* alternare. ♦ **to alternate** *vi.* alternarsi.
alternation *s.* alternazione.
alternative *agg.* alternativo. ♦ **alternative** *s.* alternativa.
alternator *s.* (*elettr.*) alternatore.
although *cong.* benché.
altimeter *s.* altimetro.
altitude *s.* 1. altitudine 2. (*aer.*) quota.
altogether *avv.* interamente.
altruism *s.* altruismo.
altruist *s.* altruista.
altruistic *agg.* altruistico.
aluminium *s.* alluminio.
always *avv.* sempre.
amalgam *s.* amalgama.
to amalgamate *vt.* amalgamare. ♦ **to amalgamate** *vi.* amalgamarsi.
amalgamation *s.* amalgamazione.
amaranth *s.* amaranto.
to amass *vt.* ammucchiare.
amateur *agg.* e *s.* amatore, dilettante.
amateurism *s.* dilettantismo.
to amaze *vt.* stupire.
amazement *s.* sorpresa.
amazing *agg.* sorprendente.
Amazon *s.* amazzone.
ambages *s. pl.* ambagi.
ambassador *s.* ambasciatore.
amber *s.* ambra.
ambient *agg.* circostante. ♦ **ambient** *s.* ambiente.
ambiguity *s.* ambiguità.
ambiguous *agg.* ambiguo.
ambit *s.* ambito.
ambition *s.* ambizione.
ambitious *agg.* ambizioso.
ambivalence *s.* ambivalenza.
ambivalent *agg.* ambivalente.
amble *s.* ambio.
ambo *s.* ambone.
ambulance *s.* ambulanza.
ambush *s.* imboscata.
to ambush *vt.* e *vi.* tendere una imboscata (a).
to ameliorate *vt.* e *vi.* migliorare.

to amend *vt.* emendare. ♦ **to amend** *vi.* emendarsi.
amendment *s.* emendamento.
amends *s.* ammenda.
amenity *s.* amenità.
American *agg.* e *s.* americano.
Americanism *s.* americanismo.
amethyst *s.* ametista.
amiability *s.* amabilità.
amiable *agg.* amabile.
amiably *avv.* amabilmente.
amianthus *s.* amianto.
amicable *agg.* amichevole.
amid *prep.* in mezzo a, tra, fra.
amiss *avv.* a male; *to take sthg.* —, aversene a male. ♦ **amiss** *agg.* inopportuno, errato.
amity *s.* amicizia.
ammonia *s.* ammoniaca.
ammunition *s.* munizioni.
amnesty *s.* amnistia.
to amnesty *vt.* amnistiare.
amoeba *s.* ameba.
among(st) *prep.* tra, fra (*più di due*); in mezzo a.
amoral *agg.* amorale.
amorality *s.* amoralità.
amorous *agg.* amoroso.
amorphous *agg.* amorfo.
to amortize *vt.* (*comm.*) ammortizzare.
amount *s.* 1. somma 2. totale 3. valore 4. quantità.
to amount *vi.* 1. ammontare 2. equivalere.
amperometer *s.* amperometro.
amphibian *agg.* e *s.* anfibio.
amphibious *agg.* anfibio.
amphitheatre *s.* anfiteatro.
amphitryon *s.* anfitrione.
amphora *s.* anfora.
ample *agg.* ampio.
amplification *s.* amplificazione.
amplifier *s.* amplificatore.
to amplify *vt.* amplificare. ♦ **to amplify** *vi.* dilungarsi.
to amputate *vt.* amputare.
amputation *s.* amputazione.
amulet *s.* amuleto.
to amuse *vt.* divertire.
amusement *s.* divertimento.
an *art.* V. *a.*
anachronic *agg.* anacronistico.
anachronism *s.* anacronismo.
anachronistic(al) *agg.* anacronistico.
anaemia *s.* anemia.
anaemic *agg.* anemico.
anaesthesia *s.* anestesia.

anaesthetic *agg.* e *s.* anestetico.
anaesthetist *s.* anestesista.
to **anaesthetize** *vt.* anestetizzare.
anagram *s.* anagramma.
anal *agg.* anale.
analgesic *agg.* e *s.* analgesico.
analogic(al) *agg.* analogico.
analogous *agg.* analogo.
analogy *s.* analogia.
to **analyse** *vt.* analizzare.
analysis *s.* (*pl.* -ses) analisi.
analyst *s.* analista.
analytic(al) *agg.* analitico.
anarchic(al) *agg.* anarchico.
anarchism *s.* anarchia.
anarchist *s.* anarchico.
anarchy *s.* anarchia.
anathema *s.* anatema.
anatomic(al) *agg.* anatomico.
anatomist *s.* anatomista.
to **anatomize** *vt.* anatomizzare.
anatomy *s.* anatomia.
ancestor *s.* antenato.
ancestral *agg.* ancestrale.
ancestry *s.* stirpe.
anchor *s.* (*mar.*) ancora.
to **anchor** *vt.* ancorare. ♦ to **anchor** *vi.* ancorarsi.
anchorage *s.* ancoraggio.
anchoret *s.* anacoreta.
anchovy *s.* acciuga.
ancient *agg.* e *s.* antico.
and *cong.* e.
androgynous *agg.* androgino.
anecdote *s.* aneddoto.
anecdotic(al) *agg.* aneddotico.
anew *avv.* di nuovo.
anfractuosity *s.* anfrattuosità.
anfractuous *agg.* anfrattuoso.
angel *s.* angelo: *guardian* —, angelo custode.
angelic(al) *agg.* angelico.
anger *s.* collera.
to **anger** *vt.* irritare.
angle *s.* (*geom.*) angolo || *at right angles*, perpendicolarmente.
to **angle** *vi.* **1.** pescare (*con l'amo*) **2.** *to* — *for*, andare in cerca di.
angler *s.* pescatore (*con l'amo*).
Anglican *agg.* e *s.* anglicano.
Anglo-Saxon *agg.* e *s.* anglosassone.
angrily *avv.* irosamente.
angry *agg.* irato, arrabbiato || *to get* —, adirarsi.
anguish *s.* angoscia.
to **anguish** *vt.* angosciare. ♦ to **anguish** *vi.* angosciarsi.
angular *agg.* angolare.
anhydride *s.* anidride.

aniline *s.* anilina.
animadversion *s.* biasimo.
to **animadvert** *vi.* criticare: *to* — *on so., sthg.*, criticare qu., qc.
animal *agg.* e *s.* animale.
to **animate** *vt.* animare.
animatedly *avv.* animatamente.
animation *s.* animazione.
animator *s.* animatore.
animism *s.* animismo.
animosity *s.* animosità.
anise *s.* anice.
ankle *s.* caviglia.
ankylosis *s.* anchilosi.
annals *s. pl.* annali.
Annelida *s. pl.* anellidi.
to **annex** *vt.* annettere.
annexation *s.* annessione.
to **annihilate** *vt.* annichilire.
annihilation *s.* annichilimento.
anniversary *s.* anniversario.
to **annotate** *vt.* e *vi.* annotare.
annotation *s.* annotazione.
to **announce** *vt.* annunciare.
announcement *s.* annuncio.
announcer *s.* annunciatore.
to **annoy** *vt.* infastidire.
annoyance *s.* fastidio.
annoying *agg.* fastidioso.
annual *agg.* annuale. ♦ **annual** *s.* annuario.
annuity *s.* rendita annuale.
to **annul** *vt.* annullare.
annulment *s.* annullamento.
to **annunciate** *vt.* annunciare.
annunciation *s.* annuncio, annunciazione.
anode *s.* anodo.
anodyne *agg.* e *s.* anodino.
to **anoint** *vt.* ungere, consacrare.
anomalous *agg.* anomalo.
anomaly *s.* anomalia.
anonym *s.* anonimo.
anonymous *agg.* anonimo.
another *agg.* e *pron.* un altro || *one* —, l'un l'altro.
answer *s.* risposta.
to **answer** *vt.* e *vi.* rispondere.
ant *s.* formica || — *-bear*, formichiere.
antagonism *s.* antagonismo.
antagonist *s.* antagonista.
Antarctic *agg.* antartico.
antecedent *agg.* e *s.* antecedente. ♦ **antecedents** *s. pl.* antenati.
to **antedate** *vt.* **1.** antidatare **2.** anticipare.
antediluvian *agg.* e *s.* antidiluviano.

antelope *s.* antilope.
anteroom *s.* anticamera.
anthem *s.* inno.
anthological *agg.* antologico.
anthology *s.* antologia.
anthracite *s.* antracite.
anthropocentric *agg.* antropocentrico.
anthropologist *s.* antropologo.
anthropology *s.* antropologia.
anthropomorphic *agg.* antropomorfo.
anthropomorphism *s.* antropomorfismo.
anthropomorphous *agg.* antropomorfo.
anthropophagous *agg.* e *s.* (*pl.* -gi) antropofago.
anthropophagy *s.* antropofagia.
antiaesthetic *agg.* antiestetico.
anti-aircraft *agg.* antiaereo.
antibiotic *agg.* e *s.* antibiotico.
antibody *s.* anticorpo.
to anticipate *vt.* 1. anticipare 2. prevedere 3. pregustare.
anticipation *s.* 1. anticipo 2. previsione 3. pregustazione.
anticlerical *agg.* anticlericale.
anticlericalism *s.* anticlericalismo.
anticonceptive *s.* antifecondativo.
anticonstitutional *agg.* anticostituzionale.
anticyclone *s.* anticiclone.
anti-dazzle *agg.* antiabbagliante.
antidote *s.* antidoto.
anti-freeze *s.* anticongelante.
anti-gas *agg.* antigas.
antimilitarism *s.* antimilitarismo.
antimilitarist *s.* antimilitarista.
antimony *s.* antimonio.
antinomy *s.* antinomia.
antiparticle *s.* antiparticella.
antipathetic(al) *agg.* avverso.
antipathy *s.* antipatia.
antiphon(y) *s.* antifona.
antipodal *agg.* degli, agli antipodi.
antipode *s.* antipodo.
antiquarian *agg.* e *s.* antiquario.
antiquary *s.* antiquario.
antiquated *agg.* antiquato.
antique *agg.* antico. ♦ **antique** *s.* antichità || — *dealer*, antiquario.
antiquity *s.* antichità.
antirheumatic *agg.* antireumatico.
anti-rust *agg.* e *s.* antiruggine.
anti-Semite *s.* antisemita.
anti-Semitism *s.* antisemitismo.
antiseptic *agg.* e *s.* antisettico.
antisocial *agg.* antisociale.

antispasmodic *agg.* e *s.* antispasmodico.
anti-tank *agg.* anticarro.
antitetanic *agg.* antitetanico.
anti-theft *agg.* e *s.* antifurto.
antithesis *s.* (*pl.* -ses) antitesi.
antithetic(al) *agg.* antitetico.
antitoxic *agg.* antitossico.
anus *s.* ano.
anvil *s.* incudine.
anxiety *s.* ansietà.
anxious *agg.* ansioso.
any *agg.* 1. qualunque 2. (*in frasi neg.; int.; dubitative*) qualche, nessuno, del || *at* — *rate*, in ogni modo. ♦ **any** *pron.* 1. alcuno, nessuno 2. ne || *have you* — *bread?*, hai del pane?; *I haven't* —, non ne ho.
anybody *pron.* 1. chiunque 2. (*in frasi neg.; int.; dubitative*) qualcuno, nessuno.
anyhow *avv.* e *cong.* comunque.
anyone *pron.* V. *anybody*.
anything *pron.* 1. qualunque cosa 2. (*in frasi neg.; int.; dubitative*) qualche cosa, niente.
anyway *avv.* in ogni modo, comunque.
anywhere *avv.* dovunque.
apace *avv.* presto.
apanage *s.* appannaggio.
apart *avv.* 1. a parte 2. lontano.
apartheid *s.* discriminazione razziale.
apartment *s.* alloggio (*in affitto*).
apathy *s.* apatia.
ape *s.* scimmia.
to ape *vt.* scimmiottare.
aperitif *s.* aperitivo.
apex *s.* apice.
aphaeresis *s.* aferesi.
aphonia *s.* afonia.
aphorism *s.* aforisma.
aphrodisiac *agg.* e *s.* afrodisiaco.
aphtha *s.* afta.
apiece *avv.* a testa.
apish *agg.* scimmiesco.
apocalypse *s.* apocalisse.
apocalyptic(al) *agg.* apocalittico.
apocrypha *s. pl.* libri apocrifi.
apocryphal *agg.* apocrifo.
apogee *s.* apogeo.
apologetic(al) *agg.* apologetico.
apologist *s.* apologista.
to apologize *vi.* scusarsi.
apologue *s.* apologo.
apology *s.* scusa.
apoplexy *s.* apoplessia.

apostasy *s.* apostasia.
apostate *agg.* e *s.* apostata.
apostle *s.* apostolo.
apostolate *s.* apostolato.
apostolic(al) *agg.* apostolico.
apostrophe *s.* apostrofo.
to **apostrophize** *vt.* apostrofare.
apothecary *s.* farmacista.
apotheosis *s.* (*pl.* -ses) apoteosi.
to **appal** *vt.* spaventare.
appalling *agg.* spaventoso.
apparatus *s.* apparato.
apparent *agg.* **1.** visibile, evidente **2.** (*giur.*) legittimo.
apparition *s.* apparizione.
appeal *s.* **1.** appello **2.** attrattiva.
to **appeal** *vi.* **1.** appellarsi **2.** attrarre.
appealing *agg.* **1.** supplichevole **2.** attraente.
to **appear** *vi.* **1.** apparire **2.** sembrare.
appearance *s.* **1.** apparenza, aspetto **2.** apparizione.
to **appease** *vt.* placare.
appeasement *s.* pacificazione, tregua.
appellative *agg.* e *s.* appellativo.
appendicitis *s.* appendicite.
appendix *s.* appendice.
appetite *s.* appetito.
appetizer *s.* aperitivo.
appetizing *agg.* appetitoso.
to **applaud** *vt.* e *vi.* applaudire.
applauding *agg.* plaudente.
applause *s.* applauso.
apple *s.* mela || — *-tree*, melo.
appliance *s.* **1.** applicazione **2.** apparecchio.
applicant *s.* richiedente.
application *s.* **1.** applicazione **2.** domanda.
to **apply** *vt.* applicare. ♦ to **apply** *vi.* **1.** applicarsi **2.** rivolgersi.
to **appoint** *vt.* **1.** fissare **2.** nominare, assegnare.
appointee *s.* persona designata.
appointment *s.* **1.** appuntamento **2.** nomina **3.** impiego.
apposition *s.* apposizione.
appraisal *s.* stima.
to **appraise** *vt.* stimare.
appreciable *agg.* apprezzabile.
to **appreciate** *vt.* **1.** apprezzare **2.** rendersi conto di. ♦ to **appreciate** *vi.* aumentare di valore.
appreciation *s.* **1.** apprezzamento **2.** aumento di valore.
to **apprehend** *vt.* assodare.

apprehension *s.* **1.** apprensione **2.** percezione **3.** arresto.
apprehensive *agg.* **1.** apprensivo **2.** perspicace.
apprentice *s.* apprendista.
apprenticeship *s.* apprendistato.
approach *s.* **1.** avvicinamento **2.** approccio **3.** impostazione (*di una pratica ecc.*).
to **approach** *vt.* avvicinare. ♦ to **approach** *vi.* avvicinarsi.
approachable *agg.* accessibile.
appropriate *agg.* appropriato.
to **appropriate** *vt.* **1.** appropriarsi di **2.** stanziare.
appropriation *s.* **1.** appropriazione **2.** stanziamento.
approval *s.* **1.** approvazione **2.** (*comm.*) prova: on —, in prova.
to **approve** *vt.* **1.** approvare **2.** mostrare.
approximate *agg.* approssimativo.
to **approximate** *vt.* approssimare. ♦ to **approximate** *vi.* approssimarsi.
approximation *s.* approssimazione.
approximative *agg.* approssimativo.
apricot *s.* albicocca || — *-tree*, albicocco.
April *s.* aprile.
apron *s.* **1.** grembiale **2.** riparo **3.** (*teat.*) proscenio.
apse *s.* abside.
apt *agg.* **1.** atto **2.** intelligente **3.** proclive.
aptitude, aptness *s.* **1.** idoneità **2.** intelligenza **3.** proprietà (*di vocabolo*).
aqualung *s.* autorespiratore.
aquamarine *s.* acquamarina.
aquarium *s.* acquario.
aquatic(al) *agg.* acquatico.
aqueduct *s.* acquedotto.
aqueous *agg.* acqueo, acquoso.
Arab *agg.* e *s.* arabo.
arabesque *s.* arabesco.
Arabian *agg.* e *s.* arabo.
Arabic *agg.* arabico.
arable *agg.* arabile.
arbiter *s.* arbitro.
arbitrage *s.* arbitraggio.
arbitrary *agg.* arbitrario.
to **arbitrate** *vt.* e *vi.* arbitrare.
arbitrator *s.* (*giur.*) arbitro.
arboreal, arboreous *agg.* arboreo.
arboriculture *s.* arboricoltura.
arbour *s.* pergolato.
arc *s.* arco.
arcade *s.* galleria.

Arcadian-*agg.* e *s.* arcadico.
arch *s.* arco.
to **arch** *vt.* **1.** fabbricare ad arco **2.** inarcare. ♦ to **arch** *vi.* inarcarsi.
archaeologic(al) *agg.* archeologico.
archaeologist *s.* archeologo.
archaeology *s.* archeologia
archaic(al) *agg.* arcaico.
archaism *s.* arcaismo.
archangel *s.* arcangelo.
archbishop *s.* arcivescovo
archduke *s.* arciduca.
archer *s.* arciere.
archetype *s.* archetipo.
archipelago *s.* arcipelago.
architect *s.* architetto.
architectonic, architectural *agg* architettonico.
architecture *s.* architettura.
archive *s.* archivio.
archivist *s.* archivista.
Arctic *agg.* e *s.* artico.
ardent *agg.* ardente.
ardour *s.* ardore.
arduous *agg.* arduo.
area *s.* area.
arena *s.* (*arch.*) arena.
Areopagus *s.* areopago.
argent *s.* argenteo.
Argentine *agg.* e *s.* argentino.
argil *s.* argilla.
to **argue** *vi.* **1.** discutere **2.** ragionare. ♦ to **argue** *vt.* dimostrare.
argument *s.* **1.** discussione **2.** argomentazione.
arid *agg.* arido.
aridity *s.* aridità.
to **arise** (**arose, arisen**) *vi.* **1.** alzarsi **2.** (*fig.*) nascere.
aristocracy *s.* aristocrazia.
aristocrat *s.* aristocratico.
aristocratic(al) *agg.* aristocratico.
Aristotelian *agg.* e *s.* aristotelico.
arithmetic *s.* aritmetica.
arithmetic(al) *agg.* aritmetico.
arm[1] *s.* braccio ‖ — -*in-* —, a braccetto.
arm[2] *s.* arma ‖ *coat of arms,* stemma.
to **arm** *vt.* armare. ♦ to **arm** *vi.* armarsi.
armament *s.* armamento.
armchair *s.* poltrona.
armful *s.* bracciata.
armistice *s.* armistizio.
armless *agg.* inerme.
armlet *s.* braccialetto.
armour *s.* corazza.
to **armour** *vt.* corazzare ‖ *armour*-

ed-car, autoblinda.
armoury *s.* **1.** arsenale **2.** armeria.
armpit *s.* ascella.
army *s.* esercito.
aromatic(al) *agg.* aromatico.
arose V. *to arise.*
around *avv.* intorno. ♦ **around** *prep.* **1.** intorno a **2.** circa.
to **arouse** *vt.* **1.** destare **2.** eccitare.
to **arrange** *vt.* **1.** accomodare **2.** predisporre **3.** (*mus.*) arrangiare.
arrangement *s.* **1.** accomodamento **2.** (*mus.*) arrangiamento **3.** dispositivo. ♦ **arrangements** *s. pl.* preparativi.
arras *s.* arazzo.
array *s.* **1.** apparato **2.** (*mil.*) spiegamento.
to **array** *vt.* **1.** ornare **2.** (*mil.*) schierare.
arrest *s.* arresto.
to **arrest** *vt.* arrestare.
arrival *s.* arrivo.
to **arrive** *vi.* arrivare.
arrogance *s.* arroganza.
arrogant *agg.* arrogante.
to **arrogate** *vt.* arrogarsi.
arrow *s.* freccia.
arsenal *s.* arsenale.
arsenic *s.* arsenico.
art *s.* arte.
arteriosclerosis *s.* arteriosclerosi.
artery *s.* arteria.
artesian *agg.* artesiano.
artful *agg.* **1.** abile **2.** artificioso **3.** astuto.
arthritic(al) *agg.* artritico.
arthritis *s.* artrite.
artichoke *s.* carciofo.
article *s.* articolo.
articulate *agg.* **1.** articolato **2.** chiaro.
to **articulate** *vt.* articolare. ♦ to **articulate** *vi.* articolarsi.
articulation *s.* articolazione.
artifice *s.* **1.** artificio **2.** abilità.
artificial *agg.* artificiale.
artificiality *s.* artificiosità.
artillery *s.* artiglieria.
artilleryman *s.* artigliere.
artist *s.* artista.
artistic(al) *agg.* artistico.
artistry *s.* abilità artistica.
artless *agg.* ingenuo.
Aryan *agg.* e *s.* ariano.
as *avv.* come ‖ — ... —, tanto ... quanto; *so* — (*con infinito*), in modo da; — *for,* quanto a; — *far* —, sin dove, fino a; — *much,* al-

trettanto; — *well*, come pure. ♦
as *cong.* **1.** poiché **2.** mentre.
asbestos *s.* asbesto.
to **ascend** *vi.* ascendere. ♦ ~
ascend *vt.* risalire, scalare.
ascendancy *s.* ascendente.
ascendant *agg.* e *s.* ascendente.
ascension *s.* ascensione.
ascent *s.* ascesa.
to **ascertain** *vt.* accertarsi di.
ascertainment *s.* accertamento.
ascetic *s.* asceta.
ascetic(al) *agg.* ascetico.
asceticism *s.* ascetismo.
to **ascribe** *vt.* ascrivere.
asepsis *s.* asepsi.
aseptic *agg.* e *s.* asettico.
asexual *agg.* asessuale.
ash *s.* cenere ‖ — *-tray*, portacenere.
ash(-tree) *s.* frassino.
ashamed *agg.* vergognoso ‖ *to be*
—, aver vergogna.
ashore *avv.* a terra.
ashy *agg.* cinereo.
Asiatic *agg.* e *s.* asiatico.
aside *avv.* a parte, da parte.
asininity *s.* asinità.
to **ask** *vt.* e *vi.* **1.** chiedere **2.** invitare ‖ *to* — *so. for sthg.*, chiedere
a qu. qc.; *to* — *for trouble*, cer-
car fastidi.
askance *avv.* di traverso.
asker *s.* interrogante.
asleep *agg.* addormentato.
asocial *agg.* asociale.
asp *s.* aspide.
asparagus *s. coll.* asparago, aspa-
ragi.
aspect *s.* aspetto.
aspen *s.* pioppo tremulo.
aspergillum *s.* aspersorio.
asperity *s.* **1.** asperità **2.** (*fig.*)
asprezza.
aspersion *s.* **1.** aspersione **2.** calunnia.
asphalt *s.* asfalto.
asphyxia *s.* asfissia.
to **asphyxiate** *vt.* asfissiare.
aspirant *agg.* e *s.* aspirante.
to **aspirate** *vt.* aspirare.
aspiration *s.* aspirazione.
aspirator *s.* aspiratore.
to **aspire** *vi.* aspirare.
aspirin *s.* aspirina.
aspiring *agg.* ambizioso.
asquint *avv.* di traverso.
ass *s.* asino ‖ *to make an* — *of one-*
self, rendersi ridicolo.
to **assail** *vt.* assalire.

assailant, assailer *s.* assalitore.
assassin *s.* assassino.
to **assassinate** *vt.* assassinare.
assassination *s.* assassinio.
assault *s.* assalto, aggressione.
to **assault** *vt.* assalire.
assaulter *s.* assalitore.
to **assay** *vt.* saggiare.
assayer *s.* (as)saggiatore.
to **assemble** *vt.* riunire. ♦ to **assemble** *vi.* riunirsi.
assembly *s.* **1.** assemblea **2.** (*mil.*)
adunata **3.** (*mecc.*) montaggio: —
line, catena di montaggio.
assent *s.* consenso.
to **assent** *vt.* approvare.
to **assert** *vt.* asserire ‖ *to* — *oneself*, farsi valere.
assertion *s.* asserzione.
assertor *s.* assertore.
to **assess** *vt.* **1.** tassare **2.** (*comm.*)
ripartire.
assessment *s.* **1.** valutazione **2.** tassazione.
assessor *s.* agente delle tasse.
asset *s.* **1.** bene, vantaggio. ♦ **assets** *s. pl.* patrimonio, attività
(*sing.*).
assiduity *s.* assiduità.
assiduous *agg.* assiduo.
to **assign** *vt.* **1.** assegnare **2.** trasferire **3.** designare.
assignation *s.* **1.** assegnazione **2.**
(*giur.*) cessione **3.** appuntamento.
assignment *s.* **1.** assegnazione **2.**
(*giur.*) cessione.
assimilable *agg.* assimilabile.
to **assimilate** *vt.* **1.** assimilare **2.**
confrontare. ♦ to **assimilate** *vi.*
assimilarsi.
assimilation *s.* **1.** assimilazione **2.**
confronto.
to **assist** *vt.* e *vi.* assistere.
assistance *s.* assistenza.
assistant *agg.* e *s.* assistente ‖ *shop*
—, commesso.
assize *s.* **1.** (*giur.*) seduta. ♦ **Assizes** *s. pl.* Assise.
associate *agg.* e *s.* associato.
to **associate** *vt.* associare. ♦ to
associate *vi.* associarsi.
association *s.* associazione.
assonance *s.* assonanza.
to **assort** *vt.* **1.** assortire **2.** classificare. ♦ to **assort** *vi.* **1.** armonizzarsi **2.** frequentare: *to* — *with
so.*, frequentare qu.
to **assume** *vt.* **1.** assumere **2.** fingere **3.** presumere.

assuming *agg.* presuntuoso.
assumption *s.* **1.** assunzione **2.** finzione **3.** supposizione **4.** presunzione.
assurance *s.* **1.** assicurazione **2.** sicurezza **3.** fiducia.
to **assure** *vt.* **1.** assicurare **2.** rassicurare.
assurer *s.* assicuratore.
asterisk *s.* asterisco.
astern *avv.* a poppa.
asteroid *s.* asteroide.
asthenia *s.* astenia.
asthma *s.* asma.
asthmatic *agg.* e *s.* asmatico.
astigmatic *agg.* astigmatico.
astigmatism *s.* astigmatismo.
astir *agg.* e *avv.* in moto.
to **astonish** *vt.* stupire.
astonishing *agg.* sorprendente
astonishment *s.* sorpresa.
to **astound** *vt.* sbalordire.
astragal(us) *s.* astragalo.
astrakhan *s.* astracan.
astral *agg.* astrale.
astray *agg.* e *avv.* fuori strada.
astride *agg.* e *avv.* a cavalcioni. ♦ **astride** *prep.* a cavalcioni di.
astringent *agg.* e *s.* astringente
astrolabe *s.* astrolabio.
astrologer *s.* astrologo.
astrology *s.* astrologia.
astronaut *s.* astronauta.
astronautics *s.* astronautica.
astronomer *s.* astronomo.
astronomic(al) *agg.* astronomico.
astronomy *s.* astronomia.
astute *agg.* astuto.
asunder *avv.* **1.** separatamente **2.** in pezzi.
asylum *s.* **1.** asilo, ricovero **2.** manicomio.
asymmetric(al) *agg.* asimmetrico.
asymmetry *s.* asimmetria.
at *prep.* (*stato, tempo, modo*) a, da, in: *to arrive — a place,* arrivare in un luogo; *— that time,* in quel momento; *— will,* a volontà.
atavistic *agg.* atavico.
atavism *s.* atavismo.
ataxy *s.* atassia.
ate V. *to eat.*
atheism *s.* ateismo.
atheist *s.* ateo.
atheistic(al) *agg.* ateistico.
athlete *s.* atleta.
athletic *agg.* atletico.
athletics *s.* atletica.
atlas *s.* atlante.

atmosphere *s.* atmosfera.
atmospheric(al) *agg.* atmosferico.
atoll *s.* atollo.
atom *s.* atomo.
atomic(al) *agg.* atomico.
atomism *s.* atomismo.
to **atomize** *vt.* nebulizzare.
atomizer *s.* atomizzatore, nebulizzatore.
atomy *s.* atomo.
to **atone** *vt.* espiare.
atonement *s.* espiazione.
atonic *agg.* **1.** atono **2.** atonico.
atrocious *agg.* atroce.
atrocity *s.* atrocità.
atrophic *agg.* atrofico.
atrophy *s.* atrofia.
to **atrophy** *vt.* atrofizzare. ♦ to **atrophy** *vi.* atrofizzarsi.
atropin(e) *s.* atropina.
to **attach** *vt.* **1.** attaccare, unire **2.** attribuire **3.** attrarre. ♦ to **attach** *vi.* attaccarsi.
attaché *s.* addetto.
attachment *s.* **1.** attaccamento **2.** (*mecc.*) accessorio.
attack *s.* attacco.
to **attack** *vt.* attaccare.
attacker *s.* assalitore.
to **attain** *vt.* raggiungere. ♦ to **attain** *vi.* giungere.
attainable *agg.* raggiungibile.
attainment *s.* **1.** raggiungimento **2.** cultura.
attempt *s.* **1.** tentativo **2.** attentato.
to **attempt** *vt.* **1.** tentare **2.** attentare a.
to **attend** *vi.* **1.** badare a **2.** obbedire ‖ *to — on,* essere al servizio di. ♦ to **attend** *vt.* **1.** assistere **2.** accompagnare **3.** frequentare.
attendance *s.* **1.** servizio **2.** assistenza **3.** frequenza.
attendant *s.* **1.** servitore **2.** assistente **3.** assiduo frequentatore.
attention *s.* attenzione: *to pay —,* fare attenzione.
attentive *agg.* **1.** attento **2.** sollecito.
to **attenuate** *vt.* **1.** assottigliare **2.** attenuare. ♦ to **attenuate** *vi.* **1.** assottigliarsi **2.** attenuarsi.
attenuation *s.* **1.** assottigliamento **2.** attenuazione.
to **attest** *vt.* attestare.
attic *agg.* e *s.* attico.
to **attire** *vt.* vestire, agghindare. ♦ to **attire** *vi.* vestirsi.
attitude *s.* atteggiamento.

attorney s. **1.** procura **2.** procuratore || — (-at-law), procuratore legale.
to **attract** vt. attrarre.
attraction s. **1.** attrazione **2.** attrattiva.
attractive agg. attraente.
attribute s. attributo.
to **attribute** vt. attribuire.
attribution s. attribuzione.
attributive agg. attributivo. ♦ **attributive** s. attributo.
aubergine s. melanzana.
auction s. asta: — sale, vendita all'asta.
to **auction** vt. vendere all'asta.
auctioneer s. banditore.
audible agg. udibile.
audience s. **1.** udienza **2.** uditorio.
audiovisual agg. audiovisivo.
audit s. verifica, revisione.
audition s. audizione.
auditory agg. e s. uditorio.
auger s. trivella, succhiello.
to **augment** vt. aumentare. ♦ to **augment** vi. crescere.
augmentative agg. e s. accrescitivo.
to **augur** vt. e vi. predire.
august agg. augusto.
August s. agosto.
aunt s. zia || great- —, prozia.
auricle s. **1.** padiglione auricolare **2.** (med.) orecchietta.
auricular agg. auricolare.
auriferous agg. aurifero.
to **auscultate** vt. auscultare.
auscultation s. auscultazione.
auscultator s. stetoscopio.
auspice s. auspicio.
auspicious agg. propizio.
austere agg. austero.
austerity s. austerità.
austral agg. australe.
Australian agg. e s. australiano.
Austrian agg. e s. austriaco.
autarky s. autarchia.
authentic(al) agg. autentico.
to **authenticate** vt. autenticare.
authentication s. autenticazione.
authenticity s. autenticità.
author s. autore.
authoress s. autrice.
authoritative agg. **1.** autoritario **2.** autorevole.
authoritativeness s. autorevolezza.
authority s. autorità.
authorization s. autorizzazione.
to **authorize** vt. autorizzare.
authorless agg. anonimo.

authorship s. paternità (di un libro).
autobiographic(al) agg. autobiografico.
autobiography s. autobiografia.
autochthon s. autoctono.
autochthonous agg. autoctono.
autocracy s. autocrazia.
autocrat s. autocrate.
autocriticism s. autocritica.
autoeducation s. autoeducazione.
autofinancing s. autofinanziamento.
autograph s. autografo.
autography s. autografia.
autolesion s. autolesione.
automatic agg. automatico. ♦ **automatic** s. arma automatica.
automation s. automazione.
automatism s. automatismo.
automaton s. automa.
autonomist s. autonomista.
autonomous agg. autonomo.
autonomy s. autonomia.
autopsy s. autopsia.
auto-suggestion s. autosuggestione.
autumn s. autunno.
autumnal agg. autunnale.
auxiliary agg. e s. ausiliare.
avail s. utilità.
to **avail** vt. e vi. servire a || to — oneself of, approfittare di.
availability s. **1.** disponibilità **2.** validità.
available agg. **1.** disponibile **2.** valevole.
avalanche s. valanga.
avarice s. **1.** avarizia **2.** cupidigia.
avaricious agg. **1.** avaro **2.** cupido.
to **avenge** vt. vendicare.
avenger s. vendicatore.
avenue s. viale.
to **aver** vt. asserire, dichiarare.
average agg. medio. ♦ **average** s. **1.** media **2.** (comm.) avaria.
averse agg. avverso.
aversion s. avversione.
to **avert** vt. sviare.
aviary s. uccelliera.
aviation s. aviazione.
aviator s. aviatore.
avid agg. avido.
avidity s. avidità.
to **avoid** vt. **1.** evitare **2.** (giur.) annullare.
avoidable agg. **1.** evitabile **2.** (giur.) annullabile.
to **avow** vt. dichiarare, ammettere.
avowal s. dichiarazione, ammissione.

to **await** *vt.* attendere.
awake *agg.* **1.** sveglio **2.** conscio.
to **awake (awoke, awoke)** *vt.*
svegliare. ♦ to **awake (awoke,
awoke)** *vi.* svegliarsi.
to **awaken** *vt.* risvegliare, far aprire
gli occhi. ♦ to **awaken** *vi.* risvegliarsi, aprire gli occhi.
awakening *s.* risveglio.
award *s.* **1.** sentenza **2.** ricompensa.
to **award** *vt.* aggiudicare.
aware *agg.* conscio.
away *avv.* via, lontano || *right* —,
subito, seduta stante.
awe *s.* timore reverenziale.
awful *agg.* **1.** terribile **2.** imponente.
awkward *agg.* **1.** goffo, imbarazzato **2.** scomodo **3.** inopportuno **4.**
delicato.
awkwardness *s.* **1.** goffaggine **2.**
imbarazzo.
awl *s.* lesina.
awning *s.* tenda.
awoke V. *to awake.*
awry *agg.* **1.** storto **2.** bieco. ♦
awry *avv.* **1.** per traverso **2.** perversamente.
ax(e) *s.* scure.
axiom *s.* assioma.
axiomatic(al) *agg.* assiomatico.
axis *s.* (*pl.* axes) asse.
axle *s.* (*mecc.*) asse.
azimuth *s.* azimut.
azote *s.* azoto.
to **azotize** *vt.* azotare.
Aztec *agg.* e *s.* azteco.
azure *agg.* e *s.* azzurro.

B

b *s.* (*mus.*) si.
babble *s.* balbettio.
to **babble** *vi.* e *vt.* **1.** balbettare **2.**
mormorare (*di acque*).
babe *s.* bambino.
babel *s.* babele.
baboon *s.* babbuino.
baby *s.* bimbo, neonato || — *-sit-
ter,* chi accudisce i bambini.
babyhood *s.* infanzia.
babyish *agg.* infantile.
baccarat *s.* baccarà.
Bacchanal *s.* **1.** baccante **2.** baccanale (*anche fig.*).
Bacchante *s.* baccante.

bacchic(al) *agg.* bacchico.
bachelor *s.* scapolo || *Bachelor of
Arts,* titolo universitario in lettere.
bachelorhood *s.* celibato.
bacillus *s.* (*pl.* -li) bacillo.
back[1] *agg.* posteriore. ♦ **back** *avv.*
dietro, indietro || *to be* —, essere
di ritorno; *to go, to come* —, ritornare.
back[2] *s.* **1.** dorso, schiena **2.** spalle
3. rovescio **4.** schienale **5.** fondo.
to **back** *vt.* **1.** sostenere **2.** fare in-
dietreggiare || *to* — *a bill,* avalla-
re una cambiale. ♦ to **back** *vi.*
indietreggiare || — *down,* abban-
donare la contesa.
to **backbite** *vt.* denigrare.
backbiter *s.* calunniatore.
backbiting *agg.* maldicente. ♦
backbiting *s.* maldicenza.
backbone *s.* **1.** spina dorsale **2.**
(*fig.*) fermezza.
backer *s.* **1.** scommettitore **2.** sostenitore.
backfire *s.* ritorno di fiamma.
background *s.* **1.** sfondo **2.** curriculum **3.** ambiente.
backing *s.* **1.** sostegno **2.** marcia indietro.
backlash *s.* rimbalzo.
backslider *s.* apostata.
backward *agg.* **1.** lento **2.** tardo.
backward(s) *avv.* indietro.
backwash *s.* risacca.
bacon *s.* lardo affumicato, pancetta.
bacterial *agg.* batterico.
bacteriology *s.* batteriologia.
bacterium *s.* (*pl.* -ia) batterio.
bad (worse, worst) *agg.* **1.** cattivo **2.** brutto. ♦ **bad** *s.* **1.** male
2. rovina.
bade V. *to bid.*
badge *s.* insegna.
badger *s.* tasso.
badly *avv.* male, malamente.
badness *s.* **1.** cattiveria **2.** cattiva
qualità.
baffle *s.* (-*plate*) deflettore, diaframma.
to **baffle** *vt.* **1.** eludere **2.** confondere.
bag *s.* **1.** sacco **2.** borsa || *sleeping-*
—, sacco a pelo.
to **bag** *vt.* **1.** gonfiare **2.** rubare **3.**
insaccare.
baggage *s.* bagaglio.
bagpipe *s.* cornamusa.
bail *s.* **1.** cauzione **2.** garante.
to **bail**[1] *vt.* **1.** dar garanzia per **2.**

affidare (*dietro cauzione*).
to **bail**[2] *vt.* e *vi.* (*mar.*) aggottare ||
to — out, lanciarsi col paracadute.
bailiff *s.* **1.** magistrato inquirente
2. ufficiale fiscale.
bain-marie *s.* bagnomaria.
bait *s.* **1.** esca **2.** sosta (*per ristoro*).
to **bait** *vt.* **1.** adescare **2.** tormentare.
♦ to **bait** *vi.* fermarsi (*per prendere ristoro*).
to **bake** *vt.* e *vi.* cuocere al forno.
baker *s.* fornaio.
bakery *s.* forno.
baking *s.* cottura al forno.
balance *s.* **1.** bilancia **2.** bilanciere
3. equilibrio **4.** bilancio.
to **balance** *vt.* **1.** pesare **2.** pareggiare. ♦ to **balance** *vi.* **1.** bilanciarsi **2.** oscillare.
balanced *agg.* equilibrato.
balancer *s.* acrobata.
balcony *s.* **1.** balcone **2.** (*teat.*).balconata.
bald *agg.* **1.** calvo, pelato **2.** povero, nudo.
baldness *s.* **1.** calvizie **2.** (*fig.*) nudità.
baldric *s.* bandoliera.
bale *s.* (*comm.*) balla.
Balkan *agg.* balcanico.
ball *s.* **1.** palla **2.** ballo || *— -bearing*, cuscinetto a sfere.
to **ball** *vt.* appallottolare. ♦ to **ball** *vi.* appallottolarsi.
ballad *s.* ballata.
ballast *s.* zavorra.
to **ballast** *vt.* zavorrare.
ballet *s.* balletto || *— -dancer*, ballerino classico.
ballistics *s.* balistica.
balloon *s.* **1.** pallone **2.** lambicco **3.** fumetto.
ballot *s.* **1.** pallina, scheda (*per votazione*) **2.** voto **3.** scrutinio || *— -box*, urna.
to **ballot** *vt.* mettere in ballottaggio.
balm *s.* balsamo.
balm-cricket *s.* (*zool.*) cicala.
balmy *agg.* balsamico.
Baltic *agg.* baltico.
balustrade *s.* balaustrata.
bamboo *s.* bambù.
ban *s.* bando.
to **ban** *vt.* proibire.
banal *agg.* banale.
banality *s.* banalità.
banana *s.* **1.** banana **2.** banano.
band *s.* **1.** legame **2.** benda **3.** nastro
4. banda.

to **band** *vt.* **1.** legare **2.** bendare.
bandage *s.* bendaggio.
to **bandage** *vt.* bendare.
banderole *s.* banderuola.
bandit *s.* bandito.
bandmaster *s.* capobanda.
bandog *s.* cane da guardia.
bandsman *s.* bandista.
bane *s.* **1.** calamità **2.** veleno.
baneful *agg.* velenoso.
bang *s.* **1.** botta **2.** detonazione.
to **bang** *vt.* e *vi.* sbattere violentemente.
banging *s.* **1.** colpi violenti **2.** detonazioni.
to **banish** *vt.* bandire, esiliare.
banishment *s.* bando, esilio.
banister *s.* ringhiera (*di scala*).
bank *s.* **1.** banca **2.** banco **3.** argine **4.** terrapieno.
to **bank** *vt.* **1.** arginare **2.** depositare in banca || *to — upon*, contare su. ♦ to **bank** *vi.* gestire una banca.
bankbook *s.* libretto bancario.
banker *s.* banchiere.
banking *agg.* bancario. ♦ **banking** *s.* tecnica, professione bancaria.
bank note *s.* banconota.
bankrupt *agg.* e *s.* fallito || *to go —*, fallire.
bankruptcy *s.* fallimento.
banner *s.* vessillo.
banns *s. pl.* pubblicazioni matrimoniali.
banquet *s.* banchetto.
to **banquet** *vi.* banchettare.
banter *s.* scherzo, beffa.
to **banter** *vt.* canzonare.
baptism *s.* battesimo.
baptist(e)ry *s.* battistero.
to **baptize** *vt.* battezzare.
bar *s.* **1.** sbarra **2.** diga **3.** striscia
4. ostacolo **5.** (*fig.*) tribunale **6.**
bar **7.** (*mus.*) battuta.
to **bar** *vt.* **1.** sbarrare **2.** ostacolare
3. proibire.
barbarian *agg.* e *s.* barbaro.
barbaric *agg.* barbarico.
barbarism *s.* **1.** barbarie **2.**
(*gramm.*) barbarismo.
barbarous *agg.* barbaro.
barbarousness *s.* barbarie.
barbecue *s.* **1.** animale arrostito intero **2.** festa campestre.
to **barbecue** *vt.* arrostire un animale intero.
barbed *agg.* dentato.
barber *s.* barbiere.

barbiturate s. barbiturico.
bard s. bardo, trovatore.
bare agg. 1. nudo 2. logoro.
to **bare** vt. 1. denudare 2. snudare 3. smascherare.
barefoot agg. scalzo.
barehanded agg. e avv. 1. a mano nuda 2. senz'armi.
bareheaded agg. a capo scoperto.
barely avv. 1. apertamente 2. appena.
bargain s. affare.
to **bargain** vt. e vi. contrattare.
bargaining s. contrattazione.
barge s. chiatta.
baritone s. baritono.
bark[1] s. corteccia.
bark[2] s. latrato.
to **bark**[1] vt. scortecciare.
to **bark**[2] vi. latrare, abbaiare.
barking[1] s. scortecciamento.
barking[2] s. abbaiamento.
barley s. orzo.
barmaid s. barista (donna).
barman s. barista.
barn s. granaio.
barometer s. barometro.
barometric(al) agg. barometrico
baron s. barone.
baroness s. baronessa.
baroque agg. e s. barocco.
barracks s. pl. caserma (sing.).
barrage s. sbarramento.
barrel s. 1. barile 2. cilindro 3. canna (di arma da fuoco) || — -organ, organetto.
to **barrel** vt. mettere in barili.
barrelled agg. double- — gun, fucile a due canne.
barren agg. sterile.
barrenness s. sterilità.
barricade s. barricata.
to **barricade** vt. barricare.
barrier s. barriera || transonic —, muro del suono.
barrister s. avvocato (che può discutere cause nelle corti superiori).
barrow s. 1. barella 2. carriola.
bartender s. barista.
barter s. baratto.
to **barter** vt. e vi. barattare.
basal agg. basilare.
basalt s. basalto.
base[1] agg. basso, vile.
base[2] s. base.
to **base** vt. basare.
baseless agg. senza base.
basement s. 1. fondamento 2. seminterrato.

baseness s. bassezza.
to **bash** vt. colpire.
bashful agg. timido.
bashfulness s. timidezza.
basic agg. 1. fondamentale 2. (chim.) basico.
basil s. basilico.
basilar agg. basilare.
basilisk s. basilisco.
basin s. 1. bacino 2. catino, lavabo || sugar —, zuccheriera.
basis s. (pl. -ses) base.
to **bask** vi. crogiolarsi (al sole, al fuoco).
basket s. cesto || —ball, pallacanestro; — -chair, poltroncina di vimini.
Basque agg. e s. basco.
bas-relief s. bassorilievo.
bass agg. e s. (mus.) basso.
bass s. pesce persico.
bassoon s. (mus.) fagotto.
bastard agg. e s. bastardo.
to **baste** vt. imbastire.
basting s. imbastitura.
bastion s. bastione.
bat[1] s. pipistrello.
bat[2] s. (sport) mazza.
batch s. 1. infornata 2. gruppo.
to **bate** vt. ridurre.
bath s. bagno || — -robe, accappatoio; — -tub, vasca da bagno.
to **bath** vt. bagnare. ♦ to **bath** vi. bagnarsi, fare il bagno.
bathe s. bagno (in mare, lago ecc.).
to **bathe** vt. bagnare. ♦ to **bathe** vi. bagnarsi, fare il bagno (in mare, lago ecc.).
bather s. bagnante.
bathing s. il bagnarsi || — -suit, costume da bagno.
bathroom s. stanza da bagno.
bathysphere s. batisfera.
batiste s. batista.
batman s. attendente.
baton s. 1. bastone 2. bacchetta (di direttore d'orchestra).
batrachian s. batrace.
batsman s. (sport) battitore.
battalion s. battaglione.
to **batten** vt. (mar.) chiudere (i boccaporti).
batter s. (cuc.) pastella.
to **batter** vt. battere || to — down, abbattere; to — in, sfondare.
battering s. cannoneggiamento.
battery s. batteria || storage —, accumulatore.
battle s. battaglia.

to **battle** vt. e vi. combattere.
battledore s. racchetta di legno ||
— and shuttlecock, volano.
battlement s. (arch.) merlo.
battleship s. nave da guerra.
bauxite s. bauxite.
bawdiness s. oscenità.
bawdy agg. osceno || — house, bordello.
bawl s. grido.
to **bawl** vt. e vi. gridare, vociare.
bay[1] s. 1. baia 2. insenatura, recesso (nelle montagne).
bay[2] s. alloro || — -tree, lauro.
bay[3] s. 1. rientranza 2. campata || — -window, bovindo.
bay[4] s. latrato || at —, senza scampo.
bay[5] agg. e s. baio.
to **bay**[1] vt. arginare.
to **bay**[2] vi. latrare.
bayonet s. baionetta.
baza(a)r s. 1. bazar 2. vendita di beneficienza.
to **be (was, been)** vi. 1. essere 2. stare 3. andare 4. costare: how much is it?, quanto costa? 5. dovere || to — in, essere in casa; to — about, stare per; so be it, così sia.
beach s. spiaggia.
beacon s. faro.
to **beacon** vt. guidare con segnalazioni luminose.
bead s. 1. goccia 2. perlina. ♦ **beads** s. pl. rosario (sing.).
to **bead** vt. imperlare. ♦ to **bead** vi. imperlarsi.
beak s. 1. becco, rostro 2. beccuccio.
to **beak** vt. beccare.
beaker s. boccale.
beam s. 1. trave 2. raggio 3. asta (di bilancia) 4. fiancata (di nave).
to **beam** vi. brillare. ♦ to **beam** vt. irradiare.
beaming agg. raggiante.
bean s. fagiolo || French —, fagiolino; coffee —, grano di caffè.
bear s. orso.
to **bear**[1] vt. e vi. speculare al ribasso (in Borsa).
to **bear**[2] (bore, born(e)) vt. 1. portare 2. sopportare 3. generare. ♦ to **bear** (bore, borne) vi. 1. resistere 2. appoggiarsi 3. pazientare || to — with, aver pazienza con.
bearable agg. sopportabile.
beard s. 1. barba 2. chioma (di cometa).
to **beard** vt. affrontare, sfidare.

bearded agg. barbuto.
beardless agg. senza barba.
bearer s. portatore.
bearing s. 1. sopportazione 2. portamento 3. condotta 4. relazione 5. sostegno 6. raccolto || to lose one's bearings, perdere l'orientamento; to take the bearings of a coast (mar.), rilevare una costa.
beast s. bestia.
beastliness s. bestialità.
beastly agg. bestiale. ♦ **beastly** avv. bestialmente.
beat s. 1. battito 2. (mus.) battuta.
to **beat (beat, beat(en))** vt. e vi. battere || to — down, abbattere; to — back, respingere.
beaten agg. abbattuto, vinto.
beater s. battitore.
beatification s. beatificazione.
beating s. 1. battito 2. bastonatura 3. sconfitta.
beatitude s. beatitudine.
beautiful agg. bello.
beautifully avv. magnificamente.
to **beautify** vt. abbellire. ♦ to **beautify** vi. abbellirsi.
beauty s. bellezza.
beaver s. castoro.
became V. to become.
because cong. perché || — of, a causa di.
beck[1] s. ruscello.
beck[2] s. cenno, gesto.
to **become (became, become)** vi. 1. divenire 2. avvenire. ♦ to **become (became, become)** vt. addirsi a.
becoming agg. adatto.
bed s. 1. letto 2. fondo 3. (geol.) strato || double —, letto matrimoniale || flower- —, aiuola; -cover, copriletto.
bedclothes s. pl. lenzuola.
bedlam s. manicomio.
bedouin agg. e s. beduino.
bedroom s. camera da letto.
bedside s. capezzale.
bedstead s. telaio del letto.
bedtime s. ora di andare a letto.
bee s. ape.
beech s. faggio || — -marten, faina.
beef s. manzo.
beefsteak s. bistecca.
beehive s. alveare.
beeline s. linea diretta, linea d'aria.
been V. to be.
beer s. birra.

beet s. barbabietola.
beetle s. coleottero, scarafaggio.
beetroot s. V. *beet.*
to **befall (befell, befallen)** vt. e vi. accadere.
before avv. prima, già || — *-mentioned,* già citato. ◆ **before** prep. 1. prima (di) 2. davanti a. ◆ **before** cong. 1. prima che 2. piuttosto che.
beforehand avv. anticipatamente.
to **beg** vt. e vi. 1. chiedere, pregare 2. elemosinare.
began V. *to begin.*
to **beget (begot, begot(ten))** vt. generare.
beggar s. mendicante.
beggarly agg. misero. ◆ **beggarly** avv. miseramente.
beggary s. mendicità.
begging agg. mendicante. ◆ **begging** s. accattonaggio.
to **begin (began, begun)** vt. e vi. cominciare || *to — with,* in primo luogo, per cominciare.
beginner s. 1. iniziatore 2. principiante.
beginning s. inizio.
begot V. *to beget.*
begotten V. *to beget.*
to **begrime** vt. insudiciare.
begun V. *to begin.*
behalf s. profitto, favore: *on — of,* da parte di, a nome di.
to **behave** vi. comportarsi: *to — oneself,* comportarsi bene || *ill -behaved,* maleducato.
behaviour s. comportamento, condotta.
to **behead** vt. decapitare.
beheld V. *to behold.*
behind avv. dietro, indietro. ◆ **behind** prep. dietro (a). ◆ **behind** s. parte posteriore.
to **behold (beheld, beheld)** vt. guardare.
beholder s. spettatore.
to **behove** vt. *imp.* convenire, essere doveroso.
being agg. presente. ◆ **being** s. 1. esistenza 2. essere vivente.
belch s. 1. rutto 2. eruzione.
to **belch** vi. ruttare. ◆ **to belch** vt. eruttare.
belfry s. campanile.
Belgian agg. e s. belga.
to **belie** vt. 1. smentire 2. deludere.
belief s. credenza, fede.
to **believe** vt. e vi. credere, aver fede.
believer s. credente.
to **belittle** vt. sminuire.
bell s. 1. campana 2. campanello || — *-boy,* fattorino d'albergo; — *-ringer,* campanaro; — *-tower,* campanile.
belligerency s. belligeranza.
belligerent agg. e s. belligerante.
bellow s. muggito.
to **bellow** vi. muggire.
bellows s. pl. mantice, soffietto (sing.).
belly s. ventre.
to **belong** vi. 1. appartenere 2. concernere.
belongings s. pl. proprietà (sing.).
beloved agg. e s. amato.
below avv. giù, al di sotto. ◆ **below** prep. sotto: — *zero,* sotto zero.
belt s. 1. cintura 2. zona.
to **belt** vt. 1. cingere 2. staffilare.
to **bemire** vt. infangare. ◆ **to bemire** vi. impantanarsi.
bench s. 1. panca 2. banco 3. seggio 4. corte giudiziaria.
bend s. 1. curva 2. curvatura 3. (mar.) nodo.
to **bend (bent, bent)** vt. 1. piegare 2. tendere. ◆ **to bend (bent, bent)** vi. piegarsi.
bending s. V. *bend.*
beneath avv. e prep. V. *below.*
benediction s. benedizione.
benefactor s. benefattore.
benefactress s. benefattrice.
benefice s. beneficio.
beneficence s. beneficenza.
beneficent agg. benefico.
beneficiary agg. e s. beneficiario.
benefit s. 1. vantaggio 2. indennità 3. (giur.) beneficio.
to **benefit** vt. giovare, beneficare. ◆ **to benefit** vi. approfittare.
benevolence s. benevolenza.
benevolent agg. benevolo.
Bengal-light s. bengala.
benign agg. benigno.
benignity s. benignità.
bent V. *to bend.* ◆ **bent** agg. risoluto. ◆ **bent** s. inclinazione.
to **benumb** vt. intorpidire.
benumbing s. intorpidimento.
benzol s. benzolo.
to **bequeath** vt. lasciare per testamento.
bequest s. lascito.
Berber agg. e s. berbero.

to bereave (bereaved, bereft) *vt.* privare.
bergamot *s.* bergamotto.
berlin(e) *s.* berlina.
berry *s.* bacca.
berth *s.* **1.** cuccetta **2.** (*mar.*) ancoraggio **3.** (*fig.*) posto.
to berth *vt.* ancorare.
beryllium *s.* berillio.
to beseech (besought, besought) *vt.* supplicare.
beseeching *s.* supplica.
to beseem *vt.* addirsi a.
beseeming *agg.* adatto.
beside *prep.* **1.** vicino a **2.** fuori di.
besides *avv.* inoltre. ♦ **besides** *prep.* oltre a.
to besiege *vt.* assediare.
besieger *s.* assediante.
besought V. *to beseech.*
to besprinkle *vt.* spruzzare.
best *agg.* (*superl. di* good) il migliore || — *-seller*, libro molto venduto. ♦ **best** *s.* il meglio. ♦ **best** *avv.* **1.** nel modo migliore **2.** maggiormente.
bestial *agg.* bestiale.
bestiality *s.* bestialità.
to bestialize *vt.* abbrutire.
to bestir *vt.* agitare.
to bestow *vt.* concedere.
bestowal *s.* conferimento.
to bestrew (bestrewed, bestrewn) *vt.* cospargere, disseminare.
bet *s.* scommessa.
to bet (bet, bet) *vt. e vi.* scommettere.
to betake (betook, betaken) *vr.* — *oneself*: dirigersi, recarsi.
to betray *vt.* tradire.
betrayal *s.* tradimento.
betrayer *s.* traditore.
betrothal *s.* fidanzamento.
betrothed *agg. e s.* fidanzato.
better[1] *s.* scommettitore.
better[2] *agg.* (*comp. di* good) migliore. ♦ **better** *avv.* meglio || *had* —, sarebbe meglio che; *all the* —, *so much the* —, tanto meglio. ♦ **better** *s.* **1.** il meglio **2.** superiore.
to better *vt. e vi.* migliorare.
between *avv.* in mezzo. ♦ **between** *prep.* tra, fra (*due cose, due persone*).
beverage *s.* bevanda.
bevy *s.* stormo, frotta.
to beware *vi.* guardarsi, diffidare.

to bewilder *vt.* sconcertare.
bewildering *agg.* sbalorditivo.
bewilderment *s.* confusione.
to bewitch *vt.* incantare.
bewitcher *s.* incantatore.
bewitching *agg.* affascinante.
beyond *avv.* più in là. ♦ **beyond** *prep.* al di là di. ♦ **beyond** *s.* l'al di là.
bias *s.* **1.** pregiudizio **2.** predisposizione.
to bias *vt.* influenzare.
bib *s.* bavaglino.
Bible *s.* Bibbia.
biblical *agg.* biblico.
bibliographic(al) *agg.* bibliografico.
bibliography *s.* bibliografia.
bicameral *agg.* bicamerale.
bicarbonate *s.* bicarbonato.
bicentennial *agg. e s.* bicentenario.
bicephalous *agg.* bicipite.
biceps *s.* bicipite.
to bicker *vi.* litigare.
bicoloured *agg.* bicolore.
biconcave *agg.* biconcavo.
bicycle *s.* bicicletta.
bid *s.* **1.** offerta (*a un'asta*) **2.** appalto.
to bid[1] **(bid, bid)** *vt.* offrire (*a un'asta*). ♦ **to bid (bid, bid)** *vi.* fare offerta di appalto.
to bid[2] **(bade, bidden)** *vt. e vi.* **1.** comandare **2.** dire || *to* — *good-bye*, accomiatarsi.
biennial *agg.* biennale.
biennium *s.* (*pl.* -biennia) biennio.
bier *s.* bara.
big *agg.* **1.** grosso **2.** gravido **3.** importante.
bigamous *agg.* bigamo.
bigamy *s.* bigamia.
bigness *s.* grossezza.
bigot *s.* bigotto.
bigoted *agg.* bigotto, fanatico.
bilateral *agg.* bilaterale.
bilberry *s.* mirtillo.
bile *s.* bile.
bilingual *agg.* bilingue.
bilious *agg.* **1.** biliare **2.** collerico.
bill[1] *s.* becco.
bill[2] *s.* **1.** progetto di legge **2.** certi- **5.** lista **6.** affisso || — *of lading*, polizza di carico; — *of rights*, dichiarazione dei diritti.
to bill *vt.* **1.** fatturare **2.** affiggere **3.** (*teat.*) mettere in programma.
billhook *s.* falcetto.
billiard *agg.* di, da bigliardo: —

-*cue*, stecca da bigliardo.
billiards *s. pl.* bigliardo (*sing.*).
billion *s.* **1.** bilione **2.** (*amer.*) miliardo.
billow *s.* onda.
bimestrial *agg.* bimestrale.
bimonthly *agg.* e *s.* bimestrale. ◆ **bimonthly** *avv.* bimestralmente.
bin *s.* recipiente || *dust-* —, bidone della spazzatura.
bind *s.* **1.** legame **2.** fascia.
to **bind** (**bound, bound**) *vt.* **1.** legare **2.** fasciare **3.** rilegare **4.** obbligare.
binder *s.* **1.** rilegatore **2.** (*mecc.*) legatrice.
binding *agg.* impegnativo. ◆ **binding** *s.* **1.** legame **2.** fasciatura **3.** rilegatura.
binocular *s.* binocolo.
binomial *s.* binomio.
biochemistry *s.* biochimica.
biographer *s.* biografo.
biographic(al) *agg.* biografico.
biography *s.* biografia.
biological *agg.* biologico.
biologist *s.* biologo.
biology *s.* biologia.
biophysics *s.* biofisica.
biosphere *s.* biosfera.
bipartite *agg.* bipartito.
bipartition *s.* bipartizione.
biped *agg.* e *s.* bipede.
biplane *s.* biplano.
bipolar *agg.* bipolare.
birch *s.* **1.** betulla **2.** verga.
bird *s.* uccello.
birdcage *s.* gabbia (*per uccelli*).
birdseed *s.* miglio.
birth *s.* **1.** nascita **2.** stirpe.
birthday *s.* compleanno.
birthmark *s.* voglia, segno caratteristico (*di persona*).
birthplace *s.* luogo di nascita.
biscuit *s.* biscotto.
bisection *s.* bisezione.
bisector *s.* bisettrice.
bisexual *agg.* ermafrodito.
bishop *s.* vescovo.
bishopric *s.* vescovato.
bismuth *s.* bismuto.
bison *s.* bisonte.
bistoury *s.* bisturi.
bistre *s.* bistro.
bit *s.* **1.** pezzettino **2.** un poco **3.** (*mecc.*) parte tagliente di un utensile **4.** morso (*del cavallo*).
bit V. *to bite.*
bitch *s.* cagna.

bite *s.* **1.** morso **2.** presa.
to **bite** (**bit, bit(ten)**) *vt.* mordere. ◆ to **bite** (**bit, bit(ten)**) *vi.* abboccare || *to* — *in*, corrodere.
biting *agg.* **1.** mordente **2.** mordace.
bitten V. *to bite.*
bitter *agg.* **1.** amaro **2.** aspro **3.** (*di clima*) rigido || — -*sweet*, agrodolce. ◆ **bitter** *s.* amaro.
bitterish *agg.* amarognolo.
bitterness *s.* **1.** amarezza **2.** rancore **3.** rigidità (*di clima*).
bitumen *s.* bitume.
bivalent *agg.* bivalente.
bivouac *s.* bivacco.
bi-weekly *agg.* e *s.* bisettimanale. ◆ **bi-weekly** *avv.* due volte alla settimana.
to **blab** *vt.* e *vi.* **1.** chiacchierare **2.** spifferare.
black *agg.* **1.** nero **2.** negro **3.** (*fig.*) malvagio, minaccioso. ◆ **black** *s.* **1.** colore nero **2.** negro.
to **black** *vt.* annerire. ◆ to **black** *vi.* annerirsi.
to **blackball** *vt.* votare contro, bocciare.
blackberry *s.* mora selvatica.
blackbird *s.* merlo.
blackboard *s* lavagna.
to **blacken** *vt.* **1.** annerire **2.** (*fig.*) diffamare. ◆ to **blacken** *vi.* diventare nero.
blackguard *s.* mascalzone.
blackish *agg.* nerastro.
blackleg *s.* **1.** truffatore **2.** crumiro.
blackmail *s.* ricatto.
to **blackmail** *vt.* ricattare.
blackmailer *s.* ricattatore.
blackness *s.* **1.** nerezza **2.** oscurità.
blackout *s.* oscuramento.
blacksmith *s.* fabbro ferraio.
bladder *s.* vescica.
blade *s.* **1.** stelo **2.** lama.
blamable *agg.* biasimevole.
blame *s.* **1.** biasimo **2.** colpa.
to **blame** *vt.* **1.** biasimare **2.** incolpare.
blameful *agg.* biasimevole.
blameless *agg.* irreprensibile.
bland *agg.* blando.
blandishment *s.* blandizie (*pl.*).
blandly *avv.* blandamente.
blank *agg.* **1.** vuoto **2.** in bianco || — *verse*, verso sciolto. ◆ **blank** *s.* **1.** vuoto **2.** spazio in bianco **3.** mira || *point-* —, di punto in bianco.
blanket *s.* coperta.

blankly *avv.* **1.** senza espressione **2.** decisamente.

blare *s.* squillo (*di tromba*).

to blaspheme *vt.* e *vi.* bestemmiare.

blasphemous *agg.* blasfemo.

blasphemously *avv.* empiamente.

blasphemy *s.* bestemmia, empietà.

blast *s.* **1.** raffica **2.** squillo **3.** scoppio **4.** flagello || — -*furnace*, altoforno.

to blast *vt.* **1.** far esplodere **2.** rovinare.

blaze *s.* **1.** fiamma **2.** scoppio.

to blaze *vi.* ardere. ♦ **to blaze** *vt.* **1.** bruciare **2.** divulgare.

blazer *s.* giacca sportiva.

blazing *s.* **1.** fiamma **2.** splendore **3.** vanteria.

blazon *s.* **1.** blasone **2.** ostentazione.

bleach *s.* imbianchimento, candeggio.

to bleach *vt.* imbiancare, candeggiare. ♦ **to bleach** *vi.* imbiancarsi.

bleacher *s.* recipiente per candeggio.

bleaching *s.* V. *bleach.*

bleak *agg.* **1.** brullo **2.** desolato **3.** incolore.

bleakness *s.* **1.** freddezza **2.** squallore.

blear *agg.* **1.** cisposo **2.** ottuso.

bleat *s.* belato.

to bleat *vi.* belare.

to bleed (bled, bled) *vi.* sanguinare. ♦ **to bleed (bled, bled)** *vt.* salassare.

bleeding *s.* **1.** emorragia **2.** salasso **3.** fuga.

blemish *s.* difetto.

blend *s.* miscela.

to blend *vt.* mescolare. ♦ **to blend** *vi.* mescolarsi.

to bless *vt.* benedire.

blessed *agg.* beato, santo.

blessing *s.* benedizione.

blew V. *to blow.*

blind *agg.* cieco. ♦ **blind** *s.* **1.** tenda **2.** persiana **3.** paraocchi **4.** finzione.

to blind *vt.* **1.** accecare **2.** oscurare **3.** nascondere.

blindness *s.* cecità.

to blink *vi.* **1.** battere le palpebre **2.** lampeggiare **3.** (*fig.*) chiudere gli occhi.

blinker *s.* **1.** lampeggiatore **2.** paraocchi.

blinking *agg.* **1.** ammiccante **2.** scintillante. ♦ **blinking** *s.* ammicco.

bliss *s.* beatitudine.

blissful *agg.* **1.** beato **2.** delizioso.

blister *s.* bolla.

blithe *agg.* gaio.

blizzard *s.* tormenta (*di neve*).

block *s.* **1.** ceppo **2.** masso **3.** isolato (*di case*) **4.** ostacolo **5.** persona stupida || — *letters*, stampatello.

to block *vt.* bloccare.

blockade *s.* blocco.

blockhead *s.* stupido.

blonde *s.* donna bionda.

blood *s.* sangue.

bloodhound *s.* segugio.

bloodless *agg.* **1.** esangue **2.** incruento **3.** (*fig.*) insensibile.

bloodshed *s.* spargimento di sangue.

bloodshot *agg.* iniettato di sangue.

bloody *agg.* **1.** sanguinante **2.** sanguinoso **3.** sanguinario **4.** maledetto.

bloom *s.* **1.** fiore **2.** rossore.

to bloom *vi.* **1.** fiorire **2.** arrossire.

blossom *s.* fiore.

to blossom *vi.* **1.** fiorire **2.** diventare.

blot *s.* macchia.

to blot *vt.* **1.** macchiare **2.** assorbire.

blotch *s.* **1.** macchia **2.** pustola.

blotting *s.* **1.** il macchiare **2.** l'asciugare || — -*paper*, carta assorbente; — -*pad*, tampone di carta assorbente.

blouse *s.* camicetta.

blow *s.* **1.** soffio **2.** colpo **3.** fioritura || *to come to blows*, venire alle mani.

to blow (blew, blown) *vt.* **1.** soffiare **2.** suonare (*strumenti a fiato*) || *to* — *up*, (far) saltare in aria. ♦ **to blow (blew, blown)** *vi.* sbocciare.

blower *s.* **1.** soffiatore **2.** sfiatatoio.

blown V. *to blow.*

blowpipe *s.* **1.** cannello per soffiare **2.** cerbottana.

blue *agg.* **1.** azzurro, blu **2.** livido **3.** triste.

bluebell *s.* campanula.

bluebottle[1] *s.* fiordaliso.

bluebottle[2] *s.* tafano.

blueprint *s.* cianografia.

bluff *s.* ripida scogliera.

bluish *agg.* bluastro.

blunder *s.* errore.

blunt *agg.* **1.** smussato **2.** ottuso **3.** schietto.

blush *s.* rossore.

to **blush** *vi.* arrossire.
board *s.* 1. asse, tavola 2. vitto 3. pensione 4. consiglio, ministero 5. (*mar.*) bordo || *on* —, a bordo; *full* —, pensione completa. ♦ **boards** *s. pl.* palcoscenico (*sing.*).
to **board** *vt.* 1. fornire di assi 2. prendere a pensione 3. (*mar.*) abbordare. ♦ to **board** *vi.* 1. essere a pensione 2. imbarcarsi.
boarder *s.* pensionante.
boarding *s.* assito || — -*house*, pensione; — -*school*, collegio.
boast *s.* vanto.
to **boast** *vt.* vantare. ♦ to **boast** *vi.* vantarsi.
boaster *s.* spaccone.
boastful *agg.* vanaglorioso.
boastfulness *s.* millanteria.
boasting *s.* vanteria.
boat *s.* barca, battello || *flying-* —, idrovolante; *sauce-* —, salsiera; *ferry-* —, traghetto.
boating *s.* canottaggio.
boatman *s.* barcaiolo.
boatswain *s.* nostromo.
to **bob** *vi.* dondolarsi, oscillare || *to* — *up*, venire a galla.
bobbin *s.* bobina.
bobsled *s.* guidoslitta.
bodice *s.* busto.
bodkin *s.* punteruolo, stiletto.
body *s.* 1. corpo 2. corporazione, ente 3. massa || — *belt*, panciera.
bodymaker *s.* carrozziere.
Boeotian *agg.* e *s.* beota.
bog *s.*
boggy *agg.* paludoso.
bogy *s.* spauracchio.
boil *s.* bollitura.
to **boil** *vt.* e *vi.* bollire, ribollire || *to* — *away*, consumarsi; *to* — *over*, traboccare bollendo.
boiler *s.* bollitore, caldaia.
boiling *agg.* bollente. ♦ **boiling** *s.* ebollizione.
boisterous *agg.* 1. rumoroso 2. violento.
boisterousness *s.* fracasso.
bold *agg.* 1. audace 2. sfacciato 3. vigoroso || — -*face*, neretto.
boldness *s.* 1. audacia 2. sfacciataggine.
bolide *s.* bolide.
Bolshevism *s.* bolscevismo.
Bolshevist *agg.* e *s.* bolscevico.
bolster *s.* 1. cuscino 2. supporto.
bolt *s.* 1. catenaccio 2. bullone 3. otturatore 4. freccia 5. fulmine.

to **bolt**[1] *vt.* 1. sprangare 2. imbullonare.
to **bolt**[2] *vt.* setacciare, vagliare.
bolter *s.* setaccio.
bomb *s.* bomba.
to **bomb** *vt.* bombardare.
to **bombard** *vt.* bombardare.
bombardier *s.* bombardiere.
bombardment *s.* bombardamento.
bombastic *agg.* ampolloso.
bomber *s.* bombardiere.
bond *s.* 1. vincolo 2. patto 3. (*comm.*) titolo 4. cauzione || — -*holder*, portatore di obbligazioni; *goods in* —, merci in attesa di sdoganamento.
bondage *s.* schiavitù.
bone *s.* 1. osso 2. lisca.
to **bone** *vt.* 1. disossare 2. spinare.
bonfire *s.* falò.
bonnet *s.* 1. cuffia 2. (*auto*) cofano.
bonus *s.* gratifica || *cost of living* —, carovita.
bony *agg.* 1. osseo 2. ossuto.
bonze *s.* bonzo.
booby *s.* sciocco.
book *s.* 1. libro 2. registro || *note-* —, taccuino; *copy-* —, quaderno.
to **book** *vt.* 1. registrare 2. prenotare.
bookbinding *s.* rilegatura.
bookcase *s.* libreria.
booking *s.* 1. registrazione 2. prenotazione || — -*office*, biglietteria.
bookish *agg.* 1. studioso 2. libresco.
bookkeeper *s.* contabile.
bookkeeping *s.* contabilità.
booklet *s.* libretto.
bookmaker *s.* allibratore.
bookseller *s.* libraio.
bookshelf *s.* (*pl.* -lves) scaffale.
bookshop *s.* libreria.
bookstall *s.* edicola, bancarella (*di libri*).
boom *s.* 1. rombo 2. periodo di prosperità.
to **boom** *vi.* 1. rimbombare 2. essere in periodo di prosperità.
boor *s.* persona zotica.
boorish *agg.* rustico.
boorishness *s.* rozzezza.
boot *s.* 1. stivale, scarpa 2. (*auto*) portabagagli.
bootblack *s.* lustrascarpe.
booth *s.* baracca || *telephone* —, cabina telefonica.
booty *s.* bottino.

border s. 1. orlo 2. frontiera.
to **border** vt. orlare || to — on, confinare con.
borderer s. abitante di confine.
bordering s. 1. il bordare 2. il confinare.
bore V. to bear.
bore[1] s. 1. buco 2. calibro (di arma).
bore[2] s. 1. seccatura 2. seccatore.
to **bore**[1] vt. forare.
to **bore**[2] vt. annoiare.
boreal agg. boreale.
boredom s. noia.
boric agg. borico.
boring[1] agg. noioso.
boring[2] s. perforazione || — test, sondaggio.
born V. to bear. ♦ **born** agg. nato, generato || to be —, nascere.
borne V. to bear.
borough s. 1. municipio 2. circoscrizione elettorale.
to **borrow** vt. prendere a prestito.
borrower s. chi prende a prestito.
bosom s. seno || — friend, amico intimo.
boss[1] s. 1. protuberanza 2. (arch.) bugna.
boss[2] s. capo, padrone.
bossy[1] agg. a bugnato.
bossy[2] agg. (gergo) prepotente.
botanist s. botanico.
botany s. botanica.
botch s. pasticcio.
to **botch** vt. 1. rattoppare 2. arruffare.
botcher s. pasticcione.
both agg. e pron. entrambi, tutti e due. ♦ **both** avv. nel medesimo tempo || — ... and, sia... sia, tanto... quanto.
bother s. seccatura.
to **bother** vt. infastidire. ♦ to **bother** vi. preoccuparsi.
bothersome agg. fastidioso.
bottle s. bottiglia || feeding- —, poppatoio; — -feeding, allattamento artificiale.
to **bottle** vt. imbottigliare.
bottling s. imbottigliamento.
bottom agg. 1. inferiore 2. basilare. ♦ **bottom** s. 1. fondo 2. fondamento 3. deretano 4. (mar.) chiglia.
to **bottom** vt. 1. mettere il fondo (a) 2. impagliare 3. capire. ♦ to **bottom** vi. posare, essere posato.
bottomless agg. 1. senza fondo 2.

senza fine.
bough s. ramo (d'albero).
bought V. to buy.
boulder s. macigno.
boulevard s. viale.
bounce s. 1. balzo 2. vanteria.
to **bounce** vt. far rimbalzare. ♦ to **bounce** vi. 1. rimbalzare 2. gloriarsi.
bouncer s. fanfarone.
bound[1] s. limite, confine.
bound[2] s. salto.
bound[3] V. to bind.
bound[4] agg. 1. destinato 2. diretto a 3. certo.
to **bound**[1] vt. confinare, limitare.
to **bound**[2] vi. balzare.
boundary s. limite, frontiera.
boundless agg. illimitato.
bounteous agg. generoso.
bounty s. generosità.
bourgeois agg. e s. borghese.
bourgeoisie s. borghesia.
bow[1] s. 1. arco 2. archetto 3. fiocco || — -window, bovindo.
bow[2] s. inchino.
bow[3] s. prua.
to **bow** vt. piegare. ♦ to **bow** vi. 1. piegarsi 2. inclinarsi.
bowels s. pl. viscere.
bower s. 1. pergolato 2. dimora.
bowl[1] s. ciotola.
bowl[2] s. boccia.
to **bowl** vt. far rotolare. ♦ to **bowl** vi. 1. rotolare 2. giocare a bocce.
bowler s. giocatore di bocce || — hat, bombetta.
bowling s. gioco delle bocce.
bowman s. arciere.
bowshot s. tiro d'arco.
box[1] s. 1. scatola 2. stanzetta 3. stalla 4. (teat.) palco 5. (giur.) banco || letter- —, buca per le lettere; money- —, salvadanaio; strong- —, cassaforte.
box[2] s. pugno, ceffone.
to **box**[1] vt. mettere in scatola.
to **box**[2] vt. schiaffeggiare. ♦ to **box** vi. fare del pugilato.
boxer s. pugile.
boxing s. pugilato.
boy s. ragazzo.
to **boycott** vt. boicottare.
boyhood s. fanciullezza.
boyish agg. fanciullesco.
bra s. reggipetto.
brace s. 1. sostegno 2. coppia, paio 3. (mar.) braccio. ♦ **braces** s. pl. bretelle.

to **brace** vt. **1.** legare **2.** fortificare.
bracelet s. braccialetto.
brachycardia s. brachicardia.
bracket s. **1.** mensola, sostegno **2.** parentesi.
brackish agg. salato, salso.
brag s. **1.** millanteria **2.** millantatore.
to **brag** vt. vantare. ♦ to **brag** vi. vantarsi.
braggart agg. e s. spaccone.
bragging s. millanteria.
braid s. **1.** treccia **2.** gallone.
to **braid** vt. **1.** intrecciare **2.** guarnire.
brain s. cervello.
brainless agg. scervellato.
brake[1] s. **1.** felce **2.** boschetto.
brake[2] s. freno.
to **brake** vt. frenare.
brakesman s. frenatore.
bramble s. rovo.
bran s. crusca.
branch s. **1.** ramo **2.** filiale.
to **branch** vt. ramificare. ♦ to **branch** vi. ramificarsi || to — out, estendersi (di attività commerciale, affari).
branching s. ramificazione.
brand s. **1.** tizzone **2.** marchio (a fuoco) **3.** marca || — -new, nuovo fiammante.
to **brand** vt. **1.** marchiare **2.** stigmatizzare.
to **brandish** vt. brandire.
brass agg. **1.** di ottone **2.** (fig.) sfacciato. ♦ **brass** s. **1.** ottone **2.** (mecc.) bronzina **3.** (fig.) sfacciataggine || — band, fanfara
brassy agg. V. brass.
bravado s. bravata.
brave agg. e s. prode, coraggioso.
bravely avv. coraggiosamente.
bravery s. **1.** coraggio **2.** splendore.
brawl s. rissa.
to **brawl** vi. rissare.
brawn s. muscolo, forza muscolare.
brawny agg. muscoloso.
bray s. raglio.
to **bray**[1] vi. **1.** ragliare **2.** (fig.) stonare.
to **bray**[2] vt. frantumare, sminuzzare.
brazen agg. V. brass.
brazier[1] s. calderaio.
brazier[2] s. braciere.
Brazilian agg. e s. brasiliar. /.
breach s. **1.** rottura **2.** breccia **3.** infrazione || — of promise, rottura di fidanzamento.

bread s. pane.
to **bread** vt. rimpanare.
breadth s. **1.** larghezza **2.** altezza (di stoffe).
breadthwise avv. in larghezza (di stoffe).
break s. **1.** rottura **2.** interruzione, intervallo **3.** infrazione || — -up, collasso, smembramento, fine.
to **break** (broke, broken) vt. **1.** rompere **2.** interrompere **3.** domare **4.** rovinare. ♦ to **break** (broke, broken) vi. **1.** rompersi **2.** irrompere || to — down, demolire, (auto) restare in panne, esaurirsi; to — off, mandare a monte; to — up, fare a pezzi.
breakdown s. **1.** collasso **2.** rottura **3.** dissesto || nervous —, esaurimento nervoso.
breaker s. **1.** rompitore **2.** violatore **3.** domatore **4.** (mecc.) macchina rompitrice **5.** (mar.) frangente **6.** (elett.) interruttore.
breakfast s. prima colazione.
to **breakfast** vi. fare la prima colazione.
breaking s. **1.** rottura **2.** (comm.) fallimento.
breakneck agg. a rotta di collo.
breakwater s. frangiflutti.
breast s. petto || — -bone, sterno.
breasted agg. dal petto || double- —, a doppio petto.
breath s. **1.** soffio **2.** respiro.
breathable agg. respirabile.
to **breathe** vi. **1.** respirare **2.** spirare. ♦ to **breathe** vt. **1.** infondere **2.** sussurrare.
breathing s. V. breath.
breathless agg. **1.** ansante **2.** esanime.
breathlessness s. affanno.
bred V. to breed. ♦ **bred** agg. ill- —, maleducato.
breech s. **1.** parte posteriore **2.** culatta (di arma).
breeches s. pl. calzoni.
breed s. razza.
to **breed** (bred, bred) vt. **1.** generare **2.** allevare. ♦ to **breed** (bred, bred) vi. nascere.
breeder s. **1.** chi genera **2.** allevatore.
breeding s. **1.** generazione **2.** allevamento **3.** educazione.
breeze s. brezza.
breezy agg. **1.** ventilato **2.** cordiale.
brethren s. pl. confratelli.

breviary s. breviario.
brevity s. brevità.
brew s. 1. mistura 2. fermentazione (di birra).
to **brew** vt. 1. mescolare 2. (fig.) macchinare. ♦ to **brew** vi. fare la birra.
brewer s. birraio.
brewery s. fabbrica di birra.
bribe s. dono (a scopo di corruzione), allettamento.
to **bribe** vt. corrompere.
briber s. corruttore.
bribery s. corruzione.
brick s. mattone.
bricklayer s. muratore.
brickwork s. muratura in mattoni.
brickyard s. mattonaia.
bride s. sposa.
bridegroom s. sposo.
bridge s. ponte || swing- —; ponte girevole; toll- —, ponte a pedaggio; — -head, testa di ponte.
bridle s. briglia, freno.
to **bridle** vt. imbrigliare.
bridling s. imbrigliamento.
brief agg. breve. ♦ **brief** s. riassunto.
to **brief** vt. 1. riassumere 2. (giur.) nominare (il proprio avvocato) 3. dare istruzioni.
briefness s. brevità, concisione.
brier s. 1. rovo 2. rosa selvatica.
brig s. brigantino.
brigade s. brigata.
bright agg. 1. chiaro, splendente 2. vivace.
to **brighten** vt. 1. far brillare 2. animare. ♦ to **brighten** vi. 1. brillare 2. animarsi.
brightness s. 1. splendore 2. gaiezza.
brill s. (itt.) rombo.
brilliance, brilliancy s. brillantezza.
brilliant agg. e s. brillante.
brilliantine s. brillantina.
brim s. 1. orlo 2. ala (di cappello).
brimful agg. colmo.
brindled agg. pezzato.
brine s. acqua salata.
to **bring** (**brought, brought**) vt. 1. portare 2. indurre || to — about, causare; to — back, richiamare alla memoria; to — forth, dare alla luce; to — up, educare, allevare.
brink s. orlo.
brisk agg. 1. vivace 2. frizzante.
briskness s. vivacità.

bristle s. setola.
to **bristle** vi. essere irto di.
bristly agg. 1. setoloso 2. ruvido.
British agg. britannico.
Briton agg. e s. britanno.
broad agg. 1. ampio 2. chiaro 3. marcato 4. volgare || — daylight, pieno giorno. ♦ **broad** s. larghezza. ♦ **broad** avv. ampiamente.
broadcast s. 1. radiodiffusione 2. radiocomunicazione.
to **broadcast** (**broadcast, broadcast**) (anche reg.) vt. e vi. radiotrasmettere.
broadcaster s. trasmettitore.
broadcasting s. radiodiffusione.
to **broaden** vt. allargare. ♦ to **broaden** vi. allargarsi, estendersi.
broadness s. 1. larghezza 2. grossolanità.
broadside s. (mar.) 1. bordo, fiancata 2. bordata.
brocade s. broccato.
bro(c)coli s. broccolo.
broil s. rissa.
to **broil** vt. cuocere alla griglia. ♦ to **broil** vi. abbrustolirsi (al sole).
broke V. to break.
broken V. to break. ♦ **broken** agg. 1. variabile (di tempo) 2. accidentato (di terreno) 3. indebolito 4. avvilito 5. scorretto.
broker s. 1. (comm.) agente 2. mediatore.
bromide s. bromuro.
bromine s. bromo.
bronchial agg. bronchiale.
bronchia s. pl. bronchi.
bronchitis s. bronchite.
broncho-pneumonia s. broncopolmonite.
bronze s. bronzo.
to **bronze** vt. abbronzare. ♦ to **bronze** vi. abbronzarsi.
brooch s. spilla.
brood s. covata.
to **brood** vt. 1. covare 2. (fig.) rimuginare, meditare.
brooding s. 1. cova 2. meditazione.
brook s. ruscello.
to **brook** vt. sopportare, tollerare.
brooklet s. ruscelletto.
broom s. 1. ginestra 2. scopa.
broth s. brodo.
brothel s. bordello.
brother s. 1. fratello 2. collega || — -in-law, cognato; half- —, fratellastro.

brotherhood *s.* 1. fratellanza 2. confraternita.
brotherlike *agg.* fraterno.
brotherly *agg.* fraterno. ◆ **brotherly** *avv.* fraternamente.
brought V. *to bring.*
brow *s.* fronte. ◆ **brows** *s. pl.* sopracciglia.
brown *agg.* 1. bruno 2. marrone. ◆ **brown** *s.* marrone.
to brown *vt.* 1. rendere bruno 2. rosolare. ◆ **to brown** *vi.* 1. diventare bruno 2. abbronzarsi
to browse *vt.* e *vi.* brucare.
bruise *s.* contusione.
to bruise *vt.* ammaccare. ◆ **to bruise** *vi.* ammaccarsi.
bruiser *s.* 1. pugilatore 2. (*fig.*) gradasso.
brush *s.* 1. spazzola, spazzolino 2. spazzolata 3. pennello 4. rissa || — -*up*, ripasso.
to brush *vt.* 1. spazzolare 2. sfiorare || *to* — *aside* (*fig.*), ignorare; *to* — *up*, ripassare.
brushwood *s.* sottobosco.
brushy *agg.* 1. ispido 2. folto (*di bosco*).
brusque *agg.* brusco.
brutal *agg.* brutale.
brutality *s.* brutalità.
to brutalize *vt.* 1. abbrutire 2. maltrattare. ◆ **to brutalize** *vi.* abbrutirsi.
brute *agg.* brutale. ◆ **brute** *s.* bruto.
brutish *agg.* brutale, rozzo.
bubble *s.* 1. bolla 2. gorgoglio.
to bubble *vi.* gorgogliare || *to* — *over*, traboccare.
bubo *s.* bubbone.
bubonic *agg.* bubbonico.
buccaneer *s.* bucaniere.
buck *s.* 1. daino 2. maschio (*di molti animali*).
to buck *vi.* sgroppare.
bucket *s.* secchio.
buckle *s.* fibbia.
to buckle *vt.* 1. affibbiare 2. piegare. ◆ **to buckle** *vi.* piegarsi.
bucolic *agg.* bucolico.
bud *s.* 1. gemma 2. germe.
to bud *vi.* germogliare.
Buddhism *s.* buddismo.
Buddhist *agg.* e *s.* buddista.
budget *s.* 1. raccolta (*di documenti*) 2. bilancio.
buffalo *s.* bufalo.
buffer *s.* respingente.

buffet[1] *s.* schiaffo.
buffet[2] *s.* credenza.
to buffet *vt.* schiaffeggiare.
buffoon *s.* buffone.
bug *s.* 1. coleottero 2. cimice || *big* —, (*gergo*) pezzo grosso.
bugbear *s.* spauracchio.
bugger *s.* sodomita.
build *s.* costruzione, struttura.
to build (built, built) *vt.* costruire || *to* — *up*, murare.
builder *s.* costruttore.
building *agg.* edilizio. ◆ **building** *s.* edificio.
built V. *to build.*
bulb *s.* 1. bulbo 2. lampadina || — *socket*, portalampada.
Bulgarian *agg.* e *s.* bulgaro.
bulge *s.* gonfiore.
to bulge *vi.* gonfiarsi. ◆ **to bulge** *vt.* 1. sporgere 2. gonfiare.
bulgy *agg.* rigonfio.
bulk *s.* 1. massa 2. carico.
bulkhead *s.* paratia.
bulky *agg.* massiccio.
bull *s.* 1. toro 2. maschio (*di alcuni mammiferi*) || —'s *eye*, oblò.
bulldog *s.* mastino.
bullet *s.* pallottola.
bulletin *s.* bollettino || *news* —, giornale radio.
bullfight *s.* corrida.
bullfighter *s.* torero.
bullock *s.* torello.
bully *agg.* borioso.
to bully *vt.* e *vi.* fare il prepotente (*verso*).
bulwark *s.* 1. bastione 2. (*mar.*) parapetto.
bumble-bee *s.* calabrone.
bump *s.* 1. urto 2. bernoccolo.
to bump *vt.* e *vi.* urtare, andare a sbattere contro.
bumper *s.* 1. paraurti 2. respingente.
bun *s.* 1. focaccia 2. crocchia.
bunch *s.* 1. mazzo 2. grappolo.
bundle *s.* 1. fagotto 2. fascio.
to bundle *vt.* riunire in fascio, fare un involto.
bung *s.* tappo.
bungler *agg.* e *s.* confusionario.
bunny *s.* coniglietto.
buoy *s.* boa.
buoyancy *s.* 1. galleggiabilità 2. ottimismo.
buoyant *agg.* 1. galleggiante 2. ottimista.
burden *s.* 1. peso 2. tonnellaggio.

to **burden** *vt.* caricare.
burdensome *agg.* gravoso.
bureau *s.* (*pl.* bureaux) ufficio.
bureaucracy *s.* burocrazia.
bureaucrat *s.* burocrate.
bureaucratic *agg.* burocratico.
burglar *s.* scassinatore (*notturno*).
burglary *s.* furto (*notturno*) con scasso.
to **burgle** *vt.* e *vi.* svaligiare con scasso.
burgomaster *s.* borgomastro.
burial *s.* sepoltura || — *-ground*, cimitero; — *-service*, ufficio funebre.
burin *s.* bulino.
burly *agg.* corpulento.
burn *s.* ustione.
to **burn** (**burnt, burnt**) (*anche reg.*) *vt.* e *vi.* bruciare, ardere.
burner *s.* bruciatore.
burning *s.* 1. incendio 2. (*metal.*) fusione.
to **burnish** *vt.* lustrare.
burnt V. *to burn.*
burrow *s.* tana, buca.
bursar *s.* economo.
bursary *s.* 1. ufficio dell'economato 2. borsa di studio.
burst *s.* 1. scoppio 2. squarcio.
to **burst** (**burst, burst**) *vt.* 1. far esplodere 2. sfondare. ♦ to **burst** (**burst, burst**) *vi.* 1. scoppiare 2. irrompere.
bursting *s.* scoppio.
to **bury** *vt.* seppellire.
bus *s.* autobus.
busby *s.* colbac.
bush *s.* cespuglio.
bushel *s.* staio.
bushy *agg.* folto.
busily *avv.* attivamente.
business *s.* 1. affare 2. mestiere 3. ditta 4. scopo || — *-man*, uomo d'affari; — *-like*, metodico, sistematico.
bust *s.* busto.
bustle *s.* trambusto.
to **bustle** *vi.* agitarsi.
busy *agg.* occupato.
to **busy** *vt.* occupare.
busybody *s.* ficcanaso.
but *cong.* ma. ♦ **but** *avv.* solo. ♦ **but** *prep.* tranne || — *for*, se non fosse per; — *that*, se non; *cannot* —, non poter far a meno di; *all* —, pressoché.
butane *s.* butano.
butcher *s.* macellaio.
butchery *s.* macello.

butler *s.* maggiordomo.
butt[1] *s.* 1. calcio (*di arma*) 2. impugnatura (*di utensile*) 3. mozzicone.
butt[2] *s.* urto.
to **butt** *vt.* e *vi.* cozzare.
butter *s.* burro.
to **butter** *vt.* imburrare.
buttercup *s.* ranuncolo.
butterfly *s.* farfalla.
buttery *agg.* burroso.
buttock *s.* natica.
button *s.* bottone.
to **button** *vt.* abbottonare.
button-hole *s.* occhiello.
to **button-hole** *vt.* 1. fare asole a 2. (*fig.*) attaccar bottone.
button-holer *s.* attaccabottoni.
buttress *s.* contrafforte.
buxom *agg.* formoso, avvenente (*di donna*).
to **buy** (**bought, bought**) *vt.* comprare || *to* — *off*, riscattare; *to* — *up*, accaparrare.
buyable *agg.* acquistabile.
buyer *s.* acquirente.
buzz *s.* ronzio.
buzzard *s.* poiana.
to **buzz** *vi.* e *vt.* ronzare, bisbigliare.
buzzer *s.* 1. insetto che ronza 2. cicala, segnale acustico.
by *avv.* 1. vicino 2. da parte, in disparte || — *and* —, fra poco; — *and large*, complessivamente. ♦ **by** *prep.* 1. (*agente, causa, mezzo*) per, da, con, di || *a book* (*written*) — *Shakespeare*, un libro di Shakespeare; *to travel* — *train*, viaggiare col treno 2. (*tempo*) entro, per, durante || *day* — *day*, di giorno in giorno; — *night*, di notte 3. (*luogo*) vicino a, a fianco di, attraverso || *a house* — *the sea*, una casa sul mare. ♦ **by** *agg.* secondario.
bye-bye *inter.* arrivederci.
bygone *agg.* e *s.* passato.
by-line *s.* (*giorn.*) firma.
byname *s.* soprannome.
by-pass *s.* 1. circonvallazione 2. deviazione.
by-product *s.* sottoprodotto.
byroad *s.* strada secondaria.
byssus *s.* bisso.
bystander *s.* spettatore.
bystreet *s.* viuzza.
byway *s.* via traversa.
byword *s.* proverbio, epiteto.
bywork *s.* lavoro supplementare (*a tempo perso*).
Byzantine *agg.* e *s.* bizantino.

C

C (*mus.*) do.
cab *s.* vettura di piazza.
cabal *s.* intrigo, cospirazione.
cabbage *s.* cavolo.
cab(b)ala *s.* cabala.
cab(b)alistic *agg.* cabalistico.
cabin *s.* 1. capanna 2. (*aer.; fer.; mar.*) cabina.
cabinet *s.* 1. stanzino 2. stipo, armadietto 3. (*pol.*) gabinetto, consiglio dei ministri || — -*maker*, ebanista; — -*minister*, membro del gabinetto.
cable *s.* 1. cavo 2. cablogramma || — -*way*, teleferica.
to cable *vt.* e *vi.* 1. fornire di cavo 2. trasmettere un cablogramma.
cablegram *s.* cablogramma.
cabman *s.* tassista.
caboose (*mar.*) cambusa.
cabotage *s.* cabotaggio.
cacao *s.* cacao.
cacophony *s.* cacofonia.
cactus *s.* cactus.
cadaverous *agg.* 1. cadaverico 2. esangue.
cadence *s.* cadenza, ritmo.
cadet *s.* cadetto.
caducity *s.* caducità.
Caesarean *agg.* cesareo, imperiale || — *operation*, parto cesareo.
caesura *s.* cesura.
café *s.* caffè (*locale pubblico*).
caffeine *s.* caffeina.
cage *s.* 1. gabbia 2. impalcatura.
to cage *vt.* mettere in gabbia.
cake *s.* torta, focaccia.
calamary *s.* calamaro.
calamitous *agg.* calamitoso.
calamity *s.* calamità.
calcareous *agg.* calcareo.
calcification *s.* calcificazione.
to calcify *vt.* calcificare. ♦ to calcify *vi.* calcificarsi.
calcination *s.* calcinazione.
to calcine V. *to calcify.*
calcite *s.* calcite.
calcium *s.* calcio.
to calculate *vt.* 1. calcolare 2. contare. ♦ to calculate *vi.* fare affidamento.
calculated *agg.* 1. calcolato 2. premeditato 3. (*fig.*) idoneo.
calculating *agg.* calcolatore || — *machine*, macchina calcolatrice.
calculation *s.* calcolo.

calculator *s.* calcolatore, calcolatrice.
calendar *s.* calendario, almanacco.
calf[1] *s.* (*pl.* calves) vitello.
calf[2] *s.* polpaccio.
to calibrate *vt.* 1. calibrare 2. (*mecc.*) tarare.
calibration *s.* calibratura, taratura.
calibre *s.* calibro.
calico *s.* calicò.
call *s.* 1. richiamo, chiamata 2. breve visita: *to pay* (*v. irr.*) *so. a* —, fare una breve visita a qu. 3. (*giur.*) appello 4. (*mil.*) adunata 5. (*mar.*) scalo || — *bird*, uccello da richiamo; — *box*, cabina telefonica; — *up*, chiamata alle armi; *trunk* —, chiamata intercontinentale.
to call *vt.* e *vi.* 1. chiamare, richiamare: *to* — *aside*, chiamare in disparte; *to* — *to arms*, chiamare alle armi; *to* — *to mind*, richiamare alla mente 2. esortare, ordinare || *to* — *into being*, creare; *to* — *out*, chiamare ad alta voce, esclamare; *to* — *up*, telefonare; *to* — *at*, fare scalo a; *to* — *for*, passare a prendere; *to* — *on*, fare una breve visita a; *to* — *upon*, implorare, invocare.
caller *s.* visitatore, visitatrice.
calligrapher *s.* calligrafo.
calligraphic *agg.* calligrafico.
calling *s.* 1. appello 2. mestiere, professione 3. vocazione.
callosity *s.* 1. callosità 2. (*fig.*) insensibilità.
callous *agg.* 1. calloso 2. (*fig.*) insensibile.
calm *agg.* calmo. ♦ calm *s.* calma.
to calm *vt.* calmare. ♦ to calm *vi.* *to* — *down*, calmarsi (*di tempesta ecc.*).
calming *agg.* calmante.
calmly *avv.* con calma.
calmness *s.* calma, tranquillità.
calorific *agg.* calorifico.
calorimeter *s.* calorimetro.
calory *s.* caloria.
to calumniate *vt.* calunniare.
Calvary *s.* Calvario.
calves V. *calf.*
Calvinism *s.* calvinismo.
Calvinist *agg.* e *s.* calvinista.
came V. *to come.*
camel *s.* cammello.
camellia *s.* camelia.
cameo *s.* cammeo.
camera *s.* 1. (*foto*) macchina foto-

grafica **2.** (*giur.*) Camera di Consiglio.

camisole *s.* corpetto, farsetto.

camouflage *s.* **1.** mascheramento **2.** (*mil.*) mimetizzazione.

to camouflage *vt.* **1.** mascherare **2.** (*mil.*) mimetizzare.

camp *s.* **1.** (*mil.*) campo **2.** campeggio || — *-bed*, brandina.

to camp *vt.* (*mil.*) accampare. ◆ **to camp** *vi.* **1.** accamparsi **2.** attendarsi.

campaign *s.* (*mil.*) campagna.

camper *s.* campeggiatore.

camphor *s.* canfora.

camping *s.* **1.** (*mil.*) accampamento **2.** campeggio.

can[1] *s.* recipiente di latta, bidone.

can[2] *v. dif.* (*ind. cong. pres.*) **could** (*ind. cong. pass. e condiz.*) potere, essere in grado di.

Canadian *agg. e s.* canadese.

canal *s.* canale.

canalization *s.* canalizzazione.

to canalize *vt.* canalizzare.

canary *agg.* giallo canarino. ◆ **canary** *s.* canarino.

to cancel *vt.* annullare, cancellare.

cancellation *s.* annullamento, cancellatura.

cancer *s.* cancro.

candid *agg.* sincero, candido.

candidate *s.* candidato.

candidature *s.* candidatura.

candidly *avv.* sinceramente, candidamente.

candied *agg.* candito.

candle *s.* candela || — *-end*, moccolo; — *-holder*, candelabro; *by* — *-light*, a lume di candela.

candlestick *s.* candeliere.

candour *s.* candore, ingenuità.

candy *s.* candito.

to candy *vt.* candire. ◆ **to candy** *vi.* cristallizzarsi (*di zucchero*).

cane *s.* **1.** giunco, canna **2.** bastone da passeggio.

to cane *vt.* bastonare (*con una canna*).

canine *s.* dente canino.

caning *s.* bastonatura.

canned *agg.* conservato in scatola.

cannibal *s.* cannibale.

cannibalism *s.* cannibalismo.

cannon *s.* **1.** cannone **2.** carambola (*al biliardo*).

to cannon *vi.* **1.** cannoneggiare **2.** far carambola.

canoe *s.* canoa.

canon *s.* **1.** canone. **2.** (*eccl.*) canonico: — *law*, diritto canonico.

canonical *agg.* canonico.

to canonize *vt.* canonizzare.

canopy *s.* **1.** baldacchino **2.** volta (*del cielo*).

cant *s.* **1.** (*arch.*) angolo esterno **2.** inclinazione **3.** gergo.

canteen *s.* **1.** (*mil.*) dispensa **2.** mensa aziendale.

canvas *s.* **1.** canovaccio **2.** (*mar.*) velatura **3.** tela **4.** tendone.

canyon *s.* burrone.

cap *s.* **1.** berretto **2.** (*arch.*) capitello **3.** (*mecc.; elettr.*) cappuccio, capsula.

capability *s.* capacità, abilità.

capable *agg.* abile, capace.

capacitor *s.* condensatore.

capacity *s.* **1.** capacità **2.** (*elettr.*) potenza (*di motore*).

cape[1] *s.* capo, promontorio.

cape[2] *s.* cappa.

caper[1] *s.* cappero.

caper[2] *s.* piroetta, capriola.

to caper *vi.* far capriole.

capercaillie *s.* gallo cedrone.

capillarity *s.* capillarità.

capillary *agg.* capillare. ◆ **capillary** *s.* (*anat.*) vaso capillare.

capital[1] *agg. e s.* capitale.

capital[2] *s.* (*arch.*) capitello.

capitalism *s.* capitalismo.

capitalist *s.* capitalista.

capitalistic *agg.* capitalistico.

to capitalize *vt.* capitalizzare.

capitular *agg.* capitolare.

capitulary *s.* capitolare.

to capitulate *vi.* capitolare.

capitulation *s.* capitolazione.

capon *s.* cappone.

caprice *s.* capriccio.

to capsize *vt.* capovolgere. ◆ **to capsize** *vi.* capovolgersi.

capstan *s.* argano.

capsule *s.* capsula.

to capsule *vt.* incapsulare.

captain *s.* **1.** capitano **2.** (*comm.*) magnate.

captious *agg.* capzioso.

to captivate *vt.* cattivare, ammaliare.

captivating *agg.* cattivante, ammaliante.

captive *s.* prigioniero: *to take* —, far prigioniero.

captivity *s.* prigionia, cattività.

capture *s.* cattura.

to capture *vt.* far prigioniero, pren-

dere (*di città ecc.*).
Capuchin *s.* **1.** (*eccl.*) Cappuccino **2.** scimmia cappuccina.
car *s.* **1.** carro **2.** automobile **3.** (*ferr.*) vagone || — -*licence*, permesso di circolazione; *dining-* —, vagone ristorante; *sleeping-* —, vagone letto.
carabin *s.* carabina.
carabineer *s.* carabiniere.
to **caracole** *vi.* caracollare.
carafe *s.* caraffa.
caramel *s.* caramello.
carat *s.* carato.
caravan *s.* **1.** carovana **2.** carro (*di zingari ecc.*).
caravel *s.* caravella.
carbon *s.* carbonio || — *paper*, carta carbone.
carbonate *s.* carbonato.
carboniferous *agg.* carbonifero
to **carbonize** *vt.* carbonizzare.
carbuncle *s.* carbonchio.
carburation *s.* carburazione.
carburetter, carburettor *s.* carburatore.
carcase *s.* carcassa.
carcinogen *s.* sostanza cancerogena.
card *s.* **1.** cartoncino, biglietto **2.** carta da giuoco.
to **card** *vt.* schedare.
cardan *s.* cardano || — *joint*, giunto cardanico.
cardboard *s.* cartone.
cardiac *agg.* cardiaco.
cardigan *s.* giacca di lana.
cardinal *agg.* e *s.* cardinale.
cardiogram *s.* cardiogramma
cardiologist *s.* cardiologo.
cardiopathy *s.* cardiopatia.
care *s.* **1.** cura, attenzione, protezione: *take* —!, attenzione!; *to take* — *of*, aver cura **2.** preoccupazione || — -*free*, senza pensieri; — -*worn*, pieno di pensieri.
to **care** *vi.* curarsi, interessarsi.
career *s.* **1.** carriera **2.** andatura veloce.
careful *agg.* **1.** accurato **2.** prudente.
carefully *avv.* **1.** accuratamente **2.** attentamente.
careless *agg.* noncurante.
carelessly *avv.* negligentemente.
carelessness *s.* trascuratezza.
caress *s.* carezza.
to **caress** *vt.* accarezzare.
caressing *agg.* carezzevole.
caretaker *s.* guardiano, custode.
caricature *s.* caricatura.

Carmelite *s.* carmelitano.
carmine *agg.* e *s.* carminio.
carnage *s.* carneficina, strage.
carnal *agg.* carnale, sensuale.
carnation *agg.* carnicino. ♦ **carnation** *s.* garofano.
carnival *s.* carnevale.
carnivore *s.* carnivoro.
carnivorous *agg.* carnivoro.
carol *s.* canto, inno.
carotid *s.* carotide.
carousel *s.* carosello.
carp *s.* carpa.
carpenter *s.* carpentiere, falegname.
carpet *s.* tappeto || *bedside* —, scendiletto.
carriage *s.* **1.** carrozza, vettura **2.** (*comm.*) trasporto.
carrier *s.* **1.** portatore, spedizioniere **2.** (*mecc.*) trasportatore **3.** supporto.
carrion *s.* carogna.
carrot *s.* carota.
carry *s.* portata (*di arma da fuoco ecc.*).
to **carry** *vt.* e *vi.* **1.** portare (*un peso*), trasportare **2.** trasmettere (*suoni*) || *to* — *about*, portare addosso; *to* — *on*, continuare; *to* — *out*, eseguire, realizzare, compiere; *to* — *through*, portare a buon fine.
carrying *s.* trasporto.
cart *s.* carro.
cartel *s.* (*econ.; pol.*) cartello.
cartilage *s.* cartilagine.
cartography *s.* cartografia.
cartomancy *s.* cartomanzia.
carton *s.* scatola di cartone.
cartoon *s.* **1.** vignetta **2.** (*cine*) disegno animato.
cartridge *s.* **1.** cartuccia **2.** (*foto*) rotolo.
to **carve** *vt.* e *vi.* scolpire, incidere, cesellare.
carver *s.* intagliatore, scultore (*in legno e avorio*).
carving *s.* scultura, intaglio (*in legno e avorio*).
caryatid *s.* cariatide.
cascade *s.* piccola cascata (*d'acqua*).
case[1] *s.* **1.** caso, avvenimento **2.** (*giur.*) causa.
case[2] *s.* **1.** astuccio **2.** cassa, cassetta.
to **case** *vt.* imballare.
casement *s.* telaio di finestra (*a due battenti*), finestra.

cash s. cassa, contanti ‖ — *on delivery*, pagamento alla consegna; *by ready* —, in contanti.
to **cash** vt. incassare, riscuotere.
cashier s. cassiere.
to **cashier** vt. destituire.
casing s. involucro, copertura.
cask s. barile, botte.
casket s. scrigno.
cassation s. cassazione.
cassock s. tunica (*del clero anglicano*).
cast s. **1.** getto, lancio **2.** (*metal.*) gettata, stampo **3.** complesso (*di attori*) ‖ — -*iron*, ghisa.
to **cast** (cast, cast) vt. e vi. **1.** gettare, lanciare **2.** (*metal.*) fondere (*in stampo*) ‖ to — *aside*, gettare da parte; to — *down*, abbassare (*gli occhi*).
castanets s. *pl.* nacchere.
castaway agg. arenato, respinto. ♦
castaway s. naufrago, reprobo.
caste s. casta.
caster s. V. *castor*.
to **castigate** vt. castigare, punire.
casting s. **1.** il gettare **2.** (*metal.*) getto, colata **3.** distribuzione (*delle parti agli attori*).
castle s. castello.
castor s. **1.** pepaiuola, saliera **2.** rotella da mobili.
castor-oil s. olio di ricino.
to **castrate** vt. castrare.
casual agg. casuale, fortuito.
casually avv. per caso.
casualness s. irregolarità, noncuranza.
casualty s. **1.** infortunio **2.** infortunato.
casuistry s. casistica.
cat s. gatto.
cataclysm s. cataclisma.
catacomb s. catacomba.
catalepsy s. catalessi.
cataleptic agg. e s. catalettico.
catalogue s. catalogo.
to **catalogue** vt. e vi. catalogare.
catalyst s. catalizzatore.
cataplasm s. cataplasma.
catapult s. catapulta.
cataract s. cateratta.
catarrh s. catarro.
catastrophe s. catastrofe, calamità.
catastrophic(al) agg. catastrofico.
catch s. **1.** presa, cattura **2.** trappola ‖ — -*as*- — -*can*, lotta libera.
to **catch** (caught, caught) vt. **1.** afferrare, acchiappare, prendere: to

— *the train*, prendere il treno **2.** pescare, sorprendere.
catching agg. **1.** attraente **2.** orecchiabile (*di melodia*) **3.** (*med.*) contagioso.
catchy agg. **1.** attraente **2.** orecchiabile (*di melodia*) **3.** insidioso.
catechism s. catechismo.
to **catechize** vt. catechizzare.
catechumen s. catecumeno.
categoric(al) agg. categorico.
category s. categoria.
to **cater** vi. **1.** provvedere cibo **2.** procurare svaghi.
caterpillar s. **1.** bruco **2.** (*mecc.*) cingolo **3.** trattore a cingoli.
catharsis s. catarsi.
cathartic agg. catartico.
cathedral s. cattedrale.
Catherine-wheel s. girandola.
cathode s. catodo.
cathodic agg. catodico.
catholic agg. e s. cattolico.
Catholicism s. cattolicesimo.
cation s. catione.
cattish agg. felino.
cattle s. bestiame, armenti ‖ — -*dealer*, negoziante di bestiame; — -*lifter*, ladro di bestiame.
caught V. *to catch*.
cauldron s. caldaia.
cauliflower s. cavolfiore.
causal agg. causale.
causality s. causalità.
causative agg. causativo.
cause s. **1.** causa, ragione, motivo **2.** (*giur.*) processo, causa.
to **cause** vt. causare, cagionare.
causeway s. strada rialzata.
caustic agg. caustico (*anche fig.*).
caustically avv. causticamente (*anche fig.*).
causticity s. causticità (*anche fig.*).
cauterization s. cauterizzazione.
to **cauterize** vt. cauterizzare.
caution s. **1.** prudenza, cautela **2.** cauzione, garanzia ‖ — -*money*, cauzione, pegno.
to **caution** vt. mettere in guardia.
cautious agg. cauto, prudente.
cautiously avv. cautamente.
cavalier s. cavaliere.
cavalry s. cavalleria.
cave s. caverna, spelonca.
to **cave** vt. e vi. scavare ‖ to — *in*, sprofondare.
cavernous agg. cavernoso (*anche fig.*).
caviar(e) s. caviale.

cavil s. cavillo.
to **cavil** vi. cavillare.
cavity s. cavità.
cavy s. cavia.
cayman s. caimano.
to **cease** vt. e vi. cessare, finire.
cedar s. cedro.
cedilla s. cediglia.
ceiling s. soffitto.
to **celebrate** vt. e vi. celebráre, solennizzare.
celebrated agg. famoso.
celebration s. celebrazione.
celebrity s. celebrità, persona fa-
mosa.
celerity s. celerità.
celery s. sedano.
celestial agg. celestiale, paradisiaco.
celibacy s. celibato.
cell s. 1. cella 2. cellula.
cellar s. cantina.
cellarman s. cantiniere.
cellular agg. cellulare, alveolare.
cellulitis s. cellulite.
celluloid agg. e s. celluloide.
cellulose s. cellulosa.
Celt s. celta.
Celtic agg. celtico.
cement s. 1. cemento 2. stucco, mastice.
to **cement** vt. cementare (anche fig.).
cemetery s. cimitero.
to **cense** vt. incensare.
censer s. turibolo.
censor s. censore.
to **censor** vt. censurare.
censorial agg. censorio.
censorship s. censura, censorato.
censure s. censura.
to **censure** vt. censurare.
census s. censo.
cent s. centesimo (di dollaro).
centaur s. centauro.
centenarian agg. e s. centenario.
centenary agg. e s. centenario.
centennial agg. centennale.
centesimal agg. centesimale.
centigrade agg. centigrado.
centigramme s. centigrammo.
centilitre s. centilitro.
centimetre s. centimetro.
central agg. 1. centrale 2. fondamentale.
centralism s. accentramento.
centralization s. concentrazione (di
poteri).
to **centralize** vt. e vi. accentrare.
centre s. centro, parte centrale, interno.

centrifugal agg. centrifugo.
centripetal agg. centripeto.
centrism s. centrismo.
to **centuplicate** vt. centuplicare.
centurion s. centurione.
century s. 1. secolo 2. (stor.) centuria.
cephalalgia s. cefalea.
ceramics s. (arte della) ceramica.
cereal agg. e s. cereale.
cerebral agg. cerebrale.
cerebro-spinal agg. cerebro-spinale.
cerebrum s. cervello.
ceremonial agg. da cerimonia. ♦
ceremonial s. cerimoniale.
ceremonious agg. cerimonioso.
ceremony s. cerimonia ‖ to stand
on —, far complimenti.
certain agg. 1. certo, sicuro 2. indeterminato, certo.
certainly avv. certamente.
certainty s. certezza.
certificate s. certificato.
to **certify** vt. certificare, attestare.
certitude s. certezza.
cervical agg. cervicale. ♦ **cervical**
s. vertebra cervicale. ♦ **cervicals**
s. pl. nervi cervicali.
cessation s. cessazione.
cession s. cessione.
cess-pit, cess-pool s. pozzo nero.
cetacean agg. di cetaceo. ♦ **cetacean** s. cetaceo.
to **chafe** vt. 1. riscaldare 2. irritare.
to **chafe** vi. 1. strofinarsi 2. irritarsi.
chaff s. 1. pula, paglia trinciata 2.
(fig.) oggetto di nessun valore.
chaffer s. contrattazione, baratto.
chain s. 1. catena 2. serie, concatenamento.
to **chain** vt. 1. incatenare 2. (fig.)
mettere in ceppi.
chain-stores s. pl. catene (di negozi o grandi magazzini).
chair s. 1. sedia: deck- —, sedia a
sdraio; easy- —, poltrona 2. cattedra (universitaria).
chairman s. presidente (di consiglio, assemblea ecc.).
chalice s. calice.
chalk s. 1. gesso 2. (min.) calcare
‖ — -drawing, disegno a pastello;
— -stone (pat.), calcolo.
chalky agg. gessoso.
challenge s. 1. sfida 2. (mil.) intimazione.
to **challenge** vt. 1. sfidare 2. (mil.)
intimare.

challenger s. sfidatore, sfidante.
chamber s. 1. sala, aula 2. (pol.; comm.) camera || — -music, musica da camera; —maid, cameriera (specialmente d'albergo).
chamberlain s. 1. ciambellano 2. tesoriere.
chameleon s. camaleonte.
chamois s. camoscio.
champion s. 1. campione 2. difensore.
championship s. campionato.
chance s. 1. avvenimento fortuito, caso 2. occasione.
to chance vi. accadere.
chancellery s. cancelleria.
chancellor s. cancelliere.
chancery s. cancelleria.
chandelier s. candeliere, lampadario.
change s. 1. cambio, mutamento || — for a —, tanto per cambiare 2. moneta spicciola.
to change vt. e vi. cambiare.
changeability s. mutabilità.
changeable agg. 1. mutabile 2. incostante (di tempo).
changing agg. cangiante, mutevole.
♦ **changing** s. cambio.
channel s. 1. canale, stretto. ♦ **channels** s. pl. vie di comunicazione.
chant s. canto, cantilena.
to channel vt. 1. fare canali 2. incanalare.
chaos s. caos.
chap¹ s. (fam.) individuo, ragazzo.
chap² s. screpolatura.
chapel s. cappella.
chaplain s. cappellano.
chaplet s. ghirlanda, corona (di fiori).
chapter s. capitolo.
to char vt. carbonizzare. ♦ **to char** vi. carbonizzarsi.
character s. 1. carattere, indole 2. scrittura 3. (lett.) personaggio.
characteristic agg. caratteristico. ♦ **characteristic** s. caratteristica.
characterization s. caratterizzazione.
to characterize vt. caratterizzare.
charade s. sciarada.
charcoal s. carbone di legna.
charge s. 1. prezzo richiesto, spesa 2. incarico, sorveglianza 3. (giur.) accusa.
to charge vt. 1. far pagare, addebitare 2. incaricare 3. accusare: to

— so. with a crime, accusare qu. di un delitto.
chargeable agg. 1. a carico di, da addebitarsi a 2. accusabile.
chariot s. cocchio.
charitable agg. caritatevole.
charitably avv. caritatevolmente.
charity s. 1. carità, benevolenza 2. istituzione benefica.
charlatan s. ciarlatano.
charm s. 1. fascino 2. incantesimo, malia.
to charm vt. 1. affascinare 2. sottoporre a magia.
charming agg. affascinante.
charmingly avv. in modo affascinante.
charnel(-house) s. ossario.
chart s. 1. grafico 2. carta marina.
charter s. 1. licenza, brevetto 2. carta costituzionale.
chartography s. cartografia.
charwoman s. domestica ad ore.
charwork s. lavoro di domestica ad ore.
chase s. 1. inseguimento, caccia 2. riserva di caccia, cacciagione.
to chase¹ vt. inseguire, cacciare.
to chase² vt. cesellare.
chaser¹ s. cacciatore, inseguitore.
chaser² s. cesellatore.
chasing s. 1. cesellatura 2. filettatura (di una vite).
chasm s. baratro, abisso.
chaste agg. casto, puro.
chastely avv. castamente, virtuosamente.
chastity s. castità.
chat s. chiacchiera.
to chat vi. chiacchierare.
chatter s. 1. chiacchiera, chiacchierio 2. il battere dei denti.
to chatter vi. 1. chiacchierare 2. battere i denti.
chatterbox s. chiacchierone, chiacchierona.
chattering s. 1. chiacchierio 2. il battere dei denti.
chauvinism s. sciovinismo.
chauvinist s. sciovinista.
cheap agg. e avv. a buon mercato.
cheaply avv. economicamente, in modo poco costoso.
cheat s. 1. frode 2. imbroglione.
to cheat vt. e vi. imbrogliare.
cheater s. truffatore, baro.
cheating s. inganno.
check¹ s. 1. scacco 2. controllo, verifica 3. scontrino, contromarca.

check² s. disegno a scacchi.
to check vi. dare scacco. ♦ to check vt. controllare, verificare.
checked agg. quadrettato.
checkmate s. scacco matto.
to checkmate vt. dare scacco matto.
cheek s. guancia.
cheekily avv. sfacciatamente.
cheeky agg. sfacciato.
to cheer vt. rallegrare, incoraggiare. ♦ to cheer vi. essere di buon umore, rallegrarsi.
cheerful agg. di buon umore.
cheerfully avv. allegramente.
cheerfulness s. buon umore.
cheering agg. incoraggiante. ♦ cheering s. acclamazioni (pl.).
cheese s. formaggio.
cheetah s. ghepardo.
chemical agg. chimico.
chemically avv. chimicamente.
chemicals s. pl. prodotti chimici.
chemisette s. camicetta.
chemist s. 1. chimico 2. farmacista.
chemistry s. chimica.
cheque s. assegno: to cash a —, cambiare un assegno; — -book, libretto d'assegni; blank —, assegno in bianco; crossed —, assegno sbarrato.
to cherish vt. 1. (fig.) nutrire 2. curare teneramente, coccolare.
cherry s. ciliegia.
cherub s. cherubino.
chess s. giuoco degli scacchi || — -board, scacchiera; — -men, pezzi degli scacchi.
chest s. 1. cassetta, cassone 2. torace.
chestnut agg. castano. ♦ chestnut s. 1. castagno 2. castagna.
to chew vt. e vi. masticare.
chicanery s. cavillo (legale).
chick s. 1. pulcino 2. (fig.) bambino.
chicken s. gallinella, pollo.
chicory s. cicoria.
to chide (chid, chid) (anche reg.) vt. e vi. redarguire, sgridare.
chief agg. principale. ♦ chief s. capo, comandante.
chiefly avv. principalmente.
chieftain s. capo (di tribù, clan ecc.).
chilblain s. gelone.
child s. (pl. children) 1. bambino, bambina 2. figlio, figlia.
childhood s. infanzia.
childish agg. infantile.

childishness s. fanciullaggine, puerilità.
childless agg. senza figli.
childlike agg. infantile.
children V. child.
Chilean agg. e s. cileno.
chill s. 1. colpo di freddo 2. (metal.) conchiglia.
to chill vt. 1. raffreddare, agghiacciare (anche fig.) 2. (metal.) fondere in conchiglia. ♦ to chill vi. raffreddarsi.
chilled agg. 1. congelato 2. (metal.) fuso in conchiglia.
chilliness s. 1. freddo 2. (fig.) freddezza.
chilly agg. 1. freddoloso (di persona) 2. fresco (di tempo).
chime s. scampanio.
to chime vt. e vi. scampanare, suonare a festa.
chiming s. lo scampanare.
chimney s. camino, comignolo || — -sweeper, spazzacamino.
chimpanzee s. scimpanzè.
chin s. mento || — -strap, sottogola.
china s. 1. porcellana fine 2. (fam.) stoviglie di porcellana.
chinchilla s. cincillà.
chine s. spina dorsale.
Chinese agg. e s. cinese.
chink s. fessura, crepa.
chip s. 1. scheggia 2. (cuc.) patatina fritta.
to chip vt. 1. scheggiare 2. rompere. ♦ to chip vi. scheggiarsi, frantumarsi.
chiromancer s. chiromante.
chiromancy s. chiromanzia.
chiropodist s. pedicure.
chirp s. 1. cinguettio, pigolio 2. stridio, il frinire (di cicale ecc.).
to chirp vi. 1. cinguettare, pigolare 2. frinire, stridere (di cicale ecc.).
chisel s. cesello.
to chisel vt. cesellare.
chiseller s. cesellatore.
chitterlings s. pl. trippa.
chivalrous agg. cavalleresco.
chivalry s. 1. cavalleria 2. condotta cavalleresca.
chloride s. cloruro.
chlorine s. cloro.
chlorite s. clorito.
chloroform s. cloroformio.
chlorophyl(l) s. clorofilla.
chock s. 1. cuneo, bietta 2. (mar.) passacavi.
chocolate agg. 1. di cioccolato 2.

color cioccolata. ♦ **chocolate** s. cioccolato: *cake of* —, tavoletta di cioccolato.

choice agg. di prima qualità, scelto. ♦ **choice** s. **1.** scelta **2.** la cosa scelta **3.** assortimento.

choir s. coro.

choke s. **1.** soffocamento **2.** strozzatura (*di tubo*).

to **choke** vt. **1.** soffocare (anche *fig.*) **2.** ingorgare. ♦ to **choke** v⁻. ostruirsi.

choker s. soffocatore.

cholera s. colera.

cholesterol s. colesterolo.

to **choose** (chose, chosen) vt. scegliere.

chooser s. chi sceglie.

chop s. **1.** (*cuc.*) braciola **2.** colpo (*di scure ecc.*).

to **chop** vt. e vi. **1.** fendere, tagliare **2.** (*cuc.*) tritare ‖ to — *down*, abbattere (*alberi*); to — *off*, tagliar via.

chopper s. **1.** ascia **2.** chi taglia con l'ascia **3.** tagliatrice.

choppy agg. **1.** screpolato **2.** increspato (*del mare*).

choral agg. corale.

chord s. **1.** (*mus.; anat.; geom.*) corda **2.** (*mus.*) accordo.

choreographer s. coreografo.

choreographic agg. coreografico.

choreography s. coreografia.

chorus s. coro ‖ — *-singer*, corista.

chose V. *to choose.*

chosen V. *to choose.*

chrism s. crisma.

to **christen** vt. battezzare.

Christendom s. cristianità.

christening s. battesimo.

Christian agg. e s. cristiano ‖ — *name*, nome di battesimo.

Christianity s. cristianesimo.

to **christianize** vt. convertire al cristianesimo.

Christmas s. Natale.

chromatic agg. cromatico.

chromatically avv. cromaticamente.

chromatism s. cromatismo.

chromatography s. cromatografia.

chrome s. cromo.

to **chrome** vt. cromare.

chromium s. cromo ‖ — *-plated*, cromato; — *-plating*, cromatura.

chromolithograph s. cromolitografia.

chromosome s. cromosoma.

chromosphere s. cromosfera.

chronic agg. cronico (anche *fig.*).

chronicle s. cronaca.

chronicler s. cronista.

chronologic(al) agg. cronologico.

chronologically avv. cronologicamente.

chronology s. cronologia.

chronometer s. cronometro.

chrysalid s. crisalide.

chrysanthemum s. crisantemo.

chubby agg. paffuto.

church s. **1.** chiesa **2.** comunità religiosa ‖ — *-going*, assiduità ai servizi religiosi; — *-living*, beneficio ecclesiastico; — *-service*, funzione religiosa.

churchman s. **1.** ecclesiastico **2.** membro della chiesa anglicana.

churchy agg. bigotto.

churchyard s. cimitero.

chyle s. (*fisiol.*) chilo.

ciborium s. ciborio.

cicada s. cicala.

to **cicatrize** vt. cicatrizzare. ♦ to **cicatrize** vi. cicatrizzarsi.

cider s. sidro.

cigar s. sigaro ‖ — *-case*, portasigari, — *-end*, mozzicone; — *-holder*, bocchino per sigari.

cigarette s. sigaretta ‖ — *-case*, portasigarette, — *-end*, mozzicone, — *-holder*, bocchino; — *paper*, cartina per sigaretta.

cilice s. cilicio.

cinder s. **1.** brace **2.** scoria.

cine-camera s. macchina da presa.

cinema s. cinematografo.

cinematograph s. **1.** proiettore cinematografico **2.** macchina da presa.

cinematographer s. **1.** operatore cinematografico **2.** cineasta.

cinematographic agg. cinematografico.

cinematography s. cinematografia.

cine-projector s. proiettore cinematografico.

cinerary agg. cinerario.

cinnabar s. cinabro.

cinnamon s. cannella.

cipher s. **1.** cifrario **2.** monogramma **3.** (*mat.; anche fig.*) zero, nullità.

to **cipher** vt. e vi. cifrare.

circle s. **1.** cerchio, circolo (anche *fig.*) **2.** orbita (*dei pianeti*) **3.** galleria (*di teatro*).

circlet s. cerchietto.

circuit s. **1.** cinta, circonvallazione **2.** rivoluzione, rotazione (*di astri*) **3.** (*elettr.; sport*) circuito.

circular *agg.* circolare. ✦ **circular** s. lettera circolare.

to **circulate** *vt.* mettere in circolazione, diffondere. ✦ to **circulate** *vi.* circolare.

circulating *agg.* circolante.

circulation s. **1.** circolazione **2.** diffusione **3.** (*giorn.*) tiratura.

circulatory *agg.* circolatorio.

to **circumcise** *vt.* circoncidere.

circumcision s. circoncisione.

circumference s. circonferenza.

circumflex *agg.* circonflesso.

circumlocution s. circonlocuzione.

to **circumnavigate** *vt.* circumnavigare.

circumnavigation s. circumnavigazione.

circumnavigator s. circumnavigatore.

to **circumscribe** *vt.* circoscrivere.

circumscription s. circoscrizione.

circumspect *agg.* circospetto.

circumspection s. circospezione.

circumstance s. circostanza.

circumstantial *agg.* **1.** circostanziale **2.** circostanziato.

circumstantiality s. abbondanza di particolari.

circumstantially *avv.* circostanziatamente.

to **circumvent** *vt.* circuire.

circumvention s. raggiro.

circumvolution s. circonvoluzione.

circus s. **1.** circo, arena **2.** piazza rotonda.

cirrhosis s. cirrosi.

cisalpine *agg.* cisalpino.

cistern s. cisterna.

citadel s. cittadella.

to **cite** *vt.* citare.

citizen s. cittadino.

citizenhood s. cittadinanza.

citizenship s. diritto di cittadinanza.

citrate s. citrato.

citric *agg.* citrico.

citron s. cedro.

city s. **1.** città (*grande*) **2.** centro di grande traffico di una città.

civic *agg.* civico.

civil *agg.* civile, cortese.

civilian *agg.* e s. civile, borghese.

civility s. civiltà, cortesia.

civilization s. civilizzazione, civiltà.

to **civilize** *vt.* civilizzare.

civilly *avv.* civilmente.

civism s. civismo.

claim s. **1.** richiesta **2.** (*giur.*) rivendicazione **3.** (*comm.*) reclamo.

to **claim** *vt.* **1.** esigere, chiedere **2.** (*giur.*) rivendicare **3.** (*comm.*) reclamare.

claimant s. **1.** rivendicatore **2.** richiedente.

clairvoyance s. chiaroveggenza.

clairvoyant *agg.* e s. chiaroveggente.

to **clamber** *vi.* arrampicarsi.

clammy *agg.* vischioso.

clamour s. clamore, vocio.

to **clamour** *vt.* e *vi.* vociferare.

clan s. gruppo familiare, tribù.

clandestine *agg.* clandestino.

to **clang** *vi.* emettere un suono, un grido. ✦ to **clang** *vt.* far risonare.

clangour s. fragore.

to **clank** *vi.* tintinnare. ✦ to **clank** *vt.* far tintinnare.

clap s. **1.** applauso **2.** rumore improvviso **3.** piccolo colpo (*con la mano*).

to **clap** *vt.* e *vi.* **1.** applaudire **2.** dare un colpo (*con la mano*) **3.** battere (*le ali*).

clapper s. **1.** battente (*di porta*) **2.** (*teat.*) membro della « claque ».

claret s. **1.** color rosso-violetto **2.** vino chiaretto.

clarification s. chiarificazione.

to **clarify** *vt.* chiarificare. ✦ to **clarify** *vi.* chiarificarsi.

clarinet s. clarinetto.

clarity s. chiarità.

clash s. **1.** cozzo, urto **2.** scontro (*d'opinioni*).

to **clash** *vt.* e *vi.* **1.** cozzare, far strepito **2.** scontrarsi (*d'opinioni*).

clasp s. fermaglio, fibbia.

to **clasp** *vt.* afferrare.

class s. **1.** classe, categoria **2.** (*scol.*) classe **3.** (*fig.*) distinzione.

classic *agg.* e s. classico.

classical *agg.* classico.

classically *avv.* classicamente.

classicism s. classicismo.

classification s. classificazione.

to **classify** *vt.* classificare.

classmate s. compagno di classe.

classroom s. aula.

classy *agg.* (*fam.*) di classe.

clatter s. fracasso.

to **clatter** *vi.* far fracasso.

clause s. clausola.

claustrophobia s. claustrofobia.

claw s. **1.** artiglio, zampa con artigli **2.** uncino **3.** chela.
to claw vt. artigliare.
clawed agg. munito di artigli.
clay s. argilla: fire- —, argilla refrattaria || — pigeon, piattello.
clayey agg. argilloso.
clean agg. **1.** pulito **2.** netto, nitido **3.** (fig.) puro, schietto.
to clean vt. pulire.
cleaner s. pulitore, pulitrice || dry- —, smacchiatore a secco.
cleaning s. pulitura.
cleanliness s. pulizia.
cleanly agg. pulito. ♦ **cleanly** avv. in modo pulito.
cleanness s. **1.** pulizia (anche fig.) **2.** nitidezza.
to cleanse vt. **1.** pulire **2.** purificare.
cleanser s. **1.** pulitore **2.** detersivo.
cleansing agg. purificante. ♦ **cleansing** s. **1.** purificazione **2.** depurazione.
clear agg. **1.** chiaro, limpido **2.** distinto, evidente || — -cut, nettamente stagliato; — -sighted, dalla vista buona.
to clear vt. **1.** chiarire, schiarire **2.** discolpare **3.** (comm.) svincolare || to — away, sparecchiare, dissiparsi (di nebbia); to — up, rassettare (una stanza), chiarire (un malinteso). ♦ **to clear** vi. schiarirsi.
clearance s. **1.** chiarificazione **2.** sgombero **3.** (comm.) sdoganamento.
clearing s. **1.** chiarimento **2.** rimozione.
clearly avv. chiaramente.
clearness s. **1.** chiarezza **2.** (fig.) limpidezza.
cleavage s. **1.** spaccatura **2.** (min.) clivaggio.
to cleave (cleft, cleft) vt. e vi. fendere, spaccare.
cleft s. fenditura.
clemency s. clemenza.
clement agg. **1.** clemente **2.** dolce, gentile (di carattere) **3.** mite (di tempo).
to clench vt. **1.** stringere (mani, denti ecc.) **2.** ribadire.
clergy s. clero.
clergyman s. ecclesiastico.
clerical agg. **1.** clericale **2.** impiegatizio.
clericalism s. clericalismo.
clerk s. impiegato || chief —, ca-
poufficio.
to clerk vi. lavorare come impiegato.
clever agg. intelligente, abile, ingegnoso.
cleverly avv. intelligentemente.
cleverness s. intelligenza, abilità, ingegnosità.
clew s. gomitolo (di filo).
click s. scatto, rumore secco.
client s. cliente.
cliff s. scogliera.
climate s. clima.
climatic agg. climatico.
climax s. apice, culmine.
climb s. **1.** rampa **2.** ascesa.
to climb vt. e vi. **1.** arrampicarsi **2.** scalare (anche fig.).
climber s. **1.** scalatore **2.** (fig.) arrivista **3.** pianta rampicante.
climbing s. **1.** scalata **2.** (fig.) arrivismo. ♦ **climbing** agg. rampicante.
to cling (clung, clung) vi. attaccarsi, aggrapparsi (anche fig.): to — to a hope, aggrapparsi ad una speranza.
clinical agg. clinico.
clinician s. clinico.
clinking s. tintinnio.
clip s. **1.** fermaglio, molletta || hair —, forcina per capelli **2.** graffa (per ferite) **3.** tosatura (di pecore).
to clip vt. **1.** tenere insieme (con un fermaglio) **2.** tosare (pecore ecc.).
clipper s. **1.** tosatore **2.** (mar.) "clipper". ♦ **clippers** s. pl. **1.** forbici **2.** macchinetta per tosare (sing.).
cloak s. **1.** mantello **2.** (fig.) manto, velo.
clock s. orologio (da muro, da tavolo) || alarm- —, sveglia.
clockwise agg. in senso orario || counter- —, in senso antiorario.
clockwork s. meccanismo a orologeria.
clod s. zolla.
clog s. **1.** impedimento, intoppo **2.** zoccolo.
to clog vt. ostruire, impedire (anche fig.). ♦ **to clog** vi. incepparsi.
cloister s. chiostro.
close agg. **1.** chiuso **2.** serrato: — combat, combattimento corpo a corpo **3.** afoso, viziato (di aria) **4.** intimo: — friend, amico intimo **5.** accurato, attento || — -fitting, aderente (di vestiti); —

-mouthed, riservato; — *-shaven*, rasato con cura.
close *s.* **1.** spazio cintato **2.** fine, termine **3.** corpo a corpo.
close *avv.* vicino, presso.
to close *vt.* chiudere ‖ *to* —· *up*, turare, sbarrare (*di strada*). ♦ **to close** *vi.* chiudersi ‖ *to* — *in*, avvicinarsi, accorciarsi (*di giorni*); *to* — *with*, venire a un accordo.
closed *agg.* chiuso.
closely *avv.* **1.** da vicino **2.** attentamente.
closeness *s.* **1.** afa, mancanza d'aria **2.** compattezza **3.** intimità **4.** vicinanza **5.** accuratezza.
closet *s.* **1.** studio, salotto privato **2.** armadio a muro **3.** gabinetto.
close-up *s.* (*cine*) primo piano.
closing *s.* chiusura (*di negozi, teatri ecc.*).
clot *s.* grumo.
to clot *vt.* raggrumare, coagulare. ♦ **to clot** *vi.* raggrumarsi, coagularsi.
cloth *s.* tessuto, stoffa, tela ‖ (*table-*) —, tovaglia.
to clothe *vt.* vestire.
clothes *s. pl.* abiti, indumenti ‖ — *-hook*, attaccapanni; — *-line*, corda (*per stendere il bucato*); — *-peg*, molletta (*fermabucato*).
clothing *s.* **1.** vestiario **2.** copertura.
cloud *s.* **1.** nuvola, nube **2.** nugolo (*di insetti*).
to cloud *vt.* e *vi.* annuvolare, oscurare ‖ *to* — (*up, over*), annuvolarsi.
clouded *agg.* **1.** coperto (*di nubi*) **2.** torbido (*di liquidi*).
cloudily *avv.* nebulosamente.
cloudy *agg.* **1.** nuvoloso **2.** torbido.
clover *s.* trifoglio.
clown *s.* pagliaccio.
clownish *agg.* pagliaccesco.
club *s.* **1.** mazza, randello **2.** circolo, associazione **3.** (*carte*) fiori.
clue *s.* **1.** indizio, traccia **2.** filo di un racconto.
clumsily *avv.* goffamente.
clumsiness *s.* goffaggine.
clumsy *agg.* goffo, senza grazia.
clung V. *to cling.*
cluster *s.* **1.** grappolo (*d'uva*), mazzo (*di fiori*), gruppo **2.** folla, capannello (*di gente*) **3.** sciame.
clutch *s.* **1.** stretta, grinfia **2.** (*auto*) frizione.

to clutch *vt.* e *vi.* afferrare, afferrarsi, agguantare.
coach *s.* **1.** carrozza, cocchio **2.** pullman **3.** carrozza ferroviaria **4.** (*sport*) allenatore, istruttore ‖ — *-house*, rimessa; *mourning-* —, carro funebre; *stage-* —, diligenza.
coachman *s.* cocchiere.
coachwork *s.* carrozzeria.
coadjutor *s.* coadiutore.
coagulant *s.* sostanza coagulante.
to coagulate *vt.* coagulare. ♦ **to coagulate** *vi.* coagularsi.
coagulation *s.* coagulazione.
coagulator *s.* coagulante.
coal *s.* carbone: — *-bed*, bacino carbonifero; — *-black*, nero come il carbone; — *-fed*, alimentato a carbone; — *-mine*, miniera di carbone.
to coalesce *vi.* **1.** coalizzarsi, unirsi **2.** fondersi.
coalition *s.* coalizione.
coarse *agg.* **1.** grossolano, rozzo **2.** ruvido, grosso (*di materiale*).
coarsely *avv.* grossolanamente.
coarseness *s.* **1.** grossolanità **2.** ruvidezza (*di stoffe ecc.*).
coast *s.* costa ‖ — *-guard*, polizia costiera.
coastal *agg.* costiero.
coaster *s.* **1.** nave cabotiera **2.** sottobicchiere.
coat *s.* **1.** giacca, soprabito **2.** manto (*anche fig.*), pelliccia (*di animale*) **3.** rivestimento, intonaco ‖ — *of arms*, stemma.
to coat *vt.* rivestire, coprire.
coating *s.* rivestimento, mano di vernice.
to coax *vt.* blandire, circuire. ♦ **to coax** *vi.* far moine.
coaxial *agg.* coassiale.
cobalt *s.* cobalto.
cobble *s.* ciottolo.
to cobble *vt.* **1.** pavimentare (*con ciottoli*) **2.** rappezzare (*scarpe*).
cobbler *s.* ciabattino.
cobra *s.* cobra.
cobweb *s.* ragnatela.
cocaine *s.* cocaina.
coccyx *s.* (*pl.* *-cyges*) coccige.
cock *s.* **1.** gallo **2.** cane di fucile.
cockade *s.* coccarda.
cockatoo *s.* cacatoa.
cockboat *s.* (*mar.*) lancia.
cockerel *s.* galletto.
cock-eyed *agg.* strabico.
cockish *agg.* sfrontato.

cockney *agg.* e *s.* dialetto londinese.

cockpit *s.* **1.** arena (*per combattimento di galli*) **2.** (*mar.*) castello di poppa.

cockroach *s.* scarafaggio.

cockscomb *s.* **1.** cresta (*di gallo*) **2.** (*fig.*) zerbinotto.

cocktail *s.* **1.** cavallo con coda mozzata **2.** cocktail.

cocoa *s.* cacao.

coconut *s.* noce di cocco.

cocoon *s.* bozzolo.

cod *s.* merluzzo.

code *s.* codice.

to code *vt.* **1.** codificare **2.** cifrare (*un dispaccio*).

codeine *s.* codeina.

codex *s.* codice, manoscritto antico.

codfish *s.* merluzzo.

codicil *s.* codicillo.

codification *s.* codificazione.

to codify *vt.* codificare.

co-director *s.* condirettore.

co-education *s.* istruzione nella scuola mista.

co-educational *agg.* (*scol.*) misto.

coefficient *agg.* e *s.* coefficiente.

coenobium *s.* cenobio.

coercible *agg.* coercibile.

coercion *s.* coercizione.

coercive *agg.* coercitivo.

coeval *agg.* e *s.* coevo.

to coexist *vi.* coesistere.

coexistence *s.* coesistenza.

coffee *s.* caffè: — *-bean*, chicco di caffè; — *-grounds*, fondi di caffè || — *-house*, caffè, bar; — *-mill*, macinino; — *-pot*, caffettiera.

coffer *s.* cassa, cofano.

coffin *s.* bara.

cog *s.* dente (*di ruota*).

cognate *agg.* e *s.* consanguineo, congiunto.

cognition *s.* cognizione.

cognitive *agg.* avente conoscenza.

cognizable *agg.* **1.** conoscibile **2.** (*giur.*) entro la giurisdizione di una corte.

to cohabit *vi.* coabitare.

cohabitation *s.* coabitazione.

coheir *s.* coerede.

coheiress *s.* (*donna*) coerede.

coherence *s.* **1.** coerenza **2.** aderenza.

coherent *agg.* **1.** coerente **2.** aderente.

coherently *avv.* coerentemente.

cohesion *s.* coesione.

cohesive *agg.* coesivo.

cohort *s.* coorte.

coil *s.* **1.** rotolo, spira **2.** (*elettr.; mecc.*) bobina.

coin *s.* moneta (*di metallo*).

to coin *vt.* coniare (*anche fig.*).

coinage *s.* conio.

to coincide *vi.* coincidere.

coincidence *s.* coincidenza.

coiner *s.* falsario.

colander *s.* colino.

cold *agg.* **1.** freddo: *to be* —, aver freddo **2.** freddo (*di carattere*), apatico: *in — blood*, a sangue freddo. ◆ **cold** *s.* **1.** freddo **2.** raffreddore: *to catch a* —, prendere il raffreddore.

coldness *s.* freddezza (*anche fig.*).

Coleoptera *s. pl.* coleotteri.

colic *s.* colica.

colitis *s.* colite.

to collaborate *vi.* collaborare.

collaboration *s.* collaborazione.

collaborationist *s.* collaborazionista.

collaborator *s.* collaboratore.

collapse *s.* **1.** crollo (*anche fig.*) **2.** collasso.

to collapse *vi.* crollare (*anche fig.*).

collar *s.* **1.** colletto **2.** collare.

to collate *vt.* **1.** collezionare, confrontare **2.** riordinare (*pagine di un'opera*).

collateral *agg.* collaterale.

colleague *s.* collega.

to collect *vt.* **1.** riunire **2.** incassare, riscuotere **3.** fare una raccolta. ◆ **to collect** *vi.* **1.** riunirsi **2.** riscuotere.

collecting *s.* il raccogliere: *stamp* —, il raccogliere francobolli.

collection *s.* **1.** raccolta, collezione **2.** riunione di persone **3.** questua, colletta.

collective *agg.* collettivo || — *title* (*tip.*), titolo generale.

collectivism *s.* collettivismo.

collectivity *s.* collettività.

collectivization *s.* collettivizzazione.

to collectivize *vt.* collettivizzare.

collector *s.* **1.** collezionista **2.** esattore.

college *s.* **1.** collegio **2.** scuola secondaria (*con internato*).

collegial *agg.* collegiale.

collier *s.* minatore.

colliery *s.* miniera di carbone.

collimator *s.* collimatore.

collision s. **1.** collisione **2.** urto, conflitto (d'interessi).

collocation s. collocazione.

colloidal agg. colloidale.

colloquial agg. d'uso corrente, familiare.

colloquialism s. espressione familiare.

colloquially avv. nella lingua parlata.

colloquy s. colloquio.

collusion s. collusione.

colon s. (gramm.) due punti.

colonel s. colonnello.

colonial agg. coloniale.

colonialism s. sistema coloniale.

colonialist s. colonialista.

colonist s. **1.** colono **2.** colonizzatore.

colonization s. colonizzazione.

to **colonize** vt. colonizzare. ◆ to **colonize** vi. stabilirsi in colonia.

colonizer s. colonizzatore.

colonnade s. colonnato.

colony s. colonia.

colossal agg. colossale.

colossus s. colosso.

colour s. **1.** colore **2.** colorito || — -bearer, portabandiera; — -blind, daltonico; — -print, stampa a colori. ◆ **colours** s. pl. bandiera (sing.) || with the —, sotto le armi.

to **colour** vt. colorare, tingere. ◆ to **colour** vi. colorirsi, prender colore.

colourable agg. verosimile.

colouration s. colorazione.

coloured agg. colorato, colorito (anche fig.).

colourful agg. colorito, pittoresco.

colouring s. **1.** colorante **2.** coloramento.

colourless agg. incolore.

colt s. **1.** puledro **2.** (fig.) novellino.

columbarium s. (pl. -ria) colombario.

column s. colonna (anche fig.).

columnist s. giornalista (che cura una rubrica).

coma s. coma.

comatose agg. comatoso.

comb s. **1.** pettine **2.** cresta (gallo, onde ecc.).

to **comb** vt. pettinare. ◆ to **comb** vi. frangersi (di onde) || to — one's hair, pettinarsi.

combat s. combattimento, lotta.

combination s. **1.** combinazione **2.** associazione.

to **combine** vt. **1.** unire **2.** (chim.) combinare **3.** contribuire. ◆ to **combine** vi. **1.** unirsi **2.** combinarsi.

combing s. pettinata.

comb-out s. rastrellamento.

combustible agg. e s. combustibile.

combustion s. combustione.

to **come** (came, come) vi. venire, arrivare, giungere, provenire || to — about, accadere; to — across, incontrare per caso; to — along (fam.), capitare; to — back, ritornare; to — down, scendere; to — in, entrare, salire (di marea); to — on, avanzare, sopraggiungere (di malattie, stagioni ecc.), entrare in scena (di attori); to — through, superare; to — under, essere soggetti, essere catalogati; to — upon, trovare per caso.

comedian s. autore, attore di commedie.

comedy s. commedia.

comeliness s. avvenenza.

comely agg. avvenente.

comer s. chi viene.

comet s. cometa.

comfit s. confetto.

comfort s. **1.** conforto **2.** comodità.

to **comfort** vt. **1.** confortare **2.** ristorare.

comfortable agg. comodo, confortevole || to be —, sentirsi a proprio agio.

comfortably avv. comodamente.

comforting agg. confortante.

comic agg. comico, buffo. ◆ **comic** s. **1.** attore comico **2.** il ridicolo, il comico. ◆ **comics** s. pl. (fam.) fumetti.

comical agg. comico, buffo.

comicality s. comicità.

coming agg. prossimo, futuro. ◆ **coming** s. **1.** venuta, arrivo || — away, partenza; — back, ritorno; — down, discesa, calo (dei prezzi).

comity s. cortesia, gentilezza.

comma s. virgola || inverted commas, virgolette.

command s. **1.** comando, ordine **2.** padronanza.

to **command** vt. e vi. **1.** comandare **2.** dominare (anche fig.).

commandant s. comandante.

commander s. comandante.

commandership s. funzioni di comandante.

commandment s. comandamento.

to **commemorate** vt. commemorare.

commemoration s. commemorazione.

commemorative agg. commemorativo.

to **commend** vt. lodare, encomiare.

commendable agg. lodevole.

commendably avv. lodevolmente.

commendation s. elogio, lode.

commendatory agg. laudativo.

commensal s. commensale.

commensurability s. commensurabilità.

commensurable agg. commensurabile.

commensurate agg. proporzionato.

comment s. 1. commento 2. critica.

to **comment** vt. e vi. commentare: to — up (on) a test, commentare un testo.

commentary s. commentario.

commentation s. annotazione, commento.

commentator s. 1. commentatore 2. radiocronista.

commerce s. commercio.

commercial agg. commerciale.

commercialism s. mercantilismo.

commercialist s. commercialista.

to **commercialize** vt. rendere commerciabile.

commercially avv. commercialmente.

commination s. comminazione.

to **commiserate** vt. e vi. commiserare.

commissary s. commissario, delegato.

commissaryship s. commissariato.

commission s. 1. commissione, comitato 2. commissione, incarico || — agent (o merchant), commissionario.

to **commission** vt. 1. commissionare 2. delegare.

commissioned agg. munito di autorità || non- — officer, sottufficiale.

commissioner s. (pol.) delegato.

to **commit** vt. 1. affidare, rimettere: to — one's soul to God, rimettere la propria anima a Dio 2. commettere.

commitment, committal s. 1. consegna 2. incarico.

committed agg. (neol.) impegnato.

committee s. comitato.

commodity s. merce, oggetto di prima necessità || free commodities, merci esenti da dogana.

common agg. 1. comune 2. solito, abituale || — law, legge consacrata dalla consuetudine.

commoner s. 1. cittadino (non nobile) 2. membro della Camera dei Comuni.

commonness s. 1. banalità 2. frequenza (di un avvenimento).

commonplace s. luogo comune.

commons s. pl. il popolo (sing.) || the House of —, la Camera dei Comuni.

commonwealth s. 1. confederazione 2. repubblica (anche fig.).

commotion s. 1. agitazione, confusione 2. insurrezione, tumulto.

communal agg. della comunità.

commune s. comune.

communicability s. comunicabilità.

communicable agg. comunicabile.

to **communicate** vt. comunicare, trasmettere (malattie, calore ecc.).

♦ to **communicate** vi. mettersi in comunicazione.

communication s. 1. comunicazione, informazione 2. relazione, rapporto.

communicative agg. comunicativo.

communicativeness s. comunicativa.

communion s. comunione, comunanza || Holy Communion, Eucarestia.

communism s. comunismo.

communist s. comunista.

communistic agg. comunista.

community s. 1. comunanza (di beni ecc.) 2. collettività, società 3. (eccl.) comunità.

commutability s. permutabilità, commutabilità.

commutable agg. permutabile, commutabile.

commutative agg. commutativo.

commutator s. commutatore.

to **commute** vt. commutare.

compact[1] s. patto, contratto.

compact[2] agg. 1. compatto 2. ridotto.

compactness s. 1. compattezza 2. concisione (di stile).

companion[1] s. compagno.

companion[2] s. (mar.) boccaporto: — -way, scaletta (di boccaporto), scalandrone.

companionable agg. socievole.

companionship s. amicizia, cameratismo.

company s. **1.** compagnia **2.** comitiva **3.** (*comm.*) società.

comparable *agg.* paragonabile.

comparative *agg.* **1.** comparativo **2.** comparato. ♦ **comparative** s. (*gramm.*) comparativo.

comparatively *avv.* **1.** comparativamente **2.** relativamente.

to **compare** *vt.* paragonare, verificare. ♦ to **compare** *vi.* competere, rivaleggiare, reggere al confronto.

comparison s. **1.** paragone, confronto **2.** (*gramm.*) comparazione.

compartment s. compartimento, scompartimento.

compass s. **1.** circonferenza, spazio, estensione **2.** bussola. ♦ **compasses** s. *pl.* (*a pair of* —) compasso (*sing.*).

to **compass** *vt.* circondare.

compassion s. compassione: *out of* —, per compassione.

compassionate *agg.* compassionevole.

to **compassionate** *vt.* compassionare.

compassionately *avv.* con compassione.

compatibility s. compatibilità.

compatible *agg.* compatibile.

compatibly *avv.* compatibilmente.

to **compel** *vt.* costringere, obbligare.

compelling *agg.* irresistibile.

compendious *agg.* compendioso.

to **compensate** *vt.* ricompensare, risarcire. ♦ to **compensate** *vi.* supplire.

compensation s. **1.** compenso **2.** (*mecc.*) compensazione **3.** indennità, risarcimento.

compensator s. compensatore.

compensatory *agg.* compensativo.

to **compete** *vi.* competere, gareggiare.

competence s. **1.** competenza **2.** mezzi sufficienti per vivere (*pl.*).

competent *agg.* competente, abile.

competently *avv.* con competenza.

competition s. **1.** competizione, gara **2.** rivalità.

competitive *agg.* **1.** di competizione **2.** (*comm.*) di concorrenza.

competitively *avv.* per mezz di concorso.

competitor s. concorrente, rivale.

compilation s. compilazione.

to **compile** *vt.* compilare.

compiler s. compilatore.

complacency s. **1.** soddisfazione **2.** compiacenza di sé.

complacent *agg.* **1.** compiacente **2.** soddisfatto di sé.

to **complain** *vi.* lagnarsi, dolersi.

complaint s. **1.** lamento **2.** reclamo.

complaisant *agg.* compiacente.

complement s. complemento.

complemental *agg.* complementare.

complementary *agg.* complementare.

complete *agg.* completo.

to **complete** *vt.* **1.** completare **2.** riempire (*moduli ecc.*).

completely *avv.* completamente.

completeness s. completezza.

completion s. compimento.

complex *agg.* **1.** complicato **2.** (*gramm.*) composto. ♦ **complex** s. complesso.

complexion s. carnagione, colorito.

complexity s. complessità.

compliance s. **1.** condiscendenza **2.** servilismo.

compliant *agg.* **1.** compiacente **2.** servile.

to **complicate** *vt.* complicare.

complicated *agg.* complicato.

complication s. complicazione.

complicity s. complicità.

compliment s. complimento: *to pay so. a* —, far un complimento a qu.

to **compliment** *vt.* complimentare, congratularsi con.

complimentary *agg.* **1.** complimentoso **2.** di favore: — *tickets*, biglietti di favore.

to **comply** *vi.* accondiscendere, conformarsi.

component *agg.* e s. componente.

to **comport** *vi.* comportarsi.

to **compose** *vt.* **1.** comporre, costituire **2.** (*mus.*) comporre || *to — a quarrel*, comporre una vertenza.

composed *agg.* **1.** composto **2.** calmo.

composer s. compositore.

composing *agg.* calmante. ♦ **composing** s. **1.** il comporre **2.** (*tip.*) composizione.

composite *agg.* composto.

composition s. **1.** composizione **2.** compromesso **3.** concordato, intesa.

compositor s. (*tip.*) compositore.

composure s. posatezza, sangue freddo.

compote *s.* conserva di frutta.
compound 1. miscela **2.** (*chim.*) composto **3.** (*gramm.*) parola composta.
to compound *vt.* e *vi.* **1.** comporre, mescolare **2.** combinare (*ingredienti, elementi ecc.*).
to comprehend *vt.* **1.** contenere **2.** capire.
comprehensibility *s.* comprensibilità.
comprehensible *agg.* **1.** comprensibile **2.** delimitato.
comprehension *s.* **1.** comprensione **2.** portata.
comprehensive *agg.* **1.** di vasta portata **2.** comprensivo.
comprehensively *avv.* comprensivamente.
compress *s.* compressa (*di garza*).
to compress *vt.* **1.** comprimere **2.** (*fig.*) condensare (*idee ecc.*).
compressibility *s.* compressibilità.
compression *s.* **1.** compressione **2.** (*fig.*) concentrazione.
to comprise *vt.* contenere, includere.
compromise *s.* compromesso.
to compromise *vt.* compromettere.
♦ **to compromise** *vi.* venire a un compromesso.
compromising *agg.* compromettente.
compulsion *s.* costrizione: *under* —, per costrizione.
compulsive *agg.* coercitivo.
compulsory *agg.* obbligatorio.
compunction *s.* compunzione.
computable *agg.* calcolabile.
computation *s.* calcolo.
to compute *vt.* computare, calcolare.
computer *s.* calcolatore.
comrade *s.* camerata, compagno.
comradeship *s.* cameratismo.
to concatenate *vt.* concatenare.
concatenation *s.* concatenazione.
concave *agg.* concavo.
to conceal *vt.* nascondere.
concealment *s.* **1.** occultamento **2.** nascondiglio.
conceit *s.* vanità, presunzione.
conceited *agg.* presuntuoso, vanitoso.
conceivability *s.* concepibilità.
conceivable *agg.* concepibile.
to conceive *vt.* **1.** concepire, generare **2.** immaginare, idee re.
to concentrate *vt.* **1.** concentrare

2. convergere. ♦ **to concentrate** *vi.* concentrarsi.
concentration *s.* **1.** concentrazione **2.** concentramento.
concentric *agg.* concentrico.
concept *s.* concetto.
conception *s.* **1.** concezione, concepimento **2.** concetto.
conceptional *agg.* concezionale.
conceptual *agg.* concettuale.
conceptualism *s.* concettualismo.
concern *s.* **1.** interesse, rapporto **2.** affare **3.** sollecitudine **4.** (*comm.*) ditta, azienda.
to concern *vt.* concernere, riguardare.
concerned *agg.* **1.** interessato **2.** ansioso, preoccupato || *as far as I am* —, per quanto mi riguarda.
concerning *prep.* riguardo a, circa.
concert *s.* **1.** concerto **2.** accordo.
concerted *agg.* **1.** (*mus.*) concertato **2.** convenuto.
concession *s.* concessione.
concessionary *agg.* e *s.* concessionario.
concettism *s.* concettismo.
conch *s.* conchiglia, mollusco.
conchoid *s.* concoide.
conchoidal *agg.* concoidale.
conciliar *agg.* conciliare.
to conciliate *vt.* conciliare.
conciliation *s.* conciliazione.
conciliator *s.* conciliatore, conciliatrice.
conciliatory *agg.* conciliante.
concise *agg.* conciso, succinto.
concision *s.* concisione.
conclave *s.* conclave.
to conclude *vt.* terminare, concludere. ♦ **to conclude** *vi.* terminare, concludersi.
conclusion *s.* conclusione.
conclusive *agg.* conclusivo.
to concoct *vt.* **1.** mescolare (*di ingredienti*) **2.** preparare, tramare.
concomitance *s.* concomitanza.
concomitant *agg.* concomitante.
concomitantly *avv.* simultaneamente.
concord *s.* **1.** concordia **2.** (*mus.*) accordo **3.** (*gramm.*) concordanza.
concordant *agg.* **1.** concorde **2.** (*mus.*) armonioso.
concordat *s.* concordato.
concourse *s.* concorso, affluenza (*di persone ecc.*).
concrete *agg.* concreto. ♦ **concrete** *s.* calcestruzzo.

concreteness *s.* concretezza.
concretion *s.* concrezione.
concubinage *s.* concubinato.
concubine *s.* concubina.
concupiscence *s.* concupiscenza.
to **concur** *vi.* concorrere, contribuire (*di cause, avvenimenti*).
concurrence *s.* **1.** concorso (*di circostanze*) **2.** cooperazione (*di persone*) **3.** (*geom.*) convergenza.
concurrent *agg.* concorrente, simultaneo.
to **concuss** *vt.* **1.** urtare **2.** (*med.*) provocare un trauma **3.** intimidire.
concussion *s.* **1.** urto **2.** (*med.*) commozione cerebrale, trauma.
to **condemn** *vt.* **1.** condannare **2.** biasimare, censurare.
condemnable *agg.* **1.** condannabile **2.** censurabile.
condemnation *s.* **1.** condanna **2.** biasimo, censura.
condensability *s.* condensabilità.
condensable *agg.* condensabile.
condensate *s.* (*fis.; chim.*) condensamento.
condensation *s.* condensazione.
to **condense** *vt.* condensare, abbreviare. ♦ to **condense** *vi.* condensarsi, concentrarsi.
condenser *s.* condensatore.
to **condescend** *vi.* accondiscendere.
condescending *agg.* condiscendente.
condescendingly *avv.* con condiscendenza.
condescension *s.* **1.** condiscendenza **2.** affabilità.
condition *s.* condizione, clausola: *on — that*, a condizione che.
to **condition** *vt.* condizionare.
conditional *agg.* e *s.* condizionale.
conditionally *avv.* condizionatamente.
conditioned *agg.* condizionato: — *air*, aria condizionata.
conditioning *s.* **1.** condizionatura (*di tessili*) **2.** condizionamento.
condolence *s.* condoglianza.
conduct *s.* **1.** condotta, comportamento **2.** metodo.
to **conduct** *vi.* **1.** condurre, guidare, dirigere **2.** (*fis.*) condurre, trasmettere. ♦ to **conduct** *vi.* **1.** comportarsi **2.** indicare la via.
conductibility *s.* conducibilità.
conductivity *s.* conducibilità.
conductor *s.* **1.** guida (*di persone*) **2.** (*mus.*) direttore **3.** bigliettario.

conduit *s.* **1.** conduttura **2.** passaggio segreto.
cone *s.* **1.** cono **2.** pigna.
to **confabulate** *vi.* confabulare.
confectionary *agg.* di pasticceria.
confectioner *s.* pasticciere.
confectionery *s.* pasticceria.
confederate *agg.* confederato. ♦
   confederate *s.* **1.** confederato **2.** complice.
to **confederate** *vt.* confederare. ♦
   to **confederate** *vi.* confederarsi.
confederation *s.* confederazione.
to **confer** *vt.* conferire, dare. ♦ to **confer** *vi.* conferire, consultarsi.
conference *s.* **1.** conferenza **2.** congresso.
to **confess** *vt.* e *vi.* confessare, professare.
confessedly *avv.* apertamente, dichiaratamente.
confession *s.* confessione, professione: — *of faith*, professione di fede.
confessional *agg.* e *s.* confessionale.
confessionary *agg.* confessionale.
confessor *s.* **1.** confessore **2.** chi si confessa.
confetti *s. pl.* coriandoli.
confidant *s.* confidente.
to **confide** *vt.* confidare. ♦ to **confide** *vi.* confidarsi: *to — in so.*, confidarsi con qu.
confidence *s.* **1.** fiducia **2.** confidenza **3.** sicurezza in se stessi.
confident *agg.* fiducioso.
confidential *agg.* confidenziale, riservato.
confidently *avv.* con sicurezza, con fiducia.
confiding *agg.* senza sospetti.
configuration *s.* configurazione.
to **configure** *vt.* configurare.
to **confine** *vt.* relegare, limitare. ♦ to **confine** *vi.* confinare, essere contiguo.
confinement *s.* **1.** reclusione **2.** limitazione **3.** puerperio.
to **confirm** *vt.* **1.** confermare **2.** cresimare.
confirmation *s.* **1.** conferma **2.** cresima **3.** (*pol.; giur.*) ratifica.
confirmatory *agg.* confermativo.
confiscable *agg.* confiscabile.
to **confiscate** *vt.* confiscare.
confiscation *s.* confisca.
conflagration *s.* conflagrazione.
conflict *s.* conflitto, contrasto.

confluence *s.* 1. confluenza 2. incrocio (*di strade ecc.*).
confluent *agg.* confluente.
to conform *vt.* conformare. ◆ to conform *vi.* conformarsi, ottemperare.
conformation *s.* 1. conformazione 2. adattamento.
conformist *s.* conformista.
conformity *s.* 1. conformità 2. conformismo.
to confound *vt.* 1. confondere, disorientare 2. sconvolgere.
confounded *agg.* attonito, confuso.
confraternity *s.* confraternita.
to confront *vt.* 1. affrontare 2. trovarsi di fronte a.
confrontation *s.* confronto.
Confucianism *s.* confucianesimo.
to confuse *vt.* 1. disorientare, sconcertare 2. confondere.
confusedly *avv.* confusamente.
confusion *s.* 1. disordine, confusione 2. turbamento.
confutation *s.* confutazione.
to confute *vt.* confutare.
to congeal *vt.* ghiacciare. ◆ to congeal *vi.* gelarsi.
congenial *agg.* 1. congeniale, affine 2. amabile, simpatico.
congeniality *s.* 1. affinità 2. carattere simpatico.
congenially *avv.* amabilmente.
congenital *agg.* congenito.
conger *s.* anguilla marina.
congeries *s.* congerie.
to congest *vt.* congestionare. ◆ to congest *vi.* congestionarsi.
congested *agg.* congestionato.
congestion *s.* congestione.
to conglobate *vt.* conglobare. ◆ to conglobate *vi.* conglobarsi.
conglobation *s.* conglobazione.
conglomerate *agg.* e *s.* conglomerato.
to conglomerate *vt.* conglomerare. ◆ to conglomerate *vi.* conglomerarsi.
conglomeration *s.* conglomerazione.
to congratulate *vt.* congratulare, congratularsi con.
congratulation *s.* congratulazione.
congratulatory *agg.* congratulatorio.
to congregate *vt.* adunare. ◆ to congregate *vi.* adunarsi.
congregation *s.* 1. unione, adunata, assemblea 2. (*relig.*) congregazione.

congregational *agg.* della congregazione.
congress *s.* congresso, riunione.
congressional *agg.* di congresso.
congruence *s.* congruenza.
congruent *agg.* congruente, conforme.
congruity *s.* conformità.
congruous *agg.* congruente, conforme.
conic(al) *agg.* conico.
conifer *s.* conifera.
coniferous *agg.* conifero.
conjecture *s.* congettura.
to conjecture *vt.* o *vi.* congetturare, ipotizzare.
conjointly *avv.* congiuntamente.
conjugal *agg.* coniugale.
conjugate *agg.* congiunto. ◆ conjugate *s.* 1. (*mat.*) coniugato 2. (*biol.*) fusione.
to conjugate *vt.* coniugare. ◆ to conjugate *vi.* coniugarsi.
conjugation *s.* coniugazione.
conjunction *s.* congiunzione.
conjunctiva *s.* (*anat.*) congiuntiva.
conjunctive *agg.* 1. (*biol.*) connettivo 2. (*gramm.*) congiuntivo. ◆ conjunctive *s.* congiuntivo.
conjunctivitis *s.* congiuntivite.
conjuncture *s.* congiuntura, circostanza.
conjuration *s.* 1. incantesimo 2. evocazione solenne.
to conjure *vt.* 1. scongiurare 2. evocare. ◆ to conjure *vi.* fare giochi di prestigio.
conjurer *s.* prestigiatore.
conjuring *s.* prestidigitazione.
connatural *agg.* connaturale.
to connect *vt.* 1. connettere, collegare, unire 2. associare (*mentalmente*). ◆ to connect *vi.* 1. avere relazioni, collegarsi 2. (*ferr.*) far coincidenza.
connecting *agg.* che connette. ◆ connecting *s.* (*elettr.*) collegamento.
connection *s.* 1. collegamento, connessione 2. relazione, parentela 3. coincidenza 4. (*comm.*) clientela.
connective *agg.* connettivo.
conning-tower *s.* (*mar.*) torretta di comando.
connivance *s.* connivenza.
to connive *vi.* essere connivente.
connotation *s.* significato implicito.
to connote *vt.* implicare, significare.

to **conquer** *vt.* conquistare.
conqueror *s.* conquistatore.
conquest *s.* conquista.
consanguine *agg.* consanguineo.
consanguinity *s.* consanguineità.
conscience *s.* coscienza: *for —'*
sake, per scrupolo di coscienza; *to*
be — -stricken, sentirsi rimordere
la coscienza.
conscienceless *agg.* senza scrupoli.
conscientious *agg.* scrupoloso || —
objector, obiettore di coscienza.
conscientiously *avv.* coscienziosamente.
conscious *agg.* consapevole, conscio.
consciousness *s.* coscienza, consapevolezza.
conscript *agg.* e *s.* coscritto.
conscription *s.* coscrizione.
to **consecrate** *vt.* consacrare, dedicare.
consecration *s.* consacrazione, dedizione.
consecutive *agg.* consecutivo.
consecutively *avv.* consecutiva-
mente.
consensual *agg.* consensuale.
consensus *s.* consenso, accordo ||
— *of opinion,* unanimità.
consent *s.* consenso, accordo || *by*
mutual —, amichevolmente.
to **consent** *vi.* acconsentire.
consequence *s.* 1. conseguenza, effetto 2. importanza.
consequent *agg.* conseguente, risultante.
consequential *agg.* consequenziale.
consequently *avv.* di conseguenza.
conservatism *s.* conservatorismo.
conservative *agg.* conservativo. ◆
Conservative *s.* conservatore.
conservator *s.* 1. conservatore 2.
sovrintendente (*di museo ecc.*).
conserve *s.* conserva di frutta.
to **consider** *vt.* considerare, riflettere, stimare.
considerable *agg.* considerevole,
importante.
considerate *agg.* rispettoso, pieno
di riguardi.
consideration *s.* 1. considerazione
2. rimunerazione 3. (*comm.*) provvigione.
considering *prep.* tenuto conto di,
considerando.
to **consign** *vt.* 1. (*comm.*) inviare,
consegnare 2. depositare (*soldi in*
banca).

consignation *s.* 1. (*comm.*) pagamento 2. consegna (*di merce*).
consignee *s.* consegnatario.
consigner *s.* mittente.
consignment *s.* 1. invio, spedizione
2. consegna, deposito.
to **consist** *vi.* consistere, essere composto.
consistence, consistency *s.* 1.
consistenza, compattezza 2. costanza.
consistent *agg.* coerente, logico.
consistently *avv.* coerentemente.
consistory *s.* concistoro.
consolation *s.* consolazione.
consolatory *agg.* consolante.
to **console** *vt.* consolare.
to **consolidate** *vt.* consolidare. ◆
to **consolidate** *vi.* consolidarsi.
consolidation *s.* consolidazione.
consoling *agg.* consolante.
consonance *s.* consonanza, accordo.
consonant *agg.* consono. ◆ **con-**
sonant *s.* consonante.
consort *s.* 1. consorte 2. compagno,
collega.
to **consort** *vi.* associarsi, unirsi. ◆
to **consort** *vt.* associare, unire.
conspicuous *agg.* cospicuo, notevole.
conspicuousness *s.* cospicuità.
conspiracy *s.* congiura.
conspirator *s.* cospiratore.
to **conspire** *vt.* e *vi.* cospirare.
constable *s.* 1. agente di polizia 2.
conestabile.
constabulary *s.* corpo della polizia.
constancy *s.* costanza.
constant *agg.* costante, fedele. ◆
constant *s.* (*mat.*) costante.
constantly *agg.* costantemente.
constellation *s.* costellazione.
consternation *s.* costernazione.
constipation *s.* stitichezza.
constituency *s.* 1. gli elettori (*pl.*)
2. circoscrizione elettorale.
constituent *agg.* costituente. ◆
constituent *s.* 1. elemento costitutivo 2. (*pol.*) elettore.
to **constitute** *vt.* 1. costituire 2.
eleggere.
constitution *s.* 1. costituzione, statuto 2. costituzione, composizione
(*del corpo, dell'aria ecc.*).
constitutional *agg.* costituzionale.
constitutionalism *s.* costituzionalismo.
constitutionality *s.* costituzionalità.

constitutive *agg.* costitutivo.
to constrain *vt.* costringere.
constrained *agg.* costretto, forzato.
constraint *s.* 1. costrizione 2. imbarazzo.
to constrict *vt.* costringere.
constriction *s.* costrizione.
to construct *vt.* costruire (*anche fig.*).
construction *s.* 1. costruzione 2. (*giur.*) interpretazione.
constructive *agg.* costruttivo.
to construe *vt.* 1. costruire grammaticalmente 2. interpretare. ♦ to construe *vi.* fare l'analisi grammaticale.
consuetudinary *agg.* consuetudinario: — *law*, diritto consuetudinario.
consul *s.* console.
consular *agg.* consolare.
consulate *s.* consolato.
to consult *vt.* consultare. ♦ to consult *vi.* consultarsi.
consultation *s.* 1. consultazione 2. consulto.
consultative *agg.* consultativo.
consulting *agg.* consulente || — -room, ambulatorio.
to consume *vt.* consumare. ♦ to consume *vi.* consumarsi.
consumer *s.* consumatore, utente.
consummate *agg.* consumato, perfetto.
consumption *s.* 1. consumo 2. sciupio 3. distruzione 4. tubercolosi.
consumptive *s.* tisico, tubercolotico.
contact *s.* contatto, relazione.
to contact *vt.* e *vi.* mettere, mettersi in contatto con, prender contatto.
contagion *s.* contagio.
contagious *agg.* contagioso.
to contain *vt.* 1. contenere, comprendere 2. reprimere, frenare (*i sentimenti*).
contained *agg.* frenato, contenuto (*di comportamento*).
container *s.* recipiente.
contamination *s.* contaminazione.
to contemplate *vt.* e *vi.* contemplare, meditare.
contemplation *s.* contemplazione.
contemplative *agg.* contemplativo.
contemplator *s.* contemplatore.
contemporaneousness *s.* contemporaneità.
contemporary *agg.* e *s.* contemporaneo.

contempt *s.* disprezzo || — *of Court* (*giur.*), vilipendio della Corte.
contemptibility *s.* spregevolezza.
contemptible *agg.* spregevole.
contemptuous *agg.* sprezzante.
contemptuously *avv.* sprezzantemente.
to contend *vi.* 1. contendere. ♦ to contend *vt.* sostenere, affermare.
contending *agg.* contendente, rivale.
content *s.* 1. volume, capacità 2. contenuto. ♦ contents *s. pl.* indice (*di libro*) (*sing.*). ♦ content *agg.* contento, soddisfatto.
to content *vt.* contentare, soddisfare.
contented *agg.* contento, pago.
contention *s.* 1. contesa 2. emulazione 3. controversia.
contentious *agg.* litigioso.
contest *s.* contestazione, contesa.
to contest *vt.* contestare, contendere. ♦ to contest *vi.* competere, rivaleggiare.
context *s.* contesto.
contiguity *s.* contiguità.
continence *s.* continenza.
continent *agg.* continente. ♦ continent *s.* (*geogr.*) continente.
continental *agg.* e *s.* continentale.
contingency *s.* contingenza, caso.
contingent *agg.* eventuale, imprevisto.
continual *agg.* continuo.
continuation *s.* continuazione, seguito.
to continue *vt.* e *vi.* continuare, far continuare.
continuity *s.* 1. continuità 2. (*cine*) sceneggiatura.
continuous *agg.* continuo.
to contort *vt.* contorcere.
contortion *s.* contorsione.
contortionist *s.* contorsionista.
contour *s.* contorno, profilo.
contraband *s.* contrabbando.
contraceptive *s.* anticoncezionale.
contract *s.* contratto, patto.
to contract *vt.* 1. contrarre (*matrimonio, amicizia ecc.*) 2. (*comm.*) contrattare 3. contrarre, restringere. ♦ to contract *vi.* contrarsi, restringersi.
contractile *agg.* contrattile.
contraction *s.* accorciamento.
contractor *s.* 1. contraente 2. appaltatore 3. imprenditore.

contractual *agg.* contrattuale.
to **contradict** *vt.* contraddire.
contradiction *s.* contraddizione.
contradictory *agg.* contraddittorio.
to **contraindicate** *vt.* controindicare.
contraindication *s.* controindicazione.
contraposition *s.* opposizione, antitesi.
contrarily *avv.* contrariamente.
contrary *agg.* contrario, opposto. ♦ **contrary** *s.* il contrario: *on the —*, al contrario. ♦ **contrary** *avv.* contrariamente, all'opposto.
contrast *s.* contrasto, opposizione.
to **contrast** *vt.* e *vi.* far contrasto, mettere in contrasto.
to **contravene** *vt.* contravvenire.
to **contribute** *vt.* contribuire. ♦ to **contribute** *vi.* collaborare (*a un giornale*).
contribution *s.* 1. contributo 2. (*comm.*) apporto di capitale 3. collaborazione (*a un giornale*).
contributor *s.* 1. contributore 2. collaboratore (*di giornale ecc.*).
contrite *agg.* contrito.
contrition *s.* contrizione.
contrivance *s.* 1. espediente 2. apparato, congegno 3. invenzione.
to **contrive** *vt.* escogitare. ♦ to **contrive** *vi.* adoperarsi, riuscire.
control *s.* autorità, influenza, dominio, controllo || — *device* (*mecc.*), dispositivo di controllo; — *room*, camera di manovra; *birth —*, limitazione delle nascite; *self —*, autocontrollo. ♦ **controls** *s. pl.* (*mecc.*) comandi.
to **control** *vt.* controllare, dirigere.
controller *s.* controllore, sovrintendente.
controversial *agg.* controverso.
controversy *s.* controversia, polemica.
controvertible *agg.* controvertibile.
contumacious *agg.* 1. insubordinato 2. contumace.
contumacy *s.* 1. ribellione 2. contumacia.
contumely *s.* onta, contumelia.
contusion *s.* contusione.
contusive *agg.* contundente.
convalescence *s.* convalescenza.
convalescent *agg.* e *s.* convalescente.
to **convene** *vt.* 1. convocare, riunire 2. (*giur.*) citare. ♦ to **convene**

vi. riunirsi, incontrarsi.
convenience *s.* 1. comodo, vantaggio. ♦ **conveniences** *s. pl.* comodità.
convenient *agg.* conveniente, comodo, adatto.
convent *s.* convento.
conventicle *s.* conventicola.
convention *s.* 1. patto, convenzione 2. assemblea 3. regola (*di gioco*). ♦ **conventions** *s. pl.* convenzioni (*sociali*).
conventional *agg.* convenzionale, comune.
conventionality *s.* convenzionalità.
conventual *agg.* e *s.* conventuale.
to **converge** *vi.* convergere. ♦ to **converge** *vt.* far convergere.
convergence *s.* convergenza.
convergent *agg.* convergente.
conversation *s.* conversazione.
converse *agg.* e *s.* inverso, contrario.
conversely *avv.* viceversa.
conversion *s.* conversione, trasformazione.
convert *s.* convertito.
to **convert** *vt.* 1. convertire 2. trasformare.
converter *s.* 1. convertitore 2. (*elettr.; mecc.*) convertitore, trasformatore.
convertible *agg.* convertibile || — *car*, automobile decappottabile.
convex *agg.* convesso.
convexity *s.* convessità.
to **convey** *vt.* 1. trasportare, convogliare 2. trasmettere (*suoni, odori ecc.*) 3. dare l'idea, suggerire.
conveyable *agg.* trasportabile, trasmissibile.
conveyance *s.* 1. trasporto 2. trasmissione 3. convogliamento.
conveyancer *s.* notaio.
conveyer *s.* 1. trasportatore 2. trasmettitore 3. convogliatore.
convict *s.* condannato, forzato.
to **convict** *vt.* condannare, dichiarare colpevole.
conviction *s.* 1. (*giur.*) verdetto di colpevolezza, condanna 2. convinzione.
to **convince** *vt.* convincere.
convincing *agg.* convincente.
convincingly *avv.* in modo convincente.
convivial *agg.* allegro, conviviale, gioviale.
conviviality *s.* giovialità.

convivially *avv.* convivialmente.
to **convocate** *vt.* convocare.
convocation *s.* convocazione.
convolution *s.* circonvoluzione.
convoy *s.* 1. (*mar.; mil.*) convoglio 2. scorta.
to **convoy** *vt.* 1. (*mar.; mil.*) convogliare 2. scortare.
convulsion *s.* 1. convulsione 2. rivolgimento.
convulsive *agg.* convulso.
to **coo** *vi.* tubare.
cook *s.* cuoco, cuoca: *head* —, capocuoco.
to **cook** *vt.* e *vi.* cucinare, cuocere.
cookery *s.* arte culinaria, cucina.
cooking *s.* 1. cottura 2. arte culinaria, cucina.
cool *agg.* 1. fresco 2. leggero (*di abito*) 3. calmo 4. freddo, senza entusiasmo 5. sfacciato.
to **cool** *vt.* 1. rinfrescare 2. calmare. ◆ to **cool** *vi.* 1. rinfrescarsi 2. calmarsi.
cooling *agg.* rinfrescante. ◆ **cooling** *s.* abbassamento di temperatura.
coolness *s.* 1. frescura 2. freddezza, calma, sangue freddo.
coop *s.* stia.
to **coop** *vt.* mettere nella stia.
cooper *s.* bottaio.
to **co-operate** *vi.* cooperare.
co-operation *s.* cooperazione.
co-operative *agg.* cooperativo.
co-operator *s.* cooperatore.
to **co-opt** *vt.* eleggere membro (*di comitato*).
co-ordinate *agg.* 1. dello stesso rango 2. coordinato. ◆ **co-ordinate** *s.* (*mat.*) coordinata.
to **co-ordinate** *vt.* coordinare.
co-ordination *s.* coordinazione.
co-ordinative *agg.* coordinativo.
co-owner *s.* comproprietario.
co-ownership *s.* comproprietà.
cop[1] *s.* cima (*di collina ecc.*).
cop[2] *s.* (*gergo*) poliziotto.
copartnership *s.* società, associazione.
to **cope** *vi.* fronteggiare, tener testa.
co-pilot *s.* (*aer.*) secondo pilota.
copper *s.* 1. rame 2. moneta di rame.
to **copper** *vt.* rivestire di rame.
copperplate *s.* 1. lastra di rame (*per incisione*) 2. incisione in rame.
Coptic *agg.* copto.

copulation *s.* copulazione.
copulative *agg.* copulativo.
copy *s.* 1. copia, trascrizione 2. riproduzione 3. esemplare || — -*book*, quaderno; — -*reader*, revisore di stampa; *fair* —, bella copia; *rough* —, brutta copia.
to **copy** *vt.* 1. copiare 2. imitare.
copyist *s.* copista.
copyright *s.* diritto d'autore, proprietà letteraria.
coquetry *s.* civetteria.
coral *s.* corallo.
cord *s.* corda, spago || *spinal* —, midollo spinale.
cordage *s.* cordame.
cordial *agg.* cordiale. ◆ **cordial** *s.* (*bevanda*) cordiale.
cordiality *s.* cordialità.
cordially *avv.* cordialmente.
cordon *s.* cordone.
core *s.* 1. torsolo 2. centro, cuore.
co-respondent *s.* (*giur.*) correo (*in adulterio*).
coriaceous *agg.* coriaceo.
cork *s.* 1. sughero 2. tappo, turacciolo || — *jacket*, cintura di salvataggio.
corkscrew *s.* cavaturaccioli.
cormorant *s.* cormorano.
corn[1] *s.* 1. grano 2. cereale || *ear of* —, spiga di grano; — -*cob*, pannocchia.
corn[2] *s.* callo, durone.
cornea *s.* cornea.
corner *s.* 1. angolo 2. (*comm.*) accaparramento (*di merci*).
to **corner** *vt.* 1. mettere, spingere in un angolo 2. (*fig.*) mettere con le spalle al muro. ◆ to **corner** *vi.* formare un angolo.
cornet *s.* cornetta.
cornice *s.* cornicione.
corolla *s.* corolla.
corollary *s.* corollario.
coronary *agg.* coronario.
coronation *s.* incoronazione.
coroner *s.* magistrato inquirente.
corporal[1] *agg.* corporale.
corporal[2] *s.* caporale.
corporation *s.* 1. corporazione 2. azienda municipale.
corporative *agg.* corporativo: — *system*, sistema corporativo.
corporeal *agg.* corporeo.
corpse *s.* cadavere.
corpulent *agg.* corpulento.
corpuscle *s.* corpuscolo.
corral *s.* recinto (*per bestiame*).

correct *agg.* corretto.

to correct *vt.* correggere.

correction *s.* correzione, rettifica.

corrective *agg.* e *s.* correttivo.

correctness *s.* correttezza.

corrector *s.* correttore: — *of the press* (*tip.*), correttore di bozze.

to correlate *vt.* essere, mettere in correlazione. ♦ **to correlate** *vi.* essere in correlazione.

correlation *s.* correlazione.

correlative *agg.* correlativo.

to correspond *vi.* 1. corrispondere, essere in rapporti epistolari 2. rispondere a (*esigenze ecc.*) 3. equivalere.

correspondence 1. corrispondenza 2. accordo, rispondenza.

correspondent *s.* corrispondente.

corridor *s.* corridoio.

corroborant *agg.* corroborante.

corroboration *s.* conferma, convalida.

to corrode *vt.* corrodere. ♦ **to corrode** *vi.* corrodersi.

corrosion *s.* corrosione.

corrosive *agg.* e *s.* corrosivo.

to corrugate *vt.* corrugare.

corrugation *s.* corrugamento.

corrupt *agg.* corrotto, guasto, depravato.

to corrupt *vt.* corrompere, alterare. ♦ **to corrupt** *vi.* corrompersi, alterarsi.

corruption *s.* corruzione.

corsair *s.* corsaro.

corset *s.* corsetto.

cortisone *s.* cortisone.

corvette *s.* corvetta.

corvine *agg.* corvino.

coryphaeus *s.* (*pl.* -aei) corifeo.

cosecant *s.* cosecante.

cosily *avv.* comodamente.

cosine *s.* coseno.

cosmetic *agg.* e *s.* cosmetico.

cosmic(al) *agg.* cosmico.

cosmogony *s.* cosmogonia.

cosmographer *s.* cosmografo.

cosmography *s.* cosmografia.

cosmology *s.* cosmologia.

cosmopolitan *agg.* e *s.* cosmopolita.

cosmopolitanism *s.* cosmopolitismo.

cosmopolite *agg.* e *s.* cosmopolita.

cosmopolitism *s.* cosmopolitismo.

cosmos *s.* cosmo.

Cossack *s.* cosacco.

cost *s.* costo, prezzo || — *of living*, carovita; *at all costs*, ad ogni costo;

extra —, spesa supplementare.

to cost (**cost, eost**) *vt.* e *vi.* costare.

costal *agg.* costale.

coster, costermonger *s.* venditore ambulante (*di frutta, verdura ecc.*).

costly *agg.* costoso.

costume *s.* 1. costume 2. abito.

cosy *agg.* comodo, intimo.

cot¹ *s.* capanna.

cot² 1. (*mar.*) cuccetta 2. culla.

cotangent *s.* cotangente.

cotenant *s.* coaffittuario.

cothurnus *s.* (*pl.*-ni) coturno.

cottage *s.* villino.

cotton *s.* cotone || — -*mill*, cotonificio; — -*spinner*, operaio di filatura; — -*wool*, ovatta; — -*waste*, cascame.

couch *s.* divano.

cough *s.* tosse.

to cough *vt.* e *vi.* tossire.

could *v.* *can.*

council *s.* 1. consiglio (*adunanza di persone*) 2. (*eccl.*) concilio.

councillor *s.* consigliere.

counsel *s.* 1. consultazione 2. consiglio 3. legale.

to counsel *vt.* e *vi.* consigliare.

counsellor *s.* 1. consigliere 2. legale.

count¹ *s.* 1. conto, calcolo 2. (*pol.*) scrutinio 3. (*giur.*) capo d'accusa.

count² *s.* conte.

to count *vt.* e *vi.* 1. contare, calcolare 2. considerare, avere importanza.

countable *agg.* numerabile.

countenance *s.* espressione del volto, aria.

counter¹ *s.* calcolatore, contatore || *revolution* —, contagiri.

counter² *s.* volta di poppa.

counter³ *s.* 1. banco, cassa (*di negozio*) 2. sportello 3. gettone (*da gioco*).

counter⁴ *agg.* contrario, opposto || — *clockwise*, in senso antiorario; — *poison*, antidoto. ♦ **counter** *avv.* in senso ontrario.

to counteract *vt.* agir contro, contrapporsi a.

counter-attack *s.* contrattacco.

to counter-attack *vt.* e *vi.* contrattaccare.

counterbalance *s.* contrappeso.

to counterbalance *vt.* controbilanciare.

counterblow *s.* contraccolpo.

countercharge s. controaccusa.
counterfeit agg. contraffatto, simulato. ◆ **counterfeit** s. contraffazione, simulazione.
counterfeiter s. 1. falsario 2. simulatore.
counterfoil s. matrice.
countermand s. revoca, contrordine.
counterpane s. copriletto.
counterpart s. 1. sostituto 2. duplicato, sosia 3. complemento.
counterpoint s. contrappunto.
countershaft s. contralbero.
countersign s. contrassegno.
counterweight s. contrappeso.
countess s. contessa.
countless agg. innumerevole.
countrified agg. campagnolo, rurale.
country s. 1. paese, regione 2. campagna 3. patria 4. nazione.
countryman s. 1. compaesano, compatriota 2. contadino.
countryside s. campagna.
countrywoman s. 1. compaesana, compatriota 2. contadina.
county s. contea, provincia.
coup s. 1. colpo 2. (fig.) impressione.
couple s. coppia, paio.
to **couple** vt. accoppiare. ◆ to **couple** vi. accoppiarsi.
coupling s. accoppiamento.
coupon s. cedola, tagliando.
courage s. coraggio, ardire.
courageous agg. coraggioso.
course s. 1. corso (del tempo), corso (di lezioni, conferenze) 2. serie 3. portata (dei pasti) 4. (sport) circuito || of —, naturalmente; in due — a tempo debito.
court s. 1. corte, cortile 2. (giur.) corte || — of justice, tribunale.
to **court** vt. corteggiare.
courtier s. cortigiano.
courting s. corteggiamento.
courtyard s. cortile.
courtship s. corteggiamento.
cousin s. cugino, cugina.
cove s. 1. insenatura 2. grotta.
covenant s. convenzione, patto.
cover s. 1. coperta, copertura 2. calotta 3. copertina (di libro) 4. riparo, ricovero 5. coperto (a tavola).
to **cover** vt. 1. coprire, ricoprire 2. proteggere 3. percorrere 4. nascondere 5. comprendere, includere.
covering s. copertura, rivestimento.

coverlet s. copriletto.
covert s. ricovero, rifugio.
covertly avv. nascostamente.
to **covet** vt. agognare.
covetousness s. cupidigia.
cow s. mucca, vacca || — bell, campanaccio; — -grass, trifoglio di campo; — -shed, stalla.
coward s. codardo, vile.
cowardice s. codardia, viltà.
cowardly agg. codardo. ◆ **cowardly** avv. vilmente.
cowboy s. bovaro.
cowherd s. vaccaro.
cowl s. 1. cappuccio, tonaca (di frate) 2. (auto; aer.) cofano del motore.
coxswain s. timoniere.
coy agg. timido, riservato.
crab s. granchio.
crabbed agg. sgarbato, bisbetico.
crack s. 1. schianto, detonazione, schiocco 2. incrinatura, rottura.
to **crack** 1. vt. schiantare, rompere, incrinare 2. schioccare. ◆ to **crack** vi. 1. screpolarsi, spezzarsi 2. scricchiolare.
cracked agg. 1. incrinato 2. fesso (di voce).
cracker s. petardo || nut-crackers, schiaccianoci; — of jokes, burlone.
crackle s. 1. crepitio 2. screpolatura, incrinatura.
to **crackle** vi. scoppiettare, scricchiolare. ◆ to **crackle** vt. screpolare.
crackling s. scoppiettio.
cradle s. culla (anche fig.).
craft s. 1. abilità, mestiere, professione 2. astuzia, inganno.
craftsman s. artigiano.
craftsmanship s. artigianato.
crafty agg. astuto, abile.
crag s. rupe, cresta.
to **cram** vt. riempire, stipare, rimpinzare. ◆ to **cram** vi. rimpinzarsi.
cramp s. crampo.
to **cramp** vt. (fig.) bloccare, paralizzare.
crane s. gru (anche mecc.).
to **crane** vt. e vi. 1. sollevare o abbassare (mediante una gru) 2. allungare (il collo).
cranium s. cranio.
crank[1] s. manovella, manubrio.
crank[2] agg. 1. piegato 2. disinnestato.

to **crank** vt. e vi. 1. piegare a gomito 2. mettere in moto (con manovella).

cranking s. avviamento (di motore).

crash s. 1. strepito, fracasso 2. caduta 3. scontro, collisione 4. rovina (anche morale).

to **crash** vt. e vi. 1. abbattere, precipitare, crollare con grande rumore 2. scontrare, scontrarsi.

crate s. cassa da imballaggio.

crater s. cratere.

to **crawl** vi. 1. strisciare, andar carponi 2. brulicare 3. avere la pelle d'oca.

crawl s. 1. strisciamento 2. (nuoto) « crawl ».

crayfish s. gambero (d'acqua dolce).

craze s. mania, smania.

craziness s. pazzia, follia.

crazy agg. 1. folle 2. maniaco, entusiasta.

to **creak** vi. cigolare, stridere.

cream s. 1. panna, crema 2. ogni sostanza densa e untuosa.

creamery s. caseificio.

creamy agg. cremoso.

crease s. piega, grinza.

to **crease** vt. fare pieghe, sgualcire. ♦ to **crease** vi. sgualcirsi.

to **create** vt. 1. creare, produrre, suscitare 2. nominare.

creation s. 1. creazione 2. universo, natura, il creato.

creative agg. creativo.

creator s. creatore.

creature s. 1. essere vivente 2. creatura (anche fig.), favorito.

credence s. credenza, fede.

credentials s. pl. credenziali.

credibility s. credibilità.

credible agg. credibile.

credit s. 1. fiducia 2. credito, reputazione, autorità 3. (comm.) fido, credito.

to **credit** vt. 1. prestar fede 2. attribuire 3. (comm.) accreditare

creditor s. creditore.

credulity s. credulità.

credulous agg. credulo.

creed s. credo, credenza religiosa.

creek s. 1. insenatura 2. (amer.) torrente.

to **creep** (crept, crept) vi. 1. strisciare, avanzare lentamente 2. arrampicarsi (di piante) || to — along, avanzare strisciando; to — away, allontanarsi strisciando.

creeper s. 1. rettile, verme 2. persona strisciante 3. pianta rampicante.

creepy agg. 1. strisciante 2. che dà i brividi.

to **cremate** vt. cremare.

cremation s. cremazione.

crematory s. crematoio.

creole agg. e s. creolo.

crept V. to creep.

crepuscular agg. crepuscolare.

crescent agg. 1. crescente 2. a mezzaluna. ♦ **crescent** s. 1. luna crescente 2. mezzaluna (emblema turco) 3. strada a semicerchio.

cress s. crescione.

crest s. 1. cresta 2. ciuffo, pennacchio 3. criniera.

to **crest** vt. ornare di pennacchio. ♦ to **crest** vi. incresparsi (di onde).

crevasse s. crepaccio.

crevice s. fessura.

crew[1] s. equipaggio, ciurma.

crew[2] V. to crow.

crib s. 1. greppia 2. presepio 3. stalla, capanna.

crick s. crampo || a — in the neck, torcicollo.

cricket s. grillo.

crime s. delitto, crimine.

criminal agg. e s. criminale.

criminalist s. penalista.

criminality s. criminalità.

criminology s. criminologia.

crimson s. cremisi.

to **cringe** vi. (fig.) farsi piccolo, umiliarsi.

cripple agg. e s. storpio, zoppo.

to **cripple** vt. storpiare. ♦ to **cripple** vi. essere zoppo.

crisis s. crisi.

crisp agg. 1. croccante 2. crespo 3. tonificante. ♦ **crisp** s. patatina fritta, croccante.

criss-cross agg. incrociato.

critic s. critico.

critical agg. critico.

criticism s. critica.

to **criticize** vt. criticare.

critique s. critica, recensione.

croak s. gracidamento.

to **croak** vt. e vi. 1. gracidare 2. (fig.) brontolare.

Croatian agg. e s. croato.

crochet s. lavoro all'uncinetto || — -hook (o — -pin), uncinetto.

crock[1] s. coccio, vaso di terracotta.

crock[2] s. 1. ronzino 2. persona vecchia e malandata.

crock³ s. fuliggine, sudiciume.
crockery s. terraglia.
crocodile s. coccodrillo.
croft s. piccolo podere, campicello.
crook s. 1. gancio, uncino 2. curva, flessione 3. (gergo) truffatore.
crookback s. gobba.
crooked agg. 1. curvo, storto, deforme 2. (fig.) perverso.
crookedly avv. 1. tortuosamente 2. indirettamente 3. perversamente.
crop s. 1. raccolto, messe 2. gozzo (di uccello) 3. (fig.) gruppo 4. rapata (di capelli).
to **crop** vt. 1. mietere 2. tosare.
cropper¹ s. mietitore.
cropper² s. (fam.) capitombolo.
cross agg. 1. obliquo, trasversale 2. adirato || — -bar, traversa; — -road, incrocio. ♦ **cross** s. 1. croce 2. tribolazione, pena.
to **cross** vt. e vi. 1. fare il segno della croce 2. attraversare 3. incrociare 4. cancellare || to — one's legs, accavallare le gambe.
crossbeam s. trave maestra.
crossbelt s. cartucciera a tracolla.
crossbow s. balestra.
crossbreed s. ibrido, incrocio.
cross-country agg. campestre.
cross-examination s. controinterrogatorio.
to **cross-examine** vt. controinterrogare.
cross-hatch s. tratteggio.
crossing s. 1. passaggio, traversata 2. incrocio || level —, passaggio a livello.
crossly avv. di malumore.
crosswise avv. 1. di traverso 2. a forma di croce.
crossword s. parole incrociate (pl.) || — puzzle, cruciverba.
crouch s. l'accovacciarsi.
to **crouch** vi. accovacciarsi, rannicchiarsi.
crow¹ s. corvo, cornacchia || a white —, una mosca bianca; to eat (v. irr.) a —, inghiottire un rospo.
crow² s. canto del gallo.
to **crow** (**crew**, **crowed**) vi. cantare (del gallo).
crowd s. folla, massa, moltitudine.
to **crowd** vi. affollare. ♦ to **crowd** vi. affollarsi, accalcarsi || to — together, stringere insieme.
crown s. 1. corona 2. cocuzzolo 3. coronamento, successo 4. (moneta) corona: half a —, mezza corona.

to **crown** vt. 1. incoronare 2. coronare, ricompensare.
crowning s. 1. incoronazione 2. coronamento.
crucial agg. cruciale.
crucible s. 1. crogiuolo 2. (fig.) dura prova.
crucifix s. crocifisso.
crucifixion s. crocifissione.
to **crucify** vt. crocifiggere.
crude agg. grezzo, rozzo, primitivo.
crudity s. asprezza.
cruel agg. crudele.
cruelty s. crudeltà.
cruet s. ampolla.
cruise s. crociera: to go on a —, fare una crociera.
cruiser s. incrociatore.
cruising s. crociera.
crumb s. 1. briciola 2. mollica.
to **crumb** vt. 1. sbriciolare 2. impanare.
to **crumble** vt. sbriciolare. ♦ to **crumble** vi. sbriciolarsi.
crumbly agg. friabile.
to **crumple** vt. spiegazzare. ♦ to **crumple** vi. spiegazzarsi.
to **crunch** vt. e vi. sgranocchiare rumorosamente.
crusade s. crociata.
crusader s. crociato.
crush s. 1. folla, calca 2. frantumazione 3. (gergo) cotta.
to **crush** vt. 1. frantumare, torchiare 2. (fig.) annientare, sconfiggere. ♦ to **crush** vi. accalcarsi, affollarsi.
crushing agg. schiacciante (anche fig.).
crust s. 1. crosta 2. incrostazione.
Crustacea s. pl. crostacei.
crutch s. 1. gruccia, stampella 2. forcella (di ramo).
cry s. grido, lamento, pianto || within —, a portata di voce.
to **cry** vt. e vi. 1. gridare 2. piangere || to — out, alzare la voce, protestare.
crypt s. cripta.
cryptogam s. crittogama.
cryptogram s. crittogramma.
cryptography s. crittografia.
crystal agg. cristallino. ♦ **crystal** s. cristallo || — work, cristalleria.
crystalline agg. cristallino (anche fig.).
crystallization s. cristallizzazione.
to **crystallize** vt. cristallizzare. ♦ to **crystallize** vi. cristallizzarsi.

crystallography s. cristallografia.
cub s. 1. volpacchiotto 2. (*fam.*) ragazzaccio.
cubage s. cubatura.
Cuban agg. e s. cubano.
cubature s. cubatura.
cube s. cubo || — *root*, radice cubica.
cubic agg. cubico.
cubism s. cubismo.
cubit s. cubito.
cuckold s. becco, cornuto.
to **cuckold** vt. tradire (*il marito*).
cuckoo s. cuculo.
cucumber s. cetriolo.
cudgel s. randello.
to **cudgel** vt. randellare.
cuff s. polsino (*di camicia*).
cuirass s. corazza.
cuirassier s. corazziere.
culinary agg. culinario.
to **cull** vt. scegliere.
culminant agg. culminante.
to **culminate** vi. culminare, giungere al culmine.
culottes s. pl. gonna pantaloni.
culprit s. 1. colpevole 2. imputato.
cult s. culto.
cultivable agg. coltivabile.
to **cultivate** vt. coltivare (*anche fig.*).
cultivation s. coltivazione.
cultural agg. culturale.
culture s. 1. coltura, coltivazione 2. cultura.
cultured agg. colto, educato.
cumbersome agg. ingombrante.
cumulative agg. cumulativo.
cumulus s. (*pl.* -li) cumulo.
cuneiform agg. cuneiforme.
cunette s. cunetta (*di trincea*).
cunning agg. astuto, furbo. ♦ **cunning** s. astuzia.
cup s. 1. tazza 2. (*sport*) coppa, trofeo || — *bearer*, coppiere; *tea- —*, tazza da tè.
cupboard s. credenza, armadio.
cupel s. coppella.
cupidity s. cupidigia.
cupreous agg. cupreo.
cupric agg. ramico.
cur s. 1. cane bastardo 2. mascalzone.
curable agg. curabile.
curacy s. vicariato, cura.
curare s. curaro.
curate s. curato, vicario.
curative agg. curativo.
curator s. direttore (*di museo, istituto ecc.*).

curb s. 1. cordone del marciapiede 2. freno (*fig.*) || — *bit*, morso della briglia.
curd s. giuncata.
to **curdle** vt. cagliare, coagulare. ♦ to **curdle** vi. cagliarsi, coagularsi.
curdy agg. cagliato, coagulato.
cure s. 1. cura, rimedio: *to take a* —, fare una cura 2. (*eccl.*) cura 3. vulcanizzazione (*di gomma*).
to **cure** vt. 1. curare, rimediare 2. salare, affumicare (*di cibi*) 3. vulcanizzare (*una gomma*). ♦ to **cure** vi. curarsi.
cureless agg. incurabile.
curette s. (*chir.*) raschiatoio.
curfew s. coprifuoco.
curio s. oggetto raro.
curiosity s. curiosità: *out of —*, per curiosità.
curious agg. 1. curioso 2. strano, singolare.
curl s. 1. ricciolo 2. curva, spirale.
to **curl** vt. 1. arricciare 2. torcere. ♦ to **curl** vi. 1. arricciarsi 2. torcersi 3. sollevarsi in spire.
curler s. ferro per arricciare i capelli, bigodino.
curly agg. 1. ricciuto 2. a spirale.
currency s. 1. (*comm.*) circolazione monetaria 2. corso, credito, voga.
current agg. corrente. ♦ **current** s. corrente (*anche fig.*) || *alternating —*, corrente alternata; *direct —*, corrente continua.
currently avv. comunemente.
curriculum s. curriculum.
to **curry** vt. 1. strigliare 2. conciare (*di cuoio*).
curry-comb s. striglia.
curse s. maledizione, anatema: *a — upon him!*, sia maledetto!
to **curse** vt. 1. maledire 2. scomunicare. ♦ to **curse** vi. imprecare, pronunciare bestemmie.
cursed agg. maledetto.
cursive agg. e s. corsivo.
to **curtail** vt. accorciare, abbreviare.
curtain s. 1. tenda, tendina 2. cortina 3. sipario || — *call*, chiamata alla ribalta.
curtain-raiser s. avanspettacolo.
curtly avv. brevemente, bruscamente.
curtsey s. riverenza, inchino (*di donna*).
curve s. curva, svolta.
to **curve** vt. curvare. ♦ to **curve** vi.

curvarsi.
curvet s. falcata.
curvilinear agg. curvilineo.
cushion s. cuscino.
cusp s. **1.** cuspide **2.** (geom.) vertice.
custard s. crema (di uova e latte).
custody s. **1.** custodia, vigilanza **2.** arresto, detenzione.
custom s. costume, consuetudine.
♦ **customs** s. pl. dogana (sing.) || — -house officer, doganiere.
customary agg. **1.** abituale, d'uso comune **2.** (giur.) consuetudinario.
customer s. cliènte, avventore.
cut s. **1.** taglio **2.** decurtazione **3.** (sport) colpo secco.
to **cut** (cut, cut) vt. e vi. **1.** tagliare, tagliarsi || to — a poor figure, fare una brutta figura **2.** (comm.) ridurre **3.** praticare un'apertura || to — down, abbattere; to — out, ritagliare; to — up, trinciare (il pollo), sradicare (alberi).
cutlet s. costoletta.
cut-off s. **1.** scorciatoia **2.** ritaglio di giornale.
cutter[1] s. **1.** tagliatore **2.** (mecc.) fresa.
cutter[2] s. (mar.) "cutter".
cut-throat agg. spietato. ♦ **cut-throat** s. tagliagole.
cutting agg. tagliente, sferzante. ♦ **cutting** s. **1.** taglio, incisione **2.** ritaglio, truciolo **3.** (comm.) riduzione.
cuttlefish s. seppia.
cyanide s. cianuro.
cybernetics s. cibernetica.
cycle s. ciclo.
cycling s. ciclismo.
cyclostyle s. ciclostile.
cyclotron s. ciclotrone.
cyclist s. ciclista.
cyclometer s. contachilometri.
cylinder s. **1.** cilindro **2.** rullo.
cylindrical agg. cilindrico.
cynic agg. e s. cinico.
cynicism s. cinismo.
cypress s. cipresso.
Cyprian agg. e s. cipriota.
Cyrillic agg. cirillico.
cyst s. cisti.
cystitis s. cistite.
cytology s. citologia.
Czar s. zar.
Czech agg. e s. ceco.
Czecho-Slovak agg. e s. cecoslovacco.

D

D s. (mus.) re.
dab s. **1.** colpo **2.** macchia.
to **dab** vt. **1.** sfiorare **2.** applicare.
to **dabble** vt. inumidire. ♦ to **dabble** vi. **1.** inumidirsi **2.** sguazzare || to — in (at), dilettarsi di.
dachshund s. cane bassotto.
dad(dy) s. (fam.) papà, babbo.
daffodil s. narciso selvatico.
daft agg. sciocco, pazzoide.
dagger s. **1.** pugnale **2.** (tip.) croce || at daggers drawn, ai ferri corti.
daguerreotype s. dagherrotipo.
daguerreotypy s. dagherrotipia.
dahlia s. dalia.
daily agg. quotidiano, giornaliero. ♦ **daily** s. (giornale) quotidiano. ♦ **daily** avv. ogni giorno.
daintily avv. delicatamente.
daintiness s. squisitezza.
dainty agg. **1.** squisito **2.** esigente **3.** raffinato (di gusti). ♦ **dainty** s. leccornia.
dairy s. latteria.
dairymaid s. lattaia.
dairyman s. lattaio.
dais s. piattaforma.
daisy s. margherita.
dalliance s. amoreggiamento.
to **dally** vi. gingillarsi, oziare.
Dalmatian agg. e s. dalmata.
daltonism s. daltonismo.
dam[1] s. diga, sbarramento.
dam[2] s. madre (di animali).
to **dam** vt. arginare.
damage s. danno. ♦ **damages** s. pl. (giur.) indennizzo, risarcimento (sing.).
to **damage** vt. danneggiare.
damaging agg. dannoso.
damask s. damasco.
to **damask** vt. damascare.
dame s. dama, gentildonna.
damn s. maledizione.
to **damn** vt. **1.** dannare **2.** (spesso scritto d-) maledire, mandare all'inferno.
damnation s. dannazione.
damnatory agg. compromettente (di prove).
damp agg. umido. ♦ **damp** s. **1.** umidità **2.** (fig.) depressione || fire-—, grisù.
to **damp** vt. **1.** inumidire **2.** (fig.) deprimere, smorzare.

damper *s.* **1.** regolatore (*di stufa, fornace ecc.*) **2.** (*mus.*) sordina.
dampness *s.* umidità.
dance *s.* danza.
to dance *vt.* e *vi.* danzare || *to — attendance on,* essere a disposizione di.
dancer *s.* ballerino.
dancing *s.* danza.
dandelion *s.* (*bot.*) soffione.
dandruff *s.* forfora.
dandy *agg.* elegante, raffinato. ♦ **dandy** *s.* zerbinotto.
Dane *s.* danese.
danger *s.* pericolo.
dangerous *agg.* pericoloso.
to dangle *vi.* ciondolare, penzolare ♦ **to dangle** *vt.* far penzolare.
dangling *agg.* penzolante.
Danish *agg.* danese.
dank *agg.* umido.
Dantean, Dantesque *agg.* dantesco.
dapple *s.* macchia || *— -grey,* leardo pomellato.
to dapple *vt.* chiazzare.
dare (dared, durst) *v. dif.* osare.
to dare *vt.* **1.** affrontare **2.** sfidare.
daredevil *s.* scavezzacollo.
daring *agg.* audace. ♦ **daring** *s.* audacia.
dark *agg.* **1.** scuro **2.** triste **3.** segreto. ♦ **dark** *s.* **1.** oscurità **2.** (*fig.*) ignoranza.
to darken *vt.* oscurare. ♦ **to darken** *vi.* oscurarsi.
darkling *agg.* oscuro. ♦ **darkling** *avv.* nell'oscurità.
darkness *s.* oscurità.
darling *agg.* e *s.* caro.
darn *s.* rammendo.
to darn *vt.* rammendare.
darnel *s.* loglio.
darner *s.* rammendatrice.
darn... : rammendo.
dart *s.* **1.** dardo **2.** slancio.
to dart *vt.* lanciare. ♦ **to dart** *vi.* lanciarsi (*in avanti*).
darting *agg.* dardeggiante.
Darwinism *s.* darwinismo.
dash *s.* **1.** slancio **2.** attacco **3.** tonfo **4.** spruzzo **5.** lineetta || *— -board,* cruscotto (*di automobili*).
to dash *vt.* **1.** frantumare **2.** macchiare. ♦ **to dash** *vi.* **1.** precipitarsi **2.** infrangersi.
dashing *agg.* impetuoso.
dastard *s.* vigliacco, furfante.
date¹ *s.* **1.** data **2.** appuntamento || *up to —,* aggiornato; *out of —,*

antiquato.
date² *s.* dattero.
to date *vt.* e *vi.* datare || *to — a girl,* dare un appuntamento a una ragazza.
dating *s.* datazione.
dative *agg.* e *s.* dativo.
datum *s.* (*pl.* data) dato, elemento.
to daub *vt.* **1.** intonacare **2.** impiastrare.
dauber *s.* imbrattatore.
daughter *s.* figlia || *— -in-law,* nuora; *grand- — (di nonni),* nipotina.
to daunt *vt.* spaventare, intimidire.
dauntless *agg.* intrepido.
to dawdle *vi.* oziare, bighellonare.
dawn *s.* alba.
to dawn *vi.* **1.** albeggiare **2.** apparire, balenare (*nella mente*).
day *s.* giorno || *— labourer,* lavoratore a giornata; *the — after tomorrow,* dopodomani; *the — before yesterday,* l'altro ieri; *this — week,* oggi a otto; *— off,* giorno di riposo; *— out,* giorno di libera uscita.
daybook *s.* (*comm.*) brogliaccio.
daybreak *s.* alba.
daydream *s.* fantasticheria.
to daydream *vi.* fantasticare.
daydreamer *s.* sognatore.
daylight *s.* luce del giorno.
daylong *agg.* che dura tutto il giorno. ♦ **daylong** *avv.* per tutto il giorno.
daytime *s.* giornata.
daze *s.* sbalordimento.
to daze *vt.* sbalordire.
dazzle *s.* abbagliamento || *— lamps* (*auto*), fari abbaglianti.
to dazzle *vt.* abbagliare.
deacon *s.* diacono.
dead *agg.* **1.** morto **2.** assoluto || *— drunk,* ubriaco fradicio. ♦ **dead** *avv.* assolutamente || *— sure,* arcisicuro.
to deaden *vt.* **1.** attutire **2.** isolare (*acusticamente*). ♦ **to deaden** *vi.* attutirsi.
deadening *s.* isolamento acustico.
deadline *s.* **1.** linea non superabile **2.** scadenza, termine massimo.
deadly *agg.* mortale. ♦ **deadly** *avv.* mortalmente.
deadness *s.* torpore.
deaf *agg.* sordo.
to deafen *vt.* assordare.
deaf-mute *s.* sordomuto.

deafness s. sordità.
deal s. 1. quantità 2. accordo 3. affare 4. mano (*del gioco delle carte*) || *a great* —, moltissimo.
to **deal** (dealt, dealt) vt. distribuire, dare. ♦ to **deal** (dealt, dealt) vi. trattare, comportarsi || *to — in*, commerciare in.
dealer s. 1. commerciante 2. mazziere (*delle carte*).
dealing s. 1. commercio 2. distribuzione 3. relazione || *double- —*, slealtà.
dealt V. *to deal*.
deambulatory agg. deambulatorio.
dean s. 1. decano 2. preside (*di facoltà universitaria*).
dear agg. caro || *— me!*, povero me!
dearly avv. 1. caramente 2. a caro prezzo.
dearness s. amorevolezza.
dearth s. penuria.
death s. morte || *— -rattles*, rantoli dell'agonia; *— -warrant*, ordine di esecuzione capitale.
deathly agg. e avv. V. *deadly*.
to **debase** vt. 1. avvilire 2. svalutare.
to **debar** vt. escludere, privare.
to **debark** vt. e vi. sbarcare.
debate s. dibattito.
to **debate** vt. e vi. 1. discutere 2. ponderare.
debauch s. intemperanza, corruzione.
debauched agg. corrotto.
debauchery s. 1. corruzione 2. dissolutezza.
debenture s. (*comm.*) obbligazione.
debit s. debito.
to **debit** vt. addebitare.
to **debouch** vi. sfociare.
debris s. detriti (*pl.*).
debt s. debito.
debtor s. debitore.
début s. debutto.
decadence s. decadenza.
decadent agg. e s. decadente.
decagram(m)e s. decagrammo.
decahedron s. decaedro.
to **decalcify** vt. decalcificare.
decalitre s. decalitro.
decalogue s. decalogo.
decametre s. decametro.
to **decamp** vi. levare le tende.
to **decant** vt. travasare.
decantation s. decantazione.
decanter s. caraffa.
to **decapitate** vt. decapitare.

decasyllabic agg. decasillabico.
decay s. 1. decadimento 2. rovina 3. carie (*dei denti*).
to **decay** vt. 1. far decadere 2. mandare in rovina. ♦ to **decay** vi. 1. decadere 2. andare in rovina 3. cariarsi.
decayable agg. deperibile.
decease s. decesso.
to **decease** vi. morire.
deceit s. 1. inganno 2. falsità.
deceitful agg. 1. ingannevole 2. falso.
to **deceive** vt. ingannare.
deceiving agg. ingannatore.
to **decelerate** vt. e vi. rallentare.
deceleration s. rallentamento.
decelerator s. rallentatore.
December s. dicembre.
decency s. decenza. ♦ **decencies** s. pl. convenienze.
decennary agg. decennale. ♦ **decennary** s. decennio.
decennial agg. e s. decennale.
decent agg. decente || *a — fellow*, un buon diavolo.
decentralization s. decentramento.
to **decentralize** vt. decentrare.
deception s. inganno.
deceptive agg. ingannevole.
to **decide** vt. decidere. ♦ to **decide** vi. decidersi, pronunciarsi.
decigram(me) s. decigrammo.
decimal agg. e s. decimale.
to **decimate** vt. decimare.
decimation s. decimazione.
decimetre s. decimetro.
to **decipher** vt. decifrare.
deciphering s. decifrazione.
decision s. decisione.
decisive agg. 1. decisivo 2. deciso.
deck s. (*mar.*) ponte, coperta || *— -chair*, sedia a sdraio; *quarter- —*, cassero.
to **deck** vt. ornare.
decker s. *double- —*, autobus a due piani.
to **declaim** vt. e vi. declamare.
declaimer s. declamatore.
declamation s. declamazione.
declamatory agg. declamatorio.
declaration s. dichiarazione.
to **declare** vt. e vi. dichiarare.
declension s. 1. declino 2. (*gramm.*) declinazione.
declinable agg. declinabile.
declination s. 1. inclinazione 2. declino.
decline s. declino, deperimento.

to **decline** vt. e vi. declinare.
declining s. 1. declinazione 2. deperimento 3. rifiuto.
declivity s. declivio.
to **decode** vt. decifrare, tradurre (testi in codice).
decolorization s. decolorazione.
decoloration s. decolorazione.
to **decolour(ize)** vt. decolorare.
decomposable agg. scomponibile.
to **decompose** vt. 1. decomporre 2. scomporre. ♦ to **decompose** vi. 1. decomporsi 2. scomporsi.
decomposition s. decomposizione.
to **deconsecrate** vt. sconsacrare.
to **decorate** vt. decorare.
decoration s. decorazione.
decorative agg. decorativo.
decorator s. decoratore.
decorous agg. decoroso.
decoy s. esca, richiamo.
decrease s. diminuzione.
to **decrease** vt. e vi. diminuire.
decree s. decreto.
to **decree** vt. decretare.
decrepit agg. decrepito.
decrepitude s. decrepitezza.
to **decry** vt. stigmatizzare, denigrare.
to **decuple** vt. decuplicare.
to **dedicate** vt. dedicare.
dedicatee s. persona a cui è dedicato qc.
dedication s. 1. dedica 2. consacrazione.
dedicative, dedicatory agg. dedicatorio.
to **deduce** vt. 1. dedurre 2. derivare.
to **deduct** vt. detrarre.
deduction s. 1. deduzione 2. detrazione.
deductive agg. deduttivo.
deed s. atto, azione.
to **deem** vt. giudicare.
deep agg. 1. profondo 2. cupo || —-freeze, surgelamento; — mourning, lutto stretto. ♦ **dcep** s. abisso, profondità. ♦ **deep** avv. profondamente || — into the night, fino a notte tarda.
to **deepen** vt. 1. approfondire 2. incupire. ♦ to **deepen** vi. 1. approfondirsi 2. incupirsi.
deeply avv. profondamente.
deepness s. profondità.
deep-rooted agg. radicato.
deer s. cervo || (fallow) —, daino.
to **deface** vt. sfregiare.

defacement s. sfregio.
defamation s. diffamazione.
defamatory agg. diffamatorio.
to **defame** vt. diffamare.
defamer s. diffamatore.
default s. 1. mancanza 2. inadempienza 3. (giur.) contumacia: judgement by —, giudizio in contumacia.
defaulting agg. (comm.) insolvente.
defeat s. 1. sconfitta 2. fallimento.
to **defeat** vt. 1. sconfiggere 2. frustrare.
defeatism s. disfattismo.
defeatist agg. e s. disfattista.
to **defecate** vt. purificare. ♦ to **defecate** vi. defecare.
defect s. difetto.
defection s. defezione.
defective agg. 1. difettoso 2. (gramm.) difettivo. ♦ **defective** s. anormale.
defence s. difesa.
defenceless agg. indifeso.
to **defend** vt. difendere.
defendant s. imputato.
defender s. difensore.
defenestration s. defenestrazione.
defensible agg. difensibile.
defensive agg. difensivo. ♦ **defensive** s. difensiva.
to **defer**[1] vt. e vi. differire || deferred payment, pagamento a rate.
to **defer**[2] vt. rimettere. ♦ to **defer** vi. rimettersi.
deference s. deferenza.
deferential agg. deferente.
deferment s. differimento.
defiance s. sfida.
defiant agg. ardito.
deficiency s. 1. deficienza 2. disavanzo.
deficient agg. e s. deficiente.
deficit s. (comm.) disavanzo.
to **defile** vi. marciare in fila. ♦ to **defile** vt. 1. insozzare 2. profanare.
defilement s. 1. contaminazione 2. profanazione.
definable agg. definibile.
to **define** vt. definire.
definite agg. definito.
definitely avv. in modo preciso.
definiteness s. precisione.
definition s. 1. definizione 2. nitidezza.
definitive agg. definitivo.
to **deflagrate** vt. far deflagrare. ♦ to **deflagrate** vi. deflagrare.

deflagration s. deflagrazione.
to **deflate** vt. sgonfiare. ◆ to **deflate** vi. sgonfiarsi.
deflation s. **1.** sgonfiamento **2.** deflazione.
to **deflect** vt. e vi. deviare.
deflection s. deviazione.
defloration s. deflorazione.
to **deflower** vt. **1.** deflorare **2.** devastare **3.** spogliare (dei fiori).
to **deforest** vt. diboscare.
deforestation s. diboscamento.
to **deform** vt. deformare. ◆ to **deform** vi. deformarsi.
deformation s. deformazione.
deformed agg. deforme.
deformity s. deformità.
to **defraud** vt. defraudare.
defrauder s. frodatore.
to **defray** vt. pagare, risarcire.
defrayal s. pagamento, risarcimento.
to **defrost** vt. sgelare.
defroster s. riscaldatore.
deft agg. abile, destro.
to **defy** vt. sfidare.
degenerate agg. e s. degenerato.
to **degenerate** vt. e vi. degenerare.
degeneration s. degenerazione.
degradation s. degradazione.
to **degrade** vt. degradare.
degree s. **1.** grado **2.** rango **3.** laurea, diploma || by degrees, gradatamente.
to **dehydrate** vt. disidratare.
dehydration s. disidratazione.
to **deify** vt. deificare.
deism s. deismo.
deity s. divinità.
to **deject** vt. abbattere, scoraggiare.
dejected agg. triste, abbattuto.
dejectedly avv. con aria abbattuta.
dejection s. abbattimento.
delation s. delazione.
delator s. delatore.
delay s. **1.** ritardo **2.** proroga.
to **delay** vt. e vi. ritardare.
delegacy s. delegazione.
delegate s. delegato.
to **delegate** vt. delegare.
delegation s. delegazione.
to **delete** vt. cancellare (anche fig.).
deliberate agg. **1.** deliberato **2.** cauto.
to **deliberate** vt. e vi. deliberare.
deliberately avv. deliberatamente.
deliberation s. **1.** deliberazione **2.** ponderatezza.
delicacy s. **1.** delicatezza **2.** ghiottoneria.

delicate agg. **1.** delicato **2.** esigente.
delicatessen s. pl. **1.** ghiottonerie **2.** salumeria (sing.).
delicious agg. delizioso.
delict s. (giur.) delitto.
delight s. delizia, gioia.
to **delight** vt. deliziare. ◆ to **delight** vi. dilettarsi.
delighted agg. lietissimo, entusiasta.
delightful agg. delizioso.
to **delimit(ate)** vt. delimitare.
delimitation s. delimitazione.
to **delineate** vt. delineare.
delineation s. delineazione.
delinquency s. **1.** delinquenza **2.** colpevolezza.
delinquent agg. colpevole. ◆ **delinquent** s. delinquente.
delirious agg. delirante.
deliriously avv. in modo delirante.
delirium s. delirio, frenesia.
to **deliver** vt. **1.** liberare **2.** consegnare **3.** partorire **4.** pronunciare (un discorso).
deliverance s. liberazione.
delivery s. **1.** liberazione **2.** consegna **3.** parto **4.** resa **5.** dizione, pronuncia || — -man, fattorino.
deltoid agg. triangolare.
to **delude** vt. ingannare.
deluge s. diluvio.
delusion s. illusione.
delusive agg. illusorio.
to **delve** vt. scavare, esumare. ◆ to **delve** vi. compiere ricerche, frugare.
demagnetization s. demagnetizzazione.
to **demagnetize** vt. demagnetizzare.
demagogic(al) agg. demagogico.
demagogue s. demagogo.
demagogy s. demagogia.
demand s. **1.** domanda **2.** esigenza || on —, a richiesta.
to **demand** vt. **1.** domandare **2.** esigere.
demarcation s. demarcazione.
demeanour s. contegno.
demerit s. demerito.
demesne s. dominio, proprietà terriera.
demigod s. semidio.
demijohn s. damigiana.
demilitarization s. smilitarizzazione.
to **demilitarize** vt. smilitarizzare.
demise s. **1.** trapasso (di proprietà)

2. decesso.
demiurge s. demiurgo.
demobilization s. smobilitazione.
to demobilize vt. smobilitare.
democracy s. democrazia.
democrat s. democratico.
democratic(al) agg. democratico.
democratization s. democratizza-zione.
to democratize vt. democratizzare.
demographic(al) agg. demografico.
demography s. demografia.
to demolish vt. demolire.
demolisher s. demolitore.
demolition s. demolizione.
demon s. demonio.
demoniac(al) agg. demoniaco.
demonology s. demonologia.
demonstrability s. dimostrabilità.
demonstrable agg. dimostrabile.
demonstrant s. dimostrante.
to demonstrate vt. e vi. dimostrare.
demonstration s. dimostrazione.
demonstrative agg. 1. dimostrativo 2. espansivo.
demonstrativeness s. 1. dimostra-zione 2. espansività.
demonstrator s. 1. dimostratore 2. dimostrante.
demoralization s. 1. depravazione 2. demoralizzazione.
to demoralize vt. 1. depravare 2. demoralizzare.
to demur vi. titubare, esitare.
demure agg. riservato, pudico.
demureness s. riservatezza, pu-dore.
den s. tana.
to denationalize vt. snazionalizzare.
to denature vt. denaturare.
deniable agg. negabile.
denial s. rifiuto || self- —, abnega-zione.
to denigrate vt. denigrare.
denigration s. denigrazione.
denigrator s. denigratore.
to denominate vt. denominare.
denomination s. 1. denominazione 2. setta 3. valore (di monete).
denominational agg. confessionale.
denominative agg. denominativo.
denominator s. denominatore.
denotation s. 1. indicazione 2. si-gnificato.
to denote vt. denotare, indicare.
to denounce vt. denunciare.
dense agg. 1. denso 2. opaco 3. stu-pido.
density s. 1. densità 2. opacità 3.

stupidità.
dent s. incavo, tacca.
dental agg. e s. dentale.
dentary agg. dentario.
dentine s. dentina.
dentist s. dentista.
dentistry s. odontoiatria.
dentition s. dentizione.
denture s. dentiera.
denudation s. denudazione.
to denude vt. denudare.
denunciation s. denunzia.
to deny vt. negare, rifiutare.
deodorant agg. e s. deodorante.
to deodorize vt. deodorare.
deontology s. deontologia.
deoxidization s. disossidazione.
to deoxidize vt. disossidare.
to depart vi. partire, allontanarsi.
department s. 1. reparto 2. (amer.) ministero || — store, grande ma-gazzino.
departure s. 1. partenza 2. allon-tanamento.
to depend vi. 1. dipendere: it all depends on circumstances, tutto di-pende dalle circostanze 2. contare: — on so., contare su qu.
dependable agg. fidato.
dependant agg. e s. dipendente.
dependence s. 1. dipendenza 2. fi-ducia.
dependency s. territorio dipen-dente.
dependent agg. dipendente.
to depict vt. dipingere.
to depilate vt. depilare.
depilatory agg. e s. depilatorio.
to deplete vt. 1. vuotare 2. esau-rire.
depletion s. esaurimento.
deplorable agg. deplorevole.
to deplore vt. deplorare.
to deploy vt. schierare, spiegare. ♦
to deploy vi. schierarsi (di trup-pe ecc.).
to depone vt. deporre (in un pro-cesso).
deponent s. testimone.
to depopulate vt. spopolare.
to deport vt. deportare || to — one-self, comportarsi.
deportation s. deportazione.
deportment s. atteggiamento.
deposal s. deposizione.
to depose vt. e vi. deporre.
deposit s. deposito.
to deposit vt. depositare.
deposition s. 1. deposizione 2. de-

posito.
depositor s. depositante.
depot s. deposito.
to **deprave** vt. depravare.
depravity s. depravazione.
deprecable agg. deprecabile.
to **deprecate** vt. disapprovare.
deprecation s. disapprovazione.
deprecative, deprecatory agg. disapprovante.
to **depreciate** vt. svalutare. ♦ to **depreciate** vi. svalutarsi.
depreciation s. 1. svalutazione 2. ammortamento: — charge, quota d'ammortamento.
depreciative, depreciatory agg. spregiativo.
depredation s. saccheggio.
depredatory agg. predatorio.
to **depress** vt. 1. deprimere 2. abbassare.
depression s. 1. depressione 2. (econ.) crisi.
depressor s. depressore.
deprivation s. privazione.
to **deprive** vt. privare.
depth s. 1. profondità 2. (mar.) fondale.
to **depurate** vt. depurare. ♦ to **depurate** vi. depurarsi.
depuration s. depurazione.
depurative agg. e s. depurativo.
depurator s. depuratore.
deputation s. delega.
to **depute** vt. deputare.
deputy s. 1. deputato 2. sostituto.
derailment s. deragliamento.
to **derange** vt. sconvolgere.
derangement s. sconvolgimento.
deratization s. derattizzazione.
to **deride** vt. deridere.
derision s. 1. derisione 2. zimbello.
derisive, derisory agg. derisorio.
derivable agg. derivabile.
derivation s. derivazione.
derivative agg. e s. derivato.
derivatively avv. per derivazione.
to **derive** vt. e vi. derivare.
derm s. derma.
dermatologist s. dermatologo.
dermatology s. dermatologia.
to **derogate** vi. derogare.
derogation s. deroga.
derogatory agg. derogatorio.
derrick s. 1. argano 2. torre di trivellazione.
descant s. 1. melodia 2. dissertazione.
to **descend** vt. e vi. (di)scendere ‖

to — upon so., aggredire qu.
descendance s. discendenza.
descendant s. discendente.
descent s. 1. discesa 2. incursione 3. lignaggio 4. caduta.
describable agg. descrivibile.
to **describe** vt. descrivere.
description s. descrizione.
descriptive agg. descrittivo.
to **descry** vt. scoprire.
to **desecrate** vt. profanare.
desert[1] agg. deserto. ♦ **desert** s. deserto.
desert[2] s. 1. merito 2. compenso.
to **desert** vt. abbandonare. ♦ to **desert** vi. disertare.
deserted agg. deserto.
deserter s. disertore.
desertion s. 1. abbandono 2. diserzione.
to **deserve** vt. meritare.
deservedly avv. meritatamente.
deserving agg. meritevole.
design s. disegno.
to **design** vt. 1. destinare 2. progettare 3. disegnare.
designate agg. designato.
to **designate** vt. 1. designare 2. indicare.
designation s. designazione.
designer s. disegnatore.
designing agg. astuto. ♦ **designing** s. 1. disegno 2. complotto.
desirable agg. desiderabile.
desire s. desiderio.
to **desire** vt. 1. desiderare 2. domandare.
desirous agg. desideroso.
to **desist** vi. desistere.
desk s. 1. scrivania 2. cassa ‖ school- master's —, cattedra (di insegnante).
desolate agg. desolato.
to **desolate** vt. 1. affliggere 2. devastare.
desolation s. desolazione.
despair s. disperazione.
to **despair** vi. disperare.
despairing agg. disperato.
desperate agg. disperato.
despicable agg. spregevole.
despicableness s. spregevolezza.
despisable agg. spregevole.
to **despise** vt. disprezzare.
despite prep. malgrado.
despiteful agg. maligno, dispettoso.
despondency s. scoraggiamento.
despondent agg. scoraggiato.
despot s. despota.

despotic(al) *agg.* dispotico.
despotism *s.* dispotismo.
destination *s.* destinazione.
to **destine** *vt.* destinare.
destiny *s.* destino.
destitute *agg.* 1. povero 2. privo.
destitution *s.* 1. povertà 2. privazione.
to **destroy** *vt.* distruggere.
destroyable *agg.* distruggibile.
destroyer *s.* 1. distruttore 2. cacciatorpediniere.
destroying *agg.* distruttore.
destruction *s.* distruzione, rovina.
destructive *agg.* distruttivo.
destructor *s.* distruttore.
desuetude *s.* disuso.
desultory *agg.* saltuario.
to **detach** *vt.* distaccare.
detachable *agg.* staccabile.
detached *agg.* 1. distaccato 2. isolato.
detachment *s.* 1. distacco 2. (*mil.*) distaccamento.
detail *s.* 1. dettaglio, particolare 2. pattuglia.
to **detail** *vt.* 1. dettagliare 2. (*mil.*) distaccare (*una pattuglia*).
to **detain** *vt.* 1. detenere 2. trattenere.
to **detect** *vt.* scoprire.
detectable *agg.* scopribile.
detection *s.* scoperta.
detective *s.* investigatore || — *novel*, romanzo poliziesco.
detector *s.* (*radio*) rivelatore.
detent *s.* (*mecc.*) arpione.
detention *s.* 1. detenzione 2. ritardo forzato.
to **deter** *vt.* trattenere.
to **deterge** *vt.* detergere.
detergent *agg. e s.* detergente, detersivo.
to **deteriorate** *vt.* deteriorare. ♦ to **deteriorate** *vi.* deteriorarsi.
deterioration *s.* deterioramento.
determinable *agg.* determinabile.
determinant *s.* causa determinante.
determinate *agg.* determinato.
determination *s.* determinazione.
determinative *agg.* determinativo.
to **determine** *vt.* determinare, decidere. ♦ to **determine** *vi.* risolversi || *to — on*, fissarsi su.
determined *agg.* deciso.
determinism *s.* determinismo.
determinist *agg. e s.* determinista.
deterrent *agg. e s.* (*neol.*) deterrente.

detersive *agg. e s.* detersivo.
to **detest** *vt.* detestare.
detestable *agg.* detestabile.
detestation *s.* 1. odio 2. esecrazione.
dethronement *s.* deposizione (*dal trono*).
to **detonate** *vt. e vi.* esplodere.
detonator *s.* detonatore.
detour *s.* deviazione, giravolta.
to **detract** *vt. e vi.* diminuire.
detraction *s.* detrazione.
detractor *s.* detrattore.
detriment *s.* detrimento.
detrimental *agg.* dannoso.
to **devaluate** *vt.* svalutare.
devaluation *s.* svalutazione.
to **devastate** *vt.* devastare.
devastation *s.* devastazione.
to **develop** *vt.* sviluppare. ♦ to **develop** *vi.* svilupparsi.
developer *s.* sviluppatore.
development *s.* sviluppo.
to **deviate** *vt. e vi.* deviare.
deviation *s.* deviazione.
deviationism *s.* deviazionismo.
device *s.* 1. trovata 2. dispositivo. ♦ **devices** *s. pl.* capriccio, inclinazione (*sing.*).
devil *s.* diavolo.
devilish *agg.* diabolico.
devious *agg.* 1. remoto 2. errante.
to **devise** *vt.* 1. escogitare 2. lasciare in eredità.
deviser *s.* inventore.
devising *s.* invenzione.
devoid *agg.* privo.
devolution *s.* 1. trasmissione (*di beni*) 2. degenerazione.
to **devolve** *vt.* trasmettere. ♦ to **devolve** *vi.* trasferirsi.
to **devote** *vt.* dedicare.
devoted *agg.* 1. devoto 2. votato.
devotion *s.* devozione.
devotional *agg.* devoto.
to **devour** *vt.* divorare.
devourer *s.* divoratore.
devout *agg.* devoto, pio, religioso.
dew *s.* rugiada.
dewy *agg.* rugiadoso.
dexterity *s.* destrezza.
dexterous *agg.* destro.
dextrin(e) *s.* destrina.
diabetes *s.* diabete.
diabetic *agg. e s.* diabetico.
diabolic(al) *agg.* diabolico.
diadem *s.* diadema.
to **diagnose** *vt.* diagnosticare.
diagnosis *s.* (*pl.* -ses) diagnosi.

diagnostic *agg.* diagnostico.
diagonal *agg. e s.* diagonale.
diagram *s.* diagramma.
dial *s.* quadrante.
to **dial** *vt.* comporre (*un numero telefonico*) || *to — so.*, telefonare a qu.
dialect *s.* dialetto.
dialectal *agg.* dialettale.
dialectic(al) *agg.* dialettico.
dialectics *s.* dialettica.
dialogue *s.* dialogo.
to **dialogue** *vt. e vi.* dialogare.
diameter *s.* diametro.
diametrically *avv.* diametralmente.
diamond *s.* **1.** diamante **2.** losanga.
diaper *s.* **1.** arabesco **2.** pannolino.
diaphanous *agg.* diafano.
diaphragm *s.* diaframma.
diapositive *s.* diapositiva.
diarchy *s.* diarchia.
diarist *s.* diarista.
diarrhoea *s.* diarrea.
diary *s.* diario.
diatribe *s.* diatriba.
dice V. *die.*
to **dice** *vt.* **1.** giocare ai dadi **2.** tagliare a dadi **3.** quadrettare.
dictaphone *s.* dittafono.
dictate *s.* dettame.
to **dictate** *vt. e vi.* dettare.
dictation *s.* **1.** dettato **2.** dettame.
dictator *s.* dittatore.
dictatorial *agg.* dittatoriale.
dictatorship *s.* dittatura.
diction *s.* **1.** stile **2.** dizione.
dictionary *s.* dizionario.
dictograph *s.* dittografo.
did V. *to do.*
didactic *agg.* didattico.
didactics *s.* didattica.
die *s.* (*pl.* dice) dado.
to **die** *vi.* morire || *to — away*, svanire; *to — out*, estinguersi.
dielectric *agg. e s.* dielettrico.
diet *s.* dieta.
to **diet** *vt.* mettere a dieta. ◆ to **diet** *vi.* essere a dieta.
dietarian *s.* chi sta a dieta.
dietary *agg.* dietetico. ◆ **dietary** *s.* dieta.
dietetic(al) *agg.* dietetico.
to **differ** *vi.* differire.
difference *s.* **1.** differenza **2.** divergenza.
different *agg.* differente.
differential *agg. e s.* differenziale.
to **differentiate** *vt.* differenziare.
◆ to **differentiate** *vi.* differenziarsi.
differentiation *s.* differenziazione.
differently *avv.* differentemente.
differing *agg.* **1.** differente, discordante.
difficult *agg.* difficile.
difficulty *s.* difficoltà.
diffidence *s.* timidezza.
diffident *agg.* esitante.
diffraction *s.* diffrazione.
diffuse *agg.* diffuso.
to **diffuse** *vt.* diffondere. ◆ to **diffuse** *vi.* diffondersi.
diffusedly, diffusely *avv.* **1.** diffusamente **2.** ovunque.
diffuser *s.* (*foto*) diffusore.
diffusion *s.* **1.** diffusione **2.** prolissità.
diffusive *agg.* **1.** diffusivo **2.** prolisso.
diffusor *s.* diffusore.
to **dig** (dug, dug) *vt.* vangare, scavare || *to — in*, affondare; *to — out*, estrarre.
digest *s.* **1.** sommario **2.** condensato.
to **digest** *vt.* classificare, condensare, redigere. ◆ to **digest** *vt. e vi.* digerire.
digestibility *s.* digeribilità.
digestible *agg.* digeribile.
digestion *s.* digestione.
digestive *agg. e s.* digestivo.
digger *s.* **1.** zappatore **2.** scavatrice.
digging *s.* **1.** scavo **2.** miniera. ◆ **diggings** *s. pl.* (*gergo*) alloggio (*sing.*).
digital *agg.* digitale.
dignified *agg.* dignitoso.
to **dignify** *vt.* elevare, nobilitare.
dignitary *s.* dignitario.
dignity *s.* **1.** dignità **2.** dignitario.
digression *s.* digressione.
digressive *agg.* digressivo.
dike *s.* diga.
to **dike** *vt.* arginare.
to **dilapidate** *vt.* dilapidare. ◆ to **dilapidate** *vi.* andare in rovina.
dilatability *s.* dilatabilità.
dilatable *agg.* dilatabile.
dilatation *s.* dilatazione.
to **dilate** *vt.* dilatare. ◆ to **dilate** *vi.* dilatarsi.
dilatory *agg.* **1.** dilatorio **2.** lento.
diligence *s.* diligenza.
diligent *agg.* diligente.
diluent *agg. e s.* diluente.
to **dilute** *vt.* diluire.
dilution *s.* **1.** diluzione **2.** sostanza

diluita.
diluvial *agg.* diluviale.
dim *agg.* 1. debole 2. appannato 3. oscuro.
to **dim** *vt.* 1. indebolire 2. oscurare.
♦ to **dim** *vi.* 1. indebolirsi 2. oscurarsi.
dime *s.* quarto di dollaro.
dimension *s.* dimensione.
dimeter *s.* dimetro.
to **diminish** *vt.* e *vi.* diminuire.
diminishable *agg.* diminuibile.
diminution *s.* diminuzione.
diminutive *agg.* minuscolo. ♦ **diminutive** *s.* diminutivo.
dimissory *agg.* dimissorio.
dimly *avv.* 1. debolmente 2. oscuramente.
dimness *s.* 1. debolezza 2. offuscamento (*di vista*).
dimple *s.* fossetta.
din *s.* baccano.
to **din** *vt.* e *vi.* rintronare.
to **dine** *vi.* pranzare.
diner *s.* commensale.
to **ding** *vt.* e *vi.* suonare, scampanellare.
dingy *agg.* scuro, sporco.
dining *s.* il pranzare || — -*room*, sala da pranzo.
dinner *s.* pranzo || — -*wagon*, carrello (*per i pasti*); — -*car*, vagone ristorante.
dinosaur *s.* dinosauro.
dint *s.* tacca || *by* — *of*, a forza di.
diocesan *agg.* e *s.* diocesano.
diocese *s.* diocesi.
diode *s.* diodo.
Dionysiac, Dionysian *agg.* dionisiaco.
diopter *s.* diottria.
dioptric *agg.* diottrico.
dioxid(e) *s.* biossido.
dip *s.* 1. bagno 2. inclinazione 3. (*aer.*) picchiata 4. tuffo.
to **dip** *vt.* 1. immergere 2. abbassare. ♦ to **dip** *vi.* 1. immergersi 2. abbassarsi 3. tuffarsi.
diphtheria *s.* difterite.
diphtheric *agg.* difterico.
diphthong *s.* dittongo.
diplomacy *s.* diplomazia.
diplomat *s.* diplomatico.
diplomatic *agg.* diplomatico.
diplomatically *avv.* diplomaticamente.
diplomatics *s.* diplomazia.
diplomatist *s.* diplomatico.
dipody *s.* dipodia.

dipper *s.* 1. tuffatore 2. mestolo || *the Big* —, l'Orsa Maggiore.
dipsomaniac *s.* dipsomane.
dipteral *agg.* dittero.
diptych *s.* dittico.
dire *agg.* terribile, orrendo.
direct *agg.* diretto.
to **direct** *vt.* 1. dirigere 2. ordinare.
direction *s.* 1. direzione 2. indicazione.
directional *agg.* direzionale.
directive *agg.* direttivo. ♦ **directive** *s.* direttiva.
directly *avv.* 1. direttamente 2. subito.
director *s.* 1. direttore 2. regista.
directorial *agg.* direttivo.
directory *agg.* direttivo. ♦ **directory** *s.* 1. (*tel.*) guida 2. (*amer.*) consiglio di amministrazione.
direful *agg.* orrendo.
dirge *s.* canto funebre.
diriment *agg.* dirimento.
dirt *s.* sporcizia.
dirtiness *s.* sozzura.
dirty *agg.* 1. sporco 2. brutto 3. sboccato.
to **dirty** *vt.* sporcare. ♦ to **dirty** *vi.* sporcarsi.
disability *s.* 1. incapacità 2. invalidità.
to **disable** *vt.* rendere incapace, inabile.
to **disabuse** *vt.* disingannare.
to **disaccustom** *vt.* disabituare.
disadvantage *s.* svantaggio.
disadvantageous *agg.* svantaggioso.
to **disagree** *vi.* dissentire.
disagreeable *agg.* sgradevole.
disagreeableness *s.* sgradevolezza.
disagreement *s.* dissenso.
to **disappear** *vi.* scomparire.
disappearance *s.* sparizione.
to **disappoint** *vt.* deludere.
disappointingly *avv.* in modo deludente.
disappointment *s.* delusione.
disapprobation, disapproval *s.* disapprovazione.
to **disapprove** *vt.* e *vi.* disapprovare.
disapprovingly *avv.* con disapprovazione.
to **disarm** *vt.* e *vi.* disarmare.
disarmament *s.* disarmo.
to **disarrange** *vt.* scompigliare.
disarrangement *s.* scompiglio.
disarray *s.* scompiglio, confusione.

to **disassemble** *vt.* smontare.
disassembling *s.* smontaggio.
disaster *s.* disastro.
disastrous *agg.* disastroso.
to **disavow** *vt.* ripudiare.
to **disband** *vt.* sciogliere. ♦ to **disband** *vi.* sbandarsi.
disbelief *s.* incredulità.
to **disbelieve** *vt.* e *vi.* non credere.
disbeliever *s.* incredulo.
disbursement *s.* pagamento.
to **discard** *vt.* scartare.
to **discern** *vt.* discernere.
discernible *agg.* visibile.
discernment *s.* discernimento.
discharge *s.* 1. scarico 2. scarica 3. congedo 4. assoluzione 5. liberazione 6. pagamento.
to **discharge** *vt.* 1. scaricare 2. congedare 3. assolvere 4. liberare. ♦ to **discharge** *vi.* scaricarsi.
disciple *s.* discepolo.
disciplinable *agg.* disciplinabile.
disciplinary *agg.* disciplinare.
discipline *s.* disciplina.
to **disclaim** *vt.* rifiutare, declinare (*responsabilità*).
disclaimer *s.* rinuncia, rifiuto.
to **disclose** *vt.* svelare.
disclosure *s.* rivelazione.
discoid *agg.* e *s.* discoide.
to **discolour** *vt.* scolorire. ♦ to **discolour** *vi.* scolorirsi.
discolouration *s.* scoloramento.
to **discomfit** *vt.* 1. sconfiggere 2. disorientare.
to **discomfort** *vt.* mettere a disagio.
to **discompose** *vt.* agitare.
to **disconcert** *vt.* turbare.
to **disconnect** *vt.* separare, disunire.
disconnected *agg.* 1. sconnesso 2. disinnestato.
disconnectedness *s.* sconnessione.
disconsolate *agg.* sconsolato.
discontent *s.* scontento.
to **discontinue** *vt.* e *vi.* cessare.
discontinuity *s.* discontinuità.
discontinuous *agg.* discontinuo.
discord *s.* 1. discordia, dissenso 2. (*mus.*) dissonanza.
discordance *s.* 1. disaccordo 2. discordanza (*di suoni*).
discordant *agg.* discorde.
discordantly *avv.* in disaccordo.
discount *s.* sconto || at a —, sottocosto.
to **discount** *vt.* 1. scontare 2. tenere in poco conto.

discountable *agg.* 1. scontabile 2. poco attendibile.
to **discourage** *vt.* scoraggiare.
discouragement *s.* scoraggiamento.
to **discover** *vt.* scoprire.
discoverer *s.* scopritore.
discovery *s.* scoperta.
discredit *s.* 1. discredito 2. dubbio.
to **discredit** *vt.* 1. screditare 2. mettere in dubbio.
discreditable *agg.* vergognoso, infamante.
discreet *agg.* prudente, discreto.
discrepancy *s.* disaccordo.
discrete *agg.* separato, distinto.
discretion *s.* 1. discrezione 2. saggezza.
discretionary *agg.* discrezionale.
discriminate *agg.* discriminato.
to **discriminate** *vt.* e *vi.* discriminare.
discriminating *agg.* 1. sagace 2. discriminante.
discrimination *s.* 1. discriminazione 2. discernimento.
discursive *agg.* divagante.
discus *s.* disco || — -thrower, discobolo.
to **discuss** *vt.* discutere.
discussion *s.* discussione.
disdain *s.* sdegno.
to **disdain** *vt.* disdegnare.
disdainful *agg.* sdegnoso.
disease *s.* malattia.
to **disembark** *vt.* e *vi.* sbarcare.
to **disembarrass** *vt.* sbarazzare.
to **disembody** *vt.* 1. disincarnare 2. congedare.
to **disembowel** *vt.* sventrare.
disembowelment *s.* sventramento.
to **disenchant** *vt.* disincantare.
disenchantment *s.* disincanto.
to **disengage** *vt.* 1. disimpegnare 2. disinnestare. ♦ to **disengage** *vi.* liberarsi.
disengagement *s.* 1. liberazione 2. disinnesto.
to **disentangle** *vt.* districare. ♦ to **disentangle** *vi.* districarsi.
disentanglement *s.* districamento.
disesteem *s.* disistima.
to **disesteem** *vt.* disprezzare.
disfavour *s.* 1. disgrazia 2. disapprovazione.
to **disfigure** *vt.* sfigurare.
disfigurement *s.* deturpamento.
to **disfranchise** *vt.* privare dei diritti (*civili o di voto*).
to **disgorge** *vt.* 1. emettere 2. vomi-

tare (*anche fig.*).
disgrace *s.* **1.** vergogna **2.** disgrazia.
to disgrace *vt.* disonorare.
disgraceful *agg.* vergognoso.
disgregation *s.* disgregazione.
disguise *s.* travestimento || *in* —,
travestito, camuffato.
to disguise *vt.* mascherare.
disgust *s.* disgusto.
to disgust *vt.* disgustare.
disgustedly *avv.* con disgusto.
disgustful, disgusting *agg.* disgustoso.
dish *s.* **1.** piatto **2.** vivanda || —
-*washer*, lavapiatti.
to dish *vt.* servire || *to* — *up*, servire in tavola.
to disharmonize *vt.* disarmonizzare.
to dishearten *vt.* scoraggiare.
disheartenment *s.* scoraggiamento.
to dishevel *vt.* arruffare.
dishonest *agg.* disonesto.
dishonesty *s.* disonestà.
dishonour *s.* **1.** disonore **2.** mancato pagamento.
to dishonour *vt.* **1.** disonorare **2.**
rifiutare di pagare.
dishonourable *agg.* disonorevole.
dishonourableness *s.* disonorabilità.
disillusion(ment) *s.* disillusione.
to disinfect *vt.* disinfettare.
disinfectant *s.* disinfettante.
disinfection *s.* disinfezione.
to disinfest *vt.* disinfestare.
disinfestation *s.* disinfestazione.
to disinherit *vt.* diseredare.
to disintegrate *vt.* disintegrare. ♦
to disintegrate *vi.* disintegrarsi.
disintegration *s.* disintegrazione.
disintegrator *s.* disintegratore.
to disinter *vt.* dissotterrare.
disinterested *agg.* disinteressato.
disinterment *s.* dissotterramento.
to disjoin *vt.* disgiungere. ♦ **to
disjoin** *vi.* disgiungersi.
to disjoint *vt.* **1.** disgregare **2.** disarticolare. ♦ **to disjoint** *vi.* disgregarsi.
disjunction *s.* separazione.
disjunctive *agg.* disgiuntivo.
disjunctively *avv.* disgiuntamente.
disk *s.* disco.
dislike *s.* avversione.
to dislike *vt.* detestare, provar avversione per.
to dislocate *vt.* **1.** spostare **2.** slogare **3.** disorganizzare.

dislocation *s.* **1.** dislocazione **2.**
slogatura **3.** disorganizzazione.
to dislodge *vt.* sloggiare.
disloyal *agg.* sleale.
disloyalty *s.* slealtà.
dismal *agg.* tetro.
to dismantle *vt.* smantellare.
dismantlement *s.* smantellamento.
to dismast *vt.* (*mar.*) disalberare.
dismay *s.* costernazione.
to dismay *vt.* costernare.
to dismember *vt.* smembrare.
dismemberment *s.* smembramento.
to dismiss *vt.* **1.** congedare **2.** licenziare **3.** bandire.
dismissal *s.* **1.** congedo **2.** licenziamento **3.** destituzione **4.** rigetto.
to dismount *vt.* e *vi.* smontare.
disobedience *s.* disubbidienza.
disobedient *agg.* disubbidiente.
to disobey *vt.* disubbidire.
to disoblige *vt.* essere scortese con.
disobliging *agg.* scortese.
disorder *s.* **1.** disordine **2.** disturbo.
to disorder *vt.* **1.** scompigliare **2.**
disturbare.
disorderly *agg.* **1.** disordinato **2.**
turbolento.
disorganization *s.* disorganizzazione.
to disorganize *vt.* disorganizzare.
to disorient(ate) *vt.* disorientare.
disorientation *s.* disorientamento.
to disown *vt.* rinnegare.
disowning *s.* rinnegamento.
to disparage *vt.* **1.** deprezzare **2.**
screditare.
disparagement *s.* **1.** deprezzamento **2.** denigrazione.
disparaging *agg.* **1.** sprezzante **2.**
denigratorio.
disparate *agg.* disparato.
disparity *s.* disparità.
dispassionate *agg.* spassionato.
dispatch *s.* **1.** spedizione **2.** dispaccio **3.** disbrigo **4.** celerità.
to dispatch *vt.* **1.** spedire **2.** sbrigare.
to dispel *vt.* dissipare.
dispensary *s.* dispensario.
dispensation *s.* **1.** (*eccl.*) dispensa **2.** distribuzione **3.** beneficio.
to dispense *vt.* dispensare. ♦ **to
dispense** *vi.* fare a meno di: *to*
— *with so.*, fare a meno di qu.
dispersal *s.* dispersione.
to disperse *vt.* disperdere. ♦ **to disperse** *vi.* disperdersi.
dispersion *s.* dispersione.

dispersive *agg.* dispersivo.
dispirited *agg.* depresso.
to **displace** *vt.* 1. spostare 2. destituire.
displacement *s.* 1. spostamento 2. sostituzione 3. (*mar.*) dislocamento.
display *s.* mostra, esibizione.
to **display** *vt.* mostrare, esporre.
to **displease** *vt.* dispiacere.
displeasing *agg.* spiacevole.
displeasure *s.* dispiacere.
disposal *s.* 1. disposizione 2. cessione.
to **dispose** *vt.* e *vi.* disporre || *to — of,* disfarsi di, smerciare.
disposition *s.* 1. disposizione 2. indole.
to **dispossess** *vt.* spogliare.
dispossession *s.* 1. spoliazione 2. (*giur.*) esproprio.
disproportion *s.* sproporzione.
disproportionate, disproportioned *agg.* sproporzionato.
to **disprove** *vt.* 1. confutare 2. dimostrare la falsità di.
disputable *agg.* discutibile.
dispute *s.* controversia, disputa.
to **dispute** *vt.* 1. disputare 2. contestare.
disqualification *s.* 1. incapacità 2. (*giur.*) interdizione 3. squalifica.
to **disqualify** *vt.* 1. rendere incapace 2. (*giur.*) interdire 3. squalificare.
disquieting *agg.* inquietante.
disquisition *s.* 1. disquisizione 2. inchiesta.
disregard *s.* noncuranza.
to **disregard** *vt.* ignorare.
disreputable *agg.* 1. sconveniente 2. screditato.
disreputably *avv.* disonorevolmente.
disrepute *s.* discredito.
disrespectful *agg.* irrispettoso.
to **disrobe** *vt.* svestire. ♦ to **disrobe** *vi.* svestirsi.
disruption *s.* rottura.
disruptive *agg.* 1. che smembra 2. dirompente.
dissatisfaction *s.* insoddisfazione.
dissatisfactory *agg.* insoddisfacente.
dissatisfied *agg.* scontento.
to **dissatisfy** *vt.* scontentare.
to **dissect** *vt.* sezionare.
dissection *s.* 1. sezionamento 2. parte sezionata.
to **dissemble** *vt.* e *vi.* dissimulare,

ignorare.
dissembling *s.* dissimulazione. ♦ **dissembling** *agg.* ipocrita.
dissemblingly *avv.* ingannevolmente.
to **disseminate** *vt.* (dis)seminare.
dissemination *s.* disseminazione.
disseminator *s.* propagatore.
dissension *s.* divergenza.
dissent *s.* 1. dissenso 2. (*relig.*) separazione, scisma.
to **dissent** *vi.* dissentire.
dissenter *s.* dissidente.
dissenting *agg.* dissenziente.
to **dissertate** *vi.* dissertare.
dissertation *s.* dissertazione.
dissertator *s.* dissertatore.
disservice *s.* cattivo servizio.
to **dissever** *vt.* scindere. ♦ to **dissever** *vi.* scindersi.
dissidence *s.* dissidio.
dissident *agg.* e *s.* dissidente.
dissimilar *agg.* dissimile.
dissimilarity *s.* dissomiglianza.
dissimilation *s.* dissimilazione.
to **dissimulate** *vt.* e *vi.* dissimulare.
dissimulation *s.* dissimulazione.
dissimulator *s.* dissimulatore.
to **dissipate** *vt.* dissipare. ♦ to **dissipate** *vi.* dissiparsi.
dissipation *s.* dissipazione.
dissociable *agg.* 1. dissociabile 2. riservato.
to **dissociate** *vt.* dissociare. ♦ to **dissociate** *vi.* dissociarsi.
dissociation *s.* 1. dissociazione 2. sdoppiamento (*della personalità*).
dissolubility *s.* dissolubilità.
dissoluble *agg.* dissolubile.
dissolute *agg.* dissoluto.
dissoluteness *s.* dissolutezza.
dissolution *s.* dissoluzione.
to **dissolve** *vt.* dissolvere. ♦ to **dissolve** *vi.* dissolversi.
dissolvent *agg.* e *s.* dissolvente.
dissonance *s.* dissonanza.
dissonant *agg.* dissonante.
to **dissuade** *vt.* dissuadere.
dissuasion *s.* dissuasione.
dissyllabic *agg.* bisillabico.
dissyllable *s.* bisillabo.
dissymmetry *s.* asimmetria.
distaff *s.* conocchia.
distance *s.* distanza || *long- — call,* telefonata interurbana; *at a —,* da lontano.
distant *agg.* 1. lontano 2. riservato.
distantly *avv.* (da) lontano.
distaste *s.* ripugnanza.

distasteful *agg.* repellente.
distemper[1] *s.* **1.** turbamento fisico **2.** cimurro **3.** tumulto.
distemper[2] *s.* tempera.
to **distend** *vt.* distendere. ♦ to **distend** *vi.* distendersi.
to **distil(l)** *vt.* e *vi.* (di)stillare.
distillate *s.* distillato.
distillation *s.* distillazione.
distiller *s.* distillatore.
distillery *s.* distilleria.
distinct *agg.* distinto.
distinction *s.* distinzione.
distinctive *agg.* distintivo.
to **distinguish** *vt.* e *vi.* distinguere.
distinguished *agg.* **1.** distinto **2.** illustre.
to **distort** *vt.* distorcere.
distortion *s.* distorsione.
to **distract** *vt.* **1.** distrarre **2.** turbare, far impazzire.
distraction *s.* **1.** distrazione **2.** follia: *to love to —*, amare alla follia.
to **distrain** *vi.* sequestrare.
distrait *agg.* distratto, smarrito.
distraught *agg.* **1.** folle **2.** sconvolto.
distress *s.* **1.** angoscia **2.** pericolo **3.** sequestro.
to **distress** *vt.* **1.** affliggere **2.** sequestrare.
distressful *agg.* penoso.
distributable *agg.* distribuibile.
to **distribute** *vt.* distribuire.
distribution *s.* distribuzione.
distributive *agg.* distributivo.
distributor *s.* distributore.
district *s.* distretto.
distrust *s.* diffidenza.
to **distrust** *vt.* diffidare di.
distrustful *agg.* diffidente.
to **disturb** *vt.* **1.** disturbare **2.** turbare.
disturbance *s.* agitazione.
disturber *s.* disturbatore.
disunion *s.* separazione.
to **disunite** *vt.* disunire. ♦ to **disunite** *vi.* separarsi.
disunited *agg.* disunito.
disuse *s.* disuso.
disused *agg.* disusato.
ditch *s.* fosso || *to die in the last —*, resistere ad oltranza.
to **ditch** *vi.* scavare fossi.
dithyramb *s.* ditirambo.
dithyrambic *agg.* ditirambico.
ditty *s.* **1.** canzone **2.** poemetto.
diuretic *agg.* e *s.* diuretico.
diurnal *agg.* **1.** diurno **2.** quotidiano.

diuturnal *agg.* diuturno.
diuturnity *s.* diuturnità.
divan *s.* divano.
dive *s.* **1.** tuffo **2.** (*aer.*) picchiata.
to **dive** *vi.* **1.** tuffarsi **2.** (*aer.*) lanciarsi in picchiata.
diver *s.* **1.** tuffatore **2.** palombaro.
to **diverge** *vi.* divergere.
divergence *s.* divergenza.
divergent *agg.* divergente.
diverse *agg.* **1.** diverso **2.** mutevole.
to **diversify** *vt.* rendere diverso.
diversion *s.* **1.** diversione **2.** passatempo.
diversity *s.* diversità.
to **divert** *vt.* **1.** deviare **2.** divertire.
to **divest** *vt.* spogliare.
to **divide** *vt.* dividere. ♦ to **divide** *vi.* dividersi.
dividend *s.* dividendo.
dividing *s.* divisione.
divination *s.* divinazione.
divinatory *agg.* divinatorio.
divine *agg.* divino. ♦ **divine** *s.* (*eccl.*) teologo.
to **divine** *vt.* e *vi.* predire.
diviner *s.* indovino || *water —*, rabdomante.
diving *s.* tuffo || *— -bell*, campana subacquea; *— -board*, trampolino.
divining *s.* divinazione.
divinity *s.* **1.** divinità **2.** teologia.
divisibility *s.* divisibilità.
divisible *agg.* divisibile.
division *s.* divisione.
divisional *agg.* di divisione.
divisor *s.* divisore.
divorce *s.* divorzio.
to **divorce** *vt.* divorziare.
divulgation *s.* divulgazione.
to **divulge** *vt.* divulgare.
divulger *s.* divulgatore.
dizzily *avv.* vertiginosamente.
dizziness *s.* vertigine.
dizzy *agg.* **1.** vertiginoso **2.** preso da vertigine **3.** stordito.
to **do** (**did, done**) *vt.* e *vi.* **1.** (*v. aus. in frasi int., neg., int.-neg.*) *— you understand English?*, capisci l'inglese?; *I do not* (*I don't*), non capisco; *he does not* (*he doesn't*) *speak English*, non parla l'inglese **2.** (*uso enfatico*) *I do study!*, studio veramente! **3.** (*sostitutivo*) *he said he would come and he did*, disse che sarebbe venuto e venne **4.** fare (*in senso generale, astratto*) *what are you doing?*, che cosa stai facendo?; *to*

— *one's duty*, fare il proprio dovere 5. bastare: *that will do*, ciò basta 6. addirsi, convenire: *this house will do me*, questa casa mi va bene || *to — without*, fare a meno.

docile *agg.* docile.

docility *s.* docilità.

dock[1] *s.* bacino: *dry- —*, bacino di carenaggio || *— -master*, capitano di porto; *wet- —*, darsena.

dock[2] *s.* banco degli imputati (*in tribunale*).

docker *s.* scaricatore.

docket *s.* 1. (*giur.*) estratto verbale 2. etichetta.

dockyard *s.* cantiere.

doctor *s.* dottore.

doctoral *agg.* dottorale.

doctorate *s.* dottorato.

doctrinaire *agg.* e *s.* dottrinario.

doctrinal *agg.* dottrinale.

doctrine *s.* dottrina.

document *s.* documento.

to document *vt.* documentare.

documentary *agg.* e *s.* documentario.

documentation *s.* documentazione.

to dodder *vi.* tremare, vacillare.

dodecagon *s.* dodecagono.

dodecahedron *s.* dodecaedro.

dodge *s.* 1. schivata 2. balzo.

to dodge *vt.* schivare. ◆ **to dodge** *vi.* scansarsi.

doe *s.* femmina (*di daino, cervo ecc.*).

doer *s.* chi agisce, chi fa.

dog *s.* 1. cane 2. (*mecc.*) gancio || *— -cart*, calesse; *— catcher*, accalappiacani; *— -days*, giorni di canicola; *— -ear*, orecchia (*a una pagina*); *— -tired*, stanco morto.

to dog *vt.* inseguire.

dogged *agg.* ostinato.

doggerel *s.* filastrocca.

dogmatic(al) *agg.* dogmatico.

dogmatism *s.* dogmatismo.

doily *s.* tovagliolino.

doings *s. pl.* azioni, imprese.

dole *s.* 1. ripartizione 2. sussidio.

doleful *agg.* triste.

dolichocephalic *agg.* dolicocefalo.

doll *s.* bambola.

dollar *s.* dollaro.

dolly *s.* 1. bambola 2. (*cine*) carrello.

dolomitic *agg.* dolomitico.

dolphin *s.* 1. delfino 2. boa.

dolt *s.* stupido.

domain *s.* dominio.

dome *s.* cupola.

domestic *agg.* 1. domestico 2. nazionale. ◆ **domestic** *s.* domestico.

domicile *s.* domicilio.

domiciliary *agg.* domiciliare.

dominant *agg.* dominante.

to dominate *vt.* e *vi.* dominare.

domination *s.* dominazione.

domineering *agg.* dispotico.

Dominican *agg.* e *s.* domenicano.

dominion *s.* dominio, possedimento (*di territori*).

donation *s.* donazione.

donative *s.* dono.

done V. *to do* || *over- —*, troppo cotto; *under- —*, poco cotto.

donjon *s.* torrione.

donkey *s.* asino.

donor *s.* donatore.

doodle *s.* ghirigoro.

doom *s.* 1. destino 2. giudizio.

to doom *vt.* condannare.

doomsday *s.* giudizio universale.

door *s.* porta, portiera || *— -keeper*, portinaio; *— -post*, stipite; *— -way*, soglia.

dope *s.* 1. vernice 2. stupefacente.

to dope *vt.* 1. verniciare 2. drogare.

doping *s.* drogaggio.

Doric *agg.* dorico.

dormer (window) *s.* abbaino.

dormitory *s.* dormitorio.

dormouse *s.* (*pl.* dormice) ghiro.

dorsal *agg.* dorsale.

dosage *s.* dosaggio.

to dose *vt.* 1. dosare 2. adulterare.

dosimeter *s.* dosatore.

dossal *s.* dossale.

dossier *s.* incartamento.

dot *s.* punto, puntino.

to dot *vt.* punteggiare.

dotage *s.* 1. rimbambimento 2. infatuazione.

dotal *agg.* dotale.

doting *agg.* 1. senile 2. infatuato. ◆ **doting** *s.* senilità.

double *agg.* doppio. ◆ **double** *s.* 1. doppio 2. (*cine*) controfigura. ◆ **double** *avv.* 1. doppiamente 2. in due.

to double *vt.* 1. raddoppiare 2. doppiare 3. piegare. ◆ **to double** *vi.* 1. raddoppiarsi 2. piegarsi.

double-dealing *s.* imbroglio.

doubleness *s.* doppiezza.

doubling *s.* raddoppiamento.

doubly *avv.* doppiamente.

doubt *s.* dubbio || *no —*, indubbiamente.

to doubt *vt.* e *vi.* dubitare.

doubtful *agg.* incerto, dubbio.
doubtfulness *s.* dubbiosità.
doubtless *agg.* indubbio. ♦ **doubt-less** *avv.* indubbiamente.
dough *s.* pasta.
dove *s.* colomba || — -*cot(e)*, colombaia.
dowdy *agg.* sciatto.
dower *s.* dote.
down[1] *s.* **1.** duna **2.** collina.
down[2] *s.* **1.** piumino **2.** lanugine.
down[3] *agg.* **1.** diretto verso il basso **2.** depresso.
down[4] *avv.* (in) giù || — *with!*, abbasso: — *with the tyrant!*, abbasso il tiranno! ♦ **down** *prep.* giù per.
to **down** *vt.* abbattere, rovesciare.
downcast *agg.* abbattuto.
downfall *s.* rovescio.
downhearted *agg.* scoraggiato.
downhill *agg.* discendente, inclinato. ♦ **downhill** *avv.* in discesa.
downpour *s.* acquazzone.
downright *agg.* vero, sincero. ♦ **downright** *avv.* completamente.
downstairs *avv.* giù. ♦ **downstairs** *agg.* dabbasso. ♦ **downstairs** *s.* pianterreno.
downtrodden *agg.* calpestato, oppresso.
downward *agg.* in giù, discendente.
downward(s) *avv.* in giù.
downy[1] *agg.* ondulato.
downy[2] *agg.* **1.** lanuginoso **2.** morbido.
dowry *s.* dote.
dowser *s.* rabdomante.
doze *s.* sonnellino.
to **doze** *vi.* sonnecchiare.
dozen *s.* dozzina.
drab *s.* **1.** sciattona **2.** sgualdrina.
draff *s.* feccia.
draft *s.* **1.** tiro **2.** sorso **3.** abbozzo **4.** corrente d'aria **5.** (*comm.*) tratta **6.** (*mar.*) pescaggio.
to **draft** *vt.* **1.** tirare **2.** abbozzare.
drag *s.* **1.** erpice **2.** (*mar.*) draga **3.** ostacolo.
to **drag** *vt.* **1.** trascinare **2.** dragare. ♦ to **drag** *vi.* trascinarsi || *to — on*, tirare in lungo.
to **draggle** *vt.* inzaccherare. ♦ to **draggle** *vi.* inzaccherarsi.
dragon *s.* drago || — -*fly*, libellula.
drain *s.* **1.** canale, fogna **2.** fuga.
to **drain** *vt.* prosciugare. ♦ to **drain** *vi.* **1.** prosciugarsi **2.** defluire.
drainage *s.* **1.** fognatura **2.** drenaggio.

draining *s.* **1.** scolatura **2.** drenaggio.
dram *s.* dramma (*unità di peso*).
drama *s.* dramma.
dramatic(al) *agg.* drammatico.
dramatics *s.* *pl.* produzioni drammatiche (*di dilettanti*).
dramatist *s.* drammaturgo.
to **dramatize** *vt.* e *vi.* drammatizzare.
dramaturgy *s.* drammaturgia.
drank V. *to drink*.
to **drape** *vt.* drappeggiare.
draper *s.* negoziante di tessuti.
drapery *s.* **1.** tessuti **2.** drappeggi.
drastic *agg.* drastico.
draught *s.* V. *draft*. ♦ **draughts** *s.* *pl.* gioco della dama (*sing.*).
draught-board *s.* scacchiera.
draw *s.* **1.** tiro **2.** estrazione **3.** attrazione.
to **draw** (**drew, drawn**) *vt.* **1.** tirare **2.** attirare **3.** disegnare **4.** estrarre **5.** (*comm.*) emettere || *to — up*, compilare. ♦ to **draw** (**drew, drawn**) *vi.* tirarsi || *to — on*, avvicinarsi; *to — in*, ritirarsi; *to — up*, fermarsi.
drawback *s.* ostacolo.
drawbridge *s.* ponte levatoio.
drawer *s.* **1.** estrattore **2.** disegnatore **3.** cassetto.
drawers *s.* *pl.* mutande.
drawing *s.* **1.** disegno **2.** estrazione **3.** attrazione || — -*pen*, tiralinee; — -*pin*, puntina da disegno.
drawing-room *s.* salotto.
to **drawl** *vt.* strascicare la voce.
drawn V. *to draw*.
dread *s.* spavento.
dreadful *agg.* terribile.
dreadnought *s.* **1.** impavido **2.** (*mar.*) corazzata.
dream *s.* sogno.
to **dream** (**dreamt, dreamt**) (*anche reg.*) *vt.* e *vi.* sognare.
dreamer *s.* sognatore.
dreamt V. *to dream*.
dreamless *agg.* senza sogni.
dreamy *agg.* **1.** sognante **2.** vago.
dreariness *s.* tristezza.
dreary *agg.* tetro, squallido.
dredge *s.* draga.
to **dredge**[1] *vt.* e *vi.* dragare.
to **dredge**[2] *vt.* cospargere, spolverizzare.
dredger[1] *s.* draga.
dredger[2] *s.* spolverizzatore.
dredging *s.* dragaggio.

dregs *s. pl.* **1.** feccia (*sing.*) **2.** sedimento (*sing.*).

to drench *vt.* inzuppare || *to get drenched,* inzupparsi.

dress *s.* abito, abbigliamento.

to dress *vt.* **1.** vestire **2.** bendare **3.** condire, rifinire. ♦ **to dress** *vi.* vestirsi.

dressing *s.* **1.** abbigliamento **2.** medicazione **3.** condimento || — -*gown,* vestaglia; — -*table,* toletta.

dressmaker *s.* sarta.

dressmaking *s.* sartoria.

drew V. *to draw.*

dribble *s.* **1.** gocciolamento **2.** (*sport*) palleggio.

to dribble *vt.* e *vi.* **1.** stillare **2.** (*sport*) palleggiare.

dribbling *s.* V. *dribble.*

drier *s.* essiccatore.

drift *s.* **1.** spinta **2.** deriva **3.** raffica **4.** (*fig.*) significato.

to drift *vt.* sospingere. ♦ **to drift** *vi.* andare alla deriva, essere trascinato.

drill *s.* **1.** trapano, trivella **2.** esercitazione.

to drill *vt.* **1.** trapanare, trivellare **2.** esercitare.

drilling *s.* **1.** trapanazione, trivellazione **2.** esercitazione || — -*machine,* trapano.

drink *s.* **1.** il bere **2.** bevanda.

to drink (drank, drunk) *vt.* e *vi.* bere.

drinkable *agg.* bevibile.

drinker *s.* bevitore.

drinking *s.* il bere.

drip *s.* gocciolamento.

to drip *vt.* e *vi.* gocciolare.

dripping *s.* gocciolio.

drive *s.* **1.** gita (*in auto*) **2.** viale (*carrozzabile*) **3.** spinta.

to drive (drove, driven) *vt.* **1.** condurre **2.** guidare **3.** azionare || *to* — *away,* scacciare; *to* — *in,* conficcare. ♦ **to drive (drove, driven)** *vi.* andare (*in veicolo*) || *to* — *off,* partire (*in veicolo*); *to* — *up,* arrivare (*in veicolo*).

drive-in *s.* cinema, banca ecc. in cui si entra in auto.

driver *s.* conducente.

driving *s* **1.** guida **2.** comando.

drizzle *s.* pioggerella.

to drizzle *vi.* piovigginare.

drizzly *agg.* piovigginoso.

droll *agg.* buffo.

drollery *s.* **1.** buffoneria **2.** scherzo.

dromedary *s.* dromedario.

drone *s.* **1.** fuco **2.** ronzio.

to drone *vt.* e *vi.* ronzare.

to droop *vt.* abbassare. ♦ **to droop** *vi.* afflosciarsi, languire.

drooping *agg.* **1.** pendente, abbassato **2.** abbattuto.

drop *s.* **1.** goccia **2.** caduta **3.** ribasso.

to drop *vt.* lasciar cadere. ♦ **to drop** *vi.* cadere || *to* — *in,* fare una visitina; *to* — *away,* scomparire.

dropper *s.* contagocce.

dropsical *agg.* idropico.

dropsy *s.* idropisia.

dross *s.* scoria.

drought *s.* siccità.

drove V. *to drive.*

to drown *vt.* **1.** annegare **2.** smorzare. ♦ **to drown** *vi.* annegare.

drowning *s.* annegamento.

to drowse *vi.* sonnecchiare, assopirsi.

drowsily *avv.* in modo sonnolento.

drowsiness *s.* sonnolenza.

drowsy *agg.* sonnolento.

to drub *vt.* percuotere, bastonare.

drudge *s.* sgobbone.

to drudge *vi.* sfacchinare.

drudgery *s.* lavoro faticoso.

drug *s.* **1.** medicina **2.** droga || — -*store,* farmacia (*in cui si vendono articoli vari*).

to drug *vt.* drogare.

druggist *s.* farmacista.

Druid *s.* druido.

drum *s.* **1.** tamburo **2.** timpano.

to drum *vi.* suonare il tamburo. ♦ **to drum** *vt.* (*fig.*) inculcare.

drummer *s.* tamburino.

drumming *s.* tambureggiamento.

drunk V. *to drink.* ♦ **drunk** *agg.* ubriaco.

drunkard *s.* ubriacone.

drunken *agg.* ubriaco.

drunkenness *s.* ubriachezza.

dry *agg.* asciutto, arido, secco || — *cleaning,* lavaggio a secco.

to dry *vt.* **1.** seccare **2.** asciugare. ♦ **to dry** *vi.* **1.** seccarsi **2.** asciugatsi || *to* — *up,* ammutolire.

dryad *s.* driade.

drying *agg.* essiccante. ♦ **drying** *s.* essiccamento.

dual *agg.* duplice.

dualism *s.* dualismo.

dualist *s.* dualista.

dualistic *agg.* dualistico.

duality s. dualità.
to **dub**[1] vt. creare cavaliere.
to **dub**[2] vt. (cine) doppiare.
dubbing s. doppiaggio.
dubious agg. 1. dubbio 2. dubbioso.
dubiousness s. dubbiosità.
dubitative agg. dubitativo.
ducal agg. ducale.
duchess s. duchessa.
duchy s. ducato.
duck[1] s. anitra.
duck[2] s. tela.
duck[3] s. tuffo.
to **duck** vt. 1. tuffare 2. piegare. ♦
   to **duck** vi. 1. tuffarsi 2. piegarsi.
duckling s. anatroccolo.
duct s. condotto.
ductile agg. duttile.
ductility s. duttilità.
due agg. e s. dovuto || to be —, dover arrivare; to fall —, scadere.
duel s. duello.
to **duel** vi. duella.e.
duet s. duetto.
dug V. to dig.
duke s. duca.
dukedom s. ducato.
dull agg. 1. tardo, sciocco 2. sordo 3. triste 4. noioso 5. opaco.
to **dull** vt. 1. istupidire 2. intorpidire 3. smorzare. ♦ to **dull** vi. 1. istupidirsi 2. intorpidirsi 3. smorzarsi.
dullard s. imbecille.
dul(l)ness s. 1. lentezza 2. noia 3. opacità 4. ottusità.
dully avv. 1. ottusamente 2. lentamente 3. in modo noioso 4. debolmente.
duly avv. debitamente.
dumb agg. muto || — -show, pantomima.
to **dumbfound** vt. confondere.
dumbness s. mutismo.
dumb-waiter s. montavivande.
dummy agg. 1. muto 2. falso. ♦ **dummy** s. fantoccio.
dump s. 1. colpo sordo 2. ammasso.
dumping s. « dumping » (tipo di vendita concorrenziale sui mercati esteri).
dunce s. ignorante.
dune s. duna.
dung s. 1. sterco 2. letame.
dungarees s. pl. tuta (da lavoro) (sing.).
dungeon s. 1. torrione 2. prigione sotterranea.
dunghill s. letamaio.

to **dunk** vt. e vi. inzuppare.
duodenal agg. duodenale.
duodenum s. (pl. -na) duodeno.
dupe s. gonzo.
duplex agg. duplice.
duplicate agg. doppio. ♦ **duplicate** s. duplicato.
to **duplicate** vt. duplicare.
duplication s. 1. raddoppiamento 2. riproduzione.
duplicator s. copialettere.
duplicity s. doppiezza.
durability s. durata.
durable agg. durevole.
durallumin s. duralluminio.
duration s. durata.
duress s. 1. prigionia 2. coercizione.
during prep. durante.
durst V. dare.
dusk s. 1. oscurità 2. crepuscolo.
dusky agg. oscuro.
dust s. polvere || — -bin, pattumiera.
to **dust** vt. 1. impolverare 2. spolverare. ♦ to **dust** vi. impolverarsi.
duster s. 1. strofinaccio (per la polvere) 2. polverizzatore.
dustman s. spazzino.
dusty agg. polveroso.
Dutch agg. olandese.
Dutchman s. olandese.
dutiful agg. rispettoso.
duty s. 1. ubbidienza 2. dovere 3. tassa.
duumvirate s. duumvirato.
dwarf s. nano.
dwarfish agg. nano.
to **dwell** (**dwelt, dwelt**) vi. 1. abitare 2. fermarsi.
dweller s. abitatore.
dwelling s. abitazione.
dwelt V. to dwell.
dye s. tintura.
to **dye** vt. tingere. ♦ to **dye** vi. tingersi.
dyer s. tintore.
dyerworks s. pl. tintoria (sing.).
dying agg. morente.
dynamic(al) agg. dinamico.
dynamics s. dinamica.
dynamism s. dinamismo.
dynamite s. dinamite.
dynamiter s. dinamitardo.
dynamo s. dinamo.
dynamometer s. dinamometro.
dynast s. dinasta.
dynastic(al) agg. dinastico.
dynasty s. dinastia.
dyne s. dina.

dysenteric *agg.* dissenterico.
dysentery *s.* dissenteria.
dyspepsia *s.* dispepsia.
dyspeptic(al) *agg.* dispeptico.

E

E (*mus.*) mi.
each *agg.* ogni, ciascuno. ♦ **each**
pron. ognuno, ciascuno || — *other*,
l'un l'altro.
eager *agg.* **1.** ardente, appassionato
2. avido, desideroso.
eagerly *avv.* **1.** ardentemente **2.** avidamente.
eagerness *s.* **1.** ardore **2.** impazienza, premura.
eagle *s.* aquila.
ear[1] orecchio || — *-ache* mal d'o-
recchi — *-drum;* timpano; —
-ring, orecchino; — *-vax,* ceru-
me; *within* — *-shot,* a portata di
voce.
ear[2] *s.* spiga (*di grano*).
earl *s.* conte.
earldom *s.* **1.** titolo di conte **2.**
contea.
early *agg.* **1.** primo, il principio, la
prima parte (*di qualsiasi tempo*)
2. mattiniero **3.** prematuro **4.** re-
moto || — *train*, treno del primo
mattino.
early *avv.* **1.** presto, di buon'ora,
per tempo **2.** al principio.
earmark *s.* **1.** marchio, caratteristica **2.** (*comm.*) contrassegno.
to earn *vt.* guadagnare, meritare.
earnest *agg.* **1.** serio, zelante **2.** ardente. ♦ **earnest** *s.* caparra, pe-
gno.
earnestly *avv.* **1.** seriamente **2.** con
ardore.
earnestness *s.* **1.** serietà **2.** ardore.
earnings *s. pl.* **1.** guadagni **2.**
(*comm.*) utili.
earth *s.* **1.** terra, mondo **2.** terreno.
earth-bound *agg.* radicato, attacca-
to ai beni terreni.
earthen *agg.* di terra, di terracotta.
earthenware *s.* terraglia.
earthly *agg.* terrestre.
earthquake *s.* terremoto.
earthworm *s.* lombrico.
earthy *agg.* terroso, di terra.
ease *s.* **1.** tranquillità (*di spirito*),

benessere **2.** facilità, agevolezza **3.**
sollievo.
to ease *vt.* e *vi.* **1.** alleviare, calmare
2. liberare, alleggerire.
ɔaseful *agg.* tranquillo.
easel *s.* cavalletto, telaio.
easily *avv.* **1.** facilmente **2.** comodamente.
easiness *s.* **1.** comodità, benessere
2. facilità.
east *s.* est, oriente: *the Far East,*
l'Estremo Oriente. ♦ **east** *avv.*
ad est, verso est.
Easter *s.* Pasqua.
easterly *agg.* dell'est, dall'est, orientale.
eastern *agg.* dell'est, orientale.
eastward *agg.* verso est.
easy *agg.* **1.** facile **2.** agiato,
modo **3.** piacevole.
easy *avv.* facilmente, comodamente.
easygoing *agg.* facilone, indolente.
to eat (ate, eaten) *vt.* e *vi.* **1.**
mangiare **2.** rodere, corrodere.
eatable *agg.* mangiabile, commesti-
bile.
eatables *s. pl.* vivande, viveri.
eaten V. *to eat.*
eater *s.* mangiatore.
eating *s.* il mangiare.
eaves *s. pl.* gronda, cornicione
(*sing.*).
to eavesdrop *vi.* origliare.
ebb *s.* **1.** riflusso, l'abbassarsi della
marea **2.** (*fig.*) decadenza || — *-tide,*
bassa marea.
ebbing *agg.* **1.** defluente **2.** in declino.
ebonist *s.* ebanista.
ebonite *s.* ebanite.
ebony *s.* ebano.
ebullition *s.* ebollizione.
eccentric *agg.* e *s.* eccentrico (*anche fig.*).
eccentricity *s.* eccentricità.
ecclesiastic *agg.* e *s.* ecclesiastico.
ecclesiastical *agg.* ecclesiastico.
echelon *s.* scaglione.
echinoderm *s.* echinoderma.
echo *s.* eco.
to echo *vt.* e *vi.* **1.** far eco (a) **2.** e-
cheggiare.
eclectic *agg.* e *s.* eclettico.
eclecticism *s.* eclettismo.
eclipse *s.* eclissi.
to eclipse *vt.* eclissare.
ecliptic *agg.* eclittico.
eclogue *s.* egloga.
ecology *s.* ecologia.

economic *agg.* economico.
economical *agg.* economico.
economics *s.* scienze economiche.
economist *s.* economista.
to **economize** *vt.* e *vi.* economizzare.
economy *s.* economia.
ecstasy *s.* estasi.
ecstatic *agg.* estatico.
ecstatically *avv.* estaticamente.
ecumenic(al) *agg.* ecumenico.
eczema *s.* eczema.
eddy *s.* 1. turbine d'aria, vortice 2. gorgo, risucchio.
edge *s.* 1. orlo, margine 2. ciglio, sponda 3. taglio (*di lama*) 4. spigolo.
to **edge** *vt.* e *vi.* 1. bordare, fare un bordo 2. affilare, arrotare, aguzzare (*anche fig.*).
edged *agg.* affilato, tagliente || *double-* —, a doppio taglio (*anche fig.*).
edgeless *agg.* 1. senza bordo 2. smussato, che non taglia.
edging *s.* orlatura, fettuccia.
edible *agg.* mangereccio.
edibles *s. pl.* commestibili.
edict *s.* editto.
edifice *s.* edificio (*anche fig.*).
edifying *agg.* edificante.
to **edit** *vt.* 1. pubblicare, curare (*un libro*) 2. redigere 3. (*cine*) montare.
editing *s.* 1. redazione, commento (*di un testo*) 2. direzione (*di un giornale, ecc.*).
edition *s.* edizione.
editor *s.* 1. commentatore, curatore (*di un testo*) 2. direttore, redattore (*di un giornale*).
editorial *s.* editoriale, articolo di fondo. ♦ **editorial** *agg.* editoriale.
editorship *s.* direzione, redazione (*di giornali*).
to **educate** *vt.* 1. istruire, educare 2. affinare, esercitare.
educated *agg.* 1. istruito, colto 2. addestrato (*di animali*).
education *s.* 1. cultura, educazione 2. istruzione, insegnamento.
educational *agg.* educativo.
educative *agg.* istruttivo.
educator *s.* educatore.
to **educe** *vt.* estrarre, sviluppare.
educible *agg.* che si può estrarre.
to **edulcorate** *vt.* dolcificare.
eel *s.* anguilla.
eerie, eery *agg.* irreale, sovrannatu-

rale.
to **efface** *vt.* cancellare, distruggere.
effect *s.* 1. effetto, risultato 2. impressione. ♦ **effects** *s. pl.* effetti personali.
to **effect** *vt.* effettuare, eseguire.
effective *agg.* 1. efficace 2. effettivo.
effectiveness *s.* efficacia.
effectual *agg.* efficace.
effectuality *s.* efficacia, validità.
effectuation *s.* effettuazione.
effeminacy *s.* effeminatezza.
effeminate *agg.* effeminato.
effervescence *s.* 1. effervescenza 2. (*fig.*) eccitamento.
effete *agg.* logoro, esaurito.
efficacious *agg.* efficace.
efficaciousness *s.* 1. efficacia 2. rendimento (*di una macchina*).
efficiency *s.* efficienza, rendimento.
efficient *agg.* 1. efficiente, di alto rendimento 2. abile, capace.
effigy *s.* effigie.
to **effloresce** *vi.* fiorire, germogliare.
effluent *agg.* defluente.
effluvium *s.* effluvio.
effort *s.* sforzo, fatica.
effortless *agg.* senza sforzo, facile.
effrontery *s.* sfrontatezza.
effulgence *s.* splendore.
effusion *s.* effusione, esuberanza.
effusive *agg.* espansivo, esuberante.
egg *s.* uovo || *boiled* —, uovo alla coque; *hard-boiled* —, uovo sodo.
to **egg** *vt. to* — *on so.*, istigare, incitare qu.
egocentric *agg.* egocentrico.
egocentrism *s.* egocentrismo.
egoism *s.* egoismo.
egoist *s.* egoista.
egoistic(al) *agg.* egoistico.
egotism *s.* egotismo.
egotist *s.* egotista.
egregious *agg.* insigne, eminente.
egress *s.* uscita.
Egyptian *agg.* e *s.* egiziano.
eider-down *s.* piumino (*da letto*).
eight *agg.* otto.
eighteen *agg.* diciotto.
eighteenth *agg.* diciottesimo.
eighth *agg.* ottavo.
eightieth *agg.* ottantesimo.
eighty *agg.* ottanta.
either *agg.* 1. l'uno o l'altro 2. ciascuno dei due, tutti e due. ♦ **either** *avv.* anche, pure. ♦ **either** *avv.* (*in frasi neg.*) neanche, neppure. ♦ **either** *cong.* (*seguito da or*) o, oppure.
to **ejaculate** *vt.* 1. eiaculare 2. e-

sclamare.
ejaculation s. **1.** eiaculazione **2.** esclamazione.
to eject vt. gettar fuori.
ejection s. **1.** espulsione **2.** (fig.) destituzione.
ejector s. espulsore.
elaborate agg. elaborato, accurato.
to elaborate vt. e vi. elaborare.
elaboration s. elaborazione.
to elapse vi. trascorrere, passare (del tempo).
elastic agg. elastico (anche fig.).
elasticity s. elasticità.
to elate vt. inebriare, esaltare.
elbow s. gomito.
to elbow vt. e vi. spingere con il gomito, andare avanti a gomitate.
elder agg. (comp. di old) maggiore, più vecchio (tra due persone). ◆
elder s. maggiore, più vecchio (fra due).
elderly agg. attempato.
eldest agg. (superl. di old) maggiore (tra fratelli), primogenito.
elect agg. eletto, scelto.
to elect vt. eleggere.
election s. **1.** elezione **2.** scelta.
elective agg. **1.** elettivo **2.** elettorale.
elector s. elettore.
electoral agg. elettorale.
electorate s. elettorato.
electric(al) agg. elettrico.
electrician s. elettricista.
electricity s. elettricità.
to electrify vt. **1.** elettrificare **2.** elettrizzare.
electrization s. elettrizzazione.
electrocardiogram s. elettrocardiogramma.
to electrocute vt. fulminare mediante elettricità.
electrocution s. elettroesecuzione.
electrode s. elettrodo.
electrodynamics s. elettrodinamica.
electrolysis s. elettrolisi.
electro-magnet s. elettromagnete.
electromagnetic agg. elettromagnetico.
electron s. elettrone.
electronic agg. elettronico.
electronics s. elettronica.
electrostatics s. elettrostatica.
elegance s. eleganza.
elegant agg. elegante, raffinato.
elegiac agg. elegiaco.
elegy s. elegia.

element s. **1.** elemento **2.** principio costitutivo.
elemental agg. **1.** dei quattro elementi **2.** elementare **3.** fondamentale.
elementary agg. elementare.
elephant s. elefante.
elephantiasis s. elefantiasi.
elephantine agg. elefantesco.
to elevate vt. innalzare, elevare (anche fig.).
elevated agg. **1.** elevato **2.** sopraelevato.
elevation s. **1.** elevazione **2.** collina, luogo alto.
elevator s. ascensore, montacarichi.
eleven agg. undici.
elevenses s. (fam.) spuntino a metà mattina.
eleventh agg. undicesimo.
elf s. (pl. elves) elfo, folletto.
elfish agg. **1.** incantato **2.** vivace.
to elicit vt. estrarre, strappare.
eligibility s. eleggibilità.
eligible agg. eleggibile.
to eliminate vt. eliminare.
elimination s. eliminazione.
elision s. elisione.
elixir s. elisir.
elk s. alce.
ellipse s. ellisse.
ellipsis s. ellissi.
elliptic(al) agg. ellittico.
elm s. olmo.
elocution s. **1.** elocuzione **2.** dizione.
to elope vi. fuggire (con un amante).
elopement s. fuga (con un amante).
eloquence s. eloquenza.
eloquent agg. eloquente (anche fig.).
else avv. (dopo avv. e pron. int., indef.) altro.
elsewhere avv. altrove.
to elude vt. eludere, schivare.
elusive agg. **1.** elusivo, ambiguo **2.** sfuggevole.
elytron s. (pl. elytra) elitra.
Elzevir agg. e s. elzeviro.
to emaciate vt. far deperire, far dimagrire.
emaciated agg. emaciato.
to emanate vi. emanare.
emanation s. emanazione.
to emancipate vt. emancipare.
emancipation s. emancipazione.
to embalm vt. **1.** imbalsamare **2.** profumare.
embalmer s. imbalsamatore.

embankment *s.* 1. argine, diga 2. alzaia.

embarcation *s.* imbarco.

embargo *s.* embargo, fermo.

to embark *vt.* imbarcare (*truppe, merci*). ♦ **to embark** *vi.* imbarcarsi.

embarkation *s.* imbarco.

to embarrass *vt.* mettere in imbarazzo.

embarrassing *agg.* imbarazzante.

embarrassment *s.* 1. imbarazzo 2. difficoltà.

embassy *s.* ambasciata.

to embattle *vt.* disporre in ordine di battaglia, fortificare.

to embed *vt.* incassare, conficcare.

to embellish *vt.* abbellire, ornare.

embellishment *s.* abbellimento, ornamento.

ember *s.* tizzone. ♦ **embers** *s. pl.* brace (*sing.*).

embezzler *s.* malversatore.

to embitter *vt.* 1. rendere amaro 2. (*fig.*) amareggiare.

embitterment *s.* amarezza, inasprimento.

to emblazon *vt.* 1. decorare 2. celebrare.

emblem *s.* emblema, simbolo (*fig.*).

emblematic(al) *agg.* emblematico.

embodiment *s.* 1. incarnazione 2. incorporamento.

to embody *vt.* 1. incarnare 2. personificare 3. incorporare.

to embolden *vt.* incoraggiare.

embolism *s.* embolia.

embolus *s.* (*pl.* -li) embolo.

to emboss *vt.* 1. scolpire 2. stampare in rilievo.

embossed *agg.* 1. sbalzato 2. fatto in rilievo.

embrace *s.* abbraccio, amplesso.

to embrace *vt.* abbracciare (*anche fig.*). ♦ **to embrace** *vi.* abbracciarsi.

embrasure *s.* 1. vano (*di porta, finestra*) 2. feritoia.

to embroider *vt.* ricamare.

embroiderer *s.* ricamatore.

embroidery *s.* ricamo.

to embroil *vt.* coinvolgere in una disputa.

embryo *s.* embrione.

embryonic *agg.* embrionale (*anche fig.*).

to emend *vt.* emendare.

emendation *s.* emendamento.

emerald *s.* smeraldo.

to emerge *vi.* 1. emergere, affiorare 2. (*fig.*) risultare.

emergency *s.* emergenza, caso imprevisto ‖ — -*door*, uscita di sicurezza; — *means*, mezzi di fortuna.

emersion *s.* emersione.

emery *s.* smeriglio ‖ — -*paper*, carta smerigliata.

emetic *agg.* e *s.* emetico.

emigrant *agg.* e *s.* emigrante.

to emigrate *vi.* emigrare.

emigration *s.* emigrazione.

eminence *s.* 1. luogo, parte eminente 2. (*anat.*) protuberanza 3. (*fig.*) eminenza, eccellenza.

eminent *agg.* eminente (*anche fig.*).

eminently *avv.* eminentemente.

emir *s.* emiro.

emissary *s.* emissario, agente segreto.

emission *s.* emissione.

to emit *vt.* 1. emettere 2. esalare.

emollient *agg.* e *s.* emolliente.

emolument *s.* remunerazione, salario.

emotion *s.* emozione, turbamento.

emotional *agg.* 1. emotivo, impressionabile 2. commovente.

emotionalism *s.* emotività.

emotionally *avv.* con emozione.

emotive *agg.* 1. commovente 2. emotivo.

emperor *s.* imperatore.

emphasis *s.* 1. accentuazione, rilievo 2. enfasi.

to emphasize *vt.* accentuare.

emphatic *agg.* 1. accentuato 2. enfatico.

emphysema *s.* enfisema.

emphyteusis *s.* enfiteusi.

empire *s.* impero.

empiric *s.* empirico.

empirical *agg.* empirico.

empiricism *s.* empirismo.

emplacement *s.* 1. collocazione 2. (*mil.*) piazzuola.

employ *s.* impiego: *out of* —, senza impiego.

to employ *vt.* 1. impiegare, adoperare 2. assumere.

employee *s.* impiegato.

employer *s.* datore di lavoro.

employment *s.* impiego, occupazione.

to empoison *vt.* avvelenare.

emporium *s.* 1. centro commerciale 2. emporio.

to empower *vt.* dare pieni poteri a.

emptiness s. 1. vuoto 2. vanità.
empty agg. 1. vuoto 2. vano 3. vacante || — -handed, a mani vuote.
to **empty** vt. vuotare. ♦ to **empty** vi. vuotarsi.
to **emulate** vt. emulare.
emulation s. emulazione.
emulator s. emulatore.
emulous agg. emulo.
to **emulsify** vt. emulsionare.
emulsion s. emulsione.
emulsive agg. emulsivo.
to **enable** vt. mettere in grado.
to **enact** vt. decretare, emanare (una legge).
enactment s. 1. promulgazione 2. legge.
enamel s. smalto.
to **enamel** vt. smaltare.
to **encamp** vi. accamparsi.
encaustic agg. encaustico.
encephalic agg. encefalico.
encephalitis s. encefalite.
to **enchant** vt. incantare, affascinare.
enchanter s. incantatore, mago.
enchanting agg. incantevole.
enchantment s. incanto, incantesimo.
enchantress s. incantatrice.
to **encircle** vt. circondare, cingere.
enclitic agg. enclitico.
to **enclose** vt. 1. racchiudere, cingere 2. accludere.
enclosed agg. 1. racchiuso, circondato 2. accluso.
enclosure s. 1. recinto, staccionata 2. allegato.
encomiast s. encomiasta.
to **encompass** vt. circondare (anche fig.).
encore avv. (teat.) bis.
to **encore** vt. chiedere il bis.
encounter s. scontro.
to **encourage** vt. incoraggiare, animare.
encouragement s. incoraggiamento.
encouraging agg. incoraggiante.
to **encroach** vt. 1. usurpare, invadere 2. (giur.) ledere.
to **encrust** vt. incrostare.
to **encumber** vt. 1. ingombrare, imbarazzare 2. ostruire.
encumbrance s. ingombro, impedimento.
encyclic(al) agg. enciclico. ♦ **encyclic(al)** s. enciclica.
encyclop(a)edia s. enciclopedia.
encyclop(a)edic(al) agg. enciclo-

pedico.
end s. 1. estremità, fine, termine 2. scopo, mira 3. morte.
to **end** vt. e vi. finire, concludere.
to **endanger** vt. mettere in pericolo, compromettere.
to **endear** vt. affezionare, rendere caro.
endearing agg. affettuoso, tenero.
endearment s. tenerezza. ♦ **endearments** s. pl. blandizie.
to **endeavo(u)r** vi. sforzarsi. ♦ to **endeavo(u)r** vt. tentare.
endemic agg. endemico.
ending agg. finale, ultimo. ♦ **ending** s. fine, conclusione.
endless agg. senza fine, eterno, continuo.
endocarditis s. endocardite.
endocardium s. endocardio.
endocarp s. endocarpo.
endocrine agg. endocrino.
endocrinology s. endocrinologia.
endogeny s. endogenesi.
to **endorse** vt. (comm.) girare, vistare.
endorsee s. (comm.) giratario.
endorsement s. (comm.) girata.
endorser s. (comm.) girante.
to **endow** vt. 1. dotare 2. fare una donazione.
endowment s. 1. costituzione di dote, donazione 2. (fig.) talento.
endurance s. 1. resistenza, sopportazione 2. durata.
to **endure** vt. tollerare, sopportare. ♦ to **endure** vi. resistere, durare.
enduring agg. 1. tollerante, paziente 2. durevole.
enema s. clistere.
enemy agg. e s. nemico.
energetic(al) agg. 1. energico 2. energetico.
to **energize** vt. infondere energia.
energumen s. energumeno.
energy s. energia, forza.
to **enervate** vt. snervare, indebolire.
enervation s. indebolimento.
to **enfeeble** vt. indebolire.
to **enfold** vt. 1. avvolgere 2. cingere.
to **enforce** vt. 1. imporre, far rispettare 2. mettere in vigore (una legge).
to **enframe** vt. incorniciare.
to **enfranchise** vt. affrancare, liberare.
enfranchisement s. affrancamento,

liberazione.

to **engage** *vt.* 1. impegnare 2. ingaggiare 3. attrarre (*l'attenzione*). ♦ to **engage** *vi.* impegnarsi ‖ *to — in conversation*, prendere parte alla conversazione.

engaged *agg.* 1. impegnato 2. fidanzato 3. occupato, riservato.

engagement *s.* 1. impegno 2. fidanzamento 3. assunzione, impiego.

engaging *agg.* attraente, avvincente.

engagingly *avv.* in modo attraente.

to **engender** *vt.* produrre, causare.

engine *s.* 1. macchina, motore 2. (*ferr.*) locomotrice ‖ *fire- —*, autopompa.

engineer *s.* 1. ingegnere 2. tecnico.

engineering *s.* 1. ingegneria 2. costruzione meccanica.

English *agg.* inglese. ♦ **English** *s.* lingua inglese.

Englishman *s.* (*uomo*) inglese.

Englishwoman *s.* (*donna*) inglese.

to **engrave** *vt.* 1. intagliare, incidere 2. (*fig.*) imprimere.

engraver *s.* incisore.

engraving *s.* arte dell'incisione ‖ *wood- —*, xilografia.

to **engross** *vt.* 1. copiare (*un atto legale*), redigere (*un documento*) 2. assorbire (*l'attenzione*).

engrossment *s.* copiatura (*di documento*).

to **enhance** *vt.* accrescere.

enigma *s.* enigma.

enigmatic(al) *agg.* enigmatico.

to **enjoy** *vt.* 1. godere, gioire 2. gùstare, provar piacere di ‖ *to — oneself*, divertirsi.

enjoyable *agg.* piacevole, gradevole.

enjoyably *avv.* piacevolmente.

enjoyment *s.* godimento, piacere.

to **enkindle** *vt.* infiammare, eccitare. ♦ to **enkindle** *vi.* infiammarsi, eccitarsi.

to **enlarge** *vt.* 1. allargare, ampliare 2. (*foto*) ingrandire. ♦ to **enlarge** *vi.* allargarsi, ampliarsi.

enlargement *s.* 1. allargamento 2. (*foto*) ingrandimento.

enlarger *s.* (*foto*) ingranditore.

to **enlighten** *vt.* rischiarare, illuminare (*anche fig.*).

enlightenment *s.* 1. spiegazione, schiarimento 2. (*lett.*) l'illuminismo.

to **enlist** *vt.* arruolare. ♦ to **enlist** *vi.* arruolarsi.

enlistment *s.* arruolamento, in-

gaggio.

to **enliven** *vt.* rianimare, ravvivare.

to **enmesh** *vt.* impegolare, irretire.

enmity *s.* ostilità, inimicizia.

to **ennoble** *vt.* nobilitare.

enormity *s.* mostruosità.

enormous *agg.* enorme, immenso.

enough *avv.* abbastanza, sufficientemente. ♦ **enough** *agg.* sufficiente. ♦ **enough** *s.* il necessario, quanto basta.

to **enrage** *vt.* far arrabbiare, esasperare.

to **enrapture** *vt.* rapire, estasiare.

to **enrich** *vt.* 1. arricchire (*anche fig.*) 2. abbellire.

enrichment *s.* 1. arricchimento 2. abbellimento.

to **enrol** *vt.* 1. arruolare, ingaggiare 2. iscrivere.

enrolment *s.* 1. arruolamento, iscrizione 2. (*giur.*) registrazione.

ensign *s.* 1. bandiera, stendardo 2. portabandiera.

to **enslave** *vt.* assoggettare, far schiavo (*anche fig.*).

enslavement *s.* asservimento, schiavitù (*anche fig.*).

to **ensnare** *vt.* adescare, intrappolare (*anche fig.*).

to **ensue** *vt.* e *vi.* seguire.

to **ensure** *vt.* assicurare, garantire.

entail *s.* eredità, ordine di successione (*vincolato*).

to **entangle** *vt.* impigliare, intralciare (*anche fig.*).

entanglement *s.* groviglio, impiccio.

to **enter** *vt.* e *vi.* 1. entrare, penetrare 2. iscrivere 3. (*comm.*) registrare ‖ *to — upon*, intraprendere (*una carriera*).

enteric *agg.* enterico.

enteritis *s.* enterite.

enterocolitis *s.* enterocolite. ·

enterogastritis *s.* gastroenterite.

enterprise *s.* 1. impresa 2. iniziativa, intraprendenza.

enterprising *agg.* intraprendente.

to **entertain** *vt.* 1. ricevere, ospitare 2. intrattenere, divertire 3. carezzare (*un'idea*), nutrire (*dubbi, speranze*).

entertainer *s.* 1. anfitrione, ospite 2. comico.

entertaining *agg.* divertente.

entertainment *s.* 1. trattenimento, spettacolo 2. ricevimento, festa 3. divertimento.

to **enthral** *vt.* (*fig.*) affascinare, incantare.

enthralment *s.* incanto, malia.

to **enthrone** *vt.* mettere sul trono.

enthronement *s.* investitura, intronizzazione.

enthusiasm *s.* entusiasmo.

enthusiast *s.* entusiasta.

enthusiastic(al) *agg.* entusiastico.

enthusiastically *avv.* entusiasticamente.

to **entice** *vt.* sedurre, allettare.

enticement *s.* **1.** attrattiva **2.** adescamento, istigazione.

enticing *agg.* seducente, attraente.

entire *agg.* intero, completo.

entirely *avv.* interamente, completamente.

to **entitle** *vt.* **1.** intitolare (*un libro*) **2.** dare un titolo.

entity *s.* entità, esistenza.

entomological *agg.* entomologico.

entomologist *s.* entomologo.

entomology *s.* entomologia.

entrails *s. pl.* intestino (*sing.*), visceri.

entrance *s.* **1.** ingresso, entrata **2.** ammissione || — *hall,* vestibolo.

to **entrap** *vt.* prendere in trappola, truffare.

to **entreat** *vt.* pregare, supplicare.

entreaty *s.* supplica, istanza.

to **entrench** *vt.* e *vi.* trincerare, fortificare (*anche fig.*) || *to* — *upon,* usurpare.

entrepreneur *s.* **1.** (*teat.*) impresario **2.** imprenditore.

to **entrust** *vt.* affidare, commettere.

entry *s.* **1.** entrata **2.** ingresso, passaggio **3.** (*comm.*) registrazione.

to **entwine** *vt.* attorcigliare, intrecciare. ♦ to **entwine** *vi.* arrotolarsi.

to **enucleate** *vt.* spiegare, chiarire.

enucleation *s.* spiegazione, chiarimento.

to **enumerate** *vt.* enumerare.

enumeration *s.* enumerazione.

enumerator *s.* numeratore.

to **enunciate** *vt.* enunciare, proclamare.

enunciation *s.* enunciazione.

to **envelop** *vt.* avvolgere, avviluppare.

envelope *s.* busta, involucro.

envelopment *s.* avvolgimento.

enviable *agg.* invidiabile.

envious *agg.* invidioso.

to **environ** *vt.* circondare, accerchiare.

environment *s.* ambiente.

environs *s. pl.* dintorni.

envy *s.* invidia.

to **envy** *vt.* invidiare.

enzyme *s.* enzima.

epaulet(te) *s.* (*mil.*) spallina.

ephebe *s.* efebo.

ephemeral *agg.* effimero.

ephemeris *s.* (*pl.* -ides) effemeride.

epic *agg.* epico. ♦ **epic** *s.* poema epico.

epically *avv.* epicamente.

epicentre *s.* epicentro.

epicurean *agg.* e *s.* epicureo.

epidemic(al) *agg.* epidemico.

epidemically *avv.* epidemicamente.

epidermal *agg.* epidermico.

epidermis *s.* epidermide.

epigastric *agg.* epigastrico.

epigram *s.* epigramma.

epigrammatic *agg.* epigrammatico.

epigrammatist *s.* epigrammista.

epigraph *s.* epigrafe.

epigraphy *s.* epigrafia.

epilepsy *s.* epilessia.

epileptic *agg.* epilettico.

epilogue *s.* epilogo.

Epiphany *s.* Epifania.

episcopacy *s.* episcopato.

episcopal *agg.* episcopale.

episcopate *s.* episcopato.

episode *s.* episodio.

episodic(al) *agg.* episodico.

epistle *s.* epistola.

epistolary *agg.* epistolare.

epitaph *s.* epitaffio.

epithalamium *s.* epitalamio.

epithet *s.* epiteto.

epitome *s.* epitome, riassunto.

epoch *s.* epoca, età.

epopee *s.* epopea.

equability *s.* uguaglianza, uniformità.

equal *agg.* uguale, simile, stesso. ♦ **equal** *s.* pari (*di rango*).

equality *s.* uguaglianza, parità.

equalization *s.* eguagliamento.

to **equalize** *vt.* e *vi.* uguagliare.

equally *avv.* ugualmente, imparzialmente.

equanimity *s.* equanimità.

equanimous *agg.* equanime.

equation *s.* **1.** equazione **2.** pareggio.

equator *s.* equatore.

equatorial *agg.* equatoriale.

equestrian *agg.* equestre.

equidistant *agg.* equidistante.

equilateral *agg.* equilatero.

equine *agg.* equino.
equinoctial *agg.* equinoziale.
equinox *s.* equinozio.
to equip *vt.* **1.** equipaggiare **2.** fornire, arredare.
equipment *s.* **1.** equipaggiamento **2.** attrezzatura.
equipoise *s.* equilibrio.
equipollent *agg.* equipollente.
equitation *s.* equitazione.
equity *s.* giustizia, equità.
equivalence *s.* equivalenza.
equivalent *agg.* e *s.* equivalente.
equivocal *agg.* **1.** ambiguo, equivoco **2.** sospetto, losco.
equivocally *avv.* **1.** ambiguamente **2.** in modo losco.
to equivocate *vi.* equivocare, giocare sull'equivoco.
equivocation *s.* **1.** l'equivocare **2.** equivoco.
equivoke *s.* **1.** gioco di parole **2.** ambiguità (*d'espressione*).
era *s.* era, epoca.
eradicable *agg.* estirpabile.
to eradicate *vt.* sradicare, estirpare.
to erase *vt.* raschiare, cancellare.
eraser *s.* **1.** raschietto **2.** gomma per cancellare.
erasure *s.* raschiatura, cancellatura.
erect *agg.* diritto, ritto.
to erect *vt.* **1.** raddrizzare **2.** costruire.
erection *s.* **1.** raddrizzamento **2.** erezione.
eremite *s.* eremita.
ermine *s.* ermellino.
to erode *vt.* corrodere, logorare.
erosion *s.* erosione.
erosive *agg.* corrosivo.
erotic *agg.* erotico.
eroticism *s.* erotismo.
to err *vi.* **1.** sbagliare **2.** errare, vagabondare.
errand *s.* commissione || — -*boy*, fattorino.
errant *agg.* **1.** errante **2.** che sbaglia.
erratic *agg.* **1.** erratico **2.** irregolare.
erratically *avv.* **1.** irregolarmente **2.** eccentricamente.
erring *agg.* **1.** errante **2.** che sbaglia.
erroneous *agg.* erroneo.
error *s.* **1.** errore **2.** torto.
erudite *agg.* erudito.
erudition *s.* erudizione.
to erupt *vi.* eruttare.
eruption *s.* eruzione.
eruptive *agg.* eruttivo.
escalade *s.* scalata.

escalator *s.* scala mobile.
escape *s.* **1.** fuga, evasione **2.** scampo, salvezza.
to escape *vt.* e *vi.* **1.** fuggire, evadere **2.** scampare.
escapism *s.* evasione dalla realtà.
escapist *s.* chi cerca di evadere dalla realtà.
eschatology *s.* escatologia.
to eschew *vt.* evitare, astenersi da.
escort *s.* scorta.
to escort *vt.* scortare, accompagnare.
Eskimo *s.* esquimese.
esoteric *agg.* esoterico.
especial *agg.* speciale.
especially *avv.* specialmente.
espionage *s.* spionaggio.
esplanade *s.* spianata.
to espy *vt.* scorgere, avvistare.
esquire *s.* (*titolo di cortesia*) John Smith Esq., egregio sig. John Smith.
essay *s.* **1.** esperimento, prova **2.** (*lett.*) saggio.
to essay *vt.* provare, mettere alla prova.
essayist *s.* saggista.
essence *s.* essenza.
essential *agg.* essenziale.
to establish *vt.* **1.** affermare (*un diritto ecc.*) **2.** instaurare **3.** (*comm.*) fondare, costituire.
established *agg.* **1.** stabilito, affermato **2.** fondato.
establishment *s.* **1.** affermazione, conferma **2.** instaurazione **3.** stabilimento, azienda.
estate *s.* **1.** terra, proprietà (*terriera*) **2.** stato, gruppo politico **3.** condizione, classe sociale || — *agent*, mediatore.
esteem *s.* stima, considerazione.
to esteem *vt.* **1.** stimare, tenere in gran conto **2.** considerare.
estimable *agg.* degno di stima.
estimate *s.* **1.** stima, giudizio **2.** (*comm.*) preventivo.
to estimate *vt.* **1.** stimare, valutare **2.** preventivare.
estimator *s.* perito, stimatore.
to estrange *vt.* alienare, alienarsi, allontanare.
estrangement *s.* alienazione, allontanamento.
estuary *s.* estuario.
etching *s.* acquaforte.
eternal *agg.* eterno.
eternity *s.* eternità.

ether *s.* etere.
ethereal *agg.* etereo.
ethic(al) *agg.* etico.
ethics *s.* etica.
Ethiopian *agg.* etiopico. ♦ **Ethiopian** *s.* etiope.
Ethiopic *agg.* etiopico.
ethnic(al) *agg.* etnico.
ethnography *s.* etnografia.
ethnologist *s.* etnologo.
ethnology *s.* etnologia.
ethylene *s.* etilene.
ethylic *agg.* etilico.
etiquette *s.* 1. etichetta 2. cerimoniale.
Etrurian, Etruscan *agg.* e *s.* etrusco.
etymologic(al) *agg.* etimologico.
etymology *s.* etimologia.
eucalyptus *s.* eucalipto.
Eucharist *s.* Eucaristia.
eucharistic(al) *agg.* eucaristico.
eugenics *s.* eugenetica.
eulogist *s.* elogiatore.
to eulogize *vt.* elogiare.
eulogy *s.* elogio, panegirico.
eunuch *s.* eunuco.
euphemism *s.* eufemismo.
euphonic *agg.* eufonico.
euphony *s.* eufonia.
euphoria *s.* euforia.
euphuism *s.* eufuismo.
euphuist *s.* affettato.
euphuistic *agg.* affettato, ricercato (*di stile*).
European *agg.* e *s.* europeo.
Eurovision *s.* eurovisione.
euthanasia *s.* eutanasia.
to evacuate *vt.* e *vi.* evacuare, sfollare.
evacuation *s.* evacuazione, sfollamento.
to evade *vt.* evitare, schivare, eludere.
to evaluate *vt.* valutare.
evaluation *s.* valutazione.
evanescent *agg.* evanescente.
evangelic(al) *agg.* evangelico.
evangelist *s.* evangelista.
evangelistic *agg.* di un evangelista, missionario.
evangelization *s.* evangelizzazione.
to evangelize *vt.* evangelizzare.
to evaporate *vi.* evaporare. ♦ **to evaporate** *vt.* far evaporare.
evaporation *s.* evaporazione.
evasion *s.* 1. evasione, scappatoia 2. scusa, pretesto.
evasive *agg.* evasivo.

evasively *avv.* evasivamente.
evasiveness *s.* ambiguità.
eve *s.* vigilia.
even *agg.* 1. uguale, uniforme, costante, regolare 2. pari, equo. ♦ **even** *avv.* 1. ancora (*con comp.*) 2. persino, anche || — *as*, nel momento in cui.
evening *s.* 1. sera, serata 2. (*fig.*) declino, fine.
evenly *avv.* in modo uguale, uniformemente.
evensong *s.* vespro.
event *s.* 1. caso, eventualità 2. avvenimento 3. (*sport*) prova.
eventful *agg.* ricco di avvenimenti, movimentato.
eventual *agg.* finale, definitivo.
eventuality *s.* eventualità.
eventually *avv.* alla fine.
ever *avv.* 1. mai 2. sempre.
evergreen *s.* sempreverde.
everlasting *agg.* eterno.
everliving *agg.* immortale.
evermore *avv.* perpetuamente.
every *agg.* ogni, ciascuno, tutti.
everybody *pron. indef.* ognuno, tutti.
everyday *agg.* di tutti i giorni, quotidiano.
everyone *pron. indef.* V. *everybody*.
everything *pron. indef.* ogni cosa, tutto.
everywhere *avv.* ovunque.
to evict *vt.* sfrattare, espellere.
eviction *s.* sfratto.
evidence *s.* 1. evidenza 2. prova.
to evidence *vt.* provare, dimostrare.
evident *agg.* evidente, chiaro.
evil *agg.* cattivo, malvagio || — -*eye*, malocchio. ♦ **evil** *s.* male, peccato.
to evirate *vt.* evirare.
to evocate *vt.* evocare.
evocation *s.* evocazione.
evocative *agg.* evocatore.
to evoke *vt.* evocare.
evolution *s.* evoluzione.
evolutional *agg.* evolutivo.
evolutionism *s.* evoluzionismo.
to evolve *vt.* evolvere. ♦ **to evolve** *vi.* evolversi.
evolvement *s.* evoluzione, sviluppo.
ewe *s.* pecora (*femmina*).
to exacerbate *vt.* esacerbare, inasprire.
exacerbation *s.* esacerbazione, inasprimento.
exact *agg.* 1. esatto, giusto 2. puntuale, rigoroso.

to **exact** vt. **1.** esigere **2.** rendere necessario.

exacting agg. **1.** esigente **2.** impegnativo.

exaction s. esazione, estorsione.

exactitude s. esattezza, precisione.

exactly avv. esattamente.

exactness s. esattezza, precisione.

to **exaggerate** vt. esagerare, ingrandire.

exaggeration s. esagerazione.

to **exalt** vt. **1.** innalzare, elevare **2.** esaltare, lodare.

exaltation s. **1.** innalzamento **2.** esaltazione.

exalted agg. **1.** elevato (di grado ecc.) **2.** esaltato, eccitato.

examination s. **1.** esame, ispezione **2.** esame scolastico **3.** (giur.) interrogatorio.

to **examine** vt. **1.** verificare, ispezionare **2.** esaminare **3.** (giur.) istruire un processo.

examiner s. esaminatore.

example s. esempio.

to **exasperate** vt. **1.** peggiorare, aggravare **2.** esasperare.

exasperatingly avv. in modo esasperante.

exasperation s. esasperazione.

to **excavate** vt. scavare, fare scavi (archeologici).

excavation s. **1.** scavo **2.** fossa, buca.

excavator s. **1.** operaio scavatore **2.** (mecc.) escavatore.

to **exceed** vt. e vi. **1.** eccedere, superare (i limiti) **2.** essere superiore.

exceeding agg. esagerato.

exceedingly avv. eccessivamente, troppo.

to **excel** vt. superare. ♦ to **excel** vi. primeggiare.

excellence s. **1.** eccellenza **2.** pregio, superiorità.

Excellency s. (titolo) Eccellenza.

excellent agg. eccellente.

except prep. eccetto, tranne.

to.**except** vt. eccettuare, escludere. ♦ to **except** vi. obiettare, sollevare eccezioni.

excepting prep. eccetto, tranne.

exception s. eccezione.

exceptional agg. eccezionale, straordinario.

excerpt s. brano scelto.

excess s. **1.** eccesso, intemperanza **2.** supplemento.

exchange s. **1.** scambio **2.** (finanza) cambio **3.** borsa, mercato ‖ bill of —, cambiale; — -broker, agente di cambio.

to **exchange** vt. cambiare, scambiare. ♦ to **exchange** vi. fare un cambio.

exchangeable agg. scambiabile.

exchanger s. cambiavalute.

exchequer s. . Tesoro, Scacchiere, fisco.

excise s. imposta indiretta ‖ — duty, dazio.

to **excise**[1] vt. tassare.

to **excise**[2] vt. estirpare, mutilare (un testo).

exciseman s. daziere, funzionario degli uffici delle imposte.

excision s. taglio, recisione.

excitability s. eccitabilità.

excitable agg. eccitabile.

excitant agg. e s. eccitante.

excitation s. eccitazione.

to **excite** vt. **1.** provocare, far nascere (una rivolta, un sentimento ecc.) **2.** eccitare, animare.

excited agg. eccitato.

excitement s. eccitazione.

to **exclaim** vt. e vi. esclamare.

exclamation s. esclamazione.

exclamatory agg. esclamativo.

to **exclude** vt. escludere.

exclusion s. esclusione.

exclusive agg. **1.** altezzoso **2.** chiuso, scelto (di ambiente) **3.** esclusivo.

exclusiveness s. esclusività.

to **excogitate** vt. escogitare.

excommunicable agg. scomunicabile.

excommunicate agg. e s. scomunicato.

to **excommunicate** vt. scomunicare.

excommunication s. scomunica.

excrement s. escremento.

excrescence s. escrescenza, protuberanza.

excruciating agg. tormentoso, straziante.

to **exculpate** vt. giustificare, scolpare.

excursion s. **1.** escursione, gita **2.** (mil.) sortita.

excursionist s. escursionista, gitante.

excusable agg. scusabile.

excuse s. **1.** scusa, giustificazione **2.**

pretesto.

to **excuse** *vt.* scusare, giustificare.

execrable *agg.* esecrabile.

to **execrate** *vt.* e *vi.* **1.** esecrare, detestare **2.** maledire.

execration *s.* **1.** esecrazione **2.** maledizione.

executant *s.* esecutore.

to **execute** *vt.* **1.** eseguire, mettere in esecuzione **2.** (*giur.*) convalidare **3.** giustiziare.

execution *s.* **1.** compimento, attuazione **2.** esecuzione.

executioner *s.* esecutore, boia.

executive *agg.* esecutivo.

executor *s.* esecutore.

exedra *s.* esedra.

exegesis *s.* (*pl.* -ses) esegesi.

exegete *s.* esegeta.

exemplary *agg.* esemplare.

exemplification *s.* esemplificazione.

to **exemplify** *vt.* esemplificare.

exempt *agg.* esente, esonerato.

to **exempt** *vt.* esentare, esonerare.

exemption *s.* esenzione, esonero.

exequies *s. pl.* esequie.

exercise *s.* esercizio, esercitazione || — -*book*, quaderno.

to **exercise** *vt.* esercitare, usare. ◆ to **exercise** *vi.* esercitarsi, allenarsi.

exercitation *s.* esercizio, uso (*di una facoltà*).

to **exert** *vt.* esercitare.

exertion *s.* **1.** esercizio (*di autorità*) **2.** sforzo.

exhalation *s.* esalazione.

to **exhale** *vt.* e *vi.* esalare, emettere.

exhaust *s.* **1.** (*mecc.*) scarico, scappamento **2.** apparato aspiratore.

to **exhaust** *vt.* e *vi.* **1.** aspirare (*aria, gas ecc.*) **2.** esaurire (*anche fig.*).

exhausted *agg.* **1.** aspirato **2.** esausto, spossato.

exhausting *agg.* che esaurisce.

exhaustion *s.* **1.** aspirazione **2.** esaurimento.

exhaustive *agg.* **1.** esauriente **2.** spossante.

exhibit *s.* **1.** insieme di oggetti in mostra **2.** (*giur.*) documento.

to **exhibit** *vt.* **1.** esibire, mostrare **2.** (*giur.*) produrre (*documenti ecc.*).

exhibition *s.* **1.** presentazione (*di documenti*) **2.** esposizione, mostra.

exhibitionism *s.* esibizionismo.

exhibitionist *s.* esibizionista.

exhibitor *s.* espositore.

to **exhilarate** *vt.* rallegrare, esilarare.

exhilarating *agg.* esilarante.

to **exhort** *vt.* esortare, ammonire.

exhortation *s.* esortazione.

exhortative *agg.* esortativo.

exhumation *s.* esumazione.

to **exhume** *vt.* esumare.

exigence *s.* **1.** esigenza, necessità **2.** situazione critica.

exigent *agg.* **1.** pressante, urgente **2.** esigente.

exigible *agg.* esigibile.

exiguity *s.* esiguità.

exiguous *agg.* esiguo.

exile *s.* **1.** esilio, bando **2.** esule.

to **exile** *vt.* esiliare.

to **exist** *vi.* esistere.

existence *s.* esistenza.

existent *agg.* esistente.

existential *agg.* esistenziale.

existentialism *s.* esistenzialismo.

existentialist *agg.* e *s.* esistenzialista.

existing *agg.* esistente, attuale.

exit *s.* uscita.

exode, exodus *s.* esodo.

exogenous *agg.* esogeno.

to **exonerate** *vt.* **1.** esonerare, dispensare **2.** giustificare.

exoneration *s.* **1.** dispensa, esonero **2.** giustificazione.

exorbitant *agg.* esorbitante.

to **exorcise** *vt.* esorcizzare.

exorciser *s.* esorcista.

exorcism *s.* esorcismo.

exorcist *s.* esorcista.

exothermic *agg.* esotermico.

exotic *agg.* esotico.

exoticism *s.* esotismo.

to **expand** *vt.* espandere, dilatare, allargare. ◆ to **expand** *vi.* espandersi, dilagare, dilatarsi, allargarsi, svilupparsi.

expanse *s.* distesa, estensione, spazio.

expansion *s.* espansione, dilatazione, allargamento.

expansionism *s.* espansionismo.

expansive *agg.* **1.** espansivo **2.** dilatabile.

to **expatiate** *vi.* **1.** errare, vagabondare **2.** parlare e scrivere diffusamente.

expatiation *s.* **1.** dissertazione **2.** prolissità.

expatriate *agg.* e *s.* espatriato.

to **expatriate** *vt.* esiliare. ◆ to

expatriate *vi.* espatriare.
expatriation *s.* espatrio.
to expect *vt.* 1. aspettare, aspettarsi 2. esigere, insistere 3. pensare, credere || *to — somebody to come,* prevedere la venuta di qu.
expectance *s.* aspettativa, attesa.
expectant *s.* 1. chi attende 2. candidato.
expectation *s.* attesa, aspettativa. ♦ **expectations** *s. pl.* speranze.
expectorant *agg.* e *s.* espettorante.
expectoration *s.* espettorazione.
expediency *s.* 1. convenienza 2. opportunismo.
expedient *s.* espediente, ripiego.
to expedite *vt.* affrettare.
expedition *s.* 1. spedizione 2. prontezza, celerità.
expeditious *s.* svelto, sbrigativo.
to expel *vt.* espellere, cacciare.
expense *s.* 1. spesa, sborso 2. (*fig.*) sacrificio, prezzo.
expensive *agg.* costoso, caro.
experience *s.* esperienza.
to experience *vt.* sperimentare, provare.
experienced *agg.* pratico, esperto.
experiment *s.* esperimento, prova.
experimental *agg.* sperimentale.
experimentation *s.* sperimentasmo.
experimentalist *s.* sperimentalista.
experimentation *s.* sperimentazione.
expert *agg.* esperto. ♦ **expert** *s.* esperto, perito, competente.
expertly *avv.* abilmente.
to expiate *vt.* espiare.
expiation *s.* espiazione.
expiatory *agg.* espiatorio.
expiration *s.* 1. fine, scadenza 2. espirazione.
expiratory *agg.* espiratorio.
to expire *vt.* e *vi.* 1. finire, scadere 2. spirare, morire.
expiring *agg.* 1. che scade 2. spirante, morente.
expiry *s.* fine, cessazione.
to explain *vt.* e *vi.* spiegare, chiarire.
explanation *s.* spiegazione, delucidazione.
expletive *agg.* espletivo, pleonastico. ♦ **expletive** *s.* 1. imprecazione 2. pleonasmo.
explicable *agg.* spiegabile.
to explicate *vt.* sviluppare (*un prin-*

cipio, un'idea ecc.).
explication *s.* spiegazione, sviluppo.
explicit *agg.* esplicito, chiaro.
to explode *vt.* esplodere, far esplodere. ♦ **to explode** *vi.* scoppiare, esplodere.
to exploit *vt.* 1. utilizzare, sfruttare 2. approfittare di.
exploitation *s.* sfruttamento, utilizzazione.
exploiter *s.* 1. chi valorizza (*idea, invenzione ecc.*) 2. sfruttatore.
exploration *s.* esplorazione.
to explore *vt.* esplorare.
explorer *s.* esploratore, esploratrice.
explosion *s.* esplosione, scoppio.
explosive *agg.* e *s.* esplosivo.
exponent *s.* 1. divulgatore 2. esponente.
exponential *agg.* esponenziale.
export *s.* esportazione.
to export *vt.* esportare.
exportation *s.* esportazione.
exporter *s.* esportatore.
to expose *vt.* 1. esporre 2. (*foto*) impressionare.
exposé *s.* esposto, resoconto.
exposition *s.* 1. spiegazione, commento 2. mostra, esposizione.
expositive *agg.* espositivo.
expositor *s.* commentatore.
expository *agg.* esplicativo.
exposure *s.* 1. esposizione (*al freddo, al caldo ecc.*) 2. mostra 3. (*foto*) (tempo di) esposizione.
to expound *vt.* spiegare (*una teoria*).
express *agg.* 1. chiaro, preciso 2. espresso, diretto. ♦ **express** *s.* espresso, corriere || *— train,* direttissimo.
to express *vt.* esprimere, manifestare.
expression *s.* espressione.
expressionism *s.* espressionismo.
expressionist *s.* espressionista.
expressive *agg.* espressivo, significativo.
expressly *avv.* espressamente.
to expropriate *vt.* espropriare.
expropriation *s.* espropriazione.
expulsion *s.* espulsione.
expulsive *agg.* espulsivo.
expunction *s.* cancellatura.
to expurgate *vt.* espurgare (*uno scritto*).
expurgation *s.* espurgazione (*di uno scritto*).

exquisite *agg.* **1.** squisito **2.** fine, sensibile. ♦ **exquisite** *s.* raffinato.

exquisiteness *s.* squisitezza, finezza.

extant *agg.* ancora esistente.

extemporaneous, extemporary *agg.* estemporaneo.

extempore *agg.* improvvisato.

extemporization *s.* improvvisazione.

to extemporize *vt.* e *vi.* improvvisare.

to extend *vt.* **1.** estendere, allungare, prolungare. ♦ **to extend** *vi.* estendersi, allungarsi, prolungarsi.

extendible *agg.* estendibile.

extensible *agg.* estensibile.

extension *s.* **1.** estensione, allungamento **2.** (*comm.*) proroga.

extensive *agg.* **1.** esteso, ampio **2.** estensivo.

extent *s.* **1.** estensione **2.** volume **3.** limite, grado.

to extenuate *vt.* attenuare.

extenuation *s.* attenuazione.

exterior *agg.* esterno, esteriore. ♦ **exterior** *s.* **1.** l'esterno **2.** esteriorità.

exteriority *s.* esteriorità.

exteriorization *s.* esteriorizzazione.

to exteriorize *vt.* esternare.

to exterminate *vt.* sterminare.

extermination *s.* sterminio.

external *agg.* esteriore, esterno.

externality *s.* superficialità.

to externalize *vt.* esternare.

externally *avv.* esternamente, esteriormente.

exterritorial *agg.* estraterritoriale.

extinct *agg.* **1.** estinto **2.** spento.

extinction *s.* estinzione.

to extinguish *vt.* **1.** estinguere, spegnere **2.** pagare, ammortizzare.

extinguisher *s.* spegnitore, estintore.

to extirpate *vt.* estirpare, sradicare.

extirpation *s.* estirpazione, sradicamento.

to extol *vt.* lodare, magnificare

to extort *vt.* estorcere, strappare.

extorter *s.* chi estorce.

extortion *s.* estorsione.

extortioner *s.* ricattatore.

extra *agg.* **1.** straordinario **2.** in più, extra. ♦ **extra** *s.* **1.** supplemento **2.** (*giorn.*) edizione straordinaria **3.** (*cine*) comparsa. ♦ **extra** *avv.* extra, di più, in più, insolitamente.

extract *s.* **1.** estratto **2.** citazione.

to extract *vt.* estrarre, togliere.

extractable *agg.* estraibile.

extraction *s.* **1.** estrazione **2.** origine, stirpe.

extractive *agg.* estrattivo.

extractor *s.* estrattore.

to extradite *vt.* estradare.

extradition *s.* estradizione.

extraneous *agg.* estraneo.

extraordinary *agg.* straordinario, eccezionale.

extraterritorial *agg.* estraterritoriale.

extraterritoriality *s.* estraterritorialità.

extravagance *s.* **1.** prodigalità, sperpero **2.** stravaganza.

extravagant *agg.* **1.** prodigo **2.** stravagante.

extreme *agg.* **1.** estremo, ultimo **2.** grave. ♦ **extreme** *s.* estremo, estremità.

extremely *avv.* estremamente.

extremism *s.* estremismo.

extremist *s.* estremista.

extremity *s.* estremità.

extrinsic(al) *agg.* estrinseco.

extrovert *s.* estroverso.

to extrude *vt.* estromettere.

exuberance *s.* esuberanza.

exuberant *agg.* **1.** copioso, abbondante **2.** esuberante, pieno di vita.

exudation *s.* essudazione.

to exude *vt.* e *vi.* trasudare.

to exult *vi.* gioire, esultare.

exultant *agg.* esultante.

exultation *s.* esultanza.

eye *s.* occhio.

eyeball *s.* bulbo oculare.

eyebrow *s.* sopracciglio.

eyeglass *s.* lente, monocolo.

eyehole *s.* orbita, occhiaia.

eyelash *s.* ciglio.

eyelet *s.* occhiello, asola.

eyelid *s.* palpebra.

eyesight *s.* vista.

eyesore *s.* cosa brutta e spiacevole.

eyewitness *s.* tèstimone oculare.

F

F *s.* (*mus.*) fa.

fable *s.* favola.

fabled *agg.* **1.** mitico **2.** inventato.

fabric *s.* **1.** tessuto **2.** manufatto **3.**

struttura **4.** fabbricazione.

to **fabricate** *vt.* **1.** fabbricare **2.** inventare.

fabrication *s.* **1.** fabbricazione **2.** invenzione.

fabulist *s.* **1.** favolista **2.** bugiardo.

fabulosity *s.* favolosità.

fabulous *agg.* favoloso.

façade *s.* facciata.

face *s.* **1.** faccia **2.** aspetto **3.** sfrontatezza **4.** facciata **5.** quadrante (*di orologio*) || *to pull faces*, fare boccacce || — *-powder*, cipria; — *value*, (*comm.*) valore nominale.

to **face** *vt.* **1.** fronteggiare **2.** affrontare **3.** ricoprire || *to — about*, fare dietro-front.

facet *s.* sfaccettatura.

facetious *agg.* faceto.

facetiousness *s.* lepidezza.

facial *agg.* facciale.

facile *agg.* **1.** facile **2.** pronto **3.** accomodante.

to **facilitate** *vt.* facilitare.

facilitation *s.* facilitazione.

facility *s.* facilità. ♦ **facilities** *s. pl.* facilitazioni.

facing *agg.* che sta di fronte. ♦ **facing** *s.* rivestimento. ♦ **facings** *s. pl.* mostrine.

fact *s.* **1.** fatto **2.** realtà || *in —*, infatti, di fatto; *as a matter of —*, effettivamente.

faction *s.* **1.** fazione **2.** faziosità.

factious *agg.* fazioso.

factiousness *s.* faziosità.

factitious *agg.* fittizio.

factitiousness *s.* artificiosità.

factor *s.* **1.** fattore **2.** agente.

factory *s.* fabbrica.

factual *agg.* effettivo.

facultative *agg.* **1.** facoltativo **2.** casuale.

faculty *s.* facoltà.

fad *s.* **1.** mania **2.** capriccio.

faddist *s.* maniaco.

faddy *agg.* capriccioso.

fade *s.* (*radio*) variazione graduale.

to **fade** *vi.* **1.** appassire **2.** sbiadire **3.** svanire || *to — in* (*cine*) aprire in dissolvenza; *to — out*, (*cine*) chiudere in dissolvenza. ♦ to **fade** *vt.* **1.** far sbiadire **2.** far svanire.

fading *s.* **1.** appassimento **2.** scolorimento **3.** affievolimento **4.** dissolvenza.

to **fag** *vt.* affaticare. ♦ to **fag** *vi.* **1.** affaticarsi **2.** sfacchinare.

fag(g)ot *s.* fascina.

faience *s.* terracotta.

fail *s.* fallo.

to **fail** *vi.* **1.** fallire **2.** mancare, venir meno **3.** indebolirsi **4.** esser bocciato. ♦ to **fail** *vt.* **1.** mancare di **2.** bocciare **3.** abbandonare.

failing[1] *agg.* debole. ♦ **failing** *s.* **1.** debolezza **2.** mancanza **3.** fallimento.

failing[2] *prep.* in mancanza di.

failure *s.* **1.** fallimento **2.** incapacità **3.** mancanza **4.** indebolimento **5.** guasto || *to be a —*, essere un fallito.

fain *agg.* contento, disposto. ♦ **fain** *avv.* volentieri || *I would — stay*, preferirei restare.

faint *agg.* **1.** debole **2.** timido **3.** vago.

faint *s.* svenimento || — *-hearted*, codardo.

to **faint** *vi.* svenire.

faintness *s.* **1.** debolezza **2.** timidezza.

fair[1] *agg.* **1.** onesto **2.** biondo **3.** gentile **4.** bello **5.** sereno (*di tempo*) **6.** (*comm.*) libero || — *-play*, comportamento leale. ♦ **fair** *avv.* **1.** con onestà **2.** con precisione.

fair[2] *s.* fiera || *fun —*, Luna Park.

fairly *avv.* **1.** onestamente **2.** abbastanza.

fairness *s.* **1.** bellezza **2.** onestà **3.** color biondo **4.** bianchezza (*di carnagione*).

fairway *s.* canale navigabile.

fairy *agg.* **1.** fatato **2.** immaginario. ♦ **fairy** *s.* fata || — *-tale*, fiaba.

fairyland *s.* paese delle fate.

fairylike *agg.* simile a fata.

faith *s.* **1.** fede **2.** promessa || — *-healer*, guaritore.

faithful *agg.* **1.** fedele **2.** degno di fiducia.

faithfulness *s.* fedeltà.

faithless *agg.* **1.** senza fede **2.** sleale.

to **fake** *vt.* (*gergo*) falsificare.

fakir *s.* fachiro.

falcon *s.* falcone.

falconry *s.* falconeria.

fall *s.* **1.** caduta, cascata **2.** (*amer.*) autunno.

to **fall** (**fell, fallen**) *vi.* **1.** cadere **2.** abbassarsi **3.** capitare in sorte **4.** dividersi || *to — back*, ritirarsi; *to — behind*, restare indietro; *to — in with*, imbattersi; *to — short*,

essere insufficiente; to — away, deperire; to — down, far fiasco; to
— due, scadere.
fallacious agg. fallace.
fallaciousness s. fallacia.
fallacy s. 1. fallacia 2. errore 3. sofisma.
fallen V. to fall.
fallibility s. fallibilità.
fallible agg. fallibile.
falling agg. cadente. ♦ **falling** s.
caduta || — back, ripiegamento; —
off, diminuzione; — short, insufficienza.
fall-out s. pioggia radioattiva.
fallow agg. incolto.
false agg. 1. falso 2. stonato 3. in-
gannevole || — bottom, doppio
fondo.
falsehood s. falsità.
falsely avv. falsamente.
falseness s. falsità.
falsifiable agg. falsificabile.
falsification s. falsificazione.
falsifier s. falsificatore.
to **falsify** vt. 1. falsificare 2. smentire.
falsity s. falsità.
to **falter** vi. vacillare. ♦ to **falter**
vt. balbettare.
fame s. fama.
famed agg. celebre.
familiar agg. familiare. ♦ **familiar**
s. amico intimo || to be — with,
esser pratico di.
familiarity s. familiarità.
familiarization s. familiarità.
to **familiarize** vt. familiarizzare.
family s. famiglia.
famine s. carestia.
to **famish** vt. far morire di fame. ♦
to **famish** vi. mòrire di fame.
famous agg. famoso.
fan[1] s. 1. ventaglio 2. ventilatore 3.
pala (d'elica).
fan[2] s. (gergo) tifoso, ammiratore.
to **fan** vt. 1. sventolare 2. (agr.) vagliare.
fanatic agg. e s. fanatico.
fanatical agg. fanatico.
fanaticism s. fanatismo.
to **fanaticize** vt. rendere fanatico.
♦ to **fanaticize** vi. agire da fanatico.
fanciful agg. 1. fantasioso 2. fantastico.
fancifulness s. 1. fantasia 2. capriccio.
fancy agg. 1. immaginario 2. stra-

vagante 3. decorato. ♦ **fancy** s.
1. fantasia 2. capriccio 3. inclina-
zione || — ball, ballo in costume;
— -dress, costume.
to **fancy** vt. 1. immaginare 2. ritenere.
fang s. 1. zanna 2. dente (velenoso).
fanning s. ventilazione.
fantastic(al) agg. 1. immaginario
2. bizzarro.
to **fantasticate** vt. e vi. fantasticare.
fantasy s. 1. fantasia 2. capriccio.
far agg. (farther, farthest)
(further, furthest) lontano. ♦
far avv. 1. lontano 2. di gran lun-
ga || — away, — off, lontano; as
— as, fino a, per quanto; so —,
finora; — -gone, a uno stadio a-
vanzato (di malattie).
farce s. farsa.
farcical agg. farsesco.
farcicality s. qualità farsesca.
fare s. 1. tariffa 2. vitto 3. passeg-
gero || bill of —, lista delle vi-
vande.
to **fare** vi. 1. andare 2. riuscire 3.
nutrirsi || to — badly, andar male.
farewell s. congedo. ♦ **farewell**
inter. addio.
farfetched agg. remoto.
farinaceous agg. farinaceo.
farinose agg. farinoso.
farm s. 1. fattoria || — -yard, aia.
to **farm** vt. coltivare. ♦ to **farm** vi.
fare l'agricoltore.
farmer s. agricoltore.
farmhouse s. casa colonica.
farming s. agricoltura.
farmstead s. cascina.
farraginous agg. farraginoso.
farrier s. maniscalco.
farsighted agg. e s. presbite.
farther agg. (comp. di far) più lontano, ulteriore. ♦ **farther** avv. 1.
(di) più 2. più lontano 3. inoltre.
farthermost agg. il più lontano.
farthest agg. (superl. di far) il più
lontano, estremo. ♦ **farthest** avv.
(il) più lontano.
farthing s. "farthing" (moneta inglese: un quarto di penny).
fascicle s. fascicolo.
to **fascinate** vt. affascinare.
fascinating agg. affascinante.
fascination s. fascino.
fascinator s. affascinatore.
fascism s. fascismo.
fascist agg. e s. fascista.

fashion s. 1. modo 2. abitudine 3. moda ||.— -*plate*, figurino; *a man of* —, un uomo di mondo.

to **fashion** vt. foggiare.

fashionable agg. 1. alla moda 2. elegante.

fast agg. 1. fermo 2. fedele 3. inalterabile 4. rapido 5. (*fig.*) dissoluto 6. in anticipo (*di orologio*). ♦ **fast** avv. 1. fermamente 2. fortemente 3. velocemente 4. in modo dissoluto.

fast s. digiuno.

to **fast** vi. digiunare.

to **fasten** vt. 1. attaccare 2. allacciare 3. chiudere 4. fissare. ♦ to **fasten** vi. 1. allacciarsi 2. chiudersi 3. fissarsi.

fastener s. 1. fermaglio 2. legaccio, chiusura || *snap* —, automatico.

fastening s. 1. legatura 2. gancio, chiavistello.

faster s. digiunatore.

fastidious agg. schizzinoso.

fastidiousness s. schizzinosità.

fastness s. 1. velocità 2. fermezza 3. solidità 4. dissolutezza.

fat agg. 1. grasso 2. (*fig.*) proficuo. ♦ **fat** s. grasso || — -*head*, zuccone.

to **fat** V. *to fatten*.

fatal agg. fatale.

fatalism s. fatalismo.

fatalist s. fatalista.

fatalistic agg. fatalistico.

fatality s. 1. fatalità 2. fatalismo.

fatally avv. 1. in modo fatale 2. fatalmente.

fate s. fato.

father s. padre || — -*in-law*, suocero.

fatherhood s. paternità.

fatherland s. madrepatria.

fatherless agg. senza padre.

fatherlike agg. paterno. ♦ **fatherlike** avv. paternamente.

fatherly agg. e avv. V. *fatherlike*.

fathom s. (*mar.*) braccio (*misura di profondità*).

to **fathom** vt. scandagliare.

fathomless agg. 1. incommensurabile 2. incomprensibile.

fatidic(al) agg. fatidico.

fatigue s. fatica.

to **fatigue** vt. affaticare. ♦ to **fatigue** vi. affaticarsi.

fatness s. grassezza.

to **fatten** vt. ingrassare. ♦ to **fatten** vi. ingrassarsi.

fattener s. ingrassatore.

fattening s. ingrassamento.

fattiness s. grassezza.

fatty agg. grasso.

fatuity s. fatuità.

fatuous agg. fatuo.

fault s. 1. fallo 2. colpa 3. difetto || — -*finder*, criticone.

faultiness s. imperfezione.

faultless agg. 1. perfetto 2. irreprensibile.

faulty agg. difettoso.

faun s. fauno.

favour s. favore.

to **favour** vt. 1. favorire 2. sostenere 3. (*fam.*) assomigliare a.

favourable agg. favorevole.

favourite agg. e s. favorito.

favouritism s. favoritismo.

fawn s. cerbiatto.

to **fawn** vt. fare le feste || *to — on*, adulare.

fawner s. adulatore.

fawning s. servilismo.

fear s. paura, timore.

to **fear** vt. e vi. temere, aver paura.

fearful agg. 1. terribile 2. timoroso.

fearfulness s. 1. aspetto terribile 2. timore.

fearless agg. intrepido.

feasibility s. fattibilità.

feasible agg. fattibile.

feast s. 1. festa 2. banchetto.

to **feast** vt. 1. rallegrare 2. festeggiare. ♦ to **feast** vi. banchettare.

feaster s. convitato.

feat s. impresa, prodezza.

feather s. penna, piuma.

to **feather** vt. 1. coprire di penne, piume 2. (*mar.*) spalare.

feathered agg. 1. pennuto 2. (*fig.*) alato.

feathering s. piumaggio.

featherless agg. implume.

feature s. 1. lineamento 2. (*cine*) attrazione 3. caratteristica || — *film*, parte principale di un film.

to **feature** vt. 1. caratterizzare 2. (*teat.*) dare una parte importante a.

featureless agg. senza caratteristiche.

febrifuge s. febbrifugo.

febrile agg. febbrile.

February s. febbraio.

fecal agg. fecale.

fecund agg. fecondo.

to **fecundate** vt. fecondare.

fecundation s. fecondazione.

fecundity s. fecondità.
fed V. to feed.
federacy s. federazione.
federal agg. federale.
federalism s. federalismo.
federate agg. confederato.
to **federate** vt. confederare. ♦ to
federate vi. confederarsi.
federation s. (con)federazione.
federative agg. federativo.
fee s. 1. onorario 2. tassa 3. (giur.)
proprietà ereditaria.
feeble agg. debole.
feebleness s. debolezza.
feed s. 1. alimentazione 2. :ascolo.
to **feed** (fed, fed) vt. 1. nutrire
2. pascere 3. rifornire ‖ to be fed
up, essere stufo. ♦ to **feed** (fed,
fed) vi. nutrirsi ‖ to — up, ingrassare.
feeder s. 1. ciò che, chi nutre 2.
cavo di alimentazione 3. affluente
4. serbatoio.
feeding s. alimentazione.
feel s. tatto.
to **feel** (felt, felt) vt. 1. sentire
(col tatto o col sentimento) 2. tastare, sondare. ♦ to **feel** (felt,
felt) vi. 1. sentirsi 2. andare a tastoni.
feeling agg. sensibile. ♦ **feeling** s.
1. sentimento 2. sensibilità 3. sensazione.
feet V. foot.
to **feign** vt. 1. inventare 2. falsificare. ♦ to **feign** vi. fingersi.
feignedly avv. simulatamente.
feigner s. simulatore.
feint s. 1. finta 2. simulazione.
to **feint** vi. fare una finta.
feldspar s. feldspato.
to **felicitate** vt. felicitarsi con ‖ to
— so. on sthg., felicitarsi con qu.
di qc.
felicitation s. felicitazione.
felicitous agg. appropriato.
feline agg. e s. felino.
fell[1] V. to fall.
fell[2] agg. 1. crudele 2. funesto.
to **fell** vt. abbattere.
felling s. taglio (di un bosco).
fellow s. 1. individuo 2. compagno,
collega ‖ — -citizen, concittadino; — -creature, simile; a good
—, un buon diavolo.
fellowship s. 1. amicizia 2. associazione.
felon agg. e s. criminale.
felony s. crimine, delitto.

felt[1] V. to feel.
felt[2] s. feltro.
to **felt** vt. feltrare.
felucca s. feluca.
female agg. 1. femminile 2. (mecc.)
femmina. ♦ **female** s. femmina.
feminine agg. e s. femminile.
femininity s. femminilità.
feminism s. femminismo.
femur s. femore.
fen s. palude ‖ — -berry, mirtillo;
— -fire, fuoco fatuo.
fence s. 1. recinto 2. scherma 3.
(fam.) ricettatore.
to **fence** vt. cintare. ♦ to **fence** vi.
tirar di scherma.
fencer s. schermidore.
fencing s. 1. cinta 2. scherma.
fender s. 1. riparo 2. paraurti 3.
(mar.) parabordo.
fennel s. finocchio.
feracity s. feracità.
feral[1] agg. ferale, funesto.
feral[2] agg. ferino.
ferial agg. feriale.
ferine agg. ferino.
ferment s. fermento.
to **ferment** vi. 1. fermentare 2. agitarsi. ♦ to **ferment** vt. 1. far fermentare 2. eccitare.
fermentation s. 1. fermentazione 2.
fermento.
fermentative agg. fermentativo.
fern s. felce.
ferocious agg. feroce.
ferocity s. ferocia.
ferreous agg. 1. ferroso 2. ferreo.
ferret[1] s. furetto.
ferret[2] s. nastro, fettuccia.
ferro-concrete s. cemento armato.
ferrous agg. ferroso.
ferruginous agg. ferruginoso.
ferry s. traghetto.
to **ferry** vt. e vi. traghettare.
ferryman s. traghettatore.
fertile agg. fertile.
fertility s. fertilità.
fertilization s. fertilizzazione.
to **fertilize** vt. 1. fertilizzare 2. fecondare.
fertilizer s. fertilizzante.
fervency s. fervore.
fervent, fervid agg. ardente.
fervour s. ardore.
festal agg. festivo.
fester s. suppurazione, piaga.
to **fester** vi. suppurare (di ferita).
festival s. 1. festa 2. festival.
festive agg. 1. festivo 2. festoso.

festivity s. festività. ✦ **festivities**
s. pl. festeggiamenti.
festoon s. festone.
to **fetch** vt. 1. andare a prendere 2.
tirare 3. fruttare, rendere || to —
back, riportare.
fetid agg. fetido.
fetish s. feticcio.
fetishism s. feticismo.
fetishist s. feticista.
fetter s. ceppo, catena.
to **fetter** vt. incatenare.
fettle s. condizione || in fine —, in
forma.
feud[1] s. ostilità.
feud[2] s. feudo.
feudal agg. feudale.
feudalism s. feudalesimo.
feudality s. 1. feudalesimo 2. feudo.
feudatory agg. e s. feudatario.
fever s. febbre || to be in a —, avere
la febbre.
feverish agg. 1. febbricitante 2. febbrile.
few agg. e pron. pochi || a —, al-
cuni; quite a —, un numero considerevole; a good —, parecchi.
fewness s. scarsità, esiguità.
fiancé s. fidanzato.
fib s. fandonia.
to **fib** vi. dire fandonie.
fibre s. fibra.
fibroid, fibrous agg. fibroso.
fickle agg. incostante.
fickleness s. incostanza.
fictile agg. fittile.
fiction s. 1. narrativa 2. finzione.
fictional agg. immaginario.
fictitious agg. fittizio.
fiddle s. violino || fit as a —, in ot-
tima salute.
to **fiddle** vi. 1. suonare il violino 2.
gingillarsi.
fiddler s. violinista.
fiddlestick s. archetto. ✦ **fiddle-
sticks** s. pl. sciocchezze.
fidelity s. fedeltà.
to **fidget** vt. agitare. ✦ to **fidget** vi.
agitarsi.
fidgety agg. irrequieto.
fiduciary agg. e s. fiduciario.
field s. campo || -glass, binoco-
lo; — -day, giorno di esercitazio-
ni; — -officer, ufficiale superiore.
fiend s. demonio.
fiendish agg. diabolico.
fierce agg. 1. fiero 2. selvaggio 3.
ardente.
fierceness s. 1. ferocia 2. ardore.

fiery agg. 1. di fuoco 2. focoso 3.
infiammabile.
fife s. piffero.
fifteen agg. e s. quindici.
fifteenth agg. e s. quindicesimo.
fifth agg. e s. quinto.
fiftieth agg. e s. cinquantesimo.
fifty agg. e s. cinquanta || — - —,
a metà.
fig[1] s. fico.
fig[2] s. tenuta, vestiario.
fight s. 1. lotta 2. spirito combattivo.
to **fight (fought, fought)** vt. e vi.
combattere || to — down, vincere;
to — off, respingere; to — shy of,
tenersi alla larga da.
fighter s. 1. combattente 2. (aer.)
caccia.
fighting s. combattimento, rissa.
figuration s. figurazione.
figurative agg. 1. figurativo 2. figurato.
figure s. 1. figura, forma 2. cifra 3.
diagramma.
to **figure** vt. raffigurare. ✦ to **figure**
vi. 1. immaginarsi 2. passare per.
figurehead s. 1. prestanome 2.
(mar.) polena.
filament s. filamento.
filamentary, filamentous agg. filamentoso.
filcher s. ladruncolo.
file[1] s. lima.
file[2] s. 1. schedario, archivio 2. fila
3. raccolta.
to **file**[1] vt. limare.
to **file**[2] vt. 1. archiviare 2. ordinare.
✦ to **file** vi. marciare in fila.
filial agg. filiale.
filiation s. filiazione.
filibuster s. filibustiere.
filigree s. filigrana.
filing[1] s. limatura.
filing[2] s. 1. archiviazione 2. sfilata.
fill s. sazietà.
to **fill** vt. 1. riempire 2. occupare
3. otturare (di denti) || to — in,
to — up, riempire, compilare. ✦
to **fill** vi. riempirsi.
fillet s. 1. nastro 2. (cuc.) filetto.
filling s. 1. riempitura 2. otturazione
3. (cuc.) ripieno || — station, sta-
zione di rifornimento.
fillip s. 1. schiocco (delle dita) 2.
stimolo.
film s. 1. pellicola 2. velo 3. membrana.
to **film** vt. 1. coprire con una pelli-

cola 2. filmare. ♦ to **film** vi. 1.
coprirsi con una pellicola 2. girare
un film.
filmy agg. velato.
filter s. filtro.
to **filter** vt. e vi. filtrare.
filth s. sozzura.
filthily avv. in modo sudicio.
filthiness s. 1. sozzura 2. corruzione morale.
filthy agg. 1. sozzo 2. corrotto.
filtration s. filtrazione.
fin s. 1. pinna 2. (mecc.) aletta.
final agg. e s. finale.
finalist s. finalista.
finality s. 1. finalità 2. carattere definitivo.
finally avv. alla fine.
finance s. finanza.
to **finance** vt. finanziare.
financial agg. finanziario.
financier s. 1. finanziere 2. finanziatore.
financing s. finanziamento.
finch s. fringuello.
find s. scoperta, ritrovamento.
to **find** (**found, found**) vt. 1. tro-
vare 2. provvedere 3. ritenere ||
to — out, scoprire.
finding s. 1. scoperta 2. sentenza.
fine[1] agg. 1. bello 2. fine. ♦ **fine**
avv. bene.
fine[2] s. multa.
to **fine**[1] vt. raffinare. ♦ to **fine** vi.
raffinarsi.
to **fine**[2] vt. multare.
finely avv. 1. bene 2. finemente.
finger s. dito || — -print, impronta
digitale; — -tip, punta delle dita;
— -post, cartello segnavia.
to **finger** vt. 1. toccare con le dita
2. rubare || to be light-fingered
(fig.), avere le mani lunghe.
finish s. 1. fine 2. finezza 3. finitura.
to **finish** vt. e vi. finire.
finished agg. (fig.) perfetto.
finishing agg. ultimo, conclusivo.
♦ **finishing** s. (ri)finitura.
finite agg. limitato.
Finn s. finlandese.
Finnic, Finnish agg. finlandese.
fir (**-tree**) s. abete || — -wood,
abetaia.
fire s. 1. fuoco 2. incendio || on —,
in fiamme; — -guard, parafuoco;
— -plug, bocca da incendio; —
station, caserma dei pompieri; —
-works, fuochi d'artificio.
to **fire** vt. 1. dar fuoco 2. far fuoco

3. (fig.) infiammare. ♦ to **fire** vi.
1. prender fuoco 2. (fig.) infiammarsi.
firedamp s. grisù.
fire escape s. 1. scala di sicurezza
2. scala dei pompieri.
firefly s. lucciola.
fireman s. pompiere.
fireplace s. caminetto.
fireproof agg. incombustibile.
fireside s. angolo del focolare.
firewood s. legna da ardere.
firing s. 1. accensione 2. sparo 3.
alimentazione (di un fuoco) || —
squad, plotone d'esecuzione.
firm[1] agg. 1. fisso 2. solido 3. deciso.
firm[2] s. azienda, ditta.
firmament s. firmamento.
firmly avv. 1. fermamente 2. solidamente.
firmness s. 1. fermezza 2. stabilità.
first agg. primo || — -aid, pronto
soccorso; — -born, primogenito;
— -class, di prima qualità; —
-name, nome di battesimo. ♦ **first**
avv. 1. prima di tutto 2. per la
prima volta || at —, sulle prime.
♦ **first** s. 1. primo 2. principio.
firth s. fiordo.
fiscal agg. fiscale.
fish s. pesce || — -hook, amo.
to **fish** vi. 1. pescare 2. cercare. ♦
to **fish** vt. pescare.
fisher s. pescatore.
fisherman s. pescatore.
fishery s. pesca.
fishing s. pesca || — -boat, pesche-
reccio; — -line, lenza.
fishmonger s. pescivendolo.
fishy agg. 1. di pesce 2. pescoso 3.
(fig.) equivoco.
fission s. fissione.
fist s. pugno.
fit[1] agg. 1. adatto 2. pronto.
fit[2] s. 1. giusta misura 2. attacco, accesso (di febbre, ira ecc.).
to **fit** vt. 1. adattare 2. andar bene
a 3. provare || to — out, equipag-
giare.
fitful agg. 1. irregolare 2. spasmodico.
fitfulness s. irregolarità.
fitness s. convenienza.
fitter s. 1. aggiustatore 2. montatore.
fitting agg. adatto, conveniente. ♦
fitting s. 1. adattamento, prova
2. equipaggiamento. ♦ **fittings**

s. pl. **1.** accessori **2.** arredamento (*sing.*).
five *agg.* e *s.* cinque.
fix *s.* **1.** difficoltà **2.** (*mar.*) punto.
to **fix** *vt.* fissare || *to — up*, sistemare, riparare. ♦ to **fix** *vi.* stabilirsi.
fixation *s.* fissazione.
fixed *agg.* **1.** fisso **2.** stabilito.
fixer *s.* **1.** montatore **2.** fissatore.
fixing *s.* **1.** collocamento **2.** messa in opera **3.** fissaggio.
fixity *s.* **1.** stabilità **2.** fissità.
fizz *s.* **1.** effervescenza **2.** bevanda effervescente.
to **fizz** *vi.* frizzare.
fjord *s.* fiordo.
flabbiness *s.* **1.** mollezza **2.** fiacchezza (*di carattere ecc.*).
flabby *agg.* **1.** floscio **2.** fiacco.
flaccid *agg.* flaccido.
flaccidness *s.* flaccidezza.
flag[1] *s.* bandiera || *— -ship*, nave ammiraglia.
flag[2] *s.* lastra di pietra (*per pavimentazione*).
to **flag**[1] *vt.* **1.** imbandierare **2.** pavesare. ♦ to **flag** *vi.* **1.** pendere **2.** avvizzire.
to **flag**[2] *vt.* lastricare.
to **flagellate** *vt.* flagellare.
flagellation *s.* flagellazione.
flagellator *s.* flagellatore.
flagrancy *s.* flagranza.
flagrant *agg.* flagrante.
flagstaff *s.* asta di bandiera.
flair *s.* fiuto, intuizione.
flake *s.* **1.** fiocco (*di neve, lana ecc.*) **2.** favilla **3.** lamina **4.** scaglia.
to **flake** *vt.* **1.** sfaldare **2.** squamare **3.** coprire di fiocchi. ♦ to **flake** *vi.* **1.** sfaldarsi **2.** squamarsi **3.** cadere in fiocchi.
flaky *agg.* **1.** a falde **2.** a lamine, a scaglie.
flame *s.* fiamma || *— -thrower*, lanciafiamme.
to **flame** *vi.* fiammeggiare.
flaming *agg.* ardente.
flange *s.* orlo, frangia.
flank *s.* fianco.
to **flank** *vt.* **1.** fiancheggiare **2.** (*mil.*) attaccare il fianco di.
flannel *s.* flanella. ♦ **flannels** *s. pl.* calzoni di flanella.
flap *s.* **1.** lembo, falda **2.** colpo, agitazione **3.** linguetta **4.** (*aer.*) alettone.
flare *s.* **1.** fiammata improvvisa **2.**

chiarore.
to **flare** *vi.* **1.** brillare (*di luce incerta*) **2.** agitarsi **3.** divampare.
flash *s.* **1.** lampo **2.** chiusa || *— -back*, scena retrospettiva; *— -light*, lampo al magnesio.
to **flash** *vt.* **1.** proiettare **2.** diffondere. ♦ to **flash** *vi.* **1.** lampeggiare **2.** muoversi rapidamente.
flashing *agg.* risplendente. ♦ **flashing** *s.* splendore, scintillio.
flask *s.* fiasca.
flat[1] *agg.* **1.** piatto, piano **2.** disteso **3.** deciso **4.** sgonfio (*di pneumatico*).
flat[2] *s.* **1.** superficie piana **2.** pianura **3.** bassofondo **4.** chiatta **5.** appartamento **6.** (*mus.*) bemolle || *— -iron*, ferro da stiro.
flatly *avv.* **1.** pianamente **2.** scialbamente **3.** recisamente.
flatness *s.* **1.** piattezza **2.** decisione.
to **flatten** *vt.* **1.** appiattire **2.** smorzare. ♦ to **flatten** *vi.* **1.** appiattirsi **2.** indebolirsi.
to **flatter** *vt.* **1.** adulare **2.** illudere.
flatterer *s.* adulatore.
flattery *s.* adulazione.
flatulence, flatulency *s.* **1.** flatulenza **2.** vanità.
flatus *s.* flatulenza.
to **flaunt** *vt.* **1.** sventolare **2.** ostentare.
flavour *s.* gusto, aroma.
to **flavour** *vt.* aromatizzare, dare gusto a.
flavoured *agg.* **1.** profumato **2.** saporito.
flavouring *s.* **1.** aroma **2.** condimento.
flavourless *agg.* insipido.
flaw *s.* **1.** screpolatura **2.** falla, pecca.
flawless *agg.* perfetto.
flax *s.* lino.
flaxen *agg.* **1.** di lino **2.** biondo.
to **flay** *vt.* **1.** scorticare **2.** criticare aspramente.
flea *s.* pulce || *— -bite* (*fig.*), inezia.
fleck *s.* **1.** macchia **2.** scaglia.
to **flee** (**fled, fled**) *vt.* **1.** abbandonare **2.** evitare, schivare. ♦ to **flee** (**fled, fled**) *vi.* **1.** fuggire **2.** svanire.
fleece *s.* vello.
fleecy *agg.* lanoso.
to **fleer** *vt.* e *vi.* far beffe (a).
fleet *s.* flotta.
fleeting *agg.* fugace.

Flemish agg. fiammingo.
flesh s. carne || to lose —, dimagrire; to put on —, ingrassare.
fleshiness s. 1. carnosità 2. corpulenza.
fleshless agg. scarno.
fleshly agg. carnale, sensuale.
flew V. to fly.
to **flex** vt. flettere, piegare. ♦ to **flex** vi. flettersi.
flexibility s. 1. flessibilità 2. docilità.
flexible agg. 1. flessibile 2. docile.
flexion s. 1. flessione 2. curva.
flexuosity s. flessuosità.
flexuous agg. flessuoso.
flicker s. tremolio, bagliore.
to **flicker** vi. 1. tremolare 2. guizzare. ♦ to **flicker** vt. far tremolare.
flight[1] s. 1. volo 2. stormo 3. rampa (di scale).
flight[2] s. fuga.
flimsiness s. leggerezza, frivolezza.
flimsy agg. leggero, sottile.
to **flinch** vi. indietreggiare, ritirarsi.
fling s. 1. getto 2. beffa 3. tentativo.
to **fling (flung, flung)** vt. gettare. || to — open, spalancare. ♦ to **fling (flung, flung)** vi. gettarsi.
flint s. selce, pietra focaia.
to **flip** vt. 1. far schioccare 2. sbattere.
flippancy s. leggerezza.
flippant agg. leggero.
flipper s. pinna.
flirt s. 1. movimento rapido 2. amoreggiamento.
to **flirt** vt. muovere rapidamente. ♦ to **flirt** vi. amoreggiare.
flirtation s. amoreggiamento.
to **flit** vi. 1. volare 2. scorrere.
float s. galleggiante.
to **float** vt. 1. trasportare 2. inondare 3. (comm.) varare (un progetto ecc.). ♦ to **float** vi. 1. galleggiare 2. spandersi.
floatage s. 1. galleggiamento 2. relitto.
floatation s. (comm.) varo.
floater s. galleggiante.
floating agg. 1. galleggiante 2. oscillante, fluttuante.
flock s. 1. bioccolo 2. gregge 3. cascame.
to **flock** vi. affollarsi.
floe s. banchisa.
to **flog** vt. fustigare || to — a dead horse, fare una fatica inutile.

flogger s. fustigatore.
flood s. inondazione, diluvio.
to **flood** vt. inondare. ♦ to **flood** vi. straripare.
flooding s. 1. inondazione 2. emorragia.
floodlight s. illuminazione con riflettore.
flood tide s. flusso della marea.
floor s. 1. pavimento 2. piano || — -lamp, lampada a stelo.
to **floor** vt. pavimentare.
flooring s. impiantito.
flop s. 1. tonfo 2. insuccesso.
floral agg. floreale.
floriculture s. floricultura.
floriculturist s. floricultore.
florid agg. 1. florido 2. fiorito (di stile).
floridity s. floridezza.
florin s. fiorino.
florist s. fiorista.
flotilla s. flottiglia.
to **flounce** vi. agitarsi || to — out, andarsene furibondo.
flour s. farina || potato- —, fecola.
to **flour** vt. 1. infarinare 2. macinare.
flourish s. 1. ornamento 2. squillo di tromba.
to **flourish** vi. 1. prosperare 2. essere attivo.
flourishing agg. 1. fiorente 2. pomposo.
floury agg. 1. farinoso 2. infarinato.
flow s. corrente, flusso.
to **flow** vi. 1. scorrere 2. derivare da. ♦ to **flow** vt. inondare.
flower s. fiore || — -bed, aiuola; — -bud, bocciuolo.
to **flower** vi. fiorire. ♦ to **flower** vt. infiorare.
flowering agg. in fiore. ♦ **flowering** s. fioritura.
flowerless agg. senza fiori.
flowery agg. fiorito.
flowing agg. 1. fluente 2. fluido.
flown V. to fly.
flu s. influenza.
to **fluctuate** vi. 1. fluttuare 2. ondeggiare.
fluctuation s. oscillazione.
flue s. condotto per l'aria.
fluency s. 1. fluidità 2. scioltezza.
fluent agg. 1. fluente 2. dalla parola facile.
fluently avv. 1. fluentemente 2. speditamente.
fluff s. peluria.

fluffy *agg.* **1.** soffice, vaporoso **2.** coperto di peluria.
fluid *agg.* e *s.* fluido.
fluidity *s.* fluidità.
flung V. *to fling.*
fluorescence *s.* fluorescenza.
fluorescent *agg.* fluorescente.
fluoride *s.* fluoruro.
fluorine *s.* fluoro.
flurry *s.* **1.** ventata **2.** agitazione.
to flurry *vt.* agitare.
flush *agg.* **1.** abbondante **2.** pieno di vita **3.** a pari livello **4.** ben fornito. ◆ **flush** *s.* **1.** flusso **2.** vampata **3.** vigore.
to flush *vt.* **1.** lavare **2.** far scorrere **3.** rianimare. ◆ **to flush** *vi.* **1.** scorrere **2.** arrossire.
flute *s.* **1.** flauto **2.** increspatura.
fluted *agg.* **1.** flautato **2.** increspato.
flutter *s.* **1.** battito, movimento rapido **2.** eccitazione.
to flutter *vt.* agitare. ◆ **to flutter** *vi.* **1.** agitarsi **2.** battere le ali.
fluttering *agg.* **1.** svolazzante **2.** palpitante. ◆ **fluttering** *s.* **1.** svolazzamento **2.** palpitazione.
fluxion *s.* flusso.
fly[1] *s.* **1.** volo **2.** calesse **3.** (*mecc.*) volano.
fly[2] *s.* mosca.
to fly (flew, flown) *vi.* volare. ◆ **to fly (flew, flown)** *vt.* **1.** far volare **2.** sventolare || *to — about,* svolazzare; *to — away,* fuggire; *to off* (*aer.*), decollare.
flying *agg.* **1.** rapido **2.** sventolante || *—boat,* idrovolante.
flypaper *s.* carta moschicida.
foam *s.* schiuma || *— rubber* gommapiuma.
to foam *vi.* spumeggiare.
foamy *agg.* spumeggiante.
focal *agg.* focale.
focus *s.* **1.** fuoco **2.** focolaio.
to focus *vt.* mettere a fuoco.
fodder *s.* foraggio.
to fodder *vt.* foraggiare.
foe *s.* nemico.
foetus *s.* feto.
fog *s.* nebbia.
foggy *agg.* nebbioso (*anche fig.*).
foible *s.* debolezza.
foil[1] *s.* **1.** fioretto **2.** traccia.
foil[2] *s.* lamina.
fold[1] *s.* ovile.
fold[2] *s.* **1.** piega **2.** spira.
to fold[1] *vt.* **1.** piegare **2.** avvolgere **3.** abbracciare. ◆ **to fold** *vi.* pie-

garsi.
to fold[2] *vt.* chiudere nell'ovile.
folder *s.* **1.** volantino **2.** cartelletta.
folding *agg.* pieghevole. ◆ **folding** *s.* **1.** piega, piegatura **2.** avvolgimento **3.** abbraccio.
foliage *s.* fogliame.
folio *s.* (*tip.*) fo(g)lio.
folk *s.* gente, popolo.
folklore *s.* folclore.
folkloristic *agg.* folcloristico.
to follow *vt.* e *vi.* seguire.
follower *s.* seguace.
following *agg.* seguente. ◆ **following** *s.* seguito.
folly *s.* follia.
to foment *vt.* fomentare.
fomentation *s.* fomentazione.
fomenter *s.* fomentatore.
fond *agg.* **1.** amante **2.** affettuoso.
to fondle *vt.* vezzeggiare.
fondly *avv.* **1.** amorevolmente **2.** ingenuamente.
fondness *s.* tenerezza, amore.
font *s.* **1.** fonte battesimale **2.** acquasantiera.
food *s.* cibo.
foodstuff *s.* alimenti (*pl.*).
fool *s.* **1.** sciocco **2.** buffone || *to make a — of,* beffarsi di.
to fool *vt.* ingannare. ◆ **to fool** *vi.* fare lo sciocco || *to — away,* sperperare.
foolery *s.* follia.
foolhardiness *s.* folle temerarietà.
foolhardy *agg.* temerario.
foolish *agg.* sciocco.
foolishness *s.* sciocchezza.
foot *s.* (*pl.* feet) **1.** piede **2.** zampa || *on —,* a piedi.
football *s.* pallone.
footballer *s.* calciatore.
foot-bath *s.* pediluvio.
footboard *s.* predellino.
footbridge *s.* cavalcavia.
footfall *s.* passo.
footing *s.* punto d'appoggio.
footlights *s. pl.* luci della ribalta.
footman *s.* domestico.
footmark *s.* orma.
footnote *s.* poscritto.
footpath *s.* sentiero.
footprint, footstep *s.* orma.
footstool *s.* sgabello.
footway *s.* passaggio pedonale.
fop *s.* damerino.
foppery *s.* fatuità.
foppish *agg.* fatuo.
for[1] *prep.* per || *— all that,* ciò no-

nostante; *as* —, in quanto a.
for[2] *cong.* poiché.
forage *s.* foraggio.
foray *s.* incursione, saccheggio.
forbade V. *to forbid.*
to forbear (forbore, forborne)
vi. **1.** astenersi **2.** essere paziente.
forbearance *s.* **1.** astensione **2.**
pazienza.
forbearing *agg.* paziente.
to forbid (forbade, forbidden)
vt. proibire, impedire.
forbidding *agg.* **1.** severo **2.** ripugnante.
forbore V. *to forbear.*
forborne V. *to forbear.*
force *s.* forza. ♦ **forces** *s. pl.* trup-
pe || *the Armed Forces*, le Forze
Armate.
to force *vt.* **1.** forzare **2.** costrin-
gere || *to* — *back*, respingere; *to*
— *in*, sfondare; *to* — *on*, far avanzare.
forceful *agg.* forte.
forceps *s.* **1.** forcipe **2.** pinza.
forcible *agg.* **1.** violento **2.** potente.
ford *s.* guado.
to ford *vt.* guadare.
fordable *agg.* guadabile.
fore *agg.* anteriore. ♦ **fore** *s.* prua.
forearm *s.* avambraccio.
to forearm *vt.* premunire.
to forebode *vt.* presagire (*un male*).
foreboding *s.* presagio.
forecast *s.* previsione.
to forecast (forecast, forecast)
vt. prevedere.
forecastle *s.* castello di prua.
forefather *s.* antenato.
forefinger *s.* indice.
foreground *s.* primo piano.
forehead *s.* fronte.
foreign *agg.* **1.** straniero **2.** estra-
neo || — *Office*, Ministero degli
Esteri.
foreigner *s.* straniero.
forelock *s.* ciuffo.
foreman *s.* caposquadra, capore-
parto.
foremast *s.* albero di trinchetto.
forename *s.* nome di battesimo.
forensic(al) *agg.* forense.
to forerun (foreran, forerun) *vt.*
precorrere.
forerunner *s.* **1.** precursore **2.** messaggero.
foresail *s.* vela di trinchetto.
to foresee (foresaw, foreseen)
vt. prevedere.

foreseeable *agg.* prevedibile.
foreseeing *s.* previsione.
foreseen V. *to foresee.*
to foreshadow *vt.* adombrare.
foreshortening *s.* scorcio.
foresight *s.* **1.** previsione **2.** previdenza.
forest *s.* foresta.
forestal *agg.* forestale.
to forestall *vt.* **1.** prevenire **2.** accaparrare.
forestalling *s.* **1.** anticipazione **2.**
accaparramento.
forester *s.* **1.** guardia forestale **2.**
abitante di foreste.
forestry *s.* **1.** foresta **2.** silvicultura.
foretaste *s.* pregustazione.
to foretaste *vt.* pregustare.
to foretell (foretold, foretold)
vt. predire.
forethought *agg.* premeditato. ♦
forethought *s.* **1.** premeditazione
2. previdenza.
foretold V. *to foretell.*
forever *avv.* per sempre.
to forewarn *vt.* avvertire.
foreword *s.* prefazione.
forfeit *s.* **1.** perdita **2.** ammenda **3.**
penitenza.
forfeiture *s.* **1.** multa **2.** confisca.
to forgather *vi.* riunirsi, associarsi.
forgave V. *to forgive.*
forge *s.* fucina.
to forge *vt.* **1.** foggiare, fabbricare
2. contraffare.
forger *s.* **1.** fabbro **2.** falsario.
forgery *s.* contraffazione.
to forget (forgot, forgotten) *vt.*
e *vi.* dimenticare, dimenticarsi.
forgetful *agg.* **1.** immemore **2.** negligente.
forgetfulness *s.* **1.** oblio **2.** negligenza.
forget-me-not *s.* non-ti-scordar-di-
-me.
to forgive (forgave, forgiven)
vt. perdonare.
forgiveness *s.* perdono.
forgot V. *to forget.*
forgotten V. *to forget.*
fork *s.* **1.** forchetta **2.** forca **3.** forcella **4.** biforcazione.
to fork *vi.* biforcarsi || *to* — *out*,
(*gergo*) pagare. ♦ **to fork** *vt.*
biforcare.
forked *agg.* biforcuto.
forlorn *agg.* abbandonato.
form *s.* **1.** forma **2.** modulo **3.**
banco.

to **form** *vt.* formare. ◆ to **form** *vi.*
formarsi.
formal *agg.* formale || — *dress*, abi-
to da cerimonia.
formalism *s.* formalismo.
formalist *s.* formalista.
formality *s.* formalità.
to **formalize** *vt.* 1. formare 2. for-
malizzare.
format *s.* formato.
formation *s.* formazione.
formative *agg.* formativo.
forme *s.* (*tip.*) forma di stampa.
former[1] *agg.* e *pron.* precedente, il
primo (*fra due*).
former[2] *s.* 1. artefice 2. stampo.
formerly *avv.* precedentemente.
formic *agg.* formico.
formidable *agg.* 1. formidabile 2.
spaventoso.
formless *agg.* informe.
formulary *s.* formulario.
to **formulate** *vt.* formulare.
formulation *s.* formulazione.
to **forsake** (**forsook, forsaken**)
vt. abbandonare.
forsaking *s.* abbandono.
forsook V. *to forsake*.
to **forswear** (**forswore, for-
sworn**) *vt.* 1. abiurare 2. spergiurare.
fort *s.* (*mil.*) fortezza.
forth *avv.* 1. avanti 2. fuori || *and
so* —, e così via.
forthcoming *agg.* prossimo.
fortieth *agg.* e *s.* quarantesimo.
fortification *s.* fortificazione.
to **fortify** *vt.* fortificare.
fortitude *s.* forza d'animo.
fortnight *s.* due settimane.
fortnightly *agg.* quindicinale. ◆
fortnightly *avv.* ogni due settimane.
fortress *s.* (*mil.*) fortezza.
fortuitous *agg.* fortuito.
fortunate *agg.* 1. fortunato 2. propizio.
fortune *s.* 1. sorte: *to tell fortunes*,
predire la sorte 2. fortuna.
fortune-teller *s.* indovino.
forty *agg.* e *s.* quaranta.
forward *agg.* 1. avanzato 2. precoce
3. pronto.
to **forward** *vt.* 1. promuovere 2.
spedire.
forwarder *s.* spedizioniere.
forwarding *s.* spedizione.
forward(s) *avv.* avanti, in avanti.
fossil *agg.* e *s.* fossile.

fossilization *s.* fossilizzazione.
to **fossilize** *vt.* fossilizzare. ◆ to
fossilize *vi.* fossilizzarsi.
to **foster** *vt.* 1. favorire 2. allevare,
nutrire.
fought V. *to fight*.
foul *agg.* 1. sporco 2. tempestoso.
foulmouthed *agg.* sboccato.
to **foul** *vt.* 1. sporcare 2. urtare. ◆
to **foul** *vi.* 1. sporcarsi 2. urtarsi.
found V. *to find*.
to **found**[1] *vt.* fondare.
to **found**[2] *vt.* fondere.
foundation *s.* 1. fondazione 2. fondamenta 3. fondamento.
founder[1] *s.* fondatore.
founder[2] *s.* fonditore.
to **founder** *vi.* crollare. ◆ to
founder *vt.* affondare.
foundling *s.* trovatello || — *-hospi-
tal*, brefotrofio.
foundry *s.* fonderia.
fountain *s.* 1. fontana 2. sorgente
|| — *-pen*, penna stilografica.
four *agg.* e *s.* quattro || — *-handed*,
quadrumane; — *-footed*, quadru-
pede.
fourscore *agg.* ottanta.
fourteen *agg.* e *s.* quattordici.
fourteenth *agg.* e *s.* quattordice-
simo.
fourth *agg.* e *s.* quarto.
fowl *s.* pollo, pollame.
fox *s.* volpe: — *-hunt*, caccia alla
volpe.
foxglove *s.* digitale.
foxy *agg.* 1. volpino 2. rossiccio 3.
scolorito 4. aspro.
foyer *s.* ridotto.
fraction *s.* frazione.
fractional *agg.* frazionario.
to **fractionize** *vt.* frazionare.
fracture *s.* frattura.
to **fracture** *vt.* fratturare. ◆ to
fracture *vi.* fratturarsi.
fragile *agg.* fragile.
fragility *s.* fragilità.
fragment *s.* frammento.
fragmentary *agg.* frammentario.
fragrance *s.* fragranza.
fragrant *agg.* fragrante.
frail *agg.* 1. debole 2. caduco.
frailness, frailty *s.* debolezza.
frame *s.* 1. cornice 2. struttura, intelaiatura.
to **frame** *vt.* 1. incorniciare 2. formare.
framework *s.* struttura.
framing *s.* incorniciatura.

franc *s.* franco.
franchise *s.* franchigia.
Franciscan *agg.* e *s.* francescano.
frank *agg.* franco.
frankness *s.* franchezza.
frantic *agg.* frenetico.
fraternal *agg.* fraterno.
fraternity *s.* **1.** fraternità **2.** confraternita.
fraternization *s.* affratellamento.
to **fraternize** *vi.* fraternizzare.
fratricidal *agg.* fratricida.
fratricide *s.* **1.** fratricida **2.** fratricidio.
fraud *s.* **1.** frode **2.** impostura **3.** (*fam.*) impostore.
fraudulence *s.* frode.
fraudulent *agg.* fraudolento.
fray *s.* zuffa.
to **fray** *vt.* consumare. ♦ to **fray** *vi.* consumarsi.
freak *s.* **1.** capriccio **2.** macchiolina.
freakish, freaky *agg.* capriccioso.
freckle *s.* lentiggine.
freckled, freckly *agg.* lentigginoso.
free *agg.* **1.** libero **2.** (*comm.*) franco **3.** abbondante **4.** gratuito || — *on board,* franco porto. ♦ **free** *avv.* gratuitamente.
to **free** *vt.* liberare.
freedom *s.* libertà.
freely *avv.* **1.** liberamente **2.** gratuitamente.
freemason *s.* massone.
freemasonry *s.* massoneria.
freethinker *s.* libero pensatore.
freethinking *s.* libertà di pensiero.
freetrade *s.* libero scambio.
freetrader *s.* libero scambista.
freeze *s.* gelo, congelamento.
to **freeze** (**froze, frozen**) *vt.* e *vi.* **1.** gelare **2.** (*imp.*) far freddo.
freezer *s.* cella frigorifera.
freezing *agg.* glaciale, congelante. ♦ **freezing** *s.* congelamento.
freight *s.* **1.** trasporto **2.** nolo.
to **freight** *vt.* **1.** trasportare **2.** noleggiare **3.** caricare.
French *agg.* francese. ♦ **French** *s.* lingua francese.
to **frenchify** *vt.* francesizzare. ♦ to **frenchify** *vi.* francesizzarsi.
Frenchman *s.* francese (*uomo*).
Frenchwoman *s.* francese (*donna*).
frenzied *agg.* frenetico.
frenzy *s.* frenesia, delirio.
frequency *s.* frequenza.
frequent *agg.* frequente.
to **frequent** *vt.* frequentare.

fresco *s.* affresco.
fresh *agg.* fresco, nuovo, puro || — *water,* acqua dolce. ♦ **fresh** *s.* sorgente.
fresh-water *agg.* d'acqua dolce.
to **freshen** *vt.* **1.** rinfrescare **2.** desalinizzare. ♦ to **freshen** *vi.* rinfrescarsi.
freshly *avv.* **1.** in modo fresco **2.** recentemente.
freshman *s.* matricola.
freshness *s.* **1.** freschezza **2.** inesperienza.
fret[1] *s.* agitazione.
fret[2] *s.* **1.** fregio **2.** traforo.
to **fret**[1] *vt.* rodere. ♦ to **fret** *vi.* **1.** affliggersi **2.** agitarsi.
to **fret**[2] *vt.* **1.** ornare **2.** traforare.
fretful *agg.* irritabile.
fretfully *avv.* con irritazione.
fretfulness *s.* irritabilità.
fretwork *s.* intaglio ornamentale.
friability *s.* friabilità.
friable *agg.* friabile.
friar *s.* frate || *Black-* —, domenicano; *Grey-* —, francescano; *White-* —, carmelitano.
friction *s.* frizione, attrito.
Friday *s.* venerdì: *Good* —, Venerdì Santo.
fried *agg.* fritto.
friend *s.* amico || *to make friends,* fare amicizia; *the Society of Friends,* i quaccheri.
friendless *agg.* senza amici.
friendliness *s.* cordialità.
friendly *agg.* amichevole. ♦ **friendly** *avv.* amichevolmente.
friendship *s.* amicizia.
frigate *s.* fregata.
fright *s.* spavento.
to **frighten** *vt.* spaventare.
frightful *agg.* spaventevole.
frightfulness *s.* spavento.
frigid *agg.* **1.** glaciale **2.** frigido.
frigidity *s.* **1.** freddezza **2.** frigidità.
frill *s.* **1.** fronzolo **2.** gala increspata.
to **frill** *vt.* ornare di gale.
fringe *s.* **1.** frangia **2.** bordo.
to **fringe** *vt.* orlare.
frippery *s.* cianfrusaglie (*pl.*).
to **frisk** *vi.* fare capriole.
frisky *agg.* gaio.
frivolity *s.* frivolezza.
frivolous *agg.* frivolo.
frizzly, frizzy *agg.* crespo.
frock *s.* **1.** abito **2.** tonaca.
frog[1] *s.* rana.

frog[2] *s.* alamaro.
frogman *s.* sommozzatore.
frolic *s.* scherzo.
frolicsome *agg.* scherzoso.
from *prep.* da, di.
front *agg.* anteriore. ◆ **front** *s.*
1. fronte 2. sfrontatezza.
to front *vt.* fronteggiare.
frontal *agg.* frontale.
frontier *s.* frontiera.
frontispiece *s.* frontespizio.
frost *s.* 1. gelo 2. brina || —*bite*,
congelamento; *hoar*- —, brinata.
to frost *vt.* 1. gelare 2. (*cuc.*) glassare 3. smerigliare.
frosty *agg.* 1. gelato 2. gelido 3.
canuto.
froth *s.* 1. schiuma 2. frivolezza.
to froth *vi.* far schiuma.
frothy *agg.* 1. schiumoso 2. leggero.
frown *s.* 1. l'aggrottare le ciglia 2.
cipiglio.
to frown *vi.* 1. aggrottare le ciglia
2. acciglarsi.
frowning *agg.* accigliato.
froze V. *to freeze*.
frozen V. *to freeze*.
fructiferous *agg.* fruttifero.
to fructify *vi.* fruttificare. ◆ **to**
fructify *vt.* fertilizzare.
frugal *agg.* frugale.
frugalist *s.* persona frugale.
frugality *s.* frugalità.
fruit *s.* 1. frutta 2. frutto.
fruiterer *s.* fruttivendolo.
fruitful *agg.* 1. fruttifero 2. fertile
3. redditizio.
fruitfulness *s.* 1. fertilità 2. vantaggio.
fruition *s.* 1. godimento 2. realizzazione.
fruitless *agg.* infruttuoso.
to frustrate *vt.* frustrare.
frustration *s.* frustrazione.
frustum *s.* (*pl.* -ta) (*geom.*) tronco.
fry *s.* fritto, frittura.
to fry *vt.* e *vi.* friggere.
fudge *s.* fandonia, sciocchezza.
to fudge *vt.* rattoppare.
fuel *s.* combustibile || — *oil*, nafta.
to fuel *vt.* alimentare di combustibile.
fugacity *s.* fugacità.
fugitive *agg.* 1. fuggitivo 2. effimero. ◆ **fugitive** *s.* 1. fuggitivo
2. rifugiato.
fugitiveness *s.* fuggevolezza.
fugue *s.* (*mus.*) fuga.
fulcrum *s.* (*pl.* fulcra) fulcro.

to fulfil *vt.* 1. compiere 2. adempiere, esaurire.
fulfilment *s.* 1. compimento 2.
adempimento, esaudimento.
fulgency *s.* fulgidezza.
fulgent *agg.* fulgente.
fulgid *agg.* fulgido.
fulguration *s.* folgorazione.
full *agg.* pieno || — *up*, completo;
— -*stop*, punto. ◆ **full** *avv.* interamente. ◆ **full** *s.* 1. intero 2.
massimo.
fullness *s.* pienezza.
fully *avv.* completamente.
fulminant *agg.* fulminante.
fulmination *s.* 1. fulminazione 2.
imprecazione.
fumarole *s.* fumarola.
to fumble *vi.* annaspare. ◆ **to fum-**
ble *vt.* maneggiare goffamente.
fume *s.* 1. fumo 2. eccitazione.
to fume *vi.* 1. fumare 2. irritarsi.
fun *s.* 1. divertimento 2. facezia ||
to make — *of so.*, canzonare qu.;
to have good —, divertirsi molto.
funambulism *s.* funambolismo.
funambulist *s.* funambolo.
function *s.* funzione.
to function *vi.* 1. funzionare 2.
fungere da.
functional *agg.* funzionale.
functionary *s.* funzionario.
fund *s.* fondo, riserva.
to fund *vt.* 1. accumulare 2. investire in obbligazioni.
fundament *s.* base.
fundamental *agg.* fondamentale. ◆
fundamental *s.* fondamento.
funeral *agg.* funebre. ◆ **funeral**
s. funerale.
funerary, funereal *agg.* funereo.
funicular *agg.* e *s.* funicolare.
funnel *s.* 1. imbuto 2. camino, ci-
miniera.
funny *agg.* 1. comico 2. strano.
fur *s.* 1. pelliccia 2. patina, rivestimento.
to fur *vt.* coprire con pelliccia.
furbelow *s.* falpalà.
furious *agg.* furioso.
to furl *vt.* 1. piegare, chiudere 2.
ammainare (*vele ecc.*). ◆ **to furl**
vi. piegarsi, chiudersi.
furnace *s.* fornace.
to furnish *vt.* 1. fornire 2. ammobiliare.
furnisher *s.* fornitore.
furnishings *s.* *pl.* arredamento
(*sing.*).

furniture s. **1.** mobilio **2.** contenuto.
furrier s. pellicciaio.
furriery s. pellicceria.
furrow s. **1.** solco **2.** scia.
to **furrow** vt. **1.** solcare **2.** arare.
further agg. (comp. di far) **1.** più lontano **2.** ulteriore. ♦ **further** avv. **1.** più in là **2.** ancora.
to **further** vt. favorire.
furthermore avv. inoltre.
furthermost agg. il più lontano.
furthest agg. (superl. di far) estremo. ♦ **furthest** avv. all'estremo limite.
furtive agg. furtivo.
furunculosis s. furuncolosi.
fury s. furia.
fuse s. **1.** valvola, fusibile **2.** spoletta **3.** miccia.
to **fuse** vt. **1.** fondere **2.** liquefare. ♦ to **fuse** vi. **1.** fondersi **2.** saltare (di valvola).
fuselage s. fusoliera.
fusible agg. fusibile.
fusion s. fusione.
fuss s. **1.** trambusto **2.** smancerie.
to **fuss** vi. far confusione. ♦ to **fuss** vt. irritare.
fussily avv. **1.** con inutile scalpore **2.** con esagerata importanza.
fussy agg. **1.** che fa confusione **2.** meticoloso.
fusty agg. stantio.
futility s. futilità.
future agg. e s. futuro.
futurism s. futurismo.
fuzz s. lanuggine.
fuzzily avv. confusamente.
fuzziness s. **1.** increspatura (di capelli) **2.** (foto) sfocatura.
fuzzy agg. **1.** lanuginoso **2.** confuso **3.** (foto) sfocato.

G

G s. (mus.) sol.
to **gabble** vt. e vi. parlare in modo confuso.
gabbler s. chiacchierone.
gable s. frontone.
gadfly s. **1.** tafano **2.** (fig.) persona irritante.
gadget s. aggeggio.
Gael s. gaelico.
Gaelic agg. e s. gaelico.

gaff s. uncino, rampone.
gag s. **1.** bavaglio **2.** improvvisazione **3.** trovata geniale.
to **gag** vt. imbavagliare. ♦ to **gag** vi. improvvisare (motti di spirito).
gage s. garanzia.
to **gage** vt. dare in pegno.
gaiety s. gaiezza. ♦ **gaieties** s. pl. divertimenti.
gaily avv. gaiamente.
gain s. **1.** guadagno **2.** aumento, miglioramento.
to **gain** vt. e vi. **1.** guadagnare **2.** aumentare || to — on, guadagnar terreno su.
gainer s. chi guadagna.
gainful agg. lucroso.
gainings s. pl. guadagni.
to **gainsay** vt. contraddire.
gainsaying s. contraddizione.
gait s. andatura.
gaiter s. ghetta.
galalith s. galalite.
galantine s. galantina.
galaxy s. galassia.
gale s. tempesta.
galenic agg. galenico.
Galilean agg. e s. galileo.
gall[1] s. bile, fiele || — -bladder, cistifellea.
gall[2] s. **1.** scorticatura **2.** irritazione.
to **gall** vt. irritare. ♦ to **gall** vi. irritarsi.
gallant agg. **1.** prode **2.** galante. ♦ **gallant** s. uomo di mondo.
gallantry s. **1.** galanteria **2.** coraggio **3.** atto, discorso amoroso.
galleon s. galeone.
gallery s. galleria || picture- —, pinacoteca.
galley s. **1.** (mar.) galea **2.** (mar.) cambusa **3.** (tip.) vantaggio || — proof (tip.), bozza in colonna; — slave, galeotto.
Gallic agg. e s. gallico.
gallicism s. francesismo.
gallinacean agg. e s. gallinaceo.
gallium s. gallio.
gallon s. gallone (misura).
galloon s. gallone (ornamento).
gallooned agg. gallonato.
gallop s. **1.** galoppo: at a —, al galoppo **2.** galoppata.
to **gallop** vt. far galoppare. ♦ to **gallop** vi. galoppare.
gallows s. pl. patibolo. (sing.).
galore s. abbondanza. ♦ **galore** avv. in abbondanza.
galosh(e) s. galoscia.

galvanic(al) *agg.* **1.** galvanico **2.** (*fig.*) galvanizzante.
galvanization *s.* galvanizzazione.
to galvanize *vt.* galvanizzare.
galvanometer *s.* galvanometro.
galvanoplastic *agg.* galvanoplastico.
gamble *s.* gioco d'azzardo.
to gamble *vt.* e *vi.* giocare (*d'azzardo*).
gambler *s.* giocatore d'azzardo.
gambling *s.* V. *gamble* || — *-house*, casa da gioco.
gambol *s.* piroetta. ◆ **game** *s.* **1.** gioco (*con regole*), mano (*in una partita*) **2.** (*fig.*) progetto **3.** selvaggina (*coll.*).
game *agg.* risoluto. ◆ **game** *s.* **1.** gioco (*con regole*), mano (*in una partita*) **2.** (*fig.*) progetto **3.** selvaggina (*coll.*).
to game V. *to gamble*.
gamekeeper *s.* guardacaccia.
gamely *avv.* coraggiosamente.
gamesome *agg.* scherzoso.
gamester *s.* giocatore.
gammon *s.* (*mar.*) trinca di bompresso.
gang *s.* **1.** squadra **2.** banda.
to gang *vt.* e *vi.* formare una banda.
ganglion *s.* (*pl.* ganglia) ganglio.
gangrene *s.* cancrena.
to gangrene *vi.* andare in cancrena.
gangster *s.* bandito.
gangsterism *s.* banditismo.
gangway *s.* **1.** passaggio (*tra file di sedie ecc.*) **2.** (*mar.*) passerella.
gaol *s.* prigione.
to gaol *vt.* imprigionare.
gaoler *s.* carceriere.
gap *s.* **1.** apertura, breccia **2.** intervallo **3.** divergenza **4.** lacuna.
gape *s.* **1.** sbadiglio **2.** apertura **3.** stupore.
to gape *vi.* **1.** spalancare la bocca **2.** sbadigliare **3.** restare a bocca aperta.
gaping *agg.* **1.** aperto **2.** stupito.
garage *s.* autorimessa || — *keeper*, garagista.
garb *s.* costume.
garbage *s.* rifiuto.
garden *s.* giardino.
to garden *vi.* fare del giardinaggio.
gardener *s.* giardiniere.
gardening *s.* giardinaggio.
gargarism *s.* gargarismo.
gargle *s.* liquido per gargarismi.
to gargle *vt.* e *vi.* gargarizzare.
gargoyle *s.* doccione.
garish *agg.* **1.** abbagliante **2.** appariscente.

garland *s.* ghirlanda.
garlic *s.* aglio.
garment *s.* abito, indumento.
garnet[1] *s.* granato.
garnet[2] *s.* (*mar.*) paranco.
to garnish *vt.* guarnire.
garnish(ment) *s.* ornamento.
garret *s.* soffitta.
garrison *s.* guarnigione.
to garrison *vt.* presidiare.
garrulity *s.* garrulità.
garrulous *agg.* garrulo.
garter *s.* giarrettiera || *knight o, the Garter*, Cavaliere dell'Ordine della Giarrettiera.
gas *s.* gas || — *-fitter*, gassista; — *-mask*, maschera antigas; — *-meter*, contatore del gas.
to gas *vt.* **1.** fornire di gas **2.** asfissiare col gas.
Gascon *agg.* e *s.* guascone.
gasconade *s.* guasconata.
gaseous *agg.* gassoso.
gash *s.* sfregio.
to gash *vt.* sfregiare.
gas oil *s.* gasolio.
gasoline *s.* (*amer.*) benzina.
gasp *s.* respiro affannoso.
to gasp *vi.* **1.** ansare **2.** restare senza fiato **3.** parlare affannosamente.
gassy *agg.* gassoso.
gastric *agg.* gastrico.
gastritis *s.* gastrite.
gastroenteritis *s.* gastroenterite.
gastronome *s.* gastronomo.
gastronomic(al) *agg.* gastronomico.
gastronomy *s.* gastronomia.
gate *s.* **1.** cancello **2.** porta.
gatekeeper *s.* portiere, custode.
gateway *s.* portone, ingresso.
to gather *vt.* **1.** raccogliere **2.** acquistare **3.** dedurre. ◆ **to gather** *vi.* raccogliersi.
gathering *s.* **1.** raccolta **2.** (*med.*) ascesso.
gaud *s.* fronzolo.
gaudiness *s.* sfarzo.
gaudy *agg.* sfarzoso. ◆ **gaudy** *s.* festa (*universitaria*).
gauge *s.* **1.** misura **2.** calibro **3.** (*ferr.*) scartamento **4.** pescaggio || *narrow* —, scartamento ridotto.
to gauge *vt.* misurare.
gaunt *agg.* scarno.
gauze *s.* garza, velo, mussolina.
gauzy *agg.* trasparente.
gave V. *to give*.
gay *agg.* **1.** gaio **2.** licenzioso.
gayety *s.* gaiezza.

gaze *s.* sguardo fisso.
to gaze *vi.* fissare.
gazelle *s.* gazzella.
gazette *s.* gazzetta.
gazetteer *s.* **1.** giornalista **2.** dizionario geografico.
gear *s.* **1.** meccanismo **2.** (*auto*) marcia, cambio **3.** (*mecc.*) ingranaggio.
to gear *vt.* ingranare || *to — up, down,* aumentare, diminuire la velocità.
gearing *s.* ingranaggio, innesto.
geese V. *goose.*
gelatin(e) *s.* gelatina.
gelatinous *agg.* gelatinoso.
to geld *vt.* castrare.
gelid *agg.* gelido.
gem *s.* gemma.
gemmy *agg.* pieno di gemme.
gender *s.* genere.
genderless *agg.* di genere comune.
genealogical *agg.* genealogico.
genealogy *s.* genealogia.
generable *agg.* generabile.
general *agg.* e *s.* generale.
generality *s.* **1.** generalità **2.** maggioranza.
generalization *s.* generalizzazione.
to generalize *vt.* e *vi.* generalizzare.
generally *avv.* generalmente.
to generate *vt.* generare.
generation *s.* generazione.
generative *agg.* generativo.
generator *s.* generatore.
generic(al) *agg.* generico.
generosity *s.* generosità.
generous *agg.* **1.** generoso **2.** abbondante.
genesis *s.* (*pl.* -ses) genesi.
genetic(al) *agg.* genetico.
genetics *s.* genetica.
genial *agg.* **1.** gioviale **2.** geniale **3.** mite (*di clima*).
geniality *s.* **1.** giovialità **2.** mitezza (*di clima*).
genital *agg.* e *s.* genitale.
genitive *agg.* e *s.* genitivo.
genius *s.* genio.
genocide *s.* genocidio.
genre *s.* genere.
genteel *agg.* raffinato.
gentian *s.* genziana.
gentile *agg.* e *s.* pagano.
gentility *s.* signorilità.
gentle *agg.* **1.** nobile **2.** garbato **3.** moderato **4.** facile.
gentleman *s.* **1.** signore **2.** gentiluomo.
gentlemanlike, gentlemanly *agg.*

da gentiluomo.
gentleness *s.* gentilezza.
gentlewoman *s.* gentildonna.
gently *avv.* **1.** gentilmente, con delicatezza **2.** gradualmente.
gentry *s.* classe gentilizia.
to genuflect *vi.* genuflettersi.
genuflection *s.* genuflessione.
genuine *agg.* **1.** autentico **2.** sincero **3.** puro.
genuineness *s.* **1.** autenticità **2.** sincerità.
genus *s.* (*pl.* -nera) genere.
geodesy *s.* geodesia.
geographer *s.* geografo.
geographic(al) *agg.* geografico.
geography *s.* geografia.
geologic(al) *agg.* geologico.
geologist *s.* geologo.
geology *s.* geologia.
geometer *s.* geometra.
geometric(al) *agg.* geometrico.
geometrician *s.* geometra.
geometry *s.* geometria.
geophysics *s.* geofisica.
geopolitics *s.* geopolitica.
georgic *agg.* georgico.
geranium *s.* geranio.
gerent *s.* gerente.
germ *s.* germe.
german *agg.* germano.
German *agg.* e *s.* tedesco.
Germanic *agg.* germanico.
Germanism *s.* germanesimo.
Germanist *s.* germanista.
germanium *s.* germanio.
germinal *agg.* germinale.
to germinate *vt.* far germinare. ◆
to germinate *vi.* germinare.
germination *s.* germinazione.
gerontology *s.* gerontologia.
gerund *s.* gerundio.
gerundial *agg.* gerundivo.
gerundive *agg.* e *s.* gerundivo.
gestation *s.* gestazione.
to gesticulate *vi.* gesticolare.
gesticulation *s.* gesticolazione.
gesture *s.* **1.** gesto **2.** il gestire.
to gesture *vi.* far gesti.
to get (got, got) *vt.* **1.** ottenere, procurare **2.** prendere **3.** portare **4.** fare. ◆ **to get (got, got)** *vi.* **1.** andare **2.** divenire || *to — off,* scendere; *to — over,* scavalcare; *to — out,* (far) uscire; *to — up,* alzarsi; *to — married,* sposarsi; *to — hold of,* impossessarsi di.
getaway *s.* **1.** fuga **2.** (*sport*) partenza.

gettable *agg.* ottenibile.

get-up *s.* 1. equipaggiamento 2. presentazione (*di libro, giornale ecc.*).

geyser *s.* 1. geyser 2. scaldabagno.

ghastliness *s.* 1. aspetto spaventoso 2. pallore spettrale.

ghastly *agg.* 1. spaventoso 2. spettrale.

gherkin *s.* cetriolo.

Ghibelline *agg.* e *s.* ghibellino.

ghost *s.* 1. spirito 2. spettro || *to give up the* —, spirare.

ghostliness *s.* 1. l'essere spettrale 2. spiritualità.

ghostly *agg.* 1. spettrale 2. spirituale.

giant *s.* gigante.

giantism *s.* gigantismo.

gibbet *s.* patibolo.

to gibbet *vt.* 1. impiccare 2. (*fig.*) mettere alla berlina.

gibbosity *s.* gibbosità.

gibbous *agg.* gibboso.

gibe *s.* scherno.

to gibe *vt.* e *vi.* schernire.

giblets *s. pl.* regaglie.

giddily *avv.* vertiginosamente.

giddiness *s.* 1. capogiro 2. (*fig.*) frivolezza.

giddy *agg.* 1. stordito 2. vertiginoso 3. frivolo.

to giddy *vt.* stordire. ♦ to giddy *vi.* aver le vertigini.

gift *s.* 1. dono 2. dote.

to gift *vt.* dotare.

gig[1] *s.* 1. calessino 2. (*mar.*) iole.

gig[2] *s.* rampone, fiocina.

gigantean, gigantic *agg.* gigantesco.

giggle *s.* risatina.

to giggle *vi.* fare risatine.

to gild (gilt, gilt) (*anche reg.*) *vt.* (in)dorare.

gilder *s.* doratore.

gilding *s.* doratura.

gill *s.* 1. branchia 2. pappagorgia.

gilt V. *to gild.*

gilt *s.* doratura.

gimlet *s.* succhiello.

gin[1] *s.* "gin" (*liquore*).

gin[2] *s.* 1. elevatore 2. trappola (*per animali*).

ginger *s.* zenzero.

gingerly *agg.* cauto. ♦ gingerly *avv.* cautamente.

gipsy *s.* zingaro.

gipsydom *s.* gli zingari (*pl.*).

gipsyish *agg.* zingaresco.

giraffe *s.* giraffa.

to gird (girt, girt) (*anche reg.*) *vt.* cingere.

girder *s.* 1. trave maestra 2. sbarra

girdle *s.* 1. cintura 2. reggicalze.

to girdle *vt.* cingere.

girl *s.* ragazza || *flower* —, fioraia.

girlhood *s.* adolescenza (*di ragazza*).

Girondist *agg.* e *s.* girondino.

girt V. *to gird.*

girth *s.* 1. circonferenza 2. cinghia.

to give (gave, given) *vt.* dare || *to* — *in*, cedere; *to* — *out*, annunciare, venir meno; *to* — *up*, smettere, abbandonare; *to* — *birth to*, generare; *to* — *oneself up*, costituirsi (*alla polizia*); *to* — *oneself up to*, dedicarsi (a); *to* — *off*, emettere (*luce ecc.*).

giver *s.* datore.

glacial *agg.* glaciale.

glaciation *s.* glaciazione.

glacier *s.* ghiacciaio.

glacis *s.* spalto.

glad *agg.* lieto.

to gladden *vt.* rallegrare. ♦ to gladden *vi.* rallegrarsi.

glade *s.* radura.

gladiator *s.* gladiatore.

gladiolus *s.* (*pl.* -li) gladiolo.

gladly *avv.* con piacere.

gladness *s.* contentezza.

glair *s.* albume.

gladsome *agg.* gioioso.

glair *s.* albume.

glamorous *agg.* affascinante.

glamour *s.* 1. fascino 2. incantesimo

glance *s.* 1. occhiata 2. colpo obliquo.

to glance *vt.* e *vi.* 1. gettare uno sguardo 2. sfiorare 3. balenare || *to* — *off*, sorvolare su.

gland *s.* 1. ghiandola 2. ghianda.

glandiferous *agg.* ghiandifero.

glandular *agg.* glandolare.

glare *s.* 1. luce abbagliante 2. sguardo truce 3. abbagliamento.

to glare *vi.* 1. splendere 2. guardare torvamente.

glaring *agg.* 1. abbagliante 2. evidente.

glass *s.* 1. vetro 2. bicchiere 3. specchio || — *-ware*, articoli in vetro; — *-work*, fabbrica di vetro; — *-paper*, carta vetrata. ♦ glasses *s. pl.* occhiali, cannocchiale (*sing.*).

to glass *vt.* 1. specchiare 2. imbottigliare.

glassy *agg.* 1. vitreo 2. cristallino.

glaucous *agg.* glauco.
glaze *s.* superficie vetrosa.
to glaze *vt.* 1. smaltare 2. mettere vetri a. ♦ **to glaze** *vi.* diventare vitreo.
glazier *s.* vetraio.
glazy *agg.* vitreo.
gleam *s.* barlume.
to gleam *vi.* scintillare.
gleamy *agg.* scintillante.
to glean *vt. e vi.* spigolare.
gleaner *s.* spigolatore.
gleaning *s.* spigolatura.
glee *s.* allegria.
gleeful *agg.* allegro.
glib *agg.* 1. liscio 2. facondo 3. sciolto.
glibness *s.* 1. disinvoltura 2. facondia.
glide *s.* scivolata.
to glide *vt.* 1. far scorrere 2. trascorrere. ♦ **to glide** *vi.* 1. scivolare 2. passare.
glider *s.* aliante.
gliding *agg.* scorrevole. ♦ **gliding** *s.* volo a vela.
glimmer *s.* barlume.
to glimmer *vi.* brillare.
glimpse *s.* 1. visione 2. occhiata 3. vaga idea.
to glimpse *vt. e vi.* intravedere.
glitter *s.* scintillio.
to glitter *vi.* scintillare.
gloaming *s.* crepuscolo.
to gloat *vi.* fissare avidamente.
global *agg.* globale.
globe *s.* 1. globo 2. pianeta.
globous, globular *agg.* sferico.
globule *s.* globulo.
gloom *s.* 1. oscurità 2. tristezza.
to gloom *vt.* 1. oscurare 2. rattristare. ♦ **to gloom** *vi.* 1. oscurarsi 2. rattristarsi.
gloomy *agg.* cupo.
glorification *s.* glorificazione.
to glorify *vt.* glorificare.
glorious *agg.* 1. glorioso 2. splendido.
gloriousness *s.* V. *glory.*
glory *s.* 1. gloria 2. splendore.
to glory *vi.* vantarsi.
gloss *s.* 1. glossa 2. lucentezza 3. apparenza.
glossarist *s.* glossatore.
glossary *s.* glossario.
glossy *agg.* lucido.
glottis *s.* glottide.
glottologist *s.* glottologo.
glottology *s.* glottologia.

glove *s.* guanto ‖ *to be hand in — with,* essere molto intimo con.
gloved *agg.* inguantato.
glover *s.* guantaio.
glow *s.* 1. calore 2. splendore 3. colorito ‖ *—worm,* lucciola.
to glow *vi.* ardere.
glucose *s.* glucosio.
glue *s.* colla.
to glue *vt.* incollare.
glut *s.* 1. scorpacciata 2. saturazione.
to glut *vt.* 1. saziare 2. saturare. ♦ **to glut** *vi.* fare una scorpacciata.
gluten *s.* glutine.
gluteus *s.* (*pl.* glutei) gluteo.
glutton *s.* ghiottone.
gluttonous *agg.* ghiottone.
gluttony *s.* ghiottoneria.
glycerin(e) *s.* glicerina.
glycogen *s.* glicogeno.
gnarled *agg.* nodoso.
to gnash *vt. e vi.* digrignare.
gnat *s.* zanzara.
to gnaw *vt.* rodere.
gnawing *agg.* 1. rosicante 2. corrodente.
gnome[1] *s.* gnomo.
gnome[2] *s.* massima.
gnomic *agg.* gnomico.
gnosis *s.* gnosi.
gnostic *agg. e s.* gnostico.
gnosticism *s.* gnosticismo.
go *s.* 1. movimento 2. energia 3. colpo ‖ — *-between,* intermediario; — *-by,* evasione; — *-cart,* girello.
to go (went, gone) *vi.* 1. andare 2. divenire ‖ *to — by,* passare; *to — for,* andare a cercare; *to — on,* continuare.
goad *s.* pungolo.
to goad *vt.* stimolare.
goal *s.* 1. traguardo 2. (*sport*) rete ‖ — *-keeper,* portiere.
goat *s.* capra.
goatish *agg.* 1. caprino 2. lascivo.
to gobble *vt.* tranguugiare, inghiottire.
goblin *s.* folletto.
god *s.* 1. dio, divinità 2. Dio.
godchild *s.* (*pl.* -children) figlioccio.
goddaughter *s.* figlioccia.
goddess *s.* dea.
godfather *s.* padrino.
godless *agg.* 1. ateo 2. empio.
godlike *agg.* divino.
godliness *s.* devozione.
godly *agg.* religioso.
godmother *s.* madrina.

godown s. deposito.
godsend s. dono del cielo.
godship s. divinità.
godson s. figlioccio.
goggle agg. 1. stralunato 2. sporgente (di occhi).
to goggle vt. stralunare. ◆ **to goggle** vi. essere sporgenti (di occhi).
goggles s. pl. occhiali di protezione.
going s. 1. l'andare 2. partenza.
goitre s. gozzo.
goitrous agg. gozzuto.
gold agg. d'oro. ◆ **gold** s. oro || — -field, zona aurifera; — -digg'', cercatore d'oro.
golden agg. dorato, d'oro.
goldfinch s. cardellino.
goldsmith s. orefice.
gone V. to go.
gonfalon s. gonfalone.
goniometer s. goniometro.
goniometry s. goniometria.
good (better, best) agg. 1. buono 2. bravo 3. bello. ◆ **good** inter. bene!
good s. 1. bene 2. utilità || for —, per sempre.
good-bye inter. e s. addio, arrivederci.
good-for-nothing s. buono a nulla.
goodly agg. bello.
goodness s. 1. bontà 2. il meglio || my —!, Dio mio!
goods s. pl. merce (sing.).
goodwill s. 1. buona volontà 2. benevolenza.
goody agg. troppo buono. ◆ **goody** inter. bene!
goose s. (pl. geese) oca.
gooseberry s. uva spina.
goose-step s. passo dell'oca.
gore s. sangue rappreso.
gorge s. gola.
to gorge V. to glut.
gorgeous agg. magnifico.
gorgeousness s. magnificenza.
gospel s. vangelo.
gossamer s. ragnatela.
gossip s. 1. pettegolezzo 2. pettegolo.
to gossip vi. far pettegolezzi.
gossiper s. pettegolo.
gossipy agg. pettegolo.
got V. to get.
Gothic agg. e s. gotico.
gothicism s. 1. stile gotico 2. rozzezza.
gouache s. guazzo.
gouge s. sgorbia.

gourd s. zucca.
gourmand s. goloso.
gourmet s. buongustaio.
gout s. 1. gotta 2. goccia.
gouty agg. gottoso.
to govern vt. 1. governare 2. controllare 3. (gramm.) reggere.
governable agg. docile.
governess s. istitutrice.
government s. governo.
governmental agg. governativo.
governor s. 1. governatore 2. regolatore.
gown s. 1. veste 2. toga || dressing-—, veste da camera; night- —, camicia da notte.
grab s. presa.
to grab vt. 1. afferrare 2. (mecc.) bloccare.
grace s. grazia.
to grace vt. adornare.
graceful agg. grazioso.
gracefulness s. grazia.
graceless agg. 1. sgraziato 2. depravato.
gracile agg. gracile.
gracility s. gracilità.
gracious agg. benigno || good —!, mio Dio!
gradation s. gradazione.
grade s. 1. grado 2. pendio.
to grade vt. 1. graduare 2. livellare.
gradient agg. che sale, scende gradatamente. ◆ **gradient** s. pendenza.
gradual agg. graduale.
graduality s. gradualità.
graduate s. laureato.
to graduate vt. 1. graduare 2. laureare. ◆ **to graduate** vi. laurearsi.
graduation s. 1. graduazione 2. laurea.
graft s. innesto.
to graft vt. innestare.
grain s. 1. granaglie (pl.) 2. chicco 3. grano.
grainy agg. 1. granuloso 2. granoso.
gram s. grammo.
Gramineae s. pl. graminacee.
grammar s. grammatica.
grammarian s. grammatico.
grammatic(al) agg. grammaticale.
gramophone s. grammofono.
granary s. granaio.
grand agg. 1. grande 2. nobile || — -aunt, prozia; — -uncle, prozio; — -nephew, pronipote (maschio); — -niece, pronipote (femmina).

grandchild s. (pl. -children) nipote (di nonni).

granddaughter s. nipote (femmina) (di nonni).

grandeur s. grandiosità.

grandfather s. nonno.

grandiloquence s. magniloquenza.

grandiloquent agg. magniloquente.

grandiose agg. grandioso.

grandiosity s. grandiosità.

grandmother s. nonna.

grandmotherly agg. protettivo.

grandparents s. pl. nonni.

grandson s. nipote (maschio) (di nonni).

grange s. fattoria, casa colonica.

granite s. granito.

granitic agg. granitico.

granivorous agg. granivoro.

grant s. concessione.

to **grant** vt. concedere || to take for granted, dare per scontato.

granular agg. granulare.

granularity s. granulosità.

to **granulate** vt. granulare. ♦ to granulate vi. granularsi.

granulation s. granulazione.

granulous agg. granuloso.

grape s. 1. acino || — -shot, mitraglia. ♦ grapes s. pl. uva.

grapefruit s. pompelmo.

grapevine s. 1. vigna 2. (fam.) notizia ufficiosa.

graph s. grafico.

graphic(al) agg. 1. grafico 2. pittoresco.

graphite s. grafite.

graphologist s. grafologo.

graphology s. grafologia.

graphomania s. grafomania.

graphomaniac s. grafomane.

grapnel s. (mar.) grappino.

to **grapple** vt. afferrare. ♦ to grapple vi. lottare.

grappling s. (mar.) aggancio || — irons, grappini d'abbordaggio.

grasp s. 1. stretta 2. manico 3. potere.

to **grasp** vt. e vi. afferrare.

grasping agg. avido.

grass s. erba.

grasshopper s. cavalletta.

grass-widow s. donna separata dal marito.

grassy agg. erboso.

grate s. 1. grata 2. graticola.

to **grate** vt. 1. fornire di grata 2. grattugiare. ♦ to grate vi. stridere.

grateful agg. grato.

gratefulness s. gratitudine.

grater s. grattugia.

to **gratify** vt. 1. ricompensare 2. appagare.

gratifying agg. soddisfacente.

grating[1] agg. 1. irritante 2. stridente. ♦ grating s. stridore.

grating[2] s. 1. grata 2. (ott.) reticolo.

gratitude s. gratitudine.

gratuitous agg. gratuito.

gratuity s. mancia.

grave[1] agg. grave.

grave[2] s. tomba.

gravel s. ghiaia.

to **gravel** vt. inghiaiare.

gravelly agg. ghiaioso.

graven agg. intagliato.

graver s. 1. incisore 2. bulino.

gravestone s. pietra tombale.

graveyard s. cimitero.

gravid agg. gravido.

to **gravitate** vi. gravitare.

gravitation s. gravitazione.

gravitational agg. gravitazionale.

gravity s. gravità.

gravy s. sugo.

gray agg. e s. grigio.

graze s. 1. colpo di striscio 2. escoriazione.

to **graze**[1] vt. e vi. 1. graffiare 2. sfiorare.

to **graze**[2] vt. e vi. pascolare, condurre al pascolo.

grazier s. allevatore (di bestiame).

grazing[1] s. abrasione.

grazing[2] s. pascolo.

grease s. grasso.

to **grease** vt. ungere, lubrificare.

greaser s. ingrassatore.

greasiness s. untuosità.

greasy agg. 1. grasso 2. unto, untuoso 3. scivoloso.

great agg. grande || -grandchild, pronipote (di nonni); — -grandfather, bisnonno; — -grandmother, bisnonna.

greatness s. grandezza.

Grecian agg. e s. greco.

greed(iness) s. avidità.

greedy agg. avido.

Greek agg. e s. greco.

green agg. 1. verde 2. inesperto 3. vigoroso 4. recente. ♦ green s. prato. ♦ greens s. pl. frasche, verdura (sing.).

greenery s. 1. vegetazione 2. serra.

greengrocer s. erbivendolo.

greenhouse s. serra.

greenish *agg.* verdastro.
greenness *s.* **1.** color verde **2.** acerbezza **3.** ingenuità **4.** vigore.
greenroom *s.* (*teat.*) camerino.
to greet *vt.* e *vi.* salutare.
greeting *s.* saluto.
Gregorian *agg.* gregoriano.
grenadier *s.* granatiere.
grenadine *s.* granatina.
grew V. *to grow.*
grey *agg.* e *s.* grigio.
greyhound *s.* levriere.
greyness *s.* grigiore.
grid *s.* griglia.
gridiron *s.* graticola.
grief *s.* **1.** dolore **2.** fallimento || *to come to* —, fare fiasco.
grievance *s.* **1.** lagnanza **2.** torto.
to grieve *vt.* affliggere. ♦ **to grieve** *vi.* affliggersi.
grievous *agg.* **1.** doloroso **2.** grave.
griffon *s.* grifone.
grill *s.* **1.** graticola **2.** cibo ai ferri || — -*room*, rosticceria.
to grill *vt.* e *vi.* arrostire (*alla graticola*).
grille *s.* inferriata.
grim *agg.* cupo.
grimace *s.* smorfia.
grime *s.* sudiciume.
to grime *vt.* insudiciare.
grimly *avv.* cupamente.
grimy *agg.* sudicio.
grin *s.* **1.** largo sorriso **2.** sogghigno.
to grin *vi.* **1.** fare un largo sorriso **2.** sogghignare.
to grind (ground, ground) *vt.* **1.** macinare **2.** molare **3.** digrignare **4.** (*fig.*) opprimere.
grinder *s.* **1.** mola **2.** molare **3.** arrotino || *organ-* —, suonatore di organetto.
grinding *agg.* irritante. ♦ **grinding** *s.* **1.** macinatura **2.** stridore **3.** affilatura **4.** (*fig.*) oppressione.
grindstone *s.* mola.
grip *s.* **1.** stretta **2.** manico **3.** (*fig.*) padronanza || *to lose one's grips*, perdere le staffe.
to grip *vt.* e *vi.* afferrare.
gripe *s.* **1.** presa **2.** freno. ♦ **gripes** *s. pl.* colica (*sing.*).
gripper *s.* pinza.
grist *s.* grano da macinare || *to bring* — *to one's mill*, tirar l'acqua al proprio mulino.
grit *s.* sabbia, arenaria.
grizzly *agg.* grigio. ♦ **grizzly** *s.* orso grigio.

groan *s.* gemito.
to groan *vi.* gemere.
groaning *s.* gemito.
grocer *s.* droghiere.
grocery *s.* drogheria. ♦ **groceries** *s. pl.* droghe e coloniali.
groggy *agg.* vacillante.
groin *s.* inguine.
groom *s.* stalliere.
to groom *vt.* strigliare.
groove *s.* solco.
to grope *vi.* brancolare.
gropingly *avv.* a tastoni.
gross *agg.* **1.** grossolano **2.** pesante **3.** lussureggiante **4.** (*comm.*) lordo.
grotesque *agg.* grottesco.
grotto *s.* grotta.
ground[1] V. *to grind.*
ground[2] *s.* **1.** suolo, terreno **2.** distanza, territorio **3.** motivi, ragioni (*general. pl.*) || — -*floor*, pianterreno.
to ground *vt.* fondare. ♦ **to ground** *vi.* **1.** fondarsi **2.** arenarsi.
grounded *agg.* interrato.
groundless *agg.* infondato.
groundlessness *s.* infondatezza.
grounds *s. pl.* **1.** fondi, sedimenti **2.** parco (*sing.*).
group *s.* gruppo.
to group *vt.* raggruppare. ♦ **to group** *vi.* raggrupparsi.
grouping *s.* raggruppamento.
grove *s.* boschetto || *olive* —, oliveto.
to grovel *vi.* **1.** strisciare a terra **2.** (*fig.*) umiliarsi.
grovelling *s.* strisciamento. ♦ **grovelling** *agg.* **1.** strisciante **2.** (*fig.*) abbietto.
to grow (grew, grown) *vi.* **1.** crescere **2.** diventare || *to* — *better*, migliorare; *to* — *old*, invecchiare; *to* — *up*, crescere, diventare maturo (*di persone*). ♦ **to grow (grew, grown)** *vt.* coltivare.
grower *s.* coltivatore.
growing *s.* coltivazione.
growl *s.* brontolio.
to growl *vt.* e *vi.* brontolare.
growler *s.* brontolone.
grown V. *to grow.*
grown-up *agg.* e *s.* adulto.
growth *s.* **1.** crescita **2.** produzione.
grub *s.* **1.** verme **2.** larva.
to grub *vt.* e *vi.* scavare.
grubby *agg.* **1.** bacato **2.** sporco.
grudge *s.* malanimo || *to bear a* — *against so.*, nutrire rancore verso

qu.

to **grudge** *vt.* **1.** dare a malincuore **2.** invidiare.

grudging *agg.* **1.** riluttante **2.** invidioso.

gruesome *agg.* raccapricciante.

gruff *agg.* burbero.

grumble *s.* brontolio.

to **grumble** *vt.* e *vi.* brontolare.

grumbler *s.* brontolone.

grumbling *s.* brontolio.

grumpy *agg.* burbero, tetro.

grunt *s.* grugnito.

to **grunt** *vt.* e *vi.* grugnire.

gruyère *s.* gruviera.

guarantee *s.* **1.** garanzia **2.** garante.

to **guarantee** *vt.* garantire.

guard *s.* **1.** guardia **2.** capotreno **3.** parapetto.

to **guard** *vt.* custodire.

guardian *s.* **1.** guardiano **2.** tutore.

guardianship *s.* **1.** protezione **2.** tutela.

guardless *agg.* indifeso.

guardrail *s.* **1.** spartitraffico **2.** corrimano (*di scala*).

Guelph *s.* guelfo.

guerrilla *s.* **1.** guerriglia **2.** guerrigliere.

guess *s.* supposizione.

to **guess** *vt.* e *vi.* **1.** supporre **2.** indovinare.

guess-work *s.* congettura.

guest *s.* ospite || — -*house*, pensione.

guffaw *s.* riso sguaiato.

guide *s.* guida.

to **guide** *vt.* guidare.

guild *s.* corporazione.

guile *s.* insidia.

guileful *agg.* insidioso.

guileless *agg.* sincero.

guillotine *s.* ghigliottina.

guilt *s.* colpa.

guiltiness *s.* colpevolezza.

guiltless *agg.* innocente.

guilty *agg.* colpevole.

guinea *s.* ghinea.

Guinea-pig *s.* cavia.

guise *s.* **1.** aspetto, apparenza **2.** falso aspetto.

guitar *s.* chitarra.

guitarist *s.* chitarrista.

gulf *s.* golfo.

gull[1] *s.* gabbiano.

gull[2] *s.* sciocco.

to **gull** *vt.* truffare.

gully *s.* condotto (*di scolo*) || —

-*hole*, tombino.

gulp *s.* **1.** boccone **2.** sorso.

to **gulp** *vt.* inghiottire.

gum[1] *s.* gengiva.

gum[2] *s.* gomma.

to **gum** *vt.* ingommare.

gummy *agg.* gommoso.

gun *s.* **1.** cannone **2.** fucile **3.** rivoltella, pistola || — -*barrel*, canna da fucile; — -*carriage*, affusto di cannone.

gunfire *s.* sparatoria.

gunner *s.* artigliere.

gunpowder *s.* polvere da sparo.

gun-room *s.* armeria.

gunshot *s.* colpo di arma da fuoco.

gunsmith *s.* armaiolo.

gurgle *s.* gorgoglio.

to **gurgle** *vi.* gorgogliare.

gush *s.* **1.** getto **2.** effusione.

to **gush** *vi.* **1.** sgorgare **2.** essere espansivo.

gusher *s.* pozzo petrolifero.

gushing *agg.* **1.** sgorgante **2.** esuberante.

gust *s.* **1.** raffica **2.** (*fig.*) impeto.

gustative, gustatory *agg.* gustativo.

gusty *agg.* ventoso.

gut *s.* budello.

to **gut** *vt.* sventrare.

gutter *s.* **1.** grondaia **2.** rigagnolo.

to **gutter** *vt.* scanalare. ♦ to **gutter** *vi.* colare.

guttural *agg.* e *s.* gutturale.

to **guzzle** *vt.* tracannare.

gymkhana *s.* gincana.

gymnasium *s.* palestra.

gymnast *s.* ginnasta.

gymnastic(al) *agg.* ginnastico.

gymnastics *s.* ginnastica.

gynaeceum *s.* (*pl.* -cea) gineceo.

gynaecologic *agg.* ginecologico.

gynaecologist *s.* ginecologo.

gynaecology *s.* ginecologia.

gypsy *s.* V. *gipsy*.

to **gyrate** *vi.* girare.

gyroscope *s.* giroscopio.

gyves *s. pl.* ceppi, catene.

H

haberdasher *s.* merciaio.

haberdashery *s.* merceria.

habit *s.* **1.** abitudine **2.** temperamen-

to **3.** costume.
habitable *agg.* abitabile.
habitation *s.* abitazione.
habitual *agg.* abituale, consueto.
habitude *s.* abitudine.
hack[1] *s.* **1.** tacca, incisione **2.** piccone, mazza **3.** tosse secca.
hack[2] *s.* **1.** ronzino **2.** (*fig.*) scribacchino.
to **hack**[1] *vt.* sminuzzare. ♦ to **hack** *vi.* tossire a colpi secchi.
to **hack**[2] *vt.* e *vi.* **1.** adoperare cavalli da nolo **2.** adibire a un lavoro da scribacchino.
hackney *s.* **1.** cavallo da nolo **2.** vettura da nolo.
hacksaw *s.* seghetto.
had V. *to have.*
haematoma *s.* ematoma.
haemoglobin *s.* emoglobina.
haemophilia *s.* emofilia.
haemoptysis *s.* emottisi.
haemorrhage *s.* emorragia.
haemorrhoids *s. pl.* emorroidi.
haemostasia *s.* emostasi.
haemostatic *agg.* e *s.* emostatico.
haft *s.* manico, impugnatura.
hag *s.* **1.** strega, megera **2.** (*zool.*) lampreda.
haggard *agg.* sparuto, emaciato.
to **haggle** *vi.* mercanteggiare.
hagiographer *s.* agiografo.
hagiography *s.* agiografia.
hail[1] *s.* grandine || — *-stone*, chicco di grandine; — *-storm*, grandinata.
hail[2] *inter.* salve!, salute!
to **hail**[1] *vi.* grandinare.
to **hail**[2] *vt.* e *vi.* salutare, chiamare.
hair *s.* **1.** capelli, capigliatura **2.** pelo, crine, setola || — *-breadth*, spessore di un capello; — *-cut*, taglio dei capelli; — *-do*, acconciatura.
hairdresser *s.* parrucchiere.
hairiness *s.* pelosità.
hairless *agg.* senza capelli.
hairpin *s.* forcella (*per capelli*).
hairy *agg.* **1.** capelluto **2.** peloso.
halation *s.* alone.
halberd *s.* alabarda.
hale *agg.* robusto, gagliardo.
half *agg.* mezzo.
half *s.* (*pl.* halves) metà, mezzo. ♦
half *avv.* a mezzo, a metà || — *-brother*, fratellastro; — *-length*, di media lunghezza; — *-mast*, a mezz'asta; — *-pay*, stipendio ridotto; — *-processed*, semilavorato; — *-sister*, sorellastra; — *-year*, se-

mestre.
halfpenny *s.* mezzo penny.
halfway *agg.* e *avv.* a mezza strada.
hall *s.* **1.** sala, salone **2.** refettorio, sala di ritrovo.
hallo! *int.* pronto (*al telefono*).
to **hallow** *vt.* santificare.
to **hallucinate** *vt.* allucinare.
hallucination *s.* allucinazione.
halo *s.* alone, aureola.
to **halt**[1] *vt.* fermare. ♦ to **halt** *vi.* fermarsi.
to **halt**[2] *vi.* zoppicare.
halter *s.* **1.** capestro **2.** cavezza.
to **halve** *vt.* dividere a metà.
halyard *s.* (*mar.*) drizza.
ham *s.* **1.** prosciutto. ♦ **hams** *s. pl.* natiche.
hamlet *s.* piccolo villaggio.
hammer *s.* martello, martelletto: — *-blow*, colpo di martello, di maglio || *to bring under the* —, mettere all'asta.
to **hammer** *vt.* e *vi.* martellare.
hammering *s.* martellamento.
hammock *s.* amaca.
hamper[1] *s.* cesta.
hamper[2] *s.* impedimento.
to **hamper** *vt.* imbarazzare, ostacolare.
to **hamstring** *vt.* azzoppare.
hand *s.* **1.** mano: *hands off!*, via le mani!; *hands up!*, mani in alto! **2.** operaio, lavoratore **3.** calligrafia || *at* —, a portata di mano; *first* —, di prima mano.
to **hand** *vt.* porgere, dare || *to* — *in*, consegnare; *to* — *out*, distribuire; *to* — *over*, rimettere.
handbag *s.* borsetta.
handbill *s.* volantino.
handbook *s.* manuale.
handcuffs *s. pl.* manette.
to **handcuff** *vt.* mettere le manette.
handful *s.* **1.** manciata **2.** piccolo numero (*di persone*).
handgrip *s.* stretta di mano, morsa della mano.
handicap *s.* svantaggio.
to **handicap** *vt.* svantaggiare, ostacolare.
handicraft *s.* **1.** lavoro manuale **2.** abilità manuale.
handicraftsman *s.* artigiano.
handily *avv.* **1.** abilmente **2.** a portata di mano.
handiwork *s.* lavoro fatto a mano.
handkerchief *s.* fazzoletto.
handle *s.* **1.** manico, impugnatura

2. (*fig.*) pretesto || — *-bar*, manubrio (*di bicicletta*).
to **handle** *vt.* **1.** maneggiare **2.** comportarsi verso.
handler *s.* manipolatore.
handling *s.* **1.** maneggiamento **2.** maniera di trattare.
handmade *agg.* fatto a mano.
handrail *s.* corrimano.
handshake *s.* stretta di mano.
handsome *agg.* bello, di bell'aspetto.
handwriting *s.* calligrafia.
handy *agg.* **1.** abile, destro **2.** a portata di mano || — *-man*, factotum.
hang *s.* inclinazione, pendio.
to **hang** (**hung, hung**) *vt.* appendere, attaccare.
to **hang** (**hung, hung**) *vi.* **1.** pendere **2.** appoggiarsi. ♦ to **hang** (*reg.*) *vt.* impiccare.
hanger *s.* gancio, uncino || — *on*, seguace, parassita; *dress-* —, attaccapanni; *paper-* —, tappezziere.
hanging *agg.* pendente, sospeso. ♦ **hanging** *s.* impiccagione.
hangman *s.* boia, carnefice.
hank *s.* matassa.
hapless *agg.* sfortunato.
to **happen** *vi.* avvenire, accadere.
happening *s.* avvenimento.
happily *avv.* felicemente.
happiness *s.* felicità.
happy *agg.* felice, contento.
harangue *s.* arringa.
to **harangue** *vt.* e *vi.* arringare, pronunciare un discorso solenne.
to **harass** *vt.* tormentare, molestare.
harbinger *s.* precursore.
harbour *s.* **1.** porto **2.** (*fig.*) rifugio.
to **harbour** *vt.* **1.** accogliere, dare asilo a **2.** nutrire (*pensieri ecc.*). ♦ to **harbour** *vi.* entrare in porto.
hard *agg.* **1.** duro **2.** severo, spietato **3.** difficile **4.** rigido (*di tempo*). ♦ **hard** *avv.* **1.** energicamente **2.** con difficoltà, duramente **3.** vicino, accanto || — *-boiled*, bollito fino a diventar duro; — *-headed*, ostinato; — *-set*, in bisogno.
to **harden** *vt.* indurire. ♦ to **harden** *vi.* indurirsi.
hardening *agg.* temprante. ♦ **hardening** *s.* tempra.
hardihood *s.* ardire, coraggio.
hardily *avv.* arditamente.
hardiness *s.* **1.** ardire **2.** robustezza.
hardly *avv.* **1.** a stento, a malapena **2.** quasi **3.** duramente, severamente.

hardness *s.* durezza (*anche fig.*).
hardship *s.* **1.** avversità **2.** stento.
hardware *s.* ferramenta.
hardy *agg.* ardito.
hare *s.* lepre || — *-brained*, scervellato; — *-lip*, labbro leporino.
to **hark** *vt.* ę *vi.* ascoltare || to — *back,* risalire a (*col pensiero*).
harlequin *s.* arlecchino.
harlequinade *s.* arlecchinata.
harlot *s.* prostituta.
harm *s.* danno (*morale e fisico*) || out of — *'s way,* in salvo.
to **harm** *vt.* far male, far torto.
harmful *agg.* nocivo, dannoso.
harmfulness *s.* l'essere nocivo.
harmless *agg.* innocuo.
harmonic *agg.* **1.** armonico, armonioso **2.** (*mat.*) in progressione.
harmonious *agg.* armonioso.
harmonium *s.* armonium.
to **harmonize** *vt.* armonizzare. ♦ to **harmonize** *vi.* armonizzarsi.
harmony *s.* armonia, accordo.
harness *s.* finimenti (*pl.*).
to **harness** *vt.* bardare, mettere i finimenti a.
harp *s.* arpa.
harpist *s.* arpista.
harpoon *s.* rampone, fiocina.
harpsichord *s.* clavicembalo.
harrow *s.* erpice.
harsh *agg.* **1.** duro, ruvido **2.** aspro **3.** discordante (*di suono*).
harshness *s.* asprezza, durezza.
harvest *s.* raccolto, messe.
harvester *s.* **1.** mietitore **2.** mietitrice meccanica.
haste *s.* fretta, rapidità || to make —, far presto.
to **haste,** to **hasten** *vt.* affrettare. ♦ to **haste,** to **hasten** *vi.* affrettarsi.
hastily *avv.* **1.** frettolosamente **2.** precipitosamente.
hasty *agg.* **1.** frettoloso, affrettato **2.** avventato, impetuoso.
hat *s.* cappello.
hatch *s.* **1.** portello, mezza porta **2.** (*mar.*) boccaporto.
hatchet *s.* accetta.
hate *s.* odio.
to **hate** *vt.* odiare, avere in odio.
hateful *agg.* **1.** odioso **2.** pieno di odio.
hatred *s.* odio.
hatstand *s.* attaccapanni.
hatter *s.* cappellaio.
haughtily *avv.* altezzosamente.

haughtiness *s.* alterigia, boria.
haughty *agg.* altezzoso, arrogante.
haul *s.* 1. trazione, tiro 2. raccolta, retata.
to haul *vt.* tirare, trainare. ♦ **to haul** *vi.* cambiare (*di vento*).
haulage *s.* 1. trasporto 2. costo del trasporto.
haunt *s.* 1. ricovero, ritiro 2. covo, tana.
to haunt *vt.* 1. frequentare assiduamente 2. perseguitare (*di ricordi, pensieri ecc.*).
haunted *agg.* 1. frequentato 2. perseguitato.
haunting *agg.* che perseguita.
to have (had, had) *vt.* 1. (*ausiliare*) avere: *I — gone*, sono andato; *I — not (I haven't) read the book*, non ho letto il libro 2. avere, possedere || *to — breakfast*, far colazione 3. dovere: *I — to go there*, devo andarci 4. ricevere, ottenere || *had better*, sarebbe meglio che; *I had rather*, preferirei.
haven *s.* (*fig.*) porto, rifugio.
havoc *s.* strage, rovina.
hawk *s.* 1. falco, sparviero 2. (*fig.*) avvoltoio.
hawker[1] *s.* falconiere.
hawker[2] venditore ambulante.
hawser *s.* gomena.
hawthorn *s.* biancospino.
hay *s.* fieno, paglia || *— -loft*, fienile; *— -making*, falciatura.
haycock *s.* mucchio di fieno.
hayseed *s.* seme di erba.
haystack *s.* mucchio di fieno.
hazard *s.* 1. azzardo, rischio 2. giuoco di dadi.
to hazard *vt.* azzardare, arrischiare.
haze *s.* foschia, nebbia.
hazel *s.* nocciuolo || *— -nut*, nocciuola.
hazily *avv.* indistintamente.
haziness *s.* 1. foschia 2. (*fig.*) confusione.
hazy *agg.* 1. nebbioso 2. indistinto (*anche fig.*).
he *pron. sogg. m.* egli, lui, colui.
head *s.* 1. testa 2. capo, direttore 3. individuo 4. parte alta di una cosa 5. capo, unità di bestiame || *— -first*, a capofitto; *— -master*, direttore di una scuola; *— -money*, taglia; *— -work*, lavoro mentale.
to head *vt.* 1. colpire con la testa 2. dirigere, comandare 3. intestare. ♦ **to head** *vi.* dirigersi.

headache *s.* mal di testa.
headed *agg.* munito di testa || *hot- —*, esaltato; *pig- —*, ostinato; *swollen- —*, tronfio; *wrong- —*, caparbio.
heading *s.* 1. intestazione, titolo (*di un capitolo*) 2. (*aer.*) rotta.
headland *s.* promontorio.
headless *agg.* senza testa (*anche fig.*).
headlight *s.* faro anteriore.
headline *s.* intestazione di capitolo, articolo.
headlong *avv.* a çapcfitto, precipitosamente.
headquarters *s. pl.* quartier generale (*sing.*).
headstone *s.* pietra tombale.
to heal *vt.* 1. guarire, curare 2. (*fig.*) sanare. ♦ **to heal** *vi.* 1. guarire 2. sanarsi.
healer *s.* guaritore.
healing *agg.* salutare.
health *s.* 1. salute 2. salvezza divina.
healthful *agg.* salubre.
healthily *avv.* salubremente.
healthiness *s.* 1. salute 2. salubrità.
healthy *agg.* 1. sano, robusto 2. salutare.
heap *s.* mucchio, cumulo.
to heap *vt.* ammucchiare, accumulare.
to hear (heard, heard) *vt. e vi.* 1. sentire, udire 2. sentir dire, venire a sapere.
hearing *s.* 1. udito 2. udienza.
hearsay *s.* diceria, voce.
hearse *s.* carro funebre.
heart *s.* 1. cuore (*anche fig.*) 2. affetto, coraggio 3. centro, parte principale || *— -beat*, pulsazione; *— -break*, crepacuore; *— -breaking*, straziante; *— -failure*, collasso cardiaco; *— -felt*, sincero, di cuore.
heartache *s.* angoscia, angustia.
heartburn *s.* bruciore di stomaco.
hearted *agg.* dal cuore, di cuore || *broken- —*, desolato; *chicken- —*, pauroso; *down- —*, depresso; *lion- —*, dal cuore di leone; *whole- —*, generoso.
to hearten *vt.* incoraggiare. ♦ **to hearten** *vi.* prendere coraggio.
hearth *s.* 1. focolare (*anche fig.*) 2. (*metal.*) crogiuolo, letto di fusione.
heartily *avv.* cordialmente.
heartiness *s.* 1. cordialità.

heartless *agg.* senza cuore.
hearty *agg.* **1.** sincero, cordiale **2.** sano, robusto.
heat *s.* **1.** calore, caldo **2.** animosità || — -*stroke*, colpo di calore; — -*wave*, ondata di calore.
to heat *vt.* **1.** scaldare **2.** animare. ♦ **to heat** *vi.* **1.** scaldarsi **2.** animarsi.
heater *s.* bollitore, riscaldatore. heath *s.* brughiera.
heath *s.* brughiera.
heathen *agg.* e *s.* pagano.
heather *s.* erica.
heating *s.* riscaldamento.
heave *s.* **1.** sforzo **2.** rigonfiamento (*di onde*) **3.** sollevamento.
heaven *s.* **1.** cielo, paradiso (*anche fig.*) **2.** stato di gioia.
heavenly *agg.* divino, celeste.
heavenward *agg.* rivolto al cielo.
heavily *avv.* pesantemente, gravemente.
heaviness *s.* pesantezza.
heavy *agg.* **1.** pesante **2.** violento, forte **3.** fangoso, pesante (*di terreno*).
Hebrew *agg.* e *s.* ebreo.
hecatomb *s.* ecatombe.
hectare *s.* ettaro.
hectic *agg.* **1.** tisico, etico **2.** febbricitante.
hectogram(me) *s.* ettogrammo.
hectolitre *s.* ettolitro.
hectometre *s.* ettometro.
hedge *s.* **1.** siepe **2.** barriera.
to hedge *vt.* circondare con una siepe. ♦ **to hedge** *vi.* essere evasivo.
hedgehog *s.* riccio, porcospino.
hedonism *s.* edonismo.
hedonist *s.* edonista.
heed *s.* attenzione, cura.
heedful *agg.* attento, vigile.
heedless *agg.* sventato.
heedlessness *s.* sventatezza, trascuratezza.
heel *s.* **1.** calcagno, tallone **2.** sperone (*di uccelli*).
Hegelian *agg.* hegeliano.
hegemony *s.* egemonia.
heifer *s.* giovenca.
heigh *inter.* ehi!
height *s.* **1.** altezza **2.** altitudine **3.** altura, collina **4.** sommità, il più alto grado.
to heighten *vt.* **1.** innalzare **2.** accrescere, intensificare. ♦ **to heighten** *vi.* innalzarsi.
heinous *agg.* atroce.

heir *s.* erede.
heiress *s.* ereditiera.
held V. *to hold*.
helicoid *agg.* elicoidale.
helicopter *s.* elicottero.
heliocentric(al) *agg.* eliocentrico.
heliotherapy *s.* elioterapia.
heliport *s.* eliporto.
helium *s.* elio.
hell *s.* inferno (*anche fig.*).
Hellenic *agg.* ellenico.
Hellenism *s.* ellenismo.
Hellenist *s.* ellenista.
hellish *agg.* infernale.
hello *inter.* salve!
helm[1] *s.* elmo, casco.
helm[2] *s.* timone (*anche fig.*).
helmet *s.* elmetto, casco.
helmsman *s.* timoniere.
help *s.* aiuto, soccorso.
to help *vt.* **1.** aiutare, soccorrere **2.** servire (*cibo*) || *cannot* —, non poter fare a meno di; *to* — *oneself to*, servirsi di (*cibo*).
helper *s.* aiutante.
helpful *agg.* utile, servizievole.
helpless *agg.* senza aiuto, indifeso.
helpmate *s.* collaboratore.
Helvetic *agg.* elvetico.
hem[1] *s.* orlo, bordo.
hem[2] *inter.* ehm!.
to hem[1] *vt.* orlare || *to* — *in*, circondare, accerchiare.
to hem[2] *vi.* schiarirsi la gola.
hemicycle *s.* emiciclo.
hemiplegia *s.* emiplegia.
hemisphere *s.* emisfero.
hemispheric(al) *agg.* emisferico.
hemlock *s.* cicuta.
hemp *s.* canapa.
hen *s.* **1.** gallina **2.** femmina (*di uccelli*) || — -*house*, pollaio.
hence *avv.* **1.** di qui, da questo momento **2.** donde.
henceforth *avv.* d'ora innanzi.
hendecasyllabic *agg.* endecasillabico.
hendecasyllable *s.* endecasillabo.
henna *s.* alcanna.
hepatic *agg.* epatico.
hepatitis *s.* epatite.
heptagon *s.* ettagono.
heptagonal *agg.* ettagonale.
her *agg. poss. f.* suo, sua, suoi, sue. ♦ **her** *pron. compl. f.* la, lei, le, colei.
herald *s.* **1.** araldo **2.** nunzio **3.** (*fig.*) precursore.

heraldic agg. araldico.
herb s. 1. erba 2. pianta medicinale.
herbaceous agg. erbaceo.
herbal agg. di erba.
herbarium s. erbario.
herbivorous agg. erbivoro.
herborist s. erborista.
Herculean agg. erculeo.
herd s. gregge, mandria.
herdsman s. mandriano.
here avv. qui, qua || — I am, eccomi.
hereabouts avv. qui intorno.
hereafter avv. d'ora innanzi.
hereby avv. 1. con questo mezzo 2. qui vicino.
hereditary agg. ereditario.
heredity s. (biol.) ereditarietà.
herein avv. 1. in questo 2. (comm.) nella presente.
heresiarch s. eresiarca.
heresy s. eresia.
heretic(al) agg. e s. eretico.
herewith avv. qui accluso.
heritable agg. ereditabile.
heritage s. eredità.
hermaphrodite agg. e s. ermafrodito.
hermeneutics s. ermeneutica.
hermetic(al) agg. ermetico.
hermetically avv. ermeticamente.
hermit s. eremita.
hermitage s. eremo, eremitaggio.
hernia s. ernia.
hernial agg. erniario.
hero s. eroe.
heroic(al) agg. eroico.
heroin s. (chim.) eroina.
heroine s. eroina.
heroism s. eroismo.
heron s. airone.
herpes s. erpete.
herring s. aringa || — -bone, spina di pesce (nei tessuti ecc.).
hers pron. poss. f. il suo, la sua, i suoi, le sue.
herself pron. r. f. 1. se stessa, sé, si 2. ella stessa.
hesitant agg. esitante.
to **hesitate** vi. esitare.
hesitatingly avv. con esitazione.
hesitation s. esitazione.
heteroclite agg. eteroclito.
heterodox agg. eterodosso.
heterodoxy s. eterodossia.
heterogeneity s. eterogeneità.
heterogeneous agg. eterogeneo.
to **hew** (**hewed, hewn**) vt. fendere, recidere || to — down, àbbat-
tere.
hexagon s. esagono.
hexagonal agg. esagonale.
hexahedron s. esaedro.
hexameter s. esametro.
hiatus s. iato.
to **hibernate** vi. (zool.) cadere in letargo invernale.
hibernation s. 1. svernamento 2. ibernazione.
hiccough, hiccup s. singhiozzo, singulto.
hid V. to hide.
hidden V. to hide.
hide[1] s. pelle, cuoio.
hide[2] s. nascondiglio || — -and-seek, rimpiattino.
to **hide**[1] (**hid, hidden**) vt. nascondere, celare. ♦ to hide (hid, hidden) vi. nascondersi, celarsi.
to **hide**[2] vt. 1. spellare, scorticare 2. frustare.
hideous agg. orrendo, odioso.
hideousness s. odiosità, aspetto orribile.
hiding s. il nascondere.
hierarchy s. gerarchia.
hieratic agg. ieratico.
hieroglyph s. geroglifico.
hieroglyphic(al) agg. geroglifico.
high agg. 1. alto, elevato (anche fig.) 2. altezzoso 3. forte, intenso (di luce, colori) || — -born, di alto lignaggio; — -class, di prim'ordine; — -coloured, dal colore acceso; — -hearted, pieno di coraggio; — -life, vita di alta società; — school, scuola media; — sea, mare aperto; — -speed, ad alta velocità. ♦ high avv. 1. alto, in alto 2. fortemente.
highbrow agg. e s. intellettuale.
highland s. regione montuosa.
highlander s. montanaro.
highly avv. 1. molto, assai 2. altamente, nobilmente.
highness s. 1. altezza, elevatezza 2. eccellenza, valore.
highway s. strada maestra.
highwayman s. bandito, rapinatore.
hilarious agg. ilare.
hill s. collina, altura.
hillock s. collinetta.
hillside s. pendio.
hilltop s. sommità della collina.
hilly agg. collinoso.
hilt s. elsa.
him pron. pers. m. lo, lui, gli, colui, sé.
himself pron. r. m. 1. si, sé, se

stesso **2.** egli stesso.
hind[1] *s.* cerva, daina.
hind[2] *s.* colono, fattore.
hind(er) *agg.* posteriore.
to **hinder** *vt.* e *vi.* **1.** impedire, ostruire **2.** imbarazzare.
hindrance *s.* ostacolo, impaccio.
Hindu *agg.* e *s.* indù.
hinge *s.* **1.** cardine **2.** (*fig.*) perno.
to **hinge** *vt.* munire di cardini. ◆ to **hinge** *vi.* **1.** girare sui cardini **2.** essere imperniato.
hint *s.* **1.** cenno, allusione **2.** consiglio.
to **hint** *vt.* e *vi.* alludere, accennare, suggerire.
hinterland *s.* retroterra.
hip *s.* anca, fianco.
hippocampus *s.* (*pl.* -pi.) ippocampo.
hippopotamus *s.* ippopotamo.
hire *s.* affitto, nolo.
to **hire** *vt.* prendere a servizio, noleggiare.
hireling *s.* mercenario.
his *agg. poss. m.* suo, sua, suoi, sue. ◆ **his** *pron. poss. m.* il suo, la sua, i suoi, le sue.
Hispanic *agg.* ispanico.
Hispanicism *s.* ispanismo.
Hispanist *s.* ispanista.
hispid *agg.* ispido.
hiss *s.* sibilo, fischio.
to **hiss** *vt.* e *vi.* **1.** sibilare **2.** fischiare.
histology *s.* istologia.
historian *s.* storico.
historic(al) *agg.* storico.
historicity *s.* storicità.
historiographer *s.* storiografo.
historiography *s.* storiografia.
history *s.* storia.
histrion *s.* istrione.
histrionic(al) *agg.* istrionico.
histrionism *s.* istrionismo.
hit *s.* **1.** colpo, botta **2.** osservazione sarcastica **3.** caso fortunato **4.** (*teat.*) successo.
to **hit** (hit, hit) *vt.* e *vi.* **1.** battere, picchiare **2.** urtare, venire a contatto **3.** (*fig.*) toccare, colpire || *to — the mark,* colpire nel segno.
hitch *s.* **1.** colpo, strattone, balzo repentino **2.** nodo.
to **hitch** *vt.* **1.** muovere a sbalzi **2.** legare, attaccare. ◆ to **hitch** *vi.* muoversi a sbalzi.
to **hitchhike** *vi.* fare l'autostop.
hitchhiker *s.* autostoppista.

hitchhiking *s.* autostop.
hive *s.* **1.** alveare, arnia **2.** sciame (*anche fig.*).
hives *s. pl.* orticaria, eruzione cutanea.
hoar *s.* candore, vecchiaia || — -*frost,* brina.
hoard *s.* gruzzolo.
to **hoard** *vt.* ammassare, ammucchiare. ◆ to **hoard** *vi.* ammucchiarsi.
hoarder *s.* incettatore.
hoarding *s.* recinto provvisorio.
hoarse *agg.* rauco, fioco.
hoarseness *s.* raucedine.
hoary *agg.* **1.** bianco, canuto **2.** venerando.
hobble *s.* **1.** zoppicamento **2.** imbarazzo.
to **hobble** *vi.* zoppicare. ◆ to **hobble** *vt.* azzoppare.
hobby *s.* svago preferito, passatempo.
hobnail *s.* chiodo (*per scarponi*).
hobnailed *agg.* chiodato.
hodman *s.* manovale.
hoe *s.* zappa.
to **hoe** *vt.* zappare, estirpare le erbacce.
hog *s.* maiale.
hogshead *s.* barilotto (*per tabacco, zucchero*).
hoist *s.* montacarichi.
to **hoist** *vt.* alzare, sollevare.
hold[1] *s.* **1.** presa **2.** (*fig.*) ascendente.
hold[2] *s.* (*mar.*) stiva.
to **hold** (held, held) *vt.* e *vi.* **1.** tenere, sostenere **2.** contenere **3.** ritenere, credere, pensare **4.** occupare una carica, possedere **5.** resistere, aggrapparsi || *to — up,* sollevare; *to — back,* esitare.
holder *s.* **1.** possessore, detentore, proprietario **2.** sostegno, supporto **3.** dente canino.
holdings *s. pl.* beni, titoli.
hold-up *s.* intoppo nel traffico, panna di automobile.
hole *s.* **1.** foro, apertura, buco **2.** antro, tana.
holiday *s.* **1.** festa, giorno festivo **2.** vacanza.
holiness *s.* santità.
hollow *agg.* **1.** concavo, infossato **2.** cupo, cavernoso **3.** (*fig.*) falso, irreale, vuoto.
to **hollow** *vt.* scavare, incavare.
hollow *avv.* (*fam.*) completamente.
hollowness *s.* **1.** cavità **2.** timbro

cavernoso (*di voce*).
holly *s.* agrifoglio.
holocaust *s.* olocausto.
holograph *agg. e s.* documento olografo.
holy *agg.* santo, sacro.
homage *s.* omaggio.
home[1] *s.* **1.** casa, focolare domestico **2.** patria **3.** rifugio, asilo, ospizio.
home[2] *agg.* domestico, casalingo.
home[3] *avv.* **1.** a casa, in patria **2.** direttamente, al segno || — -*born*, indigeno, locale; — -*bred*, allevato in casa; — -*made*, fatto in casa; — -*market*, mercato nazionale; — -*town*, città natia; — -*trade*, commercio interno
homeland *s.* patria.
homeless *agg.* senza casa.
homelike *agg.* domestico, familiare.
homely *agg.* **1.** semplice, modesto **2.** domestico.
homeopathic *agg.* omeopatico
homeopathy *s.* omeopatia.
Homeric *agg.* omerico.
homesick *agg.* nostalgico.
homesickness *s.* nostalgia.
homeward *agg. e avv.* verso casa, verso la patria.
homework *s. coll.* compiti per casa.
homicidal *agg.* omicida.
homicide *s.* omicidio.
homily *s.* omelia.
homogeneity *s.* omogeneità.
homogeneous *agg.* omogeneo.
to homogenize *vt.* omogeneizzare.
to homologate *vt.* omologare.
homologation *s.* omologazione.
homologous *agg.* omologo.
homology *s.* omologia.
homonymous *agg.* omonimo.
homonymy *s.* omonimia.
homosexual *agg. e s.* omosessuale.
homosexuality *s.* omosessualità.
homy *agg.* casalingo.
honest *agg.* **1.** onesto, integro **2.** leale.
honesty *s.* **1.** onestà, probità **2.** lealtà.
honey *s.* miele.
honeycomb *s.* favo.
honeyed *agg.* **1.** coperto di miele **2.** (*fig.*) sdolcinato, adulatorio.
honeymoon *s.* luna di miele.
honeysuckle *s.* caprifoglio.
honorary *agg.* onorario, onorifico.
honorific *agg.* onorifico.
honour *s.* **1.** onore, reputazione **2.** stima, reverenza **3.** Eccellenza.

to honour *vt.* onorare, fare onore a.
honourable *agg.* stimato, onorevole.
honourableness *s.* onorabilità.
hood *s.* cappuccio.
to hood *vt.* incappucciare, fornire di cappuccio.
hoof *s.* zoccolo (*di animale*).
hook *s.* **1.** uncino, gancio **2.** amo **3.** tagliola **4.** falce per grano || *by* — *or by crook*, di riffa o di raffa.
to hook *vt.* agganciare. ♦ **to hook** *vi.* agganciarsi.
hooked *agg.* **1.** fornito di uncini **2.** adunco, uncinato.
hoop *s.* collare, cerchio (*di botte, ruota ecc.*).
to hoop *vt.* cerchiare (*una botte*).
to hoot *vt. e vi.* **1.** urlare, gridare **2.** suonare il clacson.
hop[1] *s.* salto (*su una gamba sola*).
hop[2] *s.* luppolo.
to hop *vt. e vi.* saltare su una gamba sola.
hope *s.* speranza.
to hope *vt. e vi.* sperare, essere fiducioso.
hopeful *agg.* pieno di speranza, fiducioso.
hopefulness *s.* fiducia, buona speranza.
hopeless *agg.* senza speranza, irrimediabile.
hopelessness *s.* disperazione.
hopper *s.* persona od insetto che saltella.
horde *s.* orda.
horizon *s.* orizzonte.
horizontal *agg.* orizzontale.
horizontally *avv.* orizzontalmente.
hormone *s.* ormone.
horn *s.* **1.** corno, tentacolo, antenna **2.** (*mus.*) corno, tromba.
to horn *vt.* **1.** fornire di corna **2.** ferire con le corna.
hornet *s.* vespa, calabrone.
hornpipe *s.* cornamusa.
horology *s.* orologeria.
horoscope *s.* oroscopo: *to cast a* —, fare un oroscopo.
horrible *agg.* **1.** orribile, orrendo **2.** (*fam.*) eccessivo.
horribly *avv.* orribilmente.
horrid *agg.* orrido, orrendo.
horrific *agg.* orribile, orripilante.
to horrify *vt.* **1.** atterrire, incutere timore **2.** scandalizzare.
horror *s.* **1.** orrore, spavento **2.** cosa orribile || — -*stricken*, atterrito.

hors-d'oeuvre *s.* antipasto.
horse *s.* cavallo || — *-bean,* fava; — *-boy,* mozzo di stalla; — *-chestnut,* ippocastano; — *-doctor,* veterinario; — *-race,* corsa ippica; — *-shoe,* ferro di cavallo.
horseback *s.* dorso di cavallo || *on* —, a cavallo.
horseman *s.* cavaliere.
horticultural *agg.* attinente all'orticultura.
horticulture *s.* orticultura.
hosanna *inter.* osanna.
hose *s.* 1. idrante 2. calze *(pl.).*
hosier *s.* commerciante in calze.
hosiery *s.* maglieria.
hospice *s.* alloggio, ospizio.
hospitable *agg.* ospitale.
hospital *s.* ospedale.
hospitality *s.* ospitalità.
host[1] *s.* folla, moltitudine.
host[2] *s.* ospite, anfitrione.
hostage *s.* ostaggio.
hostel *s.* pensionato *(per giovani, studenti, militari ecc.).*
hostess *s.* 1. ospite, padrona di casa 2. assistente di volo.
hostile *agg.* ostile, nemico.
hostility *s.* inimicizia, ostilità.
hot *agg.* 1. caldo, ardente 2. forte, piccante 3. violento, impetuoso || — *-headed,* scalmanato.
hotel *s.* albergo || — *-keeper,* albergatore.
hothead *s.* testa calda.
hothouse *s.* serra.
hotly *avv.* caldamente.
hotspur *s.* persona impulsiva.
hound *s.* bracco, segugio.
to **hound** *vt.* cacciare *(con bracchi).*
hour *s.* 1. ora 2. periodo. ♦ **hours** *s. pl.* orario *(sing.).*
hourly *agg.* 1. continuo 2. all'ora 3. ad ogni ora. ♦ **hourly** *avv.* 1. continuamente 2. ad ogni ora 3. d'ora in ora.
house *s.* 1. casa, abitazione 2. albergo, pensione 3. clinica 4. convento 5. casato, dinastia 6. teatro 7. *(comm.)* ditta 8. *(mar.)* tuga.
to **house** *vt.* 1. alloggiare, ricevere in casa 2. *(fig.)* offrire un rifugio. ♦ to **house** *vi.* 1. prendere alloggio 2. rifugiarsi.
housebreaker *s.* scassinatore.
housebreaking *s.* demolizione edilizia.
household *s.* famiglia: *Royal Household,* la famiglia reale.

householder *s.* capofamiglia.
housekeeper *s.* governante, domestica.
housekeeping *s.* il governo della casa.
houseless *agg.* senza casa.
housemaid *s.* domestica, cameriera.
housewife *s.* *(pl.* -wives) massaia, casalinga.
housework *s.* lavoro domestico.
housing *s.* 1. il ricevere, l'accogliere 2. alloggio, rifugio, riparo.
hovel *s.* 1. tana 2. baracca.
to **hover** *vi.* 1. librarsi, svolazzare 2. gironzolare.
how *avv.* come, in che modo.
however *avv.* 1. comunque 2. però, tuttavia.
howitzer *s.* obice.
howl *s.* urlo, grido.
to **howl** *vt.* e *vi.* urlare, ululare.
howling *agg.* urlante, ululante.
hub *s.* mozzo di ruota.
hubbub *s.* tumulto, fracasso.
huddle *s.* calca, folla.
to **huddle** *vt.* ammucchiare. ♦ to **huddle** *vi.* affollarsi, accalcarsi.
hue *s.* tinta, colore.
hug *s.* abbraccio.
to **hug** *vt.* abbracciare *(anche fig.)* || to — *oneself,* compiacersi.
huge *agg.* enorme, vasto.
hugeness *s.* grandezza, enormità.
hull *s.* scafo.
hullabaloo *s.* tumulto, fracasso.
hullo *inter.* 1. *(fam.)* salve 2. *(tel.)* pronto.
hum *s.* ronzio, mormorio.
to **hum** *vt.* e *vi.* 1. ronzare, mormorare 2. cantare a bocca chiusa.
human *agg.* 1. umano 2. sensibile.
humane *agg.* umano, compassionevole.
humaneness *s.* benevolenza, umanità.
humanism *s.* umanesimo.
humanist *s.* umanista.
humanistic *agg.* umanistico.
humanitarian *agg.* filantropico, umanitario.
humanity *s.* 1. umanità, il genere umano 2. bontà, benevolenza.
to **humanize** *vt.* 1. rendere umano 2. adattare alla natura umana. ♦ to **humanize** *vi.* acquisire sentimenti migliori.
humankind *s.* il genere umano.
humble *agg.* umile, modesto.
to **humble** *vt.* umiliare.

humbleness s. umiltà.
humbly avv. umilmente.
humbug s. frode, impostura.
humdrum s. monotonia, tedio. ♦
humdrum agg. monotono.
humeral agg. omerale.
humerus s. (pl. -ri) omero.
humid agg. umido.
humidity s. umidità.
to **humiliate** vt. umiliare, mortificare.
humiliation s. umiliazione.
humility s. umiltà.
humming agg. ronzante. ♦ **humming** s. ronzio.
humorist s. umorista.
humorous agg. arguto, dotato di senso dell'umorismo.
humour s. 1. umorismo 2. umore.
hump s. 1. gobba, gibbosità 2. collinetta, cresta.
humpback s. 1. gobba 2. gobbo.
hunch s. gobba, gibbosità.
hunchback s. persona gobba.
hundred agg. cento. ♦ **hundred** s. centinaio.
hundredth agg. centesimo.
hung V. to hang.
Hungarian agg. e s. ungherese.
hunger s. 1. fame, appetito 2. (fig.) ingordigia.
hungrily avv. 1. con grande appetito 2. avidamente.
hungry agg. 1. affamato || to be —, aver fame 2. (fig.) avido, bramoso.
hunt s. 1. caccia 2. ricerca, inseguimento.
to **hunt** vt. e vi. 1. cacciare, andare a caccia 2. cercare affannosamente.
hunter s. cacciatore (anche fig.).
hunting s. 1. caccia 2. ricerca.
huntsman s. cacciatore.
hurdle s. ostacolo (anche fig.).
hurl s. lancio violento.
to **hurl** vt. lanciare, scagliare (anche fig.).
hurrah inter. urrah!
hurricane s. uragano, ciclone (anche fig.).
hurried agg. affrettato, precipitoso.
hurry s. fretta, precipitazione: to be in a —, aver fretta.
to **hurry** vt. affrettare. ♦ to **hurry** vi. affrettarsi || — up!, fa presto!
hurt s. lesione, ferita (anche fig.).
to **hurt (hurt, hurt)** vt. e vi. 1. dolere 2. recar dolore, offendere.
hurtful agg. 1. dannoso 2. offensivo.

husband s. marito.
husbandry s. 1. agricoltura 2. amministrazione domestica.
hush inter. silenzio.
to **hush** vt. 1. zittire, tacere 2. (fig.) calmare.
husk s. 1. guscio, baccello 2. involucro 3. (pl.) rifiuti.
to **husk** vt. sgusciare, sbucciare.
husky agg. rugoso, secco.
hussar s. ussaro.
hut s. 1. capanna, casupola 2. rifugio alpino.
hyacinth s. giacinto.
hybrid agg. e s. ibrido.
hybridism s. ibridismo.
hybridization s. ibridazione.
hydra s. idra.
hydrangea s. ortensia.
hydrant s. idrante.
hydrate s. idrato.
to **hydrate** vt. idratare.
hydraulic agg. idraulico.
hydraulics s. idraulica.
hydric agg. contenente idrogeno.
hydrocarbon s. idrocarburo.
hydrocephalus s. idrocefalo.
hydroelectric agg. idroelettrico.
hydrofluoric agg. fluoridrico.
hydrofoil boat s. aliscafo.
hydrogen s. idrogeno.
hydrology s. idrologia.
hydrolysis s. (pl. -ses) idrolisi.
hydrostatic(al) agg. idrostatico.
hyena s. iena.
hygiene s. igiene.
hygienics s. la scienza dell'igiene.
hygienist s. igienista.
hygrometry s. igrometria.
hymn s. inno.
hyperbole s. iperbole.
hyperbolic(al) agg. iperbolico.
hyperborean agg. e s. iperboreo.
hypercritical agg. ipercritico.
hypermetropy s. ipermetropia.
hypernutrition s. supernutrizione.
hypersensitive agg. ipersensibile.
hypersensitivity s. ipersensibilità.
hypertension s. ipertensione.
hypertrophy s. ipertrofia.
hyphen s. lineetta d'unione.
hypnosis s. (pl. -ses) ipnosi.
hypnotic agg. e s. ipnotico.
hypnotism s. ipnotismo.
to **hypnotize** vt. ipnotizzare.
hypochondria s. ipocondria.
hypochondriac agg. e s. ipocondriaco.
hypocrisy s. ipocrisia.

hypocrite s. ipocrita.
hypocritic(al) agg. ipocrita.
hypodermic agg. ipodermico.
hypodermoclysis s. ipodermoclisi.
hyposulphite s. iposolfito.
hypotenuse s. ipotenusa.
hypothecary agg. ipotecario.
to hypothecate vt. ipotecare.
hypothesis s. (pl. -ses) ipotesi.
to hypothesize vi. fare ipotesi.
hypothetic(al) agg. ipotetico.
hypothetically avv. ipoteticamente.
hysteria s. isterismo.
hysteric(al) agg. isterico.
hysterics s. attacco isterico.

I

I pron. pers. io.
iamb s. giambo.
iambic agg. giambico.
Iberian agg. e s. iberico.
ice s. ghiaccio || — -box, ghiacciaia; — -breaker, rompighiaccio; — -cream, gelato.
to ice vt. 1. ghiacciare 2. (cuc.) glassare.
iceboat s. nave rompighiaccio.
Icelander s. islandese.
Icelandic agg. islandese.
ichtyologist s. ittiologo.
ichthyology s. ittiologia.
icicle s. ghiacciuolo.
iciness s. gelo.
icing s. glassatura.
icon s. icona.
iconoclast s. iconoclasta.
iconoclastic agg. iconoclastico.
iconography s. iconografia.
icy agg. gelido, gelato.
idea s. idea.
ideal agg. e s. ideale.
idealism s. idealismo.
idealist s. idealista.
idealistic(al) agg. idealistico.
idealization s. idealizzazione.
to idealize vt. idealizzare.
ideally avv. idealmente.
to ideate vt. ideare.
ideation s. ideazione.
identic(al) agg. identico.
identifiable agg. identificabile.
identification s. identificazione.
to identify vt. identificare || to — oneself with, immedesimarsi con.

identity s. identità.
ideogram s. ideogramma.
ideography s. ideografia.
ideologic(al) agg. ideologico.
ideologist s. ideologo.
ideology s. ideologia.
idiocy s. idiozia.
idiom s. 1. idioma 2. idiotismo.
idiomatic(al) agg. idiomatico.
idiosyncrasy s. idiosincrasia.
idiot s. idiota.
idiotic(al) agg. idiota.
idle agg. 1. ozioso 2. vano.
to idle vi. oziare.
idleness s. 1. ozio 2. futilità.
idler s. ozioso.
idly avv. oziosamente.
idol s. idolo.
idolater s. idolatra.
to idolatrize vt. idolatrare.
idolatrous agg. idolatrico.
idolatry, idolism s. idolatria.
idyl(l) s. idillio.
idyllic agg. idillico.
if cong. se || as —, come se.
igneous agg. igneo.
to ignite vt. accendere. ♦ to ignite vi. accendersi.
ignition s. accensione || battery coil —, spinterogeno.
ignobility s. ignobilità.
ignoble agg. ignobile.
ignominious agg. ignominioso.
ignominy, ignomy s. ignominia.
ignorance s. ignoranza.
ignorant agg. ignorante.
to ignore vt. ignorare.
ilex s. leccio.
iliac agg. iliaco.
ill (worse, worst) agg. 1. ammalato 2. cattivo. ♦ ill avv. male || — -advised, sconsiderato; — -disposed, malevolo; — -fated, sfortunato; — -mannered, maleducato. ♦ ill s. male.
illation s. illazione.
illegal agg. 1. illegale 2. illecito.
illegality s. illegalità.
illegible agg. illeggibile.
illegitimacy s. illegittimità.
illegitimate agg. illegittimo.
illiberal agg. 1. illiberale 2. meschino.
illiberality s. 1. illiberalità 2. meschinità.
illicit agg. illecito.
illimitable agg. illimitato.
illiteracy s. 1. analfabetismo 2. ignoranza.

illiterate agg. e s. **1.** analfabeta **2.** ignorante.
illness s. malattia.
illogical agg. illogico.
illogicality s. illogicità.
to **ill-treat** vt. maltrattare.
to **illuminate** vt. illuminare.
illumination s. illuminazione.
to **illumine** vt. illuminare.
illuminism s. illuminismo.
ill-usage s. maltrattamento.
to **ill-use** vt. maltrattare.
illusion s. illusione.
illusionism s. illusionismo.
illusionist s. illusionista.
illusive agg. illusorio.
illusiveness s. illusorietà.
illusory agg. illusorio.
to **illustrate** vt. illustrare.
illustration s. illustrazione.
illustrative agg. illustrativo.
illustrator s. illustratore.
illustrious agg. illustre.
ill-will s. malevolenza.
ill-wisher s. malevolo.
image s. immagine.
to **image** vt. **1.** immaginare **2.** descrivere **3.** riflettere.
imagery s. raffigurazione.
imaginable agg. immaginabile.
imaginary agg. immaginario.
imagination s. immaginazione.
imaginative agg. immaginativo.
to **imagine** vt. e vi. immaginare.
imagining s. immaginazione.
imbecile agg. e s. **1.** debole **2.** imbecille.
imbecility s. **1.** debolezza **2.** imbecillità.
to **imbibe** vt. assorbire. ♦ to **imbibe** vi. imbeversi.
to **imbue** vt. impregnare.
imitable agg. imitabile.
to **imitate** vt. imitare.
imitation s. imitazione.
imitative agg. imitativo.
imitator s. imitatore.
immaculate agg. immacolato.
immanence s. immanenza.
immanent agg. immanente.
immanentism s. immanentismo.
immaterial agg. **1.** immateriale **2.** irrilevante.
immaterialism s. immaterialismo.
immaterialist s. immaterialista.
immateriality s. immaterialità.
immature agg. immaturo.
immaturity s. immaturità.
immeasurability s. incommensura-

bilità.
immeasurable agg. incommensurabile.
immediacy s. **1.** immediatezza **2.** rapporto diretto.
immediate agg. **1.** immediato **2.** diretto.
immediateness s. V. immediacy.
immemorial agg. immemorabile.
immense agg. immenso.
immenseness, immensity s. immensità.
immensurability s. immensurabilità.
immensurable agg. immensurabile.
to **immerge,** to **immerse** vt. immergere. ♦ to **immerge** vi. immergersi.
immersion s. **1.** immersione **2.** eclisse.
immigrant agg. e s. immigrante.
to **immigrate** vi. immigrare.
immigration s. immigrazione.
imminence s. **1.** imminenza **2.** pericolo.
imminent agg. **1.** imminente **2.** sovrastante.
immobile agg. immobile.
immobility s. immobilità.
immobilization s. immobilizzazione.
to **immobilize** vt. immobilizzare.
immoderate agg. smodato.
immoderateness s. smoderatezza.
immodest agg. **1.** immodesto **2.** indecente.
immodesty s. **1.** immodestia **2.** indecenza.
to **immolate** vt. immolare.
immolation s. immolazione.
immolator s. immolatore.
immoral agg. immorale.
immorality s. immoralità.
immortal agg. e s. immortale.
immortality s. immortalità.
immortalization s. l'immortalare.
to **immortalize** vt. immortalare.
immovability s. **1.** immobilità **2.** inamovibilità.
immovable agg. **1.** immobile **2.** inamovibile.
immovables s. pl. beni immobili.
immune agg. **1.** immune **2.** esente.
immunity s. **1.** immunità **2.** esenzione.
immunization s. immunizzazione.
to **immunize** vt. immunizzare.
to **immure** vt. **1.** murare **2.** impri-

gionare **3.** chiudere fra mura.
immutability *s.* immutabilità.
immutable *agg.* immutabile.
imp *s.* diavoletto.
impact *s.* urto, collisione.
to **impact** *vt.* conficcare.
to **impair** *vt.* menomare.
impairment *s.* menomazione.
to **impale** *vt.* impalare.
impalpability *s.* impalpabilità.
impalpable *agg.* impalpabile.
imparity *s.* imparità.
to **impart** *vt.* **1.** impartire **2.** rivelare.
impartial *agg.* imparziale.
impartiality *s.* imparzialità.
impassable *agg.* invalicabile, impraticabile.
impassibility *s.* impassibilità.
impassible *agg.* impassibile.
to **impassion** *vt.* appassionare.
impassionate, impassioned *agg.* eccitato, ardente.
impassive *agg.* impassibile.
impatience *s.* **1.** impazienza **2.** avversione.
impatient *agg.* **1.** impaziente **2.** intollerante.
impavid *agg.* impavido.
to **impeach** *vt.* **1.** imputare **2.** biasimare || *to — so. for high treason,* accusare qu. di alto tradimento.
impeachable *agg.* accusabile.
impeacher *s.* accusatore.
impeachment *s.* accusa.
impeccability *s.* impeccabilità.
impeccable *agg.* impeccabile.
impecunious *agg.* povero.
to **impede** *vt.* **1.** impedire **2.** ostacolare.
impediment *s.* impedimento.
to **impel** *vt.* spingere, incitare.
impellent *agg.* impellente. ♦ **impellent** *s.* incentivo.
to **impend** *vi.* incombere.
impendence *s.* imminenza.
impendent *agg.* incombente.
impenetrability *s.* impenetrabilità.
impenetrable *agg.* impenetrabile.
impenitence *s.* impenitenza.
impenitent *agg.* impenitente.
imperative *agg.* e *s.* imperativo.
imperator *s.* imperatore.
imperceptibility *s.* impercettibilità.
imperceptible *agg.* impercettibile.
imperfect *agg.* **1.** imperfetto **2.** incompiuto.
imperfection *s.* **1.** imperfezione **2.**

incompiutezza.
imperial *agg.* imperiale.
imperialism *s.* imperialismo.
imperialist *s.* imperialista.
imperialistic *agg.* imperialistico.
to **imperil** *vt.* mettere in pericolo.
imperious *agg.* **1.** imperioso **2.** impellente.
imperiousness *s.* **1.** imperiosità **2.** urgenza.
imperishability *s.* indistruttibilità.
imperishable *agg.* indistruttibile, imperituro.
impermeability *s.* impermeabilità.
impermeable *agg.* impermeabile.
impersonal *agg.* impersonale.
impersonality *s.* l'essere impersonale.
to **impersonate** *vt.* impersonare.
impersonation *s.* personificazione.
impertinence *s.* **1.** impertinenza **2.** non pertinenza.
impertinent *agg.* **1.** impertinente **2.** non pertinente.
imperturbability *s.* imperturbabilità.
imperturbable *agg.* imperturbabile.
impervious *agg.* **1.** impervio **2.** impermeabile.
to **impetrate** *vt.* impetrare.
impetration *s.* impetrazione.
impetuosity *s.* impetuosità.
impetuous *agg.* impetuoso.
impetus *s.* impeto.
impiety *s.* empietà.
impious *agg.* empio.
impish *agg.* birichino.
implacability *s.* implacabilità.
implacable *agg.* implacabile.
to **implant** *vt.* **1.** impiantare **2.** inculcare.
implement *s.* utensile.
to **implement** *vt.* **1.** compiere **2.** attrezzare.
to **implicate** *vt.* implicare.
implication *s.* implicazione.
implicit, implied *agg.* implicito.
to **implore** *vt.* implorare.
imploring *agg.* supplichevole.
to **imply** *vt.* implicare.
impolite *agg.* scortese.
impoliteness *s.* scortesia.
impolitic *agg.* impolitico.
imponderability *s.* imponderabilità.
imponderable *agg.* imponderabile.
import *s.* **1.** importanza **2.** significato **3.** *(comm.)* importazione.
to **import** *vt.* **1.** importare **2.** si-

gnificare **3.** (*comm.*) importare.
importance *s.* importanza.
important *agg.* importante.
importer *s.* importatore.
importunate, importune *agg.* urgente.
to **importune** *vt.* importunare.
importunity *s.* **1.** insistenza **2.** urgenza.
to **impose** *vt.* **1.** imporre **2.** (*tip.*) impaginare. ♦ to **impose** *vi.* imporsi || *to — on,* ingannare.
imposing *agg.* imponente.
imposition *s.* **1.** imposizione **2.** imposta **3.** inganno **4.** (*tip.*) messa in macchina.
impossibility *s.* impossibilità.
impossible *agg.* impossibile.
impostor *s.* impostore.
imposture *s.* impostura.
impotence *s.* impotenza.
impotent *agg.* impotente.
to **impoverish** *vt.* impoverire.
impoverishment *s.* impoverimento.
impracticability *s.* **1.** inattuabilità **2.** impraticabilità **3.** intrattabilità.
impracticable *agg.* **1.** inattuabile **2.** impraticabile **3.** intrattabile.
imprecation *s.* imprecazione.
imprecatory *agg.* imprecatorio.
impregnable *agg.* inespugnabile.
to **impregnate** *vt.* **1.** impregnare **2.** fecondare.
impregnation *s.* fecondazione.
to **impress** *vt.* **1.** imprimere, stampare **2.** impressionare.
impression *s.* **1.** impressione **2.** ristampa.
impressionability *s.* impressionabilità.
impressionable *agg.* impressionabile.
impressionism *s.* impressionismo.
impressionist *agg.* e *s.* impressionista.
impressive *agg.* impressionante.
imprint *s.* **1.** impronta **2.** stampa.
to **imprint** *vt.* **1.** imprimere **2.** stampare.
to **imprison** *vt.* imprigionare.
imprisonment *s.* prigionia.
improbability *s.* improbabilità.
improbable *agg.* improbabile.
improbably *avv.* improbabilmente.
impromptu *agg.* improvvisato. ♦
  impromptu *s.* improvvisazione.
improper *agg.* **1.** erroneo **2.** inadatto **3.** sconveniente, irregolare.

impropriety *s.* **1.** scorrettezza **2.** sconvenienza.
to **improve** *vt.* **1.** migliorare **2.** valorizzare. ♦ to **improve** *vi.* migliorare, perfezionarsi.
improvement *s.* miglioramento.
improvidence *s.* imprevidenza.
improvident *agg.* imprevidente.
improvisation *s.* improvvisazione.
improvisator *s.* improvvisatore.
to **improvise** *vt.* e *vi.* improvvisare.
imprudence *s.* imprudenza.
imprudent *agg.* imprudente.
impudence *s.* impudenza.
impudent *agg.* impudente.
to **impugn** *vt.* (*giur.*) impugnare.
impugnable *agg.* (*giur.*) impugnabile.
impugner *s.* oppositore.
impulse, impulsion *s.* impulso.
impulsive *agg.* impulsivo.
impulsiveness, impulsivity *s.* impulsività.
impunity *s.* impunità.
impure *agg.* impuro.
impurity *s.* impurità.
imputable *agg.* imputabile.
imputation *s.* imputazione.
to **impute** *vt.* imputare.
in *avv.* e *prep.* a, in, dentro, entro, durante || *to be — Paris,* essere a Parigi; *the best — the world,* il migliore del mondo; *— my opinion,* secondo me; *— all,* in tutto; *— that,* in quanto che.
inability *s.* incapacità.
inaccessibility *s.* inaccessibilità.
inaccessible *agg.* inaccessibile.
inaccuracy *s.* inesattezza.
inaccurate *agg.* inesatto.
inaction *s.* inattività.
inactive *agg.* inattivo.
inactivity *s.* inattività.
inadaptability *s.* inadattabilità.
inadequacy *s.* inadeguatezza.
inadequate *agg.* inadeguato.
inadmissibility *s.* inammissibilità.
inadmissible *agg.* inammissibile.
inadvertence *s.* inavvertenza.
inadvertent *agg.* **1.** disattento **2.** involontario.
inalienability *s.* inalienabilità.
inalienable *agg.* inalienabile.
inalterability *s.* inalterabilità.
inalterable *agg.* inalterabile.
inane *agg.* e *s.* vuoto.
inanimate *agg.* **1.** inanimato **2.** fiacco.
inanity *s.* inanità.

inappeasable *agg.* implacabile.
inappellable *agg.* inappellabile.
inappetence *s.* inappetenza.
inapplicable *agg.* inapplicabile.
inappropriate *agg.* inadeguato.
inapt *agg.* **1.** inadatto **2.** inetto.
inarticulate *agg.* inarticolato.
inattention *s.* **1.** disattenzione **2.** negligenza.
inattentive *agg.* **1.** disattento **2.** negligente.
inaudible *agg.* impercettibile.
inaugural *agg.* inaugurale.
to inaugurate *vt.* inaugurare.
inauguration *s.* inaugurazione.
inboard *agg.* interno. ♦ **inboard** *avv.* internamente.
inborn, inbred *agg.* innato.
incalculable *agg.* **1.** incalcolabile **2.** incerto.
incandescence *s.* incandescenza.
incandescent *agg.* incandescente.
incantation *s.* incantesimo.
incapability *s.* incapacità.
incapable *agg.* incapace.
incapacity *s.* incapacità.
to incarnate *vt.* **1.** incarnare **2.** realizzare.
incarnation *s.* incarnazione.
incatenation *s.* incatenamento.
incautious *agg.* incauto.
incendiary *agg.* e *s.* **1.** incendiario **2.** sovversivo.
incensation *s.* incensamento.
incense *s.* incenso.
to incense[1] *vt.* incensare.
to incense[2] *vt.* provocare.
incensurable *agg.* incensurabile.
incentive *agg.* stimolante. ♦ **incentive** *s.* incentivo.
incertitude *s.* incertezza.
incessant *agg.* incessante.
incest *s.* incesto.
incestuous *agg.* incestuoso.
inch *s.* pollice (*misura*).
incidence *s.* incidenza.
incident *agg.* probabile. ♦ **incident** *s.* avvenimento.
incidental *agg.* fortuito. ♦ **incidental** *s.* caso.
incipient *agg.* incipiente.
to incise *vt.* incidere.
incisive *agg.* incisivo.
incisiveness *s.* incisività.
incisor *s.* incisivo.
incitation *s.* incitamento.
to incite *vt.* incitare.
incivility *s.* villania.
inclemency *s.* inclemenza.

inclement *agg.* inclemente.
inclinable *agg.* incline.
inclination *s.* inclinazione.
to incline *vt.* inclinare. ♦ **to incline** *vi.* propendere.
inclined *agg.* **1.** inclinato **2.** incline.
to include *vt.* includere.
included *agg.* incluso, compreso.
inclusion *s.* inclusione.
inclusive *agg.* compreso.
incoherence *s.* incoerenza.
incoherent *agg.* incoerente.
incombustible *agg.* incombustibile.
income *s.* rendita, reddito || — *-tax*, imposta sul reddito.
incoming *s.* entrata. ♦ **incoming** *agg.* entrante.
incommensurability *s.* incommensurabilità.
incommensurable *agg.* incommensurabile.
incommensurate *agg.* **1.** inadeguato **2.** smisurato.
incommunicability *s.* incomunicabilità.
incommunicable *agg.* incomunicabile.
incommutable *agg.* incommutabile.
incomparable *agg.* incomparabile.
incompatibility *s.* incompatibilità.
incompatible *agg.* incompatibile.
incompetence *s.* incompetenza.
incompetent *agg.* e *s.* incompetente.
incomplete *agg.* incompleto.
incompleteness, incompletion *s.* incompletezza.
incomprehensibility *s.* incomprensibilità.
incomprehensible *agg.* incomprensibile.
incomprehension *s.* incomprensione.
inconceivability *s.* inconcepibilità.
inconceivable *agg.* inconcepibile.
inconclusive *agg.* inconcludente.
inconclusiveness *s.* inconcludenza.
incongruity *s.* incongruenza.
incongruous *agg.* incongruo.
inconsequence *s.* incongruenza.
inconsequent *agg.* incongruente.
inconsequential *agg.* **1.** incoerente **2.** irrilevante.
inconsiderate *agg.* sconsiderato.
inconsistence *s.* incoerenza.
inconsistent *agg.* incoerente.
inconsolable *agg.* inconsolabile.
inconstancy *s.* incostanza.
inconstant *agg.* incostante.

incontestability *s.* incontestabilità.
incontestable *agg.* incontestabile.
incontinence *s.* incontinenza.
incontinent *agg.* incontinente.
incontinently *avv.* smoderatamente.
incontrollable *agg.* incontrollabile.
incontrovertible *agg.* incontrovertibile.
inconvenience *s.* 1. disturbo 2. scomodità.
to **inconvenience** *vt.* scomodare. .
inconvenient *agg.* incomodo.
inconvertible *agg.* inconvertibile.
to **incorporate** *vt.* 1. incorporare 2. (*comm.*) costituire. ♦ to **incorporate** *vi.* incorporarsi.
incorporated *agg.* 1. (*comm.*) anonimo 2. incorporato.
incorporation *s.* 1. incorporazione 2. (*comm.*) costituzione.
incorporeal *agg.* incorporeo.
incorrect *agg.* scorretto.
incorrectness *s.* scorrettezza.
incorrigible *agg.* incorreggibile.
incorrupt *agg.* incorrotto.
incorruptibility *s.* incorruttibilità.
incorruptible *agg.* incorruttibile.
increase *s.* aumento.
to **increase** *vt.* e *vi.* aumentare.
increasing *agg.* crescente.
increasingly *avv.* sempre più.
incredibility *s.* incredibilità.
incredible *agg.* incredibile.
incredulity *s.* incredulità.
incredulous *agg.* incredulo.
increment *s.* incremento.
to **incriminate** *vt.* incriminare.
incrimination *s.* incriminazione.
incriminatory *agg.* incriminante.
incrustation *s.* incrostazione.
incubation *s.* incubazione.
incubator *s.* incubatrice.
to **inculcate** *vt.* inculcare.
inculcation *s.* inculcazione.
inculpable *agg.* innocente.
inculpation *s.* accusa.
incumbent *agg.* incombente.
to **incur** *vt.* incorrere in.
incurability *s.* incurabilità.
incurable *agg.* incurabile.
incursion *s.* incursione.
indebted *agg.* 1. indebitato 2. obbligato.
indecency *s.* indecenza.
indecent *agg.* indecente.
indecipherable *agg.* indecifrabile.

indecision *s.* indecisione.
indecisive *agg.* 1. indeciso 2. non decisivo.
indeclinable *agg.* indeclinabile.
indecomposable *agg.* indecomponibile.
indecorous *agg.* indecoroso.
indeed *avv.* in verità, davvero.
indefatigable *agg.* infaticabile.
indefeasible *agg.* irrevocabile.
indefinable *agg.* indefinibile.
indefinite *agg.* indefinito.
indefiniteness *s.* indeterminatezza.
indelible *agg.* indelebile.
indelicacy *s.* 1. rozzezza 2. sconvenienza.
indelicate *agg.* 1. sgarbato 2. sconveniente.
to **indemnify** *vt.* 1. indennizzare 2. assicurare.
indemnity *s.* 1. indennità 2. assicurazione.
indemonstrable *agg.* indimostrabile.
indent *s.* 1. dentellatura 2. incavo 3. (*comm.*) ordinazione 4. (*tip.*) capoverso.
to **indent** *vt.* 1. dentellare, frastagliare 2. intagliare 3. (*comm.*) ordinare (*merci*).
indentation, indention *s.* 1. dentellatura 2. incisione.
indenture *s.* 1. dentellatura 2. contratto.
independence *s.* indipendenza.
independent *agg.* e *s.* indipendente.
indescribable *agg.* indescrivibile.
indestructibility *s.* indistruttibilità.
indestructible *agg.* indistruttibile.
indeterminable *agg.* indeterminabile.
indeterminate *agg.* indeterminato.
indetermination *s.* indeterminazione.
index *s.* indice.
Indian *agg.* e *s.* indiano.
to **indicate** *vt.* indicare.
indicating *agg.* indicatore.
indication *s.* 1. indicazione 2. segno.
indicative *agg.* e *s.* indicativo.
indicator *s.* indicatore.
to **indict** *vt.* accusare.
indictment *s.* (*giur.*) accusa.
indifference *s.* 1. indifferenza 2. imparzialità 3. mancanza di valore.
indifferent *agg.* 1. indifferente 2.

imparziale 3. mediocre.
indifferentism s. indifferentismo.
indifferentist s. indifferentista.
indigence s. indigenza.
indigenous agg. indigeno.
indigent agg. indigente.
indigestible agg. indigesto.
indigestion s. dispepsia.
indignant agg. indignato.
indignation s. indignazione.
indignity s. 1. indegnità 2. offesa.
indigo s. indaco.
indirect agg. 1. indiretto 2. tortuoso.
indiscernible agg. indistinguibile.
indiscipline s. indisciplina.
indiscreet agg. 1. sconsiderato 2. indiscreto.
indiscrete agg. compatto.
indiscretion s. 1. sconsideratezza 2. indiscrezione.
indiscriminate agg. indiscriminato.
indispensable agg. indispensabile.
indisposed agg. indisposto.
indisposition s. 1. avversione 2. indisposizione.
indisputability s. indiscutibilità.
indisputable agg. indiscutibile.
indisputed agg. indiscusso.
indissolubility s. indissolubilità.
indissoluble agg. indissolubile.
indistinct agg. indistinto.
indistinguishable agg. indistinguibile.
individual agg. individuale. ♦ **individual** s. individuo.
individualism s. individualismo.
individualist agg. e s. individualista.
individualistic agg. individualistico.
individuality s. individualità.
individualization s. individualizzazione.
to **individualize** vt. individualizzare.
indivisibility s. indivisibilità.
indivisible agg. indivisibile.
indocility s. indocilità.
Indo-European agg. e s. indo-europeo.
indolence s. indolenza.
indolent agg. indolente.
indomitable agg. indomabile.
indoor agg. in casa.
indoors avv. in casa.
indraft, indraught s. risucchio, vortice.
indubitable agg. indubitabile.

to **induce** vt. indurre.
inducement s. 1. allettamento 2. movente.
induction s. 1. induzione 2. insediamento.
inductive agg. induttivo.
inductor s. induttore.
to **indulge** vt. essere indulgente verso. ♦ to **indulge** vi. indulgere.
indulgence s. 1. indulgenza 2. proroga.
indulgent agg. indulgente.
indult s. indulto.
industrial agg. industriale. ♦ **industrial** s. lavoratore dell'industria.
industrialism s. industrialismo.
industrialist s. industriale.
industrialization s. industrializzazione.
to **industrialize** vt. industrializzare.
industrious agg. industrioso.
industry s. 1. industria 2. operosità, diligenza.
inebriate agg. e s. ubriaco.
to **inebriate** vt. inebriare.
inedited agg. inedito.
ineffable agg. ineffabile.
ineffective agg. 1. inefficace 2. inefficiente.
ineffectiveness s. 1. inefficacia 2. inefficienza.
ineffectual agg. inutile.
inefficacy s. inefficacia.
inefficient agg. V. *ineffective*.
inelegance s. ineleganza.
inelegant agg. inelegante.
ineligibility s. ineleggibilità.
ineligible agg. ineleggibile.
ineluctable agg. ineluttabile.
inept agg. inadatto.
ineptitude, ineptness s. inettitudine.
inequality s. diseguaglianza.
inequity s. ingiustizia.
ineradicable agg. inestirpabile.
inerrability s. infallibilità.
inerrable agg. infallibile.
inert agg. inerte.
inertness s. inerzia.
inescapable agg. inevitabile.
inestimable agg. inestimabile.
inevitability s. inevitabilità.
inevitable agg. inevitabile.
inevitableness s. inevitabilità.
inexact agg. inesatto.
inexactitude s. inesattezza.
inexcusability s. inescusabilità.
inexcusable agg. imperdonabile.

inexecutable *agg.* ineseguibile.
inexhaustibility *s.* inesauribilità.
inexhaustible *agg.* inesauribile.
inexistence *s.* inesistenza.
inexistent *agg.* inesistente.
inexorability *s.* inesorabilità.
inexorable *agg.* inesorabile.
inexpedient *agg.* inopportuno.
inexpensive *agg.* poco costoso.
inexperience *s.* inesperienza.
inexperienced, inexpert *agg.* inesperto.
inexpiable *agg.* inespiabile.
inexplicable *agg.* inesplicabile.
inexplorable *agg.* inesplorabile.
inexpressible *agg.* inesprimibile.
inexpressive *agg.* inespressivo.
inexpressiveness *s.* inespressività.
inexpugnability *s.* inespugnabilità.
inexpugnable *agg.* inespugnabile.
inextinguishable *agg.* inestinguibile.
inextricable *agg.* inestricabile.
infallibility *s.* infallibilità.
infallible *agg.* infallibile.
infamous *agg.* infame.
infamy *s.* infamia.
infancy *s.* infanzia.
infant *agg.* infantile. ♦ **infant** *s.*
1. neonato 2. (*giur.*) minore.
infanticide *s.* 1. infanticida 2. infanticidio.
infantile *agg.* infantile.
infantilism *s.* infantilismo.
infantry *s.* fanteria || — *man*, fante.
infarct *s.* infarto.
to **infatuate** *vt.* infatuare.
infatuation *s.* infatuazione.
to **infect** *vt.* contagiare.
infection *s.* contagio.
infectious *agg.* contagioso.
infective *agg.* infettivo.
infecund *agg.* infecondo.
infelicitous *agg.* infelice.
infelicity *s.* infelicità.
to **infer** *vt.* dedurre.
inferable *agg.* deducibile.
inference *s.* deduzione.
inferior *agg. e s.* inferiore.
inferiority *s.* inferiorità.
infernal *agg.* infernale.
to **infest** *vt.* infestare.
infestation *s.* infestamento.
infidel *agg. e s.* infedele.
infidelity *s.* 1. miscredenza 2. infedeltà.
to **infiltrate** *vt.* infiltrare. ♦ to **infiltrate** *vi.* infiltrarsi. ⌄
infiltration *s.* infiltrazione.

infinite *agg. e s.* infinito.
infinitesimal *agg.* infinitesimale.
infinitive *agg. e s.* infinito.
infinitude *s.* infinità.
infinity *s.* infinità, infinito.
infirm *agg.* 1. infermo 2. irresoluto.
infirmary *s.* infermeria.
infirmity *s.* 1. infermità 2. irresolutezza.
to **inflame** *vt.* infiammare. ♦ to **inflame** *vi.* infiammarsi.
inflammability *s.* infiammabilità.
inflammable *agg.* infiammabile.
inflammation *s.* 1. l'infiammare, l'infiammarsi 2. infiammazione.
inflammatory *agg.* infiammatorio.
to **inflate** *vt.* gonfiare.
inflation *s.* 1. gonfiore, gonfiatura 2. (*comm.*) inflazione.
inflationary *agg.* inflazionistico.
to **inflect** *vt.* 1. flettere 2. modulare.
inflection *s.* 1. flessione 2. inflessione.
inflexibility *s.* inflessibilità.
inflexible *agg.* inflessibile.
to **inflict** *vt.* infliggere.
infliction *s.* 1. inflizione 2. pena.
inflorescence *s.* infiorescenza.
influence *s.* 1. influenza 2. (*elettr.*) induzione.
to **influence** *vt.* influenzare.
influential *agg.* influente.
influenza *s.* (*med.*) influenza.
influx *s.* 1. affluenza 2. sbocco (*di fiume*).
inform *agg.* informe.
to **inform** *vt.* 1. informare 2. dar forma a.
informal *agg.* non ufficiale.
informality *s.* assenza di formalità.
information *s.* (*solo sing.*) 1. informazione 2. sapere 3. accusa.
informative, informatory *agg.* informativo.
informed *agg.* istruito.
informer *s.* 1. informatore 2. accusatore.
infraction *s.* 1. infrazione 2. violazione.
infrangibility *s.* infrangibilità.
infrangible *agg.* 1. infrangibile 2. inviolabile.
infrared *agg.* infrarosso.
infrequent *agg.* raro.
to **infringe** *vt.* violare.
infringement *s.* violazione.
infringer *s.* trasgressore.
infructuous *agg.* infruttuoso.

to **infuse** *vt.* **1.** versare **2.** infondere **3.** mettere in infusione.

infusible *agg.* infusibile.

infusion *s.* **1.** infusione **2.** infuso.

ingenious *agg.* ingegnoso.

ingenuity *s.* ingegnosità.

ingenuous *agg.* **1.** ingenuo **2.** franco.

ingenuousness *s.* ingenuità.

to **ingest** *vt.* ingerire.

ingestion *s.* ingestione.

inglorious *agg.* inglorioso.

ingot *s.* lingotto.

ingratitude *s.* ingratitudine.

ingredient *s.* ingrediente.

inguen *s.* inguine.

inguinal *agg.* inguinale.

to **inhabit** *vt.* abitare.

inhabitable *agg.* abitabile.

inhabitancy *s.* domicilio.

inhabitant *s.* abitante.

inhalant *s.* **1.** inalatore **2.** sostanza da inalare.

inhalation *s.* inalazione.

to **inhale** *vt.* e *vi.* **1.** aspirare **2.** inalare.

inhaler *s.* inalatore.

inherent *agg.* inerente.

to **inherit** *vt.* e *vi.* ereditare.

inheritance *s.* eredità.

to **inhibit** *vt.* **1.** inibire **2.** interdire.

inhibition *s.* **1.** inibizione **2.** interdizione.

inhibitory *agg.* inibitorio.

inhospitable *agg.* inospitale.

inhospitality *s.* inospitalità.

inhuman *agg.* inumano.

inhumanity *s.* inumanità.

inhumation *s.* inumazione.

inimical *agg.* nemico.

inimitable *agg.* inimitabile.

iniquitous *agg.* iniquo.

iniquity *s.* iniquità.

initial *agg.* e *s.* iniziale.

to **initial** *vt.* siglare.

initiate *agg.* e *s.* iniziato.

to **initiate** *vt.* iniziare.

initiation *s.* **1.** inizio **2.** iniziazione.

initiative *agg.* introduttivo. ♦ **initiative** *s.* iniziativa.

initiator *s.* iniziatore.

to **inject** *vt.* iniettare.

injection *s.* iniezione.

injector *s.* iniettore.

injunction *s.* ingiunzione.

to **injure** *vt.* ledere, ferire.

injurer *s.* **1.** danneggiatore **2.** feritore.

injury *s.* **1.** torto, danno **2.** ferita.

injustice *s.* ingiustizia.

ink *s.* inchiostro || — *-pot*, calamaio.

inkholder *s.* calamaio.

inkling *s.* indizio.

inky *agg.* **1.** di, simile a inchiostro **2.** macchiato d'inchiostro.

inlaid V. *to inlay*.

inland *agg.* e *s.* interno. ♦ **inland** *avv.* all'interno.

inlay *s.* intarsio.

to **inlay** (**inlaid**, **inlaid**) *vt.* intarsiare.

inlet *s.* **1.** piccola insenatura **2.** apertura.

inmate *s.* **1.** inquilino **2.** ricoverato.

inmost *agg.* più interno.

inn *s.* locanda || — *-keeper*, locandiere; — *of court*, scuola di legge.

innate *agg.* innato.

innavigable *agg.* non navigabile.

inner *agg.* interno, intimo.

innermost *agg.* V. *inmost*.

innervation *s.* innervazione.

innocence *s.* innocenza.

innocent *agg.* e *s.* innocente.

innocuity *s.* innocuità.

innocuous *agg.* innocuo.

innominate *agg.* innominato.

to **innovate** *vt.* e *vi.* innovare.

innovation *s.* innovazione.

innovator *s.* innovatore.

innumerability *s.* innumerabilità.

innumerable *agg.* innumerevole.

inobservance *s.* **1.** inosservanza **2.** disattenzione.

inobservant *agg.* **1.** inosservante **2.** disattento.

to **inoculate** *vt.* **1.** inoculare **2.** inculcare.

inoculation *s.* inoculazione.

inodorous *agg.* inodoro.

inoffensive *agg.* inoffensivo.

inopportune *agg.* inopportuno.

inopportuneness *s.* inopportunità.

inordinate *agg.* smoderato.

inorganic *agg.* inorganico.

inoxidizable *agg.* inossidabile.

inpouring *agg.* affluente. ♦ **inpouring** *s.* afflusso.

input *s.* (*mecc.; elettr.*) alimentazione, entrata.

inquest *s.* **1.** inchiesta **2.** giuria.

inquietude *s.* inquietudine.

to **inquire** *vt.* e *vi.* chiedere || *to — after*, chiedere informazioni su; *to — into*, indagare su.

inquirer *s.* investigatore.

inquiring *agg.* **1.** indagatore **2.** curioso.

inquiry s. 1. ricerca 2. domanda 3. inchiesta.

inquisition s. 1. ricerca 2. inchiesta.

inquisitive agg. V. inquiring.

inquisitiveness s. curiosità

inrush s. irruzione.

insalubrity s. insalubrità.

insane agg. insano.

insanitary agg. malsano.

insanity s. insania.

insatiability s. insaziabilità.

insatiable, insatiate agg. insaziabile.

to **inscribe** vt. 1. iscrivere 2. scolpire 3. dedicare.

inscription s. 1. iscrizione 2. dedica.

inscrutability s. inscrutabilità.

inscrutable agg. inscrutabile.

inscrutableness s. inscrutabilità.

insect s. insetto.

insecticide s. insetticida.

insectivorous agg. insettivoro.

insecure agg. insicuro.

insecurity s. insicurezza.

insensate agg. 1. insensibile 2. insensato.

insensibility s. insensibilità.

insensible agg. 1. insensibile 2. inconscio.

insensitive agg. insensibile.

inseparable agg. inseparabile.

insert s. inserzione.

to **insert** vt. inserire.

insertion s. inserzione.

to **inset (inset, inset)** vt. inserire.

inside agg. e s. interno. ♦ **inside** avv. e prep. dentro.

insidious agg. insidioso.

insight s. 1. intuito 2. penetrazione.

insignificant agg. insignificante.

insincere agg. insincero.

insincerity s. falsità.

to **insinuate** vt. insinuare.

insinuation s. insinuazione.

insinuative agg. insinuante.

insipid agg. insipido.

insipidity, insipidness s. insipidezza.

insipience s. insipienza.

insipient agg. insipiente.

to **insist** vi. insistere.

insistence s. insistenza.

insistent agg. insistente.

insolation s. insolazione.

insolence s. insolenza.

insolent agg. e s. insolente.

insolubility s. insolubilità.

insoluble agg. insolubile.

insolvable agg. insolubile.

insolvency s. insolvenza.

insolvent agg. insolvente. ♦ **insolvent** s. debitore insolvente.

insomnia s. insonnia.

to **inspect** vt. ispezionare.

inspection s. ispezione.

inspector s. ispettore.

inspectoral agg. di ispettore, di ispezione.

inspectorate s. ispettorato.

inspiration s. 1. inspirazione 2. ispirazione.

to **inspire** vt. 1. inspirare 2. ispirare.

inspirer s. ispiratore.

inspiring agg. ispiratore.

instability s. instabilità.

to **install** vt. installare.

installation s. installazione.

instalment s. 1. rata 2. puntata.

instance s. 1. esempio 2. caso 3. istanza.

instancy s. 1. urgenza 2. insistenza.

instant agg. 1. urgente 2. corrente. ♦ **instant** s. istante.

instantaneous agg. istantaneo.

instantly avv. all'istante. ♦ **instantly** cong. non appena che.

instead avv. invece.

instep s. 1. collo del piede 2. collo di scarpa.

to **instigate** vt. istigare.

instigation s. istigazione.

instigator s. istigatore.

to **instil(l)** vt. instillare.

instinct agg. imbevuto. ♦ **instinct** s. istinto.

instinctive agg. istintivo.

institute s. istituto. ♦ **institutes** s. pl. istituzioni.

to **institute** vt. istituire.

institution s. istituto.

institutional agg. istituzionale.

institutor s. istitutore.

to **instruct** vt. 1. istruire 2. informare 3. ordinare.

instruction s. istruzione.

instructive agg. istruttivo.

instructor s. istruttore.

instrument s. 1. strumento 2. atto giuridico.

to **instrument** vt. 1. strumentare 2. redigere.

instrumental agg. 1. strumentale 2. utile.

instrumentation s. 1. orchestrazio-

ne 2. uso di strumenti.
insubordinate *agg.* insubordinato.
insubordination *s.* insubordinazione.
insubstantial *agg.* incorporeo.
insufferable *agg.* insopportabile.
insufficiency *s.* insufficienza.
insufficient *agg.* insufficiente.
insular *agg.* 1. insulare 2. (*fig.*) di mentalità ristretta.
to **insulate** *vt.* isolare.
insulation *s.* isolamento.
insulator *s.* isolatore.
insulin *s.* insulina.
insult *s.* insulto.
to **insult** *vt.* insultare.
insuperable *agg.* insuperabile.
insuppressible *agg.* insopprimibile.
insurance *s.* assicurazione.
insurant *s.* assicurato.
to **insure** *vt.* assicurare.
insurer *s.* assicuratore.
insurgency *s.* insurrezione.
insurgent *agg.* e *s.* insorto.
insurmountable *agg.* insormontabile.
insurrection *s.* insurrezione.
insurrectional, insurrectionary *agg.* insurrezionale.
insurrectionist *s.* insorto.
intact *agg.* intatto.
intake *s.* 1. presa 2. energia assorbita.
intangible *agg.* intangibile.
integrable *agg.* integrabile.
integral *agg.* integrale.
integrant *agg.* integrante.
to **integrate** *vt.* integrare.
integration *s.* integrazione.
integrity *s.* integrità.
intellect *s.* intelletto.
intellective *agg.* intellettivo.
intellectual *agg.* e *s.* intellettuale.
intellectualism *s.* intellettualismo.
intelligence *s.* 1. intelligenza 2. informazioni (*pl.*).
intelligent *agg.* intelligente.
intelligibility *s.* intelligibilità.
intelligible *agg.* intelligibile.
intemperance *s.* intemperanza.
intemperate *agg.* 1. smoderato 2. rigido (*di clima*).
to **intend** *vt.* 1. intendere 2. destinare.
intendant *s.* intendente.
intended *agg.* progettato.
intense *agg.* intenso.
intensification *s.* intensificazione.
to **intensify** *vt.* intensificare. ◆ to

intensify *vi.* intensificarsi.
intensity *s.* 1. intensità 2. vigore.
intensive *agg.* intensivo, intenso.
intent *agg.* intento, dedito. ◆ **intent** *s.* intenzione, scopo.
intention *s.* intenzione.
intentional *agg.* intenzionale.
intently *avv.* intensamente.
to **inter** *vt.* seppellire.
to **intercalate** *vt.* intercalare.
to **intercede** *vi.* intercedere.
to **intercept** *vt.* intercettare.
interception *s.* intercettamento.
interceptor *s.* intercettatore.
intercession *s.* intercessione.
intercessor *s.* intercessore.
interchange *s.* scambio.
to **interchange** *vt.* scambiare. ◆ to **interchange** *vi.* scambiarsi.
interchangeable *agg.* scambievole.
intercom *s.* citofono.
intercommunication *s.* intercomunicazione.
intercontinental *agg.* intercontinentale.
intercostal *agg.* intercostale.
intercourse *s.* rapporto, relazione || *trade* —, scambi commerciali.
interdependence *s.* interdipendenza.
interdependent *agg.* interdipendente.
interdict *s.* 1. interdizione 2. interdetto 3. proibizione.
to **interdict** *vt.* 1. interdire 2. proibire.
interdiction *s.* V. *interdict.*
interest *s.* interesse.
to **interest** *vt.* interessare.
interested *agg.* interessato || *those* —, gli interessati.
interesting *agg.* interessante.
to **interfere** *vi.* 1. interferire 2. scontrarsi.
interference *s.* 1. interferenza 2. collisione.
interior *agg.* e *s.* interno.
to **interject** *vt.* intromettere.
interjection *s.* intromissione.
to **interlace** *vt.* intrecciare. ◆ to **interlace** *vi.* intrecciarsi.
interlacing *s.* intreccio.
to **interline** *vt.* interlineare.
interlinear *agg.* interlineare.
interlineation *s.* interlineazione.
to **interlink** *vt.* concatenare.
to **interlock** *vt.* sincronizzare.
interlocution *s.* interlocuzione.
interlocutor *s.* interlocutore.

to **interlope** *vi.* immischiarsi.
interlude *s.* **1.** intervallo **2.** intermezzo.
intermarriage *s.* matrimonio tra membri di famiglie, razze diverse.
to **intermarry** *vt.* e *vi.* imparentarsi per mezzo di matrimonio.
to **intermeddle** *vi.* intromettersi.
intermeddler *s.* intrigante.
intermediary *agg.* intermedio, frapposto. ♦ **intermediary** *s.* **1.** intermediario, mediatore **2.** cosa intermedia.
intermediate *agg.* V. *intermediary.*
intermediation *s.* mediazione.
interment *s.* sepoltura.
interminable *agg.* interminabile.
to **intermingle** *vt.* mescolare. ♦ to **intermingle** *vi.* mescolarsi.
intermission *s.* sosta, pausa.
to **intermit** *vt.* interrompere. ♦ to **intermit** *vi.* interrompersi, essere intermittente.
intermittence *s.* intermittenza.
intermittent *agg.* intermittente.
to **intern** *vt.* internare.
internal *agg.* interno.
international *agg.* internazionale.
internationalism *s.* internazionalismo.
internationalist *s.* internazionalista.
to **internationalize** *vt.* internazionalizzare.
internment *s.* internamento.
to **interpellate** *vt.* interpellare.
interpellation *s.* interpellanza.
interphone *s.* citofono.
interplanetary *agg.* interplanetario.
interplay *s.* azione reciproca.
to **interpolate** *vt.* interpolare.
interpolation *s.* interpolazione.
to **interpose** *vt.* interporre. ♦ to **interpose** *vi.* interporsi.
interposition *s.* interposizione.
to **interpret** *vt.* interpretare. ♦ to **interpret** *vi.* fare l'interprete.
interpretation *s.* interpretazione.
interpretative *agg.* interpretativo.
interpreter *s.* interprete.
interpunction *s.* interpunzione.
interregnum *s.* **1.** interregno **2.** intervallo.
interrelation *s.* relazione.
interrelationship *s.* interdipendenza.
to **interrogate** *vt.* interrogare.
interrogation *s.* interrogazione ‖ — *-mark,* punto interrogativo.

interrogative *agg.* e *s.* interrogativo.
interrogatory *agg.* interrogativo. ♦ **interrogatory** *s.* **1.** interrogazione **2.** interrogatorio.
to **interrupt** *vt.* e *vi.* interrompere.
interrupter *s.* interruttore.
interruption *s.* interruzione.
to **intersect** *vt.* intersecare. ♦ to **intersect** *vi.* intersecarsi.
intersection *s.* intersezione.
interspace *s.* intervallo, spazio.
to **intersperse** *vt.* cospargere.
interstice *s.* interstizio.
to **intertwine** *vt.* attorcigliare. ♦ to **intertwine** *vi.* attorcigliarsi.
interurban *agg.* interurbano.
interval *s.* intervallo.
to **intervene** *vi.* intervenire.
intervener *s.* chi interviene.
intervention *s.* intervento.
interventionist *s.* interventista.
interview *s.* intervista.
to **interview** *vt.* intervistare.
interviewer *s.* intervistatore.
to **interweave (interwove, interwoven)** *vt.* intessere, intrecciare.
intestinal *agg.* intestinale.
intestine *agg.* e *s.* intestino.
intimacy *s.* intimità.
intimate *agg.* intimo. ♦ **intimate** *s.* amico intimo.
to **intimate** *vt.* **1.** intimare **2.** accennare.
intimation *s.* **1.** intimazione **2.** preannunzio.
intimidation *s.* intimidazione.
intimidatory *agg.* intimidatorio.
into *prep.* in, dentro ‖ *to go — the, park,* entrare nel parco; *far — the night,* fino a tarda notte.
intolerable *agg.* intollerabile.
intolerance *s.* intolleranza.
intolerant *agg.* e *s.* intollerante.
to **intonate** *vt.* intonare.
intonation *s.* intonazione.
to **intone** *vt.* intonare.
to **intoxicate** *vt.* inebriare.
intoxication *s.* ebbrezza.
intractable *agg.* intrattabile.
intramuscular *agg.* intramusculare.
intransgressible *agg.* che non può essere trasgredito.
intransigence *s.* intransigenza.
intransigent *agg.* e *s.* intransigente.
intransitive *agg.* intransitivo.
intravenous *agg.* endovenoso.
intrepid *agg.* intrepido.

intrepidity *s.* intrepidezza.
intricacy *s.* complicazione.
intricate *agg.* intricato.
intrigant *s.* intrigante.
intrigue *s.* intrigo.
to **intrigue** *vt.* 1. ingannare 2. rendere perplesso 3. affascinare. ♦ to **intrigue** *vi.* avere una tresca.
intriguer *s.* intrigante.
intrinsic *agg.* intrinseco.
to **introduce** *vt.* 1. introdurre 2. presentare.
introduction *s.* 1. introduzione 2. presentazione.
introductive, introductory *agg.* introduttivo.
intromission *s.* interferenza.
to **intromit** *vt.* introdurre.
to **introspect** *vi.* autoesaminarsi.
introspection *s.* introspezione.
introspective *agg.* introspettivo.
introversion *s.* introversione.
introvert *agg.* e *s.* introverso.
to **intrude** *vt.* imporre. ♦ to **intrude** *vi.* intromettersi.
intruder *s.* 1. intruso 2. importuno.
intrusion *s.* intrusione.
intrusive *agg.* 1. intruso 2. importuno.
intrusiveness *s.* indiscrezione.
intuition *s.* intuizione.
intuitional *agg.* intuitivo.
intuitionism *s.* intuizionismo.
intuitive *agg.* intuitivo.
to **inundate** *vt.* inondare.
inundation *s.* inondazione.
inurbane *agg.* inurbano.
inurbanity *s.* inurbanità.
to **inure** *vt.* abituare. ♦ to **inure** *vi.* venire in uso.
inurement *s.* abitudine.
inutility *s.* inutilità.
to **invade** *vt.* 1. invadere 2. violare.
invader *s.* invasore.
invalid *agg.* 1. invalido 2. nullo. ♦ **invalid** *s.* invalido.
to **invalid** *vt.* 1. rendere invalido 2. riformare.
to **invalidate** *vt.* invalidare.
invalidation *s.* invalidazione.
invalidity *s.* invalidità.
invaluable *agg.* inestimabile.
invariability *s.* invariabilità.
invariable *agg.* invariabile.
invasion *s.* invasione.
invective *s.* invettiva.
to **inveigh** *vi.* inveire.

to **invent** *vt.* inventare.
invention *s.* 1. invenzione 2. inventiva.
inventive *agg.* inventivo.
inventor *s.* inventore.
inventory *s.* inventario.
to **inventory** *vt.* fare l'inventario di.
inverse *agg.* e *s.* inverso.
inversion *s.* inversione.
invert *agg.* e *s.* invertito.
to **invert** *vt.* invertire.
invertebrate *agg.* e *s.* invertebrato.
invertible *agg.* invertibile.
to **invest** *vt.* 1. investire 2. rivestire.
to **investigate** *vt.* e *vi.* investigare.
investigation *s.* investigazione.
investigative *agg.* investigativo.
investigator *s.* investigatore.
investiture *s.* investitura.
investment *s.* investimento.
investor *s.* investitore.
inveterate *agg.* inveterato.
invidious *agg.* odioso.
invidiousness *s.* odiosità.
to **invigorate** *vt.* rinvigorire.
invigorative *agg.* rinforzante.
invincibility *s.* invincibilità.
invincible *agg.* invincibile.
inviolability *s.* inviolabilità.
inviolable *agg.* inviolabile.
inviolate *agg.* inviolato.
invisibility *s.* invisibilità.
invisible *agg.* invisibile.
invitation *s.* invito.
to **invite** *vt.* 1. invitare 2. provocare.
invocation *s.* invocazione.
invoice *s.* fattura.
to **invoice** *vt.* fatturare.
to **invoke** *vt.* 1. invocare 2. evocare.
involuntary *s.* involontario.
involute *agg.* 1. involuto 2. a spirale.
involution *s.* 1. involuzione 2. intrico 3. (*mat.*) elevazione a potenza.
to **involve** *vt.* 1. avvolgere 2. implicare 3. complicare.
invulnerability *s.* invulnerabilità.
invulnerable *agg.* invulnerabile.
inward *agg.* interiore.
inwardness *s.* interiorità.
inwards *avv.* internamente.
iodine *s.* iodio.
to **iodize** *vt.* iodare.
ion *s.* ione.
Ionic *agg.* ionico.

ionization s. ionizzazione.
ionosphere s. ionosfera.
Iranian agg. e s. iraniano.
Iraqi agg. e s. iracheno.
irascibility s. irascibilità.
irascible agg. irascibile.
irate agg. adirato.
ireful agg. irato.
iridescence s. iridescenza.
iridescent agg. iridescente.
iris s. iride.
Irish agg. irlandese.
Irishman s. irlandese.
irksome agg. noioso.
iron agg. di ferro. ♦ **iron** s. ferro
|| — -*foundry*, ferriera. ♦ **irons**
s. pl. catene.
to **iron** vt. 1. rivestire di ferro 2.
stirare.
ironclad agg. corazzato. ♦ **ironclad** s. corazzata.
ironic(al) agg. ironico.
ironing s. stiratura.
ironmonger s. negoziante in ferramenta.
ironsmith s. fabbro ferraio.
ironware s. ferramenta.
ironwork s. lavoro in ferro. ♦
ironworks s. pl. ferriera (*sing.*).
irony s. ironia.
to **irradiate** vt. irradiare. ♦ to **irradiate** vi. risplendere.
irradiation s. 1. illuminazione 2.
irradiazione.
irrational agg. irrazionale.
irrationalism, irrationality s. irrazionalità.
irrealizable agg. irrealizzabile.
irreconcilability s. inconciliabilità.
irreconcilable agg. irreconciliabile.
irrecoverable agg. 1. irrecuperabile 2. irrimediabile.
irredentism s. irredentismo.
irredentist s. irredentista.
irreducible agg. irriducibile.
irreflection s. irriflessione.
irreflective agg. irriflessivo.
irrefutable agg. irrefutabile.
irregular agg. e s. irregolare.
irregularity s. irregolarità.
irrelevant agg. 1. non pertinente
2. insignificante.
irreligious agg. irreligioso.
irremediable agg. irrimediabile.
irremissible agg. irremissibile.
irremovability s. irremovibilità.
irremovable agg. irremovibile.
irreparable agg. irreparabile.
irreplaceable agg. insostituibile.

irreprehensible agg. irreprensibile.
irrepressible agg. irrefrenabile.
irrepressibleness s. irrefrenabilità.
irreproachable agg. irreprensibile.
irreprovable agg. irreprensibile.
irresistible agg. irresistibile.
irresolute agg. irresoluto.
irresoluteness, irresolution s.
irresolutezza.
irresolvable agg. insolubile.
irrespective agg. noncurante.
irresponsibility s. irresponsabilità.
irresponsible agg. 1. irresponsabile 2. insolubile.
irresponsive agg. che non risponde.
irretrievable agg. irrecuperabile.
irreverence s. irriverenza.
irreverent agg. irriverente.
irreversibility s. irreversibilità.
irreversible agg. irreversibile.
irrevocable agg. irrevocabile.
irrigable agg. irrigabile.
to **irrigate** vt. irrigare.
irrigation s. irrigazione.
irritability s. irritabilità.
irritable agg. irritabile.
irritant agg. e s. irritante.
to **irritate** vt. irritare.
irritation s. irritazione.
irritative agg. irritante.
irruption s. irruzione.
Islamic agg. islamico.
Islamism s. islamismo.
island s. 1. isola 2. salvagente stradale.
islander s. isolano.
isle s. piccola isola || *the British
Isles*, le isole britanniche.
islet s. isolotto.
isochronism s. isocronismo.
to **isolate** vt. isolare.
isolation s. isolamento.
isolationism s. isolazionismo.
isolationist s. isolazionista.
isolator s. isolatore.
isomorphism s. isomorfismo.
isomorphous agg. isomorfo.
isosceles agg. isoscele.
isotherm s. isoterma.
isothermal agg. isotermico.
isotope s. isotopo.
isotrope s. isotropo.
Israeli agg. e s. israeliano.
Israelite s. israelita.
issue s. 1. uscita, sbocco, foce 2.
conclusione 3. prole, stirpe 4. problema 5. emissione, pubblicazione.
to **issue** vt. 1. emettere, pubblicare
2. rilasciare. ♦ to **issue** vi. 1.

uscire **2.** risultare **3.** discendere.
issueless *agg.* **1.** senza sbocco **2.** senza prole.
isthmus *s.* istmo.
it *pron.* *neutro* esso, essa, ciò, lo, gli, le, ne, sé || *I don't believe* —, non ci credo; — *is raining*, piove; — *is Sunday*, è domenica.
Italian *agg.* e *s.* italiano.
to **italicize** *vt.* e *vi.* **1.** stampare in corsivo **2.** sottolineare.
itch *s.* **1.** prurito **2.** scabbia.
to **itch** *vi.* **1.** prudere **2.** aver voglia di.
itching *s.* prurito.
item *s.* (*comm.*) voce.
to **itemize** *vt.* specificare, elencare.
to **iterate** *vt.* ripetere.
itinerant *agg.* ambulante.
itinerary *s.* itinerario.
its *agg.* e *pron.* *poss.* *neutro* suo, sua, suoi, sue.
itself *pron.* *r.* *neutro* esso stesso, essa stessa, sé, si || *by* —, da solo.
ivory *s.* avorio.
ivy *s.* edera.

J

jab *s.* **1.** stoccata **2.** colpo improvviso.
jack *s.* **1.** (*fam.*) marinaio **2.** fante (*gioco delle carte*) **3.** bandiera (*di nave*) **4.** maschio (*di certi animali*) **5.** uomo di fatica **6.** (*mecc.*) cricco.
jackal *s.* sciacallo.
jackass *s.* somaro.
jackdaw *s.* cornacchia.
jacket *s.* **1.** giacchetta **2.** rivestimento protettivo, isolante.
Jacobin *s.* giacobino.
jade[1] *s.* giada.
jade[2] *s.* **1.** cavallo, ronzino **2.** megera.
to **jag** *vt.* frastagliare, dentellare.
jaguar *s.* giaguaro.
jail *s.* carcere.
to **jail** *vt.* incarcerare.
jailer *s.* carceriere.
to **jam** *vt.* premere, serrare, pigiare. ♦ to **jam** *vi.* bloccarsi, incepparsi.
jam[1] *s.* marmellata.
jam[2] *s.* **1.** ammasso **2.** compressione **3.** ingorgo.
jamb *s.* stipite.

Jansenism *s.* giansenismo.
Jansenist *s.* giansenista.
January *s.* gennaio.
Japanese *agg.* e *s.* giapponese.
jar *s.* rumore aspro, stridio.
to **jar** *vi.* **1.** discordare **2.** stridere. ♦ to **jar** *vt.* **1.** far discordare **2.** far stridere.
jargon *s.* **1.** gergo **2.** linguaggio professionale.
jarring *agg.* discorde, stridente.
jasmin(e) *s.* gelsomino.
jasper *s.* diaspro.
jaundice *s.* itterizia.
javelin *s.* giavellotto.
jaw *s.* **1.** mascella, mandibola **2.** morsa, ganascia. ♦ **jaws** *s.* *pl.* stretta, gola.
jealous *agg.* geloso.
jealously *avv.* gelosamente.
jealousness, jealousy *s.* gelosia.
jeer *s.* beffa, scherno.
jelly *s.* gelatina (*anche di frutta*).
to **jeopardize** *vt.* mettere a repentaglio.
jeopardy *s.* rischio, pericolo.
jerk *s.* **1.** scatto, strattone **2.** spinta **3.** sussulto, tic nervoso.
to **jerk** *vt.* dare uno strattone. ♦ to **jerk** *vi.* sobbalzare || *to* — *along*, avanzare a scatti.
jerky *agg.* **1.** sussultante **2.** convulso.
jersey *s.* camicetta a maglia con maniche.
jest *s.* facezia, scherzo.
to **jest** *vi.* scherzare, dire delle facezie.
jester *s.* burlone.
jestful *agg.* inciine allo scherzo.
Jesuit *s.* gesuita.
Jesuitical *agg.* gesuitico.
jet[1] *agg.* nero lucido.
jet[2] *s.* **1.** getto, spruzzo **2.** spruzzatore || — *engine*, motore a reazione; — *plane*, aeroplano a reazione.
to **jet** *vt.* schizzare, sprizzare. ♦ to **jet** *vi.* slanciarsi.
jetty *s.* molo || *landing* —, imbarcadero.
Jew *s.* ebreo.
jewel *s.* gioiello.
jewelcase *s.* scrigno.
jeweller *s.* gioielliere.
jewellery *s.* **1.** gioielli **2.** commercio delle gemme.
Jewish *agg.* ebraico, ebreo.
to **jib** *vi.* recalcitrare, impuntarsi.
jig *s.* **1.** giga **2.** (*mecc.*) maschera.

Jigsaw s. sega da traforo.
to **jingle** vt. far tintinnare. ♦ to **jingle** vi. tintinnare.
job s. **1.** lavoro, impiego **2.** (fam.) faccenda, situazione.
jobber s. **1.** noleggiatore **2.** lavoratore a cottimo **3.** trafficante disonesto.
jockey s. fantino.
jocose agg. giocoso, allegro.
jocosity s. giocondità.
jocund agg. giocondo, gaio.
jocundity s. allegria, giocondità.
join s. giuntura.
to **join** vt. **1.** unire **2.** raggiungere. ♦ to **join** vi. **1.** unirsi **2.** essere contiguo.
joiner s. falegname.
joinery s. falegnameria.
joining s. congiunzione.
joint agg. unito, associato || — account, conto di partecipazione; — -heir, coerede; — -stock, capitale sociale; — -tenant, comproprietario.
joint s. **1.** giuntura, congiunzione **2.** trancio di carne **3.** articolazione.
jointer s. pialla.
jointly avv. unitamente.
joke s. scherzo, burla, facezia.
to **joke** vt. burlarsi di, canzonare. ♦ to **joke** vi. celiare.
joker s. tipo ameno, burlone.
jolly agg. gaio, vivace.
to **jolt** vt. far sobbalzare, scuotere. ♦ to **jolt** vi. traballare.
to **jostle** vt. spingere. ♦ to **jostle** vi. spingersi.
journal s. **1.** giornale **2.** diario.
journalism s. giornalismo.
journalist s. giornalista.
journalistic agg. giornalistico.
journey s. viaggio (general. per terra).
to **journey** vi. fare un viaggio.
journey-man s. operaio specializzato.
jovial agg. gioviale, allegro.
joviality s. giovialità.
jowl[1] s. **1.** mascella **2.** guancia.
jowl[2] s. gozzo.
joy s. gioia, contentezza.
joyful agg. giulivo, allegro.
joyfully avv. gaiamente, allegramente.
joyless agg. mesto, senza gioia.
joyous agg. gioioso, gaio.
joyously avv. gioiosamente.
jubilant agg. giubilante, trionfante.

to **jubilate** vi. esultare.
jubilation s. giubilo.
jubilee s. giubileo.
Judaic agg. giudaico.
Judaism s. giudaismo.
judge s. **1.** giudice **2.** intenditore.
to **judge** vt. e vi. **1.** fare da giudice, giudicare **2.** supporre, stimare.
judgement s. **1.** giudizio **2.** verdetto, sentenza **3.** parere.
judicial agg. giudiziale, giudiziario.
judiciary agg. giudiziario. ♦ **judiciary** s. magistratura.
judicious agg. giudizioso.
jug s. **1.** boccale **2.** caraffa, bricco.
juggler s. **1.** giocoliere **2.** impostore.
jugular agg. e s. giugulare.
juice s. succo (di frutta ecc.).
juiciness s. succosità.
juicy agg. succoso.
jujube s. giuggiola.
Julian agg. giuliano.
July s. luglio.
jumble s. guazzabuglio.
jump s. salto, balzo: high — (sport), salto in alto.
to **jump** vt. **1.** saltare, superare con un salto **2.** mangiare (giuoco della dama). ♦ to **jump** vi. **1.** saltare **2.** trasalire.
jumper[1] s. saltatore.
jumper[2] s. maglione.
jumping agg. saltatore.
junction s. **1.** congiunzione **2.** nodo ferroviario.
juncture s. **1.** articolazione **2.** (fig.) congiuntura, momento critico.
June s. giugno.
jungle s. giungla.
junior agg. **1.** minore, di secondaria importanza **2.** il più giovane. ♦ **junior** s. **1.** cadetto **2.** minore.
juniper s. ginepro.
junk[1] s. **1.** avanzo, rifiuto **2.** gomena vecchia **3.** carne salata.
junk[2] s. (mar.) giunca.
juridic(al) agg. giuridico.
jurisdiction s. giurisdizione.
jurisdictional agg. giurisdizionale.
jurisprudence s. giurisprudenza.
jurisprudent s. giurisprudente.
jurisprudential agg. legale.
jurist s. giurista.
jury s. giuria, giurì.
juryman s. giurato.
just agg. giusto, retto. ♦ **just** avv. appena, appunto, esattamente || — now, proprio ora; — so., proprio così; — then, proprio allora.

justice s. giustizia, imparzialità.
justiciable agg. processabile.
justiciary agg. giudiziario.
justifiability s. legittimità di difesa.
justifiable agg. giustificabile, legittimo || — homicide, omicidio per legittima difesa.
justification s. giustificazione.
justificative agg. giustificativo.
to **justify** vt. 1. giustificare 2. difendere 3. perdonare.
justly avv. giustamente, esattamente.
jut s. sporgenza.
to **jut** vt. e vi. sporgere.
jute s. iuta.
juvenile agg. giovanile.
juxtaposition s. accostamento.

K

kaleidoscope s. caleidoscopio.
kalends s. pl. calende.
kangaroo s. canguro.
kaolin(e) s. caolino.
karting s. andare in « go-kart ».
kathode s. catodo.
keel s. 1. chiglia 2. chiatta (da carbone).
to **keel** vt. 1. rovesciare 2. (mar.) carenare.
keen agg. 1. aguzzo, affilato 2. pungente 3. forte 4. appassionato 5. acuto.
keenly avv. 1. in modo penetrante 2. dolorosamente 3. avidamente 4. (comm.) al minimo.
keenness s. 1. sottigliezza 2. intensità 3. ardore 4. acume.
keep s. 1. sostentamento 2. torrione.
to **keep** (kept, kept) vi. 1. restare 2. conservarsi || to — on, continuare; to — off, tenersi in disparte. ♦ to **keep** (kept, kept) vt. 1. tenere 2. mantenere 3. custodire 4. rispettare || to — back, dissimulare; to — up, tener alto, sostenere.
keeper s. guardiano.
keeping s. 1. sorveglianza 2. mantenimento 3. armonia.
keepsake s. oggetto ricordo.
keg s. barilotto.
kennel s. 1. canile 2. muta di cani 3. rigagnolo.

to **kennel** vt. tenere in un canile. ♦ to **kennel** vi. rintanarsi.
kepi s. chepì.
kept V. to keep.
kerbstone s. cordonatura (del marciapiede).
kerchief s. fazzoletto.
kernel s. 1. gheriglio 2. seme 3. (fig.) essenza.
kettle s. bollitore, bricco.
key s. 1. chiave 2. tasto || — -money, buonuscita.
to **key** vt. 1. (mecc.) inchiavettare 2. (mus.) accordare 3. chiudere a chiave || to — up (fig.), eccitare.
keyboard s. tastiera.
keyed agg. 1. munito di chiavi 2. (mus.) a tasti.
keyhole s. buco della serratura.
keyless agg. senza chiave.
keystone s. chiave di volta.
kick s. 1. calcio 2. rinculo || — -off (sport), calcio d'inizio.
to **kick** vt. prendere a calci. ♦ to **kick** vi. 1. tirar calci 2. rinculare (di armi) 3. recalcitrare.
kicker s. chi scalcia.
kid[1] s. 1. capretto 2. bimbo.
kid[2] s. tinozza.
to **kidnap** vt. rapire.
kidnapper s. rapitore.
kidnapping s. ratto.
kidney s. 1. rene 2. temperamento || stones in the kidneys, calcoli renali.
kier s. caldaia.
to **kill** vt. 1. uccidere 2. respingere 3. smorzare 4. fermare.
killer s. uccisore || lady- —, dongiovanni.
killing agg. mortale. ♦ **killing** s. uccisione.
killjoy s. guastafeste.
kiln s. fornace.
kilo, kilogram(me) s. chilo(grammo).
kilometer s. chilometro.
kilt s. gonnellino degli scozzesi.
kin agg. consanguineo, affine. ♦ **kin** s. parentela.
kind[1] agg. gentile || very — of you, molto gentile da parte tua.
kind[2] s. specie, tipo.
to **kindle** vt. accendere. ♦ to **kindle** vi. accendersi.
kindliness s. gentilezza.
kindling s. 1. accensione 2. legna facilmente infiammabile.
kindly agg. gentile. ♦ **kindly** avv.

gentilmente.
kindness s. gentilezza.
kindred agg. **1.** imparentato **2.** affine. ♦ **kindred** s. parentela.
kinematics s. cinematica.
kinetic agg. cinetico.
kinetics s. cinetica.
king s. re || *king's English*, la lingua inglese ufficiale.
kingdom s. regno.
kinghood s. regalità.
kingly agg. regale, regio.
kingship s. regalità.
kinless agg. senza parenti.
kinsfolk s. pl. parenti.
kinship s. parentela.
kinsman s. parente.
kinswoman s. parente (*donna*).
kiosk s. chiosco || *newspaper* —, edicola.
kipper s. aringa, salmone affumicato.
to **kipper** vt. affumicare (*pesce*).
kiss s. bacio.
to **kiss** vt. baciare || *to* — *the dust*, mordere la polvere.
kit s. **1.** cassetta **2.** equipaggiamento.
kitchen s. cucina || — *garden*, orto.
kitchener s. cuciniere.
kitchenette s. cucinino.
kitchenware s. batteria da cucina.
kite s. **1.** nibbio **2.** aquilone **3.** aliante.
kitten s. gattino.
kleptomania s. cleptomania.
kleptomaniac agg. e s. cleptomane.
knack s. **1.** abilità **2.** dispositivo ingegnoso.
knapsack s. zaino (*per soldati*).
knave s. furfante.
knavery s. disonestà.
knavish agg. disonesto.
to **knead** vt. impastare.
kneader s. **1.** chi impasta **2.** impastatrice.
kneading s. impasto || — *trough*, madia.
knee s. **1.** ginocchio **2.** tubo a gomito || — -*cap*, rotula, ginocchiera.
to **kneel** (knelt, knelt) vi. inginocchiarsi.
kneeler s. **1.** chi s'inginocchia **2.** inginocchiatoio.
knell s. rintocco funebre.
to **knell** vt. chiamare a raccolta. ♦
to **knell** vi. sonare a morto.
knelt V. *to kneel.*

knew V. *to know.*
knickerbockers s. pl. calzoni alla zuava.
knick-knack s. ninnolo.
knick-knackery s. cianfrusaglie.
knife s. (*pl.* knives) **1.** coltello **2.** bisturi || *pen-* —, temperino; *pruning-* —, falcetto || — -*grinder*, arrotino.
to **knife** vt. **1.** tagliare **2.** accoltellare.
knight s. cavaliere.
knighthood s. **1.** rango di cavaliere **2.** cavalleria.
knightliness s. cavalleria.
knightly agg. cavalleresco. ♦ **knightly** avv. cavalierescamente.
to **knit** (knit, knit) (*anche reg.*) vt. **1.** lavorare a maglia **2.** corrugare **3.** unire. ♦ to **knit** (knit, knit) (*anche reg.*) vi. unirsi, saldarsi.
knitter s. **1.** magliaia **2.** telaio per maglieria.
knitting s. lavoro a maglia.
knitwear s. maglieria.
knob s. **1.** protuberanza **2.** pomo, manopola.
knobby agg. nodoso.
knock s. **1.** colpo **2.** (*mecc.*) battito in testa.
to **knock** vt. urtare. ♦ to **knock** vi. **1.** bussare **2.** detonare || *to* — *down*, abbattere; *to* — *out*, soppraffare.
knocker s. battente.
knot s. **1.** nodo **2.** coccarda **3.** gruppo **4.** difficoltà.
to **knot** vt. annodare. ♦ to **knot** vi. annodarsi.
knottiness s. **1.** nodosità **2.** (*fig.*) difficoltà.
knotty agg. **1.** nodoso **2.** (*fig.*) difficile.
to **know** (knew, known) vt. **1.** conoscere **2.** sapere **3.** riconoscere || *to* — *of*, aver sentito parlare di; *to* — *about*, essere al corrente di.
knowable agg. **1.** comprensibile **2.** riconoscibile.
knowing agg. **1.** intelligente **2.** istruito.
knowledge s. conoscenza.
known V. *to know.*
knuckle s. articolazione, nocca || — -*duster*, pugno di ferro.
to **knuckle** vi. **1.** (*fig.*) cedere **2.** applicarsi || *to* — *under*, sottomettersi.

knurl s. zigrinatura.
to knurl vt. zigrinare.
Korean agg. e s. coreano.

L

la s. (mus.) la.
label s. etichetta.
to label vt. 1. mettere l'etichetta a 2. classificare.
labial agg. e s. labiale.
laboratory s. laboratorio.
laborious agg. laborioso.
laboriousness s. laboriosità.
labour s. 1. lavoro, fatica 2. mano d'opera 3. doglie (pl.) || hard —, lavori forzati; — party, partito laborista.
to labour vi. 1. lavorare, faticare 2. avere le doglie. ♦ **to labour** vt. elaborare, sviluppare.
laboured agg. 1. elaborato 2. penoso.
labourer s. lavoratore.
labouring agg. laborioso.
labourism s. laburismo.
labourist s. laburista.
labyrinth s. labirinto.
lace s. 1. laccio 2. pizzo 3. passamaneria.
to lace vt. 1. allacciare 2. guarnire con merletti, galloni.
to lacerate vt. lacerare.
lachrymal agg. lacrimale.
lachrymator s. gas lacrimogeno.
lack s. mancanza.
to lack vt. mancare di. ♦ **to lack** vi. mancare, scarseggiare.
lacker s. 1. lacca 2. oggetto laccato.
to lacker vt. laccare.
laconic(al) agg. laconico.
to lacquer V. to lacker.
lactation s. 1. lattazione 2. allattamento.
lacteal, lacteous agg. latteo.
lactose s. lattosio.
lacunar agg. lacunoso. ♦ **lacunar** s. soffitto a cassettoni.
lacustrine agg. lacustre.
lacy agg. simile a pizzo.
lad s. ragazzo.
ladder s. 1. scala a pioli 2. smagliatura.
to ladder vt. munire di scala. ♦ to

ladder vi. smagliarsi.
to lade (laded, laden) vt. caricare.
laden agg. (fig.) oppresso.
lading s. carico: bill of —, polizza di carico.
ladle s. mestolo.
to ladle vt. versare con un mestolo.
lady s. signora || Our Lady, la Madonna; — doctor, dottoressa.
ladybird s. coccinella.
ladykiller s. (fam.) dongiovanni.
ladylike agg. signorile, raffinato.
ladyship s. 1. rango di nobildonna 2. Signoria.
lag s. ritardo, rallentamento.
to lag vi. ritardare, restare indietro.
laggard agg. e s. pigro.
lagoon s. laguna.
to laicize vt. laicizzare.
laid V. to lay.
lain V. to lie.
lair s. tana.
laity s. 1. i laici 2. i profani.
lake s. lago.
laky agg. lacustre.
lamb s. agnello.
lambent agg. 1. lambente 2. scintillante.
lame agg. 1. zoppo 2. (fig.) debole (di argomenti).
to lame vt. storpiare.
lamellar agg. lamellare.
lameness s. 1. zoppaggine 2. imperfezione.
lament s. lamento.
to lament vt. lamentare. ♦ **to lament** vi. lamentarsi.
lamentable agg. lamentevole.
lamentation s. lamento.
lamented agg. 1. deplorato 2. compianto.
to laminate vt. laminare.
lamination s. 1. laminazione 2. lamina.
lamp s. lampada || — -black, nerofumo; — -shade, paralume.
lamplight s. luce artificiale.
lampoon s. libello.
lamprey s. lampreda.
lance s. 1. lancia 2. fiocina.
to lance vt. (med.) incidere.
lancer s. lanciere.
lancet s. bisturi.
land s. 1. terra 2. paese, contrada 3. campagna, terreno || — -surveying, agrimensura; — surveyor, agrimensore.
to land vi. 1. sbarcare 2. atterrare. ♦ **to land** vt. 1. sbarcare 2. de-

porre **3.** prendere possesso di.
landed *agg.* fondiario.
landing *s.* **1.** sbarco **2.** atterraggio
3. pianerottolo || — *-stage,* pontile di sbarco; — *-strip,* pista d'atterraggio.
landlady *s.* **1.** padrona di casa **2.**
albergatrice.
landless *agg.* senza terreni.
landlord *s.* **1.** padrone di casa, di
terra **2.** albergatore.
landmark *s.* **1.** punto di riferimento **2.** pietra miliare.
landowner *s.* proprietario terriero.
landscape *s.* paesaggio || — *-painter,* paesaggista.
landslide, landslip *s.* frana.
lane *s.* **1.** viottolo, vicolo **2.** (*mar.*)
rotta **3.** corsia (*di strada*).
language *s.* linguaggio.
languid *agg.* languido.
languish *s.* languore.
to **languish** *vi.* languire.
languor *s.* languore.
languorous *agg.* languido.
lank *agg.* **1.** allampanato **2.** liscio
(*di capelli*).
lanolin(e) *s.* lanolina.
lantern *s.* lanterna.
lap[1] *s.* **1.** grembo **2.** valletta **3.** lembo.
lap[2] *s.* **1.** sovrapposizione **2.** (*sport*)
giro di pista.
to **lap** *vt.* **1.** piegare **2.** avvolgere **3.**
lambire **4.** bere avidamente. ♦ to
lap *vi.* ripiegarsi.
laparotomy *s.* laparatomia.
lapel *s.* risvolto (*di giacca, soprabito*).
lapidary *agg.* lapidario. ♦ **lapidary**
s. tagliatore di pietre.
lapidation *s.* lapidazione.
Lapp *agg.* e *s.* lappone.
lappet *s.* **1.** falda **2.** lobo dell'orecchio.
lapse *s.* **1.** errore **2.** intervallo.
to **lapse** *vi.* **1.** errare **2.** scivolare.
larboard *s.* fiancata sinistra (*di
nave*).
larceny *s.* furto.
larch *s.* larice.
lard *s.* lardo.
to **lard** *vt.* **1.** ungere con lardo **2.**
lardellare.
larder *s.* dispensa.
large *agg.* **1.** largo **2.** grande, ampio
3. generoso || *at* —, in genere; *to
be at* —, essere in libertà.
largeness *s.* **1.** ampiezza, grandezza
2. generosità.

lark *s.* allodola.
laryngitis *s.* laringite.
larynx *s.* laringe.
lascivious *agg.* lascivo.
lasciviousness *s.* lascivia.
lash *s.* **1.** frusta **2.** frustata **3.** (*eye*)-
—, ciglio.
to **lash** *vt.* frustare || *to* — *at,* sferzare.
lashing *s.* **1.** frustata **2.** legatura.
lass, lassie *s.* ragazzina.
last *agg.* (*superl. di late*) **1.** ultimo
2. scorso **3.** massimo || *the* — *but
one,* il penultimo. ♦ **last** *s.* **1.** fine **2.** ultimo. ♦ **last** *avv.* **1.** ultimo
2. l'ultima volta || *at* —, alla fine.
to **last** *vi.* durare.
lasting *agg.* durevole. ♦ **lasting** *s.*
durata.
latch *s.* chiavistello.
late (**later, latter; latest, last**)
agg. **1.** tardi **2.** in ritardo **3.** tardo
4. precedente **5.** defunto. ♦ **late**
avv. **1.** tardi **2.** in ritardo.
lately *avv.* recentemente.
latent *agg.* latente.
later *agg.* (*comp. di late*) posteriore.
♦ **later** *avv.* più tardi.
lateral *agg.* laterale.
latest *agg.* (*superl. di late*) ultimo,
recentissimo || *at the* —, al più
tardi.
latex *s.* lattice.
lathe *s.* tornio.
lather *s.* schiuma.
to **lather** *vt.* insaponare. ♦ to **lather** *vi.* schiumare.
Latin *agg.* e *s.* latino.
Latinism *s.* latinismo.
Latinist *s.* latinista.
Latinity *s.* latinità.
latitude *s.* **1.** latitudine **2.** ampiezza.
latter *agg.* (*comp. di late*) **1.** posteriore **2.** ultimo **3.** secondo.
latterly *avv.* recentemente.
lattice *s.* grata, traliccio.
latticed *agg.* munito di grata.
laudable *agg.* lodevole.
laudanum *s.* laudano.
laudatory *agg.* laudatorio.
laugh *s.* risata.
to **laugh** *vi.* ridere || *to* — *at,* deridere.
laughable *agg.* comico.
laughing *s.* risata || — *-stock,* zimbello.
laughter *s.* riso || *to burst into* —,
scoppiare a ridere.

launch¹ s. varo.
launch² s. (mar.) lancia.
to launch vt. 1. lanciare 2. varare.
to launder vt. e vi. 1. fare il bucato 2. lavare e stirare.
launderette s. lavanderia con macchine automatiche.
laundress s. lavandaia.
laundry s. 1. lavanderia 2. bucato.
laureate agg. coronato d'alloro.
laurel s. lauro, alloro.
to laurel vt. coronare d'alloro.
lavatory s. gabinetto.
lavender s. lavanda.
lavish agg. prodigo.
to lavish vt. prodigare.
lavishness s. prodigalità.
law s. 1. legge 2. professione legale 3. processo, causa || — -court, tribunale; to go to —, ricorrere in giudizio.
lawful agg. 1. legale 2. legittimo.
lawfulness s. 1. legalità 2. legittimità.
lawgiver s. legislatore.
lawless agg. 1. illegale 2. sregolato.
lawn s. prato (rasato).
lawsuit s. (giur.) processo.
lawyer s. avvocato.
lax agg. allentato.
laxative agg. e s. lassativo.
laxity s. 1. negligenza 2. rilassatezza.
lay V. to lie.
lay agg. 1. laico 2. profano || — -brother, converso; — -sister, conversa. ♦ lay s. configurazione.
to lay (laid, laid) vt. 1. porre 2. deporre 3. preparare 4. calmare || to — aside, mettere da parte; to — out, stendere, spendere.
lay-by s. piazzola di sosta.
layer s. 1. strato 2. gallina che fa uova 3. (mil.) puntatore.
laying s. 1. posa 2. covata.
layoff s. stagione morta (di lavoro).
layout s. 1. esposizione 2. schema.
lazaret s. lazzaretto.
laziness s. pigrizia.
lazy agg. pigro.
lead¹ s. 1. piombo 2. grafite || red- —, minio; white- —, biacca.
lead² s. 1. comando 2. guinzaglio 3. mano (di carte).
to lead¹ vt. impiombare.
to lead² (led, led) vt. 1. condurre, capeggiare 2. indurre.
leaden agg. di piombo, plumbeo.

leader s. 1. capo 2. articolo di fondo.
leadership s. direzione.
leading¹ agg. 1. dominante 2. primo. ♦ leading s. guida.
leading² s. impiombatura.
leaf s. (pl. leaves) 1. foglia 2. foglio.
to leaf vt. sfogliare. ♦ to leaf vi. mettere le foglie.
leafless agg. senza foglie.
leaflet s. 1. fogliolina 2. volantino.
league s. lega.
to league vi. allearsi.
leak s. 1. fessura 2. (mar.) falla 3. perdita.
to leak vi. perdere || to — out, tra pelare.
leakage s. 1. colatura 2. dispersione.
leaky agg. che cola, perde.
lean¹ agg. magro, esile.
lean² s. inclinazione.
to lean (leant, leant) (anche reg.) vt. e vi. 1. pendere 2. appoggiarsi 3. sporgersi 4. inclinare.
leaning s. 1. inclinazione 2. l'appoggiarsi.
leanness s. magrezza.
leant V. to lean.
leap s. salto || — -year, anno bisestile.
to leap (leapt, leapt) (anche reg.) vt. e vi. saltare.
to learn (learnt, learnt) (anche reg.) vt. e vi. imparare, apprendere.
learned agg. colto.
learner s. allievo.
learning s. cultura.
learnt V. to learn.
lease s. 1. contratto d'affitto 2. durata (di contratto) || on —, in affitto.
to lease vt. affittare.
leash s. guinzaglio.
to leash vt. tenere al guinzaglio.
least agg. (superl. di little) il minimo. ♦ least s. (il) meno. ♦ least avv. (il) meno.
leather s. 1. cuoio 2. oggetto in cuoio || patent —, vernice.
leathern agg. di cuoio.
leave s. 1. permesso 2. congedo.
to leave (left, left) vt. lasciare. ♦ to leave (left, left) vi. partire || to — off, smettere.
leaven s. 1. lievito 2. (fig.) fermento.
to leaven vt. far lievitare.

leaves V. *leaf.*
leaving *s.* partenza.
lecherous *agg.* lascivo.
lechery *s.* lascivia.
lecture *s.* **1.** conferenza **2.** lezione **3.** rimprovero.
to **lecture** *vt.* rimproverare. ♦ to **lecture** *vi.* fare una conferenza.
lecturer *s.* **1.** conferenziere **2.** lettore universitario.
led V. *to lead.*
ledger *s.* (*comm.*) libro mastro.
lee *s.* feccia.
leech *s.* sanguisuga (*anche fig.*).
to **leer** *vt.* e *vi.* guardare di sbieco.
leeward *agg.* e *avv.* sottovento.
leeway *s.* deriva.
left *agg.* sinistro. ♦ **left** *s.* sinistra || — *-handed,* mancino.
left V. *to leave.*
leftist *s.* (*pol.*) uomo di sinistra.
leg *s.* **1.** gamba **2.** (*cuc.*) cosciotto || *to pull so.'s* —, canzonare qu.
legacy *s.* legato.
legal *agg.* legale.
legality *s.* legalità.
legalization *s.* legalizzazione.
to **legalize** *vt.* legalizzare.
legatee *s.* legatario.
legation *s.* legazione.
legend *s.* leggenda.
legendary *agg.* leggendario.
leggins *s. pl.* gambali.
legible *agg.* leggibile.
legion *s.* legione.
legionary *agg.* e *s.* legionario.
to **legislate** *vi.* fare leggi. ♦ to **legislate** *vt.* trasformare per mezzo di leggi.
legislation *s.* legislazione.
legislative *agg.* legislativo.
legislator *s.* legislatore.
legislature *s.* **1.** legislatura **2.** corpo legislativo.
legitimacy *s.* legittimità.
legitimate *agg.* legittimo.
to **legitimate** *vt.* legittimare.
legitimation *s.* legittimazione.
legume *s.* legume.
leguminous *agg.* leguminoso.
leisure *s.* **1.** agio **2.** tempo libero.
leisurely *agg.* e *avv.* con comodo.
lemon *s.* limone.
lemonade *s.* limonata.
to **lend** (**lent, lent**) *vt.* prestare.
lender *s.* prestatore.
length *s.* **1.** lunghezza **2.** durata, spazio di tempo || *at* —, alla fine.
to **lengthen** *vt.* allungare. ♦ to

lengthen *vi.* allungarsi.
lengthy *agg.* lungo, prolisso.
lenient *agg.* **1.** emolliente **2.** mite.
lenitive *agg.* e *s.* calmante.
lens *s.* **1.** (*ott.*) lente **2.** (*foto*) obiettivo.
lent V. *to lend.*
Lent *s.* quaresima.
lentil *s.* lenticchia.
leonine *agg.* leonino.
leopard *s.* **1.** leopardo **2.** gattopardo.
leper *s.* lebbroso || — *hospital,* lebbrosario.
leporine *agg.* leporino.
leprosy *s.* lebbra.
leprous *agg.* lebbroso.
lesbian *agg.* e *s.* lesbica.
lesion *s.* lesione.
less *agg.* (*comp. di* little) minore, meno. ♦ **less** *s.* meno. ♦ **less** *avv.* meno. ♦ **less** *prep.* meno.
lessee *s.* affittuario.
to **lessen** *vt.* e *vi.* diminuire.
lesser *agg.* minore.
lesson *s.* lezione.
lest *cong.* per paura che.
to **let** (**let, let**) *vt.* **1.** lasciare, permettere **2.** affittare || *to* — *in,* far entrare; *to* — *off,* lasciar andare; *to* — *out,* lasciar uscire.
lethal *agg.* letale.
lethargy *s.* letargo.
letter *s.* lettera.
lettered *agg.* **1.** letterato **2.** intestato.
lettuce *s.* lattuga.
leucocyte *s.* leucocito.
leucocythaemia, leukemia *s.* leucemia.
levant *s.* levante.
level *agg.* **1.** livellato **2.** a livello **3.** regolato. ♦ **level** *s.* **1.** livello **2.** superficie piana **3.** livella || *on a* — *with,* sullo stesso piano di.
to **level** *vt.* **1.** livellare **2.** puntare (*un'arma*).
levelling *s.* **1.** livellamento **2.** puntamento (*di arma*).
lever *s.* **1.** manubrio **2.** leva.
to **lever** *vi.* far leva.
to **levigate** *vt.* **1.** levigare **2.** polverizzare.
levigation *s.* **1.** levigazione **2.** polverizzazione.
levity *s.* leggerezza.
levy *s.* **1.** leva **2.** imposta.
to **levy** *vt.* **1.** arruolare **2.** imporre (*di tasse*).

lewd *agg.* impudico.
lewdness *s.* impudicizia.
lexical *agg.* lessicale.
lexicographer *s.* lessicografo.
lexicography *s.* lessicografia.
lexicology *s.* lessicologia.
lexicon *s.* lessico.
liability *s.* 1. obbligo 2. tendenza 3. (*giur.*) responsabilità. ♦ **liabilities** *s. pl.* passività (*sing.*).
liable *agg.* 1. soggetto a 2. (*giur.*) responsabile.
liar *s.* bugiardo.
libation *s.* libagione.
libel *s.* 1. libello 2. (*giur.*) diffamazione.
to libel *vt.* 1. scrivere un libello contro 2. (*giur.*) sporgere querela.
liberal *agg.* 1. liberale 2. umanistico. ♦ **liberal** *s.* liberale.
liberalism *s.* liberalismo.
liberalist *s.* liberalista.
liberality *s.* liberalità.
to liberalize *vt.* rendere liberale.
to liberate *vt.* liberare.
liberation *s.* liberazione.
liberator *s.* liberatore.
liberticide *s.* 1. liberticida 2. liberticidio.
libertinage *s.* libertinaggio.
libertine *agg.* e *s.* libertino.
libertinism *s.* libertinaggio.
liberty *s.* libertà.
libidinous *agg.* libidinoso.
libido *s.* libidine.
librarian *s.* bibliotecario.
library *s.* biblioteca || *film —,* cineteca; *record —,* discoteca.
lice V. *louse.*
licence *s.* licenza || *driving —,* patente automobilistica.
to license *vt.* dare una licenza a.
licensed *agg.* autorizzato.
licentious *agg.* licenzioso.
licentiousness *s.* dissolutezza.
lichen *s.* lichene.
lick *s.* leccata.
to lick *vt.* 1. leccare 2. lambire.
lid *s.* coperchio.
lie[1] *s.* menzogna || *the —,* smentita.
lie[2] *s.* posizione.
to lie[1] *vi.* mentire.
to lie[2] **(lay, lain)** *vi.* giacere, trovarsi || *to — down,* coricarsi; *to — in,* partorire.
lieutenant *s.* tenente.
life *s.* (*pl.* lives) vita || *— -belt,* cintura di salvataggio; *— preserver,* salvagente.

lifeboat *s.* lancia di salvataggio.
lifeless *agg.* senza vita.
lifelike *agg.* vivido.
lift *s.* 1. ascensore 2. passaggio (*su un veicolo*) 3. sollevamento.
to lift *vt.* 1. alzare 2. rubare. ♦ **to lift** *vi.* alzarsi.
light[1] *agg.* 1. chiaro 2. biondo 3. leggero 4. agile 5. insignificante.
light[2] *s.* 1. luce 2. fuoco 3. lampada || *traffic lights,* semaforo.
to light (lit, lit) (*anche reg.*) *vt.* 1. accendere 2. illuminare. ♦ **to light (lit, lit)** (*anche reg.*) *vi.* 1. accendersi 2. illuminarsi 3. posarsi.
to lighten *vt.* 1. alleggerire, alleviare 2. illuminare. ♦ **to lighten** *vi.* 1. alleggerirsi 2. illuminarsi 3. (*imp.*) lampeggiare.
lighter *s.* 1. accenditore 2. (*mar.*) chiatta.
lighthouse *s.* faro.
lighting *s.* 1. accensione 2. luce (*di quadro*).
lightless *agg.* oscuro.
lightness *s.* 1. leggerezza 2. gaiezza 3. illuminazione.
lightning *s.* fulmine || *— -rod,* parafulmine.
Ligurian *agg.* e *s.* ligure.
like *agg.* 1. simile 2. caratteristico di. ♦ **like** *prep.* come || *— this, — that,* così; *to feel —,* aver voglia di; *to look —,* avere l'aria di.
like *s.* simile. ♦ **likes** *s. pl.* gusti.
to like *vt.* piacere. ♦ **to like** *vi.* volere.
likelihood *s.* probabilità.
likely *agg.* 1. probabile 2. adatto. ♦ **likely** *avv.* probabilmente.
likeness *s.* 1. somiglianza 2. immagine.
likewise *avv.* 1. allo stesso modo 2. anche.
liking *s.* 1. gusto 2. preferenza.
lilac *agg.* e *s.* lilla.
lily *agg.* bianco. ♦ **lily** *s.* giglio || *water —,* ninfea.
limb *s.* 1. membro 2. ramo.
lime[1] *s.* 1. calce 2. pania.
lime[2] *s.* cedro.
lime[3] *s.* tiglio.
to lime *vt.* 1. cementare 2. invischiare.
limelight *s.* luce della ribalta.
limestone *s.* calcare.
limit *s.* limite.
to limit *vt.* limitare.

limitary *agg.* 1. limitato 2. limitativo 3. situato alla frontiera.

limitation *s.* limitazione.

limitative *agg.* limitativo.

limited *agg.* limitato || — *company*, società a responsabilità limitata; — *monarchy*, monarchia costituzionale.

limp *agg.* molle.

to limp *vi.* zoppicare.

limpid *agg.* limpido.

limpidity *s.* limpidezza.

limping *s.* zoppicamento.

line *s.* 1. linea, riga 2. ruga 3. discendenza 4. attività 5. verso 6. (*comm.*) articolo.

to line *vt.* 1. rigare 2. fiancheggiare 3. foderare || *to — up*, allineare, allinearsi.

lineage *s.* lignaggio.

lineal *agg.* in linea diretta.

lineament *s.* lineamento.

linear *agg.* lineare.

linen *agg.* di lino. ◆ **linen** *s.* 1. tela di lino 2. biancheria.

liner *s.* 1. transatlantico 2. aereo di linea.

to linger *vt.* e *vi.* indugiare.

linguist *s.* linguista.

linguistic(al) *agg.* linguistico.

linguistics *s.* linguistica.

liniment *s.* linimento.

lining *s.* 1. rigatura 2. allineamento 3. fodera 4. rivestimento.

link *s.* 1. anello 2. (*fig.*) legame || *cuff-links*, gemelli da polso.

to link *vt.* collegare. ◆ **to link** *vi.* collegarsi.

linotyping *s.* linotipia.

linotypist *s.* linotipista.

lint *s.* garza.

lintel *s.* architrave.

lion *s.* leone.

lioness *s.* leonessa.

lip *s.* 1. labbro 2. margine || — -*stick*, rossetto per labbra.

to lip *vt.* 1. toccare (*con le labbra*) 2. sussurrare.

liquefaction *s.* liquefazione.

to liquefy *vt.* liquefare. ◆ **to liquefy** *vi.* liquefarsi.

liqueur *s.* rosolio.

liquid *agg.* 1. liquido 2. chiaro 3. armonioso 4. instabile. ◆ **liquid** *s.* liquido.

to liquidate *vt.* liquidare.

liquidation *s.* liquidazione.

liquidator *s.* liquidatore.

liquor *s.* 1. liquido 2. bevanda alcolica.

liquorice *s.* liquirizia.

to lisp *vi.* parlare bleso.

lisping *agg.* bleso. ◆ **lisping** *s.* pronuncia blesa.

list[1] *s.* 1. lista 2. striscia 3. cimosa. ◆ **lists** *s. pl.* lizza (*sing.*).

list[2] *s.* (*mar.*) sbandamento.

to list[1] *vt.* elencare, catalogare.

to list[2] *vi.* (*mar.*) sbandare.

to listen *vi.* ascoltare: *to — to so.*, ascoltare qu.; *to — in*, ascoltare la radio.

listener *s.* ascoltatore.

listening *s.* ascolto.

listless *agg.* disattento.

lit V. *to light.*

litany *s.* litania.

literal *agg.* 1. letterale 2. prosaico 3. di lettera alfabetica.

literalism *s.* interpretazione letterale.

literary *agg.* letterario.

literate *agg.* e *s.* letterato.

literature *s.* letteratura.

lithe *agg.* agile.

lithograph *s.* litografia.

to lithograph *vt.* litografare.

lithographic(al) *agg.* litografico.

lithography *s.* (*arte della*) litografia.

litigant *s.* (*giur.*) contendente.

litmus *s.* tornasole.

litre *s.* litro.

litter *s.* 1. lettiga, barella 2. strame 3. rifiuti 4. figliata.

little (less, least) *agg.* 1. piccolo 2. breve 3. poco || *a —*, un po' di. ◆ **little** *s.* poco. ◆ **little** *avv.* poco || *a —*, piuttosto.

liturgic(al) *agg.* liturgico.

liturgy *s.* liturgia.

live *agg.* 1. vivo 2. ardente 3. carico (*di armi*).

to live *vi.* e *vt.* vivere, abitare.

livelihood *s.* mezzi di sussistenza.

liveliness *s.* vivacità.

lively *agg.* vivace.

liver *s.* fegato.

livery[1] *agg.* bilioso.

livery[2] *s.* 1. livrea 2. (*giur.*) passaggio di proprietà.

lives V. *life.*

livestock *s.* bestiame.

livid *agg.* livido.

living *agg.* 1. vivo 2. perfetto (*di somiglianza*). ◆ **living** *s.* 1. mezzo di mantenimento 2. vita || — -*room*, soggiorno.

lizard s. lucertola.
llama s. (zool.) lama.
load s. 1. carico, peso 2. (elettr.) carica, tensione.
to load vt. 1. caricare 2. adulterare.
loader s. caricatore.
loading s. caricamento.
loadstar s. stella polare.
loaf s. (pl. loaves) pagnotta || sugar- —, pan di zucchero.
to loaf vi. oziare.
loafer s. fannullone.
loan s. prestito: on —, a prestito.
to loan vt. prestare.
loath agg. riluttante.
to loathe vt. detestare.
loathing s. disgusto.
loathsome agg. 1. odioso 2. disgustoso.
loaves V. loaf.
lobby s. anticamera.
lobe s. lobo.
lobster s. aragosta.
local agg. e s. locale.
locality s. località.
to localize vt. localizzare.
to locate vt. 1. situare 2. individuare 3. indicare.
location s. 1. posizione 2. locazione.
lock¹ s. 1. ricciolo 2. fiocco.
lock² s. 1. serratura 2. diga 3. otturatore (di arma).
to lock vt. serrare. ◆ **to lock** vi. (mecc.) inceparsi.
locker s. armadio, bauletto a chiave.
locket s. medaglione.
lockout s. (econ.) serrata.
locomotion s. locomozione.
locomotive agg. locomotorio. ◆ **locomotive** s. locomotiva.
locust s. locusta || — -tree, carrubo, robinia.
locution s. locuzione.
lodge s. 1. loggia 2. padiglione.
to lodge vt. 1. alloggiare 2. collocare. ◆ **to lodge** vi. 1. alloggiare 2. entrare.
lodging s. alloggio, dimora.
loftiness s. 1. altezza 2. nobiltà.
lofty agg. 1. alto, elevato 2. orgoglioso, altero.
log s. ceppo || — -book, giornale di bordo.
logarithm s. logaritmo.
logic s. logica.
logical agg. logico.
logistic(al) agg. logistico.

logistics s. pl. (mil.) logistica (sing.).
logomachy s. logomachia.
loin s. lombo. ◆ **loins** s. pl. reni.
to loiter vt. sprecare (tempo ecc.). ◆ **to loiter** vi. bighellonare, oziare.
loitering s. il bighellonare, l'andare a zonzo.
Lombard agg. e s. lombardo.
Londoner s. londinese.
Londonese agg. londinese.
loneliness s. solitudine.
lonely, lonesome agg. solo, solitario.
long agg. lungo || — -distance call, telefonata interurbana. ◆ **long** s. molto tempo. ◆ **long** avv. a lungo || how —?, quanto tempo?; all day —, tutto il giorno; as — as, fino a, purché; so —!, arrivederci!; before —, tra poco.
to long vi. desiderare ardentemente: to — for sthg., desiderare ardentemente qc.
longanimity s. longanimità.
longboat s. lancia.
longevity s. longevità.
longevous agg. longevo.
longing agg. bramoso. ◆ **longing** s. brama.
longitude s. longitudine.
longitudinal agg. longitudinale.
long-sighted agg. 1. presbite 2. preveggente.
look s. sguardo. ◆ **looks** s. pl. aspetto (sing.).
to look vi. 1. sembrare 2. guardare || to — after, badare a; to — at, guardare; to — for, cercare; to — forward to, non veder l'ora di; to — like, somigliare; to — up, consultare (orario, dizionario ecc.); to — through, esaminare attentamente; to — up to, rispettare; to — down on, disprezzare.
looker-on s. spettatore.
looking-glass s. specchio.
lookout s. 1. guardia 2. vista panoramica 3. prospettiva.
loom s. telaio.
to loom vt. tessere. ◆ **to loom** vi. apparire indistintamente.
loop s. 1. cappio 2. gancio.
loophole s. feritoia.
loose agg. 1. sciolto 2. ampio 3. vago 4. licenzioso 5. allentato.
to loose vt. 1. sciogliere 2. liberare 3. lanciare.

to **loosen** *vt.* **1.** sciogliere **2.** allentare.

looseness *s.* **1.** scioltezza **2.** ampiezza **3.** libertinaggio **4.** imprecisione.

to **lop** *vt.* potare, mozzare.

loquacious *agg.* loquace.

loquacity *s.* loquacità.

lord *s.* **1.** signore **2.** Pari || — *Mayor*, sindaco.

to **lord** *vt.* dominare.

lordly *agg.* **1.** fastoso, imponente **2.** altero.

lordship *s.* signoria, autorità.

lorry *s.* autocarro.

to **lose (lost, lost)** *vt.* e *vi.* perdere.

loser *s.* perdente.

losing, loss *s.* perdita.

lost V. *to lose*.

lot *s.* **1.** sorte **2.** parte **3.** lotto (*di terreno ecc.*) || *a — of*, una quantità di.

to **lot** *vt.* lottizzare.

lotion *s.* lozione.

lottery *s.* lotteria.

loud *agg.* forte, fragoroso, rumoroso || — *-speaker*, altoparlante. ◆ **loud(ly)** *avv.* ad alta voce.

lounge *s.* **1.** atrio (*di albergo, teat. ecc.*) **2.** lo stare in ozio.

to **lounge** *vi.* bighellonare.

lounger *s.* fannullone.

louse *s.* (*pl.* lice) pidocchio.

lousy *agg.* pidocchioso.

lovable *agg.* amabile.

love *s.* amore.

to **love** *vt.* amare.

loveless *agg.* senza amore.

loveliness *s.* bellezza.

lovely *agg.* bello.

lover *s.* amante, innamorato.

loving *agg.* amoroso.

lovingness *s.* affettuosità.

low[1] *agg.* **1.** basso **2.** debole || — *-spirited*, depresso. ◆ **low** *avv.* **1.** in basso **2.** a voce bassa **3.** a basso prezzo.

low[2] *s.* muggito.

to **low** *vi.* muggire.

to **lower** *vt.* **1.** abbassare **2.** abbattere. ◆ to **lower** *vi.* abbattersi.

lowering *s.* abbassamento.

lowland *s.* pianura.

lowly *agg.* **1.** basso **2.** umile. ◆ **lowly** *avv.* umilmente.

loyal *agg.* leale.

loyalty *s.* lealtà.

lozenge *s.* **1.** (*gèom.*) rombo **2.** pastiglia.

lubber *s.* zoticone.

lubricant *agg.* e *s.* lubrificante.

to **lubricate** *vt.* lubrificare.

lubricating, lubrication *s.* lubrificazione.

lubricator *s.* lubrificatore.

lubricity *s.* **1.** viscosità **2.** (*fig.*) lascivia.

lubricous *agg.* lubrico.

lucent *agg.* lucente.

lucid *agg.* lucido, chiaro.

lucidity *s.* lucidità, chiarezza.

luck *s.* **1.** sorte **2.** fortuna || *to be in* —, *out of* —, essere fortunato, sfortunato.

luckily *avv.* fortunatamente.

luckless *agg.* sfortunato.

lucky *agg.* fortunato.

lucrative *agg.* lucrativo.

to **lucubrate** *vi.* fare delle elucubrazioni.

lucubration *s.* elucubrazione.

ludicrous *agg.* ridicolo.

ludicrousness *s.* comicità.

luggage *s.* bagaglio.

lugubrious *agg.* lugubre.

lukewarm *agg.* tiepido, apatico.

to **lull** *vt.* **1.** cullare **2.** calmare.

lullaby *s.* ninna-nanna.

lumbago *s.* lombaggine.

lumbar *agg.* lombare.

lumber *s.* **1.** cianfrusaglie (*pl.*) **2.** legname || — *-room*, ripostiglio.

to **lumber** *vt.* **1.** ammucchiare **2.** ingombrare. ◆ to **lumber** *vi.* **1.** tagliare legname **2.** muoversi pesantemente e rumorosamente.

lumbering *s.* commercio di legname.

luminary *s.* **1.** corpo luminoso **2.** luminare.

luminous *agg.* luminoso.

luminousness *s.* luminosità.

lump *s.* **1.** mucchio **2.** gonfiore **3.** zolletta **4.** (*comm.*) blocco **5.** persona goffa.

to **lump** *vt.* ammassare. ◆ to **lump** *vi.* raggrumarsi.

lumpy *agg.* **1.** granuloso **2.** increspato (*di mare*) **3.** pesante.

lunacy *s.* pazzia.

lunar *agg.* lunare.

lunatic *agg.* e *s.* pazzo.

lunation *s.* lunazione.

lunch *s.* seconda colazione, pasto del mezzogiorno.

to **lunch** *vi.* fare la seconda colazione. ◆ to **lunch** *vt.* offrire la colazione a.

luncheon s. spuntino.
lunette s. (arch.) lunetta.
lung s. polmone: *iron* —, polmone d'acciaio.
lupine s. lupino.
lure s. esca.
to **lure** vt. adescare.
lurid agg. 1. spettrale 2. orribile.
lurk s. nascondiglio.
to **lurk** vi. nascondersi.
luscious agg. 1. dolce 2. sensuale.
lust s. 1. lussuria 2. brama.
to **lust** vi. bramare: *to — for so.*, *sthg.*, bramare qu., qc.
lustful agg. 1. sensuale 2. bramoso.
lustfulness s. 1. sensualità 2. brama.
lustral agg. lustrale.
lustre[1] s. lustro, splendore.
lustre[2] s. lustro, quinquennio.
lusty agg. vigoroso, gagliardo.
lute s. liuto.
Lutheran agg. e s. luterano.
Lutheranism s. luteranesimo.
to **luxate** vt. (med.) lussare.
luxation s. lussazione.
luxuriant agg. lussureggiante.
to **luxuriate** vi. lussureggiare ‖ *to — in*, deliziarsi di.
luxurious agg. lussuoso, sontuoso.
luxury s. 1. lusso 2. oggetto di lusso.
lye s. lisciva.
lying[1] agg. bugiardo.
lying[2] agg. giacente, situato.
lymph s. linfa.
lymphatic agg. linfatico. ♦ **lymphatic** s.· vaso linfatico.
to **lynch** vt. linciare.
lynch law s. linciaggio.
lynx s. lince.
lyre s. lira.
lyric(al) agg. lirico. ♦ **lyric** s. lirica.
lyricism, lyrism s. lirismo.
lyrist s. poeta lirico.

M

macabre agg. macabro.
macaroni s. maccheroni.
macaroon s. amaretto.
mace s. mazza ‖ — *-bearer*, mazziere.
to **macerate** vt. maccrare. ♦ to

macerate vi. macerarsi.
maceration s. macerazione.
Machiavellian agg. machiavellico.
Machiavellism s. machiavellismo.
to **machinate** vt. macchinare.
machination s. macchinazione.
machine s. macchina ‖ *sewing-* —, macchina da cucire.
to **machine** vt. e vi. lavorare a macchina.
machine-gun s. mitragliatrice.
to **machine-gun** vt. mitragliare.
machine-gunner s. mitragliere.
machinery s. 1. macchinario 2. meccanismo.
machining s. lavorazione (a macchina).
machinist s. macchinista.
mackerel s. sgombro ‖ — *sky*, cielo a pecorelle.
mackintosh s. impermeabile.
macrocephalic agg. macrocefalo.
macrocosm s. macrocosmo.
macrocosmic agg. macrocosmico.
macromulecule s. macromolecola.
macroscopic agg. macroscopico.
to **maculate** vt. maculare.
maculation s. maculamento.
mad agg. 1. pazzo 2. idrofobo ‖ *to go* —, impazzire.
madam s. signora.
madcap s. scervellato.
to **madden** vt. far impazzire. ♦ to **madden** vi. diventare matto.
madding agg. folle.
made V. *to make*.
madhouse s. manicomio.
madly avv. pazzamente.
madman s. pazzo.
madness s. 1. pazzia 2. idrofobia.
madrepore s. madrepora.
madrigal s. madrigale.
Maecenas s. mecenate.
magazine s. 1. magazzino 2. rivista 3. arsenale.
maggot s. 1. bruco 2. (fig.) capriccio.
maggoty agg. 1. bacato 2. (fig.) capriccioso.
magic s. magia.
magic(al) agg. magico.
magician s. mago.
magisterial agg. 1. di magistrato 2. autoritario.
magistracy s. magistratura.
magistrate s. magistrato.
magistrature s. magistratura.
magnanimity s. magnanimità.
magnanimous agg. magnanimo.

magnesium s. magnesio.
magnet s. magnete, calamita.
magnetic(al) agg. magnetico.
magnetism s. magnetismo.
magnetization s. 1. magnetizzazione 2. forza d'attrazione.
to **magnetize** vt. magnetizzare.
magnetizer s. magnetizzatore.
magneto s. magnete.
magnetometer s. magnetometro.
magnification s. 1. esaltazione 2. ingrandimento.
magnificence s. magnificenza.
magnificent agg. magnifico.
magnifier s. 1. esaltatore 2. lente d'ingrandimento.
to **magnify** vt. 1. esaltare 2. ingrandire.
magniloquence s. magniloquenza.
magniloquent agg. magniloquente.
magnitude s. grandezza.
magpie s. gazza.
Magyar agg. e s. magiaro.
mahogany s. mogano.
maid s. 1. fanciulla 2. cameriera || old —, zitella.
maiden[1] agg. 1. vergine, puro 2. esordiente.
maiden[2] s. fanciulla || — name, nome da ragazza.
maidenhead, maidenhood s. verginità.
maidenliness s. modestia, verecondia.
maidenly agg. verginale.
maidservant s. cameriera.
maieutics s. maieutica.
maigre agg. magro.
mail s. posta || — -train, treno postale.
to **mail** vt. mandare per posta.
to **maim** vt. storpiare.
main[1] agg. 1. principale 2. vigoroso || — road, strada maestra.
main[2] s. 1. alto mare 2. l'essenziale 3. condotto principale.
mainland s. terraferma.
mainly avv. principalmente.
mainmast s. (mar.) albero maestro.
mainsail s. vela maestra.
mainspring s. molla principale.
to **maintain** vt. 1. mantenere 2. asserire.
maintenance s. 1. mantenimento 2. manutenzione 3. difesa.
maize s. granoturco.
majestic(al) agg. maestoso.
majesty s. maestà.
major agg. maggiore, principale. ◆

major s. 1. maggiorenne 2. (mil.) maggiore.
majority s. 1. maggioranza 2. maggiore età.
make s. 1. fattura 2. costituzione 3. marca.
to **make (made, made)** vt. e vi. 1. fare 2. rendere 3. fabbricare || to — for, dirigersi; to — up, preparare, truccare; to — up for, compensare per || to — oneself understood, farsi capire; to — so. confess, obbligare qu. a confessare; to — so. do what one likes, far fare a qu. ciò che si vuole.
make-believe s. finzione.
maker s. 1. creatore 2. costruttore || — -up, truccatore.
makeshift s. espediente.
make-up s. 1. composizione 2. trucco 3. (tip.) impaginazione.
making s. 1. fattura 2. formazione.
◆ **makings** s. pl. il necessario (sing.).
maladjusted agg. 1. disadatto 2. disadattato.
maladjustment s. inadattabilità.
maladministration s. cattiva amministrazione.
maladroit agg. maldestro.
malady s. malattia.
malaise s. malessere.
Malayan agg. e s. malese.
malcontent agg. e s. malcontento.
male agg. maschio, maschile. ◆
male s. maschio.
malediction s. maledizione.
malefactor s. malfattore.
malefic agg. malefico.
maleficence s. malvagità.
maleficent agg. malefico.
malevolence s. malevolenza.
malevolent agg. malevolo.
malformation s. malformazione.
malformed agg. malformato.
malice s. 1. malignità 2. astio: to bear — to so., nutrire rancore verso qu.
malicious agg. 1. maligno 2. premeditato.
malign agg. maligno.
malignancy s. malignità.
malignant agg. maligno.
malignity s. V. malignancy.
malleability s. malleabilità.
malleable agg. malleabile.
mallet s. mazzuolo.
mallow s. malva.
malnutrition s. malnutrizione.

malpractice *s.* pratica illecita.
malt *s.* malto.
Malthusian *agg.* e *s.* maltusiano.
Malthusianism *s.* maltusianesimo.
maltose *s.* maltosio.
to **maltreat** *vt.* maltrattare.
maltreatment *s.* maltrattamento.
malversation *s.* malversazione.
mama *s.* mamma.
mamma[1] *s.* mamma.
mamma[2] *s.* mammella.
mammal *s.* mammifero.
mammalian *agg.* e *s.* mammifero.
mammiferous *agg.* mammifero.
mammoth *agg.* enorme. ♦ **mammoth** *s.* mammut.
mammy *s.* mammina.
man *s.* (*pl.* men) **1.** uomo **2.** marito
|| — -*hour*, ora lavorativa; — -*of-war*, nave da guerra.
to **man** *vt.* munire, equipaggiare (*di uomini*).
manacle *s.* manetta.
to **manacle** *vt.* ammanettare.
to **manage** *vt.* **1.** dirigere **2.** maneggiare **3.** riuscire. ♦ to **manage** *vi.* destreggiarsi, cavarsela.
manageable *agg.* **1.** maneggevole **2.** fattibile.
management *s.* **1.** direzione, amministrazione **2.** abilità.
manager *s.* **1.** direttore **2.** amministratore **3.** impresario **4.** organizzatore.
manageress *s.* **1.** direttrice **2.** amministratrice.
managerial *agg.* direttivo.
managership *s.* **1.** direzione 2. amministrazione.
managing *agg.* dirigente || — *director*, consigliere delegato.
mandarin *s.* mandarino.
mandatary *s.* mandatario.
mandate *s.* mandato.
mandator *s.* mandante.
mandatory *agg.* e *s.* mandatario.
mandible *s.* mandibola.
mandolin *s.* mandolino.
mandrake *s.* mandragora.
mandrel *s.* anima metallica.
mandrill *s.* mandrillo.
mane *s.* criniera.
manful *agg.* valoroso.
manganate *s.* manganato.
mange *s.* rogna.
manger *s.* mangiatoia.
to **mangle** *vt.* **1.** lacerare **2.** storpiare.
mangy *agg.* **1.** lacero **2.** rognoso **3.** spregevole.
to **manhandle** *vt.* manovrare (*a mano*).
manhole *s.* botola.
manhood *s.* **1.** virilità **2.** vigore **3.** genere umano.
maniac *agg.* e *s.* maniaco, pazzo.
Manich(a)eism *s.* manicheismo.
manicurist *s.* manicure.
manifest *agg.* manifesto.
to **manifest** *vt.* manifestare.
manifestant *s.* manifestante.
manifestation *s.* manifestazione.
manifold *agg.* molteplice.
manifoldness *s.* molteplicità.
manikin *s.* **1.** omiciattolo **2.** manichino.
maniple *s.* manipolo.
to **manipulate** *vt.* manipolare.
manipulation *s.* manipolazione.
manipulator *s.* manipolatore.
mankind *s.* umanità.
manlike *agg.* **1.** civile **2.** antropomorfo.
manliness *s.* virilità.
manly *agg.* maschio, virile.
manner *s.* **1.** maniera **2.** contegno.
♦ **manners** *s. pl.* **1.** modi **2.** usanze.
mannered *agg.* manierato || *ill-* —, maleducato.
mannerism *s.* manierismo.
mannerly *agg.* cortese.
manoeuvrable *agg.* manovrabile.
manoeuvre *s.* manovra.
to **manoeuvre** *vt.* manovrare. ♦ to **manoeuvre** *vi.* fare le manovre.
manoeuvrer *s.* stratega.
manometer *s.* manometro.
manor *s.* feudo || — -*house*, castello.
manorial *agg.* feudale.
mansard *s.* mansarda.
manservant *s.* domestico.
mansion *s.* palazzo.
manslaughter *s.* omicidio preterintenzionale.
mantelpiece, mantelshelf *s.* mensola di caminetto.
mantle *s.* manto, mantello.
to **mantle** *vt.* ammantare. ♦ to **mantle** *vi.* coprirsi.
manual *agg.* e *s.* manuale.
manufactory *s.* fabbrica.
manufacturable *agg.* fabbricabile.
manufacture *s.* **1.** manifattura **2.** manufatto.
to **manufacture** *vt.* fabbricare.
manufacturer *s.* fabbricante.

manufacturing *agg.* manifatturiero. ♦ **manufacturing** *s.* fabbricazione.
manure *s.* concime.
manuscript *agg.* e *s.* manoscritto.
many (more, most) *agg.* e *pron.* molti || — *a*, più di uno; — -*sided*, molteplice; *so* —, tanti; *too* —, troppi; *as* — *as*, tanti... quanti; *how* —?, quanti?
map *s.* carta geografica.
maple *s.* acero.
to **mar** *vt.* guastare.
marathon *s.* maratona.
to **maraud** *vt.* e *vi.* saccheggiare.
marauder *s.* predatore.
marble *s.* 1 marmo 2. biglia.
to **marble** *vt.* marmorizzare.
marble-cutter *s.* marmista.
March *s.* marzo.
march[1] *s.* confine.
march[2] *s.* marcia.
to **march** *vi.* 1. camminare 2. marciare || *to* — *in*, entrare marciando.
marching *agg.* in, di marcia.
marchioness *s.* marchesa.
mare *s.* cavalla.
margarine *s.* margarina.
margin *s.* margine.
marginal *agg.* marginale.
marine *agg.* marino, marittimo. ♦ **marine** *s.* 1. marina 2. fante di marina.
marital *agg.* maritale.
maritime *agg.* marittimo.
mark *s.* 1. segno 2. bersaglio 3. voto 4. marchio 5. importanza 6. marco || *question* —, punto interrogativo.
to **mark** *vt.* 1. segnare 2. dare i voti a 3. scegliere 4. osservare.
marked *agg.* notevole.
marker *s.* 1. chi segna 2. segnalibro.
market *s.* mercato.
to **market** *vt.* 1. vendere al mercato 2. introdurre sul mercato. ♦ to **market** *vi.* comprare, vendere sul mercato.
marketing *s.* 1. compra-vendita 2. « marketing » (*ricerche di mercato*).
marking *s.* segno.
marksman *s.* tiratore scelto.
marl *s.* marna.
marmalade *s.* marmellata (*d'arance*).
marmoreal *agg.* marmoreo.
marmot *s.* marmotta.

to **maroon** *vt.* abbandonare un luogo deserto.
marquee *s.* tendone.
marquess, marquis *s.* marchese.
marquise *s.* marchesa.
marriage *s.* matrimonio, unione.
married *agg.* 1. sposato 2. coniugale.
marrow *s.* midollo || (*vegetable*) —, zucca.
to **marry** *vt.* sposare. ♦ to **marry** *vi.* sposarsi.
marsh *s.* palude || — -*fever*, malaria; — *gas*, metano.
marshal *s.* maresciallo.
to **marshal** *vt.* 1. schierare 2. introdurre.
marshy *agg.* paludoso.
marsupial *agg.* e *s.* marsupiale.
marten *s.* martora.
martial *agg.* 1. marziale 2. di Marte.
Martian *agg.* e *s.* marziano.
martyr *s.* martire.
martyrdom *s.* martirio.
to **martyrize** *vt.* martirizzare.
martyrology *s.* martirologio.
marvel *s.* meraviglia.
to **marvel** *vi.* meravigliarsi.
marvellous *agg.* meraviglioso.
Marxism *s.* marxismo.
Marxist *agg.* e *s.* marxista.
marzipan *s.* marzapane.
mascot(te) *s.* mascotte.
masculine *agg.* e *s.* maschile.
masculinity *s.* mascolinità.
mash *s.* 1. mistura 2. puré.
to **mash** *vt.* 1. mescolare 2. schiacciare.
mask *s.* maschera.
to **mask** *vt.* mascherare.
masking *s.* il mascherarsi.
masochism *s.* masochismo.
mason *s.* muratore || *Free Mason*, massone.
masonry *s.* 1. arte del muratore 2. costruzione in muratura 3. massoneria.
masquerade *s.* mascherata.
to **masquerade** *vi.* 1. mascherarsi 2. fingersi.
mass[1] *s.* messa.
mass[2] *s.* massa, ammasso.
to **mass** *vt.* ammassare. ♦ to **mass** *vi.* ammassarsi.
massacre *s.* massacro.
to **massacre** *vt.* massacrare.
massage *s.* massaggio.
to **massage** *vt.* massaggiare.

masseur s. massaggiatore.
masseuse s. massaggiatrice.
massif s. massiccio.
massive agg. **1.** massiccio **2.** potente.
massiveness s. compattezza.
to **mass-produce** vt. produrre in serie.
mass-producer s. produttore in serie.
mass-production s. produzione in serie.
massy agg. massiccio.
mast s. (mar.) albero.
to **mast** vt. (mar.) alberare.
master s. **1.** padrone **2.** maestro ||
— builder, capomastro; Master of Arts, laureato in lettere.
to **master** vt. **1.** conoscere a fondo **2.** dominare.
masterful agg. **1.** autoritario **2.** abile.
masterhood s. padronanza.
masterly agg. magistrale.
masterpiece s. capolavoro.
mastership s. **1.** autorità **2.** abilità.
masterstroke s. colpo magistrale.
mastery s. **1.** maestria **2.** signoria.
mastication s. masticazione.
mastiff s. mastino.
mastitis s. mastite.
mastodon s. mastodonte.
mastoid s. mastoide.
mastoiditis s. mastoidite.
masturbation s. masturbazione.
mat s. stuoia || door- —, zerbino.
to **mat** vt. **1.** intrecciare **2.** coprire con stuoie **3.** smerigliare.
match[1] s. **1.** gara, incontro **2.** avversario **3.** l'uguale **4.** matrimonio.
match[2] s. fiammifero.
to **match** vt. **1.** accoppiare, maritare **2.** uguagliare. ♦ to **match** vi. **1.** accoppiarsi **2.** accordarsi **3.** rivaleggiare.
matchless agg. impareggiabile.
mate s. **1.** compagno **2.** aiuto **3.** (mar.) ufficiale in seconda.
to **mate** vt. accoppiare. ♦ to **mate** vi. accoppiarsi.
material agg. **1.** materiale **2.** essenziale. ♦ **material** s. **1.** materia, materiale **2.** stoffa. ♦ **materials** s. pl. articoli || raw —, materie prime.
materialism s. materialismo.
materialist agg. e s. materialista.
materialistic agg. materialistico.

materialization s. materializzazione.
to **materialize** vt. materializzare.
♦ to **materialize** vi. **1.** materializzarsi **2.** avverarsi.
maternal agg. materno.
maternity s. maternità.
mathematic(al) agg. matematico.
mathematician s. matematico.
mathematics s. matematica.
matriarchy s. matriarcato.
matricidal agg. matricida.
matricide s. **1.** matricida **2.** matricidio.
to **matriculate** vt. immatricolare.
♦ to **matriculate** vi. immatricolarsi.
matriculation s. immatricolazione.
matrimonial agg. matrimoniale.
matrimony s. matrimonio.
matrix s. **1.** matrice **2.** (anat.) utero.
matron s. **1.** matrona **2.** direttrice **3.** governante.
matronal, matronly agg. matronale.
matter s. **1.** materia **2.** faccenda ||
what is the — with you?, che cosa vi succede?; what is the —?, che succede?
to **matter** vi. **1.** importare: it matters little, poco importa **2.** (med.) suppurare.
matter-of-fact agg. pratico.
matting s. stuoia.
mattock s. piccone.
mattress s. materasso.
to **maturate** vi. **1.** maturare **2.** suppurare.
maturation s. **1.** maturazione **2.** suppurazione.
mature agg. maturo.
to **mature** vt. e vi. maturare.
maturity s. **1.** maturità **2.** (comm.) scadenza.
matutine agg. mattutino.
maudlin agg. **1.** sdolcinato **2.** querulo.
to **maunder** vi. **1.** parlare a vanvera **2.** girovagare.
mausoleum s. mausoleo.
mawkish agg. **1.** nauseante **2.** sdolcinato.
mawkishness s. **1.** sapore nauseante **2.** sdolcinatezza.
maxim s. massima.
maximalist s. massimalista.
maximum agg. e s. massimo.
May s. maggio || — Day, primo maggio.

may (might) *v. dif.* potere (*pres. ind. e congiuntivo*) || — *I go out?*, posso uscire?; *he* — *arrive to day*, può darsi che arrivi oggi; — *he live to repent it*, possa egli vivere tanto da pentirsene
maybe *avv.* forse.
maybug *s.* maggiolino.
mayflower *s.* biancospino.
mayonnaise *s.* maionese.
mayor *s.* sindaco.
maze *s.* labirinto.
to maze *vt.* disorientare, confondere.
mazily *avv.* confusamente.
mazy *agg.* intricato.
me *pron. pers.* me, mi.
meadow *s.* prato.
meagre *agg.* 1. magro 2. scarso.
meal[1] *s.* farina.
meal[2] *s.* pasto.
mealy *agg.* 1. farinoso 2. infarinato 3. pallido 4. chiazzato.
mean[1] *agg.* 1. meschino 2. mediocre.
mean[2] *s.* punto medio, mezzo. ♦ **means** *s. pl.* mezzi || *by no means*, ben lungi da.
to mean (meant, meant) *vt. e vi.* 1. intendere, significare 2. destinare.
meander *s.* meandro.
to meander *vi.* serpeggiare.
meaning *agg.* 1. disposto 2. significativo. ♦ **meaning** *s.* 1. significato 2. idea.
meaningful *agg.* significativo.
meaningless *agg.* senza senso.
meanly *avv.* 1. meschinamente 2. umilmente.
meanness *s.* meschinità.
meant V. *to mean.*
meantime *s.* frattempo. ♦ **meantime** *avv.* frattanto.
meanwhile *avv.* frattanto.
measles *s.* morbillo || *German* —, rosolia.
measurable *agg.* misurabile.
measure *s.* 1. misura 2. ritmo.
to measure *vt. e vi.* misurare.
measureless *agg.* smisurato.
measurement *s.* misurazione.
measurer *s.* misuratore.
meat *s.* carne.
meaty *agg.* 1. polposo 2. sostanzioso.
mechanic *s.* meccanico.
mechanical *agg.* meccanico.
mechanics *s.* meccanica.
mechanism *s.* 1. meccanismo 2.

tecnica.
mechanization *s.* meccanizzazione.
to mechanize *vt.* meccanizzare.
medal *s.* medaglia.
to meddle *vi.* immischiarsi.
meddler *s.* intrigante.
meddlesome *agg.* importuno.
medi(a)eval *agg.* medievale.
medi(a)evalism *s.* medievalismo.
medi(a)evalist *s.* medievalista.
medial *agg.* medio.
median *agg.* mediano.
mediate *agg.* mediato.
to mediate *vt.* conseguire con mediazione. ♦ **to mediate** *vi.* fare da intermediario.
mediation *s.* mediazione.
mediator *s.* mediatore.
medical *agg.* medico.
medicament *s.* medicamento.
medication *s.* medicazione.
medicative *agg.* curativo.
medicinal *agg.* medicinale.
medicine *s.* medicina || — *-man*, stregone.
mediocrity *s.* mediocrità.
to meditate *vt. e vi.* meditare.
meditation *s.* meditazione.
meditative *agg.* meditativo.
Mediterranean *agg.* mediterraneo.
medium *agg.* medio. ♦ **medium** *s.* mezzo.
mediumistic *agg.* medianico.
medlar *s.* nespola || — *-tree*, nespolo.
medley *agg.* misto. ♦ **medley** *s.* miscuglio.
medulla *s.* midollo.
medullar(y) *agg.* midollare.
meek *agg.* mite.
meekness *s.* mansuetudine.
to meet (met, met) *vt.* 1. incontrare 2. far fronte a. ♦ **to meet (met, met)** *vi.* incontrarsi || *to* — *with*, imbattersi in.
meeting *s.* 1. incontro 2. riunione || *political* —, comizio.
megalomaniac *s.* megalomane.
megaphone *s.* megafono.
melancholic *agg.* malinconico.
melancholy *agg.* malinconico. ♦ **melancholy** *s.* malinconia.
mellifluous *agg.* mellifluo.
mellow *agg.* 1. maturo 2. pastoso 3. ubertoso.
to mellow *vt. e vi.* maturare.
mellowness *s.* 1. maturità 2. pastosità 3. ubertosità.
melodic *agg.* melodico.

melodious *agg.* melodioso.
melodiousness *s.* melodiosità.
melodrama *s.* melodramma.
melodramatic *agg.* melodrammatico.
melody *s.* melodia.
melomaniac *s.* melomane.
melon *s.* melone || *water-* —, anguria.
melt *s.* fusione.
to **melt** *vt.* **1.** sciogliere **2.** intenerire. ♦ to **melt** *vi.* **1.** sciogliersi **2.** intenerirsi || *to* — *away*, svanire.
melter *s.* fonditore.
melting *s.* fusione || — *-pot*, crogiuolo.
meltingly *avv.* teneramente.
member *s.* membro.
membership *s.* **1.** qualifica di membro **2.** i membri.
membrane *s.* membrana.
memoirs *s. pl.* memorie.
memorable *agg.* memorabile.
memorandum *s.* (*pl.* -da) promemoria.
memorial *agg.* commemorativo. ♦ **memorial** *s.* **1.** monumento **2.** memoriale.
memorialist *s.* memorialista.
to **memorize** *vt.* imparare a memoria.
memory *s.* memoria.
men V. *man*.
menace *s.* minaccia.
to **menace** *vt.* e *vi.* minacciare.
menacing *agg.* minaccioso.
menagerie *s.* serraglio.
mend *s.* rattoppo.
to **mend** *vt.* **1.** riparare **2.** correggere. ♦ to **mend** *vi.* **1.** correggersi **2.** migliorare.
mendacious *agg.* mendace.
mendacity *s.* **1.** abitudine di mentire **2.** bugia.
mender *s.* **1.** riparatore **2.** rammendatrice.
mendicant *agg.* e *s.* mendicante.
mendicity *s.* mendicità.
mending *s.* **1.** riparazione **2.** rammendo.
menial *agg.* servile. ♦ **menial** *s.* servo.
meninx *s.* (*pl.* meninges) meninge.
meniscus *s.* menisco.
menopause *s.* menopausa.
menses *s. pl.* mestruazioni.
menstruation *s.* mestruazione.
mental *agg.* mentale || — *-hospi-tal*, manicomio.

mentality *s.* **1.** mentalità **2.** intelligenza.
menthol *s.* mentolo.
mention *s.* menzione || *don't* — *it*, non c'è di che (*risposta a* « *grazie* »).
to **mention** *vt.* nominare.
mentionable *agg.* menzionabile.
mentor *s.* mentore.
mephitic *agg.* mefitico.
mercantile *agg.* mercantile.
mercantilism *s.* mercantilismo.
mercenary *agg.* e *s.* mercenario.
merchandise *s.* merce.
to **merchandise** *vt.* e *vi.* commerciare.
merchant *s.* mercante || — *ship*, nave mercantile.
merciful *agg.* pietoso.
merciless *agg.* spietato.
mercury *s.* mercurio.
mercy *s.* pietà, misericordia.
mere[1] *agg.* **1.** mero **2.** solo.
mere[2] *s.* confine.
mere[3] *s.* laghetto, stagno.
to **merge** *vt.* assorbire. ♦ to **merge** *vi.* **1.** essere assortito **2.** immergersi.
merger *s.* (*comm.*) fusione (*di società*).
meridian *agg.* **1.** meridiano **2.** culminante. ♦ **meridian** *s.* **1.** meridiano **2.** culmine.
meridional *agg.* e *s.* meridionale.
merit *s.* merito.
to **merit** *vt.* meritare.
meritorious *agg.* meritorio.
mermaid *s.* sirena.
merman *s.* tritone.
merrily *avv.* allegramente.
merry *agg.* gaio.
merry-go-round *s.* giostra.
merrymaking *s.* festa.
mesh *s.* maglia. ♦ **meshes** *s. pl.* reti.
mesocarp *s.* mesocarpo.
mesozoic *agg.* e *s.* mesozoico.
mess *s.* **1.** mensa **2.** confusione **3.** pasticcio.
to **mess** *vt.* mettere in disordine || *to* — *up*, mettere a soqquadro.
message *s.* **1.** messaggio **2.** commissione.
messenger *s.* messaggero || — *-boy*, fattorino.
Messiah *s.* Messia.
Messianic *agg.* messianico.
mestizo *s.* meticcio.

met V. *to meet*.
metabolism *s*. metabolismo.
metal *s*. **1.** metallo **2.** pietrisco.
metallic *agg*. metallico.
metallization *s*. metallizzazione.
to **metallize** *vt*. metallizzare.
metalloid *s*. metalloide.
metallurgic(al) *agg*. metallurgico.
metallurgist *s*. metallurgico.
metallurgy *s*. metallurgia.
metamorphic *agg*. metamorfico.
metamorphism *s*. metamorfismo.
metamorphosis *s*. (*pl*. -ses) metamorfosi.
metaphor *s*. metafora.
metaphoric(al) *agg*. metaforico.
metaphysic(al) *agg*. metafisico.
metaphysics *s*. metafisica.
metapsychic(al) *agg*. metapsichico.
metapsychics *s*. metapsichica.
metastasis *s*. (*pl*. -ses) metastasi.
metayage *s*. mezzadria.
metayer *s*. mezzadro.
mete *s*. segno di confine ‖ *metes and bounds* (*giur*.), limiti e confini.
metempsychosis *s*. metempsicosi.
meteor *s*. meteora.
meteoric *agg*. **1.** meteorico **2.** transitorio.
meteoroid *s*. meteorite.
meteorologic(al) *agg*. meteorologico.
meteorologist *s*. meteorologo.
meteorology *s*. meteorologia.
meter *s*. **1.** contatore **2.** tassametro.
methane *s*. metano.
method *s*. metodo.
methodic(al) *agg*. metodico.
methodist *s*. metodista.
methodological *agg*. metodologico.
methodology *s*. metodologia.
meticulosity *s*. meticolosità.
meticulous *agg*. meticoloso.
metre *s*. **1.** metro **2.** (*mus*.) tempo.
metrical *agg*. metrico.
metrics *s*. metrica.
metronome *s*. metronomo.
metropolis *s*. metropoli.
metropolitan *agg*. metropolitano.
♦ **metropolitan** *s*. abitante di una metropoli.
mettle *s*. tempra.
mettled, mettlesome *agg*. focoso.
mew[1] *s*. gabbiano.
mew[2] *s*. miagolio.
to **mew**[1] *vt*. rinchiudere in gabbia.
to **mew**[2] *vi*. miagolare.
to **mewl** *vi*. vagire.

Mexican *agg*. e *s*. messicano.
mezzanine *s*. mezzanino.
miaul *s*. miagolio.
mice V. *mouse*.
microbe *s*. microbo.
microbial *agg*. microbico.
microbiology *s*. microbiologia.
microcosm *s*. microcosmo.
micrometer *s*. micrometro.
micrometry *s*. micrometria.
micro-organism *s*. microorganismo.
microphone *s*. microfono.
microphotography *s*. microfotografia.
microscope *s*. microscopio.
microscopic(al) *agg*. microscopico.
microscopy *s*. microscopia.
mid *agg*. medio, mezzo.
midday *s*. mezzogiorno.
middle *agg*. medio ‖ *Middle Ages*, medioevo; — *-aged*, di mezza età.
♦ **middle** *s*. **1.** mezzo **2.** cintola.
middle class *s*. borghesia.
middleman *s*. intermediario.
middling *agg*. medio.
midge *s*. moscerino.
midget *s*. nano.
midland *agg*. centrale. ♦ **midlands** *s*. *pl*. regione centrale (*sing*.).
midnight *s*. mezzanotte.
midriff *s*. **1.** diaframma **2.** costume da bagno a due pezzi.
midshipman *s*. guardiamarina.
midst *s*. mezzo.
midsummer *s*. solstizio d'estate.
midway *agg*. e *avv*. a mezza strada.
mid-week *agg*. di metà settimana.
midwife *s*. (*pl*. -wives) levatrice.
midwinter *s*. solstizio d'inverno.
mien *s*. portamento.
might *s*. potenza.
might V. *may*.
mighty *agg*. potente.
migrant *agg*. e *s*. migratore.
to **migrate** *vi*. (e)migrare.
migration *s*. (e)migrazione.
migratory *agg*. migratore.
milady *s*. nobildonna.
mild *agg*. dolce.
mildew *s*. muffa.
mildness *s*. dolcezza.
mile *s*. miglio.
milestone *s*. pietra miliare.
milfoil *s*. millefoglio.
miliary *agg*. migliare.
militant *agg*. militante. ♦ **militant** *s*. attivista.

militarily *avv.* militarmente.
militarism *s.* militarismo.
militarist *s.* militarista.
militarization *s.* militarizzazione.
to **militarize** *vt.* militarizzare.
military *agg.* e *s.* militare.
militiaman *s.* milite.
milk *s.* latte || — *-jug,* lattiera.
to **milk** *vt.* mungere. ♦ to **milk** *vi.*
1. produrre latte 2. mungere.
milker *s.* 1. mungitore 2. mucca da
latte.
milking *s.* mungitura.
milkmaid *s.* mungitrice.
milkman *s.* lattaio.
milky *agg.* 1. latteo 2. (*fig.*) genti-
le || *the Milky Way,* la Via Lat-
tea.
mill *s.* 1. mulino 2. macinino 3. fab-
brica || *saw-* —, segheria.
to **mill** *vt.* 1. macinare 2. segare 3.
frullare.
millenary *agg.* millenario. ♦ **millenary** *s.* 1. millennio 2. millenario.
millennium *s.* millennio.
millepede *s.* millepiedi.
miller *s.* 1. mugnaio 2. fresatore 3.
fresa.
millet *s.* (*bot.*) miglio.
milliard *s.* 1. miliardo 2. (*amer.*)
bilione.
milligram(me) *s.* milligrammo.
millimetre *s.* millimetro.
milliner *s.* modista.
millinery *s.* modisteria.
milling *s.* 1. macinatura 2. fresa-
tura.
million *s.* milione.
millionaire *s.* milionario.
millstone *s.* macina.
mime *s.* mimo.
to **mime** *vi.* e *vt.* mimare.
to **mimeograph** *vt.* ciclostilare.
mimetic *agg.* mimetico.
mimic *agg.* imitativo || — *art,* mi-
mica. ♦ **mimic** *s.* imitatore.
to **mimic (mimicked, mimicked)**
vt. imitare.
mimicry *s.* 1. imitazione 2. mimetismo.
minaret *s.* minareto.
minatory *agg.* minatorio.
mince *s.* carne tritata.
to **mince** *vt.* 1. tritare 2. tagliuzzare
3. mitigare. ♦ to **mince** *vi.* camminare, parlare in modo affettato.
mincer *s.* tritacarne.
mincing *agg.* affettato.

mind *s.* 1. mente 2. opinione.
to **mind** *vt.* 1. badare a 2. spiacere
|| *never* —!, non importa!; *I do
not* —, non mi preoccupo di.
minded *agg.* incline || *broad-* —, di
larghe vedute; *narrow-* —, di idee
ristrette || *if you are so* —, se la
pensate così.
mindful *agg.* memore.
mindless *agg.* 1. disattento 2. stupido.
mine[1] *pron. poss.* il mio, la mia, i
miei, le mie || *a friend of* —, un
mio amico.
mine[2] *s.* 1. miniera 2. mina || —
-sweeper, dragamine.
to **mine** *vt.* 1. scavare 2. estrarre 3.
minare.
miner *s.* minatore.
mineral *agg.* e *s.* minerale.
to **mineralize** *vt.* mineralizzare.
mineralogy *s.* mineralogia.
to **mingle** *vt.* mescolare. ♦ to **mingle** *vi.* mescolarsi.
miniature *agg.* in miniatura. ♦
miniature *s.* miniatura.
to **miniature** *vt.* e *vi.* fare miniature.
miniaturist *s.* miniaturista.
minim *s.* 1. (*mus.*) minima 2. quantità minima 3. inezia.
minimal *agg.* minimo.
to **minimize** *vt.* minimizzare.
minimum *s.* (*pl.* -ma) minimo.
mining *agg.* minerario. ♦ **mining**
s. 1. scavo 2. estrazione 3. posa
di mine.
minion *s.* favorito.
miniskirt *s.* minigonna.
minister *s.* ministro.
to **minister** *vi.* assistere.
ministerial *agg.* ministeriale.
ministry *s.* ministero.
mink *s.* visone.
minor *agg.* minore. ♦ **minor** *s.*
minorenne.
minority *s.* 1. minoranza 2. età minore.
minstrel *s.* menestrello.
mint[1] *s.* zecca.
mint[2] *s.* menta.
to **mint** *vt.* coniare.
mintage *s.* conio.
minuend *s.* minuendo.
minuet *s.* minuetto.
minus *s.* e *prep.* meno.
minute *agg.* minuto, minuscolo.
minute *s.* 1. minuto 2. nota || —
-hand, lancetta dei minuti.

minutely[1] *avv.* minutamente.
minutely[2] *avv.* di minuto in minuto.
minuteness *s.* **1.** minutezza **2.** minuziosità.
miracle *s.* miracolo.
miraculous *agg.* miracoloso.
mirage *s.* miraggio.
mire *s.* fango.
to mire *vt.* infangare. ♦ **to mire** *vi.* infangarsi.
mirror *s.* specchio || *driving-* —, specchietto retrovisore.
to mirror *vt.* rispecchiare.
mirth *s.* allegria.
mirthful *agg.* allegro.
mirthless *agg.* triste.
miry *agg.* fangoso.
misadventure *s.* disavventura.
misanthrope *s.* misantropo.
misanthropy *s.* misantropia.
misapplication *s.* applicazione erronea.
to misapply *vt.* applicare erroneamente.
misapprehension *s.* malinteso.
misbehaviour *s.* cattivo contegno.
misbelief *s.* falsa credenza.
to misbelieve *vi.* avere una falsa credenza.
misbeliever *s.* miscredente.
misbelieving *agg.* eretico.
to miscalculate *vt.* e *vi.* calcolare male.
miscarriage *s.* **1.** disguido **2.** fallimento **3.** aborto.
to miscarry *vi.* **1.** smarrirsi **2.** fallire **3.** abortire.
miscellaneous *agg.* miscellaneo.
miscellany *s.* miscellanea.
mischance *s.* sfortuna.
mischief *s.* **1.** danno, male **2.** malizia **3.** birichinata.
mischievous *agg.* **1.** nocivo **2.** malizioso.
misconduct *s.* cattiva condotta.
miscount *s.* conteggio errato.
misdeed *s.* misfatto.
misdemeanour *s.* misfatto.
to misdirect *vt.* mandare in direzione sbagliata.
misdirection *s.* indicazione sbagliata.
misdoing *s.* misfatto.
miser *s.* avaro.
miserable *agg.* **1.** triste **2.** miserabile.
miserliness *s.* avarizia.
miserly *agg.* avaro.

misery *s.* **1.** miseria **2.** sofferenza.
misfire *s.* cilecca.
misfit *s.* **1.** cosa che si adatta male **2.** (*fig.*) pesce fuor d'acqua.
misfortune *s.* sventura.
to misgive (misgave, misgiven) *vt.* preoccupare. ♦ **to misgive (misgave, misgiven)** *vi.* preoccuparsi.
misgiving *s.* **1.** presentimento **2.** timore.
to misgovern *vt.* governare male.
misgovernment *s.* malgoverno.
to misguide *vt.* **1.** guidare male **2.** traviare.
to mishandle *vt.* maltrattare.
mishap *s.* infortunio.
to misinform *vt.* informare male.
misinformation *s.* informazione sbagliata.
to misinterpret *vt.* interpretare male.
misinterpretation *s.* interpretazione errata.
to misjudge *vt.* giudicare male.
misjudgement *s.* giudizio erroneo.
to mislay (mislaid, mislaid) *vt.* smarrire.
to mislead (misled, misled) *vt.* **1.** traviare **2.** ingannare.
misogamy *s.* misogamia.
misogynist *s.* misogino.
misogyny *s.* misoginia.
misoneism *s.* misoneismo.
to misplace *vt.* collocare male, fuori posto.
misplacement *s.* spostamento.
misprint *s.* errore di stampa, refuso.
to misprint *vt.* stampare con errori.
to mispronounce *vt.* pronunciare male.
mispronunciation *s.* pronuncia scorretta.
misquotation *s.* citazione erronea.
to misquote *vt.* citare erroneamente.
to misread (misread, misread) *vt.* leggere erroneamente.
mesreading *s.* falsa interpretazione.
to misrepresent *vt.* travisare.
misrepresentation *s.* travisamento.
miss[1] *s.* **1.** colpo mancato **2.** difetto.
miss[2] *s.* signorina: *Miss Jane Smith*, la signorina Jane Smith.
to miss *vt.* **1.** mancare (*il colpo*) **2.** perdere **3.** notare, sentire la man-

canza di **4.** evitare.
missal s. messale.
missile s. missile.
missing agg. mancante || the —, i dispersi.
mission s. missione.
missionary agg. e s. missionario.
missioner s. missionario.
to **misspell** vt. sbagliare l'ortografia.
mist s. **1.** bruma **2.** pioggerella **3.** appannamento.
to **mist** vt. appannare. ♦ to **mist** vi. appannarsi.
mistakable agg. suscettibile d'errore.
mistake s. errore.
to **mistake** (**mistook, mistaken**) vt. **1.** sbagliare **2.** scambiare **3.** non capire. ·
mistaken agg. **1.** in errore **2.** erroneo.
mister s. signore: Mr. Brown, il signor Brown.
mistletoe s. vischio.
mistook V. to mistake.
mistral s. maestrale.
mistranslation s. traduzione errata.
mistress s. **1.** signora: Mrs. Brown, la signora Brown **2.** insegnante **3.** amante.
mistrust s. diffidenza.
to **mistrust** vt. e vi. diffidare di, sospettare.
mistrustful agg. diffidente.
misty agg. **1.** nebbioso **2.** confuso.
to **misunderstand** (**misunderstood, misunderstood**) vt. e vi. fraintendere.
misunderstanding s. **1.** malinteso **2.** disaccordo.
misunderstood V. to misunderstand.
misusage, misuse s. **1.** cattivo uso **2.** maltrattamento.
to **misuse** vt. **1.** usar male **2.** maltrattare.
to **miswrite** (**miswrote, miswritten**) vt. scrivere scorrettamente.
mithridatic agg. immunizzante (contro veleni).
mithridatism s. immunizzazione (contro un veleno).
to **mitigate** vt. mitigare.
mitigation s. mitigazione.
mitral agg. mitrale.
mitre s. **1.** (eccl.) mitra **2.** giunto ad angolo.

mitt(en) s. manopola, guantone.
to **mix** vt. mescolare || to — up, confondere. ♦ to **mix** vi. mescolarsi.
mixed agg. misto, eterogeneo.
mixer s. (mecc.) mescolatore.
mixing s. mescolanza.
mixture s. **1.** mescolanza **2.** miscela.
mizzen s. (mar.) mezzana.
mnemonic agg. mnemonico.
mnemonics s. mnemonica.
moan s. gemito.
to **moan** vt. e vi. gemere.
moanful agg. lamentoso.
moaning s. lamento.
moat s. fossato.
mob s. **1.** folla **2.** plebaglia.
to **mob** vt. **1.** assalire **2.** affollare.
mobile agg. **1.** mobile **2.** mutevole.
mobility s. **1.** mobilità **2.** mutevolezza.
mobilization s. mobilitazione.
to **mobilize** vt. mobilitare.
moccasin s. mocassino.
mock agg. **1.** ironico **2.** finto || —-heroic, eroicomico. ♦ **mock** s. **1.** derisione **2.** imitazione.
to **mock** vt. e vi. beffare, prendersi gioco di.
mocker s. burlone.
mockery s. **1.** derisione **2.** contraffazione.
mocking agg. beffardo.
modal agg. modale.
modality s. modalità.
model agg. modello. ♦ **model** s. **1.** modello **2.** copia.
to **model** vt. modellare.
modeller s. **1.** modellatore **2.** modellista.
modelling s. **1.** modellatura **2.** creazione di modelli.
moderate agg. e s. moderato.
to **moderate** vt. moderare. ♦ to **moderate** vi. moderarsi.
moderateness s. moderatezza.
moderation s. moderazione.
moderator s. moderatore.
modern agg. e s. moderno.
modernism s. modernismo.
modernist s. modernista.
modernity s. modernità.
modernization s. **1.** rimodernamento **2.** aggiornamento.
to **modernize** vt. modernizzare. ♦ to **modernize** vi. modernizzarsi.
modest agg. **1.** modesto **2.** pudico.

modesty *s.* **1.** modestia **2.** pudore.
modifiable *agg.* modificabile.
modification *s.* modificazione.
modifier *s.* modificatore.
to **modify** *vt.* modificare.
to **modulate** *vt.* e *vi.* modulare.
modulation *s.* modulazione.
modulator *s.* modulatore.
mofette *s.* mofeta.
Mohammedan *agg.* e *s.* maomettano.
moist *agg.* umido.
to **moisten** *vt.* inumidire. ♦ to **moisten** *vi.* inumidirsi.
moistness *s.* umidità.
moisture *s.* vapore umido.
molar *agg.* e *s.* molare.
molasses *s.* melassa.
mole[1] *s.* neo.
mole[2] *s.* talpa.
mole[3] *s.* molo.
molecular *agg.* molecolare.
molecule *s.* molecola.
moleskin *s.* **1.** pelle di talpa **2.** fustagno. ♦ **moleskins** *s. pl.* calzoni di fustagno.
to **molest** *vt.* molestare.
molestation *s.* molestia.
molester *s.* molestatore.
to **mollify** *vt.* addolcire.
mollusc *s.* mollusco.
molybdenum *s.* molibdeno.
moment *s.* **1.** momento **2.** importanza.
momentary *agg.* momentaneo.
momentous *agg.* importante.
monachal *agg.* monacale.
monad *s.* monade.
monarch *s.* monarca.
monarchic(al) *agg.* monarchico.
monarchist *s.* monarchico.
monarchy *s.* monarchia.
monastery *s.* monastero.
monastic(al) *agg.* monastico.
Monday *s.* lunedì.
monetary *agg.* monetario.
monetization *s.* monetazione.
to **monetize** *vt.* monetizzare.
money *s.* denaro || — -*bag*, portamonete; — -*order*, vaglia; *earnest* —, caparra; *paper* —, valuta cartacea; *ready* —, contanti.
moneyed *agg.* **1.** di, in denaro **2.** ricco.
moneyless *agg.* squattrinato.
monger *s.* mercante || *fish* —, pescivendolo.
Mongolian *agg.* e *s.* mongolo.
mongolism *s.* mongolismo.

mongoloid *agg.* e *s.* mongoloide.
mongrel *agg.* misto. ♦ **mongrel** *s.* **1.** bastardo **2.** incrocio.
monism *s.* monismo.
monition *s.* **1.** ammonizione **2.** (*giur.*) citazione.
monitor *s.* **1.** consigliere **2.** capoclasse **3.** dispositivo di controllo.
monitory *agg.* ammonitore.
monk *s.* monaco.
monkey *s.* scimmia.
monkeyish *agg.* scimmiesco.
monkhood *s.* monacato.
monkish *agg.* monastico, manacale.
monochromatic *agg.* monocromatico.
monochrome *s.* monocromia.
monocle *s.* monocolo.
monody *s.* monodia.
monogamist *s.* monogamo.
monogamy *s.* monogamia.
monogram *s.* monogramma.
monograph *s.* monografia.
monographic(al) *agg.* monografico.
monolith *s.* monolito.
monolithic *agg.* monolitico.
monologue *s.* monologo.
monometallic *agg.* monometallico.
monomial *s.* monomio.
monomolecular *agg.* monomolecolare.
monoplane *s.* monoplano.
monopolist *s.* monopolista.
to **monopolize** *vt.* monopolizzare.
monopoly *s.* monopolio.
monorail *s.* monorotaia.
monosyllabic *agg.* monosillabico.
monosyllable *s.* monosillabo.
monotheism *s.* monoteismo.
monotheist *s.* monoteista.
monotheistic(al) *agg.* monoteistico.
monotone *s.* tono uniforme.
monotonous *agg.* monotono.
monotony *s.* **1.** tono uniforme **2.** monotonia.
monotype *s.* monotipo.
monsoon *s.* monsone.
monster *agg.* colossale. ♦ **monster** *s.* mostro.
monstrance *s.* ostensorio.
monstrosity *s.* mostruosità.
monstrous *agg.* mostruoso.
montage *s.* montaggio.
month *s.* mese.
monthly *agg.* e *s.* mensile. ♦ **monthly** *avv.* mensilmente.
monument *s.* monumento.
monumental *agg.* monumentale.

mood *s.* **1.** umore **2.** (*gramm.*) modo.
♦ **moods** *s. pl.* capricci.
moodily *avv.* di malumore.
moodiness *s.* malumore.
moody *agg.* di malumore.
moon *s.* luna.
to **moon** *vi.* **1.** gingillarsi **2.** allunare || *to — about*, bighellonare.
mooncalf *s.* (*pl.* -lves) idiota.
mooning *s.* vagabondaggio.
moonlight *s.* chiaro di luna.
moonlit *agg.* illuminato dalla luna.
moonshine *s.* V. *moonlight.*
moonshiny *agg.* V. *moonlit.*
moony *agg.* **1.** lunare **2.** distratto.
Moor *s.* moro.
moor *s.* brughiera.
to **moor** *vt.* e *vi.* ormeggiare.
moorage *s.* ormeggio. ♦ **moorings** *s. pl.* **1.** gomena (*sing.*) **2.** ormeggi.
mop[1] *s.* **1.** scopa **2.** zazzera.
mop[2] *s.* smorfia.
to **mop**[1] *vt.* **1.** pulire **2.** asciugare || *to — up* (*mil.*), rastrellare.
to **mop**[2] *vi.* fare smorfie.
mope *s.* **1.** persona avvilita **2.** tristezza.
to **mope** *vt.* avvilire. ♦ to **mope** *vi.* avvilirsi.
mopish *agg.* avvilito.
moraine *s.* morena.
moral *agg.* morale. ♦ **moral** *s.* **1.** morale **2.** principio morale. ♦ **morals** *s. pl.* costumi.
morale *s.* il morale.
moralism *s.* moralismo.
moralist *s.* moralista.
moralistic *agg.* moralistico.
morality *s.* moralità.
moralization *s.* moralizzazione.
to **moralize** *vt.* moralizzare. ♦ to **moralize** *vi.* trarre la morale.
morass *s.* palude.
moratory *agg.* moratorio.
moratorium *s.* (*pl.* -ria) moratoria.
moray *s.* murena.
morbid *agg.* **1.** morboso **2.** patologico.
morbidity *s.* **1.** morbosità **2.** stato patologico.
mordacity, mordancy *s.* mordacità.
mordant *agg.* e *s.* mordente.
more (*comp. di* much, many) *agg.*, *pron.* e *avv.* più, di più, maggiormente || *— and —*, sempre più; *once —*, ancora una volta.
moreover *avv.* inoltre.

morganatic *agg.* morganatico.
morgue *s.* obitorio.
Mormon *agg.* e *s.* mormone.
morning *s.* mattino.
Moroccan *agg.* e *s.* marocchino.
moron *s.* deficiente.
morose *agg.* tetro.
morphia, morphine *s.* morfina.
morphinomaniac *agg.* e *s.* morfinomane.
morphologic(al) *agg.* morfologico.
morphology *s.* morfologia.
morsel *s.* boccone.
mortal *agg.* e *s.* mortale.
mortality *s.* mortalità.
mortally *avv.* mortalmente.
mortar[1] *s.* mortaio.
mortar[2] *s.* calcina.
mortgage *s.* ipoteca.
to **mortgage** *vt.* ipotecare.
mortagagee *s.* creditore ipotecario.
mortgager *s.* debitore ipotecario.
mortification *s.* mortificazione.
to **mortify** *vt.* **1.** mortificare **2.** incancrenire. ♦ to **mortify** *vi.* **1.** mortificarsi **2.** incancrenirsi.
mortuary *agg.* mortuario. ♦ **mortuary** *s.* camera mortuaria.
mosaic *agg.* musivo. ♦ **mosaic** *s.* mosaico.
Moslem *agg.* e *s.* mussulmano.
mosque *s.* moschea.
mosquito *s.* zanzara || *— -net*, zanzariera.
moss *s.* **1.** acquitrino **2.** muschio.
mossy *agg.* muscoso.
most *agg.* e *pron.* (*superl. di* much, many) il più, la maggior parte di, il massimo. ♦ **most** *avv.* **1.** il più **2.** molto **3.** maggiormente.
mostly *avv.* per lo più.
mote *s.* particella.
moth *s.* **1.** falena **2.** tignola.
mother *s.* madre || *— -country*, madrepatria; *— -in-law*, suocera.
motherhood *s.* maternità.
motherless *agg.* senza madre.
motherly *agg.* materno.
mothproof *agg.* inattaccabile dalle tarme.
motif *s.* motivo.
motion *s.* **1.** moto, movimento **2.** mozione || *— -picture*, film.
motionless *agg.* immobile.
to **motivate** *vt.* **1.** motivare **2.** stimolare.
motivation *s.* **1.** motivazione **2.** stimolo.
motive *agg.* motore. ♦ **motive** *s.*

motivo, movente.

motley *agg.* **1.** screziato **2.** eterogeneo. ♦ **motley** *s.* miscuglio.

motor *agg.* e *s.* motore || — *-cycle*, motocicletta; — *-car*, automobile, — *-boat*, motobarca; — *ship*, motonave.

to motor *vi.* andare in automobile.

motoring *s.* automobilismo.

motorist *s.* automobilista.

motorization *s.* motorizzazione.

to motorize *vt.* motorizzare.

mottle *s.* chiazza.

to mottle *vt.* chiazzare.

moufflon *s.* muflone.

mould[1] *s.* stampo.

mould[2] *s.* muffa.

mould[3] *s.* terriccio.

to mould[1] *vt.* modellare.

to mould[2] *vi.* ammuffire.

moulding *s.* **1.** il modellare **2.** cornice **3.** fusione.

mouldy *agg.* ammuffito.

mound *s.* monticello.

mount[1] *s.* monte, montagna.

mount[2] **1.** cavalcatura **2.** intelaiatura **3.** affusto di cannone **4.** montatura.

to mount *vt.* salire. ♦ **to mount** *vi.* **1.** montare **2.** ammontare.

mountain *s.* montagna.

mountaineer *s.* **1.** montanaro **2.** alpinista.

mountaineering *s.* alpinismo.

mountainous *agg.* montuoso.

mountebank *s.* ciarlatano.

mounter *s.* montatore.

to mourn *vt.* e *vi.* piangere.

mourner *s.* chi è in lutto.

mournful *agg.* lugubre.

mourning *s.* **1.** dolore **2.** lutto: *to go into* —, mettere il lutto.

mouse *s.* (*pl.* mice) topo.

moustache *s.* baffi (*pl.*).

mouth *s.* bocca.

to mouth *vt.* declamare. ♦ **to mouth** *vi.* fare smorfie.

mouthful *s.* boccone.

mouthpiece *s.* **1.** bocchino **2.** portavoce.

movable *agg.* mobile.

movables *s. pl.* beni mobili.

move *s.* **1.** movimento **2.** mossa **3.** trasloco.

to move *vt.* **1.** muovere **2.** commuovere. ♦ to **move** *vi.* **1.** muoversi

movement *s.* **1.** movimento, moto. **2.** traslocare **3.** commuoversi.

mover *s.* promotore.

movie *s.* film. ♦ **movies** *s. pl.* cinema (*sing.*).

moving *s.* **1.** spostamento **2.** trasloco.

mow *s.* covone.

to mow (mowed, mown) *vt.* falciare.

mower *s.* falciatore.

mowing *s.* falciatura.

mown V. *to mow.*

much (more, most) *agg.*, *s.* e *avv.* molto || *so* —, tanto; *too* —, troppo; *as* — *as*, tanto quanto; *how* —?, quanto?

muck *s.* letame.

mucous *agg.* mucoso.

mucus *s.* muco.

mud *s.* fango || — *-guard*, parafango.

to mud *vt.* infangare.

muddle *s.* confusione, pasticcio.

to muddle *vt.* confondere.

muddleheaded *agg.* confusionario.

muddler *s.* confusionario.

muddy *agg.* **1.** fangoso **2.** torbido **3.** infangato.

to muddy *vt.* infangare.

muff[1] *s.* manicotto.

muff[2] *s.* **1.** colpo mancato **2.** babbeo.

to muffle *vt.* **1.** avvolgere **2.** smorzare.

muffler *s.* **1.** sciarpa **2.** guantone **3.** silenziatore.

mug *s.* (*fam.*) faccia || — *shot* (*tv*), primo piano.

mulberry *s.* mora || — (*-tree*) gelso.

mule *s.* mulo.

mulish *agg.* (*fig.*) testardo.

muller *s.* pestello.

multiform *agg.* multiforme.

multimillionaire *s.* multimilionario.

multiple *agg.* e *s.* multiplo.

multiplicable *agg.* moltiplicabile.

multiplicand *s.* moltiplicando.

multiplication *s.* moltiplicazione.

multiplicity *s.* molteplicità.

multiplier *s.* moltiplicatore.

to multiply *vt.* moltiplicare. ♦ to **multiply** *vi.* moltiplicarsi.

multitude *s.* moltitudine.

multitudinous *agg.* **1.** innumerevole **2.** vasto.

mumble *s.* borbottio.

to mumble *vt.* e *vi.* borbottare.

mumbling *s.* V. *mumble.*

mummer *s.* guitto.

mummification s. mummificazione.
to **mummify** vt. mummificare.
mummy[1] s. mummia.
mummy[2] s. mammina.
mumps s. pl. orecchioni.
to **munch** vt. e vi. biascicare.
municipal agg. municipale.
municipality s. municipalità.
municipalization s. municipalizzazione.
to **municipalize** vt. municipalizzare.
munificence s. munificenza.
munificent agg. munifico.
munitions s. pl. munizioni.
mural agg. murale. ♦ **mural** s. affresco.
murder s. assassinio.
to **murder** vt. assassinare.
murderer s. assassino.
murderous agg. omicida.
muriatic agg. muriatico.
murky agg. tenebroso.
murmur s. **1.** mormorio **2.** brontolio.
to **murmur** vt. mormorare. ♦ to **murmur** vi. brontolare.
murmuring s. V. murmur.
muscat(el) s. moscato.
muscle s. muscolo.
muscled agg. muscoloso.
muscular agg. **1.** muscolare **2.** muscoloso.
musculature s. muscolatura.
Muse s. musa.
to **muse** vi. meditare.
museum s. museo.
mushroom s. fungo.
mushy agg. infrollito.
music s. musica.
musical agg. **1.** musicale **2.** appassionato di musica.
musicality s. musicalità.
musician s. musicista || street —, suonatore ambulante.
musicologist s. musicologo.
musicology s. musicologia.
musing agg. meditabondo. ♦ **musing** s. meditazione.
musk s. muschio.
musket s. moschetto.
musketeer s. moschettiere.
musky agg. muschiato.
Muslim agg. e s. mussulmano.
muslin s. mussola.
muss s. stato di confusione.
mussel s. mitilo.
must[1] s. mosto.
must[2] s. muffa.

must v. dif. (pres. ind.) dovere || he — return here, deve ritornare qui, it — be true, deve essere vero; you — know him!, non puoi non conoscerlo!
mustard s. senape.
muster s. adunata.
to **muster** vt. adunare. ♦ to **muster** vi. adunarsi.
mutability s. mutabilità.
mutable agg. mutevole.
mutation s. cambiamento.
mute agg. muto. ♦ **mute** s. **1.** muto **2.** sordina.
to **mutilate** vt. mutilare.
mutilation s. mutilazione.
mutineer s. ammutinato.
mutinous agg. ammutinato, ribelle.
mutiny s. ammutinamento.
to **mutiny** vi. ammutinarsi.
mutism s. mutismo.
to **mutter** V. to murmur.
mutton s. montone.
mutual agg. **1.** reciproco **2.** comune.
muzzle s. **1.** muso **2.** museruola **3.** bocca (di arma).
to **muzzle** vt. mettere la museruola a.
my agg. poss. mio, mia, miei, mie.
mycosis s. (pl. -ses) micosi.
myocardial agg. miocardico.
myocarditis s. miocardite.
myocardium s. miocardio.
myopia s. miopia.
myopic agg. miope.
myosote s. miosotide.
myriad s. miriade.
myriagram s. miriagrammo.
myriametre s. miriametro.
Myriapoda s. pl. miriapodi.
myrrh s. mirra.
myrtle s. mirto.
myself pron. r. io stesso, me stesso, mi.
mysterious agg. misterioso.
mystery s. mistero.
mystic agg. e s. mistico.
mystical agg. mistico.
mysticism s. misticismo.
mystification s. mistificazione.
mystifier s. mistificatore.
to **mystify** vt. **1.** disorientare **2.** avvolgere nel mistero.
myth s. mito.
mythic(al) agg. mitico.
to **mythicize** vt. volgere in mito.
mythologic(al) agg. mitologico.
to **mythologize** vi. studiare i miti.
mythology s. mitologia.

mythomania *s.* mitomania.
mythomaniac *agg.* e *s.* mitomane.

N

nabob *s.* nababbo.
nacre *s.* madreperla.
to nag *vt.* e *vi.* brontolare.
naiad *s.* naiade.
nail *s.* **1.** unghia, artiglio **2.** chiodo.
to nail *vt.* **1.** inchiodare **2.** munire di chiodi.
nailer *s.* fabbricante di chiodi.
naïve *agg.* ingenuo, semplice.
naiveté *s.* ingenuità.
naked *agg.* **1.** nudo, spogliato **2.** spoglio, indifeso.
nakedness *s.* nudità.
name *s.* **1.** nome **2.** fama, reputazione || — *-day*, onomastico; *full* —, generalità.
to name *vt.* **1.** nominare, dare un nome **2.** designare.
nameless *agg.* **1.** senza nome **2.** innominabile.
namely *avv.* cioè.
nanny *s.* bambinaia, balia.
nap[1] *s.* siesta, sonnellino.
nap[2] *s.* pelo (*di stoffe*).
to nap *vi.* schiacciare un sonnellino, sonnecchiare.
nape *s.* nuca.
naphtha *s.* nafta.
napkin *s.* **1.** tovagliolo: — *-ring,* anello per tovagliolo **2.** pannolino.
narcissism *s.* narcisismo.
narcosis, narcotism *s.* narcosi.
narcotic *agg. s.* narcotico.
narcotization *s.* narcotizzazione.
to narcotize *vt.* narcotizzare.
to narrate *vt.* narrare.
narration *s.* narrazione, racconto.
narrative *agg.* narrativo. ♦ **narrative** *s.* resoconto, narrazione.
narrator *s.* narratore.
narrow *agg.* **1.** stretto, angusto, ristretto (*anche fig.*) **2.** esatto, minuzioso || — *-minded,* di idee ristrette. ♦ **narrow** *s.* stretto, strettoia.
to narrow *vt.* stringere, ridurre. ♦ **to narrow** *vi.* stringersi, contrarsi.
narrowness *s.* strettezza, limitatezza.
narwhal *s.* narvalo.
nasal *agg.* nasale. ♦ **nasal** *s.* **1.**

suono nasale **2.** osso nasale.
nascent *agg.* nascente.
nastily *avv.* **1.** sgradevolmente **2.** con cattiveria.
nastiness *s.* **1.** cattivo gusto **2.** cattiveria.
nasty *agg.* **1.** sporco, sgradevole **2.** cattivo, tempestoso (*di tempo*).
natal *agg.* natale.
natality *s.* natalità.
natant *agg.* natante.
natation *s.* nuoto.
natatorial *agg.* natatorio.
nation *s.* nazione.
national *agg.* nazionale.
nationalism *s.* nazionalismo.
nationalist *s.* nazionalista.
nationality *s.* **1.** nazionalità **2.** patriottismo.
nationalization *s.* **1.** nazionalizzazione **2.** naturalizzazione.
to nationalize *vt.* **1.** nazionalizzare **2.** naturalizzare.
native *agg.* **1.** innato **2.** natio, indigeno. ♦ **native** *s.* indigeno, nativo.
nativity *s.* nascita, natività.
natural *agg.* **1.** naturale, fisico **2.** spontaneo **3.** istintivo, innato.
naturalism *s.* naturalismo.
naturalist *s.* naturalista.
naturalistic *agg.* naturalistico.
naturalization *s.* **1.** naturalizzazione **2.** acclimatamento.
to naturalize *vi.* **1.** naturalizzare **2.** acclimatare.
nature *s.* **1.** natura **2.** carattere, temperamento || *good* —, bontà.
natured *agg.* di natura, per natura || *good* —, buono, di buon carattere.
naturism *s.* naturismo, nudismo.
naturist *s.* naturista.
naughtily *avv.* con cattiveria.
naughtiness *s.* cattiveria.
naughty *agg.* cattivo, impertinente.
to nauseate *vt.* nauseare, disgustare. ♦ **to nauseate** *vi.* avere la nausea, disgustarsi.
nauseating *agg.* nauseabondo.
nautical *agg.* nautico.
naval *agg.* navale.
nave[1] *s.* mozzo di ruota.
nave[2] *s.* navata centrale (*di chiesa*).
navel *s.* **1.** ombelico **2.** (*fig.*) centro.
navigability *s.* navigabilità.
navigable *agg.* navigabile.
to navigate *vt.* e *vi.* **1.** navigare **2.** regolare la rotta.

navigation s. 1. navigazione 2. rotta.

navigator s. navigatore, ufficiale di rotta.

navvy s. sterratore.

navy s. marina da guerra, flotta.

nay avv. anzi, non solo.

Nazi agg. e s. nazista.

Neapolitan agg. e s. napoletano.

near agg. 1. vicino, prossimo 2. affine, intimo 3. fedele, esatto. ♦

near prep. vicino a, presso a. ♦

near avv. vicino, presso, accanto.

to **near** vt. e vi. avvicinarsi (a).

nearby agg. avv. prep. assai vicino.

nearly avv. quasi.

neat agg. 1. pulito, lindo 2. grazioso, di buon gusto 3. chiaro, conciso.

neatly avv. 1. lindamente, ordinatamente 2. con semplicità, con buon gusto 3. concisamente.

neatness s. 1. pulizia, ordine 2. grazia, armonia 3. semplicità 4. concisione.

nebula s. nebulosa.

nebular agg. nebulare.

nebulosity s. nebulosità.

nebulous agg. nebuloso, vago.

necessary agg. necessario.

to **necessitate** vt. 1. rendere necessario 2. obbligare.

necessity s. necessità.

neck s. collo || stiff —, torcicollo.

neckerchief s. fazzoletto da collo.

necklace s. collana, vezzo.

neckline s. scollatura.

necktie s. cravatta.

necrology s. necrologia.

necromancer s. negromante.

necromancy s. negromanzia.

necropolis s. necropoli.

necrosis s. (pl. -ses) necrosi.

nectar s. nettare.

need s. necessità, bisogno.

to **need** vt. e vi. essere necessario, occorrere, abbisognare, mancare di.

needful agg. necessario, indispensabile.

neediness s. bisogno, povertà.

needle s. 1. ago 2. puntina di grammofono.

to **needle** vt. 1. cucire, pungere (con un ago) 2. irritare.

needleful s. gugliata.

needless agg. inutile, superfluo.

needlewoman s. cucitrice.

needlework s. lavoro ad ago.

needs avv. necessariamente.

needy agg. povero, indigente.

ne'er avv. (contrazione di never) mai.

negation s. diniego.

negative agg. negativo. ♦ **negative** s. 1. negazione 2. qualità negativa.

neglect s. negligenza, trascuratezza.

to **neglect** vt. trascurare.

neglectful agg. negligente, noncurante.

negligence s. negligenza, trascuratezza.

negligent agg. negligente, trascurato.

negligible agg. trascurabile.

negotiable agg. negoziabile.

to **negotiate** vt. e vi. negoziare, trattare.

negotiation s. trattativa.

negress s. negra.

negro agg. e s. negro.

negroid agg. negroide.

neigh s. nitrito.

to **neigh** vi. nitrire.

neighbour s. vicino.

to **neighbour** vi. essere vicini di casa.

neighbourhood s. 1. i vicini, vicinato 2. paraggi, dintorni (pl.).

neighbouring agg. vicino, contiguo.

neither[1] agg. né l'uno né l'altro.

neither[2] avv. né, neppure, nemmeno: — ... nor, né ... né.

nemesis s. (pl. -ses) nemesi.

neo-classic(al) agg. neoclassico.

neo-classicism s. neoclassicismo.

neo-criticism s. neocriticismo.

neolithic agg. neolitico.

neologism s. neologismo.

neology s. neologia.

neon s. neon.

neophyte s. neofito.

neoplatonic agg. neoplatonico.

Neoplatonism s. neoplatonismo.

neopositivism s. neopositivismo.

neorealism s. neorealismo.

neorealist s. neorealista.

nephew s. nipote (di zio).

nephritic agg. nefritico.

nephritis s. nefrite.

nepotism s. nepotismo.

nerve s. 1. nervo 2. nervatura 3. forza, energia, sangue freddo.

to **nerve** vt. tonificare, rinvigorire.

nerveless agg. snervato, inerte.

nervous agg. 1. nervoso 2. forte, vigoroso 3. timido, apprensivo.

nervously avv. 1. nervosamente 2.

timidamente.
nervousness s. **1.** nervosismo, irritazione **2.** timidezza.
nervy agg. **1.** muscoloso, forte **2.** nervoso.
nescient agg. ignorante.
nest s. **1.** nido **2.** (fig.) covo, tana **3.** colonia (di *uccelli, insetti ecc.*).
to nest vi. fare il nido, nidificare.
to nestle vt. ospitare. ♦ **to nestle** vi. annidarsi, rifugiarsi.
nestling s. uccellino di nido.
net[1] agg. e s. netto.
net[2] s. **1.** rete **2.** (fig.) trappola.
to net vt. **1.** coprire con reti **2.** pescare con reti.
netful s. retata.
netting s. rete, reticolato.
nettle s. ortica || — *rash*, orticaria.
to nettle vt. pungere (di *ortica*).
network s. rete, reticolato.
neuralgia s. nevralgia.
neuralgic agg. nevralgico.
neurasthenia s. nevrastenia.
neurasthenic agg. nevrastenico.
neuritis s. nevrite.
neurologist s. neurologo.
neurology s. neurologia.
neuropathic agg. neuropatico.
neuropathology s. neuropatologia.
neurosis s. (pl. -ses) nevrosi.
neurotic s. neuropatico.
neuter s. parola neutra, neutro.
neutral agg. neutrale.
neutralism s. neutralismo.
neutralist s. neutralista.
neutrality s. neutralità.
neutralization s. neutralizzazione.
to neutralize vt. neutralizzare.
neutron s. neutrone.
never avv. mai, giammai || — *again*, mai più; — *mind*, non importa; *now or* —, ora o mai più; — *-ending*, eterno.
nevermore avv. mai più.
nevertheless avv. nonostante, ciò nondimeno.
new agg. nuovo, recente || — *-born*, neonato; — *-comer*, nuovo venuto; — *-made*, appena fatto.
newish agg. piuttosto nuovo.
newly avv. recentemente.
news s. notizia, notizie || — *-man*, strillone (di *giornali*); — *-reel*, cinegiornale.
newsmonger s. persona pettegola e curiosa.
newspaper s. giornale, quotidiano.
New Zealander s. neozelandese.

next agg. **1.** prossimo, vicino, il più vicino **2.** futuro, venturo **3.** primo, contiguo. ♦ **next** avv. dopo, in seguito, poi. ♦ **next** prep. presso, accanto.
nib s. pennino.
nibble s. morso.
to nibble vt. **1.** mordicchiare, sgranocchiare **2.** abboccare.
nibbler s. roditore.
nice agg. **1.** piacevole, bello, simpatico **2.** buono, gustoso **3.** accurato, minuzioso.
nicely avv. **1.** amabilmente, piacevolmente **2.** esattamente.
nicety s. **1.** finezza, precisione. ♦ **niceties** s. pl. minuzie.
niche s. nicchia.
nick s. tacca, intaccatura || *in the* — *of time*, al momento giusto.
to nick vt. **1.** intaccare **2.** colpire, afferrare al momento opportuno.
nickel s. nichel.
to nickel vt. nichelare.
nickname s. soprannome, nomignolo.
to nickname vt. soprannominare.
nicotine s. nicotina.
niece s. nipote (femmina) (di *zio*).
niggard agg. spilorcio.
niggardliness s. spilorceria.
niggardly agg. avaro, spilorcio.
nigger s. (spreg.) negro.
night s. **1.** notte, sera **2.** buio, oscurità || *by* —, di notte, *good* —, buona notte; — *-bird*, uccello notturno, nottambulo; — *-dress*, camicia da notte; — *-shift*, turno di notte.
nightcap s. berretto da notte.
nightfall s. tramonto.
nightingale s. usignolo.
nightly agg. notturno. ♦ **nightly** avv. di notte.
nightmare s. incubo.
nightpiece s. « notturno » (dipinto che rappresenta una scena notturna).
nihilism s. nichilismo.
nihilist s. nichilista.
nimble agg. **1.** agile, leggero **2.** acuto, sveglio.
nimbleness s. **1.** agilità **2.** prontezza, acutezza.
nimbly avv. **1.** agilmente, leggermente **2.** prontamente.
nine agg. nove.
ninepins s. pl. birilli.
nineteen agg. diciannove.

nineteenth *agg.* e *s.* diciannovesimo.

ninetieth *agg.* novantesimo.

ninety *agg.* novanta.

ninth *agg.* nono.

nip *s.* **1.** pizzicotto, morso **2.** stretta, presa **3.** morso (*di freddo, gelo ecc.*).

to nip *vt.* **1.** pizzicare, mordere (*anche di freddo ecc.*) **2.** stroncare.

nipple *s.* capezzolo.

nitrate *s.* nitrato.

nitric *agg.* nitrico.

nitrite *s.* (*chim.*) nitrito.

nitroglycerin(e) *s.* nitroglicerina.

no *agg.* nessuno. ♦ **no** *avv.* **1.** no **2.** in nessun modo.

nobiliary *agg.* nobiliare.

nobility *s.* nobiltà (*anche fig.*).

noble *agg.* **1.** nobile (*anche fig.*) **2.** superbo, grandioso. ♦ **noble** *s.* nobile.

nobleman *s.* nobiluomo.

nobleness *s.* nobiltà (*anche fig.*).

noblewoman *s.* nobildonna.

nobly *avv.* nobilmente.

nobody *pron. indef.* nessuno.

nocturnal *agg.* notturno.

nocturne *s.* (*pitt.; mus.*) notturno.

nod *s.* **1.** cenno del capo **2.** ordine, comando.

to nod *vt.* e *vi.* **1.** annuire col capo **2.** assopirsi, chinare il capo dal sonno **3.** inclinarsi (*di edifici ecc.*).

nodding *agg.* chinato, incliato. ♦ **nodding** *s.* cenno del capo.

nodose *agg.* nodoso.

nodosity *s.* nodosità.

nodular *agg.* a forma di nodo.

nodule *s.* nodulo.

noise *s.* rumore, fragore, chiasso.

noiseless *agg.* senza rumore, silenzioso.

noisily *avv.* rumorosamente.

noisy *agg.* **1.** rumoroso, turbolento **2.** (*fig.*) vistoso, chiassoso.

nomad *agg.* e *s.* nomade.

nomadism *s.* nomadismo.

nomenclature *s.* nomenclatura.

nominal *agg.* nominale.

nominalism *s.* nominalismo.

nominalist *s.* nominalista.

nominalistic *agg.* nominalistico.

nominative *agg.* e *s.* nominativo.

nominator *s.* nominatore.

nonagenarian *agg.* e *s.* nonagenario.

non-aligned *agg.* non allineato.

non-alignment *s.* non allineamento.

non-appearance *s.* contumacia.

non-attendance *s.* assenza.

non-commital *agg.* evasivo.

non-conducting *agg.* isolante, non conduttore.

non-conductor *s.* isolante.

nonconformist *agg.* e *s.* anticonformista.

nonconformity *s.* anticonformismo.

non-delivery *s.* mancata consegna.

none *pron. sing.* e *pl.* nessuno, non uno. ♦ **none** *avv.* affatto, niente affatto.

nonentity *s.* **1.** cosa o persona insignificante **2.** inesistenza.

non-existence *s.* inesistenza.

non-resistance *s.* resistenza passiva.

nonsense *s.* assurdità, sciocchezza.

nonsensical *agg.* assurdo, sciocco.

non-stop *agg.* continuo, senza fermate. ♦ **non-stop** *avv.* di continuo, senza fermate.

non-transferable *agg.* non trasferibile.

noodle *agg.* sciocco, gonzo.

nook *s.* **1.** cantuccio, angolo **2.** ripostiglio.

noon *s.* mezzogiorno.

noose *s.* **1.** nodo scorsoio **2.** tranello.

nor *cong.* né, neppure || *neither I — he*, né io né lui.

normal *agg.* **1.** normale, regolare **2.** perpendicolare.

normality *s.* normalità.

normalization *s.* normalizzazione.

to normalize *vt.* normalizzare.

Norman *agg.* e *s.* normanno.

normative *agg.* normativo.

north *s.* nord, settentrione || *— wind*, vento di tramontana.

north-east *s.* nord-est.

northerly *agg.* del nord, settentrionale. ♦ **northerly** *avv.* verso il nord.

northern *agg.* nordico, settentrionale.

northerner *s.* abitante del nord.

northward(s) *agg.* e *avv.* verso nord.

Norwegian *agg.* e *s.* norvegese.

nose *s.* **1.** naso **2.** muso (*di animali*) **3.** prua (*mar.*).

to nose *vt.* e *vi.* **1.** fiutare **2.** indagare **3.** ficcare il naso.

nostril *s.* narice.

not *avv.* non || *— at all*, niente affatto.

notability *s.* notabilità.
notable *agg.* degno di nota, notevole.
notarial *agg.* notarile.
notary *s.* notaio.
notation *s.* 1. (*mus.*) notazione 2. (*mat.*) numerazione.
notch *s.* tacca, dentellatura.
to **notch** *vt.* 1. intaccare 2. intagliare.
note *s.* 1. (*mus.*) nota, tono 2. marchio, segno 3. nota, appunto, commento 4. (*comm.*) cedola, acconto 5. banconota.
to **note** *vt.* notare.
notebook *s.* taccuino.
notehead *s.* intestazione.
noteless *agg.* privo di interesse.
noteworthiness *s.* importanza.
noteworthy *agg.* notevole.
nothing *pron. indef.* nulla, niente, nessuna cosa.
nothingness *s.* 1. il nulla 2. nullità.
notice *s.* 1. avviso, avvertimento 2. (*giur.*) intimazione 3. licenziamento 4. attenzione, cura 5. recensione || — -*board,* cartello pubblicitario, tabella.
to **notice** *vt.* 1. osservare, fare attenzione a 2. recensire.
noticeable *agg.* notevole.
notifiable *agg.* da denunciarsi.
notification *s.* notifica.
to **notify** *vt.* notificare; far sapere.
notion *s.* 1. nozione 2. idea, teoria.
notional *agg.* 1. immaginario 2. speculativo.
notoriety *s.* notorietà.
notorious *agg.* 1. noto, conosciuto 2. famigerato.
notoriously *avv.* notoriamente.
notwithstanding *prep.* nonostante, malgrado.
nougat *s.* torrone.
nought *s.* 1. nulla 2. (*mat.*) zero.
noumenon *s.* (*pl.* -ena) noumeno.
noun *s.* (*gramm.*) nome, sostantivo.
to **nourish** *vt.* nutrire (*anche fig.*).
nourishing *agg.* nutriente.
nourishment *s.* nutrimento.
novel *s.* romanzo.
novelist *s.* romanziere.
to **novelize** *vt.* romanzare.
novelty *s.* novità.
November *s.* novembre.
novice *s.* 1. (*eccl.*) novizio 2. apprendista.
novitiate *s.* noviziato.

now *avv.* 1. ora, adesso, subito, al presente 2. allora 3. a dire il vero. ◆ **now** *cong.* ora che. ◆ **now** *s.* ora, il presente.
nowadays *avv.* al giorno d'oggi.
nowhere *avv.* in nessun luogo.
noxious *agg.* nocivo, dannoso.
nozzle *s.* becco, beccuccio (*di teiera, pompa ecc.*).
nuclear *agg.* nucleare.
nuclein *s.* nucleina.
nucleonics *s. pl.* fisica nucleare.
nucleus *s.* (*pl.* -ei) 1. nucleo 2. nocciolo, centro.
nude *agg.* 1. nudo 2. (*fig.*) semplice. ◆ **nude** *s.* (*pitt.; scult.*) nudo.
nudism *s.* nudismo.
nudist *agg.* e *s.* nudista.
nugget *s.* pepita.
nuisance *s.* 1. noia, seccatura 2. danno.
null *agg.* nullo.
nullification *s.* annullamento.
to **nullify** *vt.* annullare.
nullity *s.* 1. nullità 2. il non essere valido.
numb *agg.* 1. intorpidito, intirizzito 2. tramortito, intontito.
to **numb** *vt.* 1. intorpidire, intirizzire 2. (*fig.*) istupidire.
number *s.* 1. numero, cifra 2. numero, quantità 3. numero di giornale.
to **number** *vt.* 1. contare, numerare 2. annoverare 3. ammontare.
numberless *agg.* innumerevole.
numbness *s.* torpore (*anche fig.*).
numerable *agg.* numerabile, calcolabile.
numeral *agg.* e *s.* numerale.
numerator *s.* numeratore.
numerical *agg.* numerico.
numerically *avv.* numericamente.
numerous *agg.* numeroso.
numismatic *agg.* numismatico.
numismatics *s.* numismatica.
numismatist *s.* numismatico.
numismatology *s.* numismatica.
nun *s.* 1. monaca, suora 2. piccione dal cappuccio.
nuncio *s.* (*eccl.*) nunzio.
nunnery *s.* convento (*di suore*).
nuptial *agg.* nuziale.
nuptials *s. pl.* nozze, sponsali.
nurse *s.* 1. nutrice, balia 2. infermiera.
to **nurse** *vt.* 1. allattare, nutrire 2. allevare 3. curare (*ammalati*).
nursling *s.* lattante.

nursery *s.* **1.** camera dei bambini **2.** scuola materna **3.** vivaio || — *rhyme*, filastrocca per bambini.
nursing *agg.* **1.** che allatta, nutre **2.** che cura || — *home*, casa di cura. ♦ **nursing** *s.* **1.** allattamento **2.** il curare **3.** professione di infermiera.
nurture *s.* vitto, nutrimento.
to **nurture** *vt.* nutrire, allevare.
nut *s.* **1.** noce **2.** (*mecc.*) dado.
nutcracker *s.* schiaccianoci.
nutmeg *s.* noce moscata.
nutrition *s.* nutrizione.
nutritive *agg.* nutritivo.
nutshell *s.* guscio di noce.
nylon *s.* nailon.
nymph *s.* ninfa.

O

oak *s.* quercia.
oakum *s.* stoppa.
oar *s.* remo || — *-blade*, pala di remo.
to **oar** *vi.* remare.
oarsman *s.* rematore.
oasis *s.* (*pl.* -ses) oasi.
oats *s. pl.* avena (*sing.*).
oath *s.* **1.** giuramento **2.** bestemmia.
obduracy *s.* **1.** inesorabilità **2.** ostinazione.
obdurate *agg.* **1.** inesorabile **2.** ostinato.
obedience *s.* ubbidienza.
obedient *agg.* ubbidiente.
obeisance *s.* riverenza.
obelisk *s.* obelisco.
obese *agg.* obeso.
obesity *s.* obesità.
to **obey** *vt.* e *vi.* ubbidire.
to **obfuscate** *vt.* **1.** offuscare **2.** confondere.
obituary *s.* necrologio.
object *s.* oggetto.
to **object** *vt.* e *vi.* obiettare.
objectification *s.* oggettivazione.
to **objectify** *vt.* oggettivare.
objection *s.* **1.** obiezione **2.** avversione.
objectionable *agg.* **1.** biasimevole **2.** sgradevole.
objective *agg.* oggettivo. ♦ **objective** *s.* obiettivo.
objectiveness *s.* oggettività.

objectivism *s.* oggettivismo.
objectivity *s.* oggettività.
objector *s.* oppositore || *conscientious* —, obiettore di coscienza.
obligation *s.* obbligo.
obligatoriness *s.* obbligatorietà.
obligatory *agg.* obbligatorio.
to **oblige** *vt.* **1.** obbligare **2.** fare un favore a.
obliging *agg.* cortese.
oblique *agg.* obliquo.
obliqueness, obliquity *s.* obliquità.
to **obliterate** *vt.* cancellare.
obliteration *s.* cancellatura.
oblivion *s.* oblio || *Act of* —, amnistia.
oblivious *agg.* dimentico.
oblong *agg.* **1.** oblungo **2.** rettangolare. ♦ **oblong** *s.* (*geom.*) rettangolo.
obnoxious *agg.* odioso.
obscene *agg.* osceno.
obscenity *s.* oscenità.
obscurantism *s.* oscurantismo.
obscurantist *agg.* e *s.* oscurantista.
obscuration *s.* oscuramento.
obscure *agg.* oscuro. ♦ **obscure** *s.* oscurità.
to **obscure** *vt.* oscurare.
obscurity *s.* oscurità.
obsecration *s.* supplica.
obsequies *s. pl.* esequie.
obsequious *agg.* ossequioso.
observable *agg.* **1.** visibile **2.** notevole.
observance *s.* **1.** osservanza **2.** (*relig.*) regola.
observant *agg.* osservante.
observation *s.* osservazione.
observatory *s.* osservatorio.
to **observe** *vt.* e *vi.* osservare.
observer *s.* osservatore.
observing *agg.* attento.
to **obsess** *vt.* ossessionare.
obsession *s.* ossessione.
obsessive *agg.* ossessivo.
obsolescence *s.* disuso.
obsolescent *agg.* che sta cadendo in disuso.
obsolete *agg.* **1.** antiquato **2.** scaduto (*di prezzi*).
obstacle *s.* ostacolo.
obstetric(al) *agg.* ostetrico.
obstetrician *s.* ostetrico.
obstetrics *s.* ostetricia.
obstinacy *s.* ostinazione.
obstinate *agg.* ostinato.
to **obstruct** *vt.* **1.** ostruire **2.** ri-

tardare **3.** intasare.
obstruction s. ostruzione, ostacolo.
obstructionism s. ostruzionismo.
obstructionist s. ostruzionista.
to obtain vt. ottenere. ♦ **to obtain** vi. prevalere.
obtainable agg. ottenibile.
to obtrude vt. imporre. ♦ **to obtrude** vi. **1.** imporsi **2.** intromettersi.
obtruder s. **1.** intruso **2.** importuno.
obtrusion s. intrusione.
obtrusive agg. **1.** intruso **2.** importuno.
obtrusiveness s. **1.** intrusione **2.** invadenza.
to obtund vt. ottundere.
obtundent agg. ottundente.
to obturate vt. otturare.
obturation s. otturazione.
obturator s. otturatore.
obtuse agg. **1.** ottuso **2.** sordo.
obtuseness s. ottusità.
to obviate vt. ovviare.
obvious agg. ovvio.
obviousness s. chiarezza.
occasion s. **1.** occasione **2.** motivo.
occasional agg. occasionale.
occident s. occidente.
occidental agg. occidentale.
occidentalism s. occidentalismo.
to occidentalize vt. occidentalizzare.
occidentally avv. all'occidentale.
occipital agg. occipitale.
occiput s. (pl. -pita) occipite.
to occlude vt. occludere.
occlusion s. occlusione.
occlusive agg. occlusivo.
occult agg. occulto.
to occult vt. occultare. ♦ **to occult** vi. occultarsi.
occultation s. occultamento.
occultism s. occultismo.
occultist s. occultista.
occupant s. occupante.
occupation s. occupazione.
occupational agg. professionale.
occupier s. occupante.
to occupy vt. occupare: to — oneself with, occuparsi di.
to occur vi. **1.** accadere **2.** venire in mente **3.** ricorrere.
occurrence s. avvenimento.
ocean s. oceano.
oceanic agg. oceanico.
oceanography s. oceanografia.
ocellus s. (pl. -li) ocello.

ochre s. ocra.
octagon s. ottagono.
octagonal agg. ottagonale.
octahedron s. ottaedro.
octane s. ottano.
octave s. ottava.
October s. ottobre.
octogenarian agg. e s. ottuagenario.
octonarian agg. e s. ottonario.
octonary agg. di otto in otto. ♦ **octonary** s. strofa di otto versi.
octopus s. (pl. -pi) polipo, piovra.
octosyllabic agg. ottosillabico.
octosyllable s. verso, parola di otto sillabe.
ocular agg. e s. oculare.
oculate(d) agg. maculato.
oculist s. oculista.
oculistic agg. oculistico.
odalisque s. odalisca.
odd agg. **1.** dispari **2.** scompagnato **3.** in più **4.** occasionale **5.** bizzarro. ♦ **odd** s. cosa extra.
oddity, oddness s. stranezza.
odds s. pl. **1.** differenza **2.** disaccordo **3.** pronostico || — and ends, rimanenze.
ode s. ode.
odious agg. odioso.
odontological agg. odontoiatrico.
odontologist s. odontoiatra.
odontology s. odontoiatria.
odoriferous agg. odorifero.
odorous agg. odoroso.
odour s. odore.
odourless agg. inodoro.
oedema s. edema.
oenologist s. enologo.
oenology s. enologia.
oesophagus s. (pl. -gi) esofago.
of prep. **1.** di **2.** (tempo) a, in **3.** da parte di: very kind — you, molto gentile da parte vostra || — late, ultimamente.
off avv. **1.** lontano, via **2.** completamente || to be —, essere finito, fermo, in libertà. ♦ **off** prep. **1.** lontano, via da **2.** giù da. ♦ **off** agg. **1.** destro **2.** esterno **3.** lontano **4.** secondario **5.** libero || — day, giorno di libertà.
offence s. **1.** offesa **2.** colpa, delitto **3.** scandalo.
offenceless agg. **1.** inoffensivo **2.** innocente.
to offend vt. offendere, ♦ **to offend** vi. **1.** peccare **2.** violare la legge.
offender s. **1.** peccatore **2.** colpevole.

offensive *agg.* **1.** offensivo **2.** sgradevole. ♦ **offensive** *s.* offensiva.
offensiveness *s.* aggressività.
offer *s.* offerta.
to offer *vt.* offrire. ♦ **to offer** *vi.* offrirsi.
offerer *s.* offerente.
offering *s.* offerta.
offertory *s.* offertorio.
offhand *agg.* **1.** improvvisato **2.** spontaneo. ♦ **offhand** *avv.* lì per lì.
office *s.* ufficio, carica || *box-* —, botteghino.
officer *s.* ufficiale, funzionario || *non-commissioned* —, sottufficiale.
official *agg.* ufficiale. ♦ **official** *s.* funzionario.
officiant *s.* ufficiante.
to officiate *vi.* **1.** esercitare le funzioni di **2.** (*relig.*) ufficiare.
officious *agg.* **1.** ufficioso **2.** intrigante.
offing *s.* (*mar.*) largo.
offscourings *s. pl.* rifiuti, scarti.
offset *s.* **1.** compenso **2.** sperone (*di monte*) **3.** germoglio, progenie **4.** (*tip.*) fotolito.
offshoot *s.* **1.** germoglio **2.** ramo.
offshore *agg.* **1.** di terra **2.** lontano dalla costa. ♦ **offshore** *avv.* al largo.
offside *s.* (*sport*) fuori gioco.
offspring *s.* **1.** prole **2.** frutto.
often *avv.* spesso || *how* —?, quante volte?
ogive *s.* ogiva.
oil *s.* **1.** olio **2.** petrolio || *— cloth*, tela cerata; *— field*, giacimento petrolifero; *— -mill*, frantoio; *— paper*, carta oleata; *— pipeline*, oleodotto.
to oil *vt.* ungere, oliare.
oiler *s.* oliatore.
oily *agg.* oleoso, untuoso.
ointment *s.* unguento.
O.K. *avv.* bene: *to be* —, andar bene.
old (**elder, older; eldest, oldest**) *agg.* vecchio || *how — are you?*, quanti anni hai?; *— -fashioned*, antiquato. ♦ **old** *s.* passato.
oldish *agg.* attempato.
oleander *s.* oleandro.
oleograph *s.* oleografia.
oleographic *agg.* oleografico.
olfactory *agg.* olfattivo.
oligarch *s.* oligarchia.
oligarchic(al) *agg.* oligarchico.

oligarchy *s.* oligarchia.
olive *agg.* **1.** d'oliva **2.** olivastro. ♦ **olive** *s.* **1.** oliva **2.** (*-tree*) olivo.
Olympiad *s.* olimpiade.
Olympian *agg.* olimpico, olimpionico. ♦ **Olympian** *s.* olimpionico.
Olympic *agg.* V. *Olympian*.
omelet(te) *s.* frittata.
omen *s.* auspicio.
ominous *agg.* di cattivo augurio.
omission *s.* omissione.
to omit *vt.* omettere.
omnipotence *s.* onnipotenza.
omnipotent *agg.* e *s.* onnipotente.
omnipresent *agg.* onnipresente.
omniscience *s.* onniscienza.
omniscient *agg.* e *s.* onnisciente.
omnivorous *agg.* onnivoro.
on *prep.* **1.** su **2.** a, in, di, per || *on purpose*, apposta. ♦ **on** *avv.* **1.** su, indosso **2.** (in) avanti || *to be* —, essere in funzione, essere rappresentato; *and so* —, eccetera.
once *avv.* una volta || *at* —, subito; *all at* —, improvvisamente. ♦ **once** *cong.* una volta che.
on-coming *agg.* prossimo.
one *agg.* **1.** uno **2.** uno solo. ♦ **one** *pron.* **1.** (*dimostr.*) questo, quello **2.** (*indef.*) (l') uno || *— by* —, uno a uno. ♦ **one** *s.* uno || *— John Brown*, un certo John Brown.
one-eyed *agg.* guercio.
oneness *s.* unità, unicità.
onerous *agg.* oneroso.
oneself *pron. r.* se stesso.
one-sided *agg.* unilaterale.
one-sidely *avv.* unilateralmente.
oneway *agg.* a senso unico.
ongoings *s. pl.* avvenimenti.
onion *s.* cipolla || *spring-* —, cipollina.
onlooker *s.* spettatore.
only *agg.* e *avv.* solo.
onomastic *agg.* onomastico.
onomatopoeia *s.* onomatopeia.
onomatopoeic *agg.* onomatopeico.
onset *s.* **1.** attacco **2.** inizio.
onto *prep.* su, in cima a.
ontological *agg.* ontologico.
ontology *s.* ontologia.
onus *s.* onere.
onward *agg.* avanzato.
onward(s) *avv.* avanti.
onyx *s.* onice.
to ooze *vt.* e *vi.* stillare || *to — out*, trapelare.
oozy *agg.* melmoso.
opacity *s.* opacità.

opal *s.* opale.
opalescent *agg.* opalescente.
opaque *agg.* opaco.
open *agg.* aperto || *wide* —, spalancato; *in the* — *air,* all'aperto.
to open *vt.* aprire. ♦ to open *vi.* aprirsi.
open-handed *agg.* generoso.
opening *s.* 1. apertura 2. radura.
openly *avv.* apertamente.
open-minded *agg.* di larghe vedute.
open-mindedness *s.* larghezza di vedute.
openness *s.* 1. apertura 2. franchezza.
opera *s.* opera lirica || — *-house,* teatro dell'opera; — *glass,* binocolo.
to operate *vt.* 1. operare 2. far funzionare 3. gestire. ♦ to operate *vi.* 1. operare 2. funzionare.
operatic *agg.* di opera.
operation *s.* 1. operazione 2. funzionamento 3. azione.
operative *agg.* 1. attivo 2. operatono, operaio (*meccanico*). sentenza. ♦ operative *s.* artigianista, telegrafista.
operator *s.* 1. operatore 2. teleforio || — *part,* dispositivo di una
ophthalmia *s.* oftalmia.
ophthalmic *agg.* oftalmico.
ophthalmology *s.* oftalmologia, oculistica.
ophthalmoscopy *s.* oftalmoscopia.
opiate *agg.* 1. oppiato 2. soporifero. ♦ opiate *s.* narcotico.
opinion *s.* opinione.
opinionated, opinionative *agg.* ostinato.
opium *s.* oppio.
opponent *s.* avversario.
opportune *agg.* opportuno.
opportunism *s.* opportunismo.
opportunist *s.* opportunista.
opportunist(ic) *agg.* opportunistico.
opportunity *s.* occasione.
opposable *agg.* opponibile.
to oppose *vt.* opporre. ♦ to oppose *vi.* opporsi.
opposed *agg.* 1. opposto 2. ostile.
opposer *s.* oppositore.
opposite *agg.* e *s.* opposto. ♦ opposite *avv.* di fronte. ♦ opposite *prep.* di fronte a, dirimpetto a.
opposition *s.* opposizione.

to oppress *vt.* opprimere.
oppression *s.* oppressione.
oppressive *agg.* opprimente.
oppressor *s.* oppressore.
opprobrious *agg.* obbrobrioso.
to opt *vi.* optare.
optic(al) *agg.* ottico.
optician *s.* ottico.
optics *s.* ottica.
optimism *s.* ottimismo.
optimist *agg.* e *s.* ottimista.
optimistic(al) *agg.* ottimistico.
option *s.* opzione.
optional *agg.* facoltativo.
opulence *s.* opulenza.
opulent. *agg.* opulento.
or *cong.* o, oppure || *either...* —, sia... sia.
oracle *s.* oracolo.
oracular *agg.* profetico.
oral *agg.* e *s.* orale.
orange *s.* 1. arancia 2. arancio.
orangeade *s.* aranciata.
orangery *s.* aranceto.
oration *s.* discorso.
orator *s.* oratore.
oratorical *agg.* oratorio.
oratory[1] *s.* oratorio.
oratory[2] *s.* oratoria.
orb *s.* 1. cerchio 2. sfera.
orbit *s.* orbita.
orbital *agg.* orbitale.
orchard *s.* frutteto.
orchestra *s.* orchestra.
orchestral *agg.* orchestrale.
to orchestrate *vt.* orchestrare.
orchestration *s.* orchestrazione.
orchid, orchis *s.* orchidea.
to ordain *vt.* ordinare (*anche eccl.*).
ordeal *s.* 1. ordalia 2. dura prova.
order *s.* 1. ordine 2. classe || *in* — *that,* affinché; *in* — *to,* allo scopo di; *postal* —, vaglia postale; *made to* —, eseguito su ordinazione. ♦ orders *s. pl.* (*relig.*) ordini: *to take* —, farsi prete.
to order *vt.* 1. ordinare 2. riordinare.
ordering *s.* ordinamento.
orderly *agg.* ordinato. ♦ orderly *s.* 1. (*mil.*) ordinanza 2. (*mil.*) attendente.
ordinal *agg.* e *s.* ordinale.
ordinance *s.* 1. ordinanza 2. (*relig.*) rito.
ordinary *agg.* ordinario. ♦ ordinary *s.* 1. condizione ordinaria 2. pranzo a prezzo fisso.
ordinate *s.* ordinata.

ordination s. 1. ordine 2. (relig.) ordinazione.

ore s. minerale.

organ s. organo || barrel- —, organetto; mouth- —, armonica.

organic agg. organico.

organism s. organismo.

organist s. organista.

organizable agg. organizzabile.

organization s. organizzazione.

to **organize** vt. organizzare. ◆ to **organize** vi. organizzarsi.

organizer s. organizzatore.

organzine s. organzino.

orgasm s. orgasmo.

orgeat s. orzata.

orgiastic agg. orgiastico.

orgy s. orgia.

orient s. oriente.

to **orient** vt. 1. orientare 2. volgere verso oriente.

oriental agg. e s. orientale.

orientalist s. orientalista.

orientation s. orientamento.

orifice s. orifizio.

origan s. origano.

origin s. origine.

original agg. e s. originale.

originality s. originalità.

originally avv. 1. originalmente 2. originariamente.

to **originate** vt. dare origine. ◆ to **originate** vi. aver origine.

originator s. iniziatore.

ornament s. ornamento.

ornamental agg. ornamentale.

ornamentation s. decorazione.

ornate agg. ornato.

ornithological agg. ornitologico.

ornithologist s. ornitologo.

ornithology s. ornitologia.

orographic(al) agg. orografico.

orography s. orografia.

orphan agg. e s. orfano.

orphanage s. 1. la condizione di orfano 2. orfanotrofio.

orthodox agg. ortodosso.

orthodoxy s. ortodossia.

orthogonal agg. ortogonale.

orthographic(al) agg. 1. ortografico 2. ortogonale.

orthography s. 1. ortografia 2. (geom.) proiezione ortogonale.

orthop(a)edic(al) agg. ortopedico.

orthop(a)edics s. ortopedia.

orthop(a)edist s. ortopedico.

to **oscillate** vi. oscillare.

oscillation s. oscillazione.

oscillator s. oscillatore.

oscillatory agg. oscillatorio.

oscillograph s. oscillografo.

osier s. vimine.

osmose, osmosis s. osmosi.

osseous agg. osseo.

ossification s. ossificazione.

to **ossify** vt. ossificare. ◆ to **ossify** vi. ossificarsi.

ostensible agg. apparente.

ostensory s. ostensorio.

ostentation s. ostentazione.

ostentatious agg. ostentato.

osteological agg. osteologico.

osteology s. osteologia.

ostracism s. ostracismo.

to **ostracize** vt. dare l'ostracismo a.

ostrich s. struzzo.

other agg. e pron. altro || each —, l'un l'altro; every — day, un giorno sì e un giorno no. ◆ **others** pron. pl. altri || some... —..., gli uni... gli altri.

otherwise agg. diverso. ◆ **otherwise** avv. altrimenti.

otherworld s. mondo ultraterreno.

otitis s. otite.

otorhinolaryngologist s. otorinolaringoiatra.

otter s. lontra.

Ottoman agg. e s. ottomano.

ought s. zero.

ought v. dif. (condiz.) dovere: you — to wait,. dovresti aspettare.

ounce s. oncia.

our agg. poss. nostro, nostra, nostri, nostre.

ours pron. poss. il nostro, la nostra, i nostri, le nostre.

ourselves pron. r. pl. noi stessi.

out agg. esterno. ◆ **out** avv. fuori. ◆ **out** (of) prep. 1. fuori (di) 2. senza 3. per || —of-date, fuori moda; — -of-work, disoccupato; — -of-the-way, remoto.

to **outbid (outbade, outbidden)** vt. offrire di più.

outboard agg. e avv. fuoribordo.

outbreak s. 1. scoppio 2. sommossa.

outburst s. scoppio.

outcast s. proscritto.

to **outclass** vt. surclassare.

outcome s. risultato.

outcry s. grido, scalpore.

outdid V. to outdo.

to **outdistance** vt. distanziare.

to **outdo (outdid, outdone)** vt. superare.

outdoor agg. all'aperto.

outdoors avv. all'aperto.

outer *agg.* esteriore.
outfit(ting) *s.* equipaggiamento.
to outfit *vt.* rifornire di equipaggiamento. ♦ **to outfit** *vi.* rifornirsi
di equipaggiamento.
outfitter *s.* fornitore.
to outfly (outflew, outflown) *vt.*
sorpassare nel volo.
outgone V. *to outgo.*
outgo *s.* uscita.
to outgo (outwent, outgone) *vt.*
sorpassare.
outgoing *agg.* uscente, in partenza.
**to outgrow (outgrew, out-
grown)** *vt.* **1.** diventare troppo
grande per **2.** sorpassare (*in statura*).
outgrowth *s.* **1.** escrescenza **2.** risultato.
outhouse *s.* **1.** tettoia **2.** dipendenza.
outing *s.* escursione || — *clothes*,
abiti sportivi.
outlandish *agg.* **1.** strano **2.** remoto.
outlaw *s.* fuorilegge.
outlawry *s.* (*giur.*) proscrizione.
outlay *s.* spesa.
outlet *s.* **1.** sbocco **2.** cortile.
outline *s.* **1.** contorno **2.** schema **3.**
lineamento.
to outline *vt.* **1.** delineare **2.** abbozzare.
outliner *s.* bozzettista.
to outlive *vt.* sopravvivere a.
outlook *s.* **1.** veduta **2.** prospettiva
3. vigilanza.
to outnumber *vt.* superare numericamente.
outpost *s.* avamposto.
outpour *s.* **1.** scroscio di pioggia
2. (*fig.*) sfogo.
output *s.* produzione, rendimento.
outrage *s.* oltraggio.
to outrage *vt.* oltraggiare.
outrageous *agg.* **1.** oltraggioso **2.**
violento.
outrageousness *s.* **1.** oltraggio **2.**
violenza.
outran V. *to outrun.*
to outrange *vt.* avere una portata
maggiore di.
to outreach *vt.* sorpassare.
outrider *s.* battistrada.
outright *agg.* **1.** franco **2.** completo. ♦ **outright** *avv.* **1.** francamente **2.** completamente.
outrightness *s.* **1.** immediatezza
2. franchezza.
outroar *s.* fracasso.

to outrun (outran, outrun) *vt.*
oltrepassare.
outrush *s.* fuga.
to outsell (outsold, outsold) *vt.*
1. vendere in quantità superiore
2. vendere a prezzo superiore.
outset *s.* esordio.
**to outshine (outshone, out-
shone)** *vt.* eclissare (*anche fig.*).
outside *agg.* e *s.* **1.** esterno **2.** massimo. ♦ **outside** *avv.* **1.** all'esterno **2.** all'aperto. ♦ **outside** *prep.*
fuori di.
outsider *s.* **1.** profano **2.** estraneo
3. (*sport*) non favorito.
outsize *agg.* fuori misura. ♦ **outsize** *s.* taglia fuori misura.
outskirt *s.* orlo. ♦ **outskirts** *s.*
pl. periferia (*sing.*).
outsold V. *to outsell.*
outspoken *agg.* franco.
**to outspread (outspread, out-
spread)** *vt.* spiegare. ♦ **to outspread (outspread, outspread)**
vi. spiegarsi.
outstanding *agg.* **1.** prominente **2.**
resistente **3.** in sospeso.
to outstretch *vt.* distendere.
to outstrip *vt.* superare (*in velocità*).
outward *agg.* e *s.* esterno. ♦ **out-
ward(s)** *avv.* esternamente.
outwent V. *to outgo.*
oval *agg.* e *s.* ovale.
ovary *s.* ovaia.
ovation *s.* ovazione.
oven *s.* forno.
over *avv.* **1.** di sopra **2.** eccessiva-
mente || *to be* —, essere finito;
— *and* — *again*, più e più volte.
♦ **over** *prep.* **1.** su **2.** più di **3.**
durante || — *there*, dall'altra parte;
— *and above*, oltre a.
overalls *s. pl.* tuta da lavoro (*sing.*).
overate V. *to overeat.*
**to overbear (overbore, over-
borne)** *vt.* dominare, sopraffare.
overbearing *agg.* imperioso.
overbearingness *s.* imperiosità.
overboard *avv.* in mare.
overbore V. *to overbear.*
overborne V. *to overbear.*
to overburden *vt.* sovraccaricare.
overcame V. *to overcome.*
overcast *agg.* scuro, nuvoloso.
to overcast (overcast, overcast)
vt. oscurare. ♦ **to overcast
(overcast, overcast)** *vi.* oscurarsi.

overcharge s. 1. sovraccarico 2. sovrapprezzo.

to **overcharge** vt. 1. sovraccaricare 2. far pagare troppo caro.

to **overcloud** vi. rannuvolarsi.

overcoat s. soprabito.

to **overcome** (overcame, overcome) vt. superare, vincere.

overcoming s. su; ...amento, vittoria.

overconfident agg. troppo sicuro di sé.

overcredulity s. credulità eccessiva.

overcrowded agg. sovraffollato.

overcrowding s. sovraffollamento.

to **overdo** (overdid, overdone) vt. 1. esagerare 2. stancare.

overdone agg. troppo cotto.

overdose s. dose eccessiva.

overdrank V. to overdrink.

to **overdraw** (overdrew, overdrawn) vt. 1. esagerare 2. scoprire il conto in banca.

to **overdrink** (overdrank, overdrunk) vi. bere troppo.

overdue agg. scaduto.

to **overeat** (overate, overeaten) vi. mangiare troppo.

to **overestimate** vt. sopravvalutare.

overexcitability s. sovreccitabilità.

overexcitable agg. sovreccitabile.

to **overexcite** vt. sovreccitare.

overexcitement s. sovreccitazione.

to **overexert** vt. stancare.

to **overexpose** vt. sovresporre.

overfeeding s. superalimentazione.

overflew V. to overfly.

to **overflow** vt. inondare. ♦ to **overflow** vi. traboccare.

overflowing s. inondazione.

to **overfly** (overflew, overflown) vt. 1. sorvolare 2. superare in volo.

overfond agg. troppo appassionato.

to **overgrow** (overgrew, overgrown) vt. 1. coprire 2. superare. ♦ to **overgrow** (overgrew, overgrown) vi. 1. coprirsi 2. crescere troppo.

overgrowth s. 1. crescita eccessiva 2. vegetazione sovrabbondante.

overhang s. sporgenza, aggetto.

to **overhang** (overhung, overhung) vt. 1. sovrastare 2. ornare con tendaggi ecc.

to **overhaul** vt. 1. revisionare 2. sorpassare.

overhaul(ing) s. revisione.

overhead agg. 1. alto 2. (comm.) generale. ♦ **overhead** avv. in alto.

to **overhear** (overheard, overheard) vt. 1. udire per caso 2. origliare.

to **overheat** vt. surriscaldare. ♦ to **overheat** vi. surriscaldarsi.

overheating s. surriscaldamento.

overhung V. to overhang.

overindulgence s. eccessiva indulgenza.

overladen agg. sovraccarico.

overland avv. via terra.

overlap s. sovrapposizione.

overlay s. copertura.

to **overleap** vt. saltare di là da.

overload s. sovraccarico.

to **overload** vt. sovraccaricare.

to **overlook** vt. 1. guardare dall'alto 2. trascurare 3. ispezionare.

overlooker s. ispettore.

overnight agg. 1. compiuto durante la notte 2. per una notte. ♦ **overnight** avv. durante la notte.

overpaid V. to overpay.

to **overpass** vt. 1. attraversare 2. sorpassare 3. trasgredire.

overpast agg. passato.

to **overpay** (overpaid, overpaid) vt. pagare più del dovuto.

overpayment s. pagamento eccessivo.

overpeopled agg. sovrappopolato.

overplus s. soprappiù.

overpopulated agg. sovrappopolato.

overpopulation s. sovrappopolazione.

to **overpower** V. to overbear.

overpowering agg. 1. schiacciante 2. prepotente.

overpressure s. sovrapressione.

to **overprint** vt. sovrastampare.

to **overprize** vt. sopravvalutare.

to **overproduce** vt. produrre in eccesso.

overproduction s. sovraproduzione.

overproud agg. troppo orgoglioso.

overran V. to overrun.

to **overrate** vt. sopravvalutare.

to **overreach** vt. 1. oltrepassare 2. imbrogliare.

to **overrule** vt. 1. dirigere 2. annullare 3. dominare.

to **overrun** (overran, overrun) vt. 1. invadere 2. devastare 3. oltrepassare.

oversaw V. *to oversee.*
oversea(s) *agg.* e *avv.* d'oltremare.
to oversee (oversaw, overseen) *vt.* ispezionare.
overseer *s.* 1. ispettore 2. capo squadra.
to overset (overset, overset) *vt.* rovesciare. ♦ **to overset (overset, overset)** *vi.* rovesciarsi.
to overshadow *vt.* 1. ombreggiare 2. adombrare 3. proteggere.
overshoe *s.* soprascarpa.
to overshoot (overshot, overshot) *vt.* lanciare di là da || *to — the mark,* passare i limiti.
overside *avv.* lungo il fianco.
oversight *s.* 1. svista 2. sorveglianza.
to oversleep (overslept, overslept) *vi.* dormire oltre l'ora fissata.
to overspread (overspread, overre. ♦ **to overspread (overspread, overspread)** *vi.* spargersi.
to overstate *vt.* esagerare.
to overtake (overtook, overtaken) *vt.* 1. cogliere 2. superare.
overtaking *s.* sorpasso: *no* —, divieto di sorpasso.
overthrew V. *to overthrow.*
overthrow *s.* 1. rovesciamento 2. disfatta.
to overthrow (overthrew, overthrown) *vt.* 1. rovesciare 2. sconfiggere.
overtime *s.* straordinario (*orario di lavoro*).
overtook V. *to overtake.*
to overturn V. *to overthrow.*
overturnable *agg.* rovesciabile.
overturn(ing) *s.* rovesciamento.
overweary *agg.* stremato.
overweight *agg.* che supera il peso. ♦ **overweight** *s.* sovraccarico.
to overwhelm *vt.* 1. sommergere 2. sopraffare.
overwhelming *agg.* schiacciante.
overwork *s.* 1. lavoro eccessivo 2. straordinario.
to overwork *vt.* 1. far lavorare troppo 2. far eccessivo uso di. ♦ **to overwork** *vi.* lavorare troppo.
to overwrite (overwrote, overwritten) *vi.* scrivere troppo.
overwrought *agg.* 1. esausto 2. ricercato (*di stile*).
ovine *agg.* ovino.
oviparous *agg.* oviparo.

ovulation *s.* ovulazione.
ovule *s.* ovulo.
to owe *vt.* dovere, essere debitore di || *you must pay what is owing,* dovete pagare il vostro debito.
owing *agg.* dovuto.
owing to *prep.* a causa di.
owl *s.* gufo.
own *agg.* e *pron.* proprio.
to own *vt.* 1. possedere 2. ammettere || *to — to,* confessare.
owner *s.* proprietario || *shipowner,* armatore.
ownership *s.* proprietà.
ox (*pl.* oxen) *s.* bue.
oxidation *s.* ossidazione.
oxide *s.* ossido.
oxidizable *agg.* ossidabile.
to oxidize *vt.* ossidare. ♦ **to oxidize** *vi.* ossidarsi.
oxygen *s.* ossigeno || — *tent,* tenda ad ossigeno.
to oxygenate *vt.* ossigenare.
oxygenation *s.* ossigenazione.
to oxygenize *vt.* ossigenare.
oxyhydrogen *agg.* ossidrico: — *blowpipe,* cannello ossidrico.
oyster *s.* 1. ostrica 2. persona silenziosa, riservata.
ozone *s.* ozono.
to ozonize *vt.* ozonizzare.

P

pace *s.* passo.
to pace *vi.* andare al passo. ♦ **to pace** *vt.* percorrere. ♦ **to pace** *vi.* andare al passo, marciare.
paced *agg.* misurato (*a passi*) || *slow-* —, a passi lenti.
pachyderm *s.* pachiderma.
pacific *agg.* pacifico.
to pacificate *vt.* pacificare.
pacification *s.* pacificazione.
pacificator, pacifier *s.* pacificatore.
pacificatory *agg.* conciliante.
pacifism *s.* pacifismo.
pacifist *agg.* e *s.* pacifista.
to pacify *vt.* pacificare.
pack *s.* 1. pacco, balla, fagotto 2. carico 3. imballaggio 4. muta (*di cani*) 5. (*med.*) impacco || — *-ice,* banchisa; — *-saddle,* basto.
to pack *vt.* 1. impacchettare 2. im-

ballare 3. raggruppare. ♦ to pack
vi. raggrupparsi || to — up, fare
i bagagli.
package s. 1. imballaggio 2. pacco.
to package vt. 1. imballare 2. impacchettare.
packer s. 1. imballatore 2. impacchettatrice (macchina).
packet s. 1. pacchetto 2. (mar.) —
(-boat), postale.
packing s. 1. imballaggio 2. (mecc.)
guarnizione 3. (mar.) baderna ||
— -free, franco d'imballaggio.
pact s. patto.
pad¹ s. 1. imbottitura 2. zampa (di
cane, lupo, volpe) 3. (med.) tampone.
pad² s. rumore sordo.
to pad vt. imbottire.
paddle s. 1. pala 2. pagaia.
to paddle vi. remare con pagaie.
paddy s. risaia.
padlock s. lucchetto.
to padlock vt. chiudere con lucchetto.
paediatric agg. pediatrico.
paediatrician s. pediatra.
paediatrics s. pediatria...
paediatrist s. pediatra.
pagan agg. e s. pagano.
paganism s. paganesimo.
page¹ s. paggio.
page² s. pagina.
to page vt. 1. (tip.) impaginare 2.
numerare le pagine.
pageant s. 1. (teat.) scena (di sacra rappresentazione) 2. parata,
corteo.
pageantry s. 1. pompa, fasto 2.
ostentazione.
to paginate vt. V. to page.
pagination s. 1. paginatura 2. impaginazione.
paid V. to pay.
pail s. secchio.
paillasse s. pagliericcio.
pain s. 1. pena 2. dolore, sofferenza.
♦ pains s. pl. doglie.
to pain vt. far male, far soffrire.
painful agg. penoso.
painless agg. indolore.
painstaking agg. diligente. ♦
painstaking s. cura.
paint s. 1. pittura 2. belletto.
to paint vt. dipingere. ♦ to paint
vi. imbellettarsi.
painter s. 1. pittore 2. imbianchino.
painting s. 1. pittura 2. dipinto,
quadro.

paintress s. pittrice.
pair s. paio, coppia.
to pair vt. accoppiare. ♦ to pair
vi. accoppiarsi.
palace s. palazzo.
paladin s. paladino.
palatable agg. 1. gustoso 2. (fig.)
gradevole.
palatal agg. e s. palatale.
palatalization s. palatalizzazione.
palate s. palato.
pale¹ agg. pallido.
pale² s. 1. palo 2. palizzata.
to pale vt. far impallidire. ♦ to
pale vi. impallidire.
paleness s. pallore.
paleochristian agg. paleocristiano.
paleographer s. paleografo.
paleography s. paleografia.
paleolithic agg. paleolitico.
paleologist s. paleologo.
paleology s. paleologia.
paleontologic(al) agg. paleontologico.
paleontologist s. paleontologo.
paleontology s. paleontologia.
paleozoic agg. paleozoico.
palette s. tavolozza.
palfrey s. palafreno.
palinode s. palinodia.
palisade s. palizzata.
pall s. 1. drappo funebre 2. (eccl.)
pallio.
to pall¹ vt. coprire con un drappo.
to pall² vt. saziare. ♦ to pall vi.
saziarsi.
pallet¹ s. pagliericcio.
pallet² s. 1. paletta 2. tavolozza.
to palliate vt. 1. attenuare 2. scusare.
palliation s. 1. attenuazione 2. scusante.
palliative agg. e s. palliativo.
pallid agg. pallido.
pallor s. pallore.
palm¹ s. palma (anche fig.).
palm² s. (anat.) palmo.
to palm vt. toccare con la mano.
palmaceous agg. (bot.) di palma.
palmar agg. palmare.
palmate, palmated, agg. palmato.
palmiped agg. e s. palmipede.
palmistry s. chiromanzia.
palmy agg. 1. coperto di palme 2.
prosperoso, vittorioso.
palpability s. palpabilità.
palpable agg. palpabile.
to palpate vt. palpare.
to palpitate vi. palpitare.

palpitation *s.* palpitazione.
palsy *s.* paralisi.
to **palsy** *vt.* paralizzare.
to **palter** *vi.* tergiversare.
paltriness *s.* meschinità.
paltry *agg.* meschino.
to **pamper** *vt.* viziare.
pamphlet *s.* opuscolo.
pamphleteer *s.* autore di opuscoli.
pan *s.* 1. padella 2. vaschetta 3. bacino 4. piatto di bilancia || *baking-* —, teglia.
pancake *s.* frittella.
panchromatic *agg.* pancromatico.
pancreatic *agg.* pancreatico.
pandemonium *s.* pandemonio.
pander *s.* mezzano, ruffiano.
to **pander** *vi.* fare il mezzano.
pane *s.* 1. lastra di vetro 2. (*edil.*) pannello 3. faccia (*di brillante*).
panegyric *s.* panegirico.
panegyric(al) *agg.* laudativo.
panel *s.* 1. pannello 2. (*neol.*) commissione, comitato 3. (*giur.*) lista di giurati.
pang *s.* 1. fitta 2. (*fig.*) stretta al cuore.
panic *agg.* e *s.* panico.
panicky *agg.* allarmato.
panicle *s.* pannocchia.
panification *s.* panificazione.
pannier *s.* paniere.
panoramic *agg.* panoramico.
pansy *s.* viola del pensiero.
pant *s.* 1. palpito 2. ansito.
to **pant** *vi.* 1. palpitare 2. ansimare.
pantagruelian *agg.* pantagruelico.
pantheism *s.* panteismo.
pantheist *s.* panteista.
pantheistic(al) *agg.* panteistico.
panther *s.* pantera.
panties *s. pl.* (*fam.*) mutandine.
panting *s.* 1. palpitazione 2. ansito 3. ansia.
pantograph *s.* pantografo.
pantomime *s.* pantomima.
pantry *s.* dispensa.
pants *s. pl.* (*fam.*) mutande.
pap *s.* pappa.
papacy *s.* papato.
papal *agg.* papale.
paper *s.* 1. carta 2. prova d'esame
paper *s.* 1. carta 2. certificato, documento 3. prova d'esame 4. giornale || — *back*, libro in brossura; — *board*, cartone; — *hanger*, tappezziere; — *hanging*, tappezzeria.
to **paper** *vt.* 1. incartare 2. tappezzare.

papery *agg.* cartaceo.
papillary *agg.* papillare.
papism *s.* papismo.
papist *s.* papista.
papyrology *s.* papirologia.
papyrus *s.* (*pl.* -ri) papiro.
parable *s.* parabola.
parabolic(al) *agg.* 1. parabolico 2. di parabola.
paraboloid *s.* paraboloide.
parachute *s.* paracadute.
to **parachute** *vt.* paracadutare. ♦
to **parachute** *vi.* paracadutarsi.
parachutism *s.* paracadutismo.
parachutist *s.* paracadutista.
parade *s.* 1. (*mil.*) parata 2. mostra, sfoggio 3. viale, passeggiata.
to **parade** *vt.* disporre in parata. ♦
to **parade** *vi.* marciare in parata.
paradigm *s.* paradigma.
paradisaic(al) *agg.* paradisiaco.
paradise *s.* paradiso.
paradisiac(al) *agg.* paradisiaco.
paradox *s.* paradosso.
paradoxical *agg.* paradossale.
paraffin *s.* paraffina.
paragon *s.* modello (*di perfezione ecc.*).
paragraph *s.* paragrafo.
to **paragraph** *vt.* dividere in paragrafi.
parallel *agg.* parallelo. ♦ **parallel** *s.* 1. parallelo 2. parallela.
to **parallel** *vt.* 1. mettere in posizione parallela 2. paragonare.
parallelepiped *s.* parallelepipedo.
parallelism *s.* parallelismo.
parallelogram *s.* parallelogramma.
paralogism *s.* paralogismo.
to **paralyse** *vt.* paralizzare.
paralysis *s.* (*pl.* -ses) paralisi.
paralytic *agg.* e *s.* paralitico.
parameter *s.* parametro.
paramount *agg.* supremo. ♦ **paramount** *s.* capo supremo.
paramour *s.* amante.
paranoia *s.* paranoia.
paranoiac *agg.* e *s.* paranoico.
paranymph *s.* paraninfo.
parapet *s.* parapetto.
paraphrase *s.* parafrasi.
to **paraphrase** *vt.* e *vi.* parafrasare.
parasite *s.* parassita.
parasitic(al) *agg.* parassitico.
parasitism *s.* parassitismo.
parasol *s.* parasole.
paratrooper *s.* paracadutista.
paratyphoid *s.* paratifo.

parcel s. **1.** pacco **2.** lotto, appezzamento di terreno **3.** gruppo.
to parcel vt. spartire.
parcelling s. spartizione.
parcener s. coerede.
to parch vt. **1.** arrostire **2.** disseccare. ♦ **to parch** vi. **1.** bruciarsi **2.** disseccarsi.
parchment s. pergamena.
pardon s. perdono.
to pardon vt. perdonare.
pardonable agg. perdonabile.
to pare vt. **1.** tagliare **2.** sbucciare.
parenchyma s. parenchima.
parent s. **1.** genitore **2.** causa, origine.
parentage s. **1.** discendenza **2.** nascita.
parental agg. paterno, materno.
parenthesis s. (pl. -ses) parentesi.
parenthetic(al) agg. parentetico.
parenthood s. paternità, maternità.
parentless agg. orfano.
paresis s. paresi.
pariah s. paria.
parietal agg. parietale.
parish s. parrocchia || — priest, parroco.
parishioner s. parrocchiano.
Parisian agg. e s. parigino.
parisyllabic agg. e s. parisillabo.
parity s. parità.
park s. **1.** parco **2.** posteggio.
to park vt. **1.** adibire a parco **2.** parcheggiare.
parking s. parcheggio || no —, divieto di sosta.
parkway s. (amer.) viale.
parley s. colloquio.
to parley vi. parlamentare.
parliament s. parlamento.
parliamentarian s. parlamentare.
parliamentarianism s. parlamentarismo.
parliamentary agg. parlamentare.
parlour s. **1.** salotto **2.** parlatorio || beauty —, istituto di bellezza.
Parmesan agg. parmigiano.
parochial agg. **1.** parrocchiale **2.** (fig.) ristretto.
parochialism s. ristrettezza di vedute.
parodist s. parodista.
parody s. parodia.
to parody vt. parodiare.
parole s. **1.** parola d'onore **2.** parola d'ordine.
paroxysm s. parossismo.
parricidal agg. parricida.

parricide s. **1.** parricidio **2.** parricida.
parrot s. pappagallo.
to parrot vt. ripetere pappagallescamente.
to parry vt. parare, schivare.
parsley s. prezzemolo.
parson s. parroco (anglicano).
parsonage s. (eccl.) canonica, parrocchia.
part s. parte.
to part vt. dividere. ♦ **to part** vi. dividersi.
to partake (partook, partaken) vi. partecipare, prendere parte.
parthenogenesis s. partenogenesi.
partial agg. parziale.
partiality s. parzialità.
partially avv. parzialmente.
participant agg. e s. partecipante.
to participate vi. **1.** partecipare **2.** condividere.
participation s. partecipazione.
participial agg. participiale.
participle s. participio.
particle s. particella (anche gramm.).
particular agg. **1.** particolare **2.** particolareggiato **3.** esigente. ♦ **particular** s. particolare.
particularism s. particolarismo.
particularist s. particolarista.
particularity s. **1.** particolarità **2.** meticolosità.
to particularize vt. e vi. dettagliare.
parting s. separazione.
partisan agg. e s. partigiano.
partition s. **1.** divisione **2.** tramezzo.
to partition vt. dividere.
partitive agg. e s. partitivo.
partly avv. in parte.
partner s. **1.** socio **2.** coniuge.
partnership s. **1.** associazione **2.** (comm.) società.
partook V. to partake.
partridge s. pernice.
parturient agg. partoriente.
parturition s. parto.
party s. **1.** parte **2.** partito **3.** brigata **4.** trattenimento **5.** pattuglia.
pasha s. pascià.
pass¹ s. passo, gola.
pass² s. **1.** passaggio **2.** trapasso **3.** promozione **4.** lasciapassare.
to pass vt. e vi. passare || to — away, sparire; to — by, passar oltre.

passable *agg.* passabile.
passage *s.* 1. passaggio 2. corridoio 3. brano.
passementerie *s.* passamaneria.
passenger *s.* passeggero.
passer *s.* — -*by*, passante.
passible *agg.* passibile.
passing *agg.* 1. passeggero 2. casuale. ♦ passing *s.* passaggio.
passion *s.* passione ‖ — -*flower*, passiflora.
passional *agg.* passionale.
passionate *agg.* appassionato, passionale.
passionless *agg.* impassibile.
passive *agg.* e *s.* passivo.
passivism, passivity *s.* passività.
passport *s.* passaporto.
password *s.* parola d'ordine.
past *agg.* passato. ♦ past *s.* passato. ♦ past *avv.* vicino. ♦ past *prep.* al di là di.
paste *s.* pasta ‖ *tooth* —, dentifricio.
to paste *vt.* 1. incollare, appiccicare 2. (*gergo*) attaccare.
pasteboard *agg.* di cartone. ♦ pasteboard *s.* cartone.
pastel *s.* pastello.
pasteurization *s.* pastorizzazione.
to pasteurize *vt.* pastorizzare.
pastime *s.* passatempo.
pastoral *agg.* e *s.* pastorale.
pastry *s.* dolci (*pl.*).
pasture *s.* pascolo.
to pasture *vt.* e *vi.* pascolare.
pasty *agg.* pastoso. ♦ pasty *s.* (*cuc.*) pasticcio.
pat *agg.* adatto. ♦ pat *avv.* esattamente. ♦ pat *s.* 1. colpetto 2. panetto di burro.
to pat *vt.* battere leggermente.
patch *s.* 1. pezza, toppa 2. macchia.
to patch *vt.* aggiustare, rattoppare, raffazzonare.
patching *s.* rattoppo.
patchy *agg.* 1. rappezzato 2. a macchie.
patent *agg.* 1. chiaro, manifesto, evidente 2. brevettato. ♦ patent *s.* brevetto.
to patent *vt.* brevettare.
patentee *s.* detentore di brevetto.
paternal *agg.* paterno.
paternalism *s* paternalismo.
paternalistic *agg.* paternalistico.
paternity *s.* paternità.
path *s.* 1. sentiero 2. pista 3. percorso, traiettoria.
pathetic *agg.* patetico.
pathfinder *s.* esploratore.
pathless *agg.* 1. senza sentieri 2. inesplorato.
pathogenic *agg.* patogeno.
pathologic(al) *agg.* patologico.
pathologist *s.* patologo.
pathology *s.* patologia.
pathway *s.* sentiero.
patience *s.* pazienza.
patient *agg.* 1. paziente 2. suscettibile. ♦ patient *s.* paziente.
patriarch *s.* patriarca.
patriarchal *agg.* patriarcale.
patriarchate *s.* patriarcato.
patrician *agg..* e *s.* patrizio.
patricide *s.* V. *parricide*.
patrimonial *agg.* patrimoniale.
patrimony *s.* patrimonio.
patriot *s.* patriota.
patriotic *agg.* patriottico.
patriotism *s.* patriottismo.
patrol *s.* pattuglia, ronda.
to patrol *vt.* e *vi.* pattugliare, fare la ronda.
patron *s.* patrono.
patronage *s.* patronato.
patronal *agg.* patronale.
patroness *s.* patronessa.
to patronize *vt.* 1. patrocinare 2. trattare con condiscendenza.
patronizing *agg.* 1. protettivo 2. condiscendente.
patter¹ *s.* gergo.
patter² *s.* picchiettio.
to patter *vi.* picchiettare.
pattern *s.* 1. modello, campione 2. disegno (*di stoffa ecc.*).
to pattern *vt.* modellare (su).
paunch *s.* pancia.
pauper *s.* povero.
pauperism *s.* povertà.
pause *s.* pausa.
to pause *vi.* 1. fare una pausa 2. esitare, indugiare.
pauseless *agg.* incessante.
to pave *vt.* 1. pavimentare 2. (*fig.*) appianare.
pavement *s.* 1. pavimentazione 2. marciapiede.
paver *s.* lastricatore.
pavilion *s.* padiglione.
paving *s.* pavimentazione.
paw *s.* zampa.
to paw *vt.* dare zampate. ♦ to paw *vi.* scalpitare (*di cavalli*).
pawn *s.* 1. pegno 2. pedina (*di scacchi*).

to **pawn** vt. impegnare (dare in pegno).

pawnbroker s. prestatore su pegno.

pawnbroking s. il prestare su pegno.

pawner s. chi dà qualcosa in pegno.

pawnshop s. agenzia di prestiti su pegno.

pay s. paga.

to **pay (paid, paid)** vt. e vi. 1. pagare 2. rendere, fruttare || to — off, liquidare.

payable agg. 1. pagabile 2. redditizio.

payee s. creditore.

payer s. pagatore.

paying out s. esborso.

payment s. pagamento.

payoff s. 1. giorno di paga 2. liquidazione.

payroll s. libro paga.

pea s. pisello || chick —, cece.

peace s. pace.

peaceable agg. pacifico.

peaceful s. pacifico, tranquillo.

peacefulness s. pace, calma.

peaceless agg. agitato.

peacemaker s. pacificatore.

peach s. (bot.) pesca.

peach-tree s. pesco.

peachy agg. simile a pesca.

peacock s. pavone.

to **peacock** vi. pavoneggiarsi.

peak s. 1. picco 2. punta 3. visiera.

peaky agg. appuntito.

peal s. 1. scampanio 2. scoppio, fragore, scroscio (di risa, applausi).

to **peal** vi. scampanare. ♦ to **peal** vt. far rimbombare.

peanut s. arachide.

pear s. pera.

pear-tree s. pero.

pearl s. perla.

to **pearl** vt. imperlare, ornare di perle. ♦ to **pearl** vi. imperlarsi.

pearly agg. 1. perlaceo 2. ricco di perle.

peasant s. contadino.

peasantry s. 1. condizione di contadino 2. i contadini (pl.).

peat s. torba || — -bog, torbiera.

pebble s. 1. ciottolo 2. cristallo di rocca.

to **pebble** vt. coprire con ciottoli.

peccary s. pecari.

peck s. beccata.

to **peck** vt. e vi. beccare.

pectoral agg. e s. pettorale.

peculation s. peculato.

peculiar agg. 1. particolare 2. strano.

peculiarity s. 1. particolarità 2. bizzarria, eccentricità.

pecuniary agg. pecuniario.

pedagogic(al) agg. pedagogico.

pedagogics s. pedagogia.

pedagogist s. pedagogista.

pedagogue s. pedagogo.

pedagogy s. pedagogia.

pedal s. pedale.

to **pedal** vt. e vi. pedalare.

pedant s. pedante.

pedantic agg. pedante.

pedantry s. pedanteria.

pedestal s. piedistallo.

pedestrian agg. pedestre. ♦ **pedestrian** s. pedone.

pediatrics ecc. V. paediatrics ecc.

pediment s. (arch.) frontone.

pedlar s. venditore ambulante.

peel s. buccia.

to **peel** vt. sbucciare. ♦ to **peel** vi. sbucciarsi.

peeling s. buccia.

peep[1] s. 1. sguardo furtivo 2. fessura.

peep[2] s. pigolio.

to **peep**[1] vi. 1. guardare furtivamente 2. far capolino.

to **peep**[2] vi. pigolare.

peeper[1] s. ficcanaso, persona curiosa.

peeper[2] s. piccioncino.

peer s. 1. pari 2. Pari, membro della Camera dei Lord.

to **peer** vt. uguagliare. ♦ to **peer** vi. 1. scrutare 2. far capolino.

peerage s. 1. i Pari 2. nobiltà.

peerless agg. senza pari.

peevish agg. irritabile.

peg s. piuolo.

to **peg** vt. fissare.

pejorative agg. e s. peggiorativo.

pelagic agg. oceanico.

pelican s. pellicano.

pellet s. 1. pallottolina (di carta ecc.) 2. pallottola 3. pillola.

pellucid agg. trasparente.

pelt[1] s. colpo (di proiettile ecc.).

pelt[2] s. pelle (di animale).

to **pelt** vt. colpire.

pelvic agg. pelvico.

pelvis s. bacino.

pen[1] s. penna || -nib, pennino; fountain- —, penna stilografica.

pen[2] s. recinto (per animali).

to **pen**[1] vt. scrivere.

to **pen**[2] vt. rinchiudere animali in un recinto.

penal *agg.* penale.
to **penalize** *vt.* (*sport.*) penalizzare.
penalty *s.* penalità, punizione.
penance *s.* penitenza.
pence *s.* V. *penny.*
pencil *s.* matita.
pendant, pendent *agg.* e *s.* pendente.
pending *prep.* 1. durante 2. fino a.
pendular *agg.* pendolare.
pendulous *agg.* pendulo.
pendulum *s.* pendolo || — *-clock,* pendola.
penetrable *agg.* penetrabile.
to **penetrate** *vt.* e *vi.* penetrare.
penetration *s.* penetrazione.
penetrative *agg.* penetrante.
penguin *s.* pinguino.
penicillin *s.* penicillina.
peninsula *s.* penisola.
peninsular *agg.* peninsulare.
penis *s.* pene.
penitence *s.* penitenza.
penitent *agg.* e *s.* penitente.
penitential *agg.* penitenziale.
penitentiary *agg.* penitenziale. ♦ **penitentiary** *s.* (*eccl.*) penitenziere 2. riformatorio 3. (*amer.*) penitenziario.
penknife *s.* (*pl.* -knives) temperino.
pennant *s.* (*mar.*) pennone.
penniless *agg.* senza un soldo.
pennon *s.* pennone.
penny *s.* (*numero delle monete*), **pence** (*loro valore*) *s.* "penny".
pension *s.* pensione.
to **pension** *vt.* pensionare.
pensionable *agg.* pensionabile.
pensioner *s.* pensionato.
pensive *agg.* pensoso.
pent *agg.* chiuso.
pentagon *s.* pentagono.
pentagonal *agg.* pentagonale.
pentagram *s.* pentagono.
pentahedron *s.* pentaedro.
pentameter *s.* pentametro.
pentane *s.* pentano.
pentathlon *s.* pentatlon.
Pentecost *s.* Pentecoste.
Pentecostal *agg.* pentecostale.
penthouse *s.* tettoia.
pentode *s.* (*elettr.*) pentodo.
pentose *s.* pentosio.
penult(imate) *agg.* e *s.* penultimo.
penury *s.* povertà.
peony *s.* peonia.
people *s.* (*costruzione al pl.*) 1. popolo 2. gente 3. folla.
to **people** *vt.* popolare.

pepper *s.* pepe || — *-mill,* macinapepe.
to **pepper** *vt.* condire con pepe.
peppercorn *s.* grano di pepe.
peppermint *s.* menta peperita.
peppery *agg.* 1. pepato 2. collerico.
pepsin(e) *s.* pepsina.
per *prep.* per: — *cent,* per cento.
peracid *s.* peracido.
to **perambulate** *vt.* 1. attraversare 2. ispezionare. ♦ to **perambulate** *vi.* passeggiare.
perambulation *s.* 1. ispezione 2. passeggiata.
perambulator *s.* carrozzella per bambini.
percale *s.* percalle.
perceivable *agg.* percettibile.
to **perceive** *vt.* percepire, scorgere. ♦ to **perceive** *vi.* accorgersi.
percentage *s.* percentuale.
perceptible *agg.* percettibile.
perception *s.* percezione.
perceptive *agg.* percettivo.
perch[1] *s.* gruccia.
perch[2] *s.* pesce persico.
to **perch** *vi.* appollaiarsi.
perchlorate *s.* perclorato.
percipience *s.* percezione.
to **percolate** *vt.* e *vi.* filtrare, colare.
percolator *s.* filtro.
percussion *s.* percussione || — *-pin,* percussore.
perdition *s.* perdizione.
perdurable *agg.* durevole.
to **peregrinate** *vi.* peregrinare.
peregrination *s.* peregrinazione.
peremptory *agg.* perentorio.
perennial *agg.* perenne.
perfect *agg.* perfetto.
to **perfect** *vt.* perfezionare.
perfectibility *s.* perfettibilità.
perfectible *agg.* perfettibile.
perfecting *s.* 1. perfezionamento 2. completamento.
perfection *s.* 1. perfezione 2. perfezionamento.
perfectionism *s.* perfezionismo.
perfectionist *s.* perfezionista.
perfectly *avv.* perfettamente.
perfidious *agg.* perfido, sleale.
perfidy *s.* perfidia, slealtà.
to **perforate** *vt.* perforare.
perforation *s.* perforazione.
to **perform** *vt.* 1. eseguire 2. (*teat.*) rappresentare.
performable *agg.* 1. eseguibile 2. rappresentabile.

performance *s.* **1.** esecuzione **2.** atto **3.** (*teat.*) rappresentazione.
performer *s.* **1** esecutore **2.** attore.
performing *agg.* ammaestrato.
perfume *s.* profumo.
to **perfume** *vt.* profumare.
perfumer *s.* profumiere.
perfumery *s.* **1.** profumeria **2.** profumi.
perfunctory *agg.* superficiale.
to **perfuse** *vt.* aspergere.
perfusion *s.* aspersione.
perhaps *avv.* forse.
pericardium *s.* pericardio.
perigee *s.* perigeo.
peril *s.* pericolo.
perilous *agg.* pericoloso.
perimeter *s.* perimetro.
period *s.* **1.** periodo **2.** ora di lezione **3.** stadio, fase (*di una malattia*) **4.** (*gramm.*) punto.
periodic *agg.* periodico.
periodical *agg.* e *s.* periodico.
periodicity *s.* periodicità.
peripheral *agg.* periferico.
periphery *s.* **1.** perimetro **2.** superficie.
periphrase, periphrasis *s.* (*pl.* -ses) perifrasi.
periphrastic *agg.* perifrastico.
periscope *s.* periscopio.
to **perish** *vi.* perire.
perishable *agg.* **1.** deperibile **2.** mortale.
perishables *s. pl.* merci deteriorabili.
peristyle *s.* peristilio.
peritonitis *s.* peritonite.
periwig *s.* parrucca.
periwigged *agg.* imparruccato.
periwinkle *s.* pervinca. .
to **perjure** *vt.* giurare falsamente.
perjurer, perjury *s.* spergiuro.
permanence *s.* permanenza.
permanent *agg.* permanente.
permanganate *s.* permanganato.
permeability *s.* permeabilità.
permeable *agg.* permeabile.
to **permeate** *vt.* permeare. ♦ to **permeate** *vi.* permearsi.
permission, permit *s.* permesso.
to **permit** *vt.* e *vi.* permettere.
to **permute** *vt.* permutare.
pernicious *agg.* pernicioso.
to **perorate** *vi.* perorare.
peroration *s.* perorazione.
peroxid(e) *s.* perossido ‖ *hydrogen* —, acqua ossigenata.
to **peroxide** *vt.* ossigenare.

perpendicular *agg.* perpendicolare.
♦ **perpendicular** *s.* **1.** perpendicolare **2.** filo a piombo.
perpendicularity *s.* perpendicolarità.
to **perpetrate** *vt.* perpetrare.
perpetration *s.* perpetrazione.
perpetual *agg.* perpetuo.
to **perpetuate** *vt.* perpetuare.
perpetuity *s.* **1.** perpetuità **2.** rendita vitalizia.
to **perplex** *vt.* **1.** rendere perplesso **2.** complicare.
perplexed *agg.* perplesso.
perplexity *s.* **1.** perplessità **2.** complicazione.
to **persecute** *vt.* perseguitare.
persecution *s.* persecuzione.
persecutor *s.* persecutore.
perseverance *s.* perseveranza.
to **persevere** *vi.* perseverare.
Persian *agg.* e *s.* persiano.
persimmon *s.* (*bot.*) cachi.
to **persist** *vi.* persistere.
persistence *s.* persistenza.
persistent *agg.* persistente.
person *s.* persona.
personable *agg.* ben fatto.
personage *s.* personaggio.
personal *agg.* personale.
personality *s.* personalità.
personalization *s.* personificazione.
to **personalize** *vt.* personificare.
personally *avv.* personalmente.
personification *s.* personificazione.
to **personify** *vt.* personificare.
personnel *s.* personale.
perspective *agg.* prospettico. ♦
perspective *s.* prospettiva.
perspicacious *agg.* perspicace.
perspicacity *s.* perspicacia.
perspicuity *s.* perspicuità.
perspicuous *agg.* perspicuo.
perspiration *s.* traspirazione.
to **perspire** *vt.* e *vi.* sudare, trasudare.
to **persuade** *vt.* persuadere.
persuasion *s.* **1.** persuasione **2.** credenza.
persuasive *agg.* persuasivo.
pert *agg.* impertinente.
to **pertain** *vi.* appartenere.
pertinacious *agg.* pertinace.
pertinacy, pertinacity *s.* pertinacia.
pertinence *s.* pertinenza.
pertinent *agg.* pertinente.
pertly *avv.* insolentemente.
pertness *s.* insolenza.

to **perturb** *vt.* perturbare.
perturbation *s.* perturbazione.
perusal *s.* lettura attenta.
to **peruse** *vt.* leggere attentamente.
to **pervade** *vt.* pervadere.
pervasion *s.* penetrazione.
pervasive *agg.* penetrante.
perverse *agg.* **1.** perverso **2.** errato
3. ostinato.
perversion *s.* perversione.
perversity *s.* perversità.
pervert *s.* **1.** pervertito **2.** apostata.
to **pervert** *vt.* pervertire.
pessimism *s.* pessimismo.
pessimist *s.* pessimista.
pessimistic *agg.* pessimistico.
pessimistically *avv.* in modo pessimistico.
pest *s.* peste *(anche fig.)*.
to **pester** *vt.* importunare.
pestiferous *agg.* pestifero.
pestilence *s.* pestilenza.
pestilent *agg.* **1.** nocivo **2.** molesto.
pestilential *agg.* pestilenziale.
pestle *s.* pestello.
pet *agg. e s.* favorito || — *name,* vezzeggiativo.
to **pet** *vt.* vezzeggiare.
petal *s.* petalo.
petard *s.* petardo.
petition *s.* petizione, istanza.
to **petition** *vt. e vi.* fare una petizione (a).
petitioner *s.* postulante.
to **petrify** *vt.* pietrificare. ♦ to **petrify** *vi.* pietrificarsi.
petrography *s.* petrografia.
petrol *s.* benzina.
petticoat *s.* sottoveste.
pettifogger *s.* azzeccagarbugli.
petty *agg.* **1.** meschino **2.** subalterno.
petulant *agg.* petulante.
pew *s.* banco *(di chiesa)*.
pewter *s.* peltro.
phagocyte *s.* fagocita.
phalanstery *s.* falansterio.
phalanx *s.* *(pl.* -ges) falange.
phallic *agg.* fallico.
phantasm *s.* fantasma.
phantasmagoria *s.* fantasmagoria.
phantasmagorial, phantasmagoric(al) *agg.* fantasmagorico.
phantom *s.* **1.** fantasma **2.** apparizione.
Pharaoh *s.* faraone.
Pharisee *s.* fariseo.
pharmaceutic(al) *agg.* farmaceutico.

pharmaceutics *s.* farmaceutica.
pharmacology *s.* farmacologia.
pharmacopoeia *s.* farmacopea.
pharmacy *s.* farmacia.
pharyngitis *s.* faringite.
pharynx *s.* *(pl.* -ges) faringe.
phase *s.* fase.
pheasant *s.* fagiano.
phenic *agg.* fenico.
phenol *s.* fenolo.
phenomenal *agg.* **1.** fenomenico **2.** fenomenale.
phenomenalism *s.* fenomenismo.
phenomenology *s.* fenomenologia.
phenomenon *s.* *(pl.* -na) fenomeno.
phial *s.* fiala.
to **philander** *vi.* fare il cascamorto.
philanderer *s.* cascamorto.
philanthrope *s.* filantropo.
philanthropic(al) *agg.* filantropico.
philanthropism *s.* filantropia.
philanthropist *s.* filantropo.
philanthropy *s.* filantropia.
philatelic(al) *agg.* filatelico.
philatelist *s.* filatelico.
philately *s.* filatelia.
philharmonic *agg.* filarmonico.
philippic *s.* filippica.
Philippine *agg.* filippino.
philologian, philologist *s.* filologo.
philology *s.* filologia.
philosopher *s.* filosofo.
philosophic(al) *agg.* filosofico.
philosophist *s.* pseudofilosofo.
to **philosophize** *vi.* filosofare.
philosophy *s.* filosofia.
phlebitis *s.* flebite.
phleboclysis *s.* fleboclisi.
phlegm *s.* flemma.
phlegmatic(al) *agg.* flemmatico.
phlegmon *s.* flemmone.
phlogistic *agg.* flogistico.
phobia *s.* fobia.
phoenix *s.* fenice.
phone *s.* V. *telephone.*
phones *s. pl.* cuffie.
phoneme *s.* fonema.
phonetics *s.* fonetica.
phonogram *s.* fonogramma.
phonograph *s.* fonografo.
phonology *s.* fonologia.
phosphate *s.* fosfato.
phosphor *s.* fosforo.
phosphorescence *s.* fosforescenza.
phosphorescent *agg.* fosforescente.
phosphoric *agg.* fosforico.
phosphorous *agg.* fosforoso.

PHOTO 204 **PILING**

photo *s.* foto.
photocell *s.* cellula fotoelettrica.
photocopy *s.* fotocopia.
photoelectric(al) *agg.* fotoelettrico.
photogenic *agg.* fotogenico.
photograph *s.* fotografia.
to photograph *vt.* fotografare.
photographer *s.* fotografo.
photography *s.* fotografia (*come arte*).
photometry *s.* fotometria.
photomontage *s.* fotomontaggio.
phrase *s.* 1. locuzione, frase 2. stile.
to phrase *vt.* esprimere.
phraseology *s.* fraseologia.
phrenetic(al) *agg.* frenetico.
phrenologist *s.* frenologo.
phrenology *s.* frenologia.
phthisiology *s.* tisiologia.
phthisis *s.* tisi.
phylloxera *s.* fillossera.
physic *s.* medicina.
physical *agg.* fisico.
physician *s.* medico.
physicist *s.* fisico.
physics *s.* fisica.
physiognomist *s.* fisionomista.
physiognomy *s.* fisionomia.
physiologic(al) *agg.* fisiologico.
physiologist *s.* fisiologo.
physiology *s.* fisiologia.
physiotherapy *s.* fisioterapia.
physique *s.* fisico.
pianist *s.* pianista.
picaresque *agg.* picaresco.
pick[1] *s.* 1. piccone 2. colpo di piccone || *tooth* —, stuzzicadenti.
pick[2] *s.* scelta, il meglio (*di qc.*).
to pick *vt.* 1. scavare 2. pulire 3. raccogliere 4. rubare.
pickax(e) *s.* piccone.
picker *s.* 1. piccone 2. zappatore 3. raccoglitore.
picket *s.* 1. piolo, palo 2. (*mil.*) picchetto.
pickle *s.* 1. salamoia 2. sottaceti (*pl.*).
to pickle *vt.* mettere in salamoia, sotto aceto.
picklock *s.* 1. scassinatore 2. grimaldello.
pickpocket *s.* borsaiolo.
pickup *s.* 1. raccolta 2. (*mecc.*) accelerazione 3. fonorivelatore.
pictorial *agg.* 1. illustrato 2. pittorico. ♦ pictorial *s.* giornale illustrato.
picture *s.* 1. quadro, dipinto, ritrat-

to 2. illustrazione. ♦ pictures *s. pl.* cinema (*sing.*) || — *fook*, libro illustrato.
to picture *vt.* dipingere || *to* — *to oneself*, immaginarsi, figurarsi.
picturesque *agg.* pittoresco.
pidgin *agg.* — *English*, inglese scorretto (*usato tra cinesi ed europei*).
pie[1] *s.* pica, gazza.
pie[2] *s.* torta, pasticcio.
pie[3] *s.* (*tip.*) refuso.
piece *s.* 1. pezzo 2. pezza (*di tessuto*) || *by the* —, a cottimo.
to piece *vt.* rappezzare, raggiustare.
piecemeal *avv.* pezzo per pezzo. ♦ piecemeal *agg.* frammentario.
piecework *s.* (*lavoro a*) cottimo.
pieceworker *s.* cottimista.
pied *agg.* screziato.
pier *s.* 1. molo 2. pilone || — *-glass*, specchiera.
to pierce *vt.* 1. forare 2. trafiggere.
piercer *s.* 1. punzone 2. punzonatore.
piercing *agg.* penetrante. ♦ piercing *s.* perforamento.
pietism *s.* pietismo.
piety *s.* pietà, reverenza.
pig *s.* 1. maiale 2. (*metal.*) lingotto.
pigeon *s.* piccione || — *-house*, piccionaia; *carrier* —, piccione viaggiatore.
pigeonhole *s.* 1. colombaia 2. casella 3. (*giur.*) casellario.
to pigeonhole *vt.* incasellare.
piggish *agg.* porcino.
pigheaded *agg.* testardo.
pigment *s.* pigmento.
pigmentation *s.* pigmentazione.
pigmy *agg.* e *s.* pigmeo.
pigsty *s.* porcile.
pike[1] *s.* picca.
pike[2] *s.* (*amer.*) pedaggio.
pilaster *s.* pilastro.
pile *s.* 1. mucchio 2. fabbricato 3. rogo 4. (*elettr.*) pila 5. (*fig.*) gruzzolo.
to pile[1] *vt.* ammucchiare. ♦ to pile *vi.* ammucchiarsi.
to pile[2] *vt.* conficcare pali in, fare palizzate.
piles *s. pl.* emorroidi.
to pilfer *vt.* e *vi.* rubacchiare.
pilferer *s.* ladruncolo.
pilgrim *s.* pellegrino.
pilgrimage *s.* pellegrinaggio.
piling[1] *s.* ammucchiamento.
piling[2] *s.* palificazione di sostegno.

pill s. pillola: *contraceptive (pill)*, pillola anticoncezionale.
pillage s. 1. saccheggio 2. bottino.
to **pillage** vt. saccheggiare.
pillar s. colonna, guanciale || — -box, cassetta delle lettere.
pillory s. berlina.
to **pillory** vt. mettere alla berlina.
pillow s. cuscino, guanciale || — -case, federa.
pilot s. pilota.
to **pilot** vt. pilotare.
pilotage s. pilotaggio.
pimple s. foruncolo.
pin s. 1. spillo 2. perno || *pins and needles*, formicolio.
to **pin** vt. 1. puntare 2. (fig.) inchiodare.
pinafore s. grembiulino.
pinaster s. pinastro.
to **pincer** vt. attanagliare.
pincers s. pl. tenaglie.
pinch s. 1. pizzico, pizzicotto 2. (fig.) angustia.
to **pinch** vt. 1. pizzicare 2. stringere 3. causare dolore. ♦ to **pinch** vi. essere avaro.
pinchbeck s. princisbecco.
pincushion s. puntaspilli.
Pindaric agg. pindarico.
pine s. pino || — -apple, ananasso; — -cone, pigna; — -wood, pineta.
to **pine** vi. struggersi.
pinion[1] s. penna remigante.
pinion[2] s. (mecc.) pignone.
to **pinion** vt. tarpare le ali a.
pink agg. rosa. ♦ **pink** s. 1. colore rosa 2. garofano 3. (fig.) quintessenza.
to **pink** vt. 1. traforare 2. trafiggere.
pinky agg. roseo.
pinnacle s. 1. pinnacolo 2. sommità.
pinpoint s. capocchia di spillo.
pint s. pinta.
pioneer s. pioniere.
pious agg. 1. pio 2. pietoso.
piousness s. pietà.
pip s. seme di frutto.
to **pip** vi. pigolare.
pipage s. 1. tubatura 2. trasporto per tubatura.
pipe s. 1. tubo 2. pipa 3. strumento a fiato 4. condotta.
to **pipe** vi. 1. suonare (piffero ecc.) 2. stridere. ♦ to **pipe** vt. 1. suonare 2. trasportare con tubature 3.

fornire di tubature.
pipeline s. oleodotto.
piper s. pifferaio.
pipet(te) s. (chim.) pipetta.
piping agg. 1. flautato 2. acuto. ♦
piping s. 1. suono (di piffero ecc.) 2. suono acuto 3. tubatura.
piquancy s. gusto piccante.
piquant agg. piccante.
pique s. ripicco, risentimento.
piracy s. 1. pirateria 2. plagio.
pirate s. 1. pirata 2. plagiario.
pirogue s. piroga.
pirouette s. piroetta.
to **pirouette** vi. piroettare.
pistil s. pistillo.
pistol s. pistola.
piston s. pistone.
pit s. 1. fossa 2. cavità 3. platea.
to **pit** vt. 1. bucare 2. mettere in una fossa.
pitch[1] s. 1. lancio 2. beccheggio 3. (mecc.) passo 4. (mus.) intonazione 5. inclinazione.
pitch[2] s. pece, bitume || — -dark, nero come la pece.
to **pitch**[1] vt. 1. sistemare 2. gettare 3. intonare. ♦ to **pitch** vi. 1. beccheggiare 2. (aer.) picchiare.
to **pitch**[2] vt. impeciare.
pitcher s. brocca.
pitchfork s. forcone.
to **pitchfork** vt. 1. rimuovere 2. spingere (col forcone).
pitching s. beccheggio.
pitchy agg. 1. impeciato 2. simile a pece.
piteous agg. pietoso.
pitfall s. trappola.
pith s. 1. midollo 2. (fig.) essenza.
pithy agg. (fig.) vigoroso.
pitiable, **pitiful** agg. pietoso.
pitiless agg. spietato.
pittance s. poco denaro.
pitted agg. butterato.
pity s. pietà || *what a —!*, che peccato!
to **pity** vt. aver pietà di, compatire.
pitying agg. pietoso.
pivot s. cardine.
to **pivot** vt. montare su cardini. ♦ to **pivot** vi. girare su cardini.
placable agg. placabile.
placard s. manifesto.
to **placate** vt. placare.
placatory agg. conciliante.
place s. 1. posto 2. brano || *to take —*, aver luogo, accadere.

to **place** vt. mettere, porre, situare.
placement s. collocamento.
placid agg. placido.
placidity s. placidità.
placing s. sistemazione.
plagiarism s. plagio.
plagiarist s. plagiario.
to **plagiarize** vt. plagiare.
plagiary s. 1. plagio 2. plagiario.
plague s. peste.
to **plague** vt. affliggere.
plaguer s. tormentatore.
plaid s. 1. mantello scozzese 2. tessuto a quadri.
plain agg. 1. piano, chiaro, evidente 2. semplice 3. comune, scialbo. ♦ **plain** avv. 1. chiaramente 2. semplicemente.
plain-clothes s. pl. abiti borghesi.
plainness s. 1. chiarezza 2. semplicità 3. aspetto scialbo.
plaint s. 1. lamento, lagnanza 2. (giur.) querela.
plaintiff s. (giur.) attore (nei processi civili).
plaintive agg. lamentoso.
plait s. 1. piega (di abiti) 2. treccia.
to **plait** vt. 1. pieghettare 2. intrecciare.
plan s. 1. piano, progetto 2. pianta (di una città).
to **plan** vt. progettare.
plane[1] agg. piano. ♦ **plane** s. 1. piano 2. aereo.
plane[2] s. pialla.
plane[3] s. — -tree, platano.
to **plane**[1] vi. volare.
to **plane**[2] vt. piallare.
planer s. (mecc.) piallatrice.
planet s. (astr.) pianeta.
planetary agg. planetario.
planimetric(al) agg. planimetrico.
planimetry s. planimetria.
planisphere s. planisfero.
plank s. tavola, asse.
to **plank** vt. coprire di tavole.
planking s. tavolato.
plankton s. plancton.
planner s. progettista.
planning s. progettazione.
plant s. 1. pianta 2. impianto, apparato 3. fabbrica, stabilimento.
to **plant** vt. (im)piantare.
plantation s. piantagione.
planter s. 1. piantatore 2. colonizzatore.
plantigrade agg. e s. plantigrado.
plaque s. placca.
plash s. pozzanghera.

plaster s. 1. cerotto 2. gesso 3. intonaco.
to **plaster** vt. 1. incerottare 2. ingessare 3. intonacare 4. ricoprire.
plastering s. 1. intonacatura 2. ingessatura.
plastic agg. plastico, malleabile.
plasticine s. plastilina.
plasticity s. plasticità.
to **plasticize** vt. rendere plastico.
plastics s. pl. materie plastiche.
plate s. 1. lastra, lamina 2. piatto 3. tavola fuori testo 4. targa 5. squama 6. vasellame.
to **plate** vt. 1. placcare 2. rivestire di piastre.
plateau s. altipiano.
platen s. 1. piastra metallica 2. rullo di macchina da scrivere.
platform s. 1. piattaforma 2. (ferr.) marciapiede 3. impalcatura 4. (amer.) programma politico.
plating s. 1. placcatura 2. rivestimento metallico.
to **platinize** vt. platinare.
platinum s. platino.
platitude s. banalità.
Platonic agg. platonico.
Platonism s. platonismo.
platoon s. plotone.
plausibility s. plausibilità.
plausible agg. plausibile.
play s. 1. gioco 2. dramma 3. (mus.) esecuzione 4. azione || — bill, cartellone teatrale; — -time, ricreazione.
to **play** vt. e vi. 1. giocare 2. recitare 3. agire 4. suonare || to — down, dare poca importanza a.
playboy s. (fam.) gaudente.
player s. 1. giocatore 2. attore 3. suonatore.
playful agg. giocoso.
playfulness s. allegria.
playground s. terreno di giochi.
playhouse s. teatro.
playing s. 1. gioco 2. rappresentazione 3. (mus.) esecuzione.
plaything s. giocattolo.
playwright, playwriter s. commediografo.
plea s. 1. giustificazione 2. (giur.) eccezione difensiva.
to **plead** vt. 1. patrocinare 2. addurre a pretesto 3. (giur.) perorare (una causa). ♦ to **plead** vi. 1. difendersi 2. supplicare.
pleader s. patrocinatore.
pleading agg. supplichevole. ♦

pleading s. difesa. ♦ **pleadings** s. pl. comparse.

pleasant agg. piacevole.

pleasantry s. piacevolezza.

to **please** vt. e vi. piacere (a) || — God, a Dio piacendo.

pleased agg. lieto.

pleasing agg. piacevole.

pleasure s. piacere.

pleat s. piega (di abiti ecc.).

to **pleat** vt. pieghettare.

plebeian agg. e s. plebeo.

plebiscitary agg. plebiscitario.

plebiscite s. plebiscito.

plectrum s. plettro.

pledge s. 1. pegno 2. promessa 3. brindisi.

to **pledge** vt. 1. impegnare 2. brindare a.

pledgee s. (giur.) creditore pignoratizio.

plenary agg. plenario || — session, seduta plenaria.

plenilune s. plenilunio.

plenipotentiary agg. e s. plenipotenziario.

plentiful agg. abbondante.

plenty s. abbondanza, quantità.

pleonasm s. pleonasma.

pleonastic agg. pleonastico.

plethora s. pletora.

plethoric agg. pletorico.

pleurisy s. pleurite.

plexus s. plesso.

pliability s. pieghevolezza.

pliable agg. pieghevole.

pliancy s. V. pliability.

pliant s. V. pliable.

pliers s. pl. pinze.

plight[1] s. situazione critica.

plight[2] s. impegno, promessa.

to **plight** vt. impegnare, promettere.

plod s. 1. passo pesante 2. lavoro faticoso.

to **plod** vt. e vi. 1. camminare faticosamente 2. sgobbare.

plodder s. 1. chi cammina faticosamente 2. sgobbone.

plot s. 1. appezzamento 2. trama 3. congiura.

to **plot** vt. e vi. 1. fare la pianta di 2. tramare.

plotter s. cospiratore.

plough s. aratro.

to **plough** vt. e vi. 1. arare 2. solcare.

ploughing s. aratura.

ploughman s. aratore.

ploughshare s. vomere.

plover s. piviere.

pluck s. 1. strappo 2. coraggio.

to **pluck** vt. 1. strappare 2. spennare 3. tirare || to — up, sradicare.

plucky agg. coraggioso.

plug s. 1. tappo (di lavandino ecc.) 2. (elettr.; tel.) spina || spark(ing)- — (mecc.), candela.

to **plug** vt. 1. tappare 2. tamponare || to — in, inserire la corrente; to — away, sgobbare.

plugging s. chiusura.

plum s. 1. prugna, susina 2. uva passa 3. (fig.) il meglio.

plumage s. piumaggio.

plumb agg. 1. a piombo 2. completo. ♦ **plumb** s. 1. filo a piombo 2. scandaglio. ♦ **plumb** avv. 1. a piombo 2. esattamente.

to **plumb** vt. 1. rendere verticale 2. scandagliare 3. impiombare.

plumber s. idraulico.

plumbery s. negozio di idraulico.

plumbing s. 1. piombatura 2. lavori idraulici.

plumbum s. piombo.

plume s. piuma, penna.

plummet s. piombino.

plump[1] agg. grassottello.

plump[2] agg. brusco, netto. ♦ **plump** avv. 1. improvvisamente 2. direttamente.

to **plump** vt. 1. ingrassare 2. far cadere. ♦ to **plump** vi. 1. ingrassare 2. cadere.

to **plunder** v.. depredare.

plunderer s. saccheggiatore.

plunge s. tuffo.

to **plunge** vt. tuffare. ♦ to **plunge** vi. tuffarsi.

plunger s. 1. tuffatore 2. stantuffo.

plunk s. colpo metallico.

to **plunk** vt. far cadere pesantemente. ♦ to **plunk** vi. cadere pesantemente.

plural agg. e s. plurale.

pluralism s. pluralismo.

plurality s. pluralità.

plus agg. 1. in più 2. (elettr.) positivo || — value, plusvalore. ♦ **plus** s. 1. più 2. quantità positiva. ♦ **plus** prep. più.

plush s. « peluche », felpa.

plutocracy s. plutocrazia.

plutocrat s. plutocrate.

ply s. piega || — -wood, compensato.

to **ply** vt. 1. maneggiare 2. importunare. ♦ to **ply** vi. 1. lavorare as-

siduamente 2. fare la spola.
pneumatic *agg.* e *s.* pneumatico.
pneumonia *s.* polmonite.
pneumothorax *s.* pneumotorace.
to poach *vt.* 1. calpestare 2. cacciare di frodo 3. interferire.
poacher *s.* bracconiere.
poaching *s.* bracconaggio.
pocket *s.* 1. tasca 2. buca (*di biliardo*) || — -*book*, lib:o tascabile.
to pocket *vt.* 1. intascare 2. nascondere, soffocare (*sentimenti ecc.*).
pocketful *s.* tascata.
pod *s.* 1. baccello 2. gruppetto.
poem *s.* 1. poesia 2. pocma.
poet *s.* pocta.
poetic(al) *agg.* poetico.
poetic(s) *s.* poetica.
poetry *s.* poesia.
pc:gnant *agg.* 1. pungente 2. commovente.
point *s.* 1. punto 2. punta, estremità 3. caratteristica.
to point *vt.* 1. indicare, segnare a dito 2. appuntire 3. dirigere || *to* — *out*, indicare, porre in rilievo.
point-blank *agg.* diretto. ♦ point-blank *avv.* direttamente.
pointed *agg.* 1. appuntito 2. mordace 3. evidente.
pointer *s.* 1. indicatore 2. lancetta (*di orologio*).
pointless *agg.* 1. spuntato 2. inutile, senza scopo.
pointsman *s.* (*ferr.*) deviatore.
poise *s.* equilibrio.
to poise *vt.* bilanciare. ♦ to poise *vi.* bilanciarsi.
poison *s.* veleno.
to poison *vt.* avvelenare.
poisoning *agg.* velenoso. ♦ poisoning *s.* avvelenamento.
poisonous *agg.* velenoso (*anche fig.*).
poke *s.* spinta, urto.
to poke *vt.* e *vi.* 1. spingere 2. andare a tastoni.
poker *s.* attizzatoio.
poky *agg.* meschino.
polar *agg.* polare.
polarity *s.* polarità.
polarization *s.* polarizzazione.
to polarize *vt.* polarizzare.
pole[1] *s.* palo.
pole[2] *s.* polo.
Pole[3] *s.* polacco.
polecat *s.* pvzzola.
polemic *s.* 1. polemica 2. polemista.
polemic(al) *agg.* polemico.

polemi(ci)st *s.* polemista.
to polemize *vi.* polemizzare.
police *s.* polizia || — -*force*, corpo di polizia.
police court *s.* pretura.
policeman *s.* poliziotto.
policy[1] *s.* 1. linea di condotta 2. sagacia.
policy[2] *s.* polizza.
polio(myelitis) *s.* poliomielite.
Polish[1] *agg.* polacco.
polish[2] *s.* 1. lucidatura 2. lucido 3. raffinatezza || *shoe* —, lucido per le scarpe.
to polish *vt.* 1. lucidare 2. raffinare. ♦ to polish *vi.* 1. divenire lucido 2. raffinarsi.
polisher *s.* 1. lucidatore 2. lucido.
polishing *s.* lucidatura.
polite *agg.* cortese.
politeness *s.* cortesia.
politic *agg.* abile.
political *agg.* politico.
politician *s.* uomo politico.
politics *s.* politica.
poll *s.* 1. votazione, scrutinio 2. referendum.
to poll *vt.* radere. ♦ to poll *vi.* votare, raccogliere voti.
pollen *s.* polline.
to pollinate *vt.* impollinare.
pollination *s.* impollinazione.
to pollute *vt.* contaminare.
pollution *s.* contaminazione.
polyandry *s.* poliandria.
polychrome *agg.* policromo.
polychromy *s.* policromia.
polyclinic *s.* policlinico.
polygamist *s.* poligamo.
polygamous *agg.* poligamo.
polygamy *s.* poligamia.
polyglot *agg.* e *s.* poliglotta.
polygon *s.* poligono.
polyhedral *agg.* poliedrico.
polyhedron *s.* poliedro.
polymerization *s.* polimerizzazione.
polymorphic *agg.* polimorfo.
polymorphism *s.* polimorfismo.
polyp *s.* polipo.
polyphonic *agg.* polifonico.
polyphony *s.* polifonia.
polysyllabic(al) *agg.* polisillabico.
polysyllable *s.* polisillabo.
polytechnic *agg.* e *s.* politecnico.
polytheism *s.* politeismo.
polytheist *s.* politeista.
polytheistic(al) *agg.* politeistico.
polyvalent *agg.* polivalente.

pomade *s.* pomata.
to pomade *vt.* impomatare.
pomegranate *s.* 1. melagrana 2. melograno.
pomp *s.* pompa, fasto.
pomposity *s.* pomposità.
pompous *agg.* pomposo.
pond *s.* stagno.
to pond *vt.* e *vi.* stagnare.
to ponder *vt.* e *vi.* ponderare.
ponderable *agg.* ponderabile.
ponderous *agg.* ponderoso.
pontiff *s.* pontefice.
pontifical *agg.* pontificio. ◆ pontifical *s.* pontificato.
pontificate *s.* pontificato.
to pontificate *vi.* pontificare.
pontoon *s.* pontone.
pony *s.* « pony », piccolo cavallo.
poodle *s.* barboncino.
pool[1] *s.* 1. stagno 2. pozza ‖ *swimming* —, piscina.
pool[2] *s.* (*comm.*) 1. fondo comune 2. (*comm.*) consorzio, sindacato.
poor *agg.* povero.
poorly *avv.* male.
poorness *s.* povertà.
pop *s.* scoppio.
to pop *vi.* scoppiare. ◆ to pop *vt.* 1. far scoppiare 2. ficcare.
popcorn *s.* fiocco di granoturco.
pope *s.* papa.
popery *s.* papismo.
poplar *s.* pioppo.
poppied *agg.* coperto di papaveri.
poppy *s.* papavero.
populace *s.* plebaglia.
popular *agg.* popolare.
popularity *s.* popolarità.
popularization *s.* popolarizzazione.
to popularize *vt.* popolarizzare.
to populate *vt.* popolare.
population *s.* popolazione.
Populism *s.* populismo.
Populist *s.* populista.
populous *agg.* popoloso.
porch *s.* portico.
porcupine *s.* porcospino.
pore *s.* poro.
to pore *vi.* esaminare.
pork *s.* carne di maiale.
pornographic *agg.* pornografico.
pornography *s.* pornografia.
porosity *s.* porosità.
porous *agg.* poroso.
porphyry *s.* porfido.
port[1] *s.* porto.
port[2] *s.* 1. (*mecc.*) apertura, foro 2. (*mar.*) portello.

port[3] *s.* fianco sinistro di nave.
portable *agg.* portatile.
portal *s.* portale.
portcullis *s.* saracinesca (*di fortezza*).
to portend *vt.* preannunciare.
portent *s.* 1. presagio 2. portento.
portentous *agg.* 1. sinistro 2. portentoso.
porter[1] *s.* facchino.
porter[2] *s.* custode, portiere.
porter[3] *s.* birra scura.
portfolio *s.* 1. cartella, busta 2. (*pol.*) portafoglio.
porthole *s.* 1. (*mar.*) portello 2. feritoia.
portion *s.* porzione, parte.
to portion *vt.* dividere, distribuire.
portrait *s.* ritratto.
portraitist *s.* ritrattista.
to portray *vt.* ritrarre.
portrayal *s.* ritratto.
portrayer *s.* ritrattista.
Portuguese *agg.* e *s.* portoghese.
pose *s.* posa.
to pose[1] *vt.* proporre.
to pose[2] *vi.* posare.
poser *s.* posatore.
position *s.* posizione.
positive *agg.* 1. positivo 2. sicuro. ◆ positive *s.* 1. realtà 2. (*foto*) positiva.
positivism *s.* positivismo.
positivist *s.* positivista.
positivistic *agg.* positivistico.
posology *s.* posologia.
to possess *vt.* possedere.
possessed *agg.* indemoniato.
possession *s.* possesso.
possessive *agg.* possessivo.
possessor *s.* possessore.
possibility *s.* possibilità.
possible *agg.* possibile.
possibly *avv.* possibilmente.
post[1] *s.* posta, corrispondenza ‖ — *card*, cartolina; *by return of* —, a giro di posta.
post[2] *s.* 1. palo, sostegno, puntello 2. stipite ‖ *sign-* —, indicatore stradale.
to post[1] *vt.* imbucare, inviare per posta.
to post[2] *vt.* affiggere.
postage *s.* spese postali (*pl.*).
postage stamp *s.* francobollo.
postal *agg.* postale.
to postdate *vt.* posdatare.
poster *s.* 1. affisso 2. attacchino.
poste-restante *s.* fermo posta.

posterior *agg.* posteriore.
posterity *s.* posterità.
postern *s.* postierla.
post-free *agg.* franco di porto.
posthumous *agg.* postumo.
postil(l)ion *s.* postiglione.
postman *s.* postino.
postmark *s.* timbro postale.
postmaster *s.* direttore di ufficio postale.
to **postpone** *vt.* rimandare.
postponement *s.* rinvio.
to **post-score** *vt.* (*cine*) sonorizzare.
postscript *s.* poscritto.
postulate *s.* postulato.
to **postulate** *vt.* **1.** porre come postulato **2.** chiedere.
postulator *s.* postulante.
posture *s.* posizione.
to **posture** *vi.* assumere una posizione.
post-war *agg.* postbellico.
posy *s.* mazzolino di fiori.
pot *s.* **1.** recipiente **2.** pentola || — -bellied, panciuto.
to **pot** *vt.* conservare (*in vaso*).
potable *agg.* potabile.
potash *s.* potassa.
potassic *agg.* potassico.
potassium *s.* potassio.
potato *s.* patata.
potent *agg.* potente.
potential *agg.* e *s.* potenziale.
potentiality *s.* potenzialità.
potion *s.* pozione.
potter *s.* vasaio.
pottery *s.* **1.** terraglie **2.** fabbrica di terraglie.
pouch *s.* borsa.
to **pouch** *vt.* intascare.
poulterer *s.* pollivendolo.
poultry *s.* pollame.
pounce *s.* balzo.
to **pounce** *vi.* avventarsi su, contro.
pound[1] *s.* **1.** libbra **2.** sterlina.
pound[2] *s.* recinto.
to **pound**[1] *vt.* e *vi.* pestare.
to **pound**[2] *vt.* rinchiudere.
pour *s.* acquazzone.
to **pour** *vt.* versare. ♦ to **pour** *vi.* **1.** versarsi **2.** diluviare.
pout *s.* broncio.
to **pout** *vi.* fare il broncio.
poverty *s.* povertà.
powder *s.* **1.** polvere **2.** cipria, talco.
to **powder** *vt.* **1.** polverizzare **2.** incipriare. ♦ to **powder** *vi.* **1.** pol-

verizzarsi **2.** incipriarsi.
powdery *agg.* **1.** friabile **2.** polveroso.
power *s.* potenza, potere || *horse* —, cavallo vapore; — -station, centrale elettrica.
to **power** *vt.* motorizzare.
powerful *agg.* potente.
powerless *agg.* debole.
pox *s.* sifilide || *chicken-* —, varicella, *small-* —, vaiolo.
practicability *s.* praticabilità.
practicable *agg.* **1.** praticabile **2.** fattibile.
practical *agg.* pratico.
practicality *s.* praticità.
practice *s.* **1.** pratica **2.** abitudine, regola **3.** esercizio **4.** professione **5.** (*coll.*) clienti (*di medico ecc.*).
to **practise** *vt.* **1.** praticare **2.** esercitare. ♦ to **practise** *vi.* esercitarsi.
practitioner *s.* professionista.
praetorian *s.* pretoriano.
pragmatic(al) *agg.* prammatico.
pragmatism *s.* pragmatismo.
pragmatist *agg.* e *s.* pragmatista.
prairie *s.* prateria.
praise *s.* lode.
to **praise** *vt.* lodare.
praiser *s.* lodatore.
praiseworthy *agg.* lodevole.
prance *s.* impennata.
prank *s.* monelleria.
to **prank** *vt.* ornare, agghindare vistosamente. ♦ to **prank** *vi.* mettersi in mostra.
prate *s.* chiacchiera, sproloquio.
to **prate** *vi.* chiacchierare, proferire parole senza senso.
prattle *s.* balbettio.
to **prattle** *vt.* e *vi.* balbettare.
praxis *s.* prassi.
to **pray** *vt.* e *vi.* pregare.
prayer *s.* preghiera.
to **preach** *vt.* e *vi.* predicare.
preacher *s.* predicatore.
to **preachify** *vi.* predicare in modo noioso.
preaching *s.* predicazione.
preachy *agg.* (*fam.*) incline a far prediche.
to **pre-announce** *vt.* preannunziare.
to **prearrange** *vt.* predisporre.
prearrangement *s.* predisposizione.
prebend *s.* prebenda.
prebendary *s.* prebendario.
precarious *agg.* precario.

precariousness s. precarietà.
precatory agg. supplichevole.
precaution s. precauzione.
precautional agg. precauzionale.
to precede vt. e vi. precedere.
precedence s. precedenza.
precedent agg. e s. precedente.
preceding agg. precedente.
precept s. precetto.
preceptive agg. istruttivo
preceptor s. precettore.
precession s. precessione.
precinct s. 1. recinto 2. limiti 3. vicinanze (pl.).
preciosity s. preziosità.
precious agg. prezioso.
preciousness s. preziosità.
precipice s. precipizio.
precipitate agg. e s. precipitato.
to precipitate vt. e vi. precipitare.
precipitation s. precipitazione.
precipitous agg. ripido.
précis s. riassunto.
precise agg. preciso.
precision s. precisione.
to preclude vt. precludere.
precocious agg. precoce.
precociousness, precocity s. precocità.
preconceived agg. preconcetto.
precursor s. precursore, predecessore.
precursory agg. 1. preliminare 2. premonitore.
predaceous agg. rapace.
to predate vt. predatare.
predatory agg. rapace.
to predecease vt. premorire a.
predecessor s. predecessore.
to predesignate vt. predesignare.
predestination s. predestinazione.
to predestine vt. predestinare.
predetermination s. predeterminazione.
to predetermine vt. predeterminare.
predicable agg. asseribile.
predicament s. situazione scabrosa.
predicate agg. e s. predicato.
to predicate vt. 1. asserire 2. implicare.
predication s. affermazione.
predicative agg. 1. predicativo 2. affermativo.
predicatory agg. predicatorio.
to predict vt. e vi. predire.
prediction s. predizione.
predilection s. predilezione.

to predispose vt. predisporre.
predisposition s. predisposizione.
predominance s. predominanza.
to predominate vi. predominare.
pre-eminence s. preminenza.
pre-eminent agg. preminente.
pre-emption s. prelazione, priorità.
to pre-engage vt. impegnare in anticipo.
to pre-establish vt. prestabilire.
to pre-exist vi. preesistere.
pre-existence s. preesistenza.
to prefabricate vt. prefabbricare.
prefabricated agg. — house, casa prefabbricata.
preface s. prefazione.
to preface vt. 1. fare una prefazione a 2. iniziare.
prefatory agg. introduttivo.
prefect s. prefetto.
prefecture s. prefettura.
to prefer vt. 1. preferire 2. promuovere, elevare.
preferable agg. preferibile.
preference s. preferenza.
preferential agg. preferenziale.
preferment s. avanzamento, promozione.
prefiguration s. prefigurazione.
to prefigure vt. prefigurare.
prefix s. prefisso.
pregnancy s. 1. gravidanza 2. (fig.) significato, importanza.
pregnant agg. 1. incinta 2. significativo, importante 3. fecondo.
prehension s. 1. prensione 2. apprendimento.
prehistoric(al) agg. preistorico.
prehistory s. preistoria.
prejudice s. pregiudizio.
to prejudice vt. 1. pregiudicare 2. influenzare.
prejudicial agg. pregiudizievole.
prelate s. prelato.
prelatic(al) agg. prelatizio.
preliminary agg. preliminare. ♦ preliminaries s. pl. preliminari.
prelude s. preludio.
to prelude vt. preludere. ♦ to prelude vi. eseguire un preludio.
premature agg. prematuro.
to premeditate vt. premeditare.
premeditation s. premeditazione.
premier s. primo ministro.
premise s. 1. premessa 2. stabile con terreni annessi.
to premise vt. premettere.
premolar agg. e s. premolare.
premonitory agg. premonitore.

preoccupation s. preoccupazione.
to preoccupy vt. 1. preoccupare 2. occupare in precedenza.
preparation s. preparazione, preparativo.
preparative, preparatory agg. preparatorio.
to prepare vt. preparare. ♦ **to prepare** vi. prepararsi.
preponderance s. preponderanza.
preponderant agg. preponderante.
preposition s. preposizione.
prepositional agg. di preposizione.
to prepossess vt. 1. occupare in precedenza 2. influenzare.
prepossessing agg. attraente.
prepossession s. prevenzione.
preposterous agg. assurdo.
prepotence s. predominio.
prepotent agg. predominante.
Pre-Raphaeli(ti)sm s. preraffaellismo.
prerogative agg. privilegiato. ♦ **prerogative** s. prerogativa.
presage s. presagio.
presbyope s. presbite.
presbyopic agg. presbite.
Presbyterian agg. e s. presbiteriano.
Presbyterianism s. presbiterianismo.
presbytery s. presbiterio.
prescience s. prescienza.
to prescribe vt. prescrivere.
prescript s. ordinanza.
prescription s. prescrizione.
presence s. presenza.
present[1] agg. presente || — -day, contemporaneo. ♦ **present** s. presente, tempo presente || at —, attualmente. ♦ **presents** s. pl. (giur.) documento (sing.).
present[2] s. dono, regalo.
to present vt. 1. presentare 2. regalare.
presentable agg. presentabile.
presentation s. 1. presentazione 2. dono.
presenter s. 1. presentatore 2. donatore.
presentiment s. presentimento.
presently avv. presto, quanto prima.
presentment s. presentazione.
preservable agg. conservabile.
preservation s. conservazione.
preservative agg. e s. preservativo.
preserve s. 1. riserva 2. conserva (di pomodoro, frutta ecc.).
to preserve vt. 1. preservare 2. conservare 3. mettere in conserva.

to preside vi. presiedere.
presidency s. presidenza.
president s. presidente.
presidential agg. presidenziale.
press s. 1. stretta, pressione 2. pressa 3. (fig.) stampa 4. calca, ressa || — conference, conferenza stampa.
to press vt. 1. premere, comprimere 2. costringere. ♦ **to press** vi. affollarsi.
pressing agg. 1. urgente 2. insistente.
pressman s. 1. cronista (di giornale) 2. (tip.) stampatore.
pressure s. pressione || — -cooker, pentola a pressione.
to pressurize vt. pressurizzare.
prestige s. prestigio.
presumable agg. presumibile.
to presume vt. e vi. 1. presumere 2. avere la presunzione di.
presuming agg. presuntuoso.
presumption s. 1. presunzione 2. supposizione.
presumptive agg. presunto.
presumptuous agg. presuntuoso.
presumptuousness s. presunzione.
to presuppose vt. presupporre.
presupposition s. presupposizione.
pretence s. 1. pretesa 2. pretesto 3. simulazione.
to pretend vi. 1. pretendere 2. fingere.
pretender s. 1. pretendente 2. simulatore.
pretension s. 1. pretesa 2. presunzione.
pretentious agg. pretenzioso.
preternatural agg. soprannaturale.
pretext s. pretesto.
prettiness s. grazia.
pretty agg. grazioso. ♦ **pretty** avv. abbastanza.
to prevail vi. prevalere.
prevailing agg. 1. prevalente 2. efficace.
prevalence s. prevalenza.
to prevaricate vi. 1. tergiversare 2. mentire.
prevarication s. 1. tergiversazione 2. menzogna.
prevaricator s. 1. chi tergiversa 2. mentitore.
to prevent vt. impedire.
prevention s. 1. impedimento 2. prevenzione.
preventive agg. preventivo.

preview *s.* anteprima.
previous *agg.* precedente.
prevision *s.* previsione.
pre-war *agg.* prebellico.
prey *s.* preda.
to **prey** *vi.* **1.** (de)predare **2.** (*fig.*) consumare.
price *s.* prezzo, costo.
to **price** *vt.* fissare il prezzo di.
priceless *agg.* inestimabile.
prick *s.* **1.** punta **2.** puntura **3.** (*fig.*) pungolo, rimorso.
to **prick** *vt.* **1.** pungere **2.** segnare **3.** rizzare le orecchie. ◆ to **prick** *vi.* **1.** formicolare **2.** pungersi.
prickle *s.* **1.** spina **2.** pungiglione.
prickly *agg.* pungente.
pride *s.* orgoglio.
to **pride** *vt.* to — *oneself upon,* essere orgoglioso di.
priest *s.* prete.
priesthood *s.* **1.** clero **2.** sacerdozio.
prig *s.* presuntuoso.
prim *agg.* affettato.
primary *agg.* primo, primario.
primate *s.* (*eccl.*) primate.
prime *agg.* **1.** primo **2.** di prima qualità. ◆ **prime** *s.* **1.** principio **2.** (*fig.*) fiore.
to **prime** *vt.* caricare, innescare.
primer[1] *s.* sillabario.
primer[2] *s.* innesco.
primeval *agg.* primordiale.
primigenial *agg.* primigenio.
priming *s.* **1.** innesco **2.** prima mano (*di vernice ecc.*).
primitive *agg.* e *s.* primitivo.
primitiveness *s.* primitività.
primogeniture *s.* primogenitura.
primordial *agg.* primordiale.
primrose *s.* primula.
prince *s.* principe.
princely *agg.* principesco.
princess *s.* principessa.
principal *agg.* principale. ◆ **principal** *s.* **1.** principale, direttore **2.** (*edil.*) trave maestra **3.** (*comm.*) mandante.
principality *s.* principato.
principle *s.* principio.
print *s.* **1.** impronta **2.** stampa **3.** stampatello **4.** (*foto*) copia.
to **print** *vt.* **1.** stampare **2.** scrivere a stampatello **3.** imprimere.
printer *s.* **1.** tipografo **2.** (*mecc.*) stampatrice.
printing *s.* **1.** stampa **2.** tiratura ‖ — -*press,* pressa tipografica.
prior *agg.* precedente. ◆ **prior** *s.*

priore. ◆ **prior** *avv.* prima.
priorate *s.* priorato.
prioress *s.* priora.
priority *s.* priorità.
prism *s.* prisma.
prismatic(al) *agg.* prismatico.
prison *s.* prigione.
prisoner *s.* prigioniero.
privacy *s.* **1.** intimità **2.** riserbo.
private *agg.* **1.** privato **2.** appartato **3.** segreto, riservato, personale. ◆ **private** *s.* soldato semplice.
privation *s.* privazione.
privative *agg.* privativo.
privilege *s.* privilegio.
to **privilege** *vt.* privilegiare.
privy *agg.* **1.** nascosto **2.** al corrente di.
prize *s.* premio.
to **prize** *vt.* stimare.
probabilism *s.* probabilismo.
probability *s.* probabilità.
probable *agg.* probabile.
probate *s.* omologazione.
probation *s.* prova.
probative *agg.* probativo.
probatory *agg.* probatorio.
probe *s.* sonda.
to **probe** *vt.* sondare.
probity *s.* probità.
problem *s.* problema.
problematic(al) *agg.* problematico.
procedural *agg.* procedurale.
procedure *s.* **1.** procedimento **2.** procedura.
to **proceed** *vi.* **1.** procedere **2.** provenire.
proceeding *s.* V. *procedure.*
proceeds *s. pl.* profitto (*sing.*).
process *s.* **1.** procedimento **2.** processo.
to **process** *vt.* **1.** processare **2.** (*chim.*) trattare.
procession *s.* processione.
processionary *s.* (*zool.*) processionaria.
proclaim *s.* proclama.
to **proclaim** *vt.* proclamare.
proclamation *s.* proclama(zione).
proconsul *s.* proconsole.
to **procrastinate** *vt.* e *vi.* procrastinare.
procrastination *s.* procrastinazione.
to **procreate** *vt.* procreare.
procreation *s.* procreazione.
procreator *s.* procreatore.
proctor *s.* **1.** censore **2.** (*giur.*) procuratore.

procurator *s.* procuratore.
to procure *vt.* 1. procurare, procurarsi 2. adescare.
procurer *s.* mezzano.
prod *s.* pungolo.
to prod *vt.* pungolare.
prodigal *agg.* e *s.* prodigo.
prodigality *s.* prodigalità.
prodigious *agg.* 1. prodigioso 2. enorme.
prodigiousness *s.* prodigiosità.
prodigy *s.* prodigio.
produce *s.* prodotto || *farm* —, prodotto agricolo; *raw* —, materia prima.
to produce *vt.* 1. produrre 2. presentare.
producer *s.* 1. produttore 2. (*teat.*) regista.
product *s.* prodotto.
production *s.* 1. esibizione 2. produzione.
productive *agg.* produttivo.
productivity *s.* produttività.
proem *s.* proemio.
profanation *s.* profanazione.
profane *agg.* 1. profano 2. empio.
to profane *vt.* profanare.
profaner *s.* profanatore.
profanity *s.* 1. profanità 2. empietà.
to profess *vt.* 1. professare 2. pretendere.
profession *s.* professione.
professional *agg.* professionale || — *man*, professionista. ♦ professional *s.* professionista.
professionalism *s.* professionismo.
professor *s.* professore (*d'università*).
professorial *agg.* professorale.
proficiency *s.* competenza || — *in English*, buona conoscenza dell'inglese.
proficient *agg.* e *s.* esperto, competente.
profile *s.* profilo.
to profile *vt.* 1. profilare 2. tracciare il profilo di.
profit *s.* profitto, guadagno.
to profit *vt.* giovare. ♦ to profit *vi.* approfittare.
profitable *agg.* vantaggioso.
profiteer *s.* profittatore.
profligacy *s.* 1. sregolatezza 2. spergero.
profligate *agg.* e *s.* 1. dissoluto 2. scialacquatore.
profound *agg.* profondo.

profuse *agg.* 1. abbondante 2. prodigo.
profusion *s.* 1. profusione 2. prodigalità.
progenitor *s.* progenitore.
progeny *s.* progenie.
prognathism *s.* prognatismo.
prognathous *agg.* prognato.
prognosis *s.* (*pl.* -ses) prognosi.
prognostic *agg.* rivelatore. ♦ prognostic *s.* 1. pronostico 2. sintomo.
prognostication *s.* 1. pronostico 2. prognosi.
program(me) *s.* programma.
to program(me) *vt.* programmare.
programming *s.* programmazione.
programmist *s.* programmista.
progress *s.* 1. progresso 2. avanzata 3. sviluppo 4. andamento, corso.
to progress *vi.* 1. progredire 2. avanzare 3. svilupparsi.
progression *s.* 1. progressione 2. avanzamento.
progressive *agg.* progressivo, progressista. ♦ progressive *s.* progressista.
to prohibit *vt.* proibire.
prohibition *s.* 1. proibizione 2. proibizionismo.
prohibitionist *s.* proibizionista.
prohibitive *agg.* proibitivo.
project *s.* progetto.
to project *vt.* 1. progettare 2. proiettare. ♦ to project *vi.* sporgere.
projectile *s.* proiettile.
projection *s.* 1. progetto 2. proiezione.
projector *s.* 1. progettista 2. proiettore.
proletarian *agg.* e *s.* proletario.
proletariat *s.* proletariato.
to proliferate *vt.* proliferare. ♦ to proliferate *vi.* moltiplicarsi.
proliferation *s.* proliferazione.
prolific *agg.* prolifico.
prolix *agg.* prolisso.
prolixity *s.* prolissità.
prologue *s.* prologo.
to prolong *vt.* 1. prolungare 2. (*comm.*) prorogare.
promenade *s.* passeggiata, passeggio pubblico, lungomare.
prominence *s.* prominenza.
prominent *agg.* prominente.
promiscuity *s.* promiscuità.
promiscuous *agg.* promiscuo.
promise *s.* promessa.
to promise *vt.* e *vi.* promettere.

promissory *agg.* contenente una promessa || — *note* (*comm.*), pagherò cambiario.
promontory *s.* promontorio.
to **promote** *vt.* 1. promuovere 2. dare impulso, favorire.
promoter *s.* promotore.
promotion *s.* 1. promozione 2. incoraggiamento.
prompt *agg.* 1. sollecito 2. (*comm.*) in contanti. ♦ **prompt** *s.* 1. (*comm.*) termine di pagamento 2. suggerimento.
to **prompt** *vt.* 1. spingere 2. suggerire.
prompter *s.* suggeritore.
promptness *s.* prontezza.
to **promulgate** *vt.* promulgare.
promulgation *s.* promulgazione.
promulgator *s.* promulgatore.
prone *agg.* prono.
prong *s.* 1. dente (*di forca*) 2. forca.
pronominal *agg.* pronominale.
pronoun *s.* pronome.
to **pronounce** *vt.* 1. pronunciare 2. dichiarare. ♦ to **pronounce** *vi.* pronunciarsi.
pronouncement *s.* dichiarazione.
pronouncing, pronunciation *s.* pronuncia.
proof *agg.* a prova di. ♦ **proof** *s.* 1. prova 2. bozza 3. gradazione alcoolica || — *-reader*, correttore di bozze; *burden of* — (*giur.*), onere della prova.
prop *s.* puntello.
to **prop** *vt.* 1. sostenere 2. appoggiare.
propaedeutic(al) *agg.* propedeutico.
propaedeutics *s.* propedeutica.
propagandist *s.* propagandista.
to **propagandize** *vt.* propagandare.
to **propagate** *vt.* propagare. ♦ to **propagate** *vi.* propagarsi.
propagation *s.* 1. propagazione 2. (*bot.*; *zool.*) riproduzione.
propagator *s.* propagatore.
propane *s.* propano.
to **propel** *vt.* spingere avanti.
propellent *agg.* e *s.* propulsore, propellente.
propeller *s.* propulsore || (*screw-*) —, elica.
propensity *s.* propensione.
proper *agg.* 1. proprio 2. adatto 3. corretto 4. propriamente detto.
property *s.* 1. proprietà 2. (*teat.*) costumi, arredi per la scena (*pl.*) ||

real —, beni immobili (*pl.*).
prophecy *s.* profezia.
to **prophesy** *vt.* e *vi.* profetizzare.
prophet *s.* profeta.
prophetic(al) *agg.* profetico.
prophylactic *agg.* e *s.* profilattico.
prophylaxis *s.* profilassi.
to **propitiate** *vt.* propiziare.
propitiation *s.* propiziazione.
propitiator *s.* propiziatore.
propitiatory *agg.* propiziatorio.
propitious *agg.* propizio.
proportion *s.* 1. proporzione 2. parte. ♦ **proportions** *s.* *pl.* dimensioni.
to **proportion** *vt.* 1. proporzionare 2. dividere in parti proporzionate.
proportional *agg.* proporzionale.
proportionality *s.* proporzionalità.
proportionate *agg.* proporzionato.
to **proportionate** V. *to proportion*.
proportioning *s.* proporzionamento.
proposal *s.* proposta.
to **propose** *vt.* proporre. ♦ to **propose** *vi.* 1. prefiggersi, intendere 2. fare richiesta di matrimonio || *to* — *the health of so.*, bere alla salute di qu.
proposition *s.* 1. proposta 2. proposizione 3. asserzione 4. problema.
proprietary *agg.* di proprietà. ♦ **proprietary** *agg.* proprietario || — *rights*, diritti di proprietà.
proprietor *s.* proprietario.
propriety *s.* 1. proprietà 2. opportunità 3. decoro, decenza. ♦ **proprieties** *s.* *pl.* convenienze.
propulsion *s.* propulsione.
propulsive *agg.* propulsivo.
propylaeum *s.* (*pl.* -laea) propileo.
propylene *s.* propilene.
prosaic *agg.* prosaico.
prosaism *s.* prosaicità.
proscenium *s.* (*pl.* -nia) proscenio.
to **proscribe** *vt.* 1. bandire 2. vietare.
proscription *s.* 1. proscrizione 2. proibizione.
prose *s.* 1. prosa 2. prosaicità || — *writer*, prosatore.
prosecutable *agg.* perseguibile.
to **prosecute** *vt.* 1. proseguire 2. perseguire.
prosecution *s.* 1. proseguimento 2. processo 3. (*giur.*) accusa.
prosecutor *s.* 1. prosecutore 2. accusatore || *Public* — (*giur.*), l'accusa pubblica.

proselyte s. proselito.
proselytism s. proselitismo.
prosiness s. 1. prosaicità 2. banalità.
prosody s. prosodia.
prospect s. 1. panorama 2. prospettiva 3. speranza, aspettativa.
to **prospect** vt. 1. esplorare 2. ricercare.
prospecting s. ricerca.
prospective agg. 1. futuro 2. eventuale.
to **prosper** vt. far prosperare. ◆ to **prosper** vi. prosperare.
prosperity s. prosperità.
prosperous agg. prospero.
prostate s. prostata.
prostatic agg. prostatico.
prosthesis s. (med.) protesi.
prostitute s. prostituta.
to **prostitute** vt. prostituire.
prostitution s. prostituzione.
prostrate agg. prostrato.
to **prostrate** vt. prostrare.
prostration s. 1. prostrazione 2. prosternazione.
prostyle agg. e s. prostilo.
prosy agg. 1. prosaico 2. noioso.
protagonist s. protagonista.
to **protect** vt. proteggere.
protection s. 1. protezione 2. salvacondotto.
protectionism s. protezionismo.
protectionist s. protezionista.
protective agg. protettivo.
protector s. protettore.
protectorate s. protettorato.
protectory s. patronato.
protein s. proteina.
protest s. 1. protesta 2. (comm.) protesto.
to **protest** vt. e vi. protestare.
protestant agg. e s. protestante.
Protestantism s. protestantesimo.
protestation s. dichiarazione.
protocol s. protocollo.
proton s. protone.
protoplasm s. protoplasma.
prototype s. prototipo.
Protozoa s. pl. protozoi.
to **protract** vt. 1. protrarre 2. rilevare.
protraction s. 1. protrazione 2. rilievo.
protractor s. 1. protrattore 2. goniometro.
to **protrude** vt. 1. sporgere 2. imporre. ◆ to **protrude** vi. 1. sporgersi 2. imporsi.

protrusion, protuberance s. protuberanza.
proud agg. orgoglioso, superbo.
to **prove** vt. 1. provare, verificare 2. omologare. ◆ to **prove** vi. risultare.
provender s. foraggio, biada.
proverb s. proverbio.
proverbial agg. proverbiale.
to **provide** vi. 1. provvedere 2. premunirsi 3. stabilire (di leggi). ◆ to **provide** vt. 1. procurare 2. rifornire.
provided cong. purché, a patto che.
providence s. 1. provvidenza 2. previdenza.
provident agg. 1. provvido 2. previdente.
providential agg. provvidenziale.
province s. 1. provincia 2. (fig.) sfera, campo d'attività.
provincial agg. e s. provinciale.
provincialism s. provincialismo.
provision s. 1. preparativo 2. provvedimento 3. clausola 4. (giur.) disposizione. ◆ **provisions** s. pl. provviste.
to **provision** vt. approvvigionare.
provisional agg. provvisorio.
provisioning s. approvvigionamento.
provocation s. provocazione.
provocative agg. 1. provocante 2. stimolante.
provocativeness s. provocazione.
to **provoke** vt. 1. provocare 2. irritare.
provoker s. provocatore.
provost s. prevosto.
prow s. prora.
prowess s. prodezza, valore.
proximity s. prossimità.
proxy s. 1. procura 2. procuratore.
prude s. persona eccessivamente pudica.
prudence s. prudenza.
prudent agg. prudente.
prudential agg. prudenziale.
prudentials s. pl. provvedimenti precauzionali.
prudery s. ritrosia eccessiva.
prudish agg. pudibondo.
prune s. prugna secca.
to **prune** vt. potare.
pruner s. potatore.
pruning s. potatura || — -hook, falcetto.
prussic agg. prussico.
pry[1] s. ficcanaso.

pry² *s.* leva.
to pry¹ *vi.* indagare.
to pry² *vt.* muovere con una leva.
psalm *s.* salmo.
psalmody *s.* salmodia.
pseudonym *s.* pseudonimo.
psyche *s.* psiche.
psychiatric(al) *agg.* psichiatrico.
psychiatrist *s.* psichiatra.
psychiatry *s.* psichiatria.
psychic *s.* 1. medium 2. psicologia.
psychic(al) *agg.* psichico.
psychoanalysis *s.* psicanalisi.
psychoanalyst *s.* psicanalista.
psychoanalytic(al) *agg.* psicanalitico.
to psychoanalyze *vt.* psicanalizzare.
psychologic(al) *agg.* psicologico.
psychologist *s.* psicologo.
psychology *s.* psicologia.
psychometry *s.* psicometria.
psychopathic *agg.* e *s.* psicopatico.
psychopathology *s.* psicopatologia.
psychopathy *s.* psicopatia.
psychosis *s.* psicosi.
psychotherapy *s.* psicoterapia.
ptisan *s.* tisana.
pub *s.* bar (*in Gran Bretagna*).
puberty *s.* pubertà.
pubis *s.* (*pl.* -bes) pube.
public *agg.* e *s.* pubblico || *the reading* —, i lettori (*pl.*).
publican *s.* 1. oste 2. (*stor.*) pubblicano.
publication *s.* pubblicazione.
publicity *s.* pubblicità.
to publish *vt.* 1. pubblicare 2. divulgare.
publishable *agg.* pubblicabile.
publisher *s.* editore.
pucker *s.* ruga, grinza.
to pucker *vt.* raggrinzare, corrugare. ♦ to pucker *vi.* raggrinzarsi, corrugarsi.
pudding *s.* 1. budino 2. pasticcio || *black* —, sanguinaccio.
puddle *s.* 1. pozzanghera 2. malta.
to puddle *vt.* 1. infangare 2. coprire di malta.
puerility *s.* puerilità.
Puerto Rican *agg.* e *s.* portoricano.
puff *s.* 1. soffio, sbuffo 2. piumino.
to puff *vi.* 1. sbuffare 2. gonfiarsi. ♦ to puff *vt.* 1. soffiare 2. gonfiare.
puffy *agg.* 1. gonfio 2. ansimante 3. paffuto, grasso.
pugilist *s.* pugile.

pugnacious *agg.* pugnace.
pugnacity *s.* combattività.
puke *s.* vomito.
to puke *vt.* e *vi.* vomitare.
pull *s.* 1. strappo 2. sforzo, tensione 3. maniglia (*di cassetto*).
to pull *vt.* 1. tirare 2. strappare || *to* — *down*, demolire. ♦ to pull *vi.* 1. trascinarsi 2. remare || *to* — *back*, ritirarsi; *to* — *up*, fermarsi.
puller *s.* (*mecc.*) estrattore.
pulley *s.* puleggia.
pulmonary *agg.* polmonare.
pulp *s.* polpa.
to pulp *vt.* ridurre in polpa. ♦ to pulp *vi.* diventare polposo.
pulpit *s.* pulpito.
pulpy *agg.* polposo.
pulsation *s.* pulsazione.
pulsatory *agg.* pulsante.
pulse *s.* 1. pulsazione, polso, battito 2. (*radio*) impulso.
to pulse *vi.* pulsare.
to pulverize *vt.* polverizzare. ♦ to pulverize *vi.* polverizzarsi.
pumice *s.* pomice.
pump *s.* pompa || *petrol* —, distributore di benzina.
to pump *vt.* e *vi.* pompare || *to* — *up*, gonfiare.
pumpkin *s.* zucca.
pun *s.* gioco di parole.
punch¹ *s.* punzone.
punch² *s.* pugno.
punch³ *s.* « punch » (*bevanda alcoolica*).
to punch¹ *vt.* (per)forare.
to punch² *vt.* prendere a pugni.
punching *s.* perforazione.
punctilio *s.* meticolosità.
punctilious *agg.* meticoloso.
punctual *agg.* puntuale.
punctuality *s.* puntualità.
punctually *avv.* puntualmente.
to punctuate *vt.* 1. punteggiare 2. (*fig.*) sottolineare.
punctuation *s.* punteggiatura.
puncture *s.* 1. puntura 2. foratura.
to puncture *vt.* 1. pungere 2. forare.
pungency *s.* 1. asprezza 2. acutezza (*di dolore*).
pungent *agg.* 1. pungente 2. acuto, cocente 3. piccante.
to punish *vt.* punire.
punishable *agg.* punibile.
punishment *s.* punizione.
punitive, punitory *agg.* punitivo.
punt *s.* chiatta.

punter *s.* puntatore (*di corse ecc.*).
puny *agg.* sparuto.
pup *s.* cucciolo.
pupil[1] *s.* **1.** allievo **2.** (*giur.*) pupillo.
pupil[2] *s.* pupilla.
pupil(l)age *s.* (*giur.*) minorità: *child in —,* bambino sotto tutela.
pupil(l)ary *agg.* (*giur.*) pupillare.
puppet *s.* burattino || — *show,* spettacolo di burattini; — *player,* burattinaio.
puppy *s.* cucciolo.
purchase *s.* acquisto.
to purchase *vt.* acquistare.
purchaser *s.* acquirente.
purchasing *s.* acquisto || — *power,* potere di acquisto.
pure *agg.* puro, schietto, casto.
purely *avv.* puramente, semplicemente.
purgative *agg.* purgativo. ♦ **purgative** *s.* purgante.
purgatory *s.* purgatorio.
purge *s.* **1.** purga **2.** epurazione.
to purge *vt.* **1.** purgare **2.** epurare. ♦ **to purge** *vi.* purgarsi.
purification *s.* purificazione.
purificatory *agg.* purificatore.
to purify *vt.* purificare.
purism *s.* purismo.
purist *s.* purista.
Puritan *agg.* e *s.* puritano.
Puritanism *s.* puritanismo.
purity *s.* purezza.
to purloin *vt.* rubare.
purloiner *s.* frodatore.
purple *agg.* **1.** purpureo, paonazzo **2.** ornato. ♦ **purple** *s.* porpora.
to purple *vt.* imporporare. ♦ **to purple** *vi.* imporpòrarsi.
purport *s.* significato.
to purport *vt.* **1.** significare **2.** pretendere.
purpose *s.* **1.** intenzione, scopo **2.** fermezza || *on —,* di proposito.
to purpose *vi.* proporsi (*di*).
purposeful *agg.* **1.** premeditato **2.** avveduto.
purposefully *avv.* intenzionalmente, espressamente.
purposeless *agg.* **1.** inutile **2.** senza intenzione.
purpurin *s.* porporina.
to purr *vi.* fare le fusa.
purse *s.* borsellino.
to purse *vt.* contrarre. ♦ **to purse** *vi.* incresparsi, contrarsi.
purser *s.* commissario di bordo.
pursuant *agg.* conforme.

to pursue *vt.* **1.** (in)seguire **2.** continuare.
pursuer *s.* **1.** inseguitore **2.** continuatore.
pursuit *s.* **1.** inseguimento **2.** occupazione, impiego.
purulence *s.* suppurazione.
purulent *agg.* purulento.
push *s.* **1.** spinta, influenza, pressione **2.** bisogno **3.** (*elettr.*) pulsante.
to push *vt.* **1.** spingere, incalzare, fare pressione **2.** lanciare (*una moda, un articolo ecc.*) ♦ **to push** *vi.* spingersi.
pusher *s.* chi, ciò che spinge.
pusillanimity *s.* pusillanimità.
pusillanimous *agg.* pusillanime.
puss(y) *s.* micino.
pustule *s.* pustola.
to put (**put, put**) *vt.* **1.** mettere, porre **2.** esporre, sottoporre || *to — off,* rimandare, togliere (*vestiti ecc.*); *to — on,* indossare, accendere; *to — through,* mettere in comunicazione telefonica; *to — up,* alzare. ♦ **to put** (**put, put**) *vi.* dirigersi.
putative *agg.* putativo.
putrefaction *s.* putrefazione.
to putrefy *vt.* putrefare. ♦ **to putrefy** *vi.* putrefarsi.
putrescence *s.* putrescenza.
putrescible *agg.* putrescibile.
putrid *agg.* putrido.
putridness *s.* putridità.
puttees *s. pl.* mollettiere.
putty *s.* mastice, stucco.
puzzle *s.* **1.** enigma **2.** imbarazzo **3.** intrigo.
to puzzle *vt.* imbarazzare. ♦ **to puzzle** *vi.* essere imbarazzato.
pygmy *agg.* e *s.* pigmeo.
pyjamas *s. pl.* pigiama (*sing.*).
pylon *s.* pilone || *steel —,* traliccio.
pylorus *s.* piloro.
pyorrh(o)ea *s.* piorrea.
pyramid *s.* piramide.
pyramidal *agg.* piramidale.
pyre *s.* pira.
pyrites *s.* pirite.
pyrography *s.* pirografia.
pyromancy *s.* piromanzia.
pyromaniac *s.* piromane.
pyrope *s.* piropo.
pyrotechnic(al) *agg.* pirotecnico.
pyrotechnics *s.* pirotecnica.
Pythagorean *agg.* e *s.* pitagorico.
python *s.* pitone.
pyx *s.* pisside.

Q

quack[1] s. ciarlatano.
quack[2] s. schiamazzare (di anitra).
to quack[1] vi. fare il ciarlatano.
to quack[2] vi. schiamazzare (di anitra).
quadrangle s. quadrangolo.
quadrangular agg. quadrangolare.
quadrant s. quadrante.
quadrennial agg. quadriennale.
quadrilateral agg. e s. quadrilatero:
quadrille s. quadriglia.
quadrumane s. quadrumane.
quadrumanous agg. quadrumane.
quadruped agg. e s. quadrupede.
quadruple agg. e s. quadruplo.
to quadruple vt. quadruplicare. ♦
to quadruple vi. quadruplicarsi.
quagmire s. pantano.
quail s. quaglia.
to quail vi. avvilirsi, sgomentarsi.
quaint agg. strano, bizzarro.
quake s. scossa, tremito.
to quake vi. 1. avere i brividi 2. tremare (anche di terra).
Quaker s. Quacchero.
quaky agg. tremante.
qualifiable agg. qualificabile.
qualification s. 1. qualificazione, capacità, requisito 2. condizione, riserva 3. qualifica.
qualified agg. 1. qualificato, competente 2. limitato || — acceptance (comm.), accettazione con riserva.
qualifier s. (gramm.) parola che modifica.
to qualify vt. 1. qualificare, definire 2. abilitare 3. (giur.) autorizzare. ♦ to qualify vi. 1. qualificarsi 2. abilitarsi.
qualitative agg. qualitativo.
quality s. qualità, caratteristica.
qualm s. 1. nausea 2. scrupolo.
qualmish agg. 1. soggetto a nausee 2. nauseante 3. scrupoloso.
quantitative agg. quantitativo.
quantity s. quantità.
quarantine s. quarantena.
quarrel s. lite, contesa.
to quarrel vi. litigare, venire a contesa.
quarreller s. attaccabrighe, contendente.
quarrelsome agg. attaccabrighe, rissoso.
quarry[1] s. 1. cava 2. (fig.) fonte d'informazione.

quarry[2] s. selvaggina, preda.
to quarry vt. 1. cavare (pietre, marmo ecc.) 2. ricavare informazioni da.
quarter s. 1. quarto: a — of an hour, un quarto d'ora 2. quartiere, rione. ♦ quarters s. pl. 1. alloggio 2. (mil.) acquartieramento.
to quarter vt. e vi. 1. dividere in quattro parti 2. alloggiare 3. (mil.) acquartierarsi.
quarterly agg. trimestrale. ♦ quarterly s. pubblicazione trimestrale. ♦ quarterly avv. trimestralmente.
quartermaster s. 1. commissario 2. quartiermastro.
quartet s. quartetto.
quartz s. quarzo.
to quash vt. (giur.) annullare.
quaternary agg. quaternario.
quatrain s. quartina.
quaver s. trillo, vibrazione.
to quaver vt. e vi. 1. vibrare, tremare (di voce) 2. gorgheggiare.
quay s. banchina, molo.
queasy agg. 1. nauseabondo 2. schizzinoso.
queen s. regina.
queenlike agg. regale.
queenly agg. regale, da regina.
queer agg. strano, eccentrico.
to queer vt. mettere in ridicolo.
queerly avv. stranamente.
to quench vt. 1. spegnere, estinguere 2. calmare.
quencher s. estintore.
quenchless agg. inestinguibile.
querulous agg. querulo, gemebondo.
query s. domanda, quesito.
to query vt. e vi. 1. chiedere, indagare 2. mettere in dubbio.
quest s. ricerca.
to quest vt. e vi. cercare, far ricerche.
question s. 1. domanda, interrogazione 2. dubbio, obiezione 3. questione, problema || — mark, punto interrogativo.
to question vt. 1. interrogare 2. mettere in dubbio.
questionable agg. incerto, discutibile.
questionably avv. discutibilmente.
questionary s. questionario.
queue s. 1. coda 2. fila di persone: to stand in a —, fare la coda.
to queue vt. e vi. fare la coda, mettere in coda.

quibble *s.* giuoco di parole, doppio senso.

to quibble *vi.* **1.** fare giuochi di parole **2.** cavillare.

quibbling *agg.* a doppio senso.

quick *agg.* **1.** rapido, veloce **2.** pronto, intelligente, acuto || — *-eyed,* dagli occhi penetranti; — *-eared,* dall'orecchio fino; — *-lime,* calce viva; — *-sighted,* dalla vista acuta; — *-tempered,* irascibile.

to quicken *vt.* **1.** affrettare **2.** animare. ♦ **to quicken** *vi.* **1.** affrettarsi **2.** animarsi.

quickly *avv.* rapidamente, prontamente.

quickness *s.* **1.** rapidità **2.** vivacità, acutezza.

quicksand *s.* sabbia mobile.

quickset *s.* siepe di sempreverdi.

quicksilver *s.* mercurio, argento vivo *(anche fig.).*

quickstep *s.* passo cadenzato.

quickthorn *s.* biancospino.

quiescence *s.* quiescenza.

quiescent *agg.* quiescente.

quiescently *avv.* tranquillamente.

quiet *agg.* **1.** quieto, tranquillo **2.** sobrio, tenue *(di colore)* **3.** docile, dolce.

to quiet *vt.* acquietare. ♦ **to quiet** *vi.* acquietarsi.

quietism *s.* quietismo.

quietist *s.* quietista.

quietly *avv.* tranquillamente, con calma.

quietness *s.* quiete, tranquillità.

quill *s.* **1.** penna, penna d'oca **2.** piccolo galleggiante *(per canna da pesca).*

to quill *vt.* pieghettare, increspare.

quilt *s.* trapunta.

to quilt *vt.* trapuntare.

quince *s.* cotogna || — *jam,* marmellata di cotogne.

quinine *s.* chinino.

quinquennial *agg.* quinquennale.

quintal *s.* quintale.

quintessence *s.* quintessenza.

quintet *s.* quintetto.

quintuple *agg.* e *s.* quintuplo.

to quintuple *vt.* quintuplicare. ♦ **to quintuple** *vi.* quintuplicarsi.

quisling *s.* collaborazionista.

to quit *vt.* **1.** abbandonare, lasciare **2.** quietanzare, saldare.

quite *avv.* **1.** completamente, interamente **2.** piuttosto, abbastanza || — *young,* giovanissimo; *to be*

— *well,* stare proprio bene.

quiver *s.* fremito, brivido.

to quiver *vt.* e *vi.* **1.** tremare, fremere **2.** palpitare.

quivering *agg.* fremente, tremolante. ♦ **quivering** *s.* tremolio.

quixotic *agg.* donchisciottesco.

quiz *s.* *(pl.* quizzes) burlone.

to quiz *vt.* burlare.

quotation *s.* **1.** citazione **2.** *(comm.)* quotazione.

quote *s.* *(fam.)* citazione. ♦ **quotes** *s. pl.* virgolette.

to quote *vt.* **1.** citare **2.** *(comm.)* quotare *(in borsa).*

quotidian *agg.* quotidiano.

quotient *s.* quoziente.

R

rabbi *s.* rabbino.

rabbit *s.* coniglio.

rabble *s.* plebaglia.

to rabble *vt.* assaltare, linciare.

rabid *agg.* **1.** rabbioso **2.** irragionevole **3.** idrofobo.

rabidity *s.* **1.** rabbia **2.** fanatismo.

rabies *s.* idrofobia.

race[1] *s.* **1.** corso **2.** corsa || — *-meeting,* concorso ippico.

race[2] *s.* razza.

to race *vi.* **1.** correre **2.** imballarsi *(di motori)* **3.** prendere parte a una corsa **4.** allevare cavalli da corsa.

racecourse *s.* ippodromo.

racehorse *s.* cavallo da corsa.

racer *s.* **1.** corridore **2.** cavallo da corsa **3.** mezzo da corsa.

racial *agg.* razziale.

racialism *s.* razzismo.

racialist *s.* razzista.

racially *avv.* dal punto di vista razziale.

racily *avv.* vivacemente.

raciness *s.* vivacità.

racing *s.* corsa || — *car,* automobile da corsa.

racism *s.* razzismo.

racist *s.* razzista.

rack[1] *s.* **1.** rastrelliera **2.** reticella portabagagli **3.** *(mecc.)* cremagliera || *clothes* —, attaccapanni.

rack[2] *s.* ruota, strumento di tortura.

rack[3] *s.* nembo, nuvolaglia.

rack[4] *s.* rovina, distruzione.

to **rack**[1] *vt*. **1.** torturare **2.** pretendere troppo.

to **rack**[2] *vi*. fuggire (*di nubi*).

racket[1] *s*. racchetta.

racket[2] *s*. **1.** fracasso **2.** baldoria **3.** (*gergo*) associazione a delinquere.

racy *agg*. **1.** genuino **2.** vivace, pungente.

radial *agg*. radiale.

radiance *s*. radiosità.

radiant *agg*. **1.** radiante **2.** raggiante.

to **radiate** *vt*. e *vi*. irradiare.

radiation *s*. (ir)radiazione.

radiator *s*. radiatore.

radical *agg*. e *s*. radicale.

radicalism *s*. radicalismo.

radio *s*. radio || — -*beacon*, radiofaro; — -*control*, radiocomando; — -*operator*, radiotelegrafista.

radioactive *agg*. radioattivo.

radioactivity *s*. radioattività.

radioengineering *s*. radiotecnica.

radiogoniometer *s*. radiogoniometro.

radiogram *s*. **1.** marconigramma **2.** radiogrammofono.

radiograph *s*. radiografia.

radiography *s*. radiografia.

radiologist *s*. radiologo.

radiology *s*. radiologia.

radioscopy *s*. radioscopia.

radiostatics *s*. *pl*. disturbi atmosferici.

radiotelegraphy *s*. radiotelegrafia.

radiotelephony *s*. radiotelefonia.

radiotherapeutics *s*. radioterapia.

radish *s*. ravanello.

radium *s*. radio.

radius *s*. raggio.

raffia *s*. rafia.

raft *s*. zattera || — -*bridge*, ponte di barche.

rag *s*. straccio.

ragamuffin *s*. pezzente.

rage *s*. **1.** furore **2.** passione.

to **rage** *vi*. infuriare || *the plague raged*, la peste infieriva.

ragged *agg*. **1.** lacero **2.** frastagliato **3.** spettinato **4.** rozzo.

raggedly *avv*. **1.** a brandelli **2.** in modo non uniforme.

raggedness *s*. **1.** cenciosità **2.** ineguaglianza.

raging *agg*. furioso.

raid *s*. incursione, scorreria.

to **raid** *vt*. e *vi*. fare un'incursione.

rail, railing *s*. **1.** sbarra **2.** ringhiera **3.** rotaia || *to go by* —, viaggiare per ferrovia.

raillery *s*. canzonatura.

railroad, railway *s*. ferrovia || — *companies*, società ferroviarie.

railwayman *s*. ferroviere.

rain *s*. pioggia || *it looks like* —, vuol piovere; *to be drenched with* —, essere inzuppato || — -*glass*, barometro.

to **rain** *v*. *imp*. piovere. ♦ to **rain** *vt*. far piovere.

rainbow *s*. arcobaleno.

raincoat *s*. impermeabile.

rainfall *s*. **1.** piovosità **2.** scroscio di pioggia.

rainproof *agg*. impermeabile.

rainy *agg*. piovoso.

raise *s*. aumento.

to **raise** *vt*. **1.** alzare **2.** innalzare **3.** allevare **4.** coltivare **5.** (*mil*.) arruolare.

raisin *s*. uva passa.

raising *s*. **1.** innalzamento **2.** aumento **3.** allevamento **4.** coltivazione **5.** educazione.

rake[1] *s*. rastrello.

rake[2] *s*. inclinazione.

rake[3] *s*. libertino.

to **rake**[1] *vt*. **1.** rastrellare **2.** raschiare || *to* — *up*, ammucchiare.

to **rake**[2] *vi*. essere inclinato.

rally[1] *s*. riunione, raduno.

rally[2] *s*. canzonatura.

to **rally**[1] *vt*. raccogliere. ♦ to **rally** *vi*. rianimarsi.

to **rally**[2] *vt*. canzonare.

ram *s*. **1.** ariete **2.** (*mar*.) sperone.

to **ram** *vt*. **1.** (*mar*.) speronare **2.** conficcare **3.** comprimere.

ramble *s*. vagabondaggio.

to **ramble** *vi*. **1.** vagare **2.** divagare.

rambler *s*. **1.** vagabondo **2.** rampicante.

rambling *agg*. **1.** errante **2.** sconnesso || — *thoughts*, divagazioni.

ramification *s*. ramificazione.

to **ramify** *vt*. ramificare. ♦ to **ramify** *vi*. ramificarsi.

rammer *s*. (*mil*.) pestello.

ramp[1] *s*. rampa.

ramp[2] *s*. (*gergo*) truffa.

rampage *s*. contegno iroso.

rampant *agg*. **1.** rampante **2.** violento **3.** predominante **4.** lussureggiante.

rampart *s*. bastione.

to **rampart** *vt*. fortificare.

ramshackle *agg*. sgangherato, che cade in rovina.

ran V. *to run.*
rancid *agg.* rancido.
rancour *s.* rancore.
rand *s.* soletta (*di scarpa*).
random *agg.* fatto a caso ‖ *at —,* a casaccio.
rang V. *to ring.*
range *s.* **1.** fila **2.** catena (*di monti*) **3.** spazio **4.** sfera, raggio **5.** gamma **6.** fornello **7.** (*aer.*) autonomia.
to range *vt.* **1.** allineare **2.** classificare **3.** puntare. ♦ **to range** *vi.* **1.** vagare **2.** avere una portata di **3.** oscillare (*di prezzi*).
ranger *s.* **1.** guardia forestale **2.** vagabondo.
rank *agg.* **1.** rigoglioso **2.** volgare **3.** puzzolente. ♦ **rank** *s.* **1.** fila **2.** rango, grado **3.** truppa.
to rank *vi.* **1.** schierarsi **2.** essere classificato.
to ransack *vt.* **1.** frugare **2.** saccheggiare.
ransom *s.* riscatto.
to ransom *vt.* riscattare.
to rant *vt. e vi.* declamare.
rap *s.* colpo.
to rap *vt. e vi.* **1.** battere **2.** bussare.
rapacious *agg.* rapace.
rapacity *s.* rapacità.
rape[1] *s.* violenza carnale.
rape[2] *s.* rapa.
to rape *vt.* violentare.
rapid *agg.* rapido. ♦ **rapid** *s.* rapida.
rapidity *s.* rapidità.
rapt *agg.* rapito.
raptorial *agg.* rapace.
rapture *s.* rapimento.
rare *agg.* **1.** raro **2.** rarefatto.
rarefaction *s.* rarefazione.
to rarefy *vt.* **1.** rarefare **2.** raffinare. ♦ **to rarefy** *vi.* rarefarsi.
rarely *avv.* **1.** raramente **2.** in modo eccellente.
rareness, rarity *s.* **1.** rarità **2.** rarefazione.
rascal *s.* furfante.
rascalism, rascality *s.* furfanteria.
rash *agg.* avventato. ♦ **rash** *s.* eruzione cutanea.
rashness *s.* avventatezza.
rasp *s.* **1.** raspa **2.** stridore.
to rasp *vt.* **1.** raspare **2.** irritare.
raspberry *s.* lampone.
rasping *agg.* stridente.
rat *s.* **1.** topo **2.** (*fig.*) traditore.
rate *s.* **1.** tasso, quota **2.** tassa **3.** prezzo, tariffa **4.** ritmo, andamento

‖ *first —,* di prim'ordine; *— of discount,* tasso di sconto.
to rate[1] *vt.* **1.** stimare **2.** tassare **3.** classificare.
to rate[2] *vt.* redarguire.
rateable *agg.* soggetto ad imposta.
ratepayer *s.* contribuente.
rather *avv.* piuttosto ‖ *I had —,* preferirei; *I would — not,* non ci tengo.
ratification *s.* ratifica.
to ratify *vt.* ratificare.
rating[1] *s.* **1.** stima **2.** tassa **3.** classificazione.
rating[2] *s.* sgridata.
ratio *s.* rapporto.
ration *s.* razione.
to ration *vt.* razionare.
rational *agg.* razionale.
rationalism *s.* razionalismo.
rationalist *s.* razionalista.
rationality *s.* razionalità.
to rationalize *vt.* **1.** razionalizzare **2.** spiegare razionalmente.
rationally *avv.* razionalmente.
rattle *s.* **1.** sonaglio **2.** rantolo **3.** tintinnio.
to rattle *vt.* far risuonare. ♦ **to rattle** *vi.* **1.** risuonare **2.** cianciare.
rattling *agg.* **1.** vivace **2.** tintinnante.
ravage *s.* rovina.
to ravage *vt.* devastare.
rave *s.* delirio.
to rave *vt.* declamare. ♦ **to rave** *vi.* delirare ‖ *to — about sthg.,* andar pazzo per qc.
ravel *s.* **1.** groviglio **2.** lembo sfilacciato.
to ravel *vt.* ingarbugliare. ♦ **to ravel** *vi.* sfilacciarsi.
raven *s.* corvo.
to raven *vt. e vi.* saccheggiare.
ravenous *agg.* vorace.
ravine *s.* burrone.
raving *agg.* delirante. ♦ **raving** *s.* delirio.
to ravish *vt.* **1.** rapire **2.** violentare.
ravisher *s.* rapitore.
ravishing *agg.* (*fig.*) affascinante.
ravishment *s.* **1.** rapimento **2.** stupro.
raw *agg.* **1.** crudo **2.** greggio **3.** inesperto **4.** a nudo. ♦ **raw** *s.* punto vivo.
rawness *s.* **1.** crudezza **2.** rozzezza **3.** inesperienza **4.** escoriazione.
ray[1] *s.* **1.** raggio **2.** lampo.

ray[2] s. (zool.) razza.
to ray vt. irradiare. ♦ to ray vi. irradiarsi.
to raze vt. radere al suolo.
razor s. rasoio || — -blade, lametta.
to reabsorb vt. riassorbire.
reach s. 1. portata 2. penetrazione || beyond my —, irraggiungibile.
to reach vt. 1. raggiungere 2. porgere. ♦ to reach vi. estendersi.
to react vi. reagire.
reaction s. reazione.
reactionary agg. e s. reazionario.
reactive agg. reattivo.
read agg. colto. ♦ read s. lettura.
to read (read, read) vt. 1. leggere 2. interpretare 3. segnare || to — over, rileggere; to — through, esaminare.
readable agg. 1. leggibile 2. interessante.
reader s. 1. lettore 2. libro di lettura.
readily avv. prontamente.
readiness s. prontezza.
reading s. 1. lettura 2. interpretazione || — -desk, leggio.
to readjust vt. riaggiustare.
readjustment s. riordinamento.
to readmit vt. riammettere.
readmittance s. riammissione.
ready agg. pronto || — -made, confezionato; — money, contanti; — -made clothes, abito preconfezionato; — -built, prefabbricato.
to ready vt. preparare.
to reaffirm vt. riaffermare.
reafforestation s. rimboschimento.
reagent s. reagente.
real agg. e s. reale || — estate, beni immobili (pl.).
realism s. realismo.
realist s. realista.
realistic agg. realistico.
reality s. 1. realtà 2. realismo.
realizable agg. realizzabile.
realization s. 1. realizzazione 2. percezione.
to realize vt. 1. accorgersi di 2. realizzare 3. capire.
really avv. realmente.
realm s. reame.
realty s. beni immobili (pl.).
ream s. (tip.) risma.
to reap vt. 1. mietere 2. fare il raccolto (anche fig.).
reaper s. mietitore.
reaping s. mietitura.

to reappear vi. riapparire.
to reappoint vt. rinominare.
rear agg. posteriore. ♦ rear s. 1. retroguardia 2. retro.
to rear vt. 1. alzare, innalzare 2. allevare 3. coltivare.
to rearm vt. riarmare.
rearmament s. riarmo.
to rearrange vt. riordinare.
rearrangement s. riordinamento.
reason s. 1. ragione 2. causa, motivo 3. raziocinio.
to reason vt. e vi. 1. ragionare 2. persuadere || to — about a subject, discutere di un argomento.
reasonable agg. ragionevole.
reasonableness s. ragionevolezza.
reasonably avv. ragionevolmente.
reasoning s. ragionamento.
to reassert vt. riasserire.
reassurance s. rassicurazione.
to reassure vt. rassicurare.
to reawaken vt. risvegliare. ♦ to reawaken vi. risvegliarsi.
rebate s. riduzione, sconto.
rebel agg. e s. ribelle.
to rebel vi. ribellarsi.
rebellion s. ribellione.
rebellious agg. ribelle.
to rebind (rebound, rebound) vt. rilegare (un libro).
rebirth s. rinascita.
reborn agg. rinato.
rebound[1] V. to rebind.
rebound[2] s. rimbalzo.
to rebound vi. rimbalzare.
rebuff s. diniego, mortificazione.
to rebuild (rebuilt, rebuilt) vt. ricostruire.
rebuke s. rimprovero.
to rebuke vt. rimproverare.
to rebut vt. respingere, rifiutare.
recalcitrant agg. recalcitrante.
to recalcitrate vi. recalcitrare.
recall s. 1. richiamo 2. revoca.
to recall vt. 1. richiamare 2. rievocare, far tornare alla memoria.
to recant vt. e vi. ritrattare.
recantation s. ritrattazione.
to recapitulate vt. e vi. ricapitolare.
recapitulation s. ricapitolazione.
recapture s. riconquista.
to recapture vt. riconquistare.
to recast (recast, recast) vt. 1. rifondere 2. rimaneggiare.
to recede vi. 1. indietreggiare 2. diminuire.

receding agg. **1.** rientrante **2.** sfuggente.

receipt s. **1.** ricevimento **2.** ricevuta **3.** ricetta.

to receipt vt. quietanzare.

to receive vt. **1.** ricevere **2.** accettare.

receiver s. **1.** ricevitore **2.** (giur.) ricettatore.

receiving s. ricezione.

recension s. revisione.

recent agg. recente.

receptacle s. ricettacolo.

reception s. **1.** ricevimento **2.** ricezione **3.** accoglienza.

receptive agg. ricettivo.

receptivity s. ricettività.

recess s. **1.** intervallo **2.** rientranza **3.** recesso.

recession s. **1.** ritiro **2.** recessione.

recessive agg. retrocedente.

recharge s. ricarica.

to recharge vt. ricaricare.

to rechristen vt. ribattezzare.

recidivism s. recidività.

recipe s. ricetta.

recipient agg. e s. ricevente.

reciprocal agg. reciproco. ♦ **reciprocal** s. (mat.) numero reciproco.

to reciprocate vt. **1.** contraccambiare **2.** muovere alternativamente. ♦ **to reciprocate** vi. muoversi alternativamente.

reciprocating agg. (mecc.) alternativo.

reciprocation s. **1.** moto alterno **2.** scambio.

reciprocity s. reciprocità.

recital s. **1.** relazione **2.** recitazione.

recitation s. **1.** recitazione **2.** recita **3.** narrazione.

recitative agg. e s. recitativo.

to recite vt. **1.** recitare **2.** riferire.

reckless agg. incurante.

recklessness s. noncuranza.

to reckon vt. **1.** contare, computare **2.** considerare.

reckoner s. calcolatore.

reckoning s. conto.

reclaim s. rivendicazione.

to reclaim vt. **1.** redimere **2.** bonificare **3.** rivendicare.

reclamation s. **1.** redenzione **2.** bonifica **3.** rivendicazione.

to recline vt. chinare. ♦ **to recline** vi. chinarsi.

reclining agg. chinato.

recluse agg. recluso. ♦ **recluse** s. eremita.

reclusion s. **1.** reclusione **2.** eremo.

recognition s. riconoscimento.

recognizable agg. riconoscibile.

to recognize vt. riconoscere.

recoil s. **1.** il ritrarsi **2.** rinculo.

to recoil vi. **1.** ritrarsi **2.** ricadere **3.** rinculare.

to recollect vt. **1.** raccogliere **2.** ricordare ‖ to — oneself, riaversi.

recollection s. ricordo.

to recommence vt. e vi. ricominciare.

to recommend vt. raccomandare.

recommendation s. raccomandazione.

recommendatory agg. raccomandatorio.

recompense s. **1.** ricompensa **2.** risarcimento.

to recompense vt. **1.** ricompensare **2.** risarcire.

to recompose vt. ricomporre.

recomposition s. ricomposizione.

to reconcile vt. (ri)conciliare ‖ to — oneself, rassegnarsi.

reconcilement s. **1.** riconciliazione **2.** rassegnazione.

reconnaissance s. ricognizione.

to reconnoitre vt. e vi. perlustrare.

to reconquer vt. riconquistare.

reconquest s. riconquista.

to reconsider vt. riconsiderare.

reconsideration s. revisione.

reconstitute vt. ricostituire.

to reconstruct vt. ricostruire.

reconstruction s. ricostruzione.

reconversion s. riconversione.

to reconvert vt. riconvertire.

record s. **1.** registrazione **2.** documento **3.** passato **4.** disco ‖ — player, giradischi.

to record vt. registrare.

recorder s. **1.** cancelliere **2.** registratore **3.** archivista ‖ tape —, magnetofono.

recording s. registrazione.

recordist s. (cine) tecnico del suono.

recourse s. ricorso.

to recover vt. ricuperare, riacquistare, riscoprire. ♦ **to recover** vi. ristabilirsi.

recoverable agg. **1.** ricuperabile **2.** guaribile.

recovery s. **1.** recupero **2.** guarigione **3.** (giur.) rivendicazione.

to recreate vt. divertire. ♦ **to recreate** vi. divertirsi.

to re-create vt. ricreare.

recreation s. ricreazione.

recreative *agg.* ricreativo.
to **recriminate** *vi.* recriminare.
recrimination *s.* recriminazione.
recrudescence *s.* recrudescenza.
recrudescent *agg.* che rincrudisce.
recruit *s.* recluta.
to **recruit** *vt.* 1. reclutare 2. rinforzare. ♦ to **recruit** *vi.* ristabilirsi.
recruitment *s.* reclutamento.
rectangle *s.* rettangolo.
rectangular *agg.* rettangolare.
rectification *s.* rettificazione.
rectifier *s.* (*mecc.*) rettificatrice.
to **rectify** *vt.* rettificare.
rectilineal *agg.* rettilineo.
rectitude *s.* rettitudine.
rector *s.* 1. rettore 2. parroco.
rectorate *s.* rettorato.
rectorship *s.* rettorato.
rectory *s.* 1. presbiterio 2. (*eccl.*) beneficio.
to **recur** *vi.* ritornare.
recurrence *s.* ricorso.
recurrent *agg.* ricorrente.
recusant *agg.* e *s.* dissidente.
red *agg.* e *s.* rosso || — -*hot*, rovente; — -*lead*, minio; — -*letter day*, giorno festivo. ♦ **Reds** *s. pl.* comunisti.
to **redact** *vt.* 1. redigere 2. revisionare.
redactor *s.* redattore.
to **redden** *vt.* arrossare. ♦ to **redden** *vi.* arrossire.
reddish *agg.* rossiccio.
to **redeem** *vt.* 1. riscattare 2. ricuperare 3. estinguere: *to — a mortgage*, estinguere un'ipoteca.
redeemable *agg.* 1. riscattabile 2. ricuperabile.
redeemer *s.* redentore.
redemption *s.* 1. redenzione 2. (*comm.*) rimborso 3. (*giur.*) riscatto.
redness *s.* rossore.
to **redouble** *vt.* e *vi.* raddoppiare.
redress *s.* riparazione.
to **redress** *vt.* riparare, rimediare.
redskin *agg.* e *s.* pellerossa.
to **reduce** *vt.* 1. ridurre 2. degradare.
reduced *agg.* ridotto.
reducer *s.* riduttore.
reduction *s.* 1. riduzione 2. degradazione.
redundance *s.* sovrabbondanza.
redundant *agg.* ridondante.
redwood *s.* sequoia.
to **re-echo** *vt.* e *vi.* riecheggiare.
reed *s.* canna || *broken* —, perso-

na infida; — -*pipe*, zampogna.
re-edification *s.* riedificazione.
to **re-edify** *vt.* riedificare.
to **re-educate** *vt.* rieducare.
reef *s.* secca || *coral-* —, banco di coralli.
to **reek** *vi.* puzzare. ♦ to **reek** *vt.* trasudare.
reel *s.* 1. bobina 2. giro vorticoso || *news-* —, cinegiornale.
to **reel** *vt.* avvolgere || *to — off*, snocciolare. ♦ to **reel** *vi.* girare.
to **re-elect** *vt.* rieleggere.
to **re-emerge** *vi.* riemergere.
to **re-enact** *vt.* richiamare in vigore (*una legge*).
to **re-enter** *vt.* rientrare.
re-entrance *s.* rientro.
re-entry *s.* 1. rientro 2. nuova registrazione.
to **re-establish** *vt.* ristabilire.
re-establishment *s.* ristabilimento.
re-examination *s.* riesame.
to **re-examine** *vt.* riesaminare.
refectory *s.* refettorio.
to **refer** *vt.* 1. attribuire 2. rimandare. ♦ to **refer** *vi.* 1. riferirsi 2. rivolgersi.
referable *agg.* riferibile.
referee *s.* arbitro.
to **referee** *vt.* e *vi.* arbitrare.
reference *s.* 1. riferimento 2. consultazione 3. referenza 4. (*giur.*) rinvio.
referential *agg.* riferentesi a.
refill *s.* ricambio.
to **refill** *vt.* riempire di nuovo.
to **refine** *vt.* raffinare. ♦ to **refine** *vi.* raffinarsi.
refined *agg.* 1. raffinato 2. colto.
refinement *s.* 1. raffinamento 2. raffinatezza.
refiner *s.* raffinatore.
refinery *s.* raffineria.
refit *s.* riparazione.
to **refit** *vt.* riparare.
to **reflect** *vt.* e *vi* 1. riflettere 2. meditare.
reflection *s.* 1. riflessione, riflesso 2. biasimo || *to cast reflections on so.*, criticare qu.
reflective *agg.* riflessivo.
reflector *s.* riflettore.
reflex *agg.* e *s.* riflesso.
reflorescence *s.* rifioritura.
reflux *s.* riflusso.
reform *s.* riforma.
to **reform** *vt.* riformare.
reformation *s.* riforma.

reformational *agg.* di riforma.
reformatory *agg.* riformativo. ♦
reformatory *s.* riformatorio.
reformer *s.* riformatore.
to **refract** *vt.* rifrangere.
refraction *s.* rifrazione.
refractivity *s.* rifrangibilità.
refractor *s.* rifrattore.
refractory *agg.* 1. refrattario 2. ostinato.
refrain *s.* ritornello.
to **refrain** *vi.* trattenersi, astenersi.
to **refresh** *vt.* 1. rinfrescare 2. rinvigorire. ♦ to **refresh** *vi.* 1. rinvigorirsi 2. rifornirsi.
refreshment *s.* ristoro. ♦ **refreshments** *s. pl.* cibo, bevanda (*sing.*).
refrigerant *agg.* e *s.* refrigerante.
to **refrigerate** *vt.* refrigerare.
refrigeration *s.* refrigerazione.
refrigerator *s.* frigorifero.
refrigeratory *agg.* refrigerante.
to **refuel** *vt.* rifornire di carburante. ♦ to **refuel** *vi.* rifornirsi di carburante.
refuge *s.* rifugio.
refugee *s.* rifugiato, profugo.
refulgence *s.* fulgore.
refulgent *agg.* rifulgente.
refund *s.* rimborso.
to **refund** *vt.* rimborsare.
refusable *agg.* rifiutabile.
refusal *s.* 1. rifiuto 2. diritto di opzione.
refuse *s.* rifiuto.
to **refuse** *vt.* rifiutare. ♦ to **refuse** *vi.* rifiutarsi.
refuser *s.* ricusante.
refutal *s.* confutazione.
to **refute** *vt.* confutare.
to **regain** *vt.* riguadagnare.
regal *agg.* regale.
regality *s.* regalità.
regally *avv.* regalmente.
regard *s.* 1. considerazione 2. sguardo ‖ *with* — *to*, riguardo a. ♦ **regards** *s. pl.* saluti.
to **regard** *vt.* 1. considerare 2. riguardare 3. osservare.
regardful *agg.* 1. attento 2. rispettoso.
regardless *agg.* senza riguardo. ♦ **regardless** *avv.* senza riguardo a, senza badare a.
regatta *s.* regata.
regelation *s.* ricongelamento.
regency *s.* reggenza.
to **regenerate** *vt.* rigenerare. ♦ to **regenerate** *vi.* rigenerarsi.

regeneration *s.* rigenerazione.
regenerative *agg.* rigeneratore.
regenerator *s.* rigeneratore.
regent *agg.* e *s.* reggente.
regicide *s.* 1. regicida 2. regicidio.
regimen *s.* regime.
regiment *s.* reggimento.
to **regiment** *vt.* 1. irreggimentare 2. disciplinare.
regimental *agg.* reggimentale.
regimentals *s. pl.* (*mil.*) uniforme (*sing.*).
region *s.* regione.
regional *agg.* regionale.
register *s.* registro.
to **register** *vt.* registrare, iscrivere. ♦ to **register** *vi.* iscriversi.
registrar *s.* 1. segretario 2. ufficiale di stato civile.
registration *s.* registrazione, iscrizione.
registry *s.* 1. registrazione 2. ufficio del Registro.
regnant *agg.* regnante.
regress *s.* retrocessione.
to **regress** *vi.* retrocedere.
regression *s.* regresso.
regressive *agg.* regressivo.
regret *s.* rammarico.
to **regret** *vt.* 1. rimpiangere 2. rammaricarsi di.
regretful *agg.* pieno di rammarico.
regular *agg.* e *s.* regolare.
regularity *s.* regolarità.
regularization *s.* regolarizzazione.
to **regularize** *vt.* regolarizzare.
regularly *avv.* regolarmente.
to **regulate** *vt.* regolare.
regulation *s.* 1. regolamento 2. regolazione.
regulative *agg.* e *s.* regolatore.
regulator *s.* regolatore.
to **rehabilitate** *vt.* 1. riabilitare 2. ripristinare.
rehabilitation *s.* 1. riabilitazione 2. ripristino.
rehearsal *s.* 1. ripetizione 2. (*teat.*) prova.
to **rehearse** *vt.* 1. ripetere 2. provare.
reign *s.* regno.
to **reign** *vi.* regnare.
to **reimburse** *vt.* rimborsare.
reimbursement *s.* rimborso.
rein *s.* redine.
to **rein** *vt.* tenere a freno.
to **reincarnate** *vt.* reincarnare.
reincarnation *s.* reincarnazione.
reindeer *s.* renna.

to **reinforce** *vt.* rinforzare.
reinforce(ment) *s.* rinforzo.
to **reinstate** *vt.* ristabilire.
to **reintegrate** *vt.* reintegrare.
reinvestment *s.* nuovo investimento.
to **reinvigorate** *vt.* rinvigorire.
reinvigoration *s.* rinvigorimento.
to **reiterate** *vt.* reiterare.
reiteration *s.* reiterazione.
reject *s.* persona, cosa rifiutata.
to **reject** *vt.* rifiutare.
rejection *s.* rifiuto.
to **rejoice** *vt.* rallegrare. ♦ to **rejoice** *vi.* rallegrarsi.
rejoicing *s.* 1. allegria 2. festa.
rejuvenation *s.* ringiovanimento.
relapse *s.* ricaduta.
to **relapse** *vi.* 1. ricadere 2. avere una ricaduta.
to **relate** *vt.* 1. narrare 2. mettere in relazione. ♦ to **relate** *vi.* aver rapporto con.
relater *s.* narratore.
relation *s.* 1. relazione 2. parente.
relationship *s.* 1. relazione 2. parentela.
relative *agg.* relativo. ♦ **relative** *s.* parente.
relativism *s.* relativismo.
relativity *s.* relatività.
to **relax** *vt.* 1. rilassare 2. allentare. ♦ to **relax** *vi.* rilassarsi.
relaxation *s.* 1. rilassamento 2. svago 3. mitigazione.
relay *s.* 1. turno 2. ricambio 3. (*radio*) collegamento.
to **relay** *vt.* (*radio*) collegare.
release *s.* 1. liberazione 2. quietanza 3. cessione 4. scarico.
to **release** *vt.* 1. liberare 2. cedere.
releasee *s.* cessionario.
to **relegate** *vt.* 1. relegare 2. rimettere.
relegation *s.* relegazione.
relentless *agg.* inflessibile.
to **relent** *vi.* impietosirsi.
relevance *s.* 1. relazione 2. pertinenza.
relevant *agg.* 1. relativo 2. pertinente.
reliability *s.* attendibilità.
reliable *agg.* attendibile, fidato.
reliance *s.* 1. fede 2. persona, cosa di fiducia.
relic *s.* reliquia.
relief[1] *s.* 1. sollievo 2. aiuto 3. esenzione 4. cambio.
relief[2] *s.* 1. rilievo 2. (*pitt.*) prospettiva.

to **relieve** *vt.* 1. alleviare, sollevare 2. aiutare 3. dare il cambio a 4. dare rilievo a.
reliever *s.* soccorritore.
relieving *agg.* 1. che allevia, soccorre 2. (*mil.*) che dà il cambio.
religion *s.* religione.
religiosity *s.* religiosità.
religious *agg.* e *s.* religioso.
to **relinquish** *vt.* abbandonare.
relinquishment *s.* abbandono.
reliquary *s.* reliquario.
reliques *s. pl.* resti.
relish *s.* 1. gusto 2. sapore, profumo, aroma 3. condimento.
to **relish** *vt.* 1. gustare 2. insaporire.
to **relive** *vt.* e *vi.* rivivere.
to **reload** *vt.* ricaricare.
to **reluct** *vi.* essere riluttante.
reluctance *s.* riluttanza.
reluctant *agg.* riluttante.
reluctantly *avv.* con riluttanza.
to **rely** *vi.* fidarsi.
remade V. *to remake*.
to **remain** *vi.* rimanere, restare.
remainder *s.* resto, avanzo, rimanenza.
remains *s. pl.* resti.
to **remake (remade, remade)** *vt.* rifare.
remark *s.* nota, osservazione, commento.
to **remark** *vt.* e *vi.* osservare.
remarkable *agg.* notevole.
remarkableness *s.* ragguardevolezza.
remarkably *avv.* notevolmente.
to **remarry** *vt.* risposare. ♦ to **remarry** *vi.* risposarsi.
remediable *agg.* rimediabile.
remedy *s.* rimedio, cura.
to **remedy** *vt.* rimediare.
to **remember** *vt.* ricordare. ♦ to **remember** *vi.* ricordarsi.
remembrance *s.* ricordo.
to **remind** *vt.* ricordare (*qc. a qu.*), far ricordare, rammentare.
reminder *s.* ricordo, promemoria.
remindful *agg.* 1. memore 2. che fa ricordare.
reminiscence *s.* ricordo.
reminiscent *agg.* che ricorda.
remise *s.* (*giur.*) cessione.
to **remise** *vt.* (*giur.*) rinunciare a, cedere (*diritti ecc.*).
remiss *agg.* negligente.
remissible *agg.* remissibile.

remission s. **1.** remissione **2.** esonero, annullamento **3.** (*med.*) remissione.

remissive *agg.* indulgente.

to **remit** *vt.* rimettere. ♦ to **remit** *vi.* diminuire, mitigarsi.

remittal s. (*giur.*) remissione (*condono*).

remittance s. rimessa (*di denaro*).

remittent *agg.* (*med.*) intermittente.

remnant *agg.* rimanente. ♦ **remnant** s. resto, rimanenza, avanzo.

to **remodel** *vt.* rimodellare.

remonstrance s. rimostranza.

to **remonstrate** *vi.* protestare.

remonstration s. rimostranza.

remorse s. rimorso.

remorseful *agg.* pieno di rimorso.

remorseless *agg.* senza rimorsi.

remote *agg.* remoto.

remoteness s. distanza, lontananza.

remotion s. rimozione, allontanamento.

remount s. rimonta (*di cavalli*).

to **remount** *vt.* e *vi.* **1.** rimontare (*a cavallo, in bicicletta*) **2.** risalire.

removable *agg.* rimovibile.

removal s. **1.** rimozione **2.** trasferimento, trasloco.

remove s. **1.** trasferimento **2.** grado (*di parentela*).

to **remove** *vt.* rimuovere. ♦ to **remove** *vi.* trasferirsi.

removed *agg.* lontano.

remover s. chi, ciò che toglie.

to **remunerate** *vt.* rimunerare.

remuneration s. rimunerazione.

remunerative *agg.* rimunerativo.

renaissance s. rinascimento.

renal *agg.* renale.

to **rename** *vt.* rinominare.

to **rend (rent, rent)** *vt.* lacerare. ♦ to **rend (rent, rent)** *vi.* lacerarsi.

to **render** *vt.* **1.** rendere **2.** consegnare.

rendering s. **1.** restituzione **2.** resa.

renegade s. rinnegato.

to **renew** *vt.* rinnovare. ♦ to **renew** *vi.* rinnovarsi.

renewable *agg.* rinnovabile.

renewal s. **1.** rinnovo **2.** ripresa.

renewer s. rinnovatore.

renitency s. riluttanza.

renitent *agg.* renitente, riluttante.

rennet s. ranetta.

to **renounce** *vt.* **1.** rinunciare a **2.** ripudiare.

renouncement s. rinuncia.

to **renovate** *vt.* rinnovare.

renown s. rinomanza, fama.

renowned *agg.* rinomato, famoso.

rent[1] s. affitto.

rent[2] s. **1.** strappo, squarcio **2.** spaccatura.

rent[3] V. *to rend.*

to **rent** *vt.* affittare. ♦ to **rent** *vi.* essere affittato.

rental s. affitto.

renunciation s. rinuncia.

to **reoccupy** *vt.* rioccupare.

to **reopen** *vt.* riaprire. ♦ to **reopen** *vi.* riaprirsi.

reopening s. riapertura.

reorganization s. riassetto, riorganizzazione.

repaid V. *to repay.*

repair s. **1.** riparazione, restaurazione **2.** stato, condizione.

to **repair** *vt.* riparare, restaurare.

repairer s. riparatore.

reparation s. riparazione.

repartee s. replica arguta.

repartition s. ripartizione.

to **repatriate** *vt.* e *vi.* rimpatriare.

repatriation s. rimpatrio.

to **repay (repaid, repaid)** *vt.* ripagare.

repayable *agg.* ripagabile.

repeal s. revoca.

to **repeal** *vt.* revocare.

repealer s. revocatore.

repeat s. ripetizione.

to **repeat** *vt.* ripetere. ♦ to **repeat** *vi.* ripetersi.

repeater s. **1.** ripetitore **2.** ripetente **3.** arma a ripetizione.

repeating *agg.* **1.** a ripetizione **2.** periodico (*di numero*).

to **repel** *vt.* respingere.

repellent *agg.* repellente.

to **repent** *vt.* e *vi.* pentirsi.

repentance s. pentimento.

repentant *agg.* pentito.

repenter s. penitente.

repercussion s. ripercussione.

repercussive *agg.* ripercussivo.

repertoire s. repertorio.

repertory s. **1.** repertorio **2.** raccolta.

repetition s. ripetizione.

to **repine** *vi.* lamentarsi.

to **replace** *vt.* **1.** ricollocare **2.** rimpiazzare, sostituire.

replaceable *agg.* sostituibile.

replacement s. **1.** ricollocamento **2.** sostituzione.

replete *agg.* pieno.
repletion *s.* pienezza.
replication *s.* replica.
reply *s.* risposta.
to reply *vi.* rispondere.
report *s.* 1. diceria 2. reputazione 3. rapporto 4. scoppio.
to report *vt.* riportare. ✦ **to report** *vi.* 1. stendere rapporto 2. fare il cronista 3. presentarsi.
reporter *s.* cronista (*di giornale*).
to repose *vt.* porre. ✦ **to repose** *vi.* riposare.
to reprehend *vt.* rimproverare.
reprehensible *agg.* biasimevole.
reprehension *s.* biasimo.
to represent *vt.* rappresentare, raffigurare.
representation *s.* 1. rappresentazione 2. rappresentanza.
representative *agg.* rappresentativo. ✦ **representative** *s.* rappresentante.
to repress *vt.* reprimere.
repressed *agg.* represso.
repressible *agg.* reprimibile.
repression *s.* repressione.
repressive *agg.* repressivo.
reprimand *s.* rimprovero.
reprint *s.* ristampa.
to reprint *vt.* ristampare.
reprisal *s.* rappresaglia.
reproach *s.* 1. rimprovero 2. discredito.
to reproach *vt.* 1. rimproverare 2. discreditare.
reproachable *agg.* riprovevole.
reproachful *agg.* di rimprovero.
reprobate *agg.* corrotto. ✦ **reprobate** *s.* reprobo.
to reprobate *vt.* 1. riprovare 2. dannare.
reprobation *s.* 1. riprovazione 2. dannazione.
to reproduce *vt.* riprodurre. ✦ **to reproduce** *vi.* riprodursi.
reproducer *s.* riproduttore.
reproducible *agg.* riproducibile.
reproduction *s.* riproduzione.
reproductive *agg.* riproduttivo.
reproof *s.* rimprovero.
to reprove *vt.* rimproverare.
reptile *agg.* strisciante. ✦ **reptile** *s.* rettile.
republic *s.* repubblica.
republican *agg.* e *s.* repubblicano.
republication *s.* ripubblicazione.
to republish *vt.* ripubblicare.
to repudiate *vt.* ripudiare.

repudiation *s.* ripudio.
repugnance *s.* 1. ripugnanza 2. incompatibilità.
repugnant *agg.* 1. ripugnante 2. incompatibile.
repulse *s.* ripulsa, rifiuto.
to repulse *vt.* respingere.
repulsion *s.* repulsione.
repulsive *agg.* ripulsivo.
reputable *agg.* onorato.
reputation *s.* reputazione.
repute *s.* fama.
to repute *vt.* reputare.
reputed *agg.* 1. supposto 2. putativo.
request *s.* richiesta.
to request *vt.* (ri)chiedere.
to require *vt.* 1. richiedere 2. ordinare, obbligare.
requirement *s.* 1. richiesta 2. requisito.
requisite *agg.* richiesto. ✦ **requisite** *s.* requisito.
requisition *s.* 1. richiesta 2. requisito 3. requisizione.
to requisition *vt.* requisire.
requital *s.* 1. contraccambio 2. ricompensa.
to requite *vt.* 1. ricompensare 2. contraccambiare.
to reread (reread, reread) *vt.* rileggere.
to rescind *vt.* rescindere.
rescission *s.* rescissione.
rescue *s.* 1. liberazione 2. soccorso.
to rescue *vt.* 1. liberare 2. riacquistare 3. soccorrere.
research *s.* ricerca || — **work**, lavoro di ricerca.
to research *vi.* fare ricerche.
researcher *s.* ricercatore.
to resell (resold, resold) *vt.* rivendere.
resemblance *s.* rassomiglianza.
to resemble *vt.* assomigliare a.
to resent *vt.* risentirsi di.
resentful *agg.* 1. risentito 2. permaloso.
resentment *s.* risentimento.
reservation *s.* 1. riserva 2. prenotazione.
reserve *s.* 1. riserva 2. riserbo.
to reserve *vt.* riservare.
reservoir *s.* serbatoio.
to reset (reset, reset) *vt.* 1. rimettere a posto 2. (*tip.*) ricomporre.
to resettle *vt.* risistemare. ✦ **to resettle** *vi.* risistemarsi.
resettlement *s.* risistemazione.

to **reshape** vt. dare nuova forma a.
to **reside** vi. risiedere.
residence s. residenza.
resident agg. e s. residente.
residential agg. residenziale.
residual agg. residuo. ◆ **residual** s. 1. residuo 2. resto.
residue s. residuo, avanzo.
to **resign** vt. 1. consegnare 2. rinunciare ‖ to — oneself, rassegnarsi. ◆ to **resign** vi. dimettersi.
resignation s. 1. dimissioni (pl.) 2. rinuncia 3. rassegnazione.
resigned agg. rassegnato.
resilience, resiliency s. elasticità.
resilient agg. elastico.
resin s. resina.
resinous agg. resinoso.
resipiscence s. resipiscenza.
resipiscent agg. resipiscente.
resist s. sostanza protettiva.
to **resist** vt. e vi. resistere.
resistance s. resistenza.
resistant, resistent agg. resistente.
resistive agg. resistente.
resold V. to resell.
to **resole** vt. risolare.
resolubile agg. (ri)solubile.
resolute agg. risoluto.
resoluteness s. risolutezza.
resolution s. 1. risolutezza 2. risoluzione 3. scissione.
resolutive agg. risolutivo.
resolvable agg. risolvibile.
resolve s. risoluzione.
to **resolve** vt. 1. risolvere 2. scindere. ◆ to **resolve** vi. risolversi.
resolvent agg. e s. solvente.
resonance s. risonanza.
resonant agg. risonante.
to **resorb** vt. riassorbire.
resorbent agg. riassorbente.
resort s. 1. ricorso 2. risorsa 3. ritrovo 4. luogo di soggiorno.
to **resort** vi. 1. ricorrere 2. recarsi.
to **resound** vi. risonare. ◆ to **resound** vt. proclamare.
resource s. risorsa.
resourceful agg. pieno di risorse.
resourceless agg. senza risorse.
respect s. 1. rispetto, stima 2. aspetto 3. punto di vista.
to **respect** vt. rispettare.
respectability s. 1. rispettabilità 2. convenzioni sociali (pl.).
respectable agg. rispettabile.
respectful agg. rispettoso.
respecting prep. rispetto a.
respective agg. rispettivo.

respiration s. respirazione.
respirator s. respiratore.
respiratory agg. respiratorio.
respite s. 1. dilazione 2. tregua.
to **respite** vt. concedere una dilazione, una tregua a.
resplendent agg. risplendente.
respond s. responsorio.
to **respond** vi. rispondere.
respondence s. rispondenza.
respondent agg. 1. rispondente 2. sensibile. ◆ **respondent** s. (giur.) convenuto.
response s. risposta.
responsibility s. responsabilità.
responsible agg. 1. responsabile 2. di responsabilità.
responsive agg. rispondente.
responsory s. responsorio.
rest[1] s. 1. riposo 2. appoggio.
rest[2] s. resto, residuo.
to **rest** vt. 1. riposare 2. appoggiare. ◆ to **rest** vi. 1. riposarsi 2. appoggiarsi.
to **restate** vt. riesporre.
restaurant s. ristorante ‖ — -car, vagone ristorante.
restful agg. tranquillo.
restfulness s. tranquillità.
resting-place s. luogo di riposo.
restitution s. restituzione.
restive agg. 1. restio 2. irrequieto.
restless agg. 1. irrequieto 2. incessante.
restlessness s. irrequietezza.
restorable agg. 1. restituibile 2. restaurabile.
restoration s. 1. restituzione 2. restauro 3. restaurazione 4. ricostruzione.
to **restore** vt. 1. restituire 2. restaurare 3. ricostruire 4. ristabilire.
to **restrain** vt. 1. trattenere 2. confinare.
restrainable agg. reprimibile.
restraint s. 1. freno 2. detenzione.
to **restrict** vt. limitare.
restrictedly avv. limitatamente.
restriction s. restrizione.
restrictive agg. restrittivo.
result s. risultato.
to **result** vi. 1. risultare 2. risolversi.
resultant agg. e s. risultante.
resultful agg. utile, efficace.
resultless agg. inutile, inefficace.
to **resume** vt. riprendere.
resummons s. nuova convocazione.
resumption s. ripresa.

resurgent *agg.* risorgente.
to **resurrect** *vt.* (*fam.*) risuscitare.
resurrection *s.* risurrezione.
resurrectional *agg.* di risurrezione.
to **resuscitate** *vt.* e *vi.* risuscitare.
resuscitation *s.* risuscitamento.
to **ret** *vt.* macerare.
retail *s.* vendita al minuto || *by* —, al minuto.
to **retail** *vt.* e *vi.* vendere al minuto.
retailer *s.* dettagliante.
to **retain** *vt.* trattenere, conservare.
retainable *agg.* trattenibile, conservabile.
retainer *s.* caparra, anticipo.
retaining *agg.* — *wall*, muro di sostegno.
retake *s.* (*cine*) replica di una ripresa.
to **retake** (**retook, retaken**) *vt.* 1. riprendere 2. (*cine*) ripetere una ripresa.
to **retaliate** *vi.* far rappresaglia.
retaliation *s.* rappresaglia.
retaliative, retaliatory *agg.* vendicativo.
retard *s.* ritardo.
to **retard** *vt.* e *vi.* ritardare.
to **retaste** *vt.* riassaggiare.
to **retch** *vi.* avere conati di vomito.
to **retell** (**retold, retold**) *vt.* ripetere.
retention *s.* 1. ritenzione 2. memoria.
retentive *agg.* 1. che trattiene 2. tenace (*di memoria*).
reticence, reticency *s.* reticenza.
reticent *agg.* reticente.
reticle *s.* (*ott.*) reticolo.
reticular *agg.* reticolare.
reticulate *agg.* reticolato.
reticulum *s.* (*pl.* -la) reticolo.
retinue *s.* seguito.
to **retire** *vt.* ritirare. ♦ to **retire** *vi.* ritirarsi.
retired *agg.* 1. ritirato 2. a riposo, in ritiro.
retirement *s.* 1. ritiro 2. collocamento a riposo 3. (*mil.*) ritirata.
retiring *agg.* 1. riservato 2. che si ritira, uscente.
retold V. *to retell.*
retook V. *to retake.*
retorsion *s.* ritorsione.
retort *s.* storta.
to **retort** *vt.* ritorcere. ♦ to **retort** *vi.* ribattere.
retort(ion) *s.* ritorsione.
retouch *s.* ritocco.

to **retouch** *vt.* ritoccare.
to **retrace** *vt.* ripercorrere, risalire.
to **retract** *vt.* 1. ritrarre 2. ritrattare. ♦ to **retract** *vi.* ritrarsi.
retractable *agg.* ritraibile 2. ritrattabile.
retractation *s.* ritrattazione.
retractile *agg.* retrattile.
retractor *s.* (*med.*) divaricatore.
to **retread** (**retrod, retrodden**) *vt.* ripercorrere.
retreat *s.* eremo, luogo appartato.
to **retreat** *vi.* ritirarsi, retrocedere.
retreating *agg.* sfuggente. ♦ **retreating** *s.* (*mil.*) ritirata.
retribution *s.* punizione.
retrievable *agg.* 1. ricuperabile 2. riparabile.
retrieval *s.* 1. ricupero (*di beni*) 2. riparazione.
to **retrieve** *vt.* 1. ricuperare 2. riparare.
retroaction *s.* 1. reazione 2. azione retroattiva.
retroactive *agg.* retroattivo.
to **retrocede**[1] *vi.* retrocedere.
to **retrocede**[2] *vt.* restituire.
retrocession[1] *s.* retrocessione.
retrocession[2] *s.* restituzione.
retrod V. *to retread.*
retrodden V. *to retread.*
retrospect(ion) *s.* sguardo retrospettivo.
retrospective *agg.* retrospettivo.
retroversion *s.* retroversione.
return *s.* 1. ritorno 2. restituzione 3. guadagno, profitto 4. relazione || — *journey*, viaggio di ritorno; *election returns*, risultati elettorali.
to **return** *vi.* 1. ritornare 2. rispondere, ricambiare, replicare. ♦ to **return** *vt.* 1. restituire, rimandare 2. produrre, fruttare 3. (*pol.*) eleggere.
reunion *s.* riunione.
to **reunite** *vt.* riunire. ♦ to **reunite** *vi.* riunirsi.
revaluation *s.* rivalutazione.
to **revalue** *vt.* rivalutare.
to **reveal** *vt.* rivelare.
revel *s.* baldoria.
to **revel** *vi.* far baldoria.
revelation *s.* rivelazione.
reveller *s.* chi fa baldoria.
revelry *s.* baldoria.
revenge *s.* vendetta.
to **revenge** *vt.* vendicare. ♦ to **revenge** *vi.* vendicarsi.
revengeful *agg.* vendicativo.

revenger s. vendicatore.
revenue s. **1.** entrata **2.** fisco.
to **reverberate** vt. e vi. riverberare.
reverberation s. riverberazione, riverbero.
to **revere** vt. riverire.
reverence s. riverenza.
to **reverence** vt. riverire.
reverend agg. reverendo.
reverent(ial) agg. riverente.
reverie s. fantasticheria.
reversal s. **1.** rovesciamento **2.** (giur.) annullamento.
reverse agg. e s. rovescio || — gear, retromarcia.
to **reverse** vt. rovesciare. ♦ to **reverse** vi. innestare la retromarcia.
reversibility s. reversibilità.
reversible agg. reversibile, rovesciabile.
reversion s. reversione.
to **revert** vi. ritornare.
review s. **1.** revisione **2.** recensione **3.** rivista, periodico **4.** (mil.) rivista.
to **review** vt. **1.** rivedere **2.** recensire **3.** (mil.) passare in rivista.
reviewal s. revisione, recensione.
reviewer s. recensore, revisore.
to **revile** vt. e vi. ingiuriare.
to **revise** vt. rivedere, modificare.
reviser s. revisore.
revision s. revisione, correzione.
revival s. **1.** ripristino **2.** ripresa **3.** rinascita.
to **revive** vt. e vi. resuscitare.
reviver s. chi, ciò che rinvigorisce.
revivification s. rinascita.
to **revivify** vt. ravvivare.
revocable agg. revocabile.
revocation s. revoca.
revocatory agg. revocatorio.
to **revoke** vt. revocare.
revolt s. rivolta.
to **revolt** vt. disgustare. ♦ to **revolt** vi. rivoltarsi.
revolution s. rivoluzione.
revolutionary agg. e s. rivoluzionario.
to **revolutionize** vt. rivoluzionare.
to **revolve** vt. meditare. ♦ to **revolve** vi. girare, rotare.
revolver s. rivoltella.
revolving agg. **1.** rotante **2.** rotativo.
revulsion s. **1.** revulsione **2.** mutamento.
revulsive agg. revulsivo.

reward s. ricompensa.
to **reward** vt. ricompensare.
rewarding agg. rimunerativo. ♦ **rewarding** s. rimunerazione.
to **rewrite (rewrote, rewritten)** vt. riscrivere.
rhagades s. pl. ragadi.
rhapsody s. rapsodia.
rheostat s. reostato.
rhetoric s. retorica.
rhetorical agg. retorico.
rhetorician s. retore.
rheumatic agg. e s. reumatico.
rheumatism s. reumatismo.
rhinitis s. rinite.
rhinoceros s. rinoceronte.
rhizome s. rizoma.
rhododendron s. rododendro.
rhomb s. rombo.
rhombic(al) agg. rombico.
rhombohedron s. (pl. -dra) romboedro.
rhomboid agg. e s. romboide.
rhubarb s. rabarbaro.
rhyme s. rima.
to **rhyme** vt. far rimare. ♦ to **rhyme** vi. rimare.
rhymer s. rimatore.
Rhynchota s. pl. rincoti.
rhythm s. ritmo.
rhythmic(al) agg. ritmico.
rib s. **1.** costola **2.** costa, nervatura **3.** stecca.
to **rib** vt. **1.** munire (di coste ecc.) **2.** scanalare.
ribbing s. **1.** nervatura **2.** rigatura.
ribbon s. nastro.
rice s. riso || —field (o — -swamp), risaia.
rich agg. ricco.
richly avv. riccamente.
richness s. ricchezza.
rick s. bica.
ricket(s) s. rachitismo.
rickety agg. **1.** rachitico **2.** malsicuro.
to **rid (rid, rid)** vt. liberare || to get — of, sbarazzarsi di.
ridden V. to ride.
riddle[1] s. indovinello.
riddle[2] s. vaglio, crivello.
to **riddle**[1] vt. risolvere.
to **riddle**[2] vt. **1.** vagliare **2.** setacciare.
ride s. passeggiata, percorso (a cavallo, su un veicolo).
to **ride (rode, ridden)** vt. **1.** montare (cavallo, bicicletta) **2.** percorrere (a cavallo, su un veicolo) **3.**

(*fig.*) opprimere. ♦ to **ride** (rode, ridden) *vi.* andare (*a cavallo, su un veicolo*).
rider *s.* cavaliere, fantino.
ridge *s.* cresta, catena di monti.
ridicule *s.* ridicolo.
to **ridicule** *vt.* schernire.
ridiculous *agg.* ridicolo.
riding *s.* corsa (*a cavallo, in veicolo*).
rifle *s.* fucile.
rifleman *s.* fuciliere.
rift *s.* crepa.
rigging *s.* attrezzatura.
right[1] *agg.* **1.** giusto **2.** (*geom.*) retto **3.** destro.
right[2] *s.* **1.** il giusto, il bene **2.** diritto **3.** destra, mano destra, lato destro.
right[3] *avv.* **1.** giustamente, bene **2.** direttamente **3.** proprio **4.** a destra.
righteous *agg.* giusto.
righteousness *s.* rettitudine.
rightful *agg.* **1.** legittimo **2.** giusto.
rightly *avv.* **1.** rettamente **2.** esattamente.
rigid *agg.* rigido.
rigidity, rigor *s.* rigidità.
rigorism *s.* rigorismo.
rigorist *s.* rigorista.
rigorous *agg.* rigido.
rigour *s.* rigore.
rim *s.* bordo, orlo.
to **rim** *vt.* bordare, cerchiare.
rind *s.* **1.** buccia **2.** corteccia **3.** crosta **4.** cotenna.
to **rind** *vt.* **1.** sbucciare **2.** scortecciare.
ring[1] *s.* **1.** anello, cerchio **2.** pista.
ring[2] *s.* **1.** scampanellata **2.** (*fig.*) accento, tono.
to **ring**[1] *vt.* circondare.
to **ring**[2] (rang, rung) *vt.* suonare || *to — up*, telefonare. ♦ to **ring** (rang, rung) *vi.* risuonare.
ringleader *s.* capobanda.
rink *s.* pista di pattinaggio.
to **rinse** *vt.* sciacquare.
rinsing *s.* risciacquatura.
riot *s.* **1.** rivolta **2.** gazzarra.
to **riot** *vi.* **1.** tumultuare **2.** gozzovigliare.
rioter *s.* rivoltoso.
riotous *agg.* **1.** tumultuante **2.** sregolato.
rip *s.* lacerazione, scucitura, strappo.
to **rip** *vt.* lacerare. ♦ to **rip** *vi.* lacerarsi.

ripe *agg.* maturo.
to **ripen** *vt.* e *vi.* maturare.
ripeness *s.* maturità.
ripple *s.* **1.** increspatura, ondulatura **2.** gorgoglio.
to **ripple** *vt.* increspare, ondulare. ♦ to **ripple** *vi.* incresparsi, ondularsi.
rise *s.* **1.** il sorgere **2.** salita, ascesa **3.** aumento **4.** sorgente.
to **rise** (rose, risen) *vi.* **1.** sorgere **2.** aumentare.
riser *s.* chi si alza.
risible *agg.* risibile.
rising *s.* **1.** sorgere **2.** salita, ascesa **3.** aumento **4.** rivolta.
risk *s.* rischio.
to **risk** *vt.* rischiare.
risky *agg.* rischioso.
rissole *s.* polpetta.
rite *s.* rito.
ritual *agg.* e *s.* rituale.
rival *agg.* e *s.* rivale.
to **rival** *vt.* rivaleggiare.
rivality, rivalry *s.* rivalità.
river *s.* fiume.
riverside *s.* lungofiume.
to **rivet** *vt.* **1.** ribadire **2.** fissare.
rivulet *s.* fiumicello.
road *s.* strada || — *-bed*, fondo stradale; — *sign*, cartello stradale.
roadstead *s.* (*mar.*) rada.
roadway *s.* carreggiata.
to **roam** *vt.* e *vi.* vagare (*per*).
roar *s.* **1.** ruggito **2.** rombo.
to **roar** *vt.* e *vi.* **1.** ruggire **2.** tuonare || *to — with laughter*, ridere fragorosamente.
roaring *agg.* **1.** rumoroso **2.** ruggente, mugghiante. ♦ **roaring** *s.* V. *roar*.
roast *agg.* e *s.* arrosto.
to **roast** *vt.* **1.** arrostire **2.** tostare. ♦ to **roast** *vi.* arrostirsi.
roasting *agg.* rovente. ♦ **roasting** *s.* **1.** arrostimento **2.** torrefazione.
to **rob** *vt.* derubare. ♦ to **rob** *vi.* rubare.
robber *s.* ladro.
robbery *s.* furto.
robe *s.* **1.** toga **2.** vestiti (*pl.*).
to **robe** *vt.* vestire. ♦ to **robe** *vi.* vestirsi.
robin *s.* pettirosso.
robust *agg.* **1.** robusto **2.** faticoso.
robustness *s.* robustezza.
rock[1] *s.* **1.** roccia **2.** rocca.
rock[2] *s.* dondolio.
to **rock** *vt.* cullare, dondolare. ♦

to **rock** vi. dondolarsi, oscillare, barcollare.

rocker s. 1. chi culla, dondola 2. dondolo (di sedia ecc.) 3. (mecc.) bilanciere.

rocket s. razzo.

rocking agg. 1. a dondolo 2. vacillante. ♦ **rocking** s. oscillazione, dondolio.

rocky agg. roccioso.

rod s. verga || fishing- —, canna da pesca.

rode V. to ride.

rodent agg. e s. roditore.

roe[1] s. capriolo maschio.

roe[2] s. uova di pesce.

rogue s. briccone.

roguery s. bricconeria.

roguish agg. bricconesco.

role s. 1. (teat.) ruolo, parte 2. funzione.

roll[1] s. 1. rotolo 2. elenco, lista 3. rullo, cilindro.

roll[2] s. 1. (mar.; aer.) rollio 2. rullo (di tamburo).

to **roll** vt. 1. far rotolare 2. arrotolare 3. spianare. ♦ to **roll** vi. 1. rotolare 2. arrotolarsi 3. ruotare 4. rollare 5. rullare.

roller s. 1. rullo, cilindro 2. cavallone || — skates, schettini.

rolling s. (ar)rotolamento || —-mill, laminatoio; — pin, matterello.

Roman agg. e s. romano.

Romance agg. romanzo, neolatino.

romance s. 1. poema cavalleresco, racconto fantastico 2. avventura romanzesca 3. idillio 4. poesia 5. (mus.) romanza.

Romanesque agg. e s. romanico.

Romanian agg. e s. romeno.

Romanic agg. romanico.

Romanist s. romanista.

Romansh agg. e s. ladino.

romantic agg. e s. romantico.

romanticism s. romanticismo.

to **romanticize** vt. romanzare.

to **romp** vi. giocare rumorosamente.

rompish agg. chiassoso.

rood s. croce.

roof s. tetto || — -garden, giardino pensile.

to **roof** vt. 1. coprire con un tetto 2. ospitare.

rook s. cornacchia.

room s. 1. stanza 2. spazio 3. possibilità.

to **room** vt. e vi. (amer.) alloggiare.

roomy agg. spazioso.

root s. radice.

to **root**[1] vt. piantare || to — away, out, up, sradicare. ♦ to **root** vi. mettere radice.

to **root**[2] vt. e vi. grufolare.

rope s. fune, corda || — -dancer, funambolo.

to **rope** vt. legare.

rosary s. 1. roseto 2. (eccl.) rosario.

rose agg. e s. rosa || — -bush, rosaio; — -diamond, rosetta; — -window, rosone.

rose V. to rise.

rosemary s. rosmarino.

roseola s. rosolia.

rosery s. roseto.

rosette s. 1. rosetta 2. (arch.) rosone 3. coccarda.

rosewood s. palissandro.

rosin s. pece greca.

rostrum s. (pl. rostra o rostrums) rostro.

rosy agg. roseo.

rot s. putrefazione.

to **rot** vt. e vi. imputridire.

rotary agg. rotante. ♦ **rotary** s. — (press), rotativa.

to **rotate** vt. e vi. rotare.

rotation s. rotazione.

rotative, rotatory agg. rotatorio.

rote s. abitudine, memoria meccanica.

rotogravure s. rotocalco.

rotor s. rotore.

rotten agg. marcio.

rottenness s. marciume.

rotund agg. 1. rotondo 2. enfatico.

rouble s. rublo.

rouge agg. rossetto.

rough agg. 1. irregolare, ruvido, scabro 2. tempestoso 3. rozzo.

to **rough** vt. irruvidire || to — il (fam.), vivere primitivamente.

to **roughen** vt. irruvidire. ♦ to **roughen** vi. irruvidirsi.

to **rough-hew** vt. abbozzare.

roughly avv. ruvidamente.

roughness s. 1. ruvidezza 2. rudezza 3. inclemenza (di tempo).

round agg. 1. rotondo 2. intero 3. franco 4. vigoroso 5. considerevole. ♦ **round** s. 1. cerchio 2. sfera 3. ciclo 4. giro, ronda.

round avv. intorno. ♦ **round** prep. intorno a.

to **round** vt. arrotondare. ♦ to **round** vi. 1. arrotondarsi 2. girare

3. svilupparsi.
roundabout *agg.* indiretto. ♦
roundabout *s.* giostra.
roundly *avv.* **1.** vigorosamente **2.**
francamente.
roundness *s.* **1.** rotondità **2.** scorrevolezza **3.** franchezza.
to **rouse** *vt.* (ri)svegliare (*anche fig.*).
♦ to **rouse** *vi.* (ri)svegliarsi.
rouser *s.* ridestatore.
rousing *agg.* stimolante.
rout *s.* **1.** plebaglia **2.** tumulto **3.**
rotta.
to **rout** *vt.* sconfiggere.
route *s.* via, rotta.
routinist *s.* abitudinario.
rove *s.* vagabondaggio.
to **rove** *vt.* e *vi.* vagare.
rover *s.* **1.** vagabondo **2.** pirata.
roving *s.* vagabondaggio.
row[1] *s.* fila.
row[2] *s.* remata, gita in barca.
to **row** *vt.* trasportare (*remando*). ♦
to **row** *vi.* remare.
rowdy *agg.* e *s.* turbolento.
rower *s.* rematore.
rowlock *s.* scalmo.
royal *agg.* regale, reale.
royalist *s.* realista.
royalty *s.* **1.** regalità **2.** i reali **3.** diritto d'autore.
rub *s.* **1.** fregata, grattata **2.** ineguaglianza **3.** ostacolo, difficoltà.
to **rub** *vt.* fregare. ♦ to **rub** *vi.* fre-
garsi.
rubber *s.* **1.** massaggiatore **2.** stro-
finaccio **3.** gomma || — *-solution,*
mastice.
rubbish *s.* rifiuti (*pl.*).
rubble *s.* pietrisco.
ruby *s.* rubino.
rucksack *s.* zaino.
rudder *s.* timone.
ruddy *agg.* rosso, rubicondo.
rude *agg.* **1.** rude, violento **2.** rudimentale **3.** grezzo.
rudeness *s.* **1.** rozzezza **2.** violenza.
rudiment *s.* rudimento.
rudimentary *agg.* rudimentale.
ruffian *agg.* brutale. ♦ **ruffian** *s.*
ribaldo.
ruffle *s.* **1.** increspatura **2.** sconvolgimento **3.** tumulto.
to **ruffle** *vt.* **1.** increspare **2.** arruffare
3. agitare.
rug *s.* **1.** coperta **2.** tappetino.
rugged *agg.* **1.** ruvido **2.** scompiglia-
to **3.** austero **4.** rozzo.
ruggedness *s.* **1.** ruvidezza **2.** auste-

rità **3.** rudezza.
ruin *s.* rovina.
to **ruin** *vt.* e *vi.* rovinare.
ruinous *agg.* **1.** rovinoso **2.** in rovina.
rule *s.* **1.** regola **2.** dominio **3.** riga
da disegno.
to **rule** *vt.* **1.** governare, dominare **2.**
rigare.
ruler *s.* **1.** dominatore **2.** regolo.
ruling *s.* **1.** governo **2.** decisione.
Rumanian *agg.* e *s.* romeno.
rumble *s.* **1.** rombo **2.** brontolio.
to **rumble** *vt.* e *vi.* **1.** rombare **2.**
brontolare.
rumbling *s.* V. *rumble.*
rumen *s.* rumine.
ruminant *agg.* e *s.* ruminante.
to **ruminate** *vt* e *vi.* ruminare.
rummage *s.* ricerca, perquisizione.
to **rummage** *vt.* e *vi.* **1.** rovistare
2. perquisire.
rumour *s.* diceria.
to **rumour** *vt.* far correre la voce.
rump *s.* **1.** posteriore **2.** resto.
to **rumple** *vt.* **1.** spiegazzare **2.** arruffare.
run *s.* **1.** corsa **2.** percorso, giro **3.**
andamento **4.** periodo **5.** richiesta.
to **run** (**ran, run**) *vi.* **1.** correre **2.**
colare **3.** diventare **4.** estendersi **5.**
essere in vigore, durare. ♦ to **run**
(**ran, run**) *vt.* **1.** far funzionare
2. dirigere **3.** seguire **4.** passare ||
to — in, rodare; *to — over,* investire.
runaway *agg.* **1.** fuggitivo **2.** decisivo. ♦ **runaway** *s.* **1.** fuggitivo
2. fuga.
rung[1] *s.* **1.** piolo **2.** raggio (*di
ruota*).
rung[2] V. *to ring.*
runnel *s.* ruscello.
runner *s.* **1.** corridore **2.** messo **3.**
passatoia **4.** pattino **5.** carrello.
running *s.* **1.** corsa **2.** esercizio **3.**
flusso || — *-in,* rodaggio.
runway *s.* pista.
rupture *s.* rottura.
rural *agg.* rurale.
rush[1] *s.* giunco.
rush[2] **1.** attacco **2.** impeto **3.** afflus-
so || — *-hours,* ore di punta.
to **rush** *vt.* spingere. ♦ to **rush** *vi.*
precipitarsi.
rushy *agg.* **1.** di giunchi **2.** folto di
giunchi.
Russian *agg.* e *s.* russo.
rust *s.* ruggine.

to **rust** *vt.* arrugginire. ♦ to **rust** *vi.* arrugginirsi.

rustic(al) *agg.* rustico. ♦ **rustic(al)** *s.* campagnolo.

rustle *s.* fruscio, stormire (*di foglie*).

to **rustle** *vt.* far frusciare. ♦ to **rustle** *vi.* frusciare.

rusty *agg.* 1. ruginoso 2. (*fig.*) ombroso.

ruthless *agg.* spietato.

ruthlessness *s.* crudeltà.

rye *s.* segale.

S

Sabbath *s.* il giorno della settimana dedicato al riposo.

sable *s.* zibellino.

sabot *s.* zoccolo.

sabotage *s.* sabotaggio.

to **sabotage** *vt. e vi.* sabotare.

saboteur *s.* sabotatore.

sabre *s.* sciabola || — *-cut*, sciabolata.

to **sabre** *vt.* sciabolare.

saccharin(e) *s.* saccarina.

saccharose *s.* saccarosio.

sacerdotal *agg.* sacerdotale.

sack[1] *s.* 1. sacco 2. (*gergo*) licenziamento.

sack[2] *s.* (*mil.*) sacco, saccheggio.

sack[3] *s.* vino bianco delle Canarie.

to **sack**[1] *vt.* 1. insaccare 2. (*gergo*) licenziare.

to **sack**[2] *vt.* (*mil.*) saccheggiare.

sacking[1] *s.* tela da sacco.

sacking[2] *s.* saccheggio.

sacral[1] *agg.* (*anat.*) sacro.

sacral[2] *agg.* rituale.

sacrament *s.* sacramento.

sacramental *agg.* sacramentale.

sacred *agg.* 1. sacro, religioso 2. consacrato, dedicato.

sacrifice *s.* 1. sacrificio 2. abnegazione.

to **sacrifice** *vt. e vi.* 1. sacrificare, immolare 2. rinunziare.

sacrilege *s.* sacrilegio.

sacrist *s.* sagrestano.

sacristy *s.* sagrestia.

sacrosanct *agg.* sacrosanto.

sad *agg.* triste, mesto || *to make so.* —, rattristare qu.

to **sadden** *vt.* rattristare. ♦ to **sad-**den *vi.* rattristarsi.

saddle *s.* 1. sella, sellino 2. giogaia.

to **saddle** *vt.* sellare, mettere in sella.

saddler *s.* sellaio.

sadism *s.* sadismo.

sadist *s.* sadico.

sadistic *agg.* sadico.

sadly *avv.* tristemente, mestamente.

sadness *s.* tristezza, mestizia.

safe *agg.* 1. sicuro, al riparo 2. salvo, intatto 3. innocuo || — *and sound*, sano e salvo; — *-conduct*, salvacondotto; — *-deposit*, cassetta di sicurezza. ♦ **safe** *s.* 1. cassaforte 2. sicura (*di armi*).

safeguard *s.* salvaguardia.

to **safeguard** *vt.* salvaguardare, difendere.

safekeeping *s.* custodia.

safety *s.* sicurezza, salvezza, scampo || — *belt*, cintura di sicurezza; — *device*, dispositivo di sicurezza; — *-pin*, spilla di sicurezza.

saffron *s.* zafferano.

sag *s.* 1. abbassamento, cedimento 2. (*mar.*) scarroccio.

sagacious *agg.* acuto, sagace.

sagaciousness, sagacity *s.* sagacia, perspicacia.

sage[1] *s.* salvia.

sage[2] *s.* saggio, dotto.

said V. *to say*.

sail[1] *s.* vela, velatura || *to set* (*v. irr.*) —, spiegare le vele, salpare; *to strike* (*v. irr.*) —, ammainare le vele.

sail[2] *s.* gita su imbarcazione a vela.

to **sail** *vt. e vi.* 1. veleggiare, navigare, costeggiare 2. salpare 3. volare, veleggiare (*di uccelli, nuvole ecc.*).

sailer *s.* veliero.

sailing *s.* 1. navigazione, traversata 2. partenza (*di navi*).

sailor *s.* marinaio.

sailplane *s.* veleggiatore.

saint *agg. e s.* santo.

to **saint** *vt.* canonizzare, santificare.

sainthood, saintliness *s.* sanità.

saintly *agg.* santo, di santo.

sake *s.* 1. amore, interesse 2. riguardo, rispetto || *for God's* —, per l'amor di Dio.

salaam *s.* riverenza, salamelecco.

salacious *agg.* salace, lascivo.

salad *s.* insalata || *fruit* —, macedonia di frutta.

salamander *s.* salamandra.

salariat s. categorie salariate.
salary s. stipendio.
sale s. 1. vendita || *bill of* —, fattura; *on* —, in vendita 2. asta: — *by auction*, vendita all'asta 3. liquidazione, svendita.
sal(e)able agg. vendibile, commerciabile.
salesman s. venditore, commesso.
saleswoman s. venditrice, commessa.
salicylate s. salicilato.
salient agg. 1. sporgente, prominente 2. saliente, notevole.
saline agg. salino, salso.
salinity s. salsedine, salinità.
saliva s. saliva.
salivary agg. salivare.
salivation s. salivazione.
sallow agg. giallastro.
sally s. 1. (*mil.*) sortita 2. escursione.
to sally vi. fare una sortita || *to* — *forth*, uscire (*per una passeggiata*).
salmon s. salmone.
saloon s. salone || *dancing* —, sala da ballo.
salt s. sale. ♦ **salt** agg. 1. salato 2. sotto sale 3. (*fig.*) amaro, piccante || — *-cellar*, saliera; — *-mine*, salina.
to salt vt. 1. salare, cospargere di sale 2. rendere piccante (*anche fig.*).
salting s. palude costiera.
saltish agg. salmastro, salaticcio.
saltness s. salsedine.
saltpetre s. salnitro.
salty agg. 1. salato, salmastro 2. piccante (*anche fig.*).
salubrious agg. salubre.
salutary agg. salutare.
salutation s. saluto.
salute s. saluto, gesto di saluto || *to fire a* —, salutare a salve.
to salute vt. salutare, dare il benvenuto.
salvage s. salvataggio (*di navi, carico ecc.*).
salvation s. salvezza (*anche relig.*).
salve s. unguento, balsamo.
same agg. medesimo, stesso, uguale || *at the* — *time*, allo stesso tempo. ♦ **same** pron. lo stesso, il medesimo.
samely agg. monotono, uniforme.
sameness s. 1. somiglianza 2. monotonia.

sample s. campione, modello, esemplare || — *book*, campionario.
sanatorium s. sanatorio.
sanatory agg. curativo.
sanctification s. santificazione.
to sanctify vt. santificare.
sanction s. 1. autorizzazione, approvazione 2. (*giur.*) ratifica 3. sanzione.
to sanction vt. 1. autorizzare 2. (*giur.*) ratificare 3. aggiungere sanzioni penali (*ad una legge*).
sanctity s. santità.
sanctuary s. 1. santuario 2. asilo, rifugio.
sand s. sabbia, rena || — *-bath*, bagno di sabbia. ♦ **sands** s. pl. spiaggia (*sing.*).
to sand vt. 1. coprire di sabbia 2. arenare 3. smerigliare.
sandal s. sandalo.
sandpaper s. carta vetrata.
sandstone s. arenaria.
sandy agg. sabbioso.
sane agg. sano di mente, sensato.
saneness, sanity s. sanità (*di mente*), equilibrio.
sang V. *to sing.*
sanguinary agg. sanguinario, crudele.
sanguine agg. sanguigno.
sanguineous agg. del sangue, sanguigno.
sanitarian s. igienista. ♦ **sanitarian** agg. igienico.
sanitarist s. igienista.
sanitary agg. igienico, sanitario.
sanity s. V. *saneness.*
sank V. *to sink.*
Sanscrit, Sanskrit agg. e s. Sanscrito.
santon s. santone.
sap s. 1. linfa, succo 2. (*fig.*) vigore.
sapful agg. 1. succoso 2. vigoroso.
sapid agg. sapido, gustoso (*anche fig.*).
sapient agg. pedante.
sapless agg. 1. secco, avvizzito 2. fiacco.
saponification s. saponificazione.
to saponify vt. saponificare.
Sapphic agg. saffico.
sapphire s. zaffiro.
saraband s. sarabanda.
Saracen agg. e s. saraceno.
sarcasm s. sarcasmo.
sarcastic agg. sarcastico.
sarcophagus s. (*pl.* -gi) sarcofago.

sardine *s.* sardina.
sardonic *agg.* sardonico.
sash[1] *s.* fascia, cintura.
sash[2] *s.* telaio scorrevole (*di finestra*).
sat V. *to sit*.
satanic(al) *agg.* satanico.
satchel *s.* cartella (*di scolaro*).
to **sate** *vt.* saziare.
satellite *s.* satellite.
satiable *agg.* saziabile.
to **satiate** *vt.* saziare, satollare.
satiety *s.* sazietà.
satin *s.* raso.
satire *s.* satira.
satiric(al) *agg.* satirico.
satirist *s.* autore di satire.
to **satirize** *vt.* satireggiare.
satisfaction *s.* **1.** soddisfazione **2.** riparazione **3.** (*giur.*) estinzione.
satisfactory *agg.* soddisfacente.
satisfiable *agg.* che può essere soddisfatto.
to **satisfy** *vt.* soddisfare, appagare ǁ *to — a claim*, accogliere un reclamo. ◆ to **satisfy** *vi.* fare ammenda.
satrap *s.* satrapo.
saturate *agg.* saturo.
to **saturate** *vt.* saturare, impregnare.
saturation *s.* saturazione.
Saturday *s.* sabato.
satyr *s.* satiro.
satyric *agg.* satiresco.
sauce *s.* salsa, intingolo.
saucepan *s.* casseruola.
saucer *s.* piattino, sottocoppa.
saucily *avv.* sfacciatamente.
saucy *agg.* sfacciato, insolente.
sauerkraut *s.* crauti.
to **saunter** *vi.* bighellonare.
saunterer *s.* bighellone.
sausage *s.* salsiccia, salame.
savage *agg.* **1.** selvaggio, barbaro **2.** feroce, crudele. ◆ **savage** *s.* selvaggio.
savagely *avv.* selvaggiamente, barbaramente.
savannah *s.* savana.
save *prep.* salvo, tranne, eccetto.
to **save** *vt.* e *vi.* **1.** salvare, difendere **2.** conservare, risparmiare.
saving *s.* liberazione, salvezza. ◆ **savings** *s. pl.* risparmi.
saviour *s.* salvatore, redentore.
to **savour** *vi.* aver sapore.
savoury *agg.* saporito, piccante.
saw *s.* sega ǁ *— -mill*, segheria.
to **saw** (sawed, sawn) *vt.* e *vi.*

segare.
saw V. *to see*.
sawdust *s.* segatura.
sawn V. *to saw*.
sawyer *s.* segatore.
Saxon *agg.* e *s.* sassone.
saxophone *s.* sassofono.
say *s.* il dire, detto, parola.
to **say** (said, said) *vt.* e *vi.* **1.** dire, affermare **2.** esprimere un'opinione ǁ *to — out*, dire apertamente.
saying *s.* proverbio, massima: *as the — goes*, come dice il proverbio.
scabbard *s.* fodero.
scabby *agg.* coperto di croste.
scabies *s.* scabbia.
scaffold *s.* **1.** impalcatura **2.** patibolo, forca.
to **scaffold** *vt.* erigere impalcature.
scaffolding *s.* impalcatura.
scald *s.* scottatura.
to **scald** *vt.* **1.** scottare **2.** sterilizzare con acqua bollente. ◆ to **scald** *vi.* scottarsi.
scale[1] *s.* piatto (*di bilancia*). ◆ **scales** *s. pl.* bilancia (*sing.*).
scale[2] *s.* scaglia.
scale[3] *s.* scala, misura, gradazione.
to **scale**[1] *vt.* e *vi.* pesare.
to **scale**[2] *vt.* squamare, scrostare. ◆ to **scale** *vi.* squamarsi, scrostarsi.
to **scale**[3] *vt.* **1.** scalare **2.** graduare ǁ *to — down*, diminuire; *to — up*, aumentare.
scalene *agg.* e *s.* scaleno.
scallop *s.* **1.** conchiglia **2.** dentellatura, festone, smerlo (*di stoffa*).
to **scallop** *vt.* **1.** tagliare a festone **2.** cuocere pesce in conchiglia.
scalp *s.* **1.** cranio, cuoio capelluto **2.** scalpo.
to **scalp** *vt.* **1.** scalpare **2.** criticare aspramente.
scalpel *s.* bisturi.
to **scan** *vt.* e *vi.* **1.** scandire (*versi*) **2.** esaminare, scrutare.
scandal *s.* **1.** scandalo **2.** maldicenza **3.** (*giur.*) diffamazione.
to **scandalize** *vt.* scandalizzare.
scandalous *agg.* scandaloso.
Scandinavian *agg.* e *s.* scandinavo.
scanning *s.* **1.** scansione (*di versi*) **2.** osservazione ǁ *— -line*, (*tv*), linea di scansione.
scansion *s.* scansione.
scantily *avv.* debolmente, scarsamente.
scantiness *s.* insufficienza, scarsezza.

scanty *agg.* **1.** scarso, insufficiente **2.** esiguo, angusto.

scapegoat *s.* capro espiatorio.

scapegrace *s.* **1.** scapestrato **2.** monello.

scapular *agg.* scapolare.

scar *s.* cicatrice, sfregio.

to **scar** *vt.* **1.** cicatrizzare **2.** sfregiare. ♦ to **scar** *vi.* cicatrizzarsi.

scarab *s.* scarabeo.

scarce *agg.* insufficiente, scarso.

scarcely *avv.* appena, a fatica, a malapena.

scare *s.* terrore, sgomento.

to **scare** *vt.* spaventare, sgomentare.

scarecrow *s.* **1.** spaventapasseri **2.** spauracchio.

scarf *s.* sciarpa, fascia.

to **scarify** *vt.* scarificare.

scarlet *agg.* scarlatto, porporino ∥ — *-fever,* scarlattina.

scarp(e) *s.* scarpata.

to **scatter** *vt.* **1.** spargere **2.** mettere in fuga, disperdere. ♦ to **scatter** *vi.* spargersi, diffondersi.

scattered *agg.* sparso, disseminato.

scattering *s.* sparpagliamento, dispersione.

scenario *s.* sceneggiatura ∥ — *writer,* sceneggiatore.

scene *s.* **1.** scena **2.** episodio **3.** scenario, quinta **4.** vista, panorama ∥ — *-painter,* scenografo.

scenery *s.* **1.** scenario **2.** prospettiva, veduta.

scenographer *s.* scenografo.

scenographic *agg.* scenografico.

scenography *s.* scenografia.

scent *s.* **1.** odore, profumo **2.** traccia, pista (*anche fig.*).

to **scent** *vt.* **1.** fiutare, seguire la traccia **2.** profumare.

scented *agg.* profumato.

scentless *agg.* inodoro.

sceptical *agg.* scettico.

scepticism *s.* scetticismo.

sceptre *s.* scettro.

schedule *s.* **1.** catalogo, distinta, elenco **2.** (*amer.*) orario **3.** inventario.

to **schedule** *vt.* comporre una lista, un catalogo.

schematic(al) *agg.* schematico.

schematism *s.* schematismo.

scheme *s.* **1.** schema **2.** piano, progetto.

to **scheme** *vt.* e *vi.* **1.** progettare, fare un piano **2.** tramare.

schism *s.* scisma.

schismatic(al) *s.* scismatico.

schizophrenic *agg.* e *s.* schizofrenico.

scholar *s.* studioso, letterato.

scholarly *agg.* dotto, istruito.

scholarship *s.* **1.** dottrina, sapere **2.** borsa di studio.

scholastic *agg.* **1.** scolastico, pedante **2.** (*fil.*) scolastico.

scholastically *avv.* scolasticamente, secondo la scolastica.

scholasticism *s.* (*fil.*) scolastica.

school *s.* **1.** scuola, classe **2.** lezione, ora di lezione ∥ — *-book,* libro di testo; — *-mate,* compagno di scuola; — *-report,* pagella; — *-term,* trimestre; — *-time,* periodo scolastico; *boarding-* —, collegio; *grammar-* —, ginnasio; *night-* —, serale.

to **school** *vt.* **1.** istruire **2.** controllare, disciplinare.

schoolboy *s.* scolaro.

schoolfellow *s.* compagno di scuola.

schoolmaster *s.* maestro, insegnante.

schoolmistress *s.* maestra, insegnante.

schoolroom *s.* aula scolastica.

schooner *s.* (*mar.*) goletta.

science *s.* scienza ∥ — *fiction,* fantascienza; *man of* —, scienziato.

scientific *agg.* scientifico.

scientifically *avv.* scientificamente.

scientism *s.* scientismo.

scientist *s.* scienziato.

scimitar *s.* scimitarra.

scion *s.* **1.** germoglio **2.** rampollo, discendente.

scission *s.* scissione, divisione.

scissors *s. pl.* forbici, cesoie.

sclerosis *s.* (*pl.* -ses) sclerosi.

sclerotic *s.* sclerotico.

scoff *s.* derisione, scherno.

to **scoff** *vt.* e *vi.* deridere, schernire ∥ to — *at so.,* farsi beffe di qu.

scold *s.* donna bisbetica.

to **scold** *vt.* sgridare, rimproverare. ♦ to **scold** *vi.* essere adirato.

scolding *s.* sgridata, rimprovero.

scoliosis *s.* scoliosi.

scooter *s.* **1.** monopattino **2.** motoretta.

scope *s.* **1.** portata, possibilità **2.** prospettiva, sfera, campo.

scorbutic *agg.* e *s.* scorbutico.

scorch *s.* bruciatura, scottatura.

to **scorch** *vt.* e *vi.* **1.** bruciacchiare **2.** inaridire (*di sole, gelo ecc.*).

scorching *agg.* **1.** bruciante, ardente **2.** (*fig.*) caustico, mordace.

score *s.* **1.** tacca, scanalatura **2.** linea, segno, linea di partenza, limite (*in corse, giuochi ecc.*) **3.** (*sport*) punteggio **4.** (*mus.*) spartito.

to score *vt.* e *vi.* **1.** intaccare, intagliare **2.** marcare, segnare **3.** (*sport*) segnare il punteggio **4.** (*mus.*) orchestrare || *to — up,* mettere in conto.

scorer *s.* (*sport*) marcatore.

scorn *s.* **1.** disprezzo, disdegno **2.** scherno.

to scorn *vt.* disprezzare, disdegnare.

scornful *agg.* sprezzante, sdegnoso.

scorpion *s.* scorpione || — *-fish,* scorfano.

Scot *s.* scozzese.

Scotch *agg.* scozzese.

Scotsman *s.* (*uomo*) scozzese.

Scottish *agg.* scozzese.

scoundrel *s.* furfante, farabutto.

scourge *s.* (*fig.*) flagello.

to scourge *vt.* sferzare, flagellare.

scout *s.* esploratore, ricognitore.

to scout *vi.* andare in esplorazione, in ricognizione. ◆ **to scout** *vt.* perlustrare.

scowl *s.* cipiglio, sguardo torvo.

to scowl *vt.* e *vi.* aggrottare le ciglia, guardare torvamente.

scramble *s.* **1.** arrampicata **2.** contesa, gara.

to scramble *vt.* **1.** arraffare **2.** mescolare alla rinfusa. ◆ **to scramble** *vi.* **1.** inerpicarsi **2.** gareggiare **3.** (*cuc.*) strapazzare (*le uova*).

scrap *s.* pezzetto, frammento || — *-heap,* mucchio di rifiuti. ◆ **scraps** *s. pl.* rimasugli, scarti.

scrape *s.* **1.** graffio, scalfittura **2.** raschio.

to scrape *vt.* e *vi.* **1.** raschiare, grattare **2.** levigare **3.** sfregare, strisciare || *to — a living,* sbarcare il lunario.

scraper *s.* **1.** raschietto **2.** strimpellatore.

scraping *s.* raschiatura.

scratch *s.* **1.** graffiatura, graffio **2.** grattata **3.** colpo fortunato (*al giuoco*).

to scratch *vt.* e *vi.* **1.** graffiare **2.** (*fig.*) scalfire **3.** grattare.

scrawl *s.* scarabocchio, sgorbio.

to scrawl *vt.* e *vi.* **1.** scarabocchiare **2.** scribacchiare.

scrawler *s.* chi scarabocchia.

scrawly *agg.* scarabocchiato || — *writing* (*fam.*), scritto a zampe di gallina.

scream *s.* grido acuto, strillo.

to scream *vt.* e *vi.* **1.** gridare, strillare **2.** fischiare (*di locomotiva*).

screamer *s.* strillone.

screaming *agg.* **1.** strillante, urlante **2.** sguaiato.

screech *s.* **1.** grido, strillo acuto **2.** stridore.

screen *s.* **1.** paravento **2.** (*cine; tv*) schermo **3.** (*mil.*) scorta.

to screen *vt.* e *vi.* **1.** riparare, schermare **2.** vagliare.

screenings *s. pl.* materiale vagliato (*sing.*).

screenplay *s.* (*cine*) sceneggiatura.

screenwriter *s.* sceneggiatore.

screw *s.* **1.** vite **2.** cavatappi, succhiello **3.** elica.

to screw *vt.* **1.** avvitare, stringere **2.** torcere. ◆ **to screw** *vi.* torcersi || *to — out,* svitare.

screwdriver *s.* cacciavite.

screwy *agg.* **1.** brillo **2.** tirchio, spilorcio.

scribble *s.* sgorbio, scarabocchio (*anche fig.*).

to scribble *vt.* e *vi.* scarabocchiare.

scribe *s.* copista.

scriber *s.* punta a tracciare.

scrip[1] *s.* **1.** pezzo di carta **2.** frammento di uno scritto.

scrip[2] *s.* certificato provvisorio, cedola.

scripture *s.* la sacra Scrittura.

to scrounge *vt.* e *vi.* rubacchiare.

scrounger *s.* ladruncolo, scroccone.

scrub *s.* **1.** boscaglia **2.** povero diavolo (*fam.*).

to scrub *vt.* e *vi.* sfregare.

scrubby *agg.* esile, debole.

scruff *s.* nuca, collottola.

scruple *s.* scrupolo.

scrupolosity *s.* scrupolosità.

scrupulous *agg.* scrupoloso.

to scrutinize *vt.* scrutinare, esaminare.

scrutiny *s.* **1.** esame minuzioso **2.** scrutinio **3.** esame (*di una legge*).

scuffle *s.* zuffa, tafferuglio.

to scuffle *vi.* azzuffarsi.

scullery *s.* retrocucina || — *-boy, -maid,* sguattero, sguattera.

sculptor *s.* scultore.

sculptress *s.* scultrice.

sculptural *agg.* scultorio, statuario.

sculpture *s.* scultura.

to sculpture *vt.* e *vi.* scolpire.

scum *s.* 1. schiuma, spuma 2. feccia (*anche fig.*).

to scum *vt.* e *vi.* 1. schiumare, far schiuma 2. produrre feccia.

scummer *s.* schiumarola.

scurf *s.* 1. squama, forfora 2. incrostazioni (*pl.*).

scurrility *s.* scurrilità, volgarità.

scurrilous *agg.* scurrile, triviale.

to scurry *vi.* precipitarsi.

scurvy *agg.* spregevole, meschino.

scuttle[1] *s.* recipiente per carbone.

scuttle[2] *s.* 1. (*mar.*) portellino 2. botola.

scuttle[3] *s.* fuga precipitosa.

to scuttle[1] *vt.* produrre falle (*in una nave*).

to scuttle[2] *vi.* correre via precipitosamente.

sea *s.* mare || — -*bear*, orso polare; — -*biscuit*, galletta; — *calf*, foca; — *fight*, battaglia navale; — *food*, frutti di mare; — *front*, lungomare; — *quake*, maremoto; — *storm*, mareggiata.

seacoast *s.* costa, spiaggia.

seafarer *s.* navigante, navigatore.

seafaring *s.* viaggi per mare.

seahorse *s.* ippocampo.

seal[1] *s.* foca.

seal[2] *s.* 1. sigillo, timbro 2. (*fig.*) suggello, vincolo.

to seal[1] *vi.* andare a caccia di foche.

to seal[2] *vt.* 1. sigillare 2. suggellare || *to* — *one's fate*, decidere la propria sorte.

sealing *s.* suggellamento || — *-wax*, ceralacca.

seam *s.* 1. cucitura 2. sutura.

to seam *vt.* 1. unire con cucitura 2. rigare, segnare.

seamen *s. pl.* equipaggio (*di una nave*).

seamanship *s.* arte della navigazione.

seamless *agg.* senza cucitura.

seamstress *s.* cucitrice.

seaplane *s.* idrovolante.

seaport *s.* porto marittimo.

search *s.* 1. ricerca, indagine 2. perquisizione, visita doganale || — *warrant*, mandato di perquisizione.

to search *vt.* e *vi.* cercare, perlustrare, perquisire || *to* — *out*, rinvenire, scovare.

searcher *s.* ricercatore.

searching *agg.* indagatore, inquisitorio. ♦ searching *s.* 1. ricerca, esame 2. sondaggio.

searchlight *s.* riflettore.

seashore *s.* spiaggia, lido.

seasickness *s.* mal di mare.

seaside *s.* spiaggia, riva.

season *s.* stagione, epoca || — *bill* (*teat.*), cartellone; — *ticket*, abbonamento stagionale.

to season *vt.* 1. stagionare 2. acclimatare 3. condire. ♦ to season *vi.* 1. stagionarsi 2. invecchiarsi (*di vino*).

seasonable *agg.* 1. di stagione 2. opportuno.

seasonal *agg.* stagionale.

seasoned *agg.* 1. stagionato 2. condito.

seasoning *s.* 1. stagionatura 2. condimento.

seat *s.* 1. sedile, posto 2. seggio 3. sede.

to seat *vt.* 1. mettere a sedere 2. insediare, collocare.

seaward *agg.* che va verso il mare.

seaweed *s.* alga marina.

sebaceous *agg.* sebaceo.

secant *agg.* e *s.* secante.

to secede *vi.* separarsi, ritirarsi.

seceder *s.* secessionista, separatista.

secession *s.* secessione, scissione.

secessionism *s.* secessionismo.

to seclude *vt.* 1. appartare, isolare 2. rinchiudere.

secluded *agg.* appartato, isolato, solitario.

seclusion *s.* 1. isolamento 2. solitudine.

seclusive *agg.* che serve ad isolare.

second[1] *s.* minuto secondo.

second[2] *agg.* secondo.

secondary *agg.* secondario.

secrecy *s.* 1. segretezza 2. riserbo.

secret *agg.* 1. segreto 2. nascosto, intimo. ♦ secret *s.* segreto.

secretariat(e) *s.* 1. segretariato 2. segreteria.

secretary *s.* 1. segretario 2. ministro (*preposto ad un dicastero*).

to secrete[1] *vt.* secernere.

to secrete[2] *vt.* occultare, nascondere.

secretion *s.* secrezione.

secretly *avv.* 1. segretamente 2. in modo reticente.

sect *s.* setta.

sectarian *s.* settario.

sectarianism *s.* spirito di setta.

sectary *s.* settario.

section *s.* **1.** sezione, parte **2.** paragrafo **3.** regione, quartiere.
to section *vt.* sezionare.
sectional *agg.* **1.** parziale, di classe **2.** a sezioni.
sector *s.* settore.
secular *agg.* **1.** secolare **2.** laico **3.** mondano, profano. ♦ **secular** *s.* laico.
secularism *s.* secolarismo.
secularist *agg. e s.* laico.
to secularize *vt.* laicizzare.
secure *agg.* **1.** sicuro, certo **2.** salvo.
to secure *vt.* **1.** assicurare, salvaguardare **2.** (*giur.; comm.*) garantire **3.** mettere al sicuro.
security *s.* **1.** sicurezza, protezione **2.** certezza **3.** garanzia, cauzione. ♦ **securities** *s. pl.* titoli, valori.
sedan *s.* — (*-chair*), portantina.
sedate *agg.* **1.** posato, composto **2.** grave, serio.
sedative *agg. e s.* sedativo.
sedentary *agg. e s.* sedentario.
sediment *s.* sedimento.
sedimentary *agg.* sedimentario.
sedimentation *s.* sedimentazione.
sedition *s.* sedizione.
seditious *agg.* sedizioso.
to seduce *vt.* sedurre, corrompere.
seduction *s.* seduzione.
sedulous *agg.* assiduo.
to see (saw, seen) *vt. e vi.* **1.** vedere, scorgere **2.** capire, rendersi conto di **3.** esaminare, giudicare **4.** fare in modo che || *to — about*, assumersi l'incarico di; *to — off*, accompagnare (*alla partenza*); *to — over*, ispezionàre; *to — through* (*fig.*), indovinare, pènetrare.
see *s.* (*eccl.*) sede, diocesi.
seed *s.* **1.** seme, semenza **2.** (*fig.*) principio, germe **3.** stirpe.
seedy *agg.* pieno di semi.
to seek (sought, sought) *vt. e vi.* **1.** cercare, andare alla ricerca di **2.** ottenere **3.** chiedere, ricorrere a || *to — for sthg.*, ricercare qc.
seeker *s.* cercatore.
to seem *vi.* sembrare, apparire.
seeming *agg.* apparente, esteriore.
seemliness *s.* decenza, decoro.
seemly *agg.* decoroso, decente.
seen V. *to see.*
segment *s.* segmento, sezione.
segmentation *s.* segmentazione.
to segregate *vt.* segregare, separare. ♦ **to segregate** *vi.* separarsi, scindersi.

segregation *s.* segregazione.
seismograph *s.* sismografo.
seismologist *s.* sismologo.
seismology *s.* sismologia.
seizable *agg.* afferrabile.
to seize *vt. e vi.* **1.** afferrare, prendere **2.** capire, comprendere **3.** (*giur.*) avere in possesso, sequestrare.
seizing *s.* **1.** atto dell'afferrare **2.** conquista, cattura.
seizure *s.* **1.** (*giur.*) confisca, sequestro **2.** conquista, cattura.
seldom *avv.* raramente.
select *agg.* **1.** scelto, selezionato **2.** schizzinoso.
to select *vt.* selezionare.
selection *s.* selezione, scelta.
selective *agg.* selettivo.
selectivity *s.* selettività.
selector *s.* selettore.
self *s.* (*pl.* selves) l'io, l'individuo. ♦ **self** *agg.* **1.** della stessa materia **2.** uniforme.
self-conceit *s.* presunzione.
self-control *s.* autocontrollo.
self-defence *s.* legittima difesa.
self-denial *s.* abnegazione.
self-determination *s.* autodeterminazione.
self-educated *agg.* autodidatta.
self-examination *s.* esame di coscienza.
self-government *s.* (*pol.*) autogoverno.
self-help *s.* (*giur.*) legittima difesa.
selfish *agg.* egoistico.
selfishness *s.* egoismo.
self-portrait *s.* autoritratto.
sell *s.* (*fam.*) delusione.
to sell (sold, sold) *vt. e vi.* **1.** vendere **2.** (*fig.*) vendere, tradire || *to — off* (*comm.*), liquidare.
seller *s.* **1.** venditore **2.** articolo che si vende.
selling *s.* vendita, smercio || *— up*, vendita fallimentare.
selves V. *self.*
semantic *agg.* semantico.
semantics *s.* semantica.
semester *s.* semestre.
semi *prefisso* semi, mezzo, metà.
semicircle *s.* semicerchio.
semicircular *agg.* semicircolare.
semicolon *s.* punto e virgola.
semifinal *agg. e s.* semifinale.
seminar *s.* seminario (*d'università*).
seminarist *s.* seminarista.
seminary *s.* seminario.
semination *s.* semina.

Semite *agg.* e *s.* semita.
Semitic *agg.* semitico.
Semitism *s.* semitismo.
semitone *s.* semitono.
semivowel *s.* semivocale.
senate *s.* senato.
senator *s.* senatore.
senatorial *agg.* senatoriale.
to send (sent, sent) *vt.* e *vi.* mandare, inviare, spedire ‖ *to — away*, congedare; *to — back*, rinviare; *to — for*, mandare a chiamare; *to — off*, inviare (*per lettera*); *to — out*, emettere.
sender *s.* **1.** mandante, mittente **2.** (*comm.*) spedizioniere **3.** (*radio, tv.*) emittente.
sending *s.* **1.** invio **2.** (*comm.*) spedizione **3.** (*radio, tv.*) trasmissione.
senescence *s.* senescenza.
senile *agg.* senile.
senility *s.* senilità.
senior *agg.* **1.** più vecchio, più anziano **2.** più ragguardevole, che ha più anzianità. ✦ **senior** *s.* **1.** decano, anziano **2.** il superiore.
seniority *s.* anzianità (*d'anni, di grado*).
sensation *s.* **1.** senso, sensazione **2.** colpo, impressione.
sensational *agg.* **1.** che dipende dai sensi **2.** sensazionale.
sense *s.* **1.** senso, sensazione, impressione **2.** conoscenza **3.** significato ‖ *common —*, buon senso. ✦ **senses** *s. pl.* facoltà mentale (*sing.*).
senseful *agg.* significativo.
senseless *agg.* **1.** inanimato **2.** insensato.
sensibility *s.* **1.** sensibilità, sensitività **2.** emotività.
sensible *agg.* **1.** sensato, giudizioso **2.** percettibile **3.** notevole, considerevole **4.** consapevole.
sensibly *avv.* **1.** assennatamente **2.** percettibilmente.
sensism *s.* sensismo.
sensist *s.* sensista.
sensitive *agg.* **1.** sensitivo, sensibile **2.** suscettibile, impressionabile.
sensitively *avv.* sensibilmente.
sensitiveness *s.* **1.** sensibilità **2.** suscettibilità.
to sensitize *vt.* sensibilizzare.
sensitizer *s.* (*foto*) sensibilizzatore.
sensorial *agg.* sensorio.
sensory *agg.* sensoriale.
sensual *agg.* sensuale.

sensualism *s.* sensualismo.
sensuality *s.* sensualità.
sensually *avv.* sensualmente, voluttuosamente.
sensuous *agg.* sensoriale, voluttuoso.
sent V. *to send.*
sentence *s.* **1.** giudizio, sentenza **2.** (*gramm.*) frase ‖ *to pass a —*, pronunciare una sentenza.
to sentence *vt.* giudicare, pronunciare una sentenza contro.
sententious *agg.* sentenzioso.
sententiously *avv.* sentenziosamente.
sentient *agg.* senziente, sensibile.
sentiment *s.* **1.** sentimento **2.** opinione, parere.
sentimental *agg.* sentimentale, romantico.
sentimentalism *s.* sentimentalismo.
sentimentalist *s.* persona sentimentale.
sentimentality *s.* sentimentalità.
sentinel *s.* sentinella, guardia.
sentry *s.* sentinella, guardia, scolta ‖ *— box*, garitta.
separate *agg.* separato, staccato.
to separate *vt.* separare. ✦ **to separate** *vi.* separarsi.
separately *avv.* separatamente.
separation *s.* separazione, divisione.
separatism *s.* separatismo.
September *s.* settembre.
septicaemia *s.* setticemia.
septuagenarian *agg.* e *s.* settuagenario.
septuagenary *agg.* settuagenario.
septum *s.* (*pl.* -ta) diaframma.
sepulchral *agg.* sepolcrale.
sepulchre *s.* sepolcro.
sequacious *agg.* pedissequo, servile.
sequel *s.* **1.** conseguenza **2.** seguito.
sequence *s.* **1.** successione, sequela **2.** sequenza.
to sequestrate *vt.* sequestrare, confiscare.
sequestration *s.* sequestro, confisca.
sequin *s.* lustrino.
seraphic(al) *agg.* serafico.
serenade *s.* serenata.
serene *agg.* **1.** sereno, senza nubi **2.** calmo, tranquillo.
serenely *avv.* serenamente.
serenity *s.* **1.** serenità, limpidezza **2.** tranquillità.
sergeant *s.* **1.** sergente **2.** brigadiere.
serial *s.* romanzo a puntate, pubblicazione periodica.

serially avv. **1.** in serie **2.** periodicamente.

sericulture s. sericoltura.

sericulturist s. sericoltore.

series s. serie, successione.

serigraphy s. serigrafia.

serious agg. **1.** serio, pensieroso **2.** grave, importante.

seriousness s. **1.** serietà **2.** gravità.

sermon s. sermone, predica.

serotherapy s. sieroterapia.

serous agg. sieroso.

serpent s. serpente.

serum s. siero.

servant s. servo, servitore.

to **serve** vt. e vi. **1.** servire, essere al servizio di **2.** servire, essere utile **3.** essere sotto le armi **4.** (giur.) notificare (di atti) || to — out, distribuire.

server s. **1.** chi serve **2.** chierico **3.** vassoio.

service s. **1.** servizio (anche militare) **2.** servigio, favore **3.** funzione religiosa **4.** (giur.) notifica. ♦ **Services** s. pl. forze armate.

serviceable agg. utile, pratico.

serviette s. tovagliolo.

servile agg. servile.

servilism s. servilismo.

servility s. servilità.

serving s. **1.** il servire **2.** servizio (di tavola).

servitude s. servitù, schiavitù.

session s. sessione, seduta. ♦ **sessions** s. pl. (giur.) udienze.

set[1] agg. **1.** fermo, fisso **2.** stabilito, prestabilito **3.** studiato, preparato. ♦ **set** s. **1.** il solidificarsi **2.** forma, serie **3.** gruppo **4.** direzione, corso **5.** (poet.) tramonto **6.** serie completa, insieme: a — of teeth, una dentiera; the complete — of Shakespeare's works, la raccolta completa delle opere di Shakespeare.

to **set** (set, set) vt. e vi. **1.** mettere, porre, collocare **2.** sistemare, mettere a punto **3.** tramontare (anche fig.) || to — about, accingersi; to — back, impedire; to — in, incominciare; to — out, esporre; to — up, fissare, installare; to — aside (giur.), annullare; to — off, compensare.

set-back s. contrattempo.

set-down s. rimprovero.

set-off s. **1.** contrasto **2.** compensazione.

setting s. **1.** messa in opera, mon-

taggio **2.** ambiente **3.** scenario, messa in scena **4.** incastonatura.

to **settle** vt. e vi. **1.** fissare, decidere, determinare **2.** saldare, liquidare (conti, questioni ecc.) **3.** sistemare, sistemarsi **4.** stabilire **5.** calmare, calmarsi **6.** depositare, depositarsi (di sedimenti ecc.) || to — down, stabilirsi (in un luogo).

settled agg. fissato, stabilito.

settlement s. **1.** determinazione **2.** saldo, liquidazione **3.** sistemazione **4.** lo stabilirsi (in un luogo) **5.** colonia, distretto **6.** (giur.) transazione || financial —, regolamento di conti.

settler s. **1.** chi decide **2.** colonizzatore.

settling s. **1.** stabilizzazione **2.** saldo, pagamento.

set-to s. zuffa.

setup s. disposizione, organizzazione.

seven agg. sette.

sevenfold agg. settuplo. ♦ **sevenfold** avv. sette volte tanto.

seventeen agg. diciassette.

seventeenth agg. diciassettesimo.

seventh agg. settimo.

seventieth agg. settantesimo.

seventy agg. settanta.

to **sever** vt. staccare, dividere. ♦ to **sever** vi. staccarsi, dividersi.

several agg. **1.** parecchi, diversi (pl.) **2.** separato, distinto. ♦ **several** pron. alcuni, diversi (pl.) || — of them, alcuni di loro.

severally avv. separatamente, individualmente.

severe agg. **1.** severo, austero **2.** violento, forte **3.** rigido (di clima).

severely avv. **1.** severamente **2.** violentemente.

severity s. **1.** severità, durezza **2.** violenza.

to **sew** (sewed, sewn) vt. e vi. cucire.

sewage s. acque di scolatura.

sewer[1] s. chi cuce, cucitrice.

sewer[2] s. **1.** canale artificiale di drenaggio **2.** fogna.

sewing s. **1.** il cucire **2.** lavoro di cucito.

sewn V. to sew.

sex s. sesso.

sexagenarian agg. e s. sessagenario.

sextet(te) s. sestetto.

sexton s. sagrestano.

sextuple agg. e s. sestuplo.

sexual agg. sessuale.

shabbiness s. 1. l'essere male in arnese 2. meschinità.

shabby agg. 1. male in arnese, cencioso 2. meschino, gretto.

shackles s. pl. 1. manette, ceppi 2. (fig.) impedimenti.

shade s. 1. ombra (anche fig.) 2. sfumatura (di colore, significato ecc.) 3. spirito, ombra 4. schermo, riparo || eye- —, visiera.

to shade vt. e vi. 1. ombreggiare, riparare (da luce, calore) 2. velare, oscurare (anche fig.).

shadiness s. ombrosità.

shading s. 1. l'ombreggiare 2. ombreggiatura, sfumatura.

shadow s. ombra (anche fig.). ♦ **shadows** s. pl. oscurità.

to shadow vt. pedinare, seguire come un'ombra.

shadowy agg. 1. ombroso, ombreggiato 2. indistinto, vago.

shady agg. ombreggiato, all'ombra.

shaft[1] s. 1. lancia, giavellotto 2. fulmine 3. gambo, stelo 4. asta, bastone 5. (mecc.) albero.

shaft[2] s. sfiatatoio, condotto.

shaggy agg. 1. ispido, irsuto 2. peloso (di tessuto) 3. incolto.

Shah s. scià.

shake s. 1. scossa, scuotimento 2. tremore, tremito 3. frullato.

to shake (shook, shaken) vt. e vi. 1. scuotere, agitare (liquidi) 2. tremare, far tremare 3. turbare 4. indebolire.

shakily avv. instabilmente.

shaking agg. tremante, vacillante. ♦ **shaking** s. scossa, scuotimento.

shaky agg. 1. instabile, tremolante 2. malsicuro.

shall v. dif. 1. (aus. per le prime pers. del fut. predicente) I — go to England next summer, andrò in Inghilterra l'estate prossima; we — work next week, lavoreremo la prossima settimana 2. (aus. per le seconde e terze pers. del fut. volitivo) you — go to bed!, andrai a letto! 3. dovere: you — wait for me, devi aspettarmi.

shallow agg. 1. poco profondo, basso 2. (fig.) superficiale.

sham s. 1. finta, inganno 2. ipocrita.

shaman s. sciamano.

shambles s. pl. 1. mattatoio (sing.) 2. carneficina (sing.).

shame s. 1. vergogna, pudore 2. disonore.

to shame vt. 1. svergognare, far arrossire 2. disonorare.

shamefaced agg. 1. vergognoso 2. timido.

shameful agg. vergognoso, disonorevole.

shameless agg. svergognato, sfacciato.

shamelessly avv. sfacciatamente.

shank s. 1. gamba, stinco 2. gambo, stelo 3. fusto (di colonna) || — -bone, tibia.

shape s. forma, figura.

to shape vt. e vi. creare, dar forma a.

shapeless agg. informe.

shapely agg. ben fatto.

share s. 1. parte, porzione 2. (comm.) azione, titolo.

to share vt. dividere, spartire. ♦ **to share** vi. partecipare, condividere.

shareholder s. azionista.

share-out s. distribuzione.

shark s. 1. squalo, pescecane 2. (fig.) profittatore.

sharp agg. 1. tagliente, affilato 2. aguzzo 3. scosceso, ripido 4. netto, chiaro 5. intelligente, acuto.

sharp avv. puntualmente, in punto.

to sharpen vt. 1. affilare, aguzzare 2. (fig.) rendere più acuto.

sharper s. imbroglione.

sharply avv. acutamente.

sharpness s. 1. filo, affilatura 2. acutezza 3. vivacità, intelligenza.

sharp-sighted agg. dalla vista acuta.

to shatter vt. frantumare. ♦ **to shatter** vi. frantumarsi.

shattering s. disintegrazione.

shave[1] s. il radersi, rasatura.

shave[2] s. pialla.

to shave[1] vt. radere. ♦ **to shave** vi. radersi.

to shave[2] vt. piallare.

shaven agg. 1. rasato 2. (eccl.) tonsurato.

shaving s. 1. il radersi 2. truciolo.

shawl s. scialle.

she pron. pers. f. ella, lei, colei. ♦ **she** attr. indicante il sesso degli animali: a — -bear, un'orsa.

sheaf s. (pl. sheaves) 1. fascio, covone 2. (geom.) fascio (di rette ecc.).

to shear (sheared, shorn) vt. 1. cesoiare, tranciare 2. tosare.

shearing *s.* recisione, taglio.
shears *s. pl.* cesoie, forbici.
sheath *s.* guaina, fodero.
to sheathe *vt.* **1.** mettere nel fodero **2.** rivestire di.
sheaves V. *sheaf.*
to shed (shed, shed) *vt.* **1.** versare, spandere **2.** lasciar cadere.
shed *s.* tettoia, capannone.
shedding *s.* **1.** spargimento **2.** perdita, caduta (*di foglie ecc.*).
sheen *s.* splendore, lucentezza.
sheep *s.* (*anche pl.*) **1.** pecora, ovino **2.** (*fig.*) persona debole, timorosa.
sheepish *agg.* timido, impacciato.
sheepskin *s.* **1.** pelle di pecora **2.** cartapecora.
sheer[1] *agg.* **1.** puro, semplice, mero **2.** liscio, non diluito (*di bevande*).
sheer[2] *s.* virata, cambiamento di rotta.
sheet *s.* **1.** lenzuolo **2.** foglio **3.** lamina, lamiera.
sheik(h) *s.* sceicco.
shelf *s.* (*pl.* shelves) mensola, scaffale.
shell *s.* **1.** conchiglia, guscio **2.** involucro, carcassa **3.** bossolo (*di cartuccia*) **4.** (*fig.*) apparenza.
to shell *vt.* e *vi.* sgusciare, sgranare.
shelter *s.* **1.** riparo, rifugio **2.** pensilina.
to shelter *vt.* riparare. ♦ **to shelter** *vi.* ripararsi.
to shelve *vt.* **1.** provvedere di scaffali **2.** mettere negli scaffali.
shelves V. *shelf.*
shelving *s.* scaffalatura.
shepherd *s.* pastore, pecoraio.
sherbet *s.* sorbetto.
shield *s.* **1.** scudo **2.** (*fig.*) protezione.
to shield *vt.* proteggere, difendere.
shift *s.* **1.** cambiamento, sostituzione **2.** risorsa, espediente **3.** turno (*di lavoro*).
to shift *vt.* **1.** spostare **2.** cambiare. ♦ **to shift** *vi.* **1.** spostarsi **2.** arrangiarsi.
shilling *s.* scellino.
to shilly-shally *vi.* tentennare.
to shimmer *vi.* luccicare, mandare bagliori.
to shine (shone, shone) *vt.* e *vi.* **1.** splendere, brillare (*anche fig.*) **2.** essere brillante.
shine *s.* **1.** splendore, luminosità **2.** luce del sole.
Shintoist *s.* scintoista.

shiny *agg.* splendente, rilucente.
ship *s.* nave, bastimento || *convoy*— —, nave scorta; *flag*- —, nave ammiraglia; *landing*- —, nave da sbarco.
to ship *vt.* **1.** imbarcare **2.** (*comm.*) spedire. ♦ **to ship** *vi.* imbarcarsi.
shipboard *s.* bordo.
shipboy *s.* mozzo.
shipbuilder *s.* costruttore navale.
shipmate *s.* compagno di bordo.
shipment *s.* imbarco, spedizione di merci.
shipping *s.* **1.** forze navali (*pl.*) **2.** imbarco, spedizione.
shipwreck *s.* naufragio.
to shipwreck *vi.* naufragare.
shipyard *s.* cantiere navale.
shirker *s.* scansafatiche.
shirt *s.* camicia (*da uomo*).
shiver[1] *s.* scheggia.
shiver[2] *s.* brivido, fremito.
to shiver[1] *vt.* frantumare. ♦ **to shiver** *vi.* frantumarsi.
to shiver[2] *vt.* e *vi.* rabbrividire, tremare.
shivering *s.* V. *shiver.*
shivery *agg.* **1.** fragile **2.** tremante.
shoal[1] *s.* secca, bassofondo.
shoal[2] *s.* banco (*di pesci*).
shock *s.* **1.** urto, collisione **2.** forte impressione, violenta emozione.
to shock *vt.* **1.** colpire, disgustare **2.** provocare un collasso. ♦ **to shock** *vi.* **1.** scandalizzarsi **2.** scontrarsi.
shocking *agg.* **1.** che colpisce **2.** disgustoso.
shoe *s.* scarpa, calzatura || *horse*— —, ferro di cavallo.
shoeblack *s.* lustrascarpe.
shoemaker *s.* calzolaio.
shoe-string *s.* laccio (*da scarpe*).
shone V. *to shine.*
shook V. *to shake.*
shoot *s.* **1.** spedizione di caccia **2.** virgulto **3.** puntura, fitta.
to shoot (shot, shot) *vt.* e *vi.* **1.** lanciare **2.** sparare, uccidere sparando **3.** cacciare **4.** fare un'istantanea.
shooter *s.* cacciatore.
shooting *s.* **1.** tiro, sparo **2.** caccia **3.** il fotografare, il girare un film.
shop *s.* **1.** bottega, negozio **2.** officina, laboratorio || — -*assistant*, commesso; — -*book*, libro dei conti; — -*lifter*, taccheggiatore; — -*window*, vetrina.

shopkeeper s. negoziante.
shopman s. commesso di negozio.
shopping s. compere, acquisti (pl.).
shore s. spiaggia, lido.
shorn V. to shear.
short agg. 1. corto, breve 2. basso, piccolo (di statura) 3. conciso 4. brusco, rude. ◆ short s. 1. compendio 2. (cine) cortometraggio.
short avv. 1. bruscamente, improvvisamente 2. (comm.) allo scoperto.
shortage s. mancanza, carenza.
short-circuit s. corto circuito.
short-cut s. scorciatoia.
short-dated agg. (comm.) a breve scadenza.
to shorten vt. accorciare, abbreviare.
shortening s. accorciamento, abbreviazione.
shorthand s. stenografia.
shortly avv. 1. fra breve 2. brevemente.
shortness s. brevità.
short-sighted agg. miope.
shot¹ V. to shoot.
shot² s. 1. sparo, colpo 2. proiettile 3. ripresa cinematografica.
shotgun s. fucile da caccia.
should s. dif. 1. (aus. per le prime pers. del condiz.) I — be very happy, sarei felicissimo 2. dovere: it — be so, dovrebbe essere così.
shoulder s. spalla.
to shoulder vt. e vi. 1. spingere con le spalle 2. portare sulle spalle.
shout s. grido, chiasso.
to shout vt. e vi. gridare, urlare.
shove s. spinta, urto.
to shove vt. spingere. ◆ to shove vi. spingersi.
shovel s. pala.
to shovel vt. spalare.
shoveller s. spalatore.
show s. 1. mostra, esibizione 2. apparenza 3. pompa, ostentazione ‖ — case, bacheca; — down, chiarificazione; — -off, esibizionismo.
to show (showed, shown) vt. e vi. 1. mostrare, far vedere 2. rappresentare, indicare 3. dimostrare, provare 4. apparire, farsi vedere ‖ to — down, mettere le carte in tavola; to — off, darsi delle arie.
shower s. acquazzone, rovescio.
showman s. presentatore.
shown V. to show.

showy agg. fastoso, appariscente.
shrank V. to shrink.
shred s. brandello, frammento.
shrew s. bisbetica.
shrewd agg. sagace, accorto.
shrewdly avv. sagacemente.
shrewdness s. sagacia, accortezza.
shrewish agg. brontolone.
shriek s. grido, strillo, suono lacerante.
to shriek vt. e vi. gridare, stridere.
shrill agg. stridulo, acuto.
to shrill vt. e vi. strillare, stridere.
shrimp s. gamberetto.
shrine s. reliquiario.
shrink s. restringimento.
to shrink (shrank, shrunk) vt. e vi. 1. restringere, restringersi, contrarre 2. indietreggiare.
shrinkable agg. restringibile.
shrinkage s. 1. diminuzione, restringimento 2. (comm.) deprezzamento.
shrinking s. contrazione, ritiro.
shroud s. sudario.
shrub s. arbusto, cespuglio.
shrubbery s. boscaglia d'arbusti.
shrug s. spallucciata.
to shrug vi. alzate le spalle.
shrunk V. to shrink.
shudder s. brivido.
to shudder vi. rabbrividire.
shuffle s. 1. passo strascicato 2. scompiglio 3. il mescolare (le carte).
to shuffle vt. e vi. 1. muoversi a fatica 2. mescolare, scompigliare.
to shun vt. sfuggire, scansare.
shunt s. 1. (elett.) derivazione 2. (ferr.) scambio.
to shunt vt. e vi. 1. (elett.) inserire in derivazione 2. (ferr.) smistare, smistarsi.
shut agg. ben chiuso.
to shut (shut, shut) vt. e vi. chiudere, serrare ‖ shut up!, tacil
shutter s. imposta, persiana.
shuttle s. spola, navetta.
shy agg. riservato, timido.
to shy vt. spaventare. ◆ to shy vi. scartare (di cavallo).
shyly avv. timidamente.
shyness s. timidezza, scontrosità.
Siberian agg. e s. siberiano.
sibilant agg. e s. sibilante.
Sibylline agg. sibillino.
Sicilian agg. e s. siciliano.
sick agg. 1. ammalato 2. nauseato ‖ to fall —, ammalarsi.

to **sicken** vt. e vi. **1.** far ammalare, ammalarsi **2.** sfiorire **3.** sentir nausea.

sickening agg. nauseabondo, rivoltante.

sickle s. falce.

sickly agg. **1.** malaticcio **2.** pallido, debole **3.** nauseante.

sickness s. malattia.

side s. **1.** lato, fianco **2.** parte, partito, fazione **3.** discendenza || — -door, porta laterale; — -face, profilo; — -look, occhiata in tralice; — -note, nota marginale; — -post, stipite.

sideboard s. credenza.

sidecar s. motocarrozzetta.

sidelong agg. laterale, obliquo.

sidereal agg. sidereo.

sideways avv. lateralmente, obliquamente.

to **sidle** vi. camminare di fianco, andare a sghembo || to — up to so., avvicinarsi furtivamente a qu.

siege s. assedio.

sieve s. setaccio, crivello.

to **sieve** vt. setacciare, crivellare.

to **sift** vt. e vi. setacciare **2.** filtrare (di luce, polvere ecc.).

sigh s. sospiro.

to **sigh** vt. e vi. **1.** sospirare **2.** sibilare.

sight s. **1.** vista, visione **2.** veduta, panorama **3.** colpo d'occhio **4.** mirino.

to **sight** vt. e vi. **1.** avvistare **2.** prendere la mira.

sighted agg. **1.** fornito di vista || long- —, presbite; short- —, miope.

sightless agg. senza vista.

sign s. **1.** segno, cenno **2.** indicazione, traccia || traffic —, segnale stradale.

to **sign** vt. e vi. firmare, segnare, sottoscrivere.

signal s. segnale, segno.

to **signal** vt. segnalare. ♦ to **signal** vi. far segnali.

signalman s. segnalatore.

signatory s. firmatario.

signature s. **1.** firma, sigla **2.** (tip.) segnatura.

signboard s. insegna (di albergo, negozio ecc.).

significant agg. espressivo, significativo.

to **signify** vt. e vi. **1.** significare, voler dire **2.** denotare, indicare, presagire **3.** importare.

silence s. silenzio.

to **silence** vt. far tacere, imporre il silenzio.

silencer s. silenziatore.

silent agg. **1.** silenzioso, taciturno **2.** muto.

silently avv. silenziosamente.

silhouette s. profilo, contorno.

silica s. silice.

silicate s. silicato.

silicon s. silicio.

silicosis s. silicosi.

silk s. seta.

silken agg. serico, di seta.

silkworm s. baco da seta || — breeding, sericoltura.

silky agg. di seta, serico.

sill s. basamento, soglia.

silliness s. stupidità, sciocchezza.

silly agg. sciocco, stupido.

to **silo** vt. conservare, mettere in silo.

silt s. melma.

silver s. argento, argenteria || — -plate, argenteria; — -plating, argentatura || quick —, mercurio.

to **silver** vt. inargentare. ♦ to **silver** vi. inargentarsi.

silverware s. oggetti d'argento.

silvery agg. argenteo.

similar agg. simile, analogo.

similarity s. somiglianza, similitudine.

similitude s. **1.** similitudine **2.** somiglianza.

simoniac agg. e s. simoniaco.

simony s. simonia.

to **simper** vi. parlare in modo affettato.

simple agg. **1.** semplice, elementare **2.** sincero **3.** autentico.

simpleton s. sempliciotto.

simplicity s. semplicità, candore.

simplification s. semplificazione.

to **simplify** vt. semplificare.

simply avv. semplicemente.

simulation s. simulazione.

simulator s. simulatore.

simultaneity s. simultaneità.

simultaneous agg. simultaneo.

sin s. **1.** peccato, colpa **2.** offesa.

to **sin** vi. peccare.

since avv. da allora, da allora in poi || long —, molto tempo fa. ♦ **since** cong. **1.** da quando **2.** poiché. ♦ **since** prep. da, fin da.

sincere agg. sincero, schietto.

sincerely avv. sinceramente || yours —, cordialmente vostro (nelle lettere).

sincerity *s.* sincerità.
sinew *s.* **1.** tendine, nervo **2.** (*fig.*) vigore, nerbo.
sinful *agg.* peccaminoso, colpevole.
sinfully *avv.* peccaminosamente.
to **sing** (**sang, sung**) *vt.* e *vi.* cantare.
to **singe** *vt.* bruciacchiare, strinare (*anche fig.*). ♦ to **singe** *vi.* bruciarsi.
singer *s.* cantante.
singing *s.* **1.** canto **2.** fischio (*del vento ecc.*).
single *agg.* **1.** solo, unico **2.** individuale, particolare **3.** celibe || *every* — *day,* tutti i giorni.
to **single** *vt.* distinguere, scegliere: *to* — *out sthg.,* scegliere qc.
singleness *s.* **1.** unicità **2.** sincerità.
singly *avv.* **1.** separatamente, ad uno ad uno **2.** da solo, senza aiuto.
singsong *s.* cantilena, canto monotono.
singular *agg.* **1.** singolare, solo **2.** eccezionale **3.** bizzarro, strano.
singularity *s.* **1.** singolarità, rarità **2.** particolarità **3.** stranezza.
singularly *avv.* singolarmente.
sinister *agg.* sinistro, funesto, di cattivo augurio.
sink *s.* **1.** lavandino, acquaio **2.** scolo.
to **sink** (**sank, sunk**) *vi.* **1.** affondare, andare a fondo **2.** sprofondare **3.** abbassare, abbassarsi, calare **4.** cadere, cedere (*di terreno, muro ecc.*).
sinner *s.* peccatore.
sinuous *agg.* sinuoso.
sinus *s.* **1.** cavità **2.** seno.
sip *s.* sorso.
to **sip** *vt.* e *vi.* sorseggiare.
siphon *s.* sifone.
sir *s.* **1.** (*vocativo*) signore **2.** « sir » (*titolo*).
siren *s.* sirena.
siroc *s.* scirocco.
sirup *s.* sciroppo.
sister *s.* **1.** sorella **2.** suora || — *-in-law,* cognata.
sisterhood *s.* congregazione religiosa di suore.
sisterly *avv.* da sorella, amorevolmente.
to **sit** (**sat, sat**) *vt.* e *vi.* **1.** sedere, stare seduto, far sedere **2.** essere in seduta **3.** appollaiarsi, posare **4.** covare || *to* — *out,* rimanere fino alla fine; *to* — *up,* rimanere al-

zato.
site *s.* area fabbricabile.
sitting *s.* **1.** posa, seduta **2.** adunanza || — *-room,* stanza di soggiorno. ♦ **sittings** *s. pl.* sessioni (*di una Corte*).
situated *agg.* **1.** situato, collocato **2.** in una certa situazione (*di persona*).
situation *s.* **1.** situazione, posizione **2.** stato, circostanza **3.** posto, impiego: *to apply for a* —, fare una domanda di impiego.
six *agg.* sei.
sixfold *agg.* sestuplo. ♦ **sixfold** *avv.* sei volte tanto.
sixpence *s.* moneta da sei « pence », mezzo scellino.
sixpenny *agg.* del valore di sei « pence ».
sixteen *agg.* sedici.
sixteenth *agg.* sedicesimo.
sixth *agg.* sesto.
sixtieth *agg.* sessantesimo.
sixty *agg.* sessanta.
size *s.* **1.** grandezza, misura, dimensione **2.** formato, taglia **3.** colla.
to **size** *vt.* allineare || *to* — *up,* valutare.
sizzle *s.* sfrigolio.
skate *s.* pattino || *roller* —, pattino a rotelle.
to **skate** *vi.* pattinare.
skating *s.* pattinaggio.
skein *s.* matassa.
skeleton *s.* scheletro (*anche fig.*).
to **skeletonize** *vt.* scheletrire. ♦ to **skeletonize** *vi.* scheletrirsi (*anche fig.*).
skeptic *agg.* e *s.* scettico.
skeptical *agg.* scettico.
skepticism *s.* scetticismo.
sketch *s.* **1.** schizzo, abbozzo **2.** scenetta.
to **sketch** *vt.* abbozzare, schizzare.
skewness *s.* asimmetria.
ski *s.* sci || — *-lift,* sciovia.
to **ski** *vi.* sciare.
skier *s.* sciatore.
skiff *s.* (*mar.*) schifo.
skilful *agg.* abile, esperto.
skilfully *avv.* abilmente.
skilfulness *s.* abilità.
skill *s.* abilità, destrezza.
skilled *agg.* esperto, abile, versato || — *worker,* operaio specializzato.
to **skim** *vt.* e *vi.* **1.** schiumare, scremare **2.** rasentare, sfiorare.
skimmer *s.* schiumarola.

skimming s. scrematura.
skin s. pelle, cute.
to **skin** vt. e vi. scuoiare || to —
over, rimarginarsi (di ferite).
skinny agg. magro, scarno.
to **skip** vt. e vi. fare un balzo, sal-
tare alla corda || to — a few pages,
saltare qualche pagina.
skirmish s. scaramuccia.·
skirt s. 1. sottana, gonna 2. orlo,
lembo.
to **skirt** vt. e vi. orlare, costeggiare.
skittish agg. capriccioso, frivolo.
skittles s. pl. birilli.
skull s. cranio, teschio || — -cap,
papalina.
sky s. cielo, firmamento.
skylark s. allodola.
skylight s. lucernario.
skyline s. linea, profilo (di montagne ecc.).
skyman s. paracadutista.
skyscraper s. grattacielo.
skyward agg. e avv. verso il cielo.
slab s. 1. lastra, piastra 2. pezzo,
fetta.
slack agg. 1. molle, allentato 2. debole, fiacco 3. (comm.) calmo, stagnante, debole. ◆ **slack** s. (comm.)
stagione morta.
to **slacken** vt. 1. allentare, mollare
2. diminuire. ◆ to **slacken** vi.
1. allentarsi 2. smorzarsi.
slacker s. fannullone.
slain V. to slay.
slam s. sbatacchiamento.
to **slam** vt. sbattere, chiudere violentemente. ◆ to **slam** vi. chiudersi violentemente.
slander s. 1. calunnia 2. (giur.) diffamazione.
to **slander** vt. 1. calunniare 2. (giur.)
diffamare.
slanderer s. 1. calunniatore 2.
(giur.) diffamatore.
slanderous agg. calunnioso, maldicente.
slang s. gergo.
slant s. pendenza, inclinazione.
to **slant** vt. e vi. essere in pendenza,
inclinare.
slanting agg. inclinato, obliquo,
sghembo.
slap s. schiaffo, ceffone.
to **slap** vt. 1. schiaffeggiare 2. sbattere.
slash s. 1. taglio, sfregio 2. frustata.
to **slash** vt. tagliare, fendere.

slate s. ardesia, tegola d'ardesia.
slaughter s. 1. macello 2. carneficina, massacro.
to **slaughter** vt. 1. macellare 2. massacrare.
slaughterer s. 1. macellatore 2.
massacratore.
slaughterhouse s. mattatoio.
Slav agg. e s. slavo.
slave s. schiavo.
slaver[1] s. schiavista.
slaver[2] s. saliva, bava.
slavery s. schiavitù.
to **slay** (slew, slain) vt. ammazzare.
sleek agg. lucido, levigato.
sleep s. sonno, dormita || — walker,
sonnambulo.
to **sleep** (slept, slept) vt. e vi. 1.
dormire, riposare 2. passare la
notte.
sleeper s. 1. dormiente, dormiglione
2. (ferr.) traversina 3. (ferr.) vettura letto.
sleepily avv. con aria assonnata.
sleeping agg. dormiente, addormen-
tato || — bag, sacco a pelo; —
-berth, cuccetta; — -car, vagone
letto; — -draught, sonnifero.
sleepless agg. insonne.
sleeplessness s. insonnia.
sleepy agg. assonnato, sonnolento.
sleet s. nevischio.
sleeve s. manica.
sleeved agg. con maniche.
sleigh s. slitta.
slender agg. 1. magro, snello 2. debole, fiacco.
slenderness s. 1. snellezza, magrezza 2. debolezza.
slept V. to sleep.
slew V. to slay.
slice s. pezzo, fetta, porzione.
to **slice** vt. affettare.
slicer s. affettatrice.
slid V. to slide.
slide s. 1. scivolata 2. pendenza 3.
scivolo 4. (mecc.) carrello, pattino.
to **slide** (slid, slid) vt. e vi. 1.
scivolare, far scivolare, scorrere,
far scorrere 2. sfuggire.
sliding agg. scorrevole.
slight agg. 1. esile, minuto, magro
2. leggero, scarso.
slim agg. 1. magro, sottile 2. debole.
slime s. melma, limo.
slimy agg. fangoso, viscoso.
sling[1] s. fionda.

sling² s. cinghia.
to sling¹ (slung, slung) vt. scagliare con la fionda.
to sling² vt. sospendere, appendere.
to slink (slunk, slunk) vi. sgattaiolare.
slip¹ s. **1.** innesto **2.** (tip.) bozza in colonna.
slip² s. **1.** scalo, molo **2.** guinzaglio **3.** sottoveste **4.** scivolone **5.** papera, lapsus.
to slip vt. e vi. **1.** scivolare, inciampare **2.** entrare, uscire furtivamente **3.** sguisciare, liberarsi || to — away, scorrere (di tempo).
slipper s. pantofola.
slippery agg. sdrucciolevole, viscido (anche fig.).
slipshod agg. **1.** scalcagnato **2.** trasandato.
slit s. fessura, fenditura.
to slit (slit, slit) vt. fendere.
slope s. pendenza, pendio.
to slope vi. essere in pendenza, inclinarsi.
sloping agg. inclinato, obliquo.
slot s. fessura, scanalatura || — -machine, distributore automatico a gettoni.
sloth s. pigrizia, indolenza.
slothful agg. pigro, indolente.
slouch s. andatura dinoccolata.
slouching agg. dinoccolato, goffo.
slovenliness s. sciatteria, sporcizia.
slovenly agg. sciatto, sudicio.
slow agg. **1.** lento **2.** tardo, ottuso || — -down, rallentamento; — -match, miccia.
to slow vt. e vi. to — up o down, rallentare.
slowly avv. lentamente.
slowness s. lentezza, pigrizia.
sluggish agg. pigro, tardo, indolente.
sluggishness s. pigrizia, indolenza.
slum s. vicolo, tugurio. ◆ **slums** s. pl. quartieri poveri (di una città).
slumber s. dormiveglia, assopimento.
to slumber vt. e vi. dormire, dormicchiare.
slung V. to sling.
slunk V. to slink.
slush s. poltiglia, fango.
sly agg. **1.** astuto, malizioso **2.** infido.
smack s. **1.** sapore, aroma **2.** schiocco **3.** schiaffo.
to smack vt. e vi. **1.** schioccare **2.** schioccare baci **3.** schiaffeggiare.

small agg. **1.** piccolo, minuto **2.** leggero, debole **3.** poco, scarso **4.** di poca importanza.
small-arms s. pl. armi portatili.
smallness s. piccolezza.
smallpox s. vaiolo.
smart agg. **1.** acuto, pungente **2.** vivace, sveglio **3.** elegante.
to smarten vt. e vi. abbellire || to — up, rianimarsi, farsi bello.
smartness s. **1.** acutezza, vivacità, brio **2.** eleganza.
smash s. **1.** urto, scontro **2.** rovina.
to smash vt. **1.** frantumare, fracassare **2.** sconfiggere; annientare. ◆
to smash vi. **1.** frantumarsi **2.** sfasciarsi **3.** crollare.
smasher s. **1.** chi frantuma **2.** (fam.) caso eccezionale.
smear s. macchia, imbrattatura.
to smear vt. macchiare, imbrattare.
smell s. **1.** odorato, olfatto **2.** odore.
to smell (smelt, smelt) vt. e vi. **1.** fiutare, sentire l'odore **2.** avere odore || to — of, sapere di; to — out, scovare.
smile s. sorriso.
to smile vt. e vi. sorridere || fortune smil'ed on you, la fortuna ti fu favorevole.
smiling agg. sorridente, sereno.
smirch s. onta, macchia.
to smite (smote, smitten) vt. e vi. **1.** colpire, percuotere **2.** sconfiggere, sgominare || to — down, abbattere.
smith s. fabbro.
smitten V. to smite.
smoke s. **1.** fumo **2.** fumata || — -stack, fumaiolo.
to smoke vt. e vi. **1.** fumare **2.** affumicare.
smoker s. fumatore, fumatrice.
smoking s. il fumare. ◆ **smoking** agg. fumante.
smoky agg. **1.** fumoso **2.** affumicato, annerito dal fumo **3.** che sa di fumo.
smooth agg. **1.** liscio, levigato **2.** omogeneo **3.** armonioso (di suono) **4.** melliffluo **5.** calmo, tranquillo (di mare).
to smooth vt. **1.** lisciare, spianare **2.** appianare.
smoothing s. lisciatura, spianatura.
smoothly avv. **1.** pianamente **2.** armonicamente **3.** in modo melliffluo.
smoothness s. **1.** levigatezza **2.** armonia (di verso, suono) **3.** affabi-

lità.

smote V. *to smite.*

to **smother** *vt.* e *vi.* **1.** soffocare, opprimere **2.** ricoprire.

to **smoulder** *vi.* ardere sotto la cenere.

to **smuggle** *vt.* e *vi.* contrabbandare.

smuggler *s.* contrabbandiere.

smuggling *s.* contrabbando.

smut *s.* fuliggine.

snack *s.* **1.** boccone, porzione **2.** spuntino || — *-bar,* tavola calda.

snail *s.* chiocciola, lumaca.

snake *s.* serpente.

snakily *avv.* **1.** tortuosamente **2.** (*fig.*) slealmente.

snaky *agg.* serpentino.

snap *s.* **1.** colpo secco, morso, schiocco **2.** scatto **3.** fermaglio, fibbia.

to **snap** *vt.* e *vi.* **1.** schioccare, far schioccare **2.** aprirsi di colpo, spezzare con un colpo secco **3.** (*foto*) scattare un'istantanea.

snapshot *s.* (*foto*) istantanea.

snare *s.* **1.** trappola, rete **2.** insidia, tentazione.

to **snare** *vt.* prendere in trappola, al laccio (*anche fig.*).

snarl *s.* ringhio.

to **snarl** *vi.* ringhiare.

snatch *s.* **1.** strappo, strattone **2.** brano, frammento.

to **snatch** *vt.* e *vi.* afferrare, ghermire || *to — off,* strappare.

sneak *s.* persona malfida.

sneer *s.* sogghigno beffardo.

to **sneer** *vt.* e *vi.* sorridere beffardamente, schernire.

sneeze *s.* starnuto.

to **sneeze** *vi.* starnutire.

to **sniff** *vt.* e *vi.* fiutare || *to — at sthg.* annusare qc.

snip *s.* **1.** ritaglio, scampolo **2.** forbiciata.

to **snip** *vt.* tagliuzzare.

snobbery *s.* snobismo.

to **snore** *vi.* russare.

snort *s.* sbuffo, rumore sbuffante.

to **snort** *vt.* e *vi.* sbuffare.

snout *s.* muso, grugno.

snow *s.* neve, nevicata || — *-plough,* spazzaneve; — *-slide,* valanga.

to **snow** *v. imp.* nevicare || *it is snowing,* nevica.

snowfall *s.* nevicata.

snowflake *s.* fiocco di neve.

snowy *agg.* **1.** nevoso, coperto di neve **2.** niveo.

snuff *s.* **1.** l'aspirare col naso **2.** tabacco da fiuto || — *-box,* tabacchiera.

to **snuff**[1] *vt.* e *vi.* **1.** annusare aspirando **2.** fiutare tabacco.

to **snuff**[2] *vt.* e *vi.* smoccolare (*una candela*).

to **snuffle** *vt.* e *vi.* pronunciare con tono nasale.

snug *agg.* **1.** comodo **2.** confortevole **3.** nascosto.

to **snuggle** *vi.* **1.** rannicchiarsi **2.** accoccolarsi.

so *avv.* così, tanto, talmente || — *far,* fino ad ora; — *long as,* a patto che; *if* —, in tal caso; *that being* —, stando così le cose.

to **soak** *vt.* **1.** immergere **2.** bagnare. ♦ to **soak** *vi.* **1.** inzupparsi, imbeversi **2.** bagnarsi.

soaking *agg.* **1.** che bagna, che inzuppa **2.** bagnato. ♦ **soaking** *s.* immersione, bagnatura.

soap *s.* sapone || — *dish,* portasapone.

to **soap** *vt.* insaponare. ♦ to **soap** *vi.* insaponarsi.

soapbox *s.* **1.** cassa per sapone **2.** (*fam.*) palco improvvisato per oratori (*da strada*).

soapsuds *s. pl.* saponata (*sing.*).

soapwort *s.* saponaria.

sob *s.* singhiozzo.

to **sob** *vt.* e *vi.* singhiozzare.

sober *agg.* **1.** sobrio (*nel bere*) **2.** calmo, composto.

sobriety *s.* **1.** sobrietà (*nel bere*) **2.** moderazione, calma.

so-called *agg.* cosiddetto.

sociability *s.* socievolezza.

sociable *agg.* socievole.

social *agg.* **1.** sociale **2.** socievole.

socialism *s.* socialismo.

socialist *s.* socialista.

sociality *s.* socievolezza.

to **socialize** *vt.* socializzare.

society *s.* **1.** società, compagnia **2.** strato sociale **3.** associazione.

sociological *agg.* sociologico.

sociologist *s.* sociologo.

sociology *s.* sociologia.

sock *s.* **1.** calzino, calza corta **2.** soletta.

socket *s.* **1.** cavità **2.** (*elett.*) presa di corrente, portalampada **3.** (*anat.*) orbita.

Socratic *agg.* e *s.* socratico.

sod *s.* zolla erbosa.

soda *s.* carbonato di sodio.

sodium s. sodio.
soft agg. 1. mòlle, tenero 2. liscio, morbido, soffice 3. dolce, mite ‖ — -boiled (egg), uovo alla coque.
to soften vt. 1. ammollire, ammorbidire 2. calmare, raddolcire. ◆ **to soften** vi. 1. ammorbidirsi 2. intenerirsi.
softening agg. che rende molle. ◆ **softening** s. 1. ammorbidimento 2. intenerimento. .
softly avv. 1. teneramente 2. sommessamente 3. pian piano.
softness s. 1. morbidezza 2. dolcezza, mitezza.
soil s. 1. suolo, terreno 2. macchia (anche fig.).
to soil vt. macchiare. ◆ **to soil** vi. macchiarsi.
sojourn s. soggiorno.
to sojourn vi. soggiornare.
solace s. sollievo, conforto.
to solace vt. consolare.
solar agg. solare.
sold V. to sell.
solder s. lega per saldatura.
to solder vt. saldare.
soldering s. saldatura.
soldier s. 1. soldato 2. stratega ‖ foot- —, soldato di fanteria; horse- —, soldato di cavalleria.
soldierlike agg. militaresco.
soldiery s. coll. soldatesca, truppe.
sole[1] agg. solo, unico.
sole[2] s. suola, pianta del piede.
sole[3] s. sogliola.
solecism s. solecismo.
solely avv. solamente.
solemn agg. solenne, serio, grave.
solemnity s. solennità.
to solemnize vt. solennizzare.
solemnly avv. solennemente.
sol-fa s. solfeggio.
to sol-fa vt. e vi. solfeggiare.
to solicit vt. 1. sollecitare 2. adescare. ◆ **to solicit** vi. fare sollecitazioni.
solicitation s. 1. sollecitazione 2. invito, adescamento.
solicitor s. 1. sollecitatore 2. procuratore legale.
solicitous agg. 1. sollecito 2. ansioso, desideroso.
solid agg. 1. solido, compatto 2. reale, fondato. ◆ **solid** s. solido.
solidarity s. solidarietà.
solidary agg. solidale.
solidification s. solidificazione.
to solidify vt. solidificare. ◆ **to so-**

lidify vi. solidificarsi.
solidity s. 1. solidità 2. (comm.) solvenza.
solidly avv. 1. solidamente 2. all'unanimità.
soliloquy s. soliloquio.
solitaire s. solitario (pietra preziosa e giuoco delle carte).
solitary agg. 1. solo, unico 2. solitario 3. isolato, romito.
solitude s. solitudine, isolamento.
soloist s. solista.
solstice s. solstizio.
solubility s. solubilità.
soluble agg. 1. solubile 2. scomponibile 3. risolvibile.
solution s. 1. (chim.) soluzione 2. risoluzione.
solvability s. 1. (comm.) solvibilità 2. solubilità 3. risolvibilità.
solvable agg. 1. (comm.) solvibile 2. solubile 3. risolvibile.
to solve vt. risolvere, chiarire.
solvency s. (comm.) solvibilità.
solvent agg. 1. (comm.) solvibile 2. solvente. ◆ **solvent** s. solvente.
somatic(al) agg. somatico.
somatology s. somatologia.
sombre agg. 1. fosco, scuro 2. (fig.) tetro, triste.
some agg. 1. qualche, alcuni, certi 2. un certo, qualsiasi 3. (partitivo) un po' di, del, della, dei, degli, delle. ◆ **some** pron. 1. alcuni, alcune 2. un po'. ◆ **some** avv. circa.
somebody pron. indef. qualcuno.
somehow avv. in qualche modo, in un modo o nell'altro.
someone pron. indef. qualcuno: — else, qualcun altro.
somersault s. 1. salto mortale, capriola 2. (aer.) capottamento 3. (auto) ribaltamento.
to somersault, **to somerset** vi. 1. fare salti mortali 2. (aer.) capottare 3. (auto.) ribaltare.
something pron. indef. qualche cosa.
sometime avv. 1. un tempo 2. presto o tardi, un giorno o l'altro.
sometimes avv. qualche volta, alcune volte.
someway avv. in un modo o nell'altro.
somewhat pron. ind. un poco.
somewhere avv. in qualche luogo.
somnambulism s. sonnambulismo.
somnambulist s. sonnambulo.

somnolent *agg.* 1. sonnolento 2. assopito.

son *s.* figlio, figliolo || — *-in-law*, genèro.

song *s.* canto, canzone.

songbook *s.* canzoniere.

songful *agg.* 1. melodioso 2. che ama cantare.

songster *s.* cantante (*uomo*).

sonnet *s.* sonetto.

sonority *s.* sonorità.

sonorous *agg.* sonoro, risonante.

sonorously *avv.* sonoramente.

soon (*comp. di* sooner) *avv.* presto, tra poco || *the sooner the better,* prima è meglio è; *sooner or later,* presto o tardi; *I had sooner,* preferirei; *as — as,* non appena.

soot *s.* fuliggine.

to soot *vt.* macchiare, sporcare di fuliggine.

to soothe *vt.* calmare, placare.

soothsayer *s.* indovino.

sooty *agg.* fuligginoso.

sophism *s.* sofisma (*anche fig.*).

sophist *s.* sofista (*anche fig.*).

sophistic(al) *agg.* sofistico, pedante.

sophisticated *agg.* 1. sofisticato, raffinato 2. adulterato.

sophistry *s.* sofisma.

sorcerer *s.* stregone, mago.

sorceress *s.* strega, maga.

sorcery *s.* stregoneria, sortilegio.

sordid *agg.* 1. sordido, avaro 2. vile, meschino.

sore *agg.* 1. doloroso, dolorante, infiammato 2. triste, addolorato 3. estremo, intenso.

sorrel *s.* sauro.

sorrow *s.* 1. dispiacere, dolore 2. rincrescimento 3. sventura.

to sorrow *vi.* affliggersi, addolorarsi.

sorrowful *agg.* 1. triste, infelice 2. penoso, doloroso.

sorry *agg.* spiacente, dolente || *sorry!,* scusate!; *to be —,* dispiacersi.

sort *s.* sorta, specie.

to sort *vt.* raggruppare, selezionare.

♦ **to sort** *vi.* accordarsi, adattarsi.

sought V. *to seek.*

soul *s.* 1. anima, animo, spirito 2. essenza, personificazione.

sound[1] *avv.* profondamente.

sound[2] *agg.* 1. sano, intero, in buono stato 2. buono, solido 3. profondo, completo || — *-headed* equilibra-

to, — *-minded,* di buon senso.

sound[3] *s.* suono, rumore || — *wave,* onda sonora.

sound[4] *s.* sondaggio.

sound[5] *s.* braccio di mare, stretto.

to sound[1] *vt.* e *vi.* 1. suonare, risuonare 2. sembrare, aver l'aria di.

to sound[2] *vt.* e *vi.* sondare, scandagliare.

sounding *agg.* sonoro, sonante, risonante.

soundless *agg.* muto, senza suono.

soundly *avv.* 1. sanamente 2. profondamente.

soundness *s.* 1. buona condizione (*di salute*) 2. solidità (*di argomento*).

soup *s.* zuppa, minestra.

sour *agg.* 1. acido, aspro, acerbo 2. bisbetico.

to sour *vt.* e *vi.* 1. inacidire 2. inasprire, esacerbare.

source *s.* 1. fonte, sorgente 2. origine.

sourdine *s.* (*mus.*) sordina.

sourish *agg.* acidulo.

sourness *s.* acidità.

south *s.* sud, mezzogiorno.

southern *agg.* del sud, meridionale.

southerner *s.* abitante del sud, meridionale.

southward *avv.* verso sud.

sovereign *s.* sovrano.

sovereignty *s.* sovranità.

sow *s.* scrofa.

to sow (sowed, sown) *vt.* e *vi.* seminare, piantare.

sowing *s.* seminagione.

sown V. *to sow.*

spa *s.* sorgente minerale.

space *s.* spazio || — *-ship,* astronave.

to space *vt.* spaziare, disporre ad intervalli.

spaceman *s.* astronauta.

spacesuit *s.* tuta spaziale.

spacial *agg.* spaziale.

spacing *s.* spaziatura, interlineatura.

spacious *agg.* spazioso, ampio.

spade *s.* vanga, badile.

span V. *to spin.*

span *s.* 1. spanna, palmo 2. breve spazio di tempo.

to span *vt.* 1. misurare a spanne 2. attraversare.

spangle *s.* lustrino.

Spaniard *s.* spagnolo.

Spanish *agg.* spagnolo.

to spank *vt.* (*fam.*) sculacciare.

spar[1] *s.* (*mar.*) antenna.

spar[2] *s.* incontro di pugilato.

spare *agg.* **1.** parco, frugale **2.** d'avanzo, disponibile, in più || — *room*, camera in più (*per gli ospiti*); — *time*, tempo disponibile; — *wheel*, ruota di scorta.

to spare *vt.* **1.** economizzare, risparmiare **2.** privarsi, fare a meno di. ◆ **to spare** *vi.* essere frugale.

sparing *agg.* **1.** parco, frugale **2.** limitato, moderato.

spark *s.* **1.** scintilla, favilla **2.** (*fig.*) lampo, barlume.

to spark *vi.* scintillare, emettere scintille.

sparkle *s.* scintilla, favilla.

to sparkle *vi.* **1.** emettere scintille (*di fuoco*) **2.** sfavillare, brillare, risplendere (*anche fig.*).

sparkler *s.* stella filante.

sparkling *agg.* scintillante, vivace (*anche fig.*).

sparrow *s.* passero || — -*hawk*, sparviero.

Spartan *agg.* e *s.* spartano.

spasm *s.* **1.** spasmo **2.** attacco, spasimo (*anche fig.*).

spasmodic(al) *agg.* spasmodico.

spastic *agg.* spastico.

spat V. *to spit.*

spatial *agg.* spaziale.

spatiality *s.* spazialità.

spatter *s.* **1.** schizzo **2.** sgocciolio.

to spatter *vt.* e *vi.* **1.** schizzare, inzaccherare **2.** gocciolare.

to speak (spoke, spoken) *vt.* e *vi.* **1.** parlare **2.** esprimere, rivelare || *to* — *at*, alludere a; *to* — *out*, parlare francamente; *to* — *to*, garantire; *to* — *up*, alzare la voce.

speaker *s.* parlatore, oratore, annunciatore || *the* — *of the House of Commons*, il Presidente della Camera dei Comuni.

speaking *agg.* parlante, espressivo, eloquente. ◆ **speaking** *s.* **1.** il parlare, discorso **2.** eloquenza, declamazione.

spear *s.* **1.** lancia, alabarda, asta **2.** fiocina.

to spear *vt.* **1.** trafiggere (*con lancia*) **2.** fiocinare.

special *agg.* **1.** speciale, particolare **2.** eccezionale, straordinario.

specialist *s.* specialista.

speciality *s.* specialità, particolarità.

to specialize *vt.* specializzare. ◆ **to**

specialize *vi.* specializzarsi.

specially *avv.* specialmente, soprattutto.

specialty *s.* **1.** (*comm.*) specialità **2.** (*giur.*) contratto sigillato.

species *s.* **1.** specie, classe **2.** sorta, genere, tipo.

specific *agg.* specifico, particolare.

specification *s.* **1.** specificazione **2.** descrizione dettagliata.

to specify *vt.* specificare, precisare.

specimen *s.* modello, esemplare.

speck *s.* **1.** macchiolina, punto **2.** granello (*di polvere ecc.*).

speckled *agg.* macchiato, screziato.

speckless *agg.* senza macchia (*anche fig.*).

spectacle *s.* spettacolo, vista. ◆ **spectacles** *s. pl.* occhiali: *to put on one's* —, mettersi gli occhiali.

spectacled *agg.* che porta gli occhiali.

spectacular *agg.* spettacolare.

spectator *s.* spettatore.

spectral *agg.* spettrale.

spectre *s.* spettro, fantasma.

specular *agg.* speculare.

to speculate *vt.* e *vi.* **1.** meditare, considerare **2.** (*comm.*) speculare.

speculation *s.* **1.** speculazione, meditazione **2.** (*comm.*) speculazione.

speculative *agg.* contemplativo, speculativo (*anche comm.*).

speculator *s.* **1.** spirito speculatore **2.** (*comm.*) speculatore.

sped V. *to speed.*

speech *s.* **1.** parola, favella **2.** discorso, arringa **3.** linguaggio.

speechless *agg.* senza parola, muto (*anche fig.*).

speed *s.* velocità, rapidità.

to speed *vi.* affrettarsi. ◆ **to speed (sped, sped)** *vt.* **1.** aiutare **2.** affrettare **3.** regolare la velocità || *to* — *up the work*, affrettare i lavori.

speedometer *s.* tachimetro.

speedway *s.* pista, circuito (*di autodromo*).

speedy *agg.* rapido, pronto.

spell[1] *s.* incantesimo.

spell[2] *s.* **1.** turno di lavoro **2.** intervallo.

to spell (spelt, spelt) (*anche reg.*) *vt.* e *vi.* compitare, sillabare.

to spellbind (spellbound, spellbound) *vt.* incantare, affascinare.

spelling *s.* **1.** compitazione **2.** ortografia.

spelt V. *to spell.*
to spend (spent, spent) *vt.* e *vi.*
1. spendere, sborsare 2. dedicare, impiegare 3. passare, trascorrere.
sperm *s.* sperma.
sphenoid *agg.* e *s.* sfenoide.
sphere *s.* sfera, globo.
spheric(al) *agg.* sferico.
sphericity *s.* sfericità.
sphincter *s.* sfintere.
Sphinx *s.* sfinge (*anche fig.*).
spice *s.* 1. aroma 2. (*fig.*) sapore, gusto 3. spezie (*pl.*).
to spice *vt.* 1. condire con spezie 2. (*fig.*) dar gusto a, rendere interessante.
spicery *s.* spezie, aromi (*pl.*).
spicily *avv.* 1. aromaticamente 2. (*fig.*) gustosamente.
spiciness *s.* 1. aroma, profumo 2. (*fam.*) arguzia.
spick-and-span *agg.* (*fam.*) lindo, lucente.
spicy *agg.* 1. aromatico, piccante 2. (*fig.*) arguto, mordace.
spider *s.* ragno.
spidery *agg.* 1. simile a ragno 2. infestato da ragni.
spike[1] *s.* punta, aculeo.
spike[2] *s.* spiga.
to spike *vt.* inchiodare || *to — so.'s guns,* guastare i piani di qu.
to spill (spilt, spilt) *vt.* 1. versare 2. disarcionare. ♦ **to spill (spilt, spilt)** *vi.* versarsi, traboccare.
spin *s.* (*aer.*) avvitamento.
to spin (span, spun) *vt.* e *vi.* 1. filare (*cotone ecc.*) 2. (*mecc.*) lavorare al tornio 3. girare, far girare.
spinach *s.* spinacio.
spinal *agg.* spinale.
spindle *s.* 1. fuso, fusello 2. (*mecc.*) asse, mandrino.
spine *s.* 1. spina, lisca 2. spina dorsale.
spineless *agg.* 1. senza spine 2. senza spina dorsale 3. (*fam.*) debole, molle.
spinner *s.* 1. ragno filatore 2. (*aer.*) ogiva 3. filatore.
spinning *s.* 1. filatura, filato 2. movimento rotatorio || *— -mill,* filanda.
spinster *s.* 1. filatrice 2. donna nubile, zitella.
spiral *agg.* spirale, a spirale. ♦ **spiral** *s.* spirale.

spire[1] *s.* guglia, cuspide.
spire[2] *s.* spira, spirale.
spirit *s.* 1. spirito, anima 2. folletto, fantasma 3. genio, intelletto 4. coraggio, vigore.
spirits[1] *s. pl.* umore, stato d'animo (*sing.*).
spirits[2] *s. pl.* bevande fortemente alcooliche.
spirited *agg.* brioso, vivace || *high- -—,* fiero; *poor- —,* depresso.
spiritism *s.* spiritismo.
spiritual *agg.* spirituale.
spiritualism *s.* 1. spiritualismo 2. spiritismo.
spiritualist *s.* 1. spiritualista 2. spiritista.
spirituality *s.* spiritualità.
spit *s.* sputo, saliva.
to spit (spat, spat) *vi.* sputare.
spite *s.* dispetto, ripicco: *out of —,* per dispetto; *in — of,* a dispetto di.
spiteful *agg.* dispettoso.
spittle V. *spit.*
spittoon *s.* sputacchiera.
splash *s.* 1. schizzo, spruzzo 2. tonfo.
to splash *vt.* e *vi.* ⒈ schizzare, spruzzare 2. inzaccherare, infangare. ♦ **to splash** *vi.* 1. spruzzare 2. cadere con un tonfo.
splashy *agg.* bagnato, fangoso.
splay *agg.* largo e piatto. ♦ **splay** *s.* (*arch.*) strombatura.
to splay *vt.* (*arch.*) strombare. ♦ **to splay** *vi.* essere in posizione obliqua.
spleen *s.* 1. milza 2. (*fig.*) malumore, umore nero.
splendid *agg.* splendido, magnifico.
splendour *s.* splendore, lustro.
splenetic *agg.* e *s.* splenetico, bilioso.
splinter *s.* scheggia, frantume.
split *agg.* spaccato, diviso. ♦ **split** *s.* 1. fessura, crepaccio 2. scissione.
to split (split, split) *vt.* 1. fendere 2. spaccare, frazionare || *to — hairs,* spaccare un capello in quattro; *to — one's sides* (*with laughing*), ridere a crepapelle. ♦ **to split (split, split)** *vi.* fendersi.
splitting *agg.* che si fende, che fende. ♦ **splitting** *s.* fessura, spaccatura.
spoil(s) *s.* spoglia, preda.

to **spoil** (**spoilt, spoilt**) *(anche reg.) vt.* e *vi.* **1.** rovinare, alterare, sciupare, viziare **2.** saccheggiare, predare.

spoilt *agg.* **1.** guasto, avariato **2.** viziato.

spoke *s.* **1.** raggio *(di ruota)* **2.** piolo *(di scala).*

spoke V. *to speak.*

spoken V. *to speak.*

spokesman *s.* portavoce.

spoliation *s.* ruberia, saccheggio.

sponge *s.* spugna, colpo di spugna.

to **sponge** *vt.* **1.** pulire, lavare con la spugna **2.** fare spugnature **3.** *(fig.; fam.)* scroccare.

sponger *s.* **1.** pescatore di spugne **2.** scroccone.

spongy *agg.* spugnoso, poroso.

sponsor *s.* **1.** padrino, madrina **2.** *(giur.)* garante, mallevadore.

to **sponsor** *vt.* **1.** essere garante di **2.** offrire *(programmi radio, tv).*

sponsorial *agg.* **1.** di garanzia **2.** di padrino, di madrina.

sponsorship *s.* **1.** garanzia **2.** qualità di padrino, di madrina.

spontaneity *s.* spontaneità.

spontaneous *agg.* spontaneo.

spontaneously *avv.* spontaneamente.

spool *s.* rocchetto, bobina.

spoon *s.* cucchiaio.

to **spoon** *vt.* prendere con un cucchiaio.

spoon-fed *agg.* coccolato, viziato.

spoonful *s.* cucchiaiata.

sporadic *agg.* sporadico, raro.

sport *s.* **1.** giuoco, divertimento **2.** scherzo **3.** sport. ♦ **sports** *s. pl* gare, incontri.

to **sport** *vi.* **1.** scherzare **2.** giocare **3.** fare dello sport.

sporting *agg.* sportivo.

sportive *agg.* **1.** gioviale **2.** sportivo.

sportsman *s.* **1.** sportivo **2.** uomo animato da spirito sportivo.

sportsmanlike *agg.* caratteristico di uno sportivo.

sportswoman *s.* donna sportiva.

spot *s.* **1.** luogo, località **2.** macchia *(anche fig.)* || *on the* —, sul colpo.

to **spot** *vt.* macchiare, punteggiare. ♦ to **spot** *vi.* macchiarsi.

spotless *agg.* senza macchia, immacolato *(anche fig.).*

spotlight *s.* riflettore, luce della ribalta.

spotty *agg.* macchiato, chiazzato.

spout *s.* **1.** tubo di scarico, grondaia **2.** getto, colonna *(d'acqua).*

to **spout** *vt.* scaricare, emettere. ♦ to **spout** *vi.* scaturire, zampillare.

sprain *s.* distorsione, strappo muscolare.

to **sprain** *vt.* storcere, slogare.

sprang V. *to spring.*

to **sprawl** *vi.* sdraiarsi in modo scomposto.

spray *s.* **1.** spruzzo, schiuma **2.** getto vaporizzato *(di acqua ecc.)* **3.** spruzzatore.

to **spray** *vt.* **1.** polverizzare, vaporizzare **2.** aspergere, spruzzare.

sprayer *s.* spruzzatore.

spread *agg.* steso, aperto, spiegato.

to **spread** (**spread, spread**) *vt.* **1.** stendere, spiegare, spalmare **2.** *(fig.)* spargere, diffondere. ♦ to **spread** (**spread, spread**) *vi.* stendersi, spiegarsi.

spreader *s.* spruzzatore.

spreading *agg.* che si propaga. ♦ **spreading** *s.* *(fig.)* propagazione.

spree *s.* baldoria.

sprig *s.* **1.** ramoscello **2.** *(fig.)* rampollo.

spring *s.* **1.** sorgente, fonte **2.** primavera **3.** salto, balzo **4.** molla, elasticità || — *-board,* trampolino; — *-head,* fontana; — *-mattress,* materasso a molle.

to **spring** (**sprang, sprung**) *vi.* **1.** nascere, discendere, scaturire *(di acqua)* **2.** saltare **3.** scattare || *to* — *up,* crescere *(di piante).* ♦ to **spring** (**sprang, sprung**) *vt.* **1.** far scattare *(con una molla)* **2.** far brillare *(una mina)* **3.** saltare.

springiness *s.* elasticità.

springy *agg.* **1.** pieno di sorgenti **2.** elastico.

sprinkle *s.* aspersione, spruzzatina.

to **sprinkle** *vt.* e *vi.* spruzzare, aspergere.

sprinkler *s.* **1.** spruzzatore, innaffiatoio **2.** aspersorio.

sprint *s.* *(sport)* scatto finale.

to **sprout** *vi.* germogliare. ♦ to **sprout** *vt.* far germogliare.

to **spruce** *vt.* adornare, agghindare.

sprung V. *to spring.* ♦ **sprung** *agg.* **1.** a molla **2.** spaccato.

spun V. *to spin.*

spur *s.* **1.** sperone **2.** *(fig.)* sprone.

to **spur** *vt.* **1.** spronare **2.** *(fig.)* incitare.

to **spurn** *vt.* e *vi.* disdegnare, trattare con disprezzo.

spurt *s.* getto, vampata.

spy *s.* spia.

to **spy** *vt.* e *vi.* spiare, fare la spia.

squabble *s.* battibecco, lite.

to **squabble** *vi.* accapigliarsi, venire a parole.

squad *s.* squadra, ... one.

squalid *agg.* squallido, miserabile.

squall *s.* urlo, strepito.

squalor *s.* squallore.

to **squander** *vt.* sprecare, scialacquare.

squanderer *s.* sciupone, sperperatore.

square *agg.* **1.** quadrato **2.** robusto, massiccio **3.** perpendicolare. ◆ **square** *s.* **1.** quadrato **2.** piazza **3.** squadra || — -*built*, tarchiato; — -*root*, radice quadrata; — -*shouldered*, dalle spalle larghe e diritte. ◆ **square** *avv.* ad angolo retto, in squadra.

to **square** *vt.* e *vi.* **1.** quadrare, squadrare **2.** pareggiare un conto **3.** elevare al quadrato.

squared *agg.* **1.** squadrato, quadrato **2.** elevato al quadrato.

squash *s.* **1.** cosa schiacciata **2.** spremuta (*di frutta*): orange- —, spremuta d'arancio.

to **squash** *vt.* **1.** schiacciare, spiaccicare **2.** spremere.

squat *agg.* rannicchiato, accoccolato.

to **squat** *vi.* accovacciarsi, accoccolarsi.

squatter *s.* pioniere.

squeak *s.* **1.** grido acuto **2.** pigolio, squittio, guaito **3.** cigolio.

to **squeak** *vt.* e *vi.* **1.** strillare in tono acuto **2.** squittire, guaire **3.** cigolare.

squeaky *agg.* **1.** che strilla **2.** che guaisce, squittisce **3.** cigolante.

squeamish *agg.* **1.** soggetto a nausee **2.** schizzinoso.

squeeze *s.* **1.** compressione **2.** spremitura **3.** stretta, abbraccio.

to **squeeze** *vt.* **1.** spremere **2.** stringere, abbracciare. ◆ to **squeeze** *vi.* accalcarsi.

squeezer *s.* **1.** ciò che preme **2.** (*mecc.*) torchio.

squid *s.* seppia.

squint *agg.* strabico. ◆ **squint** *s.* strabismo.

to **squint** *vi.* essere strabico. ◆ to **squint** *vt.* guardare di traverso.

squire *s.* gentiluomo, nobiluomo (*di campagna*).

squirrel *s.* scoiattolo.

stab *s.* coltellata, pugnalata.

to **stab** *vt.* pugnalare, accoltellare.

to **stabilize** *vt.* stabilizzare.

stabilizer *s.* stabilizzatore.

stable[1] *agg.* stabile, permanente.

stable[2] *s.* scuderia, stalla.

stack *s.* mucchio, cumulo || chimney- —, ciminiera.

to **stack** *vt.* ammucchiare, accumulare.

staff *s.* **1.** bastone, sostegno (*anche fig.*) **2.** stato maggiore **3.** personale (*di ufficio ecc.*) || editorial —, corpo redazionale; flag —, asta della bandiera.

stag *s.* cervo.

stage *s.* **1.** piattaforma **2.** palcoscenico **3.** (*fig.*) campo d'azione, scena **4.** stadio, grado **5.** tappa || — -direction, didascalia; — -director, regista (*teat.*); — -effect, effetto scenico; — -name, nome d'arte; landing- — (*mar.*), pontile.

to **stage** *vt.* **1.** mettere in scena **2.** inscenare (*una dimostrazione ecc.*).

stagger *s.* barcollamento, andatura a zig-zag.

to **stagger** *vi.* **1.** vacillare **2.** dubitare, esitare. ◆ to **stagger** *vt.* far vacillare.

staginess *s.* teatralità.

staging *s.* **1.** (*teat.*) messa in scena **2.** (*edil.*) impalcatura.

stagnancy *s.* ristagno.

stagnant *agg.* stagnante.

to **stagnate** *vi.* ristagnare.

stagnation *s.* ristagno, stasi.

staid *agg.* posato, serio.

stain *s.* **1.** scolorimento, macchia **2.** (*fig.*) taccia, onta.

to **stain** *vt.* **1.** macchiare **2.** tingere. ◆ to **stain** *vi.* macchiarsi, sporcarsi.

stained *agg.* macchiato, sporco.

stainless *agg.* senza macchia.

stair *s.* scalino, gradino. ◆ **stairs** *s. pl.* scale || winding- —, scala a chiocciola; flight of —, rampa di scale.

staircase *s.* **1.** scala, scalone **2.** tromba delle scale.

stairway *s.* scalinata.

stake[1] *s.* **1.** palo, paletto **2.** piccola incudine.

stake[2] *s.* posta, scommessa || at —, in giuoco. ◆ **stakes** *s. pl.* (*ippica*) premio, corsa.

to **stake**[1] *vt.* cintare, chiudere (*con una palizzata*).

to **stake**[2] *vt.* mettere in giuoco, scommettere.

stale *agg.* 1. vecchio, stantio 2. (*fig.*) trito, caduto in disuso.

stalk[1] *s.* stelo, gambo.

stalk[2] *s.* andatura rigida e maestosa.

stall *s.* 1. stalla 2. bancarella, chiosco.

stammer *s.* balbuzie, balbettamento.

to **stammer** *vt.* e *vi.* 1. balbettare 2. farfugliare.

stammering *agg.* balbuziente. ◆ **stammering** *s.* balbuzie.

stamp *s.* 1. impronta, segno 2. francobollo, bollo 3. stampo || — -*collector*, filatelico; — -*paper*, carta bollata.

to **stamp** *vt.* 1. imprimere, incidere 2. (*fig.*) dare l'impronta 3. timbrare || *to* — *down*, calpestare. ◆ to **stamp** *vi.* battere i piedi.

stamping *s.* 1. scalpitio 2. timbratura.

stand *s.* 1. pausa, fermata 2. punto di vista 3. posizione, luogo (*d'appostamento*) 4. palco, tribuna 5. bancarella, chiosco || *test-* —, banco di prova.

to **stand (stood, stood)** *vi.* 1. essere, stare in piedi 2. stare, trovarsi 3. fermarsi, indugiare 4. conservarsi, rimaner valido || *to* — *by*, stare accanto, restare fedele a; *to* — *for*, significare, implicare; *to* — *out*, resistere, tener duro, spiccare. ◆ to **stand (stood, stood)** *vt.* sopportare, resistere.

standard *s.* 1. stendardo, bandiera 2. modello, campione 3. livello, qualità 4. supporto, base 5. tipo.

standardization *s.* standardizzazione.

stand-by *s.* scorta, riserva.

standing *agg.* 1. eretto, che sta in piedi 2. fermo, inattivo 3. fisso, immutabile. ◆ **standing** *s.* 1. posizione eretta 2. posizione, rango 3. periodo di tempo.

standoffish *agg.* riservato, altezzoso.

standpoint *s.* 1. luogo di osservazione 2. punto di vista.

standstill *agg.* in riposo, fermo. ◆ **standstill** *s.* arresto, fermata.

stank V. *to stink.*

staple *s.* 1. prodotto principale (*di un paese ecc.*) 2. (*fig.*) argomento principale (*di una conversazione*).

star *s.* 1. stella, astro 2. (*fig.*) fortuna, destino 3. (*tip.*) asterisco.

to **star** *vt.* 1. costellare 2. segnare con un asterisco. ◆ to **star** *vi.* (*cine, teat.*) avere il ruolo di protagonista.

starboard *agg.* di dritta. ◆ **starboard** *s.* (*mar.*) dritta.

starch *s.* 1. amido 2. (*fig.*) rigidezza, formalismo.

to **starch** *vt.* 1. inamidare 2. (*fig.*) rendere formale.

starchiness *s.* 1. inamidatura 2. (*fig.*) formalismo, rigidità.

stardom *s.* divismo.

stare *s.* sguardo fisso.

to **stare** *vt.* guardare intensamente, fissare. ◆ to **stare** *vi.* sgranare gli occhi.

starfish *s.* stella di mare.

staring *agg.* 1. fisso, stupefatto 2. sgargiante, vistoso.

staringly *avv.* fissamente, con occhi sbarrati.

stark *agg.* 1. rigido, duro 2. completo, vero e proprio.

starless *agg.* senza stelle.

starlet *s.* 1. piccola stella 2. (*cine*) stellina.

starlight *agg.* stellato, stellare. ◆ **starlight** *s.* luce stellare.

starlike *agg.* simile a stella.

starlit *agg.* illuminato dalle stelle.

starred *agg.* 1. stellato, adorno di stelle 2. a stella.

starry *agg.* stellato, trapunto di stelle, brillante come una stella.

start *s.* 1. inizio, partenza 2. soprassalto || *by fits and starts*, irregolarmente 3. vantaggio dato all'inizio di una corsa 4. (*mecc.*) avviamento.

to **start** *vi.* 1. partire, mettersi in viaggio 2. cominciare 3. trasalire || *to* — *up*, *out*, aver intenzione di; *to* — *up*, spuntare all'improvviso. ◆ to **start** *vt.* 1. cominciare 2. far trasalire.

starter *s.* 1. iniziatore, fondatore 2. (*sport*) "starter", mossiere.

starting *s.* 1. inizio, partenza 2. debutto 3. (*mecc.*) messa in moto, avviamento.

startle *s.* trasalimento.

to **startle** *vt.* spaventare, far trasalire. ◆ to **startle** *vi.* spaventarsi, trasalire.

startling *agg.* impressionante, sorprendente.

starvation *s.* inedia, fame.

to starve *vi.* 1. morire di fame 2. (*fig.*) bramare. ◆ **to starve** *vt.* far morire di fame.

state *s.* 1. stato, condizione 2. governo, nazione 3. rango, dignità || — -*control*, statalizzazione; — -*documents*, documenti ufficiali; — -*prisoner*, prigioniero politico; — -*trial*, processo politico.

to state *vt.* 1. affermare, dichiarare 2. stabilire.

stateless *agg.* 1. senza patria 2. senza pompa 3. apolide.

stately *agg.* nobile, signorile.

statement *s.* 1. esposto, relazione 2. asserzione, affermazione 3. (*giur.*) deposizione, esposizione dei fatti.

statesman *s.* statista.

static(al) *agg.* statico.

statics *s.* statica.

station *s.* 1. posto, luogo, base 2. stazione 3. condizione sociale || *petrol* —, stazione di rifornimento; *through* —, stazione di transito.

stationary *agg.* stazionario.

stationer *s.* cartolaio || —'*s* (*shop*), cartoleria.

stationery *s.* articoli di cancelleria.

station house *s.* guardina.

stationmaster *s.* capostazione.

statist *s.* statista.

statistic(al) *agg.* statistico.

statistically *avv.* statisticamente.

statistics *s.* 1. scienza della statistica 2. statistiche (*pl.*).

statuary *agg.* statuario, scultorio.

statue *s.* statua.

statuesque *agg.* statuario.

stature *s.* statura.

status *s.* 1. stato, condizione sociale 2. situazione.

statute *s.* statuto, regolamento.

statutory *agg.* statutario.

to staunch *vt.* 1. arrestare 2. stagnare. ◆ **to staunch** *vi.* stagnarsi.

stave *s.* 1. doga (*di botte*) 2. piolo (*di scala*) 3. strofa.

stay[1] *s.* 1. soggiorno 2. pausa.

stay[2] *s.* 1. sostegno, supporto 2. (*mecc.*) puntello.

to stay[1] *vi.* 1. fermarsi, sostare, soggiornare 2. resistere || *to* — *away*, essere assente; *to* — *in*, stare in casa, (*mil.*) essere consegnato; *to*

— *up*, vegliare. ◆ **to stay** *vt.* 1. arrestare, fermare 2. resistere.

to stay[2] *vt.* (*mecc.*) puntellare.

steadfast *agg.* fermo, risoluto.

steadfastly *avv.* stabilmente, fermamente.

steadfastness *s.* fermezza, tenacia.

steadily *avv.* 1. saldamente, fermamente 2. costantemente.

steadiness *s.* 1. fermezza, sicurezza 2. assiduità, perseveranza.

steading *s.* tenuta agricola.

steady *agg.* 1. fermo, saldo 2. equilibrato 3. continuo, regolare 4. fedele, assiduo.

to steady *vt.* rafforzare, rendere fermo, equilibrato. ◆ **to steady** *vi.* rafforzarsi.

steak *s.* bistecca.

to steal (stole, stolen) *vt.* e *vi.* rubare || *to* — *along*, camminare furtivamente; *to* — *away*, svignarsela; *to* — *upon*, avvicinarsi pian piano.

stealing *s.* furto || *cattle* (*o borse*)- —, abigeato.

stealthily *avv.* furtivamente.

stealthy *agg.* furtivo.

steam *s.* vapore: — -*engine*, macchina a vapore.

to steam *vt.* 1. esporre al vapore 2. cucinare al vapore. ◆ **to steam** *vi.* emettere vapore.

steamboat *s.* imbarcazione a vapore.

steamer *s.* nave a vapore.

steamship *s.* piroscafo.

steamtight *agg.* a tenuta di vapore.

steamy *agg.* 1. che esala vapore 2. appannato, umido.

stearic *agg.* stearico.

steel *s.* 1. acciaio 2. arma, spada 3. acciarino || — *cap*, elmetto; — *company*, acciaieria || *stainless* —, acciaio inossidabile.

steelwork *s.* lavoro, struttura in acciaio.

steelwork *s. pl.* acciaieria (*sing.*).

steely *agg.* 1. di acciaio, simile ad acciaio 2. (*fig.*) severissimo.

steelyard *s.* stadera.

steep[1] *agg.* 1. ripido, scosceso 2. (*fig.*) ambizioso, arduo 3. esorbitante (*di prezzi*).

steep[2] *s.* macerazione, l'inzuppare.

to steep *vt.* immergere (*anche fig.*), inzuppare.

steeple *s.* guglia, campanile.

steeplechase *s.* (*ippica*) corsa ad

ostacoli.

steer s. bue giovane, manzo.

to **steer** vt. **1.** governare, manovrare **2.** dirigere. ♦ to **steer** vi. **1.** dirigersi **2.** (auto) sterzare.

steering s. guida, governo (dello sterzo, del timone).

stem s. **1.** tronco, gambo, stelo **2.** cannello (di pipa) **3.** (mar.) prua.

to **stem** vt. arrestare, arginare.

stench s. puzzo, tanfo.

step s. **1.** passo (anche fig.), andatura **2.** orma, impronta **3.** provvedimento **4.** gradino || to be in — with so., tenere il passo con qu.; — by —, gradualmente; in — (elett.), in fase.

to **step** vi. camminare || to — aside, farsi da parte; to — forward, avanzare; to — in, montare (su un veicolo). ♦ to **step** vt. misurare a passi.

stepbrother s. fratellastro.

stepchild s. (pl. -children) figliastro.

stepdaughter s. figliastra.

stepfather s. patrigno.

stepmother s. matrigna.

stepsister s. sorellastra.

stepson s. figliastro.

stereophonic agg. stereofonico.

stereophony s. stereofonia.

stereoscope s. stereoscopio.

stereotype s. stereotipo.

sterile agg. sterile.

sterility s. sterilità.

to **sterilize** vt. rendere sterile, sterilizzare.

stern[1] agg. severo, austero.

stern[2] s. (mar.) poppa.

sternly avv. severamente.

sternness s. severità, austerità.

stethoscope s. stetoscopio.

stevedore s. scaricatore (di porto).

stew s. (cuc.) umido, stufato.

to **stew** vt. e vi. cuocere in umido.

steward s. **1.** amministratore, intendente **2.** (aer., mar.) cameriere di bordo.

stewardess s. **1.** dispensiere **2.** (aer., mar.) cameriera di bordo.

stick s. **1.** bastone **2.** bastoncino **3.** barra, stecca.

to **stick** (stuck, stuck) vt. **1.** ficcare, conficcare **2.** infilare **3.** incollare, appicciare. ♦ to **stick** (stuck, stuck) vi. **1.** fissarsi, conficcarsi **2.** incollarsi.

stickiness s. viscosità, adesività.

sticky agg. **1.** appiccicaticcio, visco-

so **2.** poco accomodante.

stiff agg. **1.** rigido, duro **2.** (fig.) inflessibile **3.** indolenzito, intorpidito **4.** freddo, riservato || — collar, colletto duro; — -neck, torcicollo.

to **stiffen** vt. **1.** indurire **2.** indolenzire, intorpidire **3.** rassodare. ♦ to **stiffen** vi. **1.** indurirsi, irrigidirsi (anche fig.) **2.** rassodarsi.

stiffness s. **1.** durezza, rigidezza **2.** intorpidimento.

to **stifle** vt. **1.** soffocare **2.** (fig.) reprimere. ♦ to **stifle** vi. sentirsi soffocare.

stifling agg. soffocante.

to **stigmatize** vt. **1.** marchiare **2.** stigmatizzare.

stile s. scaletta.

still[1] agg. tranquillo, calmo, silenzioso || — -life (pitt.), natura morta.

still[2] avv. **1.** ancora, tuttora **2.** tuttavia, nondimeno.

still[3] s. alambicco.

to **still** vt. acquietare, calmare. ♦ to **still** vi. acquietarsi, calmarsi.

stillness s. calma, quiete.

stilt s. trampolo.

stimulant s. **1.** stimolante **2.** bevanda alcolica.

to **stimulate** vt. stimolare, incitare.

stimulus s. (pl.- li) stimolo, incentivo.

sting s. **1.** pungiglione, aculeo **2.** puntura d'insetto **3.** dolore acuto **4.** pungolo, stimolo.

to **sting** (stung, stung) vt. e vi. **1.** pungere **2.** colpire, ferire (anche fig.).

stinginess s. avarizia, spilorceria.

stinging agg. pungente, mordace.

stingy agg. avaro, taccagno.

stink s. puzzo, fetore.

to **stink** (stank, stunk) vt. e vi. puzzare, riempire di puzzo.

stinking agg. puzzolente, fetido.

to **stipulate** vt. e vi. stipulare.

stipulation s. stipulazione, patto.

stir s. **1.** il rimescolare, l'attizzare || to give a —, dare una rimescolata **2.** animazione, tumulto.

to **stir** vt. **1.** rimescolare **2.** muovere, agitare. ♦ to **stir** vi. muoversi, agitarsi.

stirabout agg. indaffarato.

stirrer s. incitatore, istigatore.

stirring agg. eccitante.

stirrup s. staffa.

stitch s. **1.** punto **2.** maglia.

stock s. 1. rifornimento, provvista || *to be out of* —, essere sprovvisto 2. titoli, azioni (*pl.*) 3. tronco, ceppo 4. (*fig.*) stirpe.

to stock *vt.* 1. approvvigionare 2. tenere in magazzino.

stockbroker s. agente di cambio.

stockbroking s. professione dell'agente di cambio.

stock company s. società per azioni.

Stock Exchange s. Borsa valori.

stockfish s. stoccafisso.

stockholder s. azionista.

stocking s.' calza lunga.

stoic *agg.* e s. stoico.

stoicism s. stoicismo.

stoker s. fuochista.

stole V. *to steal.*

stolen V. *to steal.*

stolid *agg.* 1. imperturbabile 2. sciocco.

stolidity s. flemma.

stomach s. stomaco: — *-ache*, mal di stomaco.

stomatitis s. stomatite.

stomatology s. stomatologia.

stone s. 1. pietra, ciottolo, sasso 2. nocciolo 3. (*med.*) calcolo || — *-blind*, completamente cieco; — *-breaker*, spaccapietre; — *cutter*, tagliapietre.

to stone *vt.* 1. lapidare 2. rivestire di pietra 3. snocciolare.

stoneless *agg.* senza nocciolo.

stoneware s. ceramica.

stony *agg.* 1. pietroso, sassoso 2. (*fig.*) duro, insensibile.

stood V. *to stand.*

stool s. sgabello, seggiolino.

stoop s. curvatura, inchino.

to stoop *vi.* 1. curvare, inchinarsi 2. (*fig.*) accondiscendere, abbassarsi.

stop s. 1. sosta, arresto 2. segno di punteggiatura || — *watch*, cronometro.

to stop *vt.* 1. fermare 2. turare, otturare 3. impedire. ♦ **to stop** *vi.* fermarsi.

stopper s. 1. tappo, turacciolo 2. otturatore.

stopping s. 1. otturazione 2. (*comm.*) cessazione, sospensione (*di pagamenti ecc.*).

storage s. 1. immagazzinamento 2. deposito, magazzino.

store s. 1. provvista, riserva 2. magazzino || — *-keeper*, magazzinie-

re; — *-ship*, nave da carico.

to store *vt.* 1. fornire, rifornire 2. immagazzinare, mettere da parte (*anche fig.*).

storehouse s. magazzino, deposito.

storey s. piano (*di edificio*).

stork s. cicogna.

storm s. 1. tempesta, temporale 2. tumulto, agitazione.

to storm *vi.* 1. infuriare, scatenarsi 2. (*fam.*) adirarsi. ♦ **to storm** *vt.* attaccare.

stormy *agg.* tempestoso, burrascoso.

story s. storia, racconto, novella, favola || *to tell stories*, contar frottole.

stoup s. acquasantiera.

stout *agg.* 1. forte, robusto, resistente 2. fermo, risoluto 3. grosso, tozzo.

stove s. 1. stufa 2. cucina economica: *gas*- —, cucina a gas.

to stove *vt.* mettere in forno, stufa.

to stow *vt.* stivare, riempire.

stowage s. (*mar.*) stivaggio.

straddle s. posizione a gambe divaricate, il mettersi a cavalcioni.

to straddle *vt.* stare a cavalcioni di. ♦ **to straddle** *vi.* mettersi a gambe divaricate.

straight[1] *agg.* 1. diritto, rettilineo 2. onesto, retto 3. ordinato || *a* — *whisky*, un whisky liscio.

straight[2] s. 1. posizione diritta 2. (*fig.*) condotta onesta.

straight[3] *avv.* 1. diritto, in linea retta 2. direttamente.

to straighten *vt.* raddrizzare. ♦ **to straighten** *vi.* raddrizzarsi.

straightforward *agg.* 1. diritto, diretto 2. schietto, leale.

straightforwardly *avv.* 1. in linea retta 2. francamente, schiettamente.

strain s. 1. tensione (*anche fig.*) 2. sforzo, fatica 3. distorsione, strappo muscolare.

to strain *vt.* 1. sottoporre a tensione 2. sforzare. ♦ **to strain** *vi.* sforzarsi.

strained *agg.* 1. teso 2. indebolito 3. non spontaneo, forzato.

strainer s. colino, filtro.

strait s. (*geogr.*) stretto. ♦ **to strand** *vi.* incagliarsi.

stranding s. incagliamento (*di una nave*).

strange *agg.* 1. strano, bizzarro 2. estraneo, sconosciuto.

stranger *s.* estraneo, sconosciuto, forestiero.
to strangle *vt.* strangolare.
strangling *s.* strangolamento.
strap *s.* **1.** cinghia, correggia **2.** maniglia a pendaglio (*su tram ecc.*).
to strap *vt.* legare con cinghia.
stratagem *s.* stratagemma.
strategic(al) *agg.* strategico.
strategist *s.* stratega.
strategy *s.* strategia.
stratification *s.* stratificazione.
to stratify *vt.* stratificare.
stratosphere *s.* stratosfera.
stratospheric *agg.* stratosferico.
stratum *s.* (*pl.* -ta) **1.** strato **2.** strato sociale.
straw *s.* **1.** paglia **2.** fuscello, cannuccia || — (*-hat*), paglietta; — *-colour*, giallo paglierino.
strawberry *s.* fragola.
stray *agg.* **1.** smarrito, randagio **2.** casuale. ♦ **stray** *s.* animale domestico smarrito.
to stray *vi.* vagare, vagabondare (*anche fig.*).
streak *s.* **1.** striscia, striatura **2.** vena (*anche fig.*).
to streak *vt.* **1.** striare **2.** venare.
stream *s.* **1.** corso d'acqua, ruscello **2.** flusso, fiotto **3.** corrente (*anche fig.*).
to stream *vi.* **1.** scorrere, fluire **2.** ondeggiare || *to — out,* effondersi. ♦ **to stream** *vt.* far scorrere.
street *s.* via, strada || *one-way* —, strada a senso unico.
streetwalker *s.* passeggiatrice.
strength *s.* **1.** forza, vigore **2.** solidità, tenacia.
to strengthen *vt.* rafforzare, irrobustire. ♦ **to strengthen** *vi.* rafforzarsi, irrobustirsi.
strengthening *agg.* fortificante.
strenuous *agg.* strenuo, energico.
strenuously *avv.* strenuamente.
strenuousness *s.* vigore.
streptococcus *s.* (*pl.* -cci) streptococco.
streptomycin *s.* streptomicina.
stress *s.* **1.** sforzo, pressione **2.** enfasi **3.** accento tonico.
to stress *vt.* **1.** forzare **2.** accentuare **3.** porre in rilievo.
stretch *s.* **1.** stiramento, tensione **2.** spazio di tempo **3.** distesa, estensione.
to stretch *vt.* tirare, tendere, stendere. ♦ **to stretch** *vi.* estendersi.

stretcher *s.* **1.** tenditore **2.** lettiga.
to strew (strewed, strewn) *vt.* spargere, sparpagliare.
strict *agg.* **1.** preciso, esatto **2.** (*fig.*) severo, rigido.
strictly *avv.* **1.** esattamente **2.** severamente.
stridden V. *to stride*.
stride *s.* passo lungo, andatura || *to make great strides,* avanzare a grandi passi.
to stride (strode, stridden) *vi.* camminare a grandi passi.
strident *agg.* stridente.
strife *s.* contesa, lotta.
strike *s.* **1.** sciopero **2.** scoperta (*di giacimento*) **3.** attacco aereo.
to strike (struck, struck) *vt.* e *vi.* **1.** battere, colpire **2.** (*fig.*) impressionare, colpire **3.** suonare le ore **4.** accendere (*un fiammifero*) **5.** scioperare || *to — down,* abbattere; *to — in,* frapporsi.
striker *s.* **1.** scioperante **2.** (*mecc.*) percussore.
striking *agg.* sorprendente.
string *s.* **1.** spago, cordicella **2.** laccio **3.** (*mus.*) corda.
to string (strung, strung) *vt.* e *vi.* **1.** legare con corde **2.** accordare (*uno strumento*) || *to — up,* impiccare.
strip *s.* striscia, nastro.
to strip *vt.* svestire. ♦ **to strip** *vi.* svestirsi.
stripe *s.* striscia, lista.
to stripe *vt.* rigare, listare.
striped *agg.* a righe, a strisce.
to strive (strove, striven) *vi.* sforzarsi.
strode V. *to stride*.
stroke *s.* **1.** colpo, percossa **2.** movimento **3.** bracciata (*al nuoto*), remata, battuta (*al tennis*) **4.** tratto (*di penna ecc.*) **5.** rintocco (*d'orologio*) **6.** (*med.*) colpo **7.** carezza.
to stroke[1] *vi.* vogare in cadenza.
to stroke[2] *vt.* accarezzare, lisciare.
stroll *s.* passeggiatina, quattro passi.
to stroll *vi.* gironzolare.
strolling *agg.* errante, girovago.
strong *agg.* forte, robusto, energico.
stronghold *s.* roccaforte.
strontium *s.* stronzio.
strove V. *to strive*.
struck V. *to strike*.
structural *agg.* strutturale.
structure *s.* **1.** struttura **2.** costruzione.

struggle s. 1. lotta, combattimento 2. sforzo || hand-to-hand —, lotta corpo a corpo.
to struggle vi. 1. lottare, divincolarsi 2. (fig.) sforzarsi.
struggler s. contendente, chi lotta.
to strum vt. e vi. strimpellare.
strumpet s. prostituta.
strung V. to string.
strut s. andatura solenne.
to strut vi. incedere con sussiego.
stub s. 1. ceppo 2. mozzicone.
stubble s. stoppia.
stubborn agg. ostinato, cocciuto, tenace, ribelle.
stubbornness s. caparbietà, tenacia.
to stucco vt. stuccare.
stuck V. to stick.
stud s. 1. chiodo a capocchia larga 2. bottoncino (da camicia).
to stud vt. guarnire di borchie.
student s. studente.
studentship s. borsa di studio.
studied agg. 1. studiato, ricercato 2. colto.
studio s. 1. studio (d'artista) 2. teatro di posa.
studious agg. studioso, diligente.
study s. 1. studio 2. esame attento, investigazione.
to study vt. e vi. 1. studiare 2. esaminare attentamente.
stuff s. 1. sostanza, materia prima 2. cosa, roba 3. stoffa, tessuto.
to stuff vt. 1. imbottire 2. (cuc.) farcire 3. rimpinzare.
stuffing s. 1. imbottitura 2. (cuc.) ripieno.
stuffy agg. afoso || — air, aria viziata.
to stumble vi. 1. inciampare 2. (fig.) fare passi falsi.
stump s. 1. ceppo, tronco 2. radice (di dente) 3. piattaforma, podio. ;
to stun vt. stordire, tramortire.
stung V. to sting.
stunk V. to stink.
stunt s. (gergo) 1. bravata, esibizione 2. trovata pubblicitaria, notizia sensazionale.
stupefaction s. 1. stupore 2. torpore provocato da stupefacenti.
to stupefy vt. 1. istupidire 2. abbrutire. ◆ to **stupefy** vi. 1. istupidirsi 2. abbrutirsi.
stupendous agg. splendido, stupendo.
stupid agg. stupido, ottuso.
stupidity s. stupidità.

stupidly avv. stupidamente.
sturdy agg. 1. vigoroso, forte 2. risoluto.
to stutter vt. e vi. balbettare.
stuttering s. balbuzie.
sty s. porcile.
style s. 1. stile (anche fig.) 2. modello, genere 3. moda.
to style vt. chiamare, denominare.
stylist s. stilista.
stylistic agg. stilistico.
stylization s. stilizzazione.
to stylize vt. stilizzare.
stylographic agg. stilografico.
stylus s. stilo.
subalpine agg. subalpino.
subaltern s. subalterno.
subaquatic agg. subacqueo.
subclass s. sottoclasse.
subcommission s. sottocommissione.
subcommissioner s. vice-commissario.
subcommittee s. sottocomitato.
subconscious agg. e s. subcosciente.
subcutaneous agg. sottocutaneo.
subdeacon s. suddiacono.
to subdivide vt. suddividere. ◆ to **subdivide** vi. suddividersi.
subdivisible agg. suddivisibile.
subdivision s. suddivisione.
subdual s. 1. soggiogamento 2. attenuazione.
to subdue vt. 1. conquistare, soggiogare 2. ridurre, attenuare.
subgovernor s. vicegovernatore.
subject[1] agg. 1. soggetto, assoggettato 2. sottoposto, esposto a.
subject[2] s. 1. argomento, materia di studio 2. (gramm.) soggetto 3. suddito.
to subject vt. 1. assoggettare 2. esporre.
subjection s. 1. assoggettamento 2. dipendenza.
subjective agg. soggettivo.
subjectivism s. soggettivismo.
subjunctive agg. congiuntivo.
sublease s. subaffitto.
to sublease vt. subaffittare.
to sublet (sublet, sublet) vt. subaffittare.
sublieutenancy s. grado di sottotenente.
sublieutenant s. sottotenente.
sublimate agg. e s. sublimato.
to sublimate vt. sublimare.
sublime agg. e s. sublime.

sublimity *s.* sublimità.
submarine *agg.* subacqueo. ♦ **sub-marine** *s.* sommergibile.
submariner *s.* sommergibilista.
to **submerge** *vt.* immergere, sommergere. ♦ to **submerge** *vi.* immergersi.
submergence *s.* sommersione.
submersible *agg.* affondabile.
submersion *s.* immersione.
submission *s.* sottomissione, docilità.
submissive *agg.* remissivo, docile.
submissively *avv.* in modo remissivo.
submissiveness *s.* sottomissione.
to **submit** *vt.* sottomettere, sottoporre. ♦ to **submit** *vi.* sottomettersi, assoggettarsi.
submultiple *agg.* e *s.* sottomultiplo.
subnormal *agg.* al di sotto della norma.
subordinacy *s.* subordinazione.
subordinate *agg.* subordinato. ♦ **subordinate** *s.* subalterno, inferiore.
to **subordinate** *vt.* subordinare.
subordination *s.* subordinazione.
to **suborn** *vt.* subornare, corrompere.
subornation *s.* subornazione.
subplot *s.* trama secondaria.
to **subscribe** *vt.* e *vi.* **1.** sottoscrivere, firmare **2.** aderire, trovarsi d'accordo **3.** abbonarsi.
subscriber *s.* **1.** *the* —, il sottoscritto **2.** abbonato.
subscription *s.* **1.** sottoscrizione **2.** abbonamento **3.** consenso.
subsequence *s.* susseguenza.
subsequent *agg.* successivo, ulteriore.
subsequently *avv.* successivamente.
to **subside** *vi.* **1.** calare, decrescere **2.** quietarsi **3.** cadere (*sul fondo*), depositare (*di liquidi*).
subsidiary *agg.* sussidiario, supplementare, ausiliario.
to **subsidize** *vt.* sussidiare.
subsidy *s.* sussidio.
to **subsist** *vt.* e *vi.* sussistere.
subsistence *s.* esistenza, sussistenza.
subsistent *agg.* sussistente.
subsoil *s.* sottosuolo.
subspecies *s.* sottospecie.
substance *s.* **1.** sostanza, essenza **2.** contenuto, l'essenziale **3.** solidità, fondamento.
substantial *agg.* **1.** sostanzioso, so-

lido **2.** importante, notevole.
substantialism *s.* sostanzialismo.
substantiality *s.* **1.** sostanzialità **2.** concretezza.
substantially *avv.* sostanzialmente.
substantive *agg.* considerevole, reale. ♦ **substantive** *s.* (*gramm.*) sostantivo.
substitute *s.* **1.** sostituto **2.** surrogato, imitazione.
to **substitute** *vt.* e *vi.* sostituire.
substitution *s.* sostituzione.
substratum *s.* (*pl.* -ta) **1.** sostrato (*anche fig.*).
subtenancy *s.* subaffitto.
subtenant *s.* subaffittuario.
subterfuge *s.* sotterfugio.
subterranean *agg.* sotterraneo.
sub-title *s.* sottotitolo, didascalia.
subtle *agg.* **1.** penetrante, acuto, sottile **2.** elusivo, indefinibile.
subtleness *s.* **1.** sottigliezza, acutezza **2.** carattere elusivo.
subtlety *s.* sottigliezza.
subtly *avv.* **1.** acutamente, sottilmente **2.** elusivamente.
to **subtract** *vt.* sottrarre, detrarre.
subtraction *s.* sottrazione.
subtractive *agg.* sottrattivo.
subtrahend *s.* sottraendo.
suburb *s.* sobborgo. ♦ **suburbs** *s. pl.* periferia (*sing.*).
suburban *agg.* suburbano, periferico.
subversion *s.* sovversione.
subversive *agg.* sovversivo.
to **subvert** *vt.* sovvertire.
subway *s.* **1.** sottopassaggio **2.** (*amer.*) metropolitana.
to **succeed** *vt.* succedere a, seguire, subentrare a. ♦ to **succeed** *vi.* **1.** succedere, seguire **2.** riuscire, aver successo.
success *s.* successo, riuscita.
successful *agg.* che ha successo.
successfully *avv.* con successo.
succession *s.* successione, serie.
successive *agg.* successivo, seguente.
successively *avv.* successivamente.
successor *s.* successore.
succint *agg.* succinto, conciso.
succulent *agg.* succulento.
to **succumb** *vi.* soccombere, soggiacere.
succursal *s.* succursale.
such *agg.* tale, simile: — *that*, — *as*, tale che, tale da. ♦ **such** *pron.* tale, tali, questo, quello, questa,

quella, questi, quelli, queste, quelle.

suchlike *agg.* simile, dello stesso genere.

suck *s.* succhiata, poppata.

to suck *vt.* e *vi.* **1.** succhiare, poppare **2.** assorbire.

sucker *s.* **1.** (*mecc.*) pistone **2.** ventosa.

to suckle *vt.* allattare.

suckling *s.* lattante.

sudden *agg.* improvviso, inaspettato. ♦ **sudden** *s.* evento improvviso.

suddenly *avv.* inaspettatamente.

suddenness *s.* subitaneità.

to sue *vt.* e *vi.* **1.** ricorrere in giudizio **2.** sollecitare.

to suffer *vt.* e *vi.* **1.** subire, patire **2.** tollerare **3.** soffrire.

suffering *s.* **1.** sofferenza, pena **2.** tolleranza.

sufficiency *s.* sufficienza.

sufficient *agg.* sufficiente.

suffix *s.* (*gramm.*) suffisso.

to suffocate *vt.* e *vi.* soffocare.

suffocation *s.* soffocamento.

suffrage *s.* **1.** suffragio, diritto di voto **2.** preghiera.

to suffuse *vt.* coprire, cospargere.

sugar *s.* **1.** zucchero **2.** (*fig.*) atteggiamento mellifluo || — *-beet*, barbabietola da zucchero; — *-cane*, canna da zucchero; — *-tongs*, mollette per lo zucchero; *lump* —, zucchero in zollette.

to sugar *vt.* **1.** inzuccherare **2.** (*fig.*) addolcire, adulare.

sugariness *s.* **1.** dolcezza **2.** mellifluità.

sugary *agg.* **1.** zuccheroso, zuccherino **2.** (*fig.*) mellifluo.

to suggest *vt.* **1.** suggerire **2.** far nascere un'idea **3.** insinuare.

suggestible *agg.* suggeribile, suggestionabile.

suggestion *s.* **1.** suggerimento **2.** suggestione **3.** associazione di idee.

suggestive *agg.* stimolante, che ispira.

suggestiveness *s.* carattere allusivo.

suicidal *agg.* suicida, che ha tendenze al suicidio.

suicide *s.* **1.** suicidio **2.** suicida.

suit *s.* **1.** domanda, preghiera **2.** (*giur.*) causa **3.** abito completo (*da uomo*) || — *-case*, valigia.

to suit *vt.* adattare, convenire a, far comodo a. ♦ **to suit** *vi.* essere conveniente, accordarsi, adattarsi.

suitability *s.* convenienza.

suitable *agg.* adatto, idoneo.

suitably *avv.* appropriatamente.

suite *s.* **1.** seguito, corteo **2.** serie.

suitor *s.* **1.** postulante **2.** corteggiatore.

sulkiness *s.* malumore.

sulks *s. pl.* malumore, broncio (*sing.*).

sulky[1] *agg.* **1.** imbronciato, scontroso **2.** tetro.

sulky[2] *s.* "sulky", sediolo.

sullen *agg.* **1.** accigliato **2.** tetro.

sullenly *avv.* accigliato, di malumore.

sulphate *s.* solfato.

sulphide *s.* solfuro.

sulphite *s.* solfito.

sulphonamide *s.* sulfamidico.

sulphur *s.* zolfo || — *-mine* (o — *-pit*), solfatara.

to sulphur, to sulphurate *vt.* solforare.

sulphuric *agg.* solforico.

sulphurous *agg.* solforoso.

sultan *s.* sultano.

sultanate *s.* sultanato.

sultriness *s.* afa, caldo soffocante.

sultry *agg.* afoso, soffocante.

sum *s.* **1.** somma, quantità (*di denaro*) **2.** addizione.

to sum *vt.* e *vi.* sommare, addizionare || *to* — *up*, riassumere.

summarily *avv.* sommariamente.

to summarize *vt.* e *vi.* riassumere.

summary *s.* sommario, ricapitolazione.

summer *s.* estate.

to summer *vi.* trascorrere l'estate.

summertime *s.* stagione estiva.

summit *s.* **1.** cima, vetta **2.** (*fig.*) culmine || *at the* — (*pol.*), al vertice.

to summon *vt.* **1.** chiamare, mandare a chiamare **2.** convocare **3.** (*giur.*) citare.

summons *s.* **1.** (*giur.*) citazione, ingiunzione **2.** convocazione.

sumptuous *agg.* sontuoso.

sumptuously *avv.* sontuosamente.

sumptuousness *s.* sontuosità.

sun *s.* sole || — *-bath*, bagno di sole; — *-glasses*, occhiali da sole.

to sun *vt.* esporre al sole. ♦ **to sun** *vi.* esporsi al sole.

to sun-bathe *vi.* fare i bagni di sole.

sunbeam *s.* raggio di sole.

sunbow *s.* arcobaleno.

sunburn *s.* **1.** abbronzatura **2.** scot-

tatura (solare).
sunburnt *agg.* **1.** abbronzato **2.** scottato dal sole.
sunburst *s.* sprazzo di sole.
Sunday *s.* domenica.
to **sunder** *vt.* separare, recidere. ♦
to **sunder** *vi.* separarsi, scindersi.
sundry *agg.* parecchi, vari.
sunflower *s.* girasole.
sung V. *to sing.*
sunk V. *to sink.*
sunlight *s.* luce del sole.
sunlit *agg.* soleggiato.
sunny *agg.* luminoso, soleggiato.
sunproof *agg.* inalterabile al sole.
sunrise *s.* il sorgere del sole.
sunset *s.* tramonto (*anche fig.*).
sunshade *s.* parasole.
sunshine *s.* luce del sole.
sunspot *s.* macchia solare.
sunstroke *s.* insolazione.
sun-worship *s.* culto del Sole.
sup *s.* sorso, goccia.
to **sup**[1] *vt.* e *vi.* sorseggiare.
to **sup**[2] *vi.* cenare.
superable *agg.* superabile.
to **superabound** *vi.* sovrabbondare.
superabundance *s.* sovrabbondanza.
superabundant *agg.* sovrabbondante.
superb *agg.* superbo, magnifico.
superciliary *agg.* sopracciliare.
supercilious *agg.* altero.
superelevation *s.* sopraelevazione.
superficial *agg.* superficiale, poco profondo.
superficiality *s.* superficialità.
superfluous *agg.* superfluo.
superhuman *agg.* sovrumano.
to **superimpose** *vt.* sovrapporre.
superintendence *s.* sovrintendenza.
superintendent *s.* sovrintendente.
superior *agg.* superiore.
superiority *s.* superiorità.
superlative *agg.* superlativo.
superman *s.* superuomo.
supermarket *s.* supermercato.
supermundane *agg.* ultraterreno.
supernatural *agg.* soprannaturale.
supernutrition *s.* supernutrizione.
to **supersede** *vt.* rimpiazzare.
supersensitive *agg.* ipersensibile.
supersensitiveness *s.* ipersensibilità.
supersession *s.* sostituzione.
supersonic *agg.* ultrasonoro, supersonico.
superstition *s.* superstizione.

superstitious *agg.* superstizioso.
superstructure *s.* sovrastruttura.
supertax *s.* soprattassa.
superterrestrial *agg.* ultraterreno.
to **supervise** *vt.* e *vi.* sovrintendere.
supervision *s.* sorveglianza, sovrintendenza.
supervisor *s.* sovrintendente.
supervisory *agg.* di controllo.
supine *agg.* supino (*anche fig.*).
supinely *avv.* supinamente.
supper *s.* cena || *to have* —, cenare; — *-time*, ora di cena.
to **supplant** *vt.* soppiantare.
supple *agg.* **1.** pieghevole, flessibile **2.** elastico (*anche fig.*).
supplement *s.* supplemento.
supplementary *agg.* supplementare.
suppliant *agg.* supplichevole. ♦
suppliant *s.* supplicante.
supply *s.* **1.** rifornimento, approvvigionamento **2.** (*comm.*) fornitura **3.** sostituto, supplente.
to **supply** *vt.* fornire, rifornire. ♦
to **supply** *vi.* fare da sostituto.
support *s.* sostegno, appoggio || *in* — *of*, in favore di.
to **support** *vt.* **1.** sostenere, reggere **2.** dare appoggio a **3.** mantenere.
supportable *agg.* sostenibile, sopportabile.
supporter *s.* **1.** sostegno **2.** fautore, sostenitore.
to **suppose** *vt.* supporre, presupporre, presumere.
supposed *agg.* presunto, supposto.
supposition *s.* supposizione, ipotesi.
suppository *s.* (*med.*) supposta.
to **suppress** *vt.* **1.** sopprimere, reprimere **2.** (*fig.*) soffocare, trattenere.
suppression *s.* **1.** soppressione **2.** il mettere a tacere.
to **suppurate** *vi.* suppurare.
suppuration *s.* suppurazione.
suprarenal *agg.* surrenale.
supremacy *s.* supremazia.
supreme *agg.* sommo, supremo.
surcharge *s.* **1.** sovraccarico **2.** soprattassa **3.** sovrapprezzo.
sure *agg.* sicuro, certo, fidato.
surely *avv.* sicuramente, certamente.
surety *s.* garanzia, pegno.
suretyship *s.* garanzia.
surf *s.* **1.** risacca **2.** spuma dei marosi.
surface *s.* superficie (*anche fig.*).
surfeit *s.* **1.** eccesso **2.** sazietà. ♦
to **surfeit** *vt.* saziare. ♦ to **sur-**

feit *vi.* saziarsi.
surge *s.* **1.** maroso, cavallone **2.** (*fig.*) impeto.
to **surge** *vi.* gonfiarsi, sollevarsi, tumultuare.
surgeon *s.* chirurgo.
surgery *s.* chirurgia.
surgical *agg.* chirurgico.
surlily *avv.* sgarbatamente.
surly *agg.* sgarbato.
to **surmount** *vt.* sormontare, superare.
surname *s.* **1.** cognome **2.** soprannome.
to **surname** *vt.* soprannominare.
to **surpass** *vt.* sorpassare, superare.
surpassing *agg.* superiore, eccellente.
surpassingly *avv.* straordinariamente.
surplus *s.* **1.** sovrappiù, eccedenza **2.** residuati di guerra.
surprise *s.* **1.** sorpresa **2.** stupore, meraviglia.
to **surprise** *vt.* **1.** sorprendere, cogliere all'improvviso **2.** stupire.
surprisedly *avv.* con sorpresa.
surprising *agg.* sorprendente.
surrealism *s.* surrealismo.
surrealist *agg.* e *s.* surrealista.
surrender *s.* **1.** resa, capitolazione **2.** abbandono, cessione.
to **surrender** *vt.* cedere, consegnare. ♦ to **surrender** *vi.* arrendersi.
surreptitious *agg.* clandestino, furtivo.
surrogate *s.* sostituto, supplente.
surround *s.* bordura, bordo.
to **surround** *vt.* **1.** circondare **2.** accerchiare.
surrounding *agg.* circostante. ♦ **surroundings** *s. pl.* dintorni.
survey *s.* esame, sguardo generale.
to **survey** *vt.* e *vi.* esaminare, fare rivelazioni.
surveyor *s.* ispettore.
survival *s.* **1.** sopravvivenza **2.** avanzo, reliquia.
to **survive** *vi.* sopravvivere. ♦ to **survive** *vt.* vivere più a lungo di.
survivor *s.* superstite.
susceptibility *s.* suscettibilità.
susceptible *agg.* **1.** suscettibile **2.** impressionabile.
suspect *agg.* sospetto. ♦ **suspect** *s.* persona sospetta.
to **suspect** *vt.* sospettare. ♦ to **suspect** *vi.* essere sospettoso.
to **suspend** *vt.* **1.** appendere, tenere

sospeso **2.** sospendere.
suspender *s.* giarrettiera, bretella.
suspense *s.* incertezza, attesa ansiosa.
suspension *s.* sospensione.
suspensive *agg.* sospensivo.
suspicion *s.* sospetto, dubbio.
suspicious *agg.* sospettoso, diffidente.
suspiciously *avv.* sospettosamente.
to **sustain** *vt.* **1.** mantenere, sostenere **2.** prolungare **3.** reggere.
sustainable *agg.* sostenibile.
sustenance *s.* mezzi di sussistenza (*pl.*).
suture *s.* sutura.
to **suture** *vt.* suturare.
swab *s.* **1.** strofinaccio **2.** (*mar.*) radazza **3.** (*med.*) tampone.
to **swab** *vt.* pulire, strofinare.
swag *s.* movimento ondeggiante.
swagger *agg.* sgargiante.
to **swagger** *vi.* **1.** pavoneggiarsi **2.** gloriarsi.
swallow[1] *s.* rondine.
swallow[2] *s.* **1.** baratro **2.** deglutizione.
to **swallow** *vt.* e *vi.* **1.** deglutire, inghiottire **2.** (*fig.*) ingoiare.
swam V. to **swim**.
swamp *s.* palude || — *-fever*, febbre malarica.
to **swamp** *vt.* inondare, inzuppare. ♦ to **swamp** *vi.* affondare (*anche fig.*).
swan *s.* cigno || — *song*, canto del cigno.
swarm *s.* sciame, folla.
to **swarm** *vi.* **1.** sciamare **2.** pullulare, brulicare, essere affollato.
swash *s.* **1.** sciacquio **2.** gradassata.
to **swash** *vi.* **1.** spruzzare, sguazzare **2.** turbinare, infrangersi. ♦ to **swash** *vt.* far sguazzare.
to **swat** *vt.* colpire, schiacciare (*mosche ecc.*).
swathe *s.* benda, fascia.
to **swathe** *vt.* bendare, fasciare.
sway *s.* **1.** oscillazione **2.** potere, potenza, preponderanza.
to **sway** *vt.* **1.** sballottolare **2.** dominare, influenzare **3.** maneggiare, impugnare **4.** (*mar.*) issare. ♦ to **sway** *vi.* **1.** ondeggiare **2.** propendere **3.** predominare.
swear *s.* bestemmia, imprecazione.
to **swear** (**swore, sworn**) *vt.* e *vi.* **1.** giurare, far giurare **2.** imprecare, bes ̄ ͛miare.

sweat *s.* sudore, traspirazione.

to sweat *vt.* e *vi.* traspirare, sudare, sfacchinare.

sweater *s.* 1. chi suda 2. maglione di lana.

sweating *s.* sudore || — -*bath*, bagno turco.

sweaty *agg.* 1. sudato 2. che fa sudare.

Swede *s.* svedese.

Swedish *agg.* svedese.

sweep *s.* 1. scopata 2. movimento circolare 3. curva, distesa.

to sweep (swept, swept) *vi.* 1. spazzare, scopare 2. muoversi rapidamente 3. estendersi. ♦ **to sweep (swept, swept)** *vt.* 1. spazzare 2. sfiorare.

sweeping *agg.* 1. vasto 2. completo 3. rapido, impetuoso (*di corrente*). ♦ **sweepings** *s. pl.* rifiuti.

sweet *agg.* 1. dolce, amabile 2. piacevole, gentile. ♦ **sweet** *s.* 1. dolce, torta 2. caramella.

to sweeten *vt.* 1. zuccherare 2. addolcire. ♦ **to sweeten** *vi.* addolcirsi.

sweetening *s.* 1. addolcimento 2. sostanza che addolcisce.

sweetheart *s.* innamorato.

sweetly *avv.* dolcemente.

sweetmeat *s.* dolciumi, frutta candita.

sweetness *s.* 1. sapore dolce 2. dolcezza, amabilità.

swell *s.* 1. rigonfiamento 2. il gonfiarsi (*dell'acqua ecc.*).

to swell (swelled, swollen) *vi.* 1. gonfiarsi 2. crescere, aumentare. ♦ **to swell (swelled, swollen)** *vt.* gonfiare.

swelling *s.* rigonfiamento, ingrossamento.

swept V. *to sweep.*

to swerve *vt.* deviare. ♦ **to swerve** *vi.* fare uno scarto.

swift *agg.* rapido, veloce.

swim *s.* nuotata.

to swim (swam, swum) *vi.* nuotare. ♦ **to swim (swam, swum)** *vt.* attraversare a nuoto.

swimmer *s.* nuotatore.

swimming *s.* nuoto || — -*belt*, salvagente; — -*pool*, piscina.

swindle *s.* truffa, frode.

to swindle *vt.* e *vi.* truffare.

swindler *s.* truffatore.

swine *s.* maiale, porco || — -*herd*, porcaro.

swing *s.* 1. oscillazione 2. libertà d'azione 3. altalena.

to swing (swung, swung) *vt.* 1. dondolare, oscillare 2. ruotare 3. camminare dondolandosi. ♦ **to swing (swung, swung)** *vt.* 1. far dondolare 2. far ruotare.

swinging *s.* dondolio.

swish *s.* 1. sibilo 2. sferzata.

Swiss *agg.* svizzero.

switch *s.* 1. verga, frustino 2. (*elett.*) interruttore.

to switch *vt.* e *vi.* 1. colpire con un frustino 2. muovere bruscamente 3. (*ferr.*) smistare || *to — off*, spegnere (*la luce*); *to — on*, accendere (*la luce*).

swollen V. *to swell.*

swoon *s.* svenimento.

to swoon *vi.* svenire.

to swoop *vi.* calare improvvisamente, abbattersi.

sword *s.* spada.

swore V. *to swear.*

sworn V. *to swear.*

swum V. *to swim.*

swung V. *to swing.*

sycamore *s.* sicomoro.

syllable *s.* sillaba.

syllogism *s.* sillogismo.

syllogistic *agg.* sillogistico.

to syllogize *vt.* e *vi.* sillogizzare.

sylph *s.* silfo, silfide.

sylvan *agg.* silvano, silvestre.

symbiosis *s.* simbiosi.

symbol *s.* simbolo.

symbolic(al) *agg.* simbolico.

symbolism *s.* simbolismo.

to symbolize *vt.* simboleggiare.

symmetric(al) *agg.* simmetrico.

symmetry *s.* simmetria.

sympathetic *agg.* 1. sensibile, comprensivo 2. congeniale, adatto.

to sympathize *vi.* condividere i sentimenti altrui.

sympathizer *s.* 1. chi è comprensivo 2. simpatizzante (*di un partito ecc.*).

sympathy *s.* 1. comprensione, partecipazione 2. condoglianze (*pl.*).

symphonic *agg.* sinfonico.

symphony *s.* sinfonia.

symposium *s.* simposio, banchetto.

symptom *s.* sintomo.

symptomatic(al) *agg.* sintomatico.

synagogue *s.* sinagoga.

synchronism *s.* sincronismo.

synchronization *s.* sincronizzazione.

to **synchronize** *vt.* e *vi.* sincronizzare.

to **syncopate** *vt.* sincopare.

syncope *s.* sincope.

syndicalism *s.* sindacalismo.

syndicate *s.* sindacato.

synod *s.* sinodo.

synonym *s.* sinonimo.

synonymous *agg.* sinonimo.

synonymy *s.* sinonimia.

synovitis *s.* sinovite.

syntactic(al) *agg.* sintattico.

syntax *s.* sintassi.

synthesis *s.* (*pl.* -ses) sintesi.

to **synthesize** *vt.* sintetizzare.

synthetic(al) *agg.* sintetico.

syntony *s.* sintonia.

syphilis *s.* sifilide.

syphilitic *agg.* sifilitico.

Syrian *agg.* e *s.* siriano.

syringe *s.* siringa.

syrup *s.* sciroppo.

syrupy *agg.* sciropposo.

system *s.* **1.** sistema **2.** metodo || *railway* —, rete ferroviaria.

systematic(al) *agg.* sistematico, metodico.

systematically *avv.* sistematicamente, metodicamente.

systematization *s.* sistemazione.

to **systematize** *vt.* ridurre a sistema.

T

tab *s.* **1.** linguetta (*di scarpa*) **2.** (*mil.*) mostrina **3.** talloncino.

tabernacle *s.* **1.** tabernacolo **2.** tempio.

table *s.* **1.** tavola **2.** tavolata **3.** tabella || —*cloth*, tovaglia; *time*—, orario.

tablet *s.* **1.** tavoletta **2.** pastiglia. compressa.

tabloid *s.* pasticca.

taboo *agg.* e *s.* tabù.

tabular *agg.* **1.** a forma di tabella **2.** catalogato **3.** piano, piatto.

tabulate *agg.* piano.

to **tabulate** *vt.* disporre in tabelle.

tabulation *s.* classificazione.

tabulator *s.* tabulatore.

tachometer *s.* tachimetro.

tachycardia *s.* tachicardia.

tacit *agg.* tacito.

taciturn *agg.* taciturno.

tack *s.* **1.** chiodo **2.** imbastitura **3.** bordata **4.** (*fig.*) linea di condotta.

to **tack** *vt.* **1.** inchiodare **2.** imbastire. ◆ to **tack** *vi.* **1.** bordeggiare **2.** virare.

tacking *s.* **1.** l'inchiodare **2.** imbastitura **3.** bordeggio.

tackle *s.* **1.** arnesi (*pl.*) **2.** (*mar.*) paranco.

to **tackle** *vt.* **1.** afferrare **2.** affrontare (*difficoltà ecc.*).

tacky *agg.* viscoso.

tact *s.* tatto.

tactful *agg.* pieno di tatto.

tactical *agg.* tattico.

tactician *s.* tattico.

tactics *s.* tattica.

tactile *agg.* **1.** tattile **2.** tangibile.

tactility *s.* **1.** tattilità **2.** tangibilità.

tactless *agg.* senza tatto.

tactlessness *s.* mancanza di tatto.

tactual *agg.* tattile.

tadpole *s.* (*zool.*) girino.

tag *s.* **1.** lembo pendente **2.** cartellino **3.** aggiunta **4.** luogo comune || *licence* —, bollo di circolazione.

to **tag** *vt.* mettere cartellini a.

tail *s.* coda || — -*coat*, marsina.

to **tail** *vt.* munire di coda. ◆ to **tail** *vi.* **1.** essere in coda **2.** seguire da presso || *to* — *away*, affievolirsi.

tailor *s.* sarto || — -*made costume*, tailleur.

to **tailor** *vi.* fare il sarto. ◆ to **tailor** *vt.* fare un abito.

taint *s.* **1.** infezione **2.** tara **3.** marchio.

to **taint** *vt.* guastare. ◆ to **taint** *vi.* guastarsi.

taintless *agg.* incontaminato.

take *s.* **1.** presa **2.** incasso **3.** (*cine*) ripresa.

to **take** (**took, taken**) *vt.* **1.** prendere **2.** portare **3.** accompagnare **4.** necessitare || *to* — *after*, assomigliare; *to* — *in*, ricevere, ridurre, capire; *to* — *off*, togliere, decollare; *to* — *on*, assumere; *to* — *to*, darsi a.

take-off *s.* (*aer.*) decollo.

taking *agg.* **1.** attraente **2.** contagioso. ◆ **taking** *s.* **1.** presa **2.** incasso.

talc(um) *s.* talco || *talcum powder*, talco in polvere.

tale s. racconto, storia novella.
talent s. talento.
talented agg. che ha talento.
talentless agg. senza talento.
tales s. pl. (giur.) giudici supplenti.
talisman s. talismano.
talk s. 1. conversazione 2. chiacchiera.
to **talk** vt. e vi. parlare, conversare, discutere || to — out, discutere a fondo.
talkative agg. loquace.
talkativeness s. loquacità.
talker s. 1. parlatore 2. chiacchierone.
talkies s. pl. (gergo) film sonoro (sing.).
talking s. conversazione.
talky agg. loquace.
tall agg. 1. alto 2. incredibile.
tallness s. altezza, statura.
tallow s. sego.
tally s. 1. tacca 2. cartellino, talloncino, etichetta.
to **tally** vt. registrare. ♦ to **tally** vi. combaciare.
tallyshop s. negozio che vende a rate.
talon s. 1. artiglio 2. (mecc.) dente 3. (comm.) matrice.
tamarind s. tamarindo.
tambourine s. tamburello.
tame agg. 1. addomesticato 2. mansueto 3. insipido, banale.
to **tame** vt. domare, addomesticare. ♦ to **tame** vi. ammansirsi.
tameable agg. addomesticabile.
tameless agg. indomito.
tamely avv. docilmente.
tameness s. 1. docilità 2. banalità.
tamer s. domatore.
taming s. addomesticamento.
to **tamp** vt. pigiare.
tamper s. pestello.
to **tamper** vi. 1. manomettere 2. immischiarsi: to — with, immischiarsi in 3. corrompere.
tamperer s. 1. falsificatore 2. corruttore 3. ficcanaso.
tampering s. 1. manomissione 2. corruzione.
tampon s. tampone.
tan agg. marrone rossiccio. ♦ **tan** s. 1. tannino 2. concia 3. abbronzatura.
to **tan** vt. 1. conciare 2. abbronzare. ♦ to **tan** vi. abbronzarsi.
tanning s. abbronzatura.

tang[1] s. 1. punta 2. odore, sapore penetrante.
tang[2] s. suono acuto.
to **tang** vt. far risuonare. ♦ to **tang** vi. risuonare.
tangency s. tangenza.
tangent agg. e s. tangente.
tangential agg. tangenziale.
tangerine s. mandarino.
tangibility s. tangibilità.
tangible agg. tangibile.
tangle s. groviglio.
to **tangle** vt. 1. aggrovigliare 2. intrappolare. ♦ to **tangle** vi. aggrovigliarsi.
tanglesome, tangly agg. ingarbugliato.
tank s. 1. serbatoio, cisterna 2. carro armato || — -truck, autobotte.
tankard s. boccale.
tanker s. nave cisterna || air —, aerocisterna; oil —, petroliera.
tanner s. conciatore.
tannery s. conceria.
tannin s. tannino.
tanning s. concia.
to **tantalize** vt. tormentare.
tantalizing agg. allettante.
tantamount agg. equivalente.
tap[1] rubinetto, spina.
tap[2] s. colpetto.
to **tap**[1] vt. 1. spillare 2. forare.
to **tap**[2] vt. battere leggermente.
tape s. nastro || — -recorder, magnetofono; recording —, nastro magnetico.
to **tape** vt. 1. legare con un nastro 2. misurare con un nastro 3. incidere su nastro magnetico.
taper agg. conico, rastremato ♦ **taper** s. 1. candela 2. conicità, rastremazione.
to **taper** vt. assottigliare. ♦ to **taper** vi. assottigliarsi, restringersi.
tapestry s. arazzo.
tapeworm s. tenia.
tapir s. tapiro.
tar s. catrame.
to **tar** vt. incatramare.
tardiness s. 1. lentezza 2. indolenza.
tardy agg. 1. lento 2. svogliato.
tare s. tara.
target s. bersaglio.
tariff s. tariffa.
tarnish s. 1. appannamento 2. macchia.
to **tarnish** vi. 1. appannarsi 2. macchiarsi. ♦ to **tarnish** vt. 1. mac-

chiare **2.** inquinare.
tarpaulin *s.* telone impermeabile.
tarry *agg.* **1.** catramato **2.** simile a c⁻trame.
to **tarry** *vi.* indugiare.
tart *agg.* aspro.
tart *s.* torta di frutta, crostata.
tartan[1] *s.* tessuto scozzese.
tartan[2] *s.* (*mar.*) tartana.
tartar *agg.* e *s.* tartaro.
tartaric *agg.* tartarico.
tartlet *s.* pasticcino.
tartly *avv.* in modo acido.
task *s.* compito, dovere, impresa.
to **task** *vt.* **1.** assegnare un compito a **2.** affaticare.
task-work *s.* lavoro a cottimo.
tassel *s.* **1.** nappa **2.** segnalibro.
to **tassel** *vt.* adornare di nappe.
taste *s.* **1.** gusto **2.** assaggio.
to **taste** *vt.* **1.** gustare **2.** assaggiare. ♦ to **taste** *vi.* sapere di.
tasteful *agg.* raffinato.
tastefulness *s.* buon gusto.
tasteless *agg.* **1.** insipido **2.** di cattivo gusto.
tastelessness *s.* **1.** scipitezza **2.** mancanza di gusto.
taster *s.* assaggiatore.
tasty *agg.* **1.** saporito **2.** (*gergo*) di buon gusto.
tatter *s.* cencio.
to **tatter** *vt.* stracciare. ♦ to **tatter** *vi.* cadere a pezzi.
tattery *agg.* stracciato.
tattle *s.* chiacchiera.
to **tattle** *vi.* chiacchierare.
tattler *s.* chiacchierone.
tattoo[1] *s.* tatuaggio.
tattoo[2] *s.* (*mil.*) **1.** ritirata **2.** carosello militare.
to **tattoo**[1] *vt.* tatuare.
to **tattoo**[2] *vi.* tamburellare.
taught V. *to teach.*
taunt *s.* sarcasmo.
to **taunt** *vt.* **1.** rimproverare **2.** schernire.
taunting *agg.* beffardo. ♦ **taunting** *s.* rimprovero sarcastico.
taut *agg.* **1.** teso **2.** in ordine.
to **tauten** *vt.* tendere. ♦ to **tauten** *vi.* tendersi.
tautness *s.* tensione.
tautologic(al) *agg.* tautologico.
tautology *s.* tautologia.
tavern *s.* taverna || — -*keeper*, oste.
taw *s.* biglia.
tawdry *agg.* sgargiante.
tawny *agg.* bruno fulvo.

tax *s.* **1.** tassa **2.** peso || — -*payer*, contribuente.
to **tax** *vt.* **1.** tassare **2.** accusare.
taxability *s.* tassabilità.
taxable *agg.* tassabile.
taxation *s.* tassazione.
taxi *s.* tassì || — -*driver*, tassista; (*aer.*) — *track*, pista di rullaggio.
to **taxi** *vi.* (*aer.*) rullare.
taxicab *s.* autopubblica.
taximeter *s.* tassametro.
tea *s.* tè || — -*pot*, teiera; *high* —, cena fredda; — -*set*, servizio da tè.
to **teach** (**taught, taught**) *vt.* insegnare.
teachable *agg.* **1.** che apprende facilmente **2.** che si insegna facilmente.
teacher *s.* insegnante.
teachership *s.* insegnamento.
teaching *agg.* che insegna. ♦ **teaching** *s.* insegnamento.
teacup *s.* tazza da tè.
team *s.* **1.** squadra **2.** tiro (*di cavalli*).
to **team** *vt.* aggiogare, accoppiarsi, raggrupparsi. ♦ to **team** *vi.* accoppiarsi, associarsi.
tear[1] *s.* **1.** lacrima **2.** goccia || — -*gas*, gas lacrimogeno.
tear[2] *s.* strappo, lacerazione.
to **tear** (**tore, torn**) *vt.* strappare, lacerare. ♦ to **tear** (**tore, torn**) *vi.* strapparsi.
tearful *agg.* lacrimoso.
tearing *agg.* violento. ♦ **tearing** *s.* strappo, lacerazione.
tear-off *s.* parte da staccare.
tease *s.* chi stuzzica.
to **tease** *vt.* **1.** stuzzicare **2.** cardare (*lana ecc.*).
teaser *s.* **1.** seccatore **2.** cardatore **3.** questione difficile.
teaspoon *s.* cucchiaino da tè.
technical *agg.* tecnico.
technicality *s.* tecnicismo.
technician *s.* tecnico.
technique *s.* tecnica.
technological *agg.* tecnologico.
technology *s.* tecnologia.
tectonics *s.* **1.** edilizia **2.** tettonica.
tedious *agg.* tedioso.
tediousness *s.* tedio.
to **teem** *vi.* brulicare.
teen-ager *s.* adolescente.
teens *s. pl.* età da tredici a diciannove anni.
teeth V. *tooth.*
teething *s.* dentizione.

teetotal(l)er s. astemio.
telecast s. teletrasmissione || — *news*, telegiornale.
to **telecast** (telecast, telecast) *vt.* teletrasmettere.
telecommunication s. telecomunicazione.
telecontrol s. telecomando.
telegram s. telegramma.
telegraph s. telegrafo.
to **telegraph** *vt.* e *vi.* telegrafare.
telegraphic *agg.* telegrafico.
telegraphist s. telegrafista.
telegraphy s. telegrafia.
telemeter s. telemetro.
telepathy s. telepatia.
telephone s. telefono || — *booth*, cabina telefonica; — *-book*, elenco telefonico.
to **telephone** *vt.* e *vi.* telefonare.
telephonist s. telefonista.
telephony s. telefonia.
telephoto s. telefoto.
telephotograph s. telefotografia.
telescope s. telescopio.
to **telescope** *vi.* incastrarsi.
teletype s. telescrivente.
teletyper s. telescriventista.
teletypewriter s. telescrivente.
to **teleview** *vt.* e *vi.* guardare la televisione.
televiewer s. telespettatore.
to **televise** *vt.* riprendere con la televisione.
television s. televisione || — *set*, televisore.
televisional *agg.* televisivo.
to **tell** (told, told) *vt.* e *vi.* **1.** dire **2.** raccontare **3.** distinguere.
teller s. **1.** narratore **2.** (*comm.*) cassiere.
telling *agg.* efficace. ♦ **telling** s. **1.** il raccontare **2.** rivelazione.
telltale s. **1.** chiacchierone **2.** (*tec.*) controllore.
telluric *agg.* tellurico.
telpher s. cabina di funivia.
telpherage s. trasporto per teleferica.
temper s. **1.** indole **2.** umore **3.** collera **4.** moderazione.
to **temper** *vt.* temperare.
temperament s. temperamento.
temperamental *agg.* capriccioso.
temperance s. temperanza.
temperate *agg.* **1.** temperato (*di clima*) **2.** moderato.
temperature s. temperatura || *to have a* —, avere la febbre.

tempered *agg.* **1.** temprato **2.** moderato **3.** di indole, umore || *quick* —, irritabile.
tempest s. tempesta.
temple[1] s. tempio.
temple[2] s. (*anat.*) tempia.
temporal *agg.* temporale.
temporariness s. temporaneità.
temporary *agg.* temporaneo.
temporization s. temporeggiamento.
to **temporize** *vi.* temporeggiare.
to **tempt** *vt.* tentare.
temptation s. tentazione.
tempter s. tentatore.
tempting *agg.* seducente.
ten *agg.* e s. dieci.
tenacious *agg.* **1.** tenace **2.** viscoso.
tenacity s. tenacia.
tenancy s. locazione.
tenant s. **1.** proprietario **2.** locatario.
to **tend**[1] *vt.* curare, badare a, custodire.
to **tend**[2] *vi.* tendere.
tendency s. tendenza.
tendential, tendentious *agg.* tendenzioso.
tender[1] *agg.* tenero || — *of*, sollecito verso.
tender[2] s. **1.** guardiano, custode **2.** nave di appoggio.
tender[3] s. offerta, proposta.
to **tender** *vt.* offrire, presentare.
tenderness s. **1.** tenerezza **2.** delicatezza.
tendon s. (*anat.*) tendine.
tendril s. viticcio.
tenebrous *agg.* tenebroso.
tenement s. **1.** podere **2.** abitazione.
tenor s. **1.** tenore (*di vita ecc.*) **2.** (*giur.*) copia esatta **3.** (*mus.*) tenore.
tense[1] *agg.* teso.
tense[2] s. (*gramm.*) tempo.
to **tense** *vt.* tendere. ♦ to **tense** *vi.* tendersi.
tension s. tensione.
tent s. tenda.
tentacle s. tentacolo.
tentative *agg.* sperimentale. ♦ **tentative** s. tentativo, prova.
tenth *agg.* e s. decimo.
tenuity s. **1.** tenuità **2.** rarefazione **3.** fluidità.
tenuous *agg.* **1.** tenue **2.** rarefatto **3.** fluido.
tenure s. **1.** possesso **2.** gestione.

tepid *agg.* tiepido.
tepidity *s.* tepidezza.
tercet *s.* terzina.
tergal *agg.* dorsale.
to **tergiversate** *vi.* tergiversare.
tergiversation *s.* tergiversazione.
term *s.* 1. termine 2. (*scol.*) trimestre 3. (*giur.*) sessione 4. condizione. ♦ **terms** *s. pl.* rapporti.
to **term** *vt.* definire.
terminable *agg.* terminabile.
terminal *agg.* estremo. ♦ **terminal** *s.* 1. estremità 2. stazione di testa, capolinea 3. (*elettr.*) morsetto.
to **terminate** *vt.* 1. limitare 2. terminare. ♦ to **terminate** *vi.* 1. essere limitato 2. terminare.
termination *s.* 1. termine 2. (*gramm.*) desinenza.
terminator *s.* 1. chi termina 2. limite.
terminology *s.* terminologia.
terminus *s.* (*pl.* -ni) 1. capolinea 2. meta.
termite *s.* (*zool.*) termite.
tern *s.* terno.
ternary *agg.* ternario.
terrace *s.* 1. terrapieno 2. terrazzo (*sul tetto*) 3. fila di case.
terraqueous *agg.* terracqueo.
terrestrial *agg.* e *s.* terrestre.
terrible *agg.* terribile.
terrific *agg.* 1. spaventoso 2. (*fam.*) straordinario.
to **terrify** *vt.* atterrire.
territorial *agg.* territoriale.
territory *s.* territorio.
terror *s.* terrore.
terrorism *s.* terrorismo.
terrorist *s.* terrorista.
terroristic *agg.* terroristico.
to **terrorize** *vt.* terrorizzare.
terse *agg.* conciso.
terseness *s.* concisione.
tertiary *agg.* e *s.* terziario.
test *s.* 1. prova, esperimento, saggio 2. "test", reattivo psicologico || — *driver*, collaudatore; — *film*, provino; — *-tube*, provetta.
to **test** *vt.* 1. controllare 2. mettere alla prova 3. analizzare.
testament *s.* testamento.
testamentary *agg.* testamentario.
tester *s.* 1. collaudatore 2. apparecchio di misura 3. baldacchino.
testicle *s.* testicolo.
to **testify** *vt.* e *vi.* testimoniare.
testimonial *s.* 1. benservito 2. dono.
testimony *s.* testimonianza.

testing *s.* collaudo, prova.
tetanic(al) *agg.* tetanico.
tetanus *s.* tetano.
tetchy *agg.* stizzoso.
tetrahedron *s.* tetraedro.
tetralogy *s.* tetralogia.
Teutonic *agg.* teutonico.
text *s.* 1. testo 2. argomento.
textile *agg.* e *s.* tessile.
textual *agg.* testuale.
texture *s.* trama, tessuto.
thallium *s.* tallio.
than *cong.* che, di, di quello che (non), di quanto (non): *he is older* — *you*, è più vecchio di te.
to **thank** *vt.* ringraziare || — *you!*, grazie!
thankful *agg.* riconoscente.
thankfulness *s.* riconoscenza.
thankless *agg.* ingrato.
thanks *s. pl.* grazie, ringraziamenti.
thanksgiving *s.* ringraziamento.
that *agg.* (*pl.* those) quello, quella. ♦ **that** *pron. dimostr.* quello, questo, ciò. ♦ **that** *pron. rel.* che, il quale, la quale, i quali, le quali.
that *cong.* 1. che 2. affinché 3. purché.
thatch *s.* copertura di paglia (*per tetti*).
to **thatch** *vt.* coprire con paglia.
thaumaturge *s.* taumaturgo.
thaumaturgic(al) *agg.* taumaturgico.
thaw *s.* sgelo, disgelo.
to **thaw** *vt.* sgelare. ♦ to **thaw** *vi.* sgelarsi.
the *art.* il, lo, la, i, gli, le.
theatre *s.* teatro.
theatrical *agg.* teatrale.
theft *s.* furto.
their *agg. poss.* loro.
theirs *pron. poss.* il, la loro; i, le loro.
theism *s.* teismo.
them *pron.* loro, li, le, sé.
thematic *agg.* tematico.
theme *s.* tema.
themselves *pron. r.* 1. se stessi, se stesse, sé, si 2. essi stessi, esse stesse.
then *avv.* 1. allora 2. poi.
theocracy *s.* teocrazia.
theocratic(al) *agg.* teocratico.
theologian *s.* teologo.
theologic(al) *agg.* teologico.
theology *s.* teologia.
theorem *s.* teorema.

theoretic(al) *agg.* teorico.
theoretics *s.* teoretica.
theorist *s.* teorico.
to theorize *vi.* teorizzare.
theory *s.* teoria.
therapeutic(al) *agg.* terapeutico.
therapeutics *s.* terapeutica.
therapy *s.* terapia.
there *avv.* 1. là, lì 2. ci, vi 3. in ciò. ✦ there *inter.* ecco! su!
thereabout(s) *avv.* 1. là vicino 2. all'incirca.
thereby *avv.* per mezzo di, perciò.
therefore *avv.* quindi, dunque.
thereupon *avv.* al che, tosto.
thermal *agg.* termico, termale.
thermic *agg.* termico.
thermionic *agg.* termoionico.
thermodynamics *s.* termodinamica.
thermoelectric *agg.* termoelettrico.
thermometer *s.* termometro.
thermonuclear *agg.* termonucleare.
thermostat *s.* termostato.
these (*pl. di* this), questi, queste.
thesis *s.* (*pl.* -ses) tesi, dissertazione.
thews *s. pl.* muscoli.
they *pron. pers.* 1. essi, esse, loro 2. (*in costruzioni impersonali*) si: — *say*, si dice.
thick *agg.* 1. spesso, grosso: *a* — *book*, un grosso libro 2. fitto, folto 3. denso, torbido.
to thicken *vt.* ispessire, addensare. ✦ to thicken *vi.* ispessirsi, addensarsi.
thickening *s.* ispessimento.
thicket *s.* boschetto.
thickly *avv.* fittamente, densamente.
thickness *s.* 1. spessore, grossezza 2. densità 3. strato.
thickset *agg.* 1. fitto, spesso 2. tarchiato.
thief *s.* (*pl.* thieves) ladro.
to thieve *vt.* e *vi.* rubare, essere ladro.
thievish *agg.* ladresco.
thigh *s.* coscia || — *bone*, femore.
thimble *s.* ditale.
thin *agg.* 1. sottile 2. magro, snello 3. rado, raro 4. fluido, rarefatto 5. debole, fiacco.
to thin *vt.* e *vi.* 1. assottigliare, assottigliarsi, dimagrire 2. diradare, sfoltire. ✦ to thin *vt.* 1. assottigliare 2. diradare, sfoltire. ✦ to thin *vi.* 1. assottigliarsi 2. diradarsi.
thing *s.* 1. cosa, oggetto 2. argomen-

to, soggetto.
to think (thought, thought) *vt.* e *vi.* 1. pensare, riflettere 2. ritenere, considerare 3. credere, aspettarsi || *to* — *of*, pensare, avere in animo di; *to* — *ill of so.*, avere una cattiva opinione di qu.; *to* — *out*, escogitare; *to* — *over*, riflettere.
thinkable *agg.* concepibile, immaginabile.
thinker *s.* pensatore.
thinking *agg.* pensante, ragionevole ✦ thinking *s.* pensiero, riflessione, opinione.
thinness *s.* sottigliezza, tenuità, magrezza, radezza.
third *agg.* e *s.* terzo.
thirdly *avv.* in terzo luogo.
third-rate *agg.* di terz'ordine.
thirst *s.* 1. sete, arsura 2. (*fig.*) avidità.
thirsty *agg.* assetato || *to be* —, aver sete; *to be* — *for* (*fig.*), bramare.
thirteen *agg.* tredici.
thirteenth *agg.* tredicesimo.
thirtieth *agg.* trentesimo.
thirty *agg.* trenta.
this *agg.* e *pron. dimostr.* (*pl.* these) questo, questa.
Thomism *s.* tomismo.
thomist *s.* tomista.
thorax *s.* torace.
thorn *s.* spina (*anche fig.*).
thorny *agg.* spinoso (*anche fig.*).
thorough *agg.* 1. completo, totale 2. perfetto, esperto 3. meticoloso.
thoroughbred *agg.* 1. purosangue (*di cavallo*) 2. di antico lignaggio. ✦ thoroughbred *s.* purosangue.
thoroughfare *s.* arteria di grande traffico || *no* —, passaggio vietato.
those (*pl. di* that) quelli, quelle.
though *avv.* comunque, tuttavia. ✦ though *cong.* benché, sebbene.
thought V. to think.
thought *s.* 1. pensiero, riflessione 2. idea, parere 3. concezione.
thoughtful *agg.* 1. pensoso, pensieroso 2. sollecito.
thoughtless *agg.* sconsiderato, sventato, negligente.
thoughtlessness *s.* sconsideratezza, negligenza.
thousand *agg.* mille. ✦ thousand *s.* migliaio.
thrall *s.* schiavo.
to thrash *vt.* e *vi.* 1. battere, sfer-

zare **2.** (*mar.*) navigare contro vento **3.** trebbiare **4.** bastonare || *to — out*, dibattere.
thrasher *s.* trebbiatore.
thrashing machine *s.* trebbiatrice.
thread *s.* **1.** filo (*anche fig.*) **2.** vena, filone.
to **thread** *vt.* **1.** infilare **2.** far passare attraverso.
threadbare *agg.* **1.** consumato, consunto **2.** (*fig.*) vieto, trito.
threading *s.* filettatura.
threadlike *agg.* filiforme.
threat *s.* minaccia.
to **threaten** *vt. e vi.* minacciare.
threatening *agg.* minaccioso.
three *agg. e s.* tre.
threescore *agg.* sessanta.
to **thresh** *vt. e vi.* trebbiare.
threshold *s.* **1.** soglia, limitare **2.** (*fig.*) esordio, inizio.
threw V. *to throw*.
thrice *avv.* tre volte.
thriftiness *s.* economia, parsimonia.
thrifty *agg.* frugale, economo.
thrill *s.* brivido, palpito.
to **thrill** *vt.* far fremere, elettrizzare. ◆ to **thrill** *vi.* fremere, vibrare, emozionarsi.
thriller *s.* (*gergo*) storia, film sensazionale, poliziesco.
thrilling *agg.* **1.** sensazionale, emozionante **2.** penetrante.
to **thrive** (**throve**, **thriven**) *vi.* **1.** prosperare, fiorire **2.** crescere vigorosamente.
thriving *agg.* **1.** prospero, fiorente **2.** rigoglioso.
throat *s.* gola || *— wash*, gargarismo; *sore —*, mal di gola.
throaty *agg.* gutturale.
throb *s.* battito, pulsazione, fremito.
to **throb** *vi.* battere, pulsare, fremere.
throbbing *agg.* palpitante, vibrante (*anche fig.*).
thrombosis *s.* trombosi.
throne *s.* trono.
throng *s.* folla, moltitudine.
to **throng** *vt.* affollare, stipare. ◆ to **throng** *vi.* affollarsi, affluire.
to **throttle** *vt.* strozzare, strangolare.
through *avv.* **1.** attraverso, da una parte all'altra **2.** (*ferr.*) direttamente || *— train*, treno diretto. ◆ **through** *prep.* **1.** attraverso, per **2.** durante, per tutta la durata di

3. per mezzo.
throughout *avv.* da un capo all'altro, dal principio alla fine. ◆ **throughout** *prep.* in ogni parte di, durante tutto il, dal principio alla fine di.
throve V. *to thrive*.
throw *s.* lancio, gittata (*di missile ecc.*), tiro.
to **throw** (**threw**, **thrown**) *vt. e vi.* **1.** gettare, scagliare, proiettare **2.** atterrare, rovesciare || *to — away*, buttar via; *to — off*, buttar fuori; *to — out* espellere.
throwback *s.* **1.** movimento brusco all'indietro **2.** ostacolo.
thrown V. *to throw*.
thrush *s.* tordo.
thrust *s.* **1.** colpo, botta **2.** colpo con arma appuntita.
to **thrust** (**thrust**, **thrust**) *vt. e vi.* **1.** spingere, ficcare **2.** frapporre **3.** forzare.
thud *s.* tonfo, rumore sordo.
to **thud** *vi.* fare un rumore sordo.
thumb *s.* pollice.
to **thumb** *vt.* **1.** lasciare ditate su (*un foglio ecc.*) **2.** strimpellare.
thump *s.* rumore sordo.
to **thump** *vt.* battere, percuotere, dar pugni.
thumping *agg.* pesante.
thunder *s.* **1.** tuono: *a peal of —*, un colpo di tuono **2.** scoppio, rombo **3.** fulmine (*anche fig.*).
to **thunder** *vt. e vi.* **1.** tuonare, rimbombare **2.** minacciare.
thunderbolt *s.* fulmine, saetta (*anche fig.*).
thundering *agg.* **1.** tonante, fulminante **2.** (*fam.*) straordinario.
thundery *agg.* minaccioso.
Thursday *s.* giovedì.
thus *avv.* così, in questo modo.
to **thwart** *vt.* opporsi a, ostacolare.
thyme *s.* timo.
thyroid *s.* tiroide.
tibia *s.* tibia.
tick *s.* tic-tac, ticchettio (*di orologio*).
to **tick** *vt. e vi.* ticchettare.
ticket *s.* **1.** biglietto, tessera, scontrino **2.** (*mil.*) congedo || *— collector*, bigliettario; *— -inspector*, controllore; *single —*, biglietto di andata.
to **ticket** *vt.* **1.** mettere il cartellino del prezzo a **2.** fornire di biglietto.

ticking s. traliccio.

tickle s. solletico.

to tickle vt. fare il solletico, solleticare (anche fig.). ♦ **to tickle** vi. prudere.

tickler s. **1.** chi solletica **2.** questione delicata.

ticklish agg. **1.** sensibile al solletico **2.** scabroso.

tide s. **1.** marea **2.** (fig.) corrente, corso || — -gauge, mareografo.

to tide vi. salire, crescere come la marea.

tidily avv. lindamente.

tidings s. pl. novità.

tidy agg. ordinato, preciso, pulito.

to tidy vt. riordinare, mettere in ordine.

tie s. **1.** laccio, legaccio **2.** cravatta **3.** (fig.) legame **4.** (ferr.) traversina.

to tie vt. **1.** legare, allacciare, congiungere (anche fig.) **2.** annodare.

tied agg. vincolato, schiavo.

tier s. ordine, fila (di posti).

to tier vt. allineare.

tiff s. stizza, bisticcio || **to be in a** —, essere in collera.

to tiff vi. essere stizzito.

tiger s. tigre.

tight agg. **1.** impermeabile, a perfetta tenuta **2.** teso, tirato **3.** stretto, aderente, attillato **4.** scarso, a corto di denaro **5.** (gergo) ubriaco. ♦ **tight** avv. **1.** ermeticamente **2.** in maniera tesa.

to tighten vt. **1.** serrare **2.** tirare, tendere. ♦ **to tighten** vi. **1.** serrarsi **2.** tendersi.

tightly avv. ermeticamente, strettamente.

tightness s. **1.** impermeabilità, tenuta **2.** tensione **3.** (gergo) ubriachezza.

tights s. pl. calzamaglia.

tigress s. tigre (femmina).

tile s. **1.** tegola, mattonella, piastrella **2.** (fam.) cappello a cilindro.

to tile vt. coprire di tegole, piastrelle.

tilemaking s. fabbricazione di tegole.

tilery s. fabbrica di tegole.

tiling s. tegolato, piastrellatura.

till[1] prep. fino a: — now, fino ad ora. ♦ **till** cong. finché, fino al momento in cui.

till[2] s. cassetto in cui si custodisce il denaro.

to till vt. dissodare, arare.

tillage s. **1.** dissodamento, aratura **2.** terreno coltivato.

tiller s. **1.** aratore **2.** (mar.) barra del timone.

tilt[1] s. tenda, tendone.

tilt[2] s. **1.** torneo, giostra **2.** contesa, disputa **3.** inclinazione, pendenza.

to tilt vt. **1.** inclinare **2.** rovesciare. ♦ **to tilt** vi. **1.** oscillare **2.** (mar.) beccheggiare.

timber s. **1.** legname da costruzione **2.** bosco con alberi d'alto fusto **3.** trave **4.** (fig.) tempra, carattere **5.** (mar.) costola || — -work, costruzione in legno.

to timber vt. rivestire di legno.

timbre s. timbro (di suoni).

time s. **1.** tempo, periodo di tempo, circostanza, epoca, età **2.** volta, volte **3.** orario, ora || with —, col passar del tempo; from — to —, di tanto in tanto; as times go, coi tempi che corrono; at times, a volte; in good —, per tempo; what — is it?, che ore sono?

to time vt. fissare l'orario di. ♦ **to time** vi. tenere il tempo.

timekeeper s. **1.** cronometro **2.** cronometrista.

timeliness s. tempestività.

timely agg. opportuno, tempestivo.

timepiece s. orologio (da tavolo).

timer s. cronometrista.

time-study agg. — engineer, analista tempi.

timid agg. timido.

timidity s. timidezza.

timing s. **1.** calcolo del tempo (di pose fotografiche ecc.) **2.** (mecc.) messa in fase.

timorous agg. timoroso.

tin s. **1.** stagno, latta **2.** recipiente.

to tin vt. **1.** stagnare **2.** conservare in scatola.

tincture s. **1.** (chim.) tintura, soluzione alcoolica **2.** tinta **3.** sfumatura, traccia **4.** gusto, aroma.

to tincture vt. **1.** tingere, colorare **2.** aromatizzare.

tinder s. esca (per fuoco).

tinge s. **1.** sfumatura, tocco **2.** (fig.) pizzico.

to tinge vt. dare una sfumatura a (anche fig.).

to tingle vt. **1.** pizzicare **2.** far tintinnare. ♦ **to tingle** vi. arrossire (di guance).

tink s. tintinnio.

tinker *s.* calderaio (*ambulante*), stagnino.
to **tinker** *vt.* rabberciare, riparare.
tinkle *s.* tintinnio.
to **tinkle** *vt.* far tintinnare. ◆ to **tinkle** *vi.* tintinnare.
tinkling *s.* tintinnio.
tinsel *agg.* vistoso, sgargiante. ◆ **tinsel** *s.* orpello (*anche fig.*).
tint *s.* tinta, colore delicato, sfumatura.
to **tint** *vt.* colorire, tinteggiare.
tiny *agg.* minuscolo.
tip[1] *s.* **1.** punta, cima **2.** puntale.
tip[2] *s.* **1.** immondezzaio **2.** inclinazione.
tip[3] *s.* mancia.
to **tip**[1] *vt.* toccare, battere leggermente.
to **tip**[2] *vt.* **1.** rovesciare **2.** inclinare. ◆ to **tip** *vi.* **1.** rovesciarsi **2.** inclinarsi.
to **tip**[3] *vt.* e *vi.* **1.** dare la mancia **2.** (*gergo*) dare, passare.
tippet *s.* mantellina.
tipsy *agg.* ubriaco.
tiptoe *s.* punta dei piedi: *on* —, in punta di piedi.
to **tiptoe** *vi.* camminare in punta di piedi.
tire *s.* **1.** cerchione di ruota **2.** pneumatico || *flat* —, gomma a terra.
to **tire**[1] *vt.* stancare, annoiare. ◆ to **tire** *vi.* stancarsi, annoiarsi.
to **tire**[2] *vt.* fornire di cerchione, di pneumatico.
tired *agg.* stanco, affaticato, esausto || *to be* — *out*, essere stanco morto.
tireless *agg.* instancabile.
tiresome *agg.* faticoso, stancante, noioso.
tissue *s.* tessuto || — *paper*, carta velina.
Titan *s.* titano, gigante.
titanic *agg.* titanico (*anche fig.*).
title *s.* **1.** titolo **2.** titolo, grado, qualifica.
to **title** *vt.* **1.** intitolare, intestare **2.** conferire un titolo.
titular *s.* titolare.
to *prep.* **1.** (*con verbo di moto*) a, in, da **2.** verso, per **3.** (*di tempo*) fino a **4.** (*paragone, rapporto*) contro a **5.** riguardo a || — *all appearances*, stando alle apparenze; — *my despair*, con mia disperazione; — *this end*, a questo scopo.
toad *s.* rospo.

toady *s.* adulatore.
to **toady** *vt.* adulare, comportarsi servilmente.
toast[1] *s.* pane abbrustolito, crostino.
toast[2] *s.* brindisi.
to **toast**[1] *vt.* abbrustolire, tostare.
to **toast**[2] *vt.* e *vi.* fare un brindisi.
toaster *s.* tostapane.
tobacco *s.* tabacco || — -*box*, tabacchiera.
tobacconist *s.* tabaccaio || — '*s shop,* tabaccheria.
tocsin *s.* segnale d'allarme.
today *s.* oggi. ◆ **today** *avv.* oggigiorno.
toddle *s.* andatura incerta, vacillante.
to **toddle** *vi.* camminare a passi incerti, passeggiare.
toe *s.* dito del piede.
together *avv.* assieme, insieme, unitamente.
toil[1] *s.* fatica, duro lavoro || — -*worn*, sfinito dalla fatica.
toil[2] *s.* laccio, trappola (*anche fig.*).
to **toil**[1] *vi.* faticare, lavorare duramente.
to **toil**[2] *vt.* prendere in trappola (*anche fig.*).
toilet *s.* **1.** toletta, pulizia **2.** abbigliamento **3.** bagno, gabinetto || — -*paper*, carta igienica.
toilsome *agg.* faticoso, laborioso.
token *s.* **1.** segno, simbolo **2.** prova, pegno, ricordo.
tolerable *agg.* **1.** tollerabile **2.** discreto.
tolerance *s.* tolleranza.
tolerant *agg.* tollerante.
to **tolerate** *vt.* tollerare, sopportare.
toleration *s.* tolleranza.
toll[1] *s.* pedaggio, dazio, gabella.
toll[2] *s.* rintocco (*di campana*).
to **toll** *vt.* suonare. ◆ to **toll** *vi.* rintoccare.
tomato *s.* pomodoro.
tomb *s.* tomba.
tomboy *s.* ragazza indiavolata.
tome *s.* tomo, volume.
tomfool *agg.* e *s.* sciocco, banale.
tommy *s.* **1.** pane, pagnotta **2.** provviste (*che l'operaio porta da casa*) (*pl.*).
tommy-gun *s.* fucile mitragliatore, mitra.
tomorrow *s.* e *avv.* domani.
ton *s.* tonnellata.
tonality *s.* tonalità.
tone *s.* tono, timbro, accento.

to **tone** vt. e vi. **1.** (mus.) dare il tono, intonare, accordare **2.** (pitt.) sfumare.

toneless agg. inespressivo, privo di colore, senza vigore.

tongs s. pl. pinze, molle, tenaglie.

tongue s. **1.** lingua **2.** lingua, linguaggio **3.** lingua (di terra, fuoco) || — -tied, muto, taciturno; — -twister, scioglilingua.

to **tongue** vt. leccare, lambire.

tonic agg. tonico, corroborante. ♦ **tonic** s. (med.) tonico, energetico.

tonight avv. e s. stanotte, stasera.

tonnage s. tonnellaggio, stazza.

tonsil s. tonsilla.

tonsillitis s. tonsillite.

tonsure s. tonsura.

to **tonsure** vt. tonsurare.

too avv. **1.** troppo **2.** anche, pure **3.** inoltre.

took V. to take.

tool s. **1.** arnese, attrezzo, utensile **2.** (fig.) strumento.

tooth s. (pl. teeth) **1.** dente, zanna **2.** dente (di pettine, forchetta ecc.) || — -paste, dentifricio; — -pick, stuzzicadenti.

toothache s. mal di denti.

toothbrush s. spazzolino da denti.

toothing s. dentatura, dentellatura.

toothless agg. sdentato.

toothy agg. dai denti sporgenti.

top[1] s. **1.** cima, sommità **2.** (fig.) apice **3.** parte superiore, "capote" di automobile.

top[2] s. trottola.

topaz s. topazio.

topic s. argomento, soggetto.

topical agg. d'attualità.

topographer s. topografo.

topographic(al) agg. topografico.

topography s. topografia.

topology s. topologia.

toponymy s. toponomastica.

topsail s. vela di gabbia.

topsyturvy agg. sottosopra, capovolto. ♦ **topsyturvy** s. capovolgimento, disordine, scompiglio. ♦ **topsyturvy** avv. sottosopra.

to **topsyturvy** vt. mettere sossopra.

toque s. berretto, tocco.

torch s. torcia, fiaccola || electric —, lampadina tascabile.

torchlight s. luce di fiaccole, torce || — procession, fiaccolata.

tore V. to tear.

torment s. tormento, tortura.

to **torment** vt. tormentare.

torn V. to tear.

tornado s. ciclone.

torpedo s. **1.** (zool.) torpedine **2.** (mar.) siluro || — -boat, torpediniera; — boat destroyer, cacciatorpediniere.

to **torpedo** vt. silurare.

torpid agg. torpido, apatico.

torpor s. torpore.

torrefaction s. torrefazione.

to **torrefy** vt. torrefare.

torrent s. torrente (anche fig.).

torrential agg. torrenziale.

torrid agg. torrido.

torsion s. torsione.

tortoise s. tartaruga.

torture s. tortura, tormento (anche fig.).

to **torture** vt. torturare, tormentare.

torturous agg. tormentoso.

toss s. **1.** lancio **2.** movimento del capo.

to **toss** vt. **1.** gettare, lanciare **2.** agitare, scuotere **3.** disarcionare. ♦ to **toss** vi. **1.** agitarsi, smaniare **2.** tirare a sorte **3.** (mar.) beccheggiare.

total agg. totale, completo. ♦ **total** s. totale.

totalitarian agg. totalitario.

totalitarianism s. totalitarismo.

totality s. totalità.

totalizator s. totalizzatore.

to **totalize** vt. e vi. totalizzare.

totalizer s. totalizzatore.

to **totter** vi. camminare barcollando.

tottering agg. vacillante, malsicuro.

touch s. **1.** tocco, colpetto **2.** tatto **3.** contatto, rapporto.

to **touch** vt. **1.** toccare **2.** sfiorare **3.** (fig.) colpire, commuovere. ♦ to **touch** vi. essere in contatto, confinare.

touchiness s. suscettibilità.

touching agg. toccante, commovente. ♦ **touching** prep. riguardo a.

touchstone s. pietra di paragone.

touchwood s. esca (per accendere il fuoco).

touchy agg. permaloso.

tough agg. **1.** duro **2.** forte, robusto **3.** (fig.) inflessibile **4.** difficile **5.** violento.

to **toughen** vt. indurire. ♦ to **toughen** vi. indurirsi.

toughness s. **1.** durezza **2.** inflessibilità.

tour s. giro, viaggio, escursione.

to **tour** vt. e vi. fare un viaggio.

tourism s. turismo.
tourist s. turista.
tourmalin(e) s. tormalina.
tournament s. torneo.
to **tousle** vt. scompigliare, arruffare.
tow s. rimorchio.
toward(s) prep. **1.** verso, in direzione di **2.** riguardo a **3.** verso, circa (di tempo).
towel s. asciugamano || — -horse, porta-asciugamano.
tower s. torre.
to **tower** vi. torreggiare.
towing s. rimorchio.
town s. **1.** città **2.** cittadinanza || — -council, consiglio comunale; — -planning, piano regolatore; chief —, capoluogo.
townhall s. municipio.
townhouse s. residenza di città.
townscape s. veduta (di città).
townsfolk s. abitanti di una città.
township s. territorio, giurisdizione di una città.
townsman s. cittadino.
townspeople s. cittadinanza.
townward(s) avv. verso la città.
toxic(al) agg. tossico.
toxicity s. tossicità.
toxicologist s. tossicologo.
toxicology s. tossicologia.
toxin s. tossina.
toy s. **1.** giocattolo **2.** bazzecola, storiella.
to **toy** vi. giocherellare, trastullarsi.
toyish agg. **1.** simile a giocattolo **2.** insignificante.
toyshop s. negozio di giocattoli.
trabeation s. trabeazione.
trace s. traccia, orma.
to **trace** vt. **1.** tracciare **2.** seguire le tracce **3.** rintracciare || to — back, risalire.
traceable agg. **1.** rintracciabile **2.** che si può tracciare.
trachea s. trachea.
tracheal agg. tracheale.
tracheitis s. tracheite.
trachyte s. trachite.
tracing s. **1.** tracciato **2.** calco, ricalco.
track s. **1.** traccia, orma **2.** sentiero, corso (anche fig.) **3.** (sport) pista **4.** (ferr.) binario || sound — (cine), colonna sonora.
to **track** vt. **1.** inseguire, pedinare **2.** tracciare un sentiero. ♦ to **track** vi. posare i binari.
tract[1] s. periodo, tratto, spazio.

tract[2] s. opuscolo.
tractability s. arrendevolezza.
tractable agg. arrendevole.
traction s. **1.** trazione **2.** contrazione.
tractor s. trattore.
trade s. **1.** mestiere **2.** commercio, traffico **3.** commercianti (pl.) || — bank, banca commerciale; — dispute, vertenza sindacale; — -mark, marchio di fabbrica; — -show (cine), anteprima per la critica; free- —, libero scambio.
to **trade** vt. e vi. commerciare, negoziare.
trader s. **1.** commerciante **2.** nave mercantile.
trading s. commercio.
tradition s. tradizione.
traditional agg. tradizionale.
traditionalism s. tradizionalismo.
traditionalist s. tradizionalista.
to **traduce** vt. calunniare.
traffic s. **1.** traffico, commercio **2.** traffico, circolazione || — lights, semaforo; — jam, ingorgo stradale.
tragedian s. **1.** tragediografo **2.** attore tragico.
tragedy s. tragedia.
tragic(al) agg. tragico.
tragicomedy s. tragicommedia.
tragicomic(al) agg. tragicomico.
trail s. **1.** traccia, striscia **2.** pista, orma **3.** cammino, sentiero.
to **trail** vt. **1.** trascinare **2.** seguire le tracce di. ♦ to **trail** vi. trascinarsi.
trailer s. **1.** inseguitore, cacciatore **2.** rimorchio **3.** (cine) film di prossima programmazione.
train s. **1.** treno: express — (o fast —), rapido; slow —, accelerato **2.** seguito, corteo **3.** serie, successione, fila.
to **train** vt. **1.** allevare, educare **2.** esercitare, allenare, addestrare. ♦ to **train** vi. **1.** esercitarsi, allenarsi **2.** viaggiare in ferrovia.
trainer s. istruttore, allenatore.
training s. educazione, ammaestramento, allenamento.
trait s. tratto, fattezza, caratteristica.
traitor s. traditore.
trajectory s. traiettoria.
tram s. **1.** tram **2.** carrello da miniera || — -conductor, tranviere.
trammel s. **1.** tramaglio **2.** intoppo.
tramp s. **1.** calpestio **2.** viaggio a piedi.

to **tramp** *vt.* **1.** camminare pesantemente **2.** viaggiare a piedi **3.** vagabondare.

trample *s.* calpestio.

to **trample** *vt.* **1.** calpestare **2.** (*fig.*) offendere. ♦ to **trample** *vi.* camminare pesantemente.

tramway *s.* tranvia.

to **tranquillize** *vt.* tranquillizzare.

tranquillizer *s.* (*med.*) tranquillante.

to **transact** *vt.* e *vi.* negoziare, trattare affari.

transaction *s.* **1.** affare, operazione **2.** (*giur.*) transazione **3.** atti (*di congresso ecc.*) (*pl.*).

transactor *s.* negoziatore.

transalpine *agg.* e *s.* transalpino.

transatlantic *agg.* transatlantico.

to **transcend** *vt.* trascendere, superare.

transcendence *s.* trascendenza.

transcendent *agg.* trascendente.

transcendental *agg.* trascendentale.

transcendentalism *s.* trascendentalismo.

transcontinental *agg.* transcontinentale.

to **transcribe** *vt.* trascrivere.

transcript *s.* riproduzione, copia.

transcription *s.* trascrizione.

transept *s.* transetto.

transfer *s.* **1.** trasferimento, cessione **2.** (*giur.*) trapasso **3.** decalcomania.

to **transfer** *vt.* trasferire, cedere.

transferable *agg.* trasferibile.

transfiguration *s.* trasfigurazione.

to **transfigure** *vt.* trasfigurare.

to **transfix** *vt.* trafiggere.

transfocator *s.* (*cine*) teleobiettivo.

to **transform** *vt.* trasformare.

transformable *agg.* trasformabile.

transformation *s.* trasformazione.

transformer *s.* trasformatore.

transformism *s.* trasformismo.

to **transfuse** *vt.* **1.** travasare **2.** fare una trasfusione (*di sangue*).

transfusion *s.* trasfusione.

to **transgress** *vt.* trasgredire. ♦ to **transgress** *vi.* commettere una violenza, peccare.

transgression *s.* trasgressione.

transgressor *s.* trasgressore.

transient *agg.* passeggero, transitorio.

transistor *s.* (*radio*) transistor.

transit *s.* **1.** transito, passaggio **2.** trasporto.

transition *s.* transizione.

transitive *agg.* transitivo.

transitory *agg.* transitorio.

translatable *agg.* traducibile.

to **translate** *vt.* tradurre.

translation *s.* **1.** traduzione **2.** trasferimento, assunzione (*al cielo*).

translator *s.* traduttore.

translucent *agg.* traslucido, diafano, trasparente.

to **transmigrate** *vi.* trasmigrare.

transmigration *s.* trasmigrazione.

transmissible *agg.* trasmissibile.

transmission *s.* trasmissione.

to **transmit** *vt.* trasmettere.

transmitter *s.* trasmettitore.

transoceanic *agg.* transoceanico.

transparence *s.* trasparenza.

transparent *agg.* **1.** trasparente, limpido **2.** chiaro, evidente.

to **transpire** *vt.* e *vi.* traspirare.

to **transplant** *vt.* trapiantare.

transplantation *s.* trapianto.

transport *s.* **1.** trasporto (*anche fig.*) **2.** mezzo di trasporto.

transportable *agg.* trasportabile.

transposal *s.* trasposizione.

transposition *s.* trasposizione (*di parole, cifre ecc.*).

transubstantiation *s.* transustanziazione.

transversal *agg.* e *s.* trasversale.

trap *s.* trappola ‖ — *-door*, botola.

to **trap** *vt.* prendere in trappola.

trapezium *s.* trapezio.

trapper *s.* chi tende trappole.

trash[1] *s.* rifiuto.

trash[2] *s.* guinzaglio.

to **trash** *vt.* sfrondare.

trashy *agg.* senza valore.

traumatic *agg.* traumatico.

travel *s.* **1.** viaggi (*pl.*): — *agency*, agenzia di viaggi **2.** (*mecc.*) corsa.

to **travel** *vi.* viaggiare.

traveller *s.* viaggiatore.

travelling *agg.* **1.** viaggiante **2.** di, da viaggio **3.** mobile. ♦ **travelling** *s.* il viaggiare.

traverse *agg.* trasversale. ♦ **traverse** *s.* **1.** trasversale **2.** traversata.

to **traverse** *vt.* **1.** traversare **2.** muovere lateralmente. ♦ to **traverse** *vi.* **1.** fare una traversata **2.** muoversi lateralmente **3.** girare su un perno.

travertin(e) *s.* travertino.

travesty *s.* parodia.

trawl *s.* (*mar.*) strascico.

trawler s. peschereccio a strascico.

tray s. vassoio || *ash-* —, portacenere.

treacherous *agg.* traditore, sleale.

treacherousness, treachery s. tradimento, slealtà.

tread s. **1.** passo **2.** suola **3.** battistrada.

to tread (trod, trodden) *vt.* e *vi.* camminare. ♦ **to tread (trod, trodden)** *vt.* **1.** percorrere **2.** calpestare.

treadle s. pedale.

treason s. tradimento.

treasure s. tesoro.

to treasure *vt.* **1.** ammassare **2.** custodire gelosamente.

treasurer s. tesoriere.

treasury s. **1.** tesoreria **2.** Ministero del Tesoro.

treat s. festa.

to treat *vt.* **1.** trattare **2.** offrire.

treatise s. trattato.

treatment s. **1.** trattamento **2.** (*med.*) cura.

treaty s. trattato.

treble *agg.* **1.** triplo, triplice **2.** (*mus.*) di soprano, parte di soprano.

to treble *vt.* triplicare. ♦ **to treble** *vi.* triplicarsi.

tree s. **1.** albero **2.** trave || — *-frog*, raganella.

trefoil s. trifoglio.

trellis s. graticcio.

tremble s. tremito.

to tremble *vi.* tremare.

trembling *agg.* tremante, tremolante. ♦ **trembling** s. tremito.

tremendous *agg.* tremendo.

tremor s. tremore.

tremulous *agg.* tremulo.

trench s. **1.** fosso **2.** trincea.

to trench *vt.* e *vi.* scavare, solcare, scavare trincee.

trenchant *agg.* tagliente, incisivo, efficace.

trencher s. tagliere.

trend s. direzione, orientamento, tendenza.

to trend *vi.* tendere.

trepan s. trapano.

to trepan *vt.* trapanare.

trepidation s. **1.** tremito **2.** trepidazione.

trespass s. **1.** trasgressione **2.** violazione.

to trespass *vi.* **1.** commettere una violazione **2.** peccare.

trespasser s. **1.** trasgressore **2.** peccatore.

trestle s. **1.** cavalletto **2.** intelaiatura.

trial s. **1.** processo **2.** prova, esperimento.

triangle s. triangolo.

triangular *agg.* triangolare.

triangulation s. triangolazione.

tribal *agg.* tribale.

tribe s. tribù.

tribune[1] s. tribuno.

tribune[2] s. tribuna.

tributary *agg.* e s. tributario.

tribute s. tributo.

trichromatic *agg.* tricromico.

trick s. **1.** trucco **2.** imbroglio **3.** mania.

to trick *vt.* ingannare.

trickery s. inganno.

trickish *agg.* scaltro.

trickle s. gocciolio.

to trickle *vi.* gocciolare.

tricky *agg.* **1.** scaltro **2.** intricato.

tricolour *agg.* e s. tricolore.

tricycle s. triciclo.

trident s. tridente.

tridimensional *agg.* tridimensionale.

triennial *agg.* triennale.

trifle s. sciocchezza.

to trifle *vi.* scherzare.

trifler s. persona leggera.

trifling *agg.* **1.** insignificante **2.** frivolo.

trigeminal *agg.* e s. trigemino.

trigeminus s. trigemino.

trigger s. grilletto.

trigonometry s. trigonometria.

trihedron s. triedro.

trill s. trillo.

to trill *vt.* e *vi.* trillare.

trillion s. **1.** trilione **2.** (*amer.*) bilione.

trilogy s. trilogia.

trim *agg.* ordinato. ♦ **trim** s. **1.** ordine **2.** assetto **3.** (*cine*) taglio.

to trim *vt.* **1.** ordinare **2.** tagliare.

trimester s. trimestre.

trimmer s. decoratore.

trimming s. **1.** guarnizione **2.** bastonatura.

trinity s. trinità.

trinket s. ninnolo.

trinomial s. trinomio.

trip s. **1.** gita, viaggio **2.** passo agile **3.** passo falso.

to trip *vi.* **1.** saltellare **2.** inciampare. ♦ **to trip** *vt.* **1.** far inciampare 2. (*mecc.*) liberare.

tripartite *agg.* tripartito.

tripartition *s.* tripartizione.

tripe *s.* 1. trippa 2. (*gergo*) ciarpame, sciocchezze (*pl.*).

triple *agg.* triplo.

to **triple** *vt.* triplicare. ◆ to **triple** *vi.* triplicarsi.

triplicate *agg.* triplicato. ◆ **triplicate** *s.* triplice copia.

to **triplicate** *vt.* triplicare.

tripod *s.* 1. treppiede 2. tripode.

tripper *s.* gitante.

triptych *s.* trittico.

trisyllabic(al) *agg.* trisillabico.

trite *agg.* trito.

to **triturate** *vt.* triturare.

triumph *s.* trionfo.

to **triumph** *vi.* trionfare.

triumphant *agg.* trionfante.

triumvir *s.* triumviro.

triumvirate *s.* triumvirato.

trivalent *agg.* trivalente.

trivial *agg.* banale.

triviality *s.* banalità.

trod V. *to tread.*

trodden V. *to tread.*

troglodyte *s.* troglodita.

troglodytic(al) *agg.* trogloditico.

trolley *s.* carrello || — *bus*, filobus; — *line*, linea tranviaria.

troop *s.* 1. gruppo 2. truppe (*pl.*).

to **troop** *vi.* 1. radunarsi 2. sfilare.

trophy *s.* trofeo.

tropic *agg.* tropico.

tropical *agg.* tropicale.

tropism *s.* tropismo.

troposphere *s.* troposfera.

trot *s.* trotto.

to **trot** *vt.* far trottare. ◆ to **trot** *vi.* trottare.

trotter *s.* trottatore.

trouble *s.* guaio, disturbo.

to **trouble** *vt.* disturbare. ◆ to **trouble** *vi.* preoccuparsi.

troublesome *agg.* fastidioso.

trough *s.* 1. truogolo 2. condotto, solco 3. depressione (*atmosferica*).

trousers *s. pl.* calzoni

trout *s.* trota.

trowel *s.* cazzuola.

truce *s.* tregua.

truck[1] *s.* baratto, scambio.

truck[1] *s.* 1. carrello 2. (*amer.*) autocarro.

to **truck**[1] *vt.* barattare.

to **truck**[2] *vt.* trasportare (*su carrello*).

trucker *s.* camionista.

truculent *agg.* truculento.

to **trudge** *vi.* camminare faticosamente.

true *agg.* vero, esatto || *ouf of* —, sfasato.

truffle *s.* tartufo.

truly *avv.* 1. veramente 2. esattamente.

to **trump** *vt.* ingannare || *to* — *up a charge*, inventare un'accusa.

trumpery *agg.* illusorio. ◆ **trumpery** *s.* orpello.

trumpet *s.* tromba.

to **trumpet** *vi.* 1. suonare la tromba 2. barrire. ◆ to **trumpet** *vt.* strombazzare.

trumpeter *s.* trombettiere.

truncate *agg.* tronco, troncato.

truncheon *s.* manganello.

trunk *s.* 1. tronco 2. baule 3. proboscide || *-call*, comunicazione interurbana. ◆ **trunks** *s. pl.* calzoni corti.

truss *s.* 1. fascio 2. (*arch.*) capriata.

trust *s.* 1. fede, fiducia 2. incarico di fiducia 3. (*econ.*) "trust", consorzio monopolistico.

to **trust** *vt.* e *vi.* confidare, fidarsi di, dar credito || *to* — *so. with sthg.*, affidare qc. a qu.

trustee *s.* 1. (*comm.*) fiduciario 2. (*giur.*) curatore.

truster *s.* chi si fida.

trustful *agg.* fiducioso.

trustworthy *agg.* degno di fiducia.

truth *s.* verità.

truthful *agg.* 1. vero 2. fedele.

try *s.* tentativo || — *-on*, prova (*di abiti*); — *-out* (*mecc.*), prova.

to **try** *vt.* provare, tentare || *to* — *for sthg.*, cercare di ottenere qc.; *to* — *on*, provare (*di abiti*); *to* — *out*, sottoporre a dura prova.

trying *agg.* 1. difficile 2. difficilmente sopportabile.

tub *s.* tinozza, vasca.

tube *s.* 1. tubo 2. camera d'aria 3. (*fam.*) ferrovia sotterranea.

tuber *s.* 1. tubero 2. tubercolo.

tubercular *agg.* 1. tubercolare 2. tubercoloso.

tuberculosis *s.* tubercolosi.

tuberculous *agg.* tubercoloso.

tubing *s.* tubatura.

tubular, tubulous *agg.* tubolare.

tuck *s.* piega (*di abito*).

to **tuck** *vt.* 1. (ri)piegare 2. pigiare || *to* — *up*, rimboccare.

Tuesday *s.* martedì.

tuff *s.* tufo vulcanico.

tuft s. 1. ciuffo 2. fiocco 3. cespuglio.

tug s. strappo || — -of-war, tiro alla fune.

to **tug** vt. e vi. 1. tirare 2. dare strattoni.

tugboat s. (mar.) rimorchiatore.

tuition s. istruzione.

tulip s. tulipano.

tumble s. 1. caduta 2. confusione.

to **tumble** vi. 1. cadere 2. agitarsi 3. precipitarsi 4. fare acrobazie. ♦ to **tumble** vt. 1. far cadere 2. scompigliare.

tumble-down agg. in rovina.

tumbler s. 1. acrobata 2. bicchiere (senza piede).

tumefaction s. tumefazione.

to **tumefy** vt. tumefare. ♦ to **tumefy** vi. tumefarsi.

tumescence s. tumescenza.

tumescent agg. gonfio.

tumid agg. tumido.

tumidity s. gonfiore.

tumour s. tumore.

tumult s. tumulto.

tumultuous agg. tumultuoso.

tumulus s. (pl. -li) tumulo.

tun s. botte.

tuna s. tonno.

tune s. 1. tono 2. accordo 3. motivo || in —, intonato; out of —, stonato.

to **tune** vt. (mus.) accordare || to — up, mettere a punto. ♦ to **tune** vi. essere in armonia.

tuneful agg. armonioso.

tuner s. 1. (mus.) accordatore 2. (radio) sintonizzatore.

tungsten s. tungsteno.

tunic s. tunica.

Tunisian agg. e s. tunisino.

to **tunnel** vi. costruire un tunnel. ♦ to **tunnel** vt. perforare.

tunny s. tonno.

turban s. turbante.

turbid agg. torbido.

turbidity s. torbidezza.

turbine s. turbina.

turbojet s. turbogetto || — engine, turboreattore.

turbulence s. turbolenza.

turbulent agg. turbolento.

tureen s. zuppiera.

turf s. 1. zolla erbosa 2. torba 3. campo da corse || — -accountant, allibratore.

turgid agg. turgido.

turgidity s. turgidezza.

Turk agg. e s. turco.

turkey s. tacchino.

Turkish agg. turco.

turmoil s. agitazione.

turn s. 1. giro 2. curva 3. turno 4. servizio 5. attitudine || — -out, assemblea, sciopero, produzione; — -table, piattaforma girevole, giradischi.

to **turn** vi. 1. girarsi, volgersi 2. diventare. ♦ to **turn** vt. 1. girare, volgere 2. mutare 3. tornire || to — off, chiudere, spegnere; to — on, aprire, accendere; to — down, abbassare; to — out, scacciare, produrre, spegnere, risultare; to — over, rovesciare.

turnabout s. 1. giostra 2. inversione (di rotta).

turncoat s. voltagabbana.

turner s. tornitore.

turning s. 1. giro, svolta 2. tornitura.

turning-point s. svolta decisiva, momento critico.

turnip s. rapa.

turnkey s. secondino.

turnout s. 1. folla 2. equipaggio.

turnover s. 1. rovesciamento 2. (comm.) giro 3. torta.

turnpike s. strada a pedaggio.

turnspit s. girarrosto.

turpentine s. trementina.

turpitude s. turpitudine.

turquoise s. turchese.

turret s. torretta.

turtle s. 1. tartaruga 2. — (-dove), tortora.

Tuscan agg. e s. toscano.

tusk s. zanna.

tussle s. zuffa.

to **tussle** vi. azzuffarsi.

tutelar(y) agg. tutelare.

tutor s. istitutore.

to **tutor** vt. 1. istruire 2. controllare.

tutorial agg. di istitutore.

tutorship s. mansione di istitutore.

twang s. 1. suono acuto 2. suono nasale.

to **twang** vi. 1. avere un suono acuto 2. parlare con voce nasale.

tweet s. cinguettio.

to **tweet** vi. cinguettare.

tweezers s. pl. pinzette.

twelfth agg. e s. dodicesimo.

twelve agg. e s. dodici.

twentieth agg. e s. ventesimo.

twenty agg. e s. venti.

twice *avv.* due volte.

twig *s.* ramoscello.

twilight *s.* **1.** crepuscolo **2.** luce fioca.

twin *agg.* e *s.* gemello.

to twin *vt.* accoppiare. ♦ to twin *vi.* accoppiarsi.

twine *s.* **1.** spago, corda **2.** groviglio.

twinge *s.* fitta, dolore.

twinkle *s.* **1.** scintillio **2.** ammicco || *in a* —, in un batter d'occhio.

to twinkle *vi.* **1.** scintillare **2.** ammiccare.

twinkling *s.* balenio.

twirl *s.* piroetta, rotazione.

to twirl *vt.* e *vi.* girare, roteare.

twist *s.* **1.** filo ritorto **2.** torsione **3.** curva.

to twist *vt.* **1.** torcere **2.** travisare. ♦ to twist *vi.* **1.** torcersi **2.** serpeggiare.

twister *s.* **1.** torcitore **2.** truffatore.

twisty *agg.* **1.** tortuoso **2.** disonesto.

to twit *vt.* biasimare.

twitch *s.* **1.** strattone **2.** tic nervoso.

twitter *s.* **1.** pigolio **2.** agitazione.

to twitter *vi.* **1.** pigolare **2.** essere ansioso.

two *agg.* e *s.* due.

twofold *agg.* doppio. ♦ twofold *avv.* doppiamente.

twopence *s.* due penny (*valore*).

tycoon *s.* (*amer.*) magnate.

type *s.* **1.** tipo **2.** simbolo **3.** (*tip.*) carattere tipografico || — *-setting* (*tip.*), composizione.

to type *vt.* **1.** rappresentare **2.** dattilografare.

written) *vt.* e *vi.* dattilografare.

to typewrite (typewrote, typewriter *s.* dattilografo.

typewriting *s.* dattilografia.

typewritten V. *to typewrite.*

typewrote V. *to typewrite.*

typhoon *s.* tifone.

typhus *s.* tifo.

typic(al) *agg.* tipico.

to typify *vt.* **1.** incarnare **2.** esemplificare.

typist *s.* dattilografo.

typographer *s.* tipografo.

typographic(al) *agg.* tipografico.

typography *s.* tipografia.

tyrannic(al) *agg.* tirannico.

tyrannicide *s.* **1.** tirannicida **2.** tirannicidio.

to tyrannize *vt.* e *vi.* tiranneggiare.

tyrannous *agg.* tirannico.

tyranny *s.* tirannia.

tyrant *s.* tiranno.

tyre *s.* V. *tire.*

Tyrrhene, Tyrrhenian *agg.* e *s.* tirreno.

Tzigane *agg.* e *s.* tzigano.

U

ubication *s.* ubicazione.

ugliness *s.* bruttezza.

ugly *agg.* **1.** brutto **2.** vile, turpe.

ulcer *s.* ulcera, piaga (*anche fig.*).

to ulcerate *vt.* ulcerare. ♦ to ulcerate *vi.* ulcerarsi.

ulceration *s.* ulcerazione.

ulcerous *agg.* ulceroso.

ulna *s.* (*pl.* -ae) (*anat.*) ulna.

ultimate *agg.* ultimo, finale, definitivo.

ultra *agg.* ultra, estremo, eccessivo. ♦ ultra *s.* estremista.

ultramarine *agg.* oltremarino.

ultramontane *agg.* e *s.* oltremontano.

ultramundane *agg.* oltremondano.

ultra-red *agg.* infrarosso.

ultrasonic *agg.* ultrasonico.

ultraviolet *agg.* ultravioletto.

umbilical *agg.* ombelicale.

umbrella *s.* ombrello || — *-stand*, portaombrelli.

umpire *s.* (*giur.; sport*) arbitro.

unabashed *agg.* imperturbato.

unabated *agg.* non diminuito, non scemato.

unable *agg.* incapace, inabile.

unabridged *agg.* non abbreviato, completo || — *edition*, edizione integrale.

unacceptable *agg.* inaccettabile.

unaccomplished *agg.* incompleto, incompiuto.

unaccountability *s.* inesplicabilità.

unaccountable *agg.* inesplicabile.

unaccustomed *agg.* non abituale, insolito.

unachievable *agg.* ineseguibile.

unacquainted *agg.* **1.** ignaro di, non al corrente di **2.** sconosciuto, poco familiare.

unacquired *agg.* non acquisito, innato.

unactive *agg.* inattivo.

unadapted *agg.* inadatto.

unadorned *agg.* disadorno.
unadvisable *agg.* non consigliabile, inopportuno.
unaffected *agg.* 1. senza affettazione, semplice 2. insensibile.
unafraid *agg.* impavido.
unalienable *agg.* inalienabile.
unallied *agg.* senza relazione, senza connessione.
unalterable *agg.* inalterabile.
unamendable *agg.* incorreggibile.
to **unanchor** *vi.* togliere l'ancora.
♦ to **unanchor** *vt.* disancorare.
unanimated *agg.* inanimato.
unanimity *s.* unanimità.
unanimous *agg.* unanime.
unannounced *agg.* non annunciato, imprevisto.
unanswerable *agg.* 1. a cui non si può rispondere 2. irrefutabile.
unanswered *agg.* senza risposta.
unappealable *agg.* inappellabile.
unappeasable *agg.* implacabile.
unappeased *agg.* insoddisfatto.
unapplied *agg.* non impiegato, inapplicato.
unappreciated *agg.* non apprezzato, ·incompreso.
unapprehensive *agg.* 1. lento nell'apprendere 2. non apprensivo.
unapproachable *agg.* inaccessibile.
unapt *agg.* 1. inadatto 2. inetto.
unargued *agg.* indiscusso.
to **unarm** *vt.* disarmare.
unarmed *agg.* disarmato, inerme.
unartful *agg.* privo di artifici, ingenuo.
unascertainable *agg.* non verificabile.
unascertained *agg.* sconosciuto, non accertato.
unasked *agg.* non richiesto.
unaspiring *agg.* senza ambizione.
unassailable *agg.* inattaccabile.
unassailed *agg.* inattaccato.
unasserted *agg.* non asserito.
unassuming *agg.* modesto, senza pretese.
unattackable *agg.* inattaccabile.
unattainable *agg.* inaccessibile.
unattempted *agg.* intentato.
unauthorized *agg.* 1. non autorizzato 2. illecito.
unavailable *agg.* 1. inutile, vano 2. non disponibile.
unavenged *agg.* impunito.
unavoidable *agg.* inevitabile.
unaware *agg.* inconsapevole, inconscio.

unawareness *s.* inconsapevolezza.
unawares *avv.* inconsapevolmente, inconsciamente.
unbalance *s.* squilibrio.
to **unbalance** *vt.* sbilanciare.
to **unbandage** *vt.* sbendare.
unbearable *agg.* insopportabile.
unbeaten *agg.* 1. insuperato, non battuto 2. non frequentato.
unbecoming *agg.* disdicevole.
unbelief *s.* incredulità, scetticismo.
unbelievable *agg.* incredibile.
unbelieving *agg.* incredulo, scettico.
to **unbend** (unbent, unbent) *vt.* 1. raddrizzare 2. allentare, slegare.
♦ to **unbend** (unbent, unbent) *vi.* raddrizzarsi.
unbias(s)ed *agg.* imparziale, senza preconcetti.
to **unbind** (unbound, unbound) *vt.* sciogliere, slegare.
to **unbolt** *vt.* disserrare, aprire.
unborn *agg.* non nato, nascituro, che deve venire.
to **unbosom** *vt.* rivelare, confidare.
♦ to **unbosom** *vi.* sfogarsi: *to — oneself to so.*, aprirsi con qu.
unbound V. to **unbind**.
unbreakable *agg.* infrangibile.
unbreathable *agg.* irrespirabile.
to **unbreech** *vt.* togliere i calzoni.
to **unbridle** *vt.* sbrigliare, dare libero corso a (anche *fig.*).
unbridled *agg.* incontrollato, senza briglia.
unbroken *agg.* 1. intatto, intero, inviolato 2. incessante.
unbruised *agg.* non· ammaccato, illeso.
to **unbuckle** *vt.* sfibbiare, slacciare.
to **unburden** *vt.* 1. scaricare, alleggerire 2. (*fig.*) alleviare.
unburied *agg.* insepolto.
to **unbury** *vt.* disseppellire.
to **unbutton** *vt.* sbottonare. ♦ to **unbutton** *vi.* sbottonarsi.
uncalled *agg.* non chiamato, non invitato: — *for*, superfluo, gratuito.
uncanny *agg.* misterioso, irreale.
uncared-for *agg.* negletto, abbandonato.
unceasing *agg.* incessante.
uncensurable *agg.* incensurabile.
uncertain *agg.* 1. incerto, malsicuro 2. irresoluto.
uncertainty *s.* 1. incertezza 2. irresolutezza.
to **unchain** *vt.* sciogliere da catene.

unchanged *agg.* immutato.
uncharged *agg.* **1.** non carico **2.** non incriminato.
uncharitable *agg.* poco caritatevole.
to **uncharm** *vt.* liberare da un incantesimo.
unchaste *agg.* impuro.
unchecked *agg.* sfrenato.
uncivil *agg.* **1.** scortese, maleducato **2.** indecoroso.
uncivilized *agg.* non civilizzato.
to **unclasp** *vt.* slacciare. ♦ to **unclasp** *vi.* allentare la stretta.
uncle *s.* zio.
uncombed *agg.* spettinato.
uncomely *agg.* **1.** sgraziato **2.** sconveniente.
uncomfortable *agg.* **1.** scomodo, a disagio **2.** spiacevole.
uncommon *agg.* insolito, raro.
uncompared *agg.* incomparato.
uncompelled *agg.* non costretto, spontaneo.
unconcerned *agg.* indifferente, noncurante.
unconcerning *agg.* irrilevante, che non interessa.
unconditional *agg.* incondizionato.
uncongenial *agg.* **1.** antipatico, spiacevole **2.** non congeniale.
unconquerable *agg.* invincibile, indomabile.
unconquered *agg.* invitto, indomito.
unconscionable *agg.* **1.** irragionevole **2.** senza scrupoli.
unconscious *agg.* **1.** inconscio, ignaro **2.** privo di sensi. ♦ **unconscious** *s.* inconscio.
unconsciousness *s.* **1.** inconsapevolezza **2.** stato di incoscienza.
unconsolable *agg.* inconsolabile.
unconstitutional *agg.* incostituzionale.
unconstrained *agg.* **1.** non costretto, libero **2.** disinvolto.
unconstraint *s.* **1.** assenza di costrizione, libertà **2.** spontaneità.
uncontrollable *agg.* incontrollabile.
uncontrolled *agg.* senza controllo, sfrenato.
unconventional *agg.* non convenzionale, disinvolto.
unconvertible *agg.* inconvertibile.
unconvincing *agg.* non convincente.
to **uncork** *vt.* sturare, stappare.

uncountable *agg.* innumerevole.
to **uncouple** *vt.* **1.** sguinzagliare **2.** staccare.
uncouth *agg.* **1.** ordinario, rozzo **2.** desolato.
to **uncover** *vt.* **1.** scoprire **2.** spogliare. ♦ to **uncover** *vi.* togliersi il cappello.
uncovered *agg.* **1.** scoperto, senza tetto **2.** spogliato **3.** senza cappello.
unction *s.* **1.** unzione **2.** unguento.
unctuous *agg.* grasso, untuoso (*anche fig.*).
uncultivable *agg.* non coltivabile.
uncultivated *agg.* incolto, non coltivato.
uncut *agg.* intonso, non tagliato.
undaunted *agg.* intrepido, impavido.
to **undeceive** *vt.* disingannare.
undecided *agg.* **1.** indeciso, non risolto **2.** indefinito **3.** irresoluto.
undeclinable *agg.* indeclinabile.
undecomposable *agg.* indecomponibile.
undefended *agg.* **1.** indifeso **2.** (*giur.*) non assistito da difesa legale.
undeniable *agg.* innegabile.
under *prep.* **1.** sotto, al di sotto di **2.** in corso di **3.** meno di. ♦ **under** *avv.* sotto, al di sotto || --age, minorenne.
underbrush *s.* sottobosco.
to **undercharge** *vt.* far pagare troppo poco.
underclothes *s. pl.* biancheria intima (*sing.*).
undercover *agg.* segreto.
undercurrent *s.* **1.** corrente sottomarina **2.** (*fig.*) attività, tendenza nascosta.
to **underdo** (**underdid, underdone**) *vt.* e *vi.* **1.** agire in modo insufficiente **2.** cuocere poco.
underdone V. to *underdo*. ♦ **underdone** *agg.* poco cotto.
to **underestimate** *vt.* sottovalutare.
underfed *agg.* denutrito.
to **underfeed** (**underfed, underfed**) *vt.* nutrire insufficientemente.
to **undergo** (**underwent, undergone**) *vt.* **1.** subire, essere sottoposto a **2.** sopportare.
undergraduate *s.* studente universitario.
underground *agg.* sotterraneo. ♦ **underground** *s.* **1.** sottosuolo **2.** metropolitana.

underground *avv.* **1.** sotterra **2.** (*pol.*) clandestinamente.

underhand *agg.* **1.** clandestino, segreto **2.** furbo, astuto. ♦ **underhand** *avv.* segretamente, clandestinamente.

to **underline** *vt.* sottolineare.

underlining *s.* sottolineatura.

undermentioned *agg.* sottoindicato.

to **undermine** *vt.* **1.** minare, scalzare **2.** (*fig.*) indebolire, insidiare.

underneath *avv.* di sotto, al di sotto.

to **underpay** (**underpaid**, **underpaid**) *vt.* pagare inadeguatamente.

to **underrate** *vt.* sottovalutare.

underscriber *s.* sottoscrittore.

undersea *agg.* sottomarino.

to **undersell** (**undersold**, **undersold**) *vt.* svendere.

undershrub *s.* sottobosco.

undersignature *s.* firma in calce.

undersold V. *to undersell.*

to **understand** (**understood**, **understood**) *vt.* e *vi.* **1.** capire, comprendere **2.** dedurre, supporre **3.** sentir dire.

understandable *agg.* comprensibile.

understanding *s.* **1.** comprensione **2.** patto, intesa ‖ *on this* —, a queste condizioni.

to **understate** *vt.* minimizzare.

understatement *s.* attenuazione del vero.

understood V. *to understand.*

to **undertake** (**undertook**, **undertaken**) *vt.* e *vi.* **1.** intraprendere **2.** incaricarsi di **3.** prendere in appalto.

undertaker *s.* **1.** impresario **2.** imprenditore di pompe funebri.

undertaking *s.* **1.** l'intraprendere **2.** (*comm.*) impresa **3.** (*giur.*) promessa, obbligazione.

undertook V. *to undertake.*

undervaluation *s.* **1.** scarsa stima **2.** svalutazione.

to **undervalue** *vt.* sottovalutare.

underwater *agg.* subacqueo ‖ *fishing* —, pesca subacquea.

underwent V. *to undergo.*

underworld *s.* **1.** bassifondi (*pl.*) **2.** oltretomba.

to **underwrite** (**underwrote**, **underwritten**) *vt.* e *vi.* **1.** sottoscrivere, firmare **2.** (*comm.*) assicurare.

undeserved *agg.* immeritato.

undeserving *agg.* immeritevole.

undesirable *agg.* indesiderabile.

undestroyable *agg.* indistruttibile.

undetected *agg.* non scoperto.

undetermined *agg.* **1.** indeterminato **2.** indeciso.

undid V. *to undo.*

undies *s.* *pl.* biancheria intima (*sing.*).

undine *s.* ondina.

undisciplined *agg.* indisciplinato.

undiscriminating *agg.* che non distingue, che non fa distinzioni.

undiscussed *agg.* indiscusso.

indisputed *agg.* incontestato.

undissembled *agg.* non dissimulato.

undistinguished *agg.* indistinto.

undisturbed *agg.* indisturbato.

undividable *agg.* indivisibile.

to **undo** (**undid**, **undone**) *vt.* **1.** disfare, sciogliere **2.** annullare, rovinare.

undoing *s.* **1.** disfacimento **2.** rovina.

undone[1] V. *to undo.* ♦ **undone** *agg.* disfatto, rovinato.

undone[2] *agg.* incompiuto.

undoubtable *agg.* indubitabile.

undoubted *agg.* indubbio.

undreamed *agg.* non sognato, impensato.

to **undress** *vt.* svestire. ♦ to **undress** *vi.* svestirsi.

undue *agg.* **1.** non dovuto, indebito **2.** inadatto.

to **undulate** *vi.* **1.** ondeggiare **2.** essere ondulato.

undulation *s.* ondulazione.

undulatory *agg.* ondulatorio.

unduly *avv.* indebitamente.

to **unearth** *vt.* **1.** dissotterrare, portare alla luce **2.** far uscire dalla tana (*un animale*).

unearthly *agg.* ultraterreno ‖ — *hour*, ora impossibile.

uneasily *avv.* **1.** a disagio, con difficoltà **2.** con ansia.

uneasiness *s.* **1.** disagio, pena **2.** ansia.

uneasy *agg.* **1.** a disagio **2.** ansioso, inquieto.

uneatable *agg.* immangiabile.

uneducated *agg.* rozzo, ignorante.

uneffected *agg.* non effettuato.

unembarrassed *agg.* a proprio agio, disinvolto.

unemployed *agg.* **1.** disoccupato **2.** non usato.

unemployment *s.* disoccupazione

|| — *benefit,* sussidio di disoccupazione.

unending *agg.* eterno, senza fine.

unequal *agg.* **1.** ineguale **2.** inadeguato, incapace.

unequalled *agg.* ineguagliato.

unerring *agg.* infallibile, sicuro.

uneven *agg.* **1.** ineguale, irregolare **2.** ruvido, non livellato.

unevenness *s.* **1.** disuguaglianza, irregolarità **2.** dislivello.

uneventful *agg.* pacifico, senza avvenimenti importanti.

unexceptionable *agg.* ineccepibile.

unexhausted *agg.* inesausto.

unexpected *agg.* inatteso.

unexpensive *agg.* poco costoso.

unexplored *agg.* inesplorato.

unextinguishable *agg.* inestinguibile.

unfadable *agg.* **1.** che non può appassire **2.** solido (*di colore*).

unfading *agg.* **1.** che non appassisce **2.** che non sbiadisce.

unfailing *agg.* **1.** infallibile, sicuro **2.** immancabile.

unfair *agg.* sleale: — *competition,* concorrenza sleale.

unfairness *s.* slealtà, ingiustizia.

unfaithful *agg.* **1.** infedele, sleale **2.** inesatto.

unfaithfulness *s.* **1.** infedeltà **2.** inesattezza.

unfaltering *agg.* fermo, non esitante.

unfamiliar *agg.* poco familiare.

unfashionable *agg.* fuori moda.

to **unfasten** *vt.* slacciare, slegare. ♦ to **unfasten** *vi.* slacciarsi, slegarsi.

unfathomable *agg.* insondabile.

unfavourable *agg.* sfavorevole.

unfeeling *agg.* insensibile, spietato.

unfinished *agg.* **1.** incompleto **2.** non rifinito.

unfit *agg.* **1.** inadatto, disadatto **2.** inabile.

unfitness *s.* **1.** inidoneità **2.** debole costituzione.

to **unfold** *vt.* **1.** aprire, schiudere **2.** svelare. ♦ to **unfold** *vi.* **1.** aprirsi, schiudersi **2.** svelarsi.

unforbearing *agg.* insofferente, impaziente.

unforeseeing *agg.* imprevidente.

unforeseen *agg.* imprevisto.

unforgettable *agg.* indimenticabile.

unforgiving *agg.* senza misericordia.

unforgotten *agg.* inobliato.

unfortunate *agg.* sfortunato.

unfortunately *avv.* sfortunatamente.

unfounded *agg.* infondato.

to **unfreeze (unfroze, unfrozen)** *vt.* disgelare, scongelare. ♦ to **unfreeze (unfroze, unfrozen)** *vi.* disgelarsi.

unfrequent *agg.* infrequente.

unfriendly *agg.* poco amichevole.

to **unfrock** *vt.* spretare.

unfroze V. *to unfreeze.*

unfrozen V. *to unfreeze.*

unfruitful *agg.* infruttuoso.

unfruitfulness *s.* infruttuosità.

to **unfurl** *vt.* e *vi.* spiegare, spiegarsi (*di bandiere ecc.*).

unfurnished *agg.* **1.** non ammobiliato **2.** sfornito.

ungainly *agg.* goffo, maldestro.

ungentlemanlike *agg.* indegno di un gentiluomo.

ungirt *agg.* senza cintura.

to **unglue** *vt.* scollare. ♦ to **unglue** *vi.* scollarsi.

ungodly *agg.* **1.** empio **2.** malvagio.

ungraceful *agg.* sgraziato.

ungrammatical *agg.* sgrammaticato.

ungrateful *agg.* ingrato.

ungrounded *agg.* **1.** infondato **2.** senza preparazione.

unguarded *agg.* sguarnito, senza difesa.

unguent *s.* unguento.

unhandy *agg.* **1.** maldestro **2.** poco maneggevole.

unhappiness *s.* infelicità.

unhappy *agg.* infelice, triste.

unharmed *agg.* intatto, illeso.

unharmful *agg.* innocuo.

unhealthily *avv.* in modo malsano, poco igienicamente.

unhealthy *agg.* **1.** malsano, insalubre **2.** (*fig.*) dannoso **3.** malaticcio.

unheard *agg.* **1.** non udito **2.** non ascoltato **3.** sconosciuto, strano || — *-of,* inaudito.

to **unhinge** *vt.* scardinare.

unholy *agg.* profano, empio.

to **unhook** *vt.* sganciare. ♦ to **unhook** *vi.* sganciarsi.

unhoped *agg.* insperato, inatteso.

to **unhorse** *vt.* **1.** disarcionare **2.** staccare i cavalli da.

unhuman *agg.* sovrumano.

unhurt *agg.* illeso, incolume.

unhurtful *agg.* innocuo.

unicellular *agg.* unicellulare.
unification *s.* unificazione.
uniform *agg.* uniforme, costante. ◆
uniform *s.* uniforme, divisa.
to uniform *vt.* uniformare.
uniformity *s.* uniformità.
to unify *vt.* unificare.
unilateral *agg.* unilaterale.
unilaterally *avv.* unilateralmente.
unimaginable *agg.* inimmaginabile.
unimpaired *agg.* inalterato, intatto.
unimpassioned *agg.* spassionato, calmo.
unimpeachable *agg.* incensurabile.
unimportance *s.* scarsa importanza.
unimportant *agg.* privo d'importanza.
unimposing *agg.* poco imponente, che non fa soggezione.
uninhabitable *agg.* inabitabile.
uninhabited *agg.* disabitato.
uninominal *agg.* uninominale.
unintelligent *agg.* stupido.
unintelligible *agg.* inintelligibile.
unintended *agg.* 1. involontario 2. (*giur.*) non intenzionale.
uninteresting *agg.* non interessante.
uninviting *agg.* poco attraente.
union *s.* unione, associazione, lega || (*trade*) —, sindacato; *the Union Jack*, la bandiera del Regno Unito.
unionism *s.* tendenza ad unirsi.
unionist *s.* unionista.
uniparous *agg.* uniparo.
unique *agg.* 1. unico, solo 2. eccezionale.
uniqueness *s.* unicità.
unisexual *agg.* unisessuale.
unison *s.* 1. (*mus.*) unisono 2. (*fig.*) concordia.
unit *s.* 1. unità, unità di misura 2. complesso, insieme.
unitary *agg.* unitario.
to unite *vt.* unire. ◆ to unite *vi.* 1. unirsi 2. mettersi d'accordo.
united *agg.* unito, collegato.
unity *s.* 1. unità 2. armonia.
universal *agg.* universale.
universality *s.* universalità.
to universalize *vt.* universalizzare.
universe *s.* universo.
university *s.* università.
univocal *agg.* univoco, non ambiguo.
to unjoint *vt.* disgiungere.
unjust *agg.* ingiusto.
unjustifiable *agg.* ingiustificabile.
unjustified *agg.* ingiustificato.
unkempt *agg.* trascurato, sciatto.

unkind *agg.* 1. sgarbato, scortese 2. crudele.
unkindness *s.* scortesia.
unknown *agg.* sconosciuto, ignoto.
unlawful *agg.* illegale.
to unlearn (unlearnt, unlearnt) (*anche reg.*) *vt.* disimparare.
unleavened *agg.* non lievitato || — *bread*, pane azzimo.
unless *cong.* a meno che, salvo che.
unlike *agg.* dissimile, diverso. ◆ unlike *avv.* diversamente. ◆ unlike *prep.* diversamente da.
unlikelihood *s.* inverosimiglianza, improbabilità.
unlikely *agg.* inverosimile, improbabile.
unlimited *agg.* illimitato, sconfinato.
to unline *vt.* sfoderare.
unlined[1] *agg.* senza fodera.
unlined[2] *agg.* senza rughe.
unliterary *agg.* non letterario.
to unload *vt.* 1. scaricare 2. (*fig.*) alleggerire.
to unlock *vt.* aprire (*con chiave*).
unlooked-for *agg.* imprevisto.
to unloose *vt.* slegare.
unlosable *agg.* che non può essere perso.
unlovable *agg.* poco amabile, antipatico.
unlucky *agg.* 1. sfortunato 2. di cattivo augurio.
to unman *vt.* 1. evirare 2. abbrutire 3. togliere forza.
unmarred *agg.* non sciupato.
unmarried *agg.* non coniugato.
to unmask *vt.* togliere la maschera (*anche fig.*). ◆ to unmask *vi.* togliersi la maschera.
unmatched *agg.* senza rivali.
unmentionable *agg.* innominabile, irripetibile.
unmerciful *agg.* spietato.
unmethodical *agg.* non metodico.
unminded *agg.* negletto.
unmindful *agg.* 1. immemore 2. incurante.
unmistakable *agg.* indubbio, inequivocabile.
to unmoor *vt.* e *vi.* togliere gli ormeggi a.
to unnail *vt.* schiodare.
unnatural *agg.* innaturale, contro natura.
unnavigable *agg.* non navigabile.
unnecessary *agg.* non necessario.
unneeded *agg.* inutile, non neces-

sario.
to **unnerve** vt. snervare.
unnoticed agg. inosservato.
unobjectionable agg. ineccepibile.
unobliging agg. poco compiacente.
unobservant agg. 1. inosservante 2. distratto.
unobserved agg. inosservato.
unobtrusive agg. discreto, modesto.
unoffending agg. inoffensivo.
unofficial agg. ufficioso.
to **unpack** vt. e vi. 1. disfare (le valigie) 2. disimballare.
unpalatable agg. di gusto sgradevole.
unpardonable agg. imperdonabile.
unpaved agg. non lastricato.
unperceivable agg. impercettibile.
unperceived agg. inavvertito.
unperishable agg. duraturo, imperituro.
unpleasant agg. spiacevole, sgradevole.
unpliable agg. poco piacevole.
unpoetic(al) agg. poco poetico.
to **unpoison** vt. svelenire.
unpolluted agg. incontaminato.
unpopular agg. impopolare.
unpopularity s. impopolarità.
unprecise agg. impreciso.
unpredictable agg. imprevedibile.
unpredicted agg. imprevisto.
unpremeditated agg. non premeditato.
unprepared agg. impreparato.
unpreparedness s. impreparazione.
unprepossessed agg. senza prevenzioni.
unprepossessing agg. senza attrattive, antipatico.
unpresentable agg. impresentabile.
unpriestly agg. che non si addice a un prete.
unprincely agg. che non si addice a un principe.
unprintable agg. non adatto ad essere pubblicato.
unproductive agg. improduttivo.
unprofitable agg. poco vantaggioso.
unprofitableness s. infruttuosità.
unpronounceable agg. impronunciabile.
unprovable agg. indimostrabile.
unpublished agg. inedito.
unqualified agg. 1. incompetente 2. non abilitato 3. (giur.) senza restrizioni.
to **unqualify** vt. 1. inabilitare 2. squalificare.

unquenchable agg. inestinguibile, insaziabile (anche fig.).
unquestionable agg. incontestabile, indiscutibile.
unquestioned agg. indiscusso.
unquiet agg. inquieto.
unquoted agg. 1. non citato 2. (comm.) non quotato (di titoli).
to **unravel** vt. districare. ♦ to **unravel** vi. districarsi.
unreachable agg. irraggiungibile.
unready agg. 1. impreparato 2. tardo, lento.
unreal agg. irreale.
unreality s. irrealtà.
unrealizable agg. irrealizzabile.
unreasonable agg. irragionevole.
unrecognizable agg. irriconoscibile.
unredeemed agg. 1. irredento 2. non controbilanciato 3. (comm.) non estinto.
unrelated agg. senza rapporti, senza legami.
unreliable agg. 1. non fidato 2. inattendibile.
unrepealed agg. (giur.) non abrogato.
unrequired agg. non richiesto.
unrest s. inquietudine.
unrestrained agg. non represso.
unrestricted agg. senza limitazioni.
unrevenged agg. invendicato.
unripe agg. immaturo, acerbo (anche fig.).
unrivalled agg. impareggiabile.
to **unroll** vt. svolgere. ♦ to **unroll** vi. svolgersi.
unruly agg. sregolato, indisciplinato.
to **unsaddle** vt. dissellare, disarcionare.
unsafe agg. malsicuro.
unsatisfied agg. 1. insoddisfatto 2. non convinto.
unsavoury agg. insipido, scipito.
unscholarly agg. 1. indegno di un letterato 2. non erudito.
to **unscrew** vt. svitare.
unscriptural agg. non conforme alle Sacre Scritture.
to **unseal** vt. dissigillare.
unseasonable agg. 1. fuori stagione 2. (fig.) intempestivo.
unseemliness s. indecenza
unseemly agg. sconveniente, indecente.
unseizable agg. inafferrabile.
unselfish agg. disinteressato.
unselfishness s. disinteresse.

unsettled *agg.* **1.** disordinato **2.** sconvolto, turbato **3.** mutevole, indeciso.

to unsew (unsewed, unsewn) *vt.* scucire.

unshaken *agg.* non scosso, fermo.

to unsheathe *vt.* sguainare.

to unshoe (unshod, unshod) *vt.* **1.** togliere le scarpe **2.** togliere i ferri a (*un cavallo*).

unshrinkable *agg.* irrestringibile.

unskilfulness *s.* incapacità, imperizia.

unskilled *agg.* inesperto, inabile.

unsocial *agg.* asociale.

unsold *agg.* invenduto.

to unsolder *vt.* dissaldare.

unsolved *agg.* insoluto.

unsound *agg.* **1.** malsano, malato **2.** guasto, avariato.

unspeakable *agg.* **1.** inesprimibile **2.** inqualificabile.

unstable *agg.* **1.** instabile **2.** (*fig.*) mutevole.

unsteadiness *agg.* incostanza, volubilità.

unsteady *agg.* instabile, incostante.

unsubstantial *agg.* **1.** inconsistente **2.** illusorio.

unsuccessful *agg.* mal riuscito, sfortunato.

unsuitable *agg.* inadatto, non appropriato.

unsure *agg.* **1.** malsicuro, precario **2.** incerto.

unsurpassed *agg.* insorpassato.

unsuspected *agg.* insospettato, non sospetto.

unsustainable *agg.* insostenibile.

untamable *agg.* indomabile.

untame *agg.* selvaggio, non addomesticato.

untaught *agg.* poco istruito, ignorante.

unteachable *agg.* **1.** difficile da insegnare **2.** non educabile.

unthinkable *agg.* inimmaginabile.

to unthread *vt.* sfilare, togliere il filo a.

untidily *avv.* disordinatamente.

untidy *agg.* disordinato, trasandato.

to untie *vt.* slegare. ♦ **to untie** *vi.* slegarsi.

until *prep.* fino a. ♦ **until** *cong.* finché.

untimeliness *s.* intempestività, inopportunità.

untimely *agg.* **1.** prematuro **2.** inopportuno. ♦ **untimely** *avv.* **1.** prematuramente **2.** inopportunamente.

untiring *agg.* instancabile.

untitled *agg.* senza titolo.

to untomb *vt.* dissotterrare.

untouchable *agg.* **1.** intoccabile **2.** (*fig.*) irraggiungibile.

untouched *agg.* **1.** non toccato, intatto **2.** illeso, indenne.

untoward *agg.* **1.** restio, caparbio **2.** infausto.

untranslatable *agg.* intraducibile.

untravelled *agg.* che non ha viaggiato.

untrodden *agg.* non calpestato, non battuto.

untrue *agg.* **1.** falso, menzognero **2.** infedele.

untrustworthy *agg.* indegno di fiducia.

to untune *vt.* scordare (*uno strumento musicale*).

unusable *agg.* inutilizzabile.

unusual *agg.* insolito, inusitato.

unutterable *agg.* indescrivibile, impronunciabile.

unvarying *agg.* invariabile.

to unveil *vt.* **1.** togliere il velo a **2.** (*fig.*) rivelare.

unwary *agg.* incauto, sconsiderato.

unwatchful *agg.* non vigilante, disattento.

unweaned *agg.* non svezzato.

unweary *agg.* non stanco, indefesso.

unwell *agg.* indisposto, ammalato.

unwieldy *agg.* **1.** ingombrante **2.** impacciato.

unwilling *agg.* **1.** riluttante **2.** involontario.

unwillingly *avv.* malvolentieri.

unwillingness *s.* **1.** riluttanza **2.** malavoglia.

to unwind (unwound, unwound) *vt.* srotolare. ♦ **to unwind (unwound, unwound)** *vi.* srotolarsi.

unwise *agg.* malaccorto.

unwitting *agg.* inconsapevole.

unworldly *agg.* spirituale, non mondano.

unworthy *agg.* indegno, spregevole.

unwound *V. to unwind.*

to unwrap *vt.* disfare, svolgere.

unwritten *agg.* non scritto || — *law*, legge tramandata oralmente.

unwrought *agg.* **1.** non lavorato **2.** grezzo.

up[1] *avv.* **1.** su, in su, in alto **2.** in piedi || — *to*, fino a; *hurry —*, spicciati; *the game is* —, tutto è perduto. ◆ **up** *prep.* su, su per, in cima a || — *now*, fino ad ora.

up² *agg.* ascendente, che va verso l'alto || — *-train*, treno per Londra.

up-and-down *agg.* **1.** che va in su e in giù **2.** oscillante.

to **upbraid** *vt.* rimproverare.

upheaval *s.* **1.** sollevamento **2.** agitazione.

uphill *agg.* **1.** in salita **2.** (*fig.*) difficile. ◆ **uphill** *avv.* in salita. ◆ **uphill** *s.* salita.

to **uphold** (**upheld**, **upheld**) *vt.* **1.** sostenere, sorreggere **2.** (*fig.*) appoggiare, patrocinare.

to **upholster** *vt.* tappezzare, imbottire.

upholsterer *s.* tappezziere.

upholstery *s.* tappezzeria, imbottitura.

upkeep *s.* mantenimento, manutenzione.

upland *agg.* montuoso. ◆ **upland** *s.* zona montuosa.

upon *prep.* V. *on*.

upper *agg.* **1.** superiore, più alto **2.** più lontano (*dall'ingresso ecc.*) || *the Upper House*, la Camera dei Lords.

uppercut *s.* (*sport*) "uppercut", colpo dal basso in alto.

upright *agg.* **1.** ritto, diritto, eretto **2.** retto, integro. ◆ **upright** *avv.* in piedi, perpendicolarmente.

uprightness *s.* **1.** perpendicolarità **2.** rettitudine.

uproar *s.* tumulto, chiasso.

uproarious *agg.* tumultuoso, chiassoso.

to **uproot** *vt.* sradicare, svellere.

ups and downs *s. pl.* **1.** ondulazioni (*del terreno*) **2.** (*fig.*) vicissitudini, alti e bassi.

to **upset** (**upset**, **upset**) *vt.* **1.** rovesciare **2.** disturbare, sconvolgere. ◆ to **upset** (**upset**, **upset**) *vi.* rovesciarsi, capovolgersi.

upset *agg.* **1.** rovesciato, capovolto **2.** (*fig.*) sconvolto, turbato. ◆ **upset** *s.* **1.** rovesciamento **2.** disordine.

upshot *s.* esito, risultato.

upside-down *avv.* capovolto, sottosopra.

upstairs *agg.* e *avv.* al piano superiore, di sopra.

upstanding *agg.* **1.** eretto, diritto **2.** (*fig.*) franco, leale.

up-to-date *agg.* aggiornato, all'ultima moda.

upward(s) *agg.* ascendente, rivolto verso l'alto. ◆ **upward** *avv.* **1.** in su, in alto **2.** al di sopra.

uranium *s.* uranio.

urban *agg.* urbano, di città.

urbane *agg.* urbano, cortese.

urbanity *s.* urbanità, cortesia.

urbanization *s.* urbanizzazione.

to **urbanize** *vt.* urbanizzare.

urchin *s.* monello.

uretic *agg.* e *s.* diuretico.

urge *s.* **1.** impulso, stimolo **2.** spinta, sprone.

to **urge** *vt.* e *vi.* **1.** spingere, stimolare **2.** consigliare, raccomandare.

urgency *s.* **1.** urgenza, premura **2.** bisogno urgente, necessità.

urgent *agg.* urgente, pressante.

uric *agg.* urico.

to **urinate** *vi.* orinare.

urine *s.* orina.

urn *s.* **1.** urna **2.** bricco.

us *pron. pers. compl. pl.* ci, noi: *three of* —, tre di noi.

usable *agg.* usabile, servibile.

usage *s.* **1.** uso, trattamento, impiego **2.** usanza.

use *s.* **1.** uso, impiego **2.** utilità, vantaggio **3.** (*giur.*) usufrutto.

to **use** *vt.* **1.** usare, adoperare **2.** trattare || *to* — *up*, consumare.

used *agg.* **1.** usato, adoperato **2.** abituato || — *-up*, esaurito.

useful *agg.* utile, pratico.

usefulness *s.* utilità, vantaggio.

useless *agg.* inutile, vano.

uselessness *s.* inutilità.

user *s.* **1.** utente **2.** (*giur.*) usufruttuario.

usher *s.* usciere.

to **usher** *vt.* precedere (*in qualità di usciere*).

usual *agg.* usuale, abituale || *as* —, come al solito.

usually *avv.* di solito, abitualmente.

usufruct *s.* (*giur.*) usufrutto.

usufructuary *agg.* e *s.* usufruttuario.

usurer *s.* usuraio.

to **usurp** *vt.* usurpare.

usurpation *s.* usurpazione.

usurper *s.* usurpatore.

usury *s.* usura (*anche fig.*).

utensil *s.* utensile, arnese.

uterine *agg.* uterino.

uterus *s.* (*pl.* -ri) utero.

utilitarian *s.* utilitarista.

utilitarianism *s.* utilitarismo.
utility *s.* utilità, vantaggio.
utilizable *agg.* utilizzabile.
utilization *s.* utilizzazione.
to **utilize** *vt.* utilizzare.
utmost *agg.* e *s.* 1. estremo, ultimo 2. massimo, sommo || *to do one's* —, fare del proprio meglio.
Utopian *s.* utopista.
utter *agg.* completo, totale.
to **utter** *vt.* 1. emettere 2. esprimere, pronunciare.
utterable *agg.* esprimibile.
utterance *s.* espressione, sfogo.
uttering *s.* 1. messa in circolazione 2. spaccio (*di assegni ecc.*).
utterly *avv.* completamente, totalmente.
uttermost *agg.* e *s.* V. *utmost.*
uxoricide *s.* 1. uxoricida 2. uxoricidio.

V

vacancy *s.* 1. vuoto, lacuna 2. posto vacante || *no* —, completo (*di alberghi ecc.*).
vacant *agg.* 1. vuoto, vacante 2. non occupato.
to **vacate** *vt.* lasciar vacante, sgomberare || *to* — *a seat,* dare le dimissioni.
vacation *s.* 1. il ritirarsi, il lasciar libero 2. vacanze: *long* —, vacanze estive (*pl.*).
to **vaccinate** *vt.* e *vi.* vaccinare.
vaccination *s.* vaccinazione.
vaccine *s.* vaccino.
to **vacillate** *vi.* 1. vacillare 2. (*fig.*) esitare.
vacillating *agg.* 1. vacillante 2. incostante, irresoluto.
vacillation *s.* 1. vacillamento 2. esitazione.
vacillatory *agg.* V. *vacillating.*
vacuity *s.* vacuità (*anche fig.*).
vacuous *agg.* 1. vacuo, vuoto 2. sciocco, ozioso.
vacuum *s.* vuoto pneumatico || — *cleaner,* aspirapolvere.
vagabond *s.* viandante, vagabondo.
vagary *s.* fantasticheria, capriccio.
vagrancy *s.* vagabondaggio, accattonaggio.
vagrant *agg.* e *s.* vagabondo.

vague *agg.* vago, impreciso.
vaguely *avv.* vagamente.
vagueness *s.* indeterminatezza.
vain *agg.* 1. vano, inutile 2. vanitoso.
vainglorious *agg.* vanaglorioso.
vainglory *s.* vanagloria.
vainly *avv.* 1. inutilmente 2. vanitosamente.
valance *s.* 1. drappeggio 2. cortina (*di un letto*).
valediction *s.* addio, commiato.
valedictory *agg.* d'addio, di saluto.
♦ **valedictory** *s.* discorso d'addio.
valence *s.* (*chim.*) valenza.
valerian *s.* valeriana.
valet *s.* valletto.
valiant *agg.* valoroso, prode.
valid *agg.* valido, legittimo.
to **validate** *vt.* render valido, convalidare.
validity *s.* validità.
validly *avv.* validamente.
valley *s.* valle, vallata.
valorization *s.* valorizzazione.
to **valorize** *vt.* valorizzare.
valour *s.* valore.
valuable *agg.* 1. di valore, prezioso 2. valutabile.
valuation *s.* 1. valutazione, stima 2. considerazione.
value *s.* 1. valore, prezzo 2. (*fig.*) pregio, importanza || — *in exchange,* valore effettivo.
to **value** *vt.* 1. valutare, stimare 2. considerare, dar valore.
valueless *agg.* di nessun valore.
valuer *s.* estimatore.
valve *s.* 1. valvola 2. valva.
vamp[1] *s.* 1. rappezzamento 2. (*mus.*) accompagnamento.
vamp[2] *s.* (*gergo*) donna fatale.
vampire *s.* vampiro.
van *s.* 1. furgone 2. vagone ferroviario || *luggage* —, bagagliaio; *prison* —, cellulare.
Vandal *agg.* e *s.* vandalo.
Vandalic *agg.* vandalico.
vandalism *s.* vandalismo.
vane *s.* 1. banderuola 2. pala (*di mulino a vento ecc.*).
vanguard *s.* avanguardia (*anche fig.*).
vanilla *s.* vaniglia.
to **vanish** *vi.* svanire, sparire.
vanishing *s.* il dileguarsi, lo sparire.
vanity *s.* vanità || — *-case,* borsetta col necessario per il trucco.

to **vanquish** *vt.* vincere, conquistare.

vanquisher *s.* conquistatore

vantage *s.* vantaggio.

vapid *agg.* insulso.

vaporization *s.* evaporazione.

to **vaporize** *vt.* far evaporare. ◆ to **vaporize** *vi.* **1.** evaporare **2.** (*fig.*) volatilizzarsi.

vaporizer *s.* vaporizzatore.

vaporous *agg.* vaporoso.

vapour *s.* vapore, esalazione.

to **vapour** *vi.* **1.** evaporare **2.** (*fig.*) vantarsi.

vapouring *agg.* che evapora. ◆ **vapouring** *s.* vanteria.

vapourish *agg.* **1.** pieno di vapori **2.** depresso.

vapours *s. pl.* depressione (*sing.*), allucinazioni.

variability *s.* variabilità, mutevolezza.

variable *agg.* variabile, incostante.

variance *s.* **1.** variazione **2.** disaccordo.

variant *agg.* differente, contrastante. ◆ **variant** *s.* variante.

variation *s.* variazione, modificazione. ◆ **variations** *s. pl.* (*mat.*) variazioni.

varicoloured *agg.* variopinto.

varicose *agg.* varicoso.

varied *agg.* **1.** vario, variato **2.** variopinto.

to **variegate** *vt.* variegare, screziare.

variegated *agg.* variegato, screziato.

variegation *s.* screziatura.

variety *s.* varietà, diversità || — *show* (*teat.*), spettacolo di varietà.

various *agg.* alcuni, molti (*pl.*).

variously *avv.* variamente.

varnish *s.* **1.** vernice, lacca **2.** (*fig.*) apparenza, aspetto esteriore || *nail* —, smalto per unghie.

to **varnish** *vt.* **1.** verniciare, laccare **2.** (*fig.*) mascherare.

varnishing *s.* verniciatura, laccatura.

to **vary** *vt.* variare, cambiare. ◆ to **vary** *vi.* essere differente.

vase *s.* vaso.

vaseline *s.* vaselina.

vassal *s.* vassallo.

vassallage *s.* vassallaggio.

vast *agg.* ampio, immenso, vasto.

vastness *s.* vastità.

vat *s.* tino, tinozza.

vault[1] *s.* **1.** volta, soffitto a volta **2.** cantina **3.** sepolcro **4.** (*fig.*) vol-

ta celeste.

vault[2] *s.* volteggio.

to **vault** *vi.* volteggiare. ◆ to **vault** *vt.* saltare.

vaulting *s.* **1.** il costruire volte **2.** costruzione a volta.

to **vaunt** *vt.* vantare. ◆ to **vaunt** *vi.* vantarsi.

veal *s.* (*cuc.*) vitello.

vector *s.* vettore.

vectorial *agg.* vettoriale.

veer *s.* **1.** cambiamento di direzione **2.** (*mar.*) virata.

to **veer** *vi.* **1.** cambiare direzione **2.** (*mar.*) virare.

vegetable *agg.* vegetale. ◆ **vegetable** *s.* **1.** vegetale **2.** ortaggio. ◆ **vegetables** *s. pl.* verdura (*sing.*).

vegetal *agg.* vegetale.

vegetarian *agg.* e *s.* vegetariano.

to **vegetate** *vi.* vegetare (*anche fig.*).

vegetation *s.* **1.** vegetazione **2.** il vegetare.

vegetative *agg.* vegetativo.

vehemence *s.* veemenza.

vehement *agg.* veemente, impetuoso.

vehicle *s.* veicolo.

veil *s.* **1.** velo, cortina **2.** (*fig.*) apparenza, pretesto.

to **veil** *vt.* **1.** velare, coprire **2.** (*fig.*) dissimulare, nascondere.

veiling *s.* **1.** il velare **2.** velo, schermo.

vein *s.* **1.** (*anat.*; *geol.*; *fig.*) vena **2.** venatura, nervatura.

to **vein** *vt.* venare, coprire di venature.

veined *agg.* **1.** venato **2.** con venature, nervature.

velleity *s.* velleità.

velocipede *s.* velocipede.

velocity *s.* velocità.

velvet *agg.* di velluto, vellutato. ◆ **velvet** *s.* velluto.

velvety *agg.* vellutato, morbido.

venal *agg.* venale.

venality *s.* venalità.

to **vend** *vt.* vendere.

vendor *s.* venditore.

to **veneer** *vt.* **1.** impiallacciare **2.** (*fig.*) mascherare.

veneer, veneering *s.* **1.** impiallacciatura **2.** (*fig.*) maschera, vernice.

venerable *agg.* venerabile.

to **venerate** *vt.* venerare.

veneration *s.* venerazione.

venereal *agg.* venereo.

Venetian *agg.* e *s.* veneziano || —

blinds, shades, persiana alla veneziana.

vengeance *s.* vendetta || *to take — on so.*, vendicarsi di qu.

vengeful *agg.* vendicativo, vendicatore.

venial *agg.* veniale.

venom *s.* veleno (*di animali*).

venomous *agg.* velenoso.

venous *agg.* **1.** venoso **2.** con nervature.

vent[1] *s.* spacco, apertura (*di abito*).

vent[2] *s.* **1.** sbocco, apertura, foro **2.** (*fig.*) sfogo || *to give — to*, dar libero corso a.

to vent *vt.* **1.** svuotare, esalare **2.** (*fig.*) sfogare.

to ventilate *vt.* **1.** ventilare **2.** (*fig.*) discutere, rendere manifesto.

ventilation *s.* **1.** ventilazione **2.** discussione.

ventral *agg.* ventrale, addominale.

ventricle *s.* ventricolo.

ventriloquism *s.* ventriloquio.

ventriloquist *s.* ventriloquo.

venture *s.* **1.** avventura, azzardo **2.** (*comm.*) speculazione.

to venture *vt.* avventurare, arrischiare. ♦ **to venture** *vi.* avventurarsi, arrischiarsi.

venturer *s.* avventuriero.

venue *s.* sede giurisdizionale.

veracious *agg.* verace.

veracity *s.* veracità.

veranda(h) *s.* veranda.

verb *s.* verbo.

verbal *agg.* **1.** verbale **2.** orale, a parole.

verbally *avv.* verbalmente, oralmente.

verbiage *s.* verbosità.

verbose *agg.* verboso, prolisso

verdant *agg.* verdeggiante.

verdict *s.* verdetto.

verdigris *s.* verderame.

verge *s.* **1.** orlo, limite || *on the — of*, sul punto di **2.** bacchetta, verga.

to verge *vi.* **1.** confinare, essere contiguo, adiacente **2.** (*fig.*) rasentare: *to — on madness*, rasentare la pazzia.

verifiable *agg.* verificabile.

verification *s.* verifica.

verifier *s.* verificatore.

to verify *vt.* **1.** verificare, controllare **2.** (*giur.*) autenticare.

verily *avv.* in verità.

verisimilar *agg.* verosimile.

verisimilitude *s.* verosimiglianza.

verism *s.* verismo.

veritable *agg.* vero, genuino.

verity *s.* verità, realtà.

vermiform *s.* vermiforme.

vermin *s. coll.* insetti parassiti.

verminous *agg.* infestato da parassiti.

vernacular *s.* vernacolo, dialetto nativo. ♦ **vernacular** *agg.* vernacolo, nativo.

versatile *agg.* versatile, multiforme.

versatility *s.* versatilità.

verse *s.* **1.** verso **2.** strofa **3.** componimento in versi.

versification *s.* versificazione.

to versify *vt.* e *vi.* **1.** comporre in versi **2.** narrare in versi.

version *s.* versione, traduzione.

vertebra *s.* (*pl.* -ae) vertebra.

vertebral *agg.* vertebrale.

vertebrate *agg.* e *s.* vertebrato.

vertex *s.* (*pl.* -tices) vertice, apice, sommità.

vertical *agg.* verticale. ♦ **vertical** *s.* piano verticale, verticale.

verticality *s.* posizione verticale, perpendicolarità.

very *agg.* **1.** vero e proprio, autentico **2.** (*uso enfatico*) esatto, stesso: *at that — moment*, in quello stesso istante. ♦ **very** *avv.* molto, assai.

vessel *s.* **1.** vaso, recipiente **2.** nave, vascello.

vest *s.* **1.** panciotto **2.** camiciola, davantino.

to vest *vt.* **1.** conferire, investire **2.** (*giur.*) assegnare **3.** parare (*di altari ecc.*). ♦ **to vest** *vi.* passare per eredità.

vestal *s.* vestale.

vestibule *s.* vestibolo, entrata, portico di chiesa.

vestige *s.* vestigio, traccia.

vestment *s.* veste (*spec. liturgica*).

vestry *s.* **1.** sagrestia **2.** assemblea parrocchiale.

vesture *s.* rivestimento, veste.

veteran *agg.* e *s.* veterano.

veterinary *s.* e *agg.* veterinario.

to vex *vt.* **1.** vessare, opprimere **2.** irritare.

vexation *s.* **1.** vessazione, oppressione **2.** irritazione.

vexatious *agg.* **1.** irritante, fastidioso **2.** (*giur.*) vessatorio.

vexed *agg.* **1.** vessato, oppresso **2.** irritato.

via *prep.* per, via, attraverso: — *air mail*, per via aerea.
viability *s.* vitalità.
viable *agg.* vitale.
viaduct *s.* viadotto.
vial *s.* fiala.
viand *s.* vivanda, cibo.
vibrant *agg.* vibrante, tremante.
to vibrate *vi.* vibrare, risuonare. ♦ to vibrate *vt.* far vibrare.
vibration *s.* vibrazione, tremolio.
vibrator *s.* vibratore.
vibratory *agg.* 1. vibratorio 2. vibrante.
vicar *s.* 1. curato (*nella Chiesa d'Inghilterra*) 2. vicario (*Chiesa Cattolica*).
vicariate *s.* vicariato.
vice[1] *s.* 1. immoralità, depravazione 2. vizio.
vice[2] *s.* (*mecc.*) morsa.
vice[3] *s.* sostituto, vice.
vice[4] *prep.* in luogo di.
viceroy *s.* viceré.
vicinity *s.* 1. vicinanza, prossimità 2. affinità.
vicious *agg.* 1. vizioso, immorale 2. maligno 3. bizzarro (*di animali*) 4. difettoso, scorretto.
vicissitude *s.* vicissitudine.
victim *s.* vittima.
victor *s.* vincitore.
victorious *agg.* vittorioso.
victory *s.* vittoria.
to victual *vt.* vettovagliare, approvvigionare. ♦ to victual *vi.* approvvigionarsi.
victualling *s.* vettovagliamento, approvvigionamento.
victuals *s. pl.* vettovaglie, viveri.
to vie *vi.* gareggiare.
view *s.* 1. vista, sguardo 2. veduta, panorama 3. opinione 4. scopo, mira 5. (*giur.*) sopralluogo ‖ *point of* —, punto di vista; — *-finder* (*foto*), mirino.
to view *vt.* 1. guardare attentamente 2. esaminare.
viewer *s.* 1. chi guarda 2. telespettatore 3. ispettore.
viewless *agg.* 1. senza vista (*di casa ecc.*) 2. invisibile.
viewpoint *s.* punto di vista.
vigil *s.* veglia.
vigilance *s.* vigilanza.
vigilant *agg.* vigilante, vigile.
vigorous *agg.* vigoroso, forte.
Viking *s.* vichingo.
vigour *s.* vigore, energia.

vigorously *avv.* vigorosamente.
vile *agg.* vile, spregevole.
vileness *s.* viltà, bassezza.
to vilify *vt.* diffamare.
villa *s.* villa.
village *s.* villaggio, paese.
villager *s.* abitante di villaggio.
villain *s.* furfante, scellerato.
villainous *agg.* scellerato, infame.
villainy *s.* scelleratezza.
to vindicate *vt.* 1. rivendicare 2. giustificare, difendere.
vindication *s.* 1. rivendicazione 2. giustificazione, difesa.
vindictive *agg.* vendicativo.
vine *s.* vite ‖ — *-leaf*, pampino; — *-dresser*, vignaiuolo.
vinegar *s.* aceto.
vinery *s.* serra per viti.
vineyard *s.* vigneto, vigna.
vintage *s.* 1. vendemmia 2. annata.
vintager *s.* vendemmiatore.
vintner *s.* vinaio.
to violate *vt.* 1. violare, trasgredire 2. profanare.
violation *s.* 1. violazione, trasgressione 2. profanazione.
violator *s.* 1. violatore, trasgressore 2. profanatore.
violence *s.* violenza, veemenza.
violent *agg.* violento, impetuoso.
violet *agg.* violetto, viola. ♦ violet *s.* viola mammola.
violin *s.* violino.
violoncellist *s.* violoncellista.
viper *s.* vipera (*anche fig.*).
virgin *agg.* e *s.* vergine.
virginal *agg.* verginale.
virginity *s.* verginità.
virile *agg.* virile.
virility *s.* virilità.
virtual *agg.* virtuale, effettivo.
virtuality *s.* potenzialità, virtualità.
virtue *s.* 1. virtù, moralità, forza d'animo 2. qualità, merito.
virtuosity *s.* virtuosismo.
virtuous *agg.* virtuoso, morale.
virulence *s.* virulenza.
virulent *agg.* virulento.
virus *s.* virus.
visa *s.* visto consolare.
to visa *vt.* vistare (*un passaporto*).
visceral *agg.* viscerale.
viscid *agg.* viscido.
viscidity *s.* viscidità.
viscose *s.* viscosa.
viscosity *s.* viscosità.
viscount *s.* visconte.
viscous *agg.* viscoso.

visibility s. visibilità.

visible agg. visibile, evidente, manifesto.

vision s. **1.** visione, immaginazione **2.** vista, capacità visiva.

visional agg. irreale.

visionary s. visionario.

visit s. visita: to pay a —, fare una visita.

to **visit** vt. e vi. visitare, fare una visita.

visitation s. **1.** visita ufficiale **2.** castigo divino.

visitor s. visitatore, ospite.

visor s. visiera.

visual agg. visuale, visivo.

to **visualize** vt. **1.** rendere visibile **2.** prospettare. ♦ to **visualize** vi. diventare visibile.

vital agg. vitale, essenziale.

vitality s. vitalità.

to **vitalize** vt. vivificare.

vitals s. pl. organi vitali.

vitamin s. vitamina.

to **vitiate** vt. **1.** viziare **2.** (giur.) invalidare.

vitiation s. **1.** corruzione **2.** (giur.) l'invalidare.

viticulture s. viticoltura.

vitreous agg. vitreo.

vitrifiable agg. vetrificabile.

vitrification s. vetrificazione.

to **vitrify** vt. vetrificare. ♦ to **vitrify** vi. vetrificarsi.

vitriol s. vetriolo.

to **vituperate** vt. vituperare.

vituperation s. invettiva, biasimo.

vivacious agg. vivace, vispo.

vivacity s. vivacità, brio.

vivid agg. **1.** vivace, vigoroso **2.** vivido, colorito.

to **vivify** vt. vivificare, animare.

viviparous agg. viviparo.

vivisection s. vivisezione.

vixen s. **1.** volpe femmina **2.** megera.

vocabulary s. vocabolario.

vocal agg. vocale.

vocalization s. vocalizzazione.

to **vocalize** vt. e vi. vocalizzare.

vocation s. **1.** vocazione **2.** attitudine, inclinazione **3.** professione.

vocational agg. professionale.

vocative agg. e s. vocativo.

vociferous agg. clamoroso, vociferante.

vogue s. voga, moda.

voice s. voce ‖ with one —, all'unanimità.

to **voice** vt. esprimere, dire.

voiced agg. **1.** dalla voce: deep- —, dalla voce profonda **2.** sonoro.

voiceless agg. senza voce, muto.

void agg. **1.** vuoto **2.** privo **3.** (giur.) nullo. ♦ **void** s. il vuoto.

to **void** vt. **1.** vuotare, liberare **2.** abrogare.

volatile agg. **1.** volatile, alato **2.** (fig.) incostante. ♦ **volatile** s. **1.** volatile **2.** (chim.) sostanza volatile.

to **volatilize** vt. volatilizzare. ♦ to **volatilize** vi. volatilizzarsi.

volcano s. vulcano.

volley s. **1.** scarica, raffica, salva ‖ — -ball, palla a volo.

voltage s. (elettr.) voltaggio, tensione.

voltameter s. voltametro.

volubility s. speditezza (di eloquio), loquacità.

voluble agg. spedito (di eloquio), loquace.

volume s. **1.** volume **2.** tomo, libro **3.** massa.

volumetric(al) agg. volumetrico.

voluminous agg. **1.** in molti volumi **2.** (fig.) fecondo (di scrittore) **3.** voluminoso.

voluntarily avv. volontariamente.

voluntary agg. **1.** volontario, spontaneo **2.** voluto, fatto di proposito **3.** mantenuto da contributi non statali. ♦ **voluntary** s. azione volontaria.

volunteer s. volontario.

to **volunteer** vi. **1.** offrirsi volontariamente **2.** arruolarsi volontario.

voluptuary agg. **1.** voluttuario **2.** voluttuoso.

voluptuous agg. voluttuoso, sensuale.

voluptuousness s. voluttà, sensualità.

volute s. voluta, spirale.

vomit s. vomito.

to **vomit** vt. e vi. vomitare (anche fig.).

voracious agg. ingordo, vorace.

vortex s. vortice, gorgo.

vortical agg. vorticoso.

votary s. seguace, devoto.

vote s. voto, votazione.

to **vote** vt. e vi. votare.

voter s. elettore.

votive agg. votivo.

to **vouch** vt. e vi. **1.** attestare, garantire **2.** (giur.) citare come garante.

voucher s. **1.** testimone **2.** documento giustificativo.
to vouchsafe vt. concedere.
vow s. voto.
to vow vi. fare un voto.
vowel s. vocale.
voyage s. viaggio (spec. per via d'acqua) || outward —, viaggio di andata; home —, viaggio di ritorno.
to voyage vi. fare una traversata, navigare.
vulcanization s. vulcanizzazione.
vulgar agg. volgare, triviale.
vulgarism, vulgarity s. volgarità.
to vulgarize vt. **1.** rendere volgare **2.** divulgare.
vulnerability s. vulnerabilità.
vulnerable agg. vulnerabile.
vulture s. avvoltoio.

W

to wabble vi. vacillare, traballare.
wad s. **1.** tampone **2.** imbottitura **3.** rotolo (di banconote).
to wad vt. **1.** tamponare **2.** imbottire.
wadable agg. guadabile.
wadding s. ovatta.
waddle s. andatura ondeggiante.
to waddle vi. camminare ondeggiando.
wade s. guado.
to wade vt. guadare. ◆ **to wade** vi. procedere faticosamente.
wader s. **1.** chi passa a guado **2.** (zool.) trampoliere. ◆ **waders** s. pl. stivaloni impermeabili.
wading s. il guadare.
wafer s. **1.** cialda **2.** disco adesivo.
waft s. soffio.
to waft vt. sospingere. ◆ **to waft** vi. fluttuare.
wag s. **1.** cenno **2.** scodinzolio.
to wag vt. scuotere. ◆ **to wag** vi. scuotersi || to have a wagging tongue, avere la lingua troppo lunga.
to wage vt. intraprendere (guerra).
to wager vt. e vi. scommettere.
wages s. pl. salario (sing.) || —-earner, salariato.
to waggle V. to wag.
wag(g)on s. carro || tea- —, car-

rello da tè.
waif s. relitto (anche fig.).
wail s. gemito.
to wail vt. e vi. gemere.
wainscot s. rivestimento in legno.
to wainscot vt. rivestire in legno.
waist s. cintola.
waistband s. cintura.
waistbelt s. cinturone.
waistcoat s. panciotto.
wait s. **1.** attesa **2.** agguato.
to wait vt. e vi. (for so., sthg.) aspettare (qu., qc.) || to — on, servire.
waiter s. **1.** cameriere **2.** vassoio.
waiting s. attesa || — -room, sala d'aspetto; to keep —, fare aspettare.
waitress s. cameriera.
to waive vt. rinunciare a, mettere da parte.
wake[1] s. **1.** scia **2.** pista.
wake[2] s. **1.** risveglio **2.** veglia (funebre).
to wake (waked e woke, waked, woke(n)) vt. svegliare. ◆ **to wake** (waked e woke, waked, woke(n)) vi. svegliarsi.
wakeful agg. sveglio.
wakefulness s. veglia.
to waken V. to wake.
wakening s. risveglio.
waking agg. sveglio. ◆ **waking** s. **1.** risveglio **2.** veglia.
walk s. **1.** passeggiata **2.** andatura **3.** (fig.) rango || to take a —, fare una passeggiata.
to walk vi. passeggiare, andare a piedi || to — off, andarsene.
walker s. camminatore.
walkie-talkie s. (radio) trasmettitore-ricevitore portatile.
walking s. il camminare || — tour, escursione a piedi.
walkover s. facile vittoria.
wall s. muro || — paper, carta da parato; main —, muro maestro.
to wall vt. circondare di mura || to — up, murare.
wallet s. portafoglio.
wall-eye s. glaucoma.
Walloon agg. e s. vallone.
to wallop vt. **1.** bastonare **2.** percuotere, sculacciare.
wallow s. pantano.
to wallow vi. sguazzare.
walnut s. noce.
walrus s. tricheco.
waltz s. valzer.

to **waltz** vi. ballare il valzer.
wan agg. pallido.
to **wan** vi. impallidire.
wand s. bacchetta magica.
wander s. vagabondaggio.
to **wander** vi. 1. vagare 2. vaneggiare.
wanderer s. vagabondo.
wandering agg. 1. errante 2. delirante. ♦ **wandering** s. 1. vagabondaggio 2. delirio.
wane s. declino.
to **wane** vi. 1. declinare 2. decrescere 3. essere in fase calante.
to **wangle** vt. ottenere con intrighi.
want s. 1. mancanza 2. bisogno: to be in — of, aver bisogno di.
to **want** vt. 1. volere 2. aver bisogno di 3. mancare.
wanted agg. ricercato: to be — by the police, essere ricercato dalla polizia.
wanting prep. senza, in mancanza di.
wanton agg. 1. licenzioso 2. capriccioso 3. arbitrario 4. lascivo.
to **wanton** vi. 1. scherzare 2. comportarsi dissolutamente.
wantonness s. 1. dissolutezza 2. capriccio.
war s. guerra: — Office, Ministero della Guerra.
to **war** vi. guerreggiare.
warble s. trillo.
to **warble** vt. e vi. trillare.
warbling agg. melodioso. ♦ **warbling** s. gorgheggio.
ward s. 1. guardia 2. reparto 3. rione 4. tutela 5. pupillo.
to **ward** vt. parare: to — off a blow, parare un colpo.
warden s. 1. guardiano 2. direttore 3. governatore.
wardenship s. carica di direttore, governatore.
warder s. 1. guardiano 2. carceriere.
wardrobe s. guardaroba.
wardroom s. (mar.) quadrato ufficiali.
wardship s. tutela.
ware agg. conscio, circospetto.
to **ware** vt. fare attenzione a.
wares s. pl. 1. articoli 2. vasellame (sing.).
warehouse s. magazzino.
to **warehouse** vt. depositare in magazzino.
warehouseman s. 1. magazziniere 2. commerciante all'ingrosso.

warfare s. operazione bellica.
warfaring agg. bellicoso.
warily avv. cautamente.
wariness s. cautela.
warlike agg. guerriero.
warlikeness s. bellicosità.
warlock s. stregone.
warm agg. 1. caldo 2. animato.
to **warm** vt. 1. scaldare 2. animare. ♦ to **warm** vi. 1. scaldarsi 2. animarsi.
warmer s. riscaldatore.
warm-hearted agg. bonario, cordiale.
warming s. riscaldamento.
warmonger s. guerrafondaio.
warmth s. calore.
to **warn** vt. avvertire || to — off, invitare ad allontanarsi.
warning s. (pre)avviso || — light, spia luminosa.
warp s. 1. ordito 2. deformazione.
to **warp** vt. 1. curvare 2. (fig.) alterare. ♦ to **warp** vi. 1. curvarsi 2. (fig.) alterarsi.
warpath s. sentiero di guerra.
warping s. deformazione, pervertimento.
warrant s. 1. garanzia, garante 2. (giur.; comm.) ordine, autorizzazione.
to **warrant** vt. 1. garantire 2. giustificare.
warrantable agg. 1. giustificabile 2. legittimo.
warrantee s. chi riceve una garanzia.
warranter, -tor s. garante.
warranty s. 1. garanzia 2. autorizzazione.
warrior s. guerriero.
warship s. nave da guerra.
wart s. verruca.
wartime s. tempo di guerra.
wary agg. cauto.
was V. to be.
wash s. 1. lavata 2. bucato 3. sciacquio 4. brodaglia 5. mano (di colore).
to **wash** vt. 1. lavare 2. bagnare 3. gettare. ♦ to **wash** vi. 1. lavarsi 2. essere lavabile || to — up, rigovernare (le stoviglie); to — over, sommergere.
washable agg. lavabile.
washbasin s. catino.
washboard s. asse per lavare.
washer s. 1. lavandaio 2. (mecc.) lavatrice 3. (mecc.) rondella.

washerwoman s. lavandaia.
washhouse s. lavanderia.
washing s. 1. lavaggio 2. bucato 3. risciacquatura ‖ — -*machine*, lavatrice.
whashout s. erosione, dilatamento.
washroom s. 1. lavanderia 2. gabinetto.
washstand s. lavabo.
washy agg. 1. annacquato 2. scialbo.
wasp s. vespa.
waspish agg. pungente.
waspishness s. irascibilità.
wastage s. logorio.
waste agg. 1. deserto 2. di scarto. ♦ **waste** s. 1. spreco 2. scarto 3. deserto ‖ — -*basket*, cestino per rifiuti; — -*paper*, carta straccia.
to waste vt. 1. consumare 2. sprecare 3. rovinare. ♦ **to waste** vi. 1. consumarsi 2. rovinarsi.
wasteful agg. 1. rovinoso 2. prodigo.
waster s. dissipatore.
wasting agg. 1. logorante 2. devastante. ♦ **wasting** s. 1. sciupio 2. deperimento 3. devastazione.
watch s. 1. orologio (*da polso*) 2. guardia ‖ — -*fire*, fuoco di bivacco; *to be on the* —, stare in guardia.
to watch vt. 1. osservare 2. stare a guardia di. ♦ **to watch** vi. 1. vegliare 2. aspettare.
watcher s. 1. spettatore 2. sorvegliante.
watchful agg. attento.
watchfulness s. 1. vigilanza 2. cautela.
watchmaker s. orologiaio.
watchman s. guardia (*notturna*).
watchword s. parola d'ordine.
water s. acqua ‖ *to hold* —, non fare acqua, (*fig.*) essere logico; — -*bottle*, borraccia; — -*colour*, acquarello; — -*colourist*, acquarellista; — -*closet*, gabinetto; — -*gate*, chiusa; — -*line*, linea di galleggiamento; — -*meadow*, marcita; — -*polo*, pallanuoto; *drinking* —, acqua potabile.
to water vt. 1. bagnare 2. diluire 3. abbeverare 4. secernere ‖ *to make one's mouth* —, far venire l'acquolina in bocca. ♦ **to water** vi. 1. abbeverarsi 2. riempirsi di acqua.
waterfall s. cascata.

watering s. 1. annaffiamento 2. diluizione 3. abbeverarsi 4. rifornimento d'acqua 5. secrezione ‖ — -*can*, — -*pot*, annaffiatoio.
waterman s. (*pl.* -men) barcaiolo.
watermark s. 1. filigrana 2. indicatore di livello 3. livello d'acqua.
watermelon s. anguria.
waterproof agg. e s. impermeabile.
to waterproof vt. impermeabilizzare.
watershed s. 1. spartiacque 2. bacino idrico.
watertight agg. stagno.
waterway s. canale navigabile.
waterworks s. pl. impianto idrico (*sing.*).
watery agg. 1. acquoso 2. lacrimoso.
wattle s. 1. fascina 2. vimine.
wave s. 1. onda, ondata 2. cenno (*della mano*).
to wave vi. 1. ondeggiare 2. far cenno (*con la mano*). ♦ **to wave** vt. 1. far ondeggiare 2. ondulare 3. chiamare (*con un cenno di mano*).
waved agg. ondulato.
wave-length s. lunghezza d'onda.
waveless agg. liscio.
wavelet s. piccola onda.
wavelike agg. ondeggiante.
to waver vi. vacillare.
wavering s. 1. oscillazione 2. esitazione.
wavily avv. a onde.
waviness s. ondulazione.
waving s. 1. ondeggiamento, ondulazione 2. sventolio 3. cenno.
wavy agg. 1. ondulato 2. ondeggiante.
wax s. 1. cera 2. paraffina.
to wax[1] vt. incerare.
to wax[2] vi. 1. crescere 2. aumentare.
waxen agg. di, come cera.
way s. 1. via 2. maniera 3. punto di vista 4. stato ‖ *to make* —, far posto; *this* —, per di qua; *in a* —, in un certo senso; *by the* —, tra parentesi; *one-* —, senso unico; *out of the* —, fuori mano.
waybill s. lista dei passeggeri.
wayfarer s. viandante.
to waylay vt. tendere un agguato a.
wayside s. margine della strada.
wayward agg. 1. indocile 2. capriccioso.
waywardness s. ostinazione.
we pron. sogg. noi.

weak *agg.* **1.** debole **2.** diluito.
to weaken *vi.* indebolirsi. ♦ **to
weaken** *vt.* indebolire.
weakling *s.* persona debole.
weakly *agg.* debole.
weakness *s.* debolezza.
weal[1] *s.* benessere, prosperità.
weal[2] *s.* livido.
wealth *s.* ricchezza.
wealthy *agg.* ricco.
to wean *vt.* **1.** svezzare **2.** togliere
il vizio a.
weaning *s.* svezzamento.
weapon *s.* arma.
wear *s.* **1.** uso, usura **2.** durata **3.**
abbigliamento.
to wear (wore, worn) *vt.* **1.** in-
dossare **2.** logorare **3.** stancare ||
to — out, logorare, stancare. ♦
to wear (wore, worn) *vi.* **1.** lo-
gorarsi **2.** stancarsi **3.** durare || *to
— out*, logorarsi, stancarsi.
wearily *avv.* stancamente.
weariness *s.* **1.** stanchezza **2.** tedio.
wearing *agg.* **1.** logorante **2.** da indossare. ♦ **wearing** *s.* **1.** logorio
2. l'indossare.
wearisome *agg.* **1.** faticoso **2.** tedioso.
weary *agg.* **1.** stanco **2.** annoiato.
to weary *vt.* **1.** affaticare **2.** annoiare. ♦ **to weary** *vi.* **1.** affaticarsi
2. annoiarsi.
weasel *s.* donnola.
weather *s.* tempo (*atmosferico*) ||
— -glass, barometro; *— -report*,
bollettino meteorologico.
to weather *vt.* **1.** esporre all'aria
2. superare || *to — a storm*, resi-
stere a una burrasca. ♦ **to weather** *vi.* alterarsi.
weathercock *s.* banderuola.
weathering *s.* alterazione (*di tempo*).
weave *s.* tessuto.
to weave (wove, woven) *vt.* **1.**
tessere, intrecciare **2.** (*fig.*) ideare.
weaver *s.* tessitore.
weaving *s.* **1.** tessitura **2.** orditura.
web *s.* **1.** tela **2.** (*fig.*) trama **3.**
membrana || *cob- —*, ragnatela.
to wed *vt.* sposare. ♦ **to wed** *vi.*
sposarsi.
wedding *s.* nozze (*pl.*) || *— -break-
fast*, rinfresco di nozze; *— -ring*,
fede nuziale.
wedge *s.* cuneo.
to wedge *vt.* **1.** incuneare **2.** fendere con cunei.

wedlock *s.* vincolo matrimoniale.
Wednesday *s.* mercoledì.
wee *agg.* minuscolo || *a — bit*, un
tantino.
weed *s.* erbaccia. ♦ **weeds** *s. pl.*
gramaglie.
to weed *vt.* **1.** sarchiare **2.** estirpare.
weeding *s.* sarchiatura.
week *s.* settimana || *today —*, oggi
a otto; *— in — out*, una settimana dopo l'altra.
weekday *s.* giorno feriale.
week-end *s.* fine settimana.
weekly *agg.* e *s.* settimanale. ♦
weekly *avv.* settimanalmente.
weep *s.* pianto.
to weep (wept, wept) *vt.* e *vi.*
1. piangere **2.** trasudare || *to —
out*, piangere disperatamente.
weeper *s.* **1.** chi piange **2.** velo,
nastro di lutto.
weeping *s.* **1.** pianto **2.** trasudamento.
weft *s.* trama (*di tessuto*).
to weigh *vt.* e *vi.* **1.** pesare **2.** (*fig.*)
ponderare || *to — down*, piegare;
to — anchor (*mar.*), levar l'ancora.
weigh-house *s.* pesa pubblica.
weighing *s.* pesatura || *— -machine*,
pesa.
weight *s.* **1.** peso **2.** importanza ||
to put on —, ingrassare
to weight *vi.* appensantire, caricare.
weightiness *s.* **1.** pesantezza **2.** (*fig.*)
importanza.
weightless *agg.* senza peso.
weighty *agg.* **1.** pesante **2.** (*fig.*)
importante.
weir *s.* chiusa, diga.
weird *agg.* **1.** fatale **2.** misterioso.
welcome *agg.* gradito. ♦ **welcome**
s. benvenuto.
to welcome *vt.* dare il benvenuto
a, gradire.
to weld *vt.* saldare. ♦ **to weld** *vi.*
saldarsi.
welding *s.* saldatura.
welfare *s.* benessere || *— contribu-
tions*, oneri previdenziali; *— state*,
stato assistenziale; *— work*, assistenza sociale.
well[1] *s.* **1.** fonte, pozzo **2.** tromba
delle scale.
well[2] *avv.* e *s.* bene || *as —*, pure;
as — as, oltre a, oltre che; *to be
—*, star bene; *to get —*, guarire.
to well *vi.* sgorgare.
well-advised *agg.* saggio.
well-being *s.* benessere.

well-bred *agg.* educato.
well-doing *s.* buona condotta.
well-done *agg.* (*cuc.*) ben cotto.
well-meaning *agg.* ben intenzionato.
well-off *agg.* agiato.
well-read *agg.* colto, ben educato.
well-timed *agg.* opportuno.
well-to-do *agg.* agiato.
Welsh *agg.* gallese.
Welshman *s.* gallese.
went V. *to go.*
wept V. *to weep.*
were V. *to be* || *as it* —, per così dire.
west *agg.* occidentale. ♦ west *avv.* a, verso ovest. ♦ west *s.* ovest.
westerly *agg.* 1. dall'ovest 2. verso ovest. ♦ westerly *avv.* verso ovest.
western *agg.* occidentale.
westerner *s.* occidentale.
to westernize *vt.* occidentalizzare. ♦ to westernize *vi.* occidentalizzarsi.
westward *agg.* e *avv.* verso ovest.
westwards *avv.* verso ovest.
wet *agg.* 1. umido 2. piovoso || — *blanket*, guastafeste. ♦ wet *s.* 1. umidità 2. tempo piovoso.
to wet *vt.* bagnare. ♦ to wet *vi.* bagnarsi.
wet-nurse *s.* nutrice.
wetting *s.* bagnatura.
whale *s.* balena || — *-boat*, baleniera.
to whale *vi.* andare a caccia di balene.
whalebone *s.* stecca di balena.
whaler *s.* 1. baleniere 2. baleniera.
wharf *s.* banchina.
to wharf *vt.* attraccare.
what *agg.* 1. (*int.*) quale? quali? che? 2. (*rel.*) (quello) ... che 3. (*escl.*) che! ♦ what *pron.* 1. (*int.*) che?, che cosa? 2. (*rel.*) ciò che 3. (*escl.*) quanto! || — *for?*, perché mai?; — *is he?*, che cosa fa? ♦ what *inter.* come!
whatever *agg.* qualunque. ♦ whatever *pron.* qualunque cosa. ♦ whatever *avv.* affatto.
whatsoever V. *whatever.*
wheat *s.* grano.
to wheedle *vt.* lusingare.
wheel *s.* 1. ruota 2. volante || *wheels within wheels*, retroscena.
to wheel *vt.* 1. far ruotare 2. spingere (*su un veicolo a ruote*). ♦

to wheel *vi.* ruotare.
wheelbarrow *s.* carriola.
wheeze *s.* respiro affannoso.
to wheeze *vi.* ansimare.
whelp *s.* cucciolo.
when *avv.* e *cong.* quando.
whence *avv.* da dove.
whenever *avv.* tutte le volte che.
where *avv.* dove.
whereabout(s) *avv.* e *cong.* dove. ♦ whereabout(s) *s.* luogo.
whereas *cong.* mentre.
whereby *avv.* 1. (*int.*) come? 2. (*rel.*) per cui.
wherefore *avv.* 1. (*int.*) perché 2. (*rel.*) perciò.
wherein *avv.* 1. (*int.*) come? dove? 2. (*rel.*) in cui.
whereof *avv.* 1. (*int.*) di che? 2. (*rel.*) di cui.
whereon *avv.* 1. (*int.*) su che? 2. (*rel.*) su cui.
whereto *avv.* 1. (*int.*) verso dove? a che scopo? 2. (*rel.*) a cui.
whereupon *avv.* 1. (*int.*) su che? 2. (*rel.*) dopo di che.
wherever *avv.* dovunque.
whet *s.* 1. affilatura 2. (*fig.*) stimolante.
to whet *vt.* 1. affilare 2. stimolare.
whether *cong.* se || — ... *or*, o...o.
whey *s.* siero (*del latte*).
which *agg.* 1. (*int.*) quale?, quali? 2. (*rel.*) il, la quale, i, le quali. ♦ which *pron.* 1. (*int.*) quale?, quali?, chi? 2. (*rel.*) il, la quale, i, le quali; il che || *I cannot tell is* —, non so distinguerli l'uno dall'altro.
whichever *agg.* qualunque. ♦ whichever *pron.* qualunque cosa.
whiff *s.* 1. soffio 2. sbuffo.
to whiff *vt.* e *vi.* 1. soffiare 2. emettere sbuffi.
whig *agg.* e *s.* (*pol. inglese*) liberale.
while *cong.* 1. mentre 2. sebbene. ♦ while *s.* momento || *once in a* —, una volta tanto; *the* —, frattanto.
to while *vt. to* — *away the time*, ammazzare il tempo.
whilst V. *while.*
whim *s.* capriccio.
whimper *s.* 1. piagnucolio 2. uggiolio.
to whimper *vi.* 1. piagnucolare 2. uggiolare.
whimsical *agg.* stravagante.

whimsicality s. stravaganza.
whimsy agg. capriccioso. ✦ **whimsy** s. capriccio.
whine s. piagnisteo.
to **whine** v. to whimper.
whinny s. nitrito.
to **whinny** vi. nitrire.
whip s. frusta.
to **whip** vt. **1.** frustare **2.** frullare. ✦ to **whip** vi. precipitarsi || to — away, partire improvvisamente; to — out, pronunciare con violenza, tirar fuori.
whipper-snapper s. gradasso.
whirl s. **1.** vortice **2.** (fig.) confusione.
to **whirl** vt. **1.** far roteare **2.** trascinare. ✦ to **whirl** vi. **1.** roteare **2.** correr via **3.** (fig.) esser confuso.
whirligig s. giostra.
whirlpool s. gorgo.
whirlwind s. turbine.
whir(r) s. **1.** ronzio **2.** frullio (d'ali) **3.** rombo (di motore).
to **whir(r)** vi. **1.** ronzare **2.** frullare (d'ali) **3.** rombare (di motore).
whisk s. **1.** scopino **2.** frullino **3.** movimento rapido.
to **whisk** vt. **1.** spazzare **2.** (cuc.) frullare **3.** agitare. ✦ to **whisk** vi. guizzare via.
whisker s. **1.** basetta **2.** baffo.
whisper s. **1.** mormorio **2.** diceria.
to **whisper** vt. e vi. mormorare, bisbigliare.
whistle s. fischio.
to **whistle** vt. e vi. **1.** fischiare **2.** chiamare con un fischio.
whistler s. **1.** chi fischia **2.** marmotta canadese.
whit s. **1.** inezia **2.** atomo.
Whit agg. di Pentecoste.
white agg. e s. bianco || — feather, viltà; — -livered, codardo.
to **whiten** vt. e vi. imbiancare.
whitener s. **1.** imbianchino **2.** candeggiante.
whiteness s. bianchezza.
whitening s. **1.** imbiancamento **2.** candeggiamento.
whitesmith s. lattoniere.
whitethorn s. biancospino.
whitewash s. **1.** calce **2.** (fig.) riabilitazione.
to **whitewash** vt. **1.** imbiancare **2.** (fig.) riabilitare.
whitewasher s. imbianchino.
whitewashing s. **1.** imbiancatura **2.** riabilitazione.

whiting s. calce.
whitish agg. biancastro.
whitlow s. patereccio.
Whitsunday s. Pentecoste.
whiz s. sibilo
who pron. **1.** (int.) chi? **2.** (rel.) il, la quale, i, le quali.
whoever pron. chiunque.
whole agg. tutto, intero. ✦ **whole** s. **1.** il tutto, l'intero **2.** il complesso || as a —, nell'insieme; on the —, nel complesso.
wholeness s. totalità.
wholesale agg. e avv. all'ingrosso. ✦ **wholesale** s. vendita all'ingrosso.
to **wholesale** vt. e vi. vendere all'ingrosso.
wholesaler s. venditore all'ingrosso.
wholesome agg. salutare.
wholly avv. totalmente.
whom pron. compl. di who.
whomever pron. compl. chiunque.
whomsoever v. whomever.
whoop s. ululato.
whooping-cough s. pertosse.
whorl s. spirale.
whose pron. **1.** (int.) di chi? **2.** (rel.) del, della quale, dei, delle quali.
whosever pron. di chiunque.
whosoever v. whoever.
why avv. **1.** (int.) perché? **2.** (rel.) per cui. ✦ **why** cong. perché. ✦ **why** inter. perbacco.
wick s. lucignolo.
wicked agg. malvagio.
wickedness s. malvagità.
wicker s. vimine.
wicket s. **1.** sportello **2.** cancelletto.
wide agg. **1.** largo **2.** alto (di tessuto) **3.** spalancato: — open, spalancato. ✦ **wide** avv. largamente.
wide-awake agg. **1.** completamente sveglio **2.** (fig.) vigilante.
widely avv. largamente.
to **widen** vt. allargare. ✦ to **widen** vi. allargarsi.
widespread agg. esteso.
widow s. vedova.
widower s. vedovo.
widowhood s. vedovanza.
width s. **1.** larghezza **2.** altezza (di stoffa).
to **wield** vt. **1.** brandire **2.** esercitare (autorità ecc.).
wife s. (pl. wives) moglie.
wig s. (fam.) sgridata.

wild *agg.* **1.** selvaggio, selvatico **2.** agitato **3.** pazzo **4.** avventato **5.** disordinato. ◆ **wild** *s.* deserto. ◆ **wild** *avv.* **1.** selvaggiamente **2.** impulsivamente **3.** sfrenatamente.

wilderness *s.* deserto.

wild-goose chase *s.* impresa vana, impossibile.

wildness *s.* **1.** selvatichezza **2.** furore.

wile *s.* astuzia.

wilful *agg.* **1.** ostinato **2.** premeditato.

wilfulness *s.* **1.** ostinazione **2.** premeditazione.

will *s.* **1.** volontà **2.** testamento || *free* —, libero arbitrio.

will *v.* ausiliare (*usato per il futuro*) *he* — *be*, egli sarà **2.** *v. dif.* volere: *I* — *go*, io voglio andare, io andrò (*futuro volitivo*).

to will *vt. e vi.* **1.** disporre **2.** lasciare per testamento.

willed *agg. strong* —, di forte volontà.

willing *agg.* **1.** volonteroso **2.** disposto || — *or not*, volente o nolente.

willingly *avv.* volentieri.

willow *s.* — -(*tree*), salice: *weeping* —, salice piangente.

willy-nilly *agg. e avv.* volente o nolente.

wily *agg.* astuto.

wimple *s.* **1.** soggolo **2.** arricciatura.

to win (won, won) *vt. e vi.* vincere || *to* — *back*, riconquistare.

wince *s.* sussulto.

to wince *vi.* trasalire.

winch *s.* **1.** argano **2.** manovella.

wind[1] *s.* **1.** vento **2.** respiro || *to get* — *of*, aver sentore di; — -*breaker*, giacca a vento; — -*cone*, manica a vento.

wind[2] *s.* **1.** svolta, curva **2.** giro di carica.

to wind[1] *vt.* **1.** fiutare **2.** sfiatare.

to wind[2] **(wound, wound)** *vt.* **1.** avvolgere **2.** (*una molla*) caricare **3.** girare || *to* — *off*, svolgere. ◆ **to wind (wound, wound)** *vi.* **1.** serpeggiare **2.** avvolgersi || *to* — *off*, svolgersi.

windbag *s.* **1.** otre (*di cornamusa*) **2.** (*fig.*) parolaio.

winder *s.* **1.** manovella **2.** avvolgitore.

winding *agg.* tortuoso. ◆ **winding** *s.* **1.** tortuosità **2.** tornante **3.** spira

4. caricamento **5.** ritorcitura.

windlass *s.* argano.

windmill *s.* mulino a vento.

window *s.* finestra, finestrino || — -*dresser*, vetrinista; *French-* —, porta finestra.

windpipe *s.* trachea.

windscreen *s.* parabrezza || — *wiper*, tergicristallo.

windshield *s.* (*amer.*) parabrezza.

windward *agg.* contro vento. ◆ **windward** *s.* sopravvento.

windy *agg.* **1.** ventoso **2.** verboso.

wine *s.* vino.

wing *s.* **1.** ala **2.** battente (*di porta*) **3.** (*teat.*) quinta || *on the* —, in volo; *to take* —, spiccare il volo.

winged *agg.* alato.

wink *s.* **1.** battito di palpebre **2.** ammicco **3.** (*fig.*) istante.

to wink *vi.* **1.** battere le palpebre **2.** ammiccare **3.** scintillare.

winner *s.* vincitore.

winning *agg.* **1.** vincitore **2.** suadente. ◆ **winning** *s.* vittoria.

to winnow *vt. e vi.* vagliare.

winsome *agg.* incantevole.

winter *s.* inverno. ◆ **winter** *agg.* invernale.

to winter *vi.* svernare.

wintered *agg.* gelato.

winterly V. *wintry.*

wintriness *s.* rigore invernale.

wintry *agg.* invernale, freddo.

wipe *s.* **1.** asciugatura **2.** spolverata.

to wipe *vt.* **1.** asciugare **2.** strofinare || *to* — *off*, cancellare.

wiper *s.* **1.** chi pulisce **2.** strofinaccio.

wire *s.* **1.** filo metallico **2.** telegramma || — *netting*, rete metallica; *barbed* —, filo spinato.

to wire *vt. e vi.* **1.** legare con filo metallico **2.** prendere in trappola **3.** telegrafare.

wired *agg.* munito di filo metallico, di rete metallica.

wireless *agg.* senza fili. ◆ **wireless** *s.* radiotelegrafia.

to wireless *vt. e vi.* radiotelegrafare.

wire-puller *s.* intrigante, eminenza grigia.

wiry *agg.* **1.** di, simile a filo metallico **2.** (*fig.*) resistente.

wisdom *s.* saggezza.

wise *agg.* **1.** saggio **2.** edotto, informato.

wise *s.* modo, maniera.

wiseacre *s.* saccente.

wisely *avv.* saggiamente.
wish *s.* **1.** desiderio **2.** augurio: *best wishes,* i migliori auguri.
to wish *vt.* e *vi.* **1.** desiderare **2.** augurare || *I wish I were,* vorrei essere; *I wish I had,* vorrei avere; *I wish I could,* vorrei potere.
wisher *s.* **1.** chi desidera **2.** chi augura.
wishful *agg.* desideroso.
wishing *agg.* desideroso. ♦ **wishing** *s.* desiderio.
wistaria *s.* glicine.
wistful *agg.* **1.** desideroso **2.** pensoso.
wistfully *avv.* **1.** con desiderio **2.** pensosamente.
wistfulness *s.* **1.** bramosia **2.** raccoglimento.
wit *s.* **1.** ingegno **2.** spirito **3.** persona di spirito || *to live by one's wits,* vivere di espedienti; *to be at one's wits' end,* non saper più cosa fare.
witch *s.* strega.
to witch *vt.* stregare.
witchcraft *s.* **1.** stregoneria *2.* fascino.
witch-doctor *s.* stregone.
witchery *s.* V. *witchcraft.*
witching *agg.* magico.
with *prep.* **1.** con **2.** presso **3.** a causa di, per, da.
to withdraw (withdrew, withdrawn) *vt.* ritirare. ♦ **to withdraw (withdrew, withdrawn)** *vi.* ritirarsi.
withdrawal *s.* **1.** ritirata, ritiro **2** ritrattazione.
withdrawn V. *to withdraw.*
withdrew V. *to withdraw.*
withe *s.* vimine.
to wither *vt.* e *vi.* avvizzire.
withering *s.* avvizzimento.
to withhold (withheld, withheld) *vt.* **1.** trattenere **2.** rifiutare **3.** nascondere.
within *prep.* entro. ♦ **within** *avv.* dentro.
without *prep.* senza, senza di. ♦ **without** *cong.* senza (che). ♦ **without** *avv.* fuori.
to withstand (withstood, withstood) *vt.* resistere a, fronteggiare.
withstander *s.* oppositore.
withstood V. *to withstand.*
witness *s.* **1.** testimone: *eye- —,* testimone oculare **2.** testimonianza.

to witness *vt.* **1.** essere testimone a **2.** mostrare. ♦ **to witness** *vi.* testimoniare.
witticism *s.* arguzia.
wittily *avv.* spiritosamente.
wittiness *s.* spirito.
wittingly *avv.* consapevolmente.
witty *agg.* spiritoso.
wives V. *wife.*
wizard *s.* mago.
to wobble V. *to wabble.*
woe *s.* dolore.
woeful *agg.* doloroso.
woke V. *to wake.*
woken V. *to wake.*
wolf *s.* (*pl.* wolves) lupo || *she- —,* lupa.
to wolf *vt.* divorare.
wolfish *agg.* da lupo.
woman, *s.* (*pl.* women) donna.
womanhood *s.* **1.** femminilità **2.** maturità (*della donna*) **3.** condizione di donna.
womanish *agg.* **1.** effeminato **2.** femminile.
womankind *s.* le donne (*in genere*).
womanlike *agg.* femminile. ♦ **womanlike** *avv.* femminilmente.
womanliness *s.* femminilità.
womanly *agg.* femminile.
womb *s.* **1.** ventre **2.** grembo **3.** utero.
women V. *woman.*
won V. *to win.*
wonder *s.* **1.** prodigio **2.** meraviglia.
to wonder *vi.* **1.** domandarsi **2.** stupirsi.
wonderful *agg.* meraviglioso.
wonderingly *avv.* con meraviglia.
wonderland *s.* paese delle meraviglie.
wondrous *agg.* mirabile.
wont *agg.* abituato. ♦ **wont** *s.* abitudine.
wonted *agg.* abituato, abituale.
to woo *vt.* corteggiare.
wood *s.* **1.** bosco **2.** legno || *— -cutter,* boscaiolo.
woodcock *s.* beccaccia.
woodcut *s.* **1.** incisione su legno **2.** xilografia.
wooden *agg.* di legno.
woodiness *s.* **1.** boscosità **2.** legnosità.
woodland *s.* terreno boscoso.
woodman *s.* **1.** guardaboschi **2.** taglialegna.
woodpecker *s.* picchio.

woodwork s. lavoro in legno.
woody agg. 1. boscoso 2. legnoso.
wooer s. corteggiatore.
wool s. 1. lana 2. peluria di animale || *cotton* —, ovatta.
wool(l)en agg. di lana. ♦ **wool(l)en** s. stoffa di lana.
woolly agg. 1. di lana, lanoso 2. (*fig.*) confuso.
word s. parola || *by* — *of mouth*, oralmente.
to word vt. esprimere.
wordiness s. verbosità.
wording s. espressione.
wordy agg. verboso.
wore V. *to wear.*
work s. lavoro || *out of* —, disoccupato. ♦ **works** s. pl. 1. meccanismo (*sing.*) 2. fabbrica, officina (*sing.*).
to work vt. 1. lavorare 2. far funzionare 3. dirigere || *to* — *in*, introdurre; *to* — *off*, liberarsi di; *to* — *out*, calcolare; *to* — *up*, elaborare. ♦ **to work** vi. 1. lavorare 2. funzionare 3. agitarsi.
workable agg. 1. eseguibile 2. lavorabile.
workaday agg. lavorativo.
workday s. giorno feriale.
worker s. lavoratore || *skilled* —, operaio qualificato.
workhouse s. ospizio di mendicità.
working agg. 1. laborioso 2. funzionante. ♦ **working** s. 1. lavorio 2. funzionamento 3. lavorazione || — *-clothes*, abiti da lavoro; — *expenses*, spese d'esercizio.
workless agg. senza lavoro.
workman s. operaio.
workmanship s. 1. abilità 2. fattura.
workroom s. laboratorio.
workshop s. officina.
workwoman s. operaia.
world s. mondo: *all over the* —, in tutto il mondo.
worldliness s. 1. condizione terrena 2. mondanità.
worldly agg. 1. terreno 2. mondano.
world-wide agg. diffuso, noto in tutto il mondo.
worm s. verme || — *-screw*, vite senza fine.
to worm vt. carpire || *to* — *one's way*, insinuarsi.
wormwood s. assenzio.
worn V. *to wear.* ♦ **worn** agg. 1.

consumato 2. indebolito || — *-out*, logoro, (*fig.*) esausto.
worried agg. 1. preoccupato 2. tormentato.
worrier s. seccatore.
worrisome agg. 1. irritante 2. preoccupato.
worry s. 1. ansia 2. guaio.
to worry vt. tormentare. ♦ **to worry** vi. preoccuparsi.
worrying agg. 1. preoccupante 2. tormentoso.
worse agg. (*comp.* di bad e ill) peggiore, peggio. ♦ **worse** avv. e s. peggio || *all the* —, tanto peggio; *so much the* — *for*, tanto peggio per; *none the* —, ugualmente; — *and* —, di male in peggio.
worship s. adorazione.
to worship vt. e vi. adorare, venerare.
worshipper s. 1. adoratore 2. fedele.
worst agg. (*superl.* di bad e ill) peggiore, pessimo. ♦ **worst** avv. e s. peggio || *at (the)* —, nella peggiore delle ipotesi.
worsted agg. di lana pettinata.
worth agg. degno. ♦ **worth** s. valore.
worthily avv. degnamente.
worthiness s. 1. valore 2. dignità.
worthless agg. 1. senza valore 2. indegno.
worthlessness s. 1. mancanza di valore 2. indegnità.
worthy agg. degno, meritevole. ♦ **worthy** s. persona illustre.
would v. dif. 1. (*ausiliare del condiz.*) *he* — *go*, egli andrebbe 2. (*passato ind. imperfetto, congiuntivo, condiz.*) volere 3. (*imperfetto ind.*) solere: *he* — *come every day*, soleva venire ogni giorno.
would-be agg. sedicente.
wound s. ferita.
to wound vt. ferire.
wound V. *to wind.*
wove V. *to weave.*
woven V. *to weave.*
wrack s. distruzione, rovina.
to wrangle vi. discutere.
wrangler s. attaccabrighe.
wrap s. sciarpa, coperta, mantello.
to wrap vt. avvolgere || *to* — *up*, impacchettare. ♦ **to wrap** vi. avvolgersi.
wrapper s. 1. imballatore 2. carta da imballo 3. copertina.

wrapping s. involucro || — *paper*, carta da imballaggio.
wrath s. ira.
wrathful agg. irato.
wrathfulness s. ira
wreath s. ghirlanda.
to wreathe vt. **1.** intrecciare 2. inghirlandare **3.** attorcigliare. ♦ *to* **wreathe** vi. innalzarsi in spire.
wreathy agg. **1.** inghirlandato **2.** a forma di ghirlanda.
wreck s. **1.** naufragio (*anche fig.*) **2.** relitto.
to wreck vt. rovinare. ♦ *to* **wreck** vi. naufragare.
wreckage V. *wreck.*
wren s. scricciolo.
wrench s. **1.** strappo **2.** (*mecc.*) chiave inglese.
to wrench, to wrest vt. **1.** strappare **2.** torcere.
wrestle s. lotta.
to wrestle vi. lottare.
wrestler s. lottatore.
wrestling s. (*sport.*) lotta
wretch s. disgraziato.
wretched agg. **1.** disgraziato **2.** scadente.
wretchedness s. **1.** disgrazia **2.** squallore.
wriggle s. contorsione.
to wriggle vt. contorcere. ♦ *to* **wriggle** vi. **1.** contorcersi **2.** (*fig.*) dar risposte evasive.
wring s. **1.** torsione **2.** dolore acuto.
to wring (wrung, wrung) vt. **1.** torcere **2.** estorcere **3.** stringere || *to — out*, spremere, (*fig.*) strappare.
wringer s. **1.** torcitore **2.** torchio.
wringing agg. lancinante (*di dolore*). ♦ **wringing** s. torcitura.
wrinkle[1] s. **1.** ruga **2.** grinza.
wrinkle[2] s. stratagemma.
to wrinkle vt. **1.** corrugare **2.** spiegazzare. ♦ *to* **wrinkle** vi. corrugarsi.
wrinkled, wrinkly agg. **1.** corrugato **2.** rugoso.
wrinkledness s. rugosità.
wrist s. polso.
wristband s. polsino.
to write (wrote, written) vt. scrivere || *to — back*, rispondere; *to — down*, annotare, descrivere; *to — off*, cancellare; *to — out*, copiare, emettere un assegno.
writer s. scrittore.
writhe s. contorcimento.

to writhe vt. contorcere. ♦ *to* **writhe** vi. **1.** contorcersi **2.** (*fig.*) fremere.
writing s. **1.** lo scrivere **2.** scrittura **3.** scritto || — *-desk*, scrivania; — *-paper*, carta da lettere.
written V. *to write.*
wrong agg. **1.** sbagliato **2.** ingiusto **3.** illegale. ♦ **wrong** avv. **1.** erroneamente **2.** ingiustamente.
wrong s. **1.** torto **2.** male || — *-doer*, peccatore, offensore; — *-doing*, peccato, offesa.
to wrong vt. **1.** far torto a **2.** imbrogliare.
wrongful agg. V. *wrong.*
wrongfulness s. ingiustizia.
wrongly avv. V. *wrong.*
wrote V. *to write.*
wrought agg. lavorato || — *-iron*, ferro battuto.
wrung V. *to wring.*
wry agg. storto.
to wry vt. contorcere. ♦ *to* **wry** vi. contorcersi.
wryly avv. per traverso.

X

xenophobe s. xenofobo.
xenophobia s. xenofobia.
xerophilous agg. xerofilo.
Xmas s. Natale.
X-ray agg. attr. a, di raggi X.
to X-ray vt. sottoporre a raggi X.
X-rays s. pl. raggi X.
xylograph s. xilografia.
xylographer s. xilografo.
xylographic(al) agg. xilografico.
xylography s. xilografia.
xylophone s. xilofono.
xylophonist s. xilofonista.

Y

yacht s. panfilo.
to yacht vi. fare crociere su panfilo.
yachtsman s. (*pl.* -men) proprietario di panfilo.
to yank vt. e vi. strappare, dare uno

strattone.
yap *s.* guaito.
to **yap** *vi.* guaire.
yard *s.* **1.** iarda **2.** cortile **3.** cantiere: *ship- —,* cantiere navale.
yarn *s.* **1.** filo **2.** *(fig.)* storia.
yawl *s.* *(naut.)* iole, piccola imbarcazione.
yawn *s.* **1.** sbadiglio **2.** apertura.
to **yawn** *vi.* **1.** sbadigliare **2.** aprirsi.
yawning *agg.* **1.** sonnolento **2.** spalancato.
yea *avv.* sì.
year *s.* anno: *— by —,* di anno in anno; *all the — round,* per tutto l'anno; *New Year's Day,* Capodanno.
yearbook *s.* annuario.
yearling *agg.* di un anno d'età. ♦
yearling *s.* animale di un anno.
yearlong *agg.* che dura un anno.
yearly *agg.* annuale. ♦ **yearly** *avv.* annualmente.
to **yearn** *vi.* languire || *to — for, after sthg.,* bramare qc.
yearning *s.* brama. ♦ **yearning** *agg.* bramoso.
yeast *s.* **1.** lievito **2.** fermento.
to **yeast** *vi.* **1.** lievitare **2.** fermentare.
yell *s.* urlo.
to **yell** *vt.* e *vi.* urlare.
yeller *s.* urlatore.
yellow *agg.* e *s.* giallo.
to **yellow** *vt.* e *vi.* ingiallire.
yellowish *agg.* giallastro.
yelp *s.* guaito.
to **yelp** *vi.* guaire.
yeoman *s.* piccolo proprietario terriero.
yes *avv.* sì.
yesterday *avv.* e *s.* ieri: *the day before —,* l'altro ieri; *— week,* ieri a otto.
yet *avv.* **1.** ancora **2.** già || *as —,* finora. ♦ **yet** *cong.* tuttavia.
yew *s.* *— (-tree)* tasso.
yield *s.* **1.** produzione **2.** *(comm.)* rendita.
to **yield** *vt.* e *vi.* **1.** produrre, rendere **2.** cedere || *to — oneself up,* arrendersi.
yielding *agg.* **1.** pieghevole **2.** docile.
yoke *s.* **1.** giogo **2.** barra *(del timone)* **3.** coppia *(di animali).*
to **yoke** *vt.* aggiogare.
yolk *s.* tuorlo.

yonder *agg.* quello là, di laggiù. ♦
yonder *avv.* là.
you *pron. pers.* **1.** tu, te, ti **2.** voi, ve, vi **3.** *(forma di cortesia)* Lei, Loro.
young *agg.* giovane || *— people,* i giovani *(in genere).*
youngster *s.* giovanetto.
your *agg. poss.* **1.** tuo **2.** vostro **3.** *(forma di cortesia)* Suo.
yours *pron. poss.* **1.** tuo **2.** vostro **3.** *(forma di cortesia)* Suo, Loro || *— truly, — faithfully,* distinti saluti.
yourself *pron. r.* **1.** tu stesso, ti, te, te stesso **2.** *(forma di cortesia)* Lei stesso.
yourselves *pron. r.* **1.** voi stessi, vi **2.** *(forma di cortesia)* Loro stessi.
youth *s.* **1.** gioventù **2.** ragazzo.
youthful *agg.* **1.** giovane **2.** giovanile.
youthfulness *s.* aspetto giovanile.
Yugoslav *agg.* e *s.* iugoslavo.

Z

zeal *s.* zelo.
zealot *s.* fanatico.
zealous *agg.* zelante.
zed *s.* zeta.
zenith *s.* zenit.
zephyr *s.* zeffiro.
zero *s.* **1.** zero **2.** *(fig.)* nullità.
zest *s.* **1.** gusto **2.** aroma.
zigzag *agg.* e *avv.* a zigzag.
to **zigzag** *vi.* andare a zigzag.
zinc *s.* zinco.
to **zinc** *vt.* zincare.
zincking *s.* zincatura.
zincograph *s.* zincografia.
to **zincograph** *vt.* imprimere su lastre di zinco.
zincographer *s.* zincografo.
zincography *s.* zincografia.
Zionism *s.* sionismo.
Zionist *s.* e *agg.* sionista.
zip *s.* fischio || *— (-fastener),* cerniera lampo.
to **zip** *vi.* sibilare.
zipper *s.* cerniera lampo.
zircon *s.* zircone.
zirconium *s.* zirconio.
zodiac *s.* zodiaco.
zodiacal *agg.* zodiacale.

zonal, zonary *agg.* zonale.
zonate(d) *agg.* a zone.
zonation *s.* zonatura.
zone *s.* zona.
zoo *s.* zoo.
zoological *agg.* zoologico.
zoologist *s.* zoologo.
zoology *s.* zoologia.
zoom *s.* **1.** rombo **2.** (*aer.*) salita a candela.
to zoom *vi.* **1.** rombare **2.** (*aer.*) salire a candela.

zoomorphic *agg.* zoomorfo.
zoomorphism *s.* zoomorfismo.
zoophilist *s.* zoofilo.
zoophilous *agg.* zoofilo.
zoophily *s.* zoofilia.
zoophobia *s.* zoofobia.
zootechnic *agg.* zootecnico.
zootechnics, zootechny *s.* zootecnica.
zootomic(al) *agg.* zootomico.
zouave *s.* zuavo.
zygoma *s.* (*pl.* zygomata) zigomo.

NOMI PROPRI, STORICI E GEOGRAFICI

Abel Abele.
Abraham Abramo.
Abyssinia .Abissinia.
Achilles Achille.
Adam Adamo.
Adolph Adolfo.
Adonis Adone.
Adriatic Sea Mar Adriatico.
Aegean Sea Mar Egeo
Aeneas Enea.
Aeschylus Eschilo.
Aesop Esopo.
Afghanistan Afganistan.
Agamemnon Agamennone.
Agatha Agata.
Agnes Agnese.
Ajax Aiace.
Albert Alberto
Aldous Aldo.
Alec, Alex *dim. di* Alexander.
Alexander Alessandro.
Alexandra Alessandra.
Alexis Alessio.
Alfred Alfredo.
Algiers Algeri.
Alps *pl.* Alpi.
Alsace Alsazia.
Amazon Rio delle Amazzoni.
Ambrose Ambrogio.
Andes *pl.* Ande.
Andrew Andrea.
Andy *dim. di* Andrew.
Angel Angelo.
Ann(e) Anna.
Annie *dim. di* Ann(e).
Antarctica Antartide.
Anthony Antonio.
Antoninus Antonino.
Antony Antonio.
Apennines *pl.* Appennini.
Aphrodite Afrodite.
Apulia Puglia.
Aragon Aragona.
Archimedes Archimede.
Ariadne Arianna.
Aristophanes Aristofane.
Aristotle Aristotele.
Armand Armando.
Arnold Arnaldo.
Arthur Arturo.
Athens Atene.
Atlantic Atlantico.

Augustin Agostino.
Augustus Augusto.
Azores *pl.* Azzorre.

Babel Babele.
Babylon Babilonia.
Bacchus Bacco.
Balearic Islands Baleari.
Balkans *pl.* Balcani.
Balthazar Baldassarre.
Baltic Sea Mar Baltico.
Baltimore Baltimora.
Baptist Battista.
Barcelona Barcellona.
Barnabas, Barnaby Barnaba.
Bartholomew Bartolomeo.
Basel Basilea.
Basil Basilio.
Beatrix Beatrice.
Belgium Belgio.
Belgrade Belgrado.
Benedict Benedetto.
Bengal Bengala.
Ben *dim. di* Benjamin.
Benjamin Beniamino.
Benny *dim. di* Benjamin.
Berlin Berlino.
Bermudas *pl.* Bermude.
Bern Berna.
Bernard Bernardo.
Bertha Berta.
Bess *dim. di* Elizabeth.
Bethlehem Betlemme.
Betty *dim. di* Elizabeth.
Bill(y) *dim. di* William.
Blanche Bianca.
Bob(by) *dim. di* Robert.
Bohemia Boemia.
Boniface Bonifacio.
Bosporus Bosforo.
Brandenburg Brandeburgo.
Brazil Brasile.
Brittany Bretagna.
Brutus Bruto.
Burma Birmania.

Cadiz Cadice.
Caesar Cesare.
Cain Caino.
Caius Caio.

Calvin Calvino.
Cambodia Cambogia.
Canada Canadà.
Capitol Campidoglio.
Caribbean Sea Mar dei Caraibi.
Caroline Carolina.
Carpathian Mountains *pl.* Carpazi.
Carthage Cartagine.
Cashmere Cascemir.
Caspian Sea Mar Caspio.
Cassiopeia Cassiopea.
Cassius Cassio.
Catherine Caterina.
Cato Catone.
Caucasus Caucaso.
Cecil Cecilio.
Channel (The) La Manica.
Charlemagne Carlomagno.
Charles Carlo.
Charlie *dim. di* Charles.
Charlotte Carlotta.
Chile Cile.
China Cina.
Christ Cristo.
Christine Cristina.
Christopher Cristoforo.
Cicero Cicerone.
Cinderella Cenerentola.
Clara Clara, Chiara.
Claude, Claudius Claudio.
Clement Clemente.
Clementine Clementina.
Clytemnestra Clitennestra.
Cologne Colonia.
Connie *dim. di* Constance.
Conrad Corrado.
Constance Costanza.
Constantine Costantino.
Constantinople Costantinopoli.
Corinth Corinto.
Cornelius Cornelio.
Cornwall Cornovaglia.
Crete Creta.
Cynthia Cinzia.
Cyprus Cipro.
Cyril Cirillo.
Cyrus Ciro.
Czechoslovakia Cecoslovacchia.

Daisy *dim. di* Margaret.
Damascus Damasco.
Damocles Damocle.
Dan *dim. di* Daniel.
Daniel Daniele.
Danny *dim. di* Daniel.
Danube Danubio.
Danzig Danzica.

Daphne Dafne.
Dardanelles *pl.* Dardanelli.
Darius Dario.
Dave *dim. di* David.
Deb(by) *dim. di* Deborah.
Deborah Debora.
Delphi Delfo.
Democritus Democrito.
Demosthenes Demostene.
Denmark Danimarca.
Dick *dim. di* Richard.
Dido Didone.
Diocletian Diocleziano.
Diogenes Diogene.
Dionysius Dionigi, Dionisio.
Dominic Domenico.
Domitian Domiziano.
Dorothy Dorotea.
Dublin Dublino.

Ed(dy) *dim. di* Edmund, Edward.
Edgar Edgardo.
Edinburgh Edimburgo.
Edmund Edmondo.
Edward Edoardo.
Egypt Egitto.
Eire (Stato Libero di) Irlanda.
Eleanor Eleonora.
Electra Elettra.
Elias, Elijah Elia.
Eliza Elisa.
Elizabeth Elisabetta.
Emanuel Emanuele.
Emily Emilia.
England Inghilterra.
Epaminondas Epaminonda.
Epicurus Epicuro.
Erasmus Erasmo.
Ernest Ernesto.
Esther Ester.
Ethiopia Etiopia.
Euclid Euclide.
Eugene Eugenio.
Euphrates Eufrate.
Euripides Euripide.
Europe Europa.
Eve Eva.
Evelyn Evelina.
Ezekiel Ezechiele.

Faust(us) Fausto.
Felix Felice.
Ferdinand Ferdinando.
Finland Finlandia.
Florence Firenze.
France Francia.
Frances Francesca.

Francis Francesco.
Frank Franco.
Frankfurt Francoforte.
Fred(dy) *dim. di* Frederic.
Frederic Federico.

Gabriel Gabriele.
Galilee Galilea.
Gascony Guascogna.
Gaule Gallia.
Geneva Ginevra.
Genoa Genova.
Geoffrey Goffredo.
George Giorgio.
Gerard Gerardo.
Germany Germania.
Gibraltar Gibilterra.
Gilbert Gilberto.
Golgotha Golgota.
Goliath Golia.
Grace Grazia.
Great Britain Gran Bretagna.
Greece Grecia.
Greenland Groenlandia.
Gregory Gregorio.
Guiana Guaiana.
Gustavus Gustavo.
Guy Guido.

Hadrian Adriano.
Hague (The) L'Aia.
Hamburg Amburgo.
Hamlet Amleto.
Hannibal Annibale.
Harold Aroldo.
Harriet Enrichetta.
Harry *dim. di* Harold, Henry.
Hebrides *pl.* Ebridi.
Hector Ettore.
Helen Elena.
Hellas Ellade.
Henrietta Enrichetta.
Henry Arrigo, Enrico.
Heraclitus Eraclito.
Herbert Erberto.
Hercules Ercole.
Hermes Ermete.
Herod Erode.
Herodotus Erodoto.
Hesiod Esiodo.
Hilary Ilario.
Himalaya Imalaia.
Hindustan Indostan.
Hippolytus Ippolito.
Holland Olanda.
Homer Omero.
Horace, Horatio Orazio.

Hubert Uberto.
Hugh Ugo.
Humbert Umberto.
Hungary Ungheria.

Icarus Icaro.
Iceland Islanda.
Ignatius Ignazio.
Innocent Innocente.
Ionian Sea Mar Ionio.
Ireland Irlanda.
Iris Iride.
Isaac Isacco.
Isabel Isabella.
Isaiah Isaia.
Ishmael Ismaele.
Isis Iside.
Israel Israele.
Italy Italia.

Jack(ie) *dim. di* John.
Jacob Giacobbe.
Jamaica Giamaica.
James Giacomo.
Jane Giovanna.
Janet *dim. di* Jane.
Japan Giappone.
Jason Giasone.
Java Giava.
Jean Giovanna.
Jeffrey Goffredo.
Jehovah Geova.
Jenny *dim. di* Jean.
Jeremiah Geremia.
Jericho Gerico.
Jerome Gerolamo.
Jerry *dim. di* Gerard, Jerome.
Jerusalem Gerusalemme.
Jesus Gesù.
Jim(my) *dim. di* James.
Jo *dim. di* Josephine.
Joan Giovanna.
Job Giobbe.
Joe *dim. di* Joseph.
John Giovanni.
Johnny *dim. di* John.
Jonah, Jonas Giona.
Jonathan Gionata.
Jordan Giordano.
Joseph Giuseppe.
Josephine Giuseppina.
Joshua Giosuè.
Jove Giove.
Judas, Jude Giuda.
Judea Giudea.
Judith Giuditta.
Judy *dim. di* Judith.

Julia Giulia.
Julian Giuliano.
Juliana Giuliana.
Julie Giulia.
Juliet Giulietta.
Julius Giulio.
Juno Giunone.
Jupiter Giove.
Juvenal Giovenale.

Kashmir Cascemir.
Kate, Kitty *dim. di* Catherine.
Korea Corea.

Lambert Lamberto.
Laocoon Laocoonte.
Lapland Lapponia.
Larry *dim. di* Lawrence.
Latium Lazio.
Launcelot Lancillotto.
Lausanne Losanna.
Lawrence Lorenzo.
Lazarus Lazzaro.
Leander Leandro.
Lebanon Libano.
Leghorn Livorno.
Leo(n) Leone.
Leonard Leonardo.
Leonidas Leonida.
Leopold Leopoldo.
Lethe Lete.
Letitia Letizia.
Lewis Luigi.
Libya Libia.
Liège Liegi.
Lisbon Lisbona
Livy Livio.
Liza, Lizzie, Liz(zy) *dim. di* Elizabeth.
Lombardy Lombardia.
London Londra.
Lou *dim. di* Louise.
Louis Luigi.
Louise Luigia, Luisa.
Louvain Lovanio.
Lucerne Lucerna.
Lucian Luciano.
Lucifer Lucifero.
Lucius Lucio.
Lucretius Lucrezio.
Lucy Lucia.
Luke Luca.
Luther Lutero.
Luxemburg Lussemburgo.
Lycurgus Licurgo.
Lydia Lidia.
Lyons Lione.

Magdalene Maddalena.
Mag(gie) *dim. di* Margaret.
Majorca Maiorca.
Malaya Malesia.
Manchuria Manciuria.
Manfred Manfredi.
Mantua Mantova.
Marathon Maratona.
Marcellus Marcello.
Margaret Margherita.
Margie *dim. di* Margaret.
Marianne Marianna.
Marius Mario.
Mark Marco.
Mars Marte.
Martha Marta.
Martial Marziale.
Martin Martino.
Mary Maria.
Matilda Matilde.
Matt *dim. di* Matthew.
Matthew Matteo.
Matty *dim. di* Martha, Matilda.
Maurice Maurizio.
Max *dim. di* Maximilian.
Maximilian Massimiliano.
May *dim. di* Mary.
Mediterranean Mediterraneo.
Meg *dim. di* Margaret.
Menelaus Menelao.
Mephistopheles Mefistofele.
Mercury Mercurio.
Merlin Merlino.
Methuselah Matusalemme.
Meuse Mosa.
Mexico Messico.
Michael Michele.
Mick(ey) *dim. di* Michael.
Midas Mida.
Mike *dim. di* Michael.
Milan Milano.
Minos Minosse.
Minotaur Minotauro.
Mithridates Mitridate.
Mohammed Maometto.
Moll(y) *dim. di* Mary.
Moluccas *pl.* Molucche.
Monaco (Principato di) Monaco.
Morocco Marocco.
Moscow Mosca.
Moses Mosè.
Mozambique Mozambico.
Munich Monaco di Baviera.
Mycenae Micene.

Naples Napoli.
Napoleon Napoleone.
Narcissus Narciso.

Nell(y) *dim. di* Helen.
Neptune Nettuno.
Nero Nerone.
Netherlands *pl.* Paesi Bassi.
Newfoundland Terranova.
New Zealand Nuova Zelanda.
Nice Nizza.
Nicholas Nicola.
Nick *dim. di* Nicholas.
Nile Nilo.
Noah Noè.
Normandy Normandia.
Norway Norvegia.

Oedipus Edipo.
Oliver Oliviero.
Olympus Olimpo.
Ophelia Ofelia.
Orestes Oreste.
Orion Orione.
Orkneys *pl.* Orcadi.
Orpheus Orfeo.
Osiris Osiride.
Oswald Osvaldo.
Othello Otello.
Ovid Ovidio.

Pacific Pacifico.
Paddy *dim. di* Patrick.
Padua Padova.
Palestine Palestina.
Pancras Pancrazio.
Papua Papuasia.
Paris[1] Paride.
Paris[2] Parigi.
Parnassus Parnaso.
Parthenon Partenone.
Pat *dim. di* Patricia, Patrick.
Patricia Patrizia.
Patrick Patrizio.
Paul Paolo.
Paula Paola.
Pauline Paolina.
Peg(gy) *dim.* di Margaret.
Peking Pechino.
Peloponnesus Peloponneso.
Pennsylvania Pensilvania.
Pericles Pericle.
Perseus Perseo.
Peru Perù.
Pete *dim. di* Peter.
Peter Pietro.
Phaedra Fedra.
Pharsalus Farsalo.
Philadelphia Filadelfia.
Philip Filippo.
Philippi Filippi.

Philippines *pl.* Filippine.
Piedmont Piemonte.
Pigmalion Pigmalione.
Pindar Pindaro.
Piraeus Pireo.
Pius Pio.
Plato Platone.
Pliny Plinio.
Plutarch Plutarco.
Poland Polonia.
Poll(y) *dim. di* Mary.
Polynesia Polinesia.
Pompey Pompeo.
Portugal Portogallo.
Prague Praga.
Prometheus Prometeo.
Ptolemy Tolomeo.
Pyrenees *pl.* Pirenei.
Pythagoras Pitagora.

Quentin Quintino.

Rachel Rachele.
Ramses Ramsete.
Raphael Raffaele, Raffaello.
Raymond Raimondo.
Remus Remo.
Rhine Reno.
Rhodes Rodi.
Rhone Rodano.
Richard Riccardo.
Rob *dim. di* Robert.
Robert Roberto.
Roderick Rodrigo.
Roger Ruggero.
Roland Orlando, Rolando.
Rome Roma.
Romulus Romolo.
Rosalie Rosalia.
Rosalind Rosalinda.
Rose Rosa.
Roumania Romania.
Roxana Rossana.
Rudolph Rodolfo.
Rudy *dim. di* Rudolph.

Sadie, Sally *dim. di* Sarah.
Sam *dim. di* Samuel.
Samson Sansone.
Samuel Samuele.
Sappho Saffo.
Sarah Sara.
Sardinia Sardegna.
Satan Satana.
Saturn Saturno.
Savoy Savoia.

Saxony Sassonia.
Scipion Scipione.
Scotland Scozia.
Sean Giovanni.
Sebastian Sebastiano.
Sibyl Sibilla.
Sicily Sicilia.
Silvester Silvestro.
Simeon Simeone.
Simon Simone.
Simplon Sempione.
Smyrna Smirne.
Socrates Socrate.
Sodom Sodoma.
Solomon Salomone.
Somaliland Somalia.
Sophia Sofia.
Sophocles Sofocle.
Soudan Sudan.
Spain Spagna.
Stephen Stefano.
Steve *dim. di* Stephen.
Stockholm Stoccolma.
Strasbourg Strasburgo.
Sue *dim. di* Susan(nah).
Sulla Silla.
Susy *dim. di* Susan(nah).
Susan(nah) Susanna.
Sweden Svezia.
Switzerland Svizzera.
Sylvia Silvia.
Syracuse Siracusa.
Syria Siria.

Tacitus Tacito.
Tangier(s) Tangeri.
Ted(dy) *dim. di* Edward.
Telemachus Telemaco.
Terence Terenzio.
Tess *dim. di* Theresa.
Thailand Tailandia.
Thames Tamigi.
Thebes Tebe.
Themistocles Temistocle.
Theodoric Teodorico.
Theresa Teresa.
Thermopylae *pl.* Termopili.
Theseus Teseo.
Thomas Tommaso.
Tiber Tevere.
Tiberius Tiberio.
Tirol Tirolo.
Titian Tiziano.
Titus Tito.
Tobias Tobia.
Toby *dim. di* Tobias.

Tom(my) *dim. di* Thomas.
Tonkin, Tonking Tonchino.
Tony *dim. di* Ant(h)ony.
Trajan Traiano.
Tristan, Tristram Tristano.
Troy Troia.
Tully Tullio.
Tunis Tunisi.
Turin Torino.
Turkey Turchia.
Tuscany Toscana.
Tyrol Tirolo.
Tyrrhenian Sea Mar Tirreno.

Ukraine Ucraina.
Ulysses Ulisse.
United States of America Stati
Uniti d'America.
Urban Urbano.
Ursula Orsola.
USA Stati Uniti d'America.
USSR URSS (Unione Repubbliche
Socialiste Sovietiche).

Valentine Valentino.
Valerius Valerio.
Vatican Vaticano.
Venetia Veneto.
Venice Venezia.
Venus Venere.
Vesuvius Vesuvio.
Victor Vittorio.
Victoria Vittoria.
Vincent Vincenzo.
Virgil Virgilio.
Vivian Viviana, Viviano.
Vulcan Vulcano.

Wales Galles.
Walter Gualtiero.
Warsaw Varsavia.
Will *dim. di* William.
William Guglielmo.
Willy *dim. di* William.

Xerxes Serse.

Yugoslavia Iugoslavia.

Zachary Zaccaria.
Zurich Zurigo.

SIGLE E ABBREVIAZIONI USATE
NEI PAESI DI LINGUA INGLESE

a., **1.** *about*: c., circa **2.** *acre*: acro **3.** *approved*: approvato, riconosciuto dallo Stato.

A.A., *Automobile Association*: A.C., Automobile Club.

A.A.R., *against all risks*: contro ogni rischio.

Abp., *Archbishop*: arcivescovo.

abr., **1.** *abridged*: ridotto (*di edizione*) **2.** *abridgment*: compendio.

A.C., *alternating current*: c.a., corrente alternata.

a/c, **ac.**, *account*: c., conto.

A.D., *Anno Domini* (= *dopo Cristo*): d.C., dopo Cristo.

adj., *adjourned*: aggiornato.

Adm., *Admiral*: ammiraglio.

adv., *advertisement*: inserzione.

A.E.C., *Atomic Energy Commission*: C.E.A., Commissione per l'energia atomica.

A.F., *Air Force*: A.M., Aeronautica Militare.

Ala., *Alabama*.

Alas., *Alaska*.

alt., **1.** *alternate*: alternata **2.** *alternating*: alternata.

a.m., *ante meridiem, before noon*: antimeridiano.

Am(er)., **1.** *America*: Am., Amer., America **2.** *American*: am., amer., americano.

anon., *anonymous*: anonimo.

A.P., *Associated Press*: Stampa Associata.

app., *appendix*: app., appendice.

approx., *approximately*: appross., approssimativamente.

Apr., *April*: apr., aprile.

apt., *apartment*: appartamento.

Ariz., *Arizona*.

Ark., *Arkansas*.

arr., **1.** *arrival*: arr., arrivo **2.** *arrived*: arr., arrivato.

ass., *association*: ass., associazione.

at. no., *atomic number*: n.a., numero atomico.

att(y)., *attorney*: proc., procuratore.

at. wt., *atomic weight*: p. at., peso atomico.

Aug., *August*: ago., agosto.

avdp., *avoirdupois*: avoirdupois.

ave., *avenue*: v.le, viale.

b., **1.** *book*: l., libro **2.** *born*: n., nato.

B.A., *Bachelor of Arts*: diplomato in lettere.

Bap(t)., *Baptist*: Battista.

B.B.C., *British Broadcasting Corporation*: Ente Radiofonico Britannico.

B.C., *Before Christ*: a.C., avanti Cristo.

B/E, **b.e.**, *bill of exchange*: cambiale.

B.E.A., *British European Airways*: Linee Aeree Europee Britanniche.

Beds., *Bedfordshire*.

Berks., *Berkshire*.

bet., *between*: fra.

B/L, *bill of lading*: polizza di carico.

blvd., *boulevard*: boulevard.

B.M., *British Museum*: Museo Britannico.

B.M.A., *British Medical Association*: Associazione Medica Britannica.

B.O.A.C., *British Overseas Airways Corporation*: Società aerea d'oltremare britannica.

B. of A., *Bank of America*: Banca d'America.

B. of E., *Bank of England*: Banca d'Inghilterra.

Bp., *Bishop*: vesc., vescovo.

bros., *brothers*: F.lli, Fratelli.

b.s., **1.** *balance sheet*: bilancio di esercizio **2.** *bill of sale*: atto di vendita.

bsh., *bushel*: staio.

Bucks., *Buckinghamshire*.

bul(l)., *bulletin*: boll., bollettino.

c., **1.** *centigrade*: c., centigrado **2.** *cent*: cent., centesimo **3.** *chapter*: cap., capitolo.

C/A, *current account*: c/c, conto corrente.

ca., **1.** *cathode*: catodo **2.** *about*: ca., circa.

Cal(if)., *California.*

Cam(b)., *Cambridge.*

Cambs., *Cambridgeshire.*

Can., **1.** *Canada*: Canada **2.** *Canadian*: canadese.

Cantab., *of Cambridge*: cantabrigense.

cap., **1.** *chapter*: cap., capitolo **2.** *capital*: capitale.

Capt., *Captain*: cap., capitano.

Card., *Cardinal*: card., cardinale.

cc., **1.** *chapters*: capp., capitoli **2.** *cubic centimetres*: cmc., centimetri cubi.

C.D., *Corps Diplomatique*: C.D., Corpo Diplomatico.

C.E.D., *Community for European Defence*: C.E.D., Comitato per la Difesa Europea.

Celt., *Celtic*: celtico.

cent., **1.** *centigrade*: c., centigrado **2.** *centimetre*: cm., centimetro **3.** *central*: centrale **4.** *century*: sec., secolo.

c.f., *cost and freight*: c.f., costo e nolo.

C.F.I., **c.f.i.**, *cost, freight and insurance*: costo, nolo e assicurazione.

Ch., **1.** *Church*: Chiesa **2.** *China*: Cina **3.** *Chinese*: cinese.

ch(ap)., *chapter*: cap., capitolo.

Ches(h)., *Cheshire.*

Chr., **1.** *Christ*: Cristo **2.** *Christian*: cristiano.

C.I.A., *Central Intelligence Agency*: Organizzazione centrale d'informazioni (Servizio segreto americano).

c.i.f., *cost, insurance, freight*: c.i.f., costo, assicurazione e nolo.

cm., *centimetre*: cm., centimetro.

Co., **1.** *Company*: s., società **2.** *County*: contea.

c/o, *care of*: c/o, presso.

C.O.D., **c.o.d.**, *cash on delivery*: pagamento alla consegna.

Col., **1.** *Colonel*: col., colonnello **2.** *Colorado.*

coll., **1.** *colleague*: collega **2.** *college*: coll., collegio **3.** *colloquial*: fam., familiare.

Colo., *Colorado.*

Conn., *Connecticut.*

Consol., *consolidated*: consolidato.

cont(d)., *continued*: continuo, ininterrotto.

coop., *co-operative*: coop., cooperativa.

corp., *corporation*: **1.** corporazione **2.** (*amer.*) s.r.l., società a responsabilità limitata.

Corn(w), *Cornwall.*

c.o.s., *cash on shipment*: pagamento alla spedizione.

C.P., *Communist Party*: P.C., Partito Comunista.

cp., *compare*: cfr., confrontare.

Ct., *Connecticut.*

cu., *cubic*: c., cubico.

Cumb., *Cumberland.*

C.U.P., *Cambridge University Press*: Edizioni dell'Università di Cambridge.

d., **1.** *date*: data **2.** *dead*: m., morto **3.** *penny, pence*: penny, pence.

d.c., *direct current*: c.c., corrente continua.

D.A.B., *Dictionary of American Biography*: Dizionario della Biografia Americana.

Dak., *Dakota.*

D.C., *District of Columbia*: Distretto della Columbia.

D.D., *Doctor of Divinity*: dottore in teologia.

dd., **d/d**, *delivered*: consegnato.

Dec., *December*: dic., dicembre.

Del., *Delaware.*

dep., **1.** *department*: reparto, ufficio; (*am.*) ministero **2.** *deputy*: deputato.

Devon., *Devonshire.*

Dir., *director*: dirett., direttore.

disc., *discount*: sconto.

D. Lit., *Doctor of Literature*: dottore in letteratura.

D.N.B., *Dictionary of National Biography*: Dizionario della Biografia Nazionale.

dol., *dollar*: dollaro.

Dorset., *Dorsetshire.*

doz., *dozen*: dozz., dozzina.

D.P., *Displaced Person*: profugo.

Dr., **1.** *Doctor*: dott., dottore **2.** *Debtor*: debitore.

dz., *dozen*: dozz., dozzina.

E., **1.** *East*: E, Est **2.** *English*: inglese.

ea., *each*: cad., cadauno.

E.B., *Encyclopaedia Britannica*: Enciclopedia Britannica.

E.C.A., *Economic Co-operation Administration*: Amministrazione della cooperazione economica.

E.C.M., *European Common Market*: M.E.C., Mercato Comune Europeo.

ed., 1. *edited*: ed., edito 2. *edition*: ed., edizione.

E.D.C., *European Defence Community*: C.E.D., Comunità per la difesa europea.

edit., V. *ed.*

Edin., *Edinburgh.*

e.g., *for example*: p. es., per esempio.

Emp., *Emperor*: imperatore.

enc(l)., *enclosure*: all., allegato.

Eng., 1. *England*: Inghilterra 2. *English*: inglese.

esp(ec)., *especially*: spec., specialmente.

Esq., *Esquire* (*titolo di cortesia usato negli indirizzi*): Egr., egregio.

etc., *and so on*: ecc., eccetera.

Eur., 1. *Europe*: Europa 2. *European*: europeo.

ex., 1. *examined*: esaminato 2. *example*: es., esempio 3. *excepted*: eccetto 4. *executive*: esecutivo.

exc., *except(ed)*: eccettuato.

F., *Fahrenheit*: F., Fahrenheit.

f., *frequency*: f., frequenza.

F.A.O., *Food and Agricultural Organization*: Organizzazione per l'agricoltura e l'alimentazione.

F.B.I., *Federal Bureau of Investigation*: Ufficio federale d'investigazione.

Feb., *February*: feb., febbraio.

Fed., 1. *Federal*: fed., federale 2. *Federation*: federazione.

Fla., **Flor.**, *Florida.*

F.O., *Foreign Office*: M.AA.EE., Ministero degli affari esteri.

F.O.B., **f.o.b.**, *free on board*: f.o.b., franco bordo.

fol., *folio*: folio.

fol(l)., *following*: seg., seguente.

Fr., 1. *Father*: P., padre 2. *France*: Francia 3. *French*: francese 4. *Friday*: ven., venerdì.

Fri., *Friday*: ven., venerdì.

ft., *foot, feet*: piede, piedi.

g., 1. *conductance*: conduttanza 2. *gender*: genere 3. *gram*: g., grammo 4. *guinea*: ghinea.

Ga., *Georgia.*

gal(l)., *gallon*: gallone.

G.B., *Great Britain*: Gran Bretagna.

Gen., *General*: gen., generale.

gen., 1. *gender*: genere 2. *generally*: gen., generalmente.

gent., *gentleman*: gentiluomo, signore.

G.H.Q., *General Headquarters*: Q.G., quartier generale.

G.I., *Government Issue*: promulgazione ministeriale.

Gloster., *Gloucestershire.*

G-Man., *Government Man*: soldato governativo.

G.O.P., *Grand Old Party* (*U.S. Republican Party*): Partito Repubblicano Americano.

G.P.O., *General Post Office*: Posta centrale.

H, *hydrogen*: H., idrogeno.

h., 1. *hour*: h., ora 2. *high*: A., alto.

H.B.M., *His* (*Her*) *Britannic Majesty*: S.M.B., Sua Maestà Britannica.

H.C., *House of Commons*: Camera dei Comuni.

H.E., *His Excellency*: S.E., Sua Eccellenza.

Hereford., *Herefordshire.*

Herts., *Hertfordshire.*

hf., *half*: metà.

H.H., 1. *His Holiness*: S.S., Sua Santità 2. *His* (*Her*) *Highness*: S.A., Sua Altezza.

hhd., *hogshead*: hogshead (*misura di capacità l. 238,5*).

H.L., *House of Lords*: Camera Alta.

H.M., *His* (*Her*) *Majesty*: V.M., Vostra Maestà.

H.M.S., *His* (*Her*) *Majesty's Service*: servizio di Sua Maestà.

Hon., *Honourable*: on., onorèvole.

H.P., 1. *high pressure*: alta pressione 2. *horse power*: H.P., cavalli vapore.

hr., *hour*: h., ora.

H.S., *High School*: scuola media superiore.

Hunts., *Huntingdonshire.*

I(a)., *Iowa.*

ib(id)., *in the same place*: ibid., nello stesso luogo.

I.D., *Intelligence Department*: reparto informazioni.

id., *the same*: id., come sopra.

Id(a)., *Idaho.*

i.e., *that is*: cioè.

Ill., *Illinois.*

in., *inch*: pollice (*misura*).

Inc., 1. *incorporated*: incorporato 2. *including*: incluso.

Inst., *instant (the present month)*: c.m., corrente mese.

I.O.U., *I owe you*: pagherò.

I.Q., *Intelligence Quotient*: Q.I., quoziente d'intelligenza.

Ire., *Ireland.*

Ja(n)., *January*: genn., gennaio.

J.P., *Justice of the Peace*: giudice di pace.

Jr., jun., *junior*: iun., junior

Kan(s)., *Kansas.*

kg., *kilogram*: kg., chilogrammo.

kilo., 1. *kilogram*: chilogrammo 2. *kilometre*: km., chilometro.

K.K.K., *Ku Klux Klan*: K.K.K., Ku Klux Klan.

km., *kilometre*: km., chilometro.

K.O., *knock out*: fuori combattimento.

kw., *kilowatt*: kw., chilowatt.

Ky., *Kentucky.*

L., *pound*: L.st., lira sterlina.

l., 1. *litre*: l., litro 2. *long*: lungo.

La., *Louisiana.*

Lancs., *Lancashire.*

Lat., *Latin*: latino.

lat., *latitude*: latitudine.

lb., *pound*: libbra.

L.C.D., *lowest common denominator*: m.c.d., minimo comun denominatore.

L.C.M., *least common multiple*: m.c.m., minimo comune multiplo.

Leics., *Leicestershire.*

L.F., *low frequency*: b.f., bassa frequenza.

Lieut., *Lieutenant*: luogotenente.

Lincs., *Lincolnshire.*

LL.D., *Doctor of Laws*: dottore in legge.

Lon., *London*: Londra.

lon(g)., *longitude*: longitudine.

L.P., 1. *Labour Party*: Partito Laburista 2. *Long Play*: microsolco.

L.R., *Lloyd's Register*: Registro dei Lloyd.

Ltd., *limited*: s.r.l., società a responsabilità limitata.

m., 1. *male*: m., maschio 2. *metre*: m., metro 3. *mile*: miglio 4. *minute*: m., minuto 5. *month*: m., mese.

M.A., *Master of Arts*: laureato in lettere.

Mad., Madm., *Madam*: sig.ra, signora.

Maj., *Major*: magg., maggiore.

Mar., *March*: mar., marzo.

Mass., *Massachusetts.*

max., *maximum*: mass., massimo.

M.C., *Member of Congress*: membro del Congresso.

Md., *Maryland.*

M.D., *Doctor of Medicine*: dottore in medicina.

Mdx., *Middlesex.*

Me., *Maine.*

M.F., *medium frequency*: m.f., media frequenza.

mg(m)., *milligram*: mg., milligrammo.

Mich., *Michigan.*

Minn., *Minnesota.*

Miss., *Mississippi.*

mm., *millimetre*: mm., millimetro.

Mo., 1. *Missouri* 2. *Monday*: lun., lunedì.

M.O., *money order*: ordine di pagamento.

Mon., *Monday*: lun., lunedì.

Mont., *Montana.*

M.P., 1. *Military Police*: Polizia militare 2. *Member of Parliament*: membro del Parlamento.

mph., *miles per hour*: miglia orarie.

Mr., *Mister*: sig., signor.

Mrs., *Mistress*: sig.ra, signora.

M/S, *motorship*: M/n, motonave.

MS., *manuscript*: ms., manoscritto.

MSS., *manuscripts*: mss., manoscritti.

Mt., *mount*: M., monte.

mus., 1. *museum*: mus., museo 2. *music*: musica.

N., *North*: N, Nord.

n., 1. *born*: n., nato 2. *number*: n., numero.

N.A.T.O., *North Atlantic Treaty Organization*: P.A., Patto atlantico.

N.B.C., *National Broadcasting Company*: Compagnia radiofonica nazionale.

N.C., *North Carolina.*

N.C.O., *non-commissioned officer*: s. uff., sottufficiale.

N. D(ak)., *North Dakota.*

Neb(r)., *Nebraska.*

Nev., *Nevada.*

New M., *New Mexico.*

N.H., *New Hampshire.*
N.J., *New Jersey.*
N. M(ex)., *New Mexico.*
no., *number*: n., numero.
Norf., *Norfolk.*
Northum(b)., *Northumberland*
nos., *numbers*: numeri.
Notts., *Nottinghamshire.*
Nov., *November*: nov., novembre.
N.Y., *New York*: Nuova York.

O., *Ohio.*
Oct., *October*: ott., ottobre.
O.E.D., *Oxford English Dictionary*: Dizionario Inglese Oxford.
Okla., *Oklahoma.*
op. cit., *in the work cited*: op. cit., opera citata.
Ore(g)., *Oregon.*
O.U.P., *Oxford University Press*: Edizioni dell'Università di Oxford.
Ox(f)., *Oxford.*
Oxon., **1.** *Oxford* **2.** *of Oxford*: ossoniese **3.** *Oxfordshire ounce*: oncia.

P., *(car-)park*: P., parcheggio.
p., **1.** *page*: p., pagina **2.** *past*: pass., passato.
Pa., *Pennsylvania.*
P.A.A., *Pan American Airways*: Linee aeree panamericane.
par., *paragraph*: parag., paragrafo.
pat., **1.** *patent*: brev., brevetto **2.** *patented*: brevettato.
P.A.Y.E., *pay as you earn (trattenuta di ricchezza mobile)*: R.M., ricchezza mobile.
pd., *paid*: pagato.
Penn(a). v. *Pa.*
Ph. D., *Doctor of Philosophy*: dottore in filosofia.
P.M., *Prime Minister*: Primo Ministro.
p.m., *post meridiem (after noon)*: pomeridiano.
P.O., **p.o.**, **1.** *Post Office*: U.P., · fficio postale **2.** *postal order*: V., vaglia.
P.O.B., *post office box*: C.P., casella postale.
p.o.d., *pay on delivery*: pagamento alla consegna.
pp., *pages*: pagg., pagine.
prep., *preparation*: preparazione.
Pres., *President*: pres., presidente.
Prof., *Professor*: prof., professore.
prox., *next*: prossimo.
P.S., *postscript*: P.S., poscritto.

p.t.o., *please turn over*: voltare pagina.

Q.M.G., *Quartermaster General*: capo dipartimento amministrazione e alloggi.
qu., **1.** *quart*: misura di capacità (1. 1.136) **2.** *quarter*: quarto.
quot., *quotation*: citazione.

R., **r.**, **1.** *river*: f., fiume **2.** *road*: strada.
R.A.C., *Royal Automobile Club*: Regio Automobile Club.
R.A.D.I.A.C., *Radioactivity Detection Identification and Computation*: Rivelazione, identificazione e calcolo della radioattività.
R.A.F., *Royal Air Force*: Regia Aviazione militare.
R.C., **1.** *Red Cross*: C.R., Croce Rossa **2.** *Roman Catholic*: Cattolico Romano.
R.C.A., *Radio Corporation of America*: Associazione Radiofonica Americana.
re., *reference* **1.** ref., referenza **2.** riferimento.
rec., **1.** *receipt*: ricevuta **2.** *record*: record.
reg., **1.** *region*: regione **2.** *register*: reg., registro **3.** *regular*: regolare.
Rev., *Reverend*: rev., reverendo.
R.H., *Royal Highness*: A.R., Altezza Reale. ·
R.N., *Royal Navy*: Regia Marina.
Rt. Hon., *Right Honourable*: molto onorevole.
Rt. Rev., *Right Reverend*: molto reverendo.
Ry., *Railway*: ferrovia.

S., *South*: S, Sud.
s., **1.** *second*: secondo **2.** *shilling*: scellino.
Sat., *Saturday*: sab., sabato.
S.C., *South Carolina.*
sch., *school*: sc., scuola.
Scot., **1.** *Scotland*: Scozia **2.** *Scottish*: scozzese.
S. D(ak)., *South Dakota.*
sec., **1.** *second*: secondo **2.** *section*: sezione **3.** *secretary*: segr., segretario
Sen., **1.** *Senate*: senato **2.** *senator*: senatore **3.** *senior*: senior.
Sept., *September*: sett., settembre.
Sergt., *sergeant*: serg., sergente.
sh., *shilling*: scellino.

S.H.A.P.E., *Supreme Headquarters Allied Powers Europe*: quartier generale delle Forze alleate in Europa.

Shrops., *Shropshire*.

So., **1.** *South*: S, Sud **2.** *Southern*: sudista.

Soc., *society*: s., società.

Somerset., *Somersetshire*.

spec., **1.** *special*: spec., speciale **2.** *specification*: specificazione.

sp. gr., *specific gravity*: gravità specifica.

sq., *square*: p.za, piazza.

Sr., **1.** *senior*: senior **2.** *Sir*: Sir **3.** *sister*: sorella.

SS, S/S, *steamship*: piroscafo.

St., **1.** *Saint*: s., santo **2.** *street*: via.

st., *stone*: misura di peso (*Kg.* 6,350).

Staffs., *Staffordshire*.

ster., **stg.**, *sterling*: L.st., lira sterlina.

St. Ex., *Stock Exchange*: Borsa valori.

Sun(d)., *Sunday*: dom., domenica.

Sup. Ct., *Supreme Court*: C.S., Corte suprema.

supp(l)., *supplement*: supplemento.

Sur., *Surrey*.

Sus., *Sussex*.

S.W., **1.** *South Wales*: Galles del sud **2.** *South West*: S.O., sud ovest.

Swit., **Swtz.**, *Switzerland*: Svizzera.

syn., *synonym*: sinonimo

Sy., *Surrey*.

t., **1.** *ton*: t., tonnellata **2.** *volume*: v., volume.

T.B., *tuberculosis*: tbc, tubercolosi.

tel., **1.** *telegram*: telegramma **2.** *telegraph*: telegrafo **3.** *telephone*: tel., telefono.

Tenn., *Tennessee*.

Tex., *Texas*.

Thur(s)., *Thursday*: giov., giovedì.

T.O., *turn over*: voltare.

T.U., *Trade-Union*: Sindacato.

Tu(es)., *Tuesday*: mar., martedì.

TV., *television*: TV, televisione.

T.W.A., *Trans World Airlines*: linee aeree intercontinentali.

U., **1.** *Union*: U., unione **2.** *University*: Università.

U.K., *United Kingdom*: R.U., Regno Unito.

U.N., *United Nations*: N.U., Nazioni Unite.

U.N.E.S.C.O., *United Nations Educational Scientific and Cultural Organization*: Organizzazione culturale, scientifica e per l'educazione delle Nazioni Unite.

U.N.I.C.E.F., *United Nations International Children's Emergency Fund*: Fondo d'emergenza internazionale per l'infanzia delle Nazioni Unite.

U.N.O., *United Nations Organization*: O.N.U., Organizzazione delle Nazioni Unite.

U.P., *United Press*: Stampa associata.

U.S., *United States*: S.U., Stati Uniti.

U.S.A., **1.** *United States of America*: S.U.A., Stati Uniti d'America **2.** *United States Army*: Esercito degli Stati Uniti.

U.S.A.E.C., *United States Atomic Energy Commission*: commissione per l'energia atomica degli Stati Uniti.

U.S.A.F., *United States Air Force*: Aviazione militare degli Stati Uniti.

U.S.I.S., *United States Information Service*: Servizio informazioni degli Stati Uniti.

U.S.N., *United States Navy*: Marina degli Stati Uniti.

U.S.S.R., *Union of Soviet Socialist Republics*: U.R.S.S., Unione delle repubbliche socialiste sovietiche.

U.S.S., *United States Ship*: nave degli Stati Uniti.

Ut., *Utah*.

v., *verse*: v., verso.

Va., *Virginia*.

Vat., *Vatican*: Vaticano.

Ven., *Venerable*: Ven., venerabile.

V.H.F., *very high frequency*: altissima frequenza.

Vic(t)., *Victoria*.

V.I.P., *Very Important Person*: Persona molto importante.

viz., *namely*: cioè.

vol., *volume*: vol., volume.

V.P., *Vice-President*: vicepresidente.

vs., *against*: contro.

Vt., *Vermont*.

Vul(g)., *Vulgate*: Vulgata.

vv., *verses*: vv., versi.

w., *watt*: W., watt.

W., 1. *West*: O, Ovest **2.** *Wa-shington.*

w., 1. *week*: settimana **2.** *wife*: moglie **3.** *with*: con.

Warwick., *Warwickshire.*

Wash., *Washington.*

W.D., *War Department*: Minįstero della Guerra.

Wed., *Wednesday*: mer., mercoledì.

Westm., *Westminster.*

Westmore., *Westmoreland.*

whf., *wharf*: pontile.

Wis(c)., *Wisconsin.*

wk., 1. *week*: settimana **2.** *work*: lavoro.

w.l., *wave length*: lunghezza d'onda.

Worcs., *Worcestershire.*

W.R.A.C., *Women's Royal Army Corps*: Regio corpo d'armata femminile.

wt., *weight*: peso.

W.Va., *West Virginia*: Virginia dell'ovest.

Wy(o)., *Wyoming.*

Xmas., *Christmas*: Natale.

y., 1. *yard*: iarda **2.** *year*: anno.

yd., *yard*: iarda.

Y.H.A., *Youth Hostels Association*: Associazione Ostelli per la gioventù.

Y.M.C.A., *Young men's Christian Association*: Associazione Cristiana per i giovani.

yr., 1. *year*: anno **2.** *your*: vostro.

Yorks., *Yorkshire.*

yrs., 1. *years*: anni **2.** *yours*: vostri.

Y.W.C.A., *Young Women's Christian Association*: Associazione Cristiana per le giovani.

Z., *atomic number*: n.a., numero atomico.

&, *and*: e.

&c., *and so forth*: etc., ecc., eccetera.

PREFACE TO THE ITALIAN-ENGLISH SECTION OF THE
PICCOLO DIZIONARIO ITALIANO-INGLESE

1. The first part of the English-Italian section of the **Compact Dictionary** contains information in Italian designed to help in its use. It gives rules of pronunciation, a list of irregular verbs, tables of comparison of the English and American units and metric system, information on the English and American currency, a list of cardinal and ordinal numbers, and an explanatory list of the abbreviations used.

A similar introduction is included here to help in the use of the Italian-English section.

2. Since Italian presents particular problems with its verbs we have provided a list of irregular verbs in general use. We have not included their compounds, as they are conjugated in the same way.

Those verbs which take *essere* as an auxiliary are indicated by means of a single star. Those which take *essere* when used intransitively and *avere* when used transitively have a double star.

With the past definite tense we have shown the 1st person singular only, since the 3rd person singular and the 3rd person plural follow the same pattern, while the 2nd person singular and plural are regular in form e.g.: *prendere* – presi, *prendesti,* prese, *prendemmo, prendeste,* presero.

3. There are two points concerning the current use of verbs which the student of Italian may well find helpful:

a) there is a tendency in modern Italian towards a more frequent use of the perfect tense to represent completed past action (though such irrefutable statements of the past as, for example, *Dante died in 1321* would still always be translated as *Dante morì . . .*);

b) though the polite form in the singular, with *Lei* and the 3rd person of the verb, is regularly used e.g.: *Lei scrive in inglese?* (Are you writing in English?), the plural form addressed to more than one person is now more frequently the 2nd person plural with *Voi*, instead of the 3rd person plural with *Loro* e.g.: *Voi scrivete in inglese?* rather than *Loro scrivono in inglese?*

4. As some Italian nouns have irregular plurals or do not change their form in the plural we have included a list of the more commonly used ones.

5. In illustrating the possible alternative translations for the Italian words listed, the following symbols have been adopted:

a) a double line (||) after the initial translation or translations indicates a grammatical change from, for example, an adjective to a noun or a pronoun to an adverb;

b) a lozenge (♦) indicates something more than just an alternative translation, showing, for example, a figurative or idiomatic use;

c) the numbers printed in large type (1., 2., 3., etc.) indicate the various alternative meanings;

d) the small numbers ([1], [2], [3], etc.) indicate words of identical form but different meaning.

The Alphabet

The Italian alphabet consists of 21 letters only. j (*i lunga*), k (*cappa*), w (*doppio vu*), x (*ics*), y (*ipsilon*) do not occur in the alphabet, though they are used for the spelling of foreign words e.g.: *judo, kimono, watt, xenofobia, yacht*. In some cases y is replaced by i, e.g. *raion* for rayon. ch replaces k, e.g. *chilogramma* for kilogram. ph is represented by f, e.g. *fobia* for phobia. x occurs in certain expressions such as *ex-presidente, extraterritoriale*, etc.

Letter	Name	Letter	Name
a	*a*	m	*emme*
b	*bi*	n	*enne*
c	*ci*	o	*o*
d	*di*	p	*pi*
e	*e*	q	*cu*
f	*effe*	r	*erre*
g	*gi*	s	*esse*
h	*acca*	t	*ti*
i	*i*	u	*u*
l	*elle*	v	*vu*
		z	*zeta*

Pronunciation

Since Italian is a phonetic language, once the rules of pronunciation are learnt, it is possible to pronounce most words correctly, though it is not always easy to tell on which syllable the tonic stress falls.

The Vowels

Italian vowels are pure sounds and should be pronounced well forward in the mouth:

A	like a in far	*gala*
close E	like a in fate	*seta*
open E	like e in ten	*pelle*
I	like i in machine	*vino*
close O	like o in store	*corte*
open O	like o in spot	*motto*
U	like oo in spoon	*uso*

The Consonants

In the case of double consonants each consonant is sounded, with the voice rising on them and falling on the following vowel.

The consonants **B, D, F, L, M, N, P, Q, T** and **V** are pronounced very much as in English. The rest are as follows:

C   1. before **a, o, u,** and consonants, including **h**: like c in cat, as in *casa, crema, chilo*;

      2. before **e** or **i**: like **ch** in chip, as in *cena, cibo*.

G   1. before **a, o, u** and consonants, including **h** but not including **l** and **n**: like g in gap, as in *gala, grido, ghiro*;

      2. before **e** or **i**: like g in gem, as in *gente, gita*.

gli   like lli in billion, as in *figlia*; (a few exceptions have the **gli** pronounced as in English, e.g. *anglicano, negligente*).

gn   like ni in onion, as in *signore*.

H   is always silent and occurs in very few words, except as shown above to harden the **c** and **g** sounds before **e** and **i**.

Q   is always followed by **u**, like qu in quick, as in *quinto*.

R   is rolled, rather as in **rr** Scottish pronunciation, as in *pera, serra*.

S   1. is voiced, like s in rose, as in *rosa, esatto*, or when followed by **b, d, g, l, m, n, r, v,** the voiceless consonants, as in *sdegno, svelto;*

      2. is unvoiced like s in sap, at the beginning of a word, or when it is doubled, as in *sega, rosso*.

sc   1. before **e** or **i** is like sh in shot, as in *scena*;

      2. before **a, o** and **u** is like sk in skate, as in *scarpa, scopo, scudo*;

      3. an **h** after it and before **e** or **i** makes it like sk, as in *schema, schiena*;

      4. an **i** after it and before **a, o** or **u** makes it like sh, as in *scialle, sciocco, sciupare*.

Z   1. voiced like ds in treads, as in *zio*;

      2. unvoiced like ts in wits, as in *forza*.

Accentuation

In printed and written Italian an accent is used to indicate when the tonı stress falls on a final vowel such as in *città* or *caffè*. It is also used to distinguish between two words which are spelt and pronounced alike but have different meanings:

     è = is   *e* = and

     dà = he gives   *da* = from, by, of, etc.

It also occurs on some monosyllabic words as in *già* and *più*.

In print the acute accent is used to indicate a stress on a final e as in *perché* or *né*, though in handwriting the grave accent is more usual. In modern Italian the grave accent is normally used elsewhere and we have followed this practice.

As a general rule the tonic stress is on the penultimate syllable, but this is not by any means always so. The grave and acute accents have been used to show where the stress falls when it does not fall on the penultimate syllable. The open and close e are distinguished in the accepted way by means of è and é, e.g. *créscere, crédere, festival, fervido,* and the grave accent is used everywhere else, e.g. *càndido, moltitùdine.*

IRREGULAR ITALIAN VERBS†

Accendere – *p. def.* accesi, *p.p.* acceso

Accludere – see alludere

Addurre – *pres.* adduco, *p. def.* addussi, *fut.* addurrò, *p.p.* addotto

Affliggere – *p. def.* afflissi, *p.p.* afflitto

Alludere – *p. def.* allusi, *p.p.* alluso

Andare* – *pres.* vado, vai, va, andiamo, andate, vanno *fut.* andrò

Annettere – *p. def.* annettei (annessi), *p.p.* annesso

Apparire* – *pres.* apparisco, *p. def.* apparii (apparvi, apparsi), *p.p.* apparso

Appendere – *p. def.* appesi, *p.p.* appeso

Ardere – *p. def.* arsi, *p.p.* arso

Aspergere – *p. def.* aspersi, *p.p.* asperso

Assalire – *pres.* assalgo (assalisco), assalgono

Assolvere – *p. def.* assolsi (assolvei, assolvetti), *p.p.* assolto

Assumere – *p. def.* assunsi, *p.p.* assunto

Bere – *pres.* bevo, *p. def.* bevvi, *fut.* berrò

Cadere* – *p. def.* caddi, *fut.* cadrò

Cedere – *p. def.* cedei (cedetti)

Chiedere – *p. def.* chiesi, *p.p.* chiesto

Chiudere – *p. def.* chiusi, *p.p.* chiuso

Cingere – *p. def.* cinsi, *p.p.* cinto

Cogliere – *pres.* colgo, colgono, *p. def.* colsi, *p.p.* colto

Comprimere – *p. def.* compressi, *p.p.* compresso

Conoscere – *p. def.* conobbi, *p.p.* conosciuto

Consumare – *p. def.* consumai (consunsi), *p.p.* consumato (consunto)

Correre** – *p. def.* corsi, *p.p.* corso

Costruire – *p.p.* costruito (costrutto)

Crescere* – *p. def.* crebbi, *p.p.* cresciuto

Cucire – *pres.* cucio

Cuocere – *pres.* cuocio, cuoci, cuoce, cociamo, cocete, cuociono, *p. def.* cossi, *p.p.* cotto

Dare – *pres.* do, dai, dà, diamo, date, danno, *p. def.* diedi (detti), desti, *fut.* darò, *p.p.* dato

† Verbs which take *essere* are indicated by one star.
     Those taking *avere* and *essere* have two stars.

Decidere – *p. def.* decisi, *p.p.* deciso
Difendere – *p. def.* difesi, *p.p.* difeso
Dipendere** – *p. def.* dipesi, *p.p.* dipeso
Dipingere – *p. def.* dipinsi, *p.p.* dipinto
Dire – *pres.* dico, dite, *p. def.* dissi, *fut.* dirò, *p.p.* detto
Dirigere – *p. def.* diressi, *p.p.* diretto
Discutere – *p. def.* discussi, *p.p.* discusso
Dissolvere – *p. def.* dissolsi (dissolvei), *p.p.* dissolto
Distinguere – *p. def.* distinsi, *p.p.* distinto
Dividere – *p. def.* divisi, *p.p.* diviso
Dolersi* – *pres.* mi dolgo, ti duoli, si duole, ci doliamo, vi dolete, si dolgono, *p. def.* mi dolsi, *fut.* mi dorrò
Dovere – *pres.* devo (debbo), devi, deve, dobbiamo, dovete, devono (debbono), *fut.* dovrò

Eccellere – *p. def.* eccelsi, *p.p.* eccelso
Emergere* – *p. def.* emersi, *p.p.* emerso
Ergere – *p. def.* ersi, *p.p.* erto
Erigere – *p. def.* eressi, *p.p.* eretto
Esigere – *p.p.* esatto
Espellere – *p. def.* espulsi, *p.p.* espulso
Esplodere** – *p. def.* esplosi, *p.p.* esploso
Evadere* – *p. def.* evasi, *p.p.* evaso

Fare – *pres.* faccio (fo), fai, fa, facciamo, fate, fanno, *imper.* facevo, *p. def.* feci, *fut.* farò, *p.p.* fatto
Fendere – *p. def.* fendei (fendetti), *p.p.* fesso (fenduto)
Figgere – *p. def.* fissi, *p.p.* fisso (fitto)
Fingere – *p. def.* finsi, *p.p.* finto
Fondere – *p. def.* fusi, *p.p.* fuso
Frangere – *p. def.* fransi, *p.p.* franto
Friggere – *p. def.* frissi, *p.p.* fritto

Giacere* – *pres.* giaccio, giacciono, *p. def.* giacqui, *p.p.* giaciuto
Giungere* – *p. def.* giunsi, *p.p.* giunto
Godere – *fut.* godrò

Incutere – *p. def.* incussi (incutei), *p.p.* incusso
Indulgere – *p. def.* indulsi, *p.p.* indulto
Intridere – *p. def.* intrisi, *p.p.* intriso
Invadere – *p. def.* invasi, *p.p.* invaso

Ledere – *p. def.* lesi, *p.p.* leso
Leggere – *p. def.* lessi, *p.p.* letto

Mettere – *p. def.* misi, *p.p.* messo

Mordere – *p. def.* morsi, *p.p.* morso
Morire * – *pres.* muoio, muori, muore, moriamo, morite, muoiono, *fut.* morrò, *p.p.* morto
Mungere – *p. def.* munsi, *p.p.* munto
Muovere – *pres.* moviamo, movete, *p. def.* mossi, *p.p.* mosso

Nascere * – *p. def.* nacqui, *p.p.* nato
Nascondere – *p. def.* nascosi, *p.p.* nascosto
Nuocere – *pres.* noccio, nociamo, nocete, nocciono, *p. def.* nocqui, *p.p.* nociuto

Offrire – *p. def.* offrii (offersi), *p.p.* offerto

Parere * – *pres.* paio, paiamo, paiono, *p. def.* parvi, *fut.* parrò, *p.p.* parso
Percuotere – *p.p.* percosso
Perdere – *p. def.* persi (perdei, perdetti), *p.p.* perduto (perso)
Persuadere – *p. def.* persuasi, *p.p.* persuaso
Piacere * – *pres.* piaccio, piaci, piace, piacciamo, piacete, piacciono, *p. def.* piacqui, *p.p.* piaciuto
Piangere – *p. def.* piansi, *p.p.* pianto
Piovere ** – *p. def.* piovve, piovvero
Porgere – *p. def.* porsi, *p.p.* porto
Porre – *pres.* pongo, poni, pone, poniamo, ponete, pongono, *p. def.* posi, *fut.* porrò, *p.p.* posto
Potere – *pres.* posso, puoi, può, possiamo, potete, possono, *fut.* potrò
Prediligere – *p. def.* predilessi, *p.p.* prediletto
Prendere – *p. def.* presi, *p.p.* preso
Proteggere – *p. def.* protessi, *p.p.* protetto
Pungere – *p. def.* punsi, *p.p.* punto

Radere – *p. def.* rasi, *p.p.* raso
Redimere – *p. def.* redensi, *p.p.* redento
Reggere – *p. def.* ressi, *p.p.* retto
Rendere – *p. def.* resi, *p.p.* reso
Ridere – *p. def.* risi, *p.p.* riso
Rifulgere ** – *p. def.* rifulsi, *p.p.* rifulso
Rispondere – *p. def.* risposi, *p.p.* risposto
Rodere – *p. def.* rosi, *p.p.* roso
Rompere – *p. def.* ruppi, *p.p.* rotto

Salire ** – *pres.* salgo, salgono
Sapere – *pres.* so, sai, sa, sappiamo, sapete, sanno, *p. def.* seppi, *fut.* saprò
Scegliere – *pres.* scelgo, scelgono, *p. def.* scelsi, *p.p.* scelto
Scendere ** – *p. def.* scesi, *p.p.* sceso
Scindere – *p. def.* scissi, *p.p.* scisso

Sciogliere – *pres.* sciolgo, sciolgono, *p. def.* sciolsi, *p.p.* sciolto

Scrivere – *p. def.* scrissi, *p.p.* scritto

Scuotere – *p. def.* scossi, *p.p.* scosso

Sedere* – *pres.* siedo (seggo), siedi, siede, sediamo, sedete, siedono (seggono)

Soddisfare – *pres.* soddisfo (soddisfaccio, soddisfò), soddisfi (soddisfai), soddisfa, soddisfiamo (soddisfacciamo), soddisfate, soddisfano (soddisfanno), *p. def.* soddisfeci, *p.p.* soddisfatto

Sorgere* – *p. def.* sorsi, *p.p.* sorto

Spargere – *p. def.* sparsi, *p.p.* sparso

Spegnere – *p. def.* spensi, *p.p.* spento

Spendere – *p. def.* spesi, *p.p.* speso

Spingere – *p. def.* spinsi, *p.p.* spinto

Stare* – *pres.* sto, stai, sta, stiamo, state, stanno, *imperf.* stavo, *p. def.* stetti, *p.p.* stato

Stringere – *p. def.* strinsi, *p.p.* stretto

Struggere – *p. def.* strussi, *p.p.* strutto

Svellere – *pres.* svello (svelgo), svellono (svelgono), *p. def.* svelsi, *p.p.* svelto

Svenire* – *p. def.* svenni

Tacere – *pres.* taccio, taci, tace, taciamo, tacete, tacciono, *p. def.* tacqui, *p.p.* taciuto

Tendere – *p. def.* tesi, *p.p.* teso

Tenere – *pres.* tengo, tieni, tiene, teniamo, tenete, tengono, *p. def.* tenni, *fut.* terrò

Tingere – *p. def.* tinsi, *p.p.* tinto

Togliere – *pres.* tolgo, tolgono, *p. def.* tolsi, *p.p.* tolto

Torcere – *p. def.* torsi, *p.p.* torto

Trarre – *pres.* traggo, trai, trae, traiamo, traete, traggono, *imperf.* traevo, *p. def.* trassi, *fut.* trarrò, *p.p.* tratto

Uccidere – *p. def.* uccisi, *p.p.* ucciso

Udire – *pres.* odo, odi, ode, udiamo, udite, odono, *fut.* udrò (udirò)

Ungere – *p. def.* unsi, *p.p.* unto

Uscire* – *pres.* esco, esci, esce, usciamo, uscite, escono

Valere** – *pres.* valgo, valgono, *p. def.* valsi, *fut.* varrò, *p.p.* valso

Vedere – *pres.* vedo (veggo), vedono (veggono), *p. def.* vidi, *fut.* vedrò, *p.p.* visto

Venire* – *pres.* vengo, vieni, viene, veniamo, venite, vengono, *p. def.* venni, *fut.* verrò

Vilipendere – *p. def.* vilipesi, *p.p.* vilipeso

Vincere – *p. def.* vinsi, *p.p.* vinto

Vivere** – *p. def.* vissi, *p.p.* vissuto

Volere – *pres.* voglio, vuoi, vuole, vogliamo, volete, vogliono, *p. def.* volli, *fut.* vorrò

Volgere – *p. def.* volsi, *p.p.* volto

IRREGULAR PLURALS OF NOUNS

l'autobus	gli autobus
il bar	i bar
il caffè	i caffè
la città	le città
la frutta	le frutta
il re	i re
il braccio	le braccia
il bue	i buoi
il centinaio	le centinaia
il dito	le dita
il ginocchio	le ginocchia
la guancia	le guance
il labbro	le labbra
il lenzuolo	le lenzuola
la mano	le mani
il migliaio	le migliaia
l'orecchio	le orecchie
il paio	le paia
l'uomo	gli uomini

ITALIAN MONEY

Italian bank notes are issued in the following denominations:

500 lire	10,000 lire
1000 lire	50,000 lire
2000 lire	100,000 lire.
5000 lire	

The one hundred thousand lire notes are not negotiable outside Italy.

Coins are issued in five, ten, twenty, fifty, one hundred and five hundred pieces.

NUMERALS

Cardinal		*Cardinal cont.*	
1	uno	3	tre
2	due	4	quattro

Cardinal

5	cinque		
6	sei		
7	sette		
8	otto		
9	nove		
10	dieci		
11	undici		
12	dodici		
13	tredici		
14	quattordici		
15	quindici		
16	sedici		
17	diciassette		
18	diciotto		
19	diciannove		
20	venti		
21	ventuno		
22	ventidue		
23	ventitré		
24	ventiquattro		
25	venticinque		
26	ventisei		
27	ventisette		
28	ventotto		

Cardinal cont.

29	ventinove
30	trenta
31	trentuno
32	trentadue
38	trentotto
40	quaranta
50	cinquanta
60	sessanta
70	settanta
80	ottanta
90	novanta
100	cento
101	centouno
105	centocinque
150	centocinquanta
200	duecento
300	trecento
1000	mille
1100	millecento
1200	milleduecento
2000	duemila
100,000	centomila
1,000,000	un milione

Ordinal

1st	primo
2nd	secondo
3rd	terzo
4th	quarto
5th	quinto
6th	sesto
7th	settimo
8th	ottavo
9th	nono
10th	decimo
11th	undicesimo or decimo primo
12th	dodicesimo or decimo secondo
20th	ventesimo
21st	ventunesimo or ventesimo primo
22nd	ventiduesimo or ventesimo secondo

30th	trentesimo°
40th	quarantesimo
50th	cinquantesimo
101st	centunesimo
200th	duecentesimo
1000th	millesimo
1205th	milleduecentocinquesimo
1,000,000th	milionesimo

ABBREVIATIONS USED IN THE DICTIONARY

abbr.	abbreviation	*(dial.)*	dialect
(aer.)	aviation	*dif.*	defective
agg.	adjective	*dim.*	diminutive
(agr.)	agriculture	*dimostr.*	demonstrative
(amer.)	American		
amm.	administrative	*ecc., etc.*	etcetera
(anat.)	anatomy	*(eccl.)*	ecclesiastical
(ant.)	archaic	*(econ.)*	economics
(arch.)	architecture	*(edil.)*	building industry
art.	article	*(elettr.)*	electricity
(arte)	art	*escl.*	exclamation
assol.	absolute		
(astr.)	astronomy	*f.*	feminine
attr.	attribute	*(fam.)*	familiar
aus.	auxiliary	*(farm.)*	pharmaceutical
(auto)	motoring	*(ferr.)*	railway
avv.	adverb	*(fig.)*	figurative
		(fil.)	philosophy
(bot.)	botany	*(fis.)*	physics
(biol.)	biology	*(foto)*	photography
		fut.	future
(chim.)	chemistry		
(chir.)	surgery	*gen.*	genitive
(cine)	cinematography	*general.*	generally
coll.	collective	*(geogr.)*	geography
(comm.)	commerce	*(geol.)*	geology
comp.	comparative	*(geom.)*	geometry
compl.	complement	*ger.*	gerund
condiz.	conditional	*(gergo)*	jargon, slang
cong.	conjunction	*(giorn.)*	journalism
(costr.)	building	*(giur.)*	legal
(cuc.)	cooking	*(gramm.)*	grammar

i.	intransitive	*pl.*	plural
id.	idem	*(poet.)*	poetical
imp.	impersonal	*(pol.)*	political
imperat.	imperative	*(pop.)*	popular
imperf.	imperfect	*poss.*	possessive
ind.	indicative	*p.p.*	past participle
indef.	indefinite	*prep.*	preposition
inf.	infinitive	*pred.*	predicate
int.	interrogative	*pres.*	present
inter.	interjection	*pron.*	pronoun
(iron.)	ironic	*prov.*	proverbial
irr.	irregular	*(psicol.)*	psychology
(itt.)	ichthyology		
		qc.	something
(lat.)	Latin, Latinism	*qu.*	someone
loc. avv.	adverbial phrase		
loc. cong.	conjunctive	*r.*	reflexive
	phrase	*(radio)*	radio
loc. prep.	prepositional	*rec.*	reciprocal
	phrase	*reg.*	regular
(lett.)	literature	*rel.*	relative
		(relig.)	religion
m.	masculine		
(mar.)	naval, maritime	*s.*	masculine and
(mat.)	mathematics		feminine noun
(mecc.)	mechanics	*semidif.*	partly defective
(med.)	medicine	*sf.*	feminine noun
(metal.)	metallurgy	*sm.*	masculine noun
(mil.)	military	*(scherz.)*	humourous
(min.)	mineralogy	*(scol.)*	scolastic
(mit.)	mythology	*(scult.)*	sculpture
(mus.)	music	*sing.*	singular
		so	someone
neg.	negative	*sogg.*	subject
(neol.)	neologism	*sost.*	noun
		spec.	especially
		(spreg.)	pejorative
ogg.	object	*sthg.*	something
(ott.)	optics	*(stor.)*	history
		superl.	superlative
p.	participle		
pass.	past		
p. def.	past definite	*t.*	transitive
pers.	personal	*(teat.)*	theatre
(pitt.)	painting	*(tec.)*	technical

(tel.)	telephony	*v. dif.*	defective verb
(teol.)	theology	*vi.*	instransitive verb
(tip.)	typography	*(v. irr.)*	irregular verb
(tv.)	television	*(volg.)*	vulgar
		vr.	reflexive verb
(us.)	usage	*v. semidif.*	partially defective verb
v.	verb	*vt.*	transitive verb
V.	cf.		
(vezz.)	diminutive	*(zool.)*	zoology

A

a, ad *prep.* **1.** (*termine*) to: *l'ho dato a te,* I gave it to you **2.** (*moto a luogo*) *vado alla stazione,* I am going to the station **3.** (*stato in luogo*) in, at: *vivo a Milano,* I live in Milan; *sono a casa,* I am at home **4.** (*tempo determinato*) at, on, in: *al mio arrivo,* on my arrival **5.** (*iterativo*): *due, tre volte al giorno,* twice, three times a day.

àbaco (*arch.*) *sm.* abacus.

abate *sm.* abbot.

abbacchiare *vt.* (*di frutta*) to beat (*v. irr.*) down. ♦ **abbacchiarsi** *vr.* to feel (*v. irr.*) down-hearted.

abbacchiato *agg.* down-hearted.

abbacinare *vt.* to dazzle.

àbbaco *sm.* elementary arithmetic book.

abbagliante *agg.* dazzling: *fari abbaglianti,* dazzling beams.

abbagliare *vt.* to dazzle, to blind (with).

abbaglio *sm.* **1.** dazzling **2.** (*errore*) blunder.

abbaiare *vi.* to bark.

abbaino *sm.*, garret.

abbandonare *vt.* **1.** to leave (*v. irr.*), to forsake (*v. irr.*), to abandon **2.** (*rinunciare*) to give (*v. irr.*) up.

abbandonato *agg.* **1.** (*trascurato*) neglected **2.** (*di casa*) deserted **3.** (*di persona*) forsaken.

abbandono *sm.* **1.** (*di persona che viene abbandonata*) forsaking **2.** (*rinuncia*) giving up.

abbarbicare *vi.* to take (*v. irr.*) root. ♦ **abbarbicarsi** *vr.* to cling (*v. irr.*) (*anche fig.*).

abbaruffarsi *vr.* to quarrel.

abbassamento *sm.* lowering || — *di temperatura,* fall (in temperature).

abbassare *vt.* **1.** to lower, to pull down || — *la . testa,* to bend (*v. irr.*) one's head **2.** (*ridurre*) to reduce. ♦ **abbassarsi** *vr.* to stoop (down).

abbasso *avv.* **1.** (*al di sotto*) below **2.** (*giù*) down **3.** (*al piano terreno, dopo aver sceso le scale*) downstairs. ♦ **abbasso!** *inter.* d wn with!

abbastanza *avv.* **1.** enough **2.** (*discretamente*) quite.

abbàttere *vt.* to pull down. ♦ **abbàttersi** *vr.* to be discouraged.

abbattimento *sm.* **1.** throwing down **2.** (*morale*) dejection.

abbattuto *agg.* disheartened.

abbazìa *sf.* abbey.

abbecedario *sm.* primer.

abbellimento *sm.* embellishment.

abbellire *vt.* to embellish.

abbeverare *vt.* to water. ♦ **abbeverarsi** *vr.* to water.

abbeveratoio *sm.* trough.

abbiccì *sm.* **1.** alphabet **2.** (*principi elementari*) primer.

abbiente *agg.* well-to-do, wealthy.

abbigliamento *sm.* clothes || *industria dell'—,* clothing industry.

abbigliare *vt.* to dress.

abbinare *vt.* to couple.

abbindolare *vt.* to cheat.

abbisognare *vi.* to need, to be necessary.

abboccamento *sm.* interview.

abboccare *vt. e vi.* **1.** to bite (*v. irr.*) **2.** (*fig.*) to be taken in. ♦ **abboccarsi** *vr.* to confer (with).

abbonacciarsi *vi.* **1.** (*di vento*) to drop **2.** (*di mare*) to smooth down.

abbonamento *sm.* **1.** subscription **2.** (*ferr.*) season-ticket.

abbonare *vt.* **1.** to make (*v. irr.*) (so.) a subscriber **2.** (*defalcare*) to make a discount. ♦ **abbonarsi** *vr.* to subscribe (to).

abbonato *sm.* **1.** subscriber **2.** (*ferr.*) season-ticket holder.

abbondante *agg.* plentiful.

abbondanza *sf.* plenty.

abbondare *vi.* to have plenty (of), to be plentiful.

abbonire *vt.* to calm.

abbordàbile *agg.* accessible.

abbordaggio *sm.* boarding.

abbordare *vt.* **1.** (*mar.*) to board **2.** (*una persona*) to open conversation (with).

abborracciare *vi.* to bungle.

abbottonare *vt.* to button (up). ♦ **abbottonarsi** *vr.* to button one's clothes (up).

abbottonatura *sf.* **1.** button-holes **2.** (*l'abbottonarsi*) buttoning.

abbozzare *vt.* to sketch || — *un sorriso,* to smile faintly.

abbozzo *sm.* sketch.

abbozzolarsi *vr.* to cocoon.

abbracciare *vt.* **1.** to embrace **2.** (*comprendere*) to include **3.** (*afferrare*) to grasp **4.** (*con lo sguardo*)

to take (*v. irr.*) in. ♦ **abbracciarsi** *vr.* to embrace.
abbraccio *sm.* embrace.
abbrancare *vt.* to grasp. ♦ **abbrancarsi** *vr.* to cling (*v. irr.*) (to).
abbreviare *vt.* to shorten, to abridge.
abbreviazione *sf.* abbreviation.
abbrivare *vt.* to get (*v. irr.*) under way.
abbrivo *sm.* freshway.
abbronzare *vt.* 1. to bronze 2. (*al sole*) to tan. ♦ **abbronzarsi** *vr.* to get (*v. irr.*) tanned.
abbronzatura *sf.* tanning.
abbruciacchiare *vt.* to scorch.
abbrustolire *vt.* to toast, to roast.
abbrutimento *sm.* brutalization.
abbrutire *vt.* to brutalize.
abbuffarsi *vr.* to stuff oneself.
abbuiarsi *vr.* to get (*v. irr.*) dark.
abbuono *sm.* allowance.
abburattare *vt.* to sift.
abdicare *vi.* to abdicate.
abdicazione *sf.* abdication.
aberrare *vi.* to stray.
aberrazione *sf.* aberration.
abetaia *sf.* fir-wood.
abete *sm.* fir-tree.
abietto *agg.* abject, base.
abiezione *sf.* abjection.
abigeato *sm.* cattle-stealing.
àbile *agg.* 1. able, skilful 2. (*a fare qc.*) clever at.
abilità *sf.* ability, skill.
abilitare *vt.* to qualify.
abilitazione *sf.* qualifica⁴ion ‖ *esame di —*, qualifying examination.
abisso *sm.* abyss.
abitàbile *agg.* inhabitable.
abitàcolo *sm.* (*aer.*) cockpit.
abitante *sm.* inhabitant.
abitare *vi.* to inhabit, to live in.
abitato *sm.* inhabited place.
abitazione *sf.* habitation, house.
àbito *sm.* 1. (*da uomo*) suit 2. (*da donna*) dress.
abituale *agg.* usual, customary.
abituare *vt.* to accustom. ♦ **abituarsi** *vr.* to get (*v. irr.*) used (to).
abitudinario *agg.* methodical. ♦ **abitudinario** *sm.* routinist.
abitùdine *sf.* habit, custom.
abituro *sm.* slum dwelling.
abiura *sf.* abjuration.
abiurare *vt.* to abjure.
ablazione *sf.* ablation.

abluzione *sf.* ablution.
abnegazione *sf.* self-denial.
abnorme *agg.* abnormal.
abolire *vt.* to abolish.
abolizione *sf.* abolition, repeal.
abominare *vt.* to loathe.
abominévole *agg.* abominable.
aborìgeni *sm. pl.* the natives.
aborrimento *sm.* abhorrence.
aborrire *vt.* to hate, to loathe.
abortire *vi.* to miscarry.
aborto *sm.* miscarriage.
abrasione *sf.* abrasion.
abrogare *vt.* 1. to abrogate 2. (*giur.*) to repeal.
abrogazione *sf.* 1. abrogation 2. (*giur.*) repeal.
àbside *sf.* apse.
abulìa *sf.* (*fig.*) lack of will-power.
abùlico *agg.* (*fig.*) lacking in will-power.
abusare *vi.* to abuse.
abusivo *agg.* abusive.
abuso *sm.* abuse.
acacia *sf.* acacia.
acanto *sm.* acanthus.
acca *sf.* letter H.
accademia *sf.* academy.
accadèmico *agg.* academical. ♦ **accadèmico** *sm.* academician.
accademismo *sm.* academism.
accadere *vi.* to happen.
accaduto *sm.* event.
accagliarsi *vr.* 1. to curdle 2. (*del sangue*) to coagulate.
accalappiacani *sm.* dog-catcher.
accalappiare *vt.* 1. to catch (*v. irr.*) 2. (*fig.*) to ensnare.
accalcarsi *vr.* to crowd.
accaldarsi *vi.* 1. to get (*v. irr.*) heated 2. (*fig.*) to get excited.
accaldato *agg.* hot.
accalorarsi *vr.* to get (*v. irr.*) excited.
accampamento *sm.* camp.
accampare *vt.* to camp: *— diritti*, to lay (*v. irr.*) claims (to).
accanimento *sm.* 1. fury 2. (*tenacia*) tenacity.
accanirsi *vr.* 1. (*infierire*) to rage 2. (*ostinarsi*) to persist.
accanito *agg.* 1. (*senza pietà*) relentless 2. obstinate.
accanto *avv.* beside, near, by ‖ *accanto a*, by, near, at the side of.
accantonare *vt.* to set (*v. irr.*) aside.
accaparrare *vt.* to buy (*v. irr.*) up.

accapigliarsi *vr.* to come (*v. irr.*) to blows, to quarrel.

accappatoio *sm.* bath-gown.

accapponarsi *vr.* to get (*v. irr.*) goose-flesh.

accarezzare *vt.* 1. to caress, to stroke 2. (*fig.*) to entertain.

accartocciare *vt.* 1. to wrap up 2. (*spiegazzare*) to crumple.

accasare *vt.* to marry, to give (*v. irr.*) in marriage. ♦ **accasarsi** *vr.* to get (*v. irr.*) married.

accasciarsi *vi.* 1. to fall (*v. irr.*) to the ground 2. (*fig.*) to lose (*v. irr.*) heart.

accatastare *vt.* to heap up.

accattivarsi *vi.* to win (*v. irr.*).

accattonaggio *sm.* begging.

accattone *sm.* beggar.

accavallare *vt.* to overlap: — *le gambe*, to cross one's legs.

accecamento *sm.* 1. blinding 2. (*fig.*) lack of perception.

accecare *vt.* to blind. ♦ **accecarsi** *vr.* to blind oneself.

accèdere *vi.* 1. to approach 2. (*entrare*) to enter 3. (*comm.*) to comply (with).

accelerare *vt.* 1. to quicken 2. (*di velocità*) to accelerate.

accelerato *sm.* (*ferr.*) slow train.

acceleratore *sm.* accelerator.

accelerazione *sf.* acceleration.

accèndere *vt.* 1. to light 2. (*di fiammiferi*) to strike (*v. irr.*) 3. (*di radio, luce ecc.*) to switch on 4. (*fig.*) to inflame. ♦ **accèndersi** *vr.* 1. to light up 2. (*prender fuoco*) to catch (*v. irr.*) fire || — *in volto*, to blush.

accendino *sm.* **accendisìgaro** *sm.* (cigarette)-lighter.

accennare *vi.* 1. to make (*v. irr.*) a sign 2. (*menzionare*) to mention 3. (*alludere*) to allude.

accenno *sm.* 1. sign 2. (*fig.*) hint.

accensione *sf.* 1. lighting 2. (*mecc.*) ignition || *chiavetta d'*—, ignition-key.

accentare *vt.* to accent, to stress.

accentazione *sf.* accentuation, stressing.

accento *sm.* 1. accent 2. (*tonico*) stress.

accentramento *sm.* centralization.

accentrare *vt.* to centralize.

accentuare *vt.* to accentuate, to stress. ♦ **accentuarsi** *vr.* to get (*v. irr.*) worse, to increase.

accerchiamento *sm.* surrounding.

accerchiare *vt.* to surround.

accertamento *sm.* 1. assurance 2. (*controllo*) verification.

accertare *vt.* 1. to assure 2. (*verificare*) to verify.

acceso *agg.* 1. lit up 2. (*in volto*) blushing 3. (*d'ira*) in a temper.

accessibile *agg.* 1. open to 2. (*di persona*) approachable.

accesso *sm.* 1. admission 2. (*di malattia, passione*) fit.

accessorio *agg.* accessory. ♦ **accessori** *sm. pl.* fittings.

accetta *sf.* hatchet.

accettare *vt.* 1. to accept 2. (*consentire*) to consent.

accetto *agg.* welcome.

accezione *sf.* meaning.

acchiappare *vt.* to catch (*v. irr.*).

acchito *sm. di primo* —, at first sight, at once.

acciacco *sm.* infirmity.

acciaierìa *sf.* steel-mill.

acciaio *sm.* steel.

acciarino *sm.* 1. flint-lock 2. (*di fucile*) gun-lock.

accidentale *agg.* accidental.

accidentato *agg.* uneven.

accidente *sm.* chance, accident.

accidenti *inter.* damn.

accidia *sf.* sloth.

accigliarsi *vr.* to frown.

accingersi *vr.* to set (*v. irr.*) about (doing).

acciottolare *vt.* to cobble.

acciottolato *sm.* cobbled paving.

acciottolìo *sm.* clatter.

acciuffare *vt.* to catch (*v. irr.*), to seize.

acciuga *sf.* anchovy.

acclamare *vt.* 1. to acclaim 2. (*applaudire*) to applaud.

acclamazione *sf.* acclamation, applause.

acclimatazione *sf.* acclimatization.

acclùdere *vt.* to enclose.

accluso *agg.* enclosed.

accoccolarsi *vr.* to squat down.

accodarsi *vr.* to follow.

accogliente *agg.* comfortable, hospitable.

accoglienza *sf.* reception, welcome.

accògliere *vt.* 1. to receive 2. (*fare buona accoglienza*) to welcome 3. (*una richiesta*) to grant.

accòlito *sm.* acolyte.

accollatura *sf.* neckline.

accoltellare *vt.* to stab.

accomiatare *vt.* **1.** to give (*v. irr.*) leave **2.** (*licenziare*) to dismiss. ♦ **accomiatarsi** *vr.* to take (*v. irr.*) leave (of).

accomodamento *sm.* **1.** adjustment **2.** (*conciliazione*) conciliation.

accomodante *agg.* yielding.

accomodare *vt.* **1.** (*riparare*) to repair **2.** (*sistemare*) to settle **3.** (*far comodo*) to suit.

accompagnamento *sm.* **1.** (*l'accompagnare*) accompanying **2.** (*seguito*) retinue **3.** (*mus.*) accompaniment.

accompagnare *vt.* **1.** to accompany **2.** (— *qu. alla stazione*) to see (*v. irr.*) so. off **3.** (*mus.*) to accompany.

accompagnatore *sm.* **1.** companion **2.** (*mus.*) accompanist.

accomunare *vt.* to join, to associate. ♦ **accomunarsi** *vr.* to join.

acconciare *vt.* **1.** to adjust, to adorn **2.** (*capelli*) to dress.

acconciatura *sf.* hair-style.

acconsentire *vi.* **1.** to consent **2.** (*annuire*) to assent.

accontentare *vt.* to satisfy. ♦ **accontentarsi** *vr.* to be content (with).

acconto *sm.* account.

accoppare *vt.* to kill.

accoppiamento *sm.* **1.** coupling **2.** (*di buoi al giogo*) yoking **3.** (*mecc.*) connection.

accoppiare *vt.* **1.** to couple **2.** (*fig.*) to match. ♦ **accoppiarsi** *vr.* to couple, to mate.

accoppiata *sf.* (*ippica*) fourecast.

accorato *agg.* sorrowful.

accorciare *vt.* to shorten.

accordare *vt.* **1.** to grant **2.** (*mus.*) to tune **3.** (*armonizzare*) to match. ♦ **accordarsi** *vr.* to agree (upon).

accordatore *sm.* tuner.

accordo *sm.* **1.** agreement ‖ *come d'—*, as agreed **2.** (*mus.*) chord **3.** (*fig.*) harmony.

accorgersi *vr.* **1.** (*percepire*) to perceive **2.** (*rendersi conto*) to realize.

accorgimento *sm.* **1.** sagacity **2.** (*stratagemma*) clever device.

accòrrere *vi.* to run (*v. irr.*), to hasten: — *in aiuto*, to rush to the help.

accortezza *sf.* sagacity.

accorto *agg.* shrewd.

accostare *vt.* **1.** to draw (*v. irr.*) near **2.** (*porte, finestre ecc.*) to set (*v. irr.*) ajar. ♦ **accostarsi** *vr.* to come (*v. irr.*) near.

accotonare *vt.* to raise.

accotonatura *sf.* raising.

accozzaglia *sf.* huddle: *un'— di gente*, a motley crowd.

accozzare *vt.* to huddle. ♦ **accozzarsi** *vr.* to huddle.

accreditamento *sm.* (*comm.*) crediting.

accreditare *vt.* to credit. ♦ **accreditarsi** *vr.* to gain credit.

accréscere *vt.* to increase.

accrescimento *sm.* increase.

accrescitivo *agg.* e *sm.* augmentative.

accucciarsi *vr.* to crouch.

accudire *vi.* to look after: — *alla casa*, to do (*v. irr.*) the house-wo k.

accumulare *vt.* to heap up.

accumulatore *sm.* accumulator.

accuratezza *sf.* accuracy, care.

accurato *agg.* careful, precise.

accusa *sf.* charge.

accusare *vt.* **1.** to accuse, to charge (with) **2.** (*sentire*) to feel (*v. irr.*) **3.** (*comm.*) to acknowledge.

accusativo *agg.* e *sm.* accusative.

accusato *sm.* accused.

accusatore *sm.* prosecutor: *pubblico —*, public prosecutor.

acerbo *agg.* **1.** unripe **2.** (*acido*) sour.

àcero *sm.* maple.

acetilene *sm.* acetylene.

aceto *sm.* vinegar.

acetone *sm.* acetone.

acidità *sf.* **1.** acidity **2.** (*di stomaco*) hyperchlorhydria.

àcido *agg.* sour. ♦ **àcido** *sm.* acid.

acìdulo *agg.* acidulous.

àcino *sm.* (*di uva*) grape.

acme *sf.* **1.** acme **2.** (*di malattia*) crisis (*pl.* -ses).

acne *sf.* acne.

aconfessionale *agg.* nondenominational.

acqua *sf.* **1.** water: — *marina*, sea water; — *piovana*, rain water; — *potabile*, drinking water **2.** (*pioggia*) rain: — *a catinelle*, heavy rain.

acquaforte *sf.* etching.

acquaio *sm.* sink.

acquamarina *sf.* aquamarine.

acquaragia *sf.* turpentine.

acquario *sm.* aquarium.

acquasanta *sf.* holy water.

acquasantiera *sf.* stoup.
acquàtico *agg.* aquatic.
acquattarsi *vr.* 1. to crouch 2. (*nascondersi*) to hide (*v. irr.*).
acquavite *sf.* brandy.
acquazzone *sm.* downpour.
acquedotto *sm.* aqueduct.
acquerellista *sm.* water-colourist.
acquerello *sm.* water-colour.
acquerùgiola *sf.* drizzle.
acquiescente *agg.* acquiescent.
acquiescenza *sf.* acquiescence.
acquirente *sm.* buyer.
acquisire *vt.* to acquire.
acquistare *vt.* 1. (*comperare*) to buy (*v. irr.*) 2. (*ottenere*) to get (*v. irr.*) 3. (*fig.*) to gain || — *terreno*, to make (*v. irr.*) progress.
acquisto *sm.* purchase || *fare acquisti*, to go (*v. irr.*) shopping.
acquitrino *sm.* marsh.
acquolina *sf.* drizzle: *far venire l'— in bocca*, to make (*v. irr.*) so.'s mouth water.
acre *agg.* 1. sour 2. (*fig.*) sarcastic 3. (*pungente*) pungent.
acrèdine *sf.* 1. acridity 2. (*fig.*) acrimony.
acrimonia *sf.* acrimony.
acròbata *s.* acrobat.
acrobàtico *agg.* acrobatic.
acrobazìa *sf.* acrobatics (*pl.*) || *fare delle acrobazie*, to perform stunts.
acròpoli *sf.* acropolis.
acuire *vt.* to sharpen: — *l'interesse*, to stimulate interest.
acùleo *sm.* 1. (*bot.*) prickle 2. (*zool.*) sting.
acume *sm.* insight.
acuminare *vt.* to sharpen.
acùstica *sf.* acoustics.
acutezza *sf.* 1. sharpness 2. (*di mente*) perspicacity.
acutizzare *vt.* to make (*v. irr.*) acute. ♦ **acutizzarsi** *vr.* to grow (*v. irr.*) acute.
acuto *agg.* 1. sharp 2. (*di angoli, accenti*) acute 3. (*intenso*) intense 4. (*di suono*) shrill. ♦ **acuto** *sm.* (*mus.*) high note.
adagiare *vt.* to lay (*v. irr.*) down with care. ♦ **adagiarsi** *vr.* to lie (*v. irr.*) down.
adagio[1] *avv.* 1. slowly 2. (*con cautela*) cautiously 3. (*con delicatezza*) gently.
adagio[2] *sm.* proverb, saying.
adamantino *agg.* adamantine.
adamìtico *agg.* adamic.

adattàbile *agg.* adaptable.
adattamento *sm.* 1. adaptation 2. (*assestamento*) adjustment.
adattare *vt.* to adapt, to fit. ♦ **adattarsi** *vr.* 1. to adapt oneself 2. (*attagliarsi*) to fit.
adatto *agg.* 1. fit, proper 2. (*che va bene*) suitable (for).
addebitare *vt.* to debit.
addébito *sm.* charge: *fare un — a qu. per qc.*, to charge so. with sthg.
addendo *sm.* addendum (*pl.* -da).
addensamento *sm.* 1. thickening 2. (*di persone*) crowding.
addensare *vt.* 1. to thicken. ♦ **addensarsi** *vr.* 1. to thicken 2. (*di folla*) to crowd.
addentare *vt.* to bite (*v. irr.*).
addentellato *sm.* 1. (*arch.*) toothing 2. (*fig.*) stepping-stone.
addentrarsi *vr.* to penetrate: — *in una questione*, to probe a question.
addentro *avv.* inside.
addestramento *sm.* 1. training 2. (*mil.*) drilling.
addestrare *vt.* 1. to train 2. (*mil.*) to drill.
addetto *agg.* employed (in). ♦ **addetto** *sm.* attaché.
addietro *avv.* 1. (*di spazio*) behind 2. (*di tempo*) before, ago || *era venuto due giorni —*, he had come two days before.
addìo *inter.* good-bye.
addirittura *avv.* 1. quite 2. (*in esclamazioni*) really!
addirsi *vr.* to become (*v. irr.*).
additare *vt.* to point at.
addizionale *agg.* additional.
addizionare *vt.* to sum up.
addizionatrice *sf.* adding-machine, adder.
addizione *sf.* addition.
addobbare *vt.* to adorn.
addobbo *sm.* 1. decoration 2. (*eccl.*) sacred ornaments (*pl.*).
addolcire *vt.* 1. to sweeten 2. (*fig.*) to soften. ♦ **addolcirsi** *vr.* to become (*v. irr.*) soft(er).
addolorare *vt.* to grieve. ♦ **addolorarsi** *vr.* to be grieved.
addolorato *agg.* grieved, sorry.
addome *sm.* abdomen.
addomesticare *vt.* to tame.
addominale *agg.* abdominal.
addormentare *vt.* 1. to send (*v. irr.*) to sleep 2. (*med.*) to anaes-

thetize. ♦ **addormentarsi** *vr.* **1.**
to fall (*v. irr.*) asleep **2.** (*fig.*) to go
(*v. irr.*) to sleep.

addossare *vt.* **1.** to lean **2.** (*attribuire*) to lay (*v. irr.*). ♦ **addos-
sarsi** *vr.* **1.** (*affollarsi*) to crowd
2. (*prendere su di sé*) to take (*v.
irr.*) upon oneself.

addosso *avv. prep.* **1.** on, upon:
mettere qc. —, to put (*v. irr.*)
sthg. on; *togliere qc. d'*—, to take
(*v. irr.*) sthg. off **2.** (*vicino a*) close to: *la casa è* — *alla montagna,*
the house is close to the mountain
‖ *dare* —, to assault, to contradict.

addottrinare *vt.* to instruct. ♦ **ad-
dottrinarsi** *vr.* to instruct oneself.

addurre *vt.* **1.** to put (*v. irr.*) forward: — *una scusa,* to plead **2.**
(*citare*) to quote.

adeguamento *sm.* **1.** proportion-
ment **2.** (*adattamento*) adaptation.

adeguare *vt.* **1.** to proportionate
2. (*adattare*) to conform. ♦ **ade-
guarsi** *vr.* to conform oneself, to
adapt oneself.

adeguato *agg.* **1.** proportionate **2.**
(*adatto*) convenient, fit **3.** (*giusto*)
fair.

adémpiere *vt.* **1.** (*compiere*) to
fulfil **2.** (*eseguire*) to carry out. ♦
adémpiersi *vr.* (*avverarsi*) to
come (*v. irr.*) true.

adempimento *sm.* **1.** fulfilment **2.**
(*esecuzione*) carrying out.

adenòidi *sf. pl.* adenoids.

adepto *sm.* **1.** adept **2.** (*seguace*)
follower.

aderente *agg.* **1.** adherent **2.** (*di
abito*) close-fitting.

aderenza *sf.* **1.** adherence **2.** (*med.*)
adhesion **3.** (*pl.*) connections.

aderire *vi.* **1.** (*stare vicino e fig.*)
to adhere, to stick **2.** (*consentire*)
to comply with **3.** (*parteggiare
per*) to take sides (with).

adescamento *sm.* **1.** enticement
2. (*seduzione*) seduction.

adescare *vt.* **1.** to entice **2.** (*sedurre*) to seduce.

adesione *sf.* adhesion: *dare la propria* — *ad un partito,* to join a
party.

adesivo *agg.* adhesive.

adesso *avv.* now, at present, at the
moment.

adiacente *agg.* adjacent.

adibire *vt.* to use as.

àdipe *sm.* fat.

adiposo *agg.* adipose.

adirarsi *vr.* to get (*v. irr.*) angry.

adirato *agg.* angry.

adire *vt.* (*giur.*) to apply to: — *le
vie legali,* to take (*v. irr.*) legal
steps.

àdito *sm.* entry: *dare* —, to give
(*v. irr.*) rise.

adocchiare *vt.* **1.** to glance **2.**
(*scorgere*) to catch (*v. irr.*) sight of.

adolescente *agg.* teen-aged, adolescent. ♦ **adolescente** *sm.* teen-
-ager.

adolescenza *sf.* adolescence.

adombrare *vt.* **1.** to shade **2.** (*nascondere*) to conceal **3.** (*simboleggiare*) to symbolize. ♦ **adom-
brarsi** *vr.* **1.** to resent **2.** (*di
cavallo*) to shy.

adoperare *vt.* to use. ♦ **adoperarsi** *vr.* to endeavour.

adoràbile *agg.* charming.

adorare *vt.* to adore, to worship.

adorazione *sf.* adoration, worship.

adornare *vt.* to adorn.

adorno *agg.* adorned.

adottare *vt.* to adopt.

adottivo *agg.* adoptive.

adozione *sf.* adoption: *patria d'*—,
adopted country.

adrenalina *sf.* adrenalin.

adulare *vt.* to flatter.

adulatore *agg.* flattering. ♦ **adulatore** *sm.* flatterer.

adulazione *sf.* flattery.

adùltera *sf.* adulteress.

adulterare *vt.* **1.** to adulterate **2.**
(*fig.*) to falsify.

adulterino *agg.* adulterine.

adulterio *sm.* adultery.

adùltero *agg.* adulterous. ♦ **adùltero** *sm.* adulterer.

adulto *agg.* e *sm.* grown-up, adult.

adunanza *sf.* meeting.

adunco *agg.* hooked.

aerare *vt.* **1.** to air **2.** (*chim.*) to
aerate.

aerazione *sf.* **1.** airing **2.** (*chim.*)
aeration.

aèreo *agg.* aerial ‖ *per via aerea,* by
air. ♦ **aèreo** *sm.* **1.** plane **2.**
(*radio*) aerial.

aerodinàmica *sf.* aerodynamics.

aeròdromo *sm.* aerodrome.

aerolito *sm.* aerolite.

aeromodello *sm.* model aircraft.

aeronàuta *sm.* aeronaut.

aeronàutica *sf.* aeronautics.

aeronave *sf.* airship.

aeronavigazione *sf.* air navigation

aeroplano *sm.* (aero)plane, aircraft || — *a razzo*, rocket plane; — *passeggeri*, passenger plane; — *da bombardamento*, bomber.

aeroporto *sm.* airport.

aerosòl *sm.* aerosol.

aerostàtica *sf.* aerostatics.

aeròstato *sm.* aerostat.

aerostazione *sf.* air-terminal.

aerotassì *sm.* airtaxi.

aerotrasportare *vt.* to air-bear.

afa *sf.* sultriness.

afasìa *sf.* aphasia.

affàbile *agg.* affable.

affabilità *sf.* affability, kindness.

affaccendarsi *vr.* to busy oneself.

affaccendato *agg.* busy.

affacciare *vt.* 1. to show (*v. irr.*) 2. (*un dubbio*) to raise. ♦ affacciarsi *vr.* 1. to show oneself 2. (*su un luogo*) to face.

affamare *vt.* to starve (out).

affamato *agg.* 1. hungry 2. (*fig.*) eager. ♦ affamato *sm.* starveling.

affamatore *sm.* starver.

affannare *vt.* to trouble, to worry. ♦ affannarsi *vr.* 1. to worry oneself 2. (*affaccendarsi*) to busy oneself.

affanno *sm.* 1. breathlessness 2. (*pena*) worry.

affannoso *agg.* 1. breathless || *respiro* —, difficult breathing 2. (*ansioso*) anxious.

affare *sm.* 1. affair, business: — *di cuore*, love affair; *questo è nostro*, this is our business 2. (*comm.*) business: *fare affari*, to do (*v. irr.*) business || (*pol.*) *affari esteri*, foreign affairs; (*in Gran Bretagna*) *Ministero degli Affari Esteri*, Foreign Office.

affarista *sm.* speculator.

affascinante *agg.* charming.

affascinare *vt.* to charm.

affaticamento *sm.* weariness.

affaticare *vt.* to tire. ♦ affaticarsi *vr.* 1. to get (*v. irr.*) tired 2. (*lavorare molto*) to work hard.

affatto *avv.* 1. completely, quite 2. (*in frasi negative*) at all: *niente* —, not at all.

affatturare *vt.* to bewitch.

affermare *vt.* 1. to affirm 2. (*fig.*) to assert. ♦ affermarsi *vr.* to make (*v. irr.*) a name for oneself.

affermativo *agg.* affirmative.

affermazione *sf.* 1. statement 2. (*successo*) achievement.

afferrare *vt.* to grasp 2. (*fig.*) to seize. ♦ afferrarsi *vr.* to grasp at, to clutch at.

affettare¹ *vt.* (*tagliare a fette*) to slice.

affettare² *vt.* (*ostentare*) to affect.

affettato¹ *agg.* sliced.

affettato² *agg.* (*ostentato*) affected.

affettatrice *sf.* slicing machine.

affettazione *sf.* affectation, show.

affettivo *agg.* emotional.

affetto¹ *sm.* affection: *portare* — *a qu.*, to set (*v. irr.*) one's affection on so.

affetto² *agg.* affected (with).

affettuosità *sf.* tenderness.

affettuoso *agg.* tender, affectionate.

affezionarsi *vr.* to grow (*v. irr.*) fond of.

affezione *sf.* 1. affection 2. (*med.*) affection, disease.

affiancare *vt.* to flank. ♦ affiancarsi *vr.* to line up (with).

affiatamento *sm.* concord.

affiatare *vt.* 1. to bring (*v. irr.*) together 2. (*mus.*) to tune. ♦ affiatarsi *vr.* to become (*v. irr.*) familiar (with).

affibbiare *vt.* 1. to buckle 2. (*fig.*) to shift (upon).

affidamento *sm.* trust, confidence: *dare* —, to inspire confidence.

affidare *vt.* 1. to entrust 2. (*consegnare*) to commit. ♦ affidarsi *vr.* to rely upon.

affievolire *vt.* to weaken. ♦ affievolirsi *vr.* to grow (*v. irr.*) weak.

affìggere *vt.* to post up: — *lo sguardo*, to fix one's eyes (on).

affilare *vt.* to sharpen. ♦ affilarsi *vr.* (*dimagrire*) to thin.

affilato *agg.* 1. sharp 2. (*di naso, viso*) thin.

affiliare *vt.* to affiliate.

affiliato *sm.* member, associate.

affiliazione *sf.* affiliation.

affinamento *sm.* 1. refining 2. (*fig.*) sharpening.

affinare *vt.* 1. to refine 2. (*assottigliare*) to make (*v. irr.*) thin. ♦ affinarsi *vr.* 1. to refine, to improve 2. (*assottigliarsi*) to become (*v. irr.*) thin.

affinché *cong.* so that, in order that.

affine *agg.* like, similar.

affinità *sf.* affinity.

affiorare *vi.* to appear on the surface.

affissare *vt.* to affix.

affissione *sf.* bill-posting.

affisso *sm.* 1. (*avviso*) bill 2. (*cartello*) placard 3. (*manifesto*) poster.

affittacàmere *sm. e sf.* landlord, landlady.

affittare *vt.* 1. (*dare in affitto*) to let (*v. irr.*) 2. (*prendere in affitto*) to rent 3. (*noleggiare*) to hire.

affitto *sm.* rent.

afflato *sm.* afflatus.

affliggere *vt.* 1. to distress 2. (*di malattie*) to afflict. ◆ **affliggersi** *vr.* to worry.

afflitto *agg.* sad, sorrowful.

afflizione *sf.* 1. affliction 2. (*flagello*) calamity.

afflosciarsi *vr.* 1. to become (*v. irr.*) flabby 2. (*fig.*) to weaken.

affluente *sm.* affluent.

affluenza *sf.* 1. (*di acque*) flow 2. (*di persone*) crowd 3. (*abbondanza*) plenty.

affluire *vi.* 1. (*di acque*) to flow 2. (*di persone*) to crowd 3. (*di cose*) to pour in.

afflusso *sm.* afflux.

affogamento *sm.* drowning.

affogare *vt.* 1. to drown 2. (*fig.*) to smother. ◆ **affogarsi** *vr.* to drown oneself.

affogato *agg.* 1. drowned 2. (*fig.*) oppressed || *uova affogate*, poached eggs.

affollamento *sm.* overcrowding, throng.

affollare *vt.* 1. to crowd 2. (*fig.*) to overwhelm. ◆ **affollarsi** *vr.* to press up.

affollato *agg.* crowded.

affondare *vt.* 1. (*sommergere*) to sink (*v. irr.*) 2. (*immergere*) to plunge.

affossamento *sm.* ditching.

affossare *vt.* to ditch. ◆ **affossarsi** *vr.* to become (*v. irr.*) hollow.

affrancamento *sm.* release.

affrancare *vt.* 1. to release 2. (*con francobollo*) to stamp. ◆ **affrancarsi** *vr.* to free oneself.

affrancato *agg.* 1. free 2. (*con francobollo*) stamped.

affrancatura *sf.* postage.

affranto *agg.* broken-hearted || (*dalla fatica*) worn out.

affratellarsi *vr.* to fraternize.

affresco *sm.* fresco.

affrettare *vt.* 1. to hasten 2. (*anticipare*) to anticipate. ◆ **affrettarsi** *vr.* to make (*v. irr.*) haste.

affrettatamente *avv.* hastily.

affrettato *agg.* 1. hasty 2. (*trascurato*) careless.

affrontare *vt.* 1. to face 2. (*fig.*) to deal (*v. irr.*) with. ◆ **affrontarsi** *vr.* (*venire alle mani*) to come (*v. irr.*) to blows.

affronto *sm.* insult.

affumicare *vt.* 1. to fill with smoke 2. (*cuc.*) to smoke.

affumicato *agg.* 1. blackened by smoke 2. (*cuc.*) smoked || *lenti affumicate*, sun-glasses.

affusolare *vt.* to taper.

afonìa *sf.* aphonia.

àfono *agg.* voiceless.

aforisma *sm.* aphorism.

afoso *agg.* sultry.

africano *agg. e sm.* African.

afroasiàtico *agg.* Afro-Asiatic.

afta *sf.* aphtha.

àgata *sf.* agate.

àgave *sf.* agave.

agenda *sf.* note-book.

agente *sm.* agent.

agenzìa *sf.* agency.

agevolare *vt.* to make (*v. irr.*) easy.

agevolazione *sf.* facilitation.

agévole *agg.* 1. easy 2. (*di strada*) smooth.

agevolmente *avv.* easily.

agganciare *vt.* 1. to hook 2. (*ferr.*) to couple up.

aggeggio *sm.* device.

aggettare *vi.* to jut out.

aggettivo *sm.* adjective.

agghiacciare *vt.* to freeze (*v. irr.*). ◆ **agghiacciarsi** *vr.* to freeze.

agghindare *vt.* to array. ◆ **agghindarsi** *vr.* to dress (oneself) up.

aggiogare *vt.* to yoke.

aggiornamento *sm.* 1. (*rinvio*) adjournment 2. (*di un libro*) revision.

aggiornare *vt.* 1. (*rinviare*) to adjourn 2. (*mettere al corrente*) to bring (*v. irr.*) up to date. ◆ **aggiornarsi** *vr.* to brush up one's knowledge.

aggiornato *agg.* up-to-date.

aggirare *vt.* to go (*v. irr.*) round || — *l'ostacolo*, to avoid an obstacle. ◆ **aggirarsi** *vr.* to wander about, to go about.

aggiudicare *vt.* to award. ◆ **ag-**

giudicarsi *vr.* to win (*v. irr.*).

aggiudicazione *sf.* award.

aggiùngere *vt.* to add. ♦ aggiùngersi *vr.* to join.

aggiunta *sf.* 1. addition 2. (*aumento*) increase.

aggiunto *agg.* added, joined. ♦ aggiunto *sm.* assistant.

aggiustare *vt.* 1. (*riparare*) to mend 2. (*sistemare*) to arrange. ♦ aggiustarsi *vr.* (*accomodarsi*) to make (*v. irr.*) oneself comfortable.

agglomerato *sm.* agglomerate.

agglutinare *vt.* to agglutinate.

aggraffare *vt.* to seize.

aggranchire *vt.* to benumb.

aggrapparsi *vr.* to cling (*v. irr.*) (to), to get (*v. irr.*) hold (of).

aggravante *agg.* aggravating. ♦ aggravante *sf.* (*giur.*) aggravating circumstance.

aggravare *vt.* to aggravate, to overburden. ♦ aggravarsi *vr.* to grow (*v. irr.*) worse.

aggravato *agg.* 1. overburdened 2. (*med.*) worse.

aggraziare *vt.* to make (*v. irr.*) graceful.

aggredire *vt.* to assault.

aggregare *vt.* to associate. ♦ aggregarsi *vr.* to join.

aggressione *sf.* aggression, assault.

aggressività *sf.* aggressiveness.

aggressivo *agg.* aggressive.

aggressore *sm.* aggressor.

aggrottare *vt.* to frown.

aggrovigliare *vt.* to entangle.

aggrovigliarsi *vr.* to get (*v. irr.*) entangled.

aggruppare *vt.* to group.

agguantare *vt.* to catch (*v. irr.*).

agguato *sm.* ambush.

agguerrire *vt.* to inure (for war). ♦ agguerrirsi *vr.* to get (*v. irr.*) inured.

agiatamente *avv.* in ease and comfort.

agiato *agg.* well-to-do.

àgile *agg.* nimble.

agilità *sf.* nimbleness.

agio *sm.* comfort, ease, leisure.

agiografia *sf.* hagiography.

agire *vi.* to act.

agitare *vt.* 1. to agitate 2. (*scuotere*) to shake (*v. irr.*) 3. to stir (*anche fig.*). ♦ agitarsi *vr.* to be agitated.

agitatore *sm.* 1. agitator 2. (*mecc.*) stirrer.

agitazione *sf.* 1. agitation 2. (*eccitazione*) excitement 3. (*di folla*) tumult.

aglio *sm.* garlic.

agnello *sm.* lamb.

agnosticismo *sm.* agnosticism.

ago *sm.* 1. needle 2. (*mecc.*) tongue.

agognare *vt.* to long (for sthg.).

agonìa *sf.* agony, pangs (*pl.*) of death.

agonismo *sm.* athletic spirit.

agonizzante *agg.* dying.

agonizzare *vi.* to be in one's death agony.

agorafobìa *sf.* agoraphobia.

agosto *sm.* August.

agraria *sf.* agriculture.

agrario *agg.* agrarian. ♦ agrario *sm.* 1. land-owner 2. (*esperto*) agriculturist.

agreste *agg.* agrestic, rustic.

agretto *agg.* sourish.

agrìcolo *agg.* agricultural.

agricoltore *sm.* farmer.

agricoltura *sf.* agriculture.

agrifoglio *sm.* holly.

agrimensore *sm.* land-surveyor.

agro *agg.* sour. ♦ agro *sm.* sourness.

agrodolce *agg.* bitter-sweet, sourish.

agronomìa *sf.* agronomy.

agronòmico *agg.* agronomical.

agrònomo *sm.* agronomist.

agrumi *sm. pl.* citrus fruit (*sing.*).

aguzzare *vt.* to sharpen.

aguzzino *sm.* 1. gaoler, jailer 2. (*fig.*) torturer.

aguzzo *agg.* sharp, pointed.

ahimè *inter.* alas.

aia *sf.* threshing-floor.

aio *sm.* tutor.

airone *sm.* heron.

aitante *agg.* vigorous, stout.

aiuola *sf.* flower-bed.

aiutante *sm.* 1. assistant 2. (*mil.*) adjutant: — di campo, aide-de-camp.

aiutare *vt.* to help. ♦ aiutarsi *vr.* (*ingegnarsi*) to make (*v. irr.*) shift. ♦ aiutarsi *vr. rec.* to help (one another).

aiuto *sm.* 1. help: *chiedere* —, to call for help 2. (*chi aiuta*) help, helper 3. (*pl.*) (*mil.*) reinforcements.

aizzare *vt.* to incite, to rouse.

ala *sf.* wing.

alabarda *sf.* halberd.

alabastro *sm.* alabaster.
àlacre *agg.* brisk, industrious.
alacrità *sf.* alacrity.
alamaro *sm.* frog.
alambicco *sm.* still.
alano *sm.* Great Dane.
alba *sf.* dawn.
albanese *agg. e sm.* Albanian.
àlbatro *sm.* albatross.
albeggiare *vi.* to dawn.
alberare *vt.* 1. to plant with trees 2. (*mar.*) to mast.
alberato *agg.* planted with trees.
alberatura *sf.* (*mar.*) masting.
albergatore *sm.* hotel-keeper.
alberghiero *agg.* hotel (*attributivo*): *industria alberghiera.* hotel trade.
albergo *sm.* hotel.
àlbero *sm.* 1. tree 2. (*mar.*) mast 3. (*mecc.*) shaft.
albicocca *sf.* apricot.
albino *agg. e sm.* albino.
albo *sm.* 1. list, roll: — *degli avvocati,* Law List; — *d'onore,* roll of honour 2. (*per fotografie ecc.*) album 3. (*tavola per affissione*) notice-board.
album *sm.* album.
albume *sm.* albumen.
albumina *sf.* albumin.
alca *sf.* auk.
alcalino *agg. e sm.* alkaline.
alce *sm.* elk.
alchimìa *sf.* alchemy.
alcòlico *agg.* alcoholic.
alcolismo *sm.* alcoholism.
alcolizzato *agg. e sm.* alcoholic.
alcool *sm.* alcohol.
alcova *sf.* alcove.
alcunché *pron.* anything, something.
alcuno *agg.* 1. (*frasi affermative*) some, a few 2. (*frasi negative*) any. ♦ **alcuno** *pron.* 1. (*frasi affermative*) somebody, someone 2. (*frasi negative*) anybody, anyone.
aldilà *sm.* hereafter.
aleatorio *agg.* aleatory.
aleggiare *vi.* 1. to flutter 2. (*fig.*) to hover (about).
alettone *sm.* aileron.
alfa *sf.* alpha.
alfabeto *sm.* alphabet.
aliiere *sm.* 1. ensign 2. (*scacchi*) bishop.
alga *sf.* seaweed.
àlgebra *sf.* algebra.
algèbrico *agg.* algebraic, algebraical.

aliante *sm.* glider.
àlibi *sm.* alibi.
alienare *vt.* to alienate, to estrange. ♦ **alienarsi** *vr.* to alienate oneself, to become (*v. irr.*) estranged.
alienato *agg.* lunatic, mad; estranged, alienated. ♦ **alienato** *sm.* 1. lunatic, madman (*pl.* -men) 2. alienated person, estranged person.
alienazione *sf.* alienation, estrangement.
alienista *sm.* alienist, psychiatrist.
alieno *agg.* averse, opposed.
alimentare[1] *vt.* to feed (*v. irr.*), to nourish.
alimentare[2] *agg.* alimentary ‖ *generi alimentari,* foodstuffs; *negozio di generi alimentari,* grocery store.
alimentazione *sf.* nourishment, feeding.
alimento *sm.* food.
alìnea *sf.* paragraph.
alìquota *sf.* aliquot, rate.
aliscafo *sm.* hydrofoil boat.
aliseo *sm.* trade-wind.
àlito *sm.* breath.
allacciare *vt.* 1. to lace, to connect 2. (*fig.*) to establish. ♦ **allacciarsi** *vr.* 1. (*abbracciarsi*) to embrace 2. (*aggrovigliarsi*) to get (*v. irr.*) entangled, to be entangled.
allagare *vt.* to flood, to inundate.
allampanato *agg.* lean, lanky.
allargamento *sm.* widening, enlargement.
allargare *vt.* to widen, to enlarge, to extend. ♦ **allargarsi** *vr.* to widen, to extend, to spread (*v. irr.*).
allarmante *agg.* alarming.
allarmare *vt.* to alarm. ♦ **allarmarsi** *vr.* to get (*v. irr.*) frightened.
allarme *sm.* alarm, warning, alert.
allattamento *sm.* breast-feeding, nursing.
allattare *vt.* to suckle, to nurse.
alleanza *sf.* alliance.
allearsi *vr.* to ally, to become (*v. irr.*) allies.
alleato *agg.* allied. ♦ **alleato** *sm.* ally.
allegare *vt.* 1. to allege 2. (*accludere*) to enclose.
allegato *sm.* enclosure.
alleggerimento *sm.* lightening, relief.
alleggerire *vt.* to lighten, to re-

lieve, to unburden. ◆ **alleggerirsi** vr. to relieve oneself.

allegorìa sf. allegory.

allegòrico agg. allegoric(al).

allegramente agg. cheerfully, merrily.

allegrìa sf. cheerfulness, mirth.

allegro agg. merry, cheerful, jolly.

allegrone sm. jolly fellow.

allenamento sm. · training.

allenare vt. to train. ◆ **allenarsi** vr. to train (oneself).

allenatore sm. trainer; (di squadre) coach.

allentamento sm. **1.** loosening **2.** (di velocità) slackening.

allentare vt. to slacken, to loosen, to relax: — il freno, to release the brake. ◆ **allentarsi** vr. to slacken.

allergìa sf. allergy.

allèrgico agg. allergic.

allestimento sm. preparation, fitting out ‖ — scenico, staging.

allestire vt. to prepare, to fit out.

allettamento sm. enticement, allurement.

allettante agg. alluring, enticing.

allettare vt. to allure, to entice.

allevamento sm. **1.** breeding, raising ‖ (di bambino) bringing up **2.** (luogo) stock-farm ‖ — di cavalli, stud-farm.

allevare vt. **1.** (bambini) to bring (v. irr.) up **2.** (animali) to breed (v. irr.), to rear.

allevatore sm. breeder.

alleviare vt. to relieve, to alleviate.

allibire vi. to be left speechless, to be struck dumb.

allibito agg. struck dumb, speechless.

allibratore sm. bookmaker.

allietare vt. to cheer. ◆ **allietarsi** vr. to cheer up.

allievo sm. **1.** pupil **2.** (mil.) cadet.

alligatore sm. alligator.

allineamento sm. **1.** alignment ‖ (tip.) — di caratteri, ranging of characters **2.** (mil.) dressing.

allineare vt. **1.** to line up, to align: — delle cifre, to tabulate figures **2.** (mil.) to dress; (in ordine di marcia) to form up. ◆ **allinearsi** vr. **1.** to get (v. irr.) into line **2.** (mil.) to dress ‖ allineatevi, draw up! **3.** (pol.) to be aligned with.

allocco sm. **1.** owl **2.** (fig.) fool.

allocuzione sf. allocution: fare un'—, to deliver a speech.

allòdola sf. skylark, lark.

allogare vt. to lodge.

allogazione sf. lease.

alloggiare vt. **1.** to lodge, to house, to put (v. irr.) up **2.** (mil.) to quarter; (in casa privata) to billet. ◆ **alloggiare** vi. **1.** to lodge, to live **2.** (mil.) to quarter; (in casa privata) to be billeted.

alloggio sm. · **1.** lodging ‖ indennità di —, living-out allowance **2.** (mil.) quarters (pl.).

allontanamento sm. **1.** removal **2.** (licenziamento) dismissal.

allontanare vt. **1.** to remove, to drive (v. irr.) away: — un pericolo, to evert a danger **2.** (licenziare) to dismiss, to turn out. ◆ **allontanarsi** vr. to go (v. irr.) away, to depart.

allora avv. **1.** then **2.** (quindi) so.

allorché cong. when.

alloro sm. laurel.

àlluce sm. big toe.

allucinare vt. **1.** to dazzle **2.** (dare allucinazioni) to hallucinate.

allucinato agg. hallucinated.

allucinazione sf. hallucination.

allùdere vi. to allude (to), to hint (at).

alluminio sm. aluminium.

allunaggio sm. mooning.

allunare vi. to moon.

allungàbile agg. extensible.

allungamento sm. lengthening, stretching.

allungare vt. **1.** to lengthen, to extend, to stretch ‖ — il passo, to quicken one's steps ‖ — il collo, to stretch one's neck ‖ — gli orecchi, to strain one's ears ‖ (fig.) — le mani su qc., to lay (v. irr.) hands on sthg. ◆ **allungarsi** vr. to lengthen, to grow (v. irr.) longer, to draw (v. irr.) out.

allusione sf. allusion, hint.

allusivo agg. allusive.

alluvionato agg. flooded ‖ zone alluvionate, flood-areas. ◆ **alluvionato** sm. flood-victim.

alluvione sf. flood.

almanaccare vi. to fantasticate.

almanacco sm. almanac.

almeno avv. at least.

alno sm. alder-tree.

aloè sm. aloe.

alone sm. halo.

alpaca sm. alpaca.

alpe sf. alp.

alpestre agg. alpine.

alpinismo sm. (mountain-)climbing, mountaineering.

alpinista s. (mountain-)climber.

alpino agg. Alpine.

alquanto avv. somewhat, rather.

altalena sf. swing.

altana sf. roof-terrace.

altare sm. altar.

alterare vt. to alter; (salute) to impair; (cibo) to adulterate. ♦ **alterarsi** vr. 1. to alter, to change 2. (andare a male) to go (v. irr.) bad 3. (turbarsi) to be upset || la sua voce si alterò, his voice faltered.

alterazione sf. 1. alteration 2. (deteriorazione) deterioration 3. (turbamento) emotion; (della voce) faltering.

alterco sm. altercation.

alterigia sf. haughtiness.

alternanza sf. alternation.

alternare vt. to alternate. ♦ **alternarsi** vr. to alternate.

alternativa sf. alternative.

alterno agg. alternate.

altero agg. lofty, proud.

altezza sf. 1. height 2. (di tessuto) width 3. (di suono) pitch 4. (fig.) essere all'— di qc., to be equal to sthg.; to be up to sthg. 5. (titolo) highness.

altezzoso agg. haughty.

alticcio agg. tight, tipsy.

altìmetro sm. altimeter.

altitùdine sf. altitude.

alto agg. 1. high, tall: un uomo —, a tall man || alta direzione, top management 2. (di suono) loud || ad alta voce, aloud, loudly 3. (profondo) deep: acqua alta, deep water 4. (geogr.) northern, upper 5. (stor.) early. ♦ **alto** sm. height || alti e bassi, ups and downs. ♦ **alto** avv. high, up || mani in —, hands up.

altoforno sm. blast-furnace.

altolocato agg. high-ranking, high-class.

altoparlante sm. loud-speaker.

altopiano sm. plateau.

altresì avv. likewise, also.

altrettanto agg. correlativo as much (...as); (pl.) as many (...as) || (neg.) as (o so) much (:..as); (pl.)

as (o so) many... (as): egli ha altrettante possibilità quanto me, he has as many chances as I. ♦ **altrettanto** pron. 1. as much; (pl.) as many 2. (lo stesso) the same: — a voi!, the same to you!. ♦ **altrettanto** avv. 1. (con agg. e avv.) as (...as); (neg.) as (o so) ...as) 2. (coi verbi) as much (as).

altrimenti avv. otherwise. ♦ **altrimenti** cong. otherwise, else.

altro agg. indef. 1. other || un —, another 2. (differente) different 3. (con pronomi int.) else: chi altro?, who else? 4. (in più) more: leggerò altri due libri, I shall read two more books 5. (susseguente) next: verrò l'altra domenica, I shall come next Sunday 6. (antecedente) last: andai l'altro mese, I went last month.

altronde 1. (nella loc. avv.) d'—, on the other hand 2. (tuttavia) however.

altrove avv. elsewhere, somewhere else.

altrui agg. other people's, someone else's. ♦ **l'altrui** sm. the property of others.

altruismo sm. unselfishness.

altruìstico agg. unselfish.

altura sf. height.

alunno sm. pupil.

alveare sm. beehive.

àlveo sm. river-bed.

alzaia sf. towing-line || strada d'—, towing-path.

alzare vt. 1. to lift, to raise 2. (erigere) to build (v. irr.) 3. (mar.) to hoist. ♦ **alzarsi** vr. (dal letto) to get (v. irr.) up 2. (in piedi) to stand (v. irr.) up 3. (in altezza) to grow (v. irr.) tall.

alzata sf. 1. raising 2. (l'alzarsi) rising.

amàbile agg. amiable.

amabilità sf. amiability.

amaca sf. hammock.

amàlgama sm. amalgam.

amalgamare vt. to amalgamate.

amante s. 1. lover 2. (fig.) fond.

amanuense sm. copyist.

amaranto sm. amaranth.

amare vt. 1. to love, to be fond of 2. (richiedere) to require.

amareggiare vt. 1. to make (v. irr.) bitter 2. (fig.) to sadden. ♦ **amareggiarsi** vr. to worry.

amarena sf. sour black cherry.

amaretto *sm.* macaroon.
amarezza *sf.* 1. bitterness 2. (*fig.*) sorrow.
amaro *agg.* bitter. ♦ **amaro** *sm.* (*liquore*) bitters (*pl.*).
amatore *sm.* 1. lover 2. (*chi si occupa d'arte per diletto*) amateur.
amàzzone *sf.* 1. Amazon 2. (*fig.*) masculine woman.
ambage *sf.* ambages (*pl.*) || *senza ambagi*, plainly.
ambasciata *sf.* 1. embassy 2. (*messaggio*) message.
ambasciatore *sm.* ambassador.
ambedue *agg.* e *pron.* both.
ambientare *vt.* 1. to acclimatize 2. (*fatti, personaggi ecc.*) to place. ♦ **ambientarsi** *vr.* to get (*v. irr.*) accustomed.
ambiente *sm.* 1. ambient 2. (*fig.*) milieu 3. (*stanza*) room.
ambiguità *sf.* ambiguity.
ambiguo *agg.* ambiguous.
ambio *sm.* amble.
ambire *vt.* to desire.
àmbito *sm.* ambit.
ambivalente *agg.* ambivalent.
ambivalenza *sf.* ambivalence.
ambizione *sf.* ambition.
ambizioso *agg.* ambitious.
ambo *sm.* ambo.
ambra *sf.* amber.
ambrosia *sf.* ambrosia.
ambulante *agg.* itinerant || *venditore* —, pedlar.
ambulanza *sf.* ambulance.
ambulatorio *sm.* surgery.
ameba *sf.* amoeba.
amebìasi *sf.* amoebiasis (*pl.* -ses).
amenità *sf.* 1. amenity 2. (*facezia*) joke.
ameno *agg.* 1. pleasant 2. (*divertente*) funny: *un tipo* —, a funny chap.
americanismo *sm.* Americanism.
americano *agg.* e *sm.* American.
ametista *sf.* amethyst.
amianto *sm.* amianthus.
amichévole *agg.* friendly.
amicizia *sf.* friendship || *fare* —, to make (*v. irr.*) friends with.
amico *sm.* friend.
amidatura *sf.* starching.
àmido *sm.* starch.
ammaccare *vt.* to bruise.
ammaccatura *sf.* bruise.
ammaestramento *sm.* 1. (*addestramento*) training 2. (*insegnamento*) teaching 3. (*di animali*) taming.
ammaestrare *vt.* 1. (*addestrare*) to train 2. (*insegnare*) to teach (*v. irr.*) 3. (*di animali*) to tame.
ammainare *vt.* to furl.
ammalarsi *vr.* to fall (*v. irr.*) ill.
ammalato *agg.* 1. (*pred.*) ill 2. (*attr.*) sick. ♦ **ammalato** *sm.* sick person, patient.
ammaliare *vt.* to bewitch.
ammaliatrice *sf.* bewitcher.
ammanco *sm.* shortage || — *di cassa*, deficit.
ammanettare *vt.* to handcuff.
ammannire *vt.* to prepare.
ammansire *vt.* 1. to tame 2. (*fig.*) to calm. ♦ **ammansirsi** *vr.* 1. to become (*v. irr.*) tamed 2. to calm down.
ammarare *vi.* 1. to alight (on water) 2. (*di capsule spaziali*) to splash down.
ammassare *vt.* to heap. ♦ **ammassarsi** *vr.* to gather.
ammasso *sm.* heap.
ammattire *vi.* to get (*v. irr.*) mad.
ammazzare *vt.* to kill.
ammazzatoio *sm.* slaughter-house.
ammenda *sf.* amends (*pl.*).
ammèttere *vt.* 1. (*lasciar entrare*) to admit, to receive 2. (*concedere, supporre*) to acknowledge, to suppose.
ammezzato *sm.* mezzanine.
ammezzire *vi.* to become (*v. irr.*) over-ripe.
ammiccare *vi.* to wink (at).
ammina *sf.* amine.
amministrare *vt.* 1. to manage 2. (*giur.; eccl.*) to administer.
amministrativo *agg.* administrative.
amministratore *sm.* manager.
amministrazione *sf.* management.
ammiràbile *agg.* admirable.
ammiraglio *sm.* admiral.
ammirare *vt.* to admire.
ammiratore *sm.* 1. admirer 2. (*di attori ecc.*) fan.
ammirazione *sf.* admiration.
ammirévole *agg.* admirable.
ammissìbile *agg.* admissible.
ammobiliamento *sm.* furnishing.
ammobiliare *vt.* to furnish.
ammodernare *vt.* to modernize.
ammodo *agg.* nice, proper.
ammogliare *vt.* to marry. ♦ **ammogliarsi** *vr.* to get (*v. irr.*) mar-

ried.

ammollare vt. 1. to soak 2. (ammorbidire) to soften.

ammollire vt. to soften.

ammonìaca sf. ammonia.

ammonire vt. 1. to admonish 2. (avvisare) to warn.

ammonizione sf. 1. admonition 2. (rimprovero) reproof 3. (avvertimento) warning.

ammontare vi. to amount.

ammonticchiare vt. to heap (up).

ammorbare vt. to taint.

ammorbidire vt. to soften.

ammortamento sm. redemption || quota d'—, depreciation allowance.

ammortire vt. to numb.

ammortizzare vt. to redeem.

ammosciare vt. to become (v. irr.) flabby.

ammucchiare vt. to heap (up).

ammuffire vi. 1. to grow (v. irr.) musty 2. (fig.) to languish: — in casa, to languish at home.

ammutinamento sm. mutiny.

ammutinarsi vr. to mutiny.

ammutinato agg. mutinous. ◆ **ammutinato** sm. mutineer.

ammutolire vi. 1. to become (v. irr.) dumb 2. (essere ammutolito da altri) to be struck dumb.

amnesìa sf. loss of memory.

amnistìa sf. amnesty.

amnistiare vt. to amnesty.

amo sm. fish-hook.

amorale agg. amoral.

amoralità .sf. amorality.

amore sm. 1. love || — di sé, selfishness 2. (persona o cosa amata) beloved || per amore di, for the sake of.

amoreggiare vi. to flirt.

amoretto sm. flirtation.

amorévole agg. loving.

amorevolezza sf. lovingness.

amorfo agg. amorphous.

amorino sm. Cupid.

amoroso agg. 1. loving 2. (fig.) amorous: poesia —, amorous verse.

amovìbile agg. movable.

amperòmetro sm. amperometer.

ampiezza sf. width, (anche fig.) breadth.

ampio agg. 1. wide 2. (di abito) comfortable.

amplesso sm. embrace.

ampliamento sm. amplification.

ampliare vt. 1. to amplify 2. (aumentare) to increase. ◆ **ampliar-**

si vr. to widen.

amplificare vt. 1. to enlarge 2. (fig.; fis.) to amplify.

amplificatore sm. amplifier.

amplificazione sf. amplification.

ampolla sf. 1. phial 2. (per olio, aceto ecc.) cruet.

ampollosità sf. pomposity.

ampolloso agg. pompous: stile —, bombastic style.

amputare vt. to amputate.

amputazione sf. amputation.

amuleto sm. amulet.

anabbaglianti sm. pl. lower beams

anabolismo sm. anabolism.

anacoreta sm. anchorite.

anacronismo sm. anachronism.

anacronìstico agg. anachronistic.

anàgrafe sf. registry office.

anagramma sm. anagram.

analcòlico agg. soft.

anale agg. anal.

analfabeta sm. illiterate.

analfabetismo sm. illiteracy.

analgèsico agg. e sm. analgesic.

anàlisi sf. analysis (pl. -ses).

analìtico agg. analytical.

analizzare vt. to analyse.

analogamente avv. likewise.

analogìa sf. analogy.

anàlogo agg. similar.

ànanas sm. pine-apple.

anarchìa sf. anarchy.

anàrchico agg. anarchic. ◆ **anàrchico** sm. anarchist.

anatema sm. anathema.

anatomìa sf. anatomy.

anatòmico agg. anatomic.

anatomista sm. anatomist.

ànatra sf. duck.

anatròccolo sm. duckling.

anca sf. hip.

ancestrale agg. ancestral.

anche avv. 1. (pure) also, too 2. (in frasi neg.) either: anch'io non verrò, I will not come either 3. (con comp.) even, still: ciò è anche peggio, it is still worse 4. (persino) even. ◆ **anche** cong. (anche se) even if, even though

ancheggiare vi. to waddle.

anchilosato agg. ankylosed.

anchilosi sf. ankylosis.

àncora sf. 1. anchor: levar l'—, to weigh anchor 2. (fig.) hope: — di salvezza, last hope.

ancora avv. 1. (tuttora) still 2. (in frasi neg.) yet 3. (di nuovo) again 4. (davanti a comp.) still, even

5. (*con pron. e agg. quantitativi*) more: — *molte persone*, many more people **6.** («*di più* » *in frasi affermative*) some more: *voglio ancora caffé*, I want some more coffee **7.** («*di più* » *in frasi neg. e dubitative*) any more: *hai ancora caffé?*, have you any more coffee? **8.** (*più a lungo*) longer: *leggi ancora un po'*, read a little longer.
ancoraggio *sm.* anchorage.
ancorare *vt.* to anchor.
ancorché *cong.* even if, even though.
andamento *sm.* **1.** (*tendenza*) trend **2.** (*procedimento*) proceeding.
andante *agg.* **1.** (*scadente*) plain **2.** (*comm.*) current **3.** (*mus.*) andante.
andare *vi.* **1.** (*anche fig.*) to go (*v. irr.*): — *a cavallo*, to go on horseback; — *a far compere*, to go shopping; — *a piedi*, to go on foot; — *a zonzo*, to lounge about; — *e venire*, to come (*v. irr.*) and go; — *in bicicletta*, to ride (*v. irr.*) a bicycle; — *in treno*, to go by train; — *a male*, to go bad **2.** (*essere molto venduto*) to be in demand **3.** (— *bene, di indumento*) to fit ‖ — *avanti* (*di orologi*), to be fast; — *indietro* (*di orologi*), to be slow. ♦ **andàrsene** *vr.* to go away.
andata *sf.* going: — *e ritorno*, going there and back ‖ *biglietto di sola* —, single ticket ‖ *biglietto di* — *e ritorno*, return ticket.
andatura *sf.* **1.** gait **2.** (*velocità*) pace.
andazzo *sm.* habit, custom.
andicappare *vt.* to handicap.
andirivieni *sm.* coming and going.
àndito *sm.* passage.
andrògino *agg.* androgynous. ♦ **andrògino** *sm.* androgyne.
androne *sm.* lobby.
aneddòtico *agg.* anecdotic.
anèddoto *sm.* anecdote.
anelare *vi.* **1.** to gasp **2.** (*fig.*) to long for.
anèlito *sm.* **1.** gasp **2.** (*fig.*) longing for.
anello *sm.* ring: — *di fidanzamento*, engagement ring; — *di matrimonio*, wedding ring ‖ — *di catena*, link of a chain.
anemìa *sf.* anaemia.
anèmico *agg.* anaemic.
anèmone *sm.* anemone.
anestesìa *sf.* anaesthesia.

anestesista *s.* anaesthetist.
anestètico *agg. e sm.* anaesthetic.
anestetizzare *vt.* to anaesthetize.
anfibio *agg.* amphibious. ♦ **anfibio** *sm.* (*zool.; mil.*) amphibian.
anfiteatro *sm.* amphitheatre.
anfitrione *sm.* amphitryon.
ànfora *sf.* amphora (*pl.* -ae).
anfrattuoso *agg.* anfractuous.
angèlico *agg.* angelic(al).
àngelo *sm.* angel.
angherìa *sf.* vexation.
angina *sf.* angina.
angioma *sm.* angioma.
anglicano *agg. e sm.* Anglican.
angolare *agg.* angular.
àngolo *sm.* **1.** corner **2.** (*fis.; geom.*) angle.
angoloso *agg.* angular.
angoscia *sf.* anguish.
angosciare *vt.* to anguish.
angoscioso *agg.* **1.** (*che dà angoscia*) distressing **2.** (*pieno di angoscia*) full of anguish.
anguilla *sf.* **1.** eel **2.** (*fig.*) elusive person.
anguria *sf.* water-melon.
angustia *sf.* **1.** narrowness **2.** (*tribolazione*) distress.
angustiare *vt.* to afflict. ♦ **angustiarsi** *vr.* to worry.
angusto *agg.* **1.** narrow **2.** (*fig.*) mean.
ànice *sm.* anise.
anidride *sf.* anhydride.
anilina *sf.* aniline.
ànima *sf.* **1.** soul ‖ *esalare l'*—, to die ‖ *vender l'*— *a caro prezzo*, to sell (*v. irr.*) one's life dearly. **2.** (*parte centrale, nerbo*) soul, heart **3.** (*cuore, sentimento*) feeling, heart **4.** (*persona*) person: *Torino ha oltre un milione di anime*, Turin has over one million persons.
animale *sm. e agg.* animal.
animalesco *agg.* beastly.
animare *vt.* to enliven, to give (*v. irr.*) life. ♦ **animarsi** *vr.* to become (*v. irr.*) lively.
animatamente *avv.* animatedly.
animato *agg.* **1.** living **2.** (*vivace*) lively.
animatore *sm.* animator.
animazione *sf.* briskness.
animismo *sm.* animism.
ànimo *sm.* **1.** mind: *ho in animo di fare ciò*, I have a mind to do that **2.** (*coraggio*) courage **3.** (*inclinazione*) disposition.

animosità *sf.* animosity.
animoso *agg.* **1.** brave **2.** (*ostile*) malevolent.
anisetta *sf.* anisette.
ànitra *sf.* duck.
annacquare *vt.* **1.** to water **2.** (*fig.*) to moderate.
annaffiare *vt.* to water.
annaffiatoio *sm.* watering-can.
annali *sm. pl.* annals.
annaspare *vi.* to grope.
annaspio *sm.* groping.
annata *sf.* **1.** year **2.** (*raccolto*) crop.
annebbiare *vt.* **1.** to dim **2.** (*fig.*) to dull. ♦ **annebbiarsi** *vr.* (*della vista*) to blur.
annegamento *sm.* drowning.
annegare *vt.* to drown. ♦ **annegarsi** *vr.* to drown oneself.
annegato *agg.* drowned.
annerimento *sm.* blackening.
annerire *vt.* to blacken.
annessione *sf.* annexation.
annesso *agg.* **1.** connected **2.** (*accluso*) enclosed.
annèttere *vt.* to annex.
annichilazione *sf.* annihilation.
annichilimento *sm.* annihilation.
annichilire *vt.* to annihilate.
annidarsi *vr.* **1.** to nestle **2.** (*nascondersi*) to hide (*v. irr.*).
annientamento *sm.* **1.** destruction **2.** (*di desideri*) frustration.
annientare *vt.* to destroy.
anniversario *agg. e sm.* anniversary.
anno *sm.* **1.** year: — *bisestile*, leap-year ‖ *Capo d'*—, New Year's Day ‖ *durante tutto l'*—, all the year round **2.** (*periodo lungo e indeterminato*) a long time **3.** (*nell'indicare l'età*) to be ... years old: *ho 10 anni*, I am 10 years old.
annodare *vt.* to knot: — *amicizie*, to make friends.
annoiare *vt.* to bore, to tire. ♦ **annoiarsi** *vr.* to be bored.
annoiato *agg.* bored.
annoiatore *sm.* tiresome person.
annoso *agg.* old.
annotare *vt.* **1.** (*corredare di note*) to annotate **2.** (*prendere nota*) to take (*v. irr.*) a note (of).
annotazione *sf.* note.
annottare *vi.* to grow (*v. irr.*) dark.
annuale *agg.* yearly.
annuario *sm.* year-book.
annuire *vi.* to nod.
annullamento *sm.* cancellation.

annullare *vt.* **1.** to annul **2.** (*comm.*) to cancel.
annunciare *vt.* **1.** to announce **2.** (*predire*) to foretell (*v. irr.*).
annunciatore *sm.* announcer.
annuncio *sm.* **1.** notice **2.** (*presagio*) presage.
ànnuo *agg.* yearly.
annusare *vt.* **1.** to smell **2.** (*tabacco*) to take (*v. irr.*) snuff.
annuvolarsi *vr.* **1.** to get (*v. irr.*) cloudy **2.** (*fig.*) to become (*v. irr.*) gloomy.
ano *sm.* anus.
anòdino *agg.* anodyne.
ànodo *sm.* anode.
anomalia *sf.* anomaly.
anòmalo *agg.* anomalous.
anònima *sf.* joint-stock company.
anònimo *agg.* anonymous. ♦ **anònimo** *sm.* anonym.
anormale *agg.* abnormal.
anormalità *sf.* abnormality.
ansa *sf.* **1.** (*insenatura*) creek **2.** (*di fiume*) bend **3.** (*manico*) handle.
ansante *agg.* panting.
ansare *vi.* to pant.
ansia *sf.* anxiety.
ansietà *sf.* anxiety.
ansimare *vi.* to pant.
ansioso *agg.* **1.** anxious **2.** (*desideroso*) eager.
ànsito *sm.* panting.
anta *sf.* **1.** shutter **2.** (*di armadio*) door.
antagonismo *sm.* antagonism.
antagonista *s.* antagonist.
antàrtico *agg.* Antarctic.
antecedente *agg.* previous. ♦ **antecedente** *sm.* antecedent.
antecessore *sm.* predecessor.
antefatto *sm.* antecedent fact.
anteguerra *sm.* pre-war time.
antenato *sm.* ancestor.
antenna *sf.* **1.** (*zool.*) antenna (*pl.* -nae) **2.** (*radio*) aerial.
anteporre *vt.* to place before, to put (*v. irr.*) before.
anteprima *sf.* preview.
anteriore *agg.* **1.** (*nello spazio*) fore **2.** (*nel tempo*) previous, former.
antiabbaglianti *sm. pl.* anti-dazzle.
antiaèreo *agg.* anti-aircraft.
antibattèrico *agg. e sm.* antibacterial.
antibiòtico *agg. e sm.* antibiotic.
anticaglia *sf.* worthless antique.
anticamente *avv.* in ancient times.
anticàmera *sf.* ante-room ‖ *fare* —,

to be kept waiting.
anticarro *agg.* anti-tank.
antichità *sf.* 1. antiquity 2. (*oggetti antichi*) antiques (*pl.*).
anticipare *vt.* 1. to anticipate 2. (*di danaro*) to pay in advance.
anticipatamente *avv.* in advance.
anticipato *agg.* 1. advanced 2. (*comm.*) in advance.
anticipazione *sf.* anticipation.
anticipo *sm.* advance: *essere in* —, to be before time 2. (*caparra*) earnest money.
anticlericale *agg. e s.* anticlerical.
anticlericalismo *sm.* anticlericalism.
antico *agg.* 1. ancient 2. (*all'antica*) old-fashioned.
anticonformista *s.* nonconformist.
anticongelante *sm.* anti-freeze.
anticorpo *sm.* antibody.
anticostituzionale *agg.* anticonstitutional.
antidatare *vt.* to antedate.
antidiluviano *agg. e sm.* antediluvian.
antidoto *sm.* antidote.
antiestetico *agg.* antiaesthetic.
antifascismo *sm.* antifascism.
antifascista *s. e agg.* antifascist.
antifebbrile *sm.* febrifuge.
antifecondativo *sm.* anti-conceptive.
antifona *sf.* antiphon: *capire l'*— to take (*v. irr.*) a hint.
antifurto *sm.* antitheft device.
antigas *agg.* anti-gas: *maschera* —, gas-mask.
antigienico *agg.* unhealthy.
antilope *sf.* antelope.
antimilitarismo *sm.* antimilitarism.
antincendio *agg.* antifire: *pompa* —, fire-pump.
antinebbia *agg. faro* —, fog-light.
antinevralgico *agg.* antineuralgic.
antinomia *sf.* antinomy.
antiparticella *sf.* antiparticle.
antipasto *sm.* hors-d'oeuvre.
antipatia *sf.* dislike.
antipatico *agg.* disagreeable.
antipodi *sm. pl.* antipodes.
antiquariato *sm.* antique-dealing.
antiquario *sm.* antique-dealer.
antiquato *agg.* old-fashioned.
antireumatico *agg.* antirheumatic.
antiruggine *agg.* anti-rust.
antisemitismo *sm.* anti-Semitism.
antisettico *agg. e sm.* antiseptic.
antispastico *agg.* antispasmodic.

antistante *agg.* before, in front of.
antitesi *sf.* antithesis (*pl.* -ses).
antitetanico *agg.* antitetanic.
antitetico *agg.* antithetic(al).
antitossico *agg.* antitoxic.
antivigilia *sf.* the day before the eve.
antologia *sf.* anthology.
antologico *agg.* anthological.
antonomasia *sf.* antonomasia || *per* —, antonomastically.
antracite *sf.* anthracite.
antro *sm.* 1. cave 2. (*tana*) den.
antropocentrismo *sm.* anthropocentrism.
antropofagia *sf.* anthropophagy.
antropofago *agg.* anthropophagous.
♦ **antropofago** *sm.* cannibal.
antropologia *sf.* anthropology.
antropologo *sm.* anthropologist.
antropomorfo *agg.* anthropomorphous.
anulare *agg.* annular. ♦ **anulare** *sm.* ring-finger.
anzi *cong.* 1. (*al contrario*) on the contrary 2. (*in più*) moreover || — *che*, rather than; — *che no*, rather.
♦ **anzi** *avv.* before: — *tempo*, before time.
anzianità *sf.* seniority.
anziano *agg.* 1. elderly 2. (*in cariche, uffici ecc.*) senior.
anziché *cong.* 1. rather than 2. (*invece di*) instead of.
anzidetto *agg.* above-mentioned.
anzitempo *avv.* before time.
aorta *sf.* aorta.
apartitico *agg.* non-sectarian.
apatia *sf.* apathy, indifference.
apatico *agg.* listless.
ape *sf.* bee.
aperitivo *sm.* aperitif.
apertamente *avv.* openly.
aperto *agg.* open.
apertura *sf.* 1. opening 2. (*di mente*) broad-mindedness 3. (*ampiezza di un arco*) span: — *alare*, wingspan.
apice *sm.* apex.
apicoltura *sf.* bee-keeping.
apnea *sf.* apnoea.
apocalisse *sf.* apocalypse.
apocalittico *agg.* apocalyptic(al).
apocrifo *agg.* apocryphal || *libri apocrifi*, Apocrypha.
apofisi *sf.* apophysis.
apogeo *sm.* apogee.
apolide *agg.* stateless. ♦ **apolide** *sm.* stateless person.

apolìtico *agg.* non-political.
apologìa *sf.* apologia.
apologista *s.* apologist.
apòlogo *sm.* apologue.
apoplessìa *sf.* apoplexy.
apoplèttico *agg.* apoplectic: *colpo* —, apoplectic fit.
apostasìa *sf.* apostasy.
apòstata *sm.* apostate.
apòstolo *sm.* apostle.
apostrofare *vt.* to apostrophize.
apòstrofe *sf.* apostrophe.
apòstrofo *sm.* apostrophe.
apoteosi *sf.* apotheosis.
appagare *vt.* 1. to satisfy, to gratify 2. (*la sete*) to quench one's thirst.
appaiare *vt.* 1. to couple 2. (*armonizzare colori, vestiario ecc.*) to match.
appallottolare *vt.* to roll into a ball.
appaltare *vt.* to give (*v. irr.*) out by contract.
appaltatore *sm.* contractor.
appalto *sm.* contract, bid.
appannaggio *sm.* apanage.
appannamento *sm.* 1. (*di metalli*) tarnishing 2. (*di vetri ecc.*) clouding 3. (*di vista*) dimming.
appannare *vt.* 1. (*di metalli*) to tarnish 2. (*di vetri ecc.*) to cloud 3. (*di vista*) to dim.
apparato *sm.* 1. apparatus 2. (*mostra*) display.
apparecchiare *vt.* to prepare: — *la tavola*, to lay (*v. irr.*) the table.
apparecchio *sm.* 1. set 2. (*aereoplano*) aeroplane || — *fotografico*, camera; — *telefonico*, telephone; — *radio*, radio set.
apparentare *vt.* to relate.
apparente *agg.* 1. (*illusorio*) seeming 2. (*chiaro*) apparent, obvious.
apparentemente *avv.* seemingly.
apparenza *sf.* 1. appearance 2. (*aspetto*) look 3. (*pompa*) show.
apparire *vi.* 1. to appear 2. (*aver l'aspetto*) to look 3. (*risultare*) to result.
appariscente *agg.* 1. striking 2. (*vistoso*) showy.
apparizione *sf.* apparition.
appartamento *sm.* flat.
appartarsi *vr.* to retire.
appartenenza *sf.* belonging.
appartenere *vi.* 1. to belong (to) 2. (*essere membro*) to be a member (of).

appassionare *vt.* to impassion. ◆ appassionarsi *vr.* to become (*v. irr.*) fond of.
appassionato *agg.* 1. passionate 2. (*di musica, arte ecc.*) keen (on).
appassire *vi.* to wither.
appellare *vt.* to name, to call. ◆ appellarsi *vr.* to appeal.
appellativo *sm.* appellative.
appello *sm.* 1. (*giur.*) appeal 2. (*chiamata*) call 3. (*esortazione*) appeal.
appena *avv.* 1. (*a fatica*) hardly 2. (*molto poco*) very little 3. (*da poco*) just: *ero* — *arrivato*, I had just arrived || *non* —, as soon as.
appèndere *vt.* to hang (*v. irr.*).
appendice *sf.* appendix || *romanzo d'*—, serial.
appendicite *sf.* appendicitis.
appesantire *vt.* to make (*v. irr.*) heavy. ◆ appesantirsi *vr.* to grow (*v. irr.*) heavy.
appestare *vt.* 1. to infect 2. (*spargere odore*) to stink (*v. irr.*).
appestato *agg.* 1. plague-stricken 2. (*fig.*) tainted. ◆ appestato *sm.* plague-stricken person.
appetenza *sf.* 1. appetite 2. (*desiderio*) longing (for sthg.).
appetibile *agg.* pleasing.
appetire *vt.* to desire.
appetito *sm.* appetite.
appezzamento *sm.* plot of land.
appianare *vt.* 1. to level 2. (*fig.*) to smooth.
appiattarsi *vr.* 1. to crouch 2. (*stare in agguato*) to lie (*v. irr.*) in wait 3. (*nascondersi*) to hide (*v. irr.*).
appiattire *vt.* to flatten.
appiccare *vt.* (*il fuoco*) to set (*v. irr.*) fire.
appiccicare *vt.* 1. to stick (*v. irr.*) 2. (*appioppare*) to palm off.
appiccicoso *agg.* sticky.
appiè *prep.* 1. (*al di sotto*) below 2. (*ai piedi*) at the foot: — *del letto*, at the foot of the bed.
appiedare *vt.* to dismount.
appiedato *agg.* dismounted.
appieno *avv.* fully.
appigliarsi *vr.* to get (*v. irr.*) hold of: — *ad un pretesto*, to take (*v. irr.*) a pretext.
appiglio *sm.* 1. support 2. (*fig.*) pretext.
appiombo *sm.* perpendicularity.
appioppare *vt.* 1. to give (*v. irr.*)

‖ — *uno schiaffo*, to slap **2.** (*affibbiare*) to palm off.

appisolarsi *vr.* to doze off.

applaudire *vt.* e *vi.* to applaud.

applauditore *sm.* applauder.

applàuso *sm.* **1.** applause (*solo sing.*) **2.** (*fig.*) praise.

applicare *vt.* **1.** to apply **2.** (*giur.*) to carry out **3.** (*accostare*) to set (*v. irr.*). ♦ **applicarsi** *vr.* to apply oneself.

applicazione *sf.* **1.** application **2.** (*fig.*) care **3.** (*guarnizione*) trimming.

appoggiare *vt.* **1.** to lean (*v. irr.*) **2.** (*posare*) to lay (*v. irr.*) **3.** (*fig.*) to back. ♦ **appoggiarsi** *vr.* **1.** to lean (*v. irr.*) **2.** (*fig.*) to rely (on).

appoggio *sm.* **1.** support **2.** (*fig.*) assistance **3.** (*colui che dà —*) supporter.

appollaiarsi *vr.* to perch.

apporre *vt.* to affix.

apportare *vt.* **1.** to bring (*v. irr.*) **2.** (*produrre*) to produce.

apporto *sm.* contribution.

appositamente *avv.* on purpose.

appòsito *agg.* **1.** special **2.** (*adatto*) fit.

apposizione *sf.* **1.** (*gramm.*) apposition **2.** (*l'apporre*) affixing.

apposta *avv.* expressly.

appostare *vt.* (*mil.*) to place. ♦ **appostarsi** *vr.* to lie (*v. irr.*) in ambush.

apprèndere *vt.* to learn (*v. irr.*).

apprendista *sm.* apprentice.

apprendistato *sm.* apprenticeship.

apprensione *sf.* **1.** concern **2.** (*l'apprendere*) learning.

appresso *avv.* near, close by. ♦ **appresso** *prep.* near, close to.

apprestamento *sm.* preparation.

apprestare *vt.* to prepare.

apprettare *vt.* to dress.

apprezzàbile *agg.* appreciable.

apprezzamento *sm.* **1.** appreciation **2.** (*giudizio*) opinion.

apprezzare *vt.* **1.** to appreciate **2.** (*valutare*) to value.

approdare *vi.* **1.** to land **2.** (*fig.*) to be of use.

approfittare *vi.* to profit (by). ♦ **approfittarsi** *vr.* **1.** to avail oneself **2.** (*abusare*) to take (*v. irr.*) undue advantage.

approfondire *vt.* **1.** to make (*v. irr.*) deeper **2.** (*fig.*) to examine

closely.

approntare *vt.* to make (*v. irr.*) ready.

appropriarsi *vr.* to take (*v. irr.*) possession of.

appropriato *agg.* fit, suitable.

appropriazione *sf.* appropriation: — *indebita*, embezzlement.

approssimarsi *vr.* **1.** to come (*v. irr.*) near **2.** (*di tempo*) to draw (*v. irr.*) near.

approssimativamente *avv.* approximately.

approssimativo *agg.* approximative.

approssimazione *sf.* approximation.

approvare *vt.* **1.** to approve (of) **2.** (*promuovere*) to pass.

approvazione *sf.* approval.

approvvigionamento *sm.* **1.** (*l'approvvigionare*) supplying **2.** (*provviste*) supplies.

approvvigionare *vt.* to supply provisions (to).

appuntamento *sm.* appointment.

appuntare *vt.* **1.** to sharpen **2.** (*prender nota*) to note **3.** (*biasimare*) to blame.

appuntellare *vt.* **1.** to prop **2.** (*fig.*) to support.

appuntino *avv.* nicely.

appuntito *agg.* pointed.

appunto[1] *sm.* **1.** note **2.** (*critica*) blame.

appunto[2] *avv.* exactly, just.

appurare *vt.* to verify.

apribottiglie *sm.* bottle-opener.

aprile *sm.* April: *pesce d'—*, April fool.

aprire *vt.* to open: — *le braccia a qc.*, to welcome so.

apriscàtole *sm.* tin-opener.

àquila *sf.* eagle.

aquilino *agg.* aquiline.

aquilone *sm.* **1.** (*vento del nord*) north wind **2.** (*giocattolo*) kite.

aquilotto *sm.* eaglet.

arabescare *vt.* to decorate with arabesques.

arabesco *sm.* arabesque.

aràbico *agg.* Arabic.

aràbile *agg.* arable.

àrabo *agg.* e *sm.* Arab.

aràchide *sf.* peanut.

aragosta *sf.* lobster.

aràldico *agg.* heraldic

araldo *sm.* herald.

arancia *sf.* orange.

aranciata *sf.* orange squash.
aranciera *sf.* orangery.
arancio *agg.* (*colore*) orange. ♦
arancio *sm.* orange-tree.
arancione *agg.* orange-coloured.
arare *vt.* to plough.
aratore *sm.* ploughman (*pl.* -men).
aratro *sm.* plough.
aratura *sf.* ploughing.
arazzo *sm.* arras.
arbitraggio *sm.* **1.** (*sport*) umpirage **2.** (*comm.*) arbitrage.
arbitrare *vt.* **1.** to arbitrate **2.** (*calcio, boxe*) to referee.
arbitrario *agg.* arbitrary.
arbitrio *sm.* **1.** will: *libero* —, free will **1.** (*atto arbitrario*) arbitrary act.
àrbitro *sm.* **1.** (*sport*) umpire **2.** (*calcio, boxe*) referee **3.** (*giur.*) arbitrator.
arboricoltore *sm.* arboriculturist.
arboricoltura *sf.* arboriculture.
arboscello *sm.* shrub.
arbusto *sm.* shrub.
arca *sf.* ark || — *di scienza*, eminent scholar.
arcàdico *agg.* e *sm.* Arcadian.
arcàico *agg.* **1.** archaic **2.** (*di parole, stile*) obsolete.
arcaismo *sm.* **1.** archaism **2.** (*parola arcaica*) obsolete word.
arcàngelo *sm.* archangel.
arcano *agg.* mysterious.
archeologìa *sf.* archaeology.
archeològico *agg.* archaeologic(al).
archeòlogo *sm.* archaeologist.
archètipo *sm.* archetype.
archetto *sm.* **1.** small arch **2.** (*mus.*) bow.
architettare *vt.* **1.** to draw (*v. irr.*) the plans **2.** (*fig.*) to devise.
architetto *sm.* architect.
architettònico *agg.* architectonic.
architettura *sf.* architecture.
architrave *sm.* architrave.
archiviare *vt.* **1.** to place in the archives **2.** (*comm.*) to file.
archivio *sm.* **1.** archives (*pl.*) **2.** (*comm.*) file.
archivista *sm.* archivist.
arciduca *sm.* archduke.
arciere *sm.* archer.
arcigno *agg.* gruff.
arcimiliardario *sm.* multimillionaire.
arcipèlago *sm.* archipelago (*pl.* -goes).
arcivescovado *sm.* archbishopric.

arcivéscovo *sm.* archbishop.
arco *sm.* **1.** (*arma*) bow **2.** (*geom.*) arc **3.** (*arch.*) arch **4.** (*mus.*) bow.
arcobaleno *sm.* rainbow.
arcolaio *sm.* wool-winder.
arcuare *vt.* **1.** to arch **2.** (*piegare*) to bend (*v. irr.*).
ardente *agg.* **1.** burning **2.** (*fig.*) passionate.
ardentemente *avv.* ardently.
àrdere *vt.* to burn (*v. irr.*).
ardesia *sf.* slate.
ardire *vi.* **1.** to dare **2.** (*avere l'impudenza*) to have the impudence.
ardito *agg.* **1.** bold **2.** (*rischioso*) risky.
ardore *sm.* **1.** fierce heat **2.** (*fig.*) passion.
àrduo *agg.* **1.** hard **2.** (*erto*) steep.
àrea *sf.* **1.** area **2.** (*sfera d'azione*) sphere.
arena *sf.* **1.** (*sabbia*) sand **2.** (*arch.*) arena.
arenarsi *vr.* to get (*v. irr.*) stranded (*anche fig.*).
arengario *sm.* tribune.
areòpago *sm.* Areopagus.
àrgano *sm.* **1.** (*mar.*) capstan **2.** (*mecc.*) windlass.
argentare *vt.* to silver.
argènteo *agg.* silvery.
argenterìa *sf.* silver ware.
argentino *agg.* silvery.
argento *sm.* silver.
argilla *sf.* clay.
argilloso *agg.* clayey.
arginare *vt.* **1.** to dam **2.** (*fig.*) to check.
àrgine *sm.* bank.
argomentare *vt.* to infer. ♦ **argomentare** *vi.* to argue.
argomentazione *sf.* reasoning.
argomento *sm.* **1.** subject **2.** (*prova a sostegno*) argument.
arguire *vt.* to deduce.
argutezza *sf.* shrewdness.
arguto *agg.* **1.** sharp **2.** (*faceto*) witty.
arguzia *sf.* wit.
aria *sf.* **1.** air: — *condizionata*, air conditioning || *corrente d'*—, draught || *camera d'*—, inner tube || *andare all'*—, to fall (*v. irr.*) through **2.** (*aspetto*) look **3.** (*mus.*) tune.
ariano *agg.* e *sm.* Aryan.
aridità *sf.* **1.** aridity **2.** (*di cuore*) lack of feeling.
àrido *agg.* **1.** arid **2.** (*di cuore*)

lacking feeling.
arieggiare *vt.* **1.** to air **2.** (*rassomigliare*) to look like **3.** (*imitare*) to imitate.
arieggiato *agg.* aired.
ariete *sm.* ram.
aringa *sf.* herring.
arioso *agg.* airy.
aristocràtico *agg.* aristocratic. ♦ **aristocràtico** *sm.* aristocrat.
aristocrazìa *sf.* aristocracy.
aristotèlico *agg. e sm.* Aristotelian.
aritmètica *sf.* arithmetic.
aritmètico *agg.* arithmetic(al).
arlecchinata *sf.* harlequinade.
arlecchino *sm.* harlequin.
arma *sf.* weapon, arm: *armi bianche*, side-arms; *armi da fuoco*, fire-arms || *galleria d'armi*, armoury.
armadietto *sm.* **1.** (*per medicinali, strumenti ecc.*) cabinet **2.** (*per abiti*) locker.
armadio *sm.* **1.** (*per stoviglie*) cupboard **2.** (*per abiti*) wardrobe.
armaiolo *sm.* armourer.
armamentario *sm.* **1.** instruments (*pl.*) **2.** (*armeria*) armoury.
armamento *sm.* arming.
armare *vt.* to arm.
armata *sf.* army.
armatore *sm.* **1.** shipbuilder **2.** (*chi possiede una nave*) shipowner.
armatura *sf.* **1.** armour **2.** (*impalcatura*) scaffolding.
armeggiare *vi.* **1.** to handle arms **2.** (*darsi da fare*) to busy oneself **3.** (*tramare*) to manoeuvre.
armeggìo *sm.* **1.** handling of arms **2.** (*l'affaccendarsi*) bustling **3.** (*intrigo*) manoeuvre.
armento *sm.* herd.
armerìa *sf.* armoury.
armiere *sm.* gunsmith.
armistizio *sm.* armistice.
armonìa *sf.* harmony.
armònica *sf.* (*a bocca*) mouth-organ.
armònico *agg.* harmonic.
armonio *sm.* harmonium.
armonioso *agg.* harmonious.
armonista *s.* harmonist.
armonizzare *vt.* to harmonize. ♦ **armonizzare** *vi.* **1.** to harmonize **2.** (*di colori*) to match.
arnese *sm.* **1.** (*strumento*) tool **2.** (*aggeggio*) gadget.
arnia *sf.* beehive.
aroma *sm.* flavour.
aromàtico *agg.* aromatic.

aromatizzare *vt.* to flavour.
arpa *sf.* harp.
arpeggiare *vi.* to play the harp.
arpeggio *sm.* arpeggio.
arpista *s.* harpist.
arra *sf.* earnest.
arrabattarsi *vr.* to bestir oneself.
arrabbiare *vi.* **1.** to become (*v. irr.*) angry **2.** (*di cane*) to be affected with rabies. ♦ **arrabbiarsi** *vr.* to get (*v. irr.*) angry.
arrabbiato *agg.* **1.** angry **2.** (*di cane*) rabid.
arrabbiatura *sf.* rage.
arraffare *vt.* to grasp.
arrampicarsi *vr.* to climb.
arrampicata *sf.* climb.
arrampicatore *sm.* **1.** mountain climber **2.** (*fig.*) social climber.
arrancare *vi.* **1.** to plod along **2.** (*zoppicare*) to limp **3.** (*affaticarsi*) to get (*v. irr.*) tired.
arrangiamento *sm.* arrangement.
arrangiare *vt.* to arrange. ♦ **arrangiarsi** *vr.* to manage.
arrecare *vt.* **1.** to bring (*v. irr.*) **2.** (*causare*) to cause.
arredamento *sm.* furnishing.
arredare *vt.* to furnish.
arredatore *sm.* internal decorator.
arredo *sm.* piece of furniture.
arrèndersi *vr.* **1.** to surrender **2.** (*fig.*) to give (*v. irr.*) it up.
arrendévole *agg.* **1.** pliant **2.** (*fig.*) docile.
arrestare *vt.* **1.** to stop **2.** (*trarre in arresto*) to arrest. ♦ **arrestarsi** *vr.* to stop.
arresto *sm.* arrest.
arretrare *vt.* **1.** to pull back **2.** (*ritirare*) to withdraw (*v. irr.*).
arretrato *agg.* backward.
arricchimento *sm.* enrichment.
arricchire *vt.* to enrich. ♦ **arricchirsi** *vr.* to grow (*v. irr.*) rich.
arricciare *vt.* to curl: — *il naso*, to turn up one's nose.
arrìdere *vi.* to be favourable.
arringare *vt.* to harangue.
arringatore *sm.* haranguer.
arrischiare *vt.* to risk. ♦ **arrischiarsi** *vr.* to venture.
arrivare *vi.* **1.** to arrive (at), (in) **2.** (*fig.*) to attain.
arrivato *agg.* (*fig.*) successful.
arrivederci *inter.* goodbye.
arrivismo *sm.* social climbing.
arrivista *sm.* social climber.
arrivo *sm.* arrival.

arrogante *agg.* arrogant.
arroganza *sf.* arrogance.
arrogarsi *vr.* to arrogate to one-self.
arrossire *vi.* to blush.
arrostire *vt.* 1. to roast 2. (*di pane*) to toast.
arrosto *sm.* roast.
arrotare *vt.* to grind (*v. irr.*): — *i denti*, to grind one's teeth.
arrotino *sm.* knife-grinder.
arrotolare *vt.* to roll up.
arrotondare *vt.* 1. to round 2. (*di cifre*) to make (*v. irr.*) a round figure.
arrovellarsi *vr.* to worry.
arroventare *vt.* to make (*v. irr.*) red-hot.
arruffare *vt.* to ruffle.
arruffone *sm.* muddler
arrugginire *vi.* to rust.
arruolare *vt.* to enrol.
arsenale *sm.* 1. (*cantiere*) ship-yard 2. (*deposito di armi*) arsenal.
arsènico *sm.* arsenic.
arsura *sf.* 1. (*siccità*) drought 2. (*sete*) parching thirst.
arte *sf.* art || *belle arti*, fine arts.
artefatto *agg.* adulterated.
artéfice *sm.* maker.
arteria *sf.* 1. artery 2. (*di traffico*) thoroughfare.
arteriosclerosi *sf.* arteriosclerosis.
artesiano *agg.* artesian.
àrtico *agg.* arctic.
articolare *vt.* to articulate.
articolazione *sf.* articulation.
artìcolo *sm.* 1. (*gramm.; di giornale*) article || — *di fondo*, editorial 2. (*comm.*) item.
artificiale *agg.* artificial.
artificio *sm.* 1. device 2. ` (*astuzia*) cunning.
artigianato *sm.* handicraft.
artigiano *sm.* craftsman (*pl.* -men).
artigliere *sm.* gunner.
artiglierìa *sf.* artillery.
artiglio *sm.* claw.
artista *sm.* artist.
artìstico *agg.* artistic(al).
arto *sm.* limb: — *artificiale*, artificial limb.
artrite *sf.* arthritis (*pl.* -ides).
artrosi *sf.* arthrosis.
arzigògolo *sm.* subtlety.
arzillo *agg.* lively, brisk.
ascella *sf.* armpit.
ascendente *sm.* 1. ascendancy 2. (*antenato*) ancestor.

ascendenza *sf.* ancestry.
ascéndere *vi.* (*anche fig.*) to rise (*v. irr.*).
ascensione *sf.* 1. ascension 2. (*scalata*) climb.
ascensore *sm.* lift.
ascesa *sf.* ascent.
ascesi *sf.* mystical practice.
ascesso *sm.* abscess.
asceta *sm.* ascetic.
ascètico *agg.* ascetical.
ascetismo *sm.* asceticism.
ascia *sf.* axe.
ascissa *sf.* abscissa (*pl.* -sae).
asciugacapelli *sm.* hair-drier.
asciugamano *sm.* towel.
asciugare *vt.* 1. to dry 2. (*con un panno*) to wipe. ◆ **asciugarsi** *vr.* to dry up.
asciugatoio *sm.* towel.
asciutto *agg.* 1. (*anche fig.*) dry 2. (*magro*) thin.
ascoltare *vt.* 1. to listen (to) 2. (*assistere*) to attend: — *le lezioni*, to attend classes.
ascolto *sm.* listening.
ascrivere *vt.* 1. to count 2. (*attribuire*) to ascribe. ◆ **ascrìversi** *vr.* to claim.
asepsi *sf.* asepsis.
asessuale *agg.* asexual.
asèttico *agg.* aseptic.
asfaltare *vt.* to asphalt.
asfalto *sm.* asphalt.
asfissìa *sf.* 1. asphyxia 2. (*da gas*) gassing.
asfissiare *vt.* 1. to asphyxiate 2. (*con gas*) to gas.
asiàtico *agg.* e *sm.* Asiatic.
asilo *sm.* 1. shelter 2. (*scuola materna*) infant-school.
asimmetrìa *sf.* asymmetry.
asimmètrico *agg.* asymmetrical.
asinerìa *sf.* stupidity.
asinità *sf.* asininity.
àsino *sm.* 1. ass 2. (*fig.*) jackass.
asma *sf.* asthma.
asmàtico *agg.* asthmatical.
asociale *agg.* asocial.
àsola *sf.* buttonhole.
aspàrago *sm.* asparagus.
aspèrgere *vt.* to sprinkle.
asperità *sf.* 1. asperity 2. (*di superfici*) unevenness 3. (*di carattere*) harshness.
aspersorio *sm.* aspergillum.
aspettare *vt.* to wait (for). ◆ **aspettarsi** *vr.* to expect.
aspettativa *sf.* 1. expectation 2.

(*esonero temporaneo*) temporary retirement.

aspetto *sm.* look || *di bell'aspetto*, good-looking || *sala d'—*, waiting-room.

àspide *sm.* asp.

aspirante *agg.* aspirant. ♦ **aspirante** *sm.* candidate, applicant.

aspirapòlvere *sm.* vacuum cleaner, hoover.

aspirare *vt.* to inspire. ♦ **aspirare** *vi.* to aspire (to).

aspiratore *sm.* aspirator.

aspirazione *sf.* 1. aspiration 2. (*mecc.*) suction.

aspirina *sf.* aspirin.

asportare *vt.* 1. to remove 2. (*med.*) to extirpate.

asportazione *sf.* 1. removal 2. (*med.*) extirpation.

asprezza *sf.* 1. sourness 2. (*fig.*) harshness.

asprigno *agg.* sourish.

aspro *agg.* 1. sour 2. (*fig.*) harsh.

assaggiare *vt.* to taste.

assaggio *sm.* 1. tasting 2. (*campione*) sample.

assai *avv.* 1. (*con agg. e avv.*) very 2. (*con comp.*) much: — *meglio*, much better.

assalire *vt.* 1. to assail 2. (*di malattia*) to attack.

assalitore *sm.* assailer.

assaltare *vt.* to assault.

assalto *sm.* assault, attack.

assaporare *vt.* 1. to savour 2. (*fig.*) to enjoy.

assassinare *vt.* to murder.

assassinio *sm.* murder.

assassino *sm.* murderer.

asse *sf.* 1. (*tavola di legno*) board 2. (*geom.*) axis (*pl.* axes) 3. (*stor.*) Axis.

assecondare *vt.* to favour.

assediare *vt.* to besiege.

assedio *sm.* siege.

assegnamento *sm.* assignment || *fare — su qualcuno*, to rely on so.

assegnare *vt.* 1. to assign 2. (*un premio*) to award.

assegno *sm.* cheque: — *al portatore*, cheque to bearer; — *circolare*, banker's draft; — *sbarrato*, crossed cheque.

assemblea *sf.* 1. meeting 2. (*corpo deliberante*) assembly.

assembramento *sm.* concourse of people.

assembrarsi *vr.* to assemble.

assennatezza *sf.* common sense.

assennato *agg.* sensible.

assenso *sm.* assent.

assentarsi *vr.* to go (*v. irr.*) away.

assente *agg.* absent.

assenteismo *sm.* absenteeism.

assentire *vi.* 1. to assent (to) 2. (*col capo*) to nod (in assent).

assenza *sf.* absence.

assenzio *sm.* absinth.

asserire *vt.* to affirm.

asserragliarsi *vr.* to barricade oneself.

asserto *sm.* assertion.

assertore *sm.* 1. assertor 2. (*difensore*) defender, champion.

asservimento *sm.* enslavement.

asservire *vt.* to enslave, to subdue.

asserzione *sf.* statement.

assessorato *sm.* assessorship.

assessore *sm.* 1. (*alle imposte*) assessor 2. (*comunale*) councillor responsible for a municipal region.

assestamento *sm.* 1. adjustment 2. (*definitivo*) settlement 3. (*del terreno*) settling.

assestare *vt.* to arrange: — *un colpo*, to deal (*v. irr.*) a blow. ♦ **assestarsi** *vr.* to settle (down).

assetato *agg.* 1. thirsty 2. (*fig.*) eager (for).

assetto *sm.* order.

assicurare *vt.* 1. (*legare*) to fasten 2. (*promettere*) to assure 3. (*affermare*) to affirm 4. (*comm.*) to insure.

assicurata *sf.* registered letter.

assicurato *agg.* insured, assured. ♦ **assicurato** *sm.* insurant.

assicuratore *sm.* insurer.

assicurazione *sf.* 1. assurance 2. (*comm.*) insurance.

assideramento *sm.* frost-bite.

assiduità *sf.* assiduity.

assiduo *agg.* assiduous.

assieme *avv.* V. *insieme*.

assieparsi *vr.* to crowd (round).

assillante *agg.* urging.

assillare *vt.* to urge.

assillo *sm.* 1. urge 2. (*fig.*) worry.

assimilàbile *agg.* assimilable.

assimilare *vt.* to assimilate, to absorb.

assimilazione *sf.* assimilation.

assioma *sm.* axiom.

assiomàtico *agg.* axiomatic.

assise *sf. pl.* assizes.

assistente *sm.* assistant.

assistenza *sf.* assistance.

assistenziale *agg.* charitable.
assìstere *vt.* **1.** to assist **2.** (*curare*) to nurse. ♦ **assìstere** *vi.* to attend (sthg.).
assito *sm.* **1.** wooden partition **2.** (*pavimento*) plank floor.
asso *sm.* **1.** (*carte*) ace **2.** (*sport*) champion || *piantare in —*, to leave (*v. irr.*) in the lurch.
associare *vt.* to join. ♦ **associarsi** *vr.* to associate.
associato *sm.* member.
associazione *sf.* association.
assodare *vt.* **1.** to consolidate **2.** (*accertare*) to ascertain.
assoggettare *vt.* to subject. ♦ **assoggettarsi** *vr.* to submit oneself.
assolato *agg.* sunny.
assoldare *vt.* to recruit.
assolo *sm.* (*mus.*) solo.
assolutamente *avv.* absolutely.
assolutismo *sm.* absolutism.
assolutista *agg. e sm.* absolutist.
assoluto *agg. e sm.* absolute.
assoluzione *sf.* **1.** (*eccl.*) absolution **2.** (*giur.*) discharge.
assòlvere *vt.* **1.** (*teol.*) to absolve **2.** (*giur.*) to discharge **3.** (*eseguire*) to accomplish.
assomigliante *agg.* like.
assomigliare *vi.* to look like.
assommare *vt. e vi.* to add, to amount (to).
assonanza *sf.* assonance.
assonnarsi *vr.* to fall (*v. irr.*) asleep.
assonnato *agg.* sleepy.
assopimento *sm.* dozing.
assopire *vt.* to make (*v. irr.*) dozy. ♦ **assopirsi** *vr.* to doze off.
assorbente *agg.* absorbing || *carta —*, blotting-paper.
assorbimento *sm.* absorption.
assorbire *vt.* to absorb.
assordante *agg.* deafening.
assordare *vt.* to deafen.
assortimento *sm.* assortment.
assortire *vt.* **1.** to stock **2.** (*fig.*) to match.
assorto *agg.* absorbed.
assottigliamento *sm.* **1.** thinning **2.** (*riduzione*) reduction.
assottigliare *vt.* **1.** to thin **2.** (*diminuire*) to reduce. ♦ **assottigliarsi** *vr.* to grow (*v. irr.*) thin.
assuefare *vt.* to accustom. ♦ **assuefarsi** *vr.* to accustom oneself.
assuefazione *sf.* custom.
assùmere *vt.* **1.** to assume **2.** (*in*

servizio) to employ **3.** (*informazioni*) to make (*v. irr.*) inquiries.
assunzione *sf.* **1.** (*ascesa*) accession **2.** (*impiego*) engagement **3.** (*teol.*) Assumption.
assurdamente *avv.* absurdly.
assurdità *sf.* absurdity.
assurdo *agg.* absurd. ♦ **assurdo** *sm.* absurdity.
assùrgere *vi.* to rise (*v. irr.*).
asta *sf.* **1.** pole **2.** (*di bandiera*) flagstaff **3.** (*di occhiali*) bar **4.** (*di bilancia*) arm (of balance) **5.** (*vendita all'asta*) auction(-sale).
astante *agg.* present. ♦ **astante** *sm.* on-looker.
astemio *agg.* abstemious. ♦ **astemio** *sm.* teetotaller.
astenersi *vr.* to abstain.
astenìa *sf.* asthenia.
astensione *sf.* abstention.
astensionista *sm.* abstentionist.
asterisco *sm.* asterisk.
asteròide *sm.* asteroid.
asticciola *sf.* pothook.
astigmàtico *agg.* astigmatic.
astigmatismo *sm.* astigmatism.
astinenza *sf.* abstinence.
astio *sm.* resentment.
astiosamente *avv.* resentfully.
astioso *agg.* resentful.
astracàn *sm.* astrakhan.
astràgalo *sm.* **1.** (*bot.*) astragalus (*pl.* -li) **2.** (*arch.*) astragal.
astrale *agg.* astral.
astrarre *vt.* to abstract. ♦ **astrarsi** *vr.* to think (*v. irr.*) about sthg. else.
astrattismo *sm.* (*arte*) abstractionism.
astratto *agg.* abstract.
astrazione *sf.* abstraction.
astringente *agg. e sm.* astringent.
astro *sm.* star.
astrolabio *sm.* astrolabe.
astrologìa *sf.* astrology.
astròlogo *sm.* astrologer.
astronàuta *sm.* astronaut.
astronave *sf.* space-ship.
astronomìa *sf.* astronomy.
astronòmico *agg.* astronomic(al).
astrònomo *sm.* astronomer.
astrusità *sf.* abstruseness.
astruso *agg.* abstruse.
astuccio *sm.* case, box: *— per occhiali*, spectacle-case.
astuto *agg.* cunning.
astuzia *sf.* **1.** (*qualità*) cunning **2.** (*atto*) trick.

atassìa *sf.* ataxy.
atàvico *agg.* atavic.
atavismo *sm.* atavism.
ateismo *sm.* atheism.
àteo *agg.* atheistic. ♦ àteo *sm.* atheist.
atleta *sm.* athlete.
atlètica *sf.* athletics.
atlètico *agg.* athletic.
atmosfera *sf.* atmosphere.
atollo *sm.* atoll.
atòmico *agg.* atomic.
atomismo *sm.* atomism.
atomìstica *sf.* atomic theory.
atomizzatore *sm.* atomizer.
àtomo *sm. (anche fig.)* atom.
atonìa *sf.* atony.
àtono *agg.* atonic.
atrio *sm.* (entrance-)hall.
atroce *agg.* dreadful.
atrocità *sf.* atrocity.
atrofìa *sf.* atrophy.
atrofizzare *vt.* to atrophy.
atrofizzato *agg.* atrophic.
atropina *sf.* atropine.
attaccabottoni *sm.* buttonholer.
attaccabrighe *sm.* quarrelsome fellow.
attaccamento *sm.* attachment: *avere dell'—*, to entertain an attachment (for).
attaccante *sm.* attacker.
attaccapanni *sm.* cloak-stand.
attaccare *vt.* 1. *(unire)* to attack 2. *(appiccicare)* to stick *(v. irr.)* 3. *(cucire)* to sew *(v. irr.)* 4. *(assalire)* to attack 5. *(mus.)* to open. ♦ attaccarsi *vr.* 1. *(appigliarsi)* to cling *(v. irr.)* 2. *(affezionarsi)* to become *(v. irr.)* fond of.
attaccatura *sf.* junction: — *della manica*, arm-hole.
attacchino *sm.* bill-poster.
attacco *sm.* 1. *(mil.)* attack 2. *(med.)* fit 3. *(mecc.)* connection ‖ — *elettrico*, connecting plug.
attagliarsi *vr.* to suit.
attanagliare *vt.* to pinch.
attardarsi *vr.* to delay.
attecchire *vi.* 1. to take *(v. irr.)* root 2. *(aver fortuna)* to find *(v. irr.)* favour.
atteggiamento *sm.* attitude.
atteggiarsi *vr.* to assume an attitude: — *a vittima*, to pose as a victim.
attempato *agg.* elderly.
attendente *sm.* orderly.

attèndere *vt.* 1. *(aspettare)* to wait for 2. *(aspettarsi)* to expect 3. *(accudire, frequentare)* to attend.
attendìbile *agg.* reliable.
attenere *vi.* to concern. ♦ attenersi *vr.* 1. to cling *(v. irr.)* (on), (to) 2. *(seguire)* to conform.
attentamente *avv.* 1. attentively 2. *(con cura)* carefully.
attentare *vi.* to attempt. ♦ attentarsi *vr.* to dare.
attentato *sm.* attempt (upon).
attenti *sm.* attention: *stare sull'—*, to stand *(v. irr.)* at attention.
attento *agg.* attentive, careful.
attenuante *agg.* extenuating.
attenuare *vt.* 1. to attenuate 2. *(giur.)* to extenuate.
attenuazione *sf.* 1. attenuation 2. *(di colpa)* extenuation.
attenzione *sf.* 1. attention 2. care: *fate* —, take care 3. *(riguardo)* regard.
atterraggio *sm.* landing.
atterrare *vt.* to knock down. ♦ atterrare *vi. (aer.)* to land.
atterrire *vt.* to terrify. ♦ atterrirsi *vr.* to take *(v. irr.)* fright.
attesa *sf.* wait.
attestare *vt.* to attest.
attestato *sm.* 1. certificate 2. *(prova)* proof.
atticciato *agg.* sturdy.
àttico *sm.* attic.
attiguo *agg.* adjoining.
attillarsi *vr.* to spruce oneself up.
attillato *agg.* close-fitting.
àttimo *sm.* moment.
attinente *agg.* pertaining.
attinenza *sf.* relationship.
attingere *vt.* to draw *(v. irr.)*: — *acqua da un pozzo*, to draw water from a well; — *denaro da qu.*, to draw on so. for money.
attirare *vt.* to attract, to draw *(v. irr.) (anche fig.)*.
attitùdine *sf.* turn, disposition.
attivare *vt.* to make *(v. irr.)* active.
attivista *s.* activist.
attività *sf.* 1. activity 2. *(comm.)* profit: — *e passività*, assets and liabilities.
attivizzare *vt.* to make *(v. irr.)* active.
attivo *agg.* active.
attizzare *vt.* to stir up.
attizzatoio *sm.* poker.
atto[1] *sm.* 1. act 2. *(azione)* action 3. *(fatto)* deed: *un — buono, a*

good deed.
atto² *agg.* fit.
attònito *agg.* astonished.
attore *sm.* actor: — *cinematografico*, screen actor.
attorniare *vt.* to surround.
attorno *avv.* e *prep.* about, round, around: *non c'è nessuno* —, there is nobody about; — *alla tavola*, round the table; *le colline* — *al villaggio*, the hills around the village ‖ *darsi d'*—, to busy oneself.
attraccaggio *sm.* mooring.
attraccare *vi.* to moor.
attraente *agg.* charming, attractive.
attrarre *vt.* to attract, to draw (*v. irr.*) (*anche fig.*).
attrattiva *sf.* attraction, appeal.
attraversamento *sm.* crossing.
attraversare *vt.* **1.** to cross **2.** (*ostacolare*) to thwart.
attraverso *avv.* **1.** (*di luogo*) across, through: — *il fiume*, across the river **2.** (*di tempo*) through.
attrazione *sf.* attraction, appeal.
attrezzare *vt.* to equip.
attrezzatura *sf.* equipment.
attrezzista *sm.* (*teat.*) property-man.
attrezzo *sm.* tool.
attribuire *vt.* **1.** to attribute **2.** (*assegnare*) to assign **3.** (*addossare*) to put (on).
attributo *sm.* attribute.
attribuzione *sf.* attribution.
attrice *sf.* actress: — *cinematografica*, screen actress.
attrito *sm.* **1.** friction **2.** (*fig.*) dissension.
attruppamento *sm.* trooping
attrupparsi *vr.* to troop.
attuàbile *agg.* feasible.
attuale *agg.* present.
attualità *sf.* the moment: *cosa d'*—, topical question.
attualmente *avv.* at present.
attuare *vt.* to carry out.
attutire *vt.* to mitigate: — *un rumore*, to deaden a noise.
audace *agg.* bold.
audacia *sf.* boldness.
audiovisivo *agg.* audiovisual.
auditore *sm.* listener.
auditorio *sm.* **1.** auditorium **2.** (*pubblico*) audience.
audizione *sf.* **1.** (*fisiol.*) hearing **2.** (*teat.*) performance.
àuge *sm.* summit: *essere in* —, to enjoy great favour.

augurale *agg.* augural.
augurare *vt.* to wish.
augurio *sm.* wish ‖ *auguri di Natale e Capodanno*, season's greetings.
augusto *agg.* august.
àula *sf.* hall, room: — *di scuola*, school-room.
aumentare *vt.* to increase.
aumento *sm.* increase.
àureo *agg.* **1.** gold **2.** (*dorato*) golden.
aurèola *sf.* halo.
aurìcola *sf.* auricle.
auricolare *agg.* auricular.
aurìfero *agg.* auriferous.
aurora *sf.* dawn (*anche fig.*).
auscultare *vt.* to auscultate.
auscultazione *sf.* auscultation.
ausiliare *agg.* auxiliary.
ausilio *sm.* **1.** help **2.** (*difesa*) defence.
auspicare *vt.* to augur.
auspicio *sm.* **1.** (*stor.*) auspice, omen: *di buon, cattivo* —, of good, ill omen **2.** (*augurio*) wish.
austerità *sf.* austerity.
austero *agg.* austere.
australe *agg.* austral.
australiano *agg.* e *sm.* Australian.
austrìaco *agg.* e *sm.* Austrian.
autarchìa *sf.* autarky.
autenticare *vt.* to certify.
autenticazione *sf.* authentication.
autenticità *sf.* authenticity.
autèntico *agg.* **1.** authentic **2.** (*genuino*) genuine.
autista *sm.* driver: — *di piazza*, taxi-driver.
àuto *sf.* car: — *da corsa*, racing car; — *aperta*, open car; — *di serie*, production-model car; — *fuori serie*, special-body car.
autoambulanza *sf.* ambulance.
auto-attrezzi *sf.* breakdown-lorry.
autobiografìa *sf.* autobiography.
autobiògrafo *sm.* autobiographer.
autoblinda *sf.* armoured car.
autobotte *sf.* tank truck.
àutobus *sm.* (motor-) bus.
autoclave *sf.* autoclave.
autocontrollo *sm.* self-control.
autòcrate *sm.* autocrat.
autocrazìa *sf.* autocracy.
autocrìtica *sf.* self-criticism.
autòctono *agg.* autochthonous. ♦ **autòctono** *sm.* native.
autodafé *sm.* auto-da-fé (*pl.* autos--da-fé).

autodeterminazione *sf.* self-determination.
autodidatta *s.* self-taught person.
autòdromo *sm.* motor-racing track.
autoeducazione *sf.* self-education.
autofinanziamento *sm.* self-financing.
autògeno *agg.* autogenous.
autogoverno *sm.* self-government.
autografare *vt.* to autograph.
autògrafo *agg.* autographic(al). ♦ **autògrafo** *sm.* autograph.
autolesione *sf.* self-injury.
autolesionismo *sm.* self-injuring.
autolettiga *sf.* ambulance.
autolìnea *sf.* bus line.
automa *sm.* automaton, robot.
automàtico *agg.* automatic: *pistola, fucile* —, automatic pistol, gun ‖ *distributore* —, slot machine.
automatismo *sm.* automatism.
automazione *sf.* automation.
automòbile *sf.* V. *auto.*
automobilismo *sm.* motoring.
automobilista *sm.* motorist.
automotrice *sf.* rail-car.
autonoleggio *sm.* car rental.
autonomìa *sf.* autonomy: — *di volo,* flight range.
autonomismo *sm.* self-government.
autònomo *agg.* self-governing.
autoparco *sm.* car-park.
autopilota *sm.* automatic pilot.
autopompa *sf.* fire-engine.
autoposteggio *sm.* parking.
autopsìa *sf.* autopsy.
autoradio *sf.* car radio-set.
autore *sm.* author.
autorespiratore *sm.* aqualung.
autorévole *agg.* authoritative.
autorevolezza *sf.* authoritativeness.
autorimessa *sf.* garage.
autorità *sf.* authority.
autoritario *agg.* authoritative.
autoritratto *sm.* self-portrait.
autorizzare *vt.* 1. (*dare autorità*) to empower 2. (*permettere*) to permit.
autorizzàzione *sf.* permission, consent.
autoscuola *sf.* driving school.
autostazione *sf.* filling station.
autostòp *sm.* hitch-hiking.
autostoppista *sm.* hitch-hiker.
autostrada *sf.* motor-way.
autosuggestione *sf.* auto-suggestion.
autotreno *sm.* motor-lorry.

autrice *sf.* authoress.
autunnale *agg.* autumnal.
autunno *sm.* autumn.
ava *sf.* 1. grandmother 2. (*antenata*) ancestress.
avallare *vt.* to guarantee.
avallo *sm.* guarantee.
avambraccio *sm.* forearm.
avamposto *sm.* outpost.
avanguardia *sf.* vanguard: *essere all'—,* to be in the van.
avannotto *sm.* fry.
avanscoperta *sf.* scouting party: *andare all'—,* to scout.
avanspettàcolo *sm.* introductory variety turn.
avanti *avv.* 1. (*di luogo*) forward: *andare* —, to move forward 2. (*a chi bussa*) « come in » 3. (*di tempo*) before ‖ (*di orologio*) fast: *il mio orologio è avanti di 20 minuti,* my watch is twenty minutes fast. ♦ **avanti** *prep.* before. ♦ **avanti che** *cong.* before (*con ger.*).
avantieri *avv.* the day before yesterday.
avanzamento *sm.* 1. advancing 2. (*progresso*) advancement 3. (*promozione*) promotion.
avanzare *vt.* 1. to advance 2. (*fig.*) to put (*v. irr.*) forward 3. (*promuovere*) to promote. ♦ **avanzare** *vi.* to advance. ♦ **avanzarsi** *vr.* to advance.
avanzata *sf.* advance.
avanzato *agg.* 1. advanced 2. (*promosso*) promoted.
avanzo *sm.* remnant ‖ — *di galera,* jail-bird ‖ — *di stoffa,* scrap of cloth.
avarìa *sf.* damage.
avariato *agg.* damaged.
avarizia *sf.* avarice.
avaro *agg.* avaricious.
avena *sf.* oats (*p*).
avere *vt.* 1. (*general. e come v. ausiliare*) to have: *ho molti libri,* I have many books; *ho letto questo giornale,* I have read this newspaper 2. (*possedere*) to own, to have got: *ha una grande casa,* he owns, has got a big house 3. (*ottenere*) to get (*v. irr.*): *ebbi quell'impiego,* I got that job 4. (*indossare*) to wear (*v. irr.*): *aveva (indosso) un abito rosso,* she was wearing a red dress 5. (*dovere*) to have to: *ho molte cose da fare,*

I have many things to do 6. (*di anni*) to be ... years old: *ho 10 anni*, I am ten years old.

aviatore *sm.* airman (*pl.* -men), pilot.

aviazione *sf.* 1. aviation 2. (*arma*) Air Force.

avicoltura *sf.* bird-rearing.

avidità *sf.* 1. avidity 2. (*ingordigia*) greed 3. (*brama*) eagerness.

àvido *agg.* 1. avid 2. (*ingordo*) greedy 3. (*desideroso*) eager.

aviere *sm.* airman (*pl.* -men).

aviogetto *sm.* jet(-plane).

aviolìnea *sf.* airline.

aviotrasportare *vt.* to air-bear (*v. irr.*).

aviotrasporto *sm.* air-transport.

avitaminosi *sf.* avitaminosis.

avito *agg.* ancestral.

avo *sm.* 1. grandfather 2. (*antenato*) ancestor 3. (*pl.*) forefathers.

avorio *sm.* ivory.

avulso *agg.* uprooted.

avvalersi *vr.* to avail oneself.

avvaloramento *sm.* strengthening.

avvalorare *vt.* 1. to give (*v. irr.*) value to 2. (*rafforzare*) to strengthen.

avvampare *vi.* to flare up (*anche fig.*).

avvantaggiare *vt.* to advantage, to better. ♦ **avvantaggiarsi** *vr.* to profit (by).

avvedersi *vr.* to perceive.

avvedutamente *avv.* shrewdly.

avvedutezza *sf.* shrewdness.

avveduto *agg.* shrewd.

avvelenamento *sm.* poisoning.

avvelenare *vt.* to poison.

avvelenatore *sm.* poisoner.

avvenente *agg.* charming, pretty.

avvenenza *sf.* charm, loveliness.

avvenimento *sm.* event.

avvenire[1] *vi. imp.* to happen.

avvenire[2] *sm.* future.

avventarsi *vr.* to throw (*v. irr.*) oneself.

avventatamente *avv.* rashly.

avventatezza *sf.* rashness.

avventato *agg.* rash.

avventizio *agg.* 1. temporary 2. (*giur.*) adventitious.

avvento *sm.* 1. (*eccl.*) Advent 2. arrival 3. (*assunzione al trono*) accession.

avventore *sm.* customer.

avventura *sf.* adventure.

avventurarsi *vr.* to venture.

avventuriero *sm.* adventurer.

avventuroso *agg.* adventurous.

avverarsi *vr.* to come (*v. irr.*) true.

avverbiale *agg.* adverbial.

avverbio *sm.* adverb.

avversare *vt.* to oppose.

avversario *agg.* contrary. ♦ **avversario** *sm.* opponent.

avversione *sf.* aversion, dislike.

avversità *sf.* adversity, misfortune.

avverso *agg.* unfavourable.

avvertenza *sf.* 1. (*avviso*) warning 2. (*attenzione, cura*) attention, care.

avvertìbile *agg.* perceptible.

avvertimento *sm.* warning.

avvertire *vt.* 1. (*avvisare*) to inform 2. (*mettere in guardia*) to warn 3. (*osservare*) to notice.

avvezzare *vt.* to accustom.

avvezzo *agg.* accustomed, used.

avviamento *sm.* starting.

avviare *vt.* to start.

avvicinamento *sm.* approach.

avvicinare *vt.* to approach. ♦ **avvicinarsi** *vr.* 1. to approach 2. (*essere simile*) to be similar.

avvicendare *vt.* to alternate. ♦ **avvicendarsi** *vr.* to alternate.

avvicendamento *sm.* alternation.

avvilente *agg.* 1. discouraging 2. (*umiliante*) humiliating.

avvilimento *sm.* 1. dejection 2. (*umiliazione*) humiliation.

avvilire *vt.* 1. (*scoraggiare*) to dishearten 2. (*umiliare*) to humiliate. ♦ **avvilirsi** *vr.* 1. to lose heart 2. (*umiliarsi*) to abase oneself.

avvilito *agg.* 1. downcast 2. (*umiliato*) humbled.

avviluppare *vt.* 1. to wrap up 2. (*aggrovigliare*) to entangle. ♦ **avvilupparsi** *vr.* 1. to wrap oneself up 2. (*aggrovigliarsi*) to get (*v. irr.*) entangled.

avvinazzarsi *vr.* to get (*v. irr.*) drunk.

avvinazzato *agg.* tipsy.

avvincente *agg.* engaging.

avvincere *vt.* to enthral.

avvinghiarsi *vr.* to cling (*v. irr.*).

avvìo *sm.* start: *prendere l'—*, to start off.

avvisaglia *sf.* (*primo segno*) foreshadowing.

avvisare *vt.* 1. to inform, to let (*v. irr.*) know 2. (*mettere in guardia*) to warn.

avviso *sm.* 1. notice 2. (*consiglio*) warning 3. (*manifesto*) poster 4.

(*opinione*) opinion.
avvistare *vt.* to sight.
avvitamento *sm.* spin.
avvitare *vt.* **1.** (*mecc.*) to screw **2.** (*aer.*) to spin.
avviticchiarsi *vr.* to twist round.
avvocato *sm.* **1.** lawyer **2.** (*civilista*) solicitor.
avvocatura *sf.* legal profession.
avvòlgere *vt.* **1.** to wrap (*anche fig.*) **2.** (*arrotolare*) to roll up.
avvolgimento *sm.* **1.** winding **2.** (*di pacchi*) wrapping up **3.** (*elettr.*) winding.
avvoltoio *sm.* vulture (*anche fig.*).
azalea *sf.* azalea.
azienda *sf.* firm, concern: — *industriale*, manufacturing concern; — *agricola*, farm.
aziendale *agg.* firm, concern.
àzimut *sm.* azimuth.
azimutale *agg.* azimuthal.
azionamento *sm.* working.
azionare *vt.* to set (*v. irr.*) in action, to work.
azionario *agg.* share: *capitale* —, share capital.
azione *sf.* **1.** action **2.** (*comm.*) share.
azionista *s.* shareholder.
azotare *vt.* to azotize.
azoto *sm.* azote.
azteco *agg. e sm.* Aztec.
azzannare *vt.* to seize in the jaws.
azzardare *vt.* to risk, to venture.
azzardo *sm.* hazard || *gioco d'*—, game of chance.
azzeccare *vt.* to guess, to hit (*v. irr.*) the mark.
àzzimo *agg.* unleavened: *pane* —, unleavened bread.
azzoppare *vt.* to lame. ♦ **azzopparsi** *vr.* to become (*v. irr.*) lame.
azzuffarsi *vr.* to come (*v. irr.*) to blows.
azzurro *agg.* blue.
azzurrògnolo *agg.* bluish.

B

babbeo *sm.* blockhead.
babbo *sm.* father, daddy.
babbuccia *sf.* slipper.
babbuino *sm.* baboon.
babele *sf.* babel.
bacare *vi.* **bacarsi** *vr.* to rot.

bacato *agg.* rotten.
bacca *sf.* berry.
baccalà *sm.* stockfish.
baccanale *sm.* bacchanal.
baccano *sm.* uproar.
baccante *sf.* Bacchante.
baccarà *sm.* baccarat.
baccellierato *sm.* bachelorship.
baccelliere *sm.* bachelor.
baccello *sm.* pod.
bacchetta *sf.* **1.** rod **2.** (*di direttore d'orchestra*) baton **3.** (*di tamburo*) drumstick.
bacchettata *sf.* rod stroke.
bacchettone *sm.* bigot.
bacchiare *vt.* to beat (*v. irr.*) down.
bàcchico *agg.* Bacchic.
bacheca *sf.* show-case.
bachelite *sf.* bakelite.
bacherozzo *sm.* **1.** (*scarafaggio*) cockroach **2.** (*bruco*) maggot.
bachicoltura *sf.* silkworm breeding.
baciamano *sm.* hand-kissing.
baciapile *sm.* bigot.
baciare *vt.* to kiss. ♦ **baciarsi** *vr. rec.* to kiss each other.
bacile *sm.* basin.
bacillo *sm.* bacillus (*pl.* -li).
bacinella *sf.* basin.
bacino *sm.* **1.** basin **2.** (*anat.*) pelvis **3.** (*mar.*) dock: — *di carenaggio*, dry dock.
bacio *sm.* kiss.
baciucchiare *vt.* to kiss repeatedly.
baco *sm.* worm: — *da seta*, silkworm.
bada *sf.* (*nella loc.*) tenere a — *qu.*, to hold (*v. irr.*) so. at bay.
badare *vi.* to mind (so., sthg.): *senza* — *a spese*, regardless of expense.
badessa *sf.* abbess.
badìa *sf.* abbey.
badilante *sm.* navvy.
badile *sm.* shovel.
baffo *sm.* **1.** moustache: *portare i baffi*, to wear (*v. irr.*) a moustache || *ridere sotto i baffi*, to laugh in one's sleeve **2.** (*sgorbio*) smear.
bagagliaio *sm.* luggage van.
bagaglio *sm.* luggage (*solo sing.*) || *fare i bagagli*, to pack || *disfare i bagagli*, to unpack.
bagarinaggio *sm.* cornering.
bagattella *sf.* trifle.
baggianata *sf.* **1.** (*azione*) foolish action **2.** (*discorso*) nonsense.
bagliore *sm.* flash.

bagnante *sm.* bather.
bagnare *vt.* 1. to wet 2. (*immergere*) to dip 3. (*di mare, fiume*) to wash. ♦ **bagnarsi** *vr.* 1. to get (*v. irr.*) wet 2. (*fare bagni in mare ecc.*) to bathe.
bagnato *agg.* wet.
bagnino *sm.* bathing attendant.
bagno *sm.* 1. bath: *far un —,* to take (*v. irr.*) a bath; *— di sole,* sun-bath 2. (*in mare ecc.*) bathe || *fare il —,* to bathe || *costume da —,* bathing-costume.
bagnomaria *sm.* bain-marie.
bagordo *sm.* revelry.
baia[1] *sf.* (*scherzo*) joke || *dare la — a qu.,* to make (*v. irr.*) fun of so.
baia[2] *sf.* (*geogr.*) bay.
baionetta *sf.* bayonet.
baita *sf.* Alpine hut.
balaustrata *sf.* balustrade.
balbettare *vt.* e *vi.* to stammer.
balbettio *sm.* stammer.
balbuzie *sf.* stammer.
balbuziente *agg.* stammering. ♦ **balbuziente** *s.* stammerer.
balconata *sf.* balcony.
balcone *sm.* balcony.
baldacchino *sm.* canopy.
baldanza *sf.* boldness.
baldanzoso *agg.* bold.
baldo *agg.* bold.
baldoria *sf.* revel: *far —,* to make (*v. irr.*) merry.
balena *sf.* whale: *stecca di —,* whalebone.
balenare *vi.* 1. to lighten 2. (*di idea*) to flash.
baleno *sm.* lightning || *in un —,* in the twinkling of an eye.
balestra *sf.* 1. crossbow 2. (*mecc.*) leaf spring.
balia *sf.* wet nurse: *— asciutta,* dry-nurse.
balìa *sf.* mercy: *in — di,* at the mercy of.
balistica *sf.* ballistics.
balla *sf.* 1. (*di cotone, di lana*) bale 2. (*volg.; fandonia*) tall story 3. (*fig.; mucchio*) heap.
ballare *vt.* e *vi.* to dance.
ballata *sf.* ballad.
ballatoio *sm.* gallery.
ballerina *sf.* 1. dancer 2. (*classica*) ballerina.
ballerino *sm.* 1. dancer 2. (*classico*) ballet-dancer.
balletto *sm.* ballet.

ballo *sm.* 1. dance 2. (*festa*) ball || *essere in —; to be on the go; tirare in —,* to call in question.
ballottaggio *sm.* second ballot.
balneare *agg.* bathing || *stazione —,* seaside resort.
balocco *sm.* toy.
balordàggine *sf.* 1. dullness 2. (*azione*) foolish action 3. (*discorso*) nonsense.
balordo *agg.* e *sm.* stupid.
balsàmico *agg.* balmy.
bàlsamo *sm.* balm.
baluardo *sm.* bulwark.
balza *sf.* 1. cliff 2. (*di vestito*) flounce.
balzano *agg.* 1. queer 2. (*di cavallo*) white-footed.
balzare *vi.* to jump.
balzo *sm.* jump: *cogliere la palla al —,* to seize an opportunity.
bambagia *sf.* cotton-wool.
bambina *sf.* 1. little girl, child (*pl.* children) 2. (*in fasce*) baby.
bambinaia *sf.* nurse.
bambino *sm.* 1. little boy, child (*pl.* children) 2. (*in fasce*) baby || *dare alla luce un —,* to bring (*v. irr.*) forth a child.
bamboccio *sm.* 1. (*bambola*) rag-doll 2. (*fig.*) simpleton.
bàmbola *sf.* doll.
bambù *sm.* bamboo.
banale *agg.* banal.
banalità *sf.* banality.
banana *sf.* banana.
banano *sm.* banana-tree.
banca *sf.* bank.
bancarella *sf.* stall.
bancario *agg.* bank: *libretto —,* passbook. ♦ **bancario** *sm.* bank clerk.
bancarotta *sf.* bankruptcy: *fare —,* to go (*v. irr.*) bankrupt.
banchetto *sm.* banquet.
banchiere *sm.* banker.
banchina *sf.* 1. (*molo*) wharf 2. (*terrapieno*) bank.
banchisa *sf.* ice-pack.
banco *sm.* 1. bench 2. (*di chiesa*) pew 3. (*di negozio*) counter 4. (*di nebbia, di sabbia, di gioco*) bank.
banconota *sf.* banknote.
banda *sf.* 1. (*lato*) side 2. (*mus.; striscia di stoffa*) band 3. (*di delinquenti*) gang.
banderuola *sf.* weathercock.
bandiera *sf.* flag, colours (*pl.*).
bandire *vt.* 1. to proclaim 2. (*esi-*

liare, eliminare) to banish.
bandito *sm.* outlaw.
bando *sm.* 1. ban 2. (*esilio*) banishment || *essere al* —, to be banished 3. (*annunzio*) announcement.
bar *sm.* bar.
bara *sf.* coffin.
baracca *sf.* hut.
baraccone *sm.* booth.
baraonda *sf.* chaos.
barare *vi.* to cheat.
bàratro *sm.* abyss.
barattare *vt.* to exchange.
baratto *sm.* barter.
baràttolo *sm.* 1. jar 2. (*di metallo*) tin.
barba *sf.* beard: *fare, farsi la* —, to shave || (*fig.*) *in — a*, in spite of.
barbabiètola *sf.* beet-root.
barbarie *sf.* 1. barbarousness 2. (*crudeltà*) barbarity.
bàrbaro *agg. e sm.* barbarian.
barbiere *sm.* barber.
barbone *sm.* 1. (*straccione*) tramp 2. (*cane*) poodle.
barbuto *agg.* bearded.
barca *sf.* boat: *andare in* —, to go (*v. irr.*) boating.
barcaiolo *sm.* boatman (*pl.* -men).
barcamenarsi *vr.* to wangle.
barcollare *vi.* to stagger.
barcone *sm.* long boat.
bardare *vt.* to harness. ♦ **bardarsi** *vr.* to dress up.
barella *sf.* stretcher.
barile *sm.* barrel.
barista *sm.* barman (*pl.* -men). ♦ **barista** *sf.* barmaid.
baritonale *agg.* baritone.
barìtono *sm.* baritone.
barlume *sm.* glimmer.
baro *sm.* cheat.
barocco *agg. e sm.* baroque.
baromètrico *agg.* barometric(al).
baròmetro *sm.* barometer.
barone *sm.* baron.
baronessa *sf.* baroness.
barra *sf.* 1. bar 2. (*mar.*) helm.
barricare *vt.* to barricade.
barricata *sf.* barricade.
barriera *sf.* 1. barrier 2. (*fig.*) obstacle.
barrire *vi.* to trumpet.
barrito *sm.* trumpet.
barroccio *sm.* cart.
baruffa *sf.* quarrel.
barzelletta *sf.* joke.
basalto *sm.* basalt.

basamento *sm.* base.
basare *vt.* to base.
basco *agg. e sm.* Basque. ♦ **basco** *sm.* (*berretto*) beret.
base *sf.* base.
basette *sf. pl.* whiskers.
bàsico *agg.* basic.
basilare *agg.* basic.
basilica *sf.* basilica.
basìlico *sm.* basil.
basilisco *sm.* basilisk.
bassezza *sf.* baseness.
basso *agg.* 1. low 2. (*di statura*) short 3. (*abietto*) base. ♦ **basso** *avv.* low. ♦ **basso** *sm.* 1. bottom 2. (*mus.*) bass.
bassofondo *sm.* shallow || *i bassifondi della società*, the underworld.
bassopiano *sm.* lowland.
bassorilievo *sm.* bas-relief.
bassotto *agg.* thick-set. ♦ **bassotto** *sm.* (*cane*) dachshund.
bassoventre *sm.* belly.
basta *inter.* stop it!: — *con*, enough of.
bastardo *agg. e sm.* 1. bastard 2. (*di animali*) mongrel.
bastare *vi.* to be enough.
bastimento *sm.* ship.
bastione *sm.* 1. rampart 2. (*mil.*) bastion.
basto *sm.* pack-saddle.
bastonare *vt.* to cane.
bastonata *sf.* blow with a cane.
bastonatura *sf.* caning.
bastone *sm.* stick, staff.
batacchio *sm.* clapper.
batisfera *sf.* bathysphere.
batista *sf.* batiste.
batosta *sf.* blow.
batrace *sm.* batrachian.
battaglia *sf.* battle, fight || (*fig.*) *cavallo di* —, favourite subject, favourite piece.
battagliare *vi.* to battle, to fight (*v. irr.*), to struggle.
battagliero *agg.* 1. warlike 2. (*fig.*) fierce.
battaglione *sm.* battalion.
battelliere *sm.* boatman (*pl.* -men).
battello *sm.* boat.
battente *sm.* 1. (*picchiotto*) knocker 2. (*di porta*) wing.
bàttere *vt.* 1. to beat (*v. irr.*), to strike (*v. irr.*) (*anche delle ore*) 2. (*scrivere a macchina*) to type || — *le mani*, to clap hands; — *i piedi*, to stamp; *in un batter d'oc-*

chio, in the twinkling of an eye. ♦ **bàttere** *vi.* **1.** to knock **2.** (*pulsare*) to throb. ♦ **bàttersi** *vr.* to fight (*v. irr.*).

batterìa *sf.* **1.** battery **2.** (*da cucina*) kitchen utensils.

battèrio *sm.* bacterium (*pl.* -ia).

batteriologìa *sf.* bacteriology.

battésimo *sm.* baptism: *nome di* —, Christian name.

battezzare *vt.* to baptize.

battibaleno *sm.* (*nella loc. avv.*) *in un* —, in a twinkling.

battibecco *sm.* squabble.

batticuore *sm.* **1.** throb **2** (*fig.*) fear.

battimano *sm.* clap.

battipanni *sm.* carpet-beater.

battistero *sm.* baptistery.

battistrada *sm.* **1.** outrider **2.** (*di pneumatico*) tread || *fare da* —, to lead (*v. irr.*) the way.

bàttito *sm.* **1.** beat **2.** (*mecc.*) knock.

battitore *sm.* **1.** beater **2.** (*cricket, baseball*) batsman (*pl.* -men).

battitura *sf.* thrashing.

battuta *sf.* **1.** beating: — *di caccia*, beating **2.** (*di spirito*) witty remark **3.** (*mus.*) bar **4.** (*teat.*) cue **5.** (*tennis*) service.

batùffolo *sm.* flock.

baule *sm.* trunk.

bauxite *sf.* bauxite.

bava *sf.* **1.** slaver **2.** (*di lumaca*) slime.

bavaglino *sm.* bib.

bavaglio *sm.* gag: *mettere il* — *a qu.* (*fig.*), to gag so.

bàvero *sm.* collar.

bazàr *sm.* bazaar.

bazza *sf.* slipper-chin.

bazzècola *sf.* trifle.

bazzicare *vt.* e *vi.* to frequent.

bazzotto *agg.* soft-boiled.

be' *inter.* well.

beare *vt.* to make (*v. irr.*) so. happy. ♦ **bearsi** *vr.* to rejoice (at).

beatificazione *sf.* beatification.

beatitùdine *sf.* beatitude.

beato *agg.* **1.** happy **2.** (*relig.*) blessed.

beccaccia *sf.* woodcock.

beccaccino *sm.* snipe.

beccare *vt.* **1.** to peck **2.** (*fam. per acchiappare*) to catch (*v. irr.*). ♦ **beccarsi** *vr.* **1.** (*procurarsi*) to get (*v. irr.*) **2.** (*litigare*) to quarrel.

beccata *sf.* peck.

beccheggiare *vi.* to pitch.

beccheggio *sm.* pitching.

becchime *sm.* birdseed.

becchino *sm.* grave-digger.

becco *sm.* **1.** beak **2.** (*caprone*) billy-goat **3.** (*fig.*) cuckold.

beccuccio *sm.* (*di teiera ecc.*) spout.

beduino *agg.* e *sm.* Bedouin.

befana *sf.* **1.** "befana" **2.** (*fig. fam.*) hag.

beffa *sf.* mockery: *farsi* — *di*, to laugh at; (*ingannare*) to make (*v. irr.*) a fool of.

beffardo *agg.* mocking. ♦ **beffardo** *sm.* mocker.

beffare *vt.* to mock. ♦ **beffarsi** *vr.* to laugh at.

beffeggiare *vt.* V. *beffare*.

bega *sf.* **1.** quarrel **2.** (*problema intricato*) entangled affair.

beghina *sf.* bigot.

begonia *sf.* (*bot.*) begonia.

belare *vi.* to bleat.

belato *sm.* bleat.

belga *agg.* e *sm.* Belgian.

bella *sf.* **1.** beauty **2.** (*innamorata*) sweetheart || *copiare in* —, to make (*v. irr.*) a fair copy.

belladonna *sf.* (*bot.; farm.*) belladonna.

belletto *sm.* rouge.

bellezza *sf.* beauty: *istituto di* —, beauty parlour.

bellicismo *sm.* warlikeness.

bèllico *agg.* **1.** war (*attributivo*) **2.** (*del tempo di guerra*) wartime.

bellicoso *agg.* warlike.

belligerante *agg.* e *sm.* belligerent.

belligeranza *sf.* belligerence.

bellimbusto *sm.* dandy.

bello *agg.* **1.** fine, beautiful **2.** (*di uomo*) handsome || *nel bel mezzo*, right in the middle. ♦ **bello** *sm.* **1.** (*la bellezza*) beauty **2.** (*innamorato*) sweetheart || *sul più* —, at the right moment; *ora viene il* —, now you'll hear the best of it.

belva *sf.* wild beast.

belvedere *sm.* **1.** observation post **2.** (*arch.*) belvedere.

bemolle *sm.* (*mus.*) flat.

benché *cong.* though.

benda *sf.* bandage.

bendaggio *sm.* bandage.

bendare *vt.* to bandage.

bene *sm.* good: *per il tuo* —, for your sake; *voler* —, to love. ♦

beni *sm. pl.* property || — *immobili*, real estate; — *di consumo*, consumer goods. ◆ **bene** *avv.* **1.** well **2.** (*molto*) very **3.** (*nientemeno*) no less than || *star* —, to be well; *andar* —, to suit.

benedetto *agg.* blessed.

benedire *vt.* to bless.

benedizione *sf.* blessing.

benefattore *sm.* benefactor.

beneficare *vt.* to help.

beneficenza *sf.* charity.

beneficiario *agg. e sm.* beneficiary.

beneficiata *sf.* benefit.

beneficio *sm.* **1.** benefit **2.** (*eccl.; giur.*) benefice.

benèfico *agg.* **1.** beneficent **2.** (*vantaggioso*) beneficial.

benemerenza *sf.* merit.

benemèrito *agg.* well-deserving.

beneplàcito *sm.* consent: *a tuo* —, as you like.

benèssere *sm.* welfare.

benestante *agg.* well-off. ◆ **benestante** *s.* well-to-do person.

benestare *sm.* assent.

benevolenza *sf.* benevolence.

benèvolo *agg.* benevolent.

bengala *sm.* Bengal light.

beniamino *sm.* darling.

benignità *sf.* **1.** benignity **2.** (*di clima*) mildness.

benigno *agg.* **1.** benign **2.** (*di clima*) mild.

beninteso *avv.* of course.

benpensante *agg.* sensible || *i benpensanti*, the right thinking.

benservito *sm.* testimonial.

bensì *cong.* but.

benvenuto *agg. sm. inter.* welcome || *dare il* — *a qu.*, to welcome so.

benvolere *vt.* to like: *farsi* —, to make (*v. irr.*) oneself liked.

benzina *sf.* petrol.

benzinaio *sm.* filling station attendant.

benzolo *sm.* benzol.

beone *sm.* drunkard.

beota *agg. e sm.* Bœotian.

bèrbero *agg. e sm.* Berber.

berciare *vi.* to bawl.

bere *vt.* to drink (*v. irr.*) || *darla a* — (*fig.*), to tell (*v. irr.*) tall stories.

bergamotto *sm.* (*bot.; farm.*) bergamot.

berillo *sm.* beryllium.

berlina *sf.* **1.** (*carrozza*) berline **2.** (*automobile*) limousine **3.** (*gogna*)

pillory: *mettere alla* —, to pillory.

bernòccolo *sm.* bump.

berretta *sf.* cap.

berretto *sm.* cap.: — *con visiera*, peaked cap.

bersagliare *vt.* **1.** to shoot (*v. irr.*) (at) **2.** (*fig.*) to torment.

bersaglio *sm.* target: *tiro al* —, target-shooting || *colpire il* —, to hit (*v. irr.*) the mark.

besciamella *sf.* cream-sauce.

bestemmia *sf.* swear.

bestemmiare *vi.* to swear (*v. irr.*).

bestia *sf.* beast || *montare in* —, to lose (*v. irr.*) one's temper.

bestiale *agg.* beastly.

bestialità *sf.* **1.** beastliness **2.** (*fig.*) foolishness || *dire* —, to talk nonsense; *fare* —, to make (*v. irr.*) blunders.

bestiame *sm.* cattle.

béttola *sf.* tavern.

betulla *sf.* birch.

bevanda *sf.* drink.

beveraggio *sm.* beverage.

bevitore *sm.* drinker.

bevuta *sf.* **1.** draught **2.** (*il bere*) drinking.

biada *sf.* fodder.

biancastro *agg.* whitish.

biancheggiare *vi. e vt.* **1.** (*essere bianco*) to be white **2.** (*diventare, far diventare bianco*) to whiten.

biancherìa *sf.* linen.

bianco *agg.* white || *in* —, blank; *di punto in* —, suddenly.

biancore *sm.* whiteness.

biancospino *sm.* hawthorn.

biascicare *vt.* to mumble.

biasimare *vt.* to blame.

biasimévole *agg.* blamable.

biàsimo *sm.* blame.

Bibbia *sf.* Bible.

bìbita *sf.* drink.

bìblico *agg.* biblical.

bibliografia *sf.* bibliography.

bibliogràfico *agg.* bibliographic(al).

biblioteca *sf.* **1.** library **2.** (*scaffale*) bookcase.

bibliotecario *sm.* librarian.

bica *sf.* stack.

bicamerale *agg.* (*pol.*) bicameral.

bicarbonato *sm.* bicarbonate.

bicchiere *sm.* glass.

bicèfalo *agg.* V. *bicipite*.

bicicletta *sf.* bicycle: *andare in* —, to cycle.

bicìpite *agg.* two-headed. ◆ **bicìpite** *sm.* biceps.

bicocca *sf.* hut.
bicolore *agg.* two-coloured.
bidè *sm.* bidet.
bidello *sm.* porter.
bidente *sm.* pitchfork.
bidone *sm.* 1. can 2. (*fam.*) swindle.
bieco *agg.* sinister.
biella *sf.* (*mecc.*) connecting rod.
biennale *agg.* biennial.
bietola *sf.* beet.
biennio *sm.* biennium (*pl.* -nia).
bifase *agg.* (*elettr.*) two-phase.
bifolco *sm.* boor.
biforcarsi *vr.* to fork.
biforcazione *sf.* fork.
biforcuto *agg.* forked.
bigamìa *sf.* bigamy.
bìgamo *agg.* bigamous. ♦ bìgamo *sm.* bigamist.
bighellonare *vi.* to lounge.
bighellone *sm.* lounger.
bigio *agg.* grey.
bigiotterìa *sf.* trinkets (*pl.*).
biglia *sf.* (biliard-)ball.
bigliettaio *sm.* 1. conductor 2. (*di stazione*) booking-clerk.
biglietterìa *sf.* 1. booking-office 2. (*di teatro*) box-office.
biglietto *sm.* 1. card: — *di visita*, visiting card 2. (*di tram ecc.*) ticket: — *di andata e ritorno*, return ticket; *mezzo* —, half-fare ticket 3. (*banconota*) bank-note.
bigodino *sm.* (hair-)curler.
bigotto *agg.* bigoted. ♦ bigotto *sm.* bigot.
bikini *sm.* bikini.
bilancia *sf.* balance, scales (*pl.*).
bilanciare *vt.* to balance.
bilanciere *sm.* 1. balance-wheel 2. (*mar.*) outrigger.
bilancio *sm.* budget: *fare il* —, to strike (*v. irr.*) the balance.
bilaterale *agg.* bilateral.
bile *sf.* 1. bile 2. (*ira*) anger.
biliardo *sm.* billiards (*pl.*).
bìlico *sm.* 1. balance 2. (*fig.*) uncertainty || *mettere in* —, to balance; *stare in* —, to be balanced.
bilingue *agg.* bilingual.
bilione *sm.* billion.
bilioso *agg.* bilious.
bimba *sf.* V. *bambina.*
bimbo *sm.* V. *bambino.*
bimensile *agg.* fortnightly.
bimestrale *agg.* bimestrial.
bimestre *sm.* (period of) two months.

bimotore *agg.* two-engined: *aereo* —, two-engined plane.
binario *sm.* track: — *morto*, dead-end track.
binòcolo *sm.* binoculars (*pl.*).
binomio *sm.* binomial.
biòccolo *sm.* flock: — *di neve*, snow-flake.
biochìmica *sf.* biochemistry.
biofìsica *sf.* biophysics.
biografìa *sf.* biography.
biogràfico *agg.* biographic(al).
biògrafo *sm.* biographer.
biologìa *sf.* biology.
biològico *agg.* biologic(al).
biòlogo *sm.* biologist.
biondo *agg.* fair.
biosfera *sf.* biosphere.
biòssido *sm.* dioxide.
bipartizione *sf.* bipartitior
bìpede *agg.* e *sm.* biped.
biplano *sm.* biplane.
bipolare *agg.* bipolar.
birba *sf.* scapegrace.
birbante *s.* rogue.
birbonata *sf.* knavery.
birbone *sm.* rogue.
bireattore *sm.* two-engined jet.
birichino *sm.* utchin. ♦ birichino *agg.* naughty.
birillo *sm.* skittle.
biro *sf.* ball-point pen.
biroccio *sm.* cart.
birra *sf.* beer.
birrerìa *sf.* 1. beer-house 2. (*fabbrica*) brewery.
bisaccia *sf.* packsack.
bisbètico *agg.* cantankerous.
bisbigliare *vt.* to whisper.
bisbiglio *sm.* whisper.
bisboccia *sf.* spree: *far* —, to revel.
bisca *sf.* gambling-house.
biscia *sf.* snake.
biscotto *sm.* biscuit.
bisessuale *agg.* bisexual.
bisestile *agg. anno* —, leap year.
bisettimanale *agg.* bi-weekly.
bisettrice *sf.* bisector.
bisìllabo *agg.* disyllabic. ♦ bisìllabo *sm.* disyllable.
bislacco *agg.* odd.
bislungo *agg.* oblong.
bismuto *sm.* bismuth.
bisnipote *s.* great-grandchild (*pl.* -children).
bisnonna *sf.* great-grandmother.
bisognare *vi. imp.* to be necessary, must.
bisnonno *sm.* great-grandfather.

bisogno *sm.* **1.** need **2.** (*povertà*) necessity ‖ *aver —*, to need.
bisognoso *agg.* needy.
bisonte *sm.* bison.
bissare *vt.* to give (*v. irr.*) an encore (of sthg.).
bistecca *sf.* beefsteak.
bisticciare *vi.* to squabble.
bisticcio *sm.* **1.** squabble **2.** (*gioco di parole*) pun.
bistrattare *vt.* to ill-treat.
bistro *sm.* bistre.
bìsturi *sm.* lancet.
bitòrzolo *sm.* bump.
bitume *sm.* bitumen.
bivacco *sm.* bivouac.
bivalente *agg.* bivalent.
bivio *sm.* **1.** fork **2.** (*fig.*) alternative.
bizantino *agg.* e *sm.* Byzantine.
bizza *sf.* freak ‖ *fare le bizze*, to be peevish.
bizzarrìa *sf.* **1.** peculiarity **2.** (*cosa*) curiosity **3.** (*atto, detto*) extravagance.
bizzarro *agg.* strange.
bizzoso *agg.* **1.** freakish **2.** (*irascibile*) irascible.
blandire *vt.* to soothe.
blandizia *sf.* blandishment.
blando *agg.* bland.
blasone *sm.* **1.** blazon **2.** (*nobiltà*) nobility.
blaterare *vi.* e *vt.* to prate.
bleso *agg.* lisping ‖ *pronuncia blesa*, lisp. ♦ **bleso** *sm.* lisper.
blindare *vt.* (*mil.*) to armour.
bloccare *vt.* to block, to stop. ♦ **bloccarsi** *vr.* to jam.
blocco *sm.* **1.** block **2.** (*mil.*) blockade.
blu *agg.* e *sm.* blue.
bluff *sm.* bluff.
blusa *sf.* blouse.
boa[1] *sf.* (*mar.*) buoy.
boa[2] *sm.* (*zool.*) boa.
bobina *sf.* bobbin.
bocca *sf.* mouth: *— da incendio*, fire-plug; *— dello stomaco*, pit of the stomach; *chiudere la — a qu.*, to silence so.
boccaccia *sf.* grimace.
boccale *sm.* jug.
boccaporto *sm.* hatchway.
boccata *sf.* mouthful.
boccheggiare *vi.* to gasp.
bocchino *sm.* mouthpiece.
boccia *sf.* **1.** water-bottle **2.** (*sport*) bowl.
bocciare *vt.* **1.** (*respingere*) to

reject **2.** (*agli esami*) to fail.
bocciatura *sf.* failure.
boccio *sm.* bud.
boccone *sm.* **1.** bit **2.** (*boccata*) mouthful **3.** (*esca*) bait.
bocconi *avv.* lying face downwards.
boia *sm.* executioner.
boicottare *vt.* to boycott.
bolgia *sf.* **1.** (*fig.*) bedlam **2.** (*di inferno*) pit.
bòlide *sm.* (*astr.*) bolide.
bolla *sf.* **1.** bubble **2.** (*vescica*) blister **3.** (*eccl.*) bull.
bollare *vt.* **1.** (*timbrare*) to stamp **2.** (*a fuoco e fig.*) to brand.
bollato *agg.* **1.** stamped: *carta bollata*, stamped paper **2.** (*a fuoco e fig.*) branded.
bollente *agg.* boiling.
bolletta *sf.* **1.** bill **2.** (*ricevuta*) receipt ‖ *essere in —* (*fig.*), to be (*v. irr.*) penniless.
bollettario *sm.* counterfoil-book.
bollettino *sm.* **1.** bulletin **2.** (*comm.*) list, note.
bollire *vi.* e *vt.* to boil.
bollito *sm.* boiled meat.
bollitore *sm.* **1.** boiler **2.** (*bricco*) kettle.
bollitura *sf.* boiling.
bollo *sm.* stamp.
bollore *sm.* **1.** boil **2.** (*fig.*) excitement.
bolscevico *agg.* e *sm.* Bolshevist.
bolscevismo *sm.* Bolshevism.
boma *sf.* (*mar.*) boom.
bomba *sf.* bomb.
bombardamento *sm.* bombardment.
bombardare *vt.* to bombard; (*generalmente da aereo*) to bomb.
bombardiere *sm.* **1.** (*soldato*) bombardier **2.** (*aereo*) bomber.
bombetta *sf.* bowler.
bòmbola *sf.* bottle.
bomboniera *sf.* candy-box.
bonaccia *sf.* dead calm.
bonaccione *agg.* good-natured. ♦ **bonaccione** *sm.* good-natured man (*pl.* men).
bonarietà *sf.* good nature.
bonario *agg.* good-natured, friendly.
bonìfica *sf.* reclamation.
bonificare *vt.* **1.** to reclaim **2.** (*comm.*) to grant an allowance.
bonomìa *sf.* good nature.
bontà *sf.* goodness.
bonzo *sm.* bonze.
borbottare *vi.* e *vt.* **1.** to mumble

2. (*lamentarsi*) to grumble.
borbottìo *sm.* **1.** mumbling **2.** (*protesta*) grumbling.
bordare *vt.* to border.
bordeggiare *vi.* to tack.
bordello *sm.* bawdyhouse.
bordo *sm.* **1.** edge **2.** (*mar.*) board: *a —*, on board.
bordura *sf.* border.
bòrea *sf.* Boreas.
boreale *agg.* boreal: *aurora —*, aurora borealis.
borgata *sf.* village.
borghese *agg.* **1.** middle-class **2.** (*comune*) plain **3.** (*civile*) civilian: *in —*, in civilian dress. ♦ **borghese** *s.* middle-class person.
borghesìa *sf.* middle class(es): *l'alta —*, the upper middle class(es); *la piccola —*, the lower middle class(es).
borgo *sm.* village.
borgomastro *sm.* burgomaster.
boria *sf.* arrogance.
bòrico *agg.* boric.
borioso *agg.* arrogant.
borotalco *sm.* talcum powder.
borraccia *sf.* flask.
borsa[1] *sf.* bag || *— per documenti*, brief case; *— di studio*, scholarship.
borsa[2] *sf.* (*comm.*) Stock Exchange.
borsaiolo *sm.* pickpocket.
borseggiare *vt.* to pick pockets.
borsellino *sm.* purse.
borsetta *sf.* (hand-)bag.
boscaglia *sf.* brushwood.
boscaiolo *sm.* woodman (*pl.* -men).
boschetto *sm.* grove.
bosco *sm.* wood.
boscoso *agg.* woody.
bòssolo *sm.* cartridge-case.
botànica *sf.* botany.
bòtola *sf.* trap-door.
botta *sf.* **1.** blow **2.** (*battuta*) sarcastic remark || *dare un sacco di botte a qu.*, to whack so.
botte *sf.* barrel.
bottega *sf.* shop.
bottegaio *sm.* shop-keeper.
bottiglia *sf.* bottle.
bottiglierìa *sf.* wine shop.
bottino *sm.* booty: *far —*, to plunder.
botto *sm.* blow || *di —*, suddenly.
bottone *sm.* button || *attaccare un — (fig.)*, to buttonhole.
bovaro *sm.* cowherd.
bovini *sm. pl.* cattle (*sing.*).

bozza *sf.* **1.** (*gonfiore*) swelling **2.** (*tip.*) proof **3.** (*abbozzo*) draft || *correggere le bozze*, to proofread.
bozzetto *sm.* sketch.
bòzzolo *sm.* cocoon.
braccare *vt.* to hunt.
braccetto (*nella loc. avv.*) *a —*, arm-in-arm.
bracciale *sm.* **1.** (*fascia che si porta al braccio*) arm-band **2.** (*braccialetto*) bracelet.
braccialetto *sm.* bracelet.
bracciante *sm.* labourer.
bracciata *sf.* **1.** armful **2.** (*di nuoto*) stroke.
braccio *sm.* arm: *essere in — a qu.*, to be in so.'s arms || *— di mare*, sound.
bracco *sm.* hound.
bracconaggio *sm.* poaching.
bracconiere *sm.* poacher.
brace *sf.* embers (*pl.*).
brache *sf. pl.* **1.** trousers **2.** (*mutande*) drawers.
brachicèfalo *agg.* brachycephalous.
braciere *sm.* brazier.
braciola *sf.* chop.
bradicardìa *sf.* (*med.*) bradycardia.
brado *agg.* wild.
brama *sf.* longing.
bramare *vt.* to long for (sthg.).
bramosìa *sf.* covetousness.
bramoso *agg.* eager for (sthg.).
branca *sf.* **1.** claw **2.** (*settore*) branch.
branchia *sf.* gill.
branco *sm.* **1.** herd **2.** (*di pecore*) flock **3.** (*di pesci*) shoal **4.** (*di lupi e fig.*) pack.
brancolare *vi.* to grope.
branda *sf.* **1.** camp-bed **2.** (*mar.*) bunk.
brandello *sm.* **1.** rag **2.** (*pezzetto*) bit || *coi vestiti a brandelli*, in rags; *fare a brandelli*, to tear (*v. irr.*) up.
brandire *vt.* to brandish.
brano *sm.* piece.
brasato *sm.* braised beef.
brasiliano *agg. e sm.* Brazilian.
bravata *sf.* bravado.
bravo *agg.* clever, good || *—!*, well done!; *su, da —!*, be a good boy!
bravura *sf.* **1.** cleverness **2.** (*coraggio*) bravery || (*mus.*) *pezzo di —*, bravura.
breccia *sf.* breach: *essere sulla —*, to stand (*v. irr.*) in the breach.
brefotrofio *sm.* foundling hospital.

bretella *sf.* brace.
breve *agg.* short.
brevettare *vt.* to patent.
brevetto *sm.* patent.
breviario *sm.* breviary.
brevità *sf.* brevity.
brezza *sf.* breeze.
bricco *sm.* kettle, pot.
bricconata *sf.* roguish trick.
briccone *sm.* rogue.
briciola *sf.* crumb.
briciolo *sm.* bit.
briga *sf.* 1. trouble 2. (*lite*) quarrel: *attaccar* —, to pick a quarrel.
brigadiere *sm.* 1. « brigadiere » 2. (*ufficiale nell'Esercito Britannico assegnato al comando di brigata*) brigadier.
brigante *sm.* robber.
brigantino *sm.* (*mar.*) brig.
brigare *vi.* to intrigue.
brigata *sf.* 1. party 2. (*mil.*) brigade.
briglia *sf.* bridle || *a* — *sciolta*, at full gallop.
brillante *agg.* e *sm.* brilliant.
brillantina *sf.* brilliantine.
brillare *vi.* to shine (*v. irr.*). ◆ **brillare** *vt.* 1. (*riso ecc.*) to hull 2. (*una mina*) to blast.
brillo *agg.* tipsy.
brina *sf.* hoarfrost.
brinare *vi.* *imp.*: *ha brinato*, there has been a frost.
brinata *sf.* hoarfrost.
brindare *vi.* to toast: — *a qu.*, to toast so.
brindello *sm.* rag.
brindisi *sm.* toast.
brio *sm.* liveliness.
brioso *agg.* lively.
britànnico *agg.* British.
brìvido *sm.* 1. shiver 2. (*di paura, orrore*) shudder.
brizzolato *agg.* grizzled.
brocca *sf.* jug.
broccato *sm.* brocade.
bròccolo *sm.* broccoli.
brodaglia *sf.* slops (*pl.*).
brodo *sm.* broth.
broglio *sm.* intrigue: — *elettorale*, gerry-mander.
bromo *sm.* bromine.
bromuro *sm.* bromide.
bronchiale *agg.* bronchial.
bronchite *sf.* bronchitis.
broncio *sm.* pout || *fare il* —, to pout.
bronco *sm.* bronchus (*pl.* -chi).

broncopolmonite *sf.* bronchopneumonia.
brontolare *vi.* e *vt.* to grumble.
brontolìo *sm.* grumbling.
brontolone *sm.* grumbler.
brontosàuro *sm.* brontosaurus.
brònzeo *agg.* 1. bronze (*attributivo*) 2. (*simile a bronzo*) bronzy.
bronzo *sm.* bronze || *faccia di* —, brazen-faced person.
brossura *sf.* paper-back binding || *in* —, paper-bound.
brucare *vt.* to browse (on).
bruciacchiare *vt.* to scorch.
bruciacchiatura *sf.* scorching.
bruciapelo (*nella loc. avv.*) *a* —, point-blank.
bruciare *vt.* e *vi.* to burn (*v. irr.*).
bruciatore *sm.* burner.
bruciatura *sf.* burn.
bruciore *sm.* burning, smart (*anche fig.*).
bruco *sm.* caterpillar.
brùffolo *sm.* pimple.
brughiera *sf.* heath.
brulicare *vi.* to swarm (with).
brulichìo *sm.* swarm.
brullo *agg.* bare.
bruma *sf.* mist.
brumoso *agg.* misty.
brunire *vt.* to burnish.
brunitura *sf.* burnishing.
bruno *agg.* brown.
bruscamente *avv.* roughly.
brusco *agg.* 1. rough 2. (*di sapore*) sour.
brusìo *sm.* buzz.
brutale *agg.* brutal.
brutalità *sf.* brutality.
bruto *agg.* e *sm.* brute.
bruttezza *sf.* ugliness.
brutto *agg.* 1. ugly 2. (*cattivo*) bad.
bruttura *sf.* 1. ugly thing 2. (*azione*) base action.
bùbbola *sf.* lie.
bubbone *sm.* bubo.
bubbònico *agg.* bubonic.
buca *sf.* hole: — *delle lettere*, letter-box.
bucaneve *sm.* snowdrop.
bucaniere *sm.* buccaneer.
bucare *vt.* 1. to pierce 2. (*una gomma*) to puncture 3. (*biglietti*) to punch.
bucato *sm.* 1. washing 2. (*i panni*) laundry.
buccia *sf.* peel.
bucherellare *vt.* to riddle.

buco *sm.* hole.
bucòlico *agg.* bucolic.
buddismo *sm.* Buddhism.
buddista *s.* Buddhist.
budello *sm.* 1. bowel 2. (*strada stretta*) alley 3. (*tubo*) narrow tube.
budino *sm.* pudding.
bue *sm.* ox (*pl.* oxen): *carne di —*, beef.
bùfalo *sm.* buffalo.
bufera *sf.* 1. storm 2. (*di vento*) gale.
buffetto *sm.* fillip: *dare un —*, to fillip.
buffo *agg.* funny || *opera buffa*, comic opera.
buffonata *sf.* buffoonery.
buffone *sm.* 1. clown, fool 2. (*di corte*) court jester 3. (*fig.*) unreliable person.
bugìa *sf.* 1. lie 2. (*portacandela*) flat candlestick.
bugiardo *agg.* false. ✦ **bugiardo** *sm.* liar.
bugigàttolo *sm.* lumber-room.
buio *agg.* e *sm.* dark: *— pesto*, pitch dark.
bulbo *sm.* 1. bulb 2. (*di occhio*) eyeball.
bùlgaro *agg.* e *sm.* Bulgarian.
bulinare *vt.* to engrave.
bulino *sm.* burin.
bullonare *vt.* (*mecc.*) to bolt.
bullone *sm.* bolt.
buonanotte *sf.* good night.
buonasera *sf.* good evening.
buoncostume *sm.*: *squadra del —*, vice squad.
buongiorno *sm.* 1. (*di mattina*) good morning 2. (*di pomeriggio*) good afternoon 3. (*a ogni ora incontrandosi, fam.*) hullo 4. (*a ogni ora lasciandosi*) goodbye.
buongustaio *sm.* gourmet.
buongusto *sm.* good taste.
buono *agg.* 1. good 2. (*di tempo*) fine || *alla buona*, informal; *a buon diritto*, by right; *di buon grado*, willingly. ✦ **buono** *sm.* 1. good 2. (*persona*) good person 3. (*comm.*) bond 4. (*tagliando*) coupon.
buonsenso *sm.* (common) sense.
buontempone *sm.* merry fellow.
buonumore *sm.* V. *umore.*
buonuomo *sm.* 1. good-natured man (*pl.* men) 2. simple man (*pl.* men).

burattinaio *sm.* puppet showman (*pl.* -men).
burattino *sm.* puppet.
burbanzoso *agg.* haughty.
bùrbero *agg.* gruff.
burla *sf.* trick || *per —*, in fun.
burlare *vt.* to play a trick on (so.). ✦ **burlarsi** *vr.* to make (*v. irr.*) fun of.
burlesco *agg.* farcical.
burlone *sm.* joker.
buròcrate *sm.* bureaucrat.
burocràtico *agg.* bureaucratic.
burocrazìa *sf.* bureaucracy; (*in Inghilterra*) Civil Service.
burrasca *sf.* storm.
burrascoso *agg.* stormy
burrificio *sm.* dairy.
burro *sm.* butter.
burrone *sm.* ravine.
burroso *agg.* buttery.
buscarsi *vr.* to get (*v. irr.*) || *buscarle*, to get a thrashing.
bussare *vi.* to knock: *— alla porta*, to knock at the door.
busse *sf. pl.* blows: *prendere le —*, to get (*v. irr.*) a thrashing.
bùssola *sf.* compass: *perdere la —* (*fig.*), to lose (*v. irr.*) one's head.
bussolotto *sm.* dice-box || *fare il giuoco dei bussolotti* (*anche fig.*), to juggle.
busta *sf.* 1. envelope 2. (*astuccio*) case.
bustarella *sf.* bribe.
bustina *sf.* (*mil.*) service cap.
busto *sm.* 1. bust 2. (*indumento per donna*) corset.
butano *sm.* (*chim.*) butane.
buttare *vt.* 1. to throw (*v. irr.*) 2. (*sprecare*) to waste || *— all'aria*, to upset (*v. irr.*); *— a terra*, to knock down.
butterato *agg.* pitted.
buzzo *sm.* belly || *di — buono*, very eagerly.

C

càbala *sf.* cab(b)ala.
cabalìstico *agg.* cab(b)alistic(al).
cabina *sf.* 1. box, hut: *— balneare*, bathing hut; *— telefonica*, telephone box 2. (*aer.; mar.*) cabin.
cablogramma *sm.* cable.

cabotaggio sm. cabotage: nave di piccolo —, coasting vessel.
cacao sm. 1. (bot.) cacao 2. (polvere, bevanda) cocoa.
cacare vi. to evacuate one's bowels.
cacarella sf. diarrhoea.
cacatoa, cacatùa sm. cockatoo.
cacca sf. excrement.
caccia sf. hunt, hunting || — grossa, big game || cane da —, sporting dog; stagione di —, shooting season; andare a —, to go (v. irr.) hunting; andare a — di uccelli, to go shooting. ♦ caccia sm. (aer.) fighter.
cacciagione sf. game.
cacciare vt. 1. to hunt 2. (mil.; mar.) to chase 3. (scacciare) to expel 4. (mettere) to put (v. irr.).
cacciatore sm. hunter (anche fig.).
cacciatorpediniere sf. (torpedo-boat) destroyer.
cacciavite sm. screwdriver.
cachi sm. persimmon.
cacio sm. cheese || essere alto come un soldo di —, to be very short.
cacofonìa sf. cacophony.
cactus sm. cactus (pl. cacti).
cadauno agg. e pron. indef. each.
cadàvere sm. corpse.
cadavèrico agg. 1. corpse-like 2. (pallido) deadly pale.
cadente agg. 1. falling 2. (di astri) setting || stella —, shooting star || età —, decrepit old age.
cadenza sf. 1. cadence 2. (ritmo) rhythm 3. (accento) accent.
cadere vi. 1. to fall (v. irr.) (anche fig.): — bocconi, to fall flat on one's face; — in mare, to fall overboard; — addormentato, to fall asleep; — a proposito, to fall in the nick of time; — dal sonno, to be overcome by sleep; — nell'errore, to fall into error || far —, to knock down; (fig.) to bring (v. irr.) about the fall of 2. (tramontare, di astri) to set (v. irr.) 3. (calare) to drop 4. (far fiasco) to fail.
cadetto agg. e sm. cadet.
caducità sf. caducity.
caduco agg. perishable, decaying.
caduta sf. 1. fall, falling 2. (fig.) downfall, ruin 3. (fis.) drop.
caffè sm. 1. coffee: — macinato, ground coffee; — nero, black coffee 2. (locale) coffee-house.
caffeina sf. caffeine.
caffettiera sf. coffee-pot.

cafone sm. boor.
cagionévole agg. sickly, weak.
cagliarsi vr. to curdle.
cagna sf. bitch.
cagnara sf. 1. furious barking 2. (fig.) uproar.
cagnesco agg. in —, surlily || guardare in —, to scowl at.
cagnolino s. 1. (cucciolo) puppy 2. (cane piccolo) small dog.
caimano sm. cayman.
cala sf. 1. creek 2. (mar.) hold.
calabrone sm. hornet.
calamaio sm. ink-stand.
calamaro sm. calamary.
calamita sf. magnet (anche fig.).
calamità sf. calamity, misfortune.
calamitare vt. to magnetize (anche fig.).
calamitoso agg. calamitous.
calandra sf. 1. (zool.) wood-lark 2. (mecc.) calender.
calare vt. to lower, to drop || cala la tela, the curtain drops. ♦ calare vi. 1. to descend 2. (di astri) to set (v. irr.) 3. (di febbre) to abate 4. (comm.) to fall (v. irr.). ♦ calarsi vr. to let (v. irr.) oneself down.
calata sf. descent.
calca sf. crowd.
calcagno sm. heel || stare alle calcagna di qu., to follow so. closely.
calcare[1] vt. 1. to tread (v. irr.) 2. (premere) to press down || — la mano (fig.), to exaggerate.
calcare[2] sm. limestone.
calcàreo agg. calcareous.
calce sf. lime || in — (loc. avv.), at the foot.
calcestruzzo sm. concrete.
calciare vi. to kick.
calciatore sm. footballer.
calcificare vt. to calcify.
calcificazione sf. calcification.
calcina sf. lime.
calcinaccio sm. debris (solo sing.).
calcinare vt. to calcine.
calcio[1] sm. 1. kick 2. (giuoco) football || — d'inizio, kick-off; — di rigore, penalty 3. (di arma) butt.
calcio[2] sm. (chim.) calcium.
calco sm. 1. (scult.) cast 2. (di disegno) drawing.
calcolàbile agg. computable.
calcolare vt. 1. to calculate, to compute 2. (prevedere) to estimate.
calcolatore sm. (electronic) computer || regolo —, slide-rule.

calcolatrice *sf.* calculating machine.
càlcolo *sm.* **1.** calculation **2.** (*med.*) stone.
calcomanìa *sf.* transfer.
caldaia *sf.* **1.** kier **2.** (*per produzione di vapore*) boiler.
caldamente *avv.* warmly.
caldeggiare *vt.* to favour.
caldeggiatore *sm.* supporter.
calderaio *sm.* tinker.
calderone *sm.* **1.** cauldron **2.** (*fig.*) medley.
caldo *agg.* **1.** warm; (*molto caldo*) hot **2.** (*fig.*) ardent. ♦ **caldo** *sm.* heat || *far —*, to be warm, to be hot.
caleidoscopio *sm.* kaleidoscope.
calendario *sm.* calendar.
calende *sf. pl.* kalends || *rimandare alle — greche*, to put off till doomsday.
calesse *sm.* gig, calash.
calessino *sm.* gig.
calibrare *vt.* to calibrate.
calibratura *sf.* calibration.
càlibro *sm.* **1.** calibre **2.** (*di persona*) caliber, importance.
càlice *sm.* **1.** (*eccl.*) chalice **2.** (*bicchiere*) goblet, drinking-cup.
calìgine *sf.* thick fog, smog.
callìfugo *sm.* corn-plaster.
calligrafìa *sf.* handwriting.
calligràfico *agg.* calligraphic.
callìgrafo *sm.* calligrapher: *perito —*, handwriting expert.
callista *sm.* chiropodist.
callo *sm.* corn.
callosità *sf.* callosity.
calloso *agg.* callous.
calma *sf.* calm.
calmante *agg.* calming, soothing. ♦ **calmante** *sm.* (*farm.*) sedative.
calmare *vt.* **1.** to calm **2.** (*metter pace*) to appease.
calmo *agg.* calm, quiet.
calo *sm.* **1.** shrinkage **2.** (*comm.*) drop.
calore *sm.* **1.** (*forte*) heat; (*moderato*) warmth **2.** (*fig.*) warmth, eagerness.
calorìa *sf.* calory.
calorìfero *sm.* heating apparatus, radiator.
caloroso *agg.* **1.** warm, hearty **2.** (*che non sente freddo*) not feeling the cold.
calotta *sf.* **1.** cap: *— cranica*, skull-cap **2.** (*geom.*) bowl.
calpestare *vt.* to tread (*v. irr.*):

vietato — l'erba, keep off the grass.
calpestìo *sm.* trampling (of feet).
calunnia *sf.* slander.
calunniare *vt.* to slander.
calunniatore *sm.* slanderer.
calvizie *sf.* baldness.
calvo *agg.* bald.
calza *sf.* **1.** (*corta*) sock; (*da donna*) stocking **2.** (*lavoro a maglia*) knitting || *fare la —*, to knit.
calzamaglia *sf.* tights (*pl.*).
calzare *vt.* to put (*v. irr.*) on. ♦ **calzare** *vi.* to fit.
calzatura *sf.* shoe || *negozio di calzature*, shoe-shop.
calzaturificio *sm.* boot factory.
calzettone *sm.* heavy sock.
calzino *sm.* sock.
calzolaio *sm.* shoemaker.
calzolerìa *sf.* shoemaker's shop.
calzoni *sm. pl.* trousers.
camaleonte *sm.* chameleon (*anche fig.*).
cambiale *sf.* bill (of exchange): *— a vista*, bill at sight; *emettere una —*, to issue a bill; *girare una —*, to endorse a bill; *protestare una —*, to note a bill || *— pagherò*, promissory note.
cambiamento *sm.* change.
cambiare *vt.* to change (*anche fig.*). ♦ **cambiarsi** *vr.* to change.
cambio *sm.* **1.** change **2.** (*econ.*) exchange **3.** (*mecc.*) change-gear **4.** (*auto*) gear || *in —*, in exchange for, instead of.
camelia *sf.* (*bot.*) camellia.
càmera *sf.* **1.** room: *— da letto*, bedroom; *— dei bambini*, nursery; *— degli ospiti*, guest-room || *musica da —*, chamber music **2.** (*pol.*) Chamber House: *camera dei deputati*, Chamber of Deputies **3.** (*tec.*) chamber || *— oscura*, dark room; *— d'aria*, inner tube.
camerata[1] *sm.* comrade, mate.
camerata[2] *sf.* dormitory.
cameratismo *sm.* comradeship.
cameriera *sf.* **1.** maid **2.** (*di albergo*) chambermaid **3.** (*di ristorante*) waitress.
cameriere *sm.* **1.** man-servant (*pl.* men-*) **2.** (*di ristorante*) waiter.
càmice *sm.* **1.** overall **2.** (*eccl.*) surplice.
camicetta *sf.* blouse.
camicia *sf.* **1.** (*da uomo*) shirt || *— da notte* (*da uomo*), night-shirt

2. (*da donna*) chemise || — *da notte* (*da donna*), night-dress **3.** (*tec.*) jacket || *è nato con la* —, he was born with a silver spoon in his mouth.

caminetto *sm.* fireplace.

camino *sm.* **1.** (*focolare*) fireplace **2.** (*comignolo*) chimney.

camion *sm.* lorry.

camioncino *sm.* van.

camionista *sm.* lorry-driver.

cammello *sm.* camel.

cammeo *sm.* cameo.

camminare *vi.* **1.** to walk || — *a grandi passi*, to stride (*v. irr.*) along; — *in punta di piedi*, to walk on tiptoe **2.** (*di meccanismi*) to go (*v. irr.*), to work **3.** (*discorsi, affari ecc.*) to proceed.

camminata *sf.* **1.** walk **2.** (*andatura*) gait.

camminatore *sm.* walker.

cammino *sm.* way.

camomilla *sf.* (*bot.*) camomile: *una tazza di* —, a cup of camomile-tea.

camoscio *sm.* chamois: *pelle di* —, chamois leather.

campagna *sf.* **1.** country: *casa di* —, country-house; *andare in* —, to go (*v. irr.*) into the country; *essere in* —, to be in the country **2.** (*tenuta*) estate **3.** (*mil.*) campaign **4.** (*villeggiatura*) holidays.

campana *sf.* bell.

campanaro *sm.* bell-ringer.

campanello *sm.* door-bell: — *d'allarme*, alarm-bell.

campanile *sm.* bell-tower.

campanilismo *sm.* parochialism.

campare *vi.* to live.

campeggiatore *sm.* camper.

campeggio *sm.* camping.

campestre *agg.* rural, rustic || *corsa* —, cross-country race.

campionario *sm.* set of samples, sample case || *fiera campionaria*, trade fair.

campionato *sm.* championship.

campione *sm.* **1.** champion **2.** (*comm.*) sample.

campo *sm.* **1.** (*mil.*) field **2.** (*sport*) sport ground || — *da tennis*, tennis court **3.** (*terreno*) field || — *di battaglia*, battle-field.

camuffare *vt.* to disguise.

canadese *agg. e sm.* Canadian.

canaglia *sf.* **1.** rabble **2.** (*di persona malvagia*) rascal.

canale *sm.* **1.** canal **2.** (*braccio di mare*) channel **3.** (*condotto*) pipe **4.** (*tv.*) channel.

cànapa *sf.* hemp.

canarino *sm.* canary.

cancellare *vt.* **1.** (*a penna*) to cross out; (*con una gomma*) to rub out; (*con un panno*) to wipe out **2.** (*fig.*) efface.

cancellatura *sf.* **1.** erasure **2.** (*fig.*) effacement.

cancellerìa *sf.* **1.** (*pol.*) chancellery **2.** (*materiale di* —) stationery articles **3.** (*giur.*) record-office.

cancelliere *sm.* **1.** (*pol.*) chancellor **2.** (*giur.*) recorder.

cancello *sm.* gate.

cancrena *sf.* gangrene.

cancro *sm.* cancer.

candeggina *sf.* chloride.

candela *sf.* **1.** candle: — *di sego*, tallow candle; *al lume di* —, by candle-light **2.** (*auto*) sparking plug.

candelabro *sm.* branched candlestick.

candeliere *sm.* candlestick.

candelotto *sm.* short thick candle: — *fumogeno*, smoke candle.

candidato *sm.* candidate.

candidatura *sf.* candidature.

càndido *agg.* **1.** snow-white **2.** (*innocente*) innocent.

candito *agg.* candied. ♦ **candito** *sm.* sugar candy.

candore *sm.* **1.** whiteness **2.** (*innocenza*) innocence.

cane *sm.* **1.** dog: — *da caccia*, sporting dog; — *pastore*, sheep dog; — *da guardia*, watch-dog **2.** (*persona spietata*) brute **3.** (*di fucile*) cock.

cànfora *sf.* camphor.

canguro *sm.* kangaroo.

canìcola *sf.* the height of summer.

canile *sm.* kennel.

canino *agg.* canine: *dente* —, canine tooth.

canna *sf.* **1.** reed **2.** (*coltivata*) cane || — *da zucchero*, sugar cane **3.** (*tubo*) pipe **4.** (*di arma*) barrel **5.** (*da pesca*) (fishing-)rod.

cannella *sf.* **1.** (*bot.*) cinnamon **2.** (*di botte*) spout.

cannello *sm.* **1.** torch **2.** (*chim.*) pipe.

canneto *sm.* canebrake.

cannìbale *sm.* cannibal.

cannocchiale *sm.* binoculars (*pl.*) || — *da campagna*, field glasses; — *da teatro*, opera glasses.

cannone *sm.* **1.** gun: — *antiaereo,* anti-aircraft gun; — *anticarro,* anti-tank gun **2.** (*fig.*) ace.

cannuccia *sf.* **1.** thin cane: — *per sorbire bibite,* straw.

cànone *sm.* canon: — *d'affitto,* rent; — *della radio,* radio-licence fee.

canònica *sf.* rectory.

canònico *agg.* canonical || *diritti canonici,* canon law. ♦ **canònico** *sm.* canon.

canonizzare *vt.* to canonize.

canoro *agg.* singing.

canottaggio *sm.* **1.** rowing, boating **2.** (*come attività*) boating.

canottiera *sf.* vest.

canotto *sm.* small boat.

canovaccio *sm.* **1.** (*per asciugare stoviglie*) dish-cloth; **2.** (*per ricamo*) canvas **3.** (*trama di un'opera*) plot.

cantante *sm.* singer.

cantare *vt.* **1.** to sing (*v. irr.*) **2.** (*del gallo*) to crow **3.** (*fare la spia*) to squeal.

cantata *sf.* song.

canterellare *vt. e vi.* to sing (*v. irr.*) softly, to hum.

càntico *sm.* hymn.

cantiere *sm.* yard.

cantilena *sf.* sing-song.

cantina *sf.* cellar.

cantiniere *sm.* cellarman (*pl.* -men).

cantino *sm.* chanterelle.

canto[1] *sm.* singing.

canto[2] *sm.* (*angolo*) corner || *dal* — *mio,* for my part; *da un* —, on one hand.

cantonata *sf.* corner: *prendere una* —, to make (*v. irr.*) a blunder.

cantone *sm.* **1.** corner **2.** (*geogr.*) canton.

cantoniera *sf.* **1.** (*mobile*) corner cupboard **2.** (*casa*) roadman's house **3.** (*ferr.*) signalman's house.

cantoniere *sm.* signalman (*pl.* -men).

canuto *agg.* hoary.

canzonare *vt.* to make (*v. irr.*) fun of.

canzone *sf.* song.

canzonetta *sf.* **1.** short song **2.** (*poet.*) canzonet.

canzonettista *s.* **1.** music-hall singer **2.** (*autore di canzoni*) songwriter.

caolino *sm.* kaolin.

caos *sm.* chaos.

capace *agg.* **1.** able **2.** (*idoneo*) fit **3.** (*abile*) clever.

capacità *sf.* **1.** ability, cleverness **2.** (*capienza*) capacity.

capanna *sf.* hut.

capanno *sm.* **1.** (*da caccia*) shooting-box **2.** (*per bagnanti*) bathing-box.

caparbierìa *sf.* stubbornness.

caparbio *agg.* stubborn.

caparra *sf.* caution-money.

capeggiare *vt.* to lead (*v. irr.*).

capello *sm.* hair (*solo sing.*) || *acconciatura dei capelli,* hairdress; *farsi tagliare i capelli,* to have one's hair cut; *avere un diavolo per* —, to be furious.

capezzale *sm.* bolster.

capézzolo *sm.* nipple.

capienza *sf.* capacity.

capigliatura *sf.* hair.

capillare *agg.* capillary.

capillarità *sf.* capillarity.

capinera *sf.* blackcap.

capire *vt.* to understand (*v. irr.*).

capitale *sm.* capital. ♦ **capitale** *agg.* **1.** (*che riguarda la vita*) capital **2.** (*principale*) main.

capitalismo *sm.* capitalism.

capitalista *s.* capitalist.

capitalizzare *vt.* to capitalize. ♦ **capitalizzare** *vi.* (*accumulare denaro*) to save.

capitano *sm.* captain, leader.

capitare *vi.* **1.** (*giungere*) to arrive **2.** (*accadere*) to happen, to befall (*v. irr.*).

capitello *sm.* (*arch.*) capital.

capitolare *vi.* to capitulate.

capitolare *sm.* capitulary. ♦ **capitolare** *agg.* capitular.

capitolo *sm.* chapter.

capitòmbolo *sm.* tumble.

capo *sm.* **1.** head || *avere mal di* —, to have a headache; *senza* — *né coda,* without rhyme or reason **2.** (*estremità*) end || *da un* — *all'altro,* from end to end; *andare a* —, new line; *in* — *a un anno,* within a year; *Capo d'Anno,* New Year's day **3.** (*geogr.*) cape **4.** (*chi comanda*) leader.

capobanda *sm.* **1.** (*mus.*) bandmaster **2.** (*di una banda di criminali*) ringleader.

capocuoco *sm.* head cook.

capocordata *sm.* first man on the rope.

capodanno *sm.* New Year's day.

capofamiglia *s.* head of a family.

capofila *sm.* file-leader.
capofitto (*nella loc. avv.*) *a* —, headlong || *cadere, tuffarsi a* —, to fall (*v. irr.*), to dive head first.
capogiro *sm.* dizziness.
capolavoro *sm.* masterpiece.
capolinea *sm.* terminus (*pl.* -ni).
capolino *sm.* small head || *far* —, to peep in.
capoluogo *sm.* main town.
caporale *sm.* corporal.
caporedattore *sm.* editor in chief.
caposaldo *sm.* **1.** datum point **2.** (*mil.*) stronghold **3.** (*fondamento*) main point.
caposcuola *sm.* leader of a movement.
capostazione *sm.* station-master.
capotare *vi.* **1.** (*di aerei*) to somersault **2.** (*di auto*) to turn over.
capoufficio *sm.* head-clerk.
capoverso *sm.* **1.** (*in poesia*) beginning of a line **2.** (*in prosa*) beginning of a paragraph.
capovòlgere *vt.* to turn upside down. ♦ **capovòlgersi** *vr.* to capsize.
cappa *sf.* **1.** (*mantello*) cloak **2.** (*di prete*) cape **3.** (*fig.*) vault || — *del camino*, chimney.
cappella *sf.* chapel.
cappellano *sm.* chaplain.
cappello *sm.* **1.** hat: — *a cilindro*, top-hat; — *di paglia*, straw hat; **2.** (*introduzione*) preamble.
càppero *sm.* caper.
cappone *sm.* capon.
cappotto *sm.* **1.** coat **2.** (*di gioco*) capot.
cappuccino *sm.* **1.** (*eccl.*) capuchin **2.** (*bevanda*) white coffee.
cappuccio *sm.* hood.
capra *sf.* goat.
capretto *sm.* kid.
capriccio *sm.* whim: *fare i capricci*, to be naughty.
caprino *agg.* goatish.
capriola[1] *sf.* caper: *far capriole*, to cut (*v. irr.*) capers.
capriola[2] *sf.* (*femmina del capriolo*) doe.
capriolo *sm.* roe-deer.
càpsula *sf.* **1.** capsule **2.** (*di dente*) crown.
captare *vt.* (*radio*) to pick up.
capzioso *agg.* captious.
carabina *sf.* carabine.
carabiniere *sm.* carabineer.
caracollare *vi.* to caracole.

caraffa *sf.* **1.** (*per acqua*) carafe **2.** (*per vino*) decanter.
caràmbola *sf.* cannon: *far* —, to cannon.
carambolare *vi.* to cannon.
caramella *sf.* sugar-drop, toffee.
caramellare *vt.* to coat with burnt sugar.
caramello *sm.* caramel.
carato *sm.* carat.
caràttere *sm.* **1.** character, temper **2.** (*caratteristica*) character **3.** (*tip.*) type.
caratterista *s.* character actor (actress).
caratterìstico *agg.* characteristic. ♦ **caratterìstica** *sf.* characteristic.
caravella *sf.* caravel.
carbonaio *sm.* coal merchant.
carbone *sm.* coal || — *di legna*, charcoal; — *fossile*, pit coal; *miniera di* —, coal-mine.
carbonerìa *sf.* Carbonarist movement.
carbonìfero *agg.* carboniferous.
carbonio *sm.* carbon.
carbonizzare *vt.* **1.** to carbonize **2.** (*di legno*) to char.
carburante *sm.* fuel.
carburatore *sm.* carburettor.
carburazione *sf.* carburation.
carcassa *sf.* carcass.
carcerazione *sf.* imprisonment.
càrcere *sm.* prison, jail.
carceriere *sm.* jailer.
carciofo *sm.* artichoke.
cardano *sm.* (*mecc.*) cardan joint.
cardare *vt.* to card.
cardìaco *agg.* cardiac || *disturbi cardiaci*, heart-disease.
cardinale *agg. e sm.* cardinal.
càrdine *sm.* **1.** hinge, pivot **2.** (*fig.*) foundation.
cardiòlogo *sm.* cardiologist.
cardiopatìa *sf.* cardiopathy.
cardo *sm.* **1.** (*bot.*) thistle **2.** (*cuc.*) cardoon **3.** (*mecc.*) carding machine.
carena *sf.* **1.** (*mar.*) keel **2.** (*aer.*) hull **3.** (*zool.*) càrina (*pl.* -nae).
carenza *sf.* want, lack.
carestìa *sf.* famine.
carezza *sf.* caress.
carezzévole *agg.* caressing.
cariàtide *sf.* caryatid.
cariato *agg.* decayed.
càrica *sf.* **1.** (*pubblico ufficio*) office: *entrare in* —, to take (*v.*

irr.) office **2.** (*mil.*) charge **3.** (*di arma da fuoco; elettr.*) charge **4.** (*di orologio*) winding up.

caricare *vt.* **1.** to load **2.** (*mil.; elettr.*) to charge **3.** (*di orologio*) to wind (*v. irr.*) up.

caricatore *sm.* **1.** loader **2.** (*di arma*) magazine.

caricatura *sf.* caricature.

càrico[1] *agg.* **1.** loaded, laden (*anche fig.*) **2.** (*di caffè*) strong **3.** (*elettr.*) charged.

càrico[2] *sm.* **1.** (*di nave*) freight; (*di veicolo*) load; (*di animale da soma*) burden **2.** (*fig.*) load, weight **3.** (*accusa*) charge || (*comm.*) essere a — di qu., to be charged to so.

carie *sf.* decay.

carino *agg.* pretty, nice.

carità *sf.* **1.** (*amore; teol.*) charity **2.** (*elemosina*) alms.

carlinga *sf.* cockpit.

carlona (*nella loc. avv.*) alla —, carelessly.

carminio *agg.* carmine.

carnagione *sf.* complexion.

carnale *agg.* carnal.

carne *sf.* **1.** flesh **2.** (*come alimento*) meat || — di manzo, beef; — di vitello, veal; — in scatola, tinned meat; — congelata, frozen meat.

carnéfice *sm.* executioner.

carneficina *sf.* slaughter.

carnevale *sm.* carnival.

carnìvoro *agg.* carnivorous.

caro *agg.* **1.** dear **2.** (*costoso*) dear, expensive.

carogna *sf.* carrion.

carosello *sm.* carousel.

carota *sf.* carrot.

caròtide *sf.* carotid.

carovana *sf.* caravan.

carovita *sm.* high cost of living.

carpa *sf.* carp.

carpentiere *sm.* carpenter.

carpire *vt.* **1.** to snatch **2.** (*con astuzia*) to swindle.

carponi *avv.* on all fours.

carràbile *agg.* cart: passo —, driveway.

carreggiata **1.** (*solco*) track **2.** (*strada*) cartway.

carrellata *sf.* dolly shot.

carrello *sm.* **1.** (*ferr.*) wag(g)on **2.** (*aer.*) landing gear **3.** (*cine; tv.*) dolly **4.** (*di macchina per scrivere*) carriage.

carriera *sf.* career || di gran —, at full speed.

carriola *sf.* wheelbarrow.

carrista *sm.* (*mil.*) tankman (*pl.* -men).

carro *sm.* **1.** (*a due ruote*) cart **2.** (*a quattro ruote*) wag(g)on || — armato, tank.

carrozza *sf.* carriage: — diretta, through coach; — viaggiatori, passenger car.

carrozzàbile *agg.* practicable.

carrozzella *sf.* **1.** cab **2.** (*per bambini*) perambulator; (*fam.*) pram.

carrozzerìa *sf.* body.

carrozziere *sm.* body-maker.

carrozzone *sm.* **1.** lumbering coach **2.** (*di zingari*) caravan.

carruba *sf.*, **carrubo** *sm.* carob.

carrùcola *sf.* pulley.

carta *sf.* paper: — da lettere, writing-paper; — carbone, carbon paper; — d'identità, identity card; — stradale, road-map.

cartaio *sm.* paper-maker.

cartamodello *sm.* dressmaker's pattern.

cartamoneta *sf.* paper-money.

cartapesta *sf.* paper-pulp.

cartavetrata *sf.* sand-paper.

carteggio *sm.* **1.** correspondence **2.** (*collezione di lettere*) collection of letters.

cartella *sf.* **1.** (*da scuola*) satchel **2.** (*di cuoio*) brief-case.

cartello *sm.* **1.** bill **2.** (*pubblicitario*) poster **3.** (*stradale*) traffic sign **4.** (*econ.*) cartel.

cartellone *sm.* **1.** (*pubblicitario*) poster **2.** (*teat.*) bill.

cartellonista *sm.* commercial artist.

cartiera *sf.* paper-mill.

cartilàgine *sf.* cartilage.

cartoccio *sm.* paper-bag.

cartografia *sf.* cartography.

cartolerìa *sf.* stationer's shop.

cartolina *sf.* postcard: — illustrata, picture postcard.

cartoncino *sm.* thin card.

cartone *sm.* cardboard || cartoni animati, cartoons.

cartuccia *sf.* cartridge || mezza — (*fig.*), shrimp.

casa *sf.* **1.** (*abitazione*) house **2.** (*ambiente familiare*) home || amico di —, family friend; donna di —, housewife; nostalgia di —, home-sickness; *andare a* —, to go (*v. irr.*) home; *restare a* —, to stay at home; *essere in* —, to be in **3.** (*stirpe*) house, dynasty, family.

casacca *sf.* coat.

casaccio (*nella loc. avv.*) *a* —, at random.

casalinga *sf.* housewife.

casalingo *agg.* homely: *cucina casalinga*, plain cooking.

casato *sm.* **1.** (*cognome*) surname **2.** (*origine, nascita*) birth.

cascame *sm.* waste.

cascamorto *sm.* spoon: *fare il* —, to run (*v. irr.*) after.

cascante *agg.* **1.** (*debole*) weak **2.** (*floscio*) flabby (*anche fig.*).

cascare *vi.* **1.** to fall (*v. irr.*) **2.** (*con rumore*) to crash || — *dalle nuvole*, to be struck with amazement; — *dal sonno*, to be overcome with sleep.

cascata *sf.* **1.** (*caduta*) fall **2.** (*d'acqua*) waterfall **3.** (*fig.*) cascade.

cascina *sf.* **1.** dairy farm **2.** (*cascinale*) farmstead.

casco *sm.* **1.** helmet **2.** (*per asciugare i capelli*) dryer.

casella *sf.*: — *postale*, post-box.

casellante *sm.* **1.** (*ferr.*) signalman (*pl.* -men) **2.** (*di passaggio a livello*) crossing keeper.

casellario *sm.* **1.** set of pigeon-holes **2.** (*giur.*) — *penale*, records-office.

casereccio *agg.* homely: *pane* —, home-made bread.

caserma *sf.* barracks (*pl.*).

caso *sm.* **1.** chance **2.** (*fatto*) case **3.** (*possibilità*) way, possibility || *a* —, at random; *per* —, by chance.

càspita *inter.* good gracious!

cassa *sf.* **1.** case, box **2.** (*comm.*) cash || *libro di* —, cash-book; *pagamento per* —, cash-payment; *sportello di* —, cashier's window **3.** (*mus.*) case || *gran* —, bass-drum.

cassaforte *sf.* safe.

cassapanca *sf.* chest.

cassazione *sf.* (*giur.*) cassation.

casseruola *sf.* saucepan.

cassetto *sm.* drawer.

cassettone *sm.* chest of drawers.

cassiere *sm.* cashier.

casta *sf.* caste.

castagna *sf.* chestnut.

castagnaccio *sm.* chestnut-tart.

castagno *sm.* chestnut-tree.

castano *agg.* nut-brown.

castellano *sm.* lord of a castle.

castello *sm.* castle.

castigare *vt.* to punish.

castigatezza *sf.* moderation.

castigato *agg.* **1.** (*casto*) chaste **2.** (*emendato*) castigated.

castigo *sm.* punishment.

castità *sf.* chastity.

casto *agg.* chaste.

castoro *sm.* beaver.

castrare *vt.* to castrate.

castrato *sm.* (*cuc.*) mutton.

castroneria *sf.* stupidity.

casuale *agg.* casual.

casualità *sf.* casualness.

cataclisma *sm.* cataclysm (*anche fig.*).

catacomba *sf.* catacomb.

catafalco *sm.* catafalque.

catafascio (*nella loc. avv.*) *andare a* —, to go (*v. irr.*) to rack and ruin; *a* —, topsyturvy.

catalessi *sf.* catalepsy.

catalizzatore *sm.* catalyst.

catalogare *vt.* to catalogue.

catàlogo *sm.* catalogue.

catapecchia *sf.* hovel.

catapulta *sf.* catapult.

catarifrangente *sm.* reflector.

catarro *sm.* catarrh.

catarsi *sf.* catharsis.

catasta *sf.* pile, heap.

catasto *sm.* cadastre.

catàstrofe *sf.* catastrophe.

catastròfico *agg.* catastrophic(al).

catechismo *sm.* catechism.

catechizzare *vt.* **1.** to catechize **2.** (*fig.*) to persuade.

catecùmeno *sm.* catechumen.

categorìa *sf.* category, class.

categòrico *agg.* categorical, absolute.

catena *sf.* **1.** chain **2.** (*fig.*) bond.

catenaccio *sm.* bolt.

cateratta *sf.* cataract.

caterva *sf.* **1.** (*di persone*) crowd **2.** (*di cose*) great quantity.

catino *sm.* basin.

catione *sm.* (*fis.*) cation.

càtodo *sm.* cathode.

catramare *vt.* to tar.

catrame *sm.* tar.

càttedra *sf.* **1.** desk **2.** (*l'ufficio dell'insegnare*) teaching post **3.** (*di università*) chair.

cattedrale *sf.* cathedral.

cattiveria *sf.* wickedness.

cattività *sf.* captivity.

cattivo *agg.* e *sm.* bad || — *scrittore*, poor writer.
cattolicésimo *sm.* catholicism.
cattòlico *agg.* catholic.
cattura *sf.* **1.** capture **2.** (*arresto*) arrest: *mandato di* —, warrant of arrest.
catturare *vt.* **1.** to capture **2.** (*arrestare*) to arrest.
caucciù *sm.* india-rubber.
càusa *sf.* **1.** cause **2.** (*giur.*) law suit || *far — a qu.*, to sue so. (for).
causare *vt.* to cause.
càustico *agg.* caustic (*anche fig.*)
cautela *sf.* caution.
cautelare *vt.* to protect. ♦ **cautelarsi** *vr.* to take (*v. irr.*) precautions.
cauterizzare *vt.* to cauterize.
càuto *agg.* cautious, prudent.
cauzione *sf.* **1.** guarantee **2.** (*per essere rilasciato dalla polizia*) bail.
cava *sf.* quarry.
cavalcare *vt.* to ride (*v. irr.*). ♦ **cavalcare** *vi.* to ride on horseback.
cavalcavìa *sm.* fly-over bridge.
cavalcioni (a) *loc. avv.* astride.
cavaliere *sm.* **1.** rider **2.** (*di ordine cavalleresco*) knight.
cavalla *sf.* mare.
cavalleresco *agg.* knightly.
cavallerìa *sf.* **1.** (*mil.*) cavalry **2.** (*stor.*) chivalry.
cavalletta *sf.* grasshopper.
cavalletto *sm.* **1.** trestle **2.** (*foto*) tripod **3.** (*per pittori*) easel.
cavallo *sm.* **1.** horse: — *da corsa*, racehorse; — *a dondolo*, rocking--horse; —. *da soma*, pack-horse; *ferro di* —, horse-shoe **2.** (*ginnastica*) vaulting-horse **3.** (*cavallo vapore*) horse-power (*abbr.* H.P.).
cavallone *sm.* (*maroso*) billow.
cavare *vt.* to take (*v. irr.*) off || — *un dente*, to pull out a tooth || *cavarsela*, to get (*v. irr.*) off.
cavatappi, cavaturàccioli *sm.* cork-screw.
caverna *sf.* cave.
cavernoso *agg.* cavernous || *voce cavernosa*, very deep voice.
cavezza *sf.* halter.
cavia *sf.* cavy.
caviale *sm.* caviar.
caviglia *sf.* ankle.
cavillare *vi.* to cavil (at).
cavillo *sm.* cavil.
cavità *sf.* cavity.

cavo *agg.* hollow, empty. ♦ **cavo** *sm.* cable, rope.
cavolfiore *sm.* cauliflower.
càvolo *sm.* cabbage.
cazzotto *sm.* punch || *fare a cazzotti*, to come (*v. irr.*) to blows.
cazzuola *sf.* trowel.
cece *sm.* chick-pea.
cecità *sf.* blindness (*anche fig.*).
cecoslovacco *agg.* e *sm.* Czechoslovak.
cèdere *vt.* e *vi.* **1.** (*dare*) to give (*v. irr.*) **2.** (*trasferire*) to hand over **3.** (*vendere*) to dispose of. ♦ **cèdere** *vi.* **1.** to surrender **2.** (*venir meno*) to subside **3.** (*essere inferiore*) to be second to.
cedimento *sm.* **1.** yielding **2.** (*fig.*) giving up.
cèdola *sf.* coupon.
cedrata *sf.* citron syrup.
cedrina *sf.* lemon-scented verbena.
cedro *sm.* **1.** citron-tree **2.** (*frutto*) citron.
cedrone *agg.* e *sm.* (*gallo*) capercaillie.
cefalea *sf.* cephalea.
cefalgìa *sf.* cephalalgy.
ceffone *sm.* slap in the face.
celare *vt.* to conceal, to hide (*v. irr.*).
celebrare *vt.* to celebrate || — *un anniversario*, to keep (*v. irr.*) an anniversary.
celebrazione *sf.* celebration.
cèlebre *agg.* celebrated.
celebrità *sf.* celebrity.
cèlere *agg.* quick, swift.
celerità *sf.* quickness.
celeste *agg.* **1.** light-blue **2.** (*del cielo*) heavenly.
celia *sf.* jest.
celiare *vi.* to jest.
celibato *sm.* bachelorhood.
cèlibe *agg.* e *sm.* single. ♦ **cèlibe** *sm.* bachelor.
cella *sf.* cell.
cèllula *sf.* cell.
cellulare *agg.* cellular || *segregazione* —, close confinement.
cellulite *sf.* cellulitis.
cellulòide *sf.* celluloid.
cellulosa *sf.* cellulose.
celta *sm.* Celt.
cèltico *agg.* Celtic.
cémbalo *sm.* **1.** (*tamburello*) tambourine **2.** (*spinetta*) spinet.
cementare *vt.* to cement (*anche fig.*).

cementazione *sf.* cementation.
cementificio *sm.* cement-factory.
cemento *sm.* cement: — *armato*, reinforced concrete.
cena *sf.* 1. (*pasto serale leggero*) supper 2. (*pranzo*) dinner || *far* —, to have supper.
cenàcolo *sm.* 1. supper-room 2. (*di artisti*) artistic coterie || *il* — *di Leonardo da Vinci,* Leonardo's Last Supper.
cenare *vi.* to have (*v. irr.*) supper.
cenciaio *sm.* ragman (*pl.* -men).
cencio *sm.* 1. rag 2. (*vestito logoro*) tatters (*pl.*).
cencioso *agg.* ragged, tattered.
cénere *sf.* ash (*general. al pl.*).
cenno *sm.* 1. (*segno*) sign 2. (*allusione*) hint 3. (*breve notizia*) notice || *fare un* — *col capo,* to nod || *a un vostro* — (*comm.*), on hearing from you.
cenobio *sm.* coenobium (*pl.* -ia).
cenone *sm.* 1. (*di Natale*) Christmas eve dinner 2. (*di Capodanno*) New Year's eve dinner.
censimento *sm.* census.
censire *vt.* 1. to take (*v. irr.*) a census of 2. (*di proprietà*) to assess.
censo *sm.* 1. (*stor.*) census 2. (*ricchezza*) wealth.
censore *sm.* 1. censor 2. (*fig.*) critic.
censorio *agg.* censorial.
censura *sf.* 1. (*ufficio di censore*) censorship 2. (*azione di censura*) censure.
censurare *vt.* 1. to censor 2. (*fig.*) to censure.
centàuro *sm.* 1. centaur 2. (*fig., motociclista*) motorcyclist.
centellinare *vt.* to sip.
centenario *agg.* e *sm.* 1. centennial 2. (*di persona*) centenarian. ◆ centenario *sm.* (*commemorazione*) centenary.
centesimale *agg.* centesimal. ◆ centèsimo *agg.* (the) hundredth ◆ centèsimo *sm.* (one) hundredth (of sthg.) 2. (*di dollaro*) cent 3. (*di franco*) centime || *non avere un* —, to be penniless.
centigrado *agg.* centigrade.
centigrammo *sm.* centigramme.
centìlitro *sm.* centilitre.
centìmetro *sm.* centimetre.
centinaio *sm.* hundred.
cento *agg.* e *num. card.* hundred || — *di questi giorni,* many happy

returns of the day.
centrale *agg.* central. ◆ centrale *sf.* 1. — *elettrica,* power station 2. — *telefonica,* exchange.
centralinista *s.* operator.
centralino *sm.* telephone exchange.
centralismo *sm.* centralism.
centrare *vt.* to hit (*v. irr.*) the centre.
centrìfuga *sf.* centrifuge.
centrìfugo *agg.* centrifugal.
centrino *sm.* doily.
centrìpeto *agg.* centripetal.
centrismo *sm.* centrism.
centro *sm.* 1. centre 2. (*istituto*) institute.
centuplicare *vt.* 1. to centuplicate 2. (*fig.*) to increase.
cèntuplo *agg.* e *sm.* centuple.
centuria *sf.* (*stor.*) century.
centurione *sm.* (*stor.*) centurion.
ceppo *sm.* 1. stump 2. (*fig.*) stock.
cera *sf.* 1. wax 2. (*aspetto*) look || *avere bella* —, to look well.
ceralacca *sf.* sealing-wax.
ceràmica *sf.* 1. (*arte*) ceramics 2. (*pezzo*) piece of pottery.
ceramista *sm.* ceramist.
cerato *agg.* waxed || *tela cerata,* wax-cloth.
cerbiatto *sm.* fawn.
cerbottana *sf.* 1. blowgun 2. (*giocattolo*) pea-shooter.
cercare *vt.* 1. to look for 2. (*per consultazione*) to look up 3. (*a tentoni*) to fumble for 4. (*chiedere*) to ask (for). ◆ cercare *vi.* to try.
cercatore *sm.* seeker: — *d'oro,* gold-digger; (*amer.*) prospector.
cerchia *sf.* circle.
cerchiare *vt.* to hoop.
cerchiatura *sf.* hooping.
cerchietto *sm.* 1. small ring 2. (*gioco*) quoit.
cerchio *sm.* 1. circle 2. (*gioco*) hoop.
cerchione *sm.* rim.
cereale *sm.* cereals (*pl.*).
cerebrale *agg.* cerebral.
cèreo *agg.* waxen.
ceretta *sf.* 1. boot polish 2. (*per depilare*) wax.
cerimonia *sf.* 1. ceremony 2. (*pompa*) pomp.
cerimoniale *sm.* ceremonial.
cerimoniere *sm.* Master of Ceremonies.
cerimonioso *agg.* ceremonious
cerino *sm.* match.

cerniera *sf.* **1.** (*di occhiali, porte, finestre*) hinge **2.** (*di borsetta*) clasp **3.** (*lampo*) zipper.

cèrnita *sf.* choice, selection.

cero *sm.* large candle.

cerone *sm.* make-up.

cerotto *sm.* plaster.

certamente *avv.* certainly, undoubtedly.

certezza *sf.* certainty.

certificare *vt.* to certify, to attest.

certificato *sm.* certificate.

certo[1] *agg. indef.* **1.** certain: *un — Mr. Smith*, a (certain) Mr. Smith **2.** (*qualche*) some: *certe persone lo riconobbero*, some people recognized him; *dopo un — tempo*, after some time **3.** (*tale, di tal genere*) such. ♦ **certi** *pron. indef. pl.* some people.

certo[2] *agg.* certain. ♦ **certo** *avv.* certainly.

certuni *pron. indef.* some.

cerùleo *agg.* sky-blue.

cerva *sf.* (*zool.*) hind.

cervella *sf.* brain.

cervelletto *sm.* cerebellum.

cervello *sm.* **1.** brain **2.** (*intelligenza, mente*) understanding, mind.

cervellòtico *agg.* far-fetched.

cervicale *agg.* cervical.

cervice *sf.* nape.

cèrvidi *sm. pl.* cervidae.

cervo *sm.* deer (*inv. al pl.*).

cesàreo *agg.* Caesarean ‖ *taglio —,* Caesarean operation.

cesarismo *sm.* Caesarism.

cesellare *vt.* to chisel (*anche fig.*).

cesellatura *sf.* chisel work.

cesello *sm.* chisel.

cesoia *sf.* shears (*pl.*).

cespuglio *sm.* bush, thicket.

cespuglioso *agg.* bushy.

cessare *vt.* e *vi.* to cease, to stop.

cessazione *sf.* cessation.

cessione *sf.* transfer.

cesso *sm.* lavatory.

cesta *sf.* basket.

cestaio *sm.* **1.** basket-maker **2.** (*chi vende*) basket-vendor.

cestinare *vt.* (*fig.*) to refuse.

cestino *sm.* small basket: — *da lavoro,* work-basket; — *da viaggio,* luncheon-basket; — *per la carta straccia,* waste-paper basket.

cesto *sm.* (*sport*) basket.

cesura *sf.* caesura.

cetàceo *agg.* e *sm.* cetacean.

ceto *sm.* ciass, rank.

cetra *sf.* cithern, lyre.

cetriolino *sm.* gherkin.

cetriolo *sm.* cucumber.

che[1] *pron. rel.* **1.** (*sogg., riferito a persone*) who, that: *l'uomo — mi parlò,* the man who (that) spoke to me **2.** (*sogg., riferito a cose e animali*) which, that: *ecco il cane — mi fu regalato,* here is the dog which (that) was given to me **3.** (*ogg., riferito a persone*) whom: *è la ragazza più graziosa — abbia mai incontrato,* she is the prettiest girl whom I ever met **4.** (*ogg., riferito a cose e animali*) which: *questo è il libro — le darò,* this is the book which I shall give her **5.** *il —,* which **6.** (*riferito a tempo*) when.

che[2] *agg. int.* **1.** what: — *musica preferisci?,* what music do you prefer? **2.** which: — *libro scegli?,* which book do you choose? ♦ **che** *pron. int.* what: — *è questo?,* what is this? ♦ **che** *agg. escl.* what, what a. ♦ **che** *pron. ind.* something.

che[3] *cong.* **1.** that **2.** (*comparativo*) than: *è più bella che intelligente,* she is more beautiful than intelligent **3.** (*correlativo*) whether: — *tu venga o no,* whether you come or not. ♦ **che** *inter.* what!

checché *pron. indef.* whatever.

checchessìa *pron. indef.* anything.

chepì *sm.* (*mil.*) kepi.

cherosene *sm.* kerosene.

cherubino *sm.* cherub.

chetamente *avv.* quietly, secretly.

chetare *vt.* to quiet. ♦ **chetarsi** *vr.* to quiet down.

chetichella (*nella loc. avv.*) *alla —,* on the sly, secretly.

cheto *agg.* quiet.

chi *pron. rel.* **1.** (*colui che*) he (*ogg.* him) who (*ogg.* whom) **2.** (*colei che*) she (*ogg.* her) who (*ogg.* whom) **3.** (*coloro che*) they (*ogg.* them) who (*ogg.* whom) **4.** (*gen.*) those, the person who(m). ♦ **chi** *pron. indef.* **1.** whoever, anyone **2.** (*qualcuno che*) someone who. ♦ **chi** *pron. int.* **1.** (*sogg.*) who **2.** (*ogg.*) whom **3.** which: — *di voi?,* which of you? **4.** (*specificazione poss.*) whose: *di — è questa casa?,* whose house is this?

chiàcchiera *sf.* chatter.

chiacchierare *vi.* to chat.

chiacchierata *sf.* chat.
chiacchierone *sm.* chatterbox.
chiamare *vt.* to call || *mandare a —*, to send (*v. irr.*) for; — *al telefono*, to call up. ◆ chiamarsi *vr.* to be called || *come ti chiami?*, what's your name?
chiamata *sf.* call, appeal.
chiara *sf.* — *d'uovo*, white (of an egg).
chiaretto *sm.* (*vino*) claret.
chiarezza *sf.* 1. clearness 2. (*fig.*) evidence.
chiarificare *vt.* to clarify.
chiarificazione *sf.* 1. clarification 2. (*fig.*) frank explanation.
chiarimento *sm.*. explanation.
chiarire *vt.* 1. to clarify, to clear up 2. (*spiegare*) to explain.
chiaro *agg.* 1. clear, evident 2. (*di luce*) light.
chiarore *sm.* 1. light 2. (*luce tenue*) faint light.
chiaroscuro *sm.* light and shade.
chiaroveggente *agg.* 1. clear-sighted 2. (*che ha facoltà divinatorie*) clairvoyant.
chiassata *sf.* row.
chiasso *sm.* noise, uproar.
chiassone *sm.* noisy person.
chiassoso *agg.* 1. noisy 2. (*fig.*) showy.
chiatta *sf.* barge.
chiavarda *sf.* bolt.
chiave *sf.* 1. key 2. (*mus.*) clef.
chiavistello *sm.* latch, bolt.
chiazza *sf.* spot, stain.
chicchessìa *pron. indef.* anyone.
chicco *sm.* 1. grain 2. (*di grandine*) hailstone 3. (*di caffè*) coffee-bean 4. (*di uva*) grape.
chièdere *vt.* 1. to ask: — *qc. a qu.*, (*per sapere*) to ask so. sthg., (*per avere*) to ask so. for sthg. 2. (*riferito a un prezzo*) to charge.
chierichetto *sm.* altar boy.
chiesa *sf.* church.
chiglia *sf.* (*mar.*) keel.
chilo[1] *sm.* (*med.*) chyle || *fare il —*, to take (*v. irr.*) a nap.
chilo[2] *sm.* kilo.
chilogrammo *sm.* kilogram.
chilometraggio *sm.* distance in kilometres.
chilòmetro *sm.* kilometre.
chilowatt *sm.* kilowatt.
chimera *sf.* chimera.
chìmica *sf.* chemistry.
chìmico *agg.* chemical. ◆ chìmico

sm. chemist.
china *sf.* slope.
chinare *vt.* to bend (*v. irr.*), to bow. ◆ chinarsi *vr.* to bend (*v. irr.*) down.
chincaglierìa *sf.* 1. small fancy articles (*pl.*) 2. (*negozio*) fancy goods shop.
chinino *sm.* quinine.
chioccia *sf.* brooding-hen.
chiòcciola *sf.* snail || *scala a —*, spiral staircase.
chiodato *agg.* nailed.
chiodo *sm.* 1. nail 2. (*fig.*) fixed idea.
chioma *sf.* hair.
chiosco *sm.* 1. kiosk 2. (*per giornali, frutta e verdura*) stand.
chiostro *sm.* cloister.
chiromante *s.* chiromancer.
chiromanzìa *sf.* chiromancy.
chirurgìa *sf.* surgery.
chirurgo *sm.* surgeon.
chissà *inter.* goodness knows.
chitarra *sf.* guitar.
chiùdere *vt.* 1. to shut (*v. irr.*) || *— a chiave*, to lock 2. (*terminare*) to close 3. (*rinchiudere*) to shut (*v. irr.*) up.
chiunque *pron.* 1. (*sogg.*) anyone who, whoever 2. (*ogg.*) whomever, anyone 3. (*specificazione possessiva*) *di —*, whosoever.
chiuso *agg.* closed, shut || *— a chiave*, locked.
chiusura *sf.* closing.
ci *pron.* 1. (*ogg.*) us: *essi — amano*, they love us 2. (*riflessivo*) ourselves: *noi — laviamo*, we wash ourselves 3. (*rec. fra due persone*) each other: *mia madre ed io — guardammo*, my mother and I looked at each other 4. (*rec. fra più persone*) one another 5. (*dimostrativo*) this, that, it: *non badarci*, pay no attention to it. ◆ ci *avv. di luogo* there (*là*), here (*qui*).
ciabatta *sf.* slipper.
ciambella *sf.* ring-shaped cake.
ciambellano *sm.* chamberlain.
ciancia *sf.* idle talk || *ciance!*, nonsense!
cianciare *vi.* to chatter.
cianografia *sf.* blueprint.
cianuro *sm.* cyanide.
ciao *inter.* 1. (*incontrandosi*) hullo 2. (*congedandosi*) bye-bye.
ciarla *sf.* 1. loquacity 2. (*notizia*

falsa) false report.
ciarlare *vi.* to talk idly.
ciarlatano *sm.* charlatan.
ciascuno *agg.* every. ♦ **ciascuno**
pron. **1.** (*con valore distributivo*)
each **2.** (*tutti*) everybody, everyone.
cibernètica *sf.* cybernetics.
cibo *sm.* food.
ciborio *sm.* ciborium (*pl.* -ia).
cicala *sf.* cicada.
cicatrice *sf.* scar.
cicatrizzare *vt.* to cicatrize, to heal.
♦ **cicatrizzarsi** *vr.* to cicatrize, to
heal.
cicerone *sm.* guide.
ciclamino *sm.* cyclamen.
cìclico *agg.* cyclic.
ciclismo *sm.* cycling.
ciclista *s*, cyclist.
ciclo *sm.* **1.** cycle **2.** (*di malattia*)
course.
ciclone *sm.* hurricane.
ciclòpico *agg.* Cyclopean.
ciclostilare *vt.* to mimeograph.
ciclostile *sm.* cyclostyle.
ciclotrone *sm.* cyclotron.
cicogna *sf.* stork.
cicuta *sf.* hemlock.
cieco *agg.* blind (*anche fig.*). ♦
cieco *sm.* blind man.
cielo *sm.* **1.** sky **2.** (*aria*) air **3.**
(*paradiso*) Heaven.
cifra *sf.* **1.** figure, number **2.** (*segno di cifrario*) cipher.
cifrare *vt.* **1.** to cipher **2.** (*ricamare
in cifra*) to mark.
ciglio *sm.* **1.** eyelash **2.** (*bordo*)
edge.
cigno *sm.* swan.
cilecca *sf.* failure || *far* —, to miss
fire, (*fig.*) to fail.
cileno *agg.* Chilean.
cilicio *sm.* **1.** hairshirt **2.** (*relig.*)
cilice.
ciliegia *sf.* cherry.
ciliegio *sm.* cherry-tree.
cilindrata *sf.* (*auto*) displacement.
cilindro *sm.* **1.** (*geom.; auto*) cylinder **2.** (*cappello*) top-hat.
cima *sf.* **1.** top, summit: *in* —,
at the top **2.** (*fig.*) genius.
cìmbali *sm. pl. essere in* —, to be
tipsy.
cimentare *vt.* to put (*v. irr.*) to
the test. ♦ **cimentarsi** *vr.* to venture upon.
cimitero *sm.* cemetery, graveyard.
cinabro *sm.* cinnabar.
cincillà *sf.* chinchilla.

cineasta *sm.* cinematographer.
cinecàmera *sf.* cine-camera.
cinedilettante *sm.* film-amateur.
cinegiornale *sm.* news-reel.
cìnema *sm.* **1.** cinema, pictures
(*pl.*) **2.** (*locale*) cinema **3.** (*amer.*)
movies (*pl.*).
cinemàtica *sf.* kinematics.
cinematografia *sf.* cinematography.
cinematògrafo *sm.* cinema.
cinèreo *agg.* cinereous, ashen-grey.
cinese *agg. e sm.* Chinese.
cineteca *sf.* film library.
cinètica *sf.* kinetics.
cìngere *vt.* **1.** to engird **2.** (*circondare*) to surround.
cinghia *sf.* **1.** strap **2.** (*mecc.*) belt.
cinghiale *sm.* (*zool.*) wild boar.
cìnico *agg.* cynical. ♦ **cìnico** *sm.*
cynic.
cinismo *sm.* cynicism.
cinocèfalo *sm.* cynocephalus (*pl.*
-ali).
cinòdromo *sm.* greyhound racing-track.
cinofilìa *sf.* dog-love.
cinquanta *agg.* fifty.
cinquantenario *sm.* fiftieth anniversary.
cinque *agg.* five.
cinquecento *agg.* five hundred.
cinta *sf.* town-walls (*pl.*): *muro di
—*, boundary walls.
cinto *sm.* belt. ♦ **cinto** *agg.*
surrounded.
cìntola *sf.* waist: *dalla — in giù*,
below the waist; *dalla — in su*,
above the waist.
cintura *sf.* belt.
cinturone *sm.* belt.
ciò *pron.* that, this, it.
ciocca *sf.* (*di capelli*) lock.
cioccolata *sf.* chocolate.
cioccolatino *sm.* chocolate.
cioccolato *sm.* chocolate.
cioè *cong.* that is.
ciondolare *vi.* **1.** to dangle **2.**
(*fig.*) to lounge.
cìondolo *sm.* pendant.
ciondoloni *avv.* dangling.
ciòtola *sf.* cup, bowl.
ciòttolo *sm.* pebble.
cipolla *sf.* onion.
cipresso *sm.* cypress.
cipria *sf.* powder: *piumino per —*,
powder puff.
circa *prep. e avv.* about, nearly ||
— a, as to.
circo *sm.* circus.

circolante *agg.* circulating: *moneta* —, currency.

circolare[1] *agg.* circular. ◆ **circolare** *sf.* circular letter.

circolare[2] *vi.* to circulate.

circolatorio *agg.* circulatory.

circolazione *sf.* **1.** circulation **2.** (*traffico*) traffic **3.** (*comm.*) currency.

circolo *sm.* **1.** circle **2.** (*associazione*) club.

circoncìdere *vt.* to circumcise.

circoncisione *sf.* circumcision.

circondare *vt.* to surround (*anche fig.*).

circonferenza *sf.* circumference.

circonflesso *agg.* circumflex.

circonlocuzione *sf.* circumlocution.

circonvallazione *sf.* ring-road.

circonvenire *vt.* to circumvent.

circonvoluzione *sf.* circumvolution.

circoscrìvere *vt.* to circumscribe.

circoscrizione *sf.* **1.** circumscription **2.** (*territorio*) area.

circospetto *agg.* circumspect.

circospezione *sf.* circumspection.

circostante *agg.* **1.** surrounding **2.** (*attr.*) neighbouring.

circostanza *sf.* circumstance, occasion: *in queste circostanze*, under these circumstances; *in quella* —, on that occasion.

circostanziale *agg.* circumstantial.

circostanziare *vt.* to detail.

circuire *vt.* **1.** to surround **2.** (*fig.*) to circumvent.

circùito *sm.* circuit.

cirìllico *agg.* cyrillic.

cirrosi *sf.* cirrhosis.

cisalpino *agg.* cisalpine.

cisposo *agg.* blear.

ciste *sf.* cyst.

cisterna *sf.* **1.** cistern **2.** (*serbatoio*) tank.

cistifèllea *sf.* gall-bladder.

cistite *sf.* cystitis.

citare *vt.* **1.** (*menzionare*) to mention **2.** (*da un libro o da un discorso ecc.*) to quote **3.** (*giur.*) to summon.

citazione *sf.* **1.** (*da un discorso, un libro ecc.*) quotation **2.** (*giur.*) summons (*pl.*).

citòfono *sm.* interphone.

citologìa *sf.* (*biol.*) cytology.

citrato *sm.* citrate.

cìtrico *agg.* citric.

città *sf.* **1.** town: — *di provincia*, country town; — *natale*, home town; *gente di* —, townspeople; *vita di* —, town life **2.** (*metropoli*) city.

cittadella *sf.* **1.** citadel **2.** (*baluardo*) stronghold.

cittadina *sf.* **1.** small town **2.** (*donna che abita in città*) woman citizen.

cittadinanza *sf.* **1.** (*abitanti*) people of the city **2.** (*nazionalità*) citizenship: *diritto di* —, right of citizenship.

cittadino *sm.* **1.** (*che abita in città*) town-dweller **2.** (*che appartiene a uno stato*) citizen. ◆ **cittadino** *agg.* town.

ciuffo *sm.* **1.** forelock **2.** (*di penne, peli, erba*) tuft.

ciurma *sf.* crew.

civetta *sf.* **1.** owl **2.** (*fig.*) coquette.

civetterìa *sf.* coquetry.

cìvico *agg.* civic.

civile *agg.* **1.** civil **2.** (*che riguarda la civiltà*) civilized **3.** (*gentile*) polite **4.** (*non ecclesiastico o non militare*) civilian.

civilizzare *vt.* to civilize.

civilizzazione *sf.* civilization.

civiltà *sf.* **1.** civilization **2.** (*cortesia*) politeness.

civismo *sm.* civic virtues (*pl.*).

clamore *sm.* uproar.

clamoroso *agg.* noisy.

clandestino *agg.* clandestine, secret.

clarinetto, clarino *sm.* clarinet.

classe *sf.* class || *di* — (*qualità*), first-rate.

classicismo *sm.* classicism.

clàssico *agg.* classical. ◆ **clàssico** *sm.* classic.

classìfica *sf.* **1.** classification **2.** (*sport*) position.

classificare *vt.* to classify.

classificazione *sf.* classification.

claudicare *vi.* to limp.

clàusola *sf.* **1.** clause **2.** (*riserva*) reserve.

claustrofobìa *sf.* claustrophobia.

clava *sf.* club.

clavicémbalo *sm.* harpsichord.

clavìcola *sf.* collar-bone.

clemente *agg.* clement, mild.

clemenza *sf.* clemency, mildness.

cleptòmane *agg. e sm.* kleptomaniac.

cleptomanìa *sf.* kleptomania.

clericale *agg.* clerical.

clero *sm.* clergy.

cliente *sm.* **1.** customer **2.** (*di medico, avvocato*) client.

clientela *sf.* **1.** customers (*pl.*) **2.** (*di medico, avvocato*) practice **3.** (*comm.*) connection.

clima *sm.* climate.

clinica *sf.* nursing-home.

clinico *agg.* clinical. ♦ **clinico** *sm* clinician.

clistere *sm.* enema.

cloaca *sf.* cloaca.

cloro *sm.* chlorine.

clorofilla *sf.* chlorophyll.

cloroformio *sm.* chloroform.

cloruro *sm.* chloride.

coabitare *vi.* to cohabit.

coabitazione *sf.* cohabitation.

coadiuvante *agg.* coadjuvant.

coadiuvare *vt.* to help.

coagulare *vt.* **1.** to coagulate **2.** (*del latte*) to curdle.

coagulazione *sf.* coagulation.

coagulo *sm.* **1.** curd **2.** (*di sangue*) blood-clot.

coalizione *sf.* alliance, coalition.

coalizzare *vt.* to unite. ♦ **coalizzarsi** *vr.* to form a coalition.

coartare *vt.* to force. .

coatto *agg.* forced: *domicilio* —, forced residence.

cobalto *sm.* cobalt.

cobelligerante *agg.* e *sm.* co-belligerent.

cobra *sm.* cobra.

cocaina *sf.* cocaine.

cocainòmane *s.* cocainist.

coccarda *sf.* cockade.

cocchiere *sm.* coachman (*pl.* -men).

cocchio *sm.* coach.

coccige *sm.* cocyx (*pl.* -yges).

coccinella *sf.* ladybird.

cocciniglia *sf.* cochineal.

coccio *sm.* **1.** (*terracotta*) crock, pot **2.** (*pezzo rotto*) fragment of pottery.

cocciutàggine *sf.* stubbornness.

cocciuto *agg.* stubborn.

cocco *sm.* **1.** (*frutto*) coconut **2.** (*albero*) coconut-tree **3.** (*fam. vezz.*) darling.

coccodrillo *sm.* crocodile.

coccolare *vt.* to pet, to fondle.

cocente *agg.* **1.** hot, scalding **2.** (*fig.*) deep, bitter.

cocòmero *sm.* water-melon.

cocùzzolo *sm.* **1.** crown **2.** (*vetta*) top.

coda *sf.* **1.** tail **2.** (*fila*) queue: *fare la* —, to queue up.

codardo *agg.* cowardly. ♦ **codardo** *sm.* coward.

codesto *agg.* **1.** that (*pl.* those) **2.** (*come* « *tale* ») such. ♦ **codesto** *pron.* that one (*pl.* those ones).

còdice *sm.* **1.** code: — *civile*, Civil Law **2.** (*manoscritto antico*) codex.

codificare *vt.* to codify.

coefficiente *sm.* coefficient.

coercitivo *agg.* coercive.

coercizione *sf.* compulsion.

coerente *agg.* coherent.

coerenza *sf.* coherence.

coesione *sf.* cohesion.

coesistenza *sf.* coexistence.

coesistere *vi.* to coexist.

coetàneo *agg.* e *sm.* contemporary ‖ *Carlo ed io siamo coetanei*, Charles and I are the same age.

cofanetto *sm.* casket: — *di gioielli*, jewel box.

còfano *sm.* **1.** coffer **2.** (*auto*) bonnet.

cògliere *vt.* **1.** to pick up, to pluck **2.** (*sorprendere*) to catch (*v. irr.*) **3.** (*colpire*) to hit (*v. irr.*) **4.** (*afferrare*) to seize: — *la palla al balzo*, to seize the opportunity.

cognata *sf.* sister-in-law.

cognato *sm.* brother-in-law.

cognizione *sf.* **1.** knowledge **2.** (*giur.*) cognizance.

cognome *sm.* surname.

coincidenza *sf.* **1.** coincidence **2.** (*ferr.*) connection.

coincidere *vi.* to coincide, to clash.

coinvolgere *vt.* to involve.

còito *sm.* coition.

colabrodo *sm.* strainer.

colaggio *sm.* **1.** (*di liquidi*) leakage **2.** (*metal.*) casting.

colare *vt.* **1.** to strain **2.** (*fondere*) to cast (*v. irr.*). ♦ **colare** *vi.* to drip.

colata *sf.* **1.** (*metal.*) casting **2.** (*quantità di metallo fuso*) cast **3.** (*di lava*) flow.

colato *agg.* strained, filtered.

colazione *sf.* **1.** (*del mattino*) breakfast **2.** (*di mezzogiorno*) lunch.

colbacco *sm.* busby.

colei *pron. dimostr.* **1.** (*sogg.*) she; (*ogg.*) her **2.** — *che*, she who, she whom (*sogg.*); her who, her whom (*ogg.*): — *che viene qui è mia sorella*, she who is coming here is my sister; — *che vedi è Maria*, she whom you see is Mary; *vedi* — *che viene?*, can you see her who is coming?; *sono stata aiutata da* —

che odiavo, I have been helped by her whom I hated.

coleòttero *sm.* coleopter.

colera *sm.* cholera.

colesterolo *sm.* cholesterol.

còlica *sf.* colic.

colino *sm.* strainer.

colite *sf.* colitis.

colla *sf.* glue || — *di farina,* paste.

collaborare *vi.* to collaborate.

collaboratore *sm.* collaborator.

collaborazione *sf.* collaboration.

collaborazionismo *sm.* collaborationism.

collaborazionista *sm.* collaborationist.

collana *sf.* **1.** necklace **2.** (*raccolta*) collection **3.** (*di libri*) series.

collare *sm.* collar.

collasso *sm.* breakdown: — *cardiaco,* heart failure.

collaterale *agg.* collateral.

collaudare *vt.* to test.

collaudatore *sm.* **1.** tester **2.** (*aer.*) test pilot **3.** (*auto*) test-driver.

collàudo *sm.* test: *fare un — di qc.,* to put (*v. irr.*) sthg. to the test.

collazionare *vt.* to collate.

colle *sm.* hill.

collega *sm.* colleague.

collegamento *sm.* **1.** connection **2.** (*mecc.*) linkwork || *essere in —,* to be in touch.

collegare *vt.* to connect, to link.

collegiale *agg.* collegial. ◆ **collegiale** *sm.* boarder.

collegio *sm.* **1.** college **2.** (*scuola con convitto*) boarding-school.

còllera *sf.* anger || *essere in —,* to be angry.

collèrico *agg.* hot-tempered.

colletta *sf.* collection.

collettivismo *sm.* collectivism.

collettività *sf.* collectivity.

collettivizzare *vt.* to collectivize.

collettivizzazione *sf.* collectivization.

collettivo *agg.* collective.

colletto *sm.* collar.

collettore *agg.* collecting. ◆ **collettore** *sm.* **1.** (*esattore; raccoglitore*) collector **2.** (*mecc.*) manifold **3.** (*elettr.*) commutator.

collezionare *vt.* to collect.

collezione *sf.* collection.

collezionista *sm.* collector.

collimare *vi.* **1.** (*essere d'accordo*) to agree (with) **2.** (*coincidere*) to coincide.

collina *sf.* hill.

collinoso *agg.* hilly.

collirio *sm.* eye-wash.

collisione *sf.* collision (*anche fig.*), impact.

collo *sm.* **1.** neck: *allungare il —,* to crane one's neck || *a rotta di —,* at breakneck speed; *tra capo e —,* unexpectedly **2.** (*pacco*) parcel, package.

collocamento *sm.* **1.** placing **2.** (*impiego*) employment || *agenzia di —,* employment bureau **3.** (*comm.*) disposal.

collocare *vt.* **1.** to place **2.** (*impiegare*) to employ **3.** (*comm.*) to sell (*v. irr.*), to dispose (of sthg.). ◆ **collocarsi** *vr.* **1.** to place oneself **2.** (*impiegarsi*) to get a situation.

collocazione *sf.* **1.** placing **2.** (*comm.*) sale **3.** (*di libri in biblioteche*) press-mark.

colloidale *agg.* colloidal.

colloquio *sm.* **1.** conversation, talk **2.** (*intervista*) interview.

collusione *sf.* collusion.

colluttazione *sf.* scuffle: *venire a —,* to come (*v. irr.*) to grips.

colmare *vt.* **1.** to fill up **2.** (*fig.*) to fill, to overwhelm.

colmo *agg.* full, brimful. ◆ **colmo** *sm.* top, summit, climax || *per — di sfortuna,* as a crowning misfortune; *è il —!,* that beats everything.

colomba *sf.* dove.

colombaia *sf.* dove-cot.

colombo *sm.* pigeon: — *viaggiatore,* carrier-pigeon.

colonia *sf.* colony.

coloniale *agg.* colonial.

colonialismo *sm.* colonialism.

colonialista *sm.* colonialist.

colonizzare *vt.* to colonize.

colonizzatore *sm.* colonizer.

colonizzazione *sf.* colonization.

colonna *sf.* column (*anche fig.*), pillar || — *d'acqua,* fall of water.

colonnato *sm.* colonnade.

colonnello *sm.* colonel.

colono *sm.* **1.** farmer **2.** (*abitante di una colonia*) settler.

colorante *agg.* colouring. ◆ **colorante** *sm.* dye.

colorare *vt.* to colour. ◆ **colorarsi** *vr.* **1.** to colour **2.** (*di persona*) to blush, to flush.

colorazione *sf.* colouring.

colore *sm.* **1.** colour ‖ *biancheria di —,* coloured linen; *gente di —,* coloured people; *colori a olio,* oil-paints **2.** *(aspetto)* look.

colorire *vt.* to colour.

colorito *sm.* complexion.

coloritura *sf.* colouring.

coloro *pron. dimostr.* **1.** they *(sogg.);* them *(compl.)* **2.** *— che,* they who, they whom *(sogg.);* them who, them whom *(compl.):* — *studiano saranno premiati,* they who study will be given a prize; — *tu vedi sono i miei amici,* they whom you see are my friends; *amerò sempre — mi amano,* I shall always love them who love me; *ti presenterò a — hai visto ieri,* I shall introduce you to them whom you saw yesterday.

colossale *agg.* colossal.

colosso *sm.* colossus *(pl.* -si).

colpa *sf.* **1.** fault **2.** *(colpevolezza)* guilt.

colpévole *agg.* guilty.

colpevolezza *sf.* guilt, guiltiness.

colpire *vt.* **1.** to hit *(v. irr.),* to strike *(v: irr.; anche fig.)* **2.** *(di arma da fuoco)* to shoot *(v. irr.).*

colpo *sm.* **1.** blow, stroke *(anche fig.):* — *di fortuna,* stroke of luck; — *apoplettico,* stroke of apoplexy ‖ — *d'aria,* draught; *a — d'occhio,* at a glance; *a — sicuro,* without any risk; *senza — ferire,* without resistance **2.** *(di arma da fuoco)* shot.

colposo *agg.* unpremeditated: *omicidio —,* manslaughter.

coltellata *sf.* stab.

coltello *sm.* knife: — *a serramanico,* jack-knife; *affilare un —,* to sharpen a knife.

coltivàbile *agg.* cultivable.

coltivare *vt.* to cultivate *(anche fig.),* to till, to farm.

coltivatore *sm.* **1.** tiller, farmer **2.** *(di patate, tabacco ecc.)* grower.

coltivazione *sf.* **1.** tilling, farming **2.** *(di patate, tabacco ecc.)* growing.

colto *agg. (istruito)* learned.

coltre *sf.* blanket, coverlet.

colui *pron. dimostr.* **1.** he *(sogg.)* him *(compl.)* **2.** *— che,* he who, he whom *(sogg.);* him who, him whom *(compl.):* — *che ti ha salutato è mio fratello,* he who has greeted you is my brother; — *che vedesti ieri è un mio vecchio ami-*

co, he whom you saw yesterday is an old friend of mine; *daranno il premio a — che studierà,* they will give the prize to him who studies; *fui aiutata da — che avevo aiutato,* I was helped by him whom I had helped.

coma *sm.* coma.

comandamento *sm.* **1.** command, precept **2.** *(relig.)* commandment.

comandante *sm.* commander.

comandare *vt.* **1.** to order, to command **2.** *(essere al comando)* to command, to be in command of.

comando *sm.* **1.** *(ordine)* order **2.** *(autorità)* command **3.** *(sede del comandante)* headquarters *(pl.).*

comatoso *agg.* comatose.

combaciare *vi.* to fit together.

combattente *sm.* **1.** fighting man **2.** *(soldato)* soldier, service man.

combattentìstico *agg.* soldier (like) *(attr.).*

combàttere *vt.* e *vi.* to fight *(v. irr.) (anche fig.).*

combattimento *sm.* **1.** combat, fight, battle **2.** *(boxe)* match.

combattività *sf.* pugnacity.

combattivo *agg.* pugnacious.

combinare *vt.* **1.** to combine **2.** *(di colori)* to match **3.** *(concludere)* to conclude **4.** *(progettare)* to plan.

combinazione *sf.* **1.** combination **2.** *(sistemazione)* arrangement **3.** *(caso, coincidenza)* chance, coincidence.

combrìccola *sf.* **1.** band **2.** *(comitiva)* party.

combustìbile *agg.* combustible. ◆ **combustìbile** *sm.* fuel.

combustione *sf.* combustion.

combutta *sf.* **1.** gang: *essere in —,* to be hand in glove **2.** *(congiura)* plot.

come *avv.* **1.** *(simile a)* like: *è proprio — suo padre,* he is just like his father **2.** *(in qualità di, modale)* as: *ti parlo — amico,* I am speaking to you as a friend **3.** *(in comp.)* as ... as; so ... as: *Carlo è studioso — me,* Charles is as studious as I; *Carlo non è studioso — me,* Charles is not so studious as I **4.** *(int.)* how: — *va?,* How are you? **5.** *(escl.)* how: — *è interessante questo libro!,* How interesting this book is! ◆ **come** *prep.* **1.** *(tempo-*

rale) as, as soon as: — *sentii la sua voce lo riconobbi*, as soon as I heard his voice I recognized him 2. (*come se*) as if: *mi guarda — se mi conoscesse*, he is looking at me as if he knew me || — *Dio volle*, in God's good time; — *segue*, as follows; — *d'accordo*, as agreed.

cometa *sf.* comet.

comicità *sf.* comicality.

còmico *agg.* comical, funny. ♦ **còmico** *sm.* comedian.

comìgnolo *sm.* chimney-pot.

cominciare *vt.* to begin (*v. irr.*), to start.

comitato *sm.* committee.

comitiva *sf.* party, company.

comizio *sm.* meeting.

comma *sm.* paragraph.

commedia *sf.* 1. comedy, play 2. (*fig.*) pretence || *recitare la* —, to play a part.

commediante *sm.* 1. player 2. (*fig.*) shammer.

commediògrafo *sm.* playwright.

commemorare *vt.* to commemorate.

commemorativo *agg.* memorial.

commemorazione *sf.* commemoration.

commendàbile *agg.* commendable.

commendatizia *sf.* letter of recommendation.

commensale *sm.* table-companion.

commentare *vt.* to comment (on).

commentario *sm.* (*lett.*) commentary.

commentatore *sm.* commentator.

commento *sm.* commentary.

commerciàbile *agg.* negotiable.

commerciale *agg.* commercial.

commercializzare *vt.* to commercialize.

commerciante *sm.* 1. trader 2. (*uomo d'affari*) business-man (*pl.* -men) || — *all'ingrosso*, wholesale dealer; — *al minuto*, retailer.

commerciare *vi.* to trade, to deal (*v. irr.*) (in).

commercio *sm.* 1. commerce, trade 2. (*affari*) business || — *all'ingrosso*, wholesale trade; — *al minuto*, retail trade; — *d'importazione, esportazione*, import, export trade; *essere in* —, to be on sale; *essere fuori* —, to be out of sale; *essere in* — (*di un commerciante*), to be in business.

commessa *sf.* shop assistant, shop-girl.

commesso *sm.* clerk, shopman (*pl.* -men), shop assistant || — *viaggiatore*, commercial traveller.

commestìbile *agg.* eatable. ♦ **commestìbili** *sm. pl.* foodstuffs.

comméttere *vt.* 1. to commit, to do (*v. irr.*), to make (*v. irr.*) 2. (*ordinare*) to order.

commiato *sm.* 1. (*preso*) leave 2. (*dato*) dismissal.

commilitone *sm.* fellow-soldier.

comminatoria *sf.* commination.

comminatorio *agg.* comminatory.

commiserare *vt.* to pity.

commiserazione *sf.* pity.

commissariato *sm.* 1. (*carica di commissario*) commissaryship 2. (*ufficio*) commissary's . office.

commissario *sm.* commissary.

commissionare *vt.* (*comm.*) to order.

commissionario *sm.* (*comm.*) commission agent.

commissione *sf.* 1. errand: *fare una* —, to go (*v. irr.*) on an errand 2. (*comm.*) commission, order 3. (*comitato*) commission, committee.

commisurare *vt.* to compare.

committente *sm.* purchaser, buyer.

commosso *agg.* moved, affected.

commovente *agg.* moving, touching, affecting.

commozione *sf.* 1. emotion 2. (*med.*) concussion: — *cerebrale*, concussion of the brain.

commuòvere *vt.* to move, to touch. ♦ **commuòversi** *vr.* to be moved.

commutàbile *agg.* commutable.

commutare *vt.* to commute.

commutativo *agg.* commutative.

commutatore *sm.* commutator.

comò *sm.* chest of drawers.

comodino *sm.* night-table.

comodità *sf.* convenience, comfort.

còmodo *agg.* 1. useful 2. (*conveniente*) convenient 3. (*confortevole*) comfortable 4. (*maneggevole*) handy.

compagnìa *sf.* 1. company: *tener* —, to keep (*v. irr.*) company 2. (*gruppo di persone*) party 3. (*società*) company.

compagno *sm.* companion, mate, comrade || — *di giuochi*, playmate; — *di stanza*, room-mate; — *di studi*, fellow-student.

compagnone *sm.* jolly good fellow.

comparàbile *agg.* comparable.

comparare *vt.* to compare.

comparativo *agg.* (*gramm.*) comparative.

comparato *agg.* comparative.

compare *sm.* 1. (*compagno*) comrade, partner 2. (*padrino*) godfather 3. (*testimone di matrimonio*) witness 4. (*complice*) accomplice.

comparire *vi.* 1. to appear 2. (*sembrare*) to show (*v. irr.*) oneself 3. (*far bella mostra*) to show (*v. irr.*) off.

comparizione *sf.* appearance: (*giur.*) *mandato di* —, summons.

comparsa *sf.* 1. appearance 2. (*teat.; cine*) supernumerary 3. (*giur.*) appearance.

compartecipare *vi.* to share in.

compartimento *sm.* 1. compartment 2. (*circoscrizione*) department.

compartizione *sf.* distribution.

compassato *agg.* 1. stiff, formal 2. (*di discorso*) restrained.

compassione *sf.* pity, commiseration.

compasso *sm.* compasses (*pl.*).

compatìbile *agg.* consistent.

compatibilità *sf.* consistency.

compatimento *sm.* pity, compassion.

compatire *vt.* to pity.

compatriota *sm.* fellow-countryman (*pl.* -men). ♦ compatriota *sf.* fellow-countrywoman (*pl.* -women).

compattezza *sf.* 1. compactness 2. (*di associazione, partito*) unity.

compatto *agg.* compact, solid.

compendiare *vt.* to abridge, to sum up.

compendio *sm.* 1. abridgement, summary.

compenetrare *vt.* to penetrate.

compensàbile *agg.* remunerable.

compensare *vt.* 1. to compensate 2. (*ricompensare*) to reward.

compensato *sm.* ply-wood.

compensazione *sf.* 1. compensation, indemnity 2. (*comm.*) clearing.

compenso *sm.* 1. compensation 2. (*rimunerazione*) reward, retribution.

còmpera *sf.* purchase.

competente *agg.* competent.

competenza *sf.* 1. competence 2. (*onorario*) fee.

compètere *vi.* 1. (*gareggiare*) to vie 2. (*spettare*) to be due, to belong.

competitivo *agg.* competitive.

competitore *sm.* competitor, rival.

competizione *sf.* competition.

compiacente *agg.* obliging.

compiacenza *sf.* 1. kindness 2. (*soddisfazione*) satisfaction.

compiacere *vt.* to please, to gratify. ♦ compiacersi *vr.* 1. to be pleased (with), to congratulate 2. (*degnarsi*) to condescend.

compiacimento *sm.* 1. satisfaction 2. (*congratulazione*) congratulation.

compiàngere *vt.* 1. to pity, to sympathize (with) 2. (*disprezzare*) to despise.

compianto *agg.* regretted. ♦ compianto *sm.* regret.

còmpiere *vt.* 1. (*finire*) to finish 2. (*eseguire*) to accomplish 3. (*adempiere*) to do (*v. irr.*): — *il proprio dovere*, to do one's duty 4. (*di età*) *ho compiuto 30 anni*, I am now 30 years old.

compilare *vt.* to compile: — *un documento*, to draw (*v. irr.*) up a document; — *una lista*, to make (*v. irr.*) a list.

compilazione *sf.* 1. compilation 2. (*comm.*) drawing up.

compimento *sm.* 1. (*il compire*) completion 2. (*conclusione*) achievement.

compitare *vt.* to spell (*v. irr.*).

compitezza *sf.* politeness, refinement.

compito *agg.* polite.

còmpito *sm.* 1. task, duty 2. (*scolastico, a casa*) homework; (*a scuola*) class-work.

compiutamente *avv.* completely.

compiutezza *sf.* completeness.

compiuto *agg.* complete.

compleanno *sm.* birthday: *buon* —!, happy birthday!.

complementare *agg.* complementary.

complemento *sm.* 1. complement 2. (*gramm.*) — *indiretto*, indirect object 3. (*mil.*) *truppe di* —, reserve.

complessato *agg.* neurotic.

complessione *sf.* constitution.

complessità *sf.* complexity.

complessivamente *avv.* on the whole.

complessivo *agg.* total, inclusive.

complesso *agg.* complex, complicated. ♦ **complesso** *sm.* **1.** whole **2.** (*industriale*) plant, set **3.** (*mus.*) band.

completamente *avv.* completely.

completare *vt.* to complete, to finish.

completezza *sf.* completeness.

completo *agg.* **1.** complete, whole **2.** (*pieno*) full. ♦ **completo** *sm.* (*vestito*) suit.

complicare *vt.* to complicate.

complicato *agg.* complicated.

complicazione *sf.* complication: *salvo complicazioni*, if no complications set in.

còmplice *s.* accomplice.

complicità *sf.* accomplicity.

complimentare *vt.* to compliment. ♦ **complimentarsi** *vr.* to congratulate (so.).

complimento *sm.* **1.** compliment **2.** (*congratulazione*) congratulation.

complottare *vi.* to plot.

complotto *sm.* plot, conspiracy.

compluvio *sm.* (*arch.*) compluvium (*pl.* -ia).

componente *agg.* component. ♦ **componente** *sm.* **1.** member **2.** (*chim.*) component.

componimento *sm.* **1.** (*lett.; mus.; scol.*) composition **2.** (*giur.*) settlement.

comporre *vt.* **1.** to compose: — *una poesia*, to write (*v. irr.*) a poem; — *un numero telefonico*, to dial a number **2.** (*chim.*) to compound **3.** (*assestare*) to arrange.

comportamento *sm.* behaviour.

comportare *vt.* to involve, to require. ♦ **comportarsi** *vr.* to behave (oneself).

compòsito *agg.* composite.

compositore *sm.* **1.** (*mus.*) composer **2.** (*tip.*) compositor.

composizione *sf.* **1.** composition **2.** (*conciliazione*) composition, agreement **3.** (*tip.*) composing.

composta *sf.* compote.

compostezza *sf.* **1.** composure **2.** (*dignità*) self-respect.

composto *agg.* **1.** compound **2.** (*ordinato*) tidy **3.** (*calmo*) calm ‖ *stare* —, to sit (*v. irr.*) still. ♦ **composto** *sm.* compound.

comprare *vt.* **1.** to buy (*v. irr.*): — *a credito*, to buy on credit; — *per contanti*, to buy for cash; — *all'ingrosso*, to buy wholesale **2.** (*corrompere*) to bribe.

compratore *sm.* buyer, purchaser.

compravéndita *sf.* marketing.

comprèndere *vt.* **1.** (*includere*) to include, to take (*v. irr.*) in **2.** (*capire*) to understand (*v. irr.*) **3.** (*rendersi conto*) to realize.

comprensìbile *agg.* intelligible.

comprensibilità *sf.* intelligibility.

comprensione *sf.* **1.** comprehension, understanding **2.** (*compassione*) sympathy.

comprensivo *agg.* **1.** comprehensive **2.** (*che capisce*) comprehending **3.** (*che prova simpatia*) sympathetic.

compressa *sf.* **1.** tablet **2.** (*di garza*) compress.

compressibilità *sf.* compressibility.

compressione *sf.* compression.

comprìmere *vt.* **1.** to compress **2.** (*fig.*) to restrain, to repress.

compromesso *sm.* compromise.

compromettente *agg.* compromising.

comprométtere *vt.* to compromise, to involve.

comproprietà *sf.* joint ownership.

comproprietario *sm.* joint owner.

comprovare *vt.* to prove.

compunto *agg.* filled with compunction, contrite.

computare *vt.* to compute.

computisterìa *sf.* book-keeping.

còmputo *sm.* reckoning.

comunale *agg.* communal, municipal.

comunardo *sm.* (*stor.*) Communard.

comune[1] *agg.* **1.** common **2.** (*abituale*) frequent, usual.

comune[2] *sm.* **1.** commune **2.** (*edificio*) Town Hall.

comunella *sf.* cabal: *far* — *con qu.*, to consort.

comunemente *avv.* commonly, usually.

comunicàbile *agg.* communicable.

comunicabilità *sf.* communicability.

comunicante *agg.* communicating.

comunicare *vt.* **1.** to communicate, to transmit **2.** (*relig.*) to communicate. ♦ **comunicarsi** *vr.* to receive Holy Communion.

comunicativa *sf.* communicativeness.

comunicativo *agg.* communicative.

comunicato *sm.* bulletin.

comunicazione *sf.* communication.

comunione *sf.* **1.** communion: —

di idee, similarity of ideas **2.** (*relig.*) Holy Communion.

comunismo *sm.* communism.

comunista *s.* communist.

comunità *sf.* community.

comunque *avv.* however, anyhow.

con *prep.* **1.** (*compagnia, unione, strumento*) with: *venne — me*, he came with me; *scrivo — questa penna*, I write with this pen **2.** (*stato, condizione*) in: — *il freddo sto meglio*, in cold weather I feel better **3.** (*mezzo di trasporto*) by: *arriverò col treno delle 3*, I shall arrive by the three o'clock train **4.** (*per mezzo di*) by means of.

conato *sm.* effort ‖ *avere conati di vomito*, to feel (*v. irr.*) sick.

conca *sf.* **1.** basin, pot **2.** (*valle*) valley.

concatenamento *sm.* concatenation.

concatenare *vt.* to concatenate.

concatenazione *sf.* concatenation.

còncavo *agg.* concave, hollow.

concèdere *vt.* **1.** to grant, to bestow **2.** (*permettere*) to allow.

concentramento *sm.* concentration: *campo di —*, concentration camp.

concentrare *vt.* to concentrate. ◆ **concentrarsi** *vr.* to concentrate.

concentrato *agg.* concentrated. ◆ **concentrato** *sm.* concentrated food.

concentrazione *sf.* concentration.

concèntrico *agg.* concentric.

concepìbile *agg.* conceivable.

concepimento *sm.* conception.

concepire *vt.* **1.** to conceive **2.** (*nutrire speranze, timori*) to entertain **3.** (*formulare*) to express.

concerìa *sf.* tannery.

concèrnere *vt.* to concern, to relate to.

concertare *vt.* **1.** (*mus.*) to harmonize **2.** (*stabilire*) to plan, to arrange.

concertato *agg.* concerted (*anche mus.*), arranged.

concertista *s.* concert artist.

concertìstico *agg.* concert.

concerto *sm.* concert.

concessionario *sm.* concessionary agent.

concessione *sf.* **1.** concession **2.** (*permesso*) permission.

concetto *sm.* concept.

concettuale *agg.* conceptual.

concezionale *agg.* conceptional.

concezione *sf.* conception.

conchiglia *sf.* shell.

concia *sf.* **1.** (*di pelli*) tanning **2.** (*di tabacco*) curing.

conciare *vt.* **1.** (*pelli*) to tan **2.** (*tabacco*) to cure **3.** (*fig.*) to ill-treat **4.** (*insudiciare*) to soil. ◆ **conciarsi** *vr.* to get (*v. irr.*) dirty.

conciatore *sm.* tanner.

conciatura *sf.* tanning.

conciliàbile *agg.* compatible, consistent.

conciliabilità *sf.* compatibility.

conciliàbolo *sm.* conventicle, secret talk.

conciliante *agg.* conciliatory.

conciliare *vt.* **1.** to reconcile **2.** (*procacciare*) to win (*v. irr.*), to gain. ◆ **conciliarsi** *vr.* to win (*v. irr.*).

conciliare *agg.* conciliar.

conciliatore *agg.* conciliatory. ◆ **conciliatore** *sm.* peacemaker ‖ *giudice —*, Justice of the Peace.

conciliazione *sf.* conciliation.

concilio *sm.* Council.

concimaia *sf.* dung-hill, dung-pit.

concimare *vt.* to dung.

concimazione *sf.* dunging.

concime *sm.* **1.** (*organico*) dung **2.** (*chimico*) fertilizer.

concio *sm.* dung.

concionare *vi.* to harangue.

concione *sf.* harangue.

concisione *sf.* concision.

conciso *agg.* concise, brief.

concistoro *sm.* (*eccl.*) concistory.

concitare *vt.* to excite, to stir (up).

concitazione *sf.* excitement, agitation.

concittadino *sm.* fellow-citizen.

conclamare *vt.* to acclaim.

conclave *sm.* (*eccl.*) conclave.

concludente *agg.* **1.** conclusive **2.** (*di persona*) energetic.

conclùdere *vt.* **1.** to conclude, to finish **2.** (*dedurre*) to infer **3.** (*fare*) to do (*v. irr.*).

conclusionale *sf.* (*giur.*) pleadings (*pl.*).

conclusione *sf.* **1.** conclusion **2.** (*risultato*) issue, result.

conclusivo *agg.* conclusive.

concomitante *agg.* concomitant.

concomitanza *sf.* concomitance.

concordanza *sf.* agreement.

concordare *vi.* to agree. ◆ **concordare** *vt.* **1.** to agree upon **2.**

(*mettere d'accordo*) to reconcile **3.** (*gramm.*) to put (*v. irr.*) in concord.

concordatario *agg.* **1.** (*eccl.*) of concordat **2.** (*giur.; comm.*) composition.

concordato *sm.* **1.** convention **2.** (*eccl.*) concordat **3.** (*giur.; comm.*) agreement, composition.

concorde *agg.* concordant, agreeing: *volontà* —, unanimous will.

concordemente *avv.* concordantly.

concordia *sf.* concord, agreement.

concorrente *agg.* **1.** concurrent **2.** (*rivale*) competing. ♦ **concorrente** *sm.* **1.** candidate **2.** (*rivale*) competitor.

concorrenza *sf.* **1.** (*affluenza*) concourse **2.** (*comm.*) competition ‖ *fare* —, to compete with; — *sleale*, unfair competition.

concorrenziale *agg.* competitive.

concòrrere *vi.* **1.** to come (*v. irr.*) together **2.** (*contribuire*) to concur, to contribute **3.** (*partecipare*) to share in **4.** (*mettersi in gara*) to compete.

concorso *sm.* **1.** (*affluenza*) rush, crowd, concourse **2.** (*gara*) competition **3.** (*sport*) contest.

concretare *vt.* **1.** to make (*v. irr.*) concrete **2.** (*concludere*) to realize.

concretezza *sf.* concreteness.

concreto *agg.* **1.** concrete, real **2.** (*solido*) solid.

concrezione *sf.* concretion.

concubina *sf.* concubine.

concubinaggio, concubinato *sm.* concubinage.

conculcare *vt.* to trample on.

concupire *vt.* to covet, to lust after.

concupiscenza *sf.* concupiscence, lust.

concussione *sf.* (*giur.*) concussion.

condanna *sf.* **1.** condemnation **2.** (*sentenza*) sentence: — *a morte*, death sentence **3.** (*pena*) penalty.

condannàbile *agg.* condemnable.

condannare *vt.* **1.** to sentence **2.** (*fig.*) to condemn **3.** (*riprovare*) to blame.

condannato *agg.* sentenced. ♦ **condannato** *sm.* condemned man.

condensàbile *agg.* condensable.

condensabilità *vt.* condensability.

condensazione *sf.* condensation.

condensare *vt.* to condense.

condensatore *sm.* condenser.

condimento *sm.* seasoning, dress-

ing.

condire *vt.* to season; (*anche fig.*) to flavour.

condirettore *sm.* joint manager.

condiscendente *agg.* complying.

condiscendenza *sf.* **1.** compliance **2.** (*degnazione*) condescension.

condiscèndere *vi.* **1.** to comply with **2.** (*degnarsi*) to condescend.

condiscépolo *sm.* schoolfellow.

condivìdere *vt.* to share (*anche fig.*).

condizionale *agg. e sm.* conditional. ♦ **condizionale** *sf.* (*giur.*) conditional sentence.

condizionamento *sm.* conditioning.

condizionare *vt.* to condition.

condizione *sf.* **1.** condition: *a* — *che*: on condition that **2.** (*ceto*) rank, station.

condoglianza *sf.* condolence.

condominio *sm.* joint ownership.

condòmino *sm.* joint-owner.

condonare *vt.* to remit.

condono *sm.* remission.

condotta *sf.* **1.** conduct, behaviour. **2.** (*gara*) competition **3.** (*sport*) contest.

condotto *agg. medico* —, doctor employed by the local authority. ♦ **condotto** *sm.* **1.** conduit, pipeline **2.** (*anat.*) duct.

conducente *sm.* driver.

conducibilità *sf.* (*fis.*) conductibility.

condurre *vt.* **1.** (*guidare*) to lead (*v. irr.*) **2.** (*accompagnare*) to take (*v. irr.*) **3.** (*governare, trattare*) to manage: — *i propri affari*, to manage one's business **4.** (*vivere*) to lead (*v. irr.*): — *una vita triste*, to lead a sad life. ♦ **condurre** *vi.* to lead (*v. irr.*): *questa strada conduce a Milano*, this route leads to Milan. ♦ **condursi** *vr.* to behave.

conduttività *sf.* conductivity.

conduttivo *agg.* conducting.

conduttore *agg.* conducting. ♦ **conduttore** *sm.* **1.** leader, guide **2.** (*di veicoli*) driver **3.** (*fis.*) conductor.

conduttura *sf.* **1.** duct, conduit **2.** (*di tubazioni*) piping.

conduzione *sf.* **1.** management **2.** (*fis.*) conduction.

confabulare *vi.* to confabulate.

confacente *agg.* suitable, proper.

confarsi *vr.* to suit, to become (*v. irr.*).

confederale *agg.* confederal.

confederare *vt.* to confederate.

confederazione *sf.* **1.** Confederation **2.** (*alleanza*) confederacy.
conferenza *sf.* **1.** lecture **2.** (*assemblea*) conference.
conferenziere *sm.* lecturer.
conferimento *sm.* bestowal.
conferire *vt.* to confer, to bestow. ♦ **conferire** *vi.* **1.** to have an interview **2.** (*giovare*) to be useful.
conferma *sf.* confirmation.
confermare *vt.* to confirm. ♦ **confermarsi** *vr.* to prove oneself.
confermazione *sf.* confirmation.
confessare *vt.* **1.** to confess **2.** (*riconoscere, ammettere*) to admit. ♦ **confessarsi** *vr.* (*eccl.*) to go (*v. irr.*) to confession.
confessionale *agg.* confessional. ♦ **confessionale** *sm.* confessional.
confessione *sf.* **1.** confession **2.** (*ammissione*) admission **3.** (*memorie*) memoirs (*pl.*).
confessore *sm.* confessor.
confetterìa *sf.* confectionery.
confettiere *sm.* confectioner.
confetto *sm.* comfit.
confettura *sf.* **1.** (*confetti*) sweetmeats (*pl.*) **2.** (*marmellata*) jam ‖ — *d'arance*, marmalade.
confezionare *vt.* **1.** to make (*v. irr.*) up **2.** (*di piatti*) to prepare **3.** (*di pacchi*) to pack up.
confezione *sf.* **1.** manufacture **2.** (*preparazione*) preparation **3.** (*pl.*) (*abiti*) ready-to-wear clothes **4.** (*imballaggio*) packing.
conficcare *vt.* to hammer, to drive (*v. irr.*). ♦ **conficcarsi** *vr.* to run (*v. irr.*) into.
confidare *vt.* to confide. ♦ **confidare** *vi.* **1.** to confide, to trust **2.** (*fare assegnamento*) to rely (on).
confidente *agg.* trustful. ♦ **confidente** *sm.* **1.** confidant **2.** (*di polizia*) police spy.
confidenza *sf.* **1.** (*fiducia*) confidence **2.** (*cosa confidata*) secret **3.** (*familiarità*) familiarity ‖ *essere in* — *con qu.*, to be on familiar terms with so.
confidenziale *agg.* confidential: *strettamente* —, strictly confidential.
confidenzialmente *avv.* confidentially.
configgere *vt.* to drive (*v. irr.*) in.
configurare *vt.* to configure, to shape.

configurazione *sf.* configuration, shape.
confinante *agg.* **1.** neighbouring **2.** (*fig.*) bordering.
confinare *vi.* to border on. ♦ **confinare** *vt.* **1.** to banish **2.** (*fig.*) to confine.
confinario *agg.* border.
confinato *agg.* interned.
confine *sm.* **1.** border, frontier **2.** (*fig.*) limit, boundary.
confino *sm.* internment, political confinement.
confisca *sf.* confiscation.
confiscàbile *agg.* confiscable.
confiscare *vt.* to confiscate.
confitto *agg.* **1.** nailed, driven in **2.** (*fig.*) fixed.
conflagrare *vi.* to break (*v. irr.*) out.
conflagrazione *sf.* **1.** conflagration **2.** (*fig.*) sudden out-break (of war).
conflitto *sm.* **1.** conflict **2.** (*fig.*) clash.
confluente *sm.* confluent.
confluenza *sf.* confluence.
confluire *vi.* to flow together.
confòndere *vt.* **1.** to confuse **2.** (*scambiare una persona per un'altra*) to mistake (*v. irr.*) **3.** (*turbare*) to confound. ♦ **confòndersi** *vr.* **1.** to get (*v. irr.*) mixed up **2.** (*mescolarsi*) to mingle **3.** (*turbarsi*) to be disconcerted.
confondìbile *agg.* liable to be confused.
conformare *vt.* to conform. ♦ **conformarsi** *vr.* to conform.
conformato *agg.* shaped.
conformazione *sf.* conformation.
conforme *agg.* **1.** conforming **2.** (*simile*) similar **3.** (*fedele*) true ‖ — *a*, in conformity with. ♦ **conforme a·** *loc. avv.* in conformity with.
conformismo *sm.* time-serving.
conformista *s.* **1.** time-server **2.** (*relig.*) conformist.
conformìstico *agg.* conformist.
conformità *sf.* conformity.
confortàbile *agg.* consolable.
confortante *agg.* consoling.
confortare *vt.* **1.** to comfort **2.** (*incoraggiare*) to encourage.
confortatore *agg.* comforting. ♦ **confortatore** *sm.* comforter.
confortatorio *agg.* comforting.
confortèvole *agg.* **1.** comforting **2.** (*comodo*) comfortable.

confortevolmente *avv.* comfortably.

conforto *sm.* 1. comfort, solace 2. (*incoraggiamento*) encouragement.

confratello *sm.* brother (*pl.* brethren).

confratèrnita *sf.* brotherhood.

confrontàbile *agg.* comparable.

confrontare *vt.* 1. to compare 2. (*giur.*) to confront.

confronto *sm.* 1. comparison 2. (*giur.*) confrontation ‖ *nei confronti di*, to, towards; *in — a*, in comparison with.

confucianésimo *sm.* confucianism.

confusamente *avv.* confusedly.

confusionario *agg.* blundering, unmethodical. ♦ **confusionario** *sm.* bungler, muddler.

confusione *sf.* confusion, medley.

confusionismo *sm.* general confusion.

confuso *agg.* 1. confused, mixed, vague 2. (*indistinto*) indistinct 3. (*imbarazzato*) embarrassed.

confutàbile *agg.* confutable.

confutare *vt.* to confute.

confutazione *sf.* confutation.

congedare *vt.* 1. to dismiss 2. (*mil.*) to discharge. ♦ **congedarsi** *vr.* to take (*v. irr.*) one's leave.

congedato *sm.* dischargee.

congedo *sm.* 1. (*commiato*) leave 2. (*mil.*) leave, discharge ‖ *essere in —*, to be on leave.

congegnare *vt.* 1. (*mecc.*) to assemble 2. (*fig.*) to devise.

congegno *sm.* 1. device, gear 2. (*fig.*) device, scheme.

congelamento *sm.* 1. freezing 2. (*med.*) congelation.

congelare *vt.* to freeze (*v. irr.*), to congeal.

congelato *agg.* congealed, frozen (*anche comm.*).

congelatore *sm.* freezer.

congènere *agg.* 1. akin (*attr.*) 2. similar (*pred.*).

congeniale *agg.* congenial.

congènito *agg.* congenital, innate.

congestionare *vt.* to congest.

congestionato *agg.* congested: *viso —*, flushed face.

congestione *sf.* congestion.

congettura *sf.* conjecture, supposition.

congetturare *vt.* to conjecture.

congiùngere *vt.* 1. to join 2. (*collegare*) to connect.

congiuntiva *sf.* conjunctiva.

congiuntivite *sf.* conjunctivitis.

congiuntivo *agg.* conjunctive. ♦ **congiuntivo** *sm.* (*gramm.*) subjunctive.

congiunto *agg.* 1. joined, united 2. (*collegato*) connected. ♦ **congiunto** *sm.* relative.

congiuntura *sf.* 1. point of junction 2. (*circostanza, situazione*) circumstance, situation 3. (*econ.*) trend, trade cycle.

congiunzione *sf.* 1. connection 2. (*gramm.; astr.*) conjunction.

congiura *sf.* conspiracy, plot.

congiurare *vi.* to conspire, to plot.

congiurato *sm.* conspirator, plotter.

conglobamento *sm.* conglobation.

conglobare *vt.* 1. to conglobate 2. (*di tasse, debiti ecc.*) to combine.

conglobazione *sf.* conglobation.

conglomerato *sm.* 1. (*geol.*) conglomerate 2. (*etnico; pol.*) grouping.

congratularsi *vr.* to congratulate.

congratulazione *sf.* congratulation.

congregazione *sf.* assembly, congregation (*anche eccl.*).

congressista *s.* member of a congress.

congresso *sm.* congress.

congruo *agg.* 1. (*coerente*) congruous 2. (*adeguato*) adequate.

conguagliare *vt.* 1. to equalize 2. (*comm.*) to balance.

coniare *vt.* to coin (*anche fig.*).

cònico *agg.* conic(al).

conìfera *sf.* conifer.

coniglio *sm.* 1. rabbit 2. (*fig.*) faint-hearted.

conio *sm.* 1. (*attrezzo per coniare*) minting die 2. (*impronta*) coin, brand 3. (*invenzione di nuove parole*) coinage.

coniugale *agg.* conjugal: *vita —*, married life.

coniugare *vt.* 1. to conjugate 2. (*unire in matrimonio*) to marry.

coniugato *agg.* married.

coniugazione *sf.* conjugation.

còniuge *sm.* husband. ♦ **còniuge** *sf.* wife.

connaturale *agg.* connatural, innate.

connaturato *agg.* deeply rooted.

connazionale *sm.* fellow-countryman (*pl.* -men). ♦ **connazionale** *sf.* fellow-countrywoman (*pl.* -women).

connessione *sf.* connection.
connesso *agg.* connected.
connèttere *vt.* 1. (*unire*) to connect, to join 2. (*fig.*) to associate, to link || *non connettere*, to talk at random.
connettivo *agg.* connective.
connivente *agg.* conniving (at).
connotato *sm.* description, feature || *i connotati*, description.
connubio *sm.* 1. marriage 2. (*fig.*) union.
cono *sm.* cone: — *gelato*, ice-cream cone.
conoscente *sm.* acquaintance.
conoscenza *sf.* 1. knowledge || *venire a — di qc.*, to become (*v. irr.*) acquainted with sthg. 2. (*persona*) acquaintance 3. (*sensi*) consciousness.
conòscere *vt.* 1. to know (*v. irr.*): — *di vista*, to know by sight; — *di fama*, to know by reputation; — *dalla voce*, to recognize by one's voice 2. (*fare la conoscenza*) to meet (*v. irr.*).
conoscìbile *agg.* 1. knowable 2. (*riconoscibile*) recognizable.
conoscitivo *agg.* cognitive.
conoscitore *sm.* expert, good judge.
conosciuto *agg.* well-known, renowned.
conquista *sf.* conquest.
conquistare *vt.* 1. to conquer 2. (*fig.*) to win (*v. irr.*).
conquistatore *sm.* 1. conqueror 2. (*rubacuori*) lady-killer.
consacrare *vt.* 1. (*eccl.*) to consecrate 2. (*dedicare*) to devote.
consacrazione *sf.* consecration.
consanguineità *sf.* consanguinity.
consanguineo *agg.* consanguine, akin. ♦ **consanguineo** *sm.* kinsman (*pl.* -men).
consapévole *agg.* aware, conscious.
consapevolezza *sf.* 1. consciousness 2. (*conoscenza*) knowledge.
conscio *agg.* conscious.
consecutivo *agg.* 1. following 2. (*di seguito*) running: *per due giorni consecutivi*, for two days running 3. (*gramm.*) consecutive.
consegna *sf.* 1. (*comm.*) delivery: — *contro assegno*, cash on delivery; — *mancata*, nondelivery; *ordine di* —, delivery-note; *effettuare la* —, to effect delivery 2. (*deposito*) consignment 3. (*mil.*) orders (*pl.*) || — *in caserma*, confi-

nement to barracks.
consegnare *vt.* 1. to deliver 2. (*mil.*) to confine to barracks.
conseguente *agg.* consequent.
conseguenza *sf.* consequence.
conseguìbile *agg.* attainable.
conseguimento *sm.* attainment.
conseguire *vt.* to attain, to achieve, to get (*v. irr.*).
consenso *sm.* 1. consent 2. (*matrimoniale*) licence.
consensuale *agg.* by mutual consent.
consentire *vi.* to consent, to agree. ♦ **consentire** *vt.* to allow.
consenziente *agg.* consenting.
conserto *agg.* interwoven, folded: *a braccia conserte*, with folded arms.
conserva *sf.* preserve || — *di frutta*, jam; — *di pomodoro*, tomato sauce.
conservare *vt.* to preserve ♦ **conservarsi** *vr.* to keep (*v. irr.*).
conservativo *agg.* conservative.
conservatore *agg.* 1. preserving 2. (*pol.*) conservative. ♦ **conservatore** *sm.* 1. preserver 2. (*pol.*) conservative.
conservatorio *sm.* academy of music.
conservazione *sf.* preservation || *istinto di* —, instinct of self-preservation.
considerare *vt.* 1. to consider, to think (*v. irr.*) of 2. (*reputare*) to deem, to judge. ♦ **considerarsi** *vr.* to consider oneself.
considerato *agg.* considerate || — *che*, considering that.
considerazione *sf.* 1. consideration 2. (*stima*) esteem, regard || *avere — per qu.*, to have regard for so.
considerévole *agg.* considerable.
consigliare *vt.* to advise. ♦ **consigliarsi** *vr.* to ask so.'s advice, to consult (with).
consigliere *sm.* 1. counsellor 2. (*membro di un consiglio*) councillor.
consiglio *sm.* 1. advice (*solo sing.*) 2. (*corpo di persone*) council.
consiliare *agg.* of a council.
consìmile *agg.* similar.
consistente *agg.* firm, substantial.
consistenza *sf.* 1. consistence 2. (*comm.*) on hand: — *di cassa*, cash on hand.
consistere *vi.* to consist.

consociare vt. to associate.
consociato agg. associated.
consociazione sf. association.
consocio sm. co-partner.
consolante agg. cheering.
consolare¹ vt. to console, to comfort. ♦ **consolarsi** vr. to be comforted.
consolare² agg. consular.
consolato sm. consulate.
consolatore agg. consoling. ♦ **consolatore** sm. consoler.
consolazione sf. consolation, solace.
cònsole sm. consul.
consolidamento sm. consolidation.
consolidare vt. to consolidate, to strengthen.
consolidato agg. consolidated.
consonante sf. consonant.
consonanza sf. consonance (anche fig.).
cònsono agg. in accordance (with).
consorella sf. (eccl.) sister.
consorte sm. consort, husband. ♦ **consorte** sf. consort, wife.
consorterìa sf. faction.
consorzio sm. society: — agrario, agricultural union.
constare vi. 1. (essere composto) to consist 2. (risultare) to be within one's knowledge || da quanto mi consta, as far as I know.
constatare vt. V. costatare.
constatazione sf. V. costatazione.
consueto agg. usual, customary.
consuetudinario agg. customary, consuetudinary.
consuetùdine sf. 1. custom, habit 2. (comm.) rule.
consulente sm. adviser.
consulenza sf. advice.
consulta sf. 1. consultation 2. (corpo consultivo) council.
consultare vt. 1. to consult 2. (esaminare) to examine.
consultazione sf. consultation: libro di —, reference book.
consultivo agg. consultative.
consulto sm. consultation.
consumare vt. 1. to consume 2. (di abiti) to wear (v. irr.) 3. (dissipare) to waste 4. (compiere) to commit.
consumato agg. 1. (perfetto) accomplished 2. (logoro) worn out 3. (divorato) consumed.
consumatore sm. consumer.
consumazione sf. 1. consumption 2. (giur.) consummation 3. (bibi-

ta) drink.
consumo sm. consumption || per proprio uso e —, for one's private use.
consuntivo agg. final: bilancio —, final balance.
consunzione sf. consumption.
contàbile agg. bookkeeping. ♦ **contàbile** sm. bookkeeper.
contabilità sf. bookkeeping.
contachilòmetri sm. speedometer.
contadino sm. countryman (pl. -men), peasant. ♦ **contadino** agg. rustic.
contado sm. countryside.
contagiare vt. to infect.
contagio sm. contagion (anche fig.), infection.
contagioso agg. contagious, infectious (anche fig.).
contagiri sm. revolution counter.
contagocce sm. dropper.
contaminare vt. 1. to pollute, to infect 2. (un testo letterario) to corrupt.
contaminazione sf. contamination (anche fig.), pollution.
contante agg. ready. ♦ **contante** sm. ready money || pagare in contanti, to pay cash.
contare vt. 1. to count, to number 2. (considerare) to consider 3. (proporsi) to think (v.: irr.) of || conto di andare a Milano domani, I think of going to Milan tomorrow 4. (aspettarsi) to expect. ♦ **contare** vi. 1. (avere importanza) to count, to be important 2. (fare assegnamento) to rely on.
contatore sm. meter: — del gas, gas-meter; — dell'acqua, water-meter; — della luce, electric power-meter.
contatto sm. 1. contact, touch: essere in —, to be in touch 2. (elettr.) contact.
conte sm. 1. Count 2. (in Gran Bretagna) Earl.
contea sf. 1. earldom 2. (divisione territoriale) county.
conteggiare vt. to count.
conteggio sm. computation.
contegno sm. 1. behaviour 2. (atteggiamento) attitude.
contegnoso agg. 1. dignified 2. (altero) stiff.
contemperamento sm. adaptation.
contemperare vt. to adapt.
contemplare vt. 1. to behold (v.

irr.), to admire **2.** (*giur.*) to consider.

contemplativo *agg.* contemplative.

contemplatore *sm.* contemplator.

contemplazione *sf.* contemplation.

contempo (*nella loc. avv.*) *nel* —, in the meantime.

contemporaneamente *avv.* at the same time.

contemporaneità *sf.* contemporaneousness.

contemporàneo *agg.* e *sm.* contemporary.

contendente *agg.* contending, opposing. ♦ **contendente** *sm.* opponent, rival.

contèndere *vt.* to contend, to refuse. ♦ **contèndersi** *vr. rec.* to contend.

contenere *vt.* **1.** to contain, to hold (*v. irr.*) **2.** (*trattenere*) to repress. ♦ **contenersi** *vr.* **1.** (*comportarsi*) to behave **2.** (*dominarsi*) to contain oneself.

contenitore *sm.* container.

contentare *vt.* to content. ♦ **contentarsi** *vr.* to be content (with).

contentezza *sf.* pleasure, joy.

contento *agg.* content, pleased.

contenuto *sm.* contents (*pl.*).

contenzioso *agg.* contentious.

conterìe *sf. pl.* glass beads.

conterràneo *sm.* fellow-countryman (*pl.* -men) ‖ (*femm.*) fellow-countrywoman (*pl.* -women).

contesa *sf.* **1.** contest **2.** (*litigio*) quarrel.

contessa *sf.* countess.

contestàbile *agg.* questionable.

contestare *vt.* **1.** to contest, to challenge, to deny **2.** (*notificare*) to declare.

contestazione *sf.* dispute, objection: *sollevare contestazioni*, to raise objections.

contesto *sm.* context.

contiguità *sf.* contiguity.

contiguo *agg.* neighbouring.

continentale *agg.* continental.

continente *agg.* moderate. ♦ **continente** *sm.* continent.

continenza *sf.* continence.

contingentamento *sm.* allotment.

contingentare *vt.* to allot.

contingenza *sf.* **1.** emergency **2.** (*circostanza*) circumstance **3.** (*fil.*) contingency.

continuamente *avv.* continuously.

continuare *vt.* e *vi.* **1.** to go (*v.*

irr.) on (with) **2.** (*riprendere*) to resume.

continuativo *agg.* continuative.

continuato *agg.* **1.** (*ininterrotto*) continuous **2.** (*che si ripete*) continual.

continuatore *sm.* continuator.

continuazione *sf.* continuation.

continuità *sf.* continuity.

continuo *agg.* **1.** (*ininterrotto*) continuous **2.** (*che si ripete*) continual.

conto *sm.* **1.** (*anche comm.*) account: *fare i conti*, to make (*v. irr.*) up accounts **2.** (*di albergo ecc.*) bill **3.** (*assegnamento*) reliance: *far — su*, to rely on **4.** (*stima*) regard ‖ *persona di poco* —, person of little account; *rendere — di*, to answer for; *rendersi* —, to realize; *mettersi per proprio* —, to set (*v. irr.*) for oneself.

contòrcere *vt.* to twist. ♦ **contòrcersi** *vr.* to twist.

contorcimento *sm.* twisting.

contornare *vt.* **1.** to surround **2.** (*con guarnizioni*) to trim.

contorno *sm.* **1.** outline **2.** (*orlo*) border **3.** (*cuc.*) vegetables (*pl.*).

contorsione *sf.* contortion.

contorsionismo *sm.* writhing.

contorsionista *s.* contorsionist.

contorto *agg.* twisted.

contrabbandare *vt.* to smuggle.

contrabbandiere *sm.* smuggler.

contrabbando *sm.* smuggling.

contrabbassista *sm.* double-bass player.

contrabbasso *sm.* double-bass.

contraccambiare *vt.* to return.

contraccambio *sm.* return ‖ *rendere il* —, to retaliate (upon).

contraccolpo *sm.* **1.** counterblow **2.** (*fig.*) reaction.

contraccusa *sf.* countercharge.

contrada *sf.* **1.** quarter **2.** (*paese*) country.

contraddanza *sf.* country-dance.

contraddire *vt.* to contradict. ♦ **contraddirsi** *vr.* to contradict oneself. ♦ **contraddirsi** *v. rec.* to contradict one another, each other.

contraddistìnguere *vt.* to mark.

contraddittore *sm.* opposer.

contraddittorio *agg.* contradictory. ♦ **contraddittorio** *sm.* debate.

contraddizione *sf.* contradiction, discrepancy.

contraente *agg.* contracting. ♦

contraente *sm.* contractor.
contraèrea *sf.* anti-aircraft artillery.
contraèreo *agg.* anti-aircraft.
contraffare *vt.* to counterfeit.
contraffatto *agg.* counterfeit.
contraffattore *sm.* 1. (*falsificatore*) counterfeiter 2. (*imitatore*) imitator.
contrafforte *sm.* buttress.
contraggenio *sm.* dislike ‖ *a* (*di*) —, unwillingly.
contràlbero *sm.* (*mecc.*) countershaft.
contralto *sm.* contralto.
contrammiraglio *sm.* rear-admiral.
contrappasso *sm.* retaliation.
contrappello *sm.* second roll-call.
contrappesare *vt.* to counterbalance.
contrappeso *sm.* counterbalance.
contrapporre *vt.* to oppose, to contrast ‖ — *qc. a qu.*, to set (*v. irr.*) sthg. against sm.
contrapposizione *sf.* contraposition.
contrapposto *agg.* opposite ‖ *per* —, on the contrary. ♦ **contrapposto** *sm.* opposite.
contrappunto *sm.* counterpoint.
contrariamente *avv.* on the contrary ‖ — *ad ogni aspettativa*, contrary to all expectation.
contrariare *vt.* 1. to oppose 2. (*irritare*) to annoy.
contrarietà *sf.* 1. opposition 2. (*avversità*) misfortune.
contrario *agg.* 1. contrary, opposed 2. (*nocivo*) harmful 3. (*riluttante*) unwilling ‖ *al* —, on the contrary. ♦ **contrario** *sm.* contrary.
contrarre *vt.* to contract.
contrassegnare *vt.* to mark.
contrassegno *sm.* 1. countersign 2. (*segno*) mark 3. (*distintivo*) badge.
contrastare *vi.* to be in contrast. ♦ **contrastare** *vt.* to oppose.
contrastato *agg.* opposed.
contrasto *sm.* 1. contrast 2. (*dissidio*) conflict.
contrattaccare *vt.* to counterattack.
contrattacco *sm.* counterattack.
contrattare *vt.* to negotiate: — *il prezzo*, to haggle about the price.
contrattazione *sf.* dealing, negotiation.
contrattempo *sm.* 1. (*incidente*) mishap 2. (*inconveniente*) inconvenience.

contràttile *agg.* contractile.
contratto *sm.* contract.
contratto *agg.* contracted.
contrattuale *agg.* contractual.
contravveleno *sm.* antidote.
contravvenire *vi.* to infringe.
contravventore *sm.* transgressor.
contravvenzione *sf.* 1. violation 2. (*multa*) fine.
contrazione *sf.* contraction.
contribuente *sm.* taxpayer.
contribuire *vi.* to contribute.
contributo *sm.* contribution.
contribuzione *sf.* contribution.
contristarsi *vr.* to grieve.
contrito *agg.* contrite.
contrizione *sf.* contrition.
contro *prep.* 1. against 2. (*in opposizione a*) contrary to ‖ — *assegno*, cash on delivery.
controbàttere *vt.* (*confutare*) to disprove, to confute.
controbilanciare *vt.* to counterbalance.
controcampo *sm.* (*cine*) reverse shot.
controcorrente *sf.* counter-current. ♦ **controcorrente** *loc. avv.* against the stream.
controffensiva *sf.* counter-offensive.
controfigura *sf.* double.
controfirmare *vt.* to countersign.
controindicare *vt.* (*med.*) to contra-indicate.
controindicazione *sf.* (*med.*) contra-indication.
controllare *vt.* 1. to control 2. (*verificare*) to verify, to check 3. (*ispezionare*) to inspect 4. (*comm.*) to audit.
controllo *sm.* 1. control 2. (*verifica*) check, verification 3. (*ispezione*) inspection 4. (*comm.*) audit.
controllore *sm.* 1. controller 2. (*ferr.*) ticket-inspector.
controluce *avv.* against the light. ♦ **controluce** *sf.* counterlight.
contromarca *sf.* pass-out check (ticket).
controparte *sf.* counter-party.
contropartita *sf.* 1. (*comm.*) counter-item 2. (*compenso*) compensation.
contropelo *sm.* wrong way of the hair ‖ *fare il* —, to shave against the lie of the hair.
controproducente *agg.* having opposite effect.

controproposta *sf.* counter-proposal.

controprova *sf.* 1. countercheck 2. (*giur.*) counter-evidence.

contròrdine *sm.* counter-order: *dare un* —, to countermand an order.

controriforma *sf.* counter-reformation.

controrivoluzione *sf.* counter-revolution.

controsenso *sm.* self-contradiction, absurdity.

controspionaggio *sm.* counter-espionage.

controstòmaco *avv.* reluctantly.

controvelaccio *sm.* (*mar.*) main royal.

controvento *avv.* against the wind.

controversia *sf.* controversy.

controverso *agg.* controversial.

controvertibile *agg.* controvertible.

controvoglia *avv.* unwillingly.

contumace *agg.* guilty of default.

contumacia *sf.* default.

contumaciale *agg.* (*giur.*) judge ment by default.

contumelia *sf.* insult, abuse.

contundente *agg.* blunt: *corpo* —, blunt instrument.

conturbare *vt.* 1. to perturb 2. (*eccitare*) to thrill.

contusione *sf.* bruise.

contuso *agg.* bruised.

convalescente *agg.* e *sm.* convalescent.

convalescenza *sf.* convalescence.

convalidare *vt.* to ratify, to confirm.

convegno *sm.* meeting.

convenévole *agg.* convenient, proper. ◆ **convenévoli** *sm. pl.* compliments.

conveniente *agg.* 1. convenient (for) 2. (*economicamente vantaggioso*) profitable.

convenienza *sf.* 1. convenience 2. (*vantaggio economico*) profit 3. (*buona creanza*) propriety.

convenire *vi.* 1. to convene 2. (*essere d'accordo*) to agree 3. (*essere utile*) to be convenient.

convento *sm.* 1. convent 2. (*di suore*) nunnery.

conventuale *agg.* conventual.

convenuto *agg.* agreed upon. ◆ **convenuto** *sm.* 1. agreement 2. *i convenuti*, the persons present.

convenzionale *agg.* conventional.

convenzionare *vt.* to make (*v. irr.*) an agreement.

convenzione *sf.* convention.

convergente *agg.* convergent.

convergenza *sf.* convergence.

convèrgere *vi.* to converge.

conversare *vi.* to talk.

conversatore *sm.* talker.

conversazione *sf.* conversation, talk.

conversione *sf.* 1. (*anche fig.*) conversion 2. (*mil.*) wheel.

convertibile *agg.* convertible.

convertire *vt.* 1. (*pol.; relig.*) to convert 2. (*mutare*) to turn, to change. ◆ **convertirsi** *vr.* to be converted.

convessità *sf.* convexity.

convesso *agg.* convex.

convincere *vt.* to convince, to persuade.

convinto *agg.* convinced, persuaded.

convinzione *sf.* persuasion, firm belief.

convitato *sm.* guest.

convito *sm.* banquet.

convitto *sm.* boarding-school.

convivente *agg.* cohabiting.

convivenza *sf.* cohabitation, life in common.

convivere *vi.* to live together.

convocare *vt.* to convene, to summon.

convocazione *sf.* convocation, summoning.

convogliare *vt.* 1. (*scortare*) to escort 2. (*trasportare*) to carry away 3. (*indirizzare*) to address.

convoglio *sm.* 1. (*treno*) train 2. (*mil.; mar.*) convoy.

convolare *vi.* to fly (*v. irr.*) together: — *a giuste nozze*, to get (*v. irr.*) married.

convulsione *sf.* convulsion.

convulso *agg.* convulsive.

cooperare *vi.* to co-operate, to collaborate.

cooperativa *sf.* 1. co-operative society 2. (*di consumo*) co-operative store.

cooperativo *agg.* co-operative.

cooperatore *sm.* co-operator.

cooperazione *sf.* co-operation, collaboration.

coordinamento *sm.* co-ordination.

coordinare *vt.* to co-ordinate.

coordinata *sf.* co-ordinate.

coordinativo *agg.* co-ordinative.

coordinato *agg.* co-ordinate.

coordinatore *agg.* co-ordinative. ♦
coordinatore *sm.* co-ordinator.
coordinazione *sf.* co-ordination.
coorte *sf.* 1. (*mil.*) cohort 2. (*folla*)
crowd.
copale *sf.* 1. copal 2. (*pelle*) patent
leather.
copeco *sm.* copeck.
coperchio *sm.* lid, cover (*anche
mecc.*).
coperta *sf.* 1. blanket: — *da viaggio*, rug; — *scozzese*, plaid 2.
(*mar.*) deck.
copertina *sf.* cover: — *di libro*,
book-cover.
coperto *agg.* 1. (*riparato*) covered,
sheltered || — *di ferro*, iron-clad;
mettere al —, to shelter from 2.
(*di cielo*) overcast 3. (*nascosto*)
hidden. ♦ **coperto** *sm.* cover.
copertone *sm.* tyre.
copertura *sf.* 1. covering 2. (*di mobili*) cover.
copia *sf.* 1. copy 2. (*foto*) print.
copiare *vt.* to copy.
copiativo *agg.* *matita copiativa*,
copying pencil.
copiatura *sf.* copying.
copione *sm.* script.
copiosamente *avv.* plentifully.
copioso *agg.* plentiful.
copista *sm.* copyist.
coppa *sf.* 1. cup 2. (*auto*) pan.
coppella *sf.* (*metal.*) cupel.
coppellare *vt.* (*metal.*) to cupel.
coppia *sf.* 1. (*di persone e cose*)
couple 2. (*di animali*) pair || *una
— di buoi*, a yoke.
copricapo *sm.* hat.
coprifuoco *sm.* curfew.
copriletto *sm.* coverlet.
coprire *vt.* 1. to cover 2. (*nascondere*) to conceal 3. (*coprire un suono*) to drown.
copto *agg.* coptic. ♦ **copto** *sm.*
copt.
copulativo *agg.* (*gramm.*) copulative.
copulazione *sf.* copulation.
coraggio *sm.* 1. courage, bravery,
heart 2. (*sfrontatezza*) impudence.
coraggiosamente *avv.* bravely.
coraggioso *agg.* brave, bold.
corale *agg.* choral.
corallifero *agg.* coralliferous.
corallo *sm.* coral.
corazza *sf.* 1. cuirass 2. (*bot.; zool.*)
armour, carapace.
corazzare *vt.* 1. to armour 2. (*fig.*)

to strengthen. ♦ **corazzarsi** *vr.*
to harden oneself.
corazzata *sf.* (*mar.*) battleship.
corazziere *sm.* cuirassier.
corbelleria *sf.* 1. foolish action 2.
(*sciocchezza*) nonsense.
corda *sf.* 1. rope 2. (*mus.*) string.
cordaio *sm.* 1. (*chi fabbrica corde*)
rope-maker 2. (*chi vende corde*)
rope-seller.
cordame *sm.* cordage.
cordata *sf.* rope: *in* —, on the rope.
cordiale *agg.* cordial, hearty. ♦
cordiale *sm.* (*liquore*) cordial.
cordialità *sf.* cordiality.
cordialmente *avv.* cordially.
cordicella *sf.* string.
cordigliera *sf.* cordillera.
cordite *sf.* cordite.
cordoglio *sm.* deep sorrow.
cordone *sm.* 1. cord 2. (*mil.*) cordon.
coreano *agg.* e *sm.* Korean.
coreografia *sf.* choreography.
coreografico *agg.* 1. choreographic
2. (*fig.*) spectacular.
coreografo *sm.* choreographer.
coriaceo *agg.* coriaceous, tough.
coriandolo *sm.* confetti (*pl.*).
coricare *vt.* to lay (*v. irr.*) down.
♦ **coricarsi** *vr.* to lie (*v. irr.*)
down.
corifeo *sm.* coryphaeus (*pl.* -aei).
corinzio *agg.* e *sm.* Corinthian.
corista *sm.* chorus-singer.
cormorano *sm.* (*zool.*) cormorant.
cornacchia *sf.* rook, crow.
cornamusa *sf.* bagpipe.
cornata *sf.* butt.
cornea *sf.* cornea.
cornetta *sf.* cornet.
cornice *sf.* frame.
cornicione *sm.* 1. (*arch.*) cornice
2. (*di finestre, porte*) label 3. (*di
gronda*) eaves (*pl.*).
cornificare *vt.* 1. (*di moglie*) to
cuckold 2. (*di marito*) to be unfaithful to.
corno *sm.* horn || (*inter.*) *un* —, not
at all.
cornuto *agg.* horned. ♦ **cornuto**
sm. (*fig.*) cuckold.
coro *sm.* 1. chorus 2. (*eccl.*) choir.
corolla *sf.* corolla.
corollario *sm.* corollary.
corona *sf.* 1. crown: — *del rosario*,
rosary crown; — *del dente*, crown
2. (*mecc.*) rim 3. (*relig.*) (*tonsura*)
tonsure.

coronamento *sm.* **1.** crowning **2.** (*completamento*) fulfilment.
coronare *vt.* to crown (*anche fig.*).
coronario *agg.* coronary.
corpo *sm.* **1.** body || *a — morto*, desperately; *combattere a — a —*, to fight (*v. irr.*) hand to hand; *passare sul — di qu.*, to pass over so. **2.** (*cadavere*) corpse **3.** (*collettività*) corps || *— insegnante*, teaching staff.
corporale *agg.* corporal.
corporativismo *sm.* (*econ.*) corporative system.
corporativo *agg.* (*econ.*) corporative.
corporatura *sf.* build, size.
corporazione *sf.* corporation.
corpòreo *agg.* corporeal.
corpulento *agg.* corpulent, stout.
corpulenza *sf.* stoutness.
corpuscolare *agg.* corpuscular.
corpùscolo *sm.* corpuscle.
corredare *vt.* **1.** to equip **2.** (*accompagnare*) to accompany.
corredino *sm.* baby's outfit.
corredo *sm.* **1.** outfit **2.** (*di sposa*) trousseau **3.** (*bagaglio*) wealth, store: *— di cultura*, store of knowledge.
corrèggere *vt.* **1.** to correct **2.** (*di bevande*) to lace. ♦ **corrèggersi** *vr.* to amend, to correct oneself.
correggia *sf.* leather strap.
correlativo *agg.* correlative.
correlazione *sf.* correlation.
corrente[1] *agg.* **1.** (*che scorre*) running **2.** (*circolante*) current **3.** (*comm.*) inst. (*abbrev. di instant*) || *conto —*, current account **4.** (*andante*) common.
corrente[2] *sf.* **1.** current (*anche fig.*), stream **2.** (*di aria*) draught.
correntemente *avv.* fluently.
còrrere *vi.* **1.** to run (*v. irr.*): *— dietro a qu.*, to run after; *— a gambe levate*, to run as hard as one can || *lasciar —*, to take (*v. irr.*) no notice of sthg. **2.** (*di tempo*) to pass **3.** (*di voci*) to be abroad.
corresponsàbile *agg.* jointly responsible.
corresponsione *sf.* payment.
correttezza *sf.* **1.** correctness **2.** (*onestà*) honesty **3.** (*decoro, educazione*) propriety, politeness.
correttivo *agg. e sm.* corrective.
corretto *agg.* **1.** correct, exact **2.** (*irreprensibile*) faultless **3.** (*di be-*

vanda) laced.
correttore *sm.* corrector || *— di bozze*, proof-reader.
correzionale *agg.* correctional.
correzione *sf.* correction || *— di bozze*, proof-reading; *casa di —*, house of correction.
corridoio *sm.* **1.** passage **2.** (*di treno*) corridor.
corridore *sm.* **1.** runner **2.** (*sport*) racer.
corriera *sf.* coach.
corriere *sm.* **1.** messenger **2.** (*chi trasporta merci*) carrier **3.** (*posta*) mail.
corrimano *sm.* handrail.
corrispettivo *agg.* correlative. ♦ **corrispettivo** *sm.* **1.** equivalent **2.** (*compenso*) compensation.
corrispondente *agg. e sm.* correspondent.
corrispondenza *sf.* correspondence.
corrispòndere *vi.* **1.** to correspond (with) **2.** (*ricambiare sentimenti ecc.*) to return. ♦ **corrispòndere** *vt.* to pay.
corrisposto *agg.* **1.** (*contraccambiato*) returned **2.** (*pagato*) paid.
corroborante *agg. e sm.* corroborant.
corroborare *vt.* to strengthen.
corròdere *vt.* to corrode.
corròmpere *vt.* **1.** to corrupt (*anche fig.*), to pollute **2.** (*con denaro*) to bribe.
corrosione *sf.* corrosion.
corrosivo *agg. e sm.* corrosive.
corrucciarsi *vr.* to get (*v. irr.*) angry.
corrucciato *agg.* angry, worried.
corruccio *sm.* anger, worry.
corrugamento *sm.* corrugation: *— della fronte*, wrinkling of the forehead.
corrugare *vt.* to wrinkle.
corruttìbile *agg.* corruptible.
corruttore *agg.* corrupting. ♦ **corruttore** *sm.* **1.** corrupter **2.** (*con denaro*) briber.
corruzione *sf.* **1.** corruption **2.** (*con denaro*) bribery.
corsa *sf.* **1.** run **2.** (*sport*) race **3.** (*su veicolo pubblico*) trip || *prezzo della —*, fare; (*ferr.*) *perdere la —*, to miss the train.
corsaro *sm.* corsair.
corsetto *sm.* corset.
corsìa *sf.* **1.** passage **2.** (*di ospedale*) ward **3.** (*di strada*) lane.

corsiero *sm.* steed.
corsivo *agg.* cursive. ♦ corsivo *sm.* (*tip.*) italics (*pl.*).
corso *sm.* 1. course (*anche fig.*) 2. (*di acque*) water-course.
corte *sf.* 1. court 2. (*cortile*) courtyard 3. (*corteggiamento*) courtship.
corteccia *sf.* 1. bark 2. (*anat.*) cortex.
corteggiare *vt.* 1. to woo 2. (*adulare*) to flatter.
corteggiatore *sm.* suitor, lover.
corteo *sm.* train, procession: — *funebre*, funeral train.
cortese *agg.* kind.
cortesìa *sf.* 1. kindness, politeness 2. (*favore*) favour || *per* —, please.
cortigiano *sm.* 1. courtier 2. (*adulatore*) flatterer.
cortile *sm.* courtyard || *animali da* —, poultry.
cortina *sf.* curtain: — *di ferro* (*pol.*), iron curtain.
cortisone *sm.* cortisone.
corto *agg.* short: *a* — *di*, short of.
cortocircùito *sm.* short circuit.
cortometraggio *sm.* short (film).
corvetta *sf.* (*mar.*) corvette.
corvino *agg.* 1. corvine 2. (*nero*) raven(-black).
corvo *sm.* raven.
cosa *sf.* 1. thing 2. (*faccenda*) matter || *nessuna* —, nothing; *ogni* —, everything; *che* —?, what?.
cosacco *agg.* e *sm.* Cossack.
coscia *sf.* 1. thigh 2. (*cuc.*) leg.
cosciente *agg.* 1. conscious 2. (*conscio*) aware.
coscienza *sf.* 1. conscience 2. (*consapevolezza*) consciousness.
coscienziosamente *avv.* conscientiously.
coscienzioso *agg.* conscientious.
cosciotto *sm.* leg: — *di manzo*, leg of beef.
coscritto *sm.* recruit.
coscrizione *sf.* conscription.
cosecante *sf.* cosecant.
coseno *sm.* (*mat.*) cosine.
così *avv.* so: *e* — *via*, and so on; — *come*, — *pure*, as well as; — *... come*, — *... quanto*, as ... as; — *da*, so ... as: *non è* — *sciocco da farlo*, he is not so foolish as to do that.
cosicché *cong.* so that.
cosiddetto *agg.* so-called.
cosiffatto *agg.* such, similar.

cosmesi *sf.* beauty culture.
cosmètico *agg.* e *sm.* cosmetic.
còsmico *agg.* cosmic.
cosmo *sm.* cosmos.
cosmogonìa *sf.* cosmogony.
cosmografia *sf.* cosmography.
cosmògrafo *sm.* cosmographer.
cosmologìa *sf.* cosmology.
cosmonàuta *s.* astronaut.
cosmonàutica *sf.* astronautics.
cosmopolita *agg.* e *sm.* cosmopolitan.
cosmopolitismo *sm.* cosmopolitanism.
coso *sm.* (*fam.*) 1. (*cosa*) thing 2. (*individuo*) fellow.
cospàrgere *vt.* 1. to strew (*v. irr.*) 2. (*sale, zucchero ecc.*) to sprinkle.
cospetto *sm.* presence: *al* — *di*, in the presence of.
cospicuità *sf.* conspicuousness.
cospicuo *agg.* 1. (*visibile*) conspicuous 2. (*notevole*) remarkable.
cospirare *vi.* to plot.
cospiratore *sm.* plotter.
cospirazione *sf.* plot.
costa *sf.* 1. coast, shore 2. (*venatura*) rib 3. (*di monte*) side 4. (*di libro*) back.
costà *avv.* there.
costaggiù *avv.* down there.
costale *agg.* costal.
costante *agg.* steady. ♦ costante *sf.* constant.
costanza *sf.* 1. firmness 2. (*perseveranza*) perseverance || *con* —, steadily.
costare *vi.* to cost (*v. irr.*).
costassù *avv.* up there.
costata *sf.* chop.
costatare *vt.* 1. (*accertare*) to ascertain 2. (*notare*) to notice.
costatazione *sf.* 1. ascertainment 2. (*osservazione*) remark.
costato *sm.* chest.
costeggiare *vt.* 1. to follow the coast of 2. (*per terra*) to skirt. ♦ costeggiare *vi.* to coast along.
costei *pron.* 1. (*sogg.*) she 2. (*compl.*) her 3. this woman, that woman.
costellare *vt.* to scatter.
costellazione *sf.* constellation.
costernare *vt.* to dismay. ♦ costernarsi *vr.* to be dismayed (at).
costernazione *sf.* dismay.
costì *avv.* there.
costiera *sf.* stretch of coast.
costiero *agg.* coastal || *nave costiera*, coaster.

costipare vt. 1. (un terreno) to tamp 2. (ammassare) to amass. ◆ **costiparsi** vr. 1. (raffreddarsi) to catch (v. irr.) a cold 2. (di intestino) to become (v. irr.) constipated.

costipato agg. essere —, to have a cold.

costipazione sf. 1. (raffreddore) cold 2. (intestinale) constipation 3. (di terreno) tamping.

costituente agg. constituent.

costituire vt. 1. to constitute, to form 2. (nominare) to appoint. ◆ **costituirsi** vr. (consegnarsi) to give (v. irr.) oneself up.

costituito agg. constituted.

costitutivo agg. constitutive.

costituto sm. (giur.) interrogation of the accused.

costituzionale agg. constitutional.

costituzionalismo sm. constitutionalism.

costituzionalità sf. constitutionality.

costituzione sf. 1. establishment 2. (pol.; med.) constitution.

costo sm. cost: ad ogni —, at all cost; a nessun —, in no case.

còstola sf. rib || stare alle costole, to watch over.

costoletta sf. cutlet.

costone sm. side.

costoro pron. 1. (sogg.) they 2. (compl.) them 3. these people, those people.

costoso agg. expensive, dear.

costringere vt. 1. (stringere) to press 2. (obbligare) to compel.

costrizione sf. 1. (restringimento) constriction 2. (obbligo) compulsion.

costruire vt. to build (v. irr.).

costruttivo agg. constructive.

costruttore agg. building. ◆ **costruttore** sm. builder.

costruzione sf. construction, building.

costui pron. 1. (sogg.) he 2. (compl.) him 3. this man, that man.

costumato agg. 1. (virtuoso) virtuous 2. (educato) polite.

costume sm. 1. (usanza) custom 2. (personale) habit 3. (condotta) morals (pl.) 4. (vestito) costume.

costumista sm. costume-designer.

cotangente sf. (mat.) cotangent.

cotenna sf. 1. pigskin 2. (del cranio) scalp 3. (del lardo) rind.

còtica sf. V. cotenna.

cotogna sf. quince.

cotognata sf. quince jam.

cotoletta sf. cutlet.

cotone sm. cotton.

cotoniere sm. cotton-spinner.

cotoniero agg. cotton.

cotonificio sm. cotton-mill.

cotonina sf. calico.

cotta[1] sf. (eccl.) surplice.

cotta[2] sf. 1. (cottura) cooking 2. (infornata) batch 3. (fam.) prendere una — per, to have a crush on.

cottimista sm. pieceworker.

còttimo sm. piecework: lavorare a —, to work by the job; lavoro a —, job-work; contratto a —, job contract.

cotto sm. brickwork.

cottura sf. 1. cooking 2. (in forno) baking.

coturno sm. cothurnus (pl. -ni).

cova sf. 1. (il covare) brooding 2. (nido) nest.

covare vt. 1. to brood 2. (fig.) to brood over 3. (di fuoco; passioni) to smoulder 4. (di malattia) to be latent.

covata sf. brood.

covo sm. den.

covone sm. sheaf (pl. sheaves).

cozza sf. mussel.

cozzare vi. 1. to strike (v. irr.) 2. (venire in collisione) to collide.

cozzo sm. 1. clash, collision 2. (conflitto) conflict.

crampo sm. cramp.

cranio sm. skull.

crasso agg. crass, gross: ignoranza crassa, gross ignorance.

cratere sm. crater.

cràuti sm. pl. sauerkraut (sing.)

cravatta sf. neck-tie.

creanza sf. politeness.

creare vt. 1. to create 2. (causare) to cause 3. (nominare) to appoint 4. (costituire) to form.

creativo agg. creative.

creato sm. creation.

creatore agg. creating. ◆ **creatore** sm. creator.

creatura sf. creature.

creazione sf. creation.

credente sm. believer.

credenza[1] sf. belief.

credenza[2] sf. (buffet) sideboard.

credenziale agg. credential: lettera —, credential.

crédere *vt.* e *vi.* **1.** (*pensare*) to think (*v. irr.*) **2.** (*prestar fede*) to believe. ♦ crédersi *vr.* to think (*v. irr.*). oneself.

credìbile *agg.* **1.** credible **2.** (*di persona*) trustworthy.

credibilità *sf.* credibility.

creditizio *agg.* credit.

crédito *sm.* **1.** (*comm.*) credit: *e* —, on credit **2.** (*stima*) esteem.

creditore *sm.* creditor.

credo *sm.* creed.

credulità *sf.* credulity.

credulone *agg.* credulous.

crema *sf.* cream.

cremagliera *sf.* rack: *ferrovia a* —, rack-railway.

cremare *vt.* to cremate.

crematorio *agg.* crematory: *forno* —, crematory.

cremazione *sf.* cremation.

cremerìa *sf.* creamery.

crèmisi *agg.* e *sm.* crimson.

crèolo *agg.* e *sm.* creole.

crepa *sf.* crack.

crepaccio *sm.* crevasse.

crepacuore *sm.* heart-break: *morire di* —, to die of a broken heart.

crepapelle (*nella loc. avv.*) *ridere a* —, to roar with laughter; *mangiare a* —, to eat to excess.

crepare *vi.* to crack.

crepella *sf.* crepoline.

crepitare *vi.* to crackle.

crepitìo *sm.* crackle.

crepuscolare *agg.* crepuscular.

crepùscolo *sm.* twilight.

crescente *agg.* growing.

crescenza *sf.* growth.

créscere *vi.* **1.** to grow (*v. irr.*) **2.** (*aumentare*) to increase.

crescione *sm.* (*bot.*) water-cress.

créscita *sf.* **1.** growth **2.** (*aumento*) increase.

crèsima *sf.* confirmation.

cresimare *vt.* to confirm.

creso *sm.* Croesus.

crespo *agg.* crisp.

cresta *sf.* **1.** crest **2.** (*di gallo*) comb.

crestina *sf.* maid-servant's cap.

creta *sf.* clay.

cretinerìa *sf.* **1.** idiocy **2.** (*azione*) foolish action **3.** (*detto*) nonsense.

cretinismo *sm.* idiocy.

cretino *agg.* e *sm.* idiot.

cricca *sf.* gang.

cricco *sm.* jack.

criminale *agg.* e *sm.* criminal.

criminalista *s.* **1.** (*avvocato*) criminal lawyer **2.** (*studioso*) criminologist.

criminalità *sf.* criminality.

crìmine *sm.* crime.

criminologìa *sf.* criminology.

criminosità *sf.* criminality.

criminoso *agg.* criminal.

crine *sm.* horse-hair.

criniera *sf.* mane.

crinolina *sf.* crinoline.

criolite *sf.* cryolite.

cripta *sf.* crypt.

crisàlide *sf.* chrysalid.

crisantemo *sm.* chrysanthemum.

crisi *sf.* **1.** crisis (*pl.* -ses) **2.** (*med.*) fit.

crisma *sm.* **1.** (*eccl.*) chrism **2.** (*fig.*) approval || *con tutti i crismi*, approved, praised.

cristallerìa *sf.* **1.** crystal-ware **2.** (*fabbrica*) crystal manufactory.

cristalliera *sf.* glass case.

cristallino *agg.* e *sm.* crystalline.

cristallizzare *vt.* e *vi.*, cristallizzarsi *vr.* to crystallize.

cristallizzazione *sf.* crystallization.

cristallo *sm.* **1.** crystal **2.** (*lastra di vetro*) plate glass.

cristallografìa *sf.* crystallography.

cristianésimo *sm.* Christianity.

cristiania *sm.* (*sport*) Christiania.

cristianità *sf.* **1.** (*i cristiani*) Christendom **2.** (*cristianesimo*) Christianity.

cristiano *agg.* e *sm.* Christian.

criterio *sm.* **1.** principle **2.** opinion **3.** (*buon senso*) sense.

crìtica *sf.* **1.** criticism **2.** (*saggio*) critical essay **3.** (*i critici*) the critics (*pl.*).

criticamente *avv.* critically.

criticare *vt.* **1.** to criticize **2.** (*biasimare*) to blame.

criticismo *sm.* **1.** criticism **2.** (*stor.*) critical philosophy.

crìtico *agg.* critical. ♦ crìtico *sm.* critic.

criticone *sm.* fault-finder.

crittògama *sf.* (*bot.*) cryptogam.

crittografìa *sf.* cryptography.

crittogramma *sm.* cryptogram.

crivellare *vt.* to riddle.

crivellatura *sf.* riddling.

crivello *sm.* riddle.

croato *agg.* e *sm.* Croatian.

croccante *agg.* crisp. ♦ croccante *sm.* almond sweetmeat.

crocchetta *sf.* croquette.
crocchia *sf.* bun.
crocchio *sm.* group.
croce *sf.* cross.
crocerossina *sf.* Red Cross nurse.
crociata *sf.* crusade.
crociato *sm.* crusader.
crocicchio *sm.* cross-road.
crociera *sf.* 1. cruise 2. (*arch.*) cross-vault.
crocifiggere *vt.* to crucify.
crocifissione *sf.* crucifixion.
crocifisso *sm.* crucifix.
croco *sm.* (*bot.*) crocus.
crogiuolo *sm.* crucible.
crollare *vi.* to fall (*v. irr.*) down.
crollo *sm.* 1. breakdown 2. (*caduta*) falling down.
croma *sf.* (*mus.*) quaver.
cromare *vt.* to chromium-plate.
cromàtico *agg.* chromatic.
cromatismo *sm.* chromatism.
cromatografia *sf.* chromatography.
cromatura *sf.* chromium plating.
cromo *sm.* chromium.
cromolitografia *sf.* chromolithography.
cromosomo *sm.* chromosome.
cronaca *sf.* 1. chronicle 2. (*di giornale*) news.
crònico *agg.* chronic. ◆ **crònico** *sm.* chronic invalid.
cronista *sm.* reporter.
cronistoria *sf.* chronicle.
cronologìa *sf.* chronology.
cronològico *agg.* chronological.
cronometraggio *sm.* time-study.
cronometrare *vt.* to time.
cronometrìa *sf.* timing.
cronòmetro *sm.* stop watch.
crosta *sf.* 1. crust 2. (*tec.*) coating.
crostàcei *sm. pl.* Crustacea.
crostata *sf.* (*cuc.*) tart.
cròtalo *sm.* rattlesnake.
crucciare *vt.*, **crucciarsi** *vr.* to worry.
cruciale *agg.* crucial.
cruciverba *sm.* cross-word puzzle.
crudele *agg.* cruel.
crudeltà *sf.* cruelty.
crudezza *sf.* 1. (*di stagione*) harshness 2. (*di parole*) coarseness 3. (*di cibo*) rawness.
crudo *agg.* 1. raw 2. (*poco cotto*) underdone 3. (*aspro, rigido*) harsh 4. (*rozzo*) coarse.
cruento *agg.* bloody.
crumiro *sm.* blackleg.
cruna *sf.* needle's eye.

crusca *sf.* bran.
cruscotto *sm.* dashboard.
cubaggio *sm.* cubage.
cubano *agg.* e *sm.* Cuban.
cubatura *sf.* cubature.
cubetto *sm.* — *di ghiaccio*, ice cube.
cùbico *agg.* cubic.
cubismo *sm.* cubism.
cubitale *agg.* a *caratteri cubitali*, in very large letters.
cùbito *sm.* 1. (*misura*) cubit 2. (*avambraccio*) forearm.
cubo *sm.* cube.
cuccagna *sf.* abundance ‖ *albero della* —, greasy pole.
cuccetta *sf.* berth.
cucchiaiata *sf.* spoonful.
cucchiaino *sm.* 1. tea-spoon, coffee-spoon 2. (*il contenuto*) tea-spoonful.
cucchiaio *sm.* spoon.
cuccia *sf.* dog-house.
cùcciolo *sm.* puppy.
cùccuma *sf.* kettle.
cucina *sf.* 1. kitchen 2. (*modo di cucinare*) cooking 3. (*culinaria*) cookery 4. (*stufa*) stove.
cucinare *vt.* to cook.
cuciniere *sm.* man-cook.
cucire *vt.* 1. to sew (*v. irr.*) 2. (*med.*) to stitch.
cucito *sm.* needlework.
cucitrice *sf.* 1. seamstress 2. (*macchinetta*) stapler.
cucitura *sf.* 1. seam 2. (*di fogli*) stapling.
cucù *sm.* (*zool.*) cuckoo.
cucùrbita *sf.* gourd.
cuffia *sf.* 1. cap. 2. (*radio*) head-phone.
cugina *sf.* cousin.
cugino *sm.* cousin.
cui *pron. rel.* 1. (*di possesso*) whose; (*di possesso, solo per animali e cose*) of which: *l'uomo la — casa*, the man whose house; *il libro le — pagine*, the book the pages of which 2. (*altri casi, per persone*) whom; (*altri casi, per animali e cose*) which: *l'uomo con — parlai*, the man to whom I spoke; *il libro di — parlai*, the book about which I spoke ‖ *in —* (*dove*), where; *in —* (*quando*) when.
culaccio *sm.* rump.
culatta *sf.* breech.
culinaria *sf.* cookery.
culinario *agg.* culinary.

culla *sf.* cradle.
cullare *vt.* to rock, to lull (*anche fig.*).
culminante *agg.* culminant: *momento* —, climax.
culminare *vi.* to culminate.
cùlmine *sm.* 1. summit 2. (*fig.*) apex.
culo *sm.* bottom; (*volg.*) ass.
culto *sm.* 1. cult 2. (*religione*) religion 3. (*adorazione*) worship.
cultore *sm.* lover.
cultura *sf.* culture.
culturale *agg.* cultural.
cumulare *vt.* to heap up.
cumulativo *agg.* cumulative.
cumulatore *sm.* hoarder.
cumulazione *sf.* hoarding.
cùmulo *sm.* 1. heap 2. (*nube*) cumulus (*pl.* -li).
cuna *sf.* cradle.
cuneiforme *agg.* cuneiform, wedge--shaped.
cùneo *sm.* wedge.
cunetta *sf.* 1. (*stradale*) road bump 2. (*scolo*) gutter.
cunìcolo *sm.* underground passage, shaft.
cuòcere *vt.* 1. to cook 2. (*in forno, fornace*) to bake.
cuoco *sm.* cook.
cuoiame *sm.* leather and hides.
cuoio *sm.* leather || — *capelluto*, scalp.
cuore *sm.* heart.
cupezza *sf.* 1. darkness 2. (*tristezza*) gloom.
cupidigia *sf.* cupidity, greed.
cùpido *agg.* greedy.
cupo *agg.* 1. dark 2. (*triste*) gloomy 3. (*profondo*) deep.
cùpola *sf.* dome.
cùpreo *agg.* cupreous.
cùprico *agg.* cupric.
cura *sf.* 1. care 2. (*med.*) treatment || *casa di* —, nursing-home.
curàbile *agg.* curable.
curante *agg. medico* —, attending physician.
curare *vt.* 1. (*aver cura di*) to take (*v. irr.*) care of 2. (*med.*) to treat 3. (*una pubblicazione*) to edit. ◆ **curarsi** *vr.* (*seguire una cura*) to follow a treatment.
curaro *sm.* curare.
curato *sm.* vicar.
curatore *sm.* trustee.
curdo *agg.* Kurdish. ◆ **curdo** *sm.* Kurd.

curia *sf.* 1. (*eccl.*) see 2. (*giur.*) court of justice.
curie *sm.* curie.
curiosare *vi.* to pry.
curiosità *sf.* 1. curiosity 2. (*stranezza*) oddity.
curioso *agg.* curious.
currìculum *sm.* curriculum (*pl.* -la).
cursore *sm.* 1. messenger 2. (*mecc.*) slider.
curva *sf.* bend.
curvare *vt.* to bend (*v. irr.*). ◆ **curvarsi** *vr.* 1. to bend (*v. irr.*) 2. (*inclinarsi*) to bow.
curvatura *sf.* 1. bending 2. (*arch.*) sweep.
curvilineo *agg.* curvilinear.
curvo *agg.* bent.
cuscinetto *sm.* small cushion || — *a sfera*, ball bearing.
cuscino *sm.* 1. cushion 2. (*guanciale*) pillow 3. (*mecc.*) pillow.
custode *sm.* keeper.
custodia *sf.* 1. care 2. (*tutela*) guardianship 3. (*astuccio*) case.
custodire *vt.* 1. to keep (*v. irr.*) 2. (*aver cura di*) to look after.
cutàneo *agg.* skin: *malattia cutanea*, skin disease.
cute *sf.* skin.

D

da *prep.* 1. (*provenienza*) from: *vengo* — *Milano*, I come from Milan 2. (*moto a luogo*) to: *andremo* — *loro*, we shall go to their house 3. (*stato in luogo*) at: *vivo* — *mia zia*, I live at my aunt's 4. (*moto per luogo*) through: *passai* — *Roma*, I passed through Rome 5. (*tempo, durata*) for: *siamo qui* — *due mesi*, we have been here for two months; (*a partire da*) since: *lo conosco dal 1955*, I have known him since 1955 6. (*agente*) by: *fu aiutato* — *sua sorella*, he was helped by his sister 7. (*come*) like: *si comportano* — *bambini*, they are behaving like children || *fare* —, to act as.
dabbasso *avv.* 1. below, down below 2. (*al piano inferiore*) downstairs.

dabbenàggine *sf.* ingenuousness.
dabbene *agg.* honest.
daccapo *avv.* over again, from the beginning.
dacché *cong.* since.
dadaismo *sm.* dadaism.
dado *sm.* 1. die (*pl.* dice) 2. (*cuc.*) cube 3. (*mecc.*) nut.
daffare *sm.* work || darsi —, to be on the go.
dagherrotipìa *sf.* daguerreotypy.
dagherròtipo *sm.* daguerreotype.
dàgli, dài *inter.* go on.
dàino *sm.* fallow-deer (*invariato al pl.*).
dalìa *sf.* dahlia.
daltònico *agg.* colour-blind.
daltonismo *sm.* colour-blindness.
d'altronde *avv.* on the other hand.
dama *sf.* 1. lady of rank 2. (*al ballo*) partner 3. (*giuoco*) draughts (*pl.*).
damasco *sm.* damask.
damerino *sm.* dandy.
damiere *sm.* draughtboard.
damigella *sf.* maid of honour.
damigiana *sf.* demijohn.
danaroso *agg.* wealthy.
danese *agg.* Danish. ♦ **danese** *sm.* Dane.
dannare *vt.* to damn || far —, to drive (*v. irr.*) so. mad. ♦ **dannarsi** 1. to be damned 2. (*fig.*) to strive (*v. irr.*) hard.
dannato *agg.* damned. ♦ **dannato** *sm.* damned soul.
dannazione *sf.* damnation: —!, damn!
danneggiamento *sm.* damage.
danneggiare *vt.* 1. to damage 2. (*di persone*) to injure.
danno *sm.* 1. damage 2. (*a persona*) injury || recare — a qu., to do (*v. irr.*) so. harm.
dànnoso *agg.* harmful.
dantesco *agg.* Dantesque.
danza *sf.* dance.
danzante *agg.* dancing: trattenimento —, dance.
danzare *vt.* e *vi.* to dance.
danzatore *sm.* dancer.
dappertutto *avv.* everywhere.
dappocàggine *sf.* ineptitude.
dappoco *agg.* inept.
dappresso *avv.* near-by.
dapprima *avv.* at first.
dardeggiare *vt.* e *vi.* to dart.
dardo *sm.* dart.
dare *sm.* debit. ♦ **dare** *vt.* to give

(*v. irr.*): — origine, luogo a qc., to give rise; — a bere a qu. che, to give so. to believe that; — ad intendere, to give to understand; — a pensare, to give food for thought || — atto di qc., to acknowledge; può darsi, maybe; — alla testa, to go (*v. irr.*) to one's head; — nell'occhio, to stand (*v. irr.*) out. ♦ **darsi** *vr.* to devote oneself || — al bere, to take (*v. irr.*) to drink; — ammalato, to pretend to be ill; — da fare, to busy oneself; darsela a gambe, to take (*v. irr.*) to one's heels.
dàrsena *sf.* wet dock.
darvinismo *sm.* Darwinism.
data *sf.* date: in — d'oggi, under to-day's date.
datare *vt.* to date.
dativo *sm.* dative.
dato *agg.* 1. given 2. (*stabilito*) stated 3. (*dedito*) addicted || — e non concesso, supposing that. ♦ **dato** *sm.* datum (*pl.* -ta). ♦ **dato che** *cong.* since, as.
datore *sm.* giver || — di lavoro, employer.
dàttero *sm.* 1. date 2. (*albero*) date-palm.
dattilografare *vt.* to typewrite.
dattilografìa *sf.* typewriting.
dattilògrafo *sm.* typist.
dattiloscritto *agg.* typewritten. ♦ **dattiloscritto** *sm.* typescript.
dattorno *avv.* round, about.
davanti *avv.* before, in front. ♦ **davanti** *sm.* front. ♦ **davanti** *agg.* front. ♦ **davanti a** (*loc. prep.*) before.
davantino *sm.* ruffle.
davanzale *sm.* window-sill.
davvero *avv.* really, indeed.
daziario *agg.* toll.
daziere *sm.* exciseman (*pl.* -men).
dazio *sm.* 1. toll, duty 2. (*ufficio daziario*) toll-house 3. (*di consumo*) excise.
dea *sf.* goddess.
deambulare *vi.* to walk about.
deambulatorio *agg.* e *sm.* deambulatory.
deambulazione *sf.* deambulation.
debellare *vt.* 1. to defeat 2. (*fig.*) to overcome (*v. irr.*).
debilitante *agg.* weakening.
debilitare *vt.* to weaken.
debilitazione debilitation.

debitamente *avv.* duly.
débito *agg.* due, proper. ♦ **débito** *sm.* debt: *fare un* —, to run (*v. irr.*) into debt.
debitore *sm.* debtor.
débole *agg.* weak.
debolezza *sf.* weakness.
debosciato *agg.* debauched.
debuttante *sm.* 1. novice 2. (*di ragazza in società*) debutante.
debuttare *vi.* 1. to make (*v. irr.*) one's debut 2. (*di ragazza in società*) to come (*v. irr.*) out.
debutto *sm.* 1. debut 2. (*di ragazza in società*) coming out.
dècade *sf.* 1. (*di giorni*) ten days 2. (*di anni*) ten years.
decadente *agg.* 1. decaying 2. (*lett.*) decadent.
decadenza *sf.* decay, decline.
decadere *vi.* to decline || — *da un diritto*, to lose (*v. irr.*) a right.
decaduto *agg.* impoverished.
decaedro *sm.* decahedron.
decagrammo *sm.* decagram.
decalcare *vt.* to transfer.
decalcificare *vt.* to decalcify.
decàlitro *sm.* decalitre.
decàlogo *sm.* decalogue.
decàmetro *sm.* decametre.
decampare *vi.* 1. to decamp 2. (*fig.*) to recede.
decano *sm.* 1. senior 2. (*eccl.*) dean.
decantare *vt.* 1. to extol 2. (*chim.*) to decant.
decantazione *sf.* (*chim.*) decantation.
decapitare *vt.* to behead.
decappottàbile *agg.* (*auto*) convertible.
decasìllabo *agg.* decasyllabic. ♦ **decasìllabo** *sm.* decasyllable.
decatissaggio *sm.* decatizing.
decèdere *vi.* to die.
decelerare *vt.* to decelerate.
decennale *agg.* decennial.
decenne *agg.* 1. ten years old (*predicativo*) 2. ten-year-old (*attributivo*).
decennio *sm.* ten-year period.
decente *agg.* decent, proper.
decentramento *sm.* decentralization.
decentrare *vt.* to decentralize.
decenza *sf.* decency.
decesso *sm.* death.
decìdere *vt.* to decide. ♦ **decìdersi** *vr.* to make (*v. irr.*) up one's

mind.
decifrare *vt.* 1. to decipher 2. (*fam.*) to make (*v. irr.*) out.
decifrazione *sf.* deciphering.
decigrammo *sm.* decigram.
decìlitro *sm.* decilitre.
decimale *agg.* e *sm.* decimal.
decimare *vt.* to decimate.
decimazione *sf.* decimation.
decìmetro *sm.* decimetre.
dècimo *agg.* tenth.
decina *sf.* ten, half-a-score.
decisione *sf.* decision.
decisivo *agg.* decisive.
deciso *agg.* 1. resolute, firm 2. (*definito*) decided.
declamare *vt.* e *vi.* to declaim.
declamatorio *agg.* declamatory.
declamazione *sf.* declamation.
declassare *vt.* to degrade.
declinàbile *agg.* declinable.
declinante *agg.* declining.
declinare *vt.* 1. to decline || — *le proprie generalità*, to say (*v. irr.*) one's name and surname. ♦ **declinare** *vi.* 1. (*del sole*) to set (*v. irr.*) 2. (*degradare*) to slope 3. (*venir meno*) to decline.
declinazione *sf.* (*gramm.*) declension.
declino *sm.* decline.
declivio *sm.* declivity.
decollaggio *sm.* (*aer.*) take-off.
decollare *vi.* to take (*v. irr.*) off.
decollo *sm.* take-off.
decolorante *agg.* decolorating. ♦ **decolorante** *sm.* decolorant.
decolorare *vt.* to decolorate.
decolorazione *sf.* decoloration || — *dei capelli*, hair bleaching.
decomponìbile *agg.* decomposable.
decomporre *vt.* to decompose.
decomposizione *sf.* 1. decomposition 2. (*putrefazione*) putrefaction.
decongelare *vt.* to defrost.
decongestionare *vt.* to decongest.
decorare *vt.* to decorate: — *al valore*, to decorate for bravery.
decorativo *agg.* decorative.
decoratore *sm.* decorator.
decorazione *sf.* decoration.
decoro *sm.* dignity.
decoroso *agg.* decorous, proper.
decorrenza *sf.* expiration: *con* — *da*, beginning from.
decòrrere *vi.* 1. to pass || *a* — *da*, to begin (*v. irr.*) from 2. (*comm.*) to run (*v. irr.*), to have effect.
decorso *sm.* 1. period 2. (*il passa-*

re) passing.
decrepitezza *sf.* decrepitude.
decrèpito *agg.* decrepit.
decréscere *vi.* to decrease.
decretare *vt.* 1. to decree 2. (*concedere*) to confer.
decreto *sm.* decree: — *legge,* Order in Council.
decuplicare *vt.* to decuple.
dècuplo *sm.* decuple, ten times as much.
decurtare *vt.* to reduce.
dèdalo *sm.* maze.
dèdica *sf.* dedication.
dedicare *vt.* to dedicate. ♦ **dedicarsi** *vr.* to devote oneself.
dedicatorio *agg.* dedicatory.
dèdito *agg.* 1. given up 2. (*a vizio*) addicted.
dedizione *sf.* devotion.
dedurre *vt.* 1. to infer, to deduce 2. (*defalcare*) to deduct.
deduttivo *agg.* deductive.
deduzione *sf.* deduction.
defalcare *vt.* to deduct.
defalco *sm.* deduction.
defecare *vi.* to defecate.
defenestrare *vt.* 1. to throw (*v. irr.*) out of the window 2. (*fig.*) to dismiss.
defenestrazione *sf.* defenestration.
deferente *agg.* deferential.
deferenza *sf.* compliance, deference.
deferire *vt.* 1. to submit 2. (*giur.*) to remit.
defezionare *vi.* to desert.
defezione *sf.* 1. defection 2. (*mil.*) desertion.
deficiente *agg.* 1. insufficient 2. (*idiota*) mentally deficient. ♦ **deficiente** *sm.* idiot.
deficienza *sf.* 1. deficiency, lack 2. (*idiozia*) mental deficiency.
dèficit *sm.* deficit.
definìbile *agg.* definable.
definire *vt.* 1. to define 2. (*determinare, risolvere*) to determine.
definitivo *agg.* final.
definito *agg.* definite.
definizione *sf.* 1. definition 2. (*risoluzione*) settlement.
deflagrante *agg.* deflagrating.
deflagrare *vi.* to deflagrate.
deflagrazione *sf.* deflagration.
deflazione *sf.* deflation.
deflèttere *vi.* to deflect.
deflettore *sm.* baffle.
deflorare *vt.* to deflower.
deflorazione *sf.* defloration.

defluire *vi.* to flow down.
deflusso *sm.* 1. downflow 2. (*di marea*) ebb-tide.
deformante *agg.* deforming.
deformare *vt.* 1. to deform, to disfigure 2. (*alterare*) to alter. ♦ **deformarsi** *vr.* 1. (*mecc.*) to warp 2. to get (*v. irr.*) deformed.
deformazione *sf.* 1. deformation 2. (*mecc.*) buckling.
deforme *agg.* deformed.
deformità *sf.* deformity.
defraudare *vt.* to defraud.
defunto *agg.* e *sm.* dead.
degenerare *vi.* to degenerate.
degenerazione *sf.* degeneration.
degènere *agg.* degenerate.
degente *sm.* patient.
degenza *sf.* stay in hospital.
deglutizione *sf.* swallowing.
degnarsi *vr.* to condescend.
degnazione *sf.* condescension.
degno *agg.* worthy, deserving.
degradante *agg.* degrading.
degradare *vt.* to degrade.
degradazione *sf.* degradation.
degustare *vt.* to taste.
deiezione *sf.* dejection.
deificare *vt.* to deify.
deismo *sm.* deism.
deità *sf.* deity.
delatore *sm.* delator.
delazione *sf.* delation, informing.
delèbile *agg.* erasable.
dèlega *sf.* 1. delegation 2. (*procura*) proxy.
delegare *vt.* to delegate.
delegato *sm.* delegate.
delegazione *sf.* 1. delegation 2. (*commissione*) committee.
deleterio *agg.* harmful.
delfino *sm.* 1. (*zool.*) dolphin 2. (*fig.*) probable successor 3. (*stor.*) dauphin.
deliberare *vt.* to decide.
deliberazione *sf.* deliberation.
delicatezza *sf.* delicacy.
delicato *agg.* 1. delicate 2. (*scrupoloso*) scrupulous 3. (*discreto*) discreet, tactful.
delimitare *vt.* to delimit.
delimitazione *sf.* delimitation.
delineare *vt.* to outline.
delineazione *sf.* delineation.
delinquente *sm.* delinquent.
delinquenza *sf.* criminality.
delìnquere *vi.* to commit an offence.
deliquio *sm.* swoon.

delirare *vi.* to rave.
delirio *sm.* delirium, frenzy (*anche* fig.).
delitto *sm.* crime.
delittuoso *agg.* criminal.
delizia *sf.* delight.
deliziare *vt.* to delight.
delizioso *agg.* 1. delightful 2. (*di sapore, profumo*) delicious.
delta *sm.* delta.
deltòide *agg.* e *sm.* deltoid.
delucidare *vt.* to explain.
delucidazione *sf.* explanation.
delùdere *vt.* to disappoint.
delusione *sf.* disappointment.
demagogìa *sf.* demagogy.
demagògico *agg.* demagogic.
demagogo *sm.* demagogue.
demandare *vt.* to commit.
demaniale *agg.* (owned by the) State.
demanio *sm.* State property.
demarcare *vt.* to mark the boundaries of.
demarcazione *sf.* demarcation.
demente *agg.* insane. ◆ **demente** *sm.* madman (*pl.* -men).
demenza *sf.* insanity.
demeritare *vt.* to forfeit. ◆ **demeritare** *vi.* to deserve censure.
demèrito *sm.* demerit.
demiurgo *sm.* demiurge.
democràtico *agg.* democratic. ◆ **democràtico** *sm.* democrat.
democratizzare *vt.* to democratize.
democrazìa *sf.* democracy.
democristiano *sm.* christian-democrat.
demografìa *sf.* demography.
demogràfico *agg.* demographic(al).
demolire *vt.* to demolish.
demolitore *sm.* 1. demolisher 2. (*fig.*) iconoclast.
demolizione *sf.* 1. demolition 2. (*fig.*) destruction.
dèmone *sm.* 1. demon 2. (*diavolo*) devil.
demonìaco *agg.* demoniac(al).
demonio *sm.* 1. devil 2. (*fig.*) demon.
demonologìa *sf.* demonology.
demoralizzare *vt.* to demoralize.
◆ **demoralizzarsi** *vr.* to lose (*v. irr.*) heart.
demoralizzazione *sf.* demoralization.
denaro *sm.* 1. money 2. (*moneta antica*) denarius (*pl.* -rii).
denaturare *vt.* to denature.

dendrologìa *sf.* dendrology.
denegare *vt.* to deny.
denicotinizzare *vt.* to denicotinize.
denigrare *vt.* to denigrate.
denigratore *sm.* denigrator.
denigrazione *sf.* denigration.
denominare *vt.* to name.
denominativo *agg.* denominative.
denominatore *sm.* denominator.
denominazione *sf.* denomination.
denotare *vt.* to signify.
densità *sf.* density.
denso *agg.* thick.
dentale *agg.* dental.
dentario *agg.* dental, tooth (*attr.*).
dentato *agg.* toothed.
dentatura *sf.* 1. set of teeth 2. (*di ingranaggio*) toothing.
dente *sm.* tooth (*pl.* teeth).
dentellare *vt.* to indent.
dentellatura *sf.* indentation.
dentello *sm.* 1. (*mecc.*) tooth 2. (*arch.*) dentil 3. (*tacca*) notch.
dentiera *sf.* dental plate.
dentifricio *agg.* tooth (*attr.*) ◆ **dentifricio** *sm.* tooth-paste.
dentina *sf.* dentine.
dentista *sm.* dentist.
dentìstico *agg.* dental: *gabinetto* —, dentist's surgery.
dentizione *sf.* teething.
dentro *avv.* in, inside. ◆ **dentro** *prep.* 1. in, inside 2. (*di tempo*) (with)in.
denudare *vt.* 1. to strip 2. (*scoprire*) to lay (*v. irr.*) bare. ◆ **denudarsi** *vr.* to strip.
denudazione *sf.* denudation.
denuncia *sf.* 1. denunciation 2. (*dichiarazione*) statement: — *dei redditi*, statement of one's income.
denunciare *vt.* 1. to denounce 2. (*dichiarare*) to report 3. (*giur.*) — *qu.*, to inform against so.
denutrito *agg.* underfed.
denutrizione *sf.* underfeeding.
deodorante *agg.* deodorizing. ◆ **deodorante** *sm.* deodorant.
deodorare *vt.* to deodorize.
deontologìa *sf.* deontology.
depauperamento *sm.* impoverishment.
depauperare *vt.* to impoverish.
depennare *vt.* to cross out.
deperìbile *agg.* perishable.
deperimento *sm.* 1. (*di salute*) wasting away 2. (*per un dolore*) pining away 3. (*di cose*) deterioration.

deperire *vi.* 1. (*di salute*) to waste away 2. (*per un dolore*) to pine. away 3. (*di cose*) to deteriorate.

depilare *vt.* to remove hair (from).

depilatore *sm.* hair-remover.

depilatorio *agg.* hair-removing.

depilazione *sf.* hair-removal.

deploràbile *agg.* deplorable.

deplorare *vt.* 1. (*essere spiacenti*) to deplore 2. (*lagnarsi di*) to complain of.

deplorazione *sf.* 1. (*biasimo*) blame 2. (*rimpianto*) regret.

deplorévole *agg.* 1. deplorable 2. (*biasimevole*) blamable.

deporre *vt.* 1. to lay (*v. irr.*) 2. (*da una carica*) to remove from (an) office 3. (*depositare*) to deposit 4. (*giur.*) to witness. ♦ **deporre** *vi.* (*giur.*) to give (*v. irr.*) evidence.

deportare *vt.* to deport.

deportato *agg.* deported. ♦ **deportato** *sm.* convict.

deportazione *sf.* deportation.

depositante *sm.* depositor.

depositare *vt.* to deposit: — *merci*, to store goods.

depositario *sm.* trustee.

depòsito *sm.* 1. deposit 2. (*luogo in cui depositare*) warehouse 3. (*per bagagli*) left-luggage room.

deposizione *sf.* deposition.

depravare *vt.* to corrupt.

depravazione *sf.* corruption.

deprecàbile *agg.* deprecable.

deprecare *vt.* to deprecate.

deprecativo *agg.* deprecatory.

deprecazione *sf.* deprecation.

depredamento *sm.* plunder.

depredare *vt.* to plunder, to ravage.

depressione *sf.* depression.

depressivo *agg.* depressing.

depresso *agg.* depressed.

depressore *sm.* depressor.

deprezzamento *sm.* depreciation.

deprezzare *vt.* to depreciate.

deprimente *agg.* depressing.

deprìmere *vt.* to depress.

depurare *vt.* to depurate.

depurativo *agg.* depurative.

depuratore *sm.* 1. depurator 2. (*mecc.*) cleaner.

depurazione *sf.* purification, depuration.

deputare *vt.* to depute.

deputato *sm.* deputy.

deputazione *sf.* deputation.

deragliamento *sm.* derailment.

deragliare *vi.* to go (*v. irr.*) off the rails.

derattizzare *vt.* to clear by deratization.

derattizzazione *sf.* deratization.

derelitto *agg.* forlorn.

deretano *sm.* posterior.

deridere *vt.* to laugh at, to make (*v. irr.*) fun of.

derisìbile *agg.* laughable.

derisione *sf.* mockery.

derisorio *agg.* derisory.

deriva *sf.* drift.

derivare *vi.* 1. to derive 2. (*originarsi*) to rise (*v. irr.*). ♦ **derivare** *vt.* to derive.

derivativo *agg.* derivative.

derivato *agg.* derived. ♦ **derivato** *sm.* 1. derivative 2. (*sottoprodotto*) by-product.

derivazione *sf.* 1. derivation 2. (*elettr.*) shunt.

derma *sm.* derm.

dermatologìa *sf.* dermatology.

dermatològico *agg.* dermatological.

dermatòlogo *sm.* dermatologist.

dèroga *sf.* derogation.

derogare *vi.* to derogate.

derrata *sf.* 1. victual 2. (*alimentare*) food-stuff.

derubare *vt.* to rob (so. of).

desco *sm.* dinner table.

descrittivo *agg.* descriptive.

descrìvere *vt.* to describe.

descrivìbile *agg.* describable.

descrizione *sf.* description.

desèrtico *agg.* desert.

deserto *agg. e sm.* desert.

desideràbile *agg.* desirable.

desiderare *vt.* 1. to wish 2. (*desiderare di avere*) to wish for.

desiderio *sm.* wish.

desideroso *agg.* desirous, eager (for).

designare *vt.* to appoint.

designazione *sf.* designation.

desinare *vi.* to dine, to have dinner. ♦ **desinare** *sm.* dinner.

desinenza *sf.* ending.

desistere *vi.* to cease, to leave (*v. irr.*) off.

desolare *vt.* 1. to desolate 2. (*addolorare*) to distress.

desolato *agg.* (*spiacente*) sorry.

desolazione *sf.* 1. desolation 2. (*dolore*) grief, sorrow.

dèspota *sm.* despot.

destare *vt.* 1. to wake (*v. irr.*) 2.

(*suscitare*) to rouse. ♦ **destarsi** *vr.* to wake (*v. irr.*) up.
destinare *vt.* 1. to destine 2. (*devolvere*) to assign.
destinatario *sm.* addressee.
destinazione *sf.* destination.
destino *sm.* 1. destiny 2. (*sorte*) lot.
destituire *vt.* to dismiss.
destituzione *sf.* dismissal.
desto *agg.* awake.
destra *sf.* 1. right hand 2. (*parte destra*) right, right side: *alla tua* —, on your right; *tenere la* —, to keep (*v. irr.*) right.
destramente *avv.* skilfully.
destreggiarsi *vr.* to manage.
destrezza *sf.* dexterity.
destriero *sm.* steed.
destrina *sf.* dextrine.
destro *agg.* 1. right 2. (*abile*) clever. ♦ **destro** *sm.* opportunity.
desueto *agg.* unusual, obsolete.
desuetùdine *sf.* disuse.
desùmere *vt.* 1. to infer 2. (*trarre*) to draw (*v. irr.*).
detenere *vt.* 1. to hold (*v. irr.*) 2. (*tener prigioniero*) to keep (*v. irr.*) in prison.
detentore *sm.* holder.
detenuto *agg.* imprisoned. ♦ **detenuto** *sm.* prisoner.
detenzione *sf.* 1. possession 2. (*il detenere*) holding 3. (*galera*) detention.
detergente *agg. e sm.* detergent.
detèrgere *vt.* to cleanse.
deterioramento *sm.* deterioration.
deteriorare *vt.* 1. to deteriorate 2. (*danneggiare*) to damage.
deteriore *agg.* worse.
determinàbile *agg.* determinable.
determinante *agg.* determinant.
determinare *vt.* 1. to determine 2. (*causare*) to cause.
determinativo *agg.* determinative || *articolo* —, definite article.
determinato *agg.* 1. determinate 2. (*particolare*) special 3. (*deciso*) resolute.
determinazione *sf.* determination.
determinismo *sm.* determinism.
deterrente *sm.* deterrent.
detersivo *agg. e sm.* detersive.
detestàbile *agg.* detestable.
detestare *vt.* to loathe.
detettore *sm.* detector.
detonante *agg.* explosive.
detonare *vi.* to detonate.

detonatore *sm.* detonator.
detonazione *sf.* explosion.
detrarre *vt.* to deduct.
detrattore *sm.* detractor.
detrazione *sf.* 1. deduction 2. (*fig.*) detraction.
detrimento *sm.* detriment.
detrìtico *agg.* detrital.
detrito *sm.* rubble, debris.
detronizzare *vt.* to depose.
detronizzazione *sf.* dethronement.
detta (*nella loc. avv.*) *a* — *di qu.*, according to what so. says.
dettagliante *sm.* retailer.
dettagliare *vt.* to detail.
dettagliatamente *avv.* in detail.
dettaglio *sm.* 1. detail 2. (*comm.*) retail.
dettame *sm.* dictate.
dettare *vt.* 1. to dictate 2. (*suggerire*) to suggest || — *la legge*, to lay (*v. irr.*) down the law.
dettato *sm.* dictation.
detto *agg.* 1. called 2. (*sopraddetto*) said, above-mentioned. ♦ **detto** *sm.* saying.
deturpare *vt.* to disfigure.
deturpazione *sf.* disfigurement.
devalutazione *sf.* depreciation.
devastare *vt.* to ravage, to ruin.
devastatore *agg.* ravaging. ♦ **devastatore** *sm.* ravager.
devastazione *sf.* devastation.
deviare *vi.* to deviate || *non* —! (*non cambiare discorso*), stick to the point! ♦ **deviare** *vt.* to divert.
deviazione *sf.* 1. deviation 2. (*stradale*) detour || — *ferroviaria*, shunting.
deviazionismo *sm.* deviationism.
devoluzione *sf.* devolution.
devòlvere *vt.* 1. (*giur.*) to devolve, to assign 2. (*adoperare*) to employ.
devoto *agg.* 1. devout, affectionate 2. (*relig.*) pious, religious.
devozione *sf.* devotion, piety.
di *prep.* 1. of 2. (*partitivo*) some, any: *dammi del pane*, give me some bread; *hai dello zucchero?*, have you any sugar? 3. (*tempo*) in, during: — *mattina*, in the morning 4. (*argomento*) of, about 5. (*paragone coi comparativi*) than: *è più graziosa* — *sua sorella*, she is prettier than her sister 6. (*nei superl.*) of, in 7. (*modo*) with, in.
dì *sm.* day.
diabete *sm.* diabetes.
diabètico *agg. e sm.* diabetic.

diabòlico *agg.* diabolic(al).
diàcono *sm.* deacon.
diadema *sm.* diadem.
diàfano *agg.* diaphanous.
diaframma *sm.* diaphragm.
diàgnosi *sf.* diagnosis (*pl.* -ses).
diagnosticare *vt.* to diagnose.
diagnòstico *agg.* diagnostic.
diagonale *agg.* diagonal. ♦ **diagonale** *sf.* diagonal.
diagonalmente *avv.* diagonally.
diagramma *sm.* diagram.
dialettale *agg.* dialectal.
dialèttica *sf.* dialectics.
dialèttico *agg.* dialectic. ♦ **dialèttico** *sm.* dialectic.
dialetto *sm.* dialect.
diàlisi *sf.* dialysis (*pl.* -ses).
dialogare *vi.* to hold (*v. irr.*) a dialogue.
diàlogo *sm.* dialogue.
diamante *sm.* diamond.
diametralmente *avv.* diametrically.
diàmetro *sm.* diameter.
diàmine *inter.* good heavens!
dianzi *avv.* just, just now.
diapositiva *sf.* slide.
diarchìa *sf.* diarchy.
diario *sm.* diary.
diarrea *sf.* diarrhoea.
diaspro *sm.* jasper.
diatonìa *sf.* diatony.
diatriba *sf.* diatribe.
diavolerìa *sf.* 1. devilry 2. (*fam.*) trick.
diavoletto *sm.* imp.
diàvolo *sm.* devil.
dibàttere *vt.* to debate. ♦ **dibàttersi** *vr.* to struggle.
dibàttito *sm.* debate, discussion.
dibattuto *agg.* controversial.
diboscamento *sm.* deforestation.
diboscare *vt.* to deforest.
dicastero *sm.* office.
dicembre *sm.* December.
dicerìa *sf.* gossip, rumour.
dichiarare *vt.* to declare.
dichiarato *agg.* declared.
dichiarazione *sf.* declaration.
diciannove *agg.* nineteen.
diciannovenne *agg.* 1. nineteen years old (*pred.*) 2. nineteen-year-old (*attr.*).
diciannovèsimo *agg.* nineteenth.
diciassette *agg.* seventeen.
diciassettenne *agg.* 1. seventeen years old (*pred.*) 2. seventeen-year-old (*attr.*).

diciassettèsimo *agg.* seventeenth.
diciottenne *agg.* 1. eighteen years old (*pred.*) 2. eighteen-year-old (*attr.*).
diciottèsimo *agg.* eighteenth.
diciotto *agg.* eighteen.
dicitore *sm.* speaker.
dicitura *sf.* wording.
didascalìa *sf.* 1. explanation 2. (*cine*) subtitles (*pl.*).
didascàlico *agg.* didactic.
didàttica *sf.* didactics.
didàttico *agg.* didactic(al).
didentro *sm.* inside.
didietro *sm.* back.
dieci *agg.* ten.
diecina *sf.* ten, half a score.
diedro *sm.* dihedral.
dielèttrico *agg.* dielectric.
diesis *sm.* sharp.
dieta *sf.* diet.
dietètico *agg.* dietetic.
dietòlogo *sm.* dietician.
dietro *avv.* behind. ♦ **dietro** *prep.* behind, after. ♦ **dietro** *sm.* back, rear.
dietrofrònt *sm.* about turn!
difatti *avv.* as a matter of fact.
difèndere *vt.* to defend.
difendìbile *agg.* defensible.
difensiva *sf.* defensive.
difensivo *agg.* defensive.
difensore *agg.* defending. ♦ **difensore** *sm.* 1. defender 2. (*giur.*) defending counsel 3. (*di un'idea ecc.*) supporter.
difesa *sf.* defence.
difettare *vi.* to be wanting.
difettivo *agg.* defective.
difetto *sm.* defect.
difettoso *agg.* defective.
diffamare *vt.* to defame.
diffamatore *sm.* defamer.
diffamatorio *agg.* defamatory.
diffamazione *sf.* defamation.
differente *agg.* unlike, different.
differentemente *avv.* differently.
differenza *sf.* difference.
differenziale *agg.* e *sm.* differential.
differenziare *vt.* to differentiate.
differenziato *agg.* differentiated.
differenziazione *sf.* differentiation.
differìbile *agg.* that can be deferred.
differimento *sm.* deferment.
differire *vi.* (*essere diverso*) to differ (from). ♦ **differire** *vt.* to delay.

difficile *agg.* difficult.
difficilmente *avv.* with difficulty.
difficoltà *sf.* difficulty.
difficoltoso *agg.* difficult.
diffida *sf.* warning, intimation.
diffidare *vi.* to distrust. ♦ **diffidare** *vt.* to give (*v. irr.*) warning.
diffidente *agg.* suspicious.
diffidenza *sf.* 1. distrust 2. (*sospetto*) suspicion.
diffòndere *vt.* to diffuse, to spread (*v. irr.*). ♦ **diffòndersi** *vr.* to spread (*v. irr.*).
difforme *agg.* 1. different 2. shapeless.
difformità *sf.* difference, deformity.
diffrazione *sf.* diffraction.
diffusamente *avv.* diffusely.
diffusione *sf.* 1. diffusion, spreading 2. (*di giornale*) circulation.
diffuso *agg.* diffuse.
diffusore *sm.* diffusor.
difilato *avv.* straight.
diftèrico *agg.* diphtheric.
difterite *sf.* diphtheria.
diga *sf.* dam.
digerente *agg.* digestive.
digeribile *agg.* digestible.
digeribilità *sf.* digestibility.
digerire *vt.* to digest.
digestione *sf.* digestion.
digestivo *agg.* e *sm.* digestive.
digesto *sm.* digest.
digitale *agg.* digital || *impronte digitali*, finger-prints. ♦ **digitale** *sf.* digitalis, (*fam.*) foxglove.
digiunare *vi.* to fast.
digiunatore *sm.* faster.
digiuno¹ *agg.* 1. fasting 2. (*fig.*) lacking (in).
digiuno² *sm.* fast..
dignità *sf.* dignity.
dignitario *sm.* dignitary.
dignitosamente *avv.* with dignity.
dignitoso *agg.* dignified.
digradante *agg.* 1. sloping 2. (*pitt.*) shading.
digradare *vi.* 1. to slope down 2. (*pitt.*) to shade off.
digressione *sf.* digression.
digressivo *agg.* digressive.
digrignare *vt.* to gnash.
digrossamento *sm.* 1. reducing 2. (*sbozzo*) rough-hewing.
digrossare *vt.* 1. to reduce 2. (*sbozzare*) to rough-hew.
dilacerare *vt.* to tear (*v. irr.*).
dilagare *vi.* to spread (*v. irr.*).
dilaniare *vt.* to tear (*v. irr.*) to pieces.

dilapidare *vt.* to squander.
dilapidatore *sm.* squanderer.
dilapidazione *sf.* squandering.
dilatàbile *agg.* dilatable.
dilatabilità *sf.* dilatability.
dilatare *vt.*, **dilatarsi** *vr.* 1. to dilate 2. (*fis.*) to expand.
dilatazione *sf.* dilatation.
dilatorio *agg.* dilatory.
dilavamento *sm.* washing away.
dilavare *vt.* to wash away.
dilazionare *vt.* to defer.
dilazione *sf.* delay, respite.
dileggiare *vt.* to mock.
dileggio *sm.* mockery.
dileguare *vt.* to disperse. ♦ **dileguarsi** *vr.* to disappear.
dilemma *sm.* dilemma.
dilettante *sm.* amateur.
dilettantismo *sm.* amateurism.
dilettare *vt.* to delight. ♦ **dilettarsi** *vr.* to take (*v. irr.*) delight (in).
dilettévole *agg.* delightful.
diletto *agg.* beloved. ♦ **diletto** *sm.* delight.
diligente *agg.* diligent.
diligenza *sf.* 1. diligence 2. (*carrozza*) stage-coach.
dilucidare *vt.* V. delucidare.
dilucidazione *sf.* V. delucidazione.
diluente *sm.* diluent.
diluire *vt.* 1. to dilute 2. (*fig.*) to water down.
diluizione *sf.* dilution.
dilungarsi *vr.* to speak (*v. irr.*) diffusely.
diluviale *agg.* 1. torrential 2. (*geol.*) diluvial.
diluviano *agg.* diluvial.
diluviare *vi.* 1. to pour 2. (*fig.*) to shower.
diluvio *sm.* deluge, flood.
dimagramento *sm.* thinning.
dimagrante *agg.* slimming.
dimagrare *vi.* to thin.
dimagrire *vi.* V. dimagrare.
dimenare *vt.* 1. (*la coda*) to wag 2. to wave. ♦ **dimenarsi** *vr.* to move about restlessly.
dimensione *sf.* dimension, size.
dimenticanza *sf.* 1. (*svista*) oversight 2. (*oblio*) oblivion.
dimenticare *vt.*, **dimenticarsi** *vr.* to forget (*v. irr.*).
diméntico *agg.* forgetful.
dimesso *agg.* 1. modest 2. (*trasandato*) shabby.

dimestichezza *sf.* familiarity.
dìmetro *sm.* dimeter.
diméttere *vt.* to dismiss ‖ — *dall'ospedale*, to discharge. ♦ **diméttersi** *vr.* to resign.
dimezzamento *sm.* halving.
dimezzare *vt.* to halve.
diminuendo *sm.* 1. (*mat.*) minuend 2. (*mus.*) diminuendo.
diminuìbile *agg.* diminishable.
diminuire *vt.* e *vi.* to lessen, to diminish.
diminutivo *agg.* e *sm.* diminutive.
diminuzione *sf.* lessening, reduction.
dimissionare *vt.* to oblige (so.) to resign.
dimissionario *agg.* resigning.
dimissione *sf.* resignation ‖ *dare le dimissioni*, to resign.
dimissoria *sf.* dimissory letter.
dimodoché *cong.* so that.
dimora *sf.* residence, lodgings (*pl.*).
dimorare *vi.* to stay, to live.
dimorfismo *sm.* dimorphism.
dimorfo *agg.* dimorphic.
dimostràbile *agg.* demonstrable.
dimostrabilità *sf.* demonstrability.
dimostrante *sm.* demonstrant.
dimostrare *vt.* 1. to show (*v. irr.*) 2. (*provare*) to demonstrate. ♦ **dimostrarsi** *vr.* to show oneself.
dimostrativo *agg.* e *sm.* demonstrative.
dimostratore *sm.* demonstrator.
dimostrazione *sf.* demonstration.
dina *sf.* dyne.
dinàmica *sf.* dynamics.
dinamicamente *avv.* dynamically.
dinamicità *sf.* dynamism, energy.
dinàmico *agg.* 1. dynamic 2. (*fig.*) energetic.
dinamismo *sm.* 1. dynamism 2. (*fig.*) energy.
dinamitardo *sm.* dynamiter.
dinamite *sf.* dynamite.
dìnamo *sf.* dynamo.
dinamòmetro *sm.* dynamometer.
dinanzi *prep.* before, in front of. ♦ **dinanzi** *avv.* before, in front, forward.
dìnaro *sm.* dinar.
dinasta *sm.* dynast.
dinastìa *sf.* dynasty.
dinàstico *agg.* dynastic(al).
dindo *sm.* turkey.
diniego *sm.* denial.
dinoccolato *agg.* slouching.
dinosàuro *sm.* dinosaur.

dintorni *sm. pl.* surroundings.
dintorno *avv.* e *prep.* 1. round, round about 2. (*circa*) about.
dio *sm.* god: *Marte, il* — *della guerra*, Mars, the god of war. ♦ **Dio** *sm.* God: — *ci-assista!*, — *non voglia!*, God help us, God forbid.
diocesano *agg.* diocesan.
diòcesi *sf.* diocese.
diodo *sm.* diode.
dionea *sf.* dionaea.
dionisìaco *agg.* Dionysiac.
diorama *sm.* diorama.
diorite *sf.* diorite.
diottrìa *sf.* diopter.
diòttrica *sf.* dioptrics.
diòttrico *agg.* dioptric.
dipanamento *sm.* winding into a ball.
dipanare *vt.* 1. to wind (*v. irr.*) into a ball 2. (*fig.*) to disentangle.
dipanatoio *sm.* skein-winder.
dipartimentale *agg.* departmental.
dipartimento *sm.* department.
dipartire *vi.* to depart. ♦ **dipartirsi** *vr.* 1. to go (*v. irr.*) away 2. (*morire*) to pass away.
dipartita *sf.* 1. departure 2. (*morte*) death.
dipendente *agg.* dependent (on). ♦ **dipendente** *sm.* employee.
dipendenza *sf.* dependence (on).
dipèndere *vi.* 1. (*derivare*) to be due 2. (*essere subordinato, vivere a carico*) to depend (on).
dipìngere *vt.* to paint.
dipinto *agg.* painted. ♦ **dipinto** *sm.* painting.
diplegìa *sf.* diplegia.
diplococco *sm.* diplococcus (*pl.* -ci).
diploma *sm.* diploma.
diplomare *vt.* to confer a diploma (upon so.). ♦ **diplomarsi** *vr.* to get (*v. irr.*) a diploma.
diplomàtica *sf.* diplomatics.
diplomaticamente *avv.* diplomatically.
diplomàtico *agg.* diplomatic. ♦ **diplomàtico** *sm.* diplomat.
diplomato *agg.* holding a diploma. ♦ **diplomato** *sm.* graduate.
diplomazìa *sf.* diplomacy.
diplopìa *sf.* diplopia.
dipnoi *sm. pl.* Dipnoi.
dipodìa *sf.* dipody.
dipoi *avv.* then.
diporto *sm.* recreation, diversion ‖

viaggiare per —, to travel on pleasure.

dipresso (*nella loc. avv.*) *a un* —, approximately.

dìptero *agg.* dipteral.

diradamento *sm.* 1. thinning 2. (*di nebbia, gas*) rarefaction.

diradare *vt.* 1. to thin out 2. (*rendere meno frequente*) to do (*v. irr.*) less frequent. ♦ **diradarsi** *vr.* 1. to clear away 2. (*divenire meno frequente*) to become (*v. irr.*) less frequent.

diramare *vt.* to issue, to spread (*v. irr.*).

diramazione *sf.* 1. branching 2. (*diffusione*) diffusion 3. (*per radio*) broadcasting.

dire *vt.* 1. (*nel senso di enunciare e quando introduce il discorso diretto*) to say (*v. irr.*): *dice che ha sonno,* he says he is sleepy; «*venite*», *ci disse,* «come», he said to us 2. (*nel senso di raccontare e quando è enunciata la persona cui si parla*) to tell (*v. irr.*): *gli dissi di venire,* I told him to come ‖ *si dice,* they say; *mi si dice,* I am told; *inutile — che,* it goes without saying that; *vale a* —, that is to say; *sentir* —, to hear (*v. irr.*); *voler* —, to mean (*v. irr.*).

dire *sm.* words (*pl.*), speech.

direttamente *avv.* directly.

direttìssima *sf. per* —, summarily.

direttìssimo *sm.* (*ferr.*) fast train.

direttiva *sf.* directions (*pl.*).

direttivo *agg.* 1. leading 2. (*comm.*) managing.

diretto *agg.* direct, straight.

direttore *sm.* 1. (*comm.; amm.*) manager 2. (*di scuola*) headmaster.

direttoriale *agg.* directorial.

direttorio *sm.* executive board.

direttrice *sf.* 1. (*comm.; amm.*) manageress 2. (*di scuola*) headmistress.

direzionale *agg.* directional ‖ *centro* —, office district.

direzione *sf.* 1. direction, course 2. (*di società*) management 3. (*di giornale*) editorship 4. (*di scuola*) headmastership 5. (*sede*) administrative office.

dirigente *agg.* directing, leading. ♦ **dirigente** *sm.* director, manager, leader.

dirìgere *vt.* 1. (*indirizzare*) to direct

2. (*guidare*) to lead (*v. irr.*) 3. (*sovraintendere*) to supervise. ♦ **dirìgersi** *vr.* to turn one's steps towards.

dirigìbile *sm.* airship.

dirigismo *sm.* state planning.

dirigista *sm.* supporter of state planning.

dirimente *agg.* diriment.

dirìmere *vt.* to settle.

dirimpettaio *sm.* person living just opposite.

dirimpetto *avv.* face to face, opposite.

diritta *sf.* right, right-hand: *a* —, on the right.

dirittamente *avv.* straight.

diritto *agg.* straight, upright ‖ *rigare* —, to behave properly. ♦ **diritto** *sm.* 1. right 2. (*tassa, tributo*) due 3. (*legge*) law.

dirittura *sf.* 1. straight line 2. (*rettitudine*) uprightness 3. (*sport*) — *d'arrivo,* home stretch.

dirizzare *vt.* 1. to direct 2. (*erigere*) to raise 3. (*raddrizzare; fig.*) to put (*v. irr.*) right, to straighten.

dirizzone *sm.* inconsiderate action.

diroccamento *sm.* demolition.

diroccare *vt.* to demolish.

diroccato *agg.* 1. (*demolito*) dismantled 2. (*in rovina*) crumbled.

dirompente *agg.* disruptive.

dirómpere *vt.* 1. (*di lino, canapa ecc.*) to scutch 2. (*rompere*) to break (*v. irr.*).

dirottare *vt.* to divert. ♦ **dirottare** *vi.* to change course.

dirotto *agg.* excessive: *pianto* —, desperate crying; *piove a* —, it is pouring.

dirozzamento *sm.* 1. (*lo sbozzare*) rough-hewing 2. (*fig.*) refinement.

dirozzare *vt.* 1. (*sbozzare*) to rough-hew 2. (*fig.*) to refine.

dirugginire *vt.* to remove the rust from.

dirupamento *sm.* 1. falling down 2. (*di luogo*) abruptness.

dirupato *agg.* 1. abrupt 2. (*roccioso*) rocky.

dirupo *sm.* precipice.

disabbellire *vt.* to spoil the beauty of. ♦ **disabbellirsi** *vr.* to lose (*v. irr.*) one's beauty.

disabitato *agg.* 1. uninhabited 2. (*abbandonato*) deserted.

disabituare *vt.* to disaccustom. ♦ **disabituarsi** *vr.* to give (*v. irr.*)

up the habit of.

disaccordo *sm.* disagreement.

disacerbare *vt.* to appease.

disadatto *agg.* **1.** unfit **2.** (*che non si addice*) unbecoming.

disadornare *vt.* to disadorn.

disadorno *agg.* **1.** unadorned **2.** (*spoglio*) bare.

disaffezionarsi *vr.* to lose (*v. irr.*) one's affection (for).

disaffezionato *agg.* estranged.

disaffezione *sf.* estrangement.

disagévole *agg.* uncomfortable.

disagiatamente *avv.* uncomfortably.

disagiato *agg.* **1.** uncomfortable **2.** (*povero*) needy.

disagio *sm.* **1.** uneasiness || *essere a —*, to be uneasy **2.** (*disturbo*) inconvenience **3.** (*pl.; privazioni*) privations.

disamare *vt.* to cease to love.

disàmina *sf.* examination.

disaminare *vt.* to examine carefully.

disancorarsi *vr.* **1.** to weigh anchor **2.** (*fig.*) to break (*v. irr.*) all connections (with).

disanimarsi *vr.* to lose (*v. irr.*) heart.

disappetenza *sf.* lack of appetite.

disapprèndere *vt.* to forget (*v. irr.*).

disapprovare *vt.* to disapprove (of).

disapprovazione *sf.* disapproval.

disappunto *sm.* disappointment.

disarcionare *vt.* to unsaddle.

disarmare *vt.* to disarm.

disarmato *agg.* disarmed.

disarmo *sm.* disarmament.

disarmonìa *sf.* discord.

disarmonicamente *avv.* discordantly.

disarmònico *agg.* discordant.

disarmonizzare *vt.* to disharmonize.

disarticolare *vt.* to disjoint.

disarticolazione *sf.* disjointing.

disastro *sm.* disaster.

disastroso *agg.* disastrous.

disattento *agg.* inattentive.

disattenzione *sf.* inattention: *errore di —*, a slip of the pen.

disavanzo *sm.* deficit.

disavveduto *agg.* heedless.

disavventura *sf.* **1.** mishap **2.** (*sfortuna*) misfortune.

disavvertenza *sf.* inadvertence.

disavvezzo *agg.* unaccustomed.

disazotare *vt.* to remove nitrogen from.

disborso *sm.* disbursement.

disbrigo *sm.* dispatch.

disbrogliare *vt.* to disentangle.

discacciare *vt.* to turn out.

discapitare *vi.* to suffer damage.

discàpito *sm.* disadvantage.

discàrico *sm.* **1.** discharge **2.** (*scusa*) defence.

discendente *agg.* descending. ◆
discendente *sm.* descendant.

discendenza *sf.* **1.** descent **2.** (*discendenti*) offspring.

discéndere *vt.* **1.** to descend, to go (*v. irr.*) down **2.** (*di astri*) to sink (*v. irr.*) **3.** (*di prezzi*) to fall (*v. irr.*).

discépolo *sm.* disciple.

discèrnere *vt.* **1.** to discern **2.** (*distinguere*) to distinguish.

discernìbile *agg.* discernible.

discernimento *sm.* discernment.

discesa *sf.* **1.** descent **2.** (*declivio*) slope **3.** (*caduta*) fall **4.** (*invasione*) invasion.

dischiùdere *vt.* to disclose.

dischiuso *agg.* disclosed.

discinto *agg.* ungirt.

disciplina *sf.* **1.** (*materia di studio*) doctrine **2.** (*regola*) discipline.

disciplinàbile *agg.* disciplinable.

disciplinare[1] *vt.* to discipline.

disciplinare[2] *agg.* disciplinary.

disciplinarmente *avv.* with discipline.

disciplinatamente *avv.* with discipline.

disciplinato *agg.* disciplined.

disco *sm.* **1.** disk **2.** (*mus.*) record **3.** (*sport*) discus **4.** (*ferr.*) disk signal.

discòbolo *sm.* discus-thrower.

discòide *agg.* discoid.

dìscolo *sm.* wild boy, little scamp.

discolpa *sf.* excuse.

discolpare *vt.* to clear.

disconoscente *aff.* ungrateful.

disconoscenza *sf.* ungratitude.

disconòscere *vt.* to refuse to recognize.

disconoscimento *sm.* **1.** refusal to recognize **2.** (*ingratitudine*) ingratitude.

discontinuità *sf.* discontinuity.

discontinuo *agg.* discontinuous.

discordante *agg.* **1.** discordant **2.** (*diverso*) different **3.** (*di colori*)

clashing.
discordanza *sf.* discordance.
discordare *vi.* 1. to disagree 2. (*di colori*) to clash 3. (*di suoni*) to jar.
discorde *agg.* discordant (with).
discordemente *avv.* discordantly.
discordia *sf.* discord.
discòrrere *vi.* to talk.
discorsivo *agg.* talkative.
discorso *sm.* speech.
discostare *vt.* to shift.
discosto *agg.* far, distant. ♦ **discosto** *avv.* at some distance.
discoteca *sf.* record library.
discreditare *vt.* to discredit.
discrédito *sm.* discredit.
discrepante *agg.* differing.
discrepanza *sf.* discrepancy.
discretamente *avv.* 1. (*con discrezione*) discreetly 2. (*sufficientemente*) fairly 3. (*piuttosto*) rather.
discreto *agg.* 1. (*che ha discrezione*) discreet 2. (*moderato*) moderate 3. (*abbastanza buono*) fairly good.
discrezionale *agg.* discretionary.
discrezione *sf.* discretion.
discriminante *agg.* discriminating.
discriminare *vt.* to discriminate.
discriminazione *sf.* discrimination.
discussione *sf.* discussion.
discusso *agg.* discussed.
discùtere *vt.* to discuss.
discutìbile *agg.* questionable.
disdegnare *vt.* to disdain.
disdegno *sm.* disdain.
disdegnosamente *avv.* disdainfully.
disdegnoso *agg.* disdainful.
disdetta *sf.* 1. (*giur.*) notice of leave 2. (*sfortuna*) bad luck.
disdettare *vt.* to give (*v. irr.*) notice.
disdicévole *agg.* unbecoming.
disdire *vt.* 1. (*ritrattare*) to take (*v. irr.*) back, to retract 2. (*annullare*) to cancel.
disegnare *vt.* 1. to draw (*v. irr.*) 2. (*progettare*) to plan.
disegnatore *sm.* designer.
disegno *sm.* 1. drawing 2. (*di tessuto*) pattern 3. (*di edificio*) plan 4. (*schizzo*) sketch 5. (*fig.*) design, plan.
diseredare *vt.* to disinherit.
diseredato *agg.* 1. poor, destitute 2. (*privato di eredità*) disinherited.

disertare *vt.* 1. to desert 2. (*abbandonare*) to leave (*v. irr.*).
disertore *sm.* deserter.
diserzione *sf.* desertion.
disfacimento *sm.* 1. (*il disfare*) undoing 2. (*decadimento*) decay.
disfare *vt.* 1. to undo (*v. irr.*) 2. (*slegare*) to untie.
disfasia *sf.* dysphasia.
disfatta *sf.* defeat.
disfattismo *sm.* defeatism.
disfattista *agg. e s.* defeatist.
disfatto *agg.* 1. (*distrutto*) ruined 2. (*slegato*) undone 3. (*molto stanco*) worn out.
disfavore *sm.* disfavour.
disfida *sf.* challenge.
disfunzione *sf.* disorder.
disgelare *vt. e vi.* to thaw.
disgelo *sm.* thaw.
disgiùngere *vt.* to disjoin.
disgiungimento *sm.* disjoining.
disgiuntamente *avv.* separately.
disgiuntivamente *avv.* disjunctively.
disgiuntivo *agg.* disjunctive.
disgiunto *agg.* disjoined.
disgiunzione *sf.* disjunction.
disgrazia *sf.* 1. misfortune 2. (*sfavore*) disfavour || *cadere in* —, to lose (*v. irr.*) so.'s favour 3. (*fatto involontario*) accident.
disgraziatamente *avv.* unfortunately.
disgraziato *agg.* 1. unlucky, wretched 2. (*deforme*) misshapen.
disgregamento *sm.* disintegration.
disgregare *vt.* to disgregate, to break (*v. irr.*) up.
disgregazione *sf.* disgregation.
disguido *sm.* miscarriage.
disgustare *vt.* to disgust, to sicken. ♦ **disgustarsi** *vr.* to become (*v. irr.*) disgusted (with).
disgusto *sm.*, 1. disgust 2. (*avversione*) dislike.
disgustoso *agg.* disgusting.
disidratare *vt.* to dehydrate.
disidratazione *sf.* dehydration.
disillùdere *vt.* to undeceive.
disillusione *sf.* disillusion.
disilluso *agg.* undeceived, disappointed.
disimballaggio *sm.* unpacking.
disimballare *vt.* to unpack.
disimpacciare *vt.* to disembarrass.
disimparare *vt.* to forget (*v. irr.*).
disimpegnare *vt.* 1. to redeem 2. (*liberare da un impegno*) to re-

lease. ♦ **disimpegnarsi** *vr.* **1.** to disengage oneself **2.** (*cavarsela*) to manage.

disimpegno *sm.* **1.** redemption **2.** (*il liberarsi da un impegno*) disengagement.

disincagliare *vt.* to get (*v. irr.*) afloat.

disincantare *vt.* to disenchant.

disincantato *agg.* disenchanted.

disincanto *sm.* disenchantment.

disinfestare *vt.* to disinfest.

disinfettante *sm.* disinfectant.

disinfettare *vt.* to disinfect.

disinfezione *sf.* disinfection.

disingannare *vt.* to undeceive.

disinganno *sm.* **1.** undeceiving **2.** (*delusione*) disappointment.

disinnescare *vt.* to defuse.

disinnestare *vt.* to disengage.

disinnesto *sm.* disengagement, release.

disinserire *vt.* to disconnect.

disintegrare *vt.* to disintegrate.

disintegratore *sm.* disintegrator.

disintegrazione *sf.* disintegration.

disinteressare *vt.* **1.** to disinterest **2.** (*comm.*) to buy (*v. irr.*) out. ♦ **disinteressarsi** *vr.* to take (*v. irr.*) no interest (in).

disinteressato *agg.* **1.** disinterested **2.** (*altruistico*) unselfish.

disinteresse *sm.* **1.** indifference **2.** (*altruismo*) unselfishness.

disintossicare *vt.* to unpoison.

disintossicazione *sf.* unpoisoning.

disinvolto *agg.* unconstrained, free-and-easy.

disinvoltura *sf.* unconstraint, free-and-easy way.

disistima *sf.* disesteem.

disistimare *vt.* to disesteem.

dislivello *sm.* **1.** difference of level **2.** (*di acque*) rise **3.** (*di strade*) gradient **4.** (*ineguaglianza*) inequality.

dislocamento *sm.* **1.** displacement **2.** (*mil.*) dislocation.

dislocare *vt.* **1.** to displace **2.** (*mil.*) to dislocate.

dislocazione *sf.* removal, dislocation.

dismisura *sf.* excess ‖ *a —*, excessively.

disobbedire *vi.* V. *disubbidire*.

disobbligare *vt.* to release from duty. ♦ **disobbligarsi** *vr.* to free oneself from duty.

disoccupato *agg.* unemployed. ♦

disoccupato *sm.* unemployed person.

disoccupazione *sf.* unemployment.

disonestà *sf.* **1.** dishonesty **2.** (*atto disonesto*) fraud.

disonesto *agg.* dishonest, fraudulent.

disonorante *agg.* shameful.

disonorare *vt.* to dishonour.

disonore *sm.* dishonour, shame.

disonorévole *agg.* dishonourable.

disopra *avv.* **1.** above, over **2.** (*in cima*) on top **3.** (*ai piani superiori*) upstairs. ♦ **disopra** *sm.* top, upper part. ♦ **al disopra di**, **disopra a** *prep.* above.

disordinare *vt.* to disorder.

disordinatamente *avv.* untidily.

disordinato *agg.* untidy, disorderly.

disòrdine *sm.* **1.** disorder, untidiness **2.** (*sregolatezza*) disorderliness **3.** (*tumulto*) disorder, tumult.

disorgànico *agg.* inorganic.

disorganizzare *vt.* to disorganize.

disorganizzato *agg.* disorganized.

disorganizzazione *sf.* disorganization.

disorientamento *sm.* disorientation, confusion.

disorientare *vt.* **1.** to disorientate **2.** (*sconcertare*) to bewilder.

disorientato *agg.* bewildered, puzzled.

disormeggiare *vt.* to unmoor.

disossare *vt.* to bone.

disossidante *sm.* deoxidizer.

disossidare *vt.* to deoxidize.

disossidazione *sf.* deoxidation.

disotto *avv.* **1.** below, underneath **2.** (*al piano inferiore*) downstairs. ♦ **disotto** *sm.* underside, lower part. ♦ **al disotto di**, **disotto a** *prep.* under, beneath, below.

dispaccio *sm.* dispatch.

disparato *agg.* disparate.

disparere *sm.* difference of opinion.

dìspari *agg.* odd.

disparità *sf.* disparity.

disparte *avv.* aside, apart: *starsene in —*, to stand (*v. irr.*) aside; (*fig.*) to stand aloof; *mettere in —*, to put (*v. irr.*) aside; (*per uno scopo*) to put by.

dispendio *sm.* **1.** heavy expense **2.** (*di forza, tempo*) waste.

dispendioso *agg.* expensive.

dispensa *sf.* **1.** pantry **2.** (*mobile*) sideboard **3.** (*pubblicazione perio-*

dica) number **4.** (*esenzione; eccl.*) dispensation.

dispensare *vt.* **1.** (*distribuire*) to deal (*v. irr.*) out **2.** (*esentare*) to exempt, to dispense.

dispensario *sm.* dispensary.

dispensato *agg.* exempted.

dispensatore *sm.* distributor, dispenser.

dispepsìa *sf.* dyspepsia.

dispèptico *agg.* dyspeptic.

disperare *vi.* to despair, to lose (*v. irr.*) all hope. ♦ **disperarsi** *vr.* to give (*v. irr.*) oneself up to despair.

disperatamente *avv.* desperately.

disperato *agg.* **1.** despairing **2.** (*senza speranza*) hopeless || *essere — (di malato),* to be far gone. ♦ **disperato** *sm.* **1.** (*miserabile*) destitute **2.** (*forsennato*) madman (*pl.* -men).

disperazione *sf.* despair.

dispèrdere *vt.* to disperse **2.** (*consumare*) to waste.

dispersione *sf.* **1.** dispersion **2.** (*elettr.*) leak.

dispersivo *agg.* dispersive.

disperso *agg.* missing, lost.

dispetto *sm.* **1.** spite: *a — di,* in spite of **2.** (*stizza*) vexation.

dispettoso *agg.* spiteful.

dispiacere [1] *vi.* **1.** to dislike || *mi dispiace,* I am sorry; (*in espressioni di cortesia*) *se non vi dispiace,* if you please **2.** (*essere sgradevole*) to be disagreeable.

dispiacere [2] *sm.* **1.** regret **2.** (*disapprovazione*) displeasure **3.** (*fastidio*) trouble.

dispiegare *vt.* **1.** (*allargare*) to spread (*v. irr.*) out **2.** (*le vele*) to unfurl.

displuvio *sm.* **1.** watershed || *linea di —,* ridge **2.** (*arch.*) hip.

disponìbile *agg.* available.

disponibilità *sf.* availability.

disporre *vt.* **1.** to arrange **2.** (*preparare*) to dispose **3.** (*deliberare*) to order.

dispositivo *sm.* (*mecc.*) device.

disposizione *sf.* **1.** disposition, arrangement **2.** (*ordine*) order, direction || *a —,* at one's disposal **3.** (*inclinazione*) bent.

disposto *agg.* **1.** ready, willing **2.** (*ben disposto fisicamente*) strong.

dispòtico *agg.* despotic.

dispotismo *sm.* despotism.

dispregiativamente *avv.* disparagingly.

dispregiativo *agg.* depreciative. ♦ **dispregiativo** *sm.* (*gramm.*) pejorative.

dispregiatore *sm.* contemner.

dispregio *sm.* contempt.

disprezzàbile *agg.* despicable.

disprezzare *vt.* **1.** to despise **2.** (*considerare di poco conto*) to look down on.

disprezzo *sm.* contempt.

dìsputa *sf.* discussion.

disputàbile *agg.* disputable.

disputare *vi.* e *vt.* to discuss.

disquisizione *sf.* disquisition.

dissaldare *vt.* to unsolder.

dissanguamento *sm.* **1.** bleeding **2.** (*fig.*) impoverishment.

dissanguare *vt.* **1.** to bleed **2.** (*fig.*) to impoverish. ♦ **dissanguarsi** *vr.* (*fig.*) to become (*v. irr.*) impoverished.

dissanguato *agg.* **1.** bloodless **2.** (*fig.*) impoverished.

dissanguatore *sm.* (*fig.*) bloodsucker.

dissapore *sm.* disagreement.

dissecare *vt.* to dissect.

disseccamento *sm.* drying up.

disseccante *agg.* drying up. ♦ **disseccante** *sm.* desiccative.

disseccare *vt.* **1.** to dry up **2.** (*cibo*) to desiccate.

disselciare *vt.* to unpave.

disseminare *vt.* to disseminate.

disseminato *agg.* strewn.

disseminatore *agg.* disseminating. ♦ **disseminatore** *sm.* disseminator.

disseminazione *sf.* dissemination.

dissennatamente *avv.* madly.

dissennatezza *sf.* **1.** madness **2.** (*avventatezza*) rashness.

dissennato *agg.* **1.** mad **2.** (*avventato*) rash.

dissensione *sf.* dissension.

dissenso *sm.* dissent.

dissenterìa *sf.* dysentery.

dissentèrico *agg.* dysenteric.

dissentire *vi.* to dissent.

dissenziente *agg.* dissenting. ♦ **dissenziente** *sm.* dissenter.

disseppellimento *sm.* disinterment.

disseppellire *vt.* **1.** to disinter **2.** (*fig.*) to revive.

disserrare *vt.* to unfasten.

dissertare *vi.* to dissertate (on).

dissertatore *sm.* dissertator.

dissertazione *sf.* dissertation.
dissestare *vt.* 1. (*finanziariamente*) to ruin 2. (*mettere fuori posto*) to derange.
dissestato *agg.* (*di persona*) ruined.
dissesto *sm.* 1. trouble 2. (*fallimento*) bankruptcy.
dissetante *agg.* refreshing: *bibita* —, refreshing drink.
dissetare *vt.* to quench the thirst of. ♦ dissetarsi *vr.* 1. to quench one's thirst 2. (*bere*) to drink (*v. irr.*); (*di animali*) to water.
dissezione *sf.* dissection.
dissidente *agg. e sm.* dissident.
dissidenza *sf.* dissidence.
dissidio *sm.* 1. dissension, disagreement 2. (*litigio*) quarrel.
dissigillare *vt.* to unseal.
dissìmile *agg.* unlike.
dissimmetrìa *sf.* dissymetry.
dissimulare *vt.* to dissemble.
dissimulatamente *avv.* dissemblingly.
dissimulatore *sm.* dissimulator.
dissimulazione *sf.* dissimulation.
dissipare *vt.* to dissipate. ♦ dissiparsi *vr.* to dissipate, to vanish.
dissipatezza *sf.* dissipation.
dissipatore *sm.* waster.
dissipazione *sf.* dissipation.
dissociàbile *agg.* dissociable.
dissociare *vt.* to dissociate.
dissociazione *sf.* dissociation.
dissodamento *sm.* tillage.
dissodare *vt.* to till.
dissolùbile *agg.* dissoluble.
dissolubilità *sf.* dissolubility.
dissolutezza *sf.* dissoluteness.
dissoluto *agg.* dissolute.
dissoluzione *sf.* dissolution.
dissolvente *agg. e sm.* dissolvent.
dissòlvere *vt.* 1. to dissolve 2. (*disperdere*) to dispel. ♦ dissòlversi *vr.* to dissolve.
dissolvimento *sm.* dissolution.
dissomigliante *agg.* dissimilar (to).
dissomiglianza *sf.* dissimilarity.
dissomigliare *vi.* to be unlike. ♦ dissomigliarsi *vr.* to differ from.
dissonante *agg.* dissonant.
dissonanza *sf.* 1. dissonance 2. (*fig.*) discordance.
dissonare *vi.* 1. to be out of tune 2. (*fig.*) to discord (with).
dissotterramento *sm.* disinterment.
dissotterrare *vt.* to disinter.

dissuadere *vt.* to dissuade.
dissuasione *sf.* dissuasion.
distaccamento *sm.* 1. detaching 2. (*mil.*) detachment.
distaccare *vt.* to detach. ♦ distaccarsi *vr.* to come (*v. irr.*) off.
distacco *sm.* 1. detaching 2. (*partenza*) leaving 3. (*indifferenza*) unconcern.
distante *agg.* distant. ♦ distante *avv.* far, far off, far away.
distanza *sf.* distance.
distanziare *vt.* 1. to space 2. (*lasciare indietro*) to distance.
distanziato *agg.* 1. spaced 2. (*sport*) outdistanced.
distare *vi.* to be far: *quanto dista?*, how far is it?
distèndere *vt.* 1. (*allungare*) to stretch 2. (*spalmare*) to spread (*v. irr.*) 3. (*porre, stendere*) to spread (*v. irr.*). ♦ distèndersi *vr.* 1. to spread (*v. irr.*) 2. (*sdraiarsi*) to lie (*v. irr.*) down 3. (*rilassarsi*) to relax.
distensione *sf.* 1. (*di nervi, tensione*) relaxation 2. (*pol.*) distension.
distensivo *agg.* relaxing.
distesa *sf.* expanse || *a* —, continuously.
distesamente *avv.* diffusely.
disteso *agg.* 1. (*teso*) extended 2. (*giacente*) lying 3. (*esteso*) extensive || *per* —, diffusely.
dìstico *sm.* couplet.
distillare *vt.* to distil.
distillato *agg.* distilled. ♦ distillato *sm.* distillate.
distillatoio *sm.* still.
distillatore *sm.* distiller.
distillazione *sf.* distillation.
distillerìa *sf.* distillery.
distìnguere *vt.* 1. to distinguish 2. (*contrassegnare*) to mark.
distinta *sf.* list.
distintivo *agg.* distinctive. ♦ distintivo *sm.* badge.
distinto *agg.* 1. distinct 2. (*garbato*) distinguished.
distinzione *sf.* 1. distinction 2. (*riguardo*) regard 3. (*raffinatezza*) refinement.
distogliere *vt.* 1. (*dissuadere*) to dissuade 2. (*distrarre*) to divert. ♦ distògliersi *vr.* to be distracted.
distorsione *sf.* distortion.
distrarre *vt.* 1. (*distogliere*) to divert 2. (*divertire*) to entertain.

distrattamente *avv.* **1.** absent-mindedly **2.** (*inavvertitamente*) inadvertently.

distratto *agg.* **1.** absent-minded **2.** (*disattento*) inattentive.

distrazione *sf.* **1.** absent-mindedness **2.** (*disattenzione*) inattention **3.** (*divertimento*) recreation.

distretta *sf.* urgent need.

distretto *sm.* district || — *militare*, recruiting centre.

distrettuale *agg.* district.

distribuìbile *agg.* distributable.

distribuire *vt.* to distribute.

distributivo *agg.* e *sm.* distributive.

distributore *agg.* distributing. ◆ **distributore** *sm.* distributor || — *di benzina*, petrol pump.

distribuzione *sf.* distribution.

districare *vt.* to disentangle.

distrùggere *vt.* **1.** to destroy **2.** (*struggere*) to consume. ◆ **distrùggersi** *vr.* (*consumarsi*) to pine (away).

distruggìbile *agg.* destroyable.

distruttivo *agg.* destroying.

distrutto *agg.* destroyed.

distruttore *agg.* destroying. ◆ **distruttore** *sm.* destroyer.

distruzione *sf.* destruction.

disturbare *vt.* to disturb.

disturbato *agg.* **1.** disturbed **2.** (*indisposto*) unwell.

disturbatore *sm.* disturber.

disturbo *sm.* **1.** trouble, inconvenience **2.** (*malattia*) trouble, illness **3.** (*radio*) disturbance.

disubbidiente *agg.* disobedient.

disubbidienza *sf.* disobedience.

disubbidire *vi.* to disobey.

disuguaglianza *sf.* **1.** inequality **2.** (*di terreno*) unevenness.

disuguale *agg.* **1.** unequal **2.** (*irregolare*) irregular **3.** (*differente*) different.

disumanamente *avv.* inhumanly.

disumanare *vt.* to divest of humanity.

disumanità *sf.* inhumanity.

disumano *agg.* inhuman.

disumidire *vt.* to dry.

disunione *sf.* disunion.

disunire *vt.* to disunite. ◆ **disunirsi** *vr.* to become (*v. irr.*) disunited.

disunito *agg.* disunited.

disusare *vt.* to disuse.

disusato *agg.* disused.

disuso *sm.* disuse.

ditale *sm.* thimble.

ditata *sf.* finger-mark.

ditiràmbico *agg.* dithyrambic.

ditirambo *sm.* dithyramb.

dito *sm.* **1.** finger **2.** (*del piede* toe.

ditta *sf.* firm.

dittàfono *sm.* dictaphone.

dittatore *sm.* dictator.

dittatoriale *agg.* dictatorial.

dittatorio *agg.* dictatorial.

dittatura *sf.* dictatorship.

dìttico *sm.* diptych.

dittongo *sm.* diphthong.

diuresi *sf.* diuresis.

diurètico *agg.* diuretic.

diurno *agg.* diurnal, daytime.

diuturnamente *avv.* for a long time.

diuturno *agg.* diuturnal.

diva *sf.* **1.** goddess **2.** (*cine*) star.

divagare *vi.* to wander **2.** (*divertire*) to amuse. ◆ **divagarsi** *vr.* **1.** to be distracted **2.** (*divertirsi*) to amuse oneself.

divagazione *sf.* digression.

divampare *vi.* to blaze.

divano *sm.* divan, sofa.

divaricamento *sm.* straddle.

divaricare *vt.* to open wide || — *le gambe*, to part one's legs wide.

divario *sm.* difference.

divedere *vt.* **1.** (*nella loc. avv.*) *dare a* —, to show (*v. irr.*) clearly **2.** (*dar a credere*) to make (*v. irr.*) believe.

divèllere *vt.* to uproot.

divenire[1] *vi.* **1.** to become (*v. irr.*) **2.** (*mutarsi lentamente*) to grow (*v. irr.*).

divenire[2] *sm.* becoming: *l'essere e il* —, being and becoming.

diverbio *sm.* quarrel.

divergente *agg.* divergent.

divergenza *sf.* divergence.

divèrgere *vi.* **1.** to diverge **2.** (*scostarsi*) to wander.

diversamente *avv.* **1.** differently **2.** (*altrimenti*) otherwise.

diversificare *vt.* to diversify. ◆ **diversificarsi** *vr.* to differ.

diversione *sf.* diversion.

diversità *sf.* diversity.

diversivo *agg.* **1.** deviating **2.** (*che distrae*) diverting. ◆ **diversivo** *sm.* diversion, distraction.

diverso *agg.* different.

divertente *agg.* amusing.

divertimento *sm.* amusement.
divertire *vt.* to amuse, to entertain
♦ **divertirsi** *vr.* to enjoy oneself,
to have a good time.
divezzamento *sm.* weaning.
divezzare *vt.* to wean.
dividendo *sm.* dividend.
divìdere *vt.* **1.** to divide **2.** (*condividere*) to share.
divieto *sm.* prohibition.
divinamente *avv.* divinely.
divinare *vt.* to divine.
divinatore *sm.* diviner.
divinatorio *agg.* divinatory.
divinazione *sf.* divination.
divincolarsi *vr.* to wriggle.
divinità *sf.* divinity.
divinizzare *vt.* to deify.
divino *agg.* divine.
divisa *sf.* **1.** uniform **2.** (*valuta*)
currency.
divisare *vt.* to plan.
divisìbile *agg.* divisible.
divisibilità *sf.* divisibility.
divisionale *agg.* divisional.
divisione *sf.* **1.** division **2.** (*amm.*)
department.
divisionismo *sm.* pointillism.
divisionista *s.* pointillist.
divismo *sm.* stardom, star worship.
diviso *agg.* **1.** divided **2.** (*separato*)
separated **3.** (*condiviso*) shared.
divisore *sm.* divisor.
divisorio *agg.* dividing.
divo *sm.* **1.** deity **2.** (*cine*) star.
divorare *vt.* to devour.
divoratore *agg.* devouring.
divorziare *vi.* to divorce, to be divorced.
divorziato *agg.* divorced. ♦ **divorziato** *sm.* divorcee.
divorzio *sm.* divorce (*anche fig.*).
divulgàbile *agg.* that may be di-
vulged.
divulgare *vt.* to spread (*v. irr.*).
divulgativo *agg.* divulging.
divulgatore *sm.* divulger.
divulgazione *sf.* divulgation, spreading.
dizionario *sm.* dictionary.
dizionarista *s.* lexicographer.
dizione *sf.* **1.** diction **2.** (*pronuncia*)
pronunciation.
do *sm.* (*mus.*) C.
doccia *sf.* shower.
docente *agg.* teaching. ♦ **docente**
sm. teacher || *libero* —, fully
established university lecturer.
docenza *sf.* teaching.

dòcile *agg.* docile.
docilità *sf.* docility.
documentare *vt.* to document.
documentario *sm.* documentary.
documentarista *s.* documentary
film-maker.
documentato *agg.* documented.
documentazione *sf.* **1.** documentation **2.** *pl.* (*documenti*) papers.
documento *sm.* document.
dodecaedro *sm.* dodecahedron.
dodecafonìa *sf.* dodecaphony.
dodecafònico *agg.* dodecaphonic.
dodecàgono *sm.* dodecagon.
dodecasìllabo *sm.* dodecasyllable.
dodicèsimo *agg.* twelfth.
dòdici *agg.* twelve.
doga *sf.* stave.
dogana *sf.* customs (*pl.*).
doganale *agg.* customs (*attr.*): *dichiarazione* —, customs entry.
doganiere *sm.* customs officer.
doge *sm.* doge.
doglia *sf.* **1.** sharp pains **2.** (*pl.*,
med.) throes.
dogma *sm.* dogma.
dogmàtico *agg.* dogmatic(al).
dogmatismo *sm.* dogmatism.
dolce *agg.* **1.** sweet **2.** (*mite*) mild
3. (*tec.*) soft. ♦ **dolce** *sm.* **1.**
sweet **2.** (*torta*) cake.
dolcezza *sf.* **1.** sweetness **2.** (*di
clima*) mildness.
dolciario *agg.* confectionary.
dolciastro *agg.* sweetish.
dolcificare *vt.* **1.** to sweeten **2.**
(*fig.*) to mitigate.
dolcificazione *sf.* sweetening.
dolciumi *sm. pl.* sweets.
dolente *agg.* **1.** afflicted, grieved **2.**
(*spiacente*) sorry.
dolere *vi.* **1.** to ache **2.** (*rincrescere*)
to regret. ♦ **dolersi** *vr.* to regret.
dolicocèfalo *agg.* dolichocephalic.
dòllaro *sm.* dollar.
dolmen *sm.* dolmen.
dolo *sm.* fraud.
dolomite *sf.* dolomite.
dolomìtico *agg.* dolomitic.
dolorante *agg.* aching.
dolore *sm.* **1.** pain, ache **2.** (*fig.*)
sorrow, grief.
dolorosamente *avv.* **1.** painfully
2. (*morale*) sadly.
doloroso *agg.* **1.** painful **2.** (*che
causa dolore*) grievous.
doloso *agg.* fraudulent.
domàbile *agg.* tamable.
domanda *sf.* **1.** question, request

2. (*richiesta scritta*) application.
domandare *vt.* to ask (so. for sthg.). ♦ **domandarsi** *vr.* to wonder.
domani *avv.* tomorrow.
domare *vt.* **1.** to tame **2.** (*sotto-mettere*) to subdue.
domatore *sm.* tamer.
domattina *avv.* tomorrow morning.
doménica *sf.* Sunday.
domenicale *agg.* Sunday (*attr.*).
domenicano *agg.* dominican.
domèstica *sf.* maid.
domèstico *agg.* e *sm.* domestic || *lavori domestici,* household duties.
domiciliare *agg.* domiciliary.
domiciliarsi *vr.* to settle (in).
domiciliato *agg.* resident, living.
domicilio *sm.* **1.** house, dwelling **2.** (*giur.*) domicile.
dominante *agg.* dominant.
dominare *vt.* to dominate.
dominatore *sm.* ruler.
dominazione *sf.* domination.
dominio *sm.* **1.** domination **2.** (*ter-ritorio*) dominion **3.** (*giur.*) domain || *di — pubblico,* known to everybody.
dòmino *sm.* domino.
donare *vt.* to give (*v. irr.*) ♦ **donare** *vi.* (*addirsi*) to suit.
donatore *sm.* donor.
donazione *sf.* **1.** donation **2.** (*somma elargita per uno scopo*) grant.
donchisciottesco *agg.* quixotic.
donde *avv.* whence, from where || *ne ha ben —,* he has good reason for it.
dondolamento *sm.* swinging.
dondolare *vt.* e *vi.* to swing (*v. irr.*). ♦ **dondolarsi** *vr.* to swing, to rock.
dondolìo *sm.* swinging.
dòndolo *sm.* **1.** (*altalena*) swing || *a —,* rocking.
donna *sf.* woman (*pl.* women).
donnaiolo *sm.* ladies' man (*pl.* men).
donnesco *agg.* womanlike.
dònnola *sf.* weasel.
dono *sm.* gift.
donzella *sf.* damsel.
dopo *avv.* **1.** (*di luogo*) after, next **2.** (*dietro*) behind **3.** (*di tempo*) after, then **4.** (*più tardi*) later. ♦ **dopo** *prep.* (*di luogo e tempo*) after.
dopodomani *avv.* the day after tomorrow.
dopoguerra *sm.* post-war period.
dopopranzo *sm.* afternoon.
dopotutto *avv.* after all.
doppiaggio *sm.* (*cine*) dubbing.
doppiamente *avv.* **1.** doubly **2.** (*con inganno*) deceitfully.
doppiare *vt.* **1.** to double **2.** (*cine*) to dub.
doppiato *agg.* **1.** doubled **2.** (*cine*) dubbed.
doppiatura *sf.* doubling.
doppietta *sf.* double-barrelled gun.
doppiezza *sf.* **1.** doubleness **2.** (*am-biguità*) double-dealing.
doppio *agg.* **1.** double **2.** (*ambiguo*) double-faced. ♦ **doppio** *sm.* twice as much, twice as many.
doppiofondo *sm.* double bottom.
doppione *sm.* **1.** double **2.** (*di pa-rola*) doublet.
doppiopetto *sm.* double-breasted.
dorare *vt.* to gild.
dorato *agg.* **1.** gilded **2.** (*color oro*) golden.
doratore *sm.* gilder.
doratura *sf.* gilding.
dòrico *agg.* doric.
dorìfora *sf.* potato-beetle.
dormicchiare *vi.* to doze.
dormiente *agg.* sleeping. ♦ **dor-miente** *sm.* sleeper.
dormiglione *sm.* sleepy-head.
dormire *vi.* **1.** to sleep (*v. irr.*) || *— tra due guanciali,* to set (*v. irr.*) one's mind at rest **2.** (*fig.*) to remain inactive.
dormita *sf.* sleep.
dormitorio *sm.* dormitory.
dormiveglia *sm.* drowsiness.
dorsale *agg.* dorsal: *spina —,* backbone.
dorso *sm.* **1.** back **2.** (*di monte*) ridge.
dosàbile *agg.* measurable.
dosaggio *sm.* dosage.
dosare *vt.* to proportion: *— le parole,* to weigh one's words.
dosatura *sf.* dosage.
dose *sf.* dose: *una buona — di,* a good deal of.
dossale *sm.* dossal.
dosso *sm.* back: *togliersi di —,* to take (*v. irr.*) off.
dotare *vt.* **1.** to give (*v. irr.*) a dowry **2.** (*fornire di una rendita*) to endow **3.** (*fornire*) to provide (with).
dotato *agg.* **1.** gifted (with) **2.** (*e-*

quipaggiato) provided (with).
dotazione *sf.* endowment.
dote *sf.* **1.** dowry **2.** (*qualità*) endowment.
dotto[1] *agg.* learned. ♦ **dotto** *sm.* scholar.
dotto[2] *sm.* (*anat.*) duct.
dottorale *agg.* doctoral.
dottorato *sm.* doctorate.
dottore *sm.* **1.** doctor **2.** (*laureato*) graduate.
dottoressa *sf.* **1.** (*laureata*) graduate **2.** (*in medicina*) lady doctor.
dottrina *sf.* doctrine.
dottrinale *agg.* doctrinal.
dottrinario *sm.* doctrinaire.
dottrinarismo *sm.* doctrinairism.
dove *avv.* where.
dovere[1] *vi.* **1.** (*obbligo*) must (*v. dif.*): *devi lavorare*, you must work **2.** to have to **3.** (*possibilità, predestinazione*) to be to: *doveva diventare un grande scrittore*, he was to become a great writer **4.** (*devo?, dobbiamo?, nel senso di: vuoi che?*) shall (*v. dif.*): *devo aprire la finestra?*, shall I open the window? **5.** (*al condizionale*) ought to, should (*v. dif.*): *dovresti essere gentile*, you ought to be kind; *dovremmo partire*, we should leave **6.** (*al congiuntivo*) should, were to: *se dovesse venire*, if he should come, if he were to come **7.** (*essere obbligati*) to be obliged, to be forced **8.** (*essere da attribuire, dover arrivare*) to be due: *lo si deve al mio ritardo*, this is due to my being late; *il treno deve arrivare alle 4*, the train is due at 4 a.m. ♦ **dovere** *vt.* (*essere debitore in tutti i sensi*) to owe: *ti devo 1000 lire*, I owe you one thousand lire; *ti devo la vita*, I owe you my life.
dovere[2] *sm.* duty: *fare il proprio —*, to do (*v. irr.*) one's duty.
doverosamente *avv.* dutifully.
doveroso *agg.* dutiful.
dovizia *sf.* plenty.
dovizioso *agg.* abundant.
dovunque *avv.* **1.** everywhere **2.** (*seguito da verbo*) wherever.
dovuto *agg.* **1.** due **2.** (*equo*) fair. ♦ **dovuto** *sm.* due.
dozzina *sf.* dozen.
dozzinale *agg.* cheap, common.
draconiano *agg.* draconian.
draga *sf.* dredger.

dragaggio *sm.* dredging.
dragamine *sm.* mine-sweeper.
dragare *vt.* to dredge.
draglia *sf.* stay.
drago *sm.* dragon.
dragona *sf.* sword-knot.
dragone *sm.* dragon.
dramma *sm.* drama.
drammàtica *sf.* dramatics.
drammaticamente *avv.* dramatically.
drammaticità *sf.* tragicalness.
drammàtico *agg.* dramatic.
drammatizzare *vt.* to dramatise.
drammaturgìa *sf.* dramaturgy.
drammaturgo *sm.* dramatist.
drappeggiare *vt.* to drape.
drappeggio *sm.* draping.
drappello *sm.* squad.
drapperìa *sf.* drapery.
drappo *sm.* cloth.
dràstico *agg.* drastic.
drenaggio *sm.* drainage.
drenare *vt.* to drain.
drìade *sf.* **1.** (*mit.*) dryad **2.** (*bot.*) dryas (*pl.* -ades).
dribblare *vt.* to dribble.
dritta *sf.* **1.** right hand, right **2.** (*mar.*) starboard.
dritto *agg.* **1.** (*non storto*) straight **2.** (*eretto, onesto*) upright. ♦ **dritto** *sm.* right side.
drizza *sf.* halyard.
drizzare *vt.* to straighten.
droga *sf.* **1.** drug **2.** (*spezia*) spices (*pl.*).
drogare *vt.* **1.** to drug **2.** (*condire*) to spice.
drogherìa *sf.* grocery.
droghiere *sm.* grocer.
dromedario *sm.* dromedary.
drùido *sm.* druid.
drupa *sf.* drupe.
dualismo *sm.* dualism.
dualità *sf.* duality.
dubbiezza *sf.* dubiousness.
dubbio *sm.* doubt: *mettere in —*, to question. ♦ **dubbio** *agg.* dubious.
dubbioso *agg.* doubtful.
dubitare *vi.* to doubt.
dubitativo *agg.* dubitative.
duca *sm.* duke.
ducale *agg.* ducal.
ducato *sm.* **1.** dukedom **2.** (*moneta*) ducat.
duchessa *sf.* duchess.
due *agg.* two.
duecentèsimo *agg.* two hundredth.

duecentesco *agg.* thirteenth century (*attr.*).

duecento *sm.* two hundred ‖ *il* —, the thirteenth century.

duellare *vi.* to duel.

duello *sm.* duel: — *all'ultimo sangue*, duel to the death.

duetto *sm.* duet.

duna *sf.* dune.

dunque *cong.* 1. (*perciò*) therefore 2. (*rafforzativo*) well, then. ♦ dunque *sm. venire al* —, to come (*v. irr.*) to the point.

duodenale *agg.* duodenal.

duodeno *sm.* duodenum.

duomo *sm.* cathedral.

duplicare *vt.* to duplicate.

duplicato *sm.* duplicate.

dùplice *agg.* twofold.

duplicità *sf.* double-dealing.

durabilità *sf.* durability.

duralluminio *sm.* duralumin.

durante *prep.* during.

durare *vi.* 1. to last 2. (*perseverare*) to persist 3. (*resistere*) to hold (*v. irr.*) out. ♦ durare *vt.* to endure ‖ *chi la dura la vince*, slow and steady wins the race.

durata *sf.* 1. duration, length 2. (*periodo*) term 3. (*di un oggetto*) endurance.

duraturo *agg.* lasting.

durévole *agg.* durable.

durezza *sf.* 1. hardness 2. (*rigidità*) stiffness.

duro *agg.* 1. hard 2. (*di voce*) harsh ‖ *avere il sonno* —, to sleep (*v. irr.*) like a log; *avere la testa dura*, to be a block-head, to be stubborn.

durone *sm.* hard skin.

dùttile *agg.* ductile.

duttilità *sf.* ductility.

E

e *cong.* and: *e... e*, both... and.

ebanista *sm.* cabinet-maker.

ebanisterìa *sf.* 1. (*bottega*) cabinet-maker's shop 2. (*arte*) cabinet-making.

ebanite *sf.* ebonite.

èbano *sm.* ebony.

ebbene *cong.* well: —?, what about it?

ebbrezza *sf.* 1. drunkenness 2. (*fig.*) elation.

ebbro *agg.* 1. drunken 2. (*fig.*) mad.

ebdomadario *agg.* weekly. ♦ ebdomadario *sm.* weekly paper.

èbete *agg.* idiotic. ♦ èbete *sm.* idiot.

ebollizione *sf.* boiling.

ebràico *agg.* Hebrew.

ebreo *agg.* Hebrew, Jewish. ♦ ebreo *sm.* Hebrew, Jew.

ecatombe *sf.* massacre.

eccedente *agg.* excessive, in excess (*pred.*). ♦ eccedente *sm.* (*comm.*) exceeding.

eccedenza *sf.* excess, surplus: — *di peso*, overweight.

eccèdere *vt.* to exceed. ♦ eccèdere *vi.* to go (*v. irr.*) too far.

eccellente *agg.* excellent.

eccellenza *sf.* 1. excellence 2. (*titolo*) excellency.

eccèllere *vi.* to excel.

eccelso *agg.* sublime.

eccentricità *sf.* eccentricity.

eccèntrico *agg.* eccentric.

eccepire *vi.* to object.

eccessivo *agg.* excessive.

eccesso *sm.* excess.

eccètera *sm.* et cetera (*abbr.* etc.), and so on.

eccetto *prep.* except, but, save. ♦ eccetto che *cong.* 1. except that 2. (*purché*) provided that.

eccettuare *vt.* to except.

eccettuato *agg.* excluded.

eccezionale *agg.* exceptional.

eccezione *sf.* exception.

ecchìmosi *sf.* bruise.

eccidio *sm.* bloodshed.

eccitàbile *agg.* excitable.

eccitabilità *sf.* excitability.

eccitamento *sm.* excitement.

eccitante *agg.* e *sm.* excitant.

eccitare *vt.* to excite. ♦ eccitarsi *vr.* to get (*v. irr.*) excited.

eccitatore *agg.* excitative. ♦ eccitatore *sm.* exciter.

eccitazione *sf.* excitement.

ecclesiàstico *agg.* ecclesiastical.

ecco *avv.* here, there (*in unione con le voci del verbo* to be *al pres. ind.*): — *il mio cappello!*, here is my hat! ‖ — *tutto*, that's all; *quand'* —, when suddenly.

eccome *inter.* and how!

echeggiare *vi.* to echo (with sthg.).

echinoderma *sm.* echinoderm.

eclèttico *agg.* e *sm.* eclectic.

eclettismo *sm.* eclecticism.
eclissare *vt.* **1.** to eclipse **2.** (*fig.*) to overshadow.
eclisse, eclissi *sf.* eclipse.
eclìttica *sf.* ecliptic.
eclìttico *agg.* ecliptic.
eco *sf.* echo.
economato *sm.* **1.** steward's office **2.** (*in università*) bursar's office.
economìa *sf.* **1.** economy **2.** (*scienza*) economics.
econòmico *agg.* **1.** economic **2.** (*a buon prezzo*) cheap.
economista *s.* economist.
economizzare *vt.* to economize.
ecònomo *agg.* economical. ◆ **ecònomo** *sm.* **1.** steward **2.** (*di università*) bursar.
ecumènico *agg.* ecumenical.
eczema *sm.* eczema.
edema *sm.* oedema.
eden *sm.* Eden.
èdera *sf.* ivy.
edìcola *sf.* newspaper kiosk.
edicolista *sm.* news-agent.
edificante *agg.* edifying.
edificare *vt.* **1.** to build (*v. irr.*) (up) **2.** (*fig.*) to edify.
edificatore *sm.* **1.** builder **2.** (*fig.*) edifier.
edificazione *sf.* **1.** building **2.** (*fig.*) edification.
edificio *sm.* building.
edile *agg.* building: *perito* —, master-builder. ◆ **edile** *sm.* (*stor. romana*) aedile.
edilizia *sf.* building industry.
edilizio *agg.* building (*attr.*).
èdito *agg.* published.
editore *sm.* publisher.
editorìa *sf.* book industry.
editoriale *agg.* e *sm.* editorial.
editrice *agg.*: *casa* —, publishing house.
editto *sm.* edict.
edizione *sf.* edition, issue.
edonismo *sm.* hedonism.
edonista *s.* hedonist.
edotto *agg.* aware: *rendere* —, to inform.
educanda *sf.* boarding-school girl.
educandato *sm.* girls' boarding-school.
educare *vt.* **1.** to educate **2.** (*allevare*) to bring (*v. irr.*) up.
educativo *agg.* educational.
educato *agg.* well-bred, polite.
educatore *sm.* educator.
educazione *sf.* **1.** education **2.**

(*buone maniere*) good manners (*pl.*).
edulcorare *vt.* to edulcorate.
efebo *sm.* ephebe.
efèlide *sf.* freckle.
effemèride *sf.* ephemeris (*pl.* -ides).
effeminare *vt.* to effeminate. ◆ **effeminarsi** *vr.* to become (*v. irr.*) effeminate.
effeminatezza *sf.* effeminacy.
efferatezza *sf.* brutality.
efferato *agg.* brutal.
effervescente *agg.* sparkling.
effervescenza *sf.* effervescence.
effettivamente *avv.* actually, indeed.
effettivo *agg.* actual.
effetto *sm.* **1.** effect, result ‖ *in effetti*, as a matter of fact **2.** (*comm.*) bill.
effettuàbile *agg.* feasible.
effettuare *vt.* to carry out: — *un piano*, to carry out a plan. ◆ **effettuarsi** *vr.* (*aver luogo*) to take (*v. irr.*) place.
effettuazione *sf.* accomplishment.
efficace *agg.* effective, efficacious.
efficacia *sf.* efficacy.
efficiente *agg.* efficient.
efficienza *sf.* efficiency.
effigiare *vt.* to portray.
effigie *sf.* image.
effìmera *sf.* (*fam.*) mayfly.
effìmero *agg.* ephemeral.
effluvio *sm.* exhalation.
effòndere *vt.* to pour forth. ◆ **effòndersi** *vr.* to spread (*v. irr.*) (about).
effrazione *sf.* (*giur.*) house-breaking, burglary.
effusione *sf.* **1.** shedding **2.** (*cordialità*) cordiality **3.** (*pl., manifestazioni*) effusions.
effusivo *agg.* effusive.
egemonìa *sf.* hegemony.
egemònico *agg.* hegemonic.
ègida *sf.* **1.** aegis **2.** (*fig.*) protection.
egiziano *agg.* e *sm.* Egyptian.
egli *pron.* he: — *stesso*, he himself.
ègloga *sf.* eclogue.
egocèntrico *agg.* egocentric. ◆ **egocèntrico** *sm.* egocentric man.
egocentrismo *sm.* egocentrism.
egoismo *sm.* selfishness.
egoista *agg.* e *sm.* egoist.
egotismo *sm.* self-conceit.
egregiamente *avv.* eminently.
egregio *agg.* eminent ‖ (*nelle lettere*) — *Signore*, Dear Sir.

eguaglianza, eguagliare, eguale ecc. V. *uguaglianza, uguagliare, uguale* ecc.

egualità *sf.* equality.

eiaculare *vi.* to ejaculate.

eiaculazione *sf.* ejaculation.

eiezione *sf.* ejection.

elaborare *vt.* to elaborate.

elaborato *agg.* elaborate.

elaborazione *sf.* 1. elaboration 2. (*di piano*) formulation.

elargire *vt.* to lavish.

elargizione *sf.* donation.

elasticità *sf.* 1. elasticity 2. (*agilità*) nimbleness.

elasticizzare *vt.* to make (*v. irr.*) elastic.

elàstico *agg.* 1. elastic 2. (*agile*) nimble. ◆ **elàstico** *sm.* rubber band.

elce *sm.* ilex.

elefante *sm.* elephant.

elefantesco *agg.* elephantine.

elefantìasi *sf.* elephantiasis.

elegante *agg.* elegant, smart.

eleganza *sf.* smartness.

elèggere *vt.* 1. to elect 2. (*nominare*) to appoint.

eleggìbile *agg.* eligible.

eleggibilità *sf.* eligibility.

elegìa *sf.* elegy.

elegìaco *agg.* elegiac.

elementare *agg.* elementary: *scuola* —, primary school.

elemento *sm.* 1. element 2. (*componente*) component 3. (*pl., rudimenti*) rudiments 4. (*persona*) person.

elemòsina *sf.* alms: *chiedere l'*—, to beg.

elemosinare *vt.* e *vi.* to beg (for).

elencare *vt.* to list.

elenco *sm.* list: — *telefonico*, telephone directory.

elettivo *agg.* elective.

eletto *agg.* elect, chosen.

elettorale *agg.* electoral.

elettorato *sm.* electorate.

elettore *sm.* voter.

elettràuto *sm.* 1. (*officina*) car electrical repairs (*pl.*) 2. (*meccanico*) car electrician.

elettricista *sm.* electrician.

elettricità *sf.* electricity.

elèttrico *agg.* electric.

elettrificare *vt.* to electrify.

elettrificazione *sf.* electrification.

elettrizzare *vt.* to electrify.

elettrocalamita *sf.* electro-magnet.

elettrocardìogramma *sm.* electrocardiogram.

elettrodinàmica *sf.* electrodynamics.

elèttrodo *sm.* electrode.

elettrodomèstici *sm. pl.* electrical household appliances.

elettrògeno *agg.* generating electricity.

elettròlisi *sf.* electrolysis.

elettromagnètico *agg.* electro-magnetic.

elettromotore *sm.* dynamo.

elettromotrice *sf.* electric rail car.

elettrone *sm.* electron.

elettrònica *sf.* electronics.

elettrònico *agg.* electronic.

elettrotècnica *sf.* electrical technology.

elettrotreno *sm.* electric train.

elevamento *sm.* elevation.

elevare *vt.* 1. to elevate 2. (*erigere*) to erect 3. (*mat.*) to raise. ◆ **elevarsi** *vr.* to rise (*v. irr.*).

elevatezza *sf.* loftiness.

elevato *agg.* elevated, high.

elevatore *sm.* elevator.

elevazione *sf.* 1. elevation 2. (*l'elevare*) rising 3. (*mat.*) raising.

elezione *sf.* election.

èlica *sf.* 1. (*aer.*) propeller 2. (*mar.*) screw.

elicoidale *agg.* helicoidal.

elicòttero *sm.* helicopter.

elìdere *vt.* to annul. ◆ **elìdersi** *vr. rec.* to annul each other.

eliminare *vt.* to eliminate. ◆ **eliminarsi** *vr.* to be eliminated.

eliminatoria *sf.* preliminary heat.

eliminazione *sf.* elimination, expulsion.

elio *sm.* helium.

eliocèntrico *agg.* heliocentric.

eliografia *sf.* heliography.

elioterapìa *sf.* heliotherapy.

eliotipìa *sf.* heliotypy.

eliporto *sm.* heliport.

elisione *sf.* elision.

elisìr *sm.* elixir.

èlitra *sf.* elytrum (*pl.* -ra).

ella *pron.* she: — *stessa*, she herself.

ellènico *agg.* Hellenic.

ellenismo *sm.* Hellenism.

ellenista *s.* Hellenist.

ellisse *sf.* ellipse.

ellissi *sf.* ellipsis (*pl.* -ses).

ellìttico *sm.* elliptic(al).

elmetto *sm.* helmet.

elmo *sm.* helmet.
elocuzione *sf.* elocution.
elogiàbile *agg.* praiseworthy.
elogiare *vt.* to eulogize, to praise.
elogiatore *sm.* eulogist.
elogio *sm.* eulogy, praise.
eloquente *agg.* eloquent.
eloquenza *sf.* eloquence.
elucubrare *vt.* to lucubrate: — *su*, *intorno a qc.*, to lucubrate on, about sthg.
elucubrazione *sf.* lucubration.
elùdere *vt.* to elude.
elusivo *agg.* elusive.
elvètico *agg.* Helvetic.
elzeviro *sm.* 1. elzevir 2. (*giorn.*) leading literary article.
emaciare *vt.* to emaciate. ♦ **emaciarsi** *vr.* to become (*v. irr.*) emaciated.
emaciato *agg.* emaciated.
emanare *vt.* 1. to issue 2. (*vapori, profumi*) to exhale.
emanazione *sf.* emanation.
emancipare *vt.* to emancipate.
emancipato *agg.* emancipated.
emancipazione *sf.* emancipation.
emàtico *agg.* haematic.
ematoma *sm.* haematoma (*pl.* -ata).
ematosi *sf.* haematosis.
embargo *sm.* embargo.
emblema *sm.* 1. emblem 2. (*simbolo*) symbol.
emblemàtico *agg.* emblematic.
embolìa *sf.* embolism.
èmbolo *sm.* embolus (*pl.* -li).
embrionale *agg.* embryonic.
embrione *sm.* embryo.
emendamento *sm.* 1. amendment 2. (*correzione*) emendation.
emendare *vt.* 1. to amend 2. (*correggere*) to emend.
emergenza *sf.* emergency.
emèrgere *vi.* 1. to emerge 2. (*fig.*) to emerge, to appear.
emèrito *agg.* emeritus.
emeroteca *sf.* newspaper library.
emersione *sf.* emersion.
eméttere *vt.* 1. to emit 2. (*di suono*) to utter 3. (*emanare*) to deliver 4. (*banconote*) to issue.
emiciclo *sm.* hemicycle.
emicrania *sf.* headache.
emigrante *agg. e sm.* emigrant.
emigrare *vi.* to emigrate.
emigrato *sm.* emigrant.
emigrazione *sf.* emigration.
eminente *agg.* outstanding, eminent.
eminenza *sf.* eminence.

emiro *sm.* emir.
emisfèrico *agg.* hemispheric(al).
emisfero *sm.* hemisphere.
emissario *sm.* emissary.
emissione *sf.* 1. emission 2. (*econ.*) issue.
emistichio *sm.* hemistich.
emittente *agg.* issuing ‖ *stazione* — (*radio*), broadcasting station.
emofilìa *sf.* haemophilia.
emoglobina *sf.* haemoglobin.
emolliente *agg.* emollient.
emolumento *sm.* emolument.
emorragìa *sf.* haemorrhage.
emorròidi *sf. pl.* haemorrhoids.
emòstasi *sf.* haemostasis.
emostàtico *agg.* haemostatic.
emoteca *sf.* blood bank.
emotività *sf.* emotionality.
emotivo *agg.* emotional.
emottisi *sf.* haemoptysis.
emozionante *agg.* touching, exciting, thrilling.
emozionare *vt.* to move. ♦ **emozionarsi** *vr.* to get (*v. irr.*) excited.
emozione *sf.* emotion, thrill.
empiastro *sm.* plaster.
empietà *sf.* impiety.
empio *agg.* impious.
empire *vt.* to fill.
empìrico *agg. e sm.* empiric.
empirismo *sm.* empiricism.
emporio *sm.* department store.
emulare *vt.* to emulate.
emulazione *sf.* emulation.
èmulo *sm.* rival.
emulsionare *vt.* to emulsify.
emulsione *sf.* emulsion.
encefalite *sf.* encephalitis.
encèfalo *sm.* encephalon (*pl.* -ala).
encìclica *sf.* encyclic.
enciclopedìa *sf.* encyclopaedia.
enciclopèdico *agg.* encyclopaedic.
enclìtico *agg.* enclitic.
encomiàbile *agg.* praiseworthy.
encomiare *vt.* to commend.
encomio *sm.* panegyric.
endecasìllabo *agg.* hendecasyllabic. ♦ **endecasìllabo** *sm.* hendecasyllable.
endèmico *agg.* endemic.
endocardio *sm.* endocardium.
endocardite *sf.* endocarditis.
endòcrino *agg.* endocrine.
endocrinologìa *sf.* endocrinology.
endovenoso *agg.* intravenous. ♦ **endovenosa** *sf.* intravenous injection.

energètico *agg.* e *sm.* tonic.
energìa *sf.* energy.
energicamente *avv.* energetically.
enèrgico *agg.* energetic(al).
energùmeno *sm.* energumen.
ènfasi *sf.* emphasis.
enfàtico *agg.* emphatic.
enfiagione *sf.* swelling.
enfisema *sm.* emphysema.
enfitèusi *sf.* emphyteusis.
enigma *sm.* enigma, puzzle.
enigmàtico *agg.* puzzling.
enigmista *sm.* enigmatographer.
enigmìstica *sf.* enigmatography.
enigmìstico *agg.* puzzle (*attr.*).
ennèsimo *agg.* nth: *ennesima potenza*, nth power.
enologìa *sf.* oenology.
enòlogo *sm.* oenologist.
enorme *agg.* huge.
enormità *sf.* **1.** hugeness **2.** (*fig.*) absurdity.
ente *sm.* **1.** being **2.** (*comm.*) body, corporation.
enterite *sf.* enteritis.
enteroclisma *sm.* enema.
enterocolite *sf.* enterocolitis.
entità *sf.* entity.
entomologìa *sf.* entomology.
entomòlogo *sm.* entomologist.
entrambi *pron.* e *agg.* both.
entrante *agg.* (*con espressioni di tempo*) next, coming.
entrare *vi.* to enter, to come (*v. irr.*) in, to go (*v. irr.*) in || *non c'entra*, this has got nothing to do with it; — *correndo*, to run (*v. irr.*) in; — *in carica*, to come (*v. irr.*) into office; — *in società*, to go into partnership (with); — *precipitosamente*, to rush in; — *in giuoco*, to come into play; — *in vigore*, to come into force.
entrata *sf.* **1.** entrance, entry **2.** (*rendita*) income.
entratura *sf.* entrance.
entro *prep.* **1.** (*luogo*) inside **2.** (*tempo*) in, within, by: — *due giorni*, within two days; — *lunedì*, by Monday.
entrobordo *sm.* inboard.
entroterra *sm.* inland.
entusiasmante *agg.* exciting.
entusiasmare *vt.* to raise enthusiasm in. ♦ **entusiasmarsi** *vr.* to become (*v. irr.*) enthusiastic.
entusiasmo *sm.* enthusiasm
entusiasta *agg.* enthusiast: *essere* — *di qc.*, to be crazy about sthg.

entusiàstico *agg.* enthusiastic(al).
enucleare *vt.* to enucleate.
enucleazione *sf.* enucleation.
enumerare *vt.* to enumerate.
enumerazione *sf.* enumeration.
enunciare *vt.* to state: — *un teorema*, to enunciate a theorem.
enunciato *sm.* proposition, terms (*pl.*).
enunciazione *sf.* enunciation.
enuresi *sf.* enuresis.
enzima *sm.* enzyme.
eòlico *agg.* Aeolian.
epàtico *agg.* hepatic.
epatite *sf.* hepatitis.
èpica *sf.* epic.
epicentro *sm.* epicentre.
èpico *agg.* epic.
epicureismo *sm.* **1.** epicurism **2.** (*fil.*) epicureanism.
epicureo *agg.* e *sm.* Epicurean.
epidemìa *sf.* epidemic.
epidèmico *agg.* epidemical.
epidèrmico *agg.* epidermic.
epidèrmide *sf.* epidermis, skin.
Epifanìa *sf.* Epiphany, Twelfth Night.
epìgono *sm.* imitator, follower.
epìgrafe *sf.* epigraph.
epigrafìa *sf.* epigraphy.
epigramma *sm.* epigram.
epigrammista *s.* epigrammatist.
epilessìa *sf.* epilepsy.
epilèttico *agg.* e *sm.* epileptic.
epìlogo *sm.* epilogue.
episcopale *agg.* episcopal.
episcopato *sm.* episcopacy.
episòdico *agg.* episodic(al).
episodio *sm.* episode.
epìstola *sf.* epistle.
epistolare *agg.* epistolary.
epistolario *sm.* letters (*pl.*).
epitaffio *sm.* epitaph.
epitalamio *sm.* epithalamium (*pl.* -ia).
epitelio *sm.* epithelium.
epìteto *sm.* epithet.
epìtome *sf.* epitome.
època *sf.* **1.** epoch **2.** (*età*) age **3.** (*data*) date || *far* —, to mark an epoch.
epopea *sf.* **1.** epopee **2.** (*serie di fatti eroici*) epos.
eppure *cong.* yet.
epulone *sm.* glutton.
epurare *vt.* to purge.
epurazione *sf.* purge.
equamente *avv.* fairly.
equànime *agg.* equanimous.

equanimità *sf.* equanimity, impartiality.

equatore *sm.* equator.

equatoriale *agg.* equatorial.

equazione *sf.* equation.

equestre *agg.* equestrian.

equidistante *agg.* equidistant.

equidistanza *sf.* equidistance.

equilàtero *agg.* equilateral.

equilibrare *vt.* to balance.

equilibrato *agg.* **1.** balanced **2.** (*fig.*) well-balanced.

equilibrio *sm.* balance, equilibrium.

equilibrismo *sm.* acrobatics (*pl.*).

equilibrista *s.* acrobat.

equino *agg.* equine.

equinozio *sm.* equinox.

equipaggiamento *sm.* equipment, outfit.

equipaggiare *vt.* to equip, to fit out.

equipaggio *sm.* (*mar.; aer.*) crew.

equiparàbile *agg.* comparable.

equiparare *vt.* to equalize.

equiparazione *sf.* equalization.

equipollente *agg.* equipollent.

equipollenza *sf.* equipollence.

equità *sf.* equity, fairness.

equitazione *sf.* riding.

equivalente *agg.* equivalent.

equivalenza *sf.* equivalence.

equivalere *vi.* to be equivalent. ♦ **equivalersi** *vr.* to be equivalent.

equivocàbile *agg.* mistakable.

equivocare *vi.* to misunderstand (*v. irr.*).

equivoco *agg.* equivocal, ambiguous. ♦ **equivoco** *sm.* equivocation.

equo *agg.* fair.

era *sf.* era, epoch.

erariale *agg.* fiscal.

erario *sm.* Treasury.

erba *sf.* grass || *in* —, green; (*fig.*) budding: *un poeta in* —, a budding poet.

erbaccia *sf.* weed.

erbàceo *agg.* herbaceous.

erbaggio *sm.* vegetable.

erbario *sm.* herbarium.

erbetta *sf.* new grass.

erbivéndolo *sm.* greengrocer.

erbivoro *agg.* herbivorous.

erborista *s.* herborist.

erboso *agg.* grassy.

èrcole *sm.* Hercules.

ercùleo *agg.* Herculean.

erede *sm.* heir. ♦ **erede** *sf.* heiress.

eredità *sf.* inheritance.

ereditare *vt.* to inherit.

ereditarietà *sf.* hereditariness.

ereditario *agg.* hereditary.

ereditiera *sf.* heiress.

eremita *sm.* hermit.

eremitaggio *sm.* hermitage.

èremo *sm.* hermitage.

eresia *sf.* heresy.

erètico *agg.* heretical.

erèttile *agg.* erectile.

eretto *agg.* **1.** upright **2.** (*costruito*) built.

erezione *sf.* **1.** erection **2.** (*costruzione*) building.

ergastolano *sm.* convict (serving a life sentence).

ergàstolo *sm.* life imprisonment.

èrgere *vt.* to raise. ♦ **èrgersi** *vr.* to rise (*v. irr.*).

èrica *sf.* heather.

erìgere *vt.* to erect, to build (*v. irr.*). ♦ **erìgersi** *vr.* to set up (for).

erma *sf.* herma (*pl.* -ae).

ermafrodito *agg.* hermaphrodite.

ermellino *sm.* ermine.

ermenèuta *sm.* hermeneut.

ermenèutica *sf.* hermeneutics.

ermètico *agg.* **1.** (*tec.*) airtight **2.** (*oscuro*) obscure.

ermetismo *sm.* obscurity.

ernia *sf.* hernia.

erniario *agg.* hernial.

erodere *vt.* to wear (*v. irr.*) away.

eroe *sm.* hero.

erogare *vt.* **1.** to distribute **2.** (*elett.; idraulica*) to deliver.

erogazione *sf.* **1.** distribution **2.** (*elettr.; idraulica*) delivery.

eròico *agg.* heroic.

eroina *sf.* **1.** heroine **2.** (*farm.*) heroin.

eroismo *sm.* heroism.

eròmpere *vi.* to burst (*v. irr.*) forth.

erosione *sf.* erosion.

erosivo *agg.* erosive.

eròtico *agg.* erotic.

erotismo *sm.* eroticism.

erotòmane *s.* erotomaniac.

èrpete *sm.* herpes.

érpice *sm.* harrow.

errabondo *agg.* wandering.

errante *agg.* errant.

errare *vi.* **1.** (*vagare*) to wander **2.** (*sbagliare*) to err.

erràtico *agg.* erratic.

errato *agg.* wrong.

erròneo *agg.* erroneous.

errore *sm.* error, mistake.

erta *sf.* steep || *stare all'*—, to be on the look-out.

erto *agg.* steep.

erudire *vt.* to teach (*v. irr.*). ◆ **erudirsi** *vr.* to get (*v. irr.*) educated.

erudito *agg.* learned. ◆ **erudìto** *sm.* scholar.

erudizione *sf.* erudition, learning.

eruttare *vt.* to erupt.

eruttivo *agg.* eruptive.

eruzione *sf.* eruption.

esacerbare *vt.* to embitter.

esacerbazione *sf.* embitterment.

esaedro *sm.* hexahedron.

esagerare *vt.* to exaggerate. ◆ **esagerare** *vi.* to go (*v. irr.*) too far, to exceed.

esagerato *agg.* 1. exaggerated 2. (*di prezzo*) exorbitant.

esagerazione *sf.* exaggeration.

esagitare *vt.* to stir violently.

esagonale *agg.* hexagonal.

esàgono *sm.* hexagon.

esalare *vt.* to exhale. ◆ **esalare** *vi.* to exhale, to rise (*v. irr.*).

esalazione *sf.* exhalation.

esaltare *vt.* to exalt. ◆ **esaltarsi** *vr.* 1. (*vantarsi*) to boast 2. (*infervorarsi*) to become (*v. irr.*) excited.

esaltato *agg.* excited. ◆ **esaltato** *sm.* hot-head.

esaltazione *sf.* 1. exaltation 2. (*eccitazione*) excitement.

esame *sm.* examination: *dare un* —, to take (*v. irr.*) an examination; *essere respinto ad un* —, to fail in an examination.

esàmetro *sm.* hexameter.

esaminando *sm.* candidate.

esaminare *vt.* to examine.

esaminatore *sm.* examiner.

esangue *agg.* bloodless.

esànime *agg.* lifeless.

esasperare *vt.* to exasperate. ◆ **esasperarsi** *vr.* to become (*v. irr.*) irritated.

esasperato *agg.* exasperated.

esasperazione *sf.* exasperation.

esattamente *avv.* exactly, just.

esattezza *sf.* exactitude.

esatto *agg.* exact, right.

esattore *sm.* collector.

esattorìa *sf.* collector's office.

esaudimento *sm.* satisfaction.

esaudire *vt.* to grant.

esauriente *agg.* exhaustive.

esaurimento *sm.* exhaustion.

esaurire *vt.* to exhaust. ◆ **esaurirsi** *vr.* to get (*v. irr.*) exhausted.

esaurito *agg.* 1. exhausted 2. (*di persona*) worn out 3. (*che ha l'esaurimento nervoso*) suffering from a nervous breakdown 4. (*di libro*) out of print.

esàusto *agg.* exhausted.

esautorare *vt.* to deprive of authority.

esazione *sf.* collection.

esborso *sm.* outlay.

esca *sf.* 1. bait 2. (*materiale infiammabile*) tinder 3. (*di esplosivo*) fuse.

escandescenza *sf.* outburst of rage || *dare in escandescenze*, to lose (*v. irr.*) one's temper.

escatologìa *sf.* eschatology.

escavatore *sm.* digger.

escavatrice *sf.* digger.

escavazione *sf.* digging out.

eschimese *agg.* e *sm.* Eskimo.

esclamare *vi.* to exclaim.

esclamativo *agg.* exclamatory: *punto* —, exclamation mark.

esclamazione *sf.* exclamation.

esclùdere *vt.* to exclude, to leave (*v. irr.*) out.

esclusione *sf.* exclusion || *ad* — *di*, except.

esclusiva *sf.* 1. patent 2. (*diritto esclusivo*) sole right.

esclusività *sf.* exclusiveness.

esclusivo *agg.* exclusive, sole.

escluso *agg.* 1. excluded 2. (*eccettuato*) excepted.

escogitare *vt.* to contrive.

escoriare *vt.* to graze.

escoriazione *sf.* abrasion.

escremento *sm.* excrement.

escrescenza *sf.* excrescence.

escursione *sf.* excursion, trip.

escursionista *s.* excursionist.

escussione *sf.* examination.

esecràbile *agg.* execrable.

esecrare *vt.* to execrate.

esecrazione *sf.* execration.

esecutivo *agg.* executive.

esecutore *sm.* 1. executor 2. (*di musica*) performer 3. (*carnefice*) executioner.

esecuzione *sf.* 1. execution 2. (*mus.*) performance.

esedra *sf.* exedra (*pl.* -ae).

esegesi *sf.* exegesis (*pl.* -ses).

esegeta *s.* exegete.

eseguìbile *agg.* feasible.

eseguire vt. 1. to execute, to carry out 2. (mus.) to perform.

esempio sm. 1. example, instance 2. (modello perfetto) pattern.

esemplare agg. exemplary. ◆ **esemplare** sm. 1. pattern, specimen 2. (di libro) copy.

esemplificare vt. to exemplify.

esemplificazione sf. exemplification.

esentare vt. to exempt.

esente agg. exempt, free.

esenzione sf. exemption.

esequie sf. pl. exequies.

esercente sm. shop-keeper.

esercire vt. to manage (a business) || — un negozio, to keep (v. irr.) a shop.

esercitare vt. 1. to exercise 2. (una professione) to practice 3. (addestrare) to train. ◆ **esercitarsi** vr. to practice.

esercitazione sf. 1. exercise 2. (allenamento) training 3. (mil.) drill.

esercito sm. army.

esercizio sm. 1. exercise 2. (negozio) shop 3. (comm.) — finanziario, financial year.

esibire vt. to exhibit, to show (v. irr.).

esibizione sf. exhibition, show.

esibizionismo sm. exhibitionism, showing-off.

esibizionista s. exhibitionist.

esigente agg. exacting.

esigenza sf. 1. demand, exigence 2. (pretesa) pretension.

esigere vt. 1. (comm.) to collect 2. (richiedere con autorità) to insist on 3. (pretendere) to exact.

esigibile agg. 1. exigible 2. (riscuotibile) collectable.

esiguità sf. exiguity.

esiguo agg. exiguous, scanty.

esilarante agg. exhilarating.

esilarare vt. to exhilarate.

esile agg. slender.

esiliare vt. to exile. ◆ **esiliarsi** vr. to go (v. irr.) into exile.

esiliato agg. banished. ◆ **esiliato** sm. exile.

esilio sm. exile.

esimere vt. to free, to excuse. ◆ **esimersi** vr. to evade (sthg.).

esimio agg. excellent.

esistente agg. 1. existing 2. (di cose) extant.

esistenza sf. existence.

esistenziale agg. existential.

esistenzialismo sm. existentialism.

esistenzialista agg. e s. existentialist.

esistere vi. to exist.

esitante agg. hesitating: voce —, faltering voice.

esitare vi. 1. to hesitate 2. (di voce) to falter.

esitazione sf. hesitation: senza —, unhesitatingly.

esito sm. result, outcome.

esiziale agg. ruinous.

esodo sm. exodus.

esofago sm. oesophagus.

esogeno agg. exogenous.

esonerare vt. to exonerate.

esonero sm. exoneration.

esorbitante agg. exorbitant.

esorbitanza sf. exorbitance.

esorbitare vi. to exceed.

esorcismo sm. exorcism.

esorcista sm. exorcist.

esorcizzare vt. to exorcize.

esorcizzatore sm. exorcizer.

esordiente agg. beginning. ◆ **esordiente** sm. beginner.

esordio sm. preamble, beginning.

esordire vi. 1. to begin (v. irr.) 2. (in arte) to make (v. irr.) one's debut.

esortare vt. to exhort.

esortativo agg. exhortative.

esortazione sf. exhortation.

esosità sf. greediness.

esoso agg. greedy.

esoterico agg. esoteric.

esotermico agg. exothermic.

esotico agg. exotic.

esotismo sm. exoticism.

espandere vt. to spread (v. irr.) (out). ◆ **espandersi** vr. to spread.

espansione sf. expansion.

espansionismo sm. expansionism.

espansività sf. effusiveness.

espansivo agg. effusive.

espatriare vi. to emigrate.

espatrio sm. expatriation.

espediente sm. expedient.

espellere vt. to expel.

esperanto sm. Esperanto.

esperienza sf. experience.

esperimento sm. 1. experiment 2. (esame) test 3. (tentativo) trial.

esperire vt. to try.

esperto agg. e sm. expert.

espettorante agg. e sm. expectorant.

espettorare vt. to expectorate.

espettorazione *sf.* expectoration.
espiare *vt.* to expiate.
espiatorio *agg.* expiatory: *capro* —, scapegoat.
espiazione *sf.* expiation.
espirare *vt.* e *vi.* to expire.
espirazione *sf.* expiration.
espletare *vt.* to dispatch.
espletazione *sf.* dispatching.
esplicare *vt.* to explicate: — *un'attività*, to have an activity.
esplicativo *agg.* explanatory.
esplicazione *sf.* explication.
esplicito *agg.* explicit.
esplòdere *vi.* to explode, to burst (*v. irr.*).
esplorare *vt.* 1. to explore 2. (*mil.*) to scout.
esploratore *sm.* 1. explorer 2. (*mil.*) scout.
esplorazione *sf.* 1. exploration 2. (*mil.*) scouting expedition.
esplosione *sf.* 1. explosion, blast 2. (*fig.*) outbreak.
esplosivo *agg.* e *sm.* explosive.
esponente *sm.* exponent.
esporre *vt.* 1. to show (*v. irr.*) 2. (*a rischio*) to venture 3. (*spiegare*) to expound 4. (*mettere in vista*) to display. ◆ **esporsi** *vr.* to expose oneself.
esportare *vt.* to export.
esportatore *agg.* exporting. ◆ **esportatore** *sm.* exporter.
esportazione *sf.* export, exportation.
esposìmetro *sm.* exposure-meter.
espositore *sm.* exhibitor.
esposizione *sf.* 1. exposure 2. (*mostra*) exhibition 3. (*eloquio*) exposition.
esposto *sm.* petition.
espressamente *avv.* 1. expressly 2. (*appositamente*) on purpose.
espressione *sf.* expression.
espressionismo *sm.* expressionism.
espressionista *s.* expressionist.
espressivo *agg.* expressive.
espresso *agg.* express.
esprìmere *vt.* to express.
esprimìbile *agg.* expressible.
espropriare *vt.* to dispossess.
espropriazione *sf.* expropriation.
espugnare *vt.* to conquer.
espugnatore *sm.* conqueror.
espugnazione *sf.* conquest.
espulsione *sf.* expulsion.
espulsivo *agg.* e *sm.* expulsive.

espulsore *sm.* ejector.
espùngere *vt.* to expunge.
espurgare *vt.* 1. to expurgate 2. (*un libro*) to bowdlerize.
espurgazione *sf.* 1. expurgation 2. (*un libro*) to bowdlerize.
essa *pron.* 1. (*sogg.*) she, (*compl.*) her 2. (*riferito a cose o animali*) it.
esse *sf.* letter S.: *a* —, S-shaped.
essenza *sf.* essence.
essenziale *agg.* essential.
essenzialità *sf.* essentiality.
èssere *vi.* to be ‖ *c'è, ci sono*, there is, there are.
èssere *sm.* 1. being 2. (*esistenza*) existence.
essi *pron.* (*sogg.*) they, (*compl.*) them.
essiccare *vt.* to dry.
essiccatoio *sm.* drier.
essiccazione *sf.* drying process.
esso *pron.* 1. (*sogg.*) he, (*compl.*) him 2. (*per cose o animali*) it.
essudato *sm.* exudate.
essudazione *sf.* exudation.
est *sm.* east.
èstasi *sf.* ecstasy: *andare in* —, to go (*v. irr.*) into ecstasies; *mandare in* —, to throw (*v. irr.*) into ecstasies.
estasiare *vt.* to enrapture. ◆ **estasiarsi** *vr.* to be enraptured.
estate *sf.* summer.
estàtico *agg.* ecstatic.
estemporàneo *agg.* extempore.
estèndere *vt.* to extend.
estendìbile *agg.* extensible.
estensione *sf.* 1. extension 2. (*distesa*) expanse, extent 3. (*mus.*) range.
estensivo *agg.* extensive.
estensore *sm.* 1. compiler 2. (*giur.*) drafts-man (*pl.* -men) 3. (*sport*) chest-expander.
estenuante *agg.* exhausting.
estenuare *vt.* to tire out.
estenuazione *sf.* exhaustion.
esteriore *agg.* outward. ◆ **esteriore** *sm.* exterior, outside.
esteriorità *sf.* outward appearance.
esternamente *avv.* externally, outside.
esternare *vt.* to express, to utter.
esterno *agg.* outer, external.
èstero *agg.* foreign. ◆ **èstero** *sm.* foreign countries (*pl.*) ‖ *all'*—, abroad.
esterofilìa *sf.* xenomania.

esterrefatto *agg.* aghast, amazed.
esteso *agg.* large, wide || *per —*, in detail.
esteta *s.* aesthete.
estètica *sf.* aesthetics.
estètico *agg.* aesthetic.
estetismo *sm.* aestheticism.
èstimo *sm.* estimate.
estìnguere *vt.* **1.** to put (*v. irr.*) out **2.** (*saldare*) to extinguish || *— la propria sete*, to slake one's thirst. ♦ **estìnguersi** *vr.* (*finire*) to die.
estinguìbile *agg.* extinguishable.
estinto *agg.* **1.** extinct **2.** (*morto*) dead. ♦ **estinto** *sm.* deceased man.
estintore *sm.* extinguisher.
estinzione *sf.* **1.** extinction **2.** (*di sete*) quenching **3.** (*di debito*) paying off.
estirpare *vt.* **1.** to extirpate **2.** (*di denti*) to pull out.
estirpazione *sf.* **1.** extirpation **2.** (*di denti*) extraction.
estivo *agg.* summer (*attr.*).
estòrcere *vt.* to extort.
estorsione *sf.* extortion.
estradare *vt.* to extradite.
estradizione *sf.* extradition.
estràneo *agg.* extraneous, alien. ♦ **estràneo** *sm.* stranger.
estraniare *vt.* to estrange. ♦ **estraniarsi** *vr.* to get (*v. irr.*) estranged.
estrarre *vt.* to draw (*v. irr.*) out: *— a sorte*, to draw by lot.
estrattivo *agg.* extractive.
estratto *sm.* **1.** extract **2.** (*riassunto*) excerpt **3.** (*comm.*) *— conto*, statement of account.
estrattore *sm.* extractor.
estrazione *sf.* **1.** extraction **2.** (*di lotteria*) drawing.
estremamente *avv.* extremely.
estremismo *sm.* extremism.
estremista *s.* extremist: *— di destra*, extreme rightist; *— di sinistra*, extreme leftist.
estremità *sf.* extremity, end.
estremo *agg.* **1.** utmost **2.** (*eccessivo*) intense **3.** (*drastico*) drastic. ♦ **estremo** *sm.* extreme.
estrinsecare *vt.* to express. ♦ **estrinsecarsi** *vr.* to be expressed.
estrinsecazione *sf.* expression.
estrìnseco *agg.* extrinsic(al).
estro *sm.* **1.** inspiration **2.** (*capriccio*) whim.

estrométtere *vt.* to turn out.
estromissione *sf.* expulsion.
estroso *agg.* **1.** (*ispirato*) inspired **2.** freakish.
estroverso *agg.* extroverted.
estuario *sm.* estuary.
esuberante *agg.* exuberant.
esuberanza *sf.* exuberance.
esulare *vi.* **1.** to go (*v. irr.*) into exile **2.** (*fig.*) to be beyond.
esulcerare *vt.* to exulcerate.
esulcerazione *sf.* exulceration.
èsule *sm.* **1.** exile **2.** (*profugo*) refugee.
esultante *agg.* rejoicing.
esultanza *sf.* exultation.
esultare *vi.* to rejoice.
esumare *vt.* to exhume.
esumazione *sf.* exhumation.
età *sf.* age || *che — hai?*, how old are you?; *avere la stessa —*, to be the same age; *una persona di mezza —*, a middle-aged person.
ètere *sm.* ether.
etèreo *agg.* ethereal.
eternare *vt.* to make (*v. irr.*) eternal.
eternità *sf.* eternity.
eterno *agg.* eternal, everlasting.
eteròclito *agg.* **1.** heteroclite **2.** (*fig.*) irregular.
eterodossìa *sf.* heterodoxy.
eterodosso *agg.* heterodox.
eterogeneità *sf.* heterogeneity.
eterogèneo *agg.* heterogeneous.
ètica *sf.* ethics.
etichetta *sf.* **1.** label **2.** (*galateo*) etiquette.
etichettare *vt.* to stick (*v. irr.*) a label (on).
ètico *agg.* ethical.
etilene *sm.* ethylene.
etìlico *agg.* ethylic.
etilismo *sm.* alcoholism.
etimologìa *sf.* etymology.
etimològico *agg.* etymologic(al).
ètnico *agg.* ethnic(al).
etnografia *sf.* ethnography.
etnologìa *sf.* ethnology.
etnòlogo *sm.* ethnologist.
etrusco *agg. e sm.* Etruscan.
ettàgono *sm.* heptagon.
èttaro *sm.* hectare.
etto *sm.* hectogram.
ettòlitro *sm.* hectolitre.
ettòmetro *sm.* hectometre.
eucalipto *sm.* eucalyptus.
eucaristìa *sf.* Eucharist, Holy Communion.

eucarìstico *agg.* Eucharistic.
eufemismo *sm.* euphemism.
eufonìa *sf.* euphony.
eufònico *agg.* euphonic(al).
euforbia *sf.* Euphorbia.
eurforìa *sf.* euphoria.
eufòrico *agg.* euphoric.
eunuco *sm.* eunuch.
euritmìa *sf.* eurhythmy.
europeismo *sm.* Europeanism.
europeo *agg.* e *sm.* European.
eurovisione *sf.* Eurovision.
eutanasìa *sf.* euthanasia.
evacuare *vt.* to evacuate.
evacuazione *sf.* evacuation.
evàdere *vi.* to escape. ◆ **evàdere**
vt. (*burocratico*) **1.** to dispatch **2.**
(*eludere*) to evade.
evanescente *agg.* vanishing.
evangèlico *agg.* evangelic(al).
evangelista *sm.* evangelist.
evangelizzare *vt.* to evangelize.
evaporare *vi.* to evaporate.
evaporazione *sf.* evaporation.
evasione *sf.* **1.** escape **2.** (*comm.*)
dare — a una pratica, to dispatch
a business.
evasivo *agg.* evasive.
evaso *sm.* runaway.
evasore *sm.* evader: — *fiscale*, **tax**
evader.
evenienza *sf.* event, occurrence:
per ogni —, for any occasion.
evento *sm.* event.
eventuale *agg.* possible.
eventualità *sf.* eventuality.
eventualmente *avv.* in case.
evidente *agg.* evident, obvious,
clear.
evidenza *sf.* evidence.
evìncere *vt.* (*giur.*) to evict.
evirare *vt.* to evirate.
evitàbile *agg.* avoidable.
evitare *vt.* **1.** to avoid **2.** (*sfuggire*)
to escape.
evo *sm.* age: *il Medio Evo*, the
Middle Ages.
evocare *vt.* to evoke, to recall.
evocativo *agg.* evocative.
evocazione *sf.* evocation.
evolutivo *agg.* evolutive.
evoluto *agg.* well-developed, modern.
evoluzione *sf.* evolution.
evoluzionismo *sm.* evolutionism.
evòlvere *vt.* to evolve.
evviva *inter.* hurray.
ex libris *sm.* ex libris.
extra *agg.* extra.

extraterritoriale *agg.* extraterritorial.
eziologìa *sf.* aetiology.

F

fa¹ *sm.* (*mus.*) F.
fa² *avv.* ago: *un anno —*, a year ago.
fabbisogno *sm.* needs (*pl.*).
fàbbrica *sf.* **1.** factory ‖ *— di au-*
tomobili, motor works; *— di*
mattoni, brickyard; *— di carta,*
paper-mill; *capo —*, fore-man (*pl.*
-men); *marchio di —*, trade-mark
2. (*fabbricazione*) manufacture.
fabbricàbile *agg.* manufacturable ‖
area —, housing area.
fabbricante *sm.* manufacturer.
fabbricare *vt.* **1.** (*produrre*) to
manufacture **2.** (*costruire*) to build
(*v. irr.*) **3.** (*fare*) to make (*v. irr.*).
fabbricato *sm.* building ‖ *imposta*
sui fabbricati, house tax.
fabbricazione *sf.* **1.** manufacture,
make **2.** (*costruzione*) building.
fabbro *sm.* blacksmith.
fabbroferraio *sm.* blacksmith.
faccenda *sf.* matter; business (*solo*
sing.) ‖ *— di stato*, state affair
2. (*lavori domestici*) housework
(*solo sing.*).
faccendiere *sm.* busybody.
faccetta *sf.* little face **2.** (*geom.*)
facet.
facchinaggio *sm.* porterage.
facchino *sm.* porter.
faccia *sf.* **1.** face: *che — tosta!*,
what a face!; *a — a —*, face to face
2. (*aspetto*) look, expression **3.** (*la-*
to, superficie) face, side.
facciale *agg.* facial.
facciata *sf.* **1.** front, façade **2.** (*pa-*
gina) page.
face *sf.* torch.
faceto *agg.* facetious, witty.
facezia *sf.* witty remark, joke: *di-*
re delle facezie, to crack jokes.
fachiro *sm.* fakir.
fàcile *agg.* **1.** easy **2.** (*trattabile*)
docile **3.** (*pronto*) ready **4.** (*incli-*
ne) inclined **3.** (*probabile*) likely.
facilità *sf.* **1.** facility **2.** (*attitudi-*
ne) aptitude.
facilitare *vt.* to make (*v. irr.*)
easier

facilitazione *sf.* **1.** facilitation **2.** (*agevolazione*) facility.

facilone *sm.* slipshod fellow.

facinoroso *agg.* lawless. ♦ **facinoroso** *sm.* lawless man.

facoltà *sf.* faculty.

facoltativo *agg.* facultative: *fermata facoltativa*, request stop.

facoltoso *agg.* wealthy.

facondia *sf.* eloquence.

facondo *agg.* eloquent.

facsìmile *sm.* facsimile.

factotum *sm.* factotum.

faggeto *sm.* beech-wood.

faggio *sm.* beech.

fagiano *sm.* pheasant.

fagiolino *sm.* French bean.

fagiolo *sm.* bean.

fagocita, fagocito *sm.* phagocyte.

fagocitare *vt.* **1.** to phagocyte **2.** (*fig.*) to absorb.

fagocitosi *sf.* phagocytosis.

fagotto[1] *sm.* bundle.

fagotto[2] *sm.* (*mus.*) bassoon.

faina *sf.* beech-marten.

falange *sf.* phalanx (*pl.* -nges).

falcata *sf.* **1.** curvet **2.** (*di persona*) stride.

falce *sf.* **1.** sickle **2.** (*da fieno*) scythe **3.** (*di luna*) crescent.

falciare *vt.* **1.** to mow (*v. irr.*) **2.** (*fig.*) to mow down.

falciatore *sm.* mower.

falciatrice *sf.* mowing-machine.

falciatura *sf.* mowing.

falcidiare *vt.* to reduce.

falco *sm.* hawk: *avere occhi di —*, to be hawk-eyed.

falconerìa *sf.* falconry.

falconiere *sm.* hawker.

falda *sf.* **1.** (*strato*) stratum (*pl.* -ta) **2.** (*di neve*) flake **3.** (*di cappello*) brim **4.** (*di monte*) slope.

falegname *sm.* joiner.

falegnamerìa *sf.* **1.** joinery **2.** (*bottega*) joiner's shop.

falena *sf.* moth.

falla *sf.* leak.

fallace *agg.* false, disappointing.

fallacia *sf.* fallacy.

fallìbile *agg.* liable to make mistakes.

fàllico *agg.* phallic.

fallimentare *agg.* bankruptcy.

fallimento *sm.* **1.** bankruptcy **2.** (*fig.*) failure.

fallire *vi.* **1.** to fail **2.** (*comm.*) to go (*v. irr.*) bankrupt **3.** (*fam.*) to go under.

fallito *agg.* **1.** (*comm.*) bankrupt **2.** (*fig.*) unsuccessful. ♦ **fallito** *sm.* **1.** (*comm.*) bankrupt **2.** (*fig.*) failure.

fallo *sm.* **1.** fault: *senza —*, without fail **2.** (*anat.*) phallus (*pl.* -li).

falò *sm.* bonfire.

falpalà *sm.* furbelow.

falsare *vt.* **1.** to misrepresent **2.** (*falsificare*) to falsify.

falsariga *sf.* **1.** ruling paper **2.** (*fig.*) pattern, model.

falsario *sm.* **1.** forger **2.** (*di monete*) coiner.

falsetto *sm.* falsetto.

falsificàbile *agg.* falsifiable.

falsificare *vt.* to falsify, to counterfeit.

falsificatore *sm.* **1.** falsifier **2.** (*di monete*) coiner.

falsificazione *sf.* falsification, forgery.

falsità *sf.* **1.** falseness **2.** (*menzogna*) falsehood **3.** (*ipocrisia*) insincerity.

falso *agg.* **1.** false **2.** (*falsificato*) forged.

fama *sf.* fame, renown, reputation: *acquistarsi —*, to win (*v. irr.*) fame; *avere cattiva —*, to have a bad reputation.

fame *sf.* **1.** hunger: *avere —*, to be hungry: *far morire di —*, to starve **2.** (*carestia*) famine.

famèlico *agg.* ravenous.

famigerato *agg.* ill-famed.

famiglia *sf.* family.

familiare *agg.* **1.** domestic, homely **2.** (*intimo, anche fig.*) familiar **3.** (*senza cerimonie*) informal. ♦ **familiare** *sm.* relative.

familiarità *sf.* familiarity: *avere — con qu.*, to be familiar with so.

famoso *agg.* famous, celebrated.

fanale *sm.* **1.** lamp **2.** (*auto*) light: *— anteriore*, head-light; *— di coda*, (*aer.*) tail light, (*auto*) rear lamp; *— di posizione*, parking lights (*pl.*).

fanàtico *agg.* fanatical. ♦ **fanàtico** *sm.* **1.** fanatic **2.** (*fam.*) fan.

fanatismo *sm.* fanaticism.

fanatizzare *vt.* to fanaticize.

fanciulla *sf.* young girl.

fanciullàggine *sf.* **1.** childishness **2.** (*azione infantile*) childish action.

fanciullesco *agg.* childish.

fanciullezza *sf.* childhood.

fanciullo *sm.* young boy, child (*pl.* children).

fandonia *sf.* lie.

fanello *sm.* linnet.

fanfara *sf.* 1. brass band 2. (*suono di trombe*) fanfare.

fanfaronata *sf.* boasting.

fanfarone *sm.* boaster.

fangaia *sf.* muddy road.

fanghiglia *sf.* slush.

fango *sm.* 1. mud: *gettare del —*
addosso a qu., to throw (*v. irr.*) mud at so.; *cadere nel —*, to fall (*v. irr.*) very low 2. (*med.*) mud-baths (*pl.*).

fangoso *agg.* muddy.

fannullone *sm.* idler.

fanone *sm.* whalebone.

fantaccino *sm.* foot-soldier.

fantascienza *sf.* science fiction.

fantasìa *sf.* 1. imagination, fancy 2. (*inventiva*) inventiveness 3. (*articoli fantasia*) fancy goods.

fantasioso *agg.* fanciful.

fantasma *sm.* ghost.

fantasmagorìa *sf.* phantasmagoria.

fantasmagòrico *agg.* phantasmagoric.

fantasticare *vt.* to daydream.

fantasticherìa *sf.* daydream.

fantàstico *agg.* 1. fanciful 2. (*bizzarro*) queer 3. (*fam.*) extraordinary.

fante *sm.* 1. infantryman (*pl.* -men) 2. (*delle carte*) knave, jack.

fanterìa *sf.* infantry.

fantesca *sf.* maid-servant.

fantino *sm.* jockey.

fantoccio *sm.* puppet (*anche fig.*).

fantomàtico *agg.* mysterious.

farabutto *sm.* blackguard.

faraona *sf.* guinea-hen.

faraone *sm.* Pharaoh.

farcire *vt.* to stuff.

farcito *agg.* stuffed.

fardello *sm.* 1. bundle 2. (*fig.*) burden.

fare *vt.* 1. (*in senso generale*) to do (*v. irr.*): *cosa fai?*, what are you doing?; *ecco fatto!*, that's done!; *— del proprio meglio*, to do one's best; 2. (*fabbricare, produrre*) to make (*v. irr.*): *— amicizia*, to make friends; *— un errore*, to make a mistake; *— in fretta*, to make haste 3. (*essere, esercitare una professione*) to be: *faccio l'insegnante*, I am a teacher 4. (*reputare*) to think (*v. irr.*): *la facevo*

più intelligente, I thought she was more intelligent 5. (*segnare le ore*): *che ora fa il tuo orologio?*, what time is it by your watch? 6. (*praticare*) to go (*v. irr.*) in for || *— le carte*, to shuffle; *— fagotto*, to pack up; *— una passeggiata*, to go for a walk; *— colazione*, to have breakfast; *— bella, brutta figura*, to cut (*v. irr.*) a fine, a poor figure; *— compassione*, to rouse compassion; *— aspettare qu.*, to keep (*v. irr.*) so. waiting; *— avere, sapere, vedere a qu.*, to let (*v. irr.*) so. have, know, see. ♦

fare *vi.* 1. (*di condizioni atmosferiche*): *che tempo fa?*, what is the weather like? 2. (*far caldo, freddo*) to be hot, cold 3. (*essere adatto*) to suit. ♦ **farsi** *vr.* to become (*v. irr.*), to grow (*v. irr.*) || *— animo*, to take (*v. irr.*) courage.

fare *sm.* manners (*pl*).

faretra *sf.* quiver.

farfalla *sf.* butterfly.

farfugliare *vt.* to mumble.

farina *sf.* meal, flour.

farinàceo *agg.* farinaceous.

faringe *sf.* pharynx (*pl.* -nges)

faringite *sf.* pharyngitis.

farinoso *agg.* mealy, floury.

fariseo *agg.* e *sm.* Pharisee.

farmacèutico *agg.* pharmaceutic.

farmacìa *sf.* 1. pharmacy 2. (*negozio*) chemist's shop.

farmacista *sm.* chemist.

fàrmaco *sm.* medicine, remedy (*anche fig.*).

farmacologìa *sf.* pharmacology.

farmacopea *sf.* pharmacopoeia.

farneticare *vi.* to rave.

faro *sm.* 1. lighthouse 2. (*auto*) headlight.

farràgine *sf.* medley, mixture.

farraginoso *agg.* confused.

farsa *sf.* farce.

farsesco *agg.* farcical.

fascetta *sf.* 1. small band 2. (*med.*) bandage 3. (*edit.*) wrapper.

fascia *sf.* 1. band 2. (*med.*) bandage 3. (*dei bambini*) swaddling-band.

fasciame *sm.* planking.

fasciare *vt.* 1. to bind (*v. irr.*) (up) 2. (*dei neonati*) to swaddle.

fasciatura *sf.* 1. dressing 2. (*di neonato*) swaddling.

fascìcolo *sm.* booklet.

fascina *sf.* faggot.

fàscino *sm.* charm, fascination.
fascio *sm.* 1. bundle 2. (*geom.*) sheaf 3. (*di luce*) beam.
fascismo *sm.* Fascism.
fascista *agg. e s.* Fascist.
fase *sf.* 1. stage 2. (*elettr.*) phase 3. (*auto*) stroke.
fastello *sm.* faggot.
fastidio *sm.* 1. trouble: *dare — a qu.*, to give (*v. irr.*) so. trouble 2. (*contrarietà*) annoyance.
fastidioso *agg.* tiresome.
fastigio *sm.* 1. pediment 2. (*fig.*) height.
fasto *sm.* pomp.
fastosità *sf.* pomp, splendour.
fastoso *agg.* magnificent.
fasullo *agg.* false.
fata *sf.* fairy.
fatale *agg.* fatal, inevitable.
fatalismo *sm.* fatalism.
fatalista *agg. e s.* fatalist.
fatalità *sf.* fatality.
fatica *sf.* weariness, fatigue.
faticare *vi.* to toil, to work hard.
faticata *sf.* drudgery.
faticoso *agg.* hard, tiring.
fatìdico *agg.* fatidical.
fato *sm.* 1. fate, destiny 2. (*sorte*) lot.
fatta *sf.* kind, sort.
fattìbile *agg.* practicable.
fattispecie *sf.* case in point: *nella —*, in this case.
fattivo *agg.* 1. effective 2. (*attivo*) busy.
fatto *sm.* 1. fact 2. (*azione*) deed 3. (*avvenimento*) event ‖ *sapere il — proprio*, to know (*v. irr.*) one's business; *venire al` —*, to go (*v. irr.*) to the point; *in — di*, as regards.
fattore *sm.* 1. factor 2. (*agr.*) farmer.
fattorìa *sf.* farm.
fattorino *sm.* errand-boy.
fattucchiere *sm.* wizard.
fattura *sf.* 1. making 2. (*lavorazione*) work 3. (*comm.*) invoice 4. (*stregoneria*) sorcery.
fatturare *vt.* 1. to adulterate 2. (*comm.*) to invoice.
fatturazione *sf.* (*comm.*) invoicing.
fatuità *sf.* fatuity.
fatuo *agg.* 1. fatuous 2. (*vanitoso*) vain ‖ *fuoco —*, will-o'-the-visp.
fàuci *sf. pl.* 1. jaws 2. (*di persona*) throat (*sing.*).
fàuna *sf.* fauna.

fàuno *sm.* faun.
fàusto *agg.* propitious.
fautore *sm.* supporter.
fava *sf.* broad bean ‖ *pigliare due piccioni con una —*, to kill two birds with one stone.
favella *sf.* speech.
favellare *vi.* to speak (*v. irr.*).
favilla *sf.* spark (*anche fig.*).
favo *sm.* 1. honeycomb 2. (*med.*) favus.
fàvola *sf.* 1. fable 2. (*frottola*) idle story 3. (*oggetto di pettegolezzo*) byword.
favoloso *agg.* fabulous.
favore *sm.* favour.
favoreggiamento *sm.* favouring.
favoreggiare *vt.* to favour.
favoreggiatore *sm.* abettor.
favorévole *agg.* favourable.
favorire *vt.* 1. to favour 2. (*aiutare*) to help 3. (*promuovere*) to foster.
favoritismo *sm.* favouritism.
favorito *agg. e sm.* favourite.
fazione *sf.* faction.
fazioso *agg.* factious.
fazzoletto *sm.* 1. handkerchief 2. (*da collo*) neckerchief.
febbraio *sm.* February.
febbre *sf.* fever.
febbricitante *agg.* feverish.
febbrìfugo *agg.* febrifugal. ♦ **febbrìfugo** *sm.* febrifuge.
febbrile *agg.* feverish.
fecale *agg.* fecal.
feccia *sf.* dregs (*pl.*) (*anche fig.*).
feci *sf. pl.* excrement (*sing.*).
fècola *sf.* starch.
fecondare *vt.* to fecundate.
fecondazione *sf.* fecundation.
fecondità *sf.* fecundity.
fecondo *agg.* fecund.
fede *sf.* 1. faith, belief 2. (*fiducia*) trust.
fedele *agg.* faithful.
fedeltà *sf.* fidelity.
fèdera *sf.* pillow-case.
federale *agg.* federal.
federalismo *sm.* federalism.
federativo *agg.* federative.
federato *agg.* federate.
federazione *sf.* federation.
fedìfrago *sm.* traitor.
fedina *sf.* criminal record.
fégato *sm.* 1. liver 2. (*fig.*) courage.
fegatoso *agg.* 1. bilious 2. (*fig.*) irritable.
felce *sf.* fern.
feldspato *sm.* felspar.

felice *agg.* 1. happy 2. (*fortunato*) lucky 3. (*piacevole*) pleasant.
felicità *sf.* happiness.
felicitarsi *vr.* to congratulate (so. on sthg.).
felicitazioni *sf. pl.* congratulation (*sing.*).
felino *agg.* e *sm.* feline.
fellone *sm.* villain, traitor.
fellonìa *sf.* felony, treason.
felpato *agg.* 1. plushy 2. (*fig.*) soft || *a passi felpati*, stealthily.
feltro *sm.* felt.
feluca *sf.* 1. (*mar.*) felucca 2. (*cappello*) cocked hat.
fémmina *sf.* female || *mala —*, bad woman.
femminile *agg.* 1. female 2. (*da donna*) feminine.
femminilità *sf.* womanliness.
femminismo *sm.* feminism.
femminuccia *sf.* 1. simple woman 2. (*uomo senza coraggio*) coward.
fèmore *sm.* thigh-bone.
fendente *sm.* cutting blow.
fèndere *vt.* to rend (*v. irr.*).
fenditura *sf.* cleft, fissure.
fenice *sf.* phoenix.
fènico *agg.* phenic.
fenolo *sm.* phenol.
fenomenale *agg.* phenomenal.
fenomenismo *sm.* phenomenalism.
fenòmeno *sm* phenomenon (*pl.* -na).
fenomenologìa *sf.* phenomenology.
ferace *agg.* fruitful, rich (*anche fig.*).
ferale *agg.* feral, deadly.
fèretro *sm.* coffin.
ferie *sf. pl.* holidays.
feriale *agg.* working: *giorno —*, working-day.
ferimento *sm.* wounding.
ferino *agg.* ferine, wild.
ferire *vt.* to wound, to hurt (*v. irr.*).
ferita *sf.* wound (*anche fig.*).
ferito *agg.* wounded, injured.
feritoia *sf.* loophole.
ferma *sf.* 1. (*mil.*) service 2. (*caccia*) pointing.
fermacarte *sm.* paper-weight.
fermaglio *sm.* 1. clasp 2. (*per gioielli*) brooch 3. (*per carte*) clip.
fermare *vt.* 1. to stop, to arrest 2. (*fissare*) to fix (*anche fig.*) 3. (*giur.*) to hold (*v. irr.*). ◆ **fermarsi** *vr.* 1. to stop 2. (*soggiornare*) to stay 3. (*fare una pausa*) to pause.

fermata *sf.* 1. stop 2. (*pausa*) pause.
fermentare *vi.* to ferment (*anche fig.*).
fermentazione *sf.* fermentation.
fermento *sm.* 1. ferment 2. (*fig.*) turmoil, ferment.
fermezza *sf.* firmness, strength.
fermo *agg.* 1. still 2. (*irremovibile*) steady, firm || *mano ferma*, firm hand; *volontà ferma*, unfaltering will. ◆ **fermo** *sm.* 1. (*mecc.*) lock, catch, stop 2. (*giur.*) provisional arrest.
fermoposta *sm.* poste-restante.
feroce *agg.* fierce, cruel.
ferocia *sf.* fierceness.
ferraglia *sf.* scrap-iron.
ferragosto *sm.* 1. August holiday 2. (*in Inghilterra*) August Bank holiday.
ferraio *sm.* blacksmith.
ferramenta *sf. pl.* hardware (*sing.*).
ferramento *sm.* iron tool.
ferrare *vt.* 1. to fit with iron 2. (*di cavalli*) to shoe.
ferrato *agg.* 1. ironshod 2. (*di scarpe*) hobnailed 3. (*strada ferrata*) railway 4. (*fig.*) well read.
ferratura *sf.* shoeing.
fèrreo *agg.* iron (*attr.*).
ferriera *sf.* iron-foundry.
ferro *sm.* iron: — *battuto*, wrought iron; — *da stiro*, flat-iron; — *da calza*, knitting needle || *i ferri del mestiere*, the tools of the trade; *tocca —!*, touch wood!
ferroso *agg.* ferrous.
ferrovìa *sf.* railway.
ferroviario *agg.* railway (*attr.*).
ferroviere *sm.* railwayman (*pl.* -men).
ferruginoso *agg.* ferruginous.
fèrtile *agg.* fertile (*anche fig.*).
fertilità *sf.* fertility.
fertilizzante *agg.* fertilizing. ◆ **fertilizzante** *sm.* fertilizer.
fertilizzare *vt.* to fertilize.
fèrula *sf.* rod.
fervente *agg.* burning, ardent (*anche fig.*).
fèrvido *agg.* fervid, ardent || *fervidi auguri*, best wishes.
fervore *sm.* fervour, heat.
fessura *sf.* 1. crack 2. (*per liquidi*) leak.
festa *sf.* 1. (*giorno di riposo*) holiday 2. (*religiosa*) feast 3. (*anniversario*) birthday 4. (*onomasti-*

co) Saint's day **5.** (*banchetto, ballo*) feast, ball || *giorno di* —, festal day.

festaiolo *sm.* reveller.

festante *agg.* rejoicing.

festeggiamento *sm.* celebration.

festeggiare *vt.* **1.** to celebrate **2.** (*accogliere festosamente*) to give (*v. irr.*) a hearty welcome.

festévole *agg.* festive.

festino *sm.* feast.

fèstival *sm.* festival.

festività *sf.* festivity.

festivo *agg.* **1.** festive **2.** (*domenicale*) Sunday (*attr.*).

festone *sm.* festoon.

festoso *agg.* joyous.

festuca *sf.* straw.

feticcio *sm.* fetish.

feticismo *sm.* fetishism.

feticista *s.* fetishist.

fètido *agg.* foetid, foul.

feto *sm.* foetus.

fetore *sm.* stink.

fetta *sf.* **1.** slice **2.** (*piccolo pezzo*) piece.

fettuccia *sf.* tape.

feudale *agg.* feudal.

feudalésimo *sm.* feudalism.

feudatario *sm.* feudatory.

fèudo *sm.* feud.

fiaba *sf.* **1.** fable **2.** (*falsità*) falsehood.

fiabesco *agg.* fairy-like.

fiacca *sf.* weariness || *battere la* — (*fam.*), to be sluggish.

fiaccare *vt.* to exhaust. ♦ **fiaccarsi** *vr.* to break (*v. irr.*) down.

fiacchezza *sf.* weakness, weariness.

fiacco *agg.* weak, exhausted.

fiàccola *sf.* torch.

fiaccolata *sf.* torchlight procession.

fiala *sf.* phial.

fiamma *sf.* **1.** flame **2.** (*molto viva*) blaze.

fiammante *agg.* **1.** flaming **2.** (*fig.*) bright || *nuovo* —, brand-new.

fiammata *sf.* blaze.

fiammeggiante *agg.* blazing, burning.

fiammeggiare *vi.* to blaze, to flame, to burn.

fiammìfero *sm.* match: *accendere un* —, to strike (*v. irr.*) a match.

fiammingo *agg.* Flemish. ♦ **fiammingo** *sm.* Fleming.

fiancata *sf.* **1.** side **2.** (*mar.*) broadside.

fiancheggiare *vt.* **1.** to flank **2.** (*fig.*) to support.

fiancheggiatore *sm.* flanker, supporter.

fianco *sm.* **1.** hip, side (*anche fig.*) **2.** (*di animali; mil.*) flank.

fiasca *sf.* flask.

fiasco *sm.* flask || *fare* —, to fail utterly.

fiatare *vi.* to breathe: *senza* —, without speaking.

fiato *sm.* breath.

fibbia *sf.* buckle.

fibra *sf.* **1.** fibre **2.** (*costituzione*) constitution.

fibroma *sm.* fibroma (*pl.* -ata).

fibroso *agg.* fibrous.

fibula *sf.* **1.** fibula **2.** (*med.*) splint-bone.

ficcanaso *sm.* meddler.

ficcare *vt.* to thrust (*v. irr.*); to drive (*v. irr.*) (in). ♦ **ficcarsi** *vr.* to interfere || — *in testa qc.*, to get (*v. irr.*) sthg. into one's head.

fico *sm.* fig.

fidanzamento *sm.* engagement.

fidanzare *vt.* to engage. ♦ **fidanzarsi** *vr.* to become (*v. irr.*) engaged (to so.).

fidanzata *sf.* fiancée.

fidanzato *sm.* fiancé.

fidare *vi.* to trust. ♦ **fidarsi** *vr.* to trust (upon so., sthg.).

fidato *agg.* reliable.

fideiussione *sf.* suretyship.

fidente *agg.* confiding.

fido *agg.* faithful. ♦ **fido** *sm.* **1.** devoted follower **2.** (*comm.*) credit.

fiducia *sf.* trust, confidence: — *in se stessi*, self-confidence.

fiduciario *agg.* fiduciary. ♦ **fiduciario** *sm.* fiduciary, trustee.

fiducioso *agg.* trusting, hopeful.

fiele *sm.* **1.** gall **2.** (*fig.*) hatred.

fienagione *sf.* haymaking.

fienile *sm.* hay-loft.

fieno *sm.* hay: *asma da* —, hay-asthma.

fiera *sf.* **1.** fair **2.** (*esposizione*) exhibition || — *campionaria*, samples fair.

fierezza *sf.* fierceness.

fiero *agg.* proud.

fièvole *agg.* **1.** feeble **2.** (*di luce, suono*) dim.

figgere *vt.* to fix.

figlia *sf.* daughter.

figliare *vt.* to bring (*v. irr.*) forth.

figliastra *sf.* step-daughter.
figliastro *sm.* step-son.
figlio *sm.* son.
figlioccia *sf.* goddaughter.
figlioccio *sm.* godson.
figliolanza *sf.* children (*pl.*), family.
figliolo *sm.* son.
figura *sf.* 1. figure 2. (*illustrazione*) illustration, picture 3. (*personaggio di romanzi, opere teatrali ecc.*) character || *fare una bella, brutta* —, to cut (*v. irr.*) a fine, poor figure.
figurare *vt.* 1. to represent 2. (*far figura*) to look smart 3. (*apparire*) to appear.
figurativo *agg.* figurative.
figurato *agg.* 1. (*illustrato*) illustrated 2. (*di linguaggio, senso*) figurative.
figurazione *sf.* figuration.
figurinista *s.* dress-designer.
figurino *sm.* fashion-plate.
figuro *sm.* scoundrel.
fila *sf.* 1. row, file 2. (*coda*) queue: *fare la* —, to queue (up).
filaccia *sf.* lint.
filamento *sm.* filament.
filamentoso *agg.* filamentous.
filanda *sf.* spinning-mill.
filandaia *sf.* spinner.
filante *agg.*: *stella* — 1. (*astr.*) falling-star 2. (*di carta*) (paper) streamer.
filantropìa *sf.* philanthropy.
filàntropo *sm.* philanthrope.
filare[1] *vt.* 1. to spin (*v. irr.*) 2. (*correre*) to run (*v. irr.*) 3. (*amoreggiare*) to flirt.
filare[2] *sm.* row, line.
filarmònico *agg.* e *sm.* philharmonic.
filastrocca *sf.* nursery rhyme.
filatelìa *sf.* stamp-collecting.
filatèlico *agg.* philatelic. ◆ **filatèlico** *sm.* philatelist.
filato *agg.* 1. spun 2. (*di seguito*) running.
filatura *sf.* spinning.
filettare *vt.* (*mecc.*) to thread.
filettatura *sf.* (*mecc.*) threading.
filetto *sm.* 1. (*filo sottile*) thin thread 2. (*mecc.*) thread || — *della lingua*, fraenum.
filiale *agg.* filial. ◆ **filiale** *sf.* branch house.
filiazione *sf.* filiation.
filibustiere *sm.* 1. filibuster 2. (*fig.*) adventurer, rascal.

filiera *sf.* 1. (*mecc.*) screw cutting die 2. (*ind. tess.*) spinneret.
filiforme *agg.* threadlike.
filigrana *sf.* 1. filigree 2. (*di carta*) watermark.
filìppica *sf.* philippic.
fillòssera *sf.* phylloxera.
film *sm.* picture || *girare un* —, to shoot (*v. irr.*) a picture.
filmare *vt.* to film.
filo *sm.* 1. thread 2. (*ind. tessile*) yarn 3. (*tec.*) wire || *un — d'acqua*, a fine stream of water; *un — d'aria*, a breath of air.
filobus *sm.* trolley-bus.
filologìa *sf.* philology.
filòlogo *sm.* philologist.
filone *sm.* 1. (*di pane*) long loaf 2. (*min.*) vein.
filosofare *vi.* to philosophize.
filosofia *sf.* philosophy.
filòsofo *sm.* philosopher.
filovìa *sf.* trolley-bus line.
filtrare *vt.* to filter, to strain.
filtro *sm.* 1. filter 2. (*colino*) strainer.
filza *sf.* 1. string 2. (*fig.*) series (*pl.*) 3. (*cucito*) running stitch.
finale *agg.* last, final.
finalità *sf.* aim, end.
finalmente *avv.* 1. at last 2. (*in conclusione*) finally.
finanche *avv.* even.
finanza *sf.* finance.
finanziamento *sm.* financing.
finanziare *vt.* to finance.
finanziario *agg.* financial.
finanziatore *sm.* financing capitalist.
finanziere *sm.* financier.
finché *cong.* 1. till, until 2. (*per tutto il tempo che*) as long as.
fine[1] *sf.* end || *alla fin* —, after all. ◆ **fine** *sm.* (*scopo*) purpose.
fine[2] *agg.* fine, thin.
finestra *sf.* window.
finestrino *sm.* window.
finezza *sf.* 1. thinness 2. (*acume*) subtlety 3. (*raffinatezza*) refinement 4. (*gentilezza*) kindness.
fingere *vi.* to pretend. ◆ **fingersi** *vr.* to feign oneself.
finimenti *sm. pl.* harness (*sing.*).
finimondo *sm.* 1. end of the world 2. (*fig.*) catastrophe.
finire *vi.* 1. to finish, to end 2. (*interrompersi*) to stop || — *con*, to end by: *finii con l'andare*, I ended by going.
finitezza *sf.* perfection.

finìtimo *agg.* bordering.

finito *agg.* 1. finished, ended 2. (*rovinato*) done for.

finitura *sf.* finishing.

fino *prep.* 1. (*di tempo*) till, until, up to: — *a dicembre*, till December 2. (*di spazio*) as far as: *andammo fino a Roma*, we went as far as Rome 3. (*fino da*) from 4. (*a partire da*) since.

finocchio *sm.* fennel.

finora *avv.* till now, so far.

finta *sf.* 1. sham 2. (*scherma*) feint.

fintantoché *avv.* V. *finché*.

finto *agg.* false.

finzione *sf.* pretence, duplicity.

fio *sm.* penalty: *pagare il —*, to pay (*v. irr.*) the penalty (of).

fioccare *vi.* 1. to snow 2. (*fig.*) to shower.

fiocco *sm.* 1. ribbon 2. (*di lana*) staple 3. (*falda*) flake 4. (*di neve*) snowflake.

fiòcina *sf.* harpoon.

fioco *agg.* 1. (*rauco*) hoarse 2. (*debole*) weak 3. (*di luce*) dim 4. (*di voce*) faint.

fionda *sf.* sling.

fioraio *sm.* florist.

fiorame *sm.* floral design.

fiordaliso *sm.* bluebottle.

fiordo *sm.* fjord.

fiore *sm.* 1. flower 2. (*fioritura*) bloom: *essere in —* (*anche fig.*), to be in bloom 3. (*parte scelta*) the best part 4. (*nelle carte*) clubs (*pl.*).

fiorente *agg.* 1. blooming 2. (*fig.*) flourishing.

fioretto *sm.* 1. little flower 2. (*relig.*) act of mortification 3. (*scherma*) foil.

fioricultore *sm.* floriculturist.

fiorino *sm.* florin.

fiorire *vi.* 1. to flower, to bloom, to blossom 2. (*fig.*) to flourish.

fiorista *s.* florist.

fiorito *agg.* 1. flowery 2. (*in fiore*) in bloom.

fioritura *sf.* 1. flowering 2. (*fig.*) flourishing.

fiotto *sm.* wave, stream: *a fiotti*, in streams.

firma *sf.* signature.

firmamento *sm.* firmament.

firmare *vt.* to sign.

firmatario *sm.* 1. signatory 2. (*comm.*) signer.

fisarmònica *sf.* accordion.

fisarmonicista *s.* accordionist.

fiscale *agg.* 1. fiscal 2. (*inquisitorio*) strict.

fiscalismo *sm.* rigorism.

fischiare *vi.* 1. to whistle 2. (*di segnale acustico*) to hoot 3. (*di serpente; per disapprovare*) to hiss 4. (*nelle orecchie*) to buzz 5. (*di proiettili*) to whiz.

fischiata *sf.* 1. whistling 2. (*di disapprovazione*) hissing.

fischiettare *vt.* to whistle softly.

fischietto *sm.* whistle.

fischio *sm.* 1. whistle 2. (*di serpente; di disapprovazione*) hiss 3. (*segnali acustici*) hoot 4. (*nelle orecchie*) buzzing.

fisco *sm.* public treasury.

fisica *sf.* physics.

fisico *agg.* physical, bodily. ♦ **fisico** *sm.* 1. (*scienziato*) physicist 2. (*costituzione*) physique.

fisima *sf.* caprice, whim.

fisiologia *sf.* physiology.

fisiològico *agg.* physiologic(al).

fisiòlogo *sm.* physiologist.

fisionomìa *sf.* 1. features (*pl.*) 2. (*carattere*) character.

fisionomista *sm.* physiognomist.

fisioterapìa *sf.* physiotherapy.

fissaggio *sm.* fixing.

fissare *vt.* 1. to fix 2. (*guardare fisso*) to gaze 3. (*prenotare*) to book. ♦ **fissarsi** *vr.* 1. to be fixed 2. (*stabilirsi*) to settle down.

fissato *agg.* 1. fixed 2. (*fam.*) obsessed.

fissatore *sm.* 1. fixer 2. (*foto*) fixing bath.

fissazione *sf.* fixed idea.

fissione *sf.* fission.

fissità *sf.* fixity.

fisso *agg.* fixed.

fìstola *sf.* 1. Pan-pipe 2. (*patol.*) fistula.

fitologìa *sf.* phytology.

fitta *sf.* stitch.

fittàvolo *sm.* tenant farmer.

fittizio *agg.* fictitious.

fitto[1] *agg.* 1. (*conficcato*) driven in 2. (*denso*) thick.

fitto[2] *sm.* rent.

fiumana *sf.* 1. broad stream 2. (*fig.*) crowd, stream.

fiume *sm.* 1. river 2. (*fig.*) flood.

fiutare *vt.* 1. to smell (*v. irr.*) 2. (*fig.*) to guess.

fiuto *sm.* 1. scent, smell 2. (*fig.*) intuition.

flàccido *agg.* flabby.

flacone *sm.* vial.

flagellare *vt.* 1. to flagellate 2. (*fig.*) to scourge.

flagellazione *sf.* flagellation.

flagello *sm.* 1. scourge, whip 2. (*fig.*) scourge, plague.

flagrante *agg.* flagrant || *cogliere qu. in* —, to catch (*v. irr.*) so. in the open act.

flagranza *sf.* flagrancy.

flanella *sf.* flannel.

flato *sm.* flatus.

flatulenza *sf.* flatulence.

flautato *agg.* fluted.

flautista *sm.* flute-player.

flàuto *sm.* flute.

flèbile *agg.* plaintive, feeble.

flebite *sf.* phlebitis.

fleboclisi *sf.* phleboclysis.

flebòtomo *sm.* phlebotomist.

flemma *sf.* coolness, phlegm.

flemmàtico *agg.* phlegmatic.

flèmmone *sm.* phlegmon.

flessìbile *agg.* flexible, pliant (*anche fig.*).

flessibilità *sf.* flexibility.

flessione *sf.* flexion, bending.

flessuosità *sf.* 1. flexuosity 2. (*di corpo*) suppleness.

flessuoso *agg.* 1. flexuous 2. (*di corpo*) supple.

flèttere *vt.* to bend (*v. irr.*).

flirtare *vi.* to flirt.

flogìstico *agg.* (*med.*) phlogistic.

flora *sf.* flora.

floreale *agg.* floral.

floricoltore *sm.* floriculturist.

floricoltura *sf.* floriculture.

floridezza *sf.* prosperity.

flòrido *agg.* 1. prosperous 2. (*fig.*) buxom 3. (*di colorito*) ruddy.

florilegio *sm.* florilegium (*pl.* -ia).

floscio *agg.* flabby.

flotta *sf.* fleet: — *metropolitana* (*in Gran Bretagna*), the Home Fleet.

flottante *agg.* floating.

flottiglia *sf.* flotilla.

fluente *agg.* fluent (*anche fig.*).

fluidità *sf.* fluency.

flùido *agg.* e *sm.* fluid.

fluire *vi.* to flow.

fluorescente *agg.* fluorescent.

fluorescenza *sf.* 1. (*fig.*) fluorescence 2. (*elettr.*) glow.

fluorìdrico *agg.* hydrofluoric.

fluorite *sf.* fluorite.

fluoro *sm.* fluorine.

fluoruro *sm.* fluoride.

flussione *sf.* fluxion.

flusso *sm.* 1. (*di marea*) flood(-tide) 2. (*fig.*) flux.

flutto *sm.* wave.

fluttuante *agg.* 1. fluctuating, floating 2. (*incerto*) irresolute.

fluttuare *vi.* to fluctuate, to waver.

fluttuazione *sf.* fluctuation.

fluviale *agg.* river (*attr.*).

fobìa *sf.* phobia, aversion.

foca *sf.* seal.

focaccia *sf.* cake || *rendere pan per* —, to give (*v. irr.*) tit for tat.

focaia *sf. pietra* —, flint.

focale *agg.* focal.

foce *sf.* mouth.

focolaio *sm.* centre of infection.

focolare *sm.* 1. hearth 2. (*caminetto*) fireplace 3. (*fig.*) home.

focoso *agg.* hot, fiery.

fòdera *sf.* lining.

foderare *vt.* to line.

fòdero *sm.* scabbard, sheath.

foga *sf.* impetuosity.

foggia *sf.* 1. (*moda*) fashion 2. (*maniera*) way 3. (*forma*) shape.

foggiare *vt.* to shape.

foglia *sf.* leaf (*pl.* leaves) || *mangiare la* —, to take (*v. irr.*) the hint.

fogliame *sm.* foliage, leafage.

foglio *sm.* sheet.

fogna *sf.* sewer.

fognatura *sf.* sewage.

foia *sf.* lust.

fola *sf.* 1. fable 2. (*fandonia*) fib.

folata *sf.* (*di vento*) gust.

folclore *sm.* folklore.

folcloristico *agg.* folkloristic.

folgorante *agg.* flashing, dazzling.

folgorare *vt.* to strike (*v. irr.*) with lightning.

folgorazione *sf.* 1. (*elettr.*) electrocution 2. (*fig.*) fulmination.

fòlgore *sf.* thunderbolt.

folla *sf.* crowd.

folle *agg.* 1. mad 2. (*mecc.*) idle 3. (*auto*) neutral.

folleggiare *vi.* 1. to behave foolishly 2. (*divertirsi*) to make (*v. irr.*) merry.

folletto *sm.* 1. imp 2. (*ragazzo*) restless child.

follìa *sf.* madness || *amare qu. alla* —, to be madly in love with so.

folto *agg.* thick. ◆ folto *sm.* thick.

fomentare *vt.* to foster.

fomentatore *sm.* fomenter.

fomento *sm.* fomentation.

fonda sf. anchorage || *nave alla —*, ship at anchor.

fòndaco sm. draper's shop.

fondale sm. **1.** (*teat.*) background **2.** (*mar.*) depth.

fondamentale agg. fundamental.

fondamento sm. **1.** foundation: *gettare le fondamenta*, to lay (v. irr.) the foundation **2.** (*fig.*) basis, ground.

fondare vt. to found. ♦ **fondarsi** vr. to base oneself on.

fondatezza sf. foundation, ground.

fondato agg. well-grounded.

fondatore sm. founder.

fondazione sf. **1.** foundation **2.** (*istituzione*) institution.

fòndere vt. **1.** to melt **2.** (*fondere in forma*) to cast (v. irr.) **3.** (*unire*) to blend.

fonderìa sf. foundry.

fondiario agg. land (*attr.*).

fondista sm. long-distance runner.

fonditore sm. melter, caster.

fonditura sf. **1.** melting **2.** (*colata*) casting.

fondo agg. deep. ♦ **fondo** sm. **1.** (*parte inferiore*) bottom **2.** (*estremità*) end **3.** (*indole*) nature **4.** (*possedimento*) estate **5.** (*capitale*) fund || *articolo di —*, leading article.

fonema sm. phoneme.

fonètica sf. phonetics.

fonogramma sm. phonogram.

fonologìa sf. phonology.

fontana sf. fountain.

fontanella sf. (*anat.*) fontanel.

fonte sf. spring, source (*anche fig.*).

foraggio sm. forage.

foràneo agg. **1.** rural **2.** (*mar.*) outer.

forare vt. **1.** to pierce **2.** (*di pneumatico*) to puncture **3.** (*di biglietti*) to punch.

foratura sf. **1.** piercing **2.** (*di pneumatico*) puncture.

fòrbici sf. pl. scissors.

forbire vt. **1.** to clean **2.** (*di stile*) to polish.

forbito agg. **1.** elegant **2.** (*di stile*) polished.

forca sf. **1.** fork **2.** (*patibolo*) gallows.

forcella sf. **1.** forked stick **2.** (*mecc.*) fork **3.** (*per capelli*) hairpin.

forchetta sf. fork.

forcina sf. hairpin.

fòrcipe sm. forceps (*pl.*).

forcuto agg. forked.

forense agg. forensic.

foresta sf. forest. (*anche fig.*), wood.

forestale agg. forestal: *guardia —*, forester.

foresterìa sf. guest-rooms (*pl.*).

forestiero agg. foreign. ♦ **forestiero** sm. foreigner.

fòrfora sf. dandruff, scurf.

forgiare vt. **1.** to forge **2.** (*modellare*) to shape.

forma sf. **1.** form, shape **2.** (*tec.*) mould.

formaggio sm. cheese.

formale agg. **1.** formal **2.** (*solenne*) solemn.

formalismo sm. formalism.

formalista agg. e s. formalist.

formalità sf. formality.

formalizzarsi vr. to be shocked (at, by).

formare vt. **1.** to form **2.** (*fare*) to make (v. irr.), to create **3.** (*modellare*) to shape **4.** (*addestrare*) to train. ♦ **formarsi** vr. **1.** to form **2.** (*crescere, affinarsi*) to grow (v. irr.), to develop.

formativo agg. formative.

formato sm. **1.** form **2.** (*misura*) size **3.** (*di libro*) format.

formazione sf. formation.

formica sf. ant.

formichiere sm. ant-eater.

formicolare vi. **1.** to swarm **2.** (*sentire un formicolio*) to tingle.

formicolìo sm. **1.** swarming **2.** (*intorpidimento*) tingling.

formidàbile agg. formidable.

fòrmula sf. formula (*pl.* -ae).

formulare vt. to formulate.

fornace sf. furnace.

fornaio sm. **1.** baker **2.** (*negozio*) baker's shop.

fornello sm. stove.

fornire vt. **1.** to supply (with), to provide (with) **2.** (*equipaggiare*) to equip (with).

fornito agg. **1.** furnished (with), supplied (with) **2.** (*equipaggiato*) equipped (with).

fornitore sm. furnisher, supplier.

fornitura sf. **1.** (*il fornire*) supplying **2.** (*attrezzatura*) furniture, fitting.

forno sm. **1.** (*da cucina*) oven **2.** (*metal.*) furnace.

foro[1] sm. hole.

foro[2] sm. **1.** court of justice **2.** (*gli avvocati*) the Bar **3.** (*stor.*) forum.

forse *avv.* **1.** perhaps, maybe **2.** (*circa*) about.

forsennato *agg.* mad, frantic.

forte *agg.* **1.** strong (*anche fig.*) **2.** (*di mali*) severe **3.** (*violento*) heavy **4.** (*di suono*) loud. ♦ **forte** *sm.* **1.** strong man **2.** (*punto di forza*) strong point **3.** (*fortezza*) fortress. ♦ **forte** *avv.* strongly.

fortezza *sf.* stronghold, fortress.

fortificare *vt.* to strengthen, to fortify (*anche fig.*).

fortificazione *sf.* fortification.

fortino *sm.* block-house.

fortùito *agg.* fortuitous, accidental.

fortuna *sf.* **1.** luck **2.** (*ricchezza*) fortune, wealth **3.** (*riuscita*) success **4.** (*emergenza*) emergency.

fortunale *sm.* storm.

fortunato *agg.* lucky.

fortunoso *agg.* **1.** stormy **2.** (*fig.*) eventful.

forùncolo *sm.* boil.

foruncolosi *sf.* furunculosis.

forviare *vt.* to lead (*v. irr.*) astray.

forza *sf.* **1.** strength **2.** (*fig.*) power || — *di volontà*, will-power; *a* — *di*, by dint of **3.** (*mil.*) force.

forzare *vt.* **1.** to force, to compel **2.** (*scassinare*) to pick the lock of.

forzato *agg.* forced. ♦ **forzato** *sm.* convict.

forziere *sm.* coffer.

forzoso *agg.* forced.

foschìa *sf.* haze, mist.

fosco *agg.* **1.** dark, hazy **2.** (*di aspetto*) gloomy.

fosfato *sm.* phosphate.

fosforescente *agg.* phosphorescent.

fosforescenza *sf.* phosphorescence.

fòsforo *sm.* **1.** phosphorus **2.** (*fig.*) intelligence.

fossa *sf.* **1.** ditch **2.** (*cavità*) hollow **3.** (*tomba*) grave.

fossato *sm.* ditch.

fòssile *agg. e sm.* fossil || *carbon* —, pit-coal.

fosso *sm.* ditch.

foto *sf.* photo.

fotocèllula *sf.* photoelectric cell.

fotocopia *sf.* photocopy.

fotogènico *agg.* photogenic.

fotografare *vt.* to photograph.

fotografìa *sf.* **1.** (*arte fotografica*) photography **2.** (*immagine fotografica*) photograph || — *istantanea*, snapshot; *fare una* —, to take (*v. irr.*) a photograph.

fotògrafo *sm.* photographer.

fotomontaggio *sm.* photomontage.

fra *prep.* V. *tra.*

fra' *sm.* (*relig.*) Brother.

frac *sm.* tail-coat.

fracassare *vt.* to smash, to shatter.

fracasso *sm.* **1.** noise, hubbub **2.** (*di cose rotte*) crash.

fracco *sm.* **1.** a great deal **2.** (*di botte*) a good thrashing.

fràdicio *agg.* **1.** rotten **2.** (*bagnato*) wet through.

fràgile *agg.* **1.** fragile **2.** (*fig.*) frail.

fragilità *sf.* fragility (*anche fig.*).

fràgola *sf.* strawberry.

fragore *sm.* loud noise.

fragoroso *agg.* noisy.

fragrante *agg.* fragrant.

fragranza *sf.* fragrance.

fraintèndere *vt.* to misunderstand (*v. irr.*).

frammassone *sm.* freemason.

frammassonerìa *sf.* freemasonry.

frammentario *agg.* fragmentary.

frammento *sm.* fragment.

framméttere *vt.* to interpose. ♦ **framméttersi** *vr.* to interpose, to intrude.

frammezzare *vt.* to intersperse.

frammezzo *prep.* V. *tra.*

frammischiare *vt.* to intermingle. ♦ **frammischiarsi** *vr.* to intermingle.

frana *sf.* landslide.

franare *vi.* **1.** (*di terreno*) to slide (*v. irr.*) down **2.** (*di casa*) to fall (*v. irr.*) in.

francescano *agg. e sm.* Franciscan.

francese *agg.* French. ♦ **francese** *sm.* Frenchman (*pl.* -men).

francesismo *sm.* Gallicism.

franchezza *sf.* frankness, outspokenness.

franchigia *sf.* **1.** immunity **2.** (*postale*) post-free **3.** (*mar.*) furlough.

franco[1] *agg.* **1.** frank, outspoken **2.** (*libero; comm.*) free: *un porto* —, a free port; — *a bordo*, free on board; — *di spese*, free of charge.

franco[2] *sm.* franc.

francobollo *sm.* stamp.

francotiratore *sm.* sharp-shooter.

frangente *sm.* **1.** (*mar.*) breaker **2.** (*situazione difficile*) emergency.

fràngere *vt.* **1.** to break (*v. irr.*) **2.** (*schiacciare*) to crush.

frangetta *sf.* fringe.

frangia *sf.* **1.** fringe **2.** (*fig.*) embellishment.

frangiare *vt.* to fringe.
frangibile *agg.* frangible.
frangibilità *sf.* frangibility.
frangiflutti *agg.* e *sm.* breakwater.
frangizolle *sm.* (*agr.*) clod-smasher.
franoso *agg.* crumbling.
frantoio *sm.* oil-mill.
frantumare *vt.* to shatter.
frantume *sm.* fragment || *andare in frantumi*, to break (*v. irr.*) into fragments.
frappé *sm.* shake.
frapporre *vt.* to interpose. ◆ **frapporsi** *vr.* to interpose.
frasario *sm.* jargon.
frasca *sf.* 1. leafy branch 2. (*donna leggera*) coquette.
frascheggiare *vi.* 1. to rustle 2. (*civettare*) to flirt.
fraschetta *sf.* 1. twig 2. (*fig.*) frivolous girl.
frase *sf.* sentence.
fraseggiare *vi.* to phrase.
fraseologia *sf.* phraseology.
fràssino *sm.* ash-tree.
frastagliare *vt.* to indent.
frastagliato *agg.* indented.
frastaglio *sm.* indentation.
frastornare *vt.* to disturb.
frastuono *sm.* noise, uproar, hubbub.
frate *sm.* 1. friar 2. (*come appellativo*) Brother.
fratellanza *sf.* brotherhood, fraternity.
fratellastro *sm.* half-brother.
fratello *sm.* brother || *fratelli siamesi*, Siamese twins.
fraternità *sf.* brotherhood, fraternity.
fraternizzare *vi.* to fraternize.
fraternizzazione *sf.* fraternization.
fraterno *agg.* brotherly.
fratricida *agg.* fratricidal. ◆ **fratricida** *s.* fratricide.
fratricidio *sm.* fratricide.
fratta *sf.* thicket.
frattaglie *sf. pl.* chitterlings.
frattanto *avv.* meantime, meanwhile.
frattempo (*nella loc. avv.*) *nel* —, in the meanwhile.
fratto *agg.* broken, crushed.
frattura *sf.* fracture.
fratturare *vt.* to fracture, to break (*v. irr.*). ◆ **fratturarsi** *vr.* to fracture, to break.
fraudolento *agg.* fraudulent.
fraudolenza *sf.* fraudulence.

frazionamento *sm.* division.
frazionare *vt.* to divide.
frazionario *agg.* fractional.
frazione *sf.* fraction.
freccia *sf.* arrow.
frecciata *sf.* (*fig.*) gibe.
freddare *vt.* 1. to cool 2. (*ammazzare*) to kill.
freddezza *sf.* coldness, coldheartedness.
freddo *agg.* cold. ◆ **freddo** *sm.* cold: *avere* —, to be cold; *tremare di* —, to shiver with cold.
freddoloso *agg.* sensitive to cold.
freddura *sf.* pun.
fregagione *sf.* massage.
fregare *vt.* 1. to rub 2. (*imbrogliare; volg.*) to swindle.
fregata[1] *sf.* rubbing.
fregata[2] *sf.* (*nave*) frigate.
fregatura *sf.* swindle.
fregiare *vt.* to decorate, to adorn.
fregio *sm.* 1. ornament 2. (*arch.*) frieze.
frego *sm.* stroke: *tirare un* — *su qc.*, to cross sthg. out.
frégola *sf.* heat.
fremente *agg.* quivering: — *d'ira*, fuming.
frèmere *vi.* to quiver, to tremble.
frèmito *sm.* quiver, thrill.
frenare *vt.* 1. to brake 2. (*trattenere*) to restrain.
frenata *sf.* braking.
frenesìa *sf.* 1. frenzy 2. (*desiderio sfrenato*) immoderate desire.
frenètico *agg.* 1. frantic 2. (*entusiastico*) enthusiastic.
freno *sm.* 1. brake || *bloccare i freni*, to jam the brakes; *togliere il* —, to release the brake 2. (*ritegno*) check restraint || *mordere il* —, to fret under restraint; *stringere i freni*, to shorten the reins 3. (*di cavallo*) bit.
frenologìa *sf.* phrenology.
frequentare *vt.* 1. to frequent 2. (*di scuola*) to attend 3. (*di luogo pubblico*) to patronize.
frequentato *agg.* 1. frequented 2. (*di scuola*) attended 3. (*di luogo pubblico*) patronized.
frequentatore *sm.* 1. frequenter 2. (*cliente assiduo*) regular customer.
frequente *agg.* frequent.
frequenza *sf.* 1. frequency 2. (*affluenza*) concourse 3. (*assiduità*) attendance.

fresa *sf.* milling machine.
fresatrìce *sf.* milling machine.
freschezza *sf.* freshness (*anche fig.*), coolness.
fresco *agg.* 1. fresh 2. (*di temperatura*) cool.
frescura *sf.* coolness.
fretta *sf.* haste, hurry: *avere —.* to be in a hurry.
frettoloso *agg.* hurried.
freudiano *agg.* Freudian.
friàbile *agg.* crumbly.
friabilità *sf.* friability.
fricassea *sf.* fricassee.
friggere *vt.* to fry || *andare a farsi —*, to go (*v. irr.*) to the devil.
friggitoria *sf.* fried food shop.
frigidezza, frigidità *sf.* frigidity.
frigido *agg.* frigid (*anche fig.*).
frignare *vi.* to whimper.
frigorìfero *agg.* refrigerant. ♦ **frigorìfero** *sm.* 1. refrigerator 2. (*fam.*) fridge.
fringuello *sm.* finch.
frittata *sf.* omelette.
frittella *sf.* pancake.
fritto *agg.* fried.
frittura *sf.* fry.
frivolezza *sf.* 1. frivolity 2. (*cosa frivola*) trifle.
frìvolo *agg.* frivolous.
frizionare *vt.* to rub, to massage.
frizione *sf.* 1. rub, rubbing, massage 2. (*auto*) clutch.
frizzante *agg.* 1. biting 2. (*di bevanda*) sparkling.
frizzare *vi.* 1. to tingle 2. (*di bevanda*) to sparkle.
frizzo *sm.* 1. witticism 2. (*scherno*) gibe.
frodare *vt.* to defraud.
frodatore *sm.* defrauder.
frode *sf.* fraud, swindle.
frodo *sm.* smuggling || *cacciare di —*, to poach; *cacciatore di —*, poacher.
frollare *vt.* to hang. ♦ **frollare** *vi.* to become (*v. irr.*) tender.
frollatura *sf.* hanging.
frollo *agg.* tender, high || *pasta frolla*, pastry.
fronda[1] *sf.* leafy branch.
fronda[2] *sf.* (*rivolta*) rebellion: *vento di —*, trouble brewing.
frondoso *agg.* leafy.
frontale *agg.* frontal.
fronte *sf.* 1. forehead: *— ampia, sfuggente*, broad, receding forehead 2. (*arch.*) front || *di — a*, in front of; *far — a*, to face. ♦ **fronte** *sm.* 1. (*mil.*) front 2. (*pol.*) union.
fronteggiare *vt.* to face.
frontespizio *sm.* 1. (*arch.*) frontispiece 2. (*di libro*) title page.
frontiera *sf.* frontier, border.
frontone *sm.* 1. pediment 2. (*di porta, finestra*) gable.
frònzolo *sm.* frill || *senza fronzoli*, plain.
frotta *sf.* 1. crowd 2. (*di animali*) flock.
fròttola *sf.* fib.
frugacchiare *vi.* to rummage.
frugale *agg.* frugal.
frugalità *sf.* frugality.
frugare *vi.* to search, to rummage.
frùgolo *sm.* lively child.
fruire *vi.* to enjoy, to avail oneself of.
fruizione *sf.* fruition.
frullare *vi.* 1. to whip, to beat (*v. irr.*) up 2. (*di ali*) to whir.
frullato *sm.* — *di frutta*, fruit-shake.
frullatore *sm.* mill.
frullino *sm.* whisk.
frullìo *sm.* whirring.
frullo *sm.* whir.
frumento *sm.* wheat.
frusciare *vi.* to rustle.
fruscìo *sm.* rustle.
frusta *sf.* 1. whip 2. (*cuc.*) whisk.
frustare *vt.* to whip, to lash.
frustata *sf.* lash.
frustino *sm.* riding-whip.
frusto *agg.* worn-out, thread-bare.
frustrare *vt.* to frustrate.
frutta *sf.* fruit: — *candita*, candied fruit; — *sciroppata*, fruit in syrup; — *cotta*, compote.
fruttare *vi.* 1. to bear (*v. irr.*) fruit, to pay (*v. irr.*) 2. (*comm.*) to yield.
frutteto *sm.* orchard.
frutticultura *sf.* fruit-growing.
fruttiera *sf.* fruit-dish.
fruttìfero *agg.* 1. fruitful 2. (*econ.* interest-bearing: *buono —*, interest-bearing security.
fruttificare *vi.* to bear (*v. irr.* fruit.
fruttivéndolo *sm.* greengrocer.
frutto *sm.* fruit || *frutti di mare*, edible mussels.
fruttuoso *agg.* fruitful, profitable.
fu *agg.* late.
fucilare *vt.* to shoot (*v. irr.*).
fucilata *sf.* shot.
fucilazione *sf.* shooting.

fucile sm. rifle, gun: — ad aria compressa, air-gun; — da caccia, shotgun; calcio del —, butt; canna del —, gun-barrel; caricare un —, to load a gun.

fucileria sf. **1.** rifle fire **2.** (insieme di fucili) musketry.

fuciliere sm. rifleman (pl. -men).

fucina sf. forge.

fucinare vt. to forge.

fuco sm. **1.** drone **2.** (bot.) fucus.

fucsia sf. fuchsia.

fuga sf. **1.** flight, escape **2.** (di innamorati) elopement **3.** (falla, apertura) escape, leak **4.** (mus.) fugue.

fugace agg. short-lived, transient.

fugacità sf. fugacity.

fugare vt. **1.** to put (v. irr.) to flight, to disperse **2.** (scacciare) to dispel.

fuggévole agg. flying, ephemeral.

fuggiasco agg. e sm. runaway.

fuggire vi. **1.** to run (v. irr.) away, to flee (v. irr.) **2.** (di innamorati) to elope. ♦ **fuggire** vt. to shun.

fuggitivo agg. e sm. fugitive.

fulcro sm. fulcrum (pl. -ra).

fulgido agg. shining.

fulgore sm. brightness.

fuliggine sf. soot.

fuligginoso agg. sooty.

fulminante agg. fulminant. ♦ **fulminante** sm. **1.** (chim.) fulminate **2.** (di arma) primer.

fulminare vt. **1.** to strike (v. irr.) by lightning **2.** (colpire) to strike.

fulminato agg. **1.** struck by lightning **2.** (fig.) thunder-struck.

fùlmine sm. lightning.

fulmineo agg. flashing.

fulvo agg. tawny.

fumaiolo sm. smoke-stack.

fumante agg. smoking, steaming.

fumare vt. e vi. to smoke.

fumarola sf. fumarole.

fumata sf. **1.** smoke **2.** (segnale) smoke signal.

fumatore sm. smoker.

fumetto sm. strip cartoon || giornali a fumetti, comics.

fumista s. stove-repairer.

fumo sm. **1.** smoke || venditore di —, windbag; andare in —, to end in smoke **2.** (vapore) fume (anche fig.) **3.** (di pentole) steam.

fumògeno agg. smoke-producing.

fumoso agg. smoky.

funàmbolo sm. rope-dancer.

fune sf. **1.** rope **2.** (cavo) cable.

fùnebre agg. **1.** funeral: canto —, dirge; carro —, hearse **2.** (cupo) gloomy.

funerale sm. funeral || i funerali, the obsequies.

funerario agg. funerary.

funèreo agg. funereal.

funestare vt. to afflict.

funesto agg. baneful, woeful.

fungaia sf. mushroom-bed.

fùngere vi. to act (as).

fungo sm. mushroom.

funicolare sf. funicular.

funivìa sf. telpherage.

funzionale agg. functional.

funzionamento sm. working.

funzionare vi. **1.** to act (as) **2.** (andar bene) to work.

funzionario sm. official.

funzione sf. **1.** function **2.** (carica) office **3.** (relig.) service.

fuochista sm. stoker.

fuoco sm. **1.** fire **2.** (cine; foto; mat.) focus: mettere a —, to focus.

fuorché cong. except, but.

fuori avv. **1.** out, outdoors **2.** (all'estero) abroad. ♦ **fuori (di)** prep. out of, outside.

fuoribordo sm. outboard motor.

fuoriclasse sm. first-rater.

fuorigioco sm., agg. e avv. off-side.

fuorilegge sm. outlaw.

fuoriserie agg. e sm. special body car.

fuoruscito sm. exile, refugee.

fuorviare vt. to lead (v. irr.) astray.

furberìa sf. cunning.

furbo agg. cunning, shrewd.

furente agg. furious, mad.

fureria sf. orderly room.

furetto sm. ferret.

furfante sm. rascal, scamp.

furgoncino sm. small van.

furgone sm. van.

furia sf. fury: montare su tutte le furie, to fly (v. irr.) into a fury.

furibondo agg. furious.

furioso agg. **1.** furious **2.** (violento) violent.

furore sm. fury: far —, to be a hit.

furoreggiare vi. to be all the rage.

furtivo agg. stealthy.

furto sm. theft.

fuscello sm. **1.** twig, straw **2.** (fig.) thin person.

fusibile sm. fuse.

fusione sf. **1.** fusion **2.** (di società comm.) merging.

fuso *sm.* spindle || — *orario*, time zone.

fusoliera *sf.* fuselage.

fustigare *vt.* to flog.

fusto *sm.* **1.** (*bot.*) stalk **2.** (*tronco umano*) trunk **3.** (*per benzina*) drum **4.** (*di legno per liquori*) barrel **5.** (*giovane prestante*) muscle--man (*pl.* -men) **6.** (*di colonna*) shaft.

fùtile *agg.* trifling.

futilità *sf.* trifle.

futurismo *sm.* futurism.

futurista *agg.* e *sm.* futurist.

futuro *agg.* e *sm.* future.

G

gabbamondo *sm.* swindler.

gabbare *vt.* to swindle.

gabbia *sf.* **1.** cage **2.** (*per imballaggio*) crate.

gabbiano *sm.* sea-gull.

gabellare *vt.* (*far credere*) to pass off as.

gabinetto *sm.* **1.** (*studio*) study **2.** (*pol.*) cabinet **3.** (*latrina*) water-closet, toilet.

gagà *sm.* dandy.

gagliardamente *avv.* vigorously.

gagliardetto *sm.* pennon.

gagliardo *agg.* vigorous.

gag'ioffo *sm.* rascal.

gaiezza *sf.* **1.** cheerfulness **2.** (*di colore*) brightness.

gaio *agg.* **1.** cheerful **2.** (*di colore*) bright.

gala *sf.* **1.** (*trina*) frill **2.** (*festa*) gala: *abito di* —, gala dress.

galante *agg.* e *sm.* gallant || *lettera* —, love letter; *fare il* —, to flirt.

galanterìa *sf.* **1.** gallantry **2.** (*complimento*) compliment.

galantina *sf.* galantine.

galantuomo *sm.* honest man.

galassia *sf.* galaxy.

galateo *sm.* **1.** good manners (*pl.*) **2.** (*libro*) book of manners.

galena *sf.* galena.

galeone *sm.* galleon.

galeotto *sm.* **1.** convict **2.** (*mezzano*) pander **3.** (*mar.*) galley-slave.

galera *sf.* **1.** jail **2.** (*mar.*) galley.

galileo *agg.* e *sm.* Galilean.

galla[1] (*nella loc. avv.*) *a* —, afloat || *stare a* —, to float; *venire a* —, to come (*v. irr.*) to the surface; (*fig.*) to come to light.

galla[2] *sf.* (*bot.*) gall.

galleggiamento *sm.* floating: *linea di* —, water-line.

galleggiante *agg.* floating, afloat (*pred.*). ♦ **galleggiante** *sm.* **1.** float **2.** (*boa*) buoy.

galleggiare *vi.* to float.

gallerìa *sf.* **1.** tunnel **2.** (*d'arte, in teatro*) gallery.

gallese *agg.* Welsh. ♦ **gallese** *sm.* Welshman (*pl.* -men).

galletta *sf.* biscuit.

gallina *sf.* **1.** hen **2.** (*cibo*) chicken.

gallinàceo *agg.* e *sm.* gallinacean.

gallio *sm.* gallium.

gallismo *sm.* cocksure behaviour (towards women).

gallo *sm.* **1.** cock **2.** (*stor.*) Gaul.

gallonato *agg.* gallooned.

gallone *sm.* **1.** braid, galloon **2.** (*mil.*) chevron stripes (*pl.*) **3.** (*misura*) gallon.

galoppante *agg.* galloping.

galoppare *vi.* to gallop.

galoppata *sf.* gallop.

galoppatoio *sm.* riding-track.

galoppino *sm.* **1.** errand-boy **2.** (*tirapiedi*) drudge.

galoppo *sm.* gallop: *al* —, at a gallop, (*fig.*) at full speed; *andare al gran* —, to ride (*v. irr.*) full gallop.

galoscia *sf.* galosh.

galvànico *agg.* galvanic.

galvanizzare *vt.* **1.** to galvanize **2.** (*rivestire di metallo*) to electroplate.

galvanizzazione *sf.* **1.** galvanization **2.** (*rivestitura di metallo*) electroplating.

galvanoplàstica *sf.* galvanoplastics.

gamba *sf.* leg || *avere le gambe lunghe*, to be long-legged; *male in* —, down at heel; *in* — (*fig.*), smart.

gambale *sm.* **1.** legging **2.** (*di armatura*) jamb.

gamberetto *sm.* shrimp.

gàmbero *sm.* **1.** (*di mare*) lobster **2.** (*d'acqua dolce*) crayfish || *andare come un* —, to go (*v. irr.*) backwards.

gambo *sm.* stem.

gamma *sf.* range: — *di lunghezza d'onda*, waveband.

ganascia *sf.* jaw || *mangiare a quattro ganasce*, to eat (*v. irr.*) voraciously.

gancio *sm.* hook.

ganga *sf.* gang.

gànghero *sm.* hinge || *andare fuori dai gangheri*, to lose (*v. irr.*) one's temper.

ganglio *sm.* ganglion (*pl.* -ia).

gangsterismo *sm.* gangsterism.

ganimede *sm.* dandy.

gara *sf.* competition.

garagista *sm.* garage keeper.

garante *sm.* 1. warranter 2. (*per un imputato*) bail || *essere* —, to answer for.

garantire *vt.* 1. to warrant 2. (*farsi garante per*) to answer for 3. (*un imputato*) to go (*v. irr.*) bail for.

garanzìa *sf.* 1. warranty, guarantee 2. (*somma di* —) security 3. (*cauzione*) bail || *dare, non dare* —, to be reliable, unreliable; *a — di*, as a guarantee for.

garbare *vi.* to like.

garbatamente *avv.* politely.

garbatezza *sf.* politeness.

garbato *agg.* polite.

garbo *sm.* politeness || *con bel* —, with a good grace.

garbuglio *sm.* entanglement.

gardenia *sf.* gardenia.

gareggiare *vi.* to compete.

garganella (*nella loc. avv.*) *bere a* —, to gulp down.

gargarismo *sm.* gargle.

gargarizzare *vi.* to gargle.

garibaldino *agg.* e *sm.* Garibaldian.

garitta *sf.* 1. sentry-box 2. (*torretta*) look-out turret 3. (*di guardiano*) cabin.

garòfano *sm.* carnation || *chiodo di* —, clove.

garrese *sm.* withers (*pl.*).

garretto *sm.* 1. back of heel 2. (*di animale*) hock.

garrire *vi.* 1. (*di bandiere*) to flutter, to flap 2. (*di uccelli*) to chirp.

gàrrulo *agg.* talkative.

garza *sf.* gauze.

garzone *sm.* shop-boy, apprentice.

gas *sm.* gas.

gasolio *sm.* gas oil.

gasometro *sm.* gasholder.

gassare *vt.* to gas.

gassato *agg.* aerated || *acqua gassata*, soda-water.

gassista *sm.* gas-fitter.

gassògeno *sm.* gas producer.

gassoso *agg.* 1. gaseous 2. (*gassato*) aerated.

gàstrico *agg.* gastric.

gastrite *sf.* gastritis.

gastroenterite *sf.* gastroenteritis.

gastronomìa *sf.* gastronomy.

gastronòmico *agg.* gastronomic(al).

gatta *sf.* she-cat.

gattabuia *sf.* jail.

gatto *sm.* cat.

gattopardo *sm.* leopard.

gaudente *agg.* 1. jolly 2. (*dissipato*) fast. ♦ **gaudente** *sm.* fast person.

gàudio *sm.* joy.

gavetta *sf.* mess-tin.

gavitello *sm.* buoy.

gazza *sf.* magpie.

gazzarra *sf.* din.

gazzella *sf.* gazelle.

gazzetta *sf.* gazette.

gelare *vt.* e *vi.* to freeze (*v. irr.*).

gelata *sf.* frost.

gelataio *sm.* ice-cream vendor.

gelaterìa *sf.* ice-cream shop.

gelatina *sf.* 1. (*cuc.*) jelly 2. (*chim.*) gelatine.

gelatinoso *agg.* gelatinous.

gelato *agg.* frozen, icy. ♦ **gelato** *sm.* ice-cream.

gèlido *agg.* icy (*anche fig.*).

gelo *sm.* 1. intense cold 2. (*fig.*) chill 3. (*ghiaccio*) ice 4. (*brina*) frost.

gelone *sm.* chilblain.

gelosìa *sf.* 1. jealousy 2. (*cura*) care 3. (*persiana*) shutter.

geloso *agg.* jealous.

gelso *sm.* mulberry(-tree).

gelsomino *sm.* jasmine.

gemebondo *agg.* groaning.

gemelli *sm. pl.* (*di polsino*) cuff-links.

gemello *agg.* e *sm.* twin.

gèmere *vi.* to groan.

gèmito *sm.* groan.

gemma *sf.* 1. gem 2. (*bot.*) bud.

gemmare *vi.* (*bot.*) to bud.

gendarme *sm.* policeman (*pl.* -men).

gendarmerìa *sf.* 1. police-force 2. (*caserma*) police-station.

genealogìa *sf.* genealogy.

genealògico *agg.* genealogical.

generàbile *agg.* generable.

generale[1] *agg.* general || *quartier* —, headquarters (*pl.*).

generale[2] *sm.* general.
generalità *sf.* generality || *dare le proprie* —, to give (*v. irr.*) one's particulars.
generalizzare *vt.* to generalize.
generalizzazione *sf.* generalization.
generare *vt.* 1. to beget (*v. irr.*) 2. (*produrre, anche tec.*) to produce.
♦ **generarsi** *vr.* to be born.
generatore *agg.* generative. ♦ **generatore** *sm.* generator.
generazione *sf.* generation.
gènere *sm.* 1. kind 2. (*gramm.*) gender 3. (*letterario*) genre 4. (*prodotto*) product || *generi alimentari*, foodstuffs; *generi di prima necessità*, commodities.
genèrico *agg.* generic, vague.
gènero *sm.* son-in-law.
generosità *sf.* generosity.
generoso *agg.* generous.
gènesi *sf.* genesis (*pl.* -ses).
genètica *sf.* genetics.
genètico *agg.* genetic.
genetlìaco *sm.* birthday.
gengiva *sf.* gum.
genìa *sf.* 1. race 2. (*spreg.*) tribe.
geniale *agg.* clever.
genialità *sf.* 1. cleverness 2. (*genio*) genius.
genio *sm.* genius || *andare a* —, to please.
genitale *agg.* e *sm.* genital.
genitivo *sm.* genitive.
genitore *sm.* 1. parent 2. (*padre*) father.
genitrice *sf.* mother.
gennaio *sm.* January.
genocidio *sm.* genocide.
gentaglia *sf.* rabble.
gente *sf.* people: *c'è molta* —, there are a lot of people; *le genti dell'Asia*, the peoples of Asia.
gentildonna *sf.* lady.
gentile *agg.* 1. kind 2. (*cortese*) polite || *è* — *da parte sua*, it is kind of him.
gentilezza *sf.* 1. kindness 2. (*cortesia*) politeness 3. (*favore*) favour.
gentilizio *agg.* noble: *stemma* —, coat of arms.
gentiluomo *sm.* gentleman (*pl.* -men).
genuflessione *sf.* genuflection.
genuflèttersi *vr.* to kneel down.
genuinità *sf.* genuineness.
genuino *agg.* genuine.
genziana *sf.* gentian.
geodesìa *sf.* geodesy.

geofìsica *sf.* geophysics.
geografìa *sf.* geography.
geogràfico *agg.* geographic(al) || *carta geografica*, map.
geògrafo *sm.* geographer.
geologìa *sf.* geology.
geològico *agg.* geologic(al).
geòlogo *sm.* geologist.
geòmetra *sm.* 1. geometer 2. (*agrimensore*) land-surveyor.
geometrìa *sf.* geometry.
geomètrico *agg.* geometric(al).
geopolìtica *sf.* geopolitics.
geòrgico *agg.* georgic.
geranio *sm.* geranium.
gerarca *sm.* leader.
gerarchìa *sf.* hierarchy.
gerente *sm.* manager.
gerenza *sf.* management.
gergo *sm.* 1. slang 2. (*di una classe professionale*) jargon.
germànico *agg.* Germanic.
germanio *sm.* germanium.
germanismo *sm.* Germanism.
germanista *s.* Germanist.
germanìstica *sf.* Germanic studies.
germano[1] *agg.* e *sm.* German.
germano[2] *agg.* german: *fratello* —, brother-german.
germe *sm.* germ.
germicida *agg.* germicidal. ♦ **germicida** *sm.* germicide.
germinare *vi.* V. *germogliare*.
germinazione *sf.* germination.
germogliare *vi.* 1. to sprout 2. (*fig.*) to spring (*v. irr.*) (up).
germoglio *sm.* germ.
geroglifico *sm.* hieroglyphic.
gerontologìa *sf.* gerontology.
gerundio *sm.* gerund.
gessetto *sm.* chalk.
gesso *sm.* 1. chalk 2. (*med.; scult.; edil.*) plaster.
gesta *sf. pl.* deeds.
gestante *sf.* pregnant woman.
gestazione *sf.* gestation.
gesticolare *vi.* to gesticulate.
gestione *sf.* management.
gestire[1] *vt.* to manage.
gestire[2] *vi.* to gesture.
gesto *sm.* gesture || *un bel* —, a noble deed.
gestore *sm.* manager.
gesuita *sm.* Jesuit.
gesuìtico *agg.* Jesuitic(al).
gettare *vt.* 1. to throw (*v. irr.*), (*anche metal.; edil.*) to cast (*v. irr.*) 2. (*bot.*) to sprout 3. (*fruttare*) to yield || — *le fondamenta*,

to lay (*v. irr.*) the foundations; — *un grido*, to utter a cry. ♦ **gettarsi** *vr.* (*di fiume*) to flow.

gettata *sf.* **1.** throw **2.** (*edil.; metal.*) cast **3.** (*di arma*) range **4.** (*molo*) jetty.

gèttito *sm.* (*delle imposte*) yield.

getto *sm.* **1.** throw **2.** (*mecc.; di liquidi*) jet **3.** (*bot.*) sprout **4.** (*metal.; edil.*) casting || *di* —, effortlessly; *a* — *continuo*, continuously.

gettone *sm.* **1.** counter: — *telefonico*, telephone counter **2.** (*contromarca*) check || *macchina a* —, slot-machine.

geyser *sm.* geyser.

gheriglio *sm.* kernel.

gherminella *sf.* trick: *fare una* —, to play a trick (on).

ghermire *vt.* to clutch.

ghette *sf. pl.* spats.

ghetto *sm.* **1.** ghetto **2.** (*insieme degli ebrei*) Jewry.

ghiacciaia *sf.* **1.** ice-box **2.** (*stanza*) ice-house.

ghiacciaio *sm.* glacier.

ghiacciare *vi* e *vt.* to freeze (*v. irr.*).

ghiacciato *agg.* **1.** frozen **2.** (*molto freddo*) icy.

ghiaccio *sm.* ice.

ghiacciolo *sm.* icicle.

ghiaia *sf.* gravel.

ghiaioso *agg.* gravelly.

ghianda *sf.* acorn.

ghiàndola *sf.* gland.

ghibellino *agg.* e *sm.* Ghibelline.

ghigliottina *sf.* guillotine.

ghigliottinare *vt.* to guillotine.

ghignare *vi.* to grin.

ghigno *sm.* grin.

ghingheri (*nella loc. avv.*) *mettersi in* —, to dress up.

ghiotto *agg.* **1.** greedy **2.** (*appetitoso*) dainty.

ghiottone *sm.* glutton.

ghiottonerìa *sf.* **1.** gluttony **2.** (*cibo prelibato*) dainty.

ghiribizzo *sm.* whim.

ghirigoro *sm.* doodle.

ghirlanda *sf.* wreath.

ghiro *sm.* dormouse (*pl.* dormice) || *dormire come un* —, to sleep (*v. irr.*) like a log.

ghisa *sf.* cast iron.

già *avv.* **1.** already **2.** (*un tempo*) once **3.** (*certamente*) of course.

giacca *sf.* coat, jacket.

giacché *cong.* as, since.

giacente *agg.* **1.** lying **2.** (*di capitale*) uninvested **3.** (*di posta*) unclaimed.

giacenza *sf.* lying || *capitale in* —, uninvested capital; *lettera in* —, unclaimed letter; *merci in* —, goods in stock.

giacere *vi.* to lie (*v. irr.*).

giaciglio *sm.* couch.

giacimento *sm.* (*min.*) deposit: — *di petrolio*, oil-field.

giacinto *sm.* hyacinth.

giacobino *sm.* e *agg.* Jacobin.

giada *sf.* jade.

giaggiolo *sm.* iris.

giaguaro *sm.* jaguar.

giallastro *agg.* yellowish.

giallo *agg.* yellow || *romanzo*, *film*, *dramma* —, thriller.

giammai *avv.* never.

giansenismo *sm.* Jansenism.

giansenista *s.* Jansenist.

giapponese *agg.* e *sm.* Japanese (*invariato al pl.*).

giara *sf.* jar.

giardinaggio *sm.* gardening.

giardinetta *sf.* station wagon.

giardiniere *sm.* gardener.

giardino *sm.* garden || — *d'infanzia*, nursery-school.

giarrettiera *sf.* garter.

giavellotto *sm.* javelin: *lancio del* —, javelin throwing.

gibbosità *sf.* hump.

giberna *sf.* cartridge-pouch.

gigante *sm.* giant || *fare passi da* —, to make (*v. irr.*) rapid progress.

giganteggiare *vi.* to tower.

gigantesco *agg.* gigantic.

gigantismo *sm.* giantism.

gigione *sm.* ham.

giglio *sm.* lily.

gilè *sm.* waistcoat.

gincana *sf.* gymkhana.

gineceo *sm.* gynaeceum (*pl.* -ea).

ginecologìa *sf.* gynaecology.

ginecòlogico *agg.* gynaecological.

ginecòlogo *sm.* gynaecologist.

ginepraio *sm.* **1.** juniper thicket **2.** (*fig.*) fix: *ficcarsi in un* —, to get (*v. irr.*) into a scrape.

ginepro *sm.* juniper.

ginestra *sf.* broom.

gingillarsi *vr.* to dawdle.

gingillo *sm.* **1.** knick-knack **2.** (*balocco*) plaything.

ginnasio *sm.* **1.** grammar school **2.**

(*in Italia e stor.*) gymnasium (*pl.* -ia).

ginnasta *sm.* athlete.

ginnàstica *sf.* gymnastics.

gìnnico *agg.* gymnastic, athletic.

ginocchiata *sf.* blow with the knee.

ginocchiera *sf.* 1. knee-guard 2. (*mecc.*) toggle.

ginocchio *sm.* 1. knee: *in* —, on one's knees 2. (*mecc.*) bend.

ginocchioni *avv.* on one's knees.

giocare *vi.* 1. to play 2. (*d'azzardo*) to gamble 3. (*scommettere*) to bet (*v. irr.*) 4. (*in borsa*) to speculate. ◆ **giocare** *vt.* 1. to play 2. (*ingannare*) to deceive. ◆ **giocarsi** *vr.* (*beffarsi*) to trifle (with).

giocata *sf.* 1. game 2. (*puntata*) stake.

giocatore *sm.* 1. player 2. (*d'azzardo*) gambler 3. (*in borsa*) stock--jobber.

giocàttolo *sm.* toy.

giocherellare *vi.* to toy.

gioco *sm.* 1. play 2. (*regolato da norme*) game 3. (*d'azzardo*) gambling 4. (*scherzo*) joke || *per* —, for fun; — *di pazienza*, puzzle; — *di parole*, pun; *essere in* —, to be involved.

giocoforza *sm.* necessary: *è* —, it is absolutely necessary.

giocoliere *sm.* juggler.

giocondità *sf.* gaiety.

giocondo *agg.* gay.

giocosità *sf.* playfulness.

giocoso *agg.* playful.

giogaia *sf.* mountain range.

giogo *sm.* 1. yoke 2. (*di monte*) summit.

gioia *sf.* 1. joy 2. (*gioiello*) jewel.

gioiellerìa *sf.* 1. jewelry 2. (*negozio*) jeweller's shop.

gioielliere *sm.* jeweller

gioiello *sm.* jewel

gioioso *agg.* joyful.

gioire *vi.* to rejoice (at).

giornalaio *sm.* newsman (*pl.* -men).

giornale *sm.* 1. newspaper 2. (*comm.*) journal || — *radio*, news bulletin; *cine* —, news-reel.

giornaliero *agg.* daily.

giornalismo *sm.* 1. journalism 2. (*la stampa*) press.

giornalista *s.* journalist, reporter.

giornalìstico *agg.* journalistic || *ambiente* —, press.

giornalmente *avv.* daily.

giornata *sf.* day: *lavorare a* —, to work by the day || *donna a* —, charwoman (*pl.* -women).

giorno *sm.* day: *di* —, by day; *a giorni*, in a few days' time; *due volte al* —, twice a day; *un* — (*avv.*), one day || — *festivo*, holiday.

giovamento *sm.* benefit || *trarre* — *da*, to benefit by.

giòvane *agg.* young. ◆ **giòvane** *sm.* young man (*pl.* -men). ◆ **giòvane** *sf.* young woman (*pl.* women).

giovanetta *sf.* girl.

giovanetto *sm.* boy.

giovanile *agg.* 1. juvenile 2. (*da giovane*) youthful.

giovanotto *sm.* young man (*pl.* men).

giovare *vi.* to be of use. ◆ **giovare** *vt.* to be good (for). ◆ **giovarsi** *vr.* to benefit (by).

giovedì *sm.* Thursday.

giovenca *sf.* heifer.

gioventù *sf.* youth.

gioviale *agg.* jolly.

giovialità *sf.* jollity.

giovinastro *sm.* hooligan.

giovincello *sm.* lad.

giovinezza *sf.* youth.

giràbile *agg.* endorsable.

giradischi *sm.* record player.

giradito *sm.* whitlow.

giraffa *sf.* giraffe.

giramento *sm.* turning: — *di capo*, giddiness; *avere un* —, to feel (*v. irr.*) giddy.

giramondo *sm.* 1. wanderer 2. (*turista*) globe-trotter.

giràndola *sf.* 1. (*fuoco d'artificio*) Catherine-wheel 2. (*fig.*) fickle person.

girandolare *vi.* to saunter.

girandolone *sm.* saunterer.

girante *sm.* 1. (*comm.*) endorser 2. (*mecc.*) impeller (*di pompa*), wheel (*di turbina*).

girare *vi. e vt.* 1. to turn 2. (*evitare*) to avoid 3. (*viaggiare*) to tour 4. (*vagare*) to stroll 5. (*comm.*) to endorse 6. (*riprendere un film*) to shoot (*v. irr.*). ◆ **girarsi** *vr.* to turn.

girarrosto *sm.* spit.

girasole *sm.* sunflower.

girata *sf.* 1. turn 2. (*comm.*) endorsement.

giratario *sm.* (*comm.*) endorsee.

giravolta *sf.* **1.** turning **2.** (*fig.*) shift || *fare una —*, to turn round.

girello *sm.* **1.** (*per bambini*) go-cart **2.** (*parte di bue*) rump.

giretto *sm.* stroll: *fare un —*, to take (*v. irr.*) a short walk.

girévole *agg.* revolving.

girino *sm.* tadpole.

giro *sm.* **1.** turn **2.** (*viaggio*) tour **3.** (*passeggiata*) stroll **4.** (*percorso*) round || *a — di posta*, by return of post; *— d'affari*, turnover; *nel — di pochi giorni*, in a few days' time; *fare un — in auto*, to go (*v. irr.*) for a drive in a car; *fare un — in bicicletta*, to take (*v. irr.*) a ride on a bicycle.

girondino *agg.* e *sm.* Girondist

gironzolare *vi.* to stroll.

giroscopio *sm.* gyroscope.

girotondo *sm.* round dance.

girovagare *vi.* to wander.

giròvago *agg.* wandering. ♦ **giròvago** *sm.* tramp || *venditore —*, pedlar.

gita *sf.* trip: *fare una —*, to take (*v. irr.*) a trip.

gitano *sm.* Spanish gipsy.

gitante *s.* tripper.

giù *avv.* **1.** down **2.** (*dabbasso*) downstairs || *— per*, down; *su per —*, approximately.

giubba *sf.* coat.

giubbetto *sm.* **1.** jacket **2.** (*da donna*) bodice.

giubbotto *sm.* (heavy) coat.

giubilare *vi.* to exult.

giubileo *sm.* jubilee.

giùbilo *sm.* rejoicing.

giudàico *agg.* Judaic.

giudaismo *sm.* Judaism.

giudeo *agg.* Jewish. ♦ **giudeo** *sm.* Jew. ♦ **giudea** *sf.* Jewess.

giudicare *vt.* **1.** to judge **2.** (*pensare*) to think (*v. irr.*).

giùdice *sm.* judge || *i giudici*, the Bench.

giudiziario *agg.* judicial.

giudizio *sm.* **1.** judgement **2.** (*causa*) trial **3.** (*sentenza*) sentence **4.** (*buon senso*) common sense || *far —*, to behave oneself; *rinviare a —*, to commit for trial.

giudizioso *agg.* sensible.

giùggiola *sf.* jujube || *andare in brodo di giuggiole*, to be extremely pleased.

giuggiolone *sm.* simpleton.

giugno *sm.* June.

giugulare *agg.* jugular.

giuliano *agg.* Julian.

giulivo *agg.* cheerful.

giullare *sm.* jester.

giumenta *sf.* (*cavalla*) mare.

giunca *sf.* junk.

giunco *sm.* reed.

giùngere *vi.* **1.** to arrive (at), to reach (sthg.) **2.** (*riuscire*) to succeed (in). ♦ **giùngere** *vt.* (*congiungere*) to join.

giungla *sf.* jungle.

giunta¹ *sf.* **1.** addition: *per —*, in addition **2.** (*di peso*) make-weight.

giunta² *sf.* *— comunale*, town council.

giunto *sm.* (*mecc.*) joint.

giuntura *sf.* juncture.

giunzione *sf.* **1.** connection **2.** (*giunto*) joint || *fare una —*, to joint.

giuramento *sm.* oath: *sotto —*, on oath.

giurare *vt.* to swear (*v. irr.*).

giurato *sm.* juryman (*pl.* -men) || *i giurati*, the jury (*sing.*).

giurìa *sf.* jury.

giurìdico *agg.* juridical: *stato —*, legal status.

giurisdizione *sf.* jurisdiction.

giurisprudenza *sf.* law.

giurista *sm.* jurist.

giustezza *sf.* **1.** exactness **2.** (*tip.*) measure.

giustificàbile *agg.* justifiable.

giustificare *vt.* to justify.

giustificazione *sf.* justification.

giustizia *sf.* justice.

giustiziare *vt.* to execute.

giustiziato *sm.* executed man.

giustiziere *sm.* **1.** executioner **2.** (*vendicatore*) avenger.

giusto *agg.* **1.** just **2.** (*esatto*) right **3.** (*legittimo*) legitimate.

glabro *agg.* hairless.

glaciale *agg.* icy: *regione —*, ice region.

glaciazione *sf.* glaciation.

gladiatore *sm.* gladiator.

gladìolo *sm.* gladiolus.

glande *sm.* glans (*pl.* -ndes).

glàndola *sf.* V. *ghiandola*.

glandolare *agg.* glandular.

glassare *vt.* **1.** (*con zucchero*) to ice **2.** (*con gelatina*) to glaze.

glàuco *agg.* glaucous.

glaucoma *sm.* glaucoma.

gleba *sf.* clod || *servo della —*, serf.

gli[1] *art.* **1.** the **2.** (*in senso generico non si traduce*): — *stranieri amano l'Italia*, foreigners love Italy **3.** (*si traduce col possessivo coi capi di vestiario ecc.*): *si tolse* — *occhiali*, he took off his glasses.

gli[2] *pron.* **1.** (*per persona*) him, to him **2.** (*per cosa*) it, to it || — *mandai un libro*, I sent him a book, I sent a book to him.

glicerina *sf.* glycerine.

glicine *sm.* wistaria.

glicògeno *sm.* glycogen.

glielo *pron.* it (to) him; it (to) her; him to him; him to her; it to it.

globale *agg.* total.

globo *sm.* globe.

globulare *agg.* globular.

glòbulo *sm.* (*biol.*) corpuscle.

gloria *sf.* glory.

gloriarsi *vr.* to glory (in).

glorificare *vt.* to glorify.

glorificazione *sf.* glorification.

glorioso *agg.* glorious.

glossa *sf.* gloss.

glossario *sm.* glossary.

glòttide *sf.* glottis.

glottologìa *sf.* glottology.

glottològico *agg.* glottological.

glottòlogo *sm.* glottologist.

glucosio *sm.* glucose.

glùteo *sm.* gluteus (*pl.* -ei).

glutinato *agg.* gluten (*attr.*).

glùtine *sm.* gluten.

gnomo *sm.* gnome.

gnosticismo *sm.* gnosticism.

gnòstico *agg.* e *sm.* gnostic.

gobba *sf.* **1.** hump (*anche fig.*) **2.** (*donna* —) humpbacked woman.

gobbo *agg.* **1.** humpbacked **2.** (*curvo*) bent. ♦ **gobbo** *sm.* humpback.

goccia *sf.* **goccio** *sm.* drop.

gocciolare *vi.* e *vt.* to drip.

gocciolìo *sm.* dripping.

godere *vi.* e *vt.* to enjoy || *goderse-la*, to have a good time.

godereccio *agg.* **1.** (*amante dei godimenti*) pleasure-loving **2.** (*che dà godimento*) pleasant.

godimento *sm.* enjoyment.

goffàggine *sf.* **1.** clumsiness **2.** (*atto goffo*) clumsy action.

goffo *agg.* clumsy.

gogna *sf.* pillory: *mettere alla* —, to pillory.

ʒola *sf.* **1.** throat: *aver mal di* —, to have a sorethroat **2.** (*golosità*) gluttony: *far* —, to tempt **3.** (*geogr.*) gorge.

goletta *sf.* (*mar.*) schooner.

golf *sm.* **1.** jersey **2.** (*gioco*) golf.

golfo *sm.* gulf.

goliàrdico *agg.* of students.

goliardo *sm.* university student.

golosità *sf.* **1.** greediness **2.** (*cibo prelibato*) dainty.

goloso *agg.* greedy. ♦ **goloso** *sm.* glutton.

gòmena *sf.* rope.

gomitata *sf.* nudge || *farsi avanti a gomitate*, to elbow one's way.

gòmito *sm.* **1.** elbow **2.** (*di strada*) sharp bend || — *a* —, side by side.

gomìtolo *sm.* clew.

gomma *sf.* **1.** rubber **2.** (*sostanza resinosa*) gum **3.** (*pneumatico*) tyre.

gommapiuma *sf.* foam rubber.

gòndola *sf.* gondola.

gonfalone *sm.* standard.

gonfiare *vt.* **1.** to swell (*v. irr.*) **2.** (*esagerare*) to exaggerate. ♦ **gonfiarsi** *vr.* to swell (*anche fig.*).

gonfiatura *sf.* **1.** swelling **2.** (*esagerazione*) exaggeration.

gonfio *agg.* **1.** swollen **2.** (*di stile*) bombastic.

gonfiore *sm.* swelling.

gong *sm.* gong.

gongolante *agg.* rejoicing (at).

gongolare *vi.* to rejoice (at).

goniòmetro *sm.* goniometer.

gonna *sf.* **1.** skirt **2.** (*di costume storico anche maschile*) gown.

gonnellino *sm.* — *scozzese*, kilt.

gonzo *sm.* blockhead.

gorgheggiare *vi.* to trill.

gorgheggio *sm.* trill.

gorgo *sm.* whirlpool.

gorgogliare *vi.* to gurgle.

gorgoglio *sm.* gurgling.

gorilla *sm.* gorilla.

gota *sf.* cheek.

gòtico *agg.* Gothic.

gotta *sf.* gout.

governàbile *agg.* governable.

governante *sm.* **1.** ruler **2.** (*statista*) statesman (*pl.* -men). ♦ **governante** *sf.* **1.** housekeeper **2.** (*bambinaia*) nurse.

governare *vt.* **1.** to govern, to rule **2.** (*badare a*) to look after **3.** (*mar.*) to steer.

governativo *agg.* government (*attributivo*).

governatore *sm.* governor.

governo *sm.* **1.** government **2.** (*dominio*) rule **3.** (*comm.*) management **4.** (*mar.*) steerage || — *della*

casa, housekeeping.
gozzo *sm.* **1.** goitre **2.** (*di uccello*) crop.
gozzoviglia *sf.* revelry.
gozzovigliare *vi.* to revel.
gozzuto *agg.* goitrous.
gracchiare *vi.* to croak.
gracidare *vi.* to croak.
gracidìo *sm.* croaking.
gràcile *agg.* frail.
gracilità *sf.* frailty.
gradassata *sf.* boastfulness, brag.
gradasso *sm.* boaster, braggart.
gradatamente *avv.* gradually.
gradazione *sf.* **1.** gradation **2.** (*sfumatura*) shade.
gradévole *agg.* agreeable.
gradimento *sm.* **1.** pleasure **2.** satisfaction **3.** (*approvazione*) approval.
gradinata *sf.* **1.** flight of steps **2.** (*negli stadi*) tiers of seats.
gradino *sm.* **1.** step **2.** (*di stadio*) stage.
gradire *vt.* **1.** to like **2.** (*accettare*) to accept.
gradito *agg.* **1.** (*piacevole*) pleasant **2.** (*ben accetto*) welcome.
grado *sm.* **1.** degree **2.** (*mil.*) rank || *essere in* —, to be able; *di buon* —, willingly.
graduale *agg.* gradual.
gradualità *sf.* graduality.
graduare *vt.* to graduate.
graduato *agg.* **1.** graded **2.** (*di strumento*) graduated. ♦ **graduato** *sm.* non-commissioned officer.
graduatoria *sf.* **1.** classification **2.** (*sport*) position.
graduazione *sf.* graduation.
graffa *sf.* clip.
graffiare *vt.* to scratch.
graffiatura *sf.* scratch.
graffio *sm.* scratch.
graffito *sm.* graffito (*pl.* -ti).
grafìa *sf.* **1.** writing **2.** (*ortografia*) spelling.
gràfico *agg.* graphic. ♦ **gràfico** *sm.* graph.
grafite *sf.* graphite.
grafologìa *sf.* graphology.
grafòlogo *sm.* graphologist.
grafòmane *s.* graphomaniac.
grafomanìa *sf.* graphomania.
gragnuola *sf.* **1.** hail **2.** (*fig.*) shower.
gramaglie *sf. pl.* mourning (*sing.*): *mettersi in* —, to go (*v. irr.*) into mourning.

gramigna *sf.* couch-grass.
graminàcee *sf. pl.* Gramineae.
grammàtica *sf.* grammar.
grammaticale *agg.* grammatical.
grammàtico *sm.* grammarian.
grammo *sm.* gram.
grammòfono *sm.* gramophone.
gramo *agg.* **1.** miserable **2.** (*scarso*) scanty.
grana *sf.* **1.** grain **2.** (*noia*) trouble **3.** (*denaro*) dough.
granaglie *sf. pl.* corn (*sing.*).
granaio *sm.* barn.
granata¹ *sf.* (*scopa*) broom.
granata² *sf.* (*mil.*) grenade.
granatiere *sm.* grenadier.
granatina *sf.* grenadine.
granato *agg.* **1.** garnet red **2.** (*fatto a grani*) grainy.
grancassa *sf.* big drum.
granchio *sm.* crab || *prendere un* —, to make (*v. irr.*) a blunder.
grande *agg.* **1.** great **2.** (*esteso*) large **3.** (*grosso*) big **4.** (*alto*) high; (*di statura*) tall **5.** (*adulto*) grownup.
grandeggiare *vi.* **1.** to tower **2.** (*ostentare*) to show (*v. irr.*) off.
grandezza *sf.* **1.** greatness **2.** (*dimensione*) size **3.** (*estensione*) largeness **4.** (*grandiosità*) grandeur **5.** (*liberalità*) liberality **6.** (*mat.*) quantity.
grandiloquenza *sf.* magniloquence.
grandinare *vi.* to hail (*anche fig.*).
grandinata *sf.* hail-storm.
gràndine *sf.* hail.
grandiosità *sf.* grandeur.
grandioso *agg.* grand.
granduca *sm.* Grand Duke.
granducato *sm.* Grand Duchy.
granduchessa *sf.* Grand Duchess.
granello *sm.* grain.
granita *sf.* grated-ice drink.
granìtico *agg.* granitic.
granito *sm.* granite.
granìvoro *agg.* granivorous.
grano *sm.* **1.** grain **2.** (*frumento*) wheat **3.** (*ogni cereale*) corn.
granturco *sm.* maize.
granulare *agg.* granular.
granuloma *sm.* granuloma.
granuloso *agg.* granulose.
grappa¹ *sf.* (*per unire blocchi di legno ecc.*) cramp.
grappa² *sf.* (*liquore*) "grappa".
gràppolo *sm.* cluster.
grassaggio *sm.* greasing.
grassatore *sm.* robber.

grassazione *sf.* robbery.
grassetto *sm.* (*tip.*) heavytype.
grassezza *sf.* fatness.
grasso *agg.* fat. ♦ grasso *sm.* 1. fat 2. (*lubrificante*) grease.
grassoccio *agg.* plump.
grata *sf.* grating.
graticciata *sf.* trellis-work.
gratìcola *sf.* 1. grill 2. (*di forno*) grate.
graticolato *sm.* 1. trellis 2. (*inferriata*) grating.
gratìfica *sf.* bonus.
gratificare *vt.* to gratify.
gratificazione *sf.* gratuity.
gratis *avv.* free.
gratitùdine *sf.* gratitude.
grato *agg.* 1. grateful 2. (*gradito*) welcome 3. (*piacevole*) pleasant.
grattacapo *sm.* trouble.
grattacielo *sm.* skyscraper.
grattare *vt.* 1. to scratch 2. (*grattugiare*) to grate.
grattugia *sf.* grater.
grattugiare *vt.* to grate.
gratùito *agg.* 1. free 2. (*ingiustificato*) gratuitous.
gravame *sm.* 1. burden 2. (*ipoteca*) mortgage.
gravare *vi.* to weigh. ♦ gravare *vt.* to burden.
grave *agg.* 1. grave 2. (*pesante*) heavy 3. (*importante, pericoloso*) serious.
gravezza *sf.* 1. (*pesantezza*) heaviness 2. (*serietà*) gravity 3. (*stanchezza*) weariness.
gravidanza *sf.* pregnancy.
gràvido *agg.* 1. (*di femmina*) pregnant 2. (*fig.*) fraught (with).
gravità *sf.* 1. gravity 2. (*severità*) severity.
gravitare *vi.* to gravitate.
gravitazionale *agg.* gravitational.
gravitazione *sf.* gravitation.
gravosità *sf.* heaviness.
gravoso *agg.* heavy.
grazia *sf.* 1. grace 2. (*favore*) favour 3. (*clemenza*) mercy 4. (*teol.*) grace 5. *Sua, Vostra Grazia*, His, Her, Your Grace || *in — di*, owing to.
graziare *vt.* to pardon.
grazie *inter.* thank you!, thanks! *— tante*, many thanks!
grazioso *agg.* pretty, graceful.
greca *sf.* 1. (*disegno*) Greek fret 2. (*mil.*) zig-zag braid.
grecale *sm.* north-east wind.

grecismo *sm.* Hellenism.
grecista *s.* Hellenist.
greco *agg.* e *sm.* Greek.
greco-romano *agg.* Graeco-Roman.
gregario *sm.* 1. follower 2. (*aiutante*) helper.
gregge *sm.* flock.
greggio *agg.* 1. raw 2. (*di tessuto*) unbleached 3. (*di metallo e fig.*) unrefined.
gregoriano *agg.* Gregorian.
grembiale, grembiule *sm.* apron
grembo *sm.* 1. lap 2. (*ventre materno*) womb 3. (*fig.*) bosom.
gremire *vt.* to fill.
gremito *agg.* filled (with).
greppia *sf.* crib.
gres *sm.* stoneware.
greto *sm.* 1. (*di fiume*) gravel bank 2. (*di mare*) shingly shore.
grettezza *sf.* meanness.
gretto *agg.* mean, narrow-minded.
greve *agg.* heavy.
grezzo *agg.* V. *greggio.*
gridare *vt.* e *vi.* 1. to cry 2. (*gridare forte, protestare*) to cry out: *gridò per il dolore*, he cried out with pain.
grido *sm.* cry || *di —*, famous.
grifagno *agg.* 1. rapacious 2. (*fig.*) fierce.
grifo *sm.* snout.
grifone *sm.* griffin.
grigiastro *agg.* greyish.
grigio *agg.* grey: *— perla*, pearl grey.
grigiore *sm.* greyness.
griglia *sf.* 1. (*di finestra*) shutter 2. (*di forno*) grate 3. (*grata, graticola*) grill || *cuocere alla —*, to grill.
grilletto *sm.* trigger.
grillo *sm.* 1. cricket 2. (*fig.*) fancy.
grillotalpa *sm.* mole-cricket.
grimaldello *sm.* picklock.
grinfia *sf.* clutch.
grinta *sf.* grim face.
grinza *sf.* 1. (*di pelle*) wrinkle 2. (*di stoffa*) crease || (*fig.*) *non fa una —*, it is quite correct.
grinzoso *agg.* 1. (*di pelle*) wrinkly 2. (*di stoffa*) creasy.
grisù *sm.* fire-damp.
gronda *sf.* eaves (*pl.*).
grondaia *sf.* 1. gutter 2. (*tubo di discesa*) gutter pipe.
grondante *agg.* dripping.
grondare *vi.* to drip || *— sangue*, to bleed (*v. irr.*).
groppa *sf.* back.

groppo *sm.* knot: *avere un — in gola*, to have a lump in one's throat.

groppone *sm.* back: *piegare il —*, to submit.

grossa *sf. dormire della —*, to sleep (*v. irr.*) soundly.

grossezza *sf.* 1. bigness 2. (*dimensione*) size 3. (*spessore*) thickness.

grossista *s.* wholesaler.

grosso *agg.* 1. (*anche fig.*) big 2. (*denso*) thick.

grossolanità *sf.* coarseness.

grossolano *agg.* coarse: *errore —*, blunder.

grotta *sf.* cave.

grottesco *agg.* grotesque.

groviera *sf.* gruyère.

groviglio *sm.* tangle.

gru *sf.* (*zool.; mecc.*) crane.

gruccia *sf.* 1. crutch 2. (*per abiti*) dress-hanger 3. (*per uccelli*) perch.

grufolare *vi.* to root.

grugnire *vi.* to grunt.

grugnito *sm.* grunt.

grugno *sm.* snout.

grumo *sm.* clot.

grumoso *agg.* clotted.

gruppo *sm.* group.

gruzzolo *sm.* hoard; (*risparmi*) savings (*pl.*).

guadàbile *agg.* fordable.

guadagnare *vt.* 1. to gain 2. (*col lavoro*) to earn.

guadagno *sm.* 1. earnings (*pl.*) 2. (*comm.*) profits (*pl.*) 3. (*fig.*) gain.

guadare *vt.* to ford.

guado *sm.* ford.

guai *inter.* woe!

guaina *sf.* 1. (*bot.; fodero per armi*) sheath 2. (*custodia, astuccio*) case 3. (*anat.*) theca (*pl.* -ae).

guaio *sm.* trouble.

guaire *vi.* to yelp.

guaito *sm.* yelp.

gualcire *vt.* to rumple.

gualdrappa *sf.* saddle-cloth.

guancia *sf.* cheek.

guanciale *sm.* pillow || *dormire fra due guanciali*, to have no worries.

guantaio *sm.* glover.

guantiera *sf.* 1. (*scatola per guanti*) glove-box 2. (*vassoio*) tray.

guantificio *sm.* glove-factory.

guanto *sm.* glove.

guantone *sm.* boxing-glove.

guardabarriere *sm.* gate-keeper.

guardaboschi *sm.* forester.

guardacaccia *sm.* gamekeeper.

guardacoste *sm.* coastguard.

guardalìnee *sm.* (*sport*) linesman (*pl.* -men).

guardamano *sm.* (*di scala*) hand-rail.

guardapesca *sm.* fishing warden.

guardaportone *sm.* doorkeeper.

guardare *vt.* 1. to look (at) 2. (*proteggere*) to protect. ♦ **guardare** *vi.* 1. (*tentare*) to try 2. (*essere orientato*) to face. ♦ **guardarsi** *vr.* (*da*), to beware (of).

guardaroba *sm.* 1. wardrobe 2. (*in teatro ecc.*) cloak-room.

guardarobiera *sf.* 1. (*nei locali pubblici*) cloak-room attendant 2. (*in alberghi e case private*) linen maid.

guardarobiere *sm.* (*nei locali pubblici*) cloak-room attendant.

guardasala *sm.* ticket-collector.

guardasigilli *sm.* keeper of the seals.

guardavìa *sm.* guard-rail.

guardia *sf.* guard || *— medica*, first-aid station; *fare la — a*, to guard; *mettere in —*, to warn.

guardiamarina *sm.* midshipman (*pl.* -men).

guardiano *sm.* 1. keeper 2. (*di armenti*) herdsman (*pl.* -men) || *— notturno*, night watchman (*pl.* -men).

guardina *sf.* guard-room.

guardingo *agg.* wary.

guardiola *sf.* guard-room.

guarìbile *agg.* 1. curable 2. (*di ferita*) healable.

guarigione *sf.* recovery.

guarire *vt.* 1. to cure 2. (*una ferita*) to heal. ♦ **guarire** *vi.* 1. to recover 2. (*di ferita*) to heal.

guaritore *sm.* healer.

guarnigione *sf.* garrison.

guarnire *vt.* 1. to trim 2. (*cuc.*) to garnish 3. (*fornire*) to furnish 4. (*mecc.*) to pack.

guarnitura, guarnizione *sf.* 1. trimming 2. (*cuc.*) garniture 3. (*mecc.*) packing.

guasconata *sf.* gasconade.

guascone *agg. e sm.* (*anche fig.*) Gascon.

guastafeste *s.* kill-joy.

guastamestieri *sm.* bungler.

guastare *vt.* 1. to spoil (*v. irr.*) 2. (*danneggiare*) to damage.

guastatore *sm.* 1. destroyer 2. (*mil.*) sapper.

guasto *agg.* **1.** damaged **2.** (*marcio*)
rotten **3.** (*corrotto*) tainted **4.**
(*mecc.*) out of order.
guasto *sm.* **1.** damage **2.** (*mecc.*)
breakdown || *ci deve essere un* —,
there must be something wrong.
guatare *vt.* to gaze (at).
guazzabuglio *sm.* mess.
guazzare *vi.* **1.** to paddle **2.** (*rotolarsi*) to wallow **3.** (*di liquidi in
recipienti*) to splash about.
guazzo *sm.* (*pitt.*) gouache.
guelfo *agg.* e *sm.* Guelph.
guercio *agg.* squinting. ♦ **guercio**
sm. squinter.
guerra *sf.* war.
guerrafondaio *sm.* warmonger.
guerreggiante *agg.* e *sm.* belligerent.
guerreggiare *vi.* to fight (*v. irr.*),
to war.
guerresco *agg.* **1.** war (*attr.*) **2.**
(*bellicoso*) warlike.
guerriero *agg.* warlike. ♦ **guerriero** *sm.* warrior.
guerriglia *sf.* guerrilla.
guerrigliero *sm.* **1.** guerrilla **2.**
partisan.
gufo *sm.* owl.
guglia *sf.* spire.
gugliata *sf.* needleful.
guida *sf.* **1.** guide **2.** (*auto*) drive
|| *patente di* —, driving licence;
— *telefonica*, telephone book.
guidare *vt.* **1.** to guide **2.** (*auto*) to
drive (*v. irr.*).
guidatore *sm.* driver.
guidoslitta *sf.* bobsleigh.
guinzaglio *sm.* leash: *mettere al* —,
to leash.
guisa *sf.* manner || *a* — *di*, like.
guitto *sm.* strolling player.
guizzante *agg.* **1.** darting **2.** (*di luce*) flashing **3.** (*di pesci*) wriggling.
guizzare *vi.* **1.** to dart **2.** (*di luce*) to
flash **3.** (*di pesci*) to wriggle.
guizzo *sm.* **1.** dart **2.** (*di luce*) flash
3. (*di pesci*) wriggle.
guscio *sm.* shell.
gustare *vt.* **1.** to enjoy **2.** (*assaggiare*) to taste.
gustativo *agg.* gustative.
gustatore *sm.* taster.
gusto *sm.* **1.** taste **2.** (*gradimento*)
liking || *di, con* —, with relish.
gustoso *agg.* **1.** (*saporito*) tasty **2.**
(*piacevole*) pleasant.
guttaperca *sf.* gutta-percha.
gutturale *agg.* guttural.

H

harem *sm.* harem.
hascisc *sm.* hashish.
hawaiano *agg.* e *sm.* Hawaiian.
hurrà *inter.* hurrah.

i *art.* the.
iarda *sf.* yard.
iato *sm.* hiatus.
iattanza *sf.* boastfulness.
iattura *sf.* misfortune.
ibèrico *agg.* e *sm.* Iberian.
ibernazione *sf.* hibernation.
ibisco *sm.* hibiscus.
ibridazione *sf.* hybridization.
ibridismo *sm.* hybridism.
ibrido *agg.* e *sm.* hybrid.
icona *sf.* icon.
iconoclasta *sm.* iconoclast.
idea *sf.* idea.
ideàbile *agg.* imaginable.
ideale *agg.* e *sm.* ideal.
idealismo *sm.* idealism.
idealista *s.* idealist.
idealìstico *agg.* idealistic.
idealizzare *vt.* to idealize.
idealizzazione *sf.* idealization.
ideare *vt.* to conceive, to devise.
ideatore *sm.* inventor, deviser.
ideazione *sf.* ideation.
idèntico *agg.* identic.
identificàbile *agg.* identifiable.
identificare *vt.* to identify.
identificazione *sf.* identification.
identità *sf.* identity.
ideografìa *sf.* ideography.
ideogramma *sm.* ideogram.
ideologìa *sf.* ideology.
ideològico *agg.* ideologic(al).
ideologismo *sm.* ideology.
ideòlogo *sm.* ideologist.
idillìaco *agg.* idyllic.
idillio *sm.* idyl.
idioma *sm.* language.
idiomàtico *agg.* idiomatic.
idiosincrasìa *sf.* idiosyncrasy.
idiota *sm.* idiot. ♦ **idiota** *agg.*
idiotic.
idiotismo *sm.* idiom.
idiozia *sf.* idiocy.
idolatra *sm.* idolater.

idolatrare *vt.* to worship.
idolatrìa *sf.* idolatry.
ìdolo *sm.* idol.
idoneità *sf.* fitness.
idòneo *agg.* fit.
idrante *sm.* hydrant.
idratare *vt.* to hydrate.
idrato *sm.* hydrate.
idràulica *sf.* hydraulics.
idràulico *agg.* hydraulic. ♦ idràulico *sm.* plumber.
ìdrico *agg.* water.
idrocarburo *sm.* hydrocarbon.
idrocefalìa *sf.* hydrocephalus.
idrocèfalo *sm.* hydrocephalus.
idroelèttrico *agg.* hydroelectric.
idròfilo *agg.* absorbent: *cotone* —, cotton wool.
idrofobìa *sf.* rabies.
idròfobo *agg.* 1. rabid 2. (*fig.*) furious.
idrògeno *sm.* hydrogen.
idrografìa *sf.* hydrography.
idròlisi *sf.* hydrolysis (*pl.* -ses).
idrologìa *sf.* hydrology.
idròpico *agg.* dropsical.
idropisìa *sf.* dropsy.
idroscalo *sm.* seaplane station.
idrostàtica *sf.* hydrostatics.
idrovolante *sm.* seaplane.
idròvora *sf.* water-scooping machine.
iella *sf.* bad luck.
iena *sf.* 1. hyaena 2. (*fig.*) vixen.
ieràtico *agg.* hieratic(al).
ieri *avv.* yesterday.
iettatore *sm.* evil-eyed man.
iettatura *sf.* evil-eye.
igiene *sf.* 1. hygiene 2. (*sistema sanitario*) sanitation.
igiènico *agg.* sanitary.
igienista *s.* hygienist.
ignaro *agg.* ignorant.
ignavia *sf.* laziness.
ignavo *agg.* lazy.
ìgneo *agg.* igneous.
ignòbile *agg.* mean.
ignominia *sf.* ignominy.
ignominioso *agg.* ignominious.
ignorante *agg.* e *sm.* ignorant.
ignoranza *sf.* ignorance.
ignorare *vt.* to ignore.
ignoto *agg.* unknown.
ignudo *agg.* naked.
igrometrìa *sf.* hygrometry.
iguana *sf.* iguana.
il *art.* the.
ilare *agg.* cheerful.
ilarità *sf.* hilarity.

ilìaco *agg.* iliac.
illanguidire *vt.* to weaken.
illazione *sf.* illation.
illécito *agg.* illicit.
illegale *agg.* illegal.
illegalità *sf.* illegality.
illeggibile *agg.* illegible.
illegittimità *sf.* illegitimacy.
illegittimo *agg.* illegitimate.
illeso *agg.* unhurt.
illibatezza *sf.* purity.
illibato *agg.* pure.
illiberale *agg.* illiberal.
illimitato *agg.* unlimited.
illividire *vt.* to make (*v. irr.*) livid.
♦ illividire *vi.* to turn livid.
illogicità *sf.* illogicality.
illogico *agg.* illogical.
illùdere *vt.* to delude. ♦ illùdersi *vr.* to delude oneself.
illuminante *agg.* illuminating.
illuminare *vt.* to light up.
illuminazione *sf.* lighting.
illuminismo *sm.* Illuminism.
illusione *sf.* illusion.
illusionismo *sm.* illusionism.
illusionista *s.* conjurer.
illuso *agg.* deluded. ♦ illuso *sm.* day-dreamer.
illusorio *agg.* illusory.
illustrare *vt.* to illustrate.
illustrativo *agg.* illustrative.
illustrato *agg.* illustrated || *cartolina illustrata*, picture post-card.
illustrazione *sf.* illustration.
illustre *agg.* renowned.
imbacuccare *vt.* to muffle up.
imbaldanzire *vt.* to embolden. ♦ imbaldanzirsi *vr.* to grow (*v. irr.*) bold.
mballaggio *sm.* packing.
imballare *vt.* to pack (up). ♦ imballarsi *vr.* (*di motori*) to race.
imbalsamare *vt.* 1. to embalm 2. (*di animali*) to stuff.
imbalsamatore *sm.* 1. embalmer 2. (*di animali*) stuffer.
imbalsamazione *sf.* 1. embalming 2. (*di animali*) stuffing.
imbambolato *agg.* dull.
imbandierare *vt.* to deck with flags.
imbandire *vt.* 1. (*la tavola*) to lay (*v. irr.*) 2. to prepare.
imbarazzante *agg.* embarrassing.
imbarazzare *vt.* to embarrass. ♦ imbarazzarsi *vr.* to meddle.
imbarazzato *agg.* embarrassed.
imbarazzo *sm.* embarrassment.

imbarcadero sm. landing-stage.
imbarcare vt. to take (v. irr.) on board. ♦ **imbarcarsi** vr. to embark.
imbarcazione sf. boat.
imbarco sm. embarkation.
imbastardire vt. to debase.
imbastardito agg. debased.
imbastire vt. 1. to tack 2. (fig.) to put (v. irr.) together.
imbastitura sf. tacking.
imbàttersi vr. to meet (v. irr.) (with).
imbattìbile agg. invincible.
imbattibilità sf. invincibility.
imbavagliare vt. to gag.
imbeccare vt. 1. to feed (v. irr.) 2. (fig.) to prompt.
imbeccata sf. 1. beakful 2. (fig.) prompting.
imbecille agg. e sm. imbecile.
imbecillità sf. imbecility.
imbelle agg. weak.
imbellettare vt. to make (v. irr.) up.
imbellire vt. to embellish.
imberbe agg. beardless.
imbestialire vi. to get (v. irr.) furious. ♦ **imbestialirsi** vr. to get furious.
imbévere vt. to imbue with.
imbiancamento sm. whitening.
imbiancare vt. 1. to whiten 2. (i muri) to whitewash.
imbiancatura sf. 1. (di muri) whitewashing 2. (di tessuti) bleaching.
imbianchino sm. house painter.
imbiondire vt. to make (v. irr.) fair. ♦ **imbiondire** vi. to become (v. irr.) fair.
imbizzarrirsi vr. 1. to become (v. irr.) restive 2. (adirarsi) to fire up.
imboccare vt. 1. to feed (v. irr.) 2. (di strada) to enter.
imboccatura sf. 1. mouth 2. (di strumento) mouthpiece.
imbonimento sm. sales talk.
imbonire vt. to allure.
imbonitore sm. charlatan.
imborghesimento sm. getting into middle-class habits.
imborghesire vt. to give (v. irr.) middle-class habits. ♦ **imborghesirsi** vr. to acquire middle-class habits.
imboscare vt. 1. to put (v. irr.) into safe keeping 2. (mil.) to help to evade military service. ♦ **im-**

boscarsi vr. 1. to lie (v. irr.) in ambush 2. (mil.) to evade military service.
imboscata sf. ambush.
imboscato sm. shirker.
imboschimento sm. afforestation.
imboschire vt. to afforest.
imbottigliamento sm. bottling || — stradale, traffic jam.
imbottigliare vt. 1. to bottle 2. (fig.) to block.
imbottire vt. 1. to stuff 2. (di vestiti) to wad 3. (fig.) — la testa, to cram. ♦ **imbottirsi** vr. 1. to fill oneself (with), to stuff oneself (with) 2. (coprirsi) to wrap oneself (into).
imbottita sf. quilt.
imbottito agg. stuffed, filled || panino —, sandwich.
imbottitura sf. 1. stuffing 2. (di vestiti) wadding.
imbracciare vt. 1. to put (v. irr.) sthg. on one's hands 2. (di fucile) to bring (v. irr.) to firing position.
imbrancare vt. to herd.
imbrattacarte sm. scribbler.
imbrattamento sm. soiling.
imbrattare vt. to soil.
imbrattatele sm. dauber.
imbrigliamento sm. bridling.
imbrigliare vt. to bridle.
imbrigliatura sf. bridling.
imbroccare vt. 1. to hit (v. irr.) 2. (fig.) to guess.
imbrogliare vt. 1. to cheat 2. (confondere) to confuse.
imbroglio sm. cheat, swindle.
imbroglione sm. cheat, swindler.
imbronciarsi vr. to pout.
imbronciato agg. sulky.
imbrunire vi. 1. to brown 2. (farsi sera) to get (v. irr.) dark.
imbrunire sm. nightfall.
imbruttire vt. to make (v. irr.) ugly. ♦ **imbruttirsi** vr. to become (v. irr.) ugly.
imbucare vt. to post.
imburrare vt. to butter.
imbuto sm. funnel.
imene sm. hymen.
imeneo sm. wedding.
imenòttero sm. hymenopteron (pl. -ra).
imitare vt. to imitate.
imitativo agg. imitative.
imitatore sm. imitator.
imitazione sf. imitation.

immacolato *agg.* spotless.
immagazzinare *vt.* to store (up).
immaginàbile *agg.* imaginable.
immaginare *vt.* to imagine.
immaginario *agg.* imaginary.
immaginativa *sf.* imagination.
immaginativo *agg.* imaginative.
immaginazione *sf.* imagination.
immàgine *sf.* image.
immalinconire *vt.* to make (*v. irr.*) melancholy. ♦ **immalinconire** *vi.* to grow (*v. irr.*) sad.
immancàbile *agg.* unfailing.
immane *agg.* 1. huge 2. (*fig.*) frightful.
immanente *agg.* immanent.
immanenza *sf.* immanence.
immangiàbile *agg.* uneatable.
immarcescìbile *agg.* incorruptible.
immateriale *agg.* immaterial.
immaterialità *sf.* immateriality.
immatricolare *vt.* to matriculate. ♦ **immatricolarsi** *vr.* to matriculate.
immatricolazione *sf.* matriculation.
immaturità *sf.* immaturity.
immaturo *agg.* 1. (*di frutto*) unripe 2. (*di persona*) immature.
immedesimare *vt.* 1. to unify. ♦ **immedesimarsi** *vr.* to identify oneself (with).
immedesimazione *sf.* unifying.
immediatamente *avv.* at once.
immediatezza *sf.* immediateness.
immediato *agg.* immediate.
immemoràbile *agg.* immemorial.
immèmore *agg.* forgetful.
immensità *sf.* immensity.
immenso *agg.* immense.
immèrgere *vt.* to immerse. ♦ **immèrgersi** *vr.* to immerse oneself.
immeritato *agg.* undeserved.
immeritévole *agg.* undeserving.
immersione *sf.* immersion.
immèttere *vt.* to let (*v. irr.*) in. ♦ **immèttersi** *vr.* to penetrate.
immigrante *agg. e sm.* immigrant.
immigrare *vi.* to immigrate.
immigrato *agg.* immigrated. ♦ **immigrato** *sm.* immigrant.
immigrazione *sf.* immigration.
imminente *agg.* impending.
imminenza *sf.* imminence.
immischiare *vt.* to involve. ♦ **immischiarsi** *vr.* to meddle (with).
immiserimento *sm.* impoverishing.
immiserire *vt.* to impoverish. ♦

immiserirsi *vr.* 1. to become (*v. irr.*) poor 2. (*fig.*) to weaken.
immissario *sm.* affluent.
immissione *sf.* letting in.
immòbile *agg.* immobile || *beni immobili*, immovables.
immobiliare *agg.* immovable.
immobilismo *sm.* ultra-conservatism.
immobilità *sf.* immobility.
immobilizzare *vt.* 1. to immobilize 2. (*comm.*) to lock up.
immobilizzazione *sf.* 1. immobilization 2. (*comm.*) locking up.
immoderato *agg.* immoderate.
immodestia *sf.* immodesty.
immodesto *agg.* immodest.
immolare *vt.* to immolate.
immondezza *sf.* dirtiness.
immondezzaio *sm.* garbage heap.
immondizia *sf.* 1. filth 2. (*spazzatura*) garbage.
immondo *agg.* dirty.
immorale *agg.* immoral.
immoralità *sf.* immorality.
immortalare *vt.* to immortalize.
immortale *agg.* immortal.
immortalità *sf.* immortality.
immoto *agg.* motionless.
immune *agg.* immune.
immunità *sf.* immunity.
immunizzare *vt.* to immunize.
immunizzazione *sf.* immunization.
immusonirsi *vr.* to sulk.
immusonito *agg.* sulky.
immutàbile *agg.* immutable.
immutabilità *sf.* immutability.
impacchettare *vt.* to package.
impacciare *vt.* to hamper.
impacciato *agg.* 1. embarrassed 2. (*goffo*) awkward.
impaccio *sm.* hindrance.
impacco *sm.* compress.
impadronirsi *vr.* to take (*v. irr.*) possession (of).
impagàbile *agg.* priceless.
impaginare *vt.* to make-up.
impaginatore *sm.* maker-up.
impaginazione *sf.* making-up.
impagliare *vt.* 1. to cover with straw 2. (*di animali*) to stuff with straw.
impagliatore *sm.* 1. chair-mender 2. (*di animali*) stuffer.
impagliatura *sf.* 1. chair-mending 2. (*di animali*) stuffing.
impalare *vt.* to impale.
impalato *agg.* stiff.
impalcatura *sf.* 1. scaffolding 2.

(*di corna di cervo*) antlers (*pl.*).
impallidire *vi.* to turn pale.
impallinare *vt.* to shot.
impalmare *vt.* to marry.
impalpàbile *agg.* impalpable.
impalpabilità *sf.* impalpability.
impanare *vt.* 1. (*cuc.*) to bread 2. (*mecc.*) to thread.
impantanare *vt.* to swamp. ♦ **impantanarsi** *vr.* to swamp (*anche fig.*).
impaperarsi *vr.* to slip up.
impappinarsi *vr.* to stammer.
imparagonàbile *agg.* incomparable.
imparare *vt.* to learn (*v. irr.*).
impareggiàbile *agg.* unparalleled.
imparentare *vt.* to relate. ♦ **imparentarsi** *vr.* to become (*v. irr.*) related (to).
impari *agg.* unequal.
imparisìllabo *agg.* e *sm.* imparisyllabic.
imparruccato *agg.* bewigged.
impartire *vt.* to impart.
imparziale *agg.* impartial.
imparzialità *sf.* impartiality.
impassìbile *agg.* impassive, unmoved.
impassibilità *sf.* impassibility.
impastare *vt.* to knead || — *i colori*, to impaste.
impastato *agg.* 1. kneaded 2. (*fig.*) full.
impastatore *sm.* kneader.
impastatrice *sf.* kneading-machine.
impasto *sm.* 1. dough 2. (*miscuglio*) mixture.
impastoiare *vt.* (*fig.*) to impede.
impatto *sm.* impact.
impaurire *vt.* to frighten. ♦ **impaurirsi** *vr.* to get (*v. irr.*) scared.
impaurito *agg.* afraid: *sguardo* —, fearful look.
impàvido *agg.* fearless.
impaziente *agg.* impatient.
impazientirsi *vr.* to lose (*v. irr.*) one's patience.
impazienza *sf.* impatience.
impazzare *vi.* to be at one's height.
impazzata (*nella loc. avv.*) *all'*—, madly.
impazzire *vi.* to go (*v. irr.*) mad.
impeccàbile *agg.* faultless.
impeciare *vt.* to pitch.
impedimento *sm.* obstacle.
impedire *vt.* to prevent (from).
impegnare *vt.* 1. (*dare in pegno*) to pawn 2. (*prenotare*) to reserve,

to book. ♦ **impegnarsi** *vr.* to engage (oneself).
impegnativo *agg.* binding || *lavoro* —, exacting job.
impegno *sm.* engagement.
impegolarsi *vr.* (*fig.*) to get (*v. irr.*) involved.
impelagarsi *vr.* to get (*v. irr.*) in trouble.
impellente *agg.* urgent.
impellicciare *vt.* to fur.
impellicciatura *sf.* veneering.
impenetràbile *agg.* impenetrable.
impenetrabilità *sf.* impenetrableness.
impenitente *agg.* impenitent.
impennacchiare *vt.* to plume.
impennarsi *vr.* 1. (*di cavallo*) to rear 2. (*fig.*) to rear up.
impennata *sf.* (*di cavallo*) rearing 2. (*fig.*) bristling.
impensàbile *agg.* unthinkable.
impensato *agg.* unexpected.
impensierire *vt.* to worry.
imperante *agg.* ruling.
imperare *vi.* to rule (over).
imperativo *agg.* imperative.
imperatore *sm.* emperor.
imperatrice *sf.* empress.
impercettìbile *agg.* imperceptible.
impercettibilità *sf.* imperceptibility.
imperdonàbile *agg.* unpardonable.
imperfetto *agg.* 1. (*gramm.*) imperfect 2. (*fig.*) faulty.
imperfezione *sf.* imperfection.
imperiale[1] *agg.* imperial.
imperiale[2] *sm.* imperial.
imperialismo *sm.* imperialism.
imperialista *s.* imperialist.
imperialìstico *agg.* imperialistic.
imperio *sm.* command, authority.
imperioso *agg.* imperious.
imperito *agg.* unskilful.
imperituro *agg.* everlasting.
imperizia *sf.* unskilfulness.
imperlare *vt.* to bead. ♦ **imperlarsi** *vr.* to bead.
impermalirsi *vr.* to resent (sthg.).
impermeàbile *agg.* impermeable. ♦ **impermeàbile** *sm.* raincoat.
impermeabilità *sf.* impermeability.
impermeabilizzare *vt.* to waterproof.
impermeabilizzazione *sf.* waterproofing.
imperniare *vt.* to pivot (upon).
impero *sm.* empire.
imperscrutàbile *agg.* inscrutable.

imperscrutabilità sf. inscrutableness.
impersonale agg. impersonal.
impersonalità sf. impersonality.
impersonare vt. to impersonate. ♦ **impersonarsi** vr. to materialize.
impertèrrito agg. undaunted.
impertinente agg. impertinent.
impertinenza sf. impertinence.
imperturbàbile agg. impassive.
imperturbabilità sf. imperturbability.
imperturbato agg. imperturbed.
imperversare vi. to rage.
impervio agg. inaccessible.
ìmpeto sm. 1. rush, impetus 2. (impulso) impulse.
impetrare vt. to impetrate.
impettito agg. stiff.
impetuosità sf. impetuosity.
impetuoso agg. impetuous.
impiantare vt. to found.
impiantito sm. 1. (di legno) parquet floor 2. (di piastrelle) tiled floor.
impianto sm. plant, installation.
impiastricciare vt. to daub.
impiastro sm. 1. plaster 2. (fig.) bore.
impiccagione sf. hanging.
impiccare vt. to hang.
impiccato agg. hanged. ♦ **impiccato** sm. hanged man.
impicciare vt. to hinder. ♦ **impicciarsi** vr. to meddle (in).
impiccio sm. hindrance.
impiccolire vt. to make (v. irr.) smaller.
impiegare .vt. 1. to employ 2. (spendere) to spend (v. irr.) 3. (comm.) to invest.
impiegatizio agg. white-collar (attributivo).
impiegato agg. employed. ♦ **impiegato** sm. employee, clerk.
impiego sm. 1. employment 2. (uso) use.
impietosire vt. to move tò pity. ♦ **impietosirsi** vr. to feel (v. irr.) sorry (for).
impietrire vt. to petrify.
impigliare vt. to entangle.
impigrire vt. to make (v. irr.) lazy.
impinguare vt. 1. to fatten 2. (fig.) to enrich.
impiombare vt. 1. to plumb 2. (otturare) to fill 3. (coprire di piombo) to lead.
impiombatura sf. 1. plumbing 2.

(otturazione) filling 3. (copertura di piombo) leading.
implacàbile agg. implacable.
implacabilità sf. implacability.
implicare vt. to involve.
implìcito agg. implicit.
implorare vt. to implore.
implorazione˙ sf. entreaty.
implume agg. featherless.
impolìtico agg. impolitic.
impollinare vt. to pollinate.
impollinazione sf. pollination.
impoltronire vt. to make (v. irr.) lazy. ♦ **impoltronirsi** vr. to grow (v. irr.) lazy.
impolverare vt. to cover with dust.
impolverato agg. dusty.
impomatare vt. to pomade. ♦ **impomatarsi** vr. to pomade oneself.
imponderàbile agg. imponderable.
imponderabilità sf. imponderability.
imponente agg. imposing.
imponenza sf. grandeur, majesty.
imponìbile agg. taxable.
imponibilità sf. taxability.
impopolare agg. unpopular.
impopolarità sf. unpopularity.
imporporarsi vr. to purple.
imporre vt. to impose: — un nome, to give (v. irr.) a name. ♦ **imporsi** vr. 1. to impose oneself 2. (avere successo) to become (v. irr.) popular.
importante agg. important.
importanza sf. importance.
importare vi. imp. to matter, to care. ♦ **importare** vt. (comm.) to import.
importatore sm. importer.
importazione sf. import.
importo sm. amount.
importunare vt. to importune, to bother.
importunità sf. importunity.
importuno agg. boring. ♦ **importuno** sm. bore.
imposizione sf. imposition.
impossessarsi vr. to take (v. irr.) possession (of).
impossìbile agg. impossible.
impossibilità sf. impossibility.
impossibilitato agg. unable.
imposta sf. 1. tax 2. (edil.) shutter.
impostare vt. 1. to start 2. (di lettera) to post.
impostazione sf. general lines (pl.).
impostore sm. impostor.

impostura *sf.* **1.** imposture **2.** (*frode*) fraud.

impotente *agg.* powerless. ♦ **impotente** *agg.* e *sm.* (*med.*) impotent.

impotenza *sf.* impotence.

impoverimento *sm.* impoverishment.

impoverire *vt.* to impoverish. ♦ **impoverirsi** *vr.* to become (*v. irr.*) poor.

impraticàbile *agg.* impracticable: *strada* —, impassable road.

impraticabilità *sf.* impracticability.

impratichire *vt.* to train. ♦ **impratichirsi** *vr.* to get (*v. irr.*) trained.

imprecare *vi.* to curse.

imprecazione *sf.* curse.

imprecisàbile *agg.* indeterminable.

imprecisato *agg.* undetermined.

imprecisione *sf.* **1.** vagueness **2.** (*inesattezza*) inaccuracy.

impreciso *agg.* inaccurate.

impregnare *vt.* to impregnate (with). ♦ **impregnarsi** *vr.* to become (*v. irr.*) imbued (with).

imprèndere *vt.* to undertake (*v. irr.*).

imprendìbile *agg.* elusive, invincible.

imprenditore *sm.* **1.** entrepreneur **2.** (*edil.*) contractor.

impreparato *agg.* unprepared.

impreparazione *sf.* unpreparedness.

impresa *sf.* **1.** (*iniziativa*) undertaking **2.** (*gesta*) deed **3.** (*azienda*) firm, company.

impresario *sm.* **1.** contractor **2.** (*teat.*) manager.

imprescindìbile *agg.* unavoidable.

imprescrittìbile *agg.* indefeasible.

impressionàbile *agg.* impressionable.

impressionabilità *sf.* impressionability.

impressionante *agg.* frightening.

impressionare *vt.* **1.** to impress **2.** (*foto*) to expose.

impressione *sf.* impression.

impressionismo *sm.* impressionism.

impressionista *s.* impressionist.

impresso *agg.* printed.

imprestare *vt.* to lend (*v. irr.*).

imprevedìbile *agg.* unforeseeable.

impreveduto *agg.* unforeseen.

imprevidente *agg.* improvident.

imprevidenza *sf.* improvidence.

imprevisto *agg.* unexpected. ♦ **imprevisto** *sm.* unforeseen event.

impreziosire *vt.* to make (*v. irr.*) precious. ♦ **impreziosirsi** *vr.* to become (*v. irr.*) precious.

imprigionamento *sm.* imprisonment.

imprigionare *vt.* to imprison.

imprìmere *vt.* to impress.

improbàbile *agg.* improbable.

improbabilità *sf.* improbability.

ìmprobo *agg.* **1.** dishonest **2.** (*faticoso*) hard.

improduttività *sf.* unproductiveness.

improduttivo *agg.* unproductive.

impronta *sf.* **1.** impression: — *del piede, digitale*, footprint, fingerprint **2.** (*fig.*) mark.

improntare *vt.* **1.** to prepare **2.** (*fig.*) to mark.

improntitùdine *sf.* impudence.

impronunciàbile *agg.* unpronounceable.

improperio *sm.* insult.

improprietà *sf.* impropriety.

improprio *agg.* improper.

improrogàbile *agg.* undelayable.

improvvido *agg.* improvident.

improvvisamente *avv.* suddenly.

improvvisare *vt.* e *vi.* to improvise. ♦ **improvvisarsi** *vr.* to act.

improvvisata *sf.* surprise.

improvvisatore *sm.* improviser.

improvvisazione *sf.* improvisation.

improvviso *agg.* sudden.

imprudente *agg.* imprudent.

imprudenza *sf.* imprudence.

impudente *agg.* impudent.

impudenza *sf.* impudence.

impudicizia *sf.* immodesty.

impudico *agg.* shameless, immodest.

impugnàbile *agg.* (*giur.*) impugnable.

impugnabilità *sf.* (*giur.*) impugnment.

impugnare *vt.* **1.** to grasp, to hold **2.** (*giur.*) to impugn.

impugnatura *sf.* hilt.

impulsività *sf.* impulsiveness.

impulsivo *agg.* impulsive.

impulso *sm.* impulse.

impunemente *avv.* safely.

impunità *sf.* impunity.

impunito *agg.* unpunished.

impuntare *vi.* to stumble (over).

♦ **impuntarsi** *vr.* **1.** to jib **2.** (*ostinarsi*) to stick (*v. irr.*) (to).
impuntura *sf.* stitching.
impurità *sf.* impurity.
impuro *agg.* impure.
imputàbile *agg.* **1.** imputable **2.** (*giur.*) chargeable (with).
imputare *vt.* **1.** to impute **2.** (*giur.*) to charge (with).
imputato *sm.* defendant.
imputazione *sf.* imputation.
imputridimento *sm.* putrefaction.
imputridire *vi.* to rot.
in *prep.* (*stato in luogo*) in, at: *essere — campagna, — città*, to be in the country, in town; *essere — casa, — chiesa*, to be at home, at church **2.** (*moto a luogo*) to: *andò — America*, he went to America **3.** (*moto dentro luogo*) into: *va' nello studio*, go into the study **4.** (*coi mezzi di trasporto*) by: *sono venuto — treno*, I came by train.
inàbile *agg.* **1.** unable **2.** (*non idoneo*) unfit.
inabilità *sf.* **1.** inability **2.** (*inidoneità*) unfitness.
inabilitare *vt.* to disable.
inabilitazione *sf.* disability.
inabissamento *sm.* sinking.
inabissarsi *vr.* to sink (*v. irr.*).
inabitàbile *agg.* uninhabitable.
inabitabilità *sf.* uninhabitableness.
inabitato *agg.* **1.** uninhabited **2.** (*deserto*) deserted.
inaccessìbile *agg.* inaccessible.
inaccessibilità *sf.* inaccessibility.
inaccettàbile *agg.* unacceptable.
inaccettabilità *sf.* unacceptableness.
inacerbire *vt.* to exacerbate. ♦ **inacerbirsi** *vr.* to grow (*v. irr.*) bitter.
inacidire *vt.* to sour. ♦ **inacidirsi** *vr.* to turn sour.
inacidito *agg.* sour.
inadattàbile *agg.* unadaptable.
inadattabilità *sf.* inadaptability.
inadatto *agg.* **1.** unfit (for) **2.** (*sconveniente*) unbecoming.
inadeguato *agg.* inadequate.
inadempìbile *agg.* unfulfillable.
inadempiente *agg.* defaulting.
inadempienza *sf.* non-execution.
inafferràbile *agg.* unseizable.
inalare *vt.* to inhale.
inalatore *sm.* inhaler.
inalazione *sf.* inhalation.

inalberare *vt.* to hoist. ♦ **inalberarsi** *vr.* **1.** to rear up **2.** (*fig.*) to lose (*v. irr.*) one's temper.
inalienàbile *agg.* inalienable.
inalienabilità *sf.* inalienability.
inalteràbile *agg.* inalterable.
inalterabilità *sf.* inalterability.
inalterato *agg.* unaltered.
inalveare *vt.* to canalize.
inamidare *vt.* to starch.
inammissìbile *agg.* inadmissible.
inammissibilità *sf.* inadmissibility.
inamovìbile *agg.* irremovable.
inamovibilità *sf.* irremovability.
inane *agg.* inane.
inanellare *vt.* to curl.
inanimato *agg.* lifeless.
inanità *sf.* inanity.
inappagàbile *agg.* unsatisfiable.
inappagato *agg.* unsatisfied.
inappellàbile *agg.* inappellable.
inappetenza *sf.* inappetence.
inapplicàbile *agg.* inapplicable.
inapprezzàbile *agg.* priceless.
inappuntàbile *agg.* **1.** irreproachable **2.** (*nel vestire*) faultlessly dressed.
inarcamento *sm.* bending, arching.
inarcare *vt.* to bend (*v. irr.*) || *— le sopracciglia*, to raise one's brows. ♦ **inarcarsi** *vr.* to arch.
inargentare *vt.* to silver.
inaridire *vt.* to dry. ♦ **inaridirsi** *vr.* to dry up.
inarticolato *agg.* inarticulate.
inascoltato *agg.* unheard.
inaspettato *agg.* unexpected.
inasprimento *sm.* embitterment.
inasprire *vt.* to embitter. ♦ **inasprirsi** *vr.* to become (*v. irr.*) embittered.
inattaccàbile *agg.* unassailable.
inattendìbile *agg.* unreliable.
inatteso *agg.* unexpected.
inattività *sf.* inactivity.
inattivo *agg.* inactive.
inattuàbile *agg.* impracticable.
inattuale *agg.* outdated.
inaudito *agg.* unheard of.
inaugurale *agg.* inaugural.
inaugurare *vt.* to inaugurate.
inaugurazione *sf.* inauguration.
inavvedutezza *sf.* carelessness.
inavveduto *agg.* careless.
inavvertenza *sf.* inadvertence.
inavvertito *agg.* unperceived.
inazione *sf.* inaction.
incagliare *vt.* to hinder. ♦ **incagliarsi** *vr.* to strand.

incaglio *sm.* **1.** stranding **2.** (*fig.*) obstacle.

incalcolàbile *agg.* incalculable.

incallire *vi.* to harden. ♦ **incallirsi** *vr.* to harden.

incallito *agg.* hardened.

incalzante *agg.* **1.** pursuing **2.** (*fig.*) pressing.

incalzare *vt.* **1.** to pursue **2.** (*fig.*) to urge.

incameramento *sm.* confiscation.

incamerare *vt.* to confiscate.

incamminare *vt.* to set (*v. irr.*) going. ♦ **incamminarsi** *vr.* to set out (for).

incanalamento *sm.* canalization.

incanalare *vt.* to canalize.

incancellàbile *agg.* indelible.

incancrenire *vi.* to become (*v. irr.*) gangrenous.

incandescente *agg.* white-hot.

incandescenza *sf.* incandescence.

incantamento *sm.* charm.

incantare *vt.* to charm. ♦ **incantarsi** *vr.* to be charmed.

incantato *agg.* enchanted.

incantatore *agg.* enchanting. ♦ **incantatore** *sm.* enchanter.

incantésimo *sm.* spell.

incantévole *agg.* charming.

incanto[1] *sm.* enchantment.

incanto[2] *sm.* (*comm.*) auction: *vendere all'—*, to sell (*v. irr.*) by auction.

incanutire *vi.* to grow (*v. irr.*) hoary.

incapace *agg.* unable.

incapacità *sf.* incapacity.

incaparbirsi *vr.* to become (*v. irr.*) obstinate.

incappare *vi.* to get (*v. irr.*) into, to stumble.

incappucciare *vt.* to hood. ♦ **incappucciarsi** *vr.* to put (*v. irr.*) on one's hood.

incapricciarsi *vr.* to take (*v. irr.*) a fancy (to).

incapsulare *vt.* to capsule.

incarcerare *vt.* to imprison.

incarcerazione *sf.* imprisonment.

incaricare *vt.* to charge (so. with). ♦ **incaricarsi** *vr.* to charge oneself (with).

incaricato *agg.* charged (with). ♦ **incaricato** *sm.* appointee.

incàrico *sm.* task, duty.

incarnare *vt.* to embody. ♦ **incarnarsi** *vr.* to take (*v. irr.*) body.

incarnato *sm.* complexion.

incarnazione *sf.* incarnation.

incarnire *vi.* to grow (*v. irr.*) into flesh.

incartamento *sm.* dossier.

incartapecorire *vi.* to wrinkle.

incartapecorito *agg.* wrinkled with age.

incartare *vt.* to wrap in paper.

incarto *sm.* set of papers.

incartocciare *vt.* to wrap up in a cornet.

incasellare *vt.* to put (*v. irr.*) in squares.

incassamento *sm.* **1.** boxing **2.** (*mecc.; arch.*) embedding.

incassare *vt.* **1.** to box **2.** (*riscuotere*) to cash.

incassatura *sf.* hollow.

incasso *sm.* **1.** collection **2.** (*di spettacoli*) receipts (*pl.*).

incastellamento *sm.* **1.** fortifications (*pl.*) **2.** (*arch.*) scaffolding.

incastellare *vt.* to fortify with battlements.

incastellatura *sf.* **1.** frame **2.** (*arch.*) scaffolding.

incastonare *vt.* to set (*v. irr.*).

incastonatura *sf.* setting.

incastrare *vt.* **1.** to embed **2.** (*adattare*) to fit in. ♦ **incastrarsi** *vr.* **1.** to fit **2.** (*impigliarsi*) to get (*v. irr.*) stuck.

incastro *sm.* joint.

incatenamento *sm.* chaining.

incatenare *vt.* to chain. ♦ **incatenarsi** *vr.* to be linked (with).

incatramare *vt.* to tar.

incattivire *vt.* to exasperate. ♦ **incattivirsi** *vr.* to get (*v. irr.*) crossed.

incàuto *agg.* rash.

incavare *vt.* to hollow out.

incavatura *sf.* hollowness.

incavo *sm.* hollow.

incèdere *vi.* to advance.

incendiare *vt.* to set (*v. irr.*) on fire.

incendiario *agg. e sm.* incendiary.

incendio *sm.* fire.

incenerire *vt.* to reduce to ashes.

incensamento *sm.* **1.** incensation **2.** (*fig.*) flattery.

incensare *vt.* **1.** to incense **2.** (*fig.*) to flatter.

incenso *sm.* incense.

incensuràbile *agg.* irreproachable.

incensurato *agg.* blameless: *essere —*, to be a first-offender.

incentivo *sm.* incentive.

inceppamento sm. 1. obstacle 2. (mecc.) jam.

inceppare vt. 1. to clog 2. (ostacolare) to encumber. ♦ incepparsi vr. to jam.

incerare vt. to wax.

incertezza sf. uncertainty, doubt.

incerto agg. uncertain. ♦ incerto sm. uncertainty.

incespicare vi. to stumble.

incessante agg. unceasing.

incesto sm. incest.

incestuoso agg. incestuous.

incetta sf. cornering: fare — di, to make (v. irr.) a corner in.

incettare vt. to corner.

incettatore sm. cornerer.

inchiesta sf. inquiry, investigation.

inchinare vt. to bow. ♦ inchinarsi vr. to bow (down).

inchino sm. bow.

inchiodare vt. to nail.

inchiodatura sf. nailing.

inchiostro sm. ink.

inciampare vi. to stumble.

inciampo sm. obstacle.

incidentale agg. 1. incidental 2. (gramm.) parenthetic.

incidente agg. incident. ♦ incidente sm. accident.

incidenza sf. incidence.

incidere[1] vt. 1. to cut (v. irr.) 2. (intagliare) to engrave 3. (su disco, nastro ecc.) to record.

incidere[2] vi. to weigh heavily: — sul bilancio, to weigh heavily on one's budget.

incinta agg. f. pregnant.

incipiente agg. incipient.

incipriare vt. to powder. ♦ incipriarsi vr. to powder (oneself).

incirca (nella loc. avv.) all'—, about.

incisione sf. 1. cut 2. (arte) engraving 3. (su disco, nastro ecc.) recording.

incisività sf. sharpness.

incisivo agg. incisive. ♦ incisivo sm. (anat.) incisor.

inciso sm. parenthetic clause: per —, incidentally.

incisore sm. engraver.

incitamento sm. urge.

incitare vt. to urge, to stimulate.

incitrullire vi. to become (v. irr.) silly.

incivile agg. 1. uncivilized 2. (scortese) rude.

incivilimento sm. civilization.

incivilire vt. to civilize. ♦ incivilirsi vr. to become (v. irr.) civilized.

inciviltà sf. 1. barbarism 2. (fig.) rudeness.

inclassificàbile agg. unclassifiable.

inclemente agg. 1. inclement: tempo —, inclement weather 2. (spietato) merciless.

inclemenza sf. 1. (di tempo) inclemency 2. (crudeltà) mercilessness.

inclinare vt. to incline, to bend (v. irr.).

inclinato agg. inclined (anche fig.).

inclinazione sf. 1. inclination 2. (attitudine) bent.

incline agg. disposed.

inclito agg. famous.

inclùdere vt. to include.

inclusione sf. inclusion.

inclusivo agg. inclusive.

incluso agg. 1. included 2. (accluso) enclosed.

incoccare vt. to nock.

incoercìbile agg. irrepressible.

incoercibilità sf. irrepressibleness.

incoerente agg. incoherent.

incoerenza sf. incoherence.

incògnita sf. 1. (mat.) unknown quantity 2. (fig.) uncertainty.

incògnito agg. unknown. ♦ incògnito sm. incognito (pl. -tos).

incollamento sm. pasting.

incollare vt. to stick (v. irr.). ♦ incollarsi vr. to stick.

incollatrice sf. sizing-machine.

incollatura[1] sf. sticking.

incollatura[2] sf. (ippica) neck.

incollerire vi. to get (v. irr.) angry. ♦ incollerirsi vr. to get angry.

incollerito agg. angry.

incolonnamento sm. column formation.

incolonnare vt. to form into columns. ♦ incolonnarsi vr. to rank.

incolore agg. colourless.

incolpàbile agg. accusable.

incolpare vt. to charge (with), to accuse (of). ♦ incolparsi vr. to accuse oneself.

incolpévole agg. blameless.

incolto agg. uncultivated.

incòlume agg. unhurt.

incolumità sf. safety.

incombente agg. impending.

incombenza sf. errand, task.

incòmbere vi. 1. (spettare) to be

one's job **2.** (*sovrastare*) to impend (over).

incombustìbile *agg.* incombustible.

incominciare *vt.* e *vi.* V. *cominciare.*

incommensuràbile *agg.* incommensurable.

incommensurabilità *sf.* incommensurability.

incommerciàbile *agg.* not negotiable.

incommutàbile *agg.* incommutable.

incomodare *vt.* to annoy. ♦ **incomodarsi** *vr.* to trouble.

incomodità *sf.* uncomfortableness.

incomodo *agg.* uncomfortable || *essere d' —,* to be in the way.

incomparàbile *agg.* incomparable.

incompatìbile *agg.* incompatible.

incompatibilità *sf.* incompatibility.

incompetente *agg.* incompetent.

incompetenza *sf.* incompetence.

incompiuto *agg.* unfinished.

incompletezza *sf.* incompleteness.

incompleto *agg.* incomplete.

incompostezza *sf.* disorder.

incomposto *agg.* disorderly.

incomprensìbile *agg.* incomprehensibie.

incomprensibilità *sf.* incomprehensibility.

incomprensione *sf.* incomprehension.

incompreso *agg.* **1.** not understood **2.** (*non apprezzato*) unappreciated.

incomputàbile *agg.* incalculable.

incomunicàbile *agg.* incommunicable.

incomunicabilità *sf.* incommunicability.

inconcepìbile *agg.* inconceivable.

inconciliàbile *agg.* irreconcilable.

inconciliabilità *sf.* irreconcilability.

inconcludente *agg.* **1.** inconclusive **2.** (*di persona*) good-for-nothing.

inconcusso *agg.* unshaken.

incondizionato *agg.* unconditional.

inconfessàbile *agg.* unavowable.

inconfessato *agg.* unconfessed.

inconfondìbile *agg.* unmistakable.

inconfutàbile *agg.* irrefutable.

incongruente *agg.* incongruous.

incongruenza *sf.* incongruity.

incòngruo *agg.* incongruous.

inconsapévole *agg.* unconscious, unaware.

inconsapevolezza *sf.* unconsciousness, unawareness.

inconscio *agg.* e *sm.* unconscious.

inconseguente *agg.* inconsequent.

inconseguenza *sf.* inconsequence.

inconsideratezza *sf.* rashness.

inconsiderato *agg.* rash.

inconsistente *agg.* insubstantial.

inconsistenza *sf.* insubstantiality.

inconsolàbile *agg.* inconsolable.

inconsueto *agg.* unusual.

inconsulto *agg.* unadvised, rash.

incontaminato *agg.* unpolluted.

incontentàbile *agg.* insatiable.

incontentabilità *sf.* insatiability.

incontestàbile *agg.* incontestable.

incontinente *agg.* incontinent.

incontinenza *sf.* incontinence.

incontrare *vt.* to meet (*v. irr.*). ♦ **incontrarsi** *vr.* to meet || *i nostri gusti non si incontrano,* our tastes do not agree.

incontrastàbile *agg.* incontestable.

incontrastato *agg.* uncontested.

incontro[1] *sm.* **1.** meeting **2.** (*sport*) match.

incontro[2] *prep. — a,* towards, to.

incontrollàbile *agg.* uncontrollable.

incontrollato *agg.* uncontrolled.

incontrovertìbile *agg.* indisputable.

inconveniente *sm.* inconvenience, drawback.

inconvertìbile *agg.* inconvertible.

inconvertibilità *sf.* inconvertibility.

incoraggiamento *sm.* encouragement.

incoraggiante *agg.* encouraging.

incoraggiare *vt.* to encourage.

incorniciare *vt.* to frame.

incorniciatura *sf.* framing.

incoronamento *sm.* V. *coronamento.*

incoronare *vt.* V. *coronare.*

incoronazione *sf.* coronation.

incorporare *vt.* to incorporate.

incorporazione *sf.* incorporation.

incorpòreo *agg.* incorporeal.

incorreggìbile *agg.* incorrigible.

incòrrere *vi.* to incur, to suffer (sthg.).

incorretto *agg.* incorrect.

incorrotto *agg.* incorrupt.

incorruttìbile *agg.* incorruptible.

incorruttibilità *sf.* incorruptibility.

incosciente *agg.* **1.** unconscious **2.** (*irresponsabile*) reckless. ♦ **incosciente** *sm.* irresponsible.

incoscienza *sf.* **1.** unconsciousness **2.** (*spericolatezza*) rashness.

incostante *agg.* inconstant: *tempo* —, changeable weather.
incostituzionale *agg.* unconstitutional.
incostituzionalità *sf.* unconstitutionality.
incredibile *agg.* incredible.
incredibilità *sf.* incredibility.
incredulità *sf.* incredulity.
incrèdulo *agg.* incredulous.
incrementare *vt.* to increase.
incremento *sm.* increase.
increscioso *agg.* unpleasant.
increspamento *sm.* **1.** (*di acque*) rippling **2.** (*di capelli*) ruffling.
increspare *vt.*, **incresparsi** *vr.* **1.** (*di acque*) to ripple **2.** (*di capelli*) to ruffle.
incretinire *vt.* to make (*v. irr.*) stupid. ♦ **incretinirsi** *vr.* to dull.
incriminàbile *agg.* impeachable.
incriminare *vt.* to impeach.
incriminazione *sf.* **1.** (*l'accusare*) crimination **2.** (*atto d'accusa*) indictment.
incrinare *vt.* to crack. ♦ **incrinarsi** *vr.* to crack.
incrinatura *sf.* crack.
incriticàbile *agg.* uncensurable.
incrociare *vt.* to cross. ♦ **incrociarsi** *vr.* to cross.
incrociatore *sm.* cruiser.
incrocio *sm.* **1.** crossing || — *stradale*, cross-road **2.** (*di razze*) crossbreed.
incrollàbile *agg.*˙ unshakable.
incrostare *vt.* to incrust. ♦ **incrostarsi** *vr.* to become (*v. irr.*) incrusted.
incrostazione *sf.* incrustation.
incrudelimento *sm.* toughening.
incrudelire *vi.* to become (*v. irr.*) cruel || — *contro* qu., to be pitiless towards so.
incrudire *vi.* to grow (*v. irr.*) worse.
incruento *agg.* bloodless.
incubatrice *sf.* incubator.
incubazione *sf.* incubation.
incubo *sm.* nightmare.
incùdine *sf.* anvil.
inculcare *vt.* to inculcate.
incunàbolo *sm.* incunabulum.
incuneare *vt.* to wedge. ♦ **incunearsi** *vr.* to wedge oneself.
incupire *vt.* e *vi.* to darken. ♦ **incupirsi** *vr.* to become (*v. irr.*) gloomy.
incuràbile *agg.* e *sm.* incurable.

incurabilità *sf.* incurability.
incurante *agg.* careless, heedless.
incuria *sf.* heedlessness.
incuriosire *vt.* to make (*v. irr.*) curious. ♦ **incuriosirsi** *vr.* to become (*v. irr.*) curious.
incuriosito *agg.* made curious.
incursione *sf.* raid.
incurvare *vt.* e **incurvarsi** *vr.* to bend (*v. irr.*), to curve.
incurvatura *sf.* bend.
incustodito *agg.* unguarded.
incùtere *vt.* to rouse.
indaco *sm.* indigo.
indaffarato *agg.* busy.
indagare *vt.* to investigate.
indagatore *agg.* investigating.
indàgine *sf.* **1.** research, investigation **2.** (*giur.*) inquiry.
indebitare *vt.* to involve in debt. ♦ **indebitarsi** *vr.* to run (*v. irr.*) into debt.
indébito *agg.* undue.
indebolimento *sm.* weakening.
indebolire *vt.* to weaken. ♦ **indebolirsi** *vr.* to weaken.
indecente *agg.* indecent.
indecenza *sf.* indecency.
indecifràbile *agg.* **1.** indecipherable **2.** (*di calligrafia*) illegible.
indecisione *sf.* indecision.
indeciso *agg.* **1.** irresolute **2.** (*di cose*) undecided.
indeclinàbile *agg.* **1.** indeclinable **2.** (*che non si può eludere*) unavoidable.
indecoroso *agg.* unseemly.
indefesso *agg.* indefatigable.
indefinìbile *agg.* indefinable.
indefinito *agg.* indefinite.
indeformàbile *agg.* indeformable.
indegno *agg.* **1.** unworthy **2.** (*spregevole*) disgraceful.
indelèbile *agg.* indelible.
indelicatezza *sf.* indelicacy.
indelicato *agg.* tactless.
indemoniato *agg.* **1.** possessed **2.** (*fig.*) frantic. ♦ **indemoniato** *sm.* demoniac.
indenne *agg.* undamaged.
indennità *sf.* allowance.
indennizzare *vt.* to indemnify.
indennizzo *sm.* indemnity.
inderogàbile *agg.* intransgressible.
indescrivìbile *agg.* indescribable.
indesideràbile *agg.* undesirable.
indeterminàbile *agg.* indeterminable.
indeterminatezza *sf.* vagueness.

indeterminativo *agg.* (*gramm.*) indefinite.

indeterminato *agg.* indeterminate.

indeterminazione *sf.* indetermination.

indi *avv.* 1. (*di tempo*) then 2. (*di luogo*) (from) thence.

indiano *agg.* Indian: — *d'America*, Red Indian; *in fila indiana*, in Indian file.

indiavolato *agg.* frenzied, furious.

indicare *vt.* 1. to show (*v. irr.*) 2. (*col dito*) to point at.

indicativo *agg.* indicative.

indicato *agg.* 1. (*adatto*) suitable 2. (*consigliabile*) advisable.

indicatore *agg.* indicatory. ♦ **indicatore** *sm.* indicator.

indicazione *sf.* indication.

indice *sm.* 1. (*dito della mano*) forefinger 2. (*di libro, statistica ecc.*) index.

indicìbile *agg.* inexpressible.

indietreggiare *vi.* to withdraw (*v. irr.*).

indietro *avv.* (*di spazio, tempo*) back, behind.

indifendìbile *agg.* indefensible.

indifeso *agg.* undefended.

indifferente *agg.* indifferent.

indifferenza *sf.* indifference.

indifferìbile *agg.* undelayable.

indìgeno *agg.* e *sm.* native.

indigente *agg.* indigent, poor.

indigenza *sf.* indigence.

indigestione *sf.* indigestion.

indigesto *agg.* 1. indigestible 2. (*fig.*) heavy.

indignare *vt.* to make (*v. irr.*) indignant. ♦ **indignarsi** *vr.* to get (*v. irr.*) angry.

indignazione *sf.* indignation.

indimenticàbile *agg.* unforgettable.

indimostràbile *agg.* indemonstrable.

indipendente *agg.* independent (of). ♦ **indipendente** *sm.* (*pol.*) independent.

indipendenza *sf.* independence.

indire *vt.* to call, to announce.

indiretto *agg.* indirect.

indirizzare *vt.* to address. ♦ **indirizzarsi** *vr.* 1. (*dirigersi*) to set (*v. irr.*) out (for) 2. (*rivolgersi*) to address oneself (to).

indirizzo *sm.* 1. address 2. (*linea di condotta*) trend.

indisciplina *sf.* indiscipline.

indisciplinato *agg.* undisciplined.

indiscretezza *sf.* indiscretion.

indiscreto *agg.* indiscreet.

indiscrezione *sf.* indiscretion.

indiscriminato *agg.* indiscriminate.

indiscusso *agg.* undiscussed.

indiscutìbile *agg.* unquestionable.

indispensàbile *agg.* indispensable.

indispettire *vt.* to vex. ♦ **indispettirsi** *vr.* to become (*v. irr.*) vexed.

indispettito *agg.* vexed.

indisponente *agg.* irritating.

indisporre *vt.* to irritate.

indisposizione *sf.* indisposition.

indisposto *agg.* unwell (*pred.*).

indissolùbile *agg.* indissoluble.

indissolubilità *sf.* indissolubility.

indistinto *agg.* indistinct.

indistruttìbile *agg.* indestructible.

indisturbato *agg.* undisturbed.

individuale *agg.* individual.

individualismo *sm.* individualism

individualista *s.* individualist.

individualìstico *agg.* individualistic.

individuare *vt.* to single out.

individuo *sm.* individual.

indivisìbile *agg.* indivisible.

indivisibilità *sf.* indivisibility.

indiviso *agg.* undivided.

indiziare *vt.* to make (*v. irr.*) suspect.

indiziario *agg.* presumptive.

indiziato *agg.* e *sm.* suspect.

indizio *sm.* 1. indication 2. (*giur.*) circumstantial proof.

indòcile *agg.* indocile.

indocilità *sf.* indocility.

indoeuropeo *agg.* e *sm.* Indo-European.

indole *sf.* nature, disposition || *un ragazzo di buona* —, a good-natured boy.

indolente *agg.* indolent.

indolenza *sf.* indolence.

idolenzimento *sm.* numbness.

indolenzire *vt.* to numb. ♦ **indolenzirsi** *vr.* to become (*v. irr.*) numb.

indolenzito *agg.* numb.

indolore *agg.* painless.

indomàbile *agg.* untamable.

indomani *sm.* next day || *all'* —, on the day after.

indòmito *agg.* indomitable.

indorare *vt.* V. *dorare*.

indossare *vt.* 1. (*avere indosso*) to wear (*v. irr.*) 2. (*mettere indosso*) to put (*v. irr.*) on.

indossatrice *sf.* mannequin.
indosso *avv.* on.
indotto *agg.* (*spinto*) driven.
indovinare *vt.* to guess.
indovinello *sm.* riddle.
indovino *sm.* soothsayer.
indubbio *agg.* undoubted.
indubitàbile *agg.* indubitable.
indugiare *vi.* to delay, to hesitate.
indugio *sm.* delay.
indulgente *agg.* indulgent.
indulgenza *sf.* indulgence.
indùlgere *vi.* to indulge (in).
indulto *sm.* **1.** (*eccl.*) indult **2.** (*giur.*) free pardon.
indumento *sm.* garment.
indurimento *sm.* hardening.
indurire *vt.* e *vi.* to harden. ♦ **indurirsi** *vr.* to harden.
indurre *vt.* to induce, to get (*v. irr.*) ‖ — *in errore*, to mislead (*v. irr.*). ♦ **indursi** *vr.* to bring (*v. irr.*) oneself (to).
industria *sf.* industry.
industriale *agg.* industrial. ♦ **industriale** *sm.* industrialist, manufacturer.
industrialismo *sm.* industrialism.
industrializzare *vt.* to industrialize.
industrializzazione *sf.* industrialization.
industriarsi *vr.* to do (*v. irr.*) one's best.
industrioso *agg.* industrious.
induttivo *agg.* inductive.
induttore *agg.* inductor.
induzione *sf.* induction.
inebetire *vt.* e *vi.* to dull.
inebetito *agg.* dull.
inebriante *agg.* inebriating.
inebriare *vt.* **1.** to make (*v. irr.*) drunk **2.** (*fig.*) to inebriate. ♦ **inebriarsi** *vr.* **1.** to get (*v. irr.*) drunk **2.** (*fig.*) to go (*v. irr.*) into raptures.
ineccepìbile *agg.* unexceptionable.
inedia *sf.* starvation.
inèdito *agg.* unpublished.
ineducato *agg.* ill-bred.
ineffàbile *agg.* ineffable.
inefficace *agg.* ineffective.
inefficacia *sf.* inefficacy.
inefficiente *agg.* inefficient.
inefficienza *sf.* ineffectiveness.
ineguaglianza *sf.* inequality.
ineguale *agg.* **1.** unlike **2.** (*irregolare*) irregular **3.** (*di superficie*) uneven.

ineleggìbile *agg.* ineligible.
ineleggibilità *sf.* ineligibility.
ineluttàbile *agg.* ineluctable.
ineluttabilità *sf.* inevitableness.
inenarràbile *agg.* unutterable.
inequivocàbile *agg.* unmistakable
'nerente *agg.* concerning.
inerme *agg.* unarmed.
inerpicarsi *vr.* to climb (up).
inerte *agg.* inert.
inerzia *sf.* inertness.
inesattezza *sf.* inaccuracy.
inesatto *agg.* incorrect.
inesaudito *agg.* ungranted.
inesaurìbile *agg.* inexhaustible.
inesàusto *agg.* unexhausted.
ineseguìbile *agg.* inexecutable.
inesigìbile *agg.* **1.** uncollectable **2.** (*di assegno*) worthless.
inesistente *agg.* inexistent.
inesistenza *sf.* inexistence.
inesoràbile *agg.* inexorable.
inesorabilità *sf.* inexorability.
inesperienza *sf.* inexperience.
inesperto *agg.* unskilled.
inespiàbile *agg.* inexpiable.
inesplicàbile *agg.* inexplicable.
inesploràbile *agg.* inexplorable.
inesplorato *agg.* unexplored.
inespressivo *agg.* inexpressive.
inespresso *agg.* implied.
inesprimìbile *agg.* inexpressible.
inespugnàbile *agg.* inexpugnable.
inespugnabilità *sf.* inexpugnability.
inestimàbile *agg.* inestimable.
inestinguìbile *agg.* unquenchable.
inestirpàbile *agg.* ineradicable.
inestricàbile *agg.* inextricable.
inettitùdine *sf.* unfitness.
inetto *agg.* **1.** unapt **2.** (*dappoco*) good-for-nothing.
inevaso *agg.* outstanding, unanswered.
inevitàbile *agg.* inevitable.
inezia *sf.* trifle.
infagottare *vt.* to muffle up. ♦ **infagottarsi** *vr.* to muffle oneself up.
infallìbile *agg.* infallible.
infallibilità *sf.* infallibility.
infamante *agg.* shameful.
infamare *vt.* to defame, to disgrace.
infame *agg.* wicked.
infamia *sf.* infamy.
infangare *vt.* to muddy. ♦ **infangarsi** *vr.* to become (*v. irr.*) muddy.
infanticida *s.* child-murderer.

infanticidio *sm.* child-murder.
infantile *agg.* childlike, childish.
infantilismo *sm.* infantilism.
infanzia *sf.* **1.** infancy **2.** (*coll.*)
children (*pl.*).
infarcire *vt.* V. *farcire.*
infarinare *vt.* to flour. ♦ **infari-
narsi** *vr.* to get (*v. irr.*) covered
with flour.
infarinatura *sf.* **1.** flouring **2.** (*fig.*)
smattering.
infarto *sm.* infarct.
infastidire *vt.* to annoy. ♦ **infastidirsi** *vr.* to get (*v. irr.*) bored.
infaticàbile *agg.* tireless.
infatti *cong.* in fact.
infatuare *vt.* to infatuate. ♦ **infa-
tuarsi** *vr.* to get (*v. irr.*) crazy
(about).
infatuato *agg.* crazy (about).
infatuazione *sf.* infatuation.
infàusto *agg.* unlucky.
infecondità *sf.* sterility.
infecondo *agg.* steril.
infedele *agg.* unfaithful. ♦ **infedele** *sm.* infidel.
infedeltà *sf.* unfaithfulness.
infelice *agg.* **1.** unhappy **2.** (*non
appropriato*) ill-timed. ♦ **infelice**
s. wretch.
infelicità *sf.* unhappiness.
inferiore *agg.* **1.** inferior **2.** (*più
basso*) lower **3.** (*al di sotto*) below. ♦ **inferiore** *sm.* inferior.
inferiorità *sf.* inferiority.
inferire *vt.* **1.** (*dedurre*) to infer
2. (*dare*) to inflict.
infermerìa *sf.* infirmary.
infermiera *sf.* nurse.
infermiere *sm.* hospital attendant.
infermità *sf.* infirmity.
infermo *agg.* e *sm.* invalid.
infernale *agg.* **1.** infernal **2.** (*fig.*)
awful.
inferno *sm.* hell.
inferocire *vt.* to enrage. ♦ **inferocire** *vi.* to get (*v. irr.*) fierce.
inferriata *sf.* grating.
infervorare *vt.* to excite. ♦ **infervorarsi** *vr.* to get (*v. irr.*) excited.
infervorato *agg.* fervent.
infestare *vt.* to infest.
infestazione *sf.* infestation.
infettare *vt.* to infect. ♦ **infettar-
si** *vr.* to become (*v. irr.*) infected.
infettivo *agg.* contagious.
infetto *agg.* infected.
infezione *sf.* infection.
infiacchimento *sm.* weakening.

infiacchire *vt.* e *vi.* to weaken. ♦
infiacchirsi *vr.* to become (*v.
irr.*) weak.
infiammàbile *agg.* inflammable.
infiammabilità *sf.* inflammability.
infiammare *vt.* **1.** to set (*v. irr.*)
on fire **2.** (*fig.*) to inflame. ♦ **infiammarsi** *vr.* **1.** to take (*v. irr.*)
fire **2.** (*fig.*) to get (*v. irr.*) excited.
infiammato *agg.* inflamed (with).
infiammatorio *agg.* inflammatory.
infiammazione *sf.* inflammation.
infiascare *vt.* to put (*v. irr.*) into
flasks.
inficiare *vt.* **1.** to invalidate **2.**
(*giur.*) to impugn.
infido *agg.* false.
infierire *vi.* to be pitiless.
infìggere *vt.* **1.** to infix **2.** (*conficcare*) to drive (*v. irr.*) (into).
infilare *vt.* **1.** to thread **2.** (*introdurre*) to insert **3.** (*passare per*)
to enter. ♦ **infilarsi** *vr.* to slip
into.
infilata *sf.* row.
infiltrarsi *vr.* to penetrate.
infiltrazione *sf.* infiltration.
infilzare *vt.* **1.** to transfix **2.** (*conficcare*) to stick (*v. irr.*). ♦ **infil-
zarsi** *vr.* **1.** to run (*v. irr.*) oneself through **2.** (*conficcarsi*) to get
(*v. irr.*) stuck.
infilzata *sf.* string.
infimo *agg.* lowest.
infine *avv.* at last.
infingardàggine *sf.* laziness.
infingardo *agg.* lazy.
infinità *sf.* infinity.
infinitamente *avv.* infinitely.
infinitesimale *agg.* infinitesimal.
infinito *agg.* boundless. ♦ **infinito**
sm. **1.** infinite **2.** (*gramm.*) infinitive.
infioccare *vt.* to tassel.
infiorare *vt.* to flower.
infirmare *vt.* to invalidate.
infischiarsi *vr.* not to care (about).
infittire *vi.* to thicken. ♦ **infittirsi**
vr. to thicken.
inflazione *sf.* inflation.
inflazionìstico *agg.* inflationary.
inflessìbile *agg.* inflexible.
inflessibilità *sf.* inflexibility.
inflessione *sf.* inflexion.
inflìggere *vt.* to inflict.
influente *agg.* influential.
influenza *sf.* **1.** influence **2.** (*med.*)
(*fam.*) 'flu.
influenzare *vt.* to influence.

influire vi. to exert influence (on, upon, over).
influsso sm. influence.
infocare vt. 1. to heat up 2. to inflame.
infocato agg. 1. red hot 2. (fig.) inflamed.
infoltire vi. to thicken.
infondatezza sf. groundlessness.
infondato agg. groundless.
infòndere vt. to infuse.
inforcare vt. 1. to pitchfork 2. (montare a cavalcioni) to get (v. irr.) on || — gli occhiali, to put (v. irr.) on one's glasses.
informale agg. informal.
informare vt. 1. to inform 2. (dare forma) to shape. ♦ **informarsi** vr. to inquire (about).
informativo agg. informative.
informato agg. informed.
informatore sm. informer.
informazione sf. information (solo sing.), news (pl.).
informe agg. shapeless.
infornare vt. to put (v. irr.) into an oven.
infornata sf. batch.
infortunarsi vr. to get (v. irr.) injured.
infortunato agg. injured.
infortunio sm. accident.
infortunìstica sf. industrial accident research.
infossamento sm. hollow.
infossare vt. to hollow. ♦ **infossarsi** vr. to become (v. irr.) hollow.
infradiciare vt. 1. to drench 2. (marcire) to rot (v. irr.).
inframmettenza sf. interference.
inframméttere vt. to interpose. ♦ **inframméttersi** vr. to meddle (with).
infràngere vt. 1. to shatter 2. (trasgredire) to infringe. ♦ **infràngersi** vr. to break (v. irr.) (up).
infrangìbile agg. unbreakable: vetro —, shatter-proof glass.
infranto agg. 1. shattered, broken 2. (di legge) infringed.
infrarosso agg. infrared.
infrasettimanale agg. midweek.
infrastruttura sf. infrastructure.
infrazione sf. infraction.
infreddolirsi vr. to feel (v. irr.) cold.
infreddolito agg. chilly.
infrequente agg. infrequent.

infrollirsi vr. 1. to become (v. irr.) tender 2. (di selvaggina) to become (v. irr.) high.
infruttìfero agg. unfruitful.
infruttuoso agg. 1. unfruitful 2. (fig.) useless.
infuori (loc. prep.) all'—, except.
infuriare vi. to enrage. ♦ **infuriarsi** vr. to flare up.
infusione sf. infusion.
infuso agg. infused. ♦ **infuso** sm. infusion.
infusorio sm. infusorial.
ingabbiare vt. 1. to cage 2. (fig.) to lock up.
ingaggiare vt. to engage.
ingaggio sm. engagement.
ingagliardire vt. to strengthen. ♦ **ingagliardirsi** vr. to strengthen.
ingannare vt. to deceive || — il tempo, to while away the time. ♦ **ingannarsi** vr. to be mistaken.
ingannatore agg. deceiving. ♦ **ingannatore** sm. deceiver.
ingannévole agg. deceitful.
inganno sm. deception, fraud.
ingarbugliare vt. to entangle. ♦ **ingarbugliarsi** vr. to get (v. irr.) mixed up.
ingegnarsi vr. to contrive (to).
ingegnere sm. engineer.
ingegnerìa sf. engineering.
ingegno sm. talent.
ingegnosità sf. ingeniousness.
ingegnoso agg. ingenious.
ingelosire vt. to make (v. irr.) jealous. ♦ **ingelosirsi** vr. to become (v. irr.) jealous.
ingenerare vt. to engender.
ingeneroso agg. selfish.
ingente agg. huge.
ingentilire vt. to refine.
ingenuità sf. naïveness.
ingenuo agg. naïve.
ingerenza sf. interference.
ingerimento sm. swallowing.
ingerire vt. to swallow.
ingessare vt. to plaster.
ingessatura sf. 1. plastering 2. (med.) plaster cast.
inghiaiare vt. to gravel.
inghiottire vt. 1. to swallow 2. (di acque ecc.) to engulf 3. (sopportare) to lump.
inghirlandare vt. to wreathe.
ingiallire vt. e vi. to yellow.
ingigantire vt. to magnify. ♦ **ingigantire** vi. to become (v. irr.) gigantic.

inginocchiarsi *vr.* to kneel (*v. irr.*) (down).

inginocchiatoio *sm.* kneeler.

ingioiellare *vt.* to bejewel.

ingiú *avv.* down, downwards.

ingiùngere *vt.* to order.

ingiuntivo *agg.* injunctive.

ingiunzione *sf.* injunction.

ingiuria *sf.* insult.

ingiuriare *vt.* to insult.

ingiurioso *agg.* insulting.

ingiustamente *avv.* unjustly.

ingiustificàbile *agg.* unjustifiable.

ingiustificato *agg.* unjustified.

ingiustizia *sf.* unjustice.

ingiusto *agg.* unjust.

inglese *agg.* English. ♦ **inglese** *sm.* Englishman (*pl.* -men) || *gli Inglesi,* the English (people).

inglobare *vt.* to inglobe.

inglorioso *agg.* inglorious.

ingobbire *vi.* to become (*v. irr.*) humpbacked. ♦ **ingobbirsi** *vr.* to become humpbacked.

ingoiare *vt.* to swallow.

ingolfarsi *vr.* (*fig.*) to throw (*v. irr.*) oneself (into).

ingollare *vt.* to gulp down.

ingolosire *vt.* to make (*v. irr.*) greedy.

ingombrante *agg.* cumbersome.

ingombrare *vt.* to encumber.

ingombro *agg.* encumbered (with). ♦ **ingombro** *sm.* encumbrance.

ingommare *vt.* **1.** to gum **2.** (*incollare*) to stick (*v. irr.*).

ingordigia *sf.* greed.

ingordo *agg.* greedy.

ingorgare *vt.* to choke. ♦ **ingorgarsi** *vr.* to become (*v. irr.*) choked.

ingorgo *sm.* **1.** obstruction **2.** (*del traffico*) traffic jam.

ingozzare *vt.* to gulp.

ingranaggio *sm.* **1.** gear **2.** (*fig.*) mechanism.

ingranare *vt.* **1.** to put (*v. irr.*) into gear **2.** (*auto*) — *una marcia,* to engage a gear. ♦ **ingranare** *vi.* (*fam.*) to get (*v. irr.*) along (with).

ingrandimento *sm.* **1.** enlargement **2.** (*ott.*) magnification.

ingrandire *vt.* **1.** to enlarge **2.** (*ott.*) to magnify. ♦ **ingrandirsi** *vr.* to become (*v. irr.*) larger.

ingrassare *vt.* **1.** to fatten **2.** (*lubrificare*) to grease. ♦ **ingrassare** *vi.* to grow (*v. irr.*) fat.

ingrasso *sm.* fattening.

ingratitùdine *sf.* ingratitude.

ingrato *agg.* ungrateful. ♦ **ingrato** *sm.* ingrate.

ingravidare *vt.* to make (*v. irr.*) pregnant. ♦ **ingravidare** *vi.* to become (*v. irr.*) pregnant.

ingraziarsi *vr.* to get (*v. irr.*) into so.'s good graces.

ingrediente *sm.* ingredient.

ingresso *sm.* **1.** entry **2.** (*entrata*) entrance **3.** (*accesso*) admittance.

ingrossamento *sm.* enlargement.

ingrossare *vt.* e *vi.* to enlarge. ♦ **ingrossarsi** *vr.* to become (*v. irr.*) bigger.

ingrosso (*nella loc. avv.*) *all'—,* wholesale.

ingualcìbile *agg.* crease-resistant.

inguaribile *agg.* incurable.

inguinale *agg.* inguinal.

inguine *sm.* inguen.

ingurgitare *vt.* to swallow.

inibire *vt.* to inhibit.

inibito *agg.* inhibited.

inibizione *sf.* inhibition.

iniettare *vt.* to inject.

iniezione *sf.* injection.

inimicare *vt.* to alienate. ♦ **inimicarsi** *vr.* to estrange from oneself.

inimicizia *sf.* enmity.

inimitàbile *agg.* incomparable, inimitable.

inimmaginàbile *agg.* unimaginable.

inintelligìbile *agg.* unintelligible.

ininterrotto *agg.* continuous, unceasing.

iniquità *sf.* iniquity.

iniquo *agg.* **1.** unfair **2.** (*malvagio*) wicked.

iniziale *agg.* initial, starting. ♦ **iniziale** *sf.* initial.

iniziare *vt.* **1.** to begin (*v. irr.*), to start **2.** (*introdurre*) to initiate.

iniziativa *sf.* initiative.

iniziato *agg.* e *sm.* initiate.

iniziazione *sf.* initiation.

inizio *sm.* beginning.

innaffiare *vt.* to water.

innaffiatoio *sm.* watering-pot.

innalzamento *sm.* elevation.

innalzare *vt.* **1.** to raise **2.** (*rendere più alto*) to heighten. ♦ **innalzarsi** *vr.* to rise (*v. irr.*).

innamoramento *sm.* falling in love.

innamorare *vt.* to charm. ♦ **innamorarsi** *vr.* to fall (*v. irr.*) in love (with)

innamorato *agg.* in love (with).
♦ **innamorato** *sm.* lover.
innanzi *avv.* 1. forward, on 2. (*di fronte*) in front of 3. (*più avanti*) further ‖ *d'ora* —, from now on. ♦ **innanzi** *prep.* before.
innato *agg.* inborn.
innaturale *agg.* unnatural.
innegàbile *agg.* undeniable.
inneggiare *vi.* 1. to exalt 2. (*acclamare*) to cheer.
innervare *vt.* to innervate.
innervosire *vt.* to get (*v. irr.*) on so.'s nerves. ♦ **innervosirsi** *vr.* to get nervous.
innescamento *sm.* priming.
innescare *vt.* to prime.
innesco *sm.* primer.
innestare *vt.* 1. (*agr.; med.*) to graft 2. (*mecc.*) to engage.
innesto *sm.* 1. (*agr.; med.*) graft 2. (*mecc.*) clutch.
inno *sm.* hymn ‖ — *nazionale*, national anthem.
innocente *agg. e sm.* innocent.
innocenza *sf.* innocence.
innocuità *sf.* innocuousness.
innocuo *agg.* harmless.
innominàbile *agg.* unmentionable.
innovare *vt.* to innovate.
innovatore *agg.* innovating. ♦ **innovatore** *sm.* innovator.
innovazione *sf.* innovation.
innumerévole *agg.* numberless.
inoculare *vt.* to inoculate.
inoculazione *sf.* inoculation.
inodoro *agg.* odourless.
inoffensivo *agg.* harmless.
inoltrare *vt.* to forward. ♦ **inoltrarsi** *vr.* to advance.
inoltrato *agg.* advanced, late.
inoltre *avv.* moreover, besides.
inoltro *sm.* 1. (*di merci*) forwarding 2. (*di documenti*) sending on.
inondare *vt.* to flood.
inondazione *sf.* flood.
inoperosità *sf.* inactivity.
inoperoso *agg.* inactive.
inopinàbile *agg.* inconceivable.
inopinato *agg.* unexpected.
inopportunità *sf.* inopportunity.
inopportuno *agg.* inopportune.
inoppugnàbile *agg.* incontestable.
inoppugnabilità *sf.* incontestability.
inorgànico *agg.* inorganic.
inorgoglire *vt.* to make (*v. irr.*) proud. ♦ **inorgoglirsi** *vr.* to become (*v. irr.*) proud.

inorridire *vt.* to horrify. ♦ **inorridire** *vi.* to be horrified.
inospitale *agg.* inhospitable.
inosservanza *sf.* inobservance.
inosservato *agg.* unobserved.
inossidàbile *agg.* rust-proof ‖ *acciaio* —, stainless steel.
inquadramento *sm.* framing.
inquadrare *vt.* 1. to frame 2. (*fig.*) to set (*v. irr.*) 3. (*mil.*) to rank 4. (*foto, cine*) to frame.
inquadratura *sf.* (*cine*) shot.
inqualificàbile *agg.* despicable.
inquietante *agg.* worrying.
inquietare *vt.* to worry. ♦ **inquietarsi** *vr.* to get (*v. irr.*) angry.
inquieto *agg.* 1. restless 2. (*preoccupato*) worried 3. (*arrabbiato*) angry.
inquietùdine *sf.* 1. restlessness 2. (*preoccupazione*) anxiety.
inquilino *sm.* tenant.
inquinamento *sm.* defilement.
inquinare *vt.* to defile.
inquirente *agg.* investigating.
inquisire *vt.* to investigate. ♦ **inquisire** *vi.* to inquire.
inquisitore *agg.* inquiring. ♦ **inquisitore** *sm.* inquisitor.
inquisizione *sf.* inquisition.
insabbiamento *sm.* (*fig.*) hindering.
insabbiare *vt.* 1. to sand 2. (*fig.*) to hinder.
insaccare *vt.* to sack.
insalata *sf.* salad.
insalatiera *sf.* salad-bowl.
insalubre *agg.* unhealthy.
insalubrità *sf.* insalubrity.
insanàbile *agg.* incurable.
insanguinare *vt.* to cover (with blood). ♦ **insanguinarsi** *vr.* to become (*v. irr.*) bloodstained.
insano *agg.* insane.
insaponare *vt.* to soap.
insaponatura *sf.* soaping.
insaporire *vt.* to flavour.
insaporo *agg.* flavourless.
insaputa *sf.* (*nella loc. avv.*) *all'— di*, unknown (to).
insaziàbile *agg.* insatiable.
insaziabilità *sf.* insatiability.
insaziato *agg.* unappeased.
inscatolare *vt.* to tin.
inscenare *vt.* to stage.
inscindìbile *agg.* inseparable.
inscrìvere *vt.* 1. (*a una scuola, esame ecc.*) to enrol 2. (*scrivere, scolpire; geom.*) to inscribe.

insediamento *sm.* installation.
insediare *vt.* to install. ♦ **insediarsi** *vr.* to install oneself.
insegna *sf.* 1. insignia (*pl.*) 2. (*bandiera*) flag 3. (*di negozio*) sign-board.
insegnamento *sm.* 1. teaching 2. (*precetto, lezione*) precept, lesson.
insegnante *agg.* teaching. ♦ **insegnante** *s.* teacher.
insegnare *vt.* to teach (*v. irr.*).
inseguimento *sm.* pursuit.
inseguire *vt.* to pursue.
inseguitore *sm.* pursuer.
insellare *vt.* to saddle.
inselvatichire *vi.* to grow (*v. irr.*) wild.
insenatura *sf.* inlet, creek.
insensatezza *sf.* 1. craziness 2. (*atto insensato*) foolish action.
insensato *agg.* foolish, crazy.
insensibile *agg.* 1. insensible 2. (*indifferente*) indifferent 3. (*frigido*) unfeeling.
insensibilità *sf.* 1. insensibility 2. (*indifferenza*) indifference.
insensibilmente *avv.* 1. (*impercettibilmente*) imperceptibly, slightly 2. (*senza sentimento*) insensibly.
inseparabile *agg.* inseparable.
insepolto *agg.* unburied.
inserimento *sm.* insertion.
inserire *vt.* 1. to insert 2. (*elettr.*) to connect.
inserto *sm.* 1. file, dossier 2. (*cine, stampa*) insert.
inservibile *agg.* useless.
inserviente *sm.* attendant.
inserzione *sf.* 1. insertion 2. (*pubblicitaria*) advertisement.
inserzionista *sm.* advertiser.
insetticida *agg. e sm.* insecticide.
insettivoro *agg.* insectivorous. ♦ **insettivoro** *sm.* insectivore.
insetto *sm.* insect.
insicurezza *sf.* insecurity.
insidia *sf.* 1. snare 2. (*pericolo*) danger.
insidiare *vt.* to endanger ‖ — *la vita di una persona*, to attempt a person's life.
insidioso *agg.* insidious.
insieme *avv.* 1. together 2. (*allo stesso tempo*) at the same time. ♦ **insieme** *prep.* together (with). ♦ **insieme** *sm.* whole: *nell'*—, as a whole ‖ *sguardo d'*—, comprehensive view.
insigne *agg.* famous.

insignificante *agg.* insignificant.
insignire *vt.* to confer (sthg. upon).
insincerità *sf.* insincerity.
insincero *agg.* insincere.
insindacàbile *agg.* undisputable.
insinuante *agg.* insinuating.
insinuare *vt.* to hint. ♦ **insinuarsi** *vr.* to insinuate oneself.
insinuazione *sf.* hint, insinuation.
insipidezza *sf.* insipidness.
insìpido *agg.* 1. tasteless 2. (*fig.*) insipid.
insistente *agg.* 1. insistent, steady 2. (*molesto*) irritating.
insistenza *sf.* insistence.
insìstere *vi.* to insist (on).
ìnsito *agg.* inborn, inherent.
insoddisfatto *agg.* dissatisfied (with).
insoddisfazione *sf.* dissatisfaction (with).
insofferente *agg.* intolerant.
insofferenza *sf.* intolerance.
insoffrìbile *agg.* unbearable.
insolazione *sf.* sunstroke.
insolente *agg. e sm.* insolent.
insolentire *vt.* to insult.
insolenza *sf.* insolence.
insòlito *agg.* unusual.
insolùbile *agg.* insoluble.
insolubilità *sf.* insolubility.
insoluto *agg.* 1. unsolved 2. (*non pagato*) unpaid.
insolvente *agg.* insolvent.
insolvenza *sf.* insolvency.
insolvìbile *agg.* 1. (*di debito*) unpayable 2. (*di persona*) insolvent.
insolvibilità *sf.* insolvency.
insomma *avv.* finally, in short.
insondàbile *agg.* unfathomable.
insonne *agg.* sleepless.
insonnia *sf.* insomnia.
insonnolito *agg.* drowsy, sleepy.
insopportàbile *agg.* unbearable.
insopprimìbile *agg.* insuppressible.
insòrgere *vi.* 1. to rise (*v. irr.*) 2. (*protestare*) to protest, to rebel 3. (*manifestarsi*) to arise (*v. irr.*).
insormontàbile *agg.* insurmountable.
insorto *sm.* rebel.
insospettàbile *agg.* beyond suspicion.
insospettato *agg.* unsuspected.
insospettire *vt.* to make (*v. irr.*) suspicious. ♦ **insospettirsi** *vr.* to grow (*v. irr.*) suspicious.
insostenìbile *agg.* unsustainable.
insostituìbile *agg.* irreplaceable.

insozzare vt. 1. to soil 2. (fig.) to disgrace.
insperàbile agg. beyond hope.
insperato agg. unhoped for.
inspiegàbile agg. inexplicable.
inspirare vt. to breathe in.
inspirazione sf. breathing in, inhalation.
instàbile agg. unstable || tempo —, unsettled weather.
instabilità sf. 1. instability 2. (fig.) fickleness.
installare vt. to install. ♦ **installarsi** vr. to settle.
installazione sf. installation.
instancàbile agg. untiring.
instaurare vt. to set (v. irr.) up.
instaurazione sf. establishment.
instradare vt. to direct, to coach.
insú avv. up, upwards.
insubordinatezza sf. insubordination.
insubordinato agg. insubordinate.
insubordinazione sf. insubordination.
insuccesso sm. failure.
insudiciare vt. to soil.
insufficiente agg. insufficient.
insufficienza sf. 1. insufficiency 2. (scol.) low mark.
insulare agg. insular.
insulina sf. insulin.
insulsàggine sf. 1. silliness 2. (cosa insulsa) nonsense.
insulso agg. silly.
insultare vt. to insult.
insulto sm. insult.
insuperàbile agg. insuperable.
insuperato agg. unsurpassed.
insuperbire vt. to elate. ♦ **insuperbirsi** vr. to pride oneself (on).
insurrezionale agg. insurrectional.
insurrezione sf. insurrection.
insussistente agg. unfounded.
intaccare vt. 1. to notch 2. (chim.) to etch 3. (fig.) to injure.
intacco sm. notch.
intagliare vt. 1. to carve 2. (incidere) to engrave.
intaglio sm. 1. carving 2. (incisione) engraving.
intangìbile agg. intangible.
intanto avv. meanwhile.
intarsiare vt. to inlay.
intarsio sm. inlay.
intasamento sm. obstruction.
intasare vt. to obstruct.
intascare vt. to pocket.

intatto agg. intact.
intavolare vt. 1. to plank 2. (iniziare) to begin (v. irr.), to start.
integèrrimo agg. strictly honest.
integràbile agg. integrable.
integrale agg. integral: (mat.) calcolo —, integral calculus.
integrante agg. integrant.
integrare vt. to integrate.
integrazione sf. integration.
integrità sf. integrity.
ìntegro agg. 1. integral 2. (onesto) honest.
intelaiatura sf. 1. framework 2. (di finestre) sash.
intellettivo agg. intellective.
intelletto sm. intellect.
intellettuale agg. e sm. intellectual.
intellettualismo sm. intellectualism.
intelligente agg. intelligent.
intelligenza sf. intelligence.
intelligìbile agg. intelligible.
intelligibilità sf. intelligibility.
intemerata sf. reprimand.
intemerato agg. faultless.
intemperante agg. intemperate.
intemperanza sf. intemperance.
intemperie sf. pl. inclemency of the weather (sing.).
intempestività sf. untimeliness.
intempestivo agg. untimely.
intendente agg. expert. ♦ **intendente** sm. superintendent.
intendenza sf. superintendence.
intèndere vt. 1. (capire) to understand (v. irr.) 2. (significare) to mean (v. irr.) 3. (avere intenzione di) to intend to. ♦ **intèndersi** vr. 1. (avere cognizione) to be a good judge 2. (mettersi d'accordo) to come (v. irr.) to an agreement.
intendimento sm. 1. understanding 2. (intenzione) intention.
intenditore sm. 1. good judge 2. (d'arte) connoisseur.
intenerimento sm. 1. softening 2. (fig.) tenderness.
intenerire vt. 1. to soften 2. (fig.) to move to pity. ♦ **intenerirsi** vr. to be moved to pity.
intensificare vt. to intensify.
intensificazione sf. intensification.
intensità sf. intensity.
intensivo agg. intensive.
intenso agg. intense.
intentàbile agg. 1. unattemptable 2. (giur.) suable.

intentare *vt.* to bring (*v. irr.*).
intento *agg.* intent. ♦ **intento** *sm.*
aim, purpose.
intenzionale *agg.* deliberate.
intenzionato *agg.* disposed.
intenzione *sf.* intention.
intepidire *vt.* to warm, to make
(*v. irr.*) tepid. ♦ **intepidirsi** *vr.*
to get (*v. irr.*) tepid.
interamente *avv.* wholly, entirely.
intercalare *agg.* intercalary. ♦ **in-**
tercalare *sm.* pet phrase.
intercalare *vt.* to intercalate.
intercambiàbile *agg.* interchangeable.
intercèdere *vi.* to intercede, to
plead.
intercessione *sf.* intercession.
intercessore *sm.* intercessor.
intercettare *vt.* to intercept.
intercettatore *sm.* interceptor.
intercettazione *sf.* interception.
intercomunale *sf.* (*tel.*) long-distance call.
intercontinentale *agg.* intercontinental.
intercòrrere *vi.* **1.** to pass **2.** (*ac-*
cadere) to happen.
intercostale *agg.* intercostal.
interdetto. *agg.* **1.** prohibited **2.**
(*giur.*) interdicted. ♦ **interdetto**
sm. interdict.
interdipendente *agg.* interdependent.
interdipendenza *sf.* interdependence.
interdire *vt.* to interdict.
interdizione *sf.* interdiction.
interessamento *sm.* concern.
interessante *agg.* interesting.
interessare *vt.* **1.** to interest **2.** (*ri-*
guardare) to concern. ♦ **interes-**
sarsi *vr.* **1.** to be interested (in)
2. (*provvedere*) to take (*v. irr.*)
care (of).
interessato *agg.* interested.
interesse *sm.* interest.
interessenza *sf.* share, profit.
interezza *sf.* wholeness.
interferenza *sf.* interference.
interferire *vi.* to interfere.
interiezione *sf.* interjection.
interinale *agg.* temporary.
interiora *sf. pl.* entrails.
interiore *agg.* inner. ♦ **interiore**
sm. interior, inside.
interiorità *sf.* inwardness.
interiormente *avv.* **1.** (*intimamen-*
te) innerly **2.** (*nell'interno*) inside.

interlìnea *sf.* **1.** interline **2.** (*tip.*)
lead.
interlineare *vt.* **1.** to interline **2.**
(*tip.*) to lead (*v. irr.*).
interlineare *vt.* to interline.
interlocutore *sm.* interlocutor.
interlocutorio *agg.* interlocutory.
interloquire *vi.* to join in the conversation.
interludio *sm.* interlude.
intermediario *agg.* intermediary.
♦ **intermediario** *sm.* **1.** go-between **2.** (*comm.*) middleman (*pl.*
-men).
intermedio *agg.* intermediate, middle.
intermezzo *sm.* **1.** intermission **2.**
(*mus.*) intermezzo.
interminàbile *agg.* endless.
intermittente *agg.* intermittent.
intermittenza *sf.* intermittence.
internamento *sm.* internment.
internare *vt.* to intern.
internato *agg.* interned. ♦ **inter-**
nato *sm.* (*scol.*) boarding-school.
internazionale *agg.* international.
internazionalismo *sm.* internationalism.
internazionalizzare *vt.* to internationalize.
interno *agg.* **1.** internal, interior **2.**
(*interiore*) inner. ♦ **interno** *sm.*
interior.
intero *agg.* **1.** whole **2.** (*intatto*) intact.
interpellanza *sf.* interrogation.
interpellare *vt.* **1.** (*pol.*) to interpellate **2.** (*giur.*) to summon **3.**
(*chiedere*) to ask.
interplanetario *agg.* interplanetary.
interpolare *vt.* to interpolate.
interpolazione *sf.* interpolation.
interporre *vt.* to interpose.
interpretare *vt.* **1.** to interpret, to
render **2.** (*teat.*) to play.
interpretativo *agg.* interpretative.
interpretazione *sf.* **1.** interpretation **2.** (*cine*) starring **3.** (*mus.*)
performance **4.** (*teat.*) acting.
intèrprete *s.* **1.** interpreter **2.** (*teat.;*
cine) actor, player.
interpunzione *sf.* punctuation.
interramento *sm.* burial.
interrare *vt.* **1.** to bury **2.** (*riem-*
pire di terra) to fill up with earth.
interrogare *vt.* to question.
interrogativo *agg.* interrogative ‖
punto —, question mark. ♦ **inter-**
rogativo *sm.* interrogative.

interrogatore *agg.* interrogating. ♦
interrogatore *sm.* examiner.
interrogatorio *sm.* examination.
interrogazione *sf.* **1.** interrogation
2. (*scol.*) oral test.
interròmpere *vt.* to interrupt. ♦
interròmpersi *vr.* to stop.
interrotto *agg.* interrupted ‖ *strada interrotta*, blocked road.
interruttore *sm.* (*elettr.*) switch.
interruzione *sf.* interruption.
intersecare *vt.* to intersect.
intersezione *sf.* intersection.
interstizio *sm.* interstice.
intervallare *vt.* to space.
intervallo *sm.* **1.** interval **2.** (*spazio*) space.
intervenire *vi.* **1.** to intervene **2.**
(*essere presenti*) to be present.
interventismo *sm.* intervention-
ism.
interventista *s.* interventionist.
intervento *sm.* **1.** intervention **2.**
(*presenza*) presence **3.** (*chir.*) operation.
intervenuto *agg.* present. ♦ **intervenuto** *sm.* person present.
intervista *sf.* interview.
intervistare *vt.* to interview.
intesa *sf.* agreement.
inteso *agg.* **1.** agreed (upon) **2.** (*mi-
rante*) aiming (at).
intèssere *vt.* to interweave (*v. irr.*).
intestare *vt.* to head, to register. ♦
intestarsi *vr.* to be determinated.
intestatario *sm.* holder.
intestato *agg.* **1.** headed **2.** (*giur.*)
registered **3.** (*senza testamento*)
intestate **4.** (*ostinato*) stubborn.
intestazione *sf.* **1.** title **2.** (*di lettera ecc.*) heading.
intestinale *agg.* intestinal.
intestino *sm.* intestine.
intimare *vt.* **1.** (*ordinare*) to order
2. (*ingiungere*) to summon.
intimazione *sf.* **1.** order **2.** (*ingiunzione*) summons.
intimidatorio *agg.* intimidatory.
intimidazione *sf.* intimidation.
intimidire *vt.* **1.** to make (*v. irr.*)
shy **2.** (*impaurire*) to intimidate.
intimità *sf.* **1.** privacy **2.** (*familiarità*) familiarity.
intimo *agg.* **1.** intimate **2.** (*profondo*) deep. ♦ **ìntimo** *sm.* **1.** (*amico*) intimate **2.** (*animo*) soul ‖
nell'—, at heart.
intimorire *vt.* to frighten. ♦ **in-
timorirsi** *vr.* to get (*v. irr.*)

frightened.
intìngere *vt.* to dip.
intìngolo *sm.* **1.** gravy **2.** (*salsa*)
sauce.
intirizzire *vt.* to benumb.
intitolare *vt.* **1.** to entitle **2.** (*dedicare*) to dedicate.
intoccàbile *agg. e sm.* untouchable.
intolleràbile *agg.* intolerable.
intollerante *agg.* intolerant.
intolleranza *sf.* intolerance.
intonacare *vt.* to plaster.
intonacatura *sf.* plastering.
intònaco *sm.* plaster.
intonare *vt.* **1.** to tune **2.** (*cantile-
nare*) to intone. ♦ **intonarsi** *vr.*
1. to harmonize (with) **2.** (*di colori*) to match.
intonato *agg.* **1.** in tune **2.** (*di colori*) matching.
intonazione *sf.* **1.** intonation **2.** (*di
strumenti*) tuning **3.** (*di colori, voce*) tone.
intonso *agg.* (*di libri*) uncut.
intontimento *sm.* stunning.
intontire *vt.* to stun.
intoppare *vt.* to stumble (on).
intoppo *sm.* **1.** obstacle **2.** (*fig.*)
hitch.
intorbidare *vt.* to make (*v. irr.*)
muddy. ♦ **intorbidarsi** *vr.* to become (*v. irr.*) muddy.
intorno *avv.* round, around. ♦ **intorno a** *prep.* **1.** round, around
2. (*circa, su di*) about.
intorpidimento *sm.* numbness.
intorpidire *vt.* to benumb. ♦ **intorpidirsi** *vr.* to grow (*v. irr.*)
numb.
intossicare *vt.* to poison.
intossicazione *sf.* poisoning.
intraducìbile *agg.* untranslatable.
intralciare *vt.* to hinder, to interfere.
intralcio *sm.* hindrance.
intrallazzo *sm.* **1.** plotting **2.** (*imbroglio*) swindle.
intramezzare *vt.* to interpose, to
alternate.
intramontàbile *agg.* everlasting.
intramuscolare *agg.* intermuscu-
lar.
intransigente *agg.* strict, intransigent.
intransigenza *sf.* intransigence.
intransitivo *agg. e sm.* intransitive.
intrappolare *vt.* to entrap.
intraprendente *agg.* enterprising.
intraprendenza *sf.* enterprise.

intraprèndere vt. **1.** to undertake (v. irr.), to start **2.** (una professione) to go (v. irr.) in for.
intrattàbile agg. intractable.
intrattenere vt. to entertain. ◆ **intrattenersi** vr. **1.** to linger **2.** (dilungarsi) to dwell (v. irr.).
intravedere vt. **1.** (vedere di sfuggita) to catch (v. irr.) a glimpse of **2.** (vedere indistintamente) to see (v. irr.) indistinctly.
intrecciare vt. **1.** to interlace ‖ — danze, to dance **2.** (capelli, nastri) to plait.
intreccio sm. **1.** interlacement **2.** (di romanzi) plot.
intrèpido agg. brave, fearless.
intricare vt. to tangle. ◆ **intricarsi** vr. to get (v. irr.) entangled.
intrico sm. tangle.
intrìdere vt. to soak.
intrigante agg. crafty. ◆ **intrigante** sm. intriguer.
intrigare vi. to intrigue. ◆ **intrigarsi** vr. to meddle (with).
intrigo sm. intrigue, plot.
intrìnseco agg. intrinsic.
intristire vi. **1.** to pine away **2.** (incattivire) to grow (v. irr.) wicked.
introdotto agg. **1.** (importato) imported **2.** (conosciuto) well-known.
intriso agg. soaked (with), imbrued.
introdurre vt. **1.** to introduce **2.** (far entrare) to show (v. irr.) in. ◆ **introdursi** vr. to get (v. irr.) into, to slip into.
introduttivo agg. introductory.
introduzione sf. introduction.
introitare vt. to cash.
intròito sm. profit.
introméttere vt. to introduce. ◆ **introméttersi** vr. to interfere.
intromissione sf. intrusion.
intronare vt. to stun.
introspettivo agg. introspective.
introspezione sf. introspection.
introvàbile agg. not to be found.
introversione sf. introversion.
introverso agg. introverted. ◆ **introverso** sm. introvert.
intrufolarsi vr. to intrude (in).
intruglio sm. bad mixture.
intruppamento sm. trooping.
intrupparsi vr. to troop.
intrusione sf. intrusion.
intruso sm. intruder.
intuìbile agg. guessable.

intuire vt. to guess, to perceive.
intuitivo agg. intuitive.
intùito sm. intuition, insight.
intuizione sf. intuition.
inturgidimento sm. swelling.
inturgidire vi. to swell (up). **inturgidirsi** vr. to swell (up).
inuguale agg. unlike.
inumanità sf. inhumanity.
inumano agg. inhuman.
inumare vt. to inter.
inumazione sf. interment.
inumidire vt. to moisten. ◆ **inumidirsi** vr. to moisten.
inurbanità sf. incivility.
inurbano agg. uncivil.
inurbarsi vr. to inurbate.
inusitato agg. unusual.
inùtile agg. useless.
inutilità sf. uselessness.
inutilizzàbile agg. unusable.
invadente agg. intrusive.
invadenza sf. intrusiveness.
invàdere vt. to invade.
invaghimento sm. fancy (for).
invaghirsi vr. to take (v. irr.) a fancy (for), to fall (v. irr.) in love (with).
invaghito agg. fond (of), infatuated.
invalere vi. to prevail.
invalicàbile agg. impassable.
invalidare vt. to invalidate.
invalidazione sf. invalidation.
invalidità sf. invalidity.
invàlido agg. e sm. invalid.
invalso agg. prevailed.
invano avv. in vain.
invariàbile agg. **1.** invariable **2.** (di tempo) unchangeable.
invariabilità sf. invariability.
invariato agg. unchanged.
invasamento sm. obsession.
invasare vt. to possess.
invasato agg. possessed. ◆ **invasato** sm. possessed person.
invasione sf. invasion.
invasore sm. invader.
invecchiamento sm. ageing.
invecchiare vt. to make (v. irr.) old. ◆ **invecchiare** vi. to grow (v. irr.) old.
invece avv. on the contrary ‖ — di, instead of.
inveire vi. to rail (at).
invelenire vt. to embitter.
invendìbile agg. unsaleable.
invendicato agg. unavenged.
invenduto agg. unsold.

inventare vt. to invent.
inventariare vt. to inventory.
inventario sm. inventory || con beneficio d'—, with reservation.
inventiva sf. inventiveness.
inventivo agg. inventive.
inventore sm. inventor.
invenzione sf. invention.
inverdire vi. to turn green.
inverecondia sf. immodesty.
inverecondo agg. immodest.
inverificàbile agg. unverifiable.
invernale agg. 1. winter (attr.) 2. (da inverno) wintry.
invernata sf. wintertime.
inverno sm. winter.
invero avv. indeed.
inverosimiglianza sf. unlikelihood.
inverosìmile agg. unlikely.
inversione sf. inversion.
inverso agg. 1. (mat.) inverse 2. opposite, contrary. ♦ **inverso** sm. opposite, contrary.
invertebrato agg. e sm. invertebrate.
invertìbile agg. invertible.
invertire vt. to invert || — la marcia, to reverse.
invertito sm. invert.
invertitore sm. reverse gear.
investigare vt. to inquire.
investigativo agg. investigative.
investigatore sm. detective.
investigazione sf. investigation.
investimento sm. 1. investment 2. collision 3. (stradale) running down.
investire vt. 1. to invest (with) 2. (comm.) to invest 3. (assalire) to assail 4. (auto) to run (v. irr.) down.
investitore sm. (comm.) investor.
investitura sf. investiture.
inveterato agg. inveterate.
invetriata sf. glass window.
invettiva sf. invective.
inviare vt. to send (v. irr.).
inviato sm. 1. messenger 2. (in diplomazia) envoy 3. (in giornalismo) correspondent.
invidia sf. envy: per —, out of envy.
invidiàbile agg. enviable.
invidiare vt. to envy.
invidioso agg. envious.
invigorire vt. to strengthen. ♦ **invigorirsi** vr. to strengthen.
inviluppare vt. to envelop, to wrap up.
invincìbile agg. invincible.

invincibilità sf. invincibility.
invìo sm. 1. (per posta) mailing 2. (di merci) forwarding 3. (per nave) shipment 4. (di danaro) remittance.
inviolàbile agg. inviolable.
inviolabilità sf. inviolability.
inviperirsi vr. to become (v. irr.) furious.
inviperito agg. furious.
invischiare vt. 1. to lime 2. (fig.) to entangle. ♦ **invischiarsi** vr. to get (v. irr.) entangled.
invisìbile agg. invisible.
invisibilità sf. invisibility.
inviso agg. disliked.
invitante agg. inviting.
invitare vt. 1. to invite 2. (domandare) to request.
invitato agg. invited. ♦ **invitato** sm. guest.
invito sm. invitation.
invitto agg. unconquered.
invocare vt. to invoke.
invocazione sf. invocation.
invogliare vt. to tempt.
involare vt. to abduct. ♦ **involarsi** vr. to flee, to run (v. irr.) away.
involontario agg. unintentional.
involto sm. bundle, parcel.
invòlucro sm. 1. envelope 2. (bot.) involucre.
involutivo agg. involutionary.
involuto agg. involved.
involuzione sf. 1. involution 2. (decadenza) decline.
invulneràbile agg. invulnerable.
invulnerabilità sf. invulnerability.
inzaccherare vt. to muddy. ♦ **inzaccherarsi** vr. to get (v. irr.) muddy.
inzuppare vt. 1. to soak 2. (intingere) to dip.
io pron. I: — stesso, I myself.
iodato agg. iodized. ♦ **iodato** sm. iodate.
iodio sm. iodine.
iole sf. gig.
ione sm. ion.
iònico agg. Ionic.
ionizzazione sf. ionization.
ionosfera sf. ionosphere.
iosa (nella loc. avv.) a —, in plenty.
iperalimentazione sf. hypernutrition.
ipèrbole sf. hyperbole.
iperbòlico agg. hyperbolic(al).
iperbòreo agg. hyperborean.

ipercrìtico *agg.* hypercritical.
ipermetropìa *sf.* hypermetropia.
ipermètrope *agg.* hypermetropic.
ipernutrizione *sf.* hypernutrition.
ipersensìbile *agg.* hypersensitive.
ipersensibilità *sf.* hypersensitivity.
ipertensione *sf.* hypertension.
iperteso *agg.* e *sm.* hypertensive.
ipertrofìa *sf.* hypertrophy.
ipnosi *sf.* hypnosis.
ipnòtico *agg.* hypnotic.
ipnotismo *sm.* hypnotism.
ipnotizzare *vt.* to hypnotize.
ipnotizzatore *sm.* hypnotizer.
ipocondrìa *sf.* hypochondria.
ipocondrìaco *agg.* e *sm.* hypochondriac.
ipocrisìa *sf.* hypocrisy.
ipòcrita *agg.* hypocritical. ♦ **ipòcrita** *sm.* hypocrite.
ipodèrmico *agg.* hypodermic.
ipodermoclisi *sf.* hypodermoclysis.
ipòfisi *sf.* hypophysis.
ipoteca *sf.* mortgage.
ipotecare *vt.* to mortgage.
ipotenusa *sf.* hypotenuse.
ipòtesi *sf.* 1. hypothesis (*pl.* -ses) 2. (*supposizione*) supposition.
ipotètico *agg.* hypothetical.
ìppica *sf.* horse-racing.
ìppico *agg.* horse (*attr.*).
ippocampo *sm.* hippocampus (*pl.* -pi).
ippocastano *sm.* horse-chestnut.
ippòdromo *sm.* race-course.
ippopòtamo *sm.* hippopotamus.
ira *sf.* anger, rage.
iracondo *agg.* irascible.
irascìbile *agg.* irritable.
irascibilità *sf.* irritability.
irato *agg.* angry.
iridato *agg.* iridescent.
ìride *sf.* iris.
iridescente *agg.* iridescent.
iridescenza *sf.* iridescence.
irlandese *agg.* Irish.
ironìa *sf.* irony.
ìronico *agg.* ironic(al).
ironizzare *vi.* to make (*v. irr.*) ironical remarks.
iroso *agg.* wrathful.
irradiamento *sm.* irradiation.
irradiare *vt.* to irradiate.
irradiazione *sf.* V. *irradiamento.*
irraggiare *vt.* V. *irradiare.*
irraggiungìbile *agg.* unreachable.
irragionévole *agg.* unreasonable.
irrancidire *vi.* to grow (*v. irr.*) rank.

irrazionale *agg.* irrational.
irrazionalità *sf.* irrationality.
irreale *agg.* unreal.
irrealizzàbile *agg.* unrealizable.
irrealtà *sf.* unreality.
irreconciliàbile *agg.* irreconcilable.
irrecuperàbile *agg.* irrecoverable.
irrefrenàbile *agg.* unrestrainable.
irrefutàbile *agg.* irrefutable.
irregolare *agg.* irregular.
irregolarità *sf.* irregularity.
irremovìbile *agg.* 1. immovable 2. (*inflessibile*) inflexible.
irreparàbile *agg.* irreparable.
irreperìbile *agg.* elusive: *rendersi —,* to hide (*v. irr.*) oneself.
irreprensìbile *agg.* irreproachable.
irrequietezza *sf.* restlessness.
irrequieto *agg.* restless.
irresistìbile *agg.* irresistible.
irresolutezza *sf.* irresolution.
irresoluto *agg.* hesitating.
irrespiràbile *agg.* unbreathable.
irresponsàbile *agg.* irresponsible.
irresponsabilità *sf.* irresponsibility.
irrestringìbile *agg.* unshrinkable.
irretire *vt.* to snare.
irreversìbile *agg.* irreversible.
irreversibilità *sf.* irreversibility.
irrevocàbile *agg.* irrevocable.
irriconoscìbile *agg.* unrecognizable.
irrìdere *vt.* to laugh at.
irriducìbile *agg.* irreducible.
irriflessione *sf.* thoughtlessness.
irriflessivo *agg.* thoughtless.
irrigàbile *agg.* irrigable.
irrigare *vt.* to irrigate.
irrigazione *sf.* irrigation.
irrigidimento *sm.* stiffening.
irrigidire *vt.* to stiffen. ♦ **irrigidirsi** *vr.* to stiffen.
irriguo *agg.* well-watered.
irrilevante *agg.* insignificant.
irrimediàbile *agg.* irremediable.
irrisione *sf.* mockery.
irrisorio *agg.* derisory, paltry.
irrispettoso *agg.* disrespectful.
irritàbile *agg.* 1. (*di persona*) irritable 2. (*di pelle*) sensitive.
irritabilità *sf.* 1. (*di persona*) irritability 2. (*di pelle*) sensitiveness.
irritante *agg.* irritating.
irritare *vt.* to irritate. ♦ **irritarsi** *vr.* 1. to grow (*v. irr.*) angry 2. (*di pelle*) to become (*v. irr.*) irritated.
irritazione *sf.* 1. irritation 2. (*di pelle*) inflammation.

irriverente *agg.* disrespectful.
irriverenza *sf.* irreverence.
irrobustire *vt.* to strengthen. ♦
irrobustirsi *vr.* to strengthen.
irròmpere *vi.* 1. to break (*v. irr.*)
into 2. (*di acque*) to overflow.
irrorare *vt.* to sprinkle.
irroratrice *sf.* sprayer.
irruente *agg.* impetuous.
irruenza *sf.* impetuosity.
irruvidire *vt.* to roughen.
irruzione *sf.* irruption: *fare —,*
to rush into.
irsuto *agg.* shaggy.
irto *agg.* bristling (with).
iscritto *sm.* member.
iscrìvere *vt.* 1. (*a scuola, esami
ecc.*) to enrol 2. (*registrare*) to record 3. (*scolpire*) to engrave. ♦
iscrìversi *vr.* to enter, to join.
iscrizione *sf.* 1. inscription 2. (*a
scuola, esami ecc.*) entry || *do-
manda d'—,* application.
islàmico *agg.* Islamic.
islamismo *sm.* Islamism.
isocronismo *sm.* isochronism.
ìsola *sf.* island.
isolamento *sm.* 1. isolation 2.
(*elettr.*) insulation || *— acustico,*
sound-proofing.
isolano *agg.* insular. ♦ isolano *sm.*
islander.
isolante *agg.* insulating. ♦ isolante *sm.* insulator.
isolare *vt.* 1. to isolate 2. (*elettr.*)
to insulate || *— acusticamente,* to
soundproof. ♦ isolarsi *vr.* to
seclude oneself.
isolato *agg.* 1. isolated 2. (*elettr.*)
insulated. ♦ isolato *sm.* (*edil.*)
block.
isolatore *sm.* insulator.
isolazionismo *sm.* isolationism.
isolazionista *s.* isolationist.
isolotto *sm.* islet.
isomorfismo *sm.* isomorphism.
isomorfo *agg.* isomorphous.
isòscele *agg.* isosceles.
isotèrmico *agg.* isothermal.
isòtopo *sm.* isotope.
isòtropo *sm.* isotrope.
ispànico *agg.* Hispanic.
ispanismo *sm.* Hispanicism.
ispanista *s.* Hispanist.
ispettorato *sm.* inspectorate.
ispettore *sm.* inspector.
ispezionare *vt.* to inspect.
ispezione *sf.* inspection.
ispido *agg.* hispid.

ispirare *vt.* to inspire (with). ♦
ispirarsi *vr.* to draw (*v. irr.*) one's
inspiration (from).
ispirato *agg.* 1. inspired 2. (*basato*)
imbued (with).
ispiratore *agg.* inspiring. ♦ ispiratore *sm.* inspirer.
ispirazione *sf.* inspiration.
israeliano *agg. e sm.* Israeli.
israelita *agg. e s.* Israelite.
issare *vt.* to hoist.
istantànea *sf.* snapshot: *fare un'—,*
to snapshot.
istantaneità *sf.* instantaneousness.
istantàneo *agg.* instantaneous.
istante *sm.* instant || *all'—, sull'—,*
instantly.
istanza *sf.* 1. request, instance 2.
(*supplica*) entreaty 3. (*domanda
scritta*) application.
istèrico *agg.* hysteric(al). ♦ istèrico *sm.* hysterical man (*pl.* -men).
isterilire *vt.* to sterilize. ♦ isteri-
lirsi *vr.* to become (*v. irr.*) barren.
isterismo *sm.* hysteria.
istigare *vt.* to instigate.
istigatore *sm.* instigator.
istigazione *sf.* instigation.
istintivo *agg.* instinctive.
istinto *sm.* instinct.
istituire *vt.* 1. to institute 2. (*fondare*) to found 3. (*giur.*) to appoint.
istituto *sm.* 1. institute 2. (*istituzione*) institution 3. (*scuola*)
school.
istitutore *sm.* tutor.
istitutrice *sf.* governess.
istituzionale *agg.* institutional.
istituzione *sf.* institution.
istmo *sm.* isthmus (*pl.* -mi).
istologìa *sf.* histology.
ìstrice *sm.* hedgehog.
istrione *sm.* 1. (*teat.*) histrion 2.
(*ciarlatano*) quack.
istriònico *agg.* histrionic.
istruire *vt.* 1. to teach (*v. irr.*) 2.
(*dare istruzioni*) to instruct, to direct 3. (*giur.*) to institute. ♦
istruirsi *vr.* to educate oneself.
istruito *agg.* learned.
istruttivo *agg.* instructive.
istruttore *sm.* instructor: *giudice
—,* examining magistrate.
istruttoria *sf.* examination || *apri-
re ·l'—,* to open proceedings.
istruzione *sf.* 1. education 2. (*cultura*) learning 3. (*insegnamento*)
teaching 4. (*ordine*) instruction.

istupidire *vt.* to make (*v. irr.*) stupid. ♦ **istupidirsi** *v.r.* to become (*v. irr.*) stupid.
italiano *agg.* e *sm.* Italian.
itinerario *sm.* itinerary.
itterizia *sf.* jaundice.
ittiologìa *sf.* ichthyology.
ittiòlogo *sm.* ichthyologist.
iugoslavo *agg.* e *sm.* Yugoslav.
iugulare *agg.* jugular.
iuta *sf.* jute.
ivi *avv.* there.

L

la¹ *art.* the. ♦ **la** *pron.* **1.** (*per donna*) her **2.** (*per animale e cosa*) it **3.** (*forma di cortesia*) you.
la² *sm.* (*mus.*) A.
là *avv.* there ‖ *l'al di* —, the hereafter; — *per* —, on the spot; *al di* — *di*, beyond; *più in* —, (*spazio*) further on, (*tempo*) later on.
labbro *sm.* lip.
labiale *agg.* labial.
làbile *agg.* fleeting: *memoria* —, weak memory.
labirinto *sm.* labyrinth.
laboratorio *sm.* **1.** laboratory **2.** (*artigianale*) workshop.
laboriosità *sf.* laboriousness.
laborioso *agg.* laborious.
laburismo *sm.* labourism.
laburista *agg.* labour ‖ *partito* —, Labour Party. ♦ **laburista** *s.* Labourite.
lacca *sf.* lacquer.
laccare *vt.* to lacquer.
laccatura *sf.* lacquering.
laccio *sm.* **1.** string ‖ *lacci da scarpe*, shoe-laces **2.** (*trappola*) snare ‖ *prendere al* — (*fig.*), to ensnare.
laceramento *sm.* tearing.
lacerante *agg.* rending.
lacerare *vt.* to tear (*v. irr.*) (up), to rend (*v. irr.*) (*anche fig.*). ♦ **lacerarsi** *vr.* to tear.
lacerazione *sf.* laceration.
làcero *agg.* **1.** torn **2.** (*med.*) lacerated.
laconicità *sf.* laconicism.
lacònico *agg.* laconic(al).
làcrima *sf.* tear.
lacrimale *agg.* lachrymal.

lacrimare *vi.* to weep (*v. irr.*).
lacrimazione *sf.* lachrymation.
lacrimévole *agg.* tearful.
lacrimògeno *agg.* lachrymatory: *gas* —, tear-gas.
lacrimoso *agg.* tearful.
lacuna *sf.* gap.
lacunoso *agg.* lacunous.
lacustre *agg.* lacustrine.
laddove *cong.* whereas. ♦ **laddove** *avv.* (there) where.
ladra *sf.* woman thief.
ladro *agg.* thieving. ♦ **ladro** *sm.* thief: *al* —!, stop thief!
ladrocinio *sm.* theft.
ladrone *sm.* robber.
ladronerìa *sf.* robbery.
laggiù *avv.* down there.
lagna *sf.* lament.
lagnanza *sf.* complaint.
lagnarsi *vr.* to complain (of).
lago *sm.* lake.
laguna *sf.* lagoon.
lagunare *agg.* lagoon (*attr.*).
laicato *sm.* laity.
laicismo *sm.* laicism.
laicizzare *vt.* to laicize.
làico *agg.* laic. ♦ **làico** *sm.* layman (*pl.* -men).
laidezza *sf.* ugliness, foulness.
làido *agg.* **1.** dirty **2.** (*brutto*) ugly.
lama¹ *sf.* blade.
lama² *sm.* (*zool.*) llama.
lama³ *sm.* (*monaco buddista*) lama.
lambiccare *vt.* to distil ‖ *lambiccarsi il cervello*, to rack one's brains.
lambiccato *agg.* **1.** distilled **2.** (*ricercato*) over-elaborate.
lambicco *sm.* alembic.
lambire *vt.* to lick.
lamella *sf.* lamella (*pl.* -lae).
lamentare *vt.* to lament. ♦ **lamentarsi** *vr.* to moan.
lamentazione *sf.* lamentation.
lamentela *sf.* complaint.
lamentévole *agg.* mournful.
lamento *sm.* moan.
lamentoso *agg.* mournful.
lametta *sf.* razor-blade.
lamiera *sf.* sheet.
làmina *sf.* lamina (*pl.* -nae).
laminare *vt.* to laminate.
laminato *sm.* **1.** (*tessuto*) lamé **2.** (*metallo*) rolled section.
laminatoio *sm.* rolling-mill.
làmpada *sf.* lamp.
lampadario *sm.* chandelier, lamp holder.

lampadina *sf.* bulb.

lampante *agg.* glaring, evident.

lampeggiamento *sm.* 1. flashing, lightning 2. (*di fari, semafori ecc.*) winking 3. (*di auto*) to blink.

lampeggiare *vi.* 1. to flash, to lighten 2. (*di fari, semafori ecc.*) to wink.

lampeggiatore *sm.* 1. winking light 2. (*di auto*) blinker.

lampione *sm.* street-lamp.

lampo *sm.* 1. lightning 2. (*luce istantanea, anche fig.*) flash || *chiusura* —, zip-fastener.

lampone *sm.* raspberry.

lampreda *sf.* lamprey.

lana *sf.* wool.

lancetta *sf.* 1. (*di quadrante*) hand 2. (*di chirurgo*) lancet.

lancia¹ *sf.* lance.

lancia² *sf.* (*mar.*) launch || — *di salvataggio*, lifeboat.

lanciafiamme *sm.* flame-thrower.

lanciare *vt.* 1. to throw (*v. irr.*) 2. (*fig.*) to launch || — *un'occhiata*, to cast (*v. irr.*) a glance. ♦ lanciarsi *vr.* to dash.

lanciatore *sm.* thrower.

lanciere *sm.* lancer.

lancinante *agg.* piercing.

lancio *sm.* 1. throwing 2. (*pubblicitario*) launching.

landa *sf.* moor.

lànguido *agg.* languid.

languire *vi.* to languish.

languore *sm.* languor.

laniero' *agg.* woollen.

lanificio *sm.* wool factory.

lanolina *sf.* lanolin.

lanoso *agg.* woolly.

lanterna *sf.* lantern.

lanùgine *sf.* down.

laparatomìa *sf.* laparotomy.

lapidare *vt.* to stone.

lapidario *agg.* lapidary.

lapidazione *sf.* lapidation.

làpide *sf.* 1. tablet 2. (*sepolcrale*) tombstone.

lapis *sm.* pencil.

lardeilare *vt.* to lard.

lardo *sm.* lard, bacon.

larga (*nella loc. avv.*) alla —, away (from).

largheggiare *vi.* to abound (with).

larghezza *sf.* 1. breadth 2. (*liberalità*) liberality 3. (*abbondanza*) plenty.

largire *vt.* to bestow (upon).

largitore *sm.* bestower.

largizione *sf.* bestowal.

largo *agg.* broad, wide. ♦ largo *sm.* 1. (*mar.*) open sea 2. (*piazza*) square || *prendere il* —, to set (*v. irr.*) sail; (*fig.*) to run (*v. irr.*) away; *andare al* —, to take (*v. irr.*) to the open sea; *fare* —, to make (*v. irr.*) room.

làrice *sm.* larch.

laringe *sf.* larynx.

laringite *sf.* laryngitis.

larva *sf.* larva (*pl.* -ae).

lasciapassare *sm.* pass.

lasciare *vt.* 1. to leave (*v. irr.*) 2. (*permettere*) to let (*v. irr.*), to allow. ♦ lasciarsi *vr. rec.* (*separarsi*) to part.

làscito *sm.* legacy.

lascivia *sf.* lust.

lascivo *agg.* lustful.

lassativo *agg. e sm.* laxative.

lasso *sm.* lapse: *dopo un certo* — *di tempo*, after a lapse of time.

lassù *avv.* up there.

lastra *sf.* 1. (*vetro*) glass' sheet 2. (*di pietra*) slab 3. (*di metallo, foto*) plate.

lastricare *vt.* to pave.

lastricatura *sf.* paving.

làstrico *sm.* pavement || *essere sul* — (*fig.*), to be destitute.

latente *agg.* latent.

laterale *agg.* side: *via* —, by-street.

lateralmente *avv.* sideways.

laterizi *sm. pl.* bricks.

làtice *sm.* latex.

latifondista *sm.* landowner.

latifondo *sm.* large landed estate.

latinismo *sm.* Latinism.

latinista *s.* Latinist.

latinità *sf.* Latinity.

latino *agg. e sm.* Latin.

latitante *agg.* absconding: *essere* —, to be in hiding. ♦ latitante *s.* absconder.

latitanza *sf.* hiding: *darsi alla* —, to evade arrest.

latitùdine *sf.* latitude.

lato¹ *sm.* 1. side 2. (*fig.*) point of view || *d'altro* —, on the other hand; *da un* —, on the one hand.

lato² *agg.* wide || *in senso* —, in a broad sense.

latore *sm.* bearer.

latrare *vi.* to bark.

latrato *sm.* barking.

latrina *sf.* lavatory.

latta *sf.* tin.

lattaio sm. milkman (pl. -men).
lattante agg. unweaned. ♦ **lattante** s. suckling (baby).
latte sm. milk.
làtteo agg. milky.
latterìa sf. dairy.
latticini sm. pl. dairy products.
lattiera sf. milk-jug.
lattiginoso agg. 1. milky 2. (bot.) lactescent.
lattoniere sm. tinker.
lattosio sm. lactose.
lattuga sf. lettuce.
laudativo agg. laudatory.
làurea sf. degree.
laureare vt. to confer a degree (on). ♦ **laurearsi** vr. to graduate.
laureato agg. graduated. ♦ **laureato** sm. graduate || — in lettere, Doctor of Literature Degree.
làuro sm. laurel.
làuto agg. sumptuous || lauti guadagni, large profits.
lava sf. lava.
lavàbile agg. washable.
lavabo sm. washbowl.
lavaggio sm. washing: — a secco, dry cleaning.
lavagna sf. 1. blackboard 2. (ardesia) slate.
lavanda[1] sf. 1. washing 2. (med.) lavage.
lavanda[2] sf. (bot.) lavender.
lavandaia sf. laundress.
lavanderìa sf. laundry.
lavandino sm. sink.
lavapiatti s. dish-washer.
lavare vt. to wash: — a secco, to dry-clean. ♦ **lavarsi** vr. to wash (oneself).
lavata sf. wash || dare una — di capo (fig.), to scold.
lavativo sm. 1. (med.) enema 2. (fig.) lazy-bones.
lavatoio sm. 1. wash-house 2. (asse per lavare) wash-board.
lavatrice sf. 1. washer 2. (lavabiancheria) washing machine.
lavatura sf. washing.
lavina sf. landslip.
lavorante sm. worker.
lavorare vi. e vt. to work.
lavorativo agg. working || ora lavorativa, man-hour.
lavoratore agg. working. ♦ **lavoratore** sm. worker || — a giornata, day-labourer.
lavorazione sf. 1. processing 2. (fattura) work 3. (agr.) tilling || —

a mano, handwork.
lavorìo sm. intense activity.
lavoro sm. 1. work 2. (occupazione) job || — a ore, work by the hour; lavori di casa, housework; — su ordinazione, work to order; eccesso di —, overwork; — in proprio, self-employment.
lazzaretto sm. lazaretto.
lazzarone sm. slacker.
lazzo sm. joke.
le art. the. ♦ **le** pron. 1. (sing.) her, to her 2. (pl.) them 3. (forma di cortesia) you, to you.
leale agg. 1. loyal 2. (corretto) fair.
lealtà sf. 1. loyalty 2. (correttezza) fairness.
lebbra sf. leprosy.
lebbrosario sm. leper hospital.
lebbroso agg. leprous. ♦ **lebbroso** sm. leper.
leccapiedi sm. bootlicker.
leccare vt. to lick. ♦ **leccarsi** vr. to lick (oneself).
leccata sf. licking.
leccornìa sf. dainty.
lécito agg. 1. lawful 2. (giusto) right 3. (permesso) allowed. ♦ **lécito** sm. right.
lèdere vt. 1. to injure 2. (danneggiare) to damage.
lega sf. 1. league 2. (di metalli) alloy || di buona —, genuine; di cattiva —, low.
legaccio sm. string.
legale agg. legal, lawful || procedere per vie legali, to have recourse to the law. ♦ **legale** sm. lawyer.
legalità sf. legality.
legalizzare vt. 1. to legalize 2. (autenticare) to authenticate.
legalizzazione sf. 1. legalization 2. (autenticazione) authentication.
legame sm. 1. string 2. (vincolo) tie 3. (connessione) link.
legamento sm. 1. string 2. (anat.) ligament.
legare[1] vt. 1. to tie 2. (di metalli) to alloy (with) 3. (aver connessione) to be connected. ♦ **legarsi** vr. to bind (v. irr.) oneself.
legare[2] vt. (giur.) to bequeath.
legatario sm. legatee.
legato[1] sm. 1. ambassador 2. (eccl.) legate.
legato[2] sm. (giur.) legacy.
legatore sm. binder.
legatorìa sf. bookbinder's establishment.

legatura *sf.* **1.** binding **2.** (*mus.; med.*) ligature.
legazione *sf.* legation.
legge *sf.* **1.** law **2.** (*singola*) act **3.** (*regola*) rule || *progetto di* —, bill; *a norma di* —, according to the law; *a termini di* —, as bv law enacted.
leggenda *sf.* legend.
leggendario *agg.* legendary.
lèggere *vt.* to read (*v. irr.*).
leggerezza *sf.* lightness.
leggero *agg.* light.
leggiadrìa *sf.* loveliness.
leggiadro *agg.* lovely.
leggìbile *agg.* readable.
leggìo *sm.* **1.** reading-desk **2.** (*mus.*) music-stand.
legiferare *vi.* to legislate.
legionario *agg. e sm.* legionary.
legione *sf.* legion.
legislativo *agg.* legislative.
legislatore *sm.* legislator.
legislatura *sf.* legislature.
legislazione *sf.* legislation.
legittimare *vt.* to legitimate.
legittimazione *sf.* legitimation.
legittimità *sf.* legitimacy.
legìttimo *agg.* legitimate.
legna *sf.* wood || — *da ardere*, fire-wood.
legnaia *sf.* wood-store.
legname *sm.* **1.** wood **2.** (*da costruzione*) timber.
legnata *sf.* blow with a cudgel.
legno *sm.* wood || *di* —, wooden.
legnosità *sf.* woodiness.
legnoso *agg.* **1.** woody **2.** (*duro*) tough.
legume *sm.* legume.
leguminoso *agg.* leguminous.
lei *pron.* **1.** (*sogg.*) she, (*compl.*) her **2.** (*forma di cortesia*) you.
lembo *sm.* **1.** edge **2.** (*pezzo*) strip.
lemma *sm.* lemma.
lèmure *sm.* lemur. ◆ **lèmuri** *sm. pl.* (*mit.*) lemures.
lena *sf.* **1.** energy **2.** (*respiro*) breath.
lenire *vt.* to soothe.
lenone *sm.* pander.
lente *sf.* lens: — *d'ingrandimento*, magnifying lens || *lenti*, glasses.
lentezza *sf.* slowness.
lenticchia *sf.* lentil.
lentìggine *sf.* freckle.
lentigginoso *agg.* freckly.
lento *agg.* **1.** slow **2.** (*non teso*) loose.

lenza *sf.* fishing-line.
lenzuolo *sm.* sheet.
leone *sm.* lion.
leonessa *sf.* lioness.
leonino *agg.* leonine.
leopardo *sm.* leopard.
lèpido *agg.* witty.
lepidòttero *sm.* lepidopteron (*pl.* -era).
leporino *agg.* leporine || *labbro* —, hare-lip.
lepre *sf.* hare.
lercio *agg.* filthy.
lèsbica *agg. e sf.* Lesbian.
lésina *sf.* awl.
lesinare *vi.* to be stingy. ◆ **lesinare** *vt.* to grudge.
lesionare *vt.* to damage, to injure.
lesione *sf.* **1.** lesion, injury **2.** (*danno*) damage.
lesivo *agg.* harmful.
leso *agg.* **1.** injured **2.** (*danneggiato*) damaged.
lessare *vt.* to boil.
lessicale *agg.* lexical.
lèssico *sm.* lexicon.
lessicografìa *sf.* lexicography.
lessicologìa *sf.* lexicology.
lesso *agg.* boiled. ◆ **lesso** *sm.* boiled meat.
lestezza *sf.* quickness.
lesto *agg.* quick.
lestofante *sm.* swindler.
letale *agg.* lethal.
letamaio *sm.* dunghill.
letame *sm.* dung.
letàrgico *agg.* **1.** lethargic **2.** (*di animali, in inverno*) hibernating; (*id., in estate*) estivating.
letargo *sm.* **1.** lethargy **2.** (*di animali, in inverno*) hibernation; (*id., in estate*) estivation.
letizia *sf.* joy.
lèttera *sf.* letter || *alla* —, literally.
letterale *agg.* literal.
letterario *agg.* literary.
letterato *agg.* lettered. ◆ **letterato** *sm.* literary man.
letteratura *sf.* literature.
lettiga *sf.* stretcher.
letto *sm.* bed || *camera da* —, bedroom; *vagone* —, sleeping-car.
lettore *sm.* reader.
lettura *sf.* reading.
leucemìa *sf.* leukaemia.
leucociti *sm. pl.* leucocytes.
leucoma *sm.* leucoma.
leva[1] *sf.* **1.** lever **2.** (*fig.*) stimulus || *far* — *sui sentimenti di qu.*, to

play on so.'s feelings.
leva[2] *sf.* (*mil.*) draft: *essere di* —, to be due for draft.
levante *sm.* 1. east 2. (*vento*) levanter.
levare *vt.* 1. (*sollevare*) to raise 2. (*togliere*) to take (*v. irr.*) off. ♦ **levarsi** *vr.* 1. to rise (*v. irr.*) 2. (*togliersi*) to take off.
levata *sf.* 1. (*di sole*) rising 2. (*di posta*) collection || — *di scudi* rebellion.
levataccia *sf.* early rising.
levatoio *agg. ponte* —, drawbridge.
levatrice *sf.* midwife (*pl.* -wives).
levatura *sf.* intelligence.
levigare *vt.* to smooth.
levigatezza *sf.* smoothness.
levigato *agg.* smooth.
levitazione *sf.* levitation.
levriere *sm.* greyhound.
lezione *sf.* 1. lesson 2. (*universitaria*) lecture 3. (*lett.*) reading.
leziosàggine *sf.* affectation.
lezioso *agg.* affected.
lezzo *sm.* stench.
li *pron.* them.
lì *avv.* there: — *vicino*, near there; — *dentro*, in there || — *per* —, at first; *di* — *a poco*, soon after; *giù di* — (*press'a poco*), thereabouts; *essere* — *per*, to be on the point of.
liana *sf.* liana.
libagione *sf.* libation.
libbra *sf.* pound.
libeccio *sm.* Southwest wind.
libello *sm.* libel.
libèllula *sf.* dragonfly.
liberale *agg.* e *sm.* liberal.
liberalismo *sm.* liberalism.
liberalità *sf.* generosity.
liberalizzare *vt.* to liberalize.
liberare *vt.* 1. to free 2. (*da pericoli*) to rescue 3. (*sbarazzare*) to rid (*v. irr.*) (of). ♦ **liberarsi** *vr.* (*sbarazzarsi*) to get (*v. irr.*) rid (of).
liberatore *agg.* liberating. ♦ **liberatore** *sm.* deliverer.
liberazione *sf.* liberation.
libero *agg.* free.
liberoscambista *agg.* e *sm.* free-trader.
libertà *sf.* liberty, freedom.
libertario *agg.* e *sm.* libertarian.
liberticida *agg.* e *s.* liberticide.
libertinaggio *sm.* libertinage.
libertino *agg.* e *sm.* libertine.

libìdine *sf.* lust.
libidinoso *agg.* lustful.
libido *sf.* lustfulness.
libraio *sm.* bookseller.
librarsi *vr.* to hover.
librerìa *sf.* 1. bookshop 2. (*mobile*) bookcase.
libresco *agg.* bookish.
libretto *sm.* 1. booklet 2. (*d'opera*) libretto || — *di assegni*, cheque-book; — *di risparmio*, savings-book; — *personale*, record-book.
libro *sm.* book.
licenza *sf.* 1. (*abuso*) licence 2. (*permesso*) permission, leave 3. (*documento*) licence.
licenziamento *sm.* dismissal.
licenziare *vt.* to dismiss. ♦ **licenziarsi** *vr.* to give (*v. irr.*) up one's job.
licenziosità *sf.* licentiousness.
licenzioso *agg.* licentious.
lichene *sm.* lichen.
licitazione *sf.* sale by auction.
lido *sm.* shore.
lieto *agg.* glad.
lieve *agg.* slight.
lievitare *vi.* to rise (*v. irr.*). ♦ **lievitare** *vt.* to leaven.
lievitazione *sf.* leavening.
lièvito *sm.* 1. yeast 2. (*fermento*) ferment.
ligio *agg.* faithful, observant (of).
lignaggio *sm.* lineage.
ligneo *agg.* wooden.
lignite *sf.* lignite.
lillà *sm.* lilac.
lillipuziano *agg.* e *sm.* Lilliputian.
lima *sf.* file.
limaccioso *agg.* slimy.
limare *vt.* 1. to file 2. (*fig.*) to polish.
limatrice *sf.* (*mecc.*) shaping-machine.
limatura *sf.* filing.
limbo *sm.* limbo.
limitare *vt.* to limit. ♦ **limitarsi** *vr.* (*controllarsi*) to check oneself.
limitatezza *sf.* limitation.
limitativo *agg.* limitative.
limitato *agg.* limited.
limitazione *sf.* limitation: — *delle nascite*, birth-control.
limite *sm.* limit: — *di velocità*, speed-limit || — *di rottura*, breaking-point.
limìtrofo *agg.* neighbouring.
limo *sm.* slime.
limonata *sf.* lemonade.

limone *sm.* lemon.
limpidezza *sf.* clearness.
limpido *agg.* limpid, clear.
lince *sf.* lynx.
linciaggio *sm.* lynching
linciare *vt.* to lynch.
lindo *agg.* neat.
linea *sf.* line || *aereo di* —, air-liner; *mantenere la* —, to keep (*v. irr.*) one's figure.
lineamenti *sm. pl.* 1. features 2. (*linee essenziali*) outlines.
lineare *agg.* 1. linear 2. (*fig.*) unswerving.
lineetta *sf.* 1. dash 2. (*trattino d'unione*) hyphen.
linfa *sf.* (*biol.*) lymph.
linfàtico *agg.* lymphatic.
linfatismo *sm.* lymphatism.
lingotto *sm.* ingot.
lingua *sf.* 1. tongue 2. (*linguaggio*) language.
linguacciuto *agg.* talkative.
linguaggio *sm.* language.
linguetta *sf.* 1. flap 2. (*mecc.; di scarpe*) tongue.
linguista *s.* linguist.
linguistica *sf.* linguistics.
linguìstico *agg.* linguistic.
linimento *sm.* liniment.
lino *sm.* flax.
linòleum *sm.* linoleum.
linone *sm.* lawn.
linotipìa *sf.* linotyping.
linotipista *s.* linotypist.
liquefare *vt.* to liquefy. ♦ **liquefarsi** *vr.* to liquefy.
liquefazione *sf.* liquefaction.
liquidare *vt.* 1. to liquidate 2. (*comm.*) to sell (*v. irr.*) off, to settle || — *una questione*, to settle a question.
liquidatore *sm.* liquidator.
liquidazione *sf.* liquidation, sale.
liquido *agg. e sm.* liquid || *denaro* —, cash.
liquirizia *sf.* liquorice.
liquore *sm.* liqueur || *i liquori*, spirits.
liquoroso *agg.* liqueur-like.
lira *sf.* 1. (*moneta*) lira 2. (*mus.*) lyre.
lirica *sf.* 1. lyric poetry 2. (*teatro lirico*) opera.
lirico *agg.* lyric(al). ♦ **lirico** *sm.* lyrist.
lirismo *sm.* lyrism.
lisciare *vt.* 1. to smooth 2. (*adulare*) to flatter. ♦ **lisciarsi** *vr.* to sleek oneself.
liscio *agg.* 1. smooth 2. (*di bevanda*) undiluted 3. (*semplice*) plain 4. (*di capelli*) sleek.
lisciva *sf.* lye.
liso *agg.* threadbare.
lista *sf.* 1. (*elenco*) list, note 2. (*striscia*) stripe.
listare *vt.* 1. to stripe 2. (*bordare*) to border.
listino *sm.* list.
litanìa *sf.* litany.
lite *sf.* 1. quarrel, wrangle 2. (*giur.*) lawsuit.
litigante *sm.* 1. wrangler 2. (*giur.*) litigant.
litigare *vi.* 1. to quarrel 2. (*giur.*) to litigate.
litigio *sm.* quarrel.
litigioso *agg.* quarrelsome.
litografia *sf.* 1. lithography 2. (*pezzo singolo*) lithograph.
litogràfico *agg.* lithographic.
litorale *agg.* littoral. ♦ **litorale** *sm.* coast.
litro *sm.* litre.
liturgìa *sf.* liturgy.
litùrgico *agg.* liturgic(al).
liuto *sm.* lute.
livellamento *sm.* levelling.
livellare *vt.* to level.
livellatrice *sf.* bulldozer.
livello *sm.* level: *a* — *del mare*, at sea-level; *passaggio a* —, level-crossing; *essere allo stesso* — *di*, to be on a level with.
livido *agg.* livid. ♦ **livido** *sm.* bruise.
livore *sm.* 1. (*invidia*) envy 2. (*odio*) hatred.
livrea *sf.* livery.
lizza *sf.* competition, lists (*pl.*) || *essere in* — (*fig.*), to be competing.
lo *art.* the. ♦ **lo** *pron.* 1. (*per uomo*) him 2. (*per animale, cosa*) it || — *credo*, I think so.
lobo *sm.* lobe.
locale *agg.* local. ♦ **locale** *sm.* 1. room 2. (*ritrovo*) place.
località *sf.* locality, spot.
localizzare *vt.* to localize.
localizzazione *sf.* localization.
locanda *sf.* inn.
locandiere *sm.* innkeeper.
locandina *sf.* play-bill.
locare *vt.* to rent.
locatario *sm.* tenant.
locativo *agg.* locative || *valore* —, rental value.

locatore *sm.* lessor.
locazione *sf.* lease.
locomotiva *sf.* locomotive.
locomotore *agg.* e *sm.* locomotive.
locomozione *sf.* locomotion.
locusta *sf.* locust.
locuzione *sf.* locution.
lodàbile *agg.* laudable.
lodare *vt.* to praise
lodatore *sm.* praiser.
lode *sf.* praise.
lodévole *agg.* praiseworthy.
logaritmo *sm.* logarithm.
loggia *sf.* 1. (*arch.*) loggia 2. (*massonica*) lodge.
loggione *sm.* gallery.
lògica *sf.* logic.
logicità *sf.* logicality.
lògico *agg.* logical. ◆ **lògico** *sm.* logician.
logìstica *sf.* logistics.
logìstico *agg.* logistic(al).
loglio *sm.* darnel.
logomachìa *sf.* logomachy.
logoramento *sm.* 1. wear 2. (*fig.*) wasting away.
logorante *agg.* wearing.
logorare *vt.* to wear (*v. irr.*) (out, down). ◆ **logorarsi** *vr.* to wear (out, down).
logorìo *sm.* wear and tear.
lògoro *agg.* worn (out, down).
lombàggine *sf.* lumbago.
lombardo *agg.* e *sm.* Lombard.
lombare *agg.* lumbar.
lombi *sm. pl.* loins.
lombrico *sm.* earth-worm.
longànime *agg.* forbearing.
longanimità *sf.* forbearance.
longevità *sf.* longevity.
longevo *agg.* longevous.
longitudinale *agg.* longitudinal.
longitùdine *sf.* longitude.
lontananza *sf.* distance: *in —*, in the distance.
lontano *agg.* 1. far 2. (*nel tempo*) far off, distant 3. (*vago*) vague. ◆ **lontano** *avv.* far || *da —*, from afar.
lontra *sf.* otter.
loquace *agg.* talkative.
loquacità *sf.* talkativeness.
loquela *sf.* glibness.
lordare *vt.* to soil. ◆ **lordarsi** *vr.* to get (*v. irr.*) dirty.
lordo *agg.* 1. (*sporco*) filthy 2. (*di peso*) gross.
loro *agg. poss.* their. ◆ **loro** *pron. poss.* theirs. ◆ **loro** *pron. pers.*

1. (*sogg.*) they, (*compl.*) them 2. (*forma di cortesia*) you.
losanga *sf.* lozenge.
losco *agg.* 1. (*bieco*) sinister 2. (*sospetto*) suspicious.
loto *sm.* 1. (*fango*) mud 2. (*bot.*) lotus.
lotta *sf.* 1. struggle 2. (*sport*) wrestling.
lottare *vi.* 1. to struggle 2. (*sport*) to wrestle.
lottatore *sm.* 1. struggler 2. (*sport*) wrestler.
lotterìa *sf.* lottery.
lottizzare *vt.* to lot.
lottizzazione *sf.* division into lots.
lotto *sm.* 1. lot 2. (*gioco*) state lottery.
lozione *sf.* lotion.
lubricità *sf.* lubricity.
lùbrico *agg.* 1. lubricous 2. (*fig.*) lascivious.
lubrificante *agg.* lubricating. ◆ **lubrificante** *sm.* lubricant.
lubrificare *vt.* to lubricate.
lubrificazione *sf.* lubrication.
lucchetto *sm.* padlock.
luccicante *agg.* glittering.
luccicare *vi.* to glitter.
luccichìo *sm.* glitter.
lùcciola *sf.* 1. firefly 2. (*senz'ali*) glow-worm.
luce *sf.* light || *alla — del sole* (*fig.*), openly; *dare alla — un bambino*, to give (*v. irr.*) birth to a child; *mettere in —*, to show (*v. irr.*); *venire alla —* (*nascere*), to be born.
lucente *agg.* bright.
lucentezza *sf.* brightness.
lucerna *sf.* oil-lamp.
lucernario *sm.* skylight.
lucèrtola *sf.* lizard.
lucidare *vt.* to polish.
lucidatrice *sf.* 1. floor-polisher 2. (*mecc.*) polishing machine.
lucidatura *sf.* polishing.
lucidezza *sf.* 1. brightness 2. (*di mente*) lucidness.
lucidità *sf.* lucidity.
lùcido *agg.* 1. lucid 2. (*lucidato*) glossy. ◆ **lùcido** *sm.* 1. (*per scarpe*) shoe-polish 2. (*lucidezza*) shine.
lucìgnolo *sm.* wick.
lucrare *vt.* to profit.
lucrativo *agg.* profitable.
lucro *sm.* profit: *a scopo di —*, for the sake of gain.
ludibrio *sm.* mockery

luglio *sm.* July.
lùgubre *agg.* lugubrious.
lui *pron.* 1. *(sogg.)* he 2. *(compl.)* him.
lumaca *sf.* snail.
lume *sm.* light ‖ *al — di candela,* by candle-light; *perdere il — della ragione,* to be blinded by anger.
lumeggiare *vt.* *(fig.)* to put *(v. irr.)* in evidence.
luminare *sm.* luminary.
luminescenza *sf.* luminescence.
luminosità *sf.* brightness.
luminoso *agg.* bright.
luna *sf.* moon: — *calante,* waning moon; — *crescente,* waxing moon ‖ *chiaro di —,* moonlight; — *di miele,* honeymoon; *avere la —* *(fig.),* to be in the sulks.
lunare *agg.* lunar.
lunario *sm.* almanac ‖ *sbarcare il —,* to make *(v. irr.)* both ends meet.
lunàtico *agg.* moody.
lunazione *sf.* lunation.
lunedì *sm.* Monday.
lunetta *sf.* lunette.
lungàggine *sf.* slowness, delay.
lunghezza *sf.* length.
lungimirante *agg.* far-sighted.
lungo *agg.* 1. long: *a —,* long; *a — andare,* in the long run 2. *(lento)* slow ‖ *in — e in largo,* far and wide; *di gran lunga,* by far. ♦ **lungo** *prep.* 1. along 2. *(durante)* during.
lungofiume *sm.* embankment.
lungolago *sm.* lake-front.
lungomare *sm.* sea-front.
lungometraggio *sm.* feature film.
luogo *sm.* place: — *di nascita,* birthplace; *sul —,* on the spot; *aver —,* to take *(v. irr.)* place; *dar —,* to cause.
luogotenente *sm.* lieutenant.
lupa *sf.* she-wolf.
lupanare *sm.* brothel.
lupara *sf.* shotgun.
lupino *sm.* *(bot.)* lupine.
lupo *sm.* wolf ‖ — *di mare,* sea-dog; *in bocca al —!,* good luck!
lùppolo *sm.* hop.
lùrido *agg.* dirty.
luridume *sm.* dirt.
lusinga *sf.* allurement, flattery.
lusingare *vt.* to allure, to flatter.
lusinghiero *agg.* alluring, flattering.
lussare *vt.* to dislocate.
lussazione *sf.* dislocation.

lusso *sm.* luxury.
lussuoso *agg.* luxurious, rich.
lussureggiante *agg.* luxuriant.
lussureggiare *vi.* to thrive *(v. irr.).*
lussuria *sf.* lust.
lussurioso *agg.* lustful.
lustrale *agg.* lustral.
lustrare *vt.* to polish.
lustrascarpe *sm.* shoeblack.
lustratura *sf.* polish.
lustrino *sm.* spangle.
lustro *agg.* shining, shiny. ♦ **lustro** *sm.* lustre.
luteranésimo *sm.* Lutheranism.
luterano *agg. e sm.* Lutheran.
lutto *sm.* mourning: *mettere il —,* to go *(v. irr.)* into mourning.
luttuoso *agg.* mournful.

M

ma *cong.* 1. but 2. *(tuttavia)* however, still.
màcabro *agg.* macabre.
macaco *sm.* 1. macaque 2. *(fig.)* runt.
macché *inter.* you don't say it!
maccheroni *sm.* *pl.* macaroni *(sing.).*
macchia[1] *sf.* spot, stain.
macchia[2] *sf.* *(boscaglia)* bush: *darsi alla —,* to take *(v. irr.)* to the bush.
macchiare *vt.* to stain. ♦ **macchiarsi** *vr.* 1. to get *(v. irr.)* stained 2. *(fig.)* to soil oneself.
macchiato *agg.* spotted.
macchietta *sf.* 1. caricature 2. *(di persona)* character.
màcchina *sf.* 1. engine, machine: — *calcolatrice,* calculating machine; — *per cucire,* sewing-machine; — *da presa,* cine-camera; — *per scrivere,* typewriter; — *fotografica,* camera; *fatto a —,* machine-made; *andare in —* *(di giornali),* to go *(v. irr.)* to press 2. *(automobile)* car.
macchinale *agg.* mechanical.
macchinare *vt.* to plot.
macchinario *sm.* machinery.
macchinazione *sf.* machination.
macchinista *sm.* 1. *(ferr.)* engine-driver 2. *(teat.)* scene-shifter.
macchinoso *agg.* complicated.

macedonia *sf.* (*cuc.*) fruit-salad.
macellaio *sm.* butcher.
macellare *vt.* to slaughter.
macelleria *sf.* butcher's shop.
macello *sm.* 1. (*luogo dove si macella*) slaughter-house 2. (*massacro*) slaughter.
macerare *vt.* 1. to soak 2. (*di lino, canapa*) to ret. ♦ macerarsi *vr.* (*fig.*) to waste (away).
maceratoio *sm.* rettery.
macerazione *sf.* 1. soaking 2. (*industria tessile*) retting.
macerie *sf. pl.* rubble (*sing.*), ruins.
màcero *sm.* (*per canapa e lino*) retting-ground: carta da —, wastepaper.
machiavèllico *agg.* Machiavellian.
machiavellismo *sm.* Machiavellism.
macigno *sm.* boulder.
macilento *agg.* emaciated.
macilenza *sf.* emaciation.
màcina *sf.* grindstone.
macinacaffè *sm.* coffee-mill.
macinapepe *sm.* pepper-mill.
macinare *vt.* 1. to grind (*v. irr.*), to mince.
macinino *sm.* grinder.
maciullare *vt.* to crush.
macrocèfalo *agg.* macrocephalous.
macrocosmo *sm.* macrocosm.
macromolècola *sf.* macromolecule.
macroscòpico *agg.* macroscopic.
maculato *agg.* spotted.
madia *sf.* 1. kitchen cupboard 2. (*per pane*) kneading trough.
màdido *agg.* wet: — di sudore, bathed in sweat.
madonna *sf.* 1. (*titolo*) Lady, My Lady 2. (*relig.*) The Virgin Mary, Our Lady 3. (*pitt.*) Madonna.
madornale *agg.* huge.
madre *sf.* mother.
madrepatria *sf.* mother-country.
madreperla *sf.* mother-of-pearl.
madreperlàceo *agg.* pearly.
madrèpora *sf.* madrepore.
madrepòrico *agg.* madreporic.
madrevite *sf.* 1. nut screw 2. (*utensile*) die.
madrigale *sm.* madrigal.
madrina *sf.* godmother.
maestà *sf.* majesty.
maestosità *sf.* majesty.
maestoso *agg.* majestic.
maestra *sf.* (*scol.*) teacher.
maestrale *sm.* mistral.
maestranza *sf.* skilled workers (*pl.*).

maestrìa *sf.* skill, ability.
maestro *sm.* 1. (*scol.*) teacher 2. (*uomo dotto*) master 3. (*mus.*) conductor, "maestro" || albero —, mainmast.
mafia *sf.* "Mafia".
maga *sf.* sorceress.
magagna *sf.* flaw, imperfection.
magari *inter.* if only! ♦ magari *avv.* (*forse*) perhaps, maybe. ♦ magari *cong.* even if.
magazzinaggio *sm.* storage.
magazziniere *sm.* store-keeper.
magazzino *sm.* warehouse || fondi di —, unsold stock.
maggese *sm.* fallow land.
maggio *sm.* May.
maggiolino *sm.* May-bug.
maggiorana *sf.* marjoram.
maggioranza *sf.* majority, most (of).
maggiorare *vt.* to increase.
maggiorazione *sf.* increase, charge.
maggiordomo *sm.* butler.
maggiore *agg.* 1. (*più grande, ampio*) greater, larger 2. (*più vecchio*) older: il —, the oldest 3. (*di fratelli*) elder (*fra due*), eldest (*fra molti*). ♦ maggiore *sm.* 1. (*mil.*) major 2. (*superiore*) superior.
maggiorenne *agg.* of age: diventare —, to come (*v. irr.*) of age. ♦ maggiorenne *sm.* major.
maggiorente *sm.* notable.
maggioritario *agg.* majority (*attr.*).
maggiormente *avv.* more, much more.
magìa *sf.* magic.
màgiaro *agg. e sm.* Magyar.
magicamente *avv.* magically.
màgico *agg.* magical.
magistrale *agg.* 1. magisteral || scuola —, teachers' institute 2. (*eccellente*) masterly.
magistralmente *avv.* skilfully.
magistrato *sm.* Magistrate.
magistratura *sf.* magistracy.
maglia *sf.* 1. (*di lavoro a maglia*) stitch || lavorare a —, to knit (*v. irr.*) 2. (*indumento*) vest 3. (*di catena*) link.
magliaia *sf.* knitter.
maglierìa *sf.* hosiery.
maglificio *sm.* hosiery.
maglio *sm.* 1. mallet 2. (*mecc.*) hammer.
maglione *sm.* sweater.
magma *sm.* magma.
magnanimità *sf.* magnanimity.

magnànimo *agg.* magnanimous.
magnate *sm.* magnate.
magnesia *sf.* magnesia.
magnesio *sm.* magnesium. *lampo al* —, flash.
magnete *sm.* magnet.
magnètico *agg.* magnetic.
magnetismo *sm.* magnetism.
magnetite *sf.* magnetite.
magnetizzare *vt.* to magnetize.
magnetizzatore *sm.* magnetizer.
magnetizzazione *sf.* magnetization.
magnetòfono *sm.* tape-recorder.
magnetòmetro *sm.* magnetometer.
magnificamente *avv.* magnificent-ly.
magnificare *vt.* to extol, to glorify.
magnificenza *sf.* magnificence.
magnifico *agg.* magnificent.
magniloquente *agg.* magniloquent.
magniloquenza *sf.* magniloquence.
magnolia *sf.* magnolia.
mago *sm.* wizard.
magra *sf.* (*di fiumi*) low water.
magrezza *sf.* thinness.
magro *agg.* **1.** thin **2.** (*di carni*) lean.
mah *inter.* who knows!
mai *avv.* **1.** ever **2.** (*non mai*) never: — *e poi* —, never never; — *più*, never more; *caso* —, if; *non si sa* —, you never can tell; *meglio tardi che* —, better late than never.
maiale *sm.* **1.** pig **2.** (*carne*) pork.
maièutica *sf.* maieutics.
maiòlica *sf.* majolica.
maionese *sf.* mayonnaise
mais *sm.* maize.
maiùscola *sf.* capital letter.
maiuscoletto *sm.* small capitals.
maiùscolo *agg.* capital.
malaccorto *agg.* ill-advised
malachite *sf.* malachite.
malacreanza *sf.* rudeness.
malafede *sf.* bad faith.
malaffare *sm.* **1.** *donna di* —, whore **2.** *gente di* —, crooks (*pl.*).
malagévole *agg.* difficult, hard.
malagrazia *sf.* bad grace.
malalingua *sf.* backbiter.
malamente *avv.* badly.
malandato *agg.* in bad condition.
malandrino *sm.* **1.** brigand **2.** (*fam.*) rogue.
malànimo *sm.* malevolence.
malanno *sm.* **1.** calamity **2.** (*malattia*) illness.

malapena (*nella loc. avv.*) *a* —, hardly.
malaria *sf.* malaria.
malaticcio *agg.* sickly.
malato *agg.* sick, ill. ◆ **malato** *sm.* patient.
malattìa *sf.* sickness, disease.
malauguratamente *avv.* unluckily.
malaugurato *agg.* ill-fated.
malaugurio *sm.* ill-omen.
malavita *sf.* underworld.
malavoglia *sf.* unwillingness || *di* —, reluctantly.
malcapitato *agg.* unlucky. ◆ **malcapitato** *sm.* victim.
malconcio *agg.* **1.** battered **2.** (*contuso*) bruised.
malcontento *agg.* dissatisfied (with). ◆ **malcontento** *sm.* discontent.
malcostume *sm.* immorality, corruption.
maldestro *agg.* awkward.
maldicente *agg.* disparaging. ◆ **maldicente** *sf.* slanderer.
maldicenza *sf.* backbiting.
maldisposto *agg.* ill-disposed, hostile.
male *sm.* **1.** evil **2.** (*malattia*) illness, disease **3.** (*dolore fisico*) pain || — *di testa*, headache. ◆ **male** *avv.* badly, ill.
maledettamente *avv.* awfully.
maledetto *agg.* cursed.
malèdico *agg.* slanderous.
maledire *vt.* to curse.
maledizione *sf.* curse, malediction || —! (*inter.*), damn!
maleducato *agg.* rude, impolite.
maleducazione *sf.* rudeness.
malefatta *sf.* mischief.
maleficio *sm.* sorcery.
malèfico *agg.* harmful.
malerba *sf.* weed.
malese *agg. e sm.* Malay.
malèssere *sm.* **1.** malaise **2.** (*disagio*) uneasiness.
malestro *sm.* mischief.
malevolenza *sf.* malevolence.
malèvolo *agg.* malevolent.
malfamato *agg.* ill-famed.
malfatto *agg.* **1.** ill-shaped **2.** (*di abito*) ill-fitting.
malfattore *sm.* evil-doer.
malfermo *agg.* shaky || *salute malferma*, poor health.
malfido *agg.* unreliable.
malfondato *agg.* ill-grounded.

malformato *agg.* malformed.
malformazione *sf.* malformation.
malgarbo *sm.* bad grace.
malgoverno *sm.* misgovernment, misrule.
malgrado *prep. e avv.* in spite of.
♦ **malgrado (che)** *cong.* though, although.
malìa *sf.* (*fascino*) fascination.
maliarda *sf.* 1. (*donna affascinante*) fascinating woman 2. (*maga*) witch.
malignamente *avv.* maliciously.
malignare *vi.* to speak (*v. irr.*) ill (of).
malignità *sf.* malice.
maligno *agg.* malicious: *tumore —*, malignant tumor.
malinconìa *sf.* melancholy.
malinconicamente *avv.* sadly.
malincònico *agg.* melancholy.
malincuore (*nella loc. avv.*) *a —*, unwillingly.
malintenzionato *agg.* ill-disposed.
malinteso *agg.* misplaced. ♦ **malinteso** *sm.* misunderstanding.
malizia *sf.* 1. malice 2. (*astuzia*) cunning.
maliziosamente *avv.* artfully.
malizioso *agg.* malicious, mischievous.
malleàbile *agg.* malleable.
malleabilità *sf.* malleability.
malleverìa *sf.* bail.
malloppo *sm.* swag.
malmenare *vt.* to manhandle.
malmesso *ag.* poorly dressed.
malnato *agg.* ill-bred.
malocchio *sm.* evil eye.
malora *sf.* ruin || *va alla —!*, go to the devil!
malore *sm.* illness.
malpensante *agg.* wrong-thinking.
malsano *agg.* unhealthy.
malsicuro *agg.* unsafe.
malta *sf.* mortar.
maltempo *sm.* bad weather.
maltenuto *agg.* untidy.
maltese *agg. e sm.* Maltese.
malto *sm.* malt.
maltolto *agg.* ill-gotten. ♦ **maltolto** *sm.* ill-gotten property.
maltosio *sm.* maltose.
maltrattamento *sm.* maltreatment.
maltrattare *vt.* to maltreat.
maltusianismo *sm.* Malthusianism.
maltusiano *agg. e sm.* Malthusian.
malumore *sm.* ill-humour.
malva *sf.* mallow.

malvagio *agg.* wicked.
malvagità *sf.* wickedness.
malversatore *sm.* embezzler.
malversazione *sf.* embezzlement.
malvisto *agg.* unpopular (with).
malvivente *sm.* gangster.
malvivenza *sf.* delinquency.
malvolentieri *avv.* unwillingly.
malvolere *sm.* ill-will.
malvolere *vi.* to dislike.
mamma *sf.* mama, mummy.
mammalucco *sm.* (*fam.*) simpleton.
mammella *sf.* 1. mamma (*pl.* -ae) 2. (*di animali da latte*) udder.
mammìfero *agg.* mammiferous. ♦ **mammìfero** *sm.* mammal.
màmmola *sf.* sweet-smelling violet.
mammùt *sm.* mammoth.
manata *sf.* slap.
manca *sf.* 1. left hand 2. (*parte sinistra*) left || *a dritta e a —*, on all sides.
mancante *agg.* incomplete.
mancanza *sf.* 1. lack, shortage 2. (*fallo*) fault || *sentire la — di qu.*, to miss so.
mancare *vi.* 1. to be lacking (in) 2. (*non esserci*) to be missing 3. (*venir meno*) to fail 4. (*agire scorrettamente*) to wrong (so.).
mancato *agg.* unsuccessful.
manchévole *agg.* defective.
manchevolezza *sf.* defect, fault.
mancia *sf.* tip || *dare la — a qu.*, to tip so.
manciata *sf.* handful.
mancina *sf.* left-hand.
mancino *agg.* left-handed. ♦ **mancino** *sm.* left-hander.
manco *avv.* not even.
mandamento *sm.* district.
mandante *sm.* 1. instigator 2. (*giur.*) principal.
mandare *vt.* 1. to send (*v. irr.*) 2. (*spedire*) to forward 3. (*emettere*) to give (*v. irr.*) out.
mandarino *sm.* mandarin.
mandata *sf.* batch || *— di chiave*, turn.
mandatario *sm.* mandatary.
mandato *sm.* 1. mandate 2. (*comm.* ` agency 3. (*giur.*) warrant.
mandìbola *sf.* mandible.
mandola *sf.* mandola.
mandolinista *s.* mandolinist.
mandolino *sm.* mandolin.
màndorla *sf.* almond.
màndorlo *sm.* almond-tree.

mandràgora *sf.* mandrake.
mandria *sf.* herd.
mandriano *sm.* herdsman (*pl.* -men).
maneggévole *agg.* handy.
maneggiare *vt.* to handle.
maneggio *sm.* 1. (*equitazione*) riding-ground 2. (*uso*) use 3. (*intrigo*) plot.
manesco *agg.* rough, aggressive.
manette *sf. pl.* handcuff (*sing.*).
manforte *sf.* help.
manganellare *vt.* to cudgel.
manganello *sm.* cudgel.
manganese *sm.* manganese.
mangereccio *agg.* eatable.
mangiàbile *agg.* eatable.
mangiare *vt.* to eat (*v. irr.*).
mangiata *sf.* square meal.
mangiatoia *sf.* manger.
mangime *sm.* fodder.
mangiucchiare *vt.* to nibble (at).
manìa *sf.* mania.
manìaco *agg.* 1. maniac 2. (*fig.*) crazy. ♦ manìaco *sm.* maniac.
mànica *sf.* sleeve ‖ essere di — larga, stretta, to be indulgent, strict.
manicheismo *sm.* Manicheism.
manicheo *agg. e sm.* Manichean.
manichino *sm.* manikin.
mànico *sm.* handle.
manicomio *sm.* mental hospital.
manicotto *sm.* 1. muff 2. (*mecc.*) sleeve.
maniera *sf.* manner, way.
manierato *agg.* affected.
manierismo *sm.* mannerism.
maniero *sm.* castle.
manifattura *sf.* manufacture.
manifatturiero *agg.* manufacturing.
manifestante *s.* demonstrator.
manifestare *vt.* 1. to manifest, to show (*v. irr.*) 2. (*pol.*) to demonstrate.
manifestazione *sf.* 1. manifestation 2. (*pol.*) demonstration.
manifesto *agg.* manifest, clear, obvious. ♦ manifesto *sm.* 1. (*affisso*) poster 2. (*volantino*) leaflet 3. (*dichiarazione*) manifesto.
maniglia *sf.* handle.
manigoldo *sm.* scoundrel.
manioca *sf.* manioc.
manipolare *vt.* to manipulate.
manipolatore *sm.* manipulator.
manipolazione *sf.* manipulation.
manìpolo *sm.* (*eccl.; stor.*) maniple.
maniscalco *sm.* blacksmith.

manna *sf.* 1. manna 2. (*fig.*) blessing.
mannaia *sf.* 1. axe 2. (*della ghigliottina*) knife.
mannaro *agg. lupo —*, werewolf.
mano *sf.* hand: *fatto a —*, hand-made; *stringere la —*, to shake (*v. irr.*) hands with ‖ *a — armata*, by force of arms; *sotto —*, underhand.
manodòpera *sf.* labour.
manòmetro *sm.* manometer.
manométtere *vt.* to tamper with.
manomissione *sf.* tampering.
manòpola *sf.* 1. knob 2. (*impugnatura*) handle.
manoscritto *agg.* handwritten. ♦ manoscritto *sm.* manuscript.
manovale *sm.* hodman (*pl.* -men).
manovella *sf.* crank.
manovra *sf.* manoeuvre, operation.
manovràbile *agg.* manoeuvrable.
manovrare *vt.* 1. to manoeuvre 2. (*mecc.*) to operate.
manovratore *sm.* operator, driver.
manrovescio *sm.* back-handed slap.
mansarda *sf.* mansard.
mansione *sf.* function.
mansuefare *vt.* to tame.
mansueto *agg.* meek, mild.
mansuetùdine *sf.* meekness.
mantella *sf.* cape.
mantello *sm.* cloak.
mantenere *vt.* to keep (*v. irr.*), to maintain: *— la parola*, to keep one's word.
mantenimento *sm.* maintenance.
màntice *sm.* bellows (*pl.*).
manto *sm.* cloak.
manuale *agg.* manual. ♦ manuale *sm.* handbook.
manubrio *sm.* 1. handle 2. (*di bicicletta ecc.*) handle-bar.
manufatto *agg.* hand-made. ♦ manufatto *sm.* hand-manufactured article.
manutèngolo *sm.* abettor.
manutenzione *sf.* maintenance, servicing.
manzo *sm.* 1. (*zool.*) steer 2. (*carne*) beef.
maomettano *agg. e sm.* Mohammedan.
mappa *sf.* map.
mappamondo *sm.* globe.
marachella *sf.* trick.
marasma *sm.* 1. (*med.*) marasmus 2. (*fig.*) decadence.
maratona *sf.* marathon race.

marca *sf.* brand: — *di fabbrica*, trade mark.

marcare *vt.* **1.** to mark **2.** (*sport*) to score.

marcato *agg.* marked, branded.

marcatore *sm.* **1.** marker **2.** (*sport*) scorer.

marcatura *sf.* **1.** marking **2.** (*sport*) scoring.

marchesa *sf.* **1.** marchioness **2.** (*se non è inglese*) marquise.

marchesato *sm.* marquisate.

marchese *sm.* marquis.

marchiano *agg.* enormous, glaring.

marchiare *vt.* to brand.

marchiatura *sf.* branding.

marchio *sm.* **1.** stamp **2.** (*a fuoco*) brand **3.** (*fig.; comm.*) mark.

marcia *sf.* **1.** (*auto*) gear **2.** (*mil.; mus.*) march.

marciapiede *sm.* **1.** pavement **2.** (*ferr.*) platform.

marciare *vi.* to march.

marciatore *sm.* (*sport*) road-walker.

marcio *agg.* **1.** rotten **2.** (*fig.*) corrupted. ◆ **marcio** *sm.* (*fig.*) corruption.

marcire *vi.* **1.** (*guastarsi*) to go (*v. irr.*) bad **2.** (*decomporsi*) to rot (*v. irr.*).

marciume *sm.* rottenness.

marco *sm.* mark.

marconigrafia *sf.* marconigraphy.

mare *sm.* sea.

marea *sf.* tide.

mareggiata *sf.* sea-storm.

maremma *sf.* maremma (*pl.* -me).

maremoto *sm.* seaquake.

mareògrafo *sm.* tide-gauge.

maresciallo *sm.* marshal.

margarina *sf.* margarine.

margherita *sf.* daisy.

marginale *agg.* marginal.

marginare *vt.* **1.** to border **2.** (*tip.*) to margin.

marginatura *sf.* **1.** edging **2.** (*tip.*) furniture.

màrgine *sm.* **1.** border, edge **2.** (*fig.*) margin.

marina *sf.* **1.** navy **2.** (*costa*) sea-shore **3.** (*pitt.*) sea-scape.

marinaio *sm.* sailor.

marinara *sf.* **1.** (*cappotto*) duffle coat **2.** (*cappello*) sailor hat.

marinare *vt.* (*cuc.*) to pickle || — *la scuola*, to play truant.

marinaresco *agg.* sailor-like.

marinaro *agg.* **1.** maritime **2.** sail-or-like. ◆ **marinaro** *sm.* sailor.

marinerìa *sf.* **1.** seamanship **2.** (*marina*) navy.

marino *agg.* sea (*attr.*).

mariolo *sm.* rogue.

marionetta *sf.* puppet.

maritale *agg.* marital.

maritare *vt.* to marry. ◆ **maritarsi** *vr.* to get (*v. irr.*) married.

marito *sm.* husband.

marìttimo *agg.* maritime || *città marìttima*, sea-town; *commercio* —, shipping business. ◆ **marìttimo** *sm.* seafarer || *i marìttimi*, seafolk (*sing.*).

marmaglia *sf.* rabble.

marmellata *sf.* **1.** jam **2.** (*d'arance*) marmalade.

marmista *sm.* marble-cutter.

marmitta *sf.* **1.** (*cuc.*) stock-pot **2.** (*auto*) silencer's muffler.

marmo *sm.* marble.

marmocchio *sm.* kid.

marmòreo *agg.* marble.

marmotta *sf.* **1.** marmot **2.** (*di persona*) lazy-bones.

marna *sf.* marl.

marocchino *agg.* Moroccan. ◆ **marocchino** *sm.* **1.** (*persona*) Moroccan **2.** (*cuoio*) Morocco leather.

maroso *sm.* billow.

marra *sf.* **1.** (*agr.*) hoe **2.** (*mar.*) fluke.

marrone *agg.* brown. ◆ **marrone** *sm.* chestnut.

martedì *sm.* Tuesday.

martellamento *sm.* hammering.

martellare *vt.* **1.** to hammer **2.** (*mil.*) to pound **3.** (*pulsare*) to throb.

martellata *sf.* hammer-blow.

martello *sm.* hammer.

martinetto *sm.* jack.

martingala *sf.* half-belt.

màrtire *sm.* martyr.

martirio *sm.* martyrdom.

martirizzare *vt.* to martyrize.

martirologio *sm.* martyrology.

màrtora *sf.* marten.

martoriare *vt.* to torture.

marxismo *sm.* Marxism.

marxista *agg. e s.* Marxist.

marzapane *sm.* marzipan.

marziale *agg.* martial.

marziano *sm.* Martian.

marzo *sm.* March.

mascalzonata *sf.* knavery.

mascalzone *sm.* rascal.

mascella *sf.* jaw.

mascellare *agg.* jaw (*attr.*).
màschera *sf.* 1. mask 2. (*figura mascherata*) masker 3. (*cosmesi*) face-pack 4. (*inserviente di cinema, teatro*) usher.
mascheramento *sm.* masking.
mascherare *vt.* to mask.
mascherata *sf.* masquerade.
maschietto *sm.* male.
maschile *agg.* male.
maschio[1] *agg.* 1. male 2. (*virile*) manly. ♦ **maschio** *sm.* 1. (*di animale*) (*uccelli*) cock, (*mammiferi*) bull (*attributivi*) 2. (*di uomo*) male 3. (*bambino*) boy.
maschio[2] *sm.* (*torre*) donjon.
mascolinità *sf.* masculinity.
masnada *sf.* gang.
masnadiere *sm.* highwayman (*pl.* -men).
masochismo *sm.* masochism.
masonite *sf.* masonite.
massa *sf.* mass, heap.
massacrante *agg.* exhausting.
massacrare *vt.* to massacre.
massacratore *sm.* slaughterer.
massacro *sm.* massacre.
massaggiare *vt.* to massage.
massaggiatore *sm.* masseur.
massaggiatrice *sf.* masseuse.
massaggio *sm.* massage.
massaia *sf.* housewife (*pl.* -wives).
massello *sm.* ingot.
masserìa *sf.* farm.
masserizie *sf. pl.* household goods.
massicciata *sf.* road-bed.
massiccio *agg.* solid. ♦ **massiccio** *sm.* massif.
màssima *sf.* maxim, rule || *in linea* —, on the whole; *accordo di* —, general agreement.
massimalismo *sm.* Maximalism.
massimalista *s.* Maximalist.
màssimo *agg.* 1. greatest, highest 2. (*l'estremo*) utmost 3. (*il più lungo*) longest. ♦ **màssimo** *sm.* 1. most 2. (*il meglio*) best 3. (*mat.; fis.*) maximum.
masso *sm.* boulder.
massone *sm.* freemason.
massonerìa *sf.* freemasonry.
mastello *sm.* tub.
masticare *vt.* to chew.
masticazione *sf.* mastication.
màstice *sm.* rubber.
mastino *sm.* mastiff.
mastite *sf.* mastitis.
mastodonte *sm.* 1. (*zool.*) mastodon 2. (*fig.*) giant.

mastodòntico *agg.* colossal.
mastòide *sf.* mastoid.
mastoidite *sf.* mastoiditis.
mastro *sm.* 1. (*libro*) ledger 2. (*appellativo*) Master.
masturbazione *sf.* masturbation.
matassa *sf.* 1. hank 2. (*fig.*) tangle.
matemàtica *sf.* mathematics.
matemàtico *agg.* mathematical. ♦ **matemàtico** *sm.* mathematician.
materasso *sm.* mattress.
materia *sf.* matter, subject.
materiale *agg.* 1. material 2. (*rozzo*) rough. ♦ **materiale** *sm.* material.
materialismo *sm.* materialism.
materialista *s.* materialist.
materialìstico *agg.* materialistic.
materializzare *vt.* to materialize.
maternità *sf.* maternity.
materno *agg.* motherly, maternal || *scuola materna*, nursery-school.
matita *sf.* pencil.
matriarcato *sm.* matriarchy.
matrice *sf.* 1. matrix (*pl.* matrices) 2. (*comm.*) counterfoil.
matricida *s.* matricide.
matricidio *sm.* matricide.
matrìcola *sf.* 1. matricula, register || *numero di* —, matriculation number 2. (*scol.*) freshman (*pl.* -men).
matricolato *agg.* matriculated || *briccone* —, arrant knave.
matrigna *sf.* stepmother.
matrimoniale *agg.* matrimonial.
matrimonio *sm.* 1. marriage 2. (*cerimonia nuziale*) wedding.
matrona *sf.* matron.
matta *sf.* 1. mad woman (*pl.* women) 2. (*al gioco*) jolly joker.
mattacchione *sm.* joker.
mattatoio *sm.* slaughter-house.
matterello *sm.* rolling-pin.
mattina *sf.* morning.
mattinata *sf.* 1. morning 2. (*teat.*) matinée.
mattiniero *agg.* early-rising.
mattino *sm.* morning.
matto[1] *agg.* mad, crazy. ♦ **matto** *sm.* madman (*pl.* -men).
matto[2] *agg.* 1. (*non lucido*) mat 2. (*di gioielli*) false.
mattone *sm.* 1. brick 2. (*fig.*) bore.
mattonella *sf.* tile.
mattutino *agg.* morning (*attr.*). ♦ **mattutino** *sm.* (*eccl.*) matins (*pl.*).
maturare *vi. e vt.* to ripen, to mature (*anche fig.*).

maturazione *sf.* maturation, ripening (*anche fig.*).

maturità *sf.* ripening, maturity (*anche fig.*).

maturo *agg.* ripe, mature (*anche fig.*).

mausoleo *sm.* mausoleum.

mazurca *sf.* mazurka.

mazza *sf.* 1. (*clava*) club 2. (*martello di legno*) mallet.

mazzata *sf.* heavy blow (*anche fig.*).

mazziere *sm.* 1. mace-bearer 2. (*di carte*) dealer.

mazzo *sm.* 1. bunch 2. (*di carte*) pack || *fare il* —, to shuffle 3. (*di fiori*) bouquet.

mazzolino *sm.* (*di fiori*) posy.

mazzuolo *sm.* mallet.

me *pron.* 1. me 2. (*me stesso*) myself.

meandro *sm.* 1. meander 2. (*labirinto*) maze.

meato *sm.* meatus.

meccanica *sf.* mechanics.

meccanico *agg.* mechanical. ◆ **meccanico** *sm.* mechanic.

meccanismo *sm.* 1. gear 2. (*movimento*) motion.

meccanizzare *vt.* to mechanize.

meccanizzazione *sf.* mechanization.

meccanografia *sf.* mechanography.

meccanografico *agg.* mechanographic.

mecenate *sm.* Maecenas.

mecenatismo *sm.* patronage.

medaglia *sf.* medal.

medaglione *sm.* 1. locket 2. (*arch.*) medallion.

medaglista *sm.* 1. (*incisore*) medallist 2. (*collezionista*) collector of medals.

medésimo *agg.* e *pron.* V. *stesso*.

media *sf.* 1. average: *alla* — *di*, at an average of 2. (*mat.*) mean.

mediana *sf.* median line.

medianico *agg.* mediumistic.

mediano *agg.* 1. medial, middle (*attr.*) 2. (*geom.; anat; bot.*) median. ◆ **mediano** *sm.* (*sport*) half-back.

mediante *prep.* by, by means of, through.

mediato *agg.* indirect.

mediatore *sm.* 1. mediator 2. (*comm.*) broker.

mediazione *sf.* 1. mediation 2. (*comm.*) brokerage.

medicamento *sm.* medicament.

medicare *vt.* to dress.

medicastro *sm.* quack (doctor).

medicazione *sf.* 1. medication 2. (*di ferita*) dressing.

medicina *sf.* medicine.

medicinale *sm.* medicinal.

medico *agg.* medical. ◆ **medico** *sm.* physician, doctor.

medievale *agg.* medieval.

medio *sm.* 1. (*dito*) middle finger 2. (*mat.*) mean. ◆ **medio** *agg.* 1. middle 2. (*normale, che risulta da una media*) average.

mediocre *agg.* second-rate.

mediocrità *sf.* mediocrity.

medioevo *sm.* Middle Ages (*pl.*).

meditabondo *agg.* thoughtful.

meditare *vt.* 1. to ponder 2. (*avere un'intenzione*) to meditate.

meditativo *agg.* meditative.

meditazione *sf.* meditation.

mediterràneo *agg.* 1. inland 2. Mediterranean.

medium *sm.* medium.

medusa *sf.* medusa (*pl.* -ae).

mefistofèlico *agg.* satanic.

mefitico *agg.* poisonous.

megaciclo *sm.* megacycle.

megàfono *sm.* megaphone.

megalòmane *sm.* megalomaniac.

megalomania *sf.* megalomania.

megatone *sm.* megaton.

meglio *avv.* 1. (*comp.*) better 2. (*superl. rel.*) best. ◆ **meglio** *agg.* 1. (*comp.*) better: *questo vestito è* — *di quello*, this dress is better than that 2. (*superl. rel.*) best. ◆ **meglio** *sm.* best, best thing || *in mancanza di* —, for lack of anything better. ◆ **meglio** *sf.* *avere la* —, to have the better || *alla* —, as well as possible.

mela *sf.* apple.

melacotogna *sf.* quince.

melagrana *sf.* pomegranate.

melanismo *sm.* melanism.

melanzana *sf.* aubergine.

melassa *sf.* molasses (*pl.*).

melato *agg.* 1. sweetened with honey 2. (*fig.*) honeyed.

melenso *agg.* dull, silly.

mellifluo *agg.* honeyed.

melma *sf.* slime.

melmoso *agg.* slimy.

melo *sm.* apple-tree.

melodia *sf.* melody.

melòdico *agg.* melodic.

melodioso *agg.* melodious.

melodramma *sm.* 1. opera 2. (*fig.*) melodrama.

melodrammàtico *agg.* **1.** operatic **2.** (*fig.*) melodramatic.

melograno *sm.* pomegranate-tree.

melòmane *s.* melomaniac.

melomanìa *sf.* melomania.

melone *sm.* melon.

membra *sf. pl.* limbs.

membrana *sf.* membrane.

membratura *sf* structure.

membro *sm.* **1.** member **2.** (*anat.*) limb.

memoràbile *agg.* memorable.

memorandum *sm.* memorandum (*pl.* -da).

mèmore *agg.* mindful.

memoria *sf.* **1.** memory: — *di ferro*, cast-iron memory || *a* —, by heart **2.** (*ricordo*) memory, recollection.

memoriale *sm.* **1.** (*petizione*) memorial **2.** (*libro di memorie*) memoirs (*pl.*).

memorialista *s.* memorialist.

menabò *sm.* dummy.

menadito (*nella loc. avv.*) *a* —, perfectly || *sapere qc. a* —, to have sthg. at one's finger-tips.

menagramo *sm.* bearer of ill-luck.

menare *vt.* (*condurre*) to lead (*v. irr.*) || — *vanto*, to boast; — *il can per l'aia*, to beat (*v. irr.*) about the bush; — *buono, gramo*, to bring (*v. irr.*) good, bad luck.

mendace *agg.* mendacious, false.

mendacia *sf.* mendacity.

mendicante *sm.* beggar.

mendicare *vi.* to beg.

mendicità *sf.* mendicity.

mendico *agg.* e *sm.* mendicant.

menestrello *sm.* minstrel.

meninge *sf.* meninx (*pl.* meninges).

menisco *sm.* meniscus.

meno *avv.* **1.** (*comp.*) less **2.** (*superl. rel.*) least || *fare a* —, to do (*v. irr.*) without; *non poter fare a* —, cannot help: *non posso fare a — di andare*, I cannot help going **3.** (*mat.*) minus. ♦ **meno** *prep.* but for || *a — che* (*non*), unless. ♦ **meno** *agg.* **1.** (*comp. sing.*) less: *è — bella di sua sorella*, she is less beautiful than her sister **2.** (*comp. con s. pl.*) fewer: *ho — libri di te*, I have fewer books than you **3.** (*superl. rel. sing.*) the least: *è il — intelligente dei miei amici*, he is the least intelligent of my friends **4.** (*superl. rel. con s. pl.*) the fewest (*raro*).

♦ **meno** *sm.* **1.** (*comp.*) less **2.** (*superl. rel.*) the least.

menomare *vt.* to lessen.

menomato *agg.* **1.** lessened **2.** (*di vista, udito*) impaired.

menomazione *sf.* **1.** lessening **2.** (*di arti, sensi*) impairment **3.** (*di persona*) disablement.

menopàusa *sf.* menopause.

mensa *sf.* table.

mensile *agg.* monthly. ♦ **mensile** *sm.* **1.** (*salario*) month's salary **2.** (*pubblicazione mensile*) monthly.

mensilità *sf.* monthly instalment || *tredicesima* —, Christmas bonus.

mensilmente *avv.* monthly, once a month.

mènsola *sf.* **1.** bracket **2.** (*scaffale*) shelf (*pl.* -lves).

menta *sf.* mint.

mentale *agg.* mental.

mentalità *sf.* mentality.

mente *sf.* mind: *persona dalla — ristretta*, narrow-minded person; *aguzzare la* —, to sharpen one's wits.

mentecatto *agg.* insane. ♦ **mentecatto** *sm.* madman (*pl.* -men).

mentina *sf.* peppermint-drop.

mentire *vi.* to lie.

mentito *agg.* false: *sotto mentite spoglie*, under false pretences.

mentitore *sm.* liar.

mento *sm.* chin.

mentolo *sm.* menthol.

mèntore *sm.* mentor.

mentre *cong.* **1.** (*temporale*) while, as, when **2.** (*avversativo*) whereas, while **3.** (*finché*) as long as, while. ♦ **mentre** *sm.* moment: *in quel* —, at that moment.

menzionare *vt.* to mention.

menzione *sf.* mention.

menzogna *sf.* falsehood.

menzognero *agg.* **1.** (*di persona*) mendacious **2.** (*di cosa*) false.

meraviglia *sf.* wonder: *sopraffatto dalla* —, wonder-struck; *non fa — che, nessuna — che*, no wonder.

meravigliare *vt.* to astonish. ♦ **meravigliarsi** *vr.* to be astonished (at).

meravigliato *agg.* astonished.

meraviglioso *agg.* wonderful.

mercante *sm.* merchant.

mercanteggiare *vi.* (*tirare sul prezzo*) to bargain, to haggle.

mercantile *agg.* mercantile. ♦ **mercantile** *sm.* cargo boat.

mercantilismo *sm.* mercantilism.
mercanzìa *sf.* merchandise.
mercato *sm.* market ‖ *a buon* —, cheap.
merce *sf.* goods (*pl.*).
mercé *sf.* mercy.
mercede *sf.* pay, reward.
mercenario *agg.* e *sm.* mercenary.
merceologìa *sf.* technology of marketable goods.
mercerìa *sf.* 1. haberdashery 2. (*negozio*) haberdasher's shop.
mercerizzato *agg.* mercerized.
merciaio *sm.* haberdasher.
mercoledì *sm.* Wednesday: — *delle Ceneri*, Ash Wednesday.
mercurio *sm.* mercury, quicksilver.
merenda *sf.* afternoon snack.
meretrice *sf.* prostitute.
meretricio *sm.* prostitution.
meridiana *sf.* sun-dial.
meridiano *agg.* e *sm.* meridian.
meridionale *agg.* Southern. ♦ **meridionale** *sm.* Southerner.
meridione *sm.* south.
meringa *sf.* meringue.
merino *sm.* merino.
meritare *vt.* to deserve.
meritévole *agg.* deserving.
mèrito *sm.* merit ‖ *in* — *a*, as to.
meritorio *agg.* meritorious, deserving.
merletto *sm.* lace.
merlo *sm.* 1. blackbird 2. (*sciocco*) simpleton.
merluzzo *sm.* codfish.
mero *agg.* 1. pure 2. (*fig.*) mere.
mesata *sf.* 1. month 2. (*paga di un mese*) month's pay.
méscere *vt.* to pour (out).
meschinità *sf.* meanness.
meschino *agg.* mean. ♦ **meschino** *sm.* wretch.
méscita *sf.* pouring (out).
mescolanza *sf.* 1. mixing 2. (*miscuglio*) mixture.
mescolare *vt.* 1. to mix 2. (*tè, caffè, liquori, tabacco*) to blend. ♦ **mescolarsi** *vr.* to mingle.
mescolatrice *sf.* mixer.
mese *sm.* month.
messa *sf.* 1. (*eccl.*) Mass 2. (*azione del mettere*) putting, setting: — *a punto*, setting up ‖ — *a fuoco*, focusing.
messaggero *sm.* messenger.
messaggio *sm.* 1. message 2. (*allocuzione*) address.
messale *sm.* missal.

messe *sf.* crop, harvest.
messìa *sm.* Messiah.
messiànico *agg.* Messianic.
messianismo *sm.* Messianism.
messicano *agg.* e *sm.* Mexican.
messinscena *sf.* staging.
mestare *vt.* to stir.
mestiere *sm.* 1. trade 2. (*perizia*) skill 3. (*lavoro*) work.
mestizia *sf.* sadness.
méstola *sf.* ladle.
méstolo *sm.* ladle.
mestruazione *sf.* menstruation.
meta *sf.* 1. destination 2. (*scopo*) aim, purpose: *senza* —, aimless.
metà *sf.* 1. half (*pl.* halves) 2. (*parte mediana*) middle 3. (*coniuge*) *la mia* —, my better half.
metabolismo *sm.* metabolism.
metafìsica *sf.* metaphysics.
metàfora *sf.* metaphor.
metafòrico *agg.* metaphoric(al).
metàllico *agg.* metallic.
metallo *sm.* metal.
metallurgìa *sf.* metallurgy.
metallùrgico *agg.* metallurgic(al). ♦ **metallùrgico** *sm.* metallurgist.
metalmeccànico *sm.* metallurgist and mechanic.
metamòrfico *agg.* metamorphic.
metamorfismo *sm.* metamorphism.
metamòrfosi *sf.* metamorphosis (*pl.* -ses).
metano *sm.* methane.
metapsìchica *sf.* metapsychics.
metapsìchico *agg.* metapsychic(al).
metàstasi *sf.* metastasis (*pl.* -ses).
metempsicosi *sf.* metempsychosis (*pl.* -ses).
metèora *sf.* meteor.
meteòrico *agg.* meteoric.
meteorite *sm.* meteorite.
meteorologìa *sf.* meteorology.
meteorològico *agg.* meteorological ‖ *previsioni meteorologiche*, weather-forecast (*sing.*).
meteoròlogo *sm.* meteorologist.
meticcio *agg.* e *sm.* mestizo (*pl.* -za).
meticoloso *agg.* meticulous.
metodicità *sf.* methodicalness.
metòdico *agg.* methodical.
metodista *agg.* e *s.* Methodist.
mètodo *sm.* method.
metodologìa *sf.* methodology.
metodològico *agg.* methodological.
mètopa *sf.* metope.
metraggio *sm.* 1. length (in metres) 2. (*cine*) *corto, lungo* —, short, full-length film.

mètrica *sf.* prosody.
mètrico *agg.* metric.
metrite *sf.* metritis.
metro *sm.* 1. metre 2. (*strumento per misurare*) rule.
metrònomo *sm.* metronome.
metronotte *sm.* night-watch.
metròpoli *sf.* metropolis (*pl.* -ses).
metropolitana *sf.* underground.
metropolitano *agg.* metropolitan.
méttere *vt.* 1. to put (*v. irr.*) || — *in chiaro qc.*, to make (*v. irr.*) sthg. clear; — *in dubbio qc.*, to doubt sthg.; — *in serbo*, to lay (*v. irr.*) aside; — *in moto*, to start; — *in luce*, to emphasize; — *in guardia qu.*, to put so. on his guard; — *le mani su qc.*, to take (*v. irr.*) possession of; — *le mani sul fuoco per qu.*, to speak (*v. irr.*) for so. 2. (*impiegare, di tempo*) to take 3. (*indossare*) to put on 4. (*paragonare*) to compare. ♦ **mettersi** *vr.* 1. to put oneself || — *in contatto con qu.*, to get (*v. irr.*) in touch with so.; — *in testa di fare qc.*, to take into one's head to do sthg.; — *sotto*, to get down to it 2. (*incominciare*) to begin (*v. irr.*) 3. (*indossare*) to put (*v. irr.*) on.
mettifoglio *sm.* (*tip.*) feeder.
mezzadrìa *sf.* métayage.
mezzadro *sm.* métayer.
mezzaluna *sf.* 1. half-moon 2. (*emblema islamico*) crescent 3. (*cuc.*) mincing-knife.
mezzana[1] *sf.* (*mar.*) mizzen sail.
mezzana[2] *sf.* procuress.
mezzano *agg.* middle. ♦ **mezzano** *sm.* go-between.
mezzanotte *sf.* midnight.
mezzatinta *sf.* half-tone.
mezzo[1] *agg.* 1. half 2. (*medio*) middle. ♦ **mezzo** *avv.* half. ♦ **in mezzo a** *prep.* 1. in the middle of 2. (*fra molti*) among 3. (*fra due*) between.
mezzo[2] *sm.* 1. means 2. (*fis.*) medium.
mezzo[3] *agg.* (*marcio*) rotten.
mezzobusto *sm.* bust.
mezzocerchio *sm.* semicircle.
mezzodì *sm.* midday, noon.
mezzofondo *sm.* middle-distance race.
mezzogiorno *sm.* 1. midday 2. (*Sud*) South.
mezzosoprano *sm.* mezzo-soprano.

mi[1] *pron.* 1. me 2. (*me stesso*) myself 3. (*a me*) to me.
mi[2] *sm.* (*mus.*) E, mi.
miagolare *vi.* to mew
miagolìo *sm.* mewing
miasma *sm.* miasma.
mica *sf.* mica.
miccia *sf.* fuse.
michetta *sf.* roll.
micidiale *agg.* lethal,, deadly.
micino *sm.* kitten, pussy.
micosi *sf.* mycosis (*pl.* -ses).
microbio *sm.* microbe.
microbiologìa *sf.* microbiology.
microcosmo *sm.* microcosm.
microfilm *sm.* microfilm.
micròfono *sm.* microphone.
microfotografìa *sf.* microphotography.
micrometrìa *sf.* micrometry.
micròmetro *sm.* micrometer.
micron *sm.* micron.
microrganismo *sm.* microorganism.
microscopìa *sf.* microscopy.
microscòpico *agg.* microscopic(al).
microscopio *sm.* microscope.
microsolco *sm.* long-playing record.
microtelèfono *sm.* microtelephone.
midolla *sf.* crumb.
midollare *agg.* medullar.
midollo *sm.* marrow: — *spinale*, spinal cord.
miele *sm.* honey.
miètere *vt.* to reap.
mietitrice *sf.* reaper.
mietitura *sf.* reaping.
migliaio *sm.* thousand.
miglio[1] *sm.* (*bot.*) millet.
miglio[2] *sm.* (*misura di lunghezza*) mile.
miglioramento *sm.* improvement.
migliorare *vt.* to better, to improve.
migliore *agg.* 1. (*comp.*) better: *questo libro è* — *di quello*, this book is better than that 2. (*superl.*) the best: *è il* — *alunno della classe*, he is the best pupil in his class.
migliorìa *sf.* improvement.
mignatta *sf.* leech.
mìgnolo *sm.* little finger.
migrare *vi.* to migrate.
migratore *agg.* migratory. ♦ **migratore** *sm.* migrant.
migratorio *agg.* migratory.
migrazione *sf.* migration.
miliardario *sm.* multi-millionaire.

miliardo *sm.* a thousand millions.
miliare *agg. pietra* —, milestone.
milionario *sm.* millionaire.
milione *sm.* million.
milionèsimo *agg.* millionth.
militante *agg.* militant.
militare[1] *agg.* military. ♦ **militare** *sm.* soldier.
militare[2] *vi.* 1. to be a soldier 2. (*lavorare a favore di*) to support.
militaresco *agg.* soldierlike.
militarismo *sm.* militarism.
militarista *sm.* militarist.
militarizzare *vt.* to militarize.
militarizzazione *sf.* militarization.
militarmente *avv.* militarily.
mìlite *sm.* militiaman (*pl.* -men).
milizia *sf.* Army.
miliziano *sm.* militiaman (*pl.* -men).
millantare *vt.* to boast of. ♦ **millantarsi** *vr.* to boast.
millantatore *sm.* boaster.
millanterìa *sf.* boasting.
mille *agg.* one thousand.
millenario *agg.* e *sm.* millenary.
millennio *sm.* millennium.
millepiedi *sm.* millepede.
millèsimo *agg.* thousandth.
milligrammo *sm.* milligram.
millìmetro *sm.* millimetre.
milza *sf.* spleen.
mimare *vt.* e *vi.* to mime.
mimètico *agg.* mimetic.
mimetismo *sm.* 1. (*di animali*) mimicry 2. (*mil.*) camouflage.
mimetizzare *vt.* to camouflage.
mimetizzazione *sf.* camouflage.
mìmica *sf.* 1. (*teat.*) mimic art 2. (*di gesti*) gesticulation.
mìmico *agg.* miming, mimic.
mimo *sm.* mime.
mimosa *sf.* mimosa.
mina *sf.* mine.
minaccia *sf.* threat.
minacciare *vt.* to threaten.
minaccioso *agg.* threatening.
minare *vt.* 1. to mine 2. (*fig.*) undermine.
minareto *sm.* minaret.
minatore *sm.* miner.
minatorio *agg.* threatening.
minchione *sm.* simpleton.
minerale *agg.* mineral. ♦ **minerale** *sm.* mineral.
mineralizzare *vt.* to mineralize.
mineralogìa *sf.* mineralogy.
minerario *agg.* mining (*attr.*).
minestra *sf.* soup.
mingherlino *agg.* slim.

miniare *vt.* 1. to paint in miniature 2. (*di manoscritti*) to illuminate.
miniato *agg.* illuminated.
miniatura *sf.* miniature.
miniaturista *sm.* miniaturist.
miniera *sf.* mine.
minigonna *sf.* miniskirt.
minimamente *avv.* not in the least.
minimizzare *vt.* to minimize.
mìnimo *agg.* least, slightest, smallest. ♦ **mìnimo** *sm.* minimum..
minio *sm.* red lead.
ministeriale *agg.* ministerial.
ministero *sm.* ministry: — *dell'Istruzione,* ministry of Education || — *degli Esteri, dell'Interno,* Foreign, Home Office; — *del Tesoro,* Treasury.
ministro *sm.* minister.
minoranza *sf.* minority.
minorare *vt.* to diminish.
minorato *agg.* disabled.
minorazione *sf.* 1. (*diminuzione*) reduction 2. (*invalidità*) disablement.
minore *agg.* 1. (*comp.*) (*più piccolo*) smaller, less; (*più basso*) lower; (*più corto*) shorter; (*più giovane*) younger 2. (*superl.*) the smallest, least, lowest, shortest, youngest.
minorile *agg.* juvenile.
minorenne *agg.* under age. ♦ **minorenne** *s.* minor.
minorile *agg.* juvenile.
minorità *sf.* minority.
minoritario *agg.* minority (*attr.*).
minuetto *sm.* minuet.
minugia *sf.* gut.
minùscolo *agg.* small letter.
minuta *sf.* rough copy.
minutaglia *sf.* bits and pieces (*pl.*).
minuto[1] *agg.* 1. minute 2. (*dettagliato*) detailed.
minuto[2] *sm.* minute.
minuto[3] *sm.* (*comm.*) retail.
minuzia *sf.* trifle.
minuziosamente *avv.* minutely.
minuziosità *sf.* minuteness.
minuzioso *agg.* minute, detailed.
minùzzolo *sm.* crumb.
mio *agg.* my. ♦ **mio** *pron.* mine
miocardìa *sf.* myocardia.
miocardio *sm.* myocardium.
miocardite *sf.* myocarditis.
miocene *sm.* miocene.
mìope *agg.* short-sighted.
miopìa *sf.* myopia.

mira *sf.* **1.** aim: *prendere la —*, to take (*v. irr.*) aim **2.** (*fig.*) aim, design.

miràbile *agg.* admirable.

mirabilia *sf. pl.* wonders.

mirabolante *agg.* astonishing.

miràcolo *sm.* miracle: *fare miracoli*, to do (*v. irr.*) miracles, (*fig.*) to work wonders.

miracoloso *agg.* miraculous.

miraggio *sm.* mirage.

mirare *vt.* to look at. ♦ **mirare** *vi.* to aim (at).

miriade *sf.* myriad.

miriagrammo *sm.* myriagram.

miriàmetro *sm.* myriametre.

miriàpodi *sm. pl.* Myriapoda.

mirifico *agg.* wondrous.

mirino *sm.* **1.** sight **2.** (*foto*) view-finder.

mirra *sf.* myrrh.

mirtillo *sm.* bilberry.

mirto *sm.* myrtle.

misantropia *sf.* misanthropy.

misàntropo *sm.* misanthrope.

miscela *sf.* **1.** mixture **2.** (*di caffè, tè, liquori, tabacco*) blend.

miscelare *vt.* **1.** to mix **2.** (*di caffè, tabacco, liquori ecc.*) to blend.

miscellànea *sf.* miscellany.

mischia *sf.* fray.

mischiare *vt.* to mix, to mingle.

mischiatura *sf.* **1.** (*il mischiare*) mixing **2.** (*miscuglio*) mixture.

misconóscere *vt.* not to acknowledge.

miscredente *agg.* misbelieving. ♦ **miscredente** *sm.* misbeliever.

miscredenza *sf.* misbelief.

miscuglio *sm.* **1.** mixture **2.** (*amalgama*) blend.

miseràbile *agg.* **1.** miserable **2.** (*scarso*) poor **3.** (*vile*) despicable, mean. ♦ **miseràbile** *sm.* wretch.

miserando *agg.* miserable.

miserévole *agg.* miserable, pitiable.

miseria *sf.* **1.** misery, poverty **2.** (*scarsità*) lack **3.** (*inezia*) trifle.

misericordia *sf.* mercy.

misericordioso *agg.* merciful.

misero *agg.* **1.** poor, scanty **2.** (*meschino*) wretched.

misfatto *sm.* misdeed.

misoginia *sf.* misogyny.

misògino *agg.* misogynous. ♦ **misògino** *sm.* misogynist.

misoneismo *sm.* misoneism.

missaggio *sm.* mixing.

missile *sm.* missile.

missionario *sm.* missionary.

missione *sf.* mission.

missiva *sf.* letter.

misteriosamente *avv.* mysteriously.

misterioso *agg.* mysterious.

mistero *sm.* mystery.

mistica *sf.* mysticism.

misticismo *sm.* mysticism.

mistico *agg.* mystic.

mistificare *vt.* to mystify.

mistificatore *sm.* mystifier.

mistificazione *sf.* mystification.

misto *agg.* mixed.

mistura *sf.* mixture.

misura *sf.* **1.** (*misurazione, precauzione*) measure **2.** (*taglia*) size **3.** (*limite*) limit.

misuràbile *agg.* measurable.

misurare *vt.* **1.** to measure **2.** (*tec.*) to gauge **3.** (*limitare*) to limit. ♦ **misurarsi** *vr.* to compete.

misurato *agg.* measured.

misuratore *sm.* **1.** (*persona che misura*) measurer **2.** (*strumento*) gauge.

misurazione *sf.* measurement.

misurino *sm.* small measure.

mite *agg.* gentle, meek.

mitezza *sf.* gentleness, meekness.

mitico *agg.* mythical.

mitigare *vt.* **1.** to mitigate **2.** (*passioni*) to appease **3.** (*dolori*) to relieve. ♦ **mitigarsi** *vr.* to be appeased.

mitigazione *sf.* **1.** mitigation **2.** (*di passioni*) appeasement **3.** (*di dolore*) relief.

mitilo *sm.* mussel.

mito *sm.* myth.

mitologia *sf.* mythology.

mitològico *agg.* mythological.

mitòmane *s.* mythomaniac.

mitomania *sf.* mythomania.

mitra[1] *sf.* (*eccl.*) mitre.

mitra[2] *sm.* (*mil.*) tommy-gun.

mitraglia *sf.* grape-shot.

mitragliare *vt.* to machine-gun.

mitragliatore *sm.* machine-gunner.

mitragliatrice *sf.* machine-gun.

mitragliere *sm.* machine-gunner.

mitrale *agg.* mitral.

mitrato *agg.* mitred.

mitridàtico *agg.* mithridatic.

mitridatismo *sm.* mithridatism.

mittente *sm.* sender.

mnemònica *sf.* mnemonics.

mnemònico *agg.* mnemonic.

mo' (*nella loc. prep.*) *a — di*, like.

mòbile *agg.* **1.** movable || *scala* —, escalator; *beni mobili,* personal property **2.** (*mutevole*) inconstant. ♦ **mòbile** *sm.* piece of furniture.

mobilia *sf.* furniture.

mobiliare[1] *agg.* movable, personal.

mobiliare[2] *vt.* to furnish.

mobilità *sf.* **1.** mobility **2.** (*fig.*) inconstancy.

mobilitare *vt.* to mobilize.

mobilitazione *sf.* mobilization.

mocassino *sm.* moccasin.

moccioso *agg.* snivelling. ♦ **moccioso** *sm.* young scoundrel, brat.

mòccolo *sm.* **1.** candle-end **2.** (*bestemmia*) curse.

moda *sf.* **1.** fashion: *di* —, in fashion; *fuori* —, out of fashion || *alla* —, fashionable **2.** (*abitudine, modo*) manner, way: *alla* — *di,* after the manner of.

modale *agg.* modal.

modalità *sf.* modality.

modanatura *sf.* moulding.

mòdano *sm.* model.

modella *sf.* model.

modellare *vt.* to model, to shape.

modellatore *sm.* modeller.

modellazione *sf.* modelling.

modello *sm.* **1.** model, pattern **2.** (*stampo*) mould.

moderare *vt.* to moderate, to check.

moderato *agg.* moderate.

moderatore *agg.* moderating. ♦ **moderatore** *sm.* moderator.

moderazione *sf.* moderation.

modernismo *sm.* modernism.

modernità *sf.* modernity.

modernizzare *vt.* to modernize.

moderno *agg.* modern, up-to-date (*attr.*).

modestia *sf.* modesty: — *a parte,* modesty apart.

modesto *agg.* modest.

modicità *sf.* **1.** moderateness **2.** (*di prezzi*) cheapness.

mòdico *agg.* moderate: *a prezzo* —, cheap.

modifica *sf.* alteration, change.

modificare *vt.* to modify.

modificazione *sf.* V. *modifica.*

modista *sf.* milliner.

modisterìa *sf.* milliner's shop.

modo *sm.* **1.** way, manner **2.** (*gramm.*) mood **3.** (*mezzo*) means: *in nessun* —, by no means || *di* — *che,* so (that); *in* — *da,* so as to; *in che* —, how; *in qualche* —, anyhow; *oltre* —, beyond measure.

modulare *vt.* to modulate.

modulato *agg.* modulated.

modulazione *sf.* modulation.

mòdulo *sm.* form.

moffetta *sf.* skunk.

mògano *sm.* mahogany.

moggio *sm.* bushel.

mogio *agg.* depressed.

moglie *sf.* wife (*pl.* wives).

moina *sf.* simpering.

mola[1] *sf.* **1.** (*di mulino*) millstone **2.** (*per arrotare*) grindstone.

mola[2] *sf.* (*itt.*) sun-fish.

molare[1] *vt.* to grind (*v. irr.*).

molare[2] *agg.* molar. ♦ **molare** *sm.* (*dente*) molar (tooth).

molatura *sf.* grinding.

molazza *sf.* muller.

mole *sf.* **1.** mass, bulk **2.** (*dimensione*) size.

molècola *sf.* molecule.

molecolare *agg.* molecular.

molestare *vt.* to molest, to tease.

molestatore *agg.* molesting. ♦ **molestatore** *sm.* molester.

molestia *sf.* nuisance, trouble.

molesto *agg.* troublesome.

molibdeno *sm.* molybdenum.

molitorio *agg.* molinary.

molla *sf.* **1.** spring **2.** (*incentivo*) spur.

mollare *vt.* **1.** (*allentare*) to slacken **2.** (*mar.*) to let (*v. irr.*) go. ♦ **mollare** *vi.* to give (*v. irr.*) in.

molle *agg.* **1.** soft **2.** (*floscio*) flabby **3.** (*debole*) weak **4.** (*inzuppato*) soaking wet. ♦ **molle** *sf. pl.* tongs.

molleggiamento *sm.* **1.** (*elasticità*) springiness **2.** (*di veicoli*) springing system.

molleggiare *vi.* to be springy.

molleggiato *agg.* sprung.

molleggio *sm.* (*di veicoli*) suspension.

molletta *sf.* **1.** (*per il bucato*) clothes-peg **2.** (*per i capelli*) hair-pin.

mollettiere *sf. pl.* puttees.

mollettone *sm.* thick flannel.

mollezza *sf.* **1.** (*morbidezza*) softness **2.** (*debolezza*) weakness.

mollica *sf.* crumb.

mollo *agg.* damp: *mettere a* —, to steep.

mollusco *sm.* mollusc.

molo *sm.* pier, wharf.

moltéplice *agg.* manifold.

molteplicità *sf.* multiplicity.

moltiplica sf. (mecc.) chain gearing.
moltiplicando sm. multiplicand.
moltiplicare vt. to multiply.
moltiplicatore sm. multiplier.
moltiplicazione sf. multiplication.
moltissimo agg. indef. 1. very much (pl. very many) 2. (di tempo) very long. ♦ **moltissimo** avv. a great deal, very much.
moltitùdine sf. multitude.
molto agg. indef. 1. (sing.) much, a great deal of, a lot of, plenty of 2. (pl.) many, a good many, a lot of, plenty of 3. (di tempo) long. ♦ **molto** avv. 1. very 2. (con comp.) much, far 3. (di tempo) long, a long time.
momentaneamente avv. at the moment.
momentàneo agg. momentary.
momento sm. 1. moment || dal — che, since 2. (tempo, circostanza) time 3. (opportunità) chance.
mònaca sf. nun.
monacale agg. monastic.
mònaco sm. monk.
mònade sf. monad.
monarca sm. monarch.
monarchìa sf. monarchy.
monàrchico agg. monarchic.
monastero sm. monastery.
monàstico agg. monastic.
moncherino sm. stump.
monco agg. 1. maimed 2. (fig.) incomplete.
moncone sm. stump.
mondanità sf. 1. society life 2. worldliness.
mondano agg. worldly.
mondare vt. 1. to clean || — il grano, to winnow the corn 2. (fig.) to cleanse.
mondiale agg. world-wide, world (attr.).
mondina sf. rice-weeder.
mondo¹ sm. world: fare il giro del —, to go (v. irr.) round the world; da che — è —, since the world began.
mondo² agg. clean.
monellerìa sf. prank.
monello sm. little rascal, urchin.
moneta sf. 1. money (solo sing.) 2. (ogni singolo pezzo) coin 3. (spiccioli) change.
monetario agg. monetary.
monetizzare vt. to monetize.
mongolfiera sf. montgolfier.
mongolismo sm. mongolism.

mòngolo agg. Mongolian. ♦ **mòngolo** sm. Mongol.
mongolòide agg. e sm. mongoloid.
monile sm. jewel.
monismo sm. monism.
mònito sm. warning.
monoblocco sm. monobloc.
monòcolo sm. monocle.
monocromàtico agg. monochromatic.
monòcromo agg. monochrome.
monodìa sf. monody.
monogamìa sf. monogamy.
monògamo agg. monogamous. ♦ **monògamo** sm. monogamist.
monografìa sf. monograph.
monogràfico agg. monographic.
monogramma sm. monogram.
monolìtico agg. monolithic.
monòlogo sm. monologue, soliloquy.
monometallismo sm. monometallism.
monomio sm. monomial.
monopàttino sm. scooter.
monoplano sm. monoplane.
monopolio sm. monopoly.
monopolista sm. monopolist.
monopolizzare vt. to monopolize.
monoposto agg. e sm. single-seater.
monorotaia sf. monorail.
monosillàbico agg. monosyllabic.
monosillabo sm. monosyllable.
monoteismo sm. monotheism.
monoteista s. monotheist.
monoteìstico agg. monotheistic.
monotipo sm. monotype.
monotonìa sf. monotony.
monòtono agg. monotonous.
monovalente agg. monovalent.
monsignore sm. monsignor (pl. -ri).
monsone sm. monsoon.
montacàrichi sm. goods-lift.
montaggio sm. 1. assembly: linea di —, assembly line 2. (cine) editing 3. (foto) montage.
montagna sf. mountain.
montagnoso agg. mountainous.
montanaro agg. mountain (attr.). ♦ **montanaro** sm. mountaineer.
montante sm. 1. (boxe) uppercut 2. (mecc.; edil.) vertical rod.
montare vt. 1. (mettere insieme) to assemble 2. (cavalcare) to ride (v. irr.) 3. (di panna) to whip. ♦ **montare** vi. 1. to climb 2. (alzarsi, aumentare) to rise (v. irr.). ♦ **montarsi** vr. to get (v. irr.) excited.

montatore *sm.* assembler.
montatura *sf.* 1. fitting 2. (*fig.*) hot hair.
montavivande *sm.* dumb-waiter.
monte *sm.* 1. mount (*seguito dal nome*) 2. mountain || *andare a* —, to come (*v. irr.*) to nothing; *mandare a* —, to cause to fail.
montone *sm.* 1. ram 2. (*carne*) mutton.
montuosità *sf.* hilliness.
montuoso *agg.* hilly.
monumentale *agg.* monumental.
monumento *sm.* monument.
mora[1] *sf.* (*bot.*) mulberry.
mora[2] *sf.* (*giur.*) delay.
morale *agg.* moral. ♦ **morale** *sm.* morale. ♦ **morale** *sf.* 1. morals (*pl.*) 2. (*fil.*) ethics 3. (*conclusione*) moral.
moralismo *sm.* moralism.
moralista *s.* moralist.
moralistico *agg.* moralistic.
moralità *sf.* morality.
moralizzare *vt.* to moralize.
moralizzazione *sf.* moralization.
moratorio *agg.* moratory.
morbidezza *sf.* softness.
mòrbido *agg.* soft.
morbillo *sm.* measles (*pl.*).
morbo *sm.* disease, plague.
morbosità *sf.* morbidity.
morboso *agg.* morbid.
mordace *agg.* biting, pungent.
mordacità *sf.* mordacity.
mordente *sm.* 1. (*mus.*) mordent 2. (*spirito aggressivo*) bite.
mòrdere *vt.* 1. to bite (*v. irr.*) 2. (*tormentare*) to torment || — *il freno*, to strain at the leash; — *la polvere*, to bite the dust.
morena *sf.* moraine.
morènico *agg.* morainic.
morente *agg.* dying. ♦ **morente** *sm.* dying man.
moresco *agg.* Moorish.
morfina *sf.* morphine.
morfinòmane *s.* morphinomaniac.
morfologìa *sf.* morphology.
morfològico *agg.* morphologic(al).
morganàtico *agg.* morganatic.
moribondo *agg.* dying. ♦ **moribondo** *sm.* dying man.
morigeratezza *sf.* moderation.
morigerato *agg.* moderate, sober.
morire *vi.* 1. to die 2. (*di luci e colori*) to fade 3. (*di suoni*) to die out 4. (*tramontare*) to set (*v. irr.*) ♦ **morire** *sm.* death.

mormone *agg. e sm.* Mormon.
mormorare *vt.* to murmur. ♦ **mormorare** *vi.* (*parlar male*) to gossip.
mormorìo *sm.* 1. murmur 2. (*lamento*) complaining 3. (*malignità*) evil gossip.
moro *agg.* dark. ♦ **moro** *sm.* 1. moor 2. (*bot.*) mulberry-tree.
morra *sf.* "morra".
morsa *sf.* vice.
morsetto *sm.* (*mecc.*) clamp.
morsicare *vt.* to bite (*v. irr.*).
morsicatura *sf.* bite.
morsicchiare *vt.* to nibble.
morso *sm.* 1. bite 2. (*puntura, stimolo*) sting, pang 3. (*del cavallo*) bit 4. (*boccone*) morsel, bit.
mortaio *sm.* mortar.
mortale *agg.* mortal, deadly.
mortalità *sf.* mortality.
mortalmente *avv.* mortally.
mortaretto *sm.* cracker.
morte *sf.* death || *pena di* —, capital punishment; *dar la* — *a qu.*, to kill so.; *odiare a* — *qu.*, to hate so. like poison.
mortella *sf.* myrtle.
mortìfero *agg.* lethal.
mortificare *vt.* 1. to humiliate 2. (*reprimere*) to mortify.
mortificato *agg.* humiliated.
mortificazione *sf.* mortification.
morto *agg.* 1. dead || *natura morta* (*pitt.*), still life; *stanco* —, dead tired 2. (*senza vivacità*) dull. ♦ **morto** *sm.* dead man.
mortorio *sm.* funeral.
mortuario *agg.* mortuary.
mosaicista *s.* mosaicist.
mosàico *sm.* mosaic.
mosca *sf.* fly.
moscatello *sm.* muscatel.
moscato *sm.* (*vino*) muscatel. ♦ **moscato** *agg. noce moscata*, nutmeg.
moscerino *sm.* gnat.
moschea *sf.* mosque.
moschettiere *sm.* musketeer.
moschetto *sm.* musket.
moscio *agg.* flabby.
moscone *sm.* blue-bottle.
mossa *sf.* 1. movement 2. (*spostamento al gioco; fig.*) move 3. (*sport*) starting post.
mossiere *sm.* (*sport*) starter.
mosso *agg.* 1. (*di mare*) rough 2. (*di capelli*) wavy.
mosto *sm.* must.

mostra *sf.* 1. (*esposizione*) show, exhibition 2. (*vetrina*) shop-window 3. (*ostentazione*) display.

mostrare *vt.* 1. to show (*v. irr.*) 2. (*ostentare*) to show (*v. irr.*) off 3. (*dimostrare*) to prove 4. (*fingere*) to pretend.

mostrina *sf.* collar badge.

mostro *sm.* monster.

mostruosamente *avv.* monstrously.

mostruosità *sf.* monstrosity.

mostruoso *agg.* monstrous. for 2. (*giur.*) to allege.

mota *sf.* mud, mire.

motivare *vt.* 1. to state the reason

motivazione *sf.* 1. motivation 2. (*giur.*) opinion.

motivo *sm.* 1. reason || *a — di*, owing to; *senza —*, groundless 2. (*mus.*) theme.

moto *sm.* 1. motion, movement 2. (*esercizio fisico*) exercise 3. (*impulso*) impulse. ♦ **moto** *sf.* motor-cycle.

motobarca *sf.* motor-boat.

motocarrozzetta *sf.* side-car.

motocicletta *sf.* motor-cycle.

motociclismo *sm.* motor-cycling.

motociclista *s.* motor-cyclist.

motofurgone *sm.* van.

motore *agg.* motor, driving. ♦ **motore** *sm.* engine, motor.

motorista *sm.* engineer.

motorizzare *vt.* to motorize. ♦ **motorizzarsi** *vr.* to buy (*v. irr.*) a car, a motor-cycle.

motorizzazione *sf.* motorization.

motoscafo *sm.* motor-boat.

motoveicolo *sm.* motòr vehicle.

motrice *sf.* 1. tractor 2. (*ferr.*) engine.

motteggiare *vt.* to make (*v. irr.*) fun of. ♦ **motteggiare** *vi.* to joke.

motteggiatore *agg.* joking. ♦ **motteggiatore** *sm.* joker.

motteggio *sm.* 1. (*il motteggiare*) raillery 2. (*detto arguto*) joke.

mottetto *sm.* motet.

motto *sm.* 1. word 2. (*proverbio*) saying 3. (*facezia*) witticism.

movente *sm.* motive, cause.

movenza *sf.* movements (*pl.*).

movìbile *agg.* movable.

movimentare *vt.* to enliven.

movimentato *agg.* 1. lively 2. (*pieno di movimento*) eventful.

movimento *sm.* 1. movement 2.

(*traffico, trambusto*) traffic, bustle.

moviola *sf.* film-editing machine.

mozione *sf.* motion.

mozzare *vt.* to cut (*v. irr.*) off.

mozzicone *sm.* 1. stump 2. (*di sigaretta*) butt.

mozzo[1] *agg.* cut (off).

mozzo[2] *sm.* 1. (*di ruota*) hub 2. (*mar.*) ship-boy.

mucca *sf.* cow.

mucchio *sm.* heap, mass.

mùcido *agg.* mouldy. ♦ **mùcido** *sm.* mould.

muco *sm.* mucus.

mucosa *sf.* mucous membrane.

mucoso *agg.* mucous.

muffa *sf.* mould.

muffire *vi.* to mildew.

muflone *sm.* moufflon.

mugghiare *vi.* 1. to bellow 2. (*fig.*) to roar 3. (*del vento*) to howl.

mugghio *sm.* 1. bellow 2. (*fig.*) roar 3. (*del vento*) howl.

muggire *vi.* V. *mugghiare*.

muggito *sm.* V. *mugghio*.

mughetto *sm.* lily of the valley.

mugnaio *sm.* miller.

mugolare *vi.* 1. to howl 2. (*piagnucolare*) to whimper.

mugolìo *sm.* 1. howling 2. (*piagnucolio*) whimpering.

mugugnare *vi.* to mumble.

mulattiera *sf.* mule-track.

mulattiere *sm.* mule-driver.

mulatto *sm.* mulatto.

muliebre *agg.* feminine, womanly.

mulinare *vt.* 1. to whirl 2. (*fig.*) to brood (over).

mulinello *sm.* 1. (*d'acqua*) whirlpool 2. (*d'aria*) whirlwind 3. (*rapido movimento*) twirl.

mulino *sm.* mill.

mulo *sm.* mule.

multa *sf.* fine.

multare *vt.* to fine.

multicolore *agg.* many-coloured.

multiforme *agg.* multiform.

mùltiplo *agg.* e *sm.* multiple.

mummia *sf.* mummy.

mummificare *vt.* to mummify.

mummificazione *sf.* mummification.

mùngere *vt.* to milk.

mungitore *sm.* milker.

mungitura *sf.* milking.

municipale *agg.* municipal.

municipalità *sf.* municipality.

municipalizzare *vt.* to municipalize.

municipalizzazione *sf.* municipalization.

municipio *sm.* **1.** municipality **2.** (*palazzo*) townhall **3.** (*stor.*) municipium (*pl.* -ia).

munificenza *sf.* munificence.

munifico *agg.* munificent.

munire *vt.* **1.** (*fortificare*) to fortify **2.** (*provvedere*) to supply (with).

munizione *sf.* munition.

muòvere *vt.* to move. ♦ **muòversi** *vr.* to move, to stir || *muoviti!* hurry up!

mura[1] *sf.* (*mar.*) tack.

mura[2] *sf. pl.* walls.

muraglia *sf.* wall.

muraglione *sm.* massive wall.

murale *agg.* mural.

murare *vt.* **1.** to wall up **2.** (*cingere di mura*) to wall.

murario *agg.* building (*attr.*).

murata *sf.* ship's side.

muratore *sm.* bricklayer.

muratura *sf.* masonry || *lavoro in* —, brickwork.

murena *sf.* moray.

muriàtico *agg.* muriatic.

muricciolo *sm.* low wall.

murice *sm.* murex.

muro *sm.* wall || *armadio a* —, built-in cupboard; — *del suono*, sound barrier.

musa *sf.* muse.

muschiato *agg.* musky.

muschio[1] *sm.* (*sostanza odorosa*) musk.

muschio[2] *sm.* (*bot.*) moss.

muscolare *agg.* muscular.

muscolatura *sf.* musculature.

mùscolo *sm.* muscle.

muscoloso *agg.* muscular.

muscoso *agg.* mossy.

museo *sm.* museum.

museruola *sf.* muzzle.

mùsica *sf.* music.

musicale *agg.* musical.

musicalità *sf.* musicality.

musicante *sm.* musician.

musicare *vt.* to set (*v. irr.*) to music.

musicista *sm.* musician.

mùsico *sm.* musician.

musicologìa *sf.* musicology.

musicòlogo *sm.* musicologist.

musivo *agg.* mosaic (*attr.*).

muso *sm.* **1.** muzzle **2.** (*broncio*) long face: *fare il* —, to pull a long face.

musone *sm.* **1.** large muzzle **2.** (*persona che tiene il broncio*) sulky person.

musonerìa *sf.* sulkiness.

mussare *vi.* to froth.

mussolina *sf.* muslin.

mustèlidi *sm. pl.* mustelidae.

musulmano *agg. e sm.* Muslim.

muta *sf.* **1.** (*di cani*) pack of hounds **2.** (*della guardia*) change **3.** (*biol.*) moult.

mutàbile *agg.* changeable.

mutabilità *sf.* **1.** (*di cosa*) changeability **2.** (*di persona*) fickleness.

mutamento *sm.* change.

mutande *sf. pl.* drawers.

mutandine *sf. pl.* trunks.

mutare *vt.* **1.** to change **2.** (*di animali*) to shed (*v. irr.*), to moult. ♦ **mutarsi** *vr.* to change.

mutazione *sf.* change.

mutévole *agg.* changeable.

mutilare *vt.* **1.** to maim **2.** (*fig.*) to mutilate.

mutilato *agg.* **1.** maimed **2.** (*fig.*) mutilated. ♦ **mutilato** *sm.* cripple.

mutilazione *sf.* **1.** maiming **2.** (*fig.*) mutilation.

mùtilo *agg.* mutilated.

mutismo *sm.* dumbness.

muto *agg.* **1.** dumb || *carta geografica muta*, blank map **2.** (*fonetica*) mute.

mutria *sf.* stand-offishness.

mutua *sf.* national insurance || *medico della* —, panel doctor.

mutualistico *agg.* insurance (*attr.*).

mutualità *sf.* mutual help.

mutuare *vt.* **1.** (*dare in mutuo*) to lend (*v. irr.*) **2.** (*prendere a mutuo*) to borrow.

mutuatario *sm.* borrower.

mutuato *agg.* insured.

mutuo *agg.* mutual. ♦ **mutuo** *sm.* loan.

N

nababbo *sm.* nabob.

nàcchera *sf.* castanet.

nafta *sf.* **1.** oil **2.** (*chim.*) naphtha.

naftalina *sf.* moth-balls (*pl.*).

naia[1] *sf.* (*zool.*) cobra.

naia[2] *sf.* (*mil.*) *fare la* —, to do (*v. irr.*) one's bit.

nàiade sf. naiad.
nàilon sm. nylon.
nandù sm. nandu.
nanismo sm. nanism.
nano sm. dwarf.
nappa sf. tassel.
narcisismo sm. narcissism.
narcisista sm. narcissist.
narciso sm. narcissus.
narcosi sf. narcosis (pl. -ses).
narcòtico agg. e sm. narcotic.
narcotizzare vt. to narcotize.
narice sf. nostril.
narrare vt. to tell (v. irr.).
narrativa sf. fiction.
narrativo agg. narrative.
narratore sm. 1. story-teller 2. (scrittore) writer.
narrazione sf. narration.
narvalo sm. narwhal.
nasale agg. nasal.
nascente agg. rising.
nàscere vi. 1. to be born 2. (di piante) to spring (v. irr.) up 3. (di fiume; sorgere) to rise (v. irr.) 4. (avere origine) to originate || far —, to give (v. irr.) rise to.
nàscita sf. 1. birth 2. (origine) origin.
nascituro sm. unborn child.
nascòndere vt. to hide (v. irr.). ◆ **nascòndersi** vr. to hide (oneself).
nascondiglio sm. hiding-place.
nascosto agg. hidden || di —, secretly.
nasello sm. (itt.) whiting.
naso sm. nose || a lume di —, by guesswork; ficcare il — in qc., to poke one's nose into sthg.; avere buon —, to be shrewd.
nassa sf. bow-net.
nastro sm. 1. ribbon 2. (tec.) tape.
natale agg. native. ◆ **Natale** sm. Christmas.
natalità sf. birth-rate.
natalizio agg. Christmas (attr.).
natante agg. floating. ◆ **natante** sm. watercraft.
natatoia sf. fin.
natatorio agg. swimming (attr.).
nàtica sf. buttock.
natività sf. nativity.
nativo agg. 1. native 2. (innato) inborn.
nato agg. born.
natura sf. nature.
naturale agg. natural.
naturalezza sf. naturalness, simplicity.

naturalismo sm. naturalism.
naturalista s. naturalist.
naturalizzare vt. to naturalize.
naturalizzazione sf. naturalization.
naturalmente avv. naturally, of course.
naturismo sm. naturism.
naturista s. naturist.
naufragare vi. 1. to be shipwrecked 2. (fig.) to be wrecked.
naufragio sm. 1. shipwreck 2. (fig.) wreck.
nàufrago sm. shipwrecked person.
nàusea sf. disgust, nausea || avere la —, to feel (v. irr.) sick.
nauseabondo agg. nauseating.
nauseare vt. to make (v. irr.) sick.
nàutica sf. navigation.
nàutico agg. nautical.
navale agg. naval.
navata sf. 1. (centrale) nave 2. (laterale) aisle.
nave sf. ship.
navetta sf. shuttle.
navicella sf. (aer.) nacelle.
navigàbile agg. navigable.
navigabilità sf. navigability.
navigare vi. to sail.
navigato agg. (fig.) cunning.
navigatore sm. navigator.
navigazione sf. navigation.
naviglio sm. 1. fleet 2. (nave) craft.
nazionale agg. national.
nazionalismo sm. nationalism.
nazionalista s. nationalist.
nazionalità sf. nationality.
nazionalizzare vt. to nationalize.
nazionalizzazione sf. nationalization.
nazionalsocialismo sm. National Socialism.
nazione sf. nation.
nazismo sm. Nazism.
nazista agg. e sm. Nazi.
nazzareno agg. e sm. Nazarene.
ne pron. 1. of him, about him; of her, about her; of it, about it; of them, about them; of this, about this; of that, about that 2. (partitivo) some: — ho, I have some; any: non — ho, I haven't any. ◆ **ne** (particella avv. di moto da luogo) from there.
né cong. 1. neither, nor 2. (né... né...) neither... nor; (in presenza di altra negazione) either... or.
neanche avv. not even. ◆ **neanche** cong. neither, nor: essi non anda-

rono e — io, they did not go and neither did I.
nebbia *sf.* fog.
nebbioso *agg.* foggy.
nebulizzare *vt.* to nebulize.
nebulizzatore *sm.* nebulizer.
nebulosa *sf.* nebula (*pl.* -ae).
nebulosità *sf.* **1.** nebulosity **2.** (*fig.*) haziness.
nebuloso *agg.* **1.** nebulous **2.** (*fig.*) vague.
necessario *agg.* necessary. ♦ **necessario** *sm.* **1.** necessary **2.** (*l'indispensabile*) necessities (*pl.*).
necessità *sf.* **1.** necessity **2.** (*bisogno*) need.
necessitare *vi.* to need.
necrologia *sf.* obituary-notice.
necrologio *sm.* **1.** necrology **2.** (*annuncio*) obituary.
necròpoli *sf.* necropolis.
necrosi *sf.* necrosis (*pl.* -ses).
necrotizzare *vt.* to necrotize.
nefandezza *sf.* wickedness.
nefando *agg.* wicked.
nefasto *agg.* ill-omened.
nefrite *sf.* nephritis.
nefrìtico *agg.* nephritic. ♦ **nefrìtico** *sm.* nephritic subject.
negare *vt.* **1.** to deny **2.** (*rifiutare*) to refuse.
negativa *sf.* (*anche foto*) negative.
negativo *agg.* negative.
negato *agg.* **1.** refused, denied **2.** (*inadatto*) unfit (for).
negatore *agg.* negatory. ♦ **negatore** *sm.* denier.
negazione *sf.* **1.** denial **2.** (*gramm.*) negative **3.** (*cosa diametralmente opposta all'altra*) negation.
neghittoso *agg.* slothful.
negletto *agg.* **1.** neglected **2.** (*di aspetto*) slovenly.
negligente *agg.* negligent, careless.
negligenza *sf.* negligence, carelessness.
negoziàbile *agg.* negotiable.
negoziante *sm.* **1.** merchant, trader **2.** (*chi ha negozio*) shopkeeper.
negoziare *vt.* to negotiate.
negoziato *agg.* negotiated. ♦ **negoziato** *sm.* negotiation.
negozio *sm.* **1.** shop **2.** (*commercio*) trade **3.** (*faccenda*) affair.
negriero *agg.* slave (*attr.*). ♦ **negriero** *sm.* slave-trader.
negro *agg.* e *sm.* **1.** negro **2.** (*spreg.*) nigger.
negròide *agg.* e *s.* negroid.

negromante *sm.* necromancer.
negromanzia *sf.* necromancy.
nembo *sm.* **1.** raincloud **2.** (*fig.*) multitude.
nèmesi *sf.* nemesis (*pl.* -ses).
nemico *agg.* **1.** adverse **2.** (*del nemico*) enemy (*attr.*). ♦ **nemico** *sm.* enemy.
neo[1] *sm.* **1.** mole **2.** (*fig.*) flaw.
neo[2] *agg.* neo.
neocapitalismo *sm.* neo-capitalism.
neocapitalista *agg.* e *sm.* neo--capitalist.
neocapitalìstico *agg.* neo-capitalistic.
neoclassicismo *sm.* neo-classicism.
neoclàssico *agg.* neo-classic.
neofascismo *sm.* neofascism.
neofascista *agg.* e *s.* neofascist.
neòfita *sm.* **1.** neophyte **2.** (*fig.*) beginner.
neolìtico *agg.* Neolithic.
neologismo *sm.* neologism.
neon *sm.* neon: *insegna al —,* neon sign.
neonato *agg.* new-born. ♦ **neonato** *sm.* (new-born) baby.
neorealismo *sm.* Neorealism.
neorealista *agg.* e *sm.* neorealist.
neozelandese *agg.* New Zealand (*attr.*). ♦ **neozelandese** *s.* New Zealander.
nepotismo *sm.* 'nepotism.
nerastro *agg.* blackish.
nerbo *sm.* **1.** sinew **2.** (*fig.*) strength, vigour.
nerboruto *agg.* brawny.
neretto *sm.* (*tip.*) boldface.
nerezza *sf.* blackness.
nero *agg.* black.
nerofumo *sm.* lamp-black.
neRògnolo *agg.* blackish.
nerume *sm.* mass of black.
nervatura *sf.* ribbing.
nervo *sm.* nerve.
nervosamente *agg.* nervously.
nervosismo *sm.* nervousness.
nervoso *agg.* nervous, irritable.
nèspola *sf.* medlar.
nèspolo *sm.* medlar(-tree).
nesso *sm.* connection.
nessuno *agg.* **1.** no **2.** (*in presenza di altra neg.*) any. ♦ **nessuno** *pron.* **1.** (*per persone*) nobody, no one; (*per cose*) none **2.** (*in presenza di altra neg.*) anybody (*solo per persone*), anyone, any || — *di,* none of, (*in presenza di altra neg.*) any of.

nèttare sm. nectar.

nettare vt. to clean.

nettezza sf. cleanness: — urbana, municipal street cleansing.

netto agg. 1. clean, spotless (anche fig.) 2. (comm.) net.

nettunio sm. neptunium.

neurite sf. neuritis.

neurochirurgìa sf. neurosurgery.

neurologìa sf. neurology.

neuròlogo sm. neurologist.

neuropàtico agg. neuropathic. ♦ neuropàtico sm. neuropath.

neuropatologìa sf. neuropathology.

neurosi sf. neurosis (pl. -ses).

neurovegetativo agg. vegetative nervous.

neutrale agg. neutral.

neutralismo sm. neutralism.

neutralista s. neutralist.

neutralità sf. neutrality.

neutralizzare vt. to neutralize.

neutralizzazione sf. neutralization.

nèutro agg. 1. neutral 2. (gramm.; bot.; zool.) neuter.

neutrone sm. neutron.

neve sf. snow.

nevicare vi. to snow: nevica, it is snowing.

nevicata sf. snowfall.

nevischio sm. sleet.

nevoso agg. snowy.

nevralgìa sf. neuralgia.

nevràlgico agg. neuralgic.

nevrastenìa sf. neurasthenia.

nevrastènico agg. neurasthenic.

nevròtico agg. e sm. neurotic.

nibbio sm. kite.

nicchia sf. niche.

nicchiare vi. to shilly-shally.

nichel sm. nickel.

nichelare vt. to nickel.

nichelatura sf. nickel-plating.

nichelino sm. nickel coin.

nichilismo sm. nihilism.

nichilista s. nihilist.

nicotina sf. nicotine.

nidiata sf. 1. nest 2. (covata) brood || una — di bambini, a swarm of children.

nidificare vi. to nest.

nido sm. nest.

niente pron. 1. nothing 2. (in presenza di altre negazioni) anything.

nimbo sm. halo.

ninfa sf. nymph.

ninfea sf. water-lily.

ninfòmane sf. nymphomaniac.

ninnananna sf. lullaby.

ninnolo sm. 1. knick-knack 2. (balocco) plaything.

nipote sm. 1. (di nonno) grand-son 2. (di zio) nephew. ♦ nipote sf. 1. (di nonno) grand-daughter 2. (di zio) niece.

nippònico agg. e sm. Japanese.

nirvana sm. nirvana.

nitidezza sf. neatness.

nìtido agg. neat, clear.

nitrato sm. nitrate.

nìtrico agg. nitric.

nitrire vi. to whinny.

nitrito[1] sm. (di cavallo) whinny.

nitrito[2] sm. (chim.) nitrite.

nitroglicerina sf. nitroglycerin.

nìveo agg. snowy.

no avv. no.

nòbile agg. e sm. noble.

nobiliare agg. nobiliary.

nobilitare vt. to ennoble.

nobilitazione sf. ennobling.

nobilmente avv. nobly.

nobiltà sf. nobility.

nocca sf. knuckle.

nocchiere sm. helmsman (pl. -men).

nocciola sf. hazel-nut.

nòcciolo sm. 1. stone 2. (ciò che è essenziale) heart.

nocciolo sm. (bot.) hazel-tree.

noce sm. walnut-tree. ♦ noce sf. walnut || guscio di — (barchetta), cockle-shell; — moscata, nutmeg.

nocivo agg. noxious, harmful.

nodo sm. knot.

nodoso agg. knotty.

noi pron. 1. (sogg.) we 2. (compl.) us.

noia sf. 1. boredom 2. (fastidio) worry, nuisance.

noioso agg. 1. boring 2. (molesto) annoying.

noleggiante sm. (mar.) charterer.

noleggiare vt. 1. to hire 2. (di navi) to charter.

noleggiatore sm. hirer.

noleggio sm. 1. hire 2. (mar.) freight.

nolente agg. unwilling || volente o —, willy-nilly.

nolo sm. 1. hire 2. (mar.) freight.

nòmade agg. e s. nomad.

nomadismo sm. nomadism.

nome sm. 1. name 2. (di battesimo) Christian name || senza —, nameless; a — di, on behalf of; per —, by name 3. (gramm.) noun.

nomea sf. notoriety.

nomenclatura *sf.* nomenclature.
nomìgnolo *sm.* nickname.
nòmina *sf.* appointment.
nominale *agg.* nominal.
nominalismo *sm.* nominalism.
nominalista *s.* nominalist.
nominalmente *avv.* nominally.
nominare *vt.* **1.** to name **2.** (*eleggere*) to appoint.
nominativo *agg.* **1.** nominative **2.** (*comm.*) registered. ♦ **nominativo** *sm.* name.
non *avv.* not.
nona *sf.* **1.** (*eccl.*) Nones (*pl.*) **2.** (*mus.*) ninth.
nonagenario *agg.* ninety years old (*pred.*); ninety-year-old (*attr.*). ♦ **nonagenario** *sm.* nonagenarian.
nonconformista *s.* non-conformist.
noncurante *agg.* careless.
noncuranza *sf.* carelessness.
nondimeno *avv.* nevertheless.
nonna *sf.* grandmother.
nonno *sm.* grandfather: *i miei nonni*, my grandparents.
nonnulla *sm.* trifle.
nono *agg.* ninth.
nonostante *prep.* notwithstanding ‖ — *che*, though, although.
nonsenso *sm.* nonsense.
non-ti-scordar-di-me *sm.* forget-me-not.
nord *sm.* north.
nordamericano *agg.* e *sm.* North American.
nòrdico *agg.* **1.** northern **2.** (*dell'Europa settentrionale*) Nordic. ♦ **nòrdico** *sm.* **1.** Northerner **2.** (*dell'Europa settentrionale*) Nordic.
nordista *sm.* (*stor. amer.*) Federal.
norma *sf.* **1.** rule, norm **2.** (*istruzioni*) instruction, direction ‖ *a* — *di legge*, according to law.
normale *agg.* e *sm.* **1.** normal **2.** (*che dà una norma*) standard.
normalità *sf.* normality.
normalizzare *vt.* to normalize.
normalizzazione *sf.* normalization.
normalmente *avv.* usually.
normanno *agg.* e *sm.* Norman: *anglo-*—, (*stor.*) Anglo-Norman.
normativo *agg.* normative.
normògrafo *sm.* stencil.
norvegese *agg.* e *sm.* Norwegian.
nosocòmio *sm.* hospital.
nostalgìa *sf.* home-sickness.
nostàlgico *agg.* homesick.
nostrano *agg.* home (*attr.*), national.

nostro *agg.* our: *i nostri amici*, our friends. ♦ **nostro** *pron.* ours: *questa casa è nostra*, this house is ours. ♦ **nostro** *sm.* **1.** *viviamo del* —, we live on our own income **2.** *il Nostro* (*di autore*), the Author **3.** *i nostri*, our family.
nostromo *sm.* boatswain.
nota *sf.* **1.** note **2.** (*lista*) list.
notàbile *agg.* notable.
notaio *sm.* notary.
notare *vt.* to note.
notariato *sm.* profession of notary.
notarile *agg.* notarial.
notazione *sf.* notation.
notévole *agg.* remarkable, notable.
notevolmente *avv.* remarkably.
notìfica *sf.* **1.** notification **2.** (*giur.*) service.
notificare *vt.* **1.** to notify **2.** (*informare*) to inform **3.** (*giur.*) to serve.
notizia *sf.* **1.** news (*pl. con costruzione sing.*), piece of news (*solo sing.*) **2.** (*informazione*) information (*solo sing.*) **3.** (*dato*) note: *notizie biografiche*, biographical notes.
notiziario *sm.* news (*pl., con costruzione sing.*).
noto *agg.* well-known. ♦ **noto** *sm.* the known.
notoriamente *avv.* notoriously.
notorietà *sf.* notoriety.
notorio *agg.* **1.** (*in senso sfavorevole*) notorious **2.** well-known.
nottàmbulo *agg.* noctambulous. ♦ **nottàmbulo** *sm.* night-bird.
nottata *sf.* night.
notte *sf.* night.
nottetempo *avv.* by night.
notturno *agg.* night (*attr.*). ♦ **notturno** *sm.* (*mus.*) nocturne.
novanta *agg.* ninety.
novantenne *agg.* **1.** ninety years old (*pred.*) **2.** ninety-year-old (*attr.*).
novantèsimo *agg.* ninetieth.
novatore *sm.* innovator.
nove *agg.* nine.
novecento *agg.* nine hundred.
novella *sf.* short story, tale.
novellino *agg.* inexperienced. ♦ **novellino** *sm.* beginner.
novellista *s.* short-story writer.
novellìstica *sf.* story-telling.
novello *agg.* **1.** new, spring (*attr.*) **2.** (*nuovo*) second: *un* — *Raffaello*, a second Raffaello.

novembre *sm.* November.
novena *sf.* novena (*pl.* -ae).
nòvero *sm.* number 2. (*categoria*) class.
novilunio *sm.* new moon.
novità *sf.* 1. novelty 2. (*notizia*) news (*pl.* con costruzione sing.), piece of news (*solo sing.*).
noviziato *sm.* novitiate.
novizio *sm.* novice.
nozione *sf.* notion.
nozze *sf. pl.* wedding (*sing.*).
nube *sf.* cloud.
nubifragio *sm.* downpour.
nùbile *agg.* unmarried, single. ♦ **nùbile** *sf.* single woman.
nuca *sf.* nape.
nucleare *agg.* nuclear.
nucleina *sf.* nuclein.
nùcleo *sm.* nucleus (*pl.* -ei).
nudismo *sm.* nudism.
nudista *s.* nudist.
nudità *sf.* nakedness.
nudo *agg.* naked, bare.
nùgolo *sm.* cloud.
nulla *pron.* V. *niente.*
nullaosta *sm.* permit.
nullatenente *agg.* without property. ♦ **nullatenente** *s.* person without property.
nullità *sf.* 1. (*di cose*) nullity 2. (*di persone*) nonentity.
nullo *agg.* (*giur.*) null, void.
nume *sm.* numen, deity.
numeràbile *agg.* numerable.
numerabilità *sf.* numerability.
numerale *agg.* numeral.
numerare *vt.* 1. to count 2. (*segnare con numero*) to number.
numerato *agg.* 1. counted 2. (*segnato con un numero*) numbered.
numerario *agg.* numerary. ♦ **numerario** *sm.* (*comm.*) ready cash.
numeratore *sm.* (*mat.*) numerator.
numerazione *sf.* 1. numbering 2. (*mat.*) numeration.
numericamente *avv.* numerically.
numèrico *agg.* numerical.
nùmero *sm.* number.
numeroso *agg.* numerous.
numismàtica *sf.* numismatics.
numismàtico *agg.* numismatic. ♦ **numismàtico** *sm.* numismatist.
nunziatura *sf.* (*eccl.*) nunciature.
nunzio *sm.* nuncio.
nuòcere *vi.* to damage, to harm.
nuora *sf.* daughter-in-law.
nuotare *vi.* to swim (*v. irr.*).
nuotata *sf.* swim.

nuotatore *sm.* swimmer.
nuoto *sm.* swimming: *gara di —*, swimming-race.
nuova *sf.* news (*pl.* con costruzione sing.), piece of news (*solo sing.*).
nuovamente *avv.* again.
nuovo *agg.* new: — *di zecca, fiammante*, brand-new.
nutazione *sf.* nutation.
nutrice *sf.* wet-nurse.
nutriente *agg.* nourishing.
nutrimento *sm.* 1. feeding 2. (*fig.*) nourishment.
nutrire *vt.* 1. to feed (*v. irr.*) 2. (*mantenere*) to maintain 3. (*di sentimenti, passioni*) to foster. ♦ **nutrirsi** *vr.* to feed (on).
nutritivo *agg.* nourishing.
nutrito *agg.* fed, nourished.
nutrizione *sf.* 1. feeding 2. (*fig.*) nourishment.
nùvola *sf.* cloud.
nuvoloso *agg.* overcast, cloudy.
nuziale *agg.* wedding (*attr.*).

O

o *cong.* or ‖ *o ... o*, either ... or: — *tu — tua madre dovete venire*, either you or your mother must come; — *l'uno — l'altro*, either: *prendi — l'uno — l'altro*, take either.
òasi *sf.* oasis (*pl.* -ses).
obbligare *vt.* to compel. ♦ **obbligarsi** *vr.* to bind (*v. irr.*) oneself.
obbligatorietà *sf.* compulsoriness.
obbligatorio *agg.* compulsory.
obbligazione *sf.* 1. obligation 2. (*comm.*) bond.
obbligazionista *sm.* bond-holder.
òbbligo *sm.* obligation: *assumersi l'—*, to undertake (*v. irr.*).
obbrobrio *sm.* disgrace.
obbrobrioso *agg.* disgraceful.
obelisco *sm.* obelisk.
oberare *vt.* to burden.
obesità *sf.* obesity.
obeso *agg.* obese.
òbice *sm.* howitzer.
obiettare *vt.* to object.
obiettivamente *avv.* objectively.
obiettivismo *sm.* objectivism.
obiettività *sf.* objectivity.

obiettivo *agg.* objective. ♦ **obiettivo** *sm.* **1.** (*mil.*) objective **2.** (*scopo*) aim **3.** (*foto*) lens.

obiettore *sm.* objector: — *di coscienza*, conscentious objector.

obiezione *sf.* objection.

obitorio *sm.* morgue.

oblatore *sm.* donor.

oblazione *sf.* donation.

obliare *vt.* to forget (*v. irr.*).

oblìo *sm.* oblivion.

obliquamente *avv.* obliquely.

obliquità *sf.* obliquity.

obliquo *agg.* oblique.

obliterare *vt.* to obliterate.

obliterazione *sf.* obliteration.

oblò *sm.* porthole.

oblungo *agg.* oblong.

òboe *sm.* oboe.

òbolo *sm.* offering.

obsoleto *agg.* obsolete.

oca *sf.* goose (*pl.* geese): *pelle d'*—, goose flesh; *penna d'*—, goose-quill.

occasionale *agg.* occasional.

occasionalismo *sm.* occasionalism.

occasionalmente *avv.* occasionally.

occasione *sf.* occasion.

occhiaia *sf.* eye-socket ‖ *avere le occhiaie*, to have rings under one's eyes.

occhiali *sm. pl.* spectacles, glasses.

occhialuto *agg.* spectacled, wearing spectacles (*pred.*).

occhiata *sf.* look, glance.

occhiataccia *sf.* glare.

occhieggiare *vt.* to cast (*v. irr.*) glances (at). ♦ **occhieggiare** *vi.* to peep (at).

occhiello *sm.* **1.** button-hole **2.** (*mecc.*) eye.

occhietto *sm. fare l'*— *a qu.*, to wink at so.

occhio *sm.* eye ‖ *costare un* —, to be terribly expensive; *chiudere un* — *su*, to turn a blind eye to; *dare nell'*—, to strike (*v. irr.*) the eye; *tenere d'*—, to keep (*v. irr.*) an eye on; *in un batter d'*—, in the twinkling of an eye.

occidentale *agg.* west, western. ♦ **occidentale** *s.* westerner.

occidentalizzare *vt.* to occidentalize.

occidente *sm.* west.

occipitale *agg.* occipital.

occipite *sm.* occiput (*pl.* occipita).

occlusione *sf.* occlusion.

occlusivo *agg.* occlusive.

occorrente *agg.* necessary. ♦ **occorrente** *sm.* the necessary.

occorrenza *sf. all'*—, in case of need.

occòrrere *vi.* **1.** (*imp.*) to be necessary **2.** (*abbisognare*) to need.

occultamento *sm.* concealment.

occultare *vt.* to hide (*v. irr.*), to conceal. ♦ **occultarsi** *vr.* to hide.

occultatore *sm.* hider.

occultismo *sm.* occultism.

occulto *agg.* **1.** occult **2.** (*nascosto*) hidden.

occupante *agg.* occupying. ♦ **occupante** *s.* occupant.

occupare *vt.* **1.** to occupy **2.** (*ingaggiare*) to employ. ♦ **occuparsi** *vr.* **1.** (*impiegarsi*) to find (*v. irr.*) a job **2.** (*badare*) to attend (to).

occupato *agg.* engaged ‖ *essere* — (*fare un lavoro*), to work.

occupazione *sf.* **1.** occupation **2.** (*lavoro*) job.

oceànico *agg.* oceanic.

ocèano *sm.* ocean.

oceanografìa *sf.* oceanography.

ocello *sm.* ocellus (*pl.* -li).

ocra *sf.* ochre.

oculare *agg.* ocular, eye (*attr.*). ♦ **oculare** *sm.* (*fis.*) eyepiece.

oculatezza *sf.* shrewdness.

oculato *agg.* prudent.

oculista *sm.* oculist.

oculìstica *sf.* ophthalmology.

odalisca *sf.* odalisque.

ode *sf.* ode.

odiare *vt.* to hate.

odierno *agg.* of today, today's.

odio *sm.* hatred.

odioso *agg.* hateful.

odontàlgico *agg.* odontalgic.

odontoiatra *s.* odontologist, dentist.

odontoiatrìa *sf.* odontology.

odontoiàtrico *agg.* odontological.

odorare *vt.* e *vi.* to smell (*v. irr.*).

odorato *sm.* smell.

odore *sm.* smell.

odorìfero *agg.* odoriferous.

odoroso *agg.* fragrant.

offèndere *vt.* to offend. ♦ **offendersi** *vr.* to be offended (at, by); to feel (*v. irr.*) hurt (by).

offensiva *sf.* offensive.

offensivo *agg.* offensive.

offensore *sm.* offender.

offerente *s.* **1.** offerer **2.** (*a un'asta*) bidder.

offerta *sf.* offer, donation.
offesa *sf.* offence.
offeso *agg.* offended, injured.
officiare *vi.* to officiate.
officina *sf.* workshop.
officinale *agg.* officinal.
offrire *vt.* to offer. ♦ **offrirsi** *vr.* to offer (oneself).
offuscamento *sm.* 1. dimming 2. (*oscurità*) dimness.
offuscare *vt.* to dim. ♦ **offuscarsi** *vr.* to grow (*v. irr.*) dim.
oftalmìa *sf.* ophthalmia.
oftàlmico *agg.* ophthalmic.
oftalmologìa *sf.* ophthalmology.
oftalmoscopìa *sf.* ophthalmoscopy.
oftalmoscopio *sm.* ophthalmoscope.
oggettivamente *avv.* objectively.
oggettivare *vt.* to objectify.
oggettivazione *sf.* objectification.
oggettivismo *sm.* objectivism.
oggettività *sf.* objectivity.
oggettivo *agg.* objective.
oggetto *sm.* object.
oggi *avv.* today.
ogiva *sf.* ogive.
ogivale *agg.* ogival.
ogni *agg.* every, each ‖ *in — modo*, anyhow; *in — luogo*, everywhere.
ogniqualvolta *cong.* whenever.
ognuno *pron.* everybody, everyone ‖ *— di*, each of.
oleandro *sm.* oleander.
oleario *agg.* oil (*attr.*).
oleato *agg.* oiled ‖ *carta oleata*, grease-proof paper.
oleificio *sm.* oil mill.
oleodotto *sm.* oil pipeline.
oleografìa *sf.* 1. oleography 2. (*pezzo singolo*) oleograph.
oleoso *agg.* oily.
olezzare *vi.* to smell (*v. irr.*) sweetly.
olezzo *sm.* fragrance.
olfattivo *agg.* olfactory.
olfatto *sm.* smell.
oliare *vt.* to oil.
oliatore *sm.* oil-can.
oliera *sf.* cruet.
oligarca *sm.* oligarch.
oligarchìa *sf.* oligarchy.
oligàrchico *agg.* oligarchic(al).
oligocene *sm.* Oligocene.
olimpìaco *agg.* V. *olimpico*.
olimpìade *sf.* Olympiad ‖ *le Olimpiadi*, Olympic games.
olimpico *agg.* Olympic.
olimpiònico *agg.* Olympic games (*attr.*). ♦ **olimpiònico** *sm.*
Olympic champion.

olio *sm.* oil.
oliva *sf.* olive.
olivastro *agg.* olive.
oliveto *sm.* olive-grove.
olivo *sm.* olive.
olmo *sm.* elm.
olocàusto *sm.* holocaust.
ològrafo *agg.* holograph.
oltraggiare *vt.* to outrage.
oltraggio *sm.* outrage.
oltraggioso *agg.* outrageous.
oltramontano *agg.* e *sm.* ultramontane.
oltranza *sf.* (*nella loc. avv.*) *a —*, to the bitter end.
oltranzista *sm.* extremist.
oltre *avv.* 1. (*di luogo*) further, farther 2. (*di tempo*) longer. ♦ **oltre** *prep.* 1. (*di luogo*) beyond 2. (*più di*) over 3. (*in aggiunta*) in addition to. ♦ **oltre a, che** *cong.* besides.
oltrecortina *avv.* beyond the Iron Curtain.
oltremare *avv.* overseas: *d'—*, overseas (*attr.*).
oltremodo *avv.* extremely.
oltrepassare *vt.* to go (*v. irr.*) beyond ‖ *— i limiti* (*fig.*), to go (*v. irr.*) too far.
oltretomba *sm.* hereafter.
omaccione *sm.* burly man (*pl.* men).
omaggio *sm.* 1. homage 2. (*offerta*) gift.
ombelicale *agg.* umbilical.
ombelico *sm.* navel.
ombra *sf.* 1. shade (*anche spettro*) 2. (*immagine proiettata, parvenza*) shadow ‖ *dar — a qu.*, to overshadow so.
ombreggiare *vt.* to shade.
ombreggiatura *sf.* shading.
ombrella *sf.* (*bot.*) umbel.
ombrellifero *agg.* umbelliferous.
ombrellino *sm.* parasol.
ombrello *sm.* umbrella.
ombrellone *sm.* sunshade.
ombretto *sm.* eye shadow.
ombrina *sf.* umbrina.
ombrosità *sf.* 1. shadiness 2. (*di persona*) touchiness 3. (*di cavallo*) skittishness.
ombroso *agg.* 1. shady 2. (*di persona*) touchy 3. (*di cavallo*) skittish.
omega *sm.* omega.
omelìa *sf.* homily.
omeopatìa *sf.* homeopathy.

omeopàtico *agg.* homeopathic. ♦
omeopàtico *sm.* homeopath
omèrico *agg.* Homeric.
òmero *sm.* humerus (*pl.* -ri).
omertà *sf.* silence.
omesso *agg.* omitted.
ométtere *vt.* to omit, to leave out.
omicida *agg.* homicidal. ♦ omicida *s.* homicide.
omicidio *sm.* homicide.
omissione *sf.* omission.
òmnibus *sm.* bus.
omogeneità *sf.* homogeneity.
omogeneizzare *vt.* to homogenize.
omogèneo *agg.* homogeneous.
omologare *vt.* **1.** to homologate **2.**
(*sport*) to ratify.
omologazione *sf.* **1.** homologation
2. (*sport*) ratification.
omòlogo *agg.* homologous.
omonimìa *sf.* homonymy.
omònimo *agg.* homonymous. ♦
omònimo *sm.* homonym.
omosessuale *agg.* e *s.* homosexual.
omosessualità *sf.* homosexuality.
oncia *sf.* ounce.
onda *sf.* wave || *mettere in* — (*ra-
dio*), to broadcast (*v. irr.*).
ondata *sf.* wave: *a ondate*, in
waves.
onde *avv.* **1.** whence **2.** (*affinché*) so
that **3.** (*cosicché*) therefore **4.** (*da,
con cui*) from, by, with which.
ondeggiamento *sm.* **1.** waving **2.**
(*di barca*) rolling **3.** (*esitazione*)
wavering.
ondeggiante *agg.* **1.** waving **2.** (*di
barca*) rolling **3.** (*esitante*) wavering.
ondeggiare *vi.* **1.** to wave **2.** (*di
barca*) tò roll **3.** (*esitare*) to waver.
ondina *sf.* undine.
ondoso *agg.* undulatory.
ondulare *vt.* to wave.
ondulato *agg.* **1.** wavy **2.** (*tec.*) cor-
rugated.
ondulatorio *agg.* undulatory.
ondulazione *sf.* **1.** undulation **2.**
(*di capelli*) wave.
onerare *vt.* to burden.
ònere *sm.* burden || — *fiscale*, tax.
oneroso *agg.* burdensome.
onestà *sf.* **1.** honesty **2.** (*castità*)
chastity.
onesto *agg.* **1.** honest **2.** (*casto*)
chaste.
ònice *sf.* onyx.
onìrico *agg.* oneiric.

onnipotente *agg.* cmnipotent. ♦
Onnipotente (l') *sm.* the Almighty.
onnipotenza *sf.* omnipotence.
onnipresente *agg.* omnipresent.
onnisciente *agg.* omniscient.
onniscienza *sf.* omniscience.
onniveggente *agg.* omnipercipient.
onnìvoro *agg.* omnivorous. ♦ onnìvoro *sm.* omnivore.
onomàstico *agg.* onomastic. ♦
onomàstico *sm.* name-day.
onomatopea *sf.* onomatopoeia.
onomatopèico *agg.* onomatopoeic.
onoràbile *agg.* honourable.
onorabilità *sf.* honourableness.
onoranza *sf.* honour.
onorare *vt.* to honour. ♦ onorar-
si *vr.* to be proud (of).
onorario *agg.* honorary. ♦ onorario *sm.* fee.
onorato *agg.* **1.** honoured **2.** (*onesto*) honourable.
onore *sm.* honour || *farsi* —, to ex-
cel; *a onor del vero*, to tell (*v.
irr.*) the truth; *serata d'*—, gala
night.
onorévole *agg.* honourable.
onorificenza *sf.* **1.** honour **2.** (*decorazione*) decoration.
onorìfico *agg.* honorific(al).
onta *sf.* **1.** shame **2.** (*offesa*) insult
|| *ad* — *di*, in spite of.
ontano *sm.* alder.
ontologìa *sf.* ontology.
ontològico *agg.* ontological.
opacità *sf.* opacity.
opaco *agg.* **1.** opaque **2.** (*di suoni,
colori*) dull.
opale *sm.* opal.
opalescente *agg.* opalescent.
opalino *agg.* opaline.
òpera *sf.* **1.** work **2.** (*melodramma*)
opera **3.** (*istituto*) institution.
operàbile *agg.* **1.** workable.
2. (*chir.*) operable.
operaio *agg.* working. ♦ operaio
sm. worker: — *specializzato*,
skilled worker.
operante *agg.* operating.
operare *vi.* to work, to operate (*anche med.*).
operativo *agg.* operative.
operato *agg.* (*di tessuto*) diapered.
♦ operato *sm.* **1.** (*condotta*)
behaviour **2.** (*chi ha subito un'operazione*) operated patient.
operatore *sm.* **1.** operator **2.** (*cine*)
cameraman (*pl.* -men).

operatorio *agg.* operating.

operazione *sf.* operation: *fare un'— a qu.*, to perform an operation on so.; *subire un'—*, to undergo (*v. irr.*) an operation.

operetta *sf.* operetta.

operistico *agg.* opera (*attr.*).

operosità *sf.* industry.

operoso *agg.* industrious.

opificio *sm.* factory.

opimo *agg.* fertile.

opinàbile *agg.* thinkable.

opinare *vi.* to think (*v. irr.*).

opinione *sf.* opinion: *secondo l'— di qu.*, in so.'s opinion.

opossum *sm.* opossum.

oppiare *vt.* to opiate.

oppiato *agg. e sm.* opiate.

oppio *sm.* opium. ✦

oppiòmane *s.* opium-addict.

opponente *agg. e sm.* opponent.

opponìbile *agg.* opposable.

opporre *vt.* 1. to oppose 2. (*obiettare*) to object. ✦ **opporsi** *vr.* to object (to), to be opposed.

opportunismo *sm.* opportunism.

opportunista *s.* opportunist.

opportunìstico *agg.* opportunistic.

opportunità *sf.* 1. (*occasione*) opportunity 2. (*l'essere opportuno*) timeliness.

opportuno *agg.* 1. opportune 2. (*giusto*) right.

oppositore *sm.* opponent.

opposizione *sf.* opposition || *fare — (a qu., qc.)*, to oppose (so., sthg.).

opposto *agg. e sm.* opposite.

oppressione *sf.* oppression.

oppressivo *agg.* oppressive.

oppresso *agg.* oppressed.

oppressore *sm.* oppressor.

opprimente *agg.* oppressive.

opprìmere *vt.* to oppress.

oppugnare *vt.* to assail.

oppure *cong.* 1. or 2. (*altrimenti*) or else.

optare *vi.* to opt.

opulento *agg.* opulent.

opulenza *sf.* opulence.

opùscolo *sm.* pamphlet.

opzione *sf.* option.

ora[1] *sf.* 1. hour 2. (*tempo*) time: *che — è?*, what time is it?; *— di punta*, rush hour; *all'—*, by the hour; *di — in —*, hourly; *di buon'—*, early; *— legale*, summer time; *non veder l'— di*, to look forward to.

ora[2] *avv.* now || *—. come —*, at the moment; *d'— in poi*, from now on; *fino ad —*, so far; *sin d'—*, now; *prima d'—*, before; *or —*, just. ✦ **ora che** *cong.* now (that).

oràcolo *sm.* oracle.

òrafo *sm.* goldsmith.

orale *agg. e sm.* oral.

oralmente *avv.* orally.

oramai *avv.* V. *ormai*.

orango *sm.* orang-outang.

orario *agg.* 1. time (*attr.*) 2. (*all'ora*) per hour. ✦ **orario** *sm.* 1. hours (*pl.*) 2. (*tabella*) time-table || *in —*, on time.

orata *sf.* dory.

oratore *sm.* orator.

oratoria *sf.* oratory.

oratorio *sm.* oratory.

orazione *sf.* 1. oration 2. (*preghiera*) prayer.

orbare *vt.* to bereave (*v. irr.*).

orbene *avv.* well.

òrbita *sf.* orbit.

orbitale *agg.* orbital.

orbo *agg.* (*di un occhio*) one-eyed.

orchestra *sf.* orchestra.

orchestrale *agg.* orchestral. ✦ **orchestrale** *s.* member of an orchestra.

orchestrare *vt.* to orchestrate.

orchestrazione *sf.* orchestration.

orchestrina *sf.* band.

orchidea *sf.* orchid.

orcio *sm.* pitcher.

orco *sm.* ogre.

orda *sf.* horde.

ordigno *sm.* device.

ordinale *agg. e sm.* ordinal.

ordinamento *sm.* 1. arrangement 2. (*regolamento*) code, system.

ordinanza *sf.* 1. order 2. (*attendente mil.*) batman (*pl.* -men).

ordinare *vt.* 1. to order 2. (*mettere in ordine*) to put (*v. irr.*) in order 3. (*eccl.*) to ordain 4. (*med.*) to prescribe. ✦ **ordinarsi** *vr.* 1. to straighten up 2. (*mil.*) to draw (*v. irr.*) up.

ordinario *agg. e sm.* ordinary.

ordinata *sf.* 1. (*mat.*) ordinate 2. (*aer.; mar.*) frame.

ordinatamente *avv.* tidily.

ordinato *agg.* tidy, orderly.

ordinazione *sf.* 1. order 2. (*med.*) prescription 3. (*eccl.*) ordination.

òrdine *sm.* order || *— d'idee*, scheme of things; *all'— del giorno*,

on the agenda; *per — di*, by order
of; *parola d'—*, password; *di pri-
m'—*, firstclass (*attr.*).
ordire *vt*. **1.** to warp **2.** (*fig.*) to
plot.
ordito *sm*. warp.
orecchiàbile *agg*. catchy.
erecchino *sm*. earring.
orecchio *sm*. ear.
orecchioni *sm*. *pl*. mumps.
oréfice *sm*. jeweller.
oreficerìa *sf*. **1.** jeweller's art **2.**
(*negozio*) jeweller's shop.
òrfano *agg*. e *sm*. orphan.
orfanotrofio *sm*. orphanage.
organetto *sm*. barrel-organ || *suo-
natore di —*, organ-grinder.
organicità *sf*. organic unity.
orgànico[1] *agg*. organic.
orgànico[2] *sm*. staff.
organismo *sm*. **1.** organism **2.** (*ente*) body.
organista *s*. organist.
organizzàbile *agg*. organizable.
organizzare *vt*. to organize.
organizzatore *sm*. organizer.
organizzazione *sf*. organization.
òrgano *sm*. organ.
organza *sf*. organza.
organzino *sm*. organzine.
orgasmo *sm*. orgasm.
orgia *sf*. orgy.
orgiàstico *agg*. orgiastic.
orgoglio *sm*. pride.
orgoglioso *agg*. proud.
orientale *agg*. eastern.
orientalista *s*. orientalist.
orientamento *sm*. orientation ||
perdere l'—, to lose (*v. irr.*) one's
bearings.
orientare *vt*. to orient. ◆ **orientarsi** *vr*. **1.** to find (*v. irr.*) one's
bearings **2.** (*tendere*) to tend.
oriente *sm*. east.
orifiamma *sf*. oriflamme.
orifizio *sm*. orifice.
orìgano *sm*. origan.
originale *agg*. **1.** original **2.** (*strano*) odd. ◆ **originale** *sm*. **1.** original **2.** (*persona eccentrica*) eccentric.
originalità *sf*. **1.** originality **2.** (*stranezza*) oddity.
originare *vt*. e *vi*. to originate.
originariamente *avv*. originally.
originario *agg*. original.
orìgine *sf*. origin || *avere —*, to
originate; *dare —*, to cause.
origliare *vi*. to eavesdrop.

orina *sf*. urine.
orinale *sm*. chamber pot.
orinare *vi*. to urinate.
orinatoio *sm*. public lavatory.
orizzontale *agg*. horizontal.
orizzontalmente *avv*. horizontally.
orizzontare *vt*., **orizzontarsi** *vr*.
V. *orientare, orientarsi*.
orizzonte *sm*. horizon.
orlare *vt*. **1.** (*bordare*) to edge **2.**
(*fare l'orlo*) to hem.
orlatura *sf*. hemming.
orlo *sm*. **1.** (*di abito ecc.*) hem **2.**
(*bordatura*) border **3.** (*estremità*)
edge **4.** (*di oggetto rotondo*) rim
|| *— a giorno*, hem-stitch; *sull'—
della rovina*, on the verge of ruin.
orma *sf*. **1.** mark **2.** (*traccia*) trace
3. (*di piede*) footprint || *seguire le
orme di qu.*, to follow in so.'s
footsteps; *tornare sulle proprie orme*, to go (*v. irr.*) back on one's
tracks.
ormai *avv*. **1.** (by) now **2.** (*al passato*) (by) then.
ormeggiare *vt*. to moor. ◆ **or-
meggiarsi** *vr*. to moor.
ormeggio *sm*. mooring.
ormone *sm*. hormone.
ormònico *agg*. hormonic.
ornamentale *agg*. ornamental.
ornamentazione *sf*. ornamentation.
ornamento *sm*. ornament.
ornare *vt*. to adorn.
ornato *agg*. **1.** adorned (with) **2.**
(*di stile*) ornate.
ornitologìa *sf*. ornithology.
ornitològico *agg*. ornithological.
ornitòlogo *sm*. ornithologist.
oro *sm*. gold || *d'—*, golden.
orografia *sf*. orography.
orogràfico *agg*. orographic(al).
orologerìa *sf*. **1.** (*arte*) horology **2.**
(*negozio*) watchmaker's shop ||
movimento d'—, clock movement.
orologiaio *sm*. watchmaker.
orologio *sm*. **1.** watch **2.** (*a muro,
da tavolo*) clock.
oròscopo *sm*. horoscope.
orpello *sm*. tinsel.
orrendamente *avv*. dreadfully.
orrendo *agg*. dreadful.
orrìbile *agg*. horrible.
orribilmente *avv*. horribly.
òrrido *agg*. frightful.
orripilante *agg*. terrifying.
orrore *sm*. horror.
orsa *sf*. she-bear: *— Maggiore*,

Great Bear; — *Minore*, Little Bear.

orsacchiotto *sm.* 1. young bear 2. (*giocattolo*) Teddy bear.

orso *sm.* bear.

ortaggio *sm.* vegetable.

ortensia *sf.* hydrangea.

ortica *sf.* nettle.

orticaria *sf.* nettle-rash.

orticultore *sm.* horticulturist.

orticultura *sf.* horticulture.

orto *sm.* 1. kitchen garden 2. (*di orticoltore*) market garden.

ortodossia *sf.* orthodoxy.

ortodosso *agg.* orthodox.

ortofruttìcolo *agg.* horticultural.

ortogonale *agg.* orthogonal.

ortografia *sf.* orthography, spelling.

ortogràfico *agg.* orthographic(al).

ortolano *sm.* 1. market-gardener 2. (*negoziante*) greengrocer.

ortopedìa *sf.* orthopedics.

ortopèdico *agg.* orthopedic. ♦ **ortopèdico** *sm.* orthopedist.

orzaiolo *sm.* sty.

orzata *sf.* (*bibita*) orgeat.

orzo *sm.* barley.

osanna *sf.* hosanna.

osare *vi.* to dare (*v. semidif.*). ♦ **osare** *vt.* (*tentare*) to attempt.

oscenità *sf.* obscenity.

osceno *agg.* obscene.

oscillare *vi.* 1. to swing (*v. irr.*) 2. (*di fiamma; opinioni*) to waver 3. (*elettr.*) to oscillate 4. (*di prezzi*) to fluctuate.

oscillatore *sm.* oscillator.

oscillatorio *agg.* oscillatory.

oscillazione *sf.* 1. swing 2. (*di fiamma; opinioni*) wavering 3. (*elettr.*) oscillation 4. (*di prezzi*) fluctuation.

oscillògrafo *sm.* oscillograph.

oscurantismo *sm.* obscurantism.

oscurantista *agg. e s.* obscurantist.

oscurare *vt.* 1. to darken 2. (*fig.*) to overshadow. ♦ **oscurarsi** *vr.* to darken.

oscurità *sf.* 1. darkness 2. (*fig.*) obscurity.

oscuro *agg.* 1. dark 2. (*sconosciuto, umile*) obscure 3. (*difficile*) hard, difficult 4. (*sconosciuto*) unknown.

osmosi *sf.* osmosis (*pl.* -ses).

ospedale *sm.* hospital.

ospedaliero *agg.* hospital (*attr.*).

ospitale *agg.* hospitable.

ospitalità *sf.* hospitality.

ospitare *vt.* to entertain.

ospite *s.* 1. (*chi ospita, uomo*) host; (*id., donna*) hostess 2. (*chi è ospitato*) guest.

ospizio *sm.* 1. (*per poveri*) alms-house 2. (*per trovatelli*) foundling hospital 3. (*per vecchi ecc.*) home (for the old etc.).

ossario *sm.* charnel-house, ossuary.

ossatura *sf.* 1. skeleton 2. (*di edificio, discorso*) framework.

òsseo *agg.* bony.

ossequente *agg.* respectful.

ossequio *sm.* 1. homage 2. (*obbedienza*) obedience 3. (*saluti*) regards (*pl.*).

ossequiosità *sf.* deference.

ossequioso *agg.* deferential.

osservàbile *agg.* observable.

osservante *agg.* observant.

osservanza *sf.* 1. observance 2. (*ossequio*) regards (*pl.*).

osservare *vt.* 1. to observe 2. (*esaminare*) to examine.

osservatore *agg.* observing. ♦ **osservatore** *sm.* observer.

osservatorio *sm.* observatory.

osservazione *sf.* 1. observation: *in* —, under observation 2. (*rimprovero*) reproach.

ossessionante *agg.* haunting.

ossessionare *vt.* to haunt.

ossessione *sf.* obsession.

ossessivo *agg.* haunting.

ossesso *sm.* person possessed.

ossìa *cong.* (*cioè*) that is.

ossidàbile *agg.* oxidizable.

ossidare *vt.* to oxidize. ♦ **ossidarsi** *vr.* to oxidize.

ossidazione *sf.* oxidation.

òssido *sm.* oxide.

ossìdrico *agg.* oxyhydrogen.

ossificare *vt.* to ossify. ♦ **ossificarsi** *vr.* to ossify.

ossificazione *sf.* ossification.

ossigenare *vt.* 1. to oxygenate 2. (*di capelli*) to peroxide.

ossigenato *agg.* 1. oxygenated 2. (*di capelli*) peroxided ‖ *acqua ossigenata*, hydrogen peroxide.

ossìgeno *sm.* oxygen.

osso *sm.* bone ‖ *in carne e ossa*, in flesh and blood; *avere le ossa rotte*, to be aching all over.

ossuto *agg.* bony.

ostacolare *vt.* to hamper.

ostàcolo *sm.* 1. obstacle 2. (*sport*) hurdle ‖ *corsa ippica ad ostacoli*, steeple-chase.

ostaggio *sm.* hostage.

oste *sm.* innkeeper.
osteggiare *vt.* to oppose.
ostello *sm.* — *della gioventù,* (youth) hostel.
ostensorio *sm.* monstrance.
ostentare *vt.* **1.** to show (*v. irr.*) off **2.** (*fingere*) to feign.
ostentatamente *avv.* ostentatiously.
ostentazione *sf.* ostentation.
osteologìa *sf.* osteology.
osterìa *sf.* pub.
ostètrica *sf.* midwife (*pl.* -wives).
ostetricia *sf.* obstetrics.
ostètrico *sm.* obstetrician.
ostia *sf.* **1.** wafer **2.** (*eccl.*) host.
òstico *agg.* **1.** irksome **2.** (*di sapore*) unpalatable **3.** (*fig.*) difficult.
ostile *agg.* hostile.
ostilità *sf.* hostility.
ostinarsi *vr.* to persist (in).
ostinato *agg.* stubborn.
ostinazione *sf.* obstinacy.
ostracismo *sm.* ostracism.
òstrica *sf.* oyster.
ostricaio *sm.* oyster-seller.
ostricultura *sf.* oyster-breeding.
ostruire *vt.* to obstruct.
ostruzione *sf.* obstruction.
ostruzionismo *sm.* obstructionism.
ostruzionista *s.* obstructionist.
otaria *sf.* otary.
otite *sf.* otitis.
otorinolaringoiatra *s.* otorhinolaryngologist.
otorinolaringoiatrìa *sf.* otorhinolaryngology.
ottaedro *sm.* octahedron.
ottagonale *agg.* octagonal.
ottàgono *sm.* octagon.
ottanta *agg.* eighty.
ottantenne *agg.* eighty years old, eighty-year-old (*attr.*).
ottantèsimo *agg.* eightieth.
ottava *sf.* octave.
ottavo *agg. e sm.* eighth.
ottemperanza *sf.* compliance.
ottemperare *vi.* to comply (with).
ottenebrare *vt.* to cloud.
ottenere *vt.* to obtain, to get (*v. irr.*).
ottetto *sm.* octet.
òttica *sf.* optics.
òttico *agg.* optic(al). ♦ **òttico** *sm.* optician.
ottimismo *sm.* optimism.
ottimista *s.* optimist.
ottimìstico *agg.* optimistic.
òttimo *agg.* best, very good. ♦ **òttimo** *sm.* optimum (*pl.* -ma).

otto *agg.* eight.
ottobre *sm.* October.
ottocento *agg.* eight hundred. ♦ **ottocento** *sm.* l'—, the nineteenth century.
ottomana *sf.* ottoman.
ottomano *agg. e sm.* Ottoman.
ottone *sm.* brass.
ottuagenario *agg. e sm.* octogenarian.
otturare *vt.* to stop. ♦ **otturarsi** *vr.* to stop.
otturatore *sm.* (*foto*) shutter.
otturazione *sf.* stopping.
ottusità *sf.* obtuseness.
ottuso *agg.* obtuse.
ovaia *sf.* ovary.
ovale *agg. e sm.* oval.
ovatta *sf.* **1.** wadding **2.** (*cotone idrofilo*) cotton-wool.
ovattare *vt.* to stuff with wadding.
ovazione *sf.* ovation.
ove *avv.* where.
ovest *sm.* west.
ovile *sm.* fold.
ovino *agg.* ovine. ♦ **ovino** *sm.* sheep (*invariato al pl.*).
ovìparo *agg.* oviparous.
ovòide *agg.* egg-shaped.
òvolo *sm.* (*fungo*) agaric.
ovulazione *sf.* ovulation.
òvulo *sm.* ovule.
ovunque *avv.* **1.** everywhere **2.** (*in qualsiasi posto*) anywhere. ♦ **o-vunque** *cong.* wherever.
ovvero *cong.* or.
ovviare *vi.* to obviate (sthg.).
ovvio *agg.* obvious.
oziare *vi.* to loaf, to idle.
ozio *sm.* idleness.
oziosamente *avv.* idly.
ozono *sm.* ozone.

P

pacare *vt.* to calm.
pacatezza *sf.* calmness.
pacato *agg.* calm.
pacca *sf.* slap.
pacchetto *sm.* packet.
pacchia *sf.* godsend.
pacchianata *sf.* coarse action.
pacchiano *agg.* coarse.
pacco *sm.* **1.** (*postale*) parcel **2.** (*collo*) package.

paccottiglia *sf.* cheap stuff.
pace *sf.* peace || *darsi* —, to set (*v. irr.*) one's mind at rest.
pachiderma *sm.* pachyderm.
pachistano *agg.* e *sm.* Pakistani.
pacificare *vt.* **1.** to pacify **2.** (*riconciliare*) to reconcile. ♦ **pacificarsi** *vr.* to become (*v. irr.*) reconciled.
pacificazione *sf.* **1.** pacification **2.** (*riconciliazione*) reconciliation.
pacifico *agg.* **1.** pacific **2.** (*evidente*) self-evident.
pacifismo *sm.* pacifism.
pacifista *s.* pacifist.
pacioccone *sm.* easy-going person.
padella *sf.* frying-pan.
padiglione *sm.* pavilion.
padre *sm.* father.
padrino *sm.* godfather.
padronale *agg.* (*privato*) private || *casa* —, manor-house.
padronanza *sf.* mastery: — *di sé*, self-control.
padrone *sm.* **1.** master **2.** (*proprietario*) owner **3.** (*di casa, albergo*) landlord || *essere* — *di sé*, to have self-control; *padronissimo!*, do as you like!
paesaggio *sm.* landscape.
paesano *agg.* rural. ♦ **paesano** *sm.* peasant.
paese *sm.* **1.** (*nazione, territorio*) country **2.** (*villaggio*) village.
paesista *s.* landscape painter.
paffuto *agg.* chubby.
paga *sf.* pay, wages (*pl.*): *libro* —, wages book; *giorno di* —, pay day.
pagàbile *agg.* payable.
pagaia *sf.* paddle.
pagamento *sm.* payment.
paganésimo *sm.* paganism.
pagano *agg.* e *sm.* pagan.
pagare *vt.* to pay (*v. irr.*).
pagella *sf.* schoolreport.
paggio *sm.* page.
pagherò *sm.* promissory note.
pàgina *sf.* page.
paglia *sf.* straw.
pagliacciata *sf.* buffoonery.
pagliaccio *sm.* clown.
pagliaio *sm.* strawstack.
pagliericcio *sm.* paillasse.
paglierino *agg.* straw-coloured.
paglietta *sf.* **1.** (*cappello*) straw-hat **2.** (*paglia di ferro*) steel-wool **3.** (*trucioli per imballaggio*) wood--shavings (*pl.*) **4.** (*trucioli, di carta*) paper-wool.

pagnotta *sf.* round loaf (*pl.* -aves).
pagoda *sf.* pagoda.
paio *sm.* **1.** (*di cose necessariamente unite*) pair **2.** (*due*) couple.
pala *sf.* **1.** shovel **2.** (*di remo, elica*) blade **3.** (*di ruota*) paddle || — *d'altare*, altar-piece.
paladino *sm.* **1.** paladin **2.** (*fig.*) champion.
palafitta *sf.* **1.** pile **2.** (*abitazione*) pile-dwelling.
palafreniere *sm.* groom.
palafreno *sm.* palfrey.
palanchino *sm.* palanquin.
palata *sf.* **1.** shovelful **2.** (*colpo*) blow with a shovel || *a palate* (*fig.*), in plenty.
palatale *agg.* palatal.
palatino *agg.* palatine.
palato *sm.* palate.
palazzo *sm.* palace.
palco *sm.* **1.** (*di teatro*) box **2.** (*pedana*) stand.
palcoscènico *sm.* stage.
paleocristiano *agg.* paleo-christian.
paleografia *sf.* paleography.
paleògrafo *sm.* paleographer.
paleontologìa *sf.* paleontology.
paleontològico *agg.* paleontologic(al).
paleontòlogo *sm.* paleontologist.
palesare *vt.* to reveal.
palese *agg.* evident.
palestra *sf.* gymnasium.
paletta *sf.* (*di capostazione*) signal stick.
palinodìa *sf.* palinode.
palissandro *sm.* rosewood.
palizzata *sf.* palisade.
palla *sf.* **1.** ball **2.** (*pallottola*) bullet.
pallacanestro *sf.* basket-ball.
pallanuoto *sf.* water-polo.
pallavolo *sf.* volley-ball.
palleggiare *vi.* (*calcio*) to dribble. ♦ **palleggiare** *vt.* to toss. ♦ **palleggiarsi** *vr. rec.* to shift on one another.
palleggio *sm.* **1.** (*calcio*) dribbling **2.** (*tennis*) tossing.
palliativo *agg.* e *sm.* palliative.
pallidezza *sf.* paleness.
pàllido *agg.* pale.
pallino *sm.* **1.** (*di fucile*) shot **2.** (*mania*) craze.
palloncino *sm.* **1.** balloon **2.** (*lampioncino*) Chinese lantern.
pallone *sm.* ball || *gioco del* —, football.

pallore *sm.* pallor.

pallòttola *sf.* 1. pellet 2. (*mil.*) bullet.

pallottoliere *sm.* abacus (*pl.* -ci).

palma[1] *sf.* (*della mano*) palm.

palma[2] *sf.* (*albero*) palm(-tree).

palmare *agg.* 1. (*anat.*) palmar 2. (*evidente*) clear.

palmato *agg.* 1. (*bot.*) palmate 2. (*zool.*) webbed.

palmeto *sm.* palm-grove.

palmìpede *agg.* e *sm.* palmiped.

palmo *sf.* palm.

palo *sm.* 1. pole 2. (*per fondamenta, ormeggio*) pile || — *indicatore,* signpost; *fare il* —, to be on the lookout.

palombaro *sm.* diver.

palpàbile *agg.* tangible.

palpare *vt.* 1. to finger 2. (*med.*) to palpate.

pàlpebra *sf.* eyelid || *battere le palpebre,* to blink.

palpitante *agg.* 1. throbbing 2. (*fig.*) fascinating.

palpitare *vi.* to throb (with sthg.).

palpitazione *sf.* 1. throbbing 2. (*med.*) palpitation.

pàlpito *sm.* throb.

paltò *sm.* overcoat.

palude *sf.* marsh.

paludoso *agg.* marshy.

pàmpino *sm.* vine-leaf (*pl.* -leaves).

panacea *sf.* panacea.

panare *vt.* to bread

panca *sf.* bench.

pancetta *sf.* 1. (*cu persona*) pot-belly.

panchina *sf.* bench.

pancia *sf.* belly.

panciera *sf.* body-belt.

panciotto *sm.* waistcoat.

panciuto *agg.* pot-bellied.

pancotto *sm.* panada.

pàncreas *sm.* pancreas.

pancreàtico *agg.* pancreatic

pandemonio *sm.* pandemonium.

pane *sm.* bread.

panegìrico *sm.* panegyric.

panetterìa *sf.* bakery.

panettiere *sm.* baker.

pànfilo *sm.* yacht.

pangermanismo *sm.* Pan-Germanism.

pànico *agg.* e *sm.* panic.

panico *sm.* (*bot.*) millet.

paniere *sm.* basket.

panificare *vi.* to make (*v. irr.*) bread.

panificazione *sf.* bread-making.

panificio *sm.* bakery.

panino *sm.* roll: — *imbottito,* sandwich.

panna[1] *sf.* cream: — *montata,* whipped cream.

panna[2] *sf.* restare in —, to have a breakdown.

pannello *sm.* 1. (*edil.*) panel 2. (*di stoffa*) light cloth.

panno *sm.* 1. cloth (*pl.* cloths) 2. *pl.* (*vestiti*) clothes.

pannocchia *sf.* cob.

pannolino *sm.* 1. (*per bambini*) napkin 2. (*assorbente igienico*) sanitary towel.

panorama *sm.* view.

panslavismo *sm.* Pan-slavism.

pantagruèlico *agg.* Pantagruelian.

pantaloni *sm. pl.* trousers || — *corti,* shorts.

pantano *sm.* 1. mire 2. (*luogo pantanoso; fig.*) quagmire.

panteismo *sm.* pantheism.

panteista *s.* pantheist.

panteìstico *agg.* pantheistic(al).

pantera *sf.* panther.

pantòfola *sf.* slipper.

pantògrafo *sm.* pantograph.

pantomima *sf.* pantomime.

panzana *sf.* fib.

paonazzo *agg.* purple.

papa *sm.* pope.

papà *sm.* daddy.

papale *agg.* papal.

papalina *sf.* skull-cap.

papato *sm.* papacy.

papàvero *sm.* poppy || *alto* —, (*fig.*) bigwig.

pàpera *sf.* 1. (*zool.*) duckling 2. (*errore*) slip 3. (*teat.*) fluff.

papilla *sf.* papilla (*pl.* -ae).

papillare *agg.* papillary.

papiro *sm.* papyrus (*pl.* -ri).

papirologìa *sf.* papyrology.

papismo *sm.* popery.

papista *s.* papist.

pappa *sf.* pap.

pappagallo *sm.* parrot || *ripetere a* —, to parrot.

pappagorgia *sf.* double chin.

pappare *vt.* to gorge. ♦ **papparsi** *vr.* to eat up.

pàprica *sf.* paprika.

paràbola *sf.* 1. parable 2. (*geom.; mil.*) parabola.

parabòlico *agg.* parabolic.

parabrezza *sm.* windscreen.

paracadutare *vt.* to parachute. ♦

paracadutarsi *vr.* to bail out.
paracadute *sm.* parachute.
paracadutismo *sm.* parachutism.
paracadutista *sm.* **1.** parachutist **2.** (*mil.*) paratrooper.
paracarro *sm.* wayside post.
paradigma *sm.* paradigm.
paradisìaco *agg.* paradisiac(al).
paradiso *sm.* paradise.
paradossale *agg.* paradoxical.
paradosso *sm.* paradox.
parafango *sm.* mudguard.
paraffina *sf.* paraffin.
parafrasare *vt.* to paraphrase.
paràfrasi *sf.* paraphrase.
parafùlmine *sm.* lightning-rod.
paragonàbile *agg.* comparable.
paragonare *vt.* to compare.
paragone *sm.* comparison: *a — di*, in comparison with.
paràgrafo *sm.* paragraph.
paràlisi *sf.* palsy.
paralìtico *agg.* e *sm.* paralytic.
paralizzare *vt.* to paralyze.
parallela *sf.* parallel: *le parallele* (*sport*), parallel bars.
parallelepìpedo *sm.* parallelepiped (*pl.* -da).
parallelismo *sm.* parallelism.
parallelo *agg.* e *sm.* parallel.
parallelogrammo *sm.* parallelogram.
paralume *sm.* lamp-shade.
paramento *sm.* **1.** hanging **2.** (*eccl.*) vestment.
paràmetro *sm.* parameter.
paraninfo *sm.* paranymph.
paranoìa *sf.* paranoia.
paranòico *agg.* e *sm.* paranoiac.
paraocchi *sm. pl.* blinkers.
parapetto *sm.* **1.** parapet **2.** (*davanzale*) sill.
parapiglia *sm.* turmoil.
parapioggia *sm.* umbrella.
parare *vt.* **1.** (*riparare*) to shield **2.** (*evitare*) to parry **3.** (*ornare*) to decorate || *andare a —*, to drive (*v. irr.*) at. ♦ **pararsi** *vr.* **1.** (*comparire*) to appear **2.** (*adornarsi*) to deck oneself.
parasole *sm.* parasol.
parassita *agg.* parasitic. ♦ **parassita** *s.* parasite.
parassitismo *sm.* parasitism.
parastatale *agg.* State controlled || *ente —*, semi-governmental body.
parata *sf.* **1.** parade **2.** (*sport*) parry || *fare una —* (*sport*), to parry.
paratìa *sf.* bulkhead.

paratifo *sm.* paratyphoid.
parato *sm.* hanging || *carta da parati*, wallpaper.
paratoia *sf.* cataract.
paraurti *sm.* bumper.
paravento *sm.* screen.
parcella *sf.* fee.
parcheggiare *vt.* to park.
parcheggio *sm.* **1.** parking **2.** (*luogo*) car park.
parco[1] *sm.* park: *— di divertimenti*, fun-fair.
parco[2] *agg.* sparing.
parecchio *agg.* quite a lot of. ♦ **parecchio** *avv.* quite a lot, quite (+ *agg.*). ♦ **parecchio** *pron.* a good deal of it, several (*pl.*).
pareggiare *vt.* **1.** (*livellare*) to level **2.** (*comm.*) to balance **3.** (*parificare una scuola*) to recognize officially. ♦ **pareggiare** *vi.* (*sport*) to draw (*v. irr.*).
pareggio *sm.* **1.** (*comm.*) balance **2.** (*sport*) draw, tie.
parentado *sm.* V. *parentela*.
parente *sm.* relative.
parentela *sf.* **1.** relationship **2.** (*i parenti*) relatives.
parèntesi *sf.* **1.** parenthesis (*pl.* -ses) **2.** (*segno grafico*) bracket.
parere[1] *vi.* **1.** to seem **2.** (*essere simile a*) to look like **3.** (*pensare*) to think (*v. irr.*) (of).
parere[2] *sm.* opinion.
paresi *sf.* paresis.
parete *sf.* wall: *— divisoria*, partition.
pàrgolo *sm.* little child (*pl.* children).
pari *agg.* **1.** equal, same **2.** (*simile*) like **3.** (*divisibile per due*) even. ♦ **pari** *sm.* equal, peer.
paria *sm.* pariah.
parietale *agg.* parietal.
parificazione *sf.* **1.** (*comm.*) balance **2.** (*scuola*) official recognition **3.** (*livellamento*) levelling.
parigino *agg.* e *sm.* Parisian.
pariglia *sf.* pair.
parimenti *avv.* likewise.
parità *sf.* equality.
paritario *agg.* equalitarian.
parlamentare[1] *agg.* parliamentary. ♦ **parlamentare** *sm.* Member of Parliament.
parlamentare[2] *vi.* to parley.
parlamentarismo *sm.* parliamentarianism.

parlamento *sm.* parliament.
parlantina *sf.* talkativeness || *aver buona* —, to be a glib talker.
parlare *vi.* to speak (*v. irr.*), to talk.
parlare *sm.* 1. (*discorso*) speech 2. (*chiacchiere*) talk 3. (*idioma*) language.
parlato *agg. cinema* —, talkies (*pl.*).
parlatore *sm.* speaker.
parlatorio *sm.* parlour.
parlottare *vi.* to mutter.
parodìa *sf.* parody.
parodiare *vt.* to parody.
parodista *s.* parodist.
parola *sf.* 1. word 2. (*facoltà di parlare, discorso*) speech || *parole incrociate,* crosswords; *gioco di parole,* pun; *far* —, to mention; *restare senza* —, to be left speechless; *venire a parole con,* to have words with; *rivolgere la* — *a qu.,* to address so.; *avere la* — *facile,* to be a glib talker.
parolaccia *sf.* nasty word: *dire parolacce,* to swear (*v. irr.*).
parolaio *sm.* 1. chatterbox 2. (*di scrittore*) word-monger.
paroliere *sm.* « lyrics » writer.
parossismo *sm.* paroxysm.
paròtide *sf.* parotid.
parricida *s.* parricide.
parricidio *sm.* parricide.
parrocchia *sf.* parish.
parrocchiale *agg.* parish (*attr.*).
parrocchiano *sm.* parishioner.
pàrroco *sm.* 1. (*cattolico*) parish priest 2. (*protestante*) parson.
parrucca *sf.* wig.
parrucchiere *sm.* hairdresser.
parsimonia *sf.* thriftiness.
parsimonioso *agg.* thrifty.
parte *sf.* 1. part 2. (*lato*) side 3. (*porzione*) share 4. (*pol.; comm.; giur.*) party || *da* —, aside: *da* — *di,* from; *da* — *a* —, right through; *da una* — ... *dall'altra,* on one hand ... on the other; *la maggior* — *di,* most (of); *a* — *ciò,* apart from that; *farsi da* —, to get (*v. irr.*) out of the way; *fare la* — *di,* to play.
partecipante *s.* 1. sharer 2. (*chi annuncia*) spokesman (*pl.* -men) 3. (*chi presenzia*) the bystander.
partecipare *vi.* 1. to share (in) 2. (*esser presente*) to be present. ♦ **partecipare** *vt.* to announce.
partecipazione *sf.* 1. sharing 2.

(*esser presente*) presence 3. (*annuncio*) announcement 4. (*biglietto*) card.
partécipe *agg.* 1. sharing 2. (*informato*) acquainted || *rendere* — *qu. di qc.,* to acquaint so. with sthg.
parteggiare *vi.* to take (*v. irr.*) sides (with).
partenogènesi *sf.* parthenogenesis.
partenza *sf.* 1. departure, leaving 2. (*sport*) start || *punto di* —, starting-point; *essere in* —, to be leaving.
particella *sf.* particle.
participiale *agg.* participial.
participio *sm.* participle.
particolare *agg.* particular. ♦ **particolare** *sm.* detail.
particolareggiato *agg.* detailed.
particolarismo *sm.* particularism.
particolarità *sf.* 1. particularity 2. (*dettaglio*) detail.
partigiano *agg. e sm.* partisan.
partire[1] *vi.* 1. to leave (*v. irr.*) 2. (*muoversi, iniziare, anche fig.*) to start || *a* — *da,* (beginning) from.
partire[2] *vt.* to separate.
partita *sf.* 1. (*giocata*) game, match 2. (*di merce*) lot 3. (*in contabilità*) entry || *dar* — *vinta* (*fig.*), to give (*v. irr.*) in.
partitivo *agg. e sm.* partitive.
partito *sm.* party.
partitura *sf.* (*mus.*) score.
partizione *sf.* division.
parto *sm.* 1. delivery 2. (*fig.*) product.
partoriente *agg.* parturient. ♦ **partoriente** *sf.* lying-in woman.
partorire *vt.* to bring (*v. irr.*) forth, to beget (*v. irr.*) (*anche fig.*).
parvenza *sf.* 1. appearance 2. (*ombra*) shadow.
parziale *agg.* partial.
parzialità *sf.* partiality.
parzialmente *avv.* partially.
pàscere *vt. e vi.* 1. to feed (*v. irr.*) 2. (*al pascolo*) to graze. ♦ **pàscersi** *vr.* to feed (on).
pascià *sm.* pasha.
pasciuto *agg.* fed.
pascolare *vt. e vi.* to pasture.
pàscolo *sm.* pasture || *essere al* —, to be grazing.
Pasqua *sf.* Easter.
pasquale *agg.* Easter (*attr.*).
passàbile *agg.* passabl-

passabilmente *avv.* passably.
passaggio *sm.* **1.** passage **2.** (*traversata*) crossing || *dare un — in macchina*, to give (*v. irr.*) a lift; *vietato il —*, no thoroughfare; *di —*, of transition; (*incidentalmente*) incidentally.
passamanerìa *sf.* passementerie.
passamano *sm.* (*fettuccia*) braid.
passamontagna *sm.* snow-cap.
passante *sm.* **1.** (*di cinghia ecc.*) loop **2.** (*persona*) passer-by.
passaporto *sm.* passport.
passare *vi.* **1.** to pass **2.** (*andare*) to call (on so., at sthg.). ♦ **passare** *vt.* **1.** to pass **2.** (*di tempo*) to spend (*v. irr.*) **3.** (*sopportare, trafiggere*) to pass through.
passatempo *sm.* pastime.
passatista *s.* traditionalist.
passato *agg.* **1.** past **2.** (*scorso*) last. ♦ **passato** *sm.* **1.** past **2.** (*cuc.*) mash.
passaverdura *sm.* vegetable masher.
passeggero *agg.* passing. ♦ **passeggero** *sm.* passenger.
passeggiare *vi.* to walk, to take (*v. irr.*) a walk.
passeggiata *sf.* **1.** walk **2.** (*in auto*) drive **3.** (*in bicicletta, a cavallo*) ride **4.** (*lungomare*) promenade.
passeggino *sm.* perambulator.
passeggio *sm.* **1.** walk **2.** (*gente che passeggia*) promenaders (*pl.*) || *andare a —*, to go (*v. irr.*) for a walk.
passeràceo *sm. e agg.* passerine.
passerella *sf.* **1.** (*ponte pedonale*) footbridge **2.** (*provvisoria*) trestle-bridge **3.** (*mar.; edil.*) gangway **4.** (*teat.*) parade.
pàssero *sm.* sparrow.
passìbile *agg.* liable (to).
passiflora *sf.* passion-flower.
passino *sm.* strainer.
passionale *agg.* **1.** passional **2.** (*appassionato*) passionate.
passione *sf.* passion.
passivamente *avv.* passively.
passività *sf.* **1.** passivity **2.** (*comm.*) liabilities (*pl.*).
passivo *agg.* passive. ♦ **passivo** *sm.* **1.** passive **2.** (*comm.*) liabilities (*pl.*).
passo *sm.* **1.** step **2.** (*andatura*) pace **3.** (*di montagna*) pass **4.** (*brano, passaggio*) passage **5.** (*cine*)

gauge **6.** (*tec.*) pitch || *passo passo*, very slowly; *segnare il —*, to mark time; *camminare a grandi passi*, to stride (*v. irr.*).
pasta *sf.* **1.** paste **2.** (*pasticcino*) cake **3.** (*per minestre*) "pasta".
pasteggiare *vi.* to feed (*v. irr.*) (on).
pastella *sf.* (*cuc.*) batter.
pastello *sm.* pastel: *matita, disegno a —*, pastel.
pasticca *sf.* tablet.
pasticcerìa *sf.* confectionery.
pasticciare *vt. e vi.* to make (*v. irr.*) a mess (of).
pasticciere *sm.* confectioner.
pasticcino *sm.* cake.
pasticcio *sm.* **1.** (*cuc.*) pie **2.** (*fig.*) mess || *essere nei pasticci*, to be in trouble.
pasticcione *sm.* bungler.
pastificio *sm.* « pasta » factory.
pastiglia *sf.* tablet.
pasto *sm.* meal.
pastoia *sf.* hobble.
pastone *sm.* mash.
pastorale *agg.* pastoral.
pastore *sm.* **1.** shepherd **2.** (*relig.*) parson.
pastorizia *sf.* stock-raising.
pastorizzare *vt.* to pasteurize.
pastorizzazione *sf.* pasteurization.
pastosità *sf.* **1.** mellowness **2.** (*morbidezza*) doughiness.
pastoso *agg.* **1.** mellow **2.** (*morbido*) doughy.
pastrano *sm.* overcoat.
pastura *sf.* pasture.
patacca *sf.* **1.** (*macchia*) spot **2.** (*cosa senza valore*) worthless object.
patata *sf.* potato: *— americana*, sweet potato || *— fritta*, chip; (*id., croccante*) crisp.
patema *sm.* worry.
patentato *agg.* licenced.
patente *agg.* patent. ♦ **patente** *sf.* licence.
patereccio *sm.* whitlow.
paternale *sf.* scolding || *fare una — a qu.*, to lecture so.
paternalismo *sm.* paternalism.
paternalistico *agg.* paternalistic.
paternità *sf.* paternity.
paterno *agg.* paternal.
pateticamente *avv.* pathetically.
patètico *agg. e sm.* pathetic.
patibolare *agg.* sinister.
patìbolo *sm.* scaffold.
patimento *sm.* pain.
pàtina *sf.* **1.** patina **2.** (*di vernice*)

coat of varnish **3.** (*sulla lingua*) coat **4.** (*su carta, terracotta*) glaze.

patinare *vt.* **1.** to varnish **2.** (*carta, terracotta*) to glaze.

patire *vt. e vi.* to suffer: — *il freddo*, to suffer from the cold || — *la fame*, to starve.

patito *agg.* sickly. ♦ **patito** *sm.* (*fig.*) fan.

patògeno *agg.* pathogenic.

patologìa *sf.* pathology.

patològico *agg.* pathologic(al).

patòlogo *sm.* pathologist.

patria *sf.* **1.** country, fatherland **2.** (*luogo natale*) birthplace.

patriarca *sm.* patriarch.

patriarcale *agg.* patriarchal.

patriarcato *sm.* patriarchate.

patricida *s.* V. *parricida.*

patrigno *sm.* stepfather.

patrimoniale *agg.* patrimonial.

patrimonio *sm.* patrimony.

patrio *agg.* **1.** native **2.** (*paterno*) paternal.

patriota *s.* patriot.

patriottardo *sm. e agg.* jingoist.

patriòttico *agg.* patriotic.

patriottismo *sm.* patriotism.

patriziato *sm.* patriciate.

patrizio *sm. e agg.* patrician.

patrocinante *sm.* pleader.

patrocinare *vt.* **1.** (*sostenere*) to support **2.** (*giur.*) to plead.

patrocinio *sm.* **1.** support **2.** (*giur.*) pleading.

patronato *sm.* **1.** patronage **2.** (*istituto benefico*) charitable institution.

patronessa *sf.* patroness.

patrono *sm.* **1.** patron **2.** (*giur.*) counsel for the defence.

patteggiare *vi.* to come (*v. irr.*) to terms.

pattinaggio *sm.* skating.

pattinare *vi.* to skate.

pattinatore *sm.* skater.

pàttino *sm.* **1.** (*a rotelle*) roller--skate **2.** (*da ghiaccio*) ice-skate **3.** (*di slitta*) shoe **4.** (*aer.*) skid **5.** (*mecc.*) sliding-block.

patto *sm.* **1.** agreement, pact **2.** (*condizione*) term || *a — che*, provided that; *a nessun —*, by no means.

pattuglia *sf.* patrol.

pattugliare *vi.* to patrol.

pattuire *vi.* to reach an agreement (upon). ♦ **pattuire** *vt.* to agree (on).

pattume *sm.* rubbish.

pattumiera *sf.* dust-bin.

pauperismo *sm.* pauperism.

paura *sf.* **1.** fear, dread **2.** (*spavento*) fright, scare.

pauroso *agg.* fearful.

pàusa *sf.* pause.

pavesare *vt.* to dress (with flags).

pavese *sm.* (*mar.*) hoist.

pavimentare *vt.* **1.** to pave **2.** (*una stanza*) to floor.

pavimento *sm.* floor.

pavone *sm.* peacock.

pavoneggiarsi *vr.* to show (*v. irr.*) off.

pazientare *vi.* to have patience.

paziente *agg. e sm.* patient.

pazienza *sf.* patience || —*!*, never mind!

pazzesco *agg.* foolish.

pazzìa *sf.* **1.** madness **2.** (*azione, idea pazza*) folly || *fare pazzie*, to act like a fool.

pazzo *agg.* mad. ♦ **pazzo** *sm.* madman (*pl.* -men).

pecca *sf.* fault || *senza —*, faultless.

peccaminoso *agg.* sinful.

peccare *vi.* **1.** to sin **2.** (*errare*) to err **3.** (*esser manchevole*) to lack (sthg.).

peccato *sm.* sin || *che —!*, what a pity!; *è un — che*, it is a pity that.

peccatore *sm.* sinner.

pece *sf.* pitch.

pècora *sf.* **1.** sheep (*pl. invariato*) **2.** (*femmina*) ewe.

pecoraio *sm.* shepherd.

peculato *sm.* peculation.

peculiare *agg.* peculiar.

peculiarità *sf.* peculiarity.

peculio *sm.* money.

pecuniario *agg.* pecuniary.

pedaggio *sm.* toll.

pedagogìa *sf.* pedagogy.

pedagògico *agg.* pedagogic(al).

pedagogista *s.* pedagogist.

pedagogo *sm.* pedagogue.

pedalare *vi.* to pedal.

pedale *sm.* pedal.

pedaliera *sf.* **1.** (*aer.*) rudder-bar **2.** (*mus.*) pedal keyboard.

pedana *sf.* **1.** (*sport*) spring-board **2.** (*piedistallo*) stand.

pedante *agg.* pedantic. ♦ **pedante** *s.* pedant.

pedanterìa *sf.* pedantry.

pedantesco *agg.* pedantic.

pedata *sf.* **1.** kick **2.** (*impronta*) footprint.

pedemontano *agg.* piedmont.
pederasta *sm.* homosexual.
pederastìa *sf.* homosexuality.
pedestre *agg.* pedestrian.
pediatra *s.* pediatrist.
pediatrìa *sf.* pediatrics.
pedicure *s.* chiropodist.
pediluvio *sm.* foot-bath.
pedina *sf.* **1.** (*alla dama*) piece **2.** (*agli scacchi*) pawn || *muovere una* — (*anche fig.*), to make (*v. irr.*) a move.
pedinare *vt.* to shadow.
pedonale *agg.* pedestrian (*attr.*): *passaggio* —, pedestrian crossing.
pedone *sm.* pedestrian || *strada riservata ai pedoni*, footpath.
pedùncolo *sm.* stalk.
peggio *agg.* (*comp.*) worse. ♦ **peggio** *sm.* the worst. ♦ **peggio** *avv.* **1.** (*comp.*) worse **2.** (*superl. rel.*) the worst || — *per lui*, so much the worse for him; *alla* —, at worst; *avere la* —, to get (*v. irr.*) the worst of it.
peggioramento *sm.* aggravation.
peggiorare *vt.* to make (*v. irr.*) worse. ♦ **peggiorare** *vi.* to get (*v. irr.*) worse.
peggiorativo *agg. e sm.* pejorative.
peggiore *agg.* **1.** (*comp.*) worse: *questo libro è* — *di quello*, this book is worse than that **2.** (*superl. rel.*) the worst: *era il suo* — *nemico*, he was his worst enemy.
pegno *sm.* pledge || *dare qc. in* —, to pledge sthg.; *polizza di* —, pawn-ticket; *agenzia di pegni*, pawnshop.
pelàgico *agg.* pelagic.
pelame *sm.* hair.
pelapatate *sm.* potato peeler.
pelare *vt.* **1.** to unhair **2.** (*sbucciare*) to peel **3.** (*spellare*) to skin **4.** (*far pagare caro*) to fleece. ♦ **pelarsi** *vr.* to lose (*v. irr.*) one's hair.
pelato *agg.* bald.
pelatura *sf.* **1.** unhairing **2.** (*sbucciatura*) peeling.
pellaio *sm.* furrier.
pellame *sm.* hides (*pl.*).
pelle *sf.* skin; (*di animale grosso*) hide || *articoli in* —, leather articles; *amici per la* —, bosom friends.
pellegrina *sf.* (*mantella*) tippet.
pellegrinaggio *sm.* pilgrimage: *in* —, on a pilgrimage.

pellegrinare *vi.* to wander, to roam.
pellegrino *sm.* pilgrim.
pellerossa *agg. e sm.* redskin.
pelletterìa *sf.* **1.** leather goods **2.** (*negozio*) leather goods shop.
pellicano *sm.* pelican.
pelliccerìa *sf.* **1.** furriery **2.** (*negozio*) furrier's shop
pelliccia *sf.* fur.
pellicciaio *sm.* furrier.
pellicola *sf.* film: — *a passo ridotto*, substandard film.
pelo *sm.* hair: *per un* —, by a hair's breadth; *cercare il* — *nell'uovo*, to split (*v. irr.*) hairs || *non avere peli sulla lingua*, to be outspoken.
peloso *agg.* hairy.
pelota *sf.* pelota.
peltro *sm.* pewter.
peluria *sf.* down || *coperto di* —, downy.
pelvi *sf.* pelvis.
pèlvico *agg.* pelvic.
pena *sf.* **1.** (*punizione*) punishment **2.** (*dolore*) pain **3.** (*disturbo*) trouble || *essere in* —, to worry; *aver* — *di*, to pity; *a mala* —, hardly; *non ne vale la* —, it is not worth while.
penale *agg.* **1.** criminal **2.** (*relativo alla pena*) penal.
penalista *sm.* criminal lawyer.
penalità *sf.* penalty.
penalizzare *vt.* to penalize.
penare *vi.* **1.** to suffer **2.** (*far fatica*) to be hardly able.
pendaglio *sm.* pendant.
pendente *agg.* **1.** pendent **2.** (*inclinato*) leaning. ♦ **pendente** *sm.* pendant.
pendenza *sf.* **1.** slope **2.** (*grado d'inclinazione*) gradient **3.** (*giur.*) pending suit **4.** (*comm.*) outstanding account.
pèndere *vi.* **1.** to hang (*v. irr.*) **2.** (*inclinare*) to lean (*v. irr.*) **3.** (*essere in declino*) to slope **4.** (*incombere*) to overhang (*v. irr.*) **5.** (*essere incerto*) to waver.
pendìo *sm.* slope.
pèndola *sf.* pendulum-clock.
pendolare *agg.* pendular.
pèndolo *sm.* pendulum.
pèndulo *agg.* pendulous.
pene *sm.* penis.
penetràbile *agg.* penetrable.
penetrabilità *sf.* penetrability.

penetrante agg. piercing.
penetrare vi. e vt. 1. to penetrate 2. (con fatica; di freddo, suono) to pierce 3. (furtivamente) to steal (v. irr.) (into).
penetrazione sf. penetration.
penicillina sf. penicillin.
peninsulare agg. peninsular.
penìsola sf. peninsula.
penitente agg. e s. penitent.
penitenza sf. 1. (teol.) penance 2. (pentimento) repentance 3. (nei giochi) forfeit.
penitenziale agg. penitential.
penitenziario agg. penitentiary. ◆ penitenziario sm. jail.
penna sf. 1. pen 2. (di uccello) feather.
pennacchio sm. 1. plume 2. (mil.) panache.
pennecchio sm. wool on the distaff.
pennellare vi. 1. to brush 2. (med.) to paint.
pennellata sf. touch (of the brush).
pennellessa sf. flat brush.
pennello sm. brush.
pennino sm. nib.
pennone sm. (mar.) yard.
pennuto agg. feathered. ◆ pennuto sm. bird.
penombra sf. half-light
penoso agg. painful.
pensare vi. e vt. 1. to think (v. irr.) (of) 2. (badare) to look after || pensa ai fatti tuoi, mind your own business.
pensata sf. thought, idea.
pensatore sm. thinker.
pensiero sm. 1. thought 2. (opinione) mind, opinion 3. (ansia) worry.
pensieroso agg. thoughtful.
pènsile agg. hanging || giardino —, roof garden.
pensilina sf. 1. penthouse 2. (di attesa) shelter.
pensionàbile agg. pensionable.
pensionante s. boarder.
pensionato[1] agg. retired. ◆ pensionato sm. pensioner, retired person.
pensionato[2] sm. (istituto) hostel.
pensione sf. 1. (assegno vitalizio) pension || essere in —, to be retired; mettere in —, to pension off 2. (albergo) boarding-house || essere a —, to be boarding (at); — completa, full board.

pensoso agg. pensive.
pentaedro sm. pentahedron.
pentàgono sm. pentagon.
pentagramma sm. (mus.) pentagram.
pentàmetro sm. pentameter.
pentano sm. pentane.
Pentecoste sf. Pentecost, Whitsunday.
pentimento sm. repentance.
pentirsi vr. 1. to repent 2. (rimpiangere) to regret.
pèntodo sm. pentode.
péntola sf. pot.
penùltimo agg. e sm. last but one.
penuria sf. shortage, penury.
penzolare vi. to dangle.
penzoloni agg. 1. (dondolante) dangling 2. (pèndente) hanging.
peocio sm. mussel.
peonia sf. peony.
pepaiola sf. pepper-box.
pepare vt. to pepper.
pepato agg. peppery (anche fig.).
pepe sm. pepper.
peperone sm. pepper: peperoni sott'aceto, pickled peppers.
pepita sf. nugget.
peplo sm. peplum.
pepsina sf. pepsin.
peptone sm. peptone.
per prep. 1. for: fallo — me, do it for me 2. (moto per luogo) through: passai per Roma, I passed through Rome 3. (entro, per mezzo di) by: devo farlo — la fine dell'anno, I have to do it by the end of the year; — telegramma, by telegram 4. (causa) owing to, because of: non potemmo andare — la nebbia, we couldn't go owing to (because of) fog || — l'addietro, in the past; — caso, by chance; — nulla, not at all; — sempre, for ever; — tempo, early. ◆ per cong. 1. (finale) to, in order to 2. (causale) for.
pera sf. pear.
peràcido sm. peracid.
perbacco inter. by Jove.
perbene agg. respectable.
percalle sm. percale.
percentuale agg. per cent. ◆ percentuale sf. percentage.
percepìbile agg. 1. perceptible 2. (di somme) receivable.
percepire vt. 1. to perceive 2. (di stipendio) to receive.

percettìbile *agg.* perceptible.
percettivo *agg.* perceptive.
percezione *sf.* perception.
perché *cong.* 1. (*int.*) why 2. (*nelle risposte*) because 3. (*affinché*) so that. ♦ perché *sm.* reason, why: *chiedersi il* —, to wonder why.
perciò *cong.* therefore, so.
perclorato *sm.* perchlorate.
percòrrere *vt.* 1. to cover 2. (*attraversare*) to run (*v. irr.*) through.
percorso *sm.* 1. (*distanza*) distance 2. (*tragitto*) way 3. (*tracciato*) course.
percossa *sf.* blow.
percuòtere *vt.* to strike (*v. irr.*).
percussione *sf.* percussion.
percussore *sm.* percussion-pin.
perdente *agg.* losing. ♦ perdente *s.* loser.
pèrdere *vt.* 1. to lose (*v. irr.*) 2. (*di treno, occasione*) to miss 3. (*far acqua*) to leak. ♦ pèrdersi *vr.* 1. to get (*v. irr.*) lost 2. (*svanire*) to fade 3. (*rovinarsi*) to be ruined || — *d'animo*, to lose heart.
perdifiato (*nella loc. avv.*) *a* —, with all one's strength.
perdigiorno *sm.* idler.
pèrdita *sf.* 1. loss 2. (*falla, fuga*) leak.
perditempo *sm.* waste of time.
perdizione *sf.* perdition.
perdonàbile *agg.* pardonable.
perdonare *vt.* 1. to forgive (*v. irr.*) 2. (*risparmiare*) to spare. ♦ perdonarsi *vr.* to forgive oneself. ♦ perdonarsi *v. rec.* to forgive each other (one another).
perdono *sm.* forgiveness || *chiedere* —, to beg one's pardon.
perdurare *vi.* to continue.
perdutamente *avv.* desperately.
perduto *agg.* lost.
peregrinare *vi.* to wander, to roam.
peregrinazione *sf.* wandering, roaming.
peregrino *agg.* rare.
perenne *agg.* 1. perennial 2. (*eterno*) everlasting.
perennemente *avv.* 1. perennially 2. (*per sempre*) for ever.
perentorio *agg.* peremptory.
perequazione *sf.* equalization.
perfettamente *avv.* perfectly.
perfettìbile *agg.* perfectible.
perfettìbilità *sf.* perfectibility.
perfetto *agg.* perfect. ◄ perfetto

sm. (*gramm.*) perfect.
perfezionamento *sm.* perfecting.
perfezionare *vt.* 1. to perfect 2. (*migliorare*) to improve. ♦ perfezionarsi *vr.* to improve.
perfezione *sf.* perfection: *alla* —, to perfection.
perfidamente *avv.* wickedly.
perfidia *sf.* wickedness.
pèrfido *agg.* wicked.
perfino *avv.* even.
perforare *vt.* 1. to pierce 2. (*d biglietti, schede*) to punch 3. (*mecc.*) to drill, to bore.
perforatore *agg.* perforating. ♦ perforatore *sm.* perforator.
perforatrice *sf.* (*macchina*) drill; punch.
perforazione *sf.* 1. perforation 2. (*mecc.*) drilling 3. (*di biglietti, schede*) punching.
pergamena *sf.* parchment.
pèrgola *sf.* bower.
pergolato *sm.* arbour.
pericardio *sm.* pericardium (*pl.* -ia).
pericolante *agg.* tottering.
perìcolo *sm.* danger || *mettere in* —, to endanger; *correre un* —, to be in danger.
pericolosamente *avv.* dangerously.
pericoloso *agg.* dangerous.
periferìa *sf.* 1. periphery 2. (*di città*) suburbs (*pl.*).
perifèrico *agg.* 1. peripheral 2. (*suburbano*) suburban.
perìfrasi *sf.* periphrasis (*pl.* -ses).
perifràstico *agg.* periphrastic.
perigeo *sm.* perigee.
perimetro *sm.* perimeter.
periodicità *sf.* periodicity.
periòdico *agg.* e *sm.* periodical.
perìodo *sm.* period.
peripezìa *sf.* vicissitude.
pèriplo *sm.* circumnavigation.
perire *vi.* to perish.
periscopio *sm.* periscope.
peristìlio *sm.* peristyle.
perito *sm.* 1. expert 2. (*comm.*) estimator.
peritonite *sf.* peritonitis.
perituro *agg.* perishable.
perizia *sf.* 1. (*abilità*) skill 2. (*valutazione*) survey.
perla *sf.* pearl.
perlàceo *agg.* pearly.
perlìfero *agg.* pearl (*attr.*).
perlomeno *avv.* at least.
perlustrare *vt.* 1. to reconnoitre 2. (*di polizia*) to patrol.

perlustratore *sm.* scout.
perlustrazione *sf.* **1.** reconnaissance **2.** (*di polizia*) patrol || *essere in* —, to be on a reconnaissance.
permalosità *sf.* touchiness.
permaloso *agg.* touchy.
permanente *agg.* permanent. ♦ permanente *sf.* permanent wave.
permanentemente *avv.* permanently.
permanenza *sf.* **1.** permanence **2.** (*soggiorno*) stay.
permanere *vi.* **1.** to remain **2.** (*durare*) to last.
permanganato *sm.* permanganate.
permeàbile *agg.* permeable.
permeabilità *sf.* permeability.
permeare *vt.* to permeate.
permesso *agg.* allowed. ♦ permesso *sm.* **1.** leave: *in* —, on leave **2.** (*autorizzazione*) licence || *documento di* —, permit.
perméttere *vt.* to allow || *permettete?*, may I? ♦ perméttersi *vr.* (*prendersi la libertà*) to take (*v. irr.*) the liberty (of) || — *il lusso*, to afford.
pèrmuta *sf.* exchange.
permutàbile *agg.* exchangeable.
permutare *vt.* to exchange.
permutazione *sf.* permutation.
pernice *sf.* partridge.
pernicioso *agg.* pernicious.
perno *sm.* pivot.
pernottamento *sm.* overnight stay.
pernottare *vi.* to stay overnight.
pero *sm.* pear-tree.
però *cong.* but.
peronòspora *sf.* mildew.
perorare *vt.* to plead.
perorazione *sf.* pleading.
peròssido *sm.* peroxide.
perpendicolare *agg.* e *sf.* perpendicular.
perpetrare *vt.* to perpetrate.
perpetuamente *avv.* perpetually.
perpetuare *vt.* to perpetuate. ♦ perpetuarsi *vr.* to last.
perpetuità *sf.* perpetuity.
perpetuo *agg.* perpetual: *in* —, perpetually.
perplessità *sf.* perplexity.
perplesso *agg.* perplexed: *rendere* —, to perplex.
perquisire *vt.* to search.
perquisizione *sf.* search.
persecutore *sm.* persecutor.
persecuzione *sf.* persecution.
perseguìbile *agg.* (*giur.*) prosecu-

table.
perseguire *vt.* **1.** to pursue **2.** (*giur.*) to prosecute.
perseguitare *vt.* to persecute.
perseguitato *sm.* persecuted person.
perseverante *agg.* persevering.
perseveranza *sf.* perseverance.
perseverare *vi.* to persevere.
persiana *sf.* shutter.
persiano *agg.* e *sm.* Persian.
persistente *agg.* persistent.
persistenza *sf.* persistence.
persìstere *vi.* to persist.
persona *sf.* person: *di* —, personally; — *giuridica*, artificial person.
personaggio *sm.* **1.** personage **2.** (*di romanzo ecc.*) character.
personale *agg.* personal. ♦ personale *sm.* **1.** staff **2.** (*corporatura*) figure.
personalità *sf.* personality: — *giuridica*, legal status.
personalmente *avv.* personally.
personificare *vt.* **1.** to personify **2.** (*teat.*) to play.
personificazione *sf.* personification.
perspicace *agg.* shrewd.
perspicacia *sf.* shrewdness.
perspicuo *agg.* perspicuous.
persuadere *vt.* to persuade. ♦ persuadersi *vr.* to convince oneself.
persuasione *sf.* persuasion.
persuasivo *agg.* persuasive.
pertanto *cong.* therefore.
pèrtica *sf.* perch.
pertinace *agg.* pertinacious.
pertinacia *sf.* pertinacity.
pertinente *agg.* pertinent.
pertinenza *sf.* pertinence.
pertosse *sf.* whooping cough.
pertugio *sm.* hole.
perturbare *vt.* to disturb.
perturbatore *agg.* disturbing. ♦ perturbatore *sm.* disturber.
perturbazione *sf.* disturbance.
pervàdere *vt.* to pervade.
pervenire *vi.* to arrive (at).
perversione *sf.* perversion.
perversità *sf.* perversity.
perverso *agg.* perverse.
pervertire *vt.* to pervert. ♦ pervertirsi *vr.* to go (*v. irr.*) astray.
pervicace *agg.* obstinate.
pervicacia *sf.* obstinacy.
pervinca *sf.* periwinkle.
pesa *sf.* **1.** (*luogo*) weigh-house **2.** (*apparecchio*) weighing-machine.
pesante *agg.* heavy.

pesantezza *sf.* heaviness.
pesare *vt.* to weigh. ♦ pesare *vi.*
1. to weigh 2. (*fig.*) to lie (*v. irr.*)
heavy.
pesata *sf.* weighing.
pesca[1] *sf.* (*bot.*) peach.
pesca[2] *sf.* 1. (*il pescare*) fishing 2.
(*industria*) fishery 3. (*il pescato*)
catch.
pescaggio *sm.* (*mar.*) draught.
pescare *vt.* 1. to fish 2. (*fig.*) to
fish out 3. (*cogliere sul fatto*) to
catch (*v. irr.*) red-handed 4. (*carte*)
to draw (*v. irr.*). ♦ pescare *vi.*
to draw.
pescatore *sm.* 1. fisher 2. (*con len-za*) angler.
pesce *sm.* fish: — *rosso,* goldfish;
— *persico,* perch.
pescecane *sm.* shark.
peschereccio *agg.* fishing. ♦ peschereccio *sm.* fishing-boat.
pescherìa *sf.* 1. fish-shop 2. (*mer-cato*) fish-market.
peschiera *sf.* fish-pond.
pesciaiola *sf.* (*cuc.*) fish-kettle.
pesco *sm.* peach-tree.
pescoso *agg.* fishy.
pesista *sm.* weight thrower.
peso *sm.* weight: *a* —, by weight.
pessimismo *sm.* pessimism.
pessimista *agg.* pessimistic. ♦ pessimista *s.* pessimist.
pessimistico *agg.* pessimistic.
pèssimo *agg.* worst, very bad.
pesta *sf.* 1. track 2. (*difficoltà*) difficulty.
pestaggio *sm.* scuffle.
pestare *vt.* 1. to pound 2. (*picchiare*) to beat (*v. irr.*) 3. (*calpestare*) to tread (*v. irr.*) on.
pestata *sf.* 1. (*lo schiacciare*) pounding 2. (*il calpestare*) treading.
peste *sf.* plague.
pestello *sm.* pestle.
pestìfero *agg.* pestiferous.
pestilenza *sf.* plague.
pestilenziale *agg.* pestilential.
pesto *agg.* pounded: *buio* —, pitch
dark; *avere gli occhi pesti,* to have
rings under one's eyes.
pètalo *sm.* petal.
petardo *sm.* petard.
petizione *sf.* petition.
petraia *sf.* 1. (*cava*) quarry 2. (*mucchio di pietre*) heap of stones.
petrografìa *sf.* petrography.
petroliera *sf.* tanker.
petrolìfero *agg.* oil (*attr.*).

petrolio *sm.* oil.
pettégola *sf.* gossiper.
pettegolare *vi.* to gossip.
pettegolezzo *sm.* gossip.
pettégolo *agg.* gossipy. ♦ pettégolo *sm.* gossiper.
pettinare *vt.* to comb. ♦ pettinar-
si *vr.* to comb one's hair.
pettinato *sm.* worsted.
pettinatrice *sf.* 1. hairdresser 2.
(*industria tessile*) comber.
pettinatura *sf.* 1. hairdo 2. (*industria tessile*) combing.
pèttine *sm.* comb.
pettirosso *sm.* robin.
petto *sm.* 1. breast 2. (*torace*) chest
|| — *a* —, face to face; *prendere
di* —, to face.
pettorale *agg.* e *sm.* pectoral.
pettorina *sf.* stomacher.
pettoruto *agg.* 1. full-breasted 2.
(*fig.*) haughty.
petulante *agg.* pert.
petulanza *sf.* pertness.
petunia *sf.* petunia.
pezza *sf.* 1. patch 2. (*macchia*) spot
|| — *di stoffa,* roll.
pezzato *agg.* spotted.
pezzente *agg.* beggarly. ♦ pezzente *s.* ragamuffin.
pezzo *sm.* piece: *fare a pezzi,* to
tear (*v. irr.*) to pieces; *a pezzi e
bocconi,* piecemeal; — *grosso* (*fig.*),
bigwig; — *di ricambio,* spare part.
pezzuola *sf.* handkerchief.
piacente *agg.* pleasant.
piacere[1] *sm.* 1. pleasure 2. (*favore*)
favour || *per* —, please; —! (*nelle
presentazioni*), how do you do!
piacere[2] *vi.* to like: *gli piace leggere,* he likes reading, he likes to
read; *come pare e piace,* as one
pleases.
piacévole *agg.* pleasant.
piacimento *sm.* pleasure, liking: *a
—,* as much as one likes.
piaga *sf.* 1. sore 2. (*calamità*)
plague 3. (*fig.*) nuisance.
piagnisteo *sm.* moaning.
piagnucolare *vi.* to whimper.
piagnucolìo *sm.* whimper.
piagnucoloso *agg.* whimpering.
pialla *sf.* plane.
piallare *vt.* to plane.
piallatrice *sf.* planer.
piallatura *sf.* 1. planing 2. (*trucioli*) shavings (*pl.*).
piana *sf.* plane.
pianeggiante *agg.* level.

pianella *sf.* **1.** (*pantofola*) slipper **2.** (*mattonella*) flat tile.

pianeròttolo *sm.* landing.

pianeta *sm.* planet.

piangente *agg.* weeping, crying.

piàngere *vi.* to cry, to weep (*v. irr.*). ♦ **piàngere** *vt.* to weep **2.** (*un lutto*) to mourn || *— a calde lacrime*, to weep one's heart out.

pianificare *vt.* to plan.

pianificazione *sf.* planning.

pianista *s.* pianist.

piano¹ *agg.* **1.** flat **2.** (*chiaro*) clear **3.** (*semplice*) simple.

piano² *sm.* **1.** plain **2.** (*di casa*) floor, storey **3.** (*strato*) layer **4.** (*superficie piana, livello*) plane **5.** (*progetto*) plan **6.** (*cine*) primo —, close up || *— stradale*, roadway; *in primo* —, in the foreground.

piano³ *avv.* **1.** (*lentamente*) slowly **2.** (*sommessamente*) softly **3.** (*con cautela*) gently.

pianoforte *sm.* piano.

pianola *sf.* barrel-organ.

pianta *sf.* **1.** plant **2.** (*carta topografica*) map **3.** (*del piede*) sole || *di sana — (completamente)*, completely; (*di nuovo*) anew.

piantagione *sf.* plantation.

piantare *vt.* **1.** to plant **2.** (*conficcare*) to drive (*v. irr.*) **3.** (*lasciare*) to leave (*v. irr.*) || *piantarla*, to stop.

piantatore *sm.* planter.

pianterreno *sm.* ground-floor.

pianto *sm.* **1.** tears (*pl.*): *scoppiare in —*, to burst (*v. irr.*) into tears **2.** (*dolore*) grief.

piantonamento *sm.* guarding.

piantonare *vt.* to guard.

piantone¹ *sm.* soldier on guard.

piantone² *sm.* (*agr.*) shoot.

pianura *sf.* plain.

piastra *sf.* **1.** plate **2.** (*di marmo*) slab **3.** (*moneta*) piastre.

piastrella *sf.* tile.

piastrellare *vt.* to tile.

piastrellatura *sf.* tiling.

piastrina *sf.* plaque.

piattaforma *sf.* platform.

piattello *sm.* pan || *tiro al —*, trap-shooting.

piattino *sm.* saucer.

piatto¹ *agg.* flat.

piatto² *sm.* **1.** dish **2.** (*portata*) course **3.** (*di lama*) flat **4.** (*di grammofono*) turn-table.

piazza *sf.* **1.** square **2.** (*comm.*) market || *mettere qc. in —*, to make (*v. irr.*) sthg. public.

piazzaforte *sf.* stronghold.

piazzale *sm.* large square.

piazzamento *sm.* place.

piazzare *vt.* to place. ♦ **piazzarsi** *vr.* (*sport*) to be placed.

piazzista *sm.* salesman (*pl.* -men).

picaresco *agg.* picaresque.

picca *sf.* pike || *picche (alle carte*), spades (*pl.*).

piccante *agg.* **1.** piquant **2.** (*salace*) spicy.

piccarsi *vr.* to plume oneself (on).

piccato *agg.* resentful.

picchettare *vt.* **1.** to peg out **2.** (*mil.*) to picket.

picchetto *sm.* **1.** peg **2.** (*mil.*) picket: *essere di —*, to be on picket.

picchiare *vt.* e *vi.* **1.** (*percuotere*) to beat (*v. irr.*) **2.** (*battere*) to strike (*v. irr.*) **3.** (*bussare*) to knock **4.** (*aer.*) to pitch || *— in testa (di motore*), to ping. ♦ **picchiarsi** *vr. rec.* to fight (*v. irr.*).

picchiata *sf.* **1.** beating **2.** (*aer.*) dive || *scendere in —*, to dive.

picchiatello *agg.* slightly crazy.

picchiettare *vt.* **1.** (*battere*) to tap **2.** (*chiazzare*) to spot.

picchiettato *agg.* spotted.

picchiettìo *sm.* tapping.

picchio¹ *sm.* **1.** (*colpo*) blow **2.** (*alla porta*) knock.

picchio² *sm.* (*zool.*) woodpecker.

picchiotto *sm.* door-knocker.

piccinerìa *sf.* meanness.

piccino *agg.* **1.** little **2.** (*fig.*) mean.

piccionaia *sf.* **1.** pigeon-house **2.** (*teat.*) gallery.

piccione *sm.* pigeon.

picco *sm.* peak || *a —*, vertically; *colare a —, mandare a —*, to sink (*v. irr.*).

piccolezza *sf.* **1.** smallness **2.** (*meschinità*) meanness **3.** (*inezia*) trifle.

piccolo *agg.* **1.** small, little **2.** (*di statura, breve*) short **3.** (*giovane*) young **4.** (*meschino*) mean **5.** (*leggero*) light.

piccone *sm.* pick(axe).

piccozza *sf.* axe.

pidocchierìa *sf.* meanness.

pidocchio *sm.* **1.** louse (*pl.* lice) **2.** (*fig.*) miser.

pidocchioso *agg.* **1.** lousy **2.** (*fig.*) stingy.

piede sm. foot (pl. feet): a piedi, on foot ‖ a — libero, on bail; prender —, to get (v. irr.) a footing.

piedistallo sm. pedestal.

piega sf. 1. fold 2. (fatta ad arte) pleat 3. (segno) crease ‖ messa in — (di capelli), set.

piegàbile agg. folding.

piegamento sm. 1. folding 2. (flessione) flexing.

piegare vt. 1. to fold 2. (flettere, anche fig.) to bend (v. irr.). ♦ **piegare** vi. 1. (voltare) to turn 2. (curvarsi) to bend. ♦ **piegarsi** vr. to bend.

piegatrice sf. (mecc.) bending-machine.

pieghettare vt. to pleat.

pieghévole agg. 1. pliable 2. (atto a essere piegato) folding. ♦ **pieghévole** sm. folder.

pieghevolezza sf. pliability.

piena sf. 1. flood, spate 2. (folla) crowd.

pienamente avv. fully.

pienezza sf. 1. fullness 2. (massimo grado) height.

pieno agg. full: — zeppo, full up; in — (completamente), fully, (esattamente) exactly, (nel mezzo) in the middle; in — giorno, in broad daylight. ♦ **pieno** sm. (il colmo) middle ‖ fare il — (auto), to fill up.

pietà sf. 1. pity 2. (relig.) piety ‖ aver — di, to have mercy on; far —, to arouse pity; per —!, for pity's sake!

pietanza sf. 1. main course 2. (piatto) dish.

pietismo sm. pietism.

pietosamente avv. pitifully.

pietoso agg. pitiful.

pietra sf. stone: posare la prima —, to lay the foundation stone.

pietraia sf. V. petraia.

pietrificare vt. to petrify. ♦ **pietrificarsi** vr. to petrify.

pietrina sf. flint.

pietrisco sm. rubble.

pietroso agg. stony.

piffero sm. pipe.

pigiama sm. pyjamas (pl.).

pigia pigia sm. awful crush.

pigiare vt. to press. ♦ **pigiarsi** vr. to crowd.

pigione sf. rent: stare a — presso, to lodge with.

pigmentato agg. pigmented.

pigmentazione sf. pigmentation.

pigmento sm. pigment.

pigmeo sm. pigmy.

pigna sf. pinecone.

pignatta sf. pot.

pignolerìa sf. faultfinding.

pignolo sm. 1. (bot.) pine-seed 2. (fig.) faultfinder.

pignoramento sm. attachment.

pignorare vt. to distrain.

pigolare vi. to peep.

pigolìo sm. peep.

pigramente avv. 1. lazily 2. (lentamente) sluggishly.

pigrizia sf. 1. laziness 2. (lentezza) sluggishness.

pigro agg. 1. lazy 2. (lento) sluggish.

pila sf. pile: — a secco, dry battery.

pilastro sm. pillar.

pillola sf. pill: — anticoncezionale, contraceptive (pill), the "pill".

pilone sm. 1. pylon 2. (di ponte) pier ‖ — d'ormeggio, mooringmast.

piloro sm. pylorus (pl. -ri).

pilota sm. 1. pilot 2. (di auto) driver.

pilotaggio sm. pilotage: scuola di —, flying-school.

pilotare vt. 1. to pilot 2. (un'auto) to drive (v. irr.).

piluccare vt. to nibble.

piluccone sm. nibbler.

pinacoteca sf. picture-gallery.

pinastro sm. pinaster.

pindàrico agg. Pindaric.

pineta sf. pinewood.

pingue agg. 1. fat 2. (ricco) rich.

pinguèdine sf. fatness.

pinguino sm. penguin.

pinna sf. 1. fin 2. (sport) flipper.

pinnàcolo[1] sm. pinnacle.

pinnàcolo[2] sm. (gioco) pinochle.

pino sm. pine (-tree).

pinolo sm. pine-seed.

pinta sf. pint.

pinza sf. pliers (pl.), pincers (pl.).

pinzetta sf. tweezers (pl.).

pio agg. pious ‖ opera pia, charitable organization.

pioggia sf. rain: sotto la —, in the rain.

piolo sm. V. piuolo.

piombare vt. 1. to plumb 2. (tip.) to lead ‖ — un dente, to stop a tooth. ♦ **piombare** vi. 1. (cade-

re) to fall (*v. irr.*) heavily 2. (*assalire*) to assail 3. (*precipitarsi*) to rush.

piombatura *sf.* sealing, leading.

piombino *sm.* 1. plummet 2. (*sigillo*) leaden seal.

piombo *sm.* 1 lead 2. (*sigillo*) leaden seal 3. (*pallottola*) bullet || *filo a* —, plumb line; *a* —, perpendicularly; *di* —, leaden; *andare coi piedi di* —, to proceed very cautiously.

pioniere *sm.* pioneer.

pioppeto *sm.* poplargrove.

pioppo *sm.* poplar.

piorrea *sf.* pyorrhoea.

piovano *agg.* rain (*attr.*).

piovasco *sm.* shower.

piòvere *vi.* to rain, to pour (*anche fig.*).

piovigginare *vi.* to drizzle.

piovigginoso *agg.* drizzly, rainy.

piovoso *agg.* rainy.

piovra *sf.* octopus.

pipa *sf.* pipe.

pipetta *sf.* (*chim.*) pipette.

pipistrello *sm.* bat.

pipita *sf.* agnail.

pira *sf.* pyre.

piramidale *ag.* pyramidal.

piràmide *sf.* pyramid.

pirata *sm.* pirate || — *della strada*, hit-and-run driver.

piraterìa *sf.* piracy.

pìrico *agg.* *polvere pirica*, gunpowder.

pirite *sf.* pyrite(s).

piroetta *sf.* pirouette.

piroettare *vi.* to pirouette.

piroga *sf.* pirogue.

pirografìa *sf.* pyrography.

piròscafo *sm.* steamer.

pirotècnica *sf.* pyrotechnics.

pirotècnico *agg.* pyrotechnic(al): *spettacolo* —, fireworks. ◆ **pirotècnico** *sm.* pyrotechnist.

piscia *sf.* piss.

pisciare *vi.* to piss.

pisciata *sf.* piss.

pisciatoio *sm.* urinal.

piscicoltura *sf.* pisciculture.

piscina *sf.* swimming-pool.

pisello *sm.* pea.

pisolino *sm.* nap.

pista *sf.* 1. (*traccia*) track 2. (*di animale*) trail 3. (*aer.*) strip.

pistacchio *sm.* pistachio.

pistillo *sm.* pistil.

pistola *sf.* pistol

pistone *sm.* piston.

pitagòrico *agg. e sm.* Pythagorean: *tavola pitagorica*, multiplication table.

pitale *sm.* chamber pot.

pitocco *agg.* 1. mean 2. (*fig.*) stingy. ◆ **pitocco** *sm.* 1. beggar 2. (*fig.*) mean person.

pitone *sm.* python.

pitonessa *sf.* pythoness.

pittore *sm.* painter.

pittoresco *agg.* picturesque.

pittòrico *agg.* pictorial.

pittrice *sf.* paintress.

pittura *sf.* 1. painting 2. (*dipinto, descrizione*) picture 3. (*vernice*) paint.

pitturare *vt.* to paint.

più *avv.* 1. (*comp. di maggioranza con agg. polisillabi, con s., v. e avv.*) more: *questo libro è — costoso di quello*, this book is more expensive than that; *ho — libri di te*, I have more books than you; *lavoro — di te*, I work more than you 2. (*comp. di maggioranza con agg. e avv. monosillabi e bisillabi terminanti in y, er, ow*) ...er: *è — gentile di lui*, he is kinder than he is 3. (*superl. rel., corrispondente a "more"*) the most, the more (*fra due*): *è il libro — costoso di tutti*, it is the most expensive book of all; *la — bella delle due sorelle*, the more beautiful of the two sisters 4. (*superl. rel., corrispondente a "...er"*) the ...est, the ...er (*fra due*): *è la persona — felice che conosca*, she is the happiest person I know; *è la — graziosa delle due sorelle*, she is the prettier of the sisters 4. (*di tempo*) no longer, no more, not again || *mai* —, never again. ◆ **più** *agg.* 1. more 2. (*diversi*) several. ◆ **più** *sm.* most: *il — è fatto*, most of it is done || *i* —, most people (*al sing.*).

piuma *sf.* 1. feather, down 2. (*ornamento*) plume.

piumaggio *sm.* plumage.

piumino *sm.* 1. down 2. (*copriletto*) eiderdown 3. (*per la cipria*) powder-puff 4. (*per spolverare*) duster.

piuttosto *avv.* rather. ◆ **piuttosto che, di** *cong.* rather than.

piuolo *sm.* 1. peg: *scala a piuoli*, ladder 2. (*paletto*) post.

piva *sf.* bagpipe.
pivello *sm.* greenhorn.
piviere *sm.* plover.
pizzicàgnolo *sm.* delicatessen seller.
pizzicare *vt.* **1.** to pinch, to nip **2.** (*di insetti*) to bite (*v. irr.*) **3.** (*di sostanza acre*) to burn (*v. irr.*) **4.** (*con parole*) to tease **5.** (*sorprendere*) to catch (*v. irr.*). ♦ **pizzicare** *vi.* (*prudere*) to itch, to tingle.
pizzicherìa *sf.* **1.** delicatessen shop **2.** (*merci*) delicatessen.
pìzzico *sm.* **1.** pinch **2.** (*pizzicore*) itch **3.** (*fig.*) bit.
pizzicore *sm.* itch.
pizzicotto *sm.* pinch.
pizzo *sm.* **1.** lace (*solo sing.*) **2.** (*di montagna*) peak **3.** (*barba*) pointed beard.
placare *vt.* to appease: — *la fame di qu.*, to satisfy so.'s hunger; — *la sete di qu.*, to quench so.'s thirst. ♦ **placarsi** *vr.* to calm down.
placca *sf.* plaque.
placcare *vt.* to plate (sthg. with).
placcatura *sf.* plating.
placenta *sf.* placenta.
placidità *sf.* placidity.
plàcido *agg.* placid.
plaga *sf.* region.
plagiare *vt.* e *vi.* to plagiarize.
plagiario *agg.* plagiaristic. ♦ **plagiario** *sm.* plagiarist.
plagio *sm.* plagiarism.
planare *vi.* to glide down.
planata *sf.* glide.
plancia *sf.* (*mar.*) deck.
plancton *sm.* plankton.
planetario *agg.* planetary. ♦ **planetario** *sm.* planetarium (*pl.* -ia).
planimetrìa *sf.* planimetry, plan.
planimètrico *agg.* planimetric(al).
planisfero *sm.* planisphere.
plantìgrado *agg.* e *sm.* plantigrade.
plasma *sm.* plasma.
plasmare *vt.* to mould.
plàstica *sf.* **1.** (*operazione*) plastic operation **2.** (*materiale*) plastic.
plasticare *vt.* to plasticize.
plasticità *sf.* plasticity.
plàstico *agg.* plastic. ♦ **plàstico** *sm.* **1.** plastic model **2.** (*carta topografica*) relief map.
plastilina *sf.* plasticine.
plàtano *sm.* plane (-tree).
platea *sf.* pit: *poltrona di* —, stall.
plateale *agg.* coarse.

platinare *vt.* **1.** to platinize **2.** (*di capelli*) to bleach.
plàtino *sm.* platinum.
platònico *agg.* Platonic.
plaudente *agg.* applauding.
plausìbile *agg.* plausible.
plàuso *sm.* **1.** applause **2.** (*lode*) praise.
plebaglia *sf.* mob.
plebe *sf.* populace.
plebeo *agg.* e *sm.* plebeian.
plebiscitario *agg.* plebiscitary.
plebiscito *sm.* plebiscite.
plenario *agg.* plenary.
plenilunio *sm.* plenilune.
plenipotenziario *agg.* e *sm.* plenipotentiary.
pleonasmo *sm.* pleonasm.
pleonàstico *agg.* pleonastic.
plesso *sm.* plexus.
plètora *sf.* plethora.
pletòrico *agg.* plethoric.
plettro *sm.* plectrum (*pl.* -ra).
plèura *sf.* pleura (*pl.* -rae).
pleurite *sf.* pleurisy.
plico *sm.* **1.** packet **2.** (*busta*) cover: *in* — *separato*, under separate cover.
plotone *sm.* platoon.
plùmbeo *agg.* leaden.
plurale *agg.* e *sm.* plural.
pluralismo *sm.* pluralism.
pluralità *sf.* plurality.
pluricellulare *agg.* multicellular.
plusvalore *sm.* plus value.
plutòcrate *sm.* plutocrat.
plutocrazìa *sf.* plutocracy.
pneumàtico *agg.* pneumatic, inflatable. ♦ **pneumàtico** *sm.* (*di auto*) tyre.
pneumatorace *sm.* pneumothorax.
pochezza *sf.* (*scarsità, ristrettezza*) scantiness, insufficiency.
pochìssimo *agg.* e *avv.* **1.** very little **2.** (*rarissimamente*) very seldom. ♦ **pochìssimi** *sm. pl.* very few.
poco *avv.* **1.** not very (*con agg. e avv.*), little (*con comp., p. passati, verbi*): *a* — *a* —, little by little; — *per volta*, a little at a time **2.** (*di tempo*) a short time || *fra* —, soon. ♦ **poco** *agg.* **1.** little (*pl.* few) **2.** (*di tempo*) short. ♦ **poco** *pron.* e *sm.* little (*pl.* few): *un* — *di*, a little.
podere *sm.* farm.
poderoso *agg.* powerful.
podio *sm.* platform.

podismo *sm.* **1.** walking **2.** (*sport*) foot-racing.

podista *sm.* (*sport*) foot-racer.

podìstico *agg.* foot (*attr.*).

poema *sm.* poem.

poesìa *sf.* **1.** poetry **2.** (*composizione poetica*) poem.

poeta *sm.* poet.

poetare *vi.* to write (*v. irr.*) poetry.

poètico *agg.* poetic(al).

poggiapiedi *sm.* footstool.

poggiare *vi.* e *vt.* to rest. ◆ **poggiarsi** *vr.* to lean (*v. irr.*) against.

poggio *sm.* hillock.

poi *avv.* **1.** then **2.** (*più tardi*) later || *d'ora in —*, from now on.

poiché *cong.* since, as.

polacca *sf.* (*mus.*) polonaise.

polacco *agg.* Polish. ◆ **polacco** *sm.* Pole.

polare *agg.* polar || *stella —*, pole-star.

polarità *sf.* polarity.

polarizzare *vt.* to polarize.

polarizzatore *agg.* polarizing. ◆ **polarizzatore** *sm.* polarizer.

polarizzazione *sf.* polarization.

polca *sf.* polka.

polèmica *sf.* polemic.

polèmico *agg.* e *sm.* polemic.

polemista *s.* polemist.

polemizzare *vi.* to polemize.

poliandrìa *sf.* polyandry.

policlìnico *sm.* polyclinic.

policromìa *sf.* polychromy.

polìcromo *agg.* polychrome.

polièdrico *agg.* **1.** polyhedral **2.** (*fig.*) versatile.

poliedro *sm.* polyhedron.

polifonìa *sf.* polyphony.

polifònico *agg.* polyphonic.

poligamìa *sf.* polygamy.

polìgamo *agg.* polygamous. ◆ **polìgamo** *sm.* polygamist.

poliglotta *s.* polyglot.

polìgono *sm.* polygon || *— di tiro*, shooting-range.

polimerizzazione *sf.* polymerization.

polìmero *agg.* polymeric. ◆ **polìmero** *sm.* polymer.

polimorfismo *sm.* polymorphism.

poliomielite *sf.* poliomyelitis.

poliomielìtico *agg.* polio (*attr.*). ◆ **poliomielìtico** *sm.* person who has had polio.

pòlipo *sm.* polyp.

polisìllabo *agg.* polysyllabic(al). ◆ **polisìllabo** *sm.* polysyllable.

politècnico *agg.* e *sm.* polytechnic.

politeismo *sm.* polytheism.

politeista *agg.* polytheistic. ◆ **politeista** *s.* polytheist.

polìtica *sf.* **1.** politics **2.** (*linea di condotta*) policy.

politicante *sm.* petty politician.

polìtico *agg.* **1.** political **2.** (*sagace*) politic || *uomo —*, politician.

polivalente *agg.* polyvalent.

polizìa *sf.* police (*us. al pl.*).

poliziesco *agg.* **1.** police (*attr.*) **2.** (*di film ecc.*) detective (*attr.*).

poliziotto *sm.* policeman (*pl. -men*).

pòlizza *sf.* **1.** policy **2.** (*ricevuta*) bill.

polla *sf.* spring.

pollaio *sm.* hen-house.

pollame *sm.* poultry.

pollastra *sf.* pullet.

pollastro *sm.* cockerel.

pòllice *sm.* **1.** thumb **2.** (*del piede*) big toe **3.** (*misura*) inch.

pollicoltore *sm.* poultryman (*pl. -men*).

pollicoltura *sf.* poultry-farming.

pòlline *sm.* pollen.

pollivéndolo *sm.* poulterer.

pollo *sm.* **1.** chicken **2.** (*fig.*) dupe.

polmonare *agg.* pulmonary.

polmone *sm.* lung; *— d'acciaio*, iron lung.

polmonite *sf.* pneumonia.

polo[1] *sm.* pole.

polo[2] *sm.* (*sport*) polo.

polpa *sf.* **1.** (*di frutta*) pulp **2.** (*carne*) lean meat.

polpaccio *sm.* calf (*pl.* calves).

polpastrello *sm.* finger-tip.

polpetta *sf.* meat-ball, croquette.

polposo *agg.* pulpy.

polsino *sm.* cuff.

polso *sm.* **1.** wrist **2.** (*fig.*) energy **3.** (*pulsazione*) pulse **4.** (*polsino*) cuff || *tastare il — a qu.*, to feel (*v. irr.*) so.'s pulse; *uomo di —*, energetic man.

poltiglia *sf.* **1.** pulp **2.** (*fanghiglia*) mud.

poltrire *vi.* to idle.

poltrona *sf.* **1.** armchair **2.** (*teat.*) stall.

poltrone *agg.* idle. ◆ **poltrone** *sm.* idler.

poltronerìa *sf.* idleness.

pòlvere *sf.* **1.** dust **2.** (*sostanza polverizzata*) powder || *togliere la —*, to dust.

polveriera *sf.* powder-magazine.

polverizzare vt. to pulverize. ♦
polverizzarsi vr. to pulverize.
polverone sm. cloud of dust.
polveroso agg. dusty.
pomata sf. salve.
pomello sm. 1. (di porta ecc.) knob
2. (di guancia) cheek-bone.
pomeridiano agg. 1. afternoon
(attr.) 2. (con le ore) p. m. (post
meridiem): alle 5 pomeridiane,
at five o'clock.
pomeriggio sm. afternoon.
pòmice sf. pumice.
pomo sm. 1. (mela) apple 2. (di
porta ecc.) knob.
pomodoro sm. tomato.
pompa sf. 1. pump 2. (fasto) pomp
3. (ostentazione) display || impresa
di pompe funebri, undertaker's
business; far — di sé, to show (v.
irr.) off.
pompare vt. 1. to pump 2. (fig.)
to puff up.
pompelmo sm. grapefruit.
pompiere sm. fireman (pl. -men).
pomposità sf. pomposity.
pomposo agg. pompous.
ponderàbile agg. ponderable.
ponderabilità sf. ponderability.
ponderare vt. to ponder.
ponderatamente avv. after reflection.
ponderatezza sf. circumspection.
ponderato agg. pondered.
ponderazione sf. consideration.
ponderoso agg. ponderous.
ponente sm. west.
ponte sm. 1. bridge: — girevole,
swing bridge 2. (mar.) deck 3.
(impalcatura) scaffold || rompere i
ponti con (fig.), to break (v. irr.)
with.
pontéfice sm. pope.
pontificale agg. pontifical.
pontificare vi. to pontificate.
pontificato sm. pontificate.
pontificio agg. papal.
pontile sm. landing-stage.
pontone sm. pontoon.
ponzare vi. to rack one's brains.
popolamento sm. peopling.
popolano agg. common. ♦ **popola-
no** sm. man of the people || i
popolani, the common people.
popolare¹ vt. to people. ♦ **popo-
larsi** vr. to become (v. irr.) pop-
ulated.
popolare² agg. 1. popular 2. (tradizionale) folk (attr.).

popolaresco agg. popular-like.
popolarità sf. popularity.
popolarizzare vt. to popularize.
popolazione sf. population.
pòpolo sm. 1. (gente) people (pl.)
2. (nazione) people.
popoloso agg. populous.
popone sm. melon.
poppa¹ sf. 1. (mar.) stern || avere il
vento in —, to sail before the
wind; a —, astern.
poppa² sf. breast.
poppante s. suckling.
poppare vt. to suck.
poppata sf. suck: ora della —,
feeding-time.
poppatoio sm. feeding-bottle.
populismo sm. populism.
populista agg. populistic. ♦ **populista** s. populist.
porcaro sm. swineherd.
porcellana sf. china (solo sing.).
porcherìa sf. 1. dirt 2. (azione di-
sonesta) dirty trick 3. (detto indecente) obscene word 4. (atto indecente) obscene act 5. (cibo cattivo) revolting stuff 6. (cose senza
valore) rubbish.
porcile sm. pigsty.
porcino agg. pig (attr.). ♦ **porcino** sm. (fungo) boletus.
porco sm. 1. pig 2. (cuc.) pork.
porcospino sm. porcupine.
pòrfido sm. porphyry.
pòrgere vt. 1. to hand 2. (offrire)
to offer.
pornografìa sf. pornography.
pornogràfico agg. pornographic
poro sm. pore.
porosità sf. porosity.
poroso agg. porous.
pòrpora sf. purple.
porporato sm. Cardinal.
porre vt. 1. to put (v. irr.) 2. (sup-
porre) to suppose || — le fonda-
menta, to lay (v. irr.) the foundations; — mano, to begin (v. irr.).
porro sm. 1. leek 2. (med.) wart.
porta sf. 1. door 2. (di mura ecc.)
gate 3. (sport) goal.
portabagagli sm. 1. luggage-rack
2. (facchino) porter.
portabandiera sm. ensign.
portacarte sm. portfolio.
portacénere sm. ash-tray.
portachiavi sm. key-holder.
portacipria sm. compact.
portaèrei sf. aircraft carrier.
portaferiti sm. stretcher-bearer.

portafiori *sm:* flower-holder.
portafoglio *sm.* 1. wallet 2. (*pol.*) portfolio.
portafortuna *sm.* mascot.
portagioielli *sm.* jewel-case.
portalèttere *sm.* ·postman (*pl.* -men).
portamento *sm.* 1. gait 2. (*condotta*) behaviour.
portamonete *sm.* purse.
portantina *sf.* sedan-chair.
portaombrelli *sm.* umbrella-stand.
portaòrdini *sm.* messenger.
portapacchi *sm.* carrier.
portapenne *sm.* penholder.
portare *vt.* 1. (*verso chi parla o ascolta*) to bring (*v. irr.*) 2. (*lontano da chi parla, accompagnare*) to take (*v. irr.*) 3. (*trasportare*) to carry 4. (*condurre*) to lead (*v. irr.*) 5. (*indossare*) to wear (*v. irr.*) 6. (*avere*) to have.
portasapone *sm.* soap-dish.
portasigarette *sm.* cigarette-case.
portaspilli *sm.* pincushion.
portata *sf.* 1. (*di pranzo*) course 2. (*di arma, strumento ottico*) range 3. (*di fiume*) flow 4. (*di ponte, auto ecc.*) capacity 5. (*stazza*) tonnage 6. (*fig.*) importance.
portàtile *agg.* portable.
portatore *sm.* bearer.
portauovo *sm.* egg-cup.
portavoce *sm.* spokesman (*pl.* -men).
portello *sm.* hatch.
portento *sm.* prodigy.
portentosamente *avv.* prodigiously.
portentoso *agg.* prodigious.
porticato *sm.* arcade.
pòrtico *sm.* 1. (*loggia*) porch 2. (*porticato*) arcade.
portiera[1] *sf.* (*porta*) door.
portiera[2] *sf.* doorkeeper.
portiere *sm.* 1. (*sport*) goal-keeper 2. porter.
portinaio *sm.* door keeper.
portineria *sf.* porter's lodge.
porto[1] *sm.* 1. port (*anche fig.*) 2. (*bacino*) harbour (*anche fig.*).
porto[2] *sm.* (*trasporto*) carriage: *franco di* —, carriage paid || — *d'armi*, shooting licence; *condurre in* — (*fig.*), to carry out.
portoghese *agg. e sm.* Portuguese.
portone *sm.* main door.
portuale *agg.* harbour (*attr.*): *città* —, port. ◆ **portuale** *sm.* docker.

porzione *sf.* portion.
posa *sf.* 1. (*il porre*) laying 2. (*posizione*) posture 3. (*affettazione*) pose 4. (*pausa*) pause 5. (*foto*) exposure || *mettersi in* —, to pose; *senza* —, incessantly.
posare *vt.* to lay (*v. irr.*). ◆ **posare** *vi.* 1. (*aver fondamento*) to rest 2. (*assumere un atteggiamento non spontaneo*) to pose 3. (*di liquido*) to stand (*v. irr.*). ◆ **posarsi** *vr.* 1. to settle 2. (*aer.; di uccello*) to alight.
posata *sf.* 1. (*coltello*) knife (*pl.* knives) 2. (*forchetta*) fork 3. (*cucchiaio*) spoon.
posato *agg.* staid.
poscritto *sm.* postscript.
positiva *sf.* (*foto*) positive.
positivamente *avv.* positively.
positivismo *sm.* positivism.
positivista *s.* positivist.
positivo *agg.* positive.
posizione *sf.* position.
posologìa *sf.* posology.
posporre *vt.* 1. to place after 2. (*posticipare*) to postpone.
possedere *vt.* to possess.
possedimento *sm.* V. *possesso.*
possente *agg.* powerful.
possessivo *agg.* possessive.
possesso *sm.* 1. possession 2. (*proprietà*) property.
possessore *sm.* possessor, owner.
possìbile *agg.* possible: *il più presto* —, as soon as possible; *fare il* —, to do (*v. irr.*) one's best.
possibilità *sf.* 1. possibility 2. (*potere*) power || — *finanziarie*, means.
possidente *sm.* 1. man (*pl.* -men) of property 2. (*terriero*) landowner.
posta *sf.* 1. post, mail 2. (*ufficio postale*) post-office || *fermo* —, poste restante; *a giro di* —, by return of post; *per* —, by mail 3. (*al gioco*) stake.
postale *agg.* postal, post (*attr.*), mail (*attr.*): *per pacco* —, by parcel post; *spese postali*, postage.
postazione *sf.* stationing.
postbèllico *agg.* post-war (*attr.*).
postdatare *vt.* to postdate.
posteggiare *vt.* to park.
posteggiatore *sm.* 1. car-park attendant 2. (*venditore*) stall-keeper.
posteggio *sm.* car-park || — *di taxi*, taxi rank.
postelegrafònico *agg.* postal telegraph and telephone (*attr.*). ◆

postelegrafònico *sm.* post-office clerk.

postema *sf.* aposteme.

pòsteri *sm. pl.* descendants.

posteriore *agg.* 1. (*nel tempo*) following 2. (*nello spazio*) back, rear.

posterità *sf.* posterity.

posticcio *agg.* false. ♦ **posticcio** *sm.* toupee.

posticipare *vt.* to postpone.

posticipazione *sf.* deferment.

postiglione *sm.* postilion.

postilla *sf.* (marginal) note.

postillare *vt.* to annotate.

postino *sm.* postman (*pl.* -men).

posto *sm.* 1. place 2. (*spazio*) room 3. (*lavoro*) job 4. (*posto a sedere*) seat 5. (*stazione*) station || *al —di*, instead of.

postoperatorio *agg.* postoperative.

postrìbolo *sm.* brothel.

postulante *sm.* 1. petitioner 2. (*eccl.*) postulant.

postulare *vt.* to petition (for sthg.).

postulato *sm.* postulate.

pòstumo *agg.* posthumous.

potàbile *agg.* drinkable.

potare *vt.* to prune.

potassa *sf.* potash.

potàssico *agg.* potassic.

potassio *sm.* potassium.

potatore *sm.* pruner.

potatura *sf.* pruning.

potente *agg.* powerful.

potenza *sf.* power || *in — (avv.)*, potentially, (*agg.*) potential.

potenziale *agg. e sm.* potential.

potenzialità *sf.* potentiality.

potenziamento *sm.* 1. (*rafforzamento*) strengthening 2. (*sviluppo*) development.

potenziare *vt.* 1. (*rafforzare*) to strengthen 2. (*sviluppare*) to develop.

potere[1] *vi.* 1. can (*pres.*), could (*pass., condiz.*), to be able: *non può venire*, he cannot come 2. (*eventualità, augurio, permesso*) may (*pres.*), might (*pass., condiz.*), to be allowed to: *può darsi*, maybe; *può darsi che venga*, he may come.

potere[2] *sm.* power.

potestà *sf.* power, authority.

poveraccio *sm.* poor devil.

pòvero *agg.* poor.

povertà *sf.* poverty.

pozione *sf.* potion.

pozza *sf.* pool.

pozzànghera *sf.* puddle.

pozzetto *sm.* 1. (*di motore*) sump 2. (*di fognatura*) drain well.

pozzo *sm.* well: — *nero*, cesspool; — *carbonifero*, coal-pit.

pragmatismo *sm.* pragmatism.

pragmatista *s.* pragmatist.

pragmatìstico *agg.* pragmatist.

prammàtica *sf.* custom: *di —*, customary.

prammàtico *agg.* pragmatic.

pranzare *vi.* to dine.

pranzo *sm.* 1. dinner 2. (*di mezzogiorno*) lunch.

prassi *sf.* praxis.

prataiolo *agg.* field (*attr.*).

praterìa *sf.* prairie.

pràtica *sf.* 1. practice 2. (*affare*) matter 3. (*esperienza*) experience 4. (*incartamento*) file 5. (*trattativa*) dealing 6. (*passo presso un'autorità*) step || *far —*, to practise; *aver — di*, to be familiar with.

praticàbile *agg.* practicable.

praticabilità *sf.* practicability.

praticaccia *sf.* practical knowledge.

praticante *agg.* practising.

praticare *vt.* 1. to practise 2. (*frequentare*) to frequent 3. (*fare*) to make (*v. irr.*).

praticità *sf.* practicality.

pràtico *agg.* 1. practical 2. (*esperto*) skilled || *esser — di*, to be familiar with.

prativo *agg.* grass (*attr.*).

prato *sm.* 1. meadow 2. (*artificiale*) lawn.

pratolina *sf.* daisy.

pravo *agg.* perverse.

preallarme *sm.* prewarning.

preàmbolo *sm.* preface.

preannunziare *vt.* to portend.

preavvertire *vt.* to forewarn.

preavvisare *vt.* to forewarn.

preavviso *sm.* 1. forewarning 2. (*disdetta*) notice.

prebèllico *agg.* pre-war (*attr.*).

prebenda *sf.* 1. (*eccl.*) prebend 2. (*salario*) salary.

precarietà *sf.* precariousness.

precario *agg.* precarious.

precauzionale *agg.* precautionary.

precauzione *sf.* 1. precaution 2. (*cautela*) caution.

precedente *agg.* previous. ♦ **precedente** *sm.* precedent || *i precedenti* (*condotta*), record.

precedenza *sf.* precedence || *in —*, previously.

precèdere vt. to precede. ♦ **precèdere** vi. to come (v. irr.) first.

precessione sf. precession.

precettare vt. 1. (giur.) to summon 2. (mil.) to call to arms.

precetto sm. 1. precept 2. (mil.) call-up notice.

precettore sm. tutor.

precipitare vt. to precipitate. ♦ **precipitare** vi. 1. to fall (v. irr.) 2. (chim.) to precipitate. ♦ **precipitarsi** vr. to dash.

precipitato agg. e sm. precipitate.

precipitazione sf. 1. (atmosferica) precipitation 2. (furia) haste.

precipitoso agg. 1. (impetuoso) headlong 2. (frettoloso) hasty 3. (scosceso) precipitous.

precipizio sm. precipice: a — (precipitosamente), headlong; (a picco) perpendicularly.

precipuo agg. principal.

precisare vt. to specify.

precisazione sf. specification.

precisione sf. 1. precision 2. (chiarezza) clarity.

preciso agg. 1. precise 2. (accurato) careful 3. (definito) definite 4. (identico) identical 5. (di ore) sharp.

preclaro agg. prominent.

preclùdere vt. to preclude.

precoce agg. 1. precocious 2. (di frutto, stagione) early 3. (prematuro) premature.

precocità sf. precociousness.

preconcetto agg. preconceived. ♦ **preconcetto** sm. prejudice.

preconizzare vt. to foretell (v. irr.).

precordi sm. pl. praecordia.

precòrrere vt. to anticipate.

precursore agg. precursory. ♦ **precursore** sm. forerunner.

preda sf. 1. prey 2. (bottino) booty || cadere in — a, to fall (v. irr.) a prey to; far — di, to plunder.

predace agg. predacious.

predare vt. to plunder.

predatore agg. predatory. ♦ **predatore** sm. plunderer.

predatorio agg. predatory.

predecessore sm. forerunner.

predella sf. 1. platform 2. (sgabello) stool.

predellino sm. 1. (di vettura) footboard 2. (poggiapiedi) footstool.

predestinare vt. to predestine.

predestinazione sf. 1. predestina-

tion 2. (destino) destiny.

predeterminare vt. to predetermine.

predeterminazione sf. predetermination.

predetto agg. 1. (suddetto) above mentioned 2. (presagito) foretold (pred.).

prediale agg. praedial.

prèdica sf. sermon: fare la — a qu., to lecture so.

predicàbile agg. predicable.

predicare vt. e vi. to preach.

predicativo agg. predicate.

predicato sm. predicate: essere in — per, to be considered for.

predicatore sm. preacher.

predicatorio agg. preachifying.

predicazione sf. preaching.

predicozzo sm. lecture.

predigestione sf. preliminary digestion.

prediletto agg. favourite. ♦ **prediletto** sm. pet.

predilezione sf. predilection.

predilìgere vt. to prefer.

predire vt. to foretell (v. irr.).

predisporre vi. 1. to predispose 2. (provvedere) to arrange. ♦ **predisporsi** vr. to prepare oneself.

predisposizione sf. 1. (med.) predisposition 2. (inclinazione) bent.

predizione sf. prediction.

predominante agg. prevailing.

predominanza sf. prevalence.

predominare vi. to prevail.

predominio sm. predominance.

predone sm. plunderer.

preesistente agg. pre-existing.

preesistenza sf. pre-existence.

preesìstere vi. to pre-exist.

prefabbricare vt. to prefabricate.

prefazio sm. preface.

prefazione sf. preface.

preferenza sf. preference: di —, generally.

preferenziale agg. preferential.

preferìbile agg. preferable.

preferire vt. to prefer.

preferito agg. e sm. V. prediletto.

prefettizio agg. prefectorial.

prefetto sm. prefect.

prefettura sf. prefecture.

prefìggere vt. to (pre-)establish. ♦ **prefìggersi** vr. to be resolved: — uno scopo, to propose an aim to oneself.

prefigurare vt. to prefigure.

prefigurazione sf. prefiguration.

prefisso *sm.* prefix.
preformare *vt.* to preform.
pregare *vt.* 1. to pray 2. (*chiedere*) to beg.
pregévole *agg.* valuable.
preghiera *sf.* 1. prayer 2. (*domanda*) request.
pregiare *vt.* to esteem. ◆ **pregiarsi** *vr.* to beg (to).
pregiato *agg.* valuable: *vino —*, vintage wine.
pregio *sm.* 1. (*valore*) value 2. (*merito*) merit || *di —*, valuable.
pregiudicare *vt.* to prejudice.
pregiudicato *sm.* previous offender.
pregiudiziale *agg.* prejudicial
pregiudizio *sm.* prejudice.
pregnante *agg.* pregnant.
pregno *agg.* 1. pregnant (with) 2. (*pieno*) full (of).
pregustare *vt.* to foretaste.
preistoria *sf.* prehistory.
preistòrico *agg.* prehistoric.
prelatizio *agg.* prelatic.
prelato *sm.* prelate.
prelazione *sf.* pre-emption.
prelevamento *sm.* drawing: *fare un — (comm.)*, to draw (*v. irr.*).
prelevare *vt.* to draw (*v. irr.*).
prelibare *vt.* to foretaste.
prelibato *agg.* excellent.
prelievo *sm.* V. *prelevamento*.
preliminare *agg.* preliminary.
prelùdere *vi.* to prelude (sthg.), to foreshadow (sthg.).
preludiare *vi.* to prelude.
preludio *sm.* prelude.
prematuro *agg.* premature.
premeditare *vt.* to premeditate.
premeditato *agg.* premeditated.
premeditazione *sf.* premeditation.
prèmere *vi.* 1. to press 2. (*importare*) to interest 3. (*essere urgente*) to be urgent. ◆ **prèmere** *vt.* to press.
premessa *sf.* introduction.
premesso *agg.* previous.
preméttere *vt.* 1. to premise 2. (*mettere prima*) to put (*v. irr.*) before.
premiare *vt.* 1. to give (*v. irr.*) a prize 2. (*ricompensare*) to reward.
premiazione *sf.* awarding of prizes.
preminente *agg.* pre-eminent.
preminenza *sf.* pre-eminence.
premio *sm.* 1. prize 2. (*ricompensa*) reward 3. (*comm.*) premium.
prèmito *sm.* tenesmus.

premolare *agg.* e *sm.* premolar.
premonitore *agg.* premonitory.
premorire *vi.* to predecease.
premunire *vt.* to forearm. ◆ **premunirsi** *vr.* to secure.
premura *sf.* 1. (*cura*) care 2. (*fretta*) hurry 3. (*gentilezza*) kindness || *aver —*, to be in a hurry.
premuroso *agg.* 1. (*servizievole*) helpful 2. (*gentile*) obliging.
prèndere *vt.* 1. to take (*v. irr.*) 2. (*sorprendere, afferrare*) to catch (*v. irr.*) 3. (*comprare, ottenere*) to get (*v. irr.*). ◆ **prèndersi** *vr.* to take || *che ti prende?*, what's the matter with you?
prendisole *sm.* sun-suit.
prenome *sm.* praenomen (*pl.* -mina).
prenotare *vt.* to book. ◆ **prenotarsi** *vr.* to engage oneself.
prenotazione *sf.* booking.
prènsile *agg.* prehensile.
prensione *sf.* prehension.
preoccupante *agg.* worrying.
preoccupare *vt.* to worry. ◆ **preoccuparsi** *vr.* to be worried (about).
preoccupazione *sf.* worry.
preordinare *vt.* to prearrange.
preparare *vt.* to prepare. ◆ **prepararsi** *vr.* to get (*v. irr.*) ready.
preparativo *sm.* preparation.
preparato *agg.* ready. ◆ **preparato** *sm.* (*med.*) preparation.
preparatore *sm.* preparer.
preparatorio *agg.* preparatory.
preparazione *sf.* preparation.
preponderante *agg.* preponderant.
preponderanza *sf.* preponderance.
preporre *vt.* 1. to put (*v. irr.*) before 2. (*preferire*) to prefer 3. (*mettere a capo*) to put at the head.
prepositivo *agg.* prepositional.
preposizione *sf.* preposition.
preposto *sm.* 1. provost 2. (*relig., prevosto*) parish priest.
prepotente *agg.* overbearing.
prepotentemente *avv.* overbearingly.
prepotenza *sf.* 1. arrogance 2. (*azione*) overbearing action.
preraffaellismo *sm.* Pre-Raphaelitism.
preraffaellita *agg.* e *s.* Pre-Raphaelite.
prerogativa *sf.* 1. prerogative 2. (*di persona*) faculty 3. (*di cosa*) property.
presa *sf.* 1. taking 2. (*stretta*) grip

3. (*cattura*) capture **4.** (*elettr.*) plug **5.** (*pizzico*) pinch || *macchina da* —, camera; *far* — (*di cemento*), to set (*v. irr.*).
presagio *sm.* presage, omen.
presagire *vt.* **1.** to foresee (*v. irr.*) **2.** (*essere presagio di*) to forebode.
presago *agg. essere* — *di* (*prevedere*), to have a presentiment of.
presbiopìa *sf.* long-sightedness.
prèsbite *agg.* long-sighted.
presbiterianismo *sm.* Presbyterianism.
presbiteriano *agg.* e *sm.* Presbyterian.
presbiterio *sm.* presbytery.
prescégliere *vt.* to choose (*v. irr.*).
prescelto *agg.* chosen.
prescienza *sf.* prescience.
prescìndere *vi.* to leave (*v. irr.*) out of consideration: *a* — *da*, apart from.
prescritto *sm.* prescript.
prescrìvere *vt.* to prescribe.
prescrizione *sf.* **1.** regulation **2.** (*med.; giur.*) prescription: *caduto in* —, invalidated by prescription.
presentàbile *agg.* presentable.
presentare *vt.* **1.** to present **2.** (*mostrare*) to show (*v. irr.*) **3.** (*far conoscere*) to introduce. ♦ **presentarsi** *vr.* **1.** to present oneself **2.** (*capitare*) to occur.
presentatore *sm.* **1.** announcer **2.** (*teat.*) showman (*pl.* -men).
presentazione *sf.* **1.** presentation **2.** (*di una persona*) introduction.
presente *agg.* e *s.* present || *i presenti*, the people present; *la* — (*lettera*), this letter.
presentemente *avv.* now.
presentimento *sm.* presentiment.
presentire *vt.* to foresee (*v. irr.*).
presenza *sf.* **1.** presence **2.** (*frequenza*) attendance.
prèsenziare *vt.* e *vi.* to be present (at).
presepio *sm.* crib.
preservare *vt.* to preserve.
preservativo *agg.* e *sm.* preservative.
preservazione *sf.* preservation.
prèside *sm.* headmaster. ♦ **prèside** *sf.* headmistress.
presidente *sm.* **1.** president **2.** (*di assemblea*) chairman (*pl.* -men).
presidenza *sf.* **1.** presidency **2.** (*di assemblea*) chairmanship **3.** (*di società*) management **4.** (*insieme di*

direttori) board of directors **5.** (*di scuola*) headmastership.
presidenziale *agg.* presidential.
presidiare *vt.* to garrison.
presidio *sm.* garrison.
presièdere *vt.* e *vi.* to preside (over, at).
pressa *sf.* press.
pressacarte *sm.* paper-weight.
pressante *agg.* pressing.
pressantemente *avv.* pressingly.
pressappoco *avv.* approximately.
pressare *vt.* to press.
pressi *sm. pl.* **1.** neighbourhood (*sing.*) **2.** (*sobborghi*) outskirts.
pressione *sf.* pressure: *fare* — *su qu.* (*fig.*), to put (*v. irr.*) pressure on so.
presso *avv.* nearly: *a un di* —, *press'a poco*, approximately; *da* —, closely. ♦ **presso** *prep.* **1.** near **2.** (*a casa di*) at **3.** (*nell'ufficio di*) with **4.** (*fra*) among **5.** (*negli indirizzi*) c/o (care of).
pressoché *avv.* almost.
pressurizzare *vt.* to pressurize.
pressurizzazione *sf.* pressurization.
prestabilire *vt.* to pre-arrange.
prestamente *avv.* quickly.
prestanome *sm.* man of straw.
prestante *agg.* good-looking.
prestanza *sf.* fine appearance.
prestare *vt.* V. *imprestare.* ♦ **prestarsi** *vr.* to volunteer.
prestatore *sm.* lender: — *d'opera*, workman (*pl.* -men).
prestazione *sf.* **1.** (*prestito*) loan **2.** (*servizio*) service **3.** (*sport*) performance.
prestezza *sf.* quickness.
prestidigitatore *sm.* conjurer.
prestigio *sm.* prestige || *gioco di* —, conjuring trick.
prestigioso *agg.* **1.** (*affascinante*) glamorous **2.** (*favoloso*) fabulous.
prèstito *sm.* loan: *prendere in* —, to borrow; *dare in* —, to lend (*v. irr.*).
presto¹ *agg.* — *di mano*, dexterous.
presto² *avv.* **1.** soon **2.** (*di buon'ora*) early **3.** (*in fretta*) quickly || *o tardi*, sooner or later; *al più* —, as soon as possible. ♦ **presto!** *inter.* quick!
presùmere *vt.* to presume.
presumìbile *agg.* presumable.
presumibilmente *avv.* presumably.
presuntivo *agg.* presumptive.
presunto *agg.* supposed.

presuntuosamente *avv.* presumptuously.

presuntuosità *sf.* conceit.

presuntuoso *agg.* presumptuous.

presunzione *sf.* presumption.

presupporre *vt.* 1. to presuppose 2. (*supporre*) to suppose.

presupposizione *sf.* 1. presupposition 2. (*supposizione*) supposition.

presupposto *sm.* V. *presupposizione*.

prete *sm.* priest. .

pretendente *sm.* 1. pretender 2. (*corteggiatore*) suitor.

pretèndere *vt.* 1. to pretend 2. (*esigere*) to want. ♦ **pretèndere** *vi.* to claim.

pretensione *sf.* pretension.

pretenzioso *agg.* 1. pretentious 2. (*presuntuoso*) conceited.

preterintenzionale *agg.* unintentional.

pretèrito *agg.* e *sm.* past.

pretesa *sf.* 1. pretence 2. (*richiesta* claim || *avere molte pretese*, to be hard to please; *avanzare pretese su*, to claim rights over.

pretesto *sm.* 1. pretext 2. (*occasione*) occasion.

pretore *sm.* magistrate.

prettamente *avv.* purely.

pretto *agg.* pure.

pretura *sf.* magistrate's court.

prevalente *agg.* prevailing.

prevalenza *sf.* prevalence.

prevalere *vi.* to prevail.

prevaricare *vi.* 1. to prevaricate 2. (*abusare del potere*) to abuse one's office.

prevaricatore *sm.* prevaricator.

prevaricazione *sf.* 1. prevarication 2. (*abuso di potere*) abuse of office.

prevedere *vt.* 1. to foresee (*v. irr.*) 2. (*di legge, contratto*) to provide (for).

prevedìbile *agg.* foreseeable.

preveggente *agg.* foreseeing.

preveggenza *sf.* foresight.

prevenire *vt.* 1. (*precedere*) to forestall 2. (*evitare*) to prevent 3. (*avvertire*) to warn.

preventivamente *avv.* 1. beforehand 2. (*in modo preventivo*) preventively.

preventivare *vt.* to estimate.

preventivo *agg.* 1. preventive 2. (*comm.*) estimated || *bilancio* —, budget. ♦ **preventivo** *sm.* estimate

preventorio *sm.* preventive sanatorium.

prevenuto *agg. essere — contro*, to have a prejudice against.

prevenzione *sf.* 1. prejudice 2. (*il prevenire*) prevention.

previdente *agg.* provident.

previdenza *sf.* providence: — *sociale*, social security.

previdenziale *agg.* social security (*attr.*).

previo *agg.* 1. previous 2. (*soggetto a*) subject to.

previsione *sf.* 1. forecast 2. (*comm.*) estimate.

previsto *agg.* 1. foreseen 2. (*comm.*) estimated 3. (*giur.*) provided.

prevosto *sm.* V. *preposto*.

preziosismo *sm.* preciosity.

preziosità *sf.* preciousness.

prezioso *agg.* precious. ♦ **prezioso** *sm.* jewel.

prezzémolo *sm.* parsley.

prezzo *sm.* 1. price, cost 2. (*valore*) value || *a — di*, at the cost of.

prezzolare *vt.* to hire.

prezzolato *agg.* (*mercenario*) mercenary.

prigione *sf.* 1. prison 2. (*pena*) imprisonment.

prigionìa *sf.* imprisonment.

prigioniero *agg.* imprisoned. ♦ **prigioniero** *sm.* prisoner.

prillare *vi.* to twirl.

prima[1] *avv.* 1. before 2. (*in anticipo*) in advance 3. (*un tempo*) once 4. (*più presto*) earlier, sooner 5. (*per prima cosa*) first || — *o poi*, sooner or later; *quanto* —, soon. ♦ **prima** *prep.* before. ♦ **prima che, di** *cong.* before.

prima[2] *sf.* 1. (*ferr.; scuola*) first class 2. (*teat.*) première.

primario *agg.* primary. ♦ **primario** *sm.* head physician.

primate *sm.* (*eccl.*) primate.

primati *sm. pl.* (*zool.*) Primates.

primaticcio *agg.* early.

primatista *s.* record-holder.

primato *sm.* 1. supremacy 2. (*sport*) record.

primavera *sf.* spring.

primaverile *agg.* spring (*attributivo*), springlike.

primeggiare *vi.* to excel.

primigenio *agg.* primigenial.

primìpara *sf.* primipara (*pl.* -ae).

primitivo *agg.* e *sm.* primitive.

primizia *sf.* 1. (*frutta*) early fruit

2. (*verdura*) early vegetable 3. (*novità*) novelty.
primo *agg.* 1. first 2. (*principale*) chief 3. (*iniziale*) early 4. (*prossimo*) next ‖ *in un — tempo*, at first.
primogènito *agg.* e *sm.* first-born.
primogenitura *sf.* primogeniture.
primordiale *agg.* primeval.
primordi *sm. pl.* beginnings.
prìmula *sf.* primrose.
principale *agg.* principal. ♦ **principale** *sm.* master, boss.
principato *sm.* principality.
prìncipe *sm.* prince.
principesco *agg.* princely.
principessa *sf.* princess.
principiante *sm.* beginner.
principiare *vt.* e *vi.* to begin (*v. irr.*).
principio *sm.* 1. (*inizio*) beginning 2. (*norma*) principle: *per —*, on principle.
priora *sf.* prioress.
priorato *sm.* priorate.
priore *sm.* prior.
priorità *sf.* priority.
prisma *sm.* prism.
prismàtico *agg.* prismatic(al).
prìstino *agg.* former.
privare *vt.* to deprive.
privatista *s.* external student.
privativa *sf.* 1. (*esclusiva*) sole right 2. (*monopolio*) monopoly 3. (*tabaccheria*) tobacconist's shop.
privativo *agg.* privative.
privato *agg.* 1. private 2. (*privo*) deprived. ♦ **privato** *sm.* private citizen.
privazione *sf.* 1. (*disagio*) privation 2. (*perdita*) loss.
privilegiare *vt.* to privilege.
privilegiato *agg.* 1. privileged 2. (*comm.*) preferred.
privilegio *sm.* privilege.
privo *agg.* devoid: *— di padre*, fatherless; *— di madre*, motherless.
pro¹ *prep.* for.
pro² *sm. a che —?*, what is the use of?
proavo *sm.* great grandfather.
probàbile *agg.* probable.
probabilismo *sm.* probabilism.
probabilità *sf.* probability.
probante *agg.* probatory.
probativo *agg.* probative.
probità *sf.* uprightness.
probiviri *sm. pl.* arbiters.

problema *sm.* problem.
problematicità *sf.* problematic nature.
problemàtico *agg.* problematic(al).
probo *agg.* upright.
proboscidati *sm. pl.* Proboscidea.
probòscide *sf.* trunk.
procaccia *sm.* postman (*pl.* -men).
procacciare *vt.* to get (*v. irr.*). ♦ **procacciarsi** *vr.* to get.
procacciatore *sm.* procurer.
procace *agg.* 1. (*provocante*) provoking 2. (*inverecondo*) immodest.
procacità *sf.* 1. provocativeness 2. (*inverecondia*) immodesty.
pro capite *loc. avv.* each.
procèdere *vi.* 1. to proceed, to go (*v. irr.*) on 2. (*agire*) to act.
procedimento *sm.* 1. (*progressione*) course 2. (*condotta*) behaviour 3. (*giur.*) proceedings (*pl.*) 4. (*tec.*) process.
procedura *sf.* 1. procedure 2. (*giur.*) practice.
procedurale *agg.* procedural.
procella *sf.* storm.
procellaria *sf.* stormy-petrel.
procelloso *agg.* stormy.
processare *vt.* to try: *far —*, to prosecute.
processionaria *sf.* processioner.
processione *sf.* procession.
processo *sm.* 1. (*giur.*) trial 2. (*med.; chim.; tec.*) process ‖ *andare sotto —*, to be tried; *intentare un —*, to bring (*v. irr.*) an action.
processuale *agg.* trial (*attr.*).
procinto (*nella loc. avv.*) *in — di*, on the point of.
proclama *sm.* proclamation.
proclamare *vt.* to proclaim.
proclamatore *sm.* proclaimer.
proclamazione *sf.* proclamation.
proclive *agg.* inclined.
proclività *sf.* inclination.
procònsole *sm.* proconsul.
procrastinare *vt.* to postpone. ♦ **procrastinare** *vi.* to procrastinate.
procrastinazione *sf.* procrastination.
procreare *vt.* to procreate.
procreatore *sm.* procreator.
procreazione *sf.* procreation.
procura *sf.* 1. proxy: *per —*, *by* proxy 2. (*documento*) letter of attorney.
procurare *vt.* 1. to get (*v. irr.*) 2. (*causare*) to cause 3. (*cercare*) to

try. ♦ **procurarsi** *vr.* to get (*v. irr.*).
procuratore *sm.* attorney.
prode *agg.* brave.
prodezza *sf.* **1.** bravery **2.** (*azione*) brave deed.
prodiere *sm.* bowman (*pl.* -men).
prodiero *agg.* forward.
prodigalità *sf.* lavishness.
prodigare *vt.* to lavish. ♦ **prodigarsi** *vr.* to do (*v. irr.*) all one can.
prodigio *sm.* prodigy.
prodigiosità *sf.* prodigiousness
prodigioso *agg.* prodigious.
pròdigo *agg.* lavish.
proditoriamente *avv.* treacherously.
proditorio *agg.* treacherous.
prodotto *sm.* **1.** product **2.** (*risultato*) result **3.** (*agr.*) produce.
pròdromo *sm.* **1.** warning sign **2.** (*med.*) symptom.
produrre *vt.* to produce. ♦ **prodursi** *vr.* **1.** (*causarsi*) to cause oneself **2.** (*accadere*) to happen **3.** (*esibirsi*) to perform (before).
produttività *sf.* productivity.
produttivo *agg.* productive.
produttore *agg.* productive. ♦ **produttore** *sm.* producer.
produzione *sf.* production.
proemio *sm.* proem.
profanamente *avv.* profanely.
profanare *vt.* to profane.
profanatore *agg.* profaning. ♦ **profanatore** *sm.* profaner.
profanazione *sf.* profanation.
profanità *sf.* profanity.
profano *agg.* profane. ♦ **profano** *sm.* (*persona inesperta*) layman (*pl.* -men) || *i profani*, the laity.
proferire *vt.* **1.** to pronounce **2.** (*dire*) to utter.
professare *vt.* to profess.
professionale *agg.* professional: *scuola* —, vocational school.
professione *sf.* profession.
professionismo *sm.* professionalism.
professionista *sm.* **1.** professional man **2.** (*sport*) professional.
professorale *agg.* professorial.
professore *sm.* **1.** teacher **2.** (*ordinario di università*) professor.
profeta *sm.* prophet.
profetare *vt.* to prophesy.
profètico *agg.* prophetic(al).
profetizzare *vt.* V. *profetare.*

profezìa *sf.* prophecy.
profferire *vt.* **1.** (*offrire*) to offer **2.** (*pronunciare*) to utter.
profferta *sf.* offer.
proficuo *agg.* profitable.
profilare *vt.* **1.** to profile **2.** (*orlare*) to edge. ♦ **profilarsi** *vr.* **1.** to be outlined **2.** (*apparire*) to loom.
profilassi *sf.* prophylaxis.
profilato *agg.* **1.** (*delineato*) outlined **2.** (*affilato*) sharp **3.** (*orlato*) edged. ♦ **profilato** *sm.* section.
profilàttico *agg.* e *sm.* prophylactic.
profilo *sm.* **1.** (*contorno*) outline **2.** (*di viso*) profile **3.** (*studio letterario*) monograph.
profittare *vi.* **1.** (*trar profitto*) to avail oneself (of) **2.** (*progredire*) to make (*v. irr.*) progress **3.** (*guadagnare*) to make profits.
profittatore *sm.* profiteer.
profittévole *agg.* profitable.
profitto *sm.* profit: *trar* —, to profit (by); *mettere qc. a* —, to make (*v. irr.*) good use of sthg.
profluvio *sm.* flood.
profondamente *avv.* deeply: *dormire* —, to sleep (*v. irr.*) soundly.
profòndere *vt.* to lavish. ♦ **profòndersi** *vr.* to be profuse (in, of).
profondità *sf.* depth.
profondo *agg.* deep. ♦ **profondo** *sm.* depth.
pròfugo *sm.* refugee.
profumare *vt.* to scent. ♦ **profumarsi** *vr.* to spray oneself with scent.
profumatamente *avv.* (*fig.*) dearly.
profumeria *sf.* perfumery.
profumiere *sm.* perfumer.
profumo *sm.* perfume, scent.
profusamente *avv.* **1.** profusely **2.** (*lungamente*) at length.
profusione *sf.* profusion.
progenerare *vt.* to procreate.
progenie *sf.* progeny.
progenitore *sm.* ancestor.
progettare *vt.* to plan.
progettazione *sf.* planning.
progettista *s.* planner.
progetto *sm.* plan.
prognatismo *sm.* prognathism.
prognato *agg.* prognathous.
prògnosi *sf.* prognosis (*pl.* -ses).
programma *sm.* program(me).
programmare *vt.* to program(me).
programmatore *sm.* programmist.
programmazione *sf.* programming.

programmista *sm.* programmer.
progredire *vi.* **1.** to advance **2.** (*fig.*) to get (*v. irr.*) on **3.** (*far progressi*) to make (*v. irr.*) progress.
progressione *sf.* progression.
progressista *agg. e s.* progressive.
progressivamente *avv.* progressively.
progressivo *agg.* progressive.
progresso *sm.* progress.
proibire *vt.* **1.** to forbid (*v. irr.*) **2.** (*impedire*) to prevent.
proibitivo *agg.* prohibitive.
proibizione *sf.* prohibition.
proibizionismo *sm.* prohibitionism.
proibizionista *agg. e s.* prohibitionist.
proiettare *vt.* **1.** to project **2.** (*cine*) to show (*v. irr.*) ♦ **proiettare** *vi.* to project. ♦ **proiettarsi** *vr.* to be projected.
proiettile *sm.* shell.
proiettore *sm.* **1.** (*riflettore*) searchlight **2.** (*cine*) projector.
proiezione *sf.* **1.** projection **2.** (*cine*) movie show || *macchina da —*, projector; *sala di —*, projection room.
prole *sf.* issue.
proletariato *sm.* proletariat.
proletario *agg. e sm.* proletarian.
proliferare *vi.* to proliferate.
proliferazione *sf.* proliferation.
prolifico *agg.* prolific.
prolissità *sf.* prolixity.
prolisso *agg.* prolix.
prologo *sm.* prologue.
prolungàbile *agg.* extendable.
prolungamento *sm.* extension.
prolungare *vt.* **1.** to extend **2.** (*differire*) to postpone. ♦ **prolungarsi** *vr.* **1.** to extend **2.** (*dilungarsi*) to dwell (*v. irr.*) (on).
prolusione *sf.* opening lecture.
promemoria *sm.* memorandum (*pl.* -da).
promessa *sf.* promise.
promettente *agg.* promising.
prométtere *vt.* to promise: *— bene*, to be full of promise.
prominente *agg.* prominent.
prominenza *sf.* prominence.
promiscuità *sf.* promiscuity.
promiscuo *agg.* mixed, promiscuous.
promontorio *sm.* promontory.
promosso *agg.* **1.** (*a scuola*) successful **2.** (*sostenuto*) promoted.

promotore *sm.* promoter.
promozione *sf.* promotion.
promulgare *vt.* to promulgate.
promulgatore *sm.* promulgator.
promulgazione *sf.* promulgation.
promuòvere *vt.* **1.** to promote **2.** (*a scuola*) to pass.
prònao *sm.* pronaos (*pl.* -aoi).
pronipote *sm.* **1.** (*di bisnonno*) great-grandson, great-grandchild (*pl.* -children) **2.** (*di prozio*) grandnephew || *i pronipoti* (*discendenti*), descendants. ♦ **pronipote** *sf.* **1.** (*di bisnonno*) great-granddaughter, great-grandchild **2.** (*di prozio*) grandniece.
prono *agg.*· prone.
pronome *sm.* pronoun.
pronominale *agg.* pronominal.
pronosticare *vt.* **1.** to forecast (*v. irr.*) **2.** (*predire*) to foretell (*v. irr.*) **3.** (*far prevedere*) to portend.
pronòstico *sm.* forecast.
prontezza *sf.* readiness.
pronto *agg.* **1.** (*preparato*) ready **2.** (*veloce*) prompt **3.** (*al telefono*) hallo || *— soccorso*, first aid.
prontuario *sm.* handbook.
pronuncia *sf.* pronunciation.
pronunciamento *sm.* pronouncement.
pronunciare *vt.* **1.** to pronounce **2.** (*proferire*) to utter || *— un discorso*, to deliver a speech. ♦ **pronunciarsi** *vr.* to give (*v. irr.*) one's opinion.
pronunciato *agg.* pronounced.
propaganda *sf.* **1.** propaganda **2.** (*comm.*) advertising: *far — (comm.*), to advertise **3.** (*pol.*) canvass.
propagandare *vt.* **1.** to propagandize **2.** (*comm.*) to advertise.
propagandista *s.* **1.** propagandist **2.** (*comm.*) advertiser.
propagandìstico *agg.* **1.** propagandist **2.** (*comm.*) advertising.
propagare *vt.* to propagate. ♦ **propagarsi** *vr.* to propagate.
propagatore *sm.* propagator.
propagazione *sf.* propagation.
propagginare *vt.* (*agr.*) to layer.
propàggine *sf.* **1.** (*agr.*) layer **2.** (*geogr.*) ramification **3.** (*discendenza*) offspring.
propalare *vt.* to spread (*v. irr.*).
propano *sm.* propane.
propedèutica *sf.* propaedeutics.
propedèutico *agg.* propaedeutic(al).

propellente *agg.* propellent. ♦
propellente *sm.* propellant.
propèndere *vi.* to be inclined. ,
propensione *sf.* propensity.
propenso *agg.* inclined.
propilene *sm.* propylene.
propileo *sm.* propylaeum (*pl.* -laea).
propina *sf.* examiner's fee.
propinare *vt.* to give (*v. irr.*).
propiziare *vt.* to propitiate. ♦
propiziarsi *vr.* to gain so.'s favour.
propiziatore *sm.* propitiator.
propiziatorio *agg.* propitiatory.
propiziazione *sf.* propitiation.
propizio *agg.* favourable.
proponimento *sm.* resolution: *far —*, to resolve.
proporre *vt.* 1. to propose 2. (*suggerire*) to suggest. ♦ proporsi *vr.* to intend, to mean (*v. irr.*).
proporzionale *agg.* proportional.
proporzionalità *sf.* proportionality.
proporzionare *vt.* to proportion.
proporzionato *agg.* (*adeguato*) proportionate: *ben —*, well-proportioned.
proporzione *sf.* 1. proportion 2. (*rapporto*) ratio.
propòsito *sm.* 1. purpose 2. (*intenzione*) intention || *di —*, on purpose; *a — di*, with regard to; *a — (inter.*), by the way; *a — (al momento giusto)*, at the right moment.
proposizione *sf.* sentence.
proposta *sf.* proposal.
proprietà *sf.* 1. property 2. (*l'essere proprietario*) ownership 3. (*correttezza*) propriety || *— letteraria*, copyright.
proprietario *agg.* proprietary. ♦
proprietario *sm.* 1. owner 2. (*di locanda*) landlord 3. (*possidente*) man of property || *— terriero*, landowner.
proprio *agg.* 1. (*rafforzativo del poss.*) own 2. (*adatto*) suitable 3. (*mat.; gramm.*) proper || *vero e —*, real. ♦ proprio *avv.* 1. (*esattamente*) exactly 2. (*veramente*) really || *— ora*, just now; *— così*, just like that.
propugnare *vt.* to support.
propugnatore *sm.* supporter.
propulsione *sf.* propulsion.
propulsivo *agg.* propulsive.
propulsore *sm.* propeller.
prora *sf.* bow.

proravìa (*nella loc. avv.*) *a —*, at the bow.
pròroga *sf.* 1. (*giur.*) adjournment 2. (*dilazione*) extension.
prorogàbile *agg.* 1. (*giur.*) adjournable 2. extensible.
prorogare *vt.* 1. to delay, to extend 2. (*giur.*) to postpone.
prorompente *agg.* bursting (out).
proròmpere *vi.* 1. to burst-(*v. irr.*) (out) 2. (*di liquidi*) to gush out.
prosa *sf.* prose || *teatro di —*, drama; *compagnia di —*, dramatic company.
prosaicità *sf.* prosaism.
prosàico *agg.* prosaic.
prosapia *sf.* race.
prosàstico *agg.* prose (*attr.*).
prosatore *sm.* prose-writer.
proscenio *sm.* proscenium.
proscimmie *sf. pl.* lemurs.
prosciògliere *vt.* 1. (*da un obbligo*) to release 2. (*giur.*) to acquit.
proscioglimento *sm.* 1. release 2. (*giur.*) acquittal.
prosciugamento *sm.* 1. drying up 2. (*artificiale*) draining.
prosciugare *vt.* 1. to dry up 2. (*artificialmente*) to drain. ♦ prosciugarsi *vr.* to dry up.
prosciutto *sm.* ham.
proscritto *sm.* exile.
proscrivere *vt.* to banish.
proscrizione *sf.* banishment.
prosecuzione *sf.* prosecution.
proseguimento *sm.* continuation.
proseguire *vt.* to continue. ♦ proseguire *vi.* to go (*v. irr.*) on.
proselitismo *sm.* proselytism.
prosèlito *sm.* proselyte.
proseguo *sm.* course.
prosodìa *sf.* prosody.
prosopopea *sf.* (*fig.*) haughtiness.
prosperare *vi.* to prosper.
prosperità *sf.* prosperity.
pròspero *agg.* prosperous.
prosperoso *agg.* 1. prosperous 2. (*in salute*) healthy.
prospettare *vt.* 1. (*indicare*) to point out 2. (*guardare*) to look on to.
prospèttico *agg.* perspective (*attr.*).
prospettiva *sf.* 1. perspective 2. (*possibilità*) prospect.
prospetto *sm.* 1. view 2. (*fronte*) front 3. (*specchietto, programma*) prospectus.
prospezione *sf.* prospecting.
prospiciente *agg.* facing.

prossimità *sf.* closeness: *in — di,* near.

pròssimo *agg.* 1. (*vicino*) near 2. (*seguente*) next. ♦ **pròssimo** *sm.* fellow creatures (*pl.*), neighbour.

pròstata *sf.* prostate.

prosternare *vt.* to prostrate.

prostituire *vt.* to prostitute.

prostituta *sf.* prostitute.

prostituzione *sf.* prostitution.

prostrare *vt.* to prostrate. ♦ **prostrarsi** *vr.* to bow down.

prostrazione *sf.* prostration.

protagonista *s.* protagonist.

protèggere *vt.* to protect.

protèico *agg.* protein (*attr.*).

proteina *sf.* protein.

protèndere *vt.* to stretch (out): — *lo sguardo,* to gaze. ♦ **protèndersi** *vr.* to stretch oneself.

protervia *sf.* insolence.

protervo *agg.* insolent.

pròtesi *sf.* prosthesis.

protesta *sf.* protest.

protestante *agg.* e *s.* protestant.

protestantésimo *sm.* Protestantism.

protestare *vt.* e *vi.* to protest.

protesto *sm.* protest: *in —,* under protest; *lasciar andare una cambiale in —,* to dishonour a bill.

protettivo *agg.* protective.

protetto *agg.* protected. ♦ **protetto** *sm.* favourite.

protettorato *sm.* protectorate.

protettore *sm.* 1. protector 2. (*patrono*) patron.

protezione *sf.* 1. protection 2. (*patronato*) patronage.

protezionismo *sm.* protectionism.

protezionista *s.* protectionist.

proto *sm.* overseer.

protocollare *agg.* protocol (*attr.*).

protocollo *sm.* 1. protocol 2. (*registro*) record || *mettere a —,* to record; *carta —,* foolscap.

protone *sm.* proton.

protoplasma *sm.* protoplasm.

protòtipo *sm.* prototype.

protozoi *sm. pl.* Protozoa.

protrarre *vt.* 1. to protract 2. (*differire*) to defer. ♦ **protrarsi** *vr.* to go (*v. irr.*) on.

protrazione *sf.* 1. protraction 2. (*differimento*) deferment.

protuberanza *sf.* bulge.

prova *sf.* 1. proof 2. (*giur.*) evidence (*solo sing.*) 3. (*esperimento, esame*) test 4. (*tentativo*) try 5.

(*sventura*) trial 6. (*teat.*) rehearsal 7. (*di abito*) fitting || *in —,* on trial; *dar — di essere,* to prove to be; *superare una —,* to pass a test.

provare *vt.* 1. to prove 2. (*tentare, mettere alla prova*) to try 3. (*sentire*) to feel (*v. irr.*) 4. (*di abiti*) to try on 5. (*teat.*) to rehearse 6. (*collaudare*) to test. ♦ **provarsi** *vr.* 1. (*tentare*) to try 2. (*cimentarsi*) to engage (in).

provenienza *sf.* origin.

provenire *vi.* to come (*v. irr.*).

provento *sm.* 1. proceeds (*pl.*) 2. (*reddito*) income.

proverbiale *agg.* proverbial.

proverbio *sm.* proverb.

provetta *sf.* test-tube.

provetto *agg.* skilled.

provincia *sf.* province.

provinciale *agg.* e *s.* provincial: *strada —,* main road.

provincialismo *sm.* provincialism.

provino *sm.* 1. (*teat.*) tryout 2. (*cine*) test film.

provocante *agg.* 1. provocative 2. (*procace*) immodest.

provocare *vt.* 1. to provoke 2. (*causare*) to cause.

provocatore *sm.* provoker.

provocazione *sf.* provocation.

provvedere *vi.* 1. to provide (for) 2. (*badare a*) to see (*v. irr.*) (to) 3. (*aver cura di*) to take (*v. irr.*) care of. ♦ **provvedere** *vt.* 1. to provide 2. (*preparare*) to prepare.

provvedimento *sm.* measure.

provveduto *agg.* 1. provided (with) 2. (*accorto*) wary.

provvidenza *sf.* providence: *essere una —,* to be providential.

provvidenziale *agg.* providential.

pròvvido *agg.* provident.

provvigione *sf.* 1. (*comm.*) commission 2. (*provvista*) supply.

provvisorietà *sf.* temporariness.

provvisorio *agg.* temporary: *in via provvisoria,* temporarily.

provvista *sf.* supply, provision (*specialmente di cibo*).

provvisto *agg.* 1. supplied (with) 2. (*fig.*) well-off.

prua *sf.* bow.

prudente *agg.* 1. prudent 2. (*cauto*) careful.

prudenza *sf.* 1. prudence 2. (*cautela*) care 3. (*precauzione*) precaution.

prùdere *vi.* to itch.
prugna *sf.* plum.
prugno *sm.* plum-tree.
pruno *sm.* **1.** thorn-bush **2.** (*spina*) thorn.
pruriginoso *agg.* itching
prurito *sm.* itch.
prùssico *agg.* prussic.
pseudònimo *sm.* pseudonym.
psicanàlisi *sf.* psychoanalysis.
psicanalista *s.* psychoanalyst.
psicanalìtico *agg.* psychoanalytic(al).
psicanalizzare *vt.* to psychoanalyze.
psiche *sf.* psyche.
psichiatra *s.* psychiatrist.
psichiatrìa *sf.* psychiatry.
psichiàtrico *agg.* psychiatric(al).
psìchico *agg.* psychic(al).
psicologìa *sf.* psychology.
psicològico *agg.* psychologic(al).
psicòlogo *sm.* psychologist.
psicometrìa *sf.* psychometry.
psicopatìa *sf.* psychopathy.
psicopàtico *agg.* e *sm.* psychopathic.
psicopatologìa *sf.* psychopathology.
psicosi *sf.* psychosis (*pl.* -ses).
psicoterapìa *sf.* psychotherapy.
psittacosi *sf.* psittacosis.
pubblicàbile *agg.* publishable.
pubblicano *sm.* publican.
pubblicare *vt.* **1.** to publish **2.** (*di leggi ecc.*) to issue.
pubblicazione *sf.* publication: *fare le pubblicazioni di matrimonio*, to put up the banns.
pubblicista *s.* journalist.
pubblicità *sf.* **1.** publicity **2.** (*propaganda*) advertising || *fare* —, to advertise.
pubblicitario *agg.* advertising.
pùbblico *agg.* public. ♦ **pùbblico** *sm.* **1.** public **2.** (*in teatro ecc.*) audience **3.** (*cine*) moviegoers (*pl.*).
pube *sm.* pubis (*pl.* -bes).
pubertà *sf.* puberty.
pudibondo *agg.* demure.
pudicizia *sf.* demureness.
pudico *agg.* demure.
pudore *sm.* decency.
puericoltura *sf.* puericulture.
puerile *agg.* childish.
puerilità *sf.* childishness.
puèrpera *sf.* childwife (*pl.* -wives).
pugilato *sm.* boxing: *fare del* —, to box

pùgile *sm.* boxer.
pugnalare *vt.* to stab.
pugnalata *sf.* **1.** stab **2.** (*fig.*) blow.
pugnale *sm.* dagger.
pugno *sm.* **1.** fist **2.** (*colpo*) punch **3.** (*manciata*) handful || *colpire col* —, to punch; *in* —, in one's hand; *di proprio* —, in one's own handwriting; *fare a pugni*, to fight (*v. irr.*), (*fig.*) to clash.
pula *sf.* chaff.
pulce *sf.* flea: — *in un orecchio*, suspicion.
pulcino *sm.* chick.
puledro *sm.* colt.
puleggia *sf.* pulley.
pulire *vt.* to clean: *pulirsi la bocca*, to wipe one's mouth.
pulito *agg.* clean.
pulitore *sm.* cleaner.
pulizìa *sf.* **1.** (*il pulire*) cleaning **2.** (*l'essere pulito*) cleanliness.
pullulare *vi.* to swarm (with).
pùlpito *sm.* pulpit.
pulsante *sm.* push button.
pulsare *vi.* to beat (*v. irr.*)
pulsazione *sf.* beat.
pulverulento *agg.* dusty.
pulvìscolo *sm.* dust: — *atmosferico*, motes (*pl.*).
puma *sm.* puma.
pungente *agg.* **1.** prickly **2.** (*fig.*) biting.
pùngere *vt.* **1.** to sting (*v. irr.*) **2.** (*di ago*) to prick **3.** (*fig.*) to tease. ♦ **pùngersi** *vr.* to prick oneself.
pungiglione *sm.* sting.
pungitopo *sm.* (*bot.*) butcher's broom.
pungolare *vt.* to goad.
pùngolo *sm.* goad.
punìbile *agg.* punishable.
punire *vt.* to punish: — *una offesa*, to revenge an insult.
punitivo *agg.* punitive.
punitore *agg.* punitory. ♦ **punitore** *sm.* punisher.
punizione *sf.* punishment.
punta *sf.* **1.** point **2.** (*estremità*) tip **3.** (*cima*) top **4.** (*un po'*) bit **5.** (*dolore, fitta*) twinge || *sulla — dei piedi*, on tiptoe; *avere qc. sulla — delle dita*, to have sthg. at one's finger-tips.
puntale *sm.* (*di bastone ecc.*) ferrule.
puntamento *sm.* aim.
puntare *vt.* **1.** to point (at) **2.** (*mirare*) to aim (at) **3.** (*spingere*) to

push 4. (*scommettere*) to bet (*v. irr.*) || — *i piedi* (*fig.*), to put (*v. irr.*) one's foot down. ◆ **puntare** *vi.* to head.

puntata *sf.* 1. (*al gioco*) stake 2. (*di romanzo*) instalment.

puntatore *sm.* 1. (*mil.*) marksman (*pl.* -men) 2. (*al gioco*) better.

punteggiare *vt.* 1. to punctuate 2. (*nel disegno*) to dot.

punteggiatura *sf.* 1. punctuation 2. (*nel disegno*) dotting.

punteggio *sm.* (*sport*) score.

puntellare *vt.* to prop.

puntellatura *sf.* propping.

puntello *sm.* prop.

punteruolo *sm.* punch.

puntiglio *sm.* 1. punctilio 2. (*ostinazione*) obstinacy || *per* —, out of pique.

puntigliosamente *avv.* 1. punctiliously 2. (*ostinatamente*) obstinately.

puntiglioso *agg.* 1. punctilious 2. (*ostinato*) obstinate.

puntina *sf.* 1. (*da fonografo*) needle 2. (*da disegno*) drawing-pin.

puntino *sm.* dot: *puntini di sospensione*, dots || *a* —, properly.

punto[1] *sm.* 1. point 2. (*di cucito*) stitch 3. (*voto*) mark 4. (*gramm.*) full stop 5. (*macchiolina*) dot || *due punti*, colon; — *e virgola*, semicolon; *mettere a* —, to set (*v. irr.*) up.

punto[2] *avv.* not at all.

punto[3] *agg. e pron.* not ... any.

puntone *sm.* (*edil.*) strut.

puntuale *agg.* punctual.

puntualità *sf.* punctuality.

puntualizzare *vt.* to stress.

puntualmente *avv.* punctually.

puntura *sf.* 1. (*di insetto*) sting 2. (*di ago*) prick 3. (*iniezione*) injection 4. (*dolore, fitta*) pain.

puntuto *agg.* pointed.

punzecchiamento *sm.* 1. (*d'insetto*) stinging 2. (*d'ago*) pricking 3. (*fig.*) teasing.

punzecchiare *vt.* 1. (*di insetti*) to sting (*v. irr.*) 2. (*fig.*) to tease.

punzonare *vt.* to punch.

punzonatrice *sf.* (*mecc.*) punch.

punzonatura *sf.* punching.

punzone *sm.* punch.

pupàttola *sf.* doll.

pupazzetto *sm.* (*disegno*) sketch.

pupazzo *sm.* puppet.

pupilla *sf.* pupil.

pupillo *sm.* pupil.

pupo *sm.* baby.

purché *cong.* provided (that).

pure *avv.* 1. (*anche*) also, too 2. (*eppure*) yet 3. (*di concessione*) as you like, of course. ◆ **pure** *cong.* 1. (*con frasi concessive*) even though 2. (*tuttavia*) but, yet. ◆ **pure di** *cong.* if only.

purè *sm.* purée: — *di patate*, mashed potatoes; *fare un* — *di verdura*, to mash vegetables.

purezza *sf.* purity.

purga *sf.* purgative, purge.

purgante *sm.* purgative, purge.

purgare *vt.* 1. to purge 2. (*di scritti*) to expurgate.

purgativo *agg.* purgative.

purgatorio *sm.* purgatory.

purificare *vt.* to purify.

purificatore *agg.* purificatory.

purificazione *sf.* purification.

purismo *sm.* purism.

purista *s.* purist.

puritanésimo *sm.* Puritanism.

puritano *agg. e sm.* Puritan.

puro *agg.* 1. pure 2. (*mero*) mere.

purosangue *sm.* thoroughbred.

purpùreo *agg.* purple.

purpurina *sf.* purpurin.

purtroppo *avv.* unfortunately.

purulento *agg.* purulent.

pus *sm.* pus.

pusillànime *agg.* pusillanimous. ◆ **pusillànime** *s.* coward.

pusillanimità *sf.* pusillanimity.

pùstola *sf.* pustule.

putacaso *loc. avv.* supposing.

putativo *agg.* putative.

putiferio *sm.* uproar: *sollevare un* —, to make (*v. irr.*) an uproar.

putrèdine *sf.* 1. putridness 2. (*cosa putrefatta*) rot.

putrefare *vi.* to rot. ◆ **putrefarsi** *vr.* to rot.

putrefatto *agg.* rotten.

putrefazione *sf.* putrefaction.

putrella *sf.* iron beam.

putrescenza *sf.* putrescence.

putrescìbile *agg.* putréscible.

putridità *sf.* rottenness.

pùtrido *agg.* rotten.

putridume *sm.* rot.

putto *sm.* putto (*pl.* -ti).

puzza *sf.* V. *puzzo*.

puzzare *vi.* to stink (*v. irr.*).

puzzo *sm.* stench.

pùzzola *sf.* polecat.

puzzolente *agg.* stinking.

Q

qua *avv.* here: *di — di*, on this side of; *per di —*, this way; *da quando in —?*, since when?

quàcchero *agg. e sm.* Quaker.

quaderno *sm.* exercise-book.

quadrangolare *agg.* quadrangular.

quadràngolo *sm.* quadrangle.

quadrante *sm.* 1. quadrant 2. (*di orologio*) dial.

quadrare *vt.* 1. (*geom.*) to square 2. (*formare*) to shape. ♦ **quadrare** *vi.* (*corrispondere*) to suit.

quadrato *agg.* 1. square 2. (*fig.*) strong. ♦ **quadrato** *sm.* 1. square 2. (*sport*) ring.

quadratura *sf.* 1. squaring 2. (*mat.*) quadrature.

quadrettato *agg.* 1. squared 2. (*di tessuto*) chequered.

quadriennale *agg.* quadrennial.

quadriennio *sm.* quadrennium (*pl.* -ia).

quadrifoglio *sm.* four-leaved clover.

quadriglia *sf.* quadrille.

quadrilàtero *sm.* quadrilateral.

quadrimotore *sm.* four-engined aircraft.

quadrivio *sm.* cross-roads.

quadro *agg.* V. *quadrato.* ♦ **quadro** *sm.* 1. picture 2. (*tabella*) table 3. (*teat.*) scene 4. (*elettr.*) board 5. (*mil.*) cadre ‖ *galleria di quadri*, picture-gallery; — *riassuntivo*, summary; — *degli interruttori*, switch board.

quadrùmane *agg.* quadrumanous. ♦ **quadrùmane** *sm.* quadrumane.

quadrùpede *agg. e sm.* quadruped.

quadruplicare *vt.* to quadruple. ♦ **quadruplicarsi** *vr.* to quadruple.

quàdruplo *agg. e sm.* 1. quadruple 2. (*quattro volte tanto*) four times as much.

quaggiù *avv.* down here.

quaglia *sf.* quail.

qualche *agg.* (*in frasi affermative e interrogative che aspettano risposta affermativa*) some; (*in frasi interrogative, dubitative, condizionali*) any ‖ — *volta*, sometimes; *in — luogo*, somewhere; *in — modo*, somehow.

qualcosa *pron.* something, anything (*per l'uso* V. *qualche*).

qualcuno *pron.* 1. somebody, someone 2. (*alcuni*) some, any: — *di,*

some, any of (*per l'uso* V. *qualche*).

quale *pron. rel.* 1. (*per persone*) who (*sogg.*), whom (*altri casi*) 2. (*per animali, cose*) which 3. (*per tutti, solo sogg. e ogg.*) that ‖ *del — (poss.*), whose: *l'uomo la casa del —*, the man whose house. ♦ **quale** *agg. e pron. int.* 1. (*di che tipo*) what 2. (*scelta tra numero limitato*) which. ♦ **quale** *agg. escl.* what. ♦ **quale** *pron.* (*correlativo di "tale"*) as ‖ *è tale e — suo fratello*, he is just like his brother.

qualìfica *sf.* 1. qualification 2. (*titolo*) title.

qualificare *vt.* to qualify.

qualificativo *agg.* qualifying.

qualificato *agg.* qualified: *operaio —*, skilled worker.

qualificazione *sf.* qualification.

qualità *sf.* 1. quality 2. (*specie*) kind 3. (*ufficio*) capacity.

qualitativo *agg.* qualitative.

qualora *cong.* in case.

qualsìasi *agg.* V. *qualunque.*

qualunque *agg.* 1. any 2. (*quale che sia*) whatever; (*riferito a numero limitato*) whichever 3. (*comune*) ordinary ‖ *uno —*, anybody; — *cosa*, anything; *in — posto*, anywhere; *in — modo*, anyhow.

quando *avv. e cong.* when ‖ *da —*, since; *da —?*, since when?; *quand'anche*, even though; *di — in —*, now and then.

quantità *sf.* quantity: *una gran — di*, a great deal of.

quantitativo *agg.* quantitative. ♦ **quantitativo** *sm.* V. *quantità.*

quanto *agg.* how much (*pl.* how many) ‖ *tanto... —*, as much... as; *tanti... quanti*, as many... as; — *tempo?* how long? ♦ **quanto** *avv.* how, how much ‖ *tanto —*, as much as; *tanti... —*, as... as; *tanto... — (sia... sia)*, both ...and; — *più... tanto più*, the more... the more; — *più... tanto meno*, the more... the less; — *a*, as for; — *prima*, soon; *per —*, however; — *fa?*, how much is it?

quantunque *cong.* though, although.

quaranta *agg.* forty.

quarantena *sf.* quarantine.

quarantenne *agg.* forty years old, forty-year-old (*attr.*).

quarantèsimo *agg.* fortieth.

quarantina *sf.* about forty: *aver*

passato la —, to be over forty.
quarésima *sf.* Lent.
quartetto *sm.* quartet.
quartiere *sm.* **1.** (*di una città*) quarter **2.** (*rione amministrativo*) district || — *generale*, headquarters (*pl.*).
quartina *sf.* quatrain.
quarto *agg.* fourth. ◆ **quarto** *sm.* quarter.
quarzo *sm.* quartz.
quasi *avv.* almost: — *mai*, hardly ever.
quassù *avv.* up here.
quaterna *sf.* set of four numbers.
quaternario *agg.* quaternary. ◆ **quaternario** *sm.* (*verso di una poesia*) line of four syllables.
quatto *agg.* **1.** squatting **2.** (*silenzioso*) silent || — —, very quietly.
quattordicèsimo *agg.* fourteenth.
quattòrdici *agg.* fourteen.
quattrini *sm. pl.* money (*us. al sing.*): *star male a* —, to be hard up.
quattro *agg.* four || *in* — *e* — *otto*, in no time; *fare il diavolo a* —, to make (*v. irr.*) a hullabaloo; *farsi in* —, to do (*v. irr.*) one's utmost.
quattrocchi (*nella loc. avv.*) *a* —, privately.
quattrocento *agg.* four hundred. ◆ **quattrocento** *sm. il* —, the fifteenth century.
quattromila *agg.* four thousand.
quegli *agg.* V. *quelli.* ◆ **quegli** *pron.* V. *egli.*
quei *agg. e pron.* V. *quelli.*
quella *agg. e pron.* V. *quello.*
quelle *agg. e pron.* V. *quelli.*
quelli *agg.* those. ◆ **quelli** *pron.* those, the ones.
quello *agg.* that. ◆ **quello** *pron.* that, the one || — *che* (*ciò che*), what; *tutto* — *che*, all that.
quercia *sf.* oak.
querela *sf.* **1.** complaint **2.** (*giur.*) action; *sporger* —, to bring (*v. irr.*) an action.
querelante *s.* plaintiff.
querelare *vt.* to proceed (against).
querelato *sm.* defendant.
quèrulo *agg.* querulous.
quesito *sm.* question.
questa *agg. e pron.* V. *questo.*
queste *agg. e pron.* V. *questi.*
questi *agg.* these. ◆ **questi** *pron.* **1.** these **2.** (*sing.*) this (*man*).

questionare *vi.* to quarrel.
questionario *sm.* questionnaire.
questione *sf.* **1.** question **2.** (*lite*) quarrel.
questo *agg.* this. ◆ **questo** *pron.* this, that || — *...quello* (*il primo... il secondo*) the former... the latter.
questore *sm.* questor.
questua *sf.* **1.** begging **2.** (*in chiesa*) collection.
questuante *agg.* begging. ◆ **questuante** *s.* beggar.
questuare *vi.* to beg.
questura *sf.* police-headquarters (*pl.*).
questurino *sm.* cop.
qui *avv.* here: *per di* —, this way; — *vicino*, close by; *da* — *innanzi*, from now on; *di* — *a un anno*, a year from now; *di* — *a otto giorni*, a week today; *fin* — (*di tempo*), so far.
quiescenza *sf.* quiescence.
quietanza *sf.* receipt.
quietare *vt.* to quiet. ◆ **quietarsi** *vr.* to quiet down.
quiete *sf.* quiet.
quietismo *sm.* quietism.
quieto *agg.* quiet || *star* — (*zitto*), to keep (*v. irr.*) quiet; *star* — (*fermo*), to keep (*v. irr.*) still; — —, very quietly.
quindi *avv.* **1.** therefore **2.** (*poi*) then.
quindicenne *agg.* fifteen years old, fifteen-year-old (*attr.*).
quindicèsimo *agg.* fifteenth.
quìndici *agg.* fifteen.
quindicina *sf.* **1.** about fifteen **2.** (*salario*) a fortnight's wages || *una* — *di giorni*, about a fortnight.
quindicinale *agg.* fortnightly.
quinquennale *agg.* quinquennial.
quinta *sf.* (*teat.*) wing || *dietro le quinte*, behind the scenes.
quintale *sm.* quintal.
quinterno *sm.* five sheets (*pl.*).
quintessenza *sf.* quintessence.
quintetto *sm.* quintet(te).
quinto *agg.* fifth.
quintuplicare *vt.* to quintuple.
quintuplo *agg. e sm.* quintuple.
quisquilia *sf.* trifle.
quivi *avv.* here.
quota *sf.* **1.** share **2.** (*aer.*) altitude **3.** (*mar.*) depth || *perdere* —, to lose (*v. irr.*) height; *prender* —, to climb.

quotare *vt.* to quote. ♦ quotarsi *vr.* to subscribe.
quotato *agg.* 1. quoted 2. (*fig.*) esteemed.
quotazione *sf.* quotation.
quotidianamente *avv.* daily.
quotidiano *agg.* e *sm.* daily: *vita quotidiana,* everyday life.
quoziente *sm.* quotient.

R

rabàrbaro *sm.* rhubarb.
rabberciamento *sm.* patching (up).
rabberciare *vt.* to patch (up).
rabbia *sf.* 1. rage 2. (*idrofobia*) rabies || *far — a qu.,* to make (*v. irr.*) so. angry.
rabbino *sm.* rabbi.
rabbioso *agg.* 1. (*med.*) rabid 2. (*fig.*) angry.
rabbonire *vt.* to calm down.
rabbrividire *vi.* 1. (*di freddo*) to shiver 2. (*di paura ecc.*) to shudder.
rabbuffare *vt.* 1. to ruffle 2. (*rimproverare*) to reprimand.
rabbuffo *sm.* rebuke.
rabbuiarsi *vr.* to darken.
rabdomante *s.* dowser.
rabdomanzìa *sf.* dowsing.
rabesco *sm.* V. *arabesco.*
raccapezzare *vt.* 1. (*raccogliere*) to gather 2. (*capire*) to understand (*v. irr.*). ♦ raccapezzarsi *vr.* to see (*v. irr.*) one's way.
raccapricciante *agg.* horrifying.
raccapricciare *vt.* to horrify. ♦ raccapricciarsi *vr.* to be horrified.
raccapriccio *sm.* horror.
raccattare *vt.* to pick up.
racchétta *sf.* racket.
racchio *agg.* ugly.
racchiùdere *vt.* to contain.
raccògliere *vt.* 1. to pick (up) 2. (*radunare*) to gather 3. (*far collezione*) to collect 4. (*accogliere*) to shelter 5. (*agr.*) to reap. ♦ raccògliersi *vr.* 1. to gather 2. (*concentrarsi*) to collect one's thoughts.
raccoglimento *sm.* 1. concentration 2. (*meditazione*) meditation.
raccogliticcio *agg.* picked up at random.

raccoglitore *sm.* 1. picker 2. (*collezionista*) collector 3. (*cartella*) folder.
raccolta *sf.* 1. (*agr.*) harvest; (*di frutta, cotone*) picking 2. (*collezione*) collection 3. (*adunanza*) gathering || *fare la —,* to harvest; *chiamare a —,* to collect.
raccoltamente *avv.* intently
raccolto *sm.* harvest.
raccomandàbile *agg.* recommendable.
raccomandare *vt.* 1. to recommend 2. (*esortare*) to urge 3. (*di lettere, pacchi*) to register. ♦ raccomandarsi *vr.* to beg (so.).
raccomandata *sf.* registered letter: *fare una —,* to register a letter.
raccomandazione *sf.* 1. recommendation 2. (*consiglio*) advice 3. (*di lettere, pacchi*) registration.
raccomodare *vt.* to mend.
raccontare *vt.* to tell (*v. irr.*) || *si racconta,* it is said.
racconto *sm.* 1. tale 2. (*resoconto*) relation.
raccorciare *vt.* to shorten. ♦ raccorciarsi *vr.* to grow (*v. irr.*) shorter.
raccordare *vt.* to connect.
raccordo *sm.* 1. connection 2. (*mecc.*) union 3. (*ferr.*) siding.
ràchide *sf.* rachis (*pl.* -ides).
rachìtico *agg.* rickety.
rachitismo *sm.* rickets.
racimolare *vt.* to glean.
rada *sf.* roadstead.
radar *sm.* radar.
raddobbare *vt.* 1. (*mar.*) to repair 2. (*riparare*) to refit.
raddobbo *sm.* (*mar.*) repair.
raddolcimento *sm.* 1. sweetening 2. (*fig.*) softening.
raddolcire *vt.* 1. to sweeten 2. (*fig.*) to soften 3. (*alleviare*) to soothe. ♦ raddolcirsi *vr.* 1. to soften 2. (*alleviarsi*) to be soothed 3. (*mitigarsi*) to grow (*v. irr.*) milder.
raddoppiamento *sm.* doubling.
raddoppiare *vt.* to double. ♦ raddoppiarsi *vr.* to double.
raddoppio *sm.* doubling.
raddrizzamento *sm.* 1. straightening 2. (*correzione*) redressing.
raddrizzare *vt.* 1. to straighten 2. (*correggere*) to redress.
radente *agg.* 1. shaving 2. (*rasente*) grazing.

ràdere vt. 1. to shave 2. (sfiorare) to graze 3. (distruggere) to raze.

radezza sf. 1. thinness 2. (rarità) infrequency.

radiale agg. radial.

radiante agg. radiant.

radiare vt. 1. to radiate 2. (espellere) to expel 3. (un nome) to strike (v. irr.) off.

radiatore sm. radiator.

radiazione sf. 1. radiation 2. (espulsione) expulsion.

radicale agg. radical.

radicalismo sm. radicalism.

radicare vi. to root. ♦ **radicarsi** vr. to root.

radicato agg. deep-rooted.

radice sf. root.

radio[1] sm. (anat.) radius (pl. -dii).

radio[2] sm. (chim.) radium.

radio[3] sf. radio, wireless: ponte —, radiolink; alla —, on the radio; — portatile ricevente e trasmittente, walkie-talkie.

radioattività sf. radioactivity.

radioattivo agg. radioactive.

radioaudizione sf. 1. broadcasting 2. (ascolto) listening.

radiocomunicazione sf. wireless communication.

radiocrònaca sf. running commentary, radio account.

radiocronista s. radio commentator, wireless commentator.

radiodiffusione sf. broadcast.

radioestesìa sf. sensitivity to radiation.

radiofaro sm. radio beacon.

radiogoniòmetro sm. radio compass.

radiografare vt. to radiograph.

radiografìa sf. 1. radiograph 2. (scienza) radiography.

radiogramma sm. radiogram.

radiogrammòfono sm. radio-gramophone.

radiologìa sf. radiology.

radiòlogo sm. radiologist.

radioscopìa sf. radioscopy.

radioscòpico agg. radioscopic.

radiosità sf. radiance.

radioso agg. bright.

radiotècnica sf. radioengineering.

radiotècnico sm. radioengineer.

radiotelefonìa sf. radiotelephony.

radiotelèfono sm. radiotelephone.

radiotelegrafìa sf. radiotelegraphy.

radiotelegràfico agg. radiotelegraphic, wireless (attr.).

radiotelegrafista s. telegraphist.

radiotelevisione sf. radio and television.

radioterapìa sf. radiotherapy.

radiotrasméttere vt. to broadcast (v. irr.).

rado agg. 1. thin 2. (non frequente) infrequent ‖ di —, seldom.

radunare vt. to gather. ♦ **radunarsi** vr. to gather.

raduno sm. gathering.

radura sf. glade.

raffazzonare vt. to patch up.

raffermo agg. stale.

ràffica sf. 1. gust 2. (di arma) burst 3. (fig.) hail.

raffigurare vt. to represent. ♦ **raffigurarsi** vr. (immaginare) to imagine.

raffinamento sm. 1. refining 2. (fig.) refinement.

raffinare vt. to refine. ♦ **raffinarsi** vr. to become (v. irr.) refined, to refine.

raffinatamente avv. refinedly.

raffinatezza sf. refinement.

raffinato agg. refined (anche fig.).

raffinazione sf. refining.

raffinerìa sf. refinery.

raffio sm. grapnel.

rafforzamento sm. strengthening.

rafforzare vt. to strengthen. ♦ **rafforzarsi** vr. to grow (v. irr.) stronger.

raffreddamento sm. 1. cooling 2. (fig.) coolness.

raffreddare vt. 1. to cool 2. (fig.) to lessen. ♦ **raffreddarsi** vr. 1. to cool 2. (fig.) to wane 3. (prendere un raffreddore) to catch (v. irr.) a cold.

raffreddato agg. essere —, to have a cold.

raffreddatore sm. cooler.

raffreddore sm. cold.

raffrenare vt. to restrain.

raffrontare vt. to compare.

raffronto sm. comparison.

rafia sf. raffia.

ràgadi sf. pl. rhagades.

raganella sf. 1. tree-frog 2. (strumento) rattle.

ragazza sf. girl.

ragazzaglia sf. crowd of youngsters.

ragazzata sf. escapade.

ragazzo sm. boy: da —, as a boy.

raggelare vt. to freeze (v. irr.). ♦ **raggelarsi** vr. to freeze.

raggiante agg. radiant (with).

raggiare *vi.* **1.** to shine (*v. irr.*) (with sthg.) **2.** (*fig.*) to beam (with sthg.). ♦ **raggiare** *vt.* to radiate.

raggiera *sf.* halo of rays: *a* —, radially.

raggio *sm.* **1.** ray **2.** (*geom.*) radius **3.** (*d'azione*) range **4.** (*di ruota*) spoke || — *di sole*, sunbeam.

raggirare *vt.* to cheat.

raggiro *sm.* cheat.

raggiùngere *vt.* to reach.

raggiungimento *sm.* reaching.

raggiustare *vt.* **1.** to repair **2.** (*riordinare*) to rearrange.

raggomitolare *vt.* to roll up. ♦ **raggomitolarsi** *vr.* to roll oneself up.

raggranellare *vt.* to scrape together.

raggrinzire *vt.* to wrinkle. ♦ **raggrinzirsi** *vr.* to wrinkle, to become (*v. irr.*) wrinkled.

raggrumare *vt.* to clot. ♦ **raggrumarsi** *vr.* to clot.

raggruppamento *sm.* **1.** grouping **2.** (*gruppo*) group.

raggruppare *vt.* to group. ♦ **raggrupparsi** *vr.* to gather.

ragguagliare *vt.* **1.** (*livellare*) to level **2.** (*informare*) to inform **3.** (*paragonare*) to compare **4.** (*comm.*) to balance.

ragguaglio *sm.* **1.** (*informazione*) information (*solo sing.*) **2.** (*paragone*) comparison **3.** (*comm.*) balance.

ragguardévole *agg.* considerable.

ragia *sf.* resin: *acqua* —, turpentine.

ragionamento *sm.* reasoning.

ragionare *vi.* **1.** to reason (about) **2.** (*discutere*) to discuss (sthg.).

ragionatore *sm.* reasoner.

ragione *sf.* **1.** reason **2.** (*diritto*) right **2.** (*rapporto*) rate || *la* — *per cui*, the reason why; *a* — *veduta*, after due consideration; *aver* —, to be right; *a maggior* —, all the more reason; *aver* — *di qu.*, to get (*v. irr.*) the better of so.; — *sociale* (*comm.*), style.

ragioneria *sf.* bookkeeping.

ragionévole *agg.* **1.** reasonable **2.** (*di buon senso*) sensible.

ragionevolezza *sf.* reasonableness.

ragioniere *sm.* bookkeeper.

ragliare *vi.* to bray.

raglio *sm.* bray.

ragnatela *sf.* cobweb.

ragno *sm.* spider.

ragù *sm.* ragout.

raion *sm.* rayon.

rallegramenti *sm. pl.* congratulations.

rallegrare *vt.* to cheer (up). ♦ **rallegrarsi** *vr.* **1.** to rejoice (at) **2.** (*congratularsi*) to congratulate (so. on sthg.).

rallentamento *sm.* slowing down.

rallentare *vt.* to slacken. ♦ **rallentare** *vi.* **1.** to slacken **2.** (*di velocità*) to slow down. ♦ **rallentarsi** *vr.* to get (*v. irr.*) slack.

rallentatore *sm.* (*cine*) slow motion.

ramaiolo *sm.* ladle.

ramanzina *sf.* scolding.

ramare *vt.* to copper.

ramarro *sm.* green lizard.

ramazza *sf.* broom.

rame *sm.* copper.

ramìfero *agg.* copper-bearing (*attr.*).

ramificare *vi.* to ramify. ♦ **ramificarsi** *vr.* to ramify.

ramificazione *sf.* ramification.

ramingo *agg.* roving.

rammagliare *vt.* to mend a run.

rammaricare *vt.* to afflict. ♦ **rammaricarsi** *vr.* **1.** to be sorry **2.** (*lamentarsi*) to complain (of).

rammàrico *sm.* sorrow.

rammendare *vt.* to darn.

rammendatrice *sf.* darner.

rammendo *sm.* **1.** darning **2.** (*parte rammendata*) darn.

rammentare *vt.* to remember: — *qc. a qu.*, to remind so. of sthg. ♦ **rammentarsi** *vr.* to remember.

rammollimento *sm.* softening.

rammollire *vt.* to soften. ♦ **rammollirsi** *vr.* to soften, to go (*v. irr.*) soft.

rammollito *agg.* soft: *un vecchio* —, a dotard. ♦ **rammollito** *sm.* imbecile.

ramo *sm.* branch.

ramoscello *sm.* twig.

ramoso *agg.* branched.

rampa *sf.* **1.** ramp **2.** (*di scale*) flight.

rampante *agg.* rampant.

rampicante *agg.* climbing: *pianta* —, creeper.

rampino *sm.* hook.

rampogna *sf.* reproach.

rampollare *vi.* to spring (*v. irr.*).

rampollo *sm.* **1.** (*d'acqua*) spring **2.** (*di albero*) shoot **3.** (*discendente*) offspring.

rampone *sm.* **1.** (*mar.*) harpoon **2.** (*da montagna*) crampon.

rana *sf.* frog: *uomo* —, frogman (*pl.* -men); *nuotare a* —, to swim (*v. irr.*) the breast stroke.

ràncido *agg.* **1.** rancid **2.** (*fig.*) trite || *sapere di* —, to have a rancid taste.

rancio *sm.* (*mil.*) mess.

rancore *sm.* grudge.

randagio *agg.* stray.

randellare *vt.* to cudgel.

randellata *sf.* blow with a cudgel.

randello *sm.* cudgel.

ranetta *sf.* rennet.

rango *sm.* rank.

rannicchiarsi *vr.* to crouch.

rannuvolamento *sm.* clouding over.

rannuvolare *vi.* to become (*v. irr.*) cloudy, to cloud over. ♦ **rannuvolarsi** *vr.* to get (*v. irr.*) cloudy.

ranocchio *sm.* frog.

rantolare *vi.* **1.** to wheeze **2.** (*in punto di morte*) to have the death-rattle.

ràntolo *sm.* **1.** wheeze **2.** (*di morte*) death-rattle.

ranùncolo *sm.* buttercup.

rapa *sf.* turnip.

rapace *agg.* greedy. ♦ **rapace** *sm.* bird of prey.

rapacità *sf.* greed.

rapare *vt.* to crop (so.'s hair).

rapato *agg.* shorn.

ràpida *sf.* rapid.

rapidità *sf.* swiftness.

ràpido *agg.* swift. ♦ **ràpido** *sm.* express (train).

rapimento *sm.* **1.** kidnapping **2.** (*di donna*) abduction **3.** (*fig.*) rapture.

rapina *sf.* robbery.

rapinare *vt.* to rob.

rapinatore *sm.* robber.

rapire *vt.* **1.** to kidnap **2.** (*una donna*) to abduct **3.** (*fig.*) to ravish.

rapitore *sm.* **1.** kidnapper **2.** (*di donna*) abductor.

rappacificare *vt.* to reconcile. ♦ **rappacificarsi** *vr.* to become (*v. irr.*) reconciled.

rappacificazione *sf.* reconciliation.

rappezzare *vt.* to patch.

rappezzatura *sf.* **1.** patching **2.** (*parte rappezzata*) patch.

rapporto *sm.* **1.** relation **2.** (*relazione*) report **3.** (*mat.*) ratio || *chiamare a* —, to summon; *andare a*

— *da*, to report to; *essere in buoni rapporti*, to be on good terms; *sotto tutti i rapporti*, in every respect.

rapprèndere *vi.* to coagulate. ♦ **rapprèndersi** *vr.* to coagulate.

rappresaglia *sf.* retaliation: *far* —, to retaliate.

rappresentàbile *agg.* performable.

rappresentante *s.* **1.** representative **2.** (*comm.*) agent.

rappresentanza *sf.* **1.** representation **2.** (*comm.*) agency || *in* — *di*, on behalf of.

rappresentare *vt.* **1.** to represent **2.** (*comm.*) to be agent (for) **3.** (*ana parte*) to play **4.** (*un'opera teatrale*) to stage. ♦ **rappresentarsi** *vr.* to imagine.

rappresentativo *agg.* representative.

rappresentazione *sf.* **1.** representation **2.** (*teat.*) performance **3.** (*cine*) exhibition.

rapsodìa *sf.* rhapsody.

rarefare *vt.* to rarefy. ♦ **rarefarsi** *vr.* to rarefy.

rarefatto *agg.* rarefied.

rarefazione *sf.* rarefaction.

rarità *sf.* rarity.

raro *agg.* rare: *rare volte*, seldom; *una bestia rara* (*fig.*), a queer fish.

rasare *vt.* **1.** to shave **2.** (*un prato*) to mow (*v. irr.*) **3.** (*lisciare*) to smooth. ♦ **rasarsi** *vr.* to shave.

rasato *agg.* **1.** shaven **2.** (*liscio*) smooth **3.** (*simile a raso*) satin (*attributivo*).

rasatura *sf.* **1.** shave **2.** (*di prato*) mowing.

raschiamento *sm.* **1.** scraping **2.** (*med.*) curettage.

raschiare *vt.* **1.** to scrape **2.** (*med.*) to curette || *raschiarsi la gola*, to clear one's throat.

raschiata *sf.* scraping.

raschiatoio *sm.* **1.** scraper **2.** (*med.*) curette.

raschiatura *sf.* scraping.

raschietto *sm.* **1.** scraper **2.** (*per cancellare*) eraser.

rasciugare *vt.* to dry.

rasentare *vt.* **1.** to graze **2.** (*confinare*) to border (on).

rasente *prep.* close to: *passare* —, to skim.

raso *agg.* V. *rasato.* ♦ **raso** *sm.* satin.

rasoio *sm.* razor.

raspa *sf.* rasp.
raspamento *sm.* rasping.
raspare *vt.* **1.** to rasp **2.** (*con le unghie*) to scratch **3.** (*frugare*) to rummage.
rassegna *sf.* **1.** (*rivista, recensione*) review **2.** (*esame*) survey ‖ *passare in* —, to inspect.
rassegnare *vt.* to hand in: — *le dimissioni*, to resign. ♦ **rassegnarsi** *vr.* to resign oneself.
rassegnato *agg.* resigned.
rassegnazione *sf.* resignation.
rasserenare *vt.* **1.** to clear **2.** (*fig.*) to cheer up. ♦ **rasserenarsi** *vr.* to clear up.
rassettare *vt.* **1.** to tidy **2.** (*riparare*) to mend.
rassicurante *agg.* reassuring.
rassicurare *vt.* to reassure. ♦ **rassicurarsi** *vr.* to be reassured.
rassicurazione *sf.* reassurance.
rassodamento *sm.* consolidation.
rassodare *vt.* **1.** to consolidate **2.** (*indurire*) to harden. ♦ **rassodarsi** *vr.* to harden.
rassomigliante *agg.* like, alike (*pred.*).
rassomiglianza *sf.* likeness.
rassomigliare *vi.* to be like. ♦ **rassomigliarsi** *vr. rec.* to be alike.
rassottigliare *vt.* V. *assottigliare.*
rastrellamento *sm.* **1.** raking **2.** (*mil.*) mopping up **3.** (*di polizia*) combing **4.** (*dragaggio*) dragging.
rastrellare *vt.* **1.** to rake **2.** (*mil.*) to mop up **3.** (*di polizia*) to comb **4.** (*dragare*) to drag.
rastrelliera *sf.* rack.
rastrello *sm.* rake.
rastremare *vt.* to taper. ♦ **rastremarsi** *vr.* to taper.
rata *sf.* instalment: *a rate*, by instalments.
rateale *agg.* by instalments.
rateare *vt.* to divide into instalments.
ratìfica *sf.* ratification.
ratificare *vt.* to ratify.
ratificatore *sm.* ratifier.
ratificazione *sf.* V. *ratìfica.*
ratto[1] *sm.* **1.** kidnapping **2.** (*di donna*) rape.
ratto[2] *sm.* (*topo*) rat.
rattoppare *vt.* to patch (up).
rattoppo *sm.* **1.** patching up **2.** (*toppa*) patch.
rattrappimento *sm.* **1.** (*intorpidi-*

mento) benumbing **2.** (*contrazione*) contraction.
rattrappire *vt.* **1.** (*contrarre*) to contract **2.** (*intorpidire*) to benumb.
rattristare *vt.* to grieve. ♦ **rattristarsi** *vr.* **1.** (*divenir triste*) to become (*v. irr.*) sad **2.** (*essere triste*) to be sad.
raucèdine *sf.* hoarseness: *avere la* —, to have a hoarse voice.
ràuco *agg.* hoarse.
ravanello *sm.* radish.
ravvedersi *vr.* to mend one's way.
ravvedimento *sm.* reformation.
ravviamento *sm.* tidying (up).
ravviare *vt.* to tidy (up).
ravvicinamento *sm.* **1.** approach **2.** (*conciliazione*) reconciliation.
ravvicinare *vt.* **1.** to bring (*v. irr.*) closer **2.** (*riconciliare*) to reconcile **3.** (*confrontare*) to compare. ♦ **ravvicinarsi** *vr.* **1.** to draw (*v. irr.*) closer **2.** (*riconciliarsi*) to become (*v. irr.*) reconciled.
ravvisàbile *agg.* recognizable.
ravvisare *vt.* to recognize.
ravvivamento *sm.* revival.
ravvivare *vt.* **1.** to revive **2.** (*rallegrare*) to brighten up ‖ — *il fuoco*, to poke the fire. ♦ **ravvivarsi** *vr.* **1.** to revive **2.** (*rallegrarsi*) to brighten up.
raziocinante *agg.* reasoning.
raziocinio *sm.* **1.** reason **2.** (*buon senso*) common sense.
razionale *agg.* rational.
razionalismo *sm.* rationalism.
razionalista *s.* rationalist.
razionalità *sf.* rationality.
razionamento *sm.* rationing.
razionare *vt.* to ration.
razione *sf.* ration.
razza[1] *sf.* **1.** race **2.** (*di animali*) breed **3.** (*genere*) kind.
razza[2] *sf.* (*itt.*) ray.
razzìa *sf.* **1.** raid **2.** (*insetticida*) insecticide ‖ *far* —, to plunder.
razziale *agg.* racial.
razziare *vt.* to plunder.
razziatore *sm.* plunderer.
razzismo *sm.* racialism.
razzista *s.* racialist.
razzo *sm.* rocket.
razzolare *vi.* to scratch about.
re[1] *sm.* king.
re[2] *sm.* (*mus.*) D, re.
reagente *sm.* reagent.
reagire *vi.* to react.

reale[1] *agg.* real.
reale[2] *agg.* (*del re*) royal.
realismo *sm.* realism.
realista[1] *agg.* e *s.* realist.
realista[2] *agg.* e *s.* (*del re*) royalist.
realistico *agg.* realistic.
realizzàbile *agg.* realizable.
realizzare *vt.* to realize. ♦ **realizzarsi** *vr.* 1. to be realized 2. (*avverarsi*) to come (*v. irr.*) true.
realizzatore *sm.* realizer.
realizzazione *sf.* 1. realization 2. (*teat.*) staging 3. (*cine*) production.
realtà *sf.* reality.
reame *sm.* kingdom.
reato *sm.* 1. offence 2. (*crimine*) crime.
reattivo *agg.* reactive. ♦ **reattivo** *sm.* reagent.
reattore *sm.* 1. reactor 2. (*aereo*) jet.
reazionario *agg.* e *sm.* reactionary.
reazione *sf.* reaction: *motore a —*, jet engine; *aereo a —*, jet.
reboante *agg.* 1. thundering 2. (*fig.*) bombastic.
rebus *sm.* rebus.
recalcitrare *vi.* V. *ricalcitrare*.
recapitare *vt.* to deliver.
recàpito *sm.* 1. (*consegna*) delivery 2. (*indirizzo*) address.
recare *vt.* 1. to bring (*v. irr.*) 2. (*fig.*) to bear (*v. irr.*) 3. (*causare*) to cause. ♦ **recarsi** *vr.* to go (*v. irr.*).
recèdere *vi.* to withdraw (*v. irr.*).
recensione *sf.* review.
recensire *vt.* to review.
recensore *sm.* reviewer.
recente *agg.* recent.
recentemente *avv.* recently.
recentissime *sf. pl.* latest news.
recessione *sf.* recession.
recessivo *agg.* receding.
recesso *sm.* 1. recess 2. (*recessione*) recession 3. (*giur.*) withdrawal.
recettivo *agg.* V. *ricettivo*.
recezione *sf.* reception.
recìdere *vt.* to cut (*v. irr.*) off.
recidiva *sf.* relapse.
recidività *sf.* 1. (*giur.*) recidivism 2. (*med.*) relapse.
recidivo *agg.* 1. (*giur.*) recidivous 2. (*med.*) relapsing. ♦ **recidivo** *sm.* 1. (*giur.*) recidivist 2. (*med.*) relapser.
recintare *vt.* to fence.
recinto *sm.* enclosure.
recipiente *sm.* vessel.

reciprocamente *avv.* reciprocally.
reciprocità *sf.* reciprocity.
recìproco *agg.* reciprocal.
recisamente *avv.* resolutely.
recisione *sf.* excision.
reciso *agg.* 1. cut 2. (*fig.*) resolute.
rècita *sf.* performance.
recitare *vt.* 1. to recite 2. (*teat.*) to act || *— una parte*, to play a part.
recitativo *sm.* recitative.
recitazione *sf.* 1. recitation 2. (*teat.*) acting.
reclamante *sm.* claimant.
reclamare *vt.* to claim. ♦ **reclamare** *vi.* to complain.
reclamìstico *agg.* advertising.
reclamizzare *vt.* to advertise.
reclamo *sm.* complaint.
reclinare *vt.* to bow.
reclusione *sf.* 1. seclusion 2. (*prigionia*) imprisonment.
recluso *agg.* 1. secluded 2. (*imprigionato*) imprisoned. ♦ **recluso** *sm.* prisoner.
rècluta *sf.* 1. recruit 2. (*fig.*) novice.
reclutamento *sm.* enlistment.
reclutare *vt.* to enlist, to recruit.
recòndito *agg.* hidden.
recriminare *vi.* 1. to recriminate 2. (*lamentarsi*) to complain.
recriminazione *sf.* 1. recrimination 2. (*lamentela*) complaint.
recrudescente *agg.* recrudescent.
recrudescenza *sf.* recrudescence.
redarguire *vt.* to reproach.
redattore *sm.* 1. drawer 2. (*di giornale*) member of the editorial staff || *— capo*, editor.
redazionale *agg.* editorial.
redazione *sf.* 1. drawing up 2. (*di giornale*) editing 2. (*i redattori*) editorial staff 3. (*ufficio*) editorial office.
redditività *sf.* profitableness.
redditizio *agg.* profitable.
rèddito *sm.* 1. income 2. (*dello Stato*) revenue.
redento *agg.* redeemed.
redentore *sm.* redeemer.
redenzione *sf.* redemption.
redìgere *vt.* to draw (*v. irr.*) up.
redìmere *vt.* to redeem.
redimìbile *agg.* redeemable.
rèdini *sf. pl.* reins.
redivivo *agg.* 1. restored to life 2. (*nuovo*) new.
rèduce *agg.* back from. ♦ **rèduce** *sm.* veteran.

referendum *sm.* referendum.
referenza *sf.* reference.
referenziare *vt.* to give (*v. irr.*) references.
referto *sm.* report.
refettorio *sm.* refectory.
refezione *sf.* meal.
refrattario *agg.* refractory: *terra refrattaria,* fireclay.
refrigerante *agg.* e *sm.* refrigerant.
refrigerare *vt.* to refrigerate.
refrigeratore *sm.* refrigerator.
refrigerazione *sf.* refrigeration.
refrigerio *sm.* 1. cool 2. (*sollievo*) relief.
refurtiva *sf.* stolen goods (*pl.*).
refuso *sm.* misprint, wrong fount.
regalare *vt.* 1. to present (so. with sthg.) 2. (*vendere a poco prezzo*) to sell (*v. irr.*) cheap.
regalato *agg.* (*venduto a buon prezzo*) cheap.
regale *agg.* regal.
regalìa *sf.* (*mancia*) gratuity.
regalo *sm.* present: *in* —, as a present.
regata *sf.* regatta.
reggente *agg.* e *sm.* regent.
reggenza *sf.* regency.
règgere *vt.* 1. (*sorreggere*) to hold (*v. irr.*) 2. (*dirigere*) to run (*v. irr.*) 3. (*gramm.*) to govern || — *una prova,* to stand (*v. irr.*) a test. ♦ **règgere** *vi.* 1. (*resistere*) to hold (out) 2. (*stare in piedi, anche fig.*) to stand. ♦ **règgersi** *vr.* 1. (*sostenersi*) to stand 2. (*appoggiarsi a*) to hold (on, to).
reggia *sf.* royal palace.
reggicalze *sm.* girdle.
reggimento *sm.* (*mil.*) regiment.
reggipetto *sm.* bra.
reggiseno *sm.* V. *reggipetto.*
reggitore *sm.* ruler.
regìa *sf.* 1. (*teat.*) production 2. (*cine*) direction || — *di,* produced, directed by.
regicida *sm.* regicide.
regicidio *sm.* regicide.
regime *sm.* 1. regime 2. (*mecc.*) speed 3. (*dieta*) diet || *essere a* —, to be on a diet.
regina *sf.* queen.
regio *agg.* royal.
regionale *agg.* regional.
regionalismo *sm.* regionalism.
regionalista *s.* regionalist.
regione *sf.* 1. region 2. (*divisione amministrativa; fig.*) province.

regista *sm.* 1. (*teat.*) producer 2. (*cine*) director.
registràbile *agg.* registrable, recordable.
registrare *vt.* 1. to register 2. (*comm.*) to book 3. (*segnare; cine*) to record 4. (*su nastro*) to tape-record 5. (*mecc.*) to adjust.
registratore *sm.* 1. (*persona*) registrar 2. (*strumento*) register: — *di cassa,* cash-register 3. (*magnetofono*) taperecorder.
registrazione *sf.* 1. registration 2. (*comm.*) entry 3. (*di suoni*) recording.
registro *sm.* 1. register 2. (*comm.*) book 3. (*ufficio governativo*) registry.
regnante *agg.* reigning. ♦ **regnante** *s.* sovereign.
regnare *vi.* to reign.
regno *sm.* 1. reign 2. (*territorio; fig.*) kingdom.
règola *sf.* 1. rule 2. (*esempio*) example 3. (*misura*) moderation || *in* —, in order; *è di* —, it is the custom.
regolamentare *agg.* prescribed: *non essere* —, to be against the rules.
regolamentarmente *avv.* according to the rules.
regolamentazione *sf.* regulations (*pl.*).
regolamento *sm.* regulation: — *dei conti,* settlement.
regolare[1] *vt.* 1. to regulate 2. (*sistemare*) to settle 3. (*sintonizzare*) to tune (in). ♦ **regolarsi** *vr.* 1. to act 2. (*controllarsi*) to control oneself.
regolare[2] *agg.* regular.
regolarità *sf.* regularity.
regolarizzare *vt.* to regularize.
regolarizzazione *sf.* regularization.
regolatamente *avv.* 1. regularly 2. (*con moderazione*) moderately.
regolatezza *sf.* sobriety.
regolato *agg.* regular.
regolatore *agg.* regulating: *piano* —, townplan. ♦ **regolatore** *sm.* regulator.
regolazione *sf.* regulation.
règolo *sm.* rule: — *calcolatore,* slide rule.
regredire *vi.* to regress.
regressione *sf.* regression.
regressivo *agg.* regressive.
regresso *sm.* regress.

reietto agg. rejected. ♦ **reietto** sm. outcast.

reiezione sf. rejection.

reincarnare vt. to reincarnate. ♦ **reincarnarsi** vr. to be reincarnated.

reincarnazione sf. reincarnation.

reintegrare vt. 1. to restore 2. (risarcire) to indemnify.

reintegrazione sf. 1. restoration 2. (risarcimento) indemnification.

reità sf. 1. (colpevolezza) guiltiness 2. (malvagità) wickedness.

reiterare vt. to reiterate.

reiterazione sf. reiteration.

relativamente avv. comparatively: — a, as regards.

relativismo sm. relativism.

relativìstico agg. relativistic.

relatività sf. relativity.

relativo agg. 1. relative 2. (rispettivo) respective 3. (attinente) pertinent.

relatore sm. 1. relator 2. (di leggi) proposer.

relazionare vt. to relate.

relazione sf. 1. report 2. (legame) relation 3. (contatto) touch 4. (conoscenza) acquaintance || aver — con, to be connected with; essere in buone relazioni, to be on good terms; mettersi in — con, to get (v. irr.) into touch with; — amorosa, love affair.

relegare vt. to relegate.

relegazione sf. relegation.

religione sf. 1. religion 2. (culto) worship.

religiosità sf. piety.

religioso agg. e sm. religious.

relìquia sf. relic.

reliquario sm. reliquary.

relitto sm. 1. wreckage 2. (di persona) outcast.

remare vi. 1. to row 2. (con pagaia) to paddle.

remata sf. 1. row 2. (colpo di remo) stroke.

rematore sm. oarsman (pl. -men).

remiganti sf. pl. remiges.

remigare vi. 1. to row 2. (di ali) to flap.

reminiscenza sf. reminiscence.

remissione sf. (giur.) remission.

remissività sf. submissiveness.

remissivo agg. submissive.

remo sm. oar.

rèmora sf. 1. (ostacolo) obstacle 2. (indugio) delay 3. (zool.) remora.

remoto agg. remote: passato — (gramm.) past simple tense.

remunerare vt. to remunerate.

remunerativo agg. remunerative.

remunerazione sf. remuneration.

rena sf. sand.

renale agg. renal.

rèndere vt. 1. to render 2. (fruttare) to yield || — conto di, to account for; — giustizia a qu., to do (v. irr.) so. justice. ♦ **rèndersi** vr. to become (v. irr.) || — conto di, to realize.

rendiconto sm. 1. statement 2. (resoconto) report.

rendimento sm. 1. rendering 2. (resa) output 3. (efficienza) efficiency.

rèndita sf. 1. revenue 2. (privata) income.

rene sm. kidney.

renella sf. gravel.

reni sf. pl. back (sing.).

renitente agg. reluctant || essere — alla leva, to fail to appear at the draft.

renitenza sf. reluctance || — alla leva, failure to register for national service.

renna sf. reindeer (pl. invariato).

renoso agg. sandy.

reo agg. guilty. ♦ **reo** sm. culprit.

reòmetro sm. rheometer.

reòstato sm. rheostat.

reparto sm. 1. department 2. (mil.) detachment.

repellente agg. repulsive.

repentaglio sm. danger: a —, in danger.

repentino agg. sudden.

reperìbile agg. to be found (pred.).

reperire vt. to find (v. irr.).

reperto sm. 1. (giur.) evidence 2. (med.) report.

repertorio sm. (teat.) repertoire.

rèplica sf. 1. reply 2. (obiezione) objection 3. (copia) copy 4. (teat.) performance || avere molte repliche (teat.), to have a long run.

replicare vt. 1. to reply 2. (obiettare) to object 3. (ripetere) to repeat.

reprensìbile agg. reprehensible.

reprensione sf. reprehension.

repressione sf. repression.

repressivo agg. repressive.

represso agg. repressed.

reprimenda sf. reprimand.

reprìmere vt. to repress.

rèprobo *agg.* e *sm.* reprobate.
repùbblica *sf.* republic.
repubblicano *agg.* e *sm.* republican.
reputare *vt.* 1. to consider 2. (*pensare*) to think (*v. irr.*).
reputazione *sf.* reputation.
requie *sf.* rest.
requisire *vt.* to requisition.
requisito *sm.* qualification.
requisitoria *sf.* 1. indictment 2. (*giur.*) summing up.
requisizione *sf.* requisition.
resa *sf.* (*rendimento*) yield 2. (*capitolazione*) surrender || — *dei conti*, rendering of accounts.
rescìndere *vt.* to rescind.
rescindìbile *agg.* rescindable.
rescissione *sf.* rescission.
reseda *sf.* reseda.
resezione *sf.* resection.
residente *agg.* e *sm.* resident.
residenza *sf.* residence.
residenziale *agg.* residential.
residuare *vi.* to be left.
residuato *agg.* residual. ◆ resìduato *sm.* — *di guerra*, war surplus.
residuo *agg.* remaining. ◆ resìduo *sm.* residue: *residui radioattivi*, radioactive waste.
rèsina *sf.* resin.
resinoso *agg.* resinous.
resipiscenza *sf.* resipiscence.
resistente *agg.* 1. resistant 2. (*forte*) strong.
resistenza *sf.* resistance.
resìstere *vi.* 1. to resist 2. (*sopportare*) to endure.
resoconto *sm.* report.
respingente *sm.* buffer.
respingere *vt.* 1. to repel 2. (*rimandare*) to return 3. (*rifiutare*) to reject 4. (*scol.*) to pluck.
respinta *sf.* V. *parata*.
respiràbile *agg.* breathable.
respirare *vt.* e *vi.* to breathe.
respiratore *sm.* respirator.
respiratorio *agg.* respiratory.
respirazione *sf.* respiration, breathing.
respiro *sm.* 1. breath 2. (*riposo*) respite.
responsàbile *agg.* responsible (for).
responsabilità *sf.* responsibility.
responso *sm.* 1. response 2. (*opinione*) opinion.
responsorio *sm.* responsory.
ressa *sf.* crowd: *far — intorno a*

qu., to crowd round so.
resta *sf.* 1. (*di cipolla, aglio ecc.*) string 2. (*di lancia*) rest.
restante *agg.* e *sm.* V. *rimanente*.
restare *vi.* V. *rimanere*.
restaurare *vt.* to restore.
restauratore *sm.* restorer.
restaurazione *sf.* restoration.
restàuro *sm.* restoration: *in —*, under repair.
restìo *agg.* loath, reluctant.
restituire *vt.* 1. to return 2. (*reintegrare*) to restore.
restituzione *sf.* 1. return 2. (*reintegrazione*) restoration.
resto *sm.* 1. rest 2. (*mat.*) remainder 3. (*di denaro*) change || *resti*, remains; *del —*, on the other hand.
restringente *sm.* astringent.
restrìngere *vt.* 1. (*contrarre*) to contract 2. (*limitare*) to limit 3. (*un vestito*) to tighten. ◆ restrìngersi *vr.* 1. to get (*v. irr.*) narrower 2. (*contrarsi*) to contract 3. (*affollarsi*) to close up 4. (*di tessuti*) to shrink (*v. irr.*).
restringimento *sm.* 1. narrowing 2. (*contrazione*) contraction 3. (*limitazione*) limitation 4. (*di tessuto*) shrinking 5. (*di vestito*) tightening.
restrittivo *agg.* restrictive.
restrizione *sf.* restriction.
retaggio *sm.* heritage.
retata *sf.* 1. haul 2. (*di polizia*) roundup.
rete *sf.* 1. net 2. (*di letto*) wire netting 3. (*intreccio*) network.
reticella *sf.* 1. (*per capelli*) hair-net 2. (*per bagagli*) luggage-rack.
reticente *agg.* reticent.
reticenza *sf.* reticence.
reticolato *sm.* 1. (*mil.*) barbed-wire entanglement 2. (*tracciato di linee*) network.
retìcolo *sm.* 1. (*anat.*) reticulum (*pl.* -la) 2. (*ott.*) reticle.
rètina *sf.* retina.
retina *sf.* V. *reticella*.
rètore *sm.* rhetorician.
retòrica *sf.* rhetoric.
retòrico *agg.* rhetorical.
retrarre *vt.* to retract.
retràttile *agg.* retractile.
retrattilità *sf.* retractility.
retribuire *vt.* to pay (*v. irr.*).
retribuzione *sf.* payment.
retrivo *agg.* reactionary.
retro *sm.* back.

retroattività *sf.* retroactivity.
retroattivo *agg.* retroactive.
retrobottega *sm.* back of the shop.
retrocèdere *vi.* to withdraw (*v. irr.*). ♦ **retrocèdere** *vt.* 1. (*mil.*) to degrade 2. to retrocede.
retrocessione *sf.* 1. retrocession 2. (*mil.*) degradation.
retrodatare *vt.* to date back.
retrògrado *agg.* 1. out-of-date 2. (*reazionario*) reactionary.
retroguardia *sf.* rear-guard.
retromarcia *sf.* reverse-gear.
retroscena *sf.* 1. back of the stage 2. (*fig.*) intrigue.
retrospettivo *agg.* retrospective.
retrostante *agg.* at the back.
retroterra *sm.* hinterland.
retroversione *sf.* 1. retroversion 2. (*di traduzione*) back version.
retrovìe *sf. pl.* zone behind the front (*sing*).
retrovisore *sm. specchietto* —, driving mirror.
retta[1] *sf.* (*geom.*) straight line.
retta[2] *sf.* (*di pensione*) terms (*pl.*).
retta[3] *sf. dar* — *a qu.*, to listen to so.
rettale *agg.* rectal.
rettamente *avv.* 1. (*giustamente*) rightly 2. (*onestamente*) honestly.
rettangolare *agg.* rectangular.
rettàngolo *sm.* rectangle.
rettìfica *sf.* 1. rectification 2. (*mecc.*) grinding.
rettificare *vt.* 1. to rectify 2. (*mecc.*) to grind (*v. irr.*).
rettificatrice *sf.* grinder.
rettificazione *sf.* V. *rettìfica*.
rettifilo *sm.* straight, stretch.
rèttile *sm.* reptile.
rettilìneo *agg.* rectilinear. ♦ **rettilìneo** *sm.* straight, stretch.
rettitùdine *sf.* righteousness, honesty.
retto *agg.* 1. straight 2. (*geom.; giusto*) right. ♦ **retto** *sm.* (*anat.*) rectum (*pl.* -ta).
rettorato *sm.* rectorship.
rettore *sm.* 1. rector 2. (*di università*) chancellor.
rèuma *sm.* rheumatism.
reumàtico *agg. e sm.* rheumatic.
reumatismo *sm.* V. *reuma*.
reverendo *agg.* reverend. ♦ **reverendo** *sm.* clergyman (*pl.* -men).
reversìbile *agg.* reversible.
reversibilità *sf.* reversibility.
reversione *sf.* reversion.

revisionare *vt.* 1. (*mecc.*) to overhaul 2. (*comm.*) to audit.
revisione *sf.* 1. revision 2. (*mecc.*) overhaul 3. (*comm.*) audit.
revisionismo *sm.* revisionism.
revisore *sm.* 1. reviser 2. (*comm.*) auditor.
reviviscenza *sf.* reviviscence.
rèvoca *sf.* revocation.
revocàbile *agg.* revocable.
revocare *vt.* 1. (*richiamare*) to recall 2. (*giur.*) to revoke.
revocazione *sf.* revocation.
revolverata *sf.* revolver shot.
revulsione *sf.* revulsion.
revulsivo *agg.* revulsive.
riabbottonare *vt.* to button again.
riabilitare *vt.* to rehabilitate.
riabilitazione *sf.* rehabilitation.
riaccèndere *vt.* 1. to relight 2. (*radio, luce ecc.*) to turn on again. ♦ **riaccèndersi** *vr.* 1. to brighten again 2. (*riprender fuoco*) to catch (*v. irr.*) fire again.
riaccompagnare *vt.* to take (*v. irr.*) home.
riacquistare *vt.* 1. to buy (*v. irr.*) again 2. (*riprendere*) to recover.
riadattare *vt.* to adapt again. ♦ **riadattarsi** *vr.* (*rassegnarsi*) to resign oneself again.
riaddormentare *vt.* to send (*v. irr.*) to sleep again. ♦ **riaddormentarsi** *vr.* to fall (*v. irr.*) asleep again.
riaffacciare *vt.* to present again. ♦ **riaffacciarsi** *vr.* to reappear, to appear again.
riaffermare *vt.* to affirm again. ♦ **riaffermarsi** *vr.* to reaffirm oneself.
riafferrare *vt.* to grasp again. ♦ **riafferrarsi** *vr.* to catch (*v. irr.*) hold of (so., sthg.) again.
riallacciare *vt.* 1. to fasten again 2. (*riprendere*) to resume.
riallargare *vt.* to widen again. ♦ **riallargarsi** *vr.* to widen again.
rialto *sm.* rise, height.
rialzamento *sm.* 1. raising 2. (*rialzo*) rise, height.
rialzare *vt.* 1. to raise 2. (*rendere più alto*) to make (*v. irr.*) higher. ♦ **rialzarsi** *vr.* to rise (*v. irr.*) again.
rialzato *agg. piano* —, ground floor.
rialzo *sm.* 1. rise 2. (*di sostegno*) support.
riamare *vt.* to love again.

riamméttere *vt.* to readmit.
rianimare *vt.* to revive. ◆ **rianimarsi** *vr.* **1.** (*riprendere allegria*) to cheer up **2.** (*riprendere coraggio*) to take (*v. irr.*) courage again.
riapertura *sf.* reopening.
riapparire *vi.* to reappear.
riaprire *vt.* to open again. ◆ **riaprirsi** *vr.* to open again.
riarmare *vt.* to rearm. ◆ **riarmarsi** *vr.* to rearm.
riarmo *sm.* rearmament.
riarso *agg.* parched.
riassestare *vt.* to readjust. ◆ **riassestarsi** *vr.* to readjust.
riassettare *vt.* to put (*v. irr.*) in order again.
riassetto *sm.* rearrangement.
riassorbire *vt.* to reabsorb.
riassùmere *vt.* **1.** (*assumere di nuovo*) to take (*v. irr.*) on again **2.** (*riepilogare*) to sum up **3.** (*riprendere*) to resume.
riassuntivo *agg.* summarizing.
riassunto *sm.* summary.
riattaccare *vt.* **1.** (*con colla*) to stick (*v. irr.*) again **2.** (*ricucire*) to sew (*v. irr.*) **3.** (*riprendere*) to begin (*v. irr.*) again **4.** (*mil.*) to attack again **5.** (*tel.*) to hang (*v. irr.*) up. ◆ **riattaccarsi** *vr.* to stick again.
riattamento *sm.* repair.
riattare *vt.* to repair.
riattivare *vt.* to restore.
riavere *vt.* **1.** to have again **2.** (*ricuperare*) to get (*v. irr.*) back. ◆ **riaversi** *vr.* to recover.
riavvicinare *vt.* **1.** to approach again **2.** (*riconciliare*) to reconcile. ◆ **riavvicinarsi** *vr.* to approach again **2.** (*riconciliarsi*) to be reconciled.
ribadire *vt.* to rivet.
ribalderìa *sf.* rascality.
ribaldo *sm.* rascal.
ribalta *sf.* **1.** (*teat.*) footlights (*pl.*) **2.** (*fig.*) limelight.
ribaltàbile *agg.* overturnable.
ribaltare *vt.* to overturn. ◆ **ribaltarsi** *vr.* to capsize.
ribassare *vt.* to reduce. ◆ **ribassare** *vi.* to fall (*v. irr.*).
ribasso *sm.* **1.** fall **2.** (*sconto*) discount.
ribàttere *vt.* **1.** to beat (*v. irr.*) again **2.** (*ribadire*) to rivet **3.** (*confutare*) to confute. ◆ **ribàttere** *vi.* to insist.

ribattezzare *vt.* to rename.
ribellarsi *vr.* to rebel.
ribelle *agg.* rebellious. ◆ **ribelle** *s.* rebel.
ribellione *sf.* rebellion.
ribes *sm.* gooseberry.
riboccante *agg.* overflowing (with).
riboccare *vi.* to overflow (with).
ribollimento *sm.* ebullition.
ribollire *vi.* to boil.
ribollitura *sf.* reboiling.
ribrezzo *sm.* disgust: *fare —*, to disgust.
ributtante *agg.* disgusting.
ributtare *vt.* **1.** to throw (*v. irr.*) again **2.** (*respingere*) to repel **3.** (*disgustare*) to disgust.
ricacciare *vt.* **1.** (*respingere*) to push (out, back) **2.** (*ficcare di nuovo*) to thrust (*v. irr.*) again. ◆ **ricacciarsi** *vr.* to plunge again.
ricadere *vi.* **1.** to fall (*v. irr.*) again **2.** (*avere una ricaduta*) to relapse **3.** (*pendere*) to hang (*v. irr.*).
ricaduta *sf.* relapse.
ricalcare *vt.* **1.** to pull down **2.** (*un disegno*) to transfer || *— le orme di qu.*, to tread (*v. irr.*) in so.'s steps.
ricalcitrante *agg.* recalcitrant.
ricalcitrare *vi.* to recalcitrate.
ricamare *vt.* e *vi.* to embroider.
ricamatore *sm.* embroiderer.
ricamatrice *sf.* embroideress.
ricambiare *vt.* **1.** to change again **2.** (*contraccambiare*) to return.
ricambio *sm.* **1.** replacement **2.** (*med.*) metabolism || *di —*, spare (*agg. attr.*).
ricamo *sm.* embroidery: *un —*, a piece of embroidery.
ricapitolare *vt.* to summarize || *ricapitolando*, in short.
ricapitolazione *sf.* summary.
ricaricare *vt.* **1.** to reload **2.** (*di batteria*) to recharge **3.** (*di orologio*) to wind (*v. irr.*) up again.
ricascare *vi.* V. *ricadere*.
ricattare *vt.* to blackmail.
ricattatore *sm.* blackmailer.
ricattatorio *agg.* blackmailing.
ricatto *sm.* blackmail.
ricavare *vt.* **1.** to draw (*v. irr.*) **2.** (*ottenere*) to get (*v. irr.*).
ricavato *sm.* proceeds (*pl.*).
ricavo *sm.* V. *ricavato*.
riccamente *avv.* richly.
ricchezza *sf.* wealth (*solo sing.*).
riccio[1] *agg.* curly.

riccio² *sm.* **1.** curl **2.** (*bot.*) chestnut husk **3.** (*zool.*) hedgehog **4.** (*di mare*) sea-urchin.

ricciuto *agg.* curly.

ricco *agg.* rich: — *di*, rich in.

ricerca *sf.* **1.** search **2.** (*scientifica*) research **3.** (*indagine*) investigation.

ricercare *vt.* **1.** (*cercare*) to seek (*v. irr.*) for **2.** (*investigare*) to investigate **3.** (*cercare di nuovo*) to look for (so., sthg.) again.

ricercatezza *sf.* refinement.

ricercato *agg.* **1.** (*richiesto*) sought-after **2.** (*raffinato*) refined **3.** (*insolito*) far-fetched **4.** (*dalla polizia*) wanted.

ricercatore *sm.* **1.** searcher **2.** (*scientifico*) researcher.

ricetta *sf.* **1.** (*med.*) prescription **2.** (*cuc.*) recipe.

ricettàcolo *sm.* receptacle.

ricettare *vt.* (*custodire cose rubate*) to receive.

ricettario *sm.* **1.** (*med.*) book of prescriptions **2.** (*cuc.*) book of recipes.

ricettatore *sm.* receiver.

ricettazione *sf.* receiving of stolen goods.

ricettività *sf.* receptivity.

ricettivo *agg.* receptive.

ricevente *agg.* receiving. ◆ **ricevente** *s.* receiver.

ricévere *vt.* to receive.

ricevimento *sm.* **1.** receipt **2.** (*festa*) party.

ricevitore *sm.* receiver.

ricevitorìa *sf.* receiving-office.

ricevuta *sf.* receipt: *accusare* —, to acknowledge receipt.

ricezione *vt.* reception.

richiamare *vt.* **1.** to call again **2.** (*far tornare*) to recall **3.** (*attirare*) to attract **4.** (*rimproverare*) to rebuke || — *all'ordine*, to call to order. ◆ **richiamarsi** *vr.* (*riferirsi*) to refer.

richiamata *sf.* recall.

richiamato *sm.* (*mil.*) re-drafted soldier.

richiamo *sm.* **1.** recall **2.** (*allettamento*) call.

richiedente *s.* applicant.

richièdere *vt.* **1.** to ask (for sthg., so.) again **2.** (*chiedere*) to ask for **3.** (*in restituzione*) to ask (for sthg.) back **4.** (*necessitare di*) to require.

richiesta *sf.* **1.** request: *dietro* —, at request **2.** (*comm.*) demand.

richiùdere *vt.* to close again. ◆ **richiùdersi** *vr.* to close again.

rìcino *sm.* castor-oil plant: *olio di* —, castor-oil.

ricognitore *sm.* (*mil.*) scout.

ricognizione *sf.* reconnaissance.

ricollegare *vt.* to connect. ◆ **ricollegarsi** *vr.* to be connected.

ricollocamento *sm.* replacement.

ricolmare *vt.* **1.** to fill up **2.** (*fig.*) to load.

ricolmo *agg.* **1.** full **2.** (*fig.*) loaded (with).

ricominciare *vt.* to begin (*v. irr.*) again.

ricomparire *vi.* to reappear.

ricompensa *sf.* reward: *in* —, as a reward.

ricompensare *vt.* to reward.

ricomperare *vt.* to buy (*v. irr.*) again.

ricomporre *vt.* to recompose.

ricomposizione *sf.* recomposition.

riconciliare *vt.* to reconcile. ◆ **riconciliarsi** *vr.* to be reconciled.

riconciliatore *sm.* reconciler.

riconciliazione *sf.* reconciliation.

ricondurre *vt.* to take (*v. irr.*) back, to bring (*v. irr.*) back.

riconferma *sf.* reconfirmation.

riconfermare *vt.* to reconfirm.

riconfortare *vt.* to cheer up. ◆ **riconfortarsi** *vr.* to cheer up.

ricongiùngere *vt.* to join again. ◆ **ricongiùngersi** *vr.* to join again.

ricongiungimento *sm.* reunion.

riconnèttere *vt.* to connect again.

riconoscente *agg.* grateful.

riconoscenza *sf.* gratitude.

riconòscere *vt.* to recognize.

riconoscìbile *agg.* recognizable.

riconoscimento *sm.* **1.** recognition **2.** (*ammissione*) admission.

riconquista *sf.* recapture.

riconquistare *vt.* to conquer again.

riconsegna *sf.* return.

riconsegnare *vt.* to redeliver.

riconsiderare *vt.* to reconsider.

riconversione *sf.* reconversion.

riconvocare *vt.* to resummon.

riconvocazione *sf.* resummons.

ricopiare *vt.* to copy.

ricopiatura *sf.* (re)copying.

ricoprire *vt.* **1.** to cover **2.** (*coprire di nuovo*) to cover again **3.** (*fig.*) to load.

ricordare *vt.* **1.** to remember **2.** (*chiamare alla memoria altrui*) to remind (so. of sthg.) **3.** (*nominare*) to mention. ♦ **ricordarsi** *vr.* to remember.

ricordo *sm.* **1.** memory **2.** (*oggetto ricordo*) souvenir **3.** (*memorie*) (*lett.*) memoirs (*pl.*).

ricorrente *agg.* recurrent.

ricorrenza *sf.* **1.** recurrence **2.** (*anniversario*) anniversary **3.** (*occasione*) occasion.

ricòrrere *vi.* **1.** (*ripetersi*) to recur **2.** (*rivolgersi*) to apply **3.** (*fare appello*) to appeal **4.** (*valersi*) to resort.

ricorso *sm.* **1.** (*ritorno*) return **2.** (*appello*) appeal ‖ *su — di*, on a petition by.

ricostituente *agg. e sm.* tonic.

ricostituire *vt.* to form again. ♦ **ricostituirsi** *vr.* to form again.

ricostituzione *sf.* reconstitution.

ricostruire *vt.* to reconstruct.

ricostruttore *agg.* reconstructive. ♦ **ricostruttore** *sm.* reconstructor.

ricostruzione *sf.* reconstruction.

ricoverare *vt.* to shelter: — *in ospedale*, to hospitalize. ♦ **ricoverarsi** *vr.* to take (*v. irr.*) shelter.

ricòvero *sm.* **1.** sheltering **2.** (*in ospedale*) hospitalization **3.** (*ospizio*) home.

ricreare[1] *vt.* to re-create.

ricreare[2] *vt.* (*divertire*) to recreate. ♦ **ricrearsi** *vr.* to recreate.

ricreativo *agg.* recreative.

ricreazione *sf.* recreation: *ora della —*, playtime.

ricrédersi *vr.* to change one's mind.

ricréscere *vi.* to grow (*v. irr.*) again.

ricréscita *sf.* fresh growth.

ricucire *vt.* **1.** to sew (*v. irr.*) up **2.** (*cucire di nuovo*) to sew (*v. irr.*) again.

ricucitura *sf.* sewing up.

ricuòcere *vt. e vi.* **1.** to cook again **2.** (*al forno*) to bake again.

ricuperàbile *agg.* recoverable.

ricuperare *vt.* **1.** to recover **2.** (*di tempo*) to make (*v. irr.*) up for.

ricùpero *sm.* recovery.

ricurvare *vt.* **1.** to bend (*v. irr.*) **2.** (*curvare di nuovo*) to bend again.

ricurvo *agg.* bent.

ricusàbile *agg.* refusable.

ricusare *vt.* to refuse.

ridacchiare *vi.* to giggle.

ridanciano *agg.* jolly.

ridare *vt.* **1.** to give (*v. irr.*) again **2.** (*restituire*) to return.

ridda *sf.* turmoil.

ridente *agg.* **1.** smiling **2.** (*di luogo*) charming.

ridere *vi.* to laugh (at): *per —*, for fun. ♦ **ridersi** *vr.* to make (*v. irr.*) fun (of).

ridestare *vt.* **1.** to wake (*v. irr.*) (up) again **2.** (*destare*) to awaken. ♦ **ridestarsi** *vr.* **1.** to wake (up) again **2.** (*destarsi*) to awake.

ridicolàggine *sf.* nonsense (*solo sing.*).

ridìcolo *agg.* ridiculous. ♦ **ridìcolo** *sm.* ridicule.

ridimensionare *vt.* to reorganize.

ridire *vt.* **1.** to say (*v. irr.*) again, to tell (*v. irr.*) again **2.** (*riferire*) to repeat **3.** (*obiettare*) to object.

ridiscéndere *vi.* to come (*v. irr.*) down again, to go (*v. irr.*) down again.

ridiscòrrere *vi.* to talk again.

ridiventare *vi.* to become (*v. irr.*) again.

ridomandare *vt.* to ask again.

ridonare *vt.* **1.** to give (*v. irr.*) again **2.** (*restituire*) to give back.

ridondante *agg.* redundant.

ridondanza *sf.* redundancy.

ridondare *vi.* **1.** to be redundant **2.** (*risultare*) to redound.

ridosso (*nella loc. avv.*) *a — di*, close to.

ridotta *sf.* redoubt.

ridotto *agg.* **1.** reduced **2.** (*di libro*) abridged ‖ *mal —*, in a sorry plight. ♦ **ridotto** *sm.* (*teat.*) foyer.

riducente *agg.* reducing. ♦ **riducente** *sm.* reducer.

riducìbile *agg.* reducible.

ridurre *vt.* **1.** to reduce **2.** (*adattare*) to. adapt **3.** (*un libro*) to abridge. ♦ **ridursi** *vr.* **1.** to be reduced **2.** (*restringersi*) to shrink (*v. irr.*).

riduttore *agg. e sm.* V. *riducente*.

riduzione *sf.* **1.** reduction **2.** (*sconto*) discount **3.** (*cine; tv*) adaptation **4.** (*di libro*) abridgement.

riecheggiare *vt. e vi.* to re-echo.

riedificare *vt.* to rebuild (*v. irr.*).

riedificazione *sf.* rebuilding.

rieducare *vt.* to re-educate.

rieducazione *sf.* re-education.

rielaborare *vt.* to re-elaborate.

rieleggere vt. to re-elect.
rieleggibile agg. re-elegible.
rielezione sf. re-election.
riemergere vi. to re-emerge.
riemersione sf. re-emergence.
riempire vt. to fill. ♦ riempirsi vr. to fill.
riempitivo sm. filling.
rientrante agg. receding.
rientranza sf. recess.
rientrare vi. 1. to re-enter 2. (tornare) to return 3. (far parte) to be part (of) 4. (piegare in dentro) to recede.
rientro sm. 1. recess 2. (astronautica) retro-firing 3. (ritorno) return.
riepilogare vt. to recapitulate.
riepilogo sm. recapitulation.
riesame sm. re-examination.
riesaminare vt. to re-examine.
riessere vi. to be again.
riesumare vt. 1. to exhume 2. (fig.) to bring (v. irr.) to light.
rievocare vt. to recall.
rievocazione sf. recalling.
rifacimento sm. 1. reconstruction 2. (adattamento) adaptation.
rifare vt. 1. to do (v. irr.) again, to make (v. irr.) again 2. (ripercorrere) to retrace 3. (riparare) to repair 4. (imitare) to imitate 5. (indennizzare) to indemnify. ♦ rifarsi vr. 1. to make up 2. (vendicarsi) to revenge oneself 3. (risalire) to go (v. irr.) back.
rifasciare vt. 1. to bandage again 2. (un bambino) to swaddle again.
riferibile agg. 1. referable 2. (raccontabile) fit to be told.
riferimento sm. reference: linea, punto di —, datum-line, datum-point.
riferire vt. 1. to report 2. (attribuire) to ascribe. ♦ riferirsi vr. to refer.
rificcare vt. to thrust (v. irr.) again.
rifilare vt. 1. to spin again 2. (tagliare a filo) to trim 3. (appioppare) to palm off.
rifilatura sf. 1. trimming 2. (bordo) border.
rifinimento sm. finishing touch.
rifinire vt. to finish.
rifinitura sf. V. rifinimento.
rifiorire vi. 1. to blossom again 2. (fig.) to flourish again.
rifioritura sf. reflorescence.
rifiutàbile agg. refusable.

rifiutare vt. to refuse.
rifiuto sm. refusal || rifiuti, waste (solo sing.); i rifiuti della società, the dregs of society.
riflessione sf. reflection.
riflessivo agg. 1. reflective 2. (gramm.) reflexive.
riflesso agg. reflected, reflex (anche fig.). ♦ riflesso sm. 1. reflection 2. (di colore) tint 3. (med.) reflex || di —, as a consequence; per —, indirectly.
riflèttere vt. e vi. to reflect. ♦ riflèttersi vr. to be reflected.
riflettore sm. 1. reflector 2. (lampada) searchlight.
rifluire vi. 1. to flow again 2. (fluire indietro) to flow back.
riflusso sm. ebb.
rifocillare vt. to give (v. irr.) refreshment. ♦. rifocillarsi vr. to take (v. irr.) refreshment.
rifòndere vt. 1. to melt again 2. (rimborsare) to refund.
riforma sf. reformation.
riformare vt. 1. to reform 2. (mil.) to declare unfit for military service.
riformatore sm. reformer.
riformatorio sm. reformatory.
riformismo sm. reformism.
riformista s. reformist.
rifornimento sm. 1. supplying 2. (aer.; auto) refuelling 3. (scorta) supply || stazione di —, filling--station; far — di benzina, to fill up the tank.
rifornire vt. to supply (so. with).
rifornitore sm. supplier.
rifràngere vt. to refract. ♦ rifràngersi vr. to be refracted.
rifrangibilità sf. refrangibility.
rifrattore sm. refractor.
rifrazione sf. refraction.
rifritto agg. 1. fried again 2. (fig.) stale.
rifuggire vi. 1. to escape again 2. (essere alieno) to shrink (v. irr.).
rifugiarsi vr. to take (v. irr.) shelter.
rifugiato agg. e sm. refugee.
rifugio sm. 1. shelter 2. (di montagna) mountain hut.
rifùlgere vi. to shine (v. irr.) brightly (with sthg.).
rifusione sf. 1. re-melting 2. (rimborso) repayment.
riga sf. 1. line 2. (fila) row 3. (regolo) rule 4. (striscia) stripe 5. (scriminatura) parting 6. (mus.

stave ‖ *mettersi in* —, to line up.

rigaglie *sf. pl.* giblets.

rigàgnolo *sm.* 1. rivulet 2. (*scolo*) gutter.

rigare *vt.* 1. to rule 2. (*solcare*) to furrow ‖ — *diritto*, to behave well.

rigato *agg.* 1. ruled 2. (*a strisce*) striped 3. (*solcato*) furrowed.

rigattiere *sm.* second-hand dealer.

rigatura *sf.* 1. ruling 2. (*di arma*) rifling.

rigenerare *vt.* 1. to regenerate 2. (*mecc.*) to repair.

rigeneratore *agg.* regenerative. ◆ **rigeneratore** *sm.* regenerator.

rigenerazione *sf.* regeneration.

rigettare *vt.* 1. to throw (*v. irr.*) again 2. (*gettare indietro*) to throw back 3. (*vomitare*) to vomit 4. (*respingere*) to reject..

rigetto *sm.* rejection.

righello *sm.* ruler.

rigidezza *sf.* 1. stiffness 2. (*di clima*) rigour.

rigidità *sf.* V. *rigidezza.*

rìgido *agg.* 1. stiff 2. (*di clima*) rigorous.

rigirare *vt.* 1. to turn again 2. (*cambiare*) to change. ◆ **rigirare** *vi.* to walk about. ◆ **rigirarsi** *vr.* to turn about.

ʼrigiro *sm.* 1. turning round 2. (*di parole*) involved expression.

rigo *sm.* V. *riga.*

rigoglio *sm.* bloom.

rigogliosità *sf.* luxuriancy.

rigoglioso *agg.* flourishing.

rigonfiamento *sm.* swelling.

rigonfiare *vt.* to swell (*v. irr.*). ◆ **rigonfiarsi** *vr.* to swell.

rigonfio *agg.* swollen (with). ◆ **rigonfio** *sm.* swelling.

rigore *sm.* 1. rigour 2. (*esattezza*) exactness ‖ *di* —, compulsory; *a* —, according to the rules; *a* — *di termini*, in the strict sense, *area di* — (*sport*), penalty-area.

rigorismo *sm.* rigorism.

rigorista *s.* rigorist.

rigorosità *sf.* 1. rigour 2. (*esattezza*) preciseness.

rigoroso *agg.* 1. rigorous 2. (*esatto*) exact.

rigovernare *vt.* 1. to govern again 2. (*di piatti*) to wash up.

rigovernatura *sf.* washing-up.

riguadagnare *vt.* 1. to earn again

2. (*ricuperare, raggiungere*) to regain.

riguardare *vt.* 1. to look at (so., sthg.) again 2. (*esaminare*) to examine 3. (*considerare*) to regard. ◆ **riguardarsi** *vr.* to take (*v. irr.*) care of oneself.

riguardata *sf.* look.

riguardévole *agg.* 1. considerable 2. (*importante*) important.

riguardo *sm.* 1. regard 2. (*cura*) care ‖ *persona di* —, person of consequence; — *a*, as regards; *a questo* —, in this connection.

riguardoso *agg.* respectful.

rigurgitare *vi.* 1. to overflow 2. (*di stomaco*) to regurgitate 3. (*brulicare*) to swarm (with).

rigùrgito *sm.* 1. overflow 2. (*di stomaco*) regurgitation 3. (*travaso*) extravasation 4. (*gorgo*) eddy.

rilanciare *vt.* 1. to throw (*v. irr.*) again 2. (*lanciare indietro*) to throw back 3. (*un'offerta*) to raise.

rilancio *sm.* 1. new throw 2. (*di offerta*) raising.

rilasciare *vt.* 1. to release 2. (*concedere*) to grant 3. (*emettere*) to issue. ◆ **rilasciarsi** *vr.* 1. to slacken 2. (*med.*) to prolapse 3. (*rilassarsi*) to relax.

rilascio *sm.* 1. release 2. (*concessione*) granting 3. (*emissione*) issue.

rilassamento *sm.* 1. slackening 2. (*med.*) prolapse 3. (*riposo*) relaxation.

rilassare *vt.* 1. to slacken 2. (*distendere*) to relax. ◆ **rilassarsi** *vr.* 1. to slacken 2. (*distendersi*) to relax.

rilassatezza *sf.* laxity.

rilegare *vt.* 1. to tie again 2. (*libri*) to bind (*v. irr.*).

rilegatura *sf.* binding.

rilèggere *vt.* to reread (*v. irr.*), to read (*v. irr.*) again.

rilento (*nella loc. avv.*) *a* —, slowly.

rilevamento *sm.* 1. (*topografico*) survey 2. (*mar.*) bearing 3. (*cambio*) relieving.

rilevante *agg.* prominent.

rilevare *vt.* 1. to take (*v. irr.*) off again 2. (*notare*) to notice 3. (*far notare*) to point out 4. (*prendere*) to take 5. (*topografia*) to survey 6. (*sostituire*) to relieve 7. (*comm.*) to take over.

rilevazione *sf.* V. *rilievo.*
rilievo *sm.* 1. relief 2. (*importanza*) importance 3. (*osservazione*) remark 4. (*topografico*) survey 5. (*comm.*) taking over || *mettere in* —, to stress.
rilucente *agg.* glittering.
rilùcere *vi.* to glitter.
riluttante *agg.* reluctant.
riluttanza *sf.* reluctance.
riluttare *vi.* to reluct (at).
rima *sf.* rhyme || *rispondere per le rime,* to give (*v. irr.*) tit for tat.
rimandare *vt.* 1. to send (*v. irr.*) again 2. (*restituire*) to send back 3. (*posporre*) to postpone 4. (*far riferimento*) to refer 5. (*agli esami*) to make (*v. irr.*) (so.) repeat (an exam).
rimando *sm.* 1. returning 2. (*differimento*) postponement 3. (*segno di richiamo*) reference-mark.
rimaneggiamento *sm.* 1. rearrangement 2. (*di opera letteraria*) adaptation 3. (*pol.*) shuffle.
rimaneggiare *vt.* 1. to rearrange 2. (*modificare*) to change 3. (*pol.*) to shuffle.
rimanente *agg.* remaining. ♦ **rimanente** *sm.* rest.
rimanenza *sf.* remainder.
rimanere *vi.* 1. to remain 2. (*avanzare*) to be left 3. (*essere sorpreso*) to be astonished.
rimangiare *vt.* to eat (*v. irr.*) again. ♦ **rimangiarsi** *vr.* to take (*v. irr.*) back.
rimarchévole *agg.* remarkable.
rimare *vt. e vi.* to rhyme.
rimarginare *vt.* to heal. ♦ **rimarginarsi** *vr.* to heal.
rimaritare *vt.* to marry again. ♦ **rimaritarsi** *vr.* to marry again.
rimasticare *vt.* 1. to chew again 2. (*fig.*) to muse.
rimasuglio *sm.* remains (*pl.*).
rimatore *sm.* rhymer.
rimbalzare *vi.* to rebound.
rimbalzello *sm.* ducks and drakes.
rimbalzo *sm.* rebound: *di* —, on the rebound.
rimbambimento *sm.* dotage.
rimbambire *vi.* to reach one's dotage.
rimbambito *agg.* in one's dotage (*pred.*): *un vecchio* —, a dotard.
rimbeccare *vt.* to retort.
rimbecco *sm.* retort.

rimbecillire *vi.* 1. to grow (*v. irr.*) stupid 2. (*per età*) to reach one's dotage.
rimbecillito *agg.* doting.
rimboccare *vt.* to tuck up. ♦ **rimboccarsi** *vr.* to tuck up.
rimbombante *agg.* thundering.
rimbombare *vi.* 1. to thunder 2. (*risuonare*) to resound.
rimbombo *sm.* roar.
rimborsàbile *agg.* repayable.
rimborsare *vt.* to reimburse.
rimborso *sm.* reimbursement.
rimboscare *vt.* V. *rimboschire.*
rimboschimento *sm.* reafforestation.
irr.) wooded again.
rimboschire *vt.* to reafforest. ♦ **rimboschirsi** *vr.* to become (*v. irr.*)
rimbrottare *vt.* to reproach.
rimbrotto *sm.* reproach.
rimediàbile *agg.* remediable.
rimediare *vi.* to find (*v. irr.*) a remedy (for).
rimedio *sm.* remedy.
rimembranza *sf.* memory.
rimembrare *vt.* to remember.
rimeritare *vt.* to reward.
rimescolamento *sm.* 1. stir 2. (*turbamento*) shock.
rimescolare *vt.* 1. to stir again 2. (*mescolare*) to stir. ♦ **rimescolarsi** *vr.* to be upset || *gli si rimescolò il sangue* (*per rabbia*), his blood boiled, (*per paura*), his blood ran cold.
rimescolìo *sm.* confusion.
rimessa *sf.* 1. replacing 2. (*per auto*) garage 3. (*di denaro*) remittance 4. (*di merci*) consignment || — *in gioco,* throw-in.
rimesso *agg.* 1. (*falso*) false 2. (*ristabilito*) well again 3. (*perdonato*) forgiven.
rimestare *vt.* V. *rimescolare.*
riméttere *vt.* 1. to put (*v. irr.*) again, to put back 2. (*consegnare*) to hand 3. (*mandare, perdonare*) to remit 4. (*affidare*) to leave (*v. irr.*) 5. (*vomitare*) to vomit || — *in gioco,* to throw (*v. irr.*) in; *rimetterci,* to lose (*v. irr.*). ♦ **riméttersi** *vr.* 1. (*affidarsi*) to rely on 2. (*ristabilirsi*) to recover 3. (*rasserenarsi*) to clear up.
rimirare *vt.* to gaze (at). ♦ **rimirarsi** *vr.* to admire oneself.
rimisurare *vt.* to measure again.
rimodellare *vt.* to remodel.

rimodernamento sm. modernization.

rimodernare vt. to modernize. ♦ rimodernarsi vr. to become up--to-date.

rimondare vt. to clean again.

rimonta sf. 1. (mil.) remount 2. (sport) catching up.

rimontare vt. 1. to go (v. irr.) up 2. (ricomporre) to reassemble. ♦ rimontare vi. 1. to remount 2. (fig.) to go back 3. (sport) to catch (v. irr.) up || — in auto, to get (v. irr.) into a car again.

rimorchiare vt. to tow.

rimorchiatore sm. tug.

rimorchio sm. 1. tow 2. (veicolo) trailer.

rimòrdere vt. 1. to bite (v. irr.) again 2. (fig.) to prick.

rimorso sm. remorse.

rimosso agg. removed.

rimostranza sf. remonstrance: fare le proprie rimostranze, to remonstrate.

rimostrare vi. to remonstrate.

rimovìbile agg. removable.

rimozione sf. removal.

rimpacchettare vt. to package again.

rimpadronirsi vr. to seize again.

rimpagliare vt. 1. to re-cover with straw 2. (imbottire) to re-stuff with straw.

rimpallo sm. counterblow.

rimpannucciarsi vr. (fig.) to improve one's financial position.

rimpastare vt. 1. to knead again 2. (fig.) to rearrange.

rimpasto sm. 1. kneading again 2. (fig.) rearrangement 3. (pol.) reshuffle.

rimpatriare vt. to repatriate. ♦ rimpatriare vi. to return to one's country.

rimpatrio sm. repatriation.

rimpetto avv. opposite.

rimpiàngere vt. 1. to regret 2. (una perdita) to mourn.

rimpianto sm. regret.

rimpiattarsi vr. to hide (v. irr.) oneself.

rimpiattino sm. hide-and-seek.

rimpiazzare vt. to replace.

rimpiazzo sm. replacement.

rimpicciolire vt. to lessen. ♦ rimpicciolirsi vr. to lessen.

rimpiegare vt. to re-employ.

rimpiego sm. re-employment.

rimpinguare vt. 1. to fatten 2. (arricchire) to enrich. ♦ rimpinguarsi vr. 1. to fatten 2. (arricchirsi) to grow (v. irr.) rich.

rimpinzare vt. to stuff (with).

rimpolpare vt. V. rimpinguare.

rimproverare vt. to reproach.

rimpròvero sm. reproach: muovere un —, to reproach.

rimuginare vt. to brood over.

rimunerare vt. to remunerate.

rimuòvere vt. 1. to remove 2. (dissuadere) to dissuade 3. (da una carica) to dismiss.

rimutare vt. to change again.

rinascenza sf. Renaissance.

rinàscere vi. to revive.

rinascimentale agg. Renaissance (attr.).

rinascimento sm. Renaissance.

rinàscita sf. 1. rebirth 2. (fig.) revival.

rincagnarsi vr. to frown.

rincagnato agg. pug (attr.).

rincalzare vt. 1. (rimboccare) to tuck in 2. (sostenere) to prop up.

rincalzo sm. support: a — di, in support of.

rincantucciare vt. to put (v. irr.) in a corner. ♦ rincantucciarsi vr. to hide (v. irr.) in a corner.

rincarare vt. 1. to raise the price of 2. (esagerare) to exaggerate. ♦ rincarare vi. to become (v. irr.) more expensive.

rincaro sm. rise in prices.

rincasare vi. to return home.

rinchiùdere vt. to shut (v. irr.) up.

rincitrullire vt. to make (v. irr.) silly. ♦ rincitrullirsi vr. to grow (v. irr.) silly.

rincivilire vt. to civilize. ♦ rincivilirsi vr. 1. to become (v. irr.) civilized 2. (raffinarsi) to become refined.

rincollare vt. to paste again.

rincominciare vt. to begin (v. irr.) again.

rincontrare vt. to meet (v. irr.) again. ♦ rincontrarsi vr. to meet again.

rincontro sm. meeting.

rincoramento sm. encouragement.

rincorare vt. to encourage. ♦ rincorarsi vr. to pluck up courage.

rincòrrere vt. to run (v. irr.) after.

rincorsa sf. run-up.

rincréscere vi. 1. to be sorry: mi

rincresce, I am sorry 2. (*dar noia*) to mind: *ti rincresce aprire la finestra?*, do you mind opening the window?

rincrescimento *sm.* regret: *con mio —*, to my regret.

rincrudimento *sm.* aggravation.

rincrudire *vi.* 1. to aggravate 2. (*esacerbare*) to embitter 3. (*del tempo*) to get (*v. irr.*) worse.

rinculare *vi.* to recoil.

rinculo *sm.* recoil.

rinfacciare *vt.* to throw (*v. irr.*) (sthg.) in so.'s face.

rinfiancare *vt.* to support.

rinfilare *vt.* 1. to thread again 2. (*rinserire*) to insert again. ♦ **rinfilarsi** *vr.* 1. (*introdursi*) to slip again 2. (*rindossare*) to slip on again.

rinfiorare *vt.* to adorn with flowers again.

rinfittire *vt.* 1. to thicken 2. (*rendere più frequenti*) to make (*v. irr.*) more frequent. ♦ **rinfittirsi** *vr.* (*di lana*) to shrink (*v. irr.*).

rinfocolare *vt.* 1. to poke 2. (*fig.*) to stir up (again).

rinfoderare *vt.* to sheathe (again).

rinforzamento *sm.* strengthening.

rinforzare *vt.* 1. to strengthen 2. (*mecc.*) to stiffen. ♦ **rinforzarsi** *vr.* to become (*v. irr.*) stronger.

rinforzo *sm.* 1. strengthening 2. (*mil.*) reinforcements (*pl.*) 3. (*fig.*) support 4. (*mecc.*) stiffener.

rinfrancare *vt.* to encourage. ♦ **rinfrancarsi** *vr.* 1. (*migliorare*) to improve 2. (*riprendere coraggio*) to pluck up courage.

rinfrescamento *sm.* cooling.

rinfrescante *agg.* refreshing.

rinfrescare *vt.* 1. to cool 2. (*ristorare*) to refresh 3. (*rinnovare*) to renovate. ♦ **rinfrescare** *vi.* to cool.

rinfresco *sm.* 1. refreshments (*pl.*) 2. (*ricevimento*) cocktail party.

rinfusa (*nella loc. avv.*) *alla —*, in confusion.

ringalluzzire *vt.* to make (*v. irr.*) cocky. ♦ **ringalluzzirsi** *vr.* to become (*v. irr.*) cocky.

ringentilire *vt.* to refine.

ringhiare *vi.* to snarl.

ringhiera *sf.* 1. railing 2. (*di scale*) banisters (*pl.*).

ringhio *sm.* snarl.

ringhioso *agg.* snarling

ringiovanimento *sm.* rejuvenation.

ringiovanire *vt.* 1. to make (*v. irr.*) young again 2. (*far sembrare più giovane*) to make (so.) look younger. ♦ **ringiovanire** *vi.* 1. to grow (*v. irr.*) young again 2. (*sembrare più giovane*) to look younger.

ringiovanito *agg.* young again.

ringoiare *vt.* to swallow up again.

ringranare *vt.* to re-engage.

ringraziamento *sm.* thanks (*pl.*).

ringraziare *vt.* to thank.

ringuainare *vt.* V. *rinfoderare*.

rinite *sf.* rhinitis.

rinnegabile *agg.* deniable.

rinnegamento *sm.* disowning.

rinnegare *vt.* to disown.

rinnegato *agg.* e *sm.* renegade.

rinnegatore *sm.* disowner.

rinnestare *vt.* 1. (*agr.*) to graft again 2. (*mecc.*) to re-engage.

rinnesto *sm.* 1. (*agr.*) new grafting 2. (*mecc.*) re-engagement.

rinnovàbile *agg.* renewable.

rinnovamento *sm.* renewal.

rinnovare *vt.* to renew. ♦ **rinnovarsi** *vr.* (*riaccadere*) to happen again.

rinnovatore *sm.* renewer.

rinnovazione *sf.* renewal.

rinnovellare *vt.* to renew. ♦ **rinnovellarsi** *vr.* to be renewed.

rinnovo *sm.* renewal.

rinoceronte *sm.* rhinoceros.

rinolaringite *sf.* rhinolaryngitis.

rinologìa *sf.* rhinology.

rinomanza *sf.* renown.

rinomato *agg.* renowned.

rinominare *vt.* 1. to name again 2. (*designare di nuovo*) to reappoint.

rinoplàstica *sf.* rhinoplasty.

rinoscopìa *sf.* rhinoscopy.

rinoscopio *sm.* rhinoscope.

rinsaccare *vt.* to pack again. ♦ **rinsaccarsi** *vr.* to shrug one's shoulders.

rinsaldamento *sm.* consolidation.

rinsaldare *vt.* to consolidate.

rinsanguare *vt.* 1. to supply with new blood 2. (*fig.*) to reinvigorate. ♦ **rinsanguarsi** *vr.* 1. to recover 2. (*finanziariamente*) to re-establish one's financial condition.

rinsanire *vi.* 1. to recover 2. (*rinsavire*) to return to reason.

rinsavimento *sm.* return to reason.

rinsavire *vi.* to recover one's wits.

rinsecchire *vi.* 1. to dry up 2. (*di persone*) to get (*v. irr.*) thin 3.

(*avvizzire*) to wither.
rinserrare *vt.* to shut (*v. irr.*) up (again).
rintanarsi *vr.* to shut (*v. irr.*) oneself up.
rintascare *vt.* to pocket again.
rintavolare *vt.* to start again.
rintoccare *vi.* **1.** (*di orologio*) to strike (*v. irr.*) **2.** (*di campana*) to toll.
rintocco *sm.* **1.** (*di orologio*) stroke **2.** (*di campana*) toll.
rintontire *vt.* to stun. ✦ **rintontirsi** *vr.* to be stunned.
rintracciare *vt.* **1.** to trace **2.** (*trovare*) to find (*v. irr.*) out.
rintronamento *sm.* booming.
rintronare *vt.* **1.** to deafen **2.** (*stordire*) to stun. ✦ **rintronare** *vi.* to boom.
rintuzzare *vt.* **1.** to blunt **2.** (*ribattere*) to retort.
rinuncia *sf.* renouncement.
rinunciare *vi.* to renounce (sthg.).
rinunciatario *agg.* releasee.
rinvenimento *sm.* recovery.
rinvenire *vt.* to find (*v. irr.*). ✦ **rinvenire** *vi.* **1.** to recover one's senses **2.** (*riprendere freschezza*) to revive **3.** (*riprendere morbidezza*) to soften.
rinverdire *vt.* (*ravvivare*) to reawaken. ✦ **rinverdire** *vi.* **1.** to turn green again **2.** (*ravvivarsi*) to revive.
rinvestimento *sm.* reinvestment.
rinvestire *vt.* **1.** to restore to the possession of **2.** (*comm.*) to reinvest.
rinviare *vt.* **1.** to put (*v. irr.*) off **2.** (*mandare indietro*) to return.
rinvigorimento *sm.* reinvigoration.
rinvigorire *vt.* to reinvigorate. ✦ **rinvigorirsi** *vr.* to regain strength.
rinvilire *vt.* to lower. ✦ **rinvilire** *vi.* to become (*v. irr.*) cheaper.
rinvìo *sm.* **1.** postponement **2.** (*il rimandare indietro*) returning.
rinvoltare *vt.* to wrap up again.
rinzaffare *vt.* **1.** to bung again **2.** (*arch.*) to rough in.
rinzaffatura *sf.* (*arch.*) roughing-in coat.
rio[1] *sm.* rivulet.
rio[2] *agg.* evil.
rioccupare *vt.* to reoccupy.
rioccupazione *sf.* reoccupation.
rionale *agg.* local, ward (*attr.*).

rione *sm.* ward, district.
riordinare *vt.* **1.** to tidy up **2.** (*riorganizzare*) to reorganize **3.** (*comandare di nuovo*) to order again.
riordinatore *sm.* **1.** rearranger **2.** (*riorganizzatore*) reorganizer.
riordinazione *sf.* **1.** rearrangement **2.** (*riorganizzazione*) reorganization **3.** (*nuova ordinazione*) new order.
riòrdino *sm.* V. *riordinazione.*
riorganizzare *vt.* to reorganize.
riorganizzatore *sm.* reorganizer.
riorganizzazione *sf.* reorganization.
riottosità *sf.* **1.** turbulence **2.** (*indocilità*) indocility.
riottoso *agg.* **1.** turbulent **2.** (*indocile*) indocile.
ripa *sf.* **1.** bank **2.** (*scarpata*) scarp.
ripagare *vt.* **1.** to repay (*v. irr.*) **2.** (*pagare di nuovo*) to pay (*v. irr.*) again.
riparare *vt.* **1.** (*proteggere*) to shelter **2.** (*aggiustare*) to repair **3.** (*risarcire*) to redress ‖ — *un esame,* to repeat an exam. ✦ **riparare** *vi.* **1.** (*porre rimedio*) to remedy **2.** (*rifugiarsi*) to take (*v. irr.*) shelter. ✦ **ripararsi** *vr.* to take shelter.
riparatore *agg.* repairing. ✦ **riparatore** *sm.* repairer.
riparazione *sf.* **1.** repair: *in —,* under repair **2.** (*fig.*) reparation.
riparlare *vi.* to speak (*v. irr.*) again.
riparo *sm.* **1.** shelter **2.** (*rimedio*) remedy **3.** (*mecc.*) guard.
ripartire[1] *vi.* to start again.
ripartire[2] *vt.* to divide.
ripartizione *sf.* division.
ripassare *vi.* **1.** to pass again **2.** (*far visita*) to call again. ✦ **ripassare** *vt.* **1.** (*riattraversare*) to cross again **2.** (*dare di nuovo*) to pass again **3.** (*rileggere, rivedere*) to go (*v. irr.*) through **4.** (*mecc.*) to overhaul.
ripassata *sf.* **1.** (*revisione*) revision **2.** (*mecc.*) overhauling **3.** (*pulita*) cleaning **4.** (*mano di vernice*) new coat.
ripasso *sf.* **1.** (*ritorno*) return **2.** (*revisione*) revision **3.** (*di lezioni*) review.
ripensamento *sm.* reflection: *avere un —,* to change one's mind.
ripensare *vi.* **1.** to think (*v. irr.*) (of sthg., so.) again **2.** (*riconside-*

rare) to think over **3.** (*cambiar parere*) to change one's mind: *ci ho ripensato*, I have changed my mind.

ripercòrrere *vt.* to travel over (sthg.) again.

ripercuòtere *vt.* to strike (*v. irr.*) again. ♦ **ripercuòtersi** *vr.* **1.** to reverberate **2.** (*fig.*) to influence (so., sthg.).

ripercussione *sf.* repercussion.

ripescare *vt.* **1.** to catch (*v. irr.*) again **2.** (*ritrovare*) to find (*v. irr.*) again.

ripetente *s.* repeater.

ripètere *vt.* to repeat.

ripetitore *sm.* **1.** repeater **2.** (*scol.*) private tutor.

ripetizione *sf.* **1.** (*rifacimento*) repetition **2.** (*ripasso*) revision **3.** (*lezione privata*) private lesson ‖ *arma a* —, repeater.

ripetuto *agg.* repeated.

ripiano *sm.* **1.** (*terreno*) terrace **2.** (*pianerottolo*) landing **3.** (*scaffale*) shelf (*pl.* -lves).

ripicco *sm.* spite: *per* —, out of spite.

ripidezza *sf.* steepness.

rìpido *agg.* steep.

ripiegamento *sm.* **1.** folding **2.** (*il curvare*) bending **3.** (*mil.*) withdrawal.

ripiegare *vt.* **1.** to bend (*v. irr.*) again **2.** (*piegare*) to fold. ♦ **ripiegare** *vi.* **1.** to bend **2.** (*ritirarsi*) to withdraw (*v. irr.*). ♦ **ripiegarsi** *vr.* to bend.

ripiegatura *sf.* **1.** folding **2.** (*piega*) fold **2.** (*curva*) bend.

ripiego *sm.* **1.** expedient **2.** (*rimedio*) remedy.

ripienezza *sf.* fullness.

ripieno *agg.* **1.** full **2.** (*cuc.*) stuffed (with). ♦ **ripieno** *sm.* **1.** filling **2.** (*cuc.*) stuffing.

ripigliare *vt.* V. *riprendere*.

ripiombare *vt.* to plunge back. ♦ **ripiombare** *vi.* to fall (*v. irr.*) again.

ripopolamento *sm.* **1.** repeopling **2.** (*di animali*) restocking.

ripopolare *vt.* **1.** to repeople **2.** (*di animali*) to restock.

riporre *vt.* **1.** to replace **2.** (*metter via*) to put (*v. irr.*) away **3.** (*porre*) to place. ♦ **riporsi** *vr.* (*riprendere*) to resume.

riportare *vt.* **1.** to bring (*v. irr.*)

again, to take (*v. irr.*) again **2.** (*portare indietro*) to bring back, to take back **3.** (*riferire*) to report **4.** (*citare*) to quote **5.** (*ricevere*) to get (*v. irr.*) **6.** (*mat.*) to carry. ♦ **riportarsi** *vr.* (*tornare*) to go (*v. irr.*) back.

riporto *sm.* **1.** (*mat.*) carry over **2.** (*in borsa*) contango **3.** (*ornamento*) appliqué.

riposante *agg.* restful.

riposare *vt.* **1.** to rest **2.** (*posare di nuovo*) to place back. ♦ **riposare** *vi.* to rest. ♦ **riposarsi** *vr.* to rest.

riposato *agg.* **1.** (*fresco*) fresh **2.** (*tranquillo*) quiet.

riposo *sm.* rest: *andare a* —, to retire.

ripostiglio *sm.* cupboard.

riprèndere *vt.* **1.** to take (*v. irr.*) again **2.** (*riavere*) to take back **3.** (*riassumere, ricominciare*) to resume **4.** (*ricuperare*) to recover **5.** (*rimproverare*) to reprove **6.** (*teat.*) to revive **7.** (*cine*) to shoot (*v. irr.*). ♦ **riprèndersi** *vr.* **1.** to recover **2.** (*da turbamento*) to collect oneself **3.** (*correggersi*) to correct oneself.

riprensione *sf.* reprehension.

riprensivo *agg.* reprehensive.

ripresa *sf.* **1.** renewal **2.** (*teat.; rinascita*) revival **3.** (*riconquista*) recapture **4.** (*da malattia*) recovery **5.** (*cine*) shot **6.** (*auto*) acceleration **7.** (*registrazione*) recording **8.** (*di pugilato*) round **9.** (*sport*) second half.

ripresentare *vt.* to present again.

ripristinare *vt.* **1.** to restore **2.** (*rimettere in vigore*) to re-establish.

ripristino *sm.* **1.** restoration **2.** (*il rimettere in vigore*) re-establishment.

riproducibile *agg.* reproducible.

riprodurre *vt.* to reproduce. ♦ **riprodursi** *vr.* to reproduce.

riproduttivo *agg.* reproductive.

riproduttore *agg.* reproducing. ♦ **riproduttore** *sm.* reproducer.

riproduzione *sf.* reproduction.

riprométtere *vt.* to promise again. ♦ **riprométtersi** *vr.* **1.** to intend **2.** (*aspettarsi*) to expect.

riproporre *vt.* to re-propose. ♦ **riproporsi** *vr.* to re-propose.

riprova *sf.* (new) proof.

riprovare *vt.* **1.** to try again **2.** (*sentire di nuovo*) to feel (*v. irr.*)

again 3. (*disapprovare*) to criticize 4. (*scol.*) to fail.

riprovazione *sf.* reprobation.

riprovévole *agg.* **1.** blamable **2.** (*spregevole*) despicable.

ripubblicare *vt.* to republish.

ripudiare *vt.* to repudiate.

ripudio *sm.* repudiation.

ripugnante *agg.* repugnant.

ripugnanza *sf.* repugnance.

ripugnare *vi.* **1.** (*disgustare*) to disgust **2.** (*essere contrario*) to be repugnant.

ripulire *vt.* **1.** to clean again **2.** (*pulire*) to clean **3.** (*fig.*) to polish **4.** (*saccheggiare*) to ransack.

ripulita *sf.* clean: *darsi una —*, to tidy oneself up.

ripulsa *sf.* repulse.

ripulsione *sf.* repulsion.

ripulsivo *agg.* repulsive.

riquadrare *vt.* **1.** to square **2.** (*una stanza*) to decorate.

riquadratura *sf.* **1.** square **2.** (*decorazione*) decoration.

riquadro *sm.* **1.** square **2.** (*su parete*) panel.

risacca *sf.* surf.

risaia *sf.* rice-field.

risalire *vt.* **1.** to go (*v. irr.*) up again **2.** (*contro corrente*) to go up: *— la corrente*, to go upstream. ♦ **risalire** *vi.* **1.** to go up again **2.** (*nel tempo*) to go back.

risaltare[1] *vi.* **1.** to show (*v. irr.*) up **2.** (*di persona*) to stand (*v. irr.*) out.

risaltare[2] *vt.* to jump again.

risalto *sm.* **1.** prominence **2.** (*rilievo*) relief.

risanàbile *agg.* **1.** curable **2.** (*bonificabile*) reclaimable.

risanamento *sm.* **1.** curing **2.** (*guarigione*) recovery **3.** (*bonifica*) reclamation **4.** (*fig.*) reformation || *— di quartiere*, slum-clearance.

risanare *vt.* **1.** to cure **2.** (*bonificare*) to reclaim **3.** (*un quartiere*) to clear (a slum). ♦ **risanare** *vi.* to recover.

risanatore *agg.* healing. ♦ **risanatore** *sm.* healer.

risapere *vt.* to come (*v. irr.*) to know.

risaputo *agg.* well-known.

risarcìbile *agg.* that can be indemnified.

risarcimento *sm.* indemnity.

risarcire *vt.* to indemnify.

risata *sf.* laugh: *scoppiare in una —*, to burst (*v. irr.*) out laughing.

riscaldamento *sm.* heating.

riscaldare *vt.* **1.** to warm (up) **2.** (*di casa*) to heat **3.** (*fig.*) to excite. ♦ **riscaldarsi** *vr.* to warm up.

riscaldo *sm.* inflammation.

riscattàbile *agg.* redeemable.

riscattare *vt.* to redeem.

riscatto *sm.* **1.** ransom **2.** (*redenzione*) redemption.

rischiaramento *sm.* brightening.

rischiarare *vt.* to light (*v. irr.*) (up). ♦ **rischiararsi** *vr.* **1.** to light up **2.** (*diventare più chiaro*) to get (*v. irr.*) clearer **3.** (*di cielo*) to clear up.

rischiare *vt.* to risk. ♦ **rischiare** *vi.* to run (*v. irr.*) the risk (of).

rischio *sm.* risk.

rischioso *agg.* risky.

risciacquare *vt.* to rinse. ♦ **risciacquarsi** *vr.* to rinse.

risciacquata *sf.* rinse.

risciacquatura *sf.* **1.** rinsing **2.** (*acqua*) dish-water.

riscontare *vt.* to rediscount.

risconto *sm.* rediscount.

riscontrare *vt.* **1.** (*controllare*) to check **2.** (*trovare*) to find (*v. irr.*) **3.** (*confrontare*) to compare.

riscontro *sm.* **1.** (*controllo*) checking **2.** (*confronto*) comparison **3.** (*risposta*) reply **4.** (*corrispondenza simmetrica*) pendant.

riscoprire *vt.* to discover again.

riscossa *sf.* **1.** (*rivolta*) revolt **2.** (*riscatto*) redemption || *andare alla —*, to counterattack.

riscossione *sf.* collection.

riscotìbile *agg.* collectable.

riscotimento *sm.* collection.

riscrìvere *vt.* **1.** to rewrite (*v. irr.*) **2.** (*in risposta*) to write (*v. irr.*) back.

riscuòtere *vt.* **1.** (*denaro*) to collect **2.** (*conseguire*) to win (*v. irr.*) **3.** (*scuotere*) to shake (*v. irr.*). ♦ **riscuòtersi** *vr.* (*trasalire*) to start.

riseccare *vt.* to dry up. ♦ **riseccarsi** *vr.* to dry up.

risedersi *vr.* to sit (*v. irr.*) down again.

risega *sf.* **1.** (*arch.*) offset **2.** (*della pelle*) fold.

riseminare *vt.* to sow (*v. irr.*) again.

risentimento *sm.* resentment: *con —*, resentfully.

risentire *vt.* **1.** (*sentire di nuovo*) to feel (*v. irr.*) again **2.** (*riudire*) to hear (*v. irr.*) again **3.** (*sentire*) to feel ‖ — *di qc.*, to show (*v. irr.*) traces of sthg.; (*di persona*) to feel the effect of sthg. ♦ **risentirsi** *vr.* to take (*v. irr.*) offence (at).

risentito *agg.* (*sdegnato*) resentful.

riserbare *vt.* V. *riservare*.

riserbo *sm.* **1.** reserve **2.** (*discrezione*) discretion.

riserva *sf.* **1.** reserve **2.** (*di caccia, pesca*) preserve.

riservare *vt.* to reserve. ♦ **riservarsi** *vr.* (*ripromettersi*) to intend: — *la diagnosi*, to refuse to formulate a definite diagnosis.

riservatezza *sf.* reservedness.

riservato *agg.* **1.** reserved **2.** (*segreto*) private.

risibile *agg.* laughable.

risicoltore *sm.* rice-grower.

risicoltura *sf.* rice-growing.

risièdere *vi.* to reside.

risma *sf.* **1.** ream **2.** (*fig.*) kind.

riso[1] *sm.* (*bot.*) rice.

riso[2] *sm.* laugh.

risolare *vt.* to resole.

risolatura *sf.* resoling.

risollevare *vt.* **1.** to raise again **2.** (*confortare*) to cheer up. ♦ **risollevarsi** *vr.* **1.** to rise again **2.** (*confortarsi*) to cheer up.

risolutezza *sf.* resolution.

risolutivo *agg.* resolutive.

risoluto *agg.* resolute.

risoluzione *sf.* **1.** resolution **2.** (*giur.*) cancellation.

risòlvere *vt.* **1.** to resolve **2.** (*rescindere*) to rescind. ♦ **risòlversi** *vr.* **1.** (*decidersi*) to make (*v. irr.*) up one's mind **2.** (*mutarsi*) to turn (into) **3.** (*di malattia*) to clear up.

risolvìbile *agg.* **1.** resolvable **2.** (*rescindibile*) rescindable.

risonante *agg.* resonant.

risonanza *sf.* resonance.

risonare *vt.* **1.** to play again **2.** (*un campanello*) to ring (*v. irr.*) again. ♦ **risonare** *vi.* to resound.

risòrgere *vi.* **1.** to rise (*v. irr.*) again **2.** (*rifiorire*) to revive ‖ *far* —, to revive.

risorgimento *sm.* revival.

risorsa *sf.* resource.

risparmiare *vt.* **1.** to save **2.** (*evitare, salvare*) to spare.

risparmiatore *agg.* thrifty. ♦ **risparmiatore** *sm.* saver.

risparmio *sm.* saving: *senza* —, lavishly.

rispecchiare *vt.* to reflect. ♦ **rispecchiarsi** *vr.* to be reflected.

rispedire *vt.* **1.** to send (*v. irr.*) again **2.** (*spedire indietro*) to send back.

rispettàbile *agg.* respectable.

rispettabilità *sf.* respectability.

rispettare *vt.* **1.** to respect **2.** (*onorare*) to honour.

rispettivo *agg.* respective.

rispetto *sm.* respect: — *a*, as regards; *a* — *di*, in comparison to; *mancare di* — *a*, to be disrespectful to.

rispettoso *agg.* respectful.

risplendente *agg.* shining.

risplèndere *vi.* to shine (*v. irr.*).

rispolverare *vt.* **1.** to dust again **2.** (*fig.*) to brush up.

rispondente *agg.* answering (to).

rispondenza *sf.* correspondence.

rispòndere *vt. e vi.* **1.** to answer (so., sthg.) **2.** (*obbedire*) to respond ‖ — *di qu., qc.*, to answer for so., sthg.

risposare *vt.* V. *rimaritare*.

risposta *sf.* answer, reply.

rispuntare *vi.* **1.** to reappear **2.** (*risorgere*) to rise (*v. irr.*) again **3.** (*di germogli*) to sprout again.

rissa *sf.* brawl.

rissare *vi.* to brawl.

rissoso *agg.* quarrelsome.

ristabilimento *sm.* **1.** restoration **2.** (*di salute*) recovery.

ristabilire *vt.* to restore. ♦ **ristabilirsi** *vr.* **1.** to settle again **2.** (*rimettersi*) to recover.

ristagnamento *sm.* **1.** stagnation **2.** (*di sangue*) staunching.

ristagnare *vi.* to stagnate. ♦ **ristagnare** *vt.* to staunch.

ristagno *sm.* (*econ.*) slackness.

ristampa *sf.* reprint: *essere in* —, to be reprinting.

ristampare *vt.* to reprint.

ristare *vi.* **1.** (*cessare*) to stop **2.** (*rimanere*) to remain.

ristoràbile *agg.* restorable.

ristorante *sm.* restaurant.

ristorare *vt.* to refresh, to restore (*anche fig.*).

ristoratore *agg.* refreshing. ♦ **ristoratore** *sm.* restorer.

ristoro *sm.* **1.** relief **2.** (*cibo, be-*

vanda) refreshment || *luogo di* —, refreshment-room.

ristrettezza *sf.* **1.** narrowness **2.** (*insufficienza*) lack || — *di idee*, narrow-mindedness.

ristretto *agg.* **1.** narrow **2.** (*condensato*) condensed.

ristringere *vt.* **1.** to tighten again **2.** (*premere di nuovo*) to press again || — *la mano a qu.*, to shake (*v. irr.*) hands with so. again.

ristuccare *vt.* **1.** (*edil.*) to replaster **2.** (*nauseare*) to surfeit.

ristuccatura *sf.* (*edil.*) replastering.

ristudiare *vt.* to study again.

risucchiare *vt.* to suck (again).

risucchio *sm.* whirlpool.

risultante *agg. e sf.* resultant.

risultanza *sf.* result.

risultare *vi.* **1.** to result **2.** (*venire a sapere*) to turn out || *mi risulta*, I know.

risultato *sm.* result.

risurrezione *sf.* resurrection.

risuscitamento *sm.* resuscitation.

risuscitare *vt. e vi.* to resuscitate.

risvegliare *vt.* to wake (*v. irr.*) (up). ◆ **risvegliarsi** *vr.* to wake up.

risveglio *sm.* **1.** awakening **2.** (*fig.*) revival.

risvoltare *vt.* to turn up.

risvolto *sm.* **1.** (*di giacca*) lapel **2.** (*di calzoni*) turn-up.

ritagliare *vt.* **1.** to cut (*v. irr.*) out **2.** (*tagliare di nuovo*) to cut again.

ritaglio *sm.* **1.** (*di stoffa*) remnant **2.** (*di giornale*) clipping || *ritagli di tempo*, odd moments.

ritardare *vt.* to delay. ◆ **ritardare** *vi.* **1.** to be late **2.** (*di orologio*) to be slow.

ritardatario *sm.* late-comer.

ritardo *sm.* delay: *in* —, late.

ritegno *sm.* **1.** reserve **2.** (*freno*) restraint **3.** (*riluttanza*) reluctance.

ritemprare *vt.* **1.** to strengthen **2.** (*metalli*) to harden again. ◆ **ritemprarsi** *vr.* to get (*v. irr.*) stronger.

ritenere *vt.* **1.** to hold (*v. irr.*) **2.** (*giudicare*) to consider **3.** (*pensare*) to think (*v. irr.*).

ritentare *vt.* **1.** to tempt again **2.** (*riprovare*) to try again.

ritenuta *sf.* deduction.

ritenzione *sf.* retention.

ritingere *vt.* to dye again.

ritirare *vt.* **1.** to withdraw (*v. irr.*)

2. (*farsi consegnare*) to collect. ◆ **ritirarsi** *vr.* **1.** to retire **2.** (*di stoffa*) to shrink (*v. irr.*).

ritirata *sf.* **1.** retreat **2.** (*latrina*) lavatory.

ritiro *sm.* **1.** withdrawal **2.** (*il ritirarsi*) retirement **3.** (*luogo appartato*) retreat **4.** (*il farsi consegnare*) collection.

ritmare *vt.* to mark.

ritmica *sf.* rhythmic(s).

ritmico *agg.* rhythmic(al).

ritmo *sm.* rhythm.

rito *sm.* rite: *essere di* —, to be customary.

ritoccare *vt.* to retouch.

ritoccatore *sm.* retoucher.

ritocco *sm.* retouch.

ritogliere *vt.* **1.** to take (*v. irr.*) off again **2.** (*riappropriarsi*) to take back. ◆ **ritogliersi** *vr.* to take off again.

ritorcere *vt.* **1.** to twist again **2.** (*torcere*) to twist **3.** (*rivolgere*) to retort. ◆ **ritorcersi** *vr.* **1.** to get (*v. irr.*) twisted **2.** (*fig.*) to recoil (on, upon).

ritorcitura *sf.* twisting.

ritornare *vi.* to return.

ritornello *sm.* refrain.

ritorno *sm.* return: — *di fiamma*, backfire; *essere di* —, to be back.

ritorsione *sf.* retortion.

ritorto *agg.* twisted.

ritrarre *vt.* **1.** to withdraw (*v. irr.*) **2.** (*distogliere*) to turn away **3.** (*rappresentare*) to represent **4.** (*dedurre*) to understand (*v. irr.*). ◆ **ritrarsi** *vr.* to withdraw.

ritrattare *vt.* **1.** to retract **2.** (*trattare di nuovo*) to treat again.

ritrattazione *sf.* **1.** retraction **2.** (*nuova trattazione*) new treatment.

ritrattista *s.* portraitist.

ritrattistica *sf.* portraiture.

ritratto *sm.* portrait.

ritrazione *sf.* retraction.

ritrito *agg.* stale.

ritrosìa *sf.* **1.** (*riluttanza*) reluctance **2.** (*timidezza*) shyness.

ritroso *agg.* **1.** (*riluttante*) reluctant **2.** (*timido*) shy || *a* —, backwards.

ritrovamento *sm.* finding.

ritrovare *vt.* **1.** to find (*v. irr.*) again **2.** (*ricuperare*) to recover **3.** (*scoprire*) to discover. ◆ **ritrovarsi** *vr.* **1.** to find oneself **2.** (*rincontrarsi*) to meet (*v. irr.*) again.

ritrovato *sm.* **1.** invention **2.** (*scoperta*) discovery.
ritrovo *sm.* meeting-place, haunt.
ritto *agg.* upright.
rituale *agg. e sm.* ritual.
rituffare *vt.* to plunge again. ♦ **rituffarsi** *vr.* to plunge again.
riudire *vt.* to hear (*v. irr.*) again.
riunione *sf.* meeting.
riunire *vt.* **1.** to re-unite **2.** (*raccogliere*) to gather **3.** (*unire*) to join. ♦ **riunirsi** *vr.* **1.** to come (*v. irr.*) together again **2.** (*unirsi*) to unite **3.** (*incontrarsi*) to meet (*v. irr.*).
riuscire *vi.* **1.** to succeed (in), to be good (at) **2.** (*risultare*) to be **3.** (*uscire di nuovo*) to go (*v. irr.*) out again.
riuscita *sf.* **1.** issue **2.** (*successo*) success.
riutilizzare *vt.* to utilize again.
riva *sf.* **1.** (*di mare, lago*) shore **2.** (*di fiume*) bank.
rivale *agg. e sm.* rival.
rivaleggiare *vi.* to rival (so., sthg.).
rivalersi *vr.* **1.** to make (*v. irr.*) up for one's losses **2.** (*valersi di nuovo*) to make use again.
rivalicare *vt.* to recross.
rivalità *sf.* rivalry.
rivalsa *sf.* **1.** (*rivincita*) revenge **2.** (*risarcimento*) compensation **3.** (*comm.*) recourse.
rivalutare *vt.* **1.** to revalue **2.** (*elevare*) to raise.
rivalutazione *sf.* **1.** revaluation **2.** (*aumento*) rise.
rivangare *vt. e vi.* to dig (*v. irr.*) up again.
rivedere *vt.* **1.** to see (*v. irr.*) again **2.** (*revisionare*) to revise.
riveduta *sf.* look, revision.
rivelare *vt.* to reveal. ♦ **rivelarsi** *vr.* **1.** to reveal oneself **2.** (*dimostrarsi*) to prove.
rivelatore *agg.* revealing. ♦ **rivelatore** *sm.* **1.** revealer **2.** (*radio*) detector.
rivelazione *sf.* **1.** revelation **2.** (*fis.; radio*) detection.
rivéndere *vt.* **1.** to resell (*v. irr.*) **2.** (*al dettaglio*) to retail.
rivendicare *vt.* **1.** to claim **2.** (*vendicare*) to revenge.
rivendicatore *agg.* **1.** claiming **2.** (*vendicatore*) revenging. ♦ **rivendicatore** *sm.* **1.** claimant **2.** (*vendicatore*) revenger.
rivendicazione *sf.* claim.

rivéndita *sf.* **1.** resale **2.** (*spaccio*) shop.
rivenditore *sm.* retailer.
rivendùgliolo *sm.* V. *rigattiere*.
riverberare *vt.* to reverberate. ♦ **riverberarsi** *vr.* to reverberate.
rivèrbero *sm.* reverberation: *di* —, indirectly.
riverente *agg.* reverent.
riverenza *sf.* **1.** reverence **2.** (*inchino*) bow.
riverenziale *agg.* reverential.
riverire *vt.* **1.** to revere **2.** (*salutare*) to pay (*v. irr.*) one's respects (to).
riversare *vt.* **1.** to pour again **2.** (*versare*) to pour **3.** (*di fiume*) to flow. ♦ **riversarsi** *vr.* to flow.
riverso *avv.* on one's back.
rivestimento *sm.* **1.** covering **2.** (*interno*) lining.
rivestire *vt.* **1.** to dress again **2.** (*foderare*) to line (with sthg.) **3.** (*coprire*) to cover (with sthg.) **4.** (*fig.*) to hold (*v. irr.*).
riviera *sf.* coast || *la Riviera*, the Riviera.
rivierasco *agg.* coast (*attr.*).
rivincere *vt.* **1.** to win (*v. irr.*) again **2.** (*recuperare*) to win back.
rivincita *sf.* **1.** (*vendetta*) revenge **2.** (*sport*) return match **3.** (*al gioco*) return game.
rivista *sf.* **1.** review **2.** (*teat.*) revue **3.** (*mil.*) parade || *passare in* —, to review.
rivivere *vi. e vt.* to live again.
rivo *sm.* stream.
rivolere *vt.* **1.** to want again **2.** (*volere indietro*) to want back.
rivòlgere *vt.* **1.** to turn **2.** (*indirizzare*) to address. ♦ **rivòlgersi** *vr.* **1.** to turn **2.** (*parlando*) to address (so.) **3.** (*ricorrere, riferirsi*) to apply (to).
rivolgimento *sm.* **1.** upheaval **2.** (*cambio*) change.
rìvolo *sm.* streamlet.
rivolta *sf.* revolt.
rivoltante *agg.* revolting.
rivoltare *vt.* **1.** to turn (over) again **2.** (*rovesciare*) to turn **3.** (*capovolgere*) to turn upside-down **4.** (*con l'interno all'esterno*) to turn inside out **5.** (*fig.*) to upset (*v. irr.*). ♦ **rivoltarsi** *vr.* **1.** to turn round **2.** (*rigirarsi*) to turn over **3.** (*ribellarsi*) to revolt **4.** (*fig.*) to turn.
rivoltella *sf.* revolver.

rivoltoso *agg.* e *sm.* rebel.
rivoluzionare *vt.* to revolutionize.
rivoluzionario *agg.* e *sm.* revolutionary.
rivoluzione *sf.* revolution.
rizoma *sm.* rhizome.
rizzare *vt.* to raise: — *le orecchie*, to prick one's ears. ♦ **rizzarsi** *vr.* 1. to stand (*v. irr.*) up 2. (*di capelli*) to stand on end.
roba *sf.* stuff, things (*pl.*).
robaccia *sf.* rubbish.
robinia *sf.* locust-tree.
robustezza *sf.* robustness.
robusto *agg.* robust.
rocambolesco *agg.* daring.
rocca[1] *sf.* 1. stronghold 2. (*roccia*) rock.
rocca[2] *sf.* (*conocchia*) distaff.
roccaforte *sf.* stronghold.
rocchetto *sm.* 1. spool 2. (*elettr.*) coil.
rocchio *sm.* 1. (*di tronco*) log 2. (*di colonna*) drum.
roccia *sf.* rock.
rocciatore *sm.* rock-climber.
roccioso *agg.* rocky.
roco *agg.* hoarse.
rodaggio *sm.* (*auto*) running in.
rodare *vt.* to run (*v. irr.*) in.
ròdere *vt.* 1. to gnaw 2. (*corrodere*) to corrode. ♦ **ròdersi** *vr.* 1. to worry 2. (*di rabbia ecc.*) to be consumed (with).
rodimento *sm.* 1. gnawing 2. (*fig.*) anxiety.
roditore *agg.* e *sm.* rodent.
rododendro *sm.* rhododendron.
rogare *vt.* to draw (*v. irr.*) up.
rogatoria *sf.* request.
rogazioni *sf. pl.* rogations.
roggia *sf.* irrigation ditch.
rògito *sm.* deed.
rogna *sf.* 1. scabies 2. (*fig.*) trouble.
rognone *sm.* kidney.
rognoso *agg.* scabby.
rogo *sm.* 1. fire 2. (*pira*) pyre 3. (*supplizio*) stake.
rollare *vi.* to roll.
rollìo *sm.* roll.
romancio *agg.* Romansh.
romànico *agg.* 1. (*arch.*) Romanesque 2. Romanic.
romano *agg.* e *sm.* Roman.
romantcherìa *sf.* 1. (*atteggiamento*) romantic attitude 2. (*azione*) romantic deed.
romanticismo *sm.* Romanticism.
romàntico *agg.* e *sm.* romantic.

romanza *sf.* romance.
romanzare *vt.* to romanticize.
romanzesco *agg.* romantic.
romanziere *sm.* novelist.
romanzo[1] *agg.* Romance.
romanzo[2] *sm.* 1. novel 2. (*storia incredibile*) romance ‖ — *a puntate*, serial; — *a fumetti*, comics.
romba *sf.* roar.
rombare *vi.* to rumble.
ròmbico *agg.* rhombic(al).
rombo[1] *sm.* (*rumore*) rumble.
rombo[2] *sm.* (*geom.*) rhomb.
rombo[3] *sm.* (*itt.*) brill.
romboèdrico *agg.* rhombohedral.
romboedro *sm.* rhombohedron (*pl.* -ra).
romboidale *agg.* rhomboid(al).
rombòide *agg.* e *sm.* rhomboid.
romeno *agg.* e *sm.* Rumanian.
romeo *sm.* pilgrim.
romitaggio *sm.* hermitage.
ròmito *agg.* solitary. ♦ **romito** *sm.* hermit.
romitorio *sm.* hermitage.
ròmpere *vt.* to break (*v. irr.*): — *i ponti con qu.*, to break with so. ♦ **ròmpersi** *vr.* to break (up).
rompicapo *sm.* puzzle.
rompicollo *sm.* madcap: *a* —, headlong.
rompighiaccio *sm.* ice-breaker.
rompiscàtole *s.* nuisance.
rompitore *sm.* breaker.
ronca *sf.* pruning-knife (*pl.* -ives).
ronciglio *sm.* hook.
ròncola *sf.* pruning-hook.
ronda *sf.* 1. rounds (*pl.*) 2. (*pattuglia*) patrol.
rondella *sf.* washer.
ròndine *sf.* swallow: *a coda di* —, swallow-tailed.
rondinotto *sm.* young swallow.
rondò *sm.* 1. (*mus.*) rondo 2. (*poet.*) rondel 3. (*piazza circolare*) circus.
rondone *sm.* swift.
ronfare *vi.* to snore.
ronzare *vi.* 1. to buzz 2. (*fig.*) to hang (*v. irr.*) around.
ronzino *sm.* jade.
ronzio *sm.* buzz.
ròrido *agg.* 1. (*bagnato*) wet 2. (*rugiadoso*) dewy.
rosa *sf.* rose ‖ *all'acqua di rose* (*fig.*), moderate. ♦ **rosa** *agg.* e *sm.* pink.
rosàceo *agg.* rosy.
rosaio *sm.* rose-bush.
rosario *sm.* rosary.

rosato *agg.* rosy.
ròseo *agg.* rosy.
rosèola *sf.* roseola.
roseto *sm.* rose-garden.
rosetta *sf.* 1. rosette 2. (*diamante*) rose 3. (*mecc.*) washer.
rosicchiare *vt.* to gnaw.
rosmarino *sm.* rosemary.
rosolare *vt.* to brown. ♦ **rosolarsi** *vr.* 1. to get (*v. irr.*) brown 2. (*prendere il sole*) to bask.
rosolìa *sf.* German measles (*pl.*).
rosolio *sm.* rosolio.
rosone *sm.* rose-window.
rospo *sm.* toad.
rossastro *agg.* reddish.
rosseggiare *vi.* to be reddish.
rossetto *sm.* 1. (*per labbra*) lipstick 2. (*per guance*) rouge.
rossiccio *agg.* ruddy.
rosso *agg. e sm.* red: — *d'uovo*, yolk; *diventar* —, to flush.
rossore *sm.* flush.
rosticcerìa *sf.* rotisserie.
rosticciere *sm.* owner of a rotisserie.
rostro *sm.* 1. rostrum (*pl.* -ra) 2. (*becco*) beak.
rotàbile *agg.* carriage (*attr.*).
rotaia *sf.* 1. rail 2. (*solca*) rut.
rotare *vi. e vt.* to rotate, to revolve.
rotativa *sf.* rotary press.
rotativo *agg.* rotary.
rotatorio *agg.* rotating.
rotazione *sf.* rotation.
roteare *vt.* 1. to swing (*v. irr.*) 2. (*gli occhi*) to roll. ♦ **roteare** *vi.* to wheel.
rotella *sf.* small wheel.
rotocalco *sm.* 1. rotogravure 2. (*rivista*) illustrated magazine.
rotolamento *sm.* rolling.
rotolare *vt. e vi.* to roll. ♦ **rotolarsi** *vr.* to roll.
ròtolo *sm.* roll ‖ *andare a rotoli*, to go (*v. irr.*) to rack and ruin; *mandare a rotoli*, to ruin.
rotolone *sm.* V. *ruzzolone*.
rotonda *sf.* rotunda.
rotondità *sf.* roundness.
rotondo *agg.* 1. round 2. (*grassoccio*) plump.
rotore *sm.* rotor.
rotta *sf.* 1. course 2. (*rottura*) breach 3. (*sconfitta*) rout ‖ *a — di collo*, headlong; *essere in — con*, to be on bad terms with; *mettere in* —, to rout.
rottame *sm.* 1. wreck 2. (*di scarto*) scraps (*pl.*).

rotto *agg.* 1. broken 2. (*stracciato*) torn 3. (*avvezzo*) accustomed.
rottura *sf.* break(ing).
ròtula *sf.* knee-cap.
rovente *agg.* red-hot.
ròvere *sm.* oak.
rovesciamento *sm.* 1. overthrowing 2. (*cambiamento*) reversal.
rovesciare *vt.* 1. to overturn 2. (*capovolgere*) to turn upside down 3. (*gettare*) to throw (*v. irr.*) 4. (*rivoltare*) to turn inside out 5. (*versare intenzionalmente*) to pour 6. (*versare accidentalmente*) to spill 7. (*abbattere*) to overthrow (*v. irr.*). ♦ **rovesciarsi** *vr.* 1. to overturn 2. (*riversarsi*) to pour.
rovescio *sm.* 1. reverse 2. (*opposto*) opposite 3. (*di pioggia*) heavy shower 4. (*di critiche ecc.*) hail ‖ *a — (capovolto*), upside down.
roveto *sm.* bramble-bush.
rovina *sf.* ruin.
rovinare *vt.* 1. to ruin 2. (*sciupare*) to spoil (*v. irr.*). ♦ **rovinare** *vi.* to crash.
rovinìo *sm.* 1. downfall 2. (*rumore*) crash.
rovinoso *agg.* ruinous.
rovistare *vt. e vi.* to rummage.
rovo *sm.* blackberry bush.
rozza *sf.* jade.
rozzezza *sf.* roughness.
rozzo *agg.* rough.
ruba *sf.* *andare a* —, to sell (*v. irr.*) like wildfire.
rubacchiare *vt.* to pilfer.
rubacuori *agg.* bewitching. ♦ **rubacuori** *sm.* lady-killer.
rubare *vt.* to steal (*v. irr.*).
ruberìa *sf.* theft.
rubicondo *agg.* ruddy.
rubinetterìa *sf.* plumbing fixtures (*pl.*).
rubinetto *sm.* tap.
rubino *sm.* ruby.
rubizzo *agg.* hale.
rublo *sm.* rouble.
rubrica *sf.* 1. (*di giornale*) column 2. (*per indirizzi*) addressbook.
rude *agg.* rough.
rùdere *sm.* ruin.
rudezza *sf.* roughness.
rudimentale *agg.* rudimentary.
rudimento *sm.* rudiment.
ruffiano *sm.* pander.
ruga *sf.* wrinkle.
ruggente *agg.* roaring.

rùggine *sf.* **1.** rust **2.** (*fig.*) grudge.
rugginoso *agg.* rusty.
ruggire *vi.* to roar.
ruggito *sm.* roar.
rugiada *sf.* dew: *goccia di* —, dew-drop.
rugiadoso *agg.* dewy.
rugosità *sf.* **1.** wrinkledness **2.** (*scabrosità*) ruggedness.
rugoso *agg.* **1.** wrinkled **2.** (*scabro*) rugged.
rullaggio *sm. pista di* —, taxi-track.
rullare *vi.* **1.** to roll **2.** (*di aereo*) to taxi.
rullino *sm.* roll.
rullìo *sm.* roll.
rullo *sm.* **1.** roll **2.** (*mecc.*) roller.
rum *sm.* rum.
ruminante *agg. e sm.* ruminant.
ruminare *vt.* to ruminate.
ruminazione *sf.* rumination.
rùmine *sm.* rumen.
rumore *sm.* **1.** noise **2.** (*diceria*) rumour || *far* — (*fig.*), to arouse great interest.
rumoreggiare *vi.* **1.** to rumble **2.** (*fig.*) to rumour.
rumorìo *sm.* noise.
rumorista *sm.* noise-maker.
rumoroso *agg.* noisy.
ruolino *sm.* (*di marcia*) time schedule.
ruolo *sm.* **1.** roll, list **2.** (*teat.*) role **3.** (*amm.*) roster.
ruota *sf.* wheel.
rupe *sf.* cliff.
rupestre *agg.* rocky.
rurale *agg.* rural || *i rurali*, country people.
ruscello *sm.* brook.
ruspa *sf.* scraper.
ruspare *vi.* (*razzolare*) to scratch about.
russare *vi.* to snore.
russo *agg. e sm.* Russian.
rusticità *sf.* rusticity.
rùstico *agg.* **1.** rustic **2.** (*ritroso*) unsociable.
ruta *sf.* rue.
rutilante *agg.* glowing.
ruttare *vi.* to belch.
rutto *sm.* belch.
rùvido *agg.* rough.
ruzzare *vi.* to romp.
ruzzolare *vt.* to roll. ♦ **ruzzolare** *vi.* **1.** to roll **2.** (*cadere*) to tumble down.
ruzzolone *sm.* tumble: *fare un* —, to tumble down.

S

sàbato *sm.* Saturday.
sabba *sm.* witches' Sabbath.
sabbia *sf.* sand.
sabbiare *vt.* to sand.
sabbiatura *sf.* sand-bath.
sabbioso *agg.* sandy.
sabotaggio *sm.* sabotage.
sabotare *vt.* to sabotage.
sabotatore *sm.* saboteur.
sacca *sf.* bag.
saccarina *sf.* saccharine.
saccarosio *sm.* saccharose.
saccente *agg.* pedantic. ♦ **saccente** *s.* pedant.
saccheggiare *vt.* to sack.
saccheggio *sm.* sack.
sacchetto *sm.* small bag.
sacco *sm.* **1.** sack, bag || *colazione al* —, picnic; *mettere qu. nel* —, to take (*v. irr.*) so. in **2.** (*grande quantità*) a lot of.
saccoccia *sf.* pocket.
saccone *sm.* palliasse.
sacerdotale *agg.* sacerdotal.
sacerdote *sm.* priest.
sacerdozio *sm.* priesthood.
sacrale *agg.* sacral.
sacramentale *agg.* sacramental.
sacramentare *vi.* (*fig.*) to swear (*v. irr.*).
sacramento *sm.* sacrament.
sacrario *sm.* shrine.
sacrificare *vt.* to sacrifice.
sacrificio *sm.* sacrifice.
sacrilegio *sm.* sacrilege.
sacrìlego *agg.* sacrilegious.
sacrista *sm.* sacristan.
sacro *agg.* sacred, holy.
sacrosanto *agg.* **1.** sacrosanct **2.** (*indiscutibile*) absolute.
sàdico *agg.* sadistic. ♦ **sàdico** *sm.* sadist.
sadismo *sm.* sadism.
saetta *sf.* **1.** arrow **2.** (*fulmine*) thunderbolt.
saettare *vt.* **1.** to shoot (*v. irr.*) arrows at **2.** (*fig.*) to dart. ♦ **saettare** *vi.* to dart.
sàffico *agg.* Sapphic.
sagace *agg.* sagacious.
sagacia *sf.* sagacity.
saggezza *sf.* wisdom.
saggiare *vt.* to assay, to test.
saggiatore *sm.* **1.** assayer **2.** (*bilancia*) assay balance.
saggina *sf.* sorghum.

saggio[1] *agg.* wise. ♦ **saggio** *sm.* wise man (*pl.* men).

saggio[2] *sm.* 1. essay 2. (*campione*) sample 3. (*saggio ginnico*) display.

saggista *s.* essayist.

sagittario *sm.* 1. archer 2. (*astr.*) Sagittarius.

sàgoma *sf.* shape || *è una —!* (*fam.*), he is a character!

sagomare *vt.* to shape.

sagra *sf.* festival.

sagrato *sm.* church-square.

sagrestano *sm.* sacristan.

sagrestìa *sf.* sacristy.

saia *sf.* serge.

saio *sm.* habit.

sala *sf.* hall, room: — *da pranzo*, dining-room.

salace *agg.* salacious.

salacità *sf.* salacity.

salamandra *sf.* salamander.

salame *sm.* salami (*pl.*).

salamelecco *sm.* salaam.

salamoia *sf.* pickle.

salare *vt.* to salt.

salariale *agg.* salary (*attr.*).

salariato *agg.* wage-earning. ♦ **salariato** *sm.* wage-earner.

salario *sm.* wages (*pl.*).

salassare *vt.* to bleed (*v. irr.*).

salasso *sm.* 1. bleeding 2. (*fig.*) extortion.

salato *agg.* 1. salty 2. (*costoso*) dear 3. (*salace*) keen.

salatura *sf.* salting.

salda *sf.* starch-water.

saldamente *avv.* firmly.

saldare *vt.* 1. to solder, to weld 2. (*un conto*) to settle.

saldatore *sm.* solderer, welder.

saldatrice *sf.* welding machine.

saldatura *sf.* soldering, welding.

saldezza *sf.* firmness.

saldo[1] *agg.* firm.

saldo[2] *sm.* balance: — *attivo, passivo*, credit, debit balance.

sale *sm.* salt.

salesiano *agg.* e *sm.* Salesian.

salgemma *sm.* rock-salt.

sàlice *sm.* willow.

salicilato *sm.* salicylate.

saliente *agg.* important.

saliera *sf.* salt-cellar.

salina *sf.* salt-pit.

salino *agg.* saline, salt (*attr.*).

salire *vi.* 1. to rise (*v. irr.*), to go (*v. irr.*) up 2. (*di prezzi*) to increase.

saliscendi *sm.* 1. latch 2. (*alter-* *narsi di salite e discese*) ups and downs (*pl.*).

salita *sf.* 1. slope, ascent 2. (*aumento*) rise.

saliva *sf.* saliva, spittle.

salivare *agg.* salivary.

salivare *vi.* to salivate.

salivazione *sf.* salivation.

salma *sf.* corpse.

salmastro *agg.* saltish.

salmo *sm.* psalm.

salmodìa *sf.* psalmody.

salmodiare *vi.* to sing (*v. irr.*) psalms.

salmone *sm.* salmon.

salnitro *sm.* saltpetre.

salone *sm.* large hall, reception-room.

salottiero *agg.* drawing-room (*attr.*).

salotto *sm.* sitting-room.

salpare *vi.* to set (*v. irr.*) sails.

salsa *sf.* sauce.

salsèdine *sf.* saltness.

salsiccia *sf.* sausage.

salsiera *sf.* sauce-boat.

salso *agg.* salt (*attr.*).

saltare *vt.* e *vi.* to jump, to leap (*v. irr.*): — *di palo in frasca*, to jump from one subject to another; *far — una serratura*, to break (*v. irr.*) a lock.

saltatore *agg.* jumping. ♦ **saltatore** *sm.* jumper.

saltellare *vi.* to hop.

saltimbanco *sm.* tumbler.

salto *sm.* jump, leap.

saltuario *agg.* desultory.

salubre *agg.* healthy.

salubrità *sf.* healthiness.

salume *sm.* salted meat.

salumiere *sm.* delicatessen seller.

salumerìa *sf.* delicatessen.

salutare[1] *agg.* healthy.

salutare[2] *vt.* to greet, to hail.

salute *sf.* health.

saluto *sm.* greeting, salute.

salva *sf.* volley (*anche fig.*): *colpo a —*, blank shot.

salvacondotto *sm.* safe-conduct.

salvadanaio *sm.* money-box.

salvagente *sm.* 1. life-belt 2. (*marciapiede*) traffic island.

salvaguardare *vt.* to safeguard.

salvaguardia *sf.* safeguard.

salvare *vt.* 1. to save (*anche fig.*) 2. (*trarre in salvo*) to rescue. ♦ **salvarsi** *vr.* to save oneself.

salvataggio *sm.* rescue.

salvatore *sm.* saviour, saver.

salve *inter.* hail.
salvezza *sf.* salvation.
salvia *sf.* sage.
salvietta *sf.* towel.
salvo *agg.* safe. ♦ **salvo** *prep.* except, save. ♦ **salvo che** *cong.* except that, unless.
sanàbile *agg.* curable, remediable.
sanare *vt.* to heal.
sanatorio *sm.* sanatorium (*pl.* -ia).
sancire *vt.* to sanction.
sanculotto *sm.* sansculotte.
sàndalo[1] *sm.* (*calzatura*) sandal.
sàndalo[2] *sm.* (*mar.*) punt.
sandolino *sm.* small canoe.
sangue *sm.* blood: *spargimento di* —, bloodshed; *perdita di* —, bleeding; — *freddo*, coolness; *a* — *freddo*, in cold blood; *farsi cattivo* —, to worry over; *buon* — *non mente*, blood will tell.
sanguigno *agg.* sanguineous, blood (*attr.*).
sanguinaccio *sm.* blood-sausage.
sanguinante *agg.* bleeding.
sanguinare *vi.* to bleed (*v. irr.*).
sanguinario *agg. e sm.* sanguinary: *uomo* —, bloodthirsty man.
sanguinoso *agg.* bloody.
sanguisuga *sf.* leech.
sanità *sf.* soundness, sanity.
sanitario *agg.* sanitary.
sano *agg.* 1. healthy 2. (*fig.*) sound 3. (*intero, intatto*) intact.
sansa *sf.* husk.
sànscrito *sm.* Sanskrit.
santarellina *sf.* goody-goody.
santificante *agg.* sanctifying.
santificare *vt.* to canonize: — *le feste*, to observe holy days.
santificazione *sf.* sanctification.
santino *sm.* small holy picture.
santìssimo *agg.* most holy: *il* — *Sacramento*, the Blessed Sacrament.
santità *sf.* holiness.
santo *agg.* 1. holy 2. (*seguito da nome proprio*) saint. ♦ **santo** *sm.* saint.
santone *sm.* santon.
santuario *sm.* sanctuary.
sanzionare *vt.* to ratify.
sanzione *sf.* sanction.
sapere[1] *vt.* 1. to know (*v. irr.*): *non* — *che fare*, to be at a loss what to do; *chi sa!*, who knows!; *non si sa mai*, you never know; *venire a* —, to hear (*v. irr.*) 2. (*essere capace*) can, to be able: *sai parlare inglese?*, can you speak

English?; *non so farlo*, I am not able to do it. ♦ **sapere** *vi.* (*aver sapore*) to taste.
sapere[2] *sm.* 1. knowledge 2. (*cultura*) learning.
sàpido *agg.* sapid.
sapiente *agg.* wise. ♦ **sapiente** *sm.* sage.
sapienza *sf.* wisdom.
saponaria *sf.* soapwort.
saponata *sf.* lather (*solo sing.*).
sapone *sm.* soap: — *da barba*, shaving-soap; — *da bagno*, bath soap.
saponetta *sf.* cake of soap.
saponificare *vt.* to saponify.
saponificazione *sf.* saponification.
saponificio *sm.* soap-works (*pl. con costruzione sing.*).
sapore *sm.* taste, flavour (*anche fig.*).
saporire *vt.* to flavour
saporitamente *avv.* savourily || *dormire* —, to sleep (*v. irr.*) soundly.
saporito *agg.* savoury, tasty.
saputello *sm.* wiseacre.
saputo *agg.* 1. learned 2. (*noto*) well-known.
sarabanda *sf.* saraband.
saraceno *sm.* saracen.
saracinesca *sf.* rolling-shutter.
sarcasmo *sm.* sarcasm.
sarcàstico *agg.* sarcastic.
sarchiare *vt.* to weed.
sarchiatore *agg.* weeding. ♦ **sarchiatore** *sm.* weeder.
sarchiatura *sf.* weeding.
sarchio *sm.* hoe.
sarcòfago *sm.* sarcophagus (*pl.* -gi).
sardina *sf.* sardine.
sardònico *agg.* sardonic.
sarmento *sm.* runner.
sarta *sf.* dressmaker.
sartie *sf. pl.* shrouds.
sartina *sf.* grisette.
sarto *sm.* tailor.
sartorìa *sf.* 1. (*da uomo*) tailor's 2. (*da donna*) dressmaker's.
sassaia *sf.* stony place.
sassaiuola *sf.* 1. shower of stones 2. (*battaglia di sassi*) stone-fight.
sassata *sf.* blow with a stone.
sasso *sm.* stone: *a un tiro di* — *da*, within a stone's throw of.
sassofonista *sm.* saxophonist.
sassòfono *sm.* saxophone.
sassolino *sm.* pebble.
sàssone *agg. e sm.* Saxon.

sassoso *agg.* stony.
satànico *agg.* Satanic.
satèllite *sm.* satellite.
sàtira *sf.* satire.
satìrico *agg.* satirical.
sàtiro *sm.* satyr.
satollare *vt.* to satiate.
satollo *agg.* satiated.
sàtrapo *sm.* satrap.
saturare *vt.* to saturate.
saturazione *sf.* saturation.
saturnali *sm. pl.* saturnalia.
sàturo *agg.* saturated.
sàuro *agg.* sorrel.
savana *sf.* savannah.
savio *agg.* wise. ♦ savio *sm.* sage.
saziàbile *agg.* satiable.
saziare *vt.* to satisfy, to glut. ♦ saziarsi *vr.* to get (*v. irr.*) full.
sazietà *sf.* satiety: *mangiare, bere a* —, to eat (*v. irr.*), to drink (*v. irr.*) one's fill.
sazio *agg.* replete, full.
sbaciucchiare *vt.* to smother with kisses.
sbadatàggine *sf.* carelessness.
sbadato *agg.* careless.
sbadigliare *vi.* to yawn.
sbadiglio *sm.* yawn.
sbafare *vi.* to scrounge.
sbafatore *sm.* scrounger.
sbafo (*nella loc. avv.*) *prendere qc. a* —, to scrounge sthg.
sbagliare *vi.* to mistake (*v. irr.*). ♦ sbagliarsi *vr.* to make (*v. irr.*) a mistake.
sbagliato *agg.* wrong.
sbaglio *sm.* mistake.
sbalestrare *vt.* 1. to send (*v. irr.*) 2. (*fig.*) to flounder.
sballare *vt.* to unpack.
sballato *agg.* (*fig.*) foolhardy.
sballottamento *sm.* jolting.
sballottare *vt.* to jolt (about), to toss (about).
sbalordimento *sm.* amazement.
sbalordire *vt.* to amaze.
sbalorditivo *agg.* amazing.
sbalordito *agg.* amazed.
sbalzamento *sm.* 1. overthrow 2. (*fig.*) dismissal.
sbalzare[1] *vt.* to throw (*v. irr.*), to toss.
sbalzare[2] *vt.* (*arte*) to emboss.
sbalzato *agg.* (*arte*) embossed.
sbalzo *sm.* 1. bound, jump 2. (*cambio*) change.
sbancare *vt.* to leave (*v. irr.*) broke.

sbandamento *sm.* 1. dispersal 2. (*auto*) skid 3. (*mar.*) list.
sbandare *vt.* 1. to disperse 2. (*auto*) to cause a skid.
sbandata *sf.* V. *sbandamento*.
sbandato *sm.* straggler.
sbandierare *vt.* (*fig.*) to display.
sbaragliare *vt.* to rout.
sbaraglio *sm.* jeopardy: *mettere allo* —, to jeopardize.
sbarazzare *vt.* to clear up. ♦ sbarazzarsi *vr.* to get (*v. irr.*) rid (of).
sbarazzino *agg.* free and easy. ♦ sbarazzino *sm.* little scamp.
sbarbare *vt.* to shave.
sbarbatello *sm.* young colt.
sbarcare *vt. e vi.* to land, to disembark.
sbarco *sm.* 1. (*di passeggeri*) landing 2. (*di merci*) unloading.
sbarra *sf.* 1. bar 2. (*del timone*) tiller.
sbarramento *sm.* 1. barricade 2. (*di acque*) dam 3. (*mil.*) barrage.
sbarrare *vt.* 1. to bar: — *un assegno*, to cross a cheque 2. (*spalancare*) to open wide.
sbarrato *agg.* blocked || *occhi sbarrati*, wide open eyes.
sbatacchiamento *sm.* banging, slamming.
sbatacchiare *vt.* to bang, to slam.
sbàttere *vt.* 1. (*urtare contro*) to knock 2. (*scaraventare*) to throw (*v. irr.*) 3. (*chiudere violentemente*) to slam 4. (*di panna, uova*) to whip, to beat (*v. irr.*).
sbattezzare *vt.* to force to abjure Christianity.
sbattimento *sm.* banging.
sbattiuova *sm.* egg-whisk.
sbattuto *agg.* 1. depressed: *viso* —, tired face 2. (*di uova*) beaten.
sbavare *vi.* 1. to dribble 2. (*tip.*) to smudge.
sbavatura *sf.* 1. dribble 2. (*tip.*) smudge.
sbellicarsi *vr.* — *dalle risa*, to split (*v. irr.*) one's sides with laughter.
sbendare *vt.* to unbandage.
sberla *sf.* slap.
sberleffo *sm.* grimace.
sbertucciare *vt.* 1. to mock 2. (*sgualcire*) to crumple.
sbiadire *vi.* to fade.
sbiancare *vt.* to bleach. ♦ sbiancare *vi.* to turn white. ♦ sbiancarsi *vr.* to turn white.

sbieco *agg.* slanting: *guardare qu. di —*, to look askance at so.; *tagliare una stoffa di —*, to cut a (*v. irr.*) a cloth on the bias.

sbigottimento *sm.* dismay.

sbigottire *vt.* to dismay. ◆ **sbigottirsi** *vr.* to be dismayed.

sbigottito *agg.* dismayed.

sbilanciare *vt.* to unbalance. ◆ **sbilanciarsi** *vr.* 1. to lose (*v. irr.*) one's balance 2. (*fig.*) to commit oneself.

sbilancio *sm.* lack of balance; disproportion.

sbilenco *agg.* crooked.

sbirciare *vt.* to cast (*v. irr.*) a sidelong glance.

sbirraglia *sf.* police (*us. al pl.*).

sbirro *sm.* policeman (*pl.* -men).

sbizzarrirsi *vr.* to satisfy one's whims.

sbloccare *vt.* to raise the blockade: *— gli affitti*, to decontrol rents.

sblocco *sm.* 1. raising the blockade 2. (*mecc.*) releasing the brake 3. (*econ.*) decontrol.

sboccare *vi.* 1. (*di corso d'acqua*) to flow 2. (*di strada*) to lead (*v. irr.*).

sboccato *agg.* (*fig.*) coarse.

sbocciare *vi.* to open, to blossom.

sboccio *sm.* blooming.

sbocco *sm.* outlet, exit.

sbocconcellare *vt.* to nibble.

sbollire *vi.* (*fig.*) to cool down.

sbolognare *vt.* to palm off.

sbornia *sf.* drunkenness: *prendere la —*, to get (*v. irr.*) drunk.

sborsamento *sm.* paying out.

sborsare *vt.* to pay (*v. irr.*) out.

sborso *sm.* 1. payment 2. (*denaro sborsato*) outlay.

sbottare *vi.* to burst (*v. irr.*) out.

sbotto *sm.* outburst.

sbottonare *vt.* to unbutton. ◆ **sbottonarsi** *vr.* 1. to undo (*v. irr.*) one's buttons 2. (*fig.*) to disclose one's feelings.

sbozzare *vt.* to sketch out.

sbracare *vt.* to unbreech.

sbracato *agg.* (*fig.*) unseemly.

sbracciare *vi.* to gesticulate. ◆ **sbracciarsi** *vr.* 1. to roll up one's sleeves 2. (*agitarsi*) to strive (*v. irr.*).

sbracciato *agg.* (*di persona*) with bare arms.

sbraitare *vi.* to shout.

sbranamento *sm.* tearing to pieces.

sbranare *vt.* to tear (*v. irr.*) to pieces.

sbrancare *vt.* to separate. ◆ **sbrancarsi** *vr.* to scatter.

sbrattare *vt.* to clean.

sbriciolamento *sm.* crumbling.

sbriciolare *vt.* to crumble.

sbrigare *vt.* to finish off, to get (*v. irr.*) through. ◆ **sbrigarsi** *vr.* to hurry up.

sbrigativo *agg.* quick, hasty.

sbrigliare *vt.* to unbridle.

sbrinamento *sm.* defrosting.

sbrinare *vt.* to defrost.

sbrindellare *vt.* to tear (*v. irr.*) to ribbons.

sbrodolare *vt.* to spill (*v. irr.*).

sbrodolone *sm.* 1. slovenly eater 2. (*chi parla a lungo*) babbler.

sbrogliare *vt.* to disentangle. ◆ **sbrogliarsi** *vr.* to extricate oneself.

sbronza *sf.* V. *sbornia.*

sbronzarsi *vr.* to get (*v. irr.*) drunk.

sbronzo *agg.* drunk.

sbruffare *vt.* to besprinkle. ◆ **sbruffare** *vi.* (*fig.*) to brag.

sbruffo *sm.* sprinkle.

sbruffone *sm.* braggart.

sbucare *vi.* 1. to come (*v. irr.*) out 2. (*fig.*) to spring (*v. irr.*).

sbucciare *vt.* 1. to peel 2. (*sgranare*) to shell.

sbucciatura *sf.* 1. peeling 2. (*scalfittura*) scratch.

sbudellamento *sm.* stabbing.

sbudellare *vt.* to stab.

sbuffare *vi.* 1. to pant, to puff 2. (*per noia, ira*) to snort.

sbuffo *sm.* 1. puff 2. (*per noia, ira*) snort.

sbugiardare *vt.* to give (*v. irr.*) the lie to.

sbullonare *vt.* to unbolt.

scabbia *sf.* scabies.

scabbioso *agg.* scabby.

scabro *agg.* rough.

scabrosità *sf.* 1. roughness 2. (*fig.*) difficulty.

scabroso *agg.* 1. rough 2. (*fig.*) scabrous.

scacchiera *sf.* chess-board.

scacchiere *sm.* (*stor.*) Exchequer.

scacchista *sm.* chess-player.

scacciacani *sf.* dummy pistol.

scacciare *vt.* 1. to drive (*v. irr.*) away 2. (*da scuola*) to expel.

scacciata *sf.* expulsion.

scaccino *sm.* church cleaner.

scacco *sm.* **1.** (*quadratino*) square **2.** (*disegno su tessuti*) check **3.** (*giuoco*) chess || — *matto*, check-mate.

scadente *agg.* **1.** poor **2.** (*comm.*) falling due.

scadenza *sf.* (*comm.*) maturity: *a breve, lunga scadenza* (*comm.*), at short, long maturity || *a breve* —, in a short time.

scadenzario *sm.* discount bill-book.

scadere *vi.* **1.** to expire **2.** (*di pagamenti ecc.*) to become (*v. irr.*) due **3.** (*peggiorare*) to fall (*v. irr.*) off.

scadimento *sm.* decay.

scafandro *sm.* diving-suit.

scaffalare *vt.* to shelve.

scaffalatura *sf.* shelving.

scaffale *sm.* shelf (*pl.* shelves).

scafo *sm.* hull, body.

scagionare *vt.* to acquit. ♦ **scagionarsi** *vr.* to exculpate oneself.

scaglia *sf.* **1.** scale **2.** (*di legno, pietra*) chip.

scagliare *vt.* to fling (*v. irr.*), to throw (*v. irr.*).

scaglionare *vt.* to divide into groups.

scaglione *sm.* **1.** group **2.** (*mil.*) echelon.

scaglioso *agg.* scaly.

scala *sf.* **1.** stairs (*pl.*) **2.** (*trasportabile*) ladder **3.** (*scala graduata*) scale || *salire, scendere le scale*, to go (*v. irr.*) upstairs, downstairs.

scalare[1] *agg.* gradual.

scalare[2] *vt.* **1.** to climb (up) **2.** (*diminuire*) to scale down.

scalata *sf.* climbing.

scalatore *sm.* climber.

scalcagnato *agg.* down-at-heel, shabby.

scalciare *vi.* to kick.

scalcinato *agg.* **1.** unplastered **2.** (*sciatto*) shabby.

scaldabagno *sm.* water-heater.

scaldaletto *sm.* bed-warmer.

scaldapiedi *sm.* foot-warmer.

scaldare *vt.* to heat, to warm. ♦ **scaldarsi** *vr.* to warm oneself, to get (*v. irr.*) warm.

scaldavivande *sm.* dish-warmer.

scaldino *sm.* hand-warmer.

scalea *sf.* flight of stairs.

scaleno *agg.* scalene.

scalfire *vt.* to scratch.

scalfittura *sf.* scratch.

scalinata *sf.* flight of steps.

scalino *sm.* step.

scalmanarsi *vr.* (*fig.*) to get (*v. irr.*) excited.

scalmanato *agg.* out of breath, excited.

scalmo *sm.* rowlock.

scalo *sm.* **1.** (*mar.; aer.*) port of call: *volo senza* —, non-stop flight **2.** (*ferr.*) goods station || *fare* — *a*, to touch at.

scalogna *sf.* bad luck.

scalognato *agg.* unlucky.

scalone *sm.* great staircase.

scaloppina *sf.* veal cutlet.

scalpellare *vt.* to chisel.

scalpellino *sm.* stone-cutter.

scalpello *sm.* chisel.

scalpicciare *vi.* to shuffle.

scalpiccio *sm.* shuffling.

scalpitare *vi.* **1.** to paw **2.** (*di persona*) to stamp.

scalpitio *sm.* **1.** pawing **2.** (*di persona*) stamping.

scalpore *sm.* fuss, noise.

scaltrezza *sf.* shrewdness.

scaltrire *vt.* to sharpen so.'s wits. ♦ **scaltrirsi** *vr.* to become (*v. irr.*) sharp.

scaltro *agg.* shrewd.

scalzacane *sm.* **1.** (*incompetente*) botcher **2.** (*malridotto*) down-and-out.

scalzare *vt.* **1.** to take (*v. irr.*) so.'s shoes and socks off **2.** (*fig.*) to undermine.

scalzo *agg.* barefoot.

scambiare *vt.* **1.** to exchange **2.** (*sbagliarsi*) to mistake (*v. irr.*).

scambiévole *agg.* reciprocal.

scambio *sm.* **1.** exchange **2.** (*ferr.*) points (*pl.*).

scambista *sm.* (*ferr.*) pointsman (*pl.* -men).

scamiciato *agg.* shirt-sleeved (*attr.*).

scamosciare *vt.* to chamois.

scamosciato *agg.* shammy.

scampagnata *sf.* trip into the country.

scampanare *vt.* to chime.

scampanellare *vi.* to ring (*v. irr.*) long and loudly.

scampanellata *sf.* loud long ring.

scampare *vi.* to escape || *l'hai scampata bella!*, you have had a narrow escape.

scampato *sm.* survivor.

scampo[1] *sm.* escape: *via di* —, escape.

scampo[2] *sm.* (*itt.*) shrimp.
scàmpolo *sm.* remnant.
scanalare *vt.* to channel.
scanalatura *sf.* groove.
scandagliare *vt.* to sound.
scandaglio *sm.* sounding-lead.
scandalizzare *vt.* to shock.
scandalizzato *agg.* shocked.
scàndalo *sm.* scandal: *fare uno —*, to stir up a scandal.
scandaloso *agg.* scandalous, shocking.
scandire *vt.* 1. to scan 2. (*parole*) to syllabize 3. (*mus.*) to stress.
scannare *vt.* 1. to cut (*v. irr.*) so.'s throat 2. (*uccidere crudelmente*) to slaughter.
scannatoio *sm.* slaughter-house.
scanno *sm.* seat.
scansafatiche *sm.* lazy-bones.
scansare *vt.* to avoid, to shun. ♦ scansarsi *vr.* to step aside.
scansìa *sf.* shelves (*pl.*).
scantinato *sm.* basement.
scantonamento *sm.* (*l'evitare*) avoiding.
scantonare *vt.* (*evitare*) to avoid. ♦ scantonare *vi.* to turn the corner.
scanzonato *agg.* unconventional.
scapaccione *sm.* slap.
scapatàggine *sf.* recklessness.
scapestrato *agg.* e *sm.* madcap.
scapigliare *vt.* to dishevel.
scapigliato *agg.* 1. dishevelled 2. (*fig.*) unruly.
scàpito *sm.* damage, detriment: *a — di*, to the detriment of.
scàpola *sf.* shoulder-blade.
scapolare *agg.* e *sm.* scapular.
scàpolo *agg.* single. ♦ scàpolo *sm.* bachelor.
scappamento *sm.* 1. escape 2. (*di motori*) exhaust.
scappare *vi.* to escape, to run (*v. irr.*) away || *lasciarsi —*, to miss.
scappata *sf.* 1. escape 2. (*breve visita*) call.
scappatella *sf.* prank.
scappatoia *sf.* loop-hole.
scappellarsi *vr.* to take (*v. irr.*) off one's hat.
scappellata *sf.* raising one's hat.
scappellotto *sm.* slap.
scarabeo *sm.* scarab.
scarabocchiare *vt.* e *vi.* to scribble.
scarabocchio *sm.* scribble.
scarafaggio *sm.* black-beetle.
scaramanzìa *sf.* *per —*, for luck.

scaramuccia *sf.* skirmish.
scaraventare *vt.* to hurl.
scarcerare *vt.* to release (from prison).
scarcerazione *sf.* release (from prison).
scardinare *vt.* to unhinge.
scàrica *sf.* 1. (*di armi da fuoco; elettr.*) discharge 2. (*di proiettili, frecce; fig.*) shower.
scaricabarili *sm.* *fare a —*, to lay (*v. irr.*) the blame on so. else.
scaricamento *sm.* unloading.
scaricare *vt.* to discharge.
scaricatoio *sm.* 1. wharf 2. (*tubo*) waste-pipe.
scaricatore *sm.* unloader: *— di porto*, docker.
scàrico *sm.* 1. (*scolo*) drain 2. (*di merci*) discharge. ♦ scàrico *agg.* 1. (*di arma*) unloaded 2. discharged.
scarlattina *sf.* scarlet fever.
scarlatto *agg.* scarlet.
scarmigliare *vt.* to dishevel.
scarnire *vt.* to take (*v. irr.*) flesh off.
scarno *agg.* thin, lean.
scarpa *sf.* shoe: *— col tacco alto*, high-heeled shoe; *lucido per scarpe*, shoe polish.
scarpata *sf.* scarp.
scarpone *sm.* boot.
scarroccio *sm.* (*mar.*) leeway.
scarrozzare *vt.* e *vi.* to drive (*v. irr.*) about.
scarsamente *avv.* scarcely.
scarseggiare *vi.* to be lacking (in).
scarsità *vt.* shortage, lack.
scarso *agg.* scanty, lacking in.
scartabellare *vt.* to look through.
scartafaccio *sm.* note-book.
scartamento *sm.* (*ferr.*) gauge: *— ridotto*, narrow gauge.
scartare[1] *vt.* (*mettere da parte*) to reject.
scartare[2] *vi.* to unwrap.
scartare[3] *vt.* (*sport*) to swerve.
scarto[1] *sm.* 1. (*cosa scartata*) discard 2. (*lo scartare*) discarding.
scarto[2] *sm.* (*deviazione*) swerve.
scartocciare *vt.* to unwrap.
scartoffie *sf.* *pl.* heap of papers.
scassare *vt.* (*rompere*) to force open.
scassinare *vt.* to break (*v. irr.*) open.
scassinatore *sm.* 1. house-breaker 2. (*di notte*) burglar.

scasso *sm.* lock-picking, house--breaking: *furto con — (di giorno)*, house-breaking; *(di notte)* burglary.

scatenamento *sm.* *(fig.)* outburst.

scatenare *vt.* 1. *(aizzare)* to stir up 2. *(suscitare)* to rouse. ♦ **scatenarsi** *vr.* 1. to break *(v. irr.)* loose 2. *(fig.)* to break out.

scàtola *sf.* 1. box 2. *(di latta)* tin.

scatolame *sm.* 1. tins *(pl.)* 2. *(cibo in scatola)* tinned food.

scattare *vi.* 1. *(adirarsi)* to lose *(v. irr.)* one's temper 2. to go *(v. irr.)* off; to spring *(v. irr.)*. ♦ **scattare** *vt.* *(foto)* to shoot *(v. irr.)*.

scatto *sm.* 1. *(d'ira)* outburst || *di —*, suddenly; *a scatti*, in jerks 2. *(rumore)* click 3. *(di stipendio)* increase.

scaturire *vi.* 1. to spring *(v. irr.)* 2. *(derivare)* to originate.

scavalcare *vt.* 1. *(gettare da cavallo)* to unhorse 2. *(fig.)* to supplant 3. *(passare sopra)* to step, to jump over.

scavare *vt.* 1. to dig *(v. irr.)* 2. *(archeologia)* to excavate.

scavatrice *sf.* excavator.

scavezzacollo *sm.* reckless fellow.

scavo *sm.* 1. digging 2. *(archeologia)* excavation.

scégliere *vt.* to choose *(v. irr.)*, to pick out.

sceicco *sm.* sheik.

scelleratezza *sf.* 1. wickedness 2. *(atto scellerato)* misdeed.

scellerato *agg.* wicked. ♦ **scellerato** *sm.* wicked person.

scellino *sm.* shilling: *mezzo —*, sixpence.

scelta *sf.* choice.

scelto *agg.* choice, selected.

scemare *vi.* to diminish.

scemenza *sf.* stupidity.

scemo *agg.* e *sm.* stupid.

scempiare *vt.* to halve.

scempio[1] *agg.* stupid, foolish.

scempio[2] *sm.* havoc.

scena *sf.* 1. scene 2. *(palcoscenico)* stage: *colpo di —*, stage effect.

scenario *sm.* scenery.

scenata *sf.* row.

scéndere *vi.* 1. to go *(v. irr.)* down, to come *(v. irr.)* down 2. *(da un veicolo)* to get *(v. irr.)* off; *(da a cavallo)*, to dismount (from a horse) 3. *(declinare)* to slope down 4. *(di astri)* to sink *(v. irr.)* 5. *(avere origini)* to descend.

scendiletto *sm.* bedside-carpet.

sceneggiare *vt.* to arrange into scenes.

sceneggiatore *sm.* scenarist.

sceneggiatura *sf.* screenplay.

scenicamente *avv.* scenically.

scenografia *sf.* scenography.

scèrnere *vt.* to choose *(v. irr.)*.

scervellarsi *vr.* to rack one's brains.

scervellato *agg.* brainless. ♦ **scervellato** *sm.* brainless person.

scetticismo *sm.* scepticism.

scèttico *agg.* sceptical. ♦ **scèttico** *sm.* sceptic.

scettro *sm.* sceptre.

sceverare *vt.* to discern.

scevro *agg.* exempt.

scheda *sf.* card: *— elettorale*, voting-paper.

schedario *sm.* card-index.

scheggia *sf.* splinter, chip.

scheggiare *vt.* to chip, to splinter.

schelètrico *agg.* skeletal.

schèletro *sm.* skeleton.

schema *sm.* 1. scheme 2. *(tec.)* diagram.

schemàtico *agg.* schematic.

schematismo *sm.* schematism.

scherma *sf.* fencing.

schermaglia *sf.* skirmish.

schermare *vt.* 1. to screen 2. *(elettr.)* to shield.

schermirsi *vr.* to act coy.

schermitore *sm.* fencer.

schermo *sm.* 1. protection 2. *(cine)* screen 3. *(fis.)* shield 4. *(foto)* filter.

schernire *vt.* to laugh at.

scherno *sm.* mockery, derision.

scherzare *vi.* 1. to joke 2. *(considerare con leggerezza)* to trifle with.

scherzo *sm.* 1. joke: *per —*, for fun 2. *(effetto)* effects *(pl.)*.

scherzosamente *avv.* playfully.

scherzoso *agg.* playful.

schettinare *vi.* to roller-skate.

schettini *sm.* *pl.* roller-skates.

schiaccianoci *sm.* nut-cracker.

schiacciante *agg.* *(decisivo)* overwhelming.

schiacciare *vt.* to crush, to squash.

schiacciasassi *sm.* steam-roller.

schiaffare *vt.* to hurl.

schiaffeggiare *vt.* to slap.

schiaffo *sm.* 1. slap 2. *(affronto)* slap in the face.

schiamazzare *vi.* to make *(v. irr.)* a din.

schiamazzo *sm.* din, uproar.

schiantare *vt.* to break (*v. irr.*). ♦
schiantarsi *vr.* to break, to crash.
schiarimento *sm.* (*spiegazione*) explanation.
schiarire *vt.* to clear, to make (*v. irr.*) clear: — *i capelli*, to bleach one's hair. ♦ schiarirsi *vr.* (*fig.*) to brighten.
schiarita *sf.* 1. clearing 2. (*miglioramento*) improvement.
schiattare *vi.* to burst: — *di rabbia*, to burst with rage.
schiavista *sm.* 1. anti-abolitionist 2. (*mercante di schiavi*) slave-trader.
schiavitù *sf.* slavery.
schiavo *agg. e sm.* slave.
schidionata *sf.* spitful.
schidione *sm.* spit.
schiena *sf.* 1. back 2. (*di monte*) ridge.
schienale *sm.* back.
schiera *sf.* 1. formation 2. (*gruppo di persone*) group.
schieramento *sm.* array.
schierare *vt.* to array. ♦ schierarsi *vr.* 1. to draw (*v. irr.*) up 2. (*parteggiare*) to side with.
schiettezza *sf.* openness, purity.
schietto *agg.* pure, open.
schifare *vt.* to loathe. ♦ schifarsi *vr.* to feel (*v. irr.*) disgusted (at).
schifezza *sf.* disgusting thing.
schifiltoso *agg.* squeamish.
schifo[1] *sm.* disgust.
schifo[2] *sm.* (*mar.*) skiff.
schifoso *agg.* disgusting.
schioccare *vi.* 1. to crack 2. (*le dita*) to snap 3. (*le labbra*) to smack.
schiocco *sm.* 1. crack 2. (*di labbra*) smack.
schiodare *vt.* to unnail.
schiodatura *sf.* unnailing.
schioppettata *sf.* shot.
schioppo *sm.* gun.
schiùdere *vt.* to open. ♦ schiùdersi *vr.* to open.
schiuma *sf.* 1. foam 2. (*di vino, birra*) froth 3. (*di sapone*) lather.
schiumare *vt.* to skim. ♦ schiumare *vi.* 1. to foam 2. (*di bevande*) to froth.
schiumarola *sf.* skimmer.
schiumoso *agg.* 1. (*di mare*) foamy 2. (*di bevande*) frothy 3. (*di sapone*) lathery.
schiuso *agg.* open.

schivare *vt.* to avoid.
schivata *sf.* dodge.
schivo *agg.* shy, bashful.
schizofrenìa *sf.* schizophrenia.
schizofrènico *agg.* schizophrenic. ♦
schizofrènico *sm.* schizophrene.
schizzare *vt.* 1. to splash, to spatter 2. (*abbozzare*) to sketch. ♦
schizzare *vi.* to spurt.
schizzata *sf.* splashing.
schizzatoio *sm.* spray.
schizzetto *sm.* spray.
schizzinoso *agg.* squeamish, fussy.
schizzo *sm.* 1. splash, squirt 2. (*pitt.*) sketch.
sci *sm.* ski.
scia *sf.* 1. (*mar.*) wake 2. (*traccia*) trail.
scià *sm.* shah.
sciàbica *sf.* trawl.
sciàbola *sf.* sabre.
sciabolata *sf.* sabre-cut.
sciabolatore *sm.* sabreur.
sciabordare *vi.* to wash.
sciabordìo *sm.* washing, lapping.
sciacallo *sm.* 1. jackal 2. (*fig.*) profiteer.
sciacquare *vt.* to rinse (out).
sciacquatura *sf.* 1. rinsing 2. (*acqua*) rinsing-water.
sciacquìo *sm.* rinsing.
sciacquone *sm.* flush.
sciagura *sf.* misfortune.
sciagurato *agg.* 1. unlucky 2. (*malvagio*) wicked. ♦ sciagurato *sm.* wretch.
scialacquare *vt.* to squander.
scialacquatore *sm.* squanderer.
scialacquìo *sm.* squandering.
scialare *vt.* to squander money.
scialbare *vt.* to plaster.
scialbo *agg.* pale, wan.
scialle *sm.* shawl.
scialo *sm.* waste.
scialuppa *sf.* boat.
sciamannato *agg.* slovenly.
sciamano *sm.* shaman.
sciamare *vi.* to swarm.
sciame *sm.* swarm.
sciancarsi *vr.* to become (*v. irr.*) lame.
sciancato *agg.* lame.
sciarada *sf.* charade.
sciare[1] *vi.* to ski.
sciare[2] *vi.* (*mar.*) to back water.
sciarpa *sf.* scarf.
sciàtica *sf.* sciatica.
sciàtico *agg.* sciatic.
sciatore *sm.* skier.

sciatterìa *sf.* slovenliness.

sciatto *agg.* 1. slovenly, untidy 2. (*di ·stile ecc.*) careless.

scìbile *sm.* knowledge.

sciccherìa *sf.* smartness.

scientìfico *agg.* scientific.

scienza *sf.* science.

scienziato *sm.* scientist.

scilinguàgnolo *sm.* glib tongue.

scimitarra *sf.* scimitar.

scimmia *sf.* monkey, ape (*anche fig.*).

scimmiesco *agg.* monkeyish.

scimmiottare *vt.* to ape.

scimmiotto *sm.* young monkey.

scimpanzé *sm.* chimpanzee.

scimunito *agg.* silly. ♦ **scimunito** *sm.* blockhead.

scìndere *vt.* to divide: — *le questioni*, to deal (*v. irr.*) with each matter separately.

scintilla *sf.* spark.

scintillamento *sf.* sparkling.

scintillante *agg.* sparkling.

scintillare *vi.* to sparkle.

scintillìo *sm.* sparkling.

scintoismo *sm.* Shintoism.

scintoista *sm.* Shintoist.

scioccamente *avv,* foolishly.

sciocchezza *sf.* 1. foolishness 2. foolish thing 3. trifle.

sciocco *agg.* silly.

sciògliere *vt.* 1. to melt 2. (*slegare, disfare*) to untie 3. (*liberare*) to release 4. (*risolvere*) to solve. ♦ **sciògliersi** *vr.* to dissolve, to get (*v. irr.*) loose.

scioglilingua *sm.* tongue-twister.

scioglimento *sm.* 1. dissolution, breaking up 2. (*epilogo*) unravelling.

sciolina *sf.* ski wax.

scioltezza *sf.* 1. agility 2. (*spigliatezza*) ease 3. (*nel parlare*) fluency.

sciolto *agg.* 1. melted 2. (*slegato*) untied 3. (*agile*) agile 4. (*disinvolto*) easy || *capelli sciolti*, loose hair; *avere la lingua sciolta*, to have a ready tongue; — *da obblighi*, free from obligations.

scioperante *sm.* striker.

scioperare *vi.* to strike (*v. irr.*).

scioperatàggine *sf.* laziness.

scioperato *agg.* lazy. ♦ **scioperato** *sm.* lazy fellow.

sciòpero *sm.* strike.

sciorinare *vt.* to air, to display (*anche fig.*).

sciovìa *sf.* ski-lift.

sciovinismo *sm.* chauvinism.

sciovinista *sm.* chauvinist.

scipitàggine *sf.* insipidity (*anche fig.*).

scipito *agg.* insipid.

scirocco *sm.* sirocco.

sciroppare *vt.* to syrup.

sciroppato *agg.* in syrup.

sciropposo *agg.* syrupy.

scisma *sm.* schism.

scismàtico *agg.* e *sm.* schismatic.

scissione *sf.* 1. scission, split (*anche fig.*) 2. (*fis.; biol.*) fission.

scisso *agg.* divided.

scissura *sf.* 1. cleft, split 2. (*fig.*) dissension.

sciupare *vt.* 1. to spoil (*v. irr.*), to damage 2. (*sprecare*) to waste.

sciupato *agg.* 1. spoilt 2. (*sprecato*) wasted.

sciupìo *sm.* waste.

sciupone *agg.* wasteful. ♦ **sciupone** *sm.* waster.

scivolamento *sm.* sliding.

scivolare *vi.* 1. to slide (*v. irr.*) 2. (*involontariamente*) to slip.

scivolata *sf.* 1. slide 2. (*involontaria*) slip.

scìvolo *sm.* 1. (*aer.; mar.*)´slipway 2. skid.

scivolone *sm.* slip.

scivoloso *agg.* slippery.

sclerosi *sf.* sclerosis.

scleròtica *sf.* sclerotic.

scleròtico *agg.* sclerotic.

scoccare *vt.* e *vi.* 1. to shoot (*v. irr.*) 2. (*l'ora*) to strike (*v. irr.*).

scocciare *vt.* to bother.

scocciatore *sm.* bore.

scocciatura *sf.* bother.

scodella *sf.* bowl.

scodellare *vt.* to dish up.

scodinzolare *vi.* to wag the tail.

scodinzolìo *sm.* tail-wagging.

scogliera *sf.* cliff.

scoglio *sm.* 1. rock 2. (*fig.*)´difficulty.

scoiare *vt.* V. *scuoiare*.

scoiàttolo *sm.*´squirrel.

scolapasta *sm.* colander.

scolara *sf.* pupil, schoolgirl.

scolare *vt.* 1. to drain 2. (*in un colabrodo*) to strain.

scolaresca *sf.* student-body.

scolaro *sm.* pupil, schoolboy.

scolàstica *sf.* scholasticism.

scolàstico *agg.* 1. school (*attr.*) 2. (*dispregiativo*) bookish.

scolatoio *sm.* drain.

scolatura *sf.* draining.
scoliosi *sf.* scoliosis.
scollacciato *agg.* 1. (*di abito*) low-
-necked 2. (*fig.*) coarse.
scollare[1] *vt.* to cut (*v. irr.*) away
the neck of.
scollare[2] *vt.* (*staccare*) to unglue.
scollato[1] *agg.* (*di abito*) low-necked.
scollato[2] *agg.* unglued.
scollatura *sf.* neckline.
scollo *sm.* neck-opening.
scolo *sm.* draining.
scolorare *vt.* to discolour. ♦ **sco-
lorarsi** *vr.* to grow (*v. irr.*) pale.
scolorimento *sm.* discolouration.
scolorire *vt.* to bleach.
scolorito *agg.* faded, pale.
scolpare *vt.* to exculpate.
scolpire *vt.* to sculpture.
scombinare *vt.* to upset (*v. irr.*).
scombinato *agg.* screwy.
scombussolamento *sm.* upsetting.
scombussolare *vt.* to upset (*v.
irr.*).
scommessa *sf.* bet.
scomméttere *vt.* to bet (*v. irr.*).
scommettitore *sm.* bettor.
scomodamente *avv.* uncomfortably.
scomodare *vt.* to trouble, to bother.
scomodità *sf.* lack of comfort.
scòmodo *agg.* uncomfortable.
scompaginamento *sm.* upsetting,
upset.
scompaginare *vt.* to upset (*v. irr.*).
scompagnare *vt.* to break (*v. irr.*)
up (a pair).
scompagnato *agg.* odd.
scomparire *vi.* 1. to disappear 2.
(*non spiccare*) not to stand (*v.
irr.*) out.
scomparsa *sf.* 1. disappearance 2.
(*morte*) death.
scomparso *agg.* 1. disappeared 2.
(*morto*) dead.
scompartimento *sm.* 1. partition
2. (*ferr.*) compartment.
scompartire *vt.* to divide, to share
out.
scomparto *sm.* V. *scompartimento*.
scompenso *sm.* lack of balance:
— *cardiaco*, cardiac decompen-
sation.
scompiacenza *sf.* unkindness.
scompigliare *vt.* 1. to upset (*v.
irr.*) 2. (*arruffare*) to ruffle.
scompigliatamente *avv.* confusedly.

scompiglio *sm.* confusion, disorder.
scomponìbile *agg.* decomposable.
scomponimento *sm.* decomposition.
scomporre *vt.* 1. to decompose
2. (*i lineamenti*) to distort.
scompostamente *avv.* in an unseemly manner.
scompostezza *sf.* unseemliness.
scomposto *agg.* 1. (*sguaiato*) unseemly 2. decomposed.
scomùnica *sf.* excommunication.
scomunicare *vt.* to excommunicate.
scomunicato *agg.* e *sm.* excommunicate.
sconcertante *agg.* disconcerting.
sconcertare *vt.* to disconcert, to
baffle.
sconcertato *agg.* disconcerted.
sconcerto *sm.* perturbation.
sconcezza *sf.* indecency.
sconciamente *avv.* indecently.
sconcio *agg.* indecent.
sconclusionatamente *avv.* incon-
clusively.
sconclusionato *agg.* inconclusive.
scondito *agg.* 1. unseasoned 2. (*di
insalata*) undressed.
sconfessare *vt.* to disown.
sconfessione *sf.* disowning.
sconfìggere *vt.* to defeat.
sconfinamento *sm.* 1. (*in paese
straniero*) crossing the frontier 2.
(*in proprietà privata*) trespass.
sconfinare *vi.* 1. (*in paese straniero*) to cross the frontier 2. (*in
proprietà privata*) to trespass.
sconfinato *agg.* boundless.
sconfitta *sf.* defeat.
sconfitto *agg.* defeated.
sconfortante *agg.* discouraging.
sconfortare *vt.* to discourage.
sconfortato *agg.* discouraged.
sconforto *sm.* 1. discouragement
2. (*dolore*) sorrow.
scongiurare *vt.* 1. to beseech (*v.
irr.*) 2. (*evitare*) to avoid.
scongiuro *sm.* exorcism.
sconnessione *sf.* disconnectedness.
sconnesso *agg.* 1. disconnected 2.
(*fig.*) rambling.
sconnèttere *vt.* to disconnect. ♦
sconnèttere *vi.* to wander.
sconoscente *agg.* ungrateful.
sconoscenza *sf.* ingratitude.
sconòscere *vt.* to disown.
sconosciuto *agg.* unknown. ♦
sconosciuto *sm.* stranger.

sconquassare *vt.* to shatter.
sconquassato *agg.* ramshackle.
sconquasso *sm.* mess, disorder.
sconsacrare *vt.* to deconsecrate.
sconsideratezza *sf.* rashness.
sconsiderato *agg.* thoughtless.
sconsigliare *vt.* to advise against.
sconsigliato *agg.* rash.
sconsolante *agg.* discouraging.
sconsolare *vt.* to dishearten.
sconsolato *agg.* disconsolate.
scontàbile *agg.* discountable.
scontare *vt.* **1.** (*comm.*) to discount **2.** (*detrarre*) to deduct **3.** (*espiare*) to expiate.
scontato *agg.* (*previsto*) expected.
scontentare *vt.* to displease.
scontentezza *sf.* discontent.
scontento *agg.* displeased.
sconto *sm.* discount.
scontrarsi *vr.* to clash.
scontrino *sm.* ticket, check.
scontro *sm.* **1.** encounter **2.** (*di veicoli*) crash **3.** (*fig.*) clash.
scontrosamente *avv.* peevishly.
scontrosità *sf.* bad temper.
scontroso *agg.* bad-tempered.
sconveniente *agg.* **1.** unprofitable **2.** (*indecente*) unseemly.
sconvenientemente *avv.* unbecomingly.
sconvenienza *sf.* **1.** unprofitableness **2.** (*mancanza di correttezza*) unseemliness.
sconvolgente *agg.* upsetting.
sconvòlgere *vt.* to upset (*v. irr.*).
sconvolgimento *sm.* upsetting, confusion.
sconvolto *agg.* upset.
scopa *sf.* broom.
scopare *vt.* to sweep (*v. irr.*).
scoperchiare *vt.* to take (*v. irr.*) off the lid.
scoperta *sf.* discovery.
scopertamente *avv.* openly.
scoperto *agg.* uncovered ‖ *automobile scoperta*, open car; *a capo* —, bare-headed; *giocare a carte scoperte*, to act openly.
scopino *sm.* street-sweeper.
scopo *sm.* aim, purpose: *senza* —, aimless.
scopolamina *sf.* scopolamine.
scoppiare *vi.* **1.** to burst (*v. irr.*) **2.** (*di guerre, epidemie ecc.*) to break (*v. irr.*) out.
scoppiettante *agg.* crackling.
scoppiettare *vi.* to crackle.
scoppiettìo *sm.* crackling.

scoppio *sm.* **1.** burst, explosion: *motore a* —, piston-engine **2.** (*di guerre, rivoluzioni ecc.*) outbreak.
scoprimento *sm.* **1.** discovering **2.** (*di monumento*) unveiling.
scoprire *vt.* **1.** to discover **2.** (*avvistare*) to sight **3.** (*togliere ciò che copre*) to uncover **4.** (*palesare*) to show (*v. irr.*). ♦ **scoprirsi** *vr.* (*rivelarsi*) to reveal oneself.
scopritore *sm.* discoverer.
scoraggiamento *sm.* discouragement.
scoraggiante *agg.* discouraging.
scoraggiare *vt.* to discourage. ♦ **scoraggiarsi** *vr.* to get (*v. irr.*) discouraged.
scoraggiato *agg.* discouraged.
scoramento *sm.* discouragement.
scorato *agg.* disheartened.
scorbùtico *agg.* **1.** (*med.*) scorbutic **2.** (*fig.*) ill-tempered.
scorbuto *sm.* scurvy.
scorciare *vt.* to shorten.
scorciatoia *sf.* short cut.
scorcio *sm.* **1.** foreshortening **2.** (*spazio di tempo*) end, close.
scordare[1] *vt.* to forget (*v. irr.*).
scordare[2] *vt.* (*mus.*) to untune.
scordato[1] *agg.* forgotten.
scordato[2] *agg.* (*mus.*) untuned.
scòrfano *sm.* **1.** sea-scorpion **2.** (*di persona*) fright: *che* —!, what a fright!
scòrgere *vt.* to perceive, to discern.
scoria *sf.* **1.** (*metal.*) dross **2.** (*fig.*) scum.
scornare *vt.* **1.** to horn **2.** (*fig.*) to humiliate.
scornato *agg.* humiliated.
scorno *sm.* shame.
scorpacciata *sf.* blow out: *fare una* — *di*, to stuff oneself with.
scorpione *sm.* scorpion.
scorporare *vt.* to disembody.
scòrporo *sm.* breaking up.
scorrazzare *vi.* to run (*v. irr.*) about.
scòrrere *vi.* **1.** to run (*v. irr.*) **2.** (*scivolare*) to glide **3.** (*fluire*) to flow **4.** (*di tempo*) to fly (*v. irr.*).
scorrerìa *sf.* raid.
scorrettezza *sf.* incorrectness.
scorretto *agg.* **1.** incorrect **2.** (*di costumi*) dissolute **3.** (*maleducato*) rude.
scorrévole *agg.* **1.** sliding **2.** (*fig.*) fluent.

scorrevolezza *sf.* fluency.

scorribanda *sf.* incursion, raid.

scorrimento *sm.* sliding.

scorsa *sf.* glance.

scorso *agg.* last, past.

scorsoio *agg.* running.

scorta *sf.* **1.** escort **2.** (*provvista*) supply || *ruota di* —, spare wheel.

scortare *vt.* to escort.

scortecciare *vt.* **1.** to peel **2.** (*un albero*) to bark.

scortese *agg.* rude, impolite.

scortesìa *sf.* rudeness.

scorticare *vt.* to skin.

scorticatura *sf.* scratch.

scortichino *sm.* flaying-knife.

scorza *sf.* **1.** (*corteccia*) bark **2.** (*buccia*) skin, rind.

scoscéndere *vt.* to split (*v. irr.*).

scoscendimento *sm.* **1.** collapse **2.** (*di terreno*) break.

scosceso *agg* steep, sloping.

scossa *sf.* shock, shake.

scosso *agg.* **1.** shaken **2.** (*fig.*) upset.

scossone *sm.* **1.** shake **2.** (*strattone*) jerk.

scostare *vt.* to shift, to move away. ♦ **scostarsi** *vr.* **1.** to move away **2.** (*staccarsi*) to turn off.

scostumatezza *sf.* dissoluteness.

scostumato *agg.* dissolute. ♦ **scostumato** *sm.* dissolute person.

scotennare *vt.* to scalp.

scottante *agg.* burning.

scottare *vt.* **1.** to burn (*v. irr.*) **2.** (*cuc.*) to half-cook **3.** (*fig.*) to hurt (*v. irr.*).

scottatura *sf.* burn.

scotto[1] *sm.* score: *pagare lo* —, to - pay (*v. irr.*) one's piper.

scotto[2] *agg.* overdone.

scovare *vt.* **1.** to put (*v. irr.*) up **2.** (*scoprire*) to discover.

scozzare *vt.* to shuffle.

scozzese *agg.* Scotch, Scottish. ♦ **scozzese** *sm.* Scotchman (*pl.* -men).

scozzonare *vt.* **1.** to break (*v. irr.*) in **2.** (*fig.*) to teach (*v. irr.*) the first elements.

screanzatamente *avv.* rudely.

screanzato *agg.* rude, impolite. ♦ **screanzato** *sm.* rude person.

screditare *vt.* to discredit.

screditato *agg.* discredited.

scrédito *sm.* discredit.

scremare *vt.* to skim.

scremato *agg.* skimmed: *latte* —, skim-milk.

scrematura *sf.* skimming.

screpolare *vi.* **1.** to crack **2.** (*della pelle*) to get (*v. irr.*) chapped.

screpolatura *sf.* **1.** crack **2.** (*della pelle*) chap.

screziare *vt.* to variegate.

screziato *agg.* variegated.

screziatura *sf.* variegation.

screzio *sm.* disagreement.

scribacchiare *vt.* e *vi.* to scribble.

scribacchino *sm.* scribbler.

scricchiolare *vi.* **1.** to creak **2.** (*dì denti*) to grind (*v. irr.*).

scricchiolìo *sm.* **1.** creaking **2.** (*dì denti*) grinding.

scrigno *sm.* casket: — *di gioielli*, jewel-case.

scriminatura *sf.* (hair-)parting.

scriteriato *agg.* senseless.

scritta *sf.* **1.** inscription **2.** (*cartello*) notice **3.** (*dicitura*) caption.

scritto *sm.* writing.

scrittoio *sm.* writing-desk.

scrittore *sm.* writer.

scrittrice *sf.* woman writer.

scrittura *sf.* **1.** writing: — *a macchina*, typewriting; — *a mano*, handwriting **2.** (*teat.*) engagement **3.** (*giur.*) deed.

scritturare *vt.* to engage.

scrivanìa *sf.* writing-desk.

scrivano *sm.* clerk, copyist.

scrìvere *vt.* to write (*v. irr.*): — *a mano*, to write by hand; — *a penna*, *a matita*, to write in pen, in pencil; — *sotto dettatura*, to write from dictation; — *a macchina*, to typewrite (*v. irr.*) **2.** (*registrare*) to enter, to record.

scroccare *vt.* to scrounge.

scrocco *sm.* *vivere a* —, to sponge one's living.

scroccone *sm.* sponger.

scrofa *sf.* sow.

scrofoloso *agg.* scrofulous.

scrollamento *sm.* **1.** shaking **2.** (*di spalle*) shrugging.

scrollare *vt.* **1.** to shake (*v. irr.*) **2.** (*le spalle*) to shrug.

scrollata *sf.* **1.** (*di testa*) shake **2.** (*di spalle*) shrug.

scrosciante *agg.* (*di risa ecc.*) roaring: *pioggia* —, pelting rain.

scrosciare *vi.* **1.** (*di pioggia*) to pelt down **2.** (*fig.*) to roar.

scroscio *sm.* **1.** (*di cascata, torrente ecc.*) roar **2.** (*fig.*) roar, burst || — *di pioggia*, shower.

scrostamento *sm.* peeling.

scrostare vt. **1.** to take (v. irr.) the crust off, to peel off **2.** (dei muri) to remove the plaster from a wall. ♦ **scrostarsi** vr. to fall (v. irr.) off, to peel off.

scrùpolo sm. scruple.

scrupolosamente avv. scrupulously.

scrupolosità sf. scrupulosity.

scrupoloso agg. scrupulous.

scrutare vt. to search, to scan.

scrutatore agg. searching, inquisitive. ♦ **scrutatore** sm. **1.** searcher **2.** (di elezioni) scrutineer.

scrutinare vt. to scrutinize.

scrutinio sm. **1.** (di elezioni) poll **2.** (scolastico) assignment of a term's marks **3.** (attento esame) scrutiny.

scucire vt. to unsew (v. irr.), to unstitch. ♦ **scucirsi** vr. to rip.

scucito agg. **1.** unsewn **2.** (fig.) incoherent.

scucitura sf. unsewing.

scuderìa sf. stable.

scudetto sm. **1.** small shield **2.** (sport) (championship) shield.

scudiero sm. squire.

scudisciare vt. to lash.

scudisciata sf. lash.

scudiscio sm. switch, lash.

scudo sm. shield.

scuffia sf. (sbornia) drunkenness.

sculacciare vt. to spank.

sculacciata sf. spank.

sculettare vi. to waddle.

scultore sm. sculptor.

scultòreo agg. sculptural.

scultura sf. sculpture.

scuoiare vt. to skin.

scuola sf. school: — diurna, day--classes; — elementare, primary school; — media inferiore, superiore, secondary school; — pubblica, State school; maestro di —, schoolmaster.

scuòtere vt. **1.** to shake (v. irr.) (anche fig.) **2.** (agitare) to stir.

scuotimento sm. shaking.

scure sf. axe.

scurire vt. **1.** to darken **2.** (pitt.) to tone down. ♦ **scurirsi** vr. to grow (v. irr.) dark.

scuro agg. dark || faccia scura, grim face.

scurrile agg. scurrilous.

scurrilità sf. scurrility.

scusa sf. **1.** excuse, apology **2.** (pretesto) pretext.

scusàbile agg. excusable.

scusare vt. to excuse, to forgive (v. irr.) || scusi!, scusate!, sorry!, excuse me! ♦ **scusarsi** vr. to apologize.

sdebitarsi vr. **1.** to pay (v. irr.) off one's debts **2.** (disobbligarsi) to return a kindness.

sdegnare vt. **1.** to disdain **2.** (provocare lo sdegno) to enrage.

sdegnato agg. indignant.

sdegno sm. disdain, indignation.

sdegnosamente avv. disdainfully.

sdegnoso agg. **1.** (di atti e parole) disdainful **2.** (di persona) haughty.

sdentare vt. to break (v. irr.) the teeth.

sdentato agg. toothless.

sdilinquimènto sm. mawkishness.

sdilinquirsi vr. to melt away.

sdoganamento sm. clearing (through the customs).

sdolcinato agg. sugary, affected.

sdolcinatura sf. mawkishness.

sdoppiamento sm. splitting.

sdoppiare vt. to split.

sdraia sf. deck-chair.

sdraiarsi vr. to lie (v. irr.) down.

sdrucciolare vi. to slip, to slide.

sdrucciolévole agg. slippery.

sdrucciolone sm. slip.

sdrucire vt. to tear (v. irr.).

sdrucito agg. torn.

se cong. **1.** if **2.** (dubitativo) whether || — mai, in case; — non altro, at least; — non che, except that; anche —, even if.

sé pron. pers. **1.** one, him, her, it, them **2.** (riflessivi) oneself, himself, herself, itself, themselves || una donna piena di —, a conceited woman; essere fuori di —, to be beside oneself; tornare in —, to recover consciousness; amore di —, selfishness; padronanza di —, self--control; un uomo sicuro di —, a self-confident man; un uomo che si è fatto da —, a self-made man; rispetto di —, self-respect.

sebàceo agg. sebaceous.

sebbene cong. though, although.

sebo sm. sebum.

secante sf. secant.

secca sf. **1.** shoal **2.** (siccità) drought.

seccamente avv. coldly.

seccante agg. (fig.) annoying, irritating || una cosa, persona —, a nuisance.

seccare *vt.* 1. to dry up 2. (*annoia-re*) to annoy, to irritate. ♦ **sec-carsi** *vr.* (*infastidirsi*) to be annoyed (with).
seccatore *sm.* bother.
seccatura *sf.* 1. (*essicamento*) drying 2. (*noia*) bother, nuisance.
secchia *sf.* pail, bucket.
secchiello *sm.* bucket.
secchio *sm.* V. *secchia*.
secco *agg.* 1. dry 2. (*appassito*) withered 3. (*magro*) thin 4. (*brusco*) sharp 5. (*freddo*) cold.
secentesco *agg.* of the seventeenth century.
secèrnere *vt.* to secrete.
secessione *sf.* secession
secessionista *agg. e sm.* secessionist.
seco *pron.* with him, with her, with them.
secolare *agg.* 1. secular 2. (*in opposizione a ecclesiastico*) lay.
secolarizzare *vt.* to secularize.
secolarizzazione *sf.* secularization.
sècolo *sm.* 1. century 2. (*epoca*) epoch, age || *Padre Carlo, al — John Smith*, Father Charles, in the world John Smith.
seconda *sf.* (*auto*) second gear || *a — di* (*loc. prep.*), according to.
secondare *vt.* to favour.
secondario *agg.* secondary.
secondino *sm.* warder.
secondo[1] *agg.* 1. second 2. (*favorevole*) favourable. ♦ **secondo** *sm.* 1. (*minuto*) second 2. (*ufficiale in seconda*) executive officer.
secondo[2] *prep.* according to. ♦ **secondo** *avv.* second.
secrezione *sf.* secretion.
sèdano *sm.* celery.
sedare *vt.* to soothe.
sedativo *agg. e sm.* sedative.
sede *sf.* 1. seat, centre 2. (*residenza*) residence 3. (*eccl.*) see 4. (*edificio per pubblici uffici*) office.
sedentario *agg.* sedentary.
sedere[1] *vi.* 1. (*stare seduto*) to sit (*v. irr.*), to be sitting 2. (*mettersi a sedere*) to sit (down).
sedere[2] *sm.* bottom.
sedia *sf.* chair: — *a dondolo*, rocking-chair.
sedicenne *agg.* 1. (*attr.*) sixteen--year-old 2. (*pred.*) sixteen years old.
sedicente *agg.* would-be.
sedicèsimo *agg.* sixteenth.

sédici *agg.* sixteen.
sedile *sm.* seat, chair.
sedimentario *agg.* sedimentary.
sedimentazione *sf.* sedimentation.
sedimento *sm.* sediment.
sedizione *sf.* sedition.
sedizioso *agg.* seditious.
seducente *agg.* 1. alluring 2. (*affascinante*) charming.
sedurre *vt.* to seduce, to tempt.
seduta *sf.* sitting, session.
seduttore *agg.* seducing. ♦ **seduttore** *sm.* seducer.
seduzione *sf.* 1. seduction 2. (*attrazione*) attraction.
sega *sf.* saw.
ségala *sf.* rye.
segaligno *agg.* 1. rye (*attr.*) 2. (*di persona*) wiry.
segare *vt.* to saw (*v. irr.*).
segatura *sf.* sawdust.
seggio *sm.* chair, seat: — *elettorale*, poll.
sèggiola *sf.* chair.
seggiovìa *sf.* chair-lift.
segherìa *sf.* saw-mill.
seghettare *vt.* to jag.
segmentazione *sf.* segmentation.
segmento *sm.* segment.
segnalare *vt.* 1. to signal 2. (*far notare*) to point out. ♦ **segnalarsi** *vr.* to distinguish oneself.
segnalatore *sm.* 1. signaller 2. (*segnalatore di direzione*) direction indicator.
segnalazione *sf.* signal: — *stradale*, traffic signal.
segnale *sm.* signal: — *di pericolo, allarme*, danger, alarm signal; — *di linea libera, occupata* (*tel.*), ringing, engaged tone; — *di passaggio a livello*, level-crossing signal.
segnalètica *sf.* signals (*pl.*).
segnalètico *agg.* descriptive.
segnalibro *sm.* book-mark.
segnare *vt.* 1. to mark 2. (*indicare*) to show (*v. irr.*) 3. (*sport*) to score. ♦ **segnarsi** *vr.* to cross oneself.
segnatura *sf.* 1. marking 2. (*sport*) scoring.
segno *sm.* 1. sign, mark: *passare il —*, to overstep the mark 2. (*limite*) limit 3. (*simbolo*) symbol.
sego *sm.* tallow.
segregare *vt.* to segregate.
segregazione *sf.* segregation.
segreta *sf.* dungeon.

segretamente *avv.* in secret.
segretariato *sm.* secretariate.
segretario *sm.* secretary.
segreteria *sf.* 1. secretariat 2. (*di ministero*) secretariat of State.
segretezza *sf.* secrecy.
segreto *agg.* secret. ♦ **segreto** *sm.* 1. secret: *nel — del cuore*, in the depths of one's heart 2. (*parte interna, intimità*) secrecy.
seguace *sm.* follower, supporter.
seguente *agg.* following, next.
segugio *sm.* bloodhound.
seguire *vt.* e *vi.* 1. to follow 2. (*sorvegliare*) to supervise 3. (*frequentare regolarmente*) to attend.
séguito *sm.* 1. (*corteo*) retinue 2. (*successione, sequela*) series 3. (*continuazione*) continuation || *il — alla prossima puntata*, to be continued 4. (*comm.*): *a — di*, following up.
sei *agg.* six.
seicento *agg.* six hundred. ♦ **seicento** *sm.* the seventeenth century.
selce *sf.* flint.
selciare *vt.* to pave.
selciato *sm.* pavement.
selenio *sm.* selenium.
selenite *agg.* lunar. ♦ **selenite** *sf.* selenite.
selettività *sf.* selectivity.
selettivo *agg.* selective.
selettore *sm.* selector.
selezionare *vt.* to select.
selezione *sf.* selection.
sella *sf.* saddle.
sellaio *sm.* saddler.
sellare *vt.* to saddle.
sellino *sm.* saddle.
selva *sf.* 1. wood 2. (*fig.*) mass.
selvaggina *sf.* game.
selvaggio *agg.* wild, primitive. ♦ **selvaggio** *sm.* savage.
selvàtico *agg.* 1. wild 2. (*non socievole*) unsociable.
selvoso *agg.* woody.
semàforo *sm.* traffic-lights (*pl.*).
semàntica *sf.* semantics.
semàntico *agg.* semantic.
sembianza *sf.* features (*pl.*).
sembrare *vi.* 1. to seem 2. (*somigliare*) to look like.
seme *sm.* 1. seed 2. (*carte da giuoco*) suit.
sementa *sf.* 1. seeds (*pl.*) 2. (*epoca della semina*) seed-time.
semente *sf.* seeds (*pl.*).
semenza *sf.* seeds (*pl.*).

semenzaio *sm.* seed-bed.
semestrale *agg.* six-monthly (*attr.*).
semestralmente *avv.* twice a year.
semestre *sm.* half-year.
semiaperto *agg.* half-open.
semicerchio *sm.* semicircle.
semichiuso *agg.* half-closed.
semicircolare *agg.* semicircular.
semiconduttore *sm.* semiconductor.
semidiàmetro *sm.* semi-diameter.
semidìo *sm.* demigod.
semifinale *sf.* semifinal.
semilavorato *agg.* e *sm.* semi--manufactured.
sémina *sf.* sowing.
seminàbile *agg.* fit to be sown.
seminagione *sf.* sowing.
seminare *vt.* to sow (*v. irr.*).
seminario *sm.* seminary.
seminarista *sm.* seminarist.
seminato *agg.* 1. sown 2. (*fig.* strewn.
seminatore *sm.* sower.
seminfermità *sf.* partial infirmity: *— mentale*, partial insanity.
seminudo *agg.* half-naked.
semiserio *agg.* half-serious.
semisfera *sf.* hemisphere.
semita *s.* Semite.
semìtico *agg.* Semitic.
semitono *sm.* semitone.
semivivo *agg.* half-alive.
sémola *sf.* bran.
semolino *sm.* semolina.
semovente *agg.* self-moving.
sempiterno *agg.* everlasting.
sémplice *agg.* simple.
semplicione *sm.* simpleton.
semplicismo *sm.* superficiality.
semplicìstico *agg.* superficial.
semplicità *sf.* simplicity.
semplificare *vt.* to simplify.
semplificazione *sf.* simplification
sempre *avv.* 1. always: *— avanti!* always onward!; *— meglio, peggio*, better and better, worse and worse; *per —*, for ever; *una volta per —*, once for all 2. (*tuttora*) still: *vivi — qui?*, do you still live here?
sempreverde *sm.* evergreen.
sènape *sf.* mustard.
senato *sm.* senate.
senatore *sm.* senator.
senatoriale *agg.* senatorial.
senescenza *sf.* senescence.
senile *agg.* senile.
senilità *sf.* senility.
senno *sm.* sense, wisdom.

seno *sm.* **1.** breast, bosom **2.** (*grembo*) womb.
sensale *sm.* broker.
sensatezza *sf.* good sense.
sensato *agg.* sensible.
sensazionale *agg.* sensational.
sensazione *sf.* sensation, feeling.
sensìbile *agg.* sensitive.
sensibilità *sf.* sensitiveness.
sensibilizzare *vt.* to sensitize.
sensibilmente *avv.* **1.** sensitively **2.** (*notevolmente*) sensibly.
sensitività *sf.* sensitivity.
sensitivo *agg.* **1.** sensory **2.** (*sensibile*) sensitive.
senso *sm.* **1.** sense **2.** (*sensazione*) sensation **3.** (*direzione*) direction, way **4.** (*modo*) way, manner.
sensorio *agg.* sensorial.
sensuale *agg.* sensual.
sensualità *sf.* sensuality.
sensualmente *avv.* sensually.
sentenza *sf.* **1.** sentence **2.** (*massima*) saying.
sentenziare *vi.* to judge, to hold (*v. irr.*).
sentenziosamente *avv.* sententiously.
sentenzioso *agg.* sententious.
sentiero *sm.* path.
sentimentale *agg.* sentimental.
sentimentalismo *sm.* sentimentalism.
sentimentalità *sf.* sentimentality.
sentimento *sm.* **1.** sentiment **2.** (*disposizione spirituale*) feeling.
sentinella *sf.* sentry.
sentire *vt.* **1.** to feel (*v. irr.*) **2.** (*udire*) to hear (*v. irr.*) **3.** (*gustare*) to taste **4.** (*odorare*) to smell (*v. irr.*) **5.** (*ascoltare*) to listen to. ♦ **sentirsi** *vr.* to feel.
sentitamente *avv.* heartily.
sentito *agg.* **1.** heart-felt **2.** (*udito*) heard || *per — dire*, by hearsay.
sentore *sm.* inkling: *aver — di*, to suspect.
senza *prep.* without: *— scarpe*, barefoot; *— fine*, endless; *— confronto*, unrivalled; *— numero*, countless; *— testa*, thoughtless.
senzatetto *s.* homeless person.
separare *vt.* to separate. ♦ **separarsi** *vr.* to separate.
separatamente *avv.* separately.
separatismo *sm.* separatism.
separatista *s.* separatist.
separativo *agg.* separative.
separato *agg.* separated.

separazione *sf.* separation.
sepolcrale *agg.* sepulchral.
sepolcro *sm.* sepulchre, tomb.
sepolto *agg.* buried.
sepoltura *sf.* burial.
seppellimento *sm.* burial.
seppellire *vt.* to bury.
seppia *sf.* cuttle-fish.
seppure *cong.* even if.
sequela *sf.* series (*invariato al pl.*).
sequenza *sf.* **1.** series **2.** (*cine*) sequence.
sequestràbile *agg.* seizable.
sequestrare *vt.* to seize.
sequestro *sm.* **1.** seizure **2.** (*per debiti*) distress.
sequoia *sf.* sequoia.
sera *sf.* evening.
seràfico *agg.* seraphic.
serafino *sm.* seraph.
serale *agg.* evening (*attr.*).
serata *sf.* **1.** evening **2.** (*ricevimento serale*) party.
serbare *vt.* **1.** (*mettere in serbo*) to put (*v. irr.*) aside **2.** (*conservare*) to keep (*v. irr.*) || *— odio, rancore*, to nourish hatred, rancour. ♦ **serbarsi** *vr.* to keep, to remain.
serbatoio *sm.* reservoir, tank.
serbo (*nella loc.*) *tenere in —*, to keep (*v. irr.*) aside.
serenamente *avv.* serenely.
serenata *sf.* serenade.
serenìssimo *agg.* Serene Highness.
serenità *sf.* serenity.
sereno *agg.* serene, clear || *giudizio —*, objective judgement.
sergente *sm.* sergeant.
sèrico *agg.* silk (*attr.*), silky.
sericoltore *sm.* silkgrower.
sericoltura *sf.* sericulture.
serie *sf.* **1.** series (*invariato al pl.*): *in —*, mass-produced **2.** (*assieme*) set **3.** (*fila*) row.
serietà *sf.* seriousness.
serio *agg.* serious, earnest.
sermone *sm.* **1.** sermon **2.** (*rimprovero*) lecture.
seròtino *agg.* evening (*attr.*).
serpe *sf.* snake.
serpeggiante *agg.* winding.
serpeggiare *vi.* to wind (*v. irr.*).
serpente *sm.* snake, serpent.
serpentina *sf.* **1.** coil **2.** (*di strada*) winding road.
serpentino *agg.* snakelike. ♦ **serpentino** *sm.* serpentine.
serra *sf.* greenhouse.

serraglio *sm.* **1.** menagerie **2.** (*del sultano*) seraglio.

serramànico (*nella loc. avv.*) coltello a —, flick-knife.

serramento *sm.* lock.

serrare *vt.* **1.** to shut (*v. irr.*), to close **2.** (*a chiave*) to lock **3.** (*stringere*) to tighten **4.** (*concludere*) to conclude.

serrata *sf.* (*econ.*) lockout.

serratura *sf.* lock: *buco della* —, keyhole.

serva *sf.* maid-servant.

servìbile *agg.* usable.

servigio *sm.* service, favour.

servile *agg.* servile.

servilismo *sm.* servility.

servire *vt.* **1.** to serve **2.** (*di persona di servizio*) to wait on **3.** (*le carte*) to deal (*v. irr.*). ♦ **servire** *vi.* (*occorrere*) to need: *vi serve qualcosa?*, can I help you? ♦ **servirsi** *vr.* **1.** to use **2.** (*a tavola*) to help oneself (to).

servitore *sm.* servant.

servitù *sf.* **1.** servitude, slavery **2.** (*personale di servizio*) servants (*pl.*).

serviziévole *agg.* obliging.

servizio *sm.* **1.** service **2.** (*lavoro*) work: *fuori* —, off duty **3.** (*favore*) favour.

servo *sm.* **1.** servant **2.** (*schiavo*) slave.

servofreno *sm.* brake booster.

sèsamo *sm.* sesame.

sessanta *agg.* sixty.

sessantenne *agg.* **1.** (*attr.*) sixty--year-old **2.** (*pred.*) sixty years old. ♦ **sessantenne** *s.* sixty-year-old person.

sessantèsimo *agg.* sixtieth.

sessantina *sf.* about sixty: *un uomo sulla* —, a man in his sixties.

sessione *sf.* session.

sesso *sm.* sex.

sessuale *agg.* sexual.

sessualità *sf.* sexuality.

sestante *sm.* sextant.

sesterzio *sm.* sesterce.

sestetto *sm.* sextet.

sesto¹ *agg.* sixth.

sesto² *sm.* **1.** order **2.** (*arch.*) curve.

sèstuplo *agg. e sm.* sextuple.

seta *sf.* silk.

setacciare *vt.* to sieve.

setaccio *sm.* sieve.

sete *sf.* thirst: *avere* —, to be thirsty.

seterìa *sf.* **1.** silk factory **2.** (*negozio di seta*) silk shop.

setificio *sm.* silk factory.

sétola *sf.* **1.** bristle **2.** (*crine*) hair.

setta *sf.* sect.

settanta *agg.* seventy.

settantenne *agg.* **1.** (*attr.*) seventy--year-old **2.** (*pred.*) seventy years old. ♦ **settantenne** *s.* seventy--year-old person.

settantèsimo *agg.* seventieth.

settario *agg.* sectarian.

settarismo *sm.* sectarianism.

sette *agg.* seven.

settecentesco *agg.* of eighteenth century.

settecento *agg.* seven hundred. ♦ **settecento** *sm.* the eighteenth century.

settembre *sm.* September.

settentrionale *agg.* northern.

settentrione *sm.* north.

setticemìa *sf.* septicaemia.

sèttico *agg.* septic.

settimana *sf.* week.

settimanale *agg.* weekly. ♦ **settimanale** *sm.* weekly magazine.

settimino *sm.* seven months' child.

setto *sm.* septum (*pl.* -ta).

settore *sm.* **1.** (*geom.*) sector **2.** (*campo*) field.

settoriale *agg.* sectorial.

severità *sf.* severity.

severo *agg.* severe, strict.

sevizia *sf.* torture.

seviziare *vt.* to torture.

sezionamento *sm.* dissection.

sezionare *vt.* (*anat.*) to dissect.

sezione *sf.* **1.** section **2.** (*reparto*) department **3.** (*di scuola*) side.

sfaccendato *agg.* idle. ♦ **sfaccendato** *sm.* idler.

sfaccettare *vt.* to facet.

sfacchinare *vi.* to drudge.

sfacciatàggine *sf.* impudence.

sfacciato *agg.* **1.** impudent, cheeky **2.** (*di colori*) gaudy.

sfacelo *sm.* break-up.

sfaldamento *sm.* flaking.

sfaldarsi *vr.* to flake away.

sfamare *vt.* to appease so.'s hunger.

sfarfallare *vi.* to flutter about.

sfarzo *sm.* pomp.

sfarzoso *agg.* sumptuous.

sfasamento *sm.* **1.** (*mecc.; elettr.*) phase-displacement, phase-difference **2.** (*fig.*) inconsequence.

sfasato *agg.* **1.** out of phase **2.** (*fig.*) inconsequent.

sfasciare[1] *vt.* (*togliere le fasce*) to unbandage.

sfasciare[2] *vt.* to smash. ◆ **sfasciarsi** *vr.* to collapse.

sfasciato *agg.* (*rotto*) in pieces.

sfatare *vt.* to discredit.

sfaticato *agg.* lazy. ◆ **sfaticato** *sm.* lazy-bones.

sfatto *agg.* undone.

sfavillante *agg.* shining.

sfavillare *vi.* to shine (*v. irr.*), to sparkle.

sfavore *sm.* disfavour, discredit.

sfavorévole *agg.* unfavourable.

sfebbrato *agg.* without a temperature.

sfegatarsi *vr.* to wear (*v. irr.*) oneself out.

sfegatato *agg.* fanatic.

sfenòide *sm.* sphenoid.

sfera *sf.* 1. sphere 2. (*lancetta*) hand 3. (*mecc.*) ball.

sfericità *sf.* sphericity.

sfèrico *agg.* spherical.

sferragliare *vi.* to clang.

sferrare *vt.* 1. (*un attacco*) to launch 2. (*un colpo*) to land a blow. ◆ **sferrarsi** *vr.* to hurl oneself (at).

sferruzzare *vi.* to knit (*v. irr.*).

sferza *sf.* whip, lash (*anche fig.*).

sferzare *vt.* 1. to whip, to lash 2. (*fig.*) to reprimand.

sferzata *sf.* 1. lash 2. (*fig.*) sharp rebuke.

sfiancare *vt.* to wear (*v. irr.*) out.

sfiatare *vi.* to leak. ◆ **sfiatarsi** *vr.* to talk oneself hoarse.

sfiatato *agg.* out of breath.

sfiatatoio *sm.* vent.

sfibbiare *vt.* to unbuckle.

sfibramento *sm.* enfeeblement.

sfibrante *agg.* exhausting.

sfibrare *vt.* to weaken, to wear (*v. irr.*) out.

sfibratura *sf.* breaking.

sfida *sf.* challenge: *in tono di* —, defiantly.

sfidante *sm.* challenger.

sfidare *vt.* 1. to challenge 2. (*affrontare*) to face, to dare: — *la morte*, to face death.

sfiducia *sf.* mistrust: *avere* —, to mistrust.

sfiduciare *vt.* to discourage. ◆ **sfiduciarsi** *vr.* to become (*v. irr.*) discouraged.

sfiduciato *agg.* discouraged.

sfigurare *vt.* to spoil (*v. irr.*). ◆

sfigurare *vi.* to cut (*v. irr.*) a poor figure.

sfigurato *agg.* disfigured.

sfilacciare *vt.* to fray.

sfilacciato *agg.* frayed.

sfilare[1] *vt.* to unthread, to unstring (*v. irr.*).

sfilare[2] *vi.* to parade.

sfilata *sf.* 1. march, parade 2. (*fila*) line, string.

sfinge *sf.* sphinx.

sfinimento *sm.* exhaustion.

sfinire *vt.* to exhaust.

sfinitezza *sf.* extreme weakness.

sfinito *agg.* worn out.

sfintere *sm.* sphincter.

sfiorare *vt.* to graze, to touch on.

sfiorire *vi.* to wither, to fade.

sfiorito *agg.* faded, withered (*anche fig.*).

sfittare *vt.* to vacate.

sfitto *agg.* vacant.

sfocato *agg.* out of focus.

sfociare *vi.* to flow.

sfoderare *vt.* 1. to unline 2. (*sguainare*) to unsheathe 3. (*ostentare*) to display.

sfoderato *agg.* 1. unlined 2. (*sguainato*) unsheathed.

sfogare *vt.* to give (*v. irr.*) vent to. ◆ **sfogarsi** *vr.* to relieve one's feelings.

sfoggiare *vi.* to show (*v. irr.*) off.

sfoggio *sm.* show, ostentation.

sfoglia *sf.* 1. (*lamina*) foil 2. (*cuc.*) pastry.

sfogliare[1] *vt.* to pluck the petals off.

sfogliare[2] *vt.* 1. (*voltare le pagine*) to turn over the pages 2. (*dare un'occhiata*) to glance through.

sfogliata *sf.* 1. (*cuc.*) puff-pastry 2. (*di libro*) thumbing.

sfogo *sm.* vent, outlet.

sfolgoramento *sm.* blazing.

sfolgorante *agg.* flaming.

sfolgorare *vi.* to blaze.

sfolgorìo *sm.* blaze.

sfollagente *sm.* truncheon.

sfollamento *sm.* 1. dispersal 2. (*mil.*) evacuation.

sfollare *vt.* e *vi.* to disperse 2. (*mil.*) to evacuate.

sfollato *agg.* 1. evacuated. ◆ **sfollato** *sm.* evacuee.

sfoltire *vt.* to thin.

sfondamento *sm.* breaking.

sfondare *vt.* 1. (*rompere il fondo*) to break (*v. irr.*) the bottom 2.

(mil.) to break through. ♦ sfondare vi. to have success.
sfondato agg. 1. without a bottom
|| scarpe sfondate, worn-out shoes
2. (insaziabile) voracious.
sfondo sm. background.
sforbiciare vt. to cut (v. irr.) with
scissors.
sformare vt. 1. to pull out of
shape 2. (togliere dalla forma) to
remove from the mould. ♦ sfor-
marsi vr. to get (v. irr.) out of
shape.
sformato agg. shapeless.
sfornare vt. 1. to take (v. irr.) out
of the oven 2. (produrre) to bring
(v. irr.) out.
sfornito agg. destitute, lacking (in).
sfortuna sf. bad luck.
sfortunato agg. unlucky.
sforzare vt. to strain, to force. ♦
sforzarsi vr. to try hard.
sforzatamente avv. 1. with much
effort 2. (in modo forzato) for-
cedly.
sforzato agg. 1. forced 2. (fig.)
false.
sforzatura sf. (cosa sforzata) far-
-fetched thing.
sforzo sm. 1. effort 2. (mecc.) stress.
sfòttere vt. to pull so.'s legs.
sfracellare vt. to smash. ♦ sfra-
cellarsi vr. to smash.
sfrangiare vt. to undo (v. irr.), to
form a fringe. ♦ sfrangiarsi vr.
to fray.
sfrangiatura sf. fraying.
sfrattare vt. to evict.
sfratto sm. eviction.
sfrecciare vi. to dart.
sfregamento sm. rubbing.
sfregare vt. to rub.
sfregiare vt. to disfigure.
sfregiato agg. disfigured.
sfregio sm. slash, scar.
sfrenare vt. to unbridle.
sfrenatezza sf. unrestraint.
sfrenato agg. wild, unbridled.
sfrigolare vi. to sizzle.
sfrigolìo sm. sizzle.
sfringuellare vi. to twitter.
sfrondare vt. 1. to strip off leaves
2. (fig.) to curtail.
sfrontatezza sf. effrontery.
sfrontato agg. brazen, impudent. ♦
sfrontato sm. impudent fellow.
sfrusciare vi. to rustle.
sfruscìo sm. rustling.
sfruttamento sm. exploitation.

sfruttare vt. to exploit.
sfruttatore sm. profiteer.
sfuggente agg. receding: sguardo
—, elusive look.
sfuggévole agg. transitory.
sfuggire vi. to escape, to slip. ♦
sfuggire vt. to avoid.
sfuggita sf. di —, quickly: vedere
qu. di —, to have a glimpse of so.
sfumare vt. to shade. ♦ sfumare
vi. 1. to evaporate 2. (fig.) to
come (v. irr.) to nothing.
sfumatamente avv. softly.
sfumato agg. 1. vanished 2. (di colori) soft.
sfumatura sf. 1. (lo sfumare)
shading 2. (gradazione) shade.
sfuriata sf. outburst.
sgabello sm. stool.
sgabuzzino sm. closet.
sgambettare vi. to kick (one's
legs) about.
sgambetto sm. trip: fare lo —, to
trip (so.); (fig.) to supplant.
sganasciamento sm. dislocation
(of so.'s jaw).
sganasciarsi vr. — dalle risa, to
laugh oneself silly.
sganascione sm. slap.
sganciare vt. 1. to unhook 2. (ferr.)
to uncouple 3. (di bombe) to release. ♦ sganciarsi vr. (liberarsi di qu.) to get (v. irr.) away (so.).
sgangherare vt. to unhinge.
sgangherato agg. 1. unhinged 2.
(sguaiato) wild.
sgarbatamente avv. impolitely.
sgarbato agg. rude, impolite.
sgarberia sf. rudeness.
sgarbo sm. offence.
sgargiante agg. gaudy.
sgarrare vi. 1. to be wrong 2. (di
orologio) (se è avanti) to gain; (se
è indietro) to lose (v. irr.).
sgattaiolare vi. to slip away.
sgelare vi. to thaw. ♦ sgelarsi vr.
to thaw.
sgelo sm. thawing.
sghembo agg. oblique: di —, obliquely.
sgherro sm. hired assassin.
sghignazzare vi. to guffaw.
sghignazzata sf. guffaw.
sghimbescio (nella loc. avv.) di
—, awry.
sghiribizzo sm. whim.
sgobbare vi. to work hard.
sgobbone sm. 1. hard worker 2.
(studentesco) swot.

sgocciolare *vi.* to drip.
sgocciolio *sm.* dripping.
sgolarsi *vr.* to shout oneself hoarse.
sgombrare *vt.* to clear.
sgombro *agg.* **1.** clear (of) **2.** (*fig.*) free (from).
sgomentare *vt.* to dismay.
sgomento *agg.* dismayed. ◆ **sgomento** *sm.* dismay.
sgominare *vt.* to rout.
sgonfiamento *sm.* deflation.
sgonfiare *vt.* to deflate.
sgonfio *agg.* deflated.
sgorbia *sf.* gouge.
sgorbiare *vt.* to scrawl.
sgorbio *sm.* **1.** scrawl **2.** (*pittura mal fatta*) daub **3.** (*fig.*) deformed man (*pl.* men).
sgorgare *vi.* to gush, to flow.
sgozzare *vt.* to cut (*v. irr.*) so.'s throat.
sgradévole *agg.* unpleasant.
sgradito *agg.* **1.** disagreeable **2.** (*mal accetto*) unwelcome.
sgrammaticato *agg.* ungrammatical.
sgranare *vt.* **1.** to shell: — *gli occhi*, to open one's eyes wide **2.** (*mangiare*) to devour.
sgranatrice *sf.* husker.
sgranchire *vt.* to stretch.
sgranocchiare *vt.* to munch.
sgrassare *vt.* to take (*v. irr.*) the grease off: — *il brodo,* to skim the grease from the broth.
sgravare *vt.* **1.** to lighten **2.** (*fig.*) to relieve.
sgravio *sm.* **1.** lightening **2.** (*fig.*) relief.
sgraziato *agg.* awkward.
sgretolamento *sm.* pounding.
sgretolare *vt.* to pound. ◆ **sgretolarsi** *vr.* to crumble.
sgridare *vt.* to scold.
sgroppare[1] *vt.* (*sciogliere*) to untie.
sgroppare[2] *vi.* (*di cavallo*) to buck.
sgroppata *sf.* bucking.
sgrossamento *sm.* rough-shaping.
sgrossare *vt.* **1.** to rough **2.** (*dirozzare*) to refine.
sgrovigliare *vt.* to unravel.
sguaiato *agg.* **1.** unbecoming **2.** (*volgare*) coarse.
sguainare *vt.* to unsheathe.
sgualcire *vt.* to crease.
sgualdrina *sf.* harlot, whore.
sguardo *sm.* look, glance: *dare uno* —, to have a look.

sguarnire *vt.* **1.** to untrim **2.** (*mil.*) to dismantle.
sguàttero *sm.* scullery-boy.
sguazzare *vi.* to wallow.
sguinzagliare *vt.* to unleash.
sgusciare *vt.* to shell. ◆ **sgusciare** *vi.* to slip away.
si[1] *pron.* **1.** (*riflessivo*) oneself, himself, herself, itself, themselves **2.** (*rec.*) (*fra due*) each other; (*fra molti*) one another **3.** (*pron. indef.*) one, people, we, they: — *dice,* people say.
si[2] *sm.* (*mus.*) si, B.
sì *avv.* yes: *penso di* —, I think so; — *certo,* certainly; *e* — *che,* yet; *uno* —, *uno no,* every other one; *forse che* —, *forse che no,* maybe yes, maybe no.
sia *cong.* **1.** (*o l'uno o l'altro*) whether... or, either... or **2.** (*entrambi*) both... and.
siamese *agg. e s.* Siamese.
sibarita *s.* sybarite.
siberiano *agg.* Siberian.
sibilante *agg.* **1.** hissing **2.** (*fonetica*) sibilant.
sibilare *vi.* to whistle, to hiss.
sibilla *sf.* sibyl.
sibillino *agg.* sibylline.
sìbilo *sm.* hiss, whistle.
sicario *sm.* cut-throat.
sicché *cong.* **1.** so... that **2.** (*dunque*) therefore.
siccità *sf.* drought.
siccome *cong.* as, since.
siciliano *agg. e sm.* Sicilian.
sicomoro *sm.* sycamore.
sicumera *sf.* presumption.
sicura *sf.* safety belt.
sicurezza *sf.* **1.** (*certezza*) certainty **2.** (*immunità da pericoli*) safety || *dispositivo di* —, safety device; *misura di* —, precautionary measure; *uscita di* —, emergency door; *rasoio, spilla di* —, safety-razor, pin.
sicuro *agg.* **1.** (*certo*) sure: — *di sé,* self-confident **2.** (*immune da pericoli*) safe **3.** (*che non sbaglia*) unfailing **4.** (*calmo, saldo*) calm, steady **5.** (*esperto*) skilful.
siderale *agg.* sidereal.
siderurgìa *sf.* metallurgy of iron.
siderùrgico *agg.* iron (*attr.*): *stabilimento* —, iron-works (*pl.*). ◆ **siderùrgico** *sm.* iron worker.
sidro *sm.* cider.
siepe *sf.* hedge.

siero *sm.* serum.
sieroso *agg.* serous.
sieroterapìa *sf.* serotherapy.
siesta *sf.* nap.
siffatto *agg.* such.
sifilide *sf.* syphilis.
sifone *sm.* siphon.
sigaraia *sf.* cigar-seller.
sigaretta *sf.* cigarette.
sìgaro *sm.* cigar.
sigillare *vt.* to seal.
sigillatura *sf.* sealing.
sigillo *sm.* seal.
sigla *sf.* monogram.
siglare *vt.* to initial.
significare *vt.* 1. to mean (*v. irr.*) 2. (*comunicare*) to signify 3. (*simboleggiare*) to represent.
significativo *agg.* meaningful.
significato *sm.* 1. meaning 2. (*valore*) import.
signora *sf.* 1. lady, woman (*pl.* women) 2. (*seguito da cognome*) Mrs: *la — Smith*, Mrs. Smith 3. (*vocativo*) Madam: *buon giorno —*, good morning Madam 4. (*padrona*) mistress 5. (*donna ricca*) rich lady 6. (*moglie*) wife (*pl.* wives).
signore *sm.* 1. gentleman, man (*pl.* -men) 2. (*seguito da cognome*) *il — Smith*, Mr. Smith 3. (*padrone*) master 4. (*vocativo*) Sir: *sì —!* yes, Sir! 5. (*uomo ricco*) lord 6. (*Dio*) God, Lord.
signoreggiare *vt.* to rule.
signorìa *sf.* 1. (*di uomo*) Lordship; (*di donna*) Ladyship 2. (*dominio*) dominion.
signorile *agg.* 1. (*riferito a uomo*) gentlemanlike; (*riferito a donna*) ladylike 2. (*elegante*) luxury.
signorilità *sf.* distinction, high class.
signorina *sf.* 1. young lady 2. (*seguito da cognome*) Miss: *la — Smith*, Miss Smith 3. (*vocativo*) Madam: *Buon giorno —*, good morning Madam 4. (*padroncina*) young mistress 5. (*donna non sposata*) unmarried woman.
signorotto *sm.* squire.
silenziatore *sm.* silencer.
silenzio *sm.* silence.
silenzioso *agg.* silent || *una strada silenziosa*, a noiseless street.
sìlfide *sf.* sylph.
silfo *sm.* sylph.
sìlice *sf.* silica.

silicio *sm.* silicon.
silicone *sm.* silicone.
silicosi *sf.* silicosis.
sìllaba *sf.* syllable.
sillabare *vt.* to syllabize.
sìllabo *sm.* summary.
sillogismo *sm.* syllogism.
sillogìstico *agg.* syllogistic.
silo *sm.* silo (*pl.* silos).
siluramento *sm.* 1. torpedoing 2. (*fig.*) firing.
silurante *sf.* torpedo-boat.
silurare *vt.* 1. to torpedo 2. (*fig.*) to dismiss.
siluriano *agg. e sm.* Silurian.
siluro *sm.* (*mil.; zool.*) torpedo.
silvestre *agg.* sylvan.
silvicoltore *sm.* forester.
silvicoltura *sf.* forestry.
simbiosi *sf.* symbiosis.
simboleggiare *vt.* to symbolize.
simbòlico *agg.* 1. symbolic 2. (*nominale*) nominal.
simbolismo *sm.* symbolism.
simbolista *agg. e sm.* symbolist.
sìmbolo *sm.* symbol.
similare *agg.* similar.
sìmile *agg.* 1. like, similar 2. (*pred.*) alike 3. (*tale*) such. ♦ **sìmile** *sm.* fellow-creature.
similitùdine *sf.* 1. likeness 2. (*lett.*) simile.
simmetrìa *sf.* symmetry.
simmètrico *agg.* symmetric(al).
simonìa *sf.* simony.
simonìaco *agg. e sm.* simoniac.
simpatìa *sf.* liking.
simpàtico *agg.* nice, pleasant.
simpatizzante *agg.* sympathizing. ♦ **simpatizzante** *s.* sympathizer.
simpatizzare *vi.* 1. to sympathize 2. (*rec.*) to take (*v. irr.*) a liking to each other.
simposio *sm.* symposium (*pl.* -ia).
simulacro *sm.* 1. simulacre 2. (*finzione*) sham.
simulare *vt.* to feign.
simulato *agg.* simulated.
simulatore *sm.* simulator.
simulazione *sf.* simulation.
simultaneità *sf.* simultaneity.
simultàneo *agg.* simultaneous (with).
sinagoga *sf.* synagogue.
sincerarsi *vr.* to make (*v. irr.*) sure.
sincerità *sf.* sincerity.
sincero *agg.* sincere, true.
sincopare *vt.* to syncopate.

sincopato *agg.* syncopated.
sìncope *sf.* **1.** (*med.*) syncope **2.** (*mus.; gramm.*) syncopation.
sincronismo *sm.* synchronism.
sincronizzare *vt.* to synchronize.
sincronizzazione *sf.* synchronization.
sindacale *agg.* trade-union (*attr.*).
sindacalismo *sm.* trade-unionism.
sindacalista *s.* trade-unionist.
sindacare *vt.* **1.** to control **2.** (*criticare*) to criticize.
sindacato *sm.* trade-union.
sìndaco *sm.* **1.** mayor **2.** (*di società*) auditor.
sìndrome *sf.* syndrome.
sinecura *sf.* sinecure.
sinfonìa *sf.* symphony.
sinfònico *agg.* symphonic.
singhiozzare *vi.* to sob.
singhiozzo *sm.* **1.** hiccup **2.** (*di pianto*) sob.
singolare *agg.* **1.** singular **2.** (*singolo*) single.
singolarità *sf.* singularity.
singolarmente *avv.* **1.** (*ad uno ad uno*) singly **2.** (*segnatamente*) particularly.
sìngolo *agg.* single, individual.
singulto *sm.* **1.** hiccup **2.** (*di pianto*) sob.
sinistra *sf.* **1.** left: *alla mia* —, on my left **2.** (*mano*) left hand **3.** (*parte*) left-hand side || *uomo di* — (*pol.*), left-winger.
sinistramente *avv.* sinisterly.
sinistrato *agg.* **1.** (*di edificio*) bomb-damaged **2.** (*di persona*) injured. ♦ **sinistrato** *sm.* (*damage*) sufferer.
sinistro *agg.* **1.** left **2.** (*truce*) sinister, grim. ♦ **sinistro** *sm.* **1.** accident, mishap **2.** (*boxe*) left.
sinòlogo *sm.* Sinologist.
sinonimìa *sf.* synonymy.
sinònimo *agg.* synonymous. ♦ **sinònimo** *sm.* synonym.
sinora *avv.* till now, so far.
sinovite *sf.* synovitis.
sintassi *sf.* syntax.
sintàttico *agg.* syntactic(al).
sìntesi *sf.* synthesis (*pl.* -ses).
sintètico *agg.* synthetic.
sintetizzare *vt.* to synthetize.
sintomàtico *agg.* symptomatic.
sìntomo *sm.* symptom.
sintonìa *sf.* syntony.
sintonizzare *vt.* to tune in.
sinuosità *sf.* winding.

sinuoso *agg.* winding.
sinusite *sf.* sinusitis.
sionismo *sm.* Zionism.
sionista *s.* Zionist.
sipario *sm.* curtain.
sirena *sf.* **1.** (*mit.*) siren, mermaid **2.** (*acustica*) hooter.
siringa *sf.* syringe.
siringare *vt.* to syringe.
sìsmico *agg.* seismic.
sismògrafo *sm.* seismograph.
sismologìa *sf.* seismology.
sismòlogo *sm.* seismologist.
sistema *sm.* system: — *di vita*, way of life.
sistemare *vt.* **1.** (*mettere in ordine*) to arrange **2.** (*definire*) to settle.
sistemàtico *agg.* systematic(al).
sistemazione *sf.* **1.** (*ordine*) arrangement **2.** (*collocazione di macchinari*) layout **3.** (*il sistemarsi*) settling **4.** (*lavoro*) job.
sito *sm.* place.
situare *vt.* to place.
situazione *sf.* situation.
slabbrare *vt.* to chip the rim of.
slabbratura *sf.* chipping.
slacciare *vt.* **1.** to untie **2.** (*sbottonare*) to unbutton.
slanciarsi *vr.* to rush.
slanciato *agg.* slim.
slancio *sm.* **1.** rush **2.** (*energia*) energy.
slargare *vt.* to widen.
slattamento *sm.* weaning.
slattare *vt.* to wean.
slavato *agg.* pale.
slavina *sf.* landslide; (*di neve*) snowslide.
slavo *agg. e sm.* Slav.
sleale *agg.* unfair.
slealtà *sf.* disloyalty.
slegare *vt.* to untie.
slegato *agg.* **1.** untied **2.** (*di discorso ecc.*) disconnected.
slitta *sf.* sleigh.
slittamento *sm.* skidding.
slittare *vi.* **1.** to slide (*v. irr.*) **2.** (*di ruote*) to skid.
slogamento *sm.* dislocation.
slogare *vt.* to dislocate.
slogatura *sf.* dislocation.
sloggiare *vi.* to clear out. ♦ **sloggiare** *vt.* to drive (*v. irr.*) out.
smaccato *agg.* sickly-sweet.
smacchiare *vt.* to clean.
smacchiatore *sm.* stain-remover.
smacchiatura *sf.* cleaning.
smacco *sm.* mortification.

smagliante agg. dazzling.
smagliare vt. to unravel. ♦ **smagliarsi** vr. (di calze) to ladder.
smagliato agg. unravelled.
smagliatura sf. 1. (di calze) ladder.
smagnetizzare vt. to demagnetize.
smagnetizzazione sf. demagnetization.
smagrire vt. e vi. to thin.
smagrito agg. thin, grown thin.
smaliziare vt. to smarten up. ♦ **smaliziarsi** vr. to wisen.
smaliziato agg. cunning.
smaltare vt. to enamel: — le unghie, to paint one's nails.
smaltato agg. 1. enamelled 2. (di unghie) painted.
smaltire vt. to digest: — la sbornia, to get (v. irr.) over one's drunkenness.
smalto sm. enamel: — per unghie, nail-polish.
smanceria sf. mawkishness.
smangiare vt. to corrode.
smania sf. 1. great desire 2. (agitazione) frenzy.
smaniare vi. 1. to yearn (for) 2. (essere agitati) to be restless.
smanioso agg. 1. eager 2. (agitato) restless.
smantellamento sm. dismantling.
smantellare vt. to dismantle.
smarcare vt. to unmark.
smargiassata sf. swagger.
smargiasseria sf. bragging.
smargiasso sm. braggart.
smarginare vt. to trim the edge.
smarrimento sm. 1. loss 2. (turbamento) bewilderment.
smarrire vt. to lose (v. irr.). ♦ **smarrirsi** vr. 1. to lose one's way 2. (di lettera, pacco) to miscarry 3. (turbarsi) to be bewildered.
smascellarsi vr. to dislocate one's jaws.
smascherare vt. to unmask.
smembramento sm. dismemberment.
smembrare vt. to dismember.
smemorataggine sf. 1. lack of memory 2. (dimenticanza) lapse of memory.
smemorato agg. absent-minded.
smentire vt. to deny. ♦ **smentirsi** vr. 1. to contradict oneself 2. (venir meno) to be untrue to oneself.
smentita sf. denial.
smeraldo sm. emerald.

smerciare vt. to sell (v. irr.) off.
smercio sm. sale.
smerigliare vt. 1. to polish with emery 2. (di vetri) to frost glass.
smerigliato agg. emery: carta smerigliata, emery paper; vetro —, frosted glass.
smeriglio sm. emery.
smerlo sm. scallop.
smesso agg. cast off.
smettere vt. to stop, to leave (v. irr.) off: — un vestito, to cast (v. irr.) off a dress.
smezzare vt. to halve.
smidollato agg. (di persona) spineless.
smilitarizzare vt. to demilitarize.
smilitarizzazione sf. demilitarization.
smilzo agg. thin.
sminuire vt. to diminish. ♦ **sminuirsi** vr. to belittle oneself.
sminuzzare vt. 1. (tritare) to mince 2. (tagliuzzare) to chop up 3. (sbriciolare) to crumble.
smistamento sm. 1. clearing 2. (ferr.) shunting 3. (di corrispondenza) sorting.
smistare vt. 1. (di corrispondenza) to sort out 2. (ferr.) to shunt.
smisuratamente avv. beyond measure.
smisurato agg. enormous, huge.
smobilitare vt. to demobilize.
smobilitazione sf. demobilization.
smoccolare vt. to snuff.
smoccolatoio sm. snuffers (pl.).
smoccolatura sf. snuffing.
smodato agg. immoderate.
smoderatezza sf. immoderateness.
smoderato agg. immoderate.
smontabile agg. demountable.
smontaggio sm. disassembling.
smontare vt. 1. (far scendere) (da cavallo) to unhorse; (da un'automobile) to drop 2. (scomporre in parti) to take (v. irr.) to pieces 3. (mecc.) to disassemble 4. (fig.) to dishearten, to cool. ♦ **smontare** vi. 1. (da un treno, tram ecc.) to get (v. irr.) off 2. (da un'automobile) to get (v. irr.) out 3. (da cavallo) to dismount 4. (dal lavoro) to go (v. irr.) off duty 5. (sbiadire) to fade.
smorfia sf. grimace.
smorfioso agg. affected.
smorto agg. pale.
smorzamento sm. 1. (di luci) shad-

ing **2.** (*di colori*) toning down **3.** (*di suoni*) lowering **4.** (*di sete; fig.*) quenching.

smorzare *vt.* **1.** (*di luci*) to shade **2.** (*di colori*) to tone down **3.** (*di suoni*) to lower **4.** (*di sete; fig.*) to quench **5.** (*spegnere*) to put (*v. irr.*) down.

smottamento *sm.* landslip.

smottare *vi.* to slip.

smozzicare *vt.* **1.** to hack to pieces **2.** (*di parole*) to clip.

smunto *agg.* pale.

smuòvere *vt.* **1.** to shift **2.** (*fig.*) to move.

smussare *vt.* **1.** to round off **2.** (*fig.*) to soften.

smussato *agg.* **1.** blunted **2.** (*fig.*) softened.

snaturare *vt.* to pervert.

snaturato *agg.* unnatural.

snazionalizzare *vt.* to denationalize.

snebbiare *vt.* **1.** to dispel the fog **2.** (*fig.*) to clear.

snellezza *sf.* slenderness.

snellire *vt.* **1.** to make (*v. irr.*) slender **2.** (*fig.*) to simplify. ◆ **snellirsi** *vr.* to grow (*v. irr.*) slender.

snello *agg.* slender.

snervante *agg.* enervating.

snervare *vt.* to enervate.

snidare *vt.* **1.** to flush **2.** (*fig.*) to dislodge.

snobbare *vt.* to snob.

snobismo *sm.* snobbery.

snocciolare *vt.* **1.** to stone **2.** (*fig.*) to tell (*v. irr.*).

snodare *vt.* **1.** to untie **2.** (*rendere agile*) to make (*v. irr.*) supple. ◆ **snodarsi** *vr.* (*di strade*) to wind (*v. irr.*).

snodato *agg.* **1.** supple **2.** (*di cosa*) jointed.

snodo *sm.* joint.

soave *agg.* sweet.

soavità *sf.* sweetness.

sobbalzare *vi.* **1.** to jerk **2.** (*trasalire*) to start.

sobbalzo *sm.* **1.** jerk **2.** (*sussulto*) start.

sobbarcarsi *vr.* to take (*v. irr.*) upon oneself.

sobborgo *sm.* suburb.

sobillare *vt.* to stir up.

sobillatore *sm.* instigator.

sobrietà *sf.* sobriety.

sobrio *agg.* sober.

socchiùdere *vt.* **1.** to half-close **2.** (*aprire un po'*) to half-open.

socchiuso *agg.* half-closed, half-open.

sòccida *sf.* agistment.

soccòmbere *vi.* to succumb.

soccòrrere *vt.* to help, to assist.

soccorritore *agg.* helpful. ◆ **soccorritore** *sm.* helper.

soccorso *sm.* help || *pronto* —, first aid.

socialdemocràtico *agg.* socialdemocratic.

socialdemocrazìa *sf.* socialdemocracy.

sociale *agg.* social.

socialismo *sm.* Socialism.

socialista *agg. e sm.* Socialist.

socialità *sf.* sociality.

socializzare *vt.* to socialize.

socializzazione *sf.* socialization.

società *sf.* **1.** society **2.** (*comm.*) company: — *anonima*, joint-stock company; — *a responsabilità limitata*, limited company || *entrare in* —, to enter into partnership.

sociévole *agg.* sociable.

socievolezza *sf.* sociability.

socio *sm.* **1.** member **2.** (*comm.*) partner.

sociologìa *sf.* sociology.

sociològico *agg.* sociological.

sociòlogo *sm.* sociologist.

socràtico *agg.* Socratic.

soda *sf.* soda.

sodalizio *sm.* **1.** society **2.** (*confraternita*) brotherhood.

sodare *vt.* to consolidate.

sodatura *sf.* (*tessile*) fulling.

soddisfacente *agg.* satisfactory.

soddisfare *vt.* **1.** to satisfy **2.** (*adempiere*) to fulfil **3.** (*far fronte a*) to discharge **4.** (*riparare*) to make (*v. irr.*) amends.

soddisfazione *sf.* satisfaction.

sodio *sm.* sodium.

sodo *agg.* solid, firm: *uovo* —, hard-boiled egg; *darle sode a qu.*, to strike (*v. irr.*) so. hard.

sofferente *agg.* **1.** suffering **2.** (*malaticcio*) poorly.

sofferenza *sf.* pain.

soffermare *vt.* to stop. ◆ **soffermarsi** *vr.* to stop.

soffiare *vt. e vi.* to blow (*v. irr.*): *soffiarsi il naso*, to blow one's nose.

soffiata *sf.* puff.

soffiato *agg.* puffed.

soffiatore *sm.* blower.
soffiatura *sf.* blowing.
sòffice *agg.* soft.
soffietto *sm.* 1. bellows (*pl.*) 2. (*edit.*) blurb.
soffio *sm.* puff, whiff.
soffione *sm.* 1. blow-pipe 2. (*geol.*) fumarole.
soffitta *sf.* garret.
soffitto *sm.* ceiling.
soffocamento *sm.* choking.
soffocante *agg.* choking: *caldo* —, sultry heat.
soffocare *vt.* 1. to choke 2. (*reprimere*) to repress.
soffocato *agg.* choked.
sòffoco *sm.* sultriness.
soffòndere *vt.* to suffuse.
soffrìggere *vt.* to fry slightly.
soffrire *vt.* 1. to suffer 2. (*sopportare*) to stand (*v. irr.*).
soffuso *agg.* suffused.
sofisma *sm.* sophism.
sofista *sm.* sophist.
sofìstica *sf.* sophistry.
sofisticare *vi.* to quibble. ♦ **sofisticare** *vt.* to adulterate.
sofisticato *agg.* 1. sophisticated 2. (*adulterato*) adulterated.
sofisticazione *sf.* adulteration.
sofisticherìa *sf.* quibbling.
sofìstico *agg.* sophistical.
soggettista *sm.* scenario writer.
soggettivismo *sm.* subjectivism.
soggettività *sf.* subjectivity.
soggettivo *agg.* subjective.
soggetto *agg. e sm.* subject.
soggezione *sf.* 1. subjection 2. (*timidezza*) shyness.
sogghignare *vi.* to sneer.
sogghigno *sm.* sneer.
soggiacere *vi.* to be subjected.
soggiogare *vt.* to subdue.
soggiornare *vi.* to stay.
soggiorno *sm.* stay: *stanza di* —, living-room.
soggiùngere *vt.* to add.
soglia *sf.* threshold.
sògliola *sf.* sole.
sognante *agg.* dreaming: *occhi sognanti*, dreamy eyes.
sognare *vt.* to dream (*v. irr.*): — *ad occhi aperti*, to have day-dreams.
sognatore *agg.* dreaming. ♦ **sognatore** *sm.* dreamer.
sogno *sm.* dream.
soia *sf.* soya.
solaio *sm.* attic.

solamente *avv.* only.
solare *agg.* 1. solar 2. (*radioso*) radiant.
solatìo *agg.* sunny.
solcare *vt.* 1. to plough 2. (*fig.*) to furrow.
solcato *agg.* 1. ploughed 2. (*fig.*) furrowed.
solcatura *sf.* ploughing, furrowing.
solco *sm.* 1. (*agr.*) furrow 2. (*ruga*) wrinkle 3. (*mar.*) wake 4. (*di ruota sul terreno*) track.
solcòmetro *sm.* log.
soldataglia *sf.* soldiery.
soldatesco *agg.* soldierly.
soldato *sm.* soldier.
soldo *sm.* 1. penny 2. (*denaro*) money 3. (*salario*) pay: *essere al* — *di qu.*, to be in so.'s pay.
sole *sm.* sun: *bagno di* —, sun-bathing; *colpo di* —, sunstroke; *un giorno di* —, *senza* —, a sunny day, a sunless day; *tramonto del* —, sunset.
soleggiare *vt.* to sun-dry.
soleggiato *agg.* sunny.
solenne *agg.* solemn.
solennità *sf.* 1. solemnity 2. (*cerimonia*) ceremony.
solennizzare *vt.* to solemnize.
solenòide *sm.* solenoid.
solere *vi.* to use (*usato solo al passato*).
solerte *agg.* diligent.
solerzia *sf.* diligence.
soletta *sf.* sole.
solfa *sf.* 1. scale 2. (*fig.*) old story.
solfara *sf.* sulphur mine.
solfare *vt.* to sulphur.
solfatara *sf.* solfatara.
solfato *sm.* sulphate.
solfeggiare *vt.* to sol-fa.
solfeggio *sm.* solfeggio.
solfito *sm.* sulphite.
solfuro *sm.* sulphide.
solidale *agg.* solid (for).
solidamente *avv.* solidly.
solidarietà *sf.* solidarity.
solidarizzare *vi.* to be solid (for).
solidificare *vt.* to solidify.
solidificazione *sf.* solidification.
solidità *sf.* 1. solidity 2. (*di colori*) fastness.
sòlido *agg.* 1. solid 2. (*di colori*) fast 3. (*fig.*) sound. ♦ **sòlido** *sm.* solid.
soliloquio *sm.* soliloquy.
solipsismo *sm.* solipsism.
solista *s.* soloist.

solitamente *avv.* usually.
solitario[1] *agg.* solitary. ♦ **solitario**
sm. 1. hermit 2.. (*brillante*) solitaire.
solitario[2] *sm.* (*a carte*) solitaire.
sòlito *agg.* usual, customary: *essere* —, to be used to (doing); *di* —, usually.
solitùdine *sf.* loneliness.
sollazzare *vt.* to amuse.
sollazzo *sm.* amusement.
sollecitante *agg.* urging.
sollecitare *vt.* 1. (*far premura*) to urge 2. (*brigare*) to solicit 3. (*affrettare*) to hurry up.
sollecitazione *sf.* 1. solicitation 2. (*preghiera*) entreaty.
sollécito *agg.* 1. (*rapido*) prompt 2. (*preoccupato*) solicitous 3. (*premuroso*) obliging.
sollecitùdine *sf.'* 1. (*rapidità*) promptness 2. (*interessamento*) concern 3. (*gentilezza*) kindness.
solleone *sm.* dog-days (*pl.*).
solleticante *agg.* alluring.
solleticare *vt.* to tickle.
sollético *sm.* 1. tickle: *soffrire il* —, to be ticklish 2. (*fig.*) itch.
sollevamento *sm.* lifting.
sollevare *vt.* 1. to lift 2. (*issare*) to hoist 3. (*fig.*) to raise 4. (*dar sollievo*) to relieve. ♦ **sollevarsi** *vr.* 1. to rise (*v. irr.*) 2. (*riaversi*) to recover 3. (*insorgere*) to rebel.
sollevato *agg.* (*rasserenato*) cheered up.
sollevazione *sf.* (*rivolta*) rising.
sollievo *sm.* relief.
sollùchero *sm.* andare in —, to go (*v. irr.*) into raptures.
solo *agg.* 1. alone (*pred.*): *da* —, by oneself. 2. (*unico*) only. ♦ **solo** *avv.* only.
solstizio *sm.* solstice.
soltanto *avv.* only.
solùbile *agg.* soluble.
solubilità *sf.* solubility.
soluzione *sf.* solution.
solvente *agg. e sm.* solvent.
solvenza *sf.* (*comm.*) solvency.
solvibile *agg.* solvent. _
solvibilità *sf.* solvency.
soma *sf.* load, burden.
somaràggine *sf.* stupidity.
somaro *sm.* ass.
somàtico *agg.* somatic.
somigliante *agg.* alike, similar.
somiglianza *sf.* likeness.
somigliare *vi.* to look like.

somma *sf.* 1. (*mat.*) addition 2. (*di denaro*) sum.
sommamente *avv.* extremely.
sommare *vt.* to add.
sommariamente *avv.* summarily.
sommario *agg. e sm.* summary.
sommèrgere *vt.* to submerge.
sommergìbile *agg.* submersible. ♦ **sommergìbile** *sm.* submarine.
sommergibilista *sm.* submariner.
sommersione *sf.* submersion.
sommerso *agg.* submerged.
sommessamente *avv.* 1. submissively 2. (*a bassa voce*) in a low voice.
sommesso *agg.* 1. submissive 2. (*di voce*) low.
somministrare *vt.* to administer.
somministratore *sm.* giver.
somministrazione *sf.* giving.
sommissione *sf.* V. *sottomissione*.
sommità *sf.* summit, top.
sommo[1] *agg.* 1. highest 2. (*fig.*) supreme.
sommo[2] *sm.* summit, top.
sommossa *sf.* rising.
sommovimento *sm.* movement, agitation.
sommozzatore *sm.* frogman (*pl.* -men).
sommuòvere *vt.* to stir up.
sonagliera *sf.* collar with bells.
sonaglio *sm.* 1. harness-bell 2. (*giocattolo*) rattle || *serpente a sonagli*, rattlesnake.
sonante *agg.* resounding || *denaro* —, ready money.
sonare *vt.* 1. to sound 2. (*musica*) to play 3. (*di orologio*) to strike (*v. irr.*). ♦ **sonare** *vi.* (*di campanello*) to ring (*v. irr.*).
sonata *sf.* (*mus.*) sonata.
sonatore *sm.* player.
sonda *sf.* 1. (*mar.*) sounding line 2. (*med.*) probe 3. (*min.*) drill.
sondaggio *sm.* 1. sounding 2. (*med.*) probing 3. (*min.*) drilling.
sondare *vt.* 1. to sound 2. (*fig.*) to throw (*v. irr.*) out.
soneria *sf.* 1. (*di orologio*) striking-mechanism 2. alarm.
sonetto *sm.* sonnet.
sonnacchiosamente *avv.* drowsily.
sonnacchioso *agg.* 1. sleepy 2. (*fig.*) torpid.
sonnambulismo *sm.* sleep-walking.
sonnàmbulo *sm.* sleep-walker.
sonnecchiare *vi.* to doze.
sonnellino *sm.* nap.

sonnìfero *sm.* sleeping pills (*pl.*).
sonno *sm.* sleep: — *profondo,* sound sleep.
sonnolento *agg.* drowsy.
sonnolenza *sf.* drowsiness.
sonoramente *avv.* sonorously.
sonorità *sf.* sonority.
sonorizzare *vt.* to post-score.
sonorizzazione *sf.* post-scoring.
sonoro *agg.* 1. sonorous 2. (*rumoroso*) loud 3. (*cine*) sound.
sontuosamente *avv.* sumptuously.
sontuosità *sf.* sumptuousness.
sontuoso *agg.* sumptuous.
soperchierìa *sf.* V. *soverchierìa.*
sopire *vt.* 1. to make (*v. irr.*) drowsy 2. (*calmare*) to soothe.
sopore *sm.* doze.
soporìfero *agg.* soporific.
sopperire *vi.* 1. to provide (for) 2. (*supplire*) to make (*v. irr.*) up (for).
soppesare *vt.* 1. to weigh in one's hand 2. (*considerare*) to weigh.
soppiantare *vt.* to supplant.
soppiatto (*nella loc. avv.*) *di* —, stealthily.
sopportàbile *agg.* bearable.
sopportabilità *sf.* bearableness.
sopportabilmente *avv.* bearably.
sopportare *vt.* to bear (*v. irr.*).
sopportazione *sf.* endurance.
soppressare *vt.* to press.
soppressione *sf.* 1. suppression 2. (*abolizione*) abolition.
soppresso *agg.* 1. suppressed 2. (*abolito*) abolished.
sopprimere *vt.* 1. to suppress 2. (*abolire*) to abolish.
sopra *prep.* 1. (*con contatto*) on, upon 2. (*senza contatto*) over 3. (*al di sopra*) above. ♦ **sopra** *avv.* 1. above 2. (*al piano superiore*) upstairs.
soprabbondanza *sf.* V. *sovrabbondanza.*
soprabbondare *vi.* V. *sovrabbondare.*
sopràbito *sm.* overcoat.
sopraccaricare *vt.* V. *sovraccaricare.*
sopraccàrico *sm.* V. *sovraccàricó.*
sopraccennato *agg.* above-mentioned.
sopracciglio *sm.* eyebrow.
sopraccitato *agg.* V. *sopraddetto.*
sopraccoperta *sf.* 1. (*di libro*) jacket 2. (*di letto*) counterpane. ♦ **sopraccoperta** *avv.* (*mar.*) on

deck.
sopraddetto *agg.* above-mentioned.
sopraelevare *vt.* 1. (*edil.*) to increase the height of 2. (*di strade, rotaie ecc.*) to bank.
sopraelevazione *sf.* 1. (*edil.*) heightening 2. (*di strade, rotaie ecc*). superelevation.
sopraffare *vt.* to overwhelm.
sopraffazione *sf.* 1. overwhelming 2. (*abuso*) abuse.
sopraffino *agg.* first-rate.
sopraggiùngere *vi.* 1. to arrive 2. (*accadere*) to happen.
sopraggiunta *sf.* addition.
sopraindicato *agg.* V. *sopraddetto.*
sopralluogo *sm.* investigation on the spot.
soprammercato (*nella loc. avv.*) *per* —, moreover.
sopramméttere *vt.* to place on.
soprammòbile *sm.* knick-knack.
soprannaturale *agg.* supernatural.
soprannome *sm.* nickname.
soprannominare *vt.* to nickname.
soprannùmero *sm.* excess.
soprano *sm.* soprano.
soprappassaggio *sm.* overbridge.
soprappensiero *avv.* lost in thought.
soprappiù *sm.* extra, addition.
soprapprezzo *sm.* extra charge.
soprascarpa *sf.* galosh.
soprascritta *sf.* inscription.
soprascritto *agg.* above-written.
soprasensìbile *agg.* supersensible.
soprassalto *sm.* jerk: *di* —, all of a sudden.
soprassedere *vi.* 1. to wait 2. (*rimandare*) to postpone.
soprassoldo *sm.* extra pay.
soprastruttura *sf.* superstructure.
soprattassa *sf.* extra tax.
soprattutto *avv.* above all.
sopravanzare *vt.* 1. (*superare*) to surpass 2. (*avanzare*) to be left over.
sopravanzo *sm.* surplus.
sopravvalutare *vt.* to overrate.
sopravvenire *vi.* 1. (*di persone*) to turn up 2. (*di cose*) to come (*v. irr.*) about.
sopravvento *sm.* 1. (*mar.*) windward 2. (*fig.*) upper hand: *prendere il* —, to get (*v. irr.*) the upper hand.
sopravvissuto *agg. e sm.* surviving. ♦ **sopravvissuto** *sm.* survivor.
sopravvivenza *sf.* survival.

sopravvìvere *vi.* to survive.
sopruso *sm.* abuse of power.
soqquadro *sm.* confusion: *a —*, topsy-turvy.
sorbettare *vt.* to freeze (*v. irr.*).
sorbetto *sm.* sherbet.
sorbire *vt.* to sip. ♦ **sorbirsi** *vr.* to put (*v. irr.*) up with.
sorcio *sm.* mouse (*pl.* mice).
sordamente *avv.* dully.
sordidamente *avv.* filthily.
sordidezza *sf.* filthiness.
sòrdido *agg.* filthy.
sordina *sf.* (*mus.*) mute: *in —* (*fig.*), on the sly.
sordità *sf.* deafness.
sordo *agg.* deaf.
sordomuto *sm.* deaf-mute.
sorella *sf.* sister.
sorellastra *sf.* half-sister.
sorgente *sf.* spring, source.
sòrgere *vi.* to rise (*v. irr.*).
sorgiva *sf.* spring-water.
sorgivo *agg.* spring (*attr.*).
soriano *agg.* syrian: *gatto —*, tabby cat.
sormontare *vt.* 1. to surmount 2. (*superare*) to overcome (*v. irr.*).
sornione *agg.* sly. ♦ **sornione** *sm.* sly person.
sorpassare *vt.* 1. to overtake (*v. irr.*) 2. (*sport*) to outrun (*v. irr.*).
sorpassato *agg.* old-fashioned.
sorpasso *sm.* overtaking.
sorprendente *agg.* surprising.
sorprèndere *vt.* 1. (*cogliere inaspettatamente*) to catch (*v. irr.*) 2. (*meravigliare*) to surprise.
sorpresa *sf.* surprise: *di —*, by surprise.
sorrèggere *vt.* to support.
sorridente *agg.* smiling.
sorrìdere *vi.* 1. to smile 2. (*attrarre*) to appeal.
sorriso *sm.* smile.
sorsata *sf.* sip.
sorseggiare *vt.* to sip.
sorso *sm.* gulp, sip.
sorta *sf.* kind, sort.
sorte *sf.* 1. destiny, lot 2. (*avvenire*) future.
sorteggiare *vt.* to draw (*v. irr.*) lots (for).
sorteggio *sm.* draw.
sortilegio *sm.* witchcraft.
sortire[1] *vt.* to get (*v. irr.*).
sortire[2] *vi.* to come (*v. irr.*) out.
sortita *sf.* sally.
sorvegliante *sm.* overseer.

sorveglianza *sf.* overseeing.
sorvegliare *vt.* to oversee (*v. irr.*).
sorvolare *vt.* 1. to fly (*v. irr.*) over 2. (*passar sopra*) to pass over.
sorvolo *sm.* flying over.
sosia *sm.* double.
sospèndere *vt.* 1. (*attaccare*) to suspend 2. (*interrompere*) to defer.
sospensione *sf.* 1. (*incertezza; chim.*) suspension 2. (*interruzione*) interruption.
sospensiva *sf.* suspension.
sospensivo *agg.* suspensive.
sospeso *agg.* 1. hanging 2. (*interrotto*) suspended.
sospettàbile *agg.* liable to suspicion.
sospettare *vt.* to suspect.
sospetto *sm.* suspicion.
sospettosamente *avv.* suspiciously.
sospettoso *agg.* suspicious.
sospìngere *vt.* to drive (*v. irr.*) || *ad ogni piè sospinto*, at every moment.
sospirare *vi.* 1. to sigh 2. (*fig.*) to pine. ♦ **sospirare** *vt.* to long (for).
sospirato *agg.* (*desiderato*) longed for.
sospiro *sm.* sigh.
sosta *sf.* 1. (*fermata*) stop 2. (*pausa*) pause.
sostantivamente *avv.* substantively.
sostantivare *vt.* to substantivize.
sostantivo *sm.* substantive, noun.
sostanza *sf.* substance || *in — (in breve)*, in short.
sostanziale *agg.* substantial.
sostanzialmente *avv.* substantially.
sostanzioso *agg.* substantial.
sostare *vi.* to stop.
sostegno *sm.* support.
sostenere *vt.* 1. to support 2. (*affermare*) to maintain 3. (*tener alto*) to keep (*v. irr.*) up.
sostenìbile *agg.* 1. supportable 2. (*di opinioni*) maintainable.
sostenimento *sm.* 1. support 2. (*sostentamento*) sustenance.
sostenitore *sm.* supporter.
sostentamento *sm.* sustenance.
sostenuto *agg.* 1. stiff, distant 2. (*comm.*) steady.
sostituìbile *agg.* replaceable.
sostituire *vt.* to replace.
sostituto *sm.* substitute.
sostituzione *sf.* replacement.
sostrato *sm.* substratum (*pl.* -ta).

sottacere *vt.* to keep (*v. irr.*) (sthg.) from.

sottaceti *sm. pl.* pickles.

sottana *sf.* 1. skirt 2. (*di prete*) cassock.

sottecchi (*nella loc. avv.*) *di* —, stealthily.

sotterfugio *sm.* subterfuge.

sotterramento *sm.* burial.

sotterrànea *sf.* underground.

sotterràneo *agg.* underground. ♦ sotterràneo *sm.* 1. (*di basilica*) vault 2. (*di castello*) dungeon.

sotterrare *vt.* to bury.

sottigliezza *sf.* 1. thinness 2. (*acutezza*) subtlety.

sottile *agg.* 1. thin 2. (*fig.*) subtle.

sottilizzare *vi.* to split (*v. irr.*) hairs.

sottilmente *avv.* 1. finely 2. (*con acutezza*) subtly.

sottintèndere *vt.* to imply.

sottinteso *agg.* implied. ♦ sottinteso *sm.* allusion.

sotto *prep.* 1. under 2. (*al di sotto, più in basso*) below, beneath 3. (*in espressioni di tempo*) — *Natale*, at Christmas; *essere — gli esami*, to be close to the exams. ♦ sotto *avv.* 1. underneath, below 2. (*al piano di sotto*) downstairs.

sottobanco *loc. avv.* underthecounter.

sottobosco *sm.* underbrush.

sottocchio *avv.* in front of: *tenere qc.* —, to keep (*v. irr.*) an eye on sthg.

sottochiave *avv.* under lock and key.

sottocoperta *sf.* (*mar.*) below deck.

sottocoppa *sf.* saucer.

sottocutàneo *agg.* subcutaneous.

sottofondo *sm.* 1. (*edil.*) foundation 2. (*sfondo*) background.

sottogamba (*nella loc. avv.*) *prendere qc.* —, to make (*v. irr.*) light of sthg.

sottolineare *vt.* 1. to underline 2. (*fig.*) to lay (*v. irr.*) stress (on).

sottolineatura *sf.* underlining.

sottomano *avv.* 1. (*di nascosto*) underhand 2. (*a portata di mano*) at hand.

sottomarino *agg. e sm.* submarine.

sottomesso *agg.* 1. subdued 2. (*obbediente*) submissive.

sottométtere *vt.* to subject. ♦ sottométtersi *vr.* to submit (oneself).

sottomissione *sf.* 1. subdual 2. (*obbedienza*) submission.

sottopassaggio *sm.* subway.

sottoporre *vt.* 1. (*al giudizio di qu.*) to submit 2. (*subire, far subire*) to subject 3. (*esporre*) to expose.

sottoposto *sm.* subordinate.

sottoprodotto *sm.* by-product.

sottoscritto *agg.* subscribed. ♦ sottoscritto *sm.* undersigned.

sottoscrivere *vt.* 1. to sign 2. (*comm.*) to underwrite. ♦ sottoscrivere *vi.* to subscribe.

sottoscrizione *sf.* subscription.

sottosegretario *sm.* under-secretary.

sottosopra *avv.* 1. upside down 2. (*in disordine*) topsy-turvy.

sottospecie *sf.* subspecies (*invariato al pl.*). ·

sottostante *agg.* below.

sottostare *vi.* 1. (*essere sotto*) to be below 2. (*essere soggetto*) to be subjected 3. (*sottomettersi*) to submit.

sottosuolo *sm.* subsoil.

sottotenente *sm.* second lieutenant.

sottotitolo *sm.* subtitle.

sottovalutare *vt.* to undervalue.

sottovento *avv.* (*mar.*) leeward.

sottoveste *sf.* petticoat.

sottovoce *avv.* in a low voice.

ottrarre *vt.* 1. (*mat.*) to subtract 2. (*portar via*) to take (*v. irr.*) away 3. (*rubare*) to steal (*v. irr.*) 4. (*salvare da*) to deliver. ♦ sottrarsi *vr.* to avoid (sthg.).

sottrazione *sf.* subtraction.

sottufficiale *sm.* non-commissioned officer.

sovente *avv.* often, frequently.

soverchiare *vi.* to overcome (*v. irr.*).

soverchieria *sf.* oppression.

soviètico *agg. e sm.* Soviet.

sovrabbondante *agg.* superabundant.

sovrabbondanza *sf.* superabundance.

sovrabbondare *vi.* to superabound.

sovraccaricare *vt.* to overload.

sovraccàrico *sm.* overload.

sovraccoperta *sf. e avv.* V. *sopraccoperta.*

sovranità *sf.* 1. sovereignty 2. (*supremazia*) supremacy.

sovrannaturale *agg.* V. *soprannaturale.*

sovrano *agg.* sovereign.
sovrappopolare *vt.* to overpopulate.
sovrappopolato *agg.* overpopulated.
sovrappopolazione *sf.* overpopulation.
sovrapporre *vt.* to superimpose.
sovrapposizione *sf.* superimposition.
sovrastampa *sf.* overprint.
sovrastante *agg.* impending, overhanging.
sovrastare *vi.* **1.** to overhang (*v. irr.*) over **2.** (*fig.*) to impend **3.** (*essere superiore*) to be superior.
sovreccedente *agg.* superabundant.
sovreccedenza *sf.* surplus.
sovreccitàbile *agg.* overexcitable.
sovreccitabilità *sf.* overexcitability.
sovreccitare *vt.* to overexcite.
sovreccitazione *sf.* overexcitement.
sovrimposta *sf.* additional tax.
sovrimpressione *sf.* (*foto; cine*) superimposure.
sovrintendente *sm.* superintendent.
sovrintendenza *sf.* superintendence.
sovrumano *agg.* superhuman.
sovvenzionare *vt.* to subsidize.
sovvenzione *sf.* subsidy.
sovversione *sf.* overthrow.
sovversivo *agg.* subversive. ◆ **sovversivo** *sm.* subverter.
sovvertimento *sm.* subversion.
sovvertire *vt.* to overthrow (*v. irr.*).
sozzo *agg.* filthy.
sozzume *sm.* filth.
spaccalegna *sm.* wood-cutter.
spaccamontagne *sm.* braggart.
spaccapietre *sm.* stone-breaker.
spaccare *vt.* **1.** to split (*v. irr.*) **2.** (*rompere*) to break (*v. irr.*) || *il mio orologio spacca il minuto*, my watch is dead right; *il sole spacca le pietre*, the sun is blazing down.
spaccatura *sf.* split, cleft.
spacchettare *vt.* to unpack.
spacciare *vt.* **1.** (*vendere*) to sell (*v. irr.*) **2.** (*mettere in circolazione*) to circulate **3.** (*far credere*) to make (*v. irr.*) (so.) believe **4.** (*uccidere*) to kill. ◆ **spacciarsi** *vr.* to pretend to be || *lo danno per spacciato* (*di malato*), they give him up.
spacciato *agg.* done for.

spacciatore *sm.* **1.** seller **2.** (*di monete false*) forger.
spaccio *sm.* **1.** shop **2.** (*vendita*) sale.
spacco *sm.* **1.** split **2.** (*di abiti*) vent.
spacconata *sf.* bluff.
spaccone *sm.* boaster.
spada *sf.* sword.
spadaccino *sm.* fencer.
spadino *sm.* court-sword.
spadroneggiare *vi.* to lord it.
spaesato *agg.* (*fig.*) lost.
spaghetto *sm.* **1.** (*piccolo spago*) string **2.** (*fam.*) (*paura*) fright.
spagliare *vt.* to take (*v. irr.*) the straw off.
spagnoletta *sf.* **1.** (*di filo*) spool **2.** (*arachide*) peanut.
spagnolismo *sm.* Hispanicism.
spagnolo *agg.* Spanish. ◆ **spagnolo** *sm.* Spaniard.
spago *sm.* string.
spaiare *vt.* to uncouple.
spaiato *agg.* odd.
spalancare *vt.* to open wide.
spalancato *agg.* wide open.
spalare *vt.* to shovel away.
spalatore *sm.* shoveller.
spalatura *sf.* shovelling.
spalla *sf.* **1.** shoulder **2.** (*pl.*) back (*sing.*) **3.** (*teat.*) stooge man || *alle spalle*, behind; *vivere alle spalle di qu.*, to live on so.
spallata *sf.* **1.** push with the shoulders **2.** (*alzata di spalle*) shrug.
spalleggiare *vt.* to back.
spalletta *sf.* parapet.
spalliera *sf.* **1.** back **2.** (*di piante*) espalier.
spallina *sf.* **1.** shoulder-strap **2.** (*mil.*) epaulette.
spalluccia *sf.* *far spallucce*, to shrug one's shoulders.
spalmare *vt.* to smear.
spalto *sm.* glacis.
spampanare *vt.* to strip a vine of its leaves.
spàndere *vt.* **1.** to spread (*v. irr.*) **2.** (*versare*) to shed (*v. irr.*) **3.** (*scialacquare*) to squander.
spanna *sf.* span.
spannare *vt.* to skim.
spannocchiare *vt.* to husk.
spappolare *vt.* to pulp. ◆ **spappolarsi** *vr.* to become (*v. irr.*) mushy.
sparare[1] *vt.* to shoot (*v. irr.*), to fire.

sparare[2] *vt.* (*squartare*) to split (*v. irr.*).

sparata *sf.* 1. discharge 2. (*spacconata*) brag.

sparato *sm.* (*di camicia*) shirt--front.

sparatore *sm.* shooter.

sparatoria *sf.* shooting.

sparecchiare *vt.* to clear.

spareggio *sm.* 1. disparity 2. (*sport*) deciding game.

spàrgere *vt.* 1. to scatter 2. (*divulgare*) to spread (*v. irr.*) 3. (*versare; di luce*) to shed (*v. irr.*).

spargimento *sm.* 1. spreading 2. (*versamento*) shedding || — *di sangue*, bloodshed.

sparigliare *vt.* to unmatch.

sparire *vi.* to disappear.

sparizione *sf.* disappearance.

sparlare *vi.* to speak (*v. irr.*) badly.

sparo *sm.* shot.

sparpagliare *vt.* to scatter. ♦ **sparpagliarsi** *vr.* to scatter.

sparso *agg.* 1. (*versato*) shed 2. (*sciolto*) loose.

spartano *agg.* Spartan.

spartiacque *sm.* watershed.

spartineve *sm.* snow-plough.

spartire *vt.* to share out.

spartito *sm.* score.

spartizione *sf.* sharing.

sparuto *agg.* lean, spare.

spàrviero *sm.* sparrow-hawk.

spasimante *sm.* wooer.

spasimare *vi.* 1. to suffer agonies 2. (*fig.*) to yearn.

spàsimo *sm.* pang.

spasmo *sm.* spasm.

spasmodicamente *avv.* spasmodically.

spasmòdico *agg.* spasmodic.

spassare *vt.* to amuse || *spassarsela*, to have a very good time.

spassionato *agg.* impartial.

spasso *sm.* 1. amusement: *che —!*, what fun! 2. (*passeggiata*) andare *a —*, -to go (*v. irr.*) for a walk; *essere a —*, to be out of work.

spassoso *agg.* funny, amusing.

spàstico *agg.* spastic.

spato *sm.* spar.

spàtola *sf.* broad knife.

spatriare *vt.* V. *espatriare*.

spauracchio *sm.* 1. scarecrow 2. (*fig.*) bugbear.

spaurire *vt.* to frighten. ♦ **spaurirsi** *vr.* to get (*v irr.*) frightened.

spaurito *agg.* frightened.

spavalderìa *sf.* boldness.

spavaldo *agg.* bold, arrogant.

spaventapàsseri *sm.* scarecrow.

spaventare *vt.* to frighten, to scare. ♦ **spaventarsi** *vr.* to be frightened.

spaventato *agg.* frightened, scared.

spavento *sm.* fright.

spaventoso *agg.* dreadful, frightful.

spaziale *agg.* space (*attr.*).

spaziare *vt.* to space. ♦ **spaziare** *vi.* to range.

spaziatura *sf.* spacing.

spazieggiare *vt.* to space.

spazientirsi *vr.* to lose (*v. irr.*) one's patience.

spazio *sm.* 1. space 2. (*posto*) room.

spazioso *agg.* wide.

spazzacamino *sm.* chimney-sweep.

spazzamine *sm.* mine-sweeper.

spazzaneve *sm.* snow-plough.

spazzare *vt.* to sweep (*v. irr.*).

spazzata *sf.* sweep.

spazzatura *sf.* (*rifiuti*) sweepings (*pl.*): *bidone della —*, dust-bin; *carro della —*, dust-cart.

spazzino *sm.* 1. road-sweeper 2. (*spazzaturaio*) dustman (*pl.* -men).

spàzzola *sf.* brush || *capelli a —*, crew-cut.

spazzolare *vt.* to brush.

spazzolata *sf.* brush.

spazzolino *sm.* (small) brush: — *da denti*, tooth-brush.

spazzolone *sm.* scrubbing-brush.

specchiarsi *vr.* 1. to look at oneself in a mirror 2. (*riflettersi*) to be mirrored.

specchiera *sf.* looking-glass.

specchietto *sm.* 1. hand-mirror 2. (*tabella*) table || — *retrovisore*, driving-mirror.

specchio *sm.* 1. mirror 2. (*prospetto*) register 3. (*modello*) model || — *d'acqua*, sheet of water.

speciale *agg.* special.

specialista *s.* specialist.

specialità *sf.* speciality.

specializzare *vt.* to specialize. ♦ **specializzarsi** *vr.* to specialize.

specializzazione *sf.* specialization.

specie *sf.* 1. kind 2. (*scientifico; teol.*) species (*pl. invariato*) || *far —*, to surprise.

specificamente *avv.* specifically.

specificare *vt.* to specify.

specificazione *sf.* specification.

specifico *agg. e sm.* specific.

specioso *agg.* specious.

speculare[1] *vi.* to speculate (on): —
al rialzo, al ribasso, to speculate
for the advance, for the fall.
speculare[2] *agg.* mirror-like.
speculativo *agg.* speculative.
speculatore *agg.* speculative. ◆
speculatore *sm.* speculator.
speculazione *sf.* speculation.
spedire *vt.* **1.** to send (*v. irr.*) **2.**
(*via mare*) to ship **3.** (*via terra*)
to forward.
speditamente *avv.* **1.** quickly **2.**
(*correntemente*) fluently.
speditezza *sf.* **1.** quickness **2.** (*nel
parlare*) fluency.
spedito *agg.* **1.** (*svelto*) quick **2.**
(*nel parlare*) fluent.
speditore *sm.* sender.
spedizione *sf.* **1.** forwarding **2.** (*per
mare*) shipment **3.** (*di lettere, pacchi*) dispatch **4.** (*scientifico; mil.*)
expedition || — *per via aerea,* air-
-freight.
spedizioniere *sm.* forwarding
agent.
spègnere *vt.* **1.** (*un fuoco*) to put
(*v. irr.*) out **2.** (*gas, luce ecc.*) to
turn off **3.** (*fig.*) to stifle || — *la
sete,* to quench one's thirst. ◆
spègnersi *vr.* **1.** to go (*v. irr.*)
out **2.** (*fig.*) to fade **3.** (*morire*) to
pass away.
spegnimento *sm.* extinction.
spegnitoio *sm.* snuffer.
spelacchiare *vt.* to tear (*v. irr.*)
out the hair of. ◆ **spelacchiarsi**
vr. to lose (*v. irr.*) one's hair.
spelacchiato *agg.* **1.** scanty-haired
2. (*di stoffe, pellicce*) worn-out.
spelare *vt.* to balden. ◆ **spelarsi**
vr. V. *spelacchiarsi.*
spelato *agg.* **1.** hairless **2.** (*di indumento*) worn.
spelatura *sf.* **1.** hairless patch **2.**
(*di indumento*) worn patch.
speleologìa *sf.* speleology.
speleològico *agg.* speleological.
speleòlogo *sm.* speleologist.
spellare *vt.* to skin. ◆ **spellarsi**
vr. to peel.
spellatura *sf.* **1.** skinning **2.** (*parte spellata*) graze.
spelonca *sf.* den.
spendaccione *sm.* spendthrift.
spèndere *vt.* to spend (*v. irr.*) (*anche fig.*).
spennacchiare *vt.* to pluck. ◆
spennacchiarsi *vr.* to lose (*v.
irr.*) one's feathers.

spennare *vt.* to pluck.
spennellare *vt.* **1.** to brush **2.**
(*med.*) to paint.
spennellata *sf.* touch of the brush.
spennellatura *sf.* (*med.*) painting.
spensieratamente *avv.* thought-
lessly.
spensieratezza *sf.* thoughtlessness.
spensierato *agg.* thoughtless.
spento *agg.* **1.** extinguished, out
(*pred.*) **2.** (*estinto*) extinct **3.** (*smorto*) duli.
speràbile *agg.* to be hoped (for).
speranza *sf.* hope.
speranzoso *agg.* hopeful.
sperare *vt. e vi.* to hope (for sthg.,
in so.).
spèrdersi *vr.* **1.** to get (*v. irr.*) lost
2. (*dileguare*) to vanish.
sperduto *agg.* **1.** scattered **2.** (*isolato*) secluded **3.** (*smarrito*) lost.
sperequazione *sf.* inequality.
spergiurare *vi.* to swear (*v. irr.*)
falsely: *giurare e* —, to swear
again and again.
spergiuro *sm.* **1.** perjury **2.** (*di persona*) perjurer.
spericolato *agg.* reckless. ◆ **spericolato** *sm.* daredevil.
sperimentale *agg.* experimental.
sperimentalismo *sm.* experimen-
talism.
sperimentalmente *avv.* experimen-
tally.
sperimentare *vt.* **1.** to experiment
(with) **2.** (*mettere alla prova*) to
test.
sperimentato *agg.* **1.** (*provato*)
tried **2.** (*esperto*) experienced.
sperimentatore *sm.* experimenter.
sperimentazione *sf.* experimentation.
sperma *sm.* sperm.
spermatozoo *sm.* spermatozoon
(*pl.* -zoa).
speronare *vt.* **1.** (*mar.*) to ram **2.**
(*un cavallo*) to spur.
speronata *sf.* **1.** (*mar.*) ramming
2. (*colpo di sperone*) spur.
sperone *sm.* V. *sprone.*
sperperamento *sm.* squandering.
sperperare *vt.* to squander.
sperperatore *sm.* squanderer.
spèrpero *sm.* dissipation.
sperticato *agg.* excessive.
spesa *sf.* **1.** expense: *far fronte a
una* —, to meet (*v. irr.*) an expense
2. (*compera*) shopping: *andare a
far spese,* to go (*v. irr.*) shopping.

spesare *vt*. to maintain.

spesato *agg. essere —*, to have all expenses paid.

spessire *vt*. to thicken. ♦ spessirsi *vr*. to thicken.

spesso[1] *agg*. 1. thick 2. (*frequente*) frequent.

spesso[2] *avv*. often.

spessore *sm*. thickness.

spettàbile *agg*. respectable.

spettàcolo *sm*. 1. spectacle 2. (*teat*.) performance.

spettacoloso *agg*. spectacular.

spettante *agg*. due.

spettanze *sf. pl*. dues.

spettare *vi*. 1. to be (for so.) 2. (*essere dovuto*) to be due.

spettatore *sm*. 1. spectator 2. (*testimone*) witness || *gli spettatori*, the audience.

spettegolare *vi*. to gossip.

spettinare *vt*. to ruffle so.'s hair. ♦ spettinarsi *vr*. to ruffle one's hair.

spettinato *agg*. uncombed.

spettrale *agg*. spectral.

spettro *sm*. 1. ghost 2. (*fis*.) spectrum (*pl*. -ra).

spettroscopìa *sf*. spectroscopy.

spettroscòpico *agg*. spectroscopic(al).

spettroscopio *sm*. spectroscope.

speziale *sm*. (*farmacista*) chemist.

spezie *sf. pl*. spices.

spezzàbile *agg*. breakable.

spezzare *vt*. to break (*v. irr*.). ♦ spezzarsi *vr*. to break.

spezzatino *sm*. stew.

spezzato *agg*. broken.

spezzettamento *sm*. chopping.

spezzettare *vt*. to chop.

spezzone *sm*. 1. (*mil*.) incendiary bomb 2. (*metal*.) cut-down size.

spia *sf*. 1. spy 2. (*indizio*) evidence 3. (*di porta*) peep-hole || — *luminosa*, warning light; *fare la —*, to play the spy.

spiaccicare *vt*. to squash. ♦ spiaccicarsi *vr*. to get (*v. irr*.) squashed.

spiacente *agg*. sorry.

spiacere *vi*. V. *dispiacere*.

spiacévole *agg*. unpleasant.

spiacevolmente *avv*. unpleasantly.

spiaggia *sf*. 1. beach 2. (*riva*) (sea)shore.

spianamento *sm*. 1. levelling 2. (*il radere al suolo*) razing.

spianare *vt*. 1. to level 2. (*radere*

al suolo) to raze 3. (*appianare, lisciare*) to smooth. ♦ spianarsi *vr*. to become (*v. irr*.) smooth.

spianata *sf*. 1. levelling 2. (*luogo spianato*) open space 3. (*arch*.) esplanade 4. (*in un bosco*) clearing.

spianato *agg*. 1. levelled 2. (*liscio*) smooth.

spiano (*nella loc. avv*.) *a tutto —*, profusely; (*sodo*) hard.

spiantare *vt*. 1. to pull out 2. (*rovinare*) to ruin. ♦ spiantarsi *vr*. (*rovinarsi*) to go (*v. irr*.) to ruin.

spiantato *agg*. (*fig*.) penniless. ♦ spiantato *sm*. (*fig*.) pauper.

spiare *vt*. 1. to spy (upon) 2. (*aspettare*) to watch (for).

spiattellare *vt*. to blab (out).

spiazzo *sm*. 1. open space 2. (*nel bosco*) clearing.

spiccare *vt*. 1. to pick 2. (*tagliare*) to cut (*v. irr*.) off 3. (*pronunciare*) to enunciate distinctly 4. (*emettere*) to issue || — *un salto*, to take (*v. irr*.) a leap; — *il volo*, to fly (*v. irr*.) up; — *una tratta*, to draw (*v. irr*.) a bill. ♦ spiccare *vi*. to stand (*v. irr*.) out.

spiccatamente *avv*. distinctly.

spiccato *agg*. 1. (*marcato*) marked 2. (*nitido*) clear.

spicchio *sm*. 1. slice 2. (*di agrumi*) segment 3. (*di aglio*) clove 4. (*geom*.) sector || *a spicchi*, sliced.

spicciare *vt*. to dispatch. ♦ spicciarsi *vr*. to hurry up.

spicciativo *agg*. V. *spiccio*.

spiccicare *vt*. 1. to detach 2. (*pronunciare*) to utter.

spiccio *agg*. 1. quick 2. (*franco*) straightforward || *andar per le spicce*, to go (*v. irr*.) straight to the point; *moneta spiccia*, small change.

spicciolata (*nella loc. avv*.) *alla —*, few at a time.

spìccioli *sm. pl*. change (*solo sing*.).

spicco *sm. far —*, to stand (*v. irr*.) out.

spidocchiare *vt*. to delouse.

spiedo *sm*. spit.

spiegàbile *agg*. explainable.

spiegamento *sm*. 1. spreading out 2. (*mil*.) deployment.

spiegare *vt*. 1. to explain 2. (*stendere*) to spread (*v. irr*.) out 3. (*di vele*) to unfurl 4. (*mil*.) to deploy. ♦ spiegarsi *vr*. 1. (*farsi capire*) to make (*v. irr.*) oneself understood **2.** (*stendersi*) to spread out.

spiegazione *sf.* explanation.
spiegazzare *vt.* to crumple.
spietatamente *avv.* ruthlessly.
spietatezza *sf.* ruthlessness.
spietato *agg.* ruthless.
spifferare *vt.* to blurt out.
spìffero *sm.* draught.
spiga *sf.* **1.** spike **2.** (*di cereali*) ear.
spigare *vi.* to ear.
spighetta *sf.* braid.
spigliatamente *avv.* easily.
spigliatezza *sf.* ease.
spigliato *agg.* easy.
spigo *sm.* lavender.
spigolare *vt.* to glean (*anche fig.*).
spigolatore *sm.* gleaner.
spigolatrice *sf.* gleaner.
spigolatura *sf.* gleaning.
spìgolo *sm.* edge.
spigoloso *agg.* edgy.
spilla *sf.* **1.** pin **2.** (*gioiello*) brooch.
spillare *vt.* **1.** to draw (*v. irr.*) **2.** (*fig.*) to worm.
spillo *sm.* pin: — *da balia*, safety-pin.
spillone *sm.* (*per cappello*) hat-pin.
spilorcerìa *sf.* stinginess.
spilorcio *agg.* stingy. ◆ **spilorcio** *sm.* miser.
spilungona *sf.* lanky woman.
spilungone *sm.* lanky man.
spina *sf.* **1.** thorn **2.** (*lisca*) fishbone **3.** (*elettr.*) plug **4.** (*mecc.*) pin **5.** (*di botte*) bung **6.** (*fig.*) sorrow, grief ‖ — *dorsale*, backbone; *a* — *di pesce*, herring-bone.
spinacio *sm.* spinach (*solo sing.*).
spinale *agg.* spinal.
spinare *vt.* (*pesce*) to bone.
spinato *agg.* (*a spina di pesce*) herring-bone ‖ *filo* —, barbed wire.
spinetta *sf.* spinet.
spìngere *vt.* **1.** to push **2.** (*condurre*) to drive (*v. irr.*) **3.** (*stimolare*) to urge **4.** (*portare*) to carry. ◆ **spìngersi** *vr.* to push.
spino *sm.* thorn.
spinone *sm.* (*cane*) griffon.
spinosità *sf.* thorniness.
spinoso *agg.* thorny.
spinta *sf.* **1.** push **2.** (*stimolo*) incentive **3.** (*mecc.; edil.*) thrust.
spinterògeno *sm.* (battery) coil ignition.
spinto *agg.* **1.** (*eccessivo*) excessive **2.** (*audace*) risky.

spintone *sm.* shove ‖ *farsi avanti a spintoni*, to elbow one's way forward.
spiombare *vt.* to unseal.
spionaggio *sm.* espionage.
spioncino *sm.* peep-hole.
spione *sm.* spy.
spiovente *agg.* **1.** drooping **2.** (*inclinato*) sloping. ◆ **spiovente** *sm.* **1.** slope **2.** (*sport*) high kick.
spiòvere *vi.* **1.** to stop raining **2.** (*ricadere*) to come (*v. irr.*) down.
spira *sf.* coil.
spiraglio *sm.* **1.** small hole **2.** (*barlume*) gleam.
spirale *sf.* **1.** spiral **2.** (*molla*) spring.
spirante *agg.* **1.** (*soffiante*) blowing **2.** (*morente*) passing away **3.** (*esalante*) exhaling.
spirare *vi.* **1.** (*soffiare*) to blow (*v. irr.*) **2.** (*morire*) to pass away **3.** (*scadere*) to expire **4.** (*emanare*) to emanate. ◆ **spirare** *vt.* to exhale.
spiritato *agg.* **1.** possessed **2.** (*spaventato*) frightened.
spirìtico *agg.* spiritualistic.
spiritismo *sm.* spiritualism.
spiritista *s.* spiritualist.
spiritìstico *agg.* V. *spiritico.*
spìrito *sm.* **1.** spirit **2.** (*fantasma*) ghost **3.** (*arguzia*) wit **4.** (*alcool*) alcohol ‖ *far dello* —, to be witty.
spiritosàggine *sf.* witticism.
spiritosamente *avv.* wittily.
spiritoso *agg.* **1.** witty **2.** (*alcoolico*) alcoholic.
spirituale *agg.* spiritual.
spiritualismo *sm.* spiritualism.
spiritualista *agg.* spiritualistic. ◆ **spiritualista** *s.* spiritualist.
spiritualità *sf.* spirituality.
spiritualizzare *vt.* to spiritualize.
spiritualmente *avv.* spiritually.
spizzicare *vt.* to nibble.
spìzzico (*nella loc. avv.*) *a* —, little by little.
splendente *agg.* bright.
splèndere *vi.* to shine (*v. irr.*).
splèndido *agg.* splendid.
splendore *sm.* splendour.
spocchia *sf.* haughtiness.
spocchioso *agg.* haughty.
spodestamento *sm.* **1.** dispossession **2.** (*da posizione autorevole*) dethronement.
spodestare *vt.* **1.** to dispossess **2.** (*detronizzare*) to dethrone.
spoetizzare *vt.* to disenchant.

spoglia *sf.* 1. (*di animale*) skin 2. (*veste*) dress 3. (*bottino*) spoils (*pl.*) || *spoglie mortali*, mortal remains.

spogliare *vt.* 1. to strip 2. (*derubare*) to rob 3. (*saccheggiare*) to plunder. ♦ spogliarsi *vr.* 1. to strip 2. (*di alberi*) to shed (*v. irr.*) 3. (*privarsi*) to strip oneself (of).

spogliarello *sm.* strip-tease.

spogliatoio *sm.* 1. dressing-room 2. (*teat. ecc.*) cloak-room.

spoglio *agg.* bare. ♦ spoglio *sm.* 1. (*computo*) counting 2. (*esame*) examination 3. (*vestito smesso*) cast-off || *fare lo* —, to go (*v. irr.*) through.

spola *sf.* shuttle.

spoletta *sf.* 1. spool 2. (*di arma*) fuse.

spoliazione *sf.* spoliation.

spolmonarsi *vr.* to talk oneself hoarse.

spolpare *vt.* 1. to take (*v. irr.*) the flesh off 2. (*fig.*) to skin.

spolpato *agg.* 1. stripped of the flesh 2. (*fig.*) skinned.

spolverare *vt.* to dust.

spolveratura *sf.* 1. dusting 2. (*fig.*) smattering.

spolverino *sm.* dust-coat.

spolverizzare *vt.* to dust.

spòlvero *sm.* 1. dusting 2. (*disegno*) perforated pattern.

sponda *sf.* 1. edge 2. (*di fiume*) bank 3. (*di mare*) shore 4. (*parapetto*) parapet.

sponsali *sm. pl.* nuptials.

spontaneamente *avv.* spontaneously.

spontaneità *sf.* spontaneity.

spontàneo *agg.* spontaneous.

spopolamento *sm.* depopulation.

spopolare *vt.* to depopulate. ♦ spopolarsi *vr.* to become (*v. irr.*) depopulated.

spopolato *agg.* (*deserto*) deserted.

spora *sf.* spore.

sporàdico *agg.* sporadic.

sporcaccione *sm.* dirty man

sporcare *vt.* to dirty.

sporcizia *sf.* dirt.

sporco *agg.* dirty.

sporgente *agg.* protruding.

sporgenza *sf.* protrusion.

spòrgere *vi.* to put (*v. irr.*) out. ♦ spòrgere *vt.* to put (*v. irr.*) out. ♦ spòrgersi *vr.* to lean (*v. irr.*) out.

sport *sm.* sport.

sporta *sf.* basket.

sportello *sm.* 1. door 2. (*di biglietteria*) ticket-window 3. (*di ufficio postale ecc.*) counter.

sportivamente *avv.* sportingly.

sportivo *agg.* sporting. ♦ sportivo *sm.* sportsman (*pl.* -men).

sporto *agg.* 1. leaning out 2. (*proteso*) outstretched.

sposa *sf.* bride.

sposalizio *sm.* wedding.

sposare *vt.* to marry. ♦ sposarsi *vr.* to get (*v. irr.*) married.

sposo *sm.* bridegroom.

spossamento *sm.* exhaustion.

spossante *agg.* exhausting.

spossare *vt.* to exhaust.

spossatezza *sf.* V. *spossamento*.

spossato *agg.* weary.

spossessare *vt.* to dispossess.

spostàbile *agg.* shiftable.

spostamento *sm.* 1. shifting 2. (*cambiamento*) change.

spostare *vt.* 1. to shift, to move 2. (*cambiare*) to change. ♦ spostarsi *vr.* to shift.

spostato *agg.* out of one's place (*pred.*). ♦ spostato *sm.* misfit.

spranga *sf.* bar.

sprangare *vt.* to bar.

sprazzo *sm.* flash: — *d'ingegno*, brain-wave.

sprecare *vt.* to waste.

spreco *sm.* waste.

sprecone *sm.* waster.

spregévole *agg.* despicable.

spregiare *vt.* to scorn.

spregiativo *agg.* 1. scornful 2. (*gramm.*) pejorative. ♦ spregiativo *sm.* (*gramm.*) pejorative.

spregio *sm.* contempt.

spregiudicatamente *avv.* open-mindedly.

spregiudicatezza *sf.* open-mindedness.

spregiudicato *agg.* open-minded.

sprèmere *vt.* 1. to squeeze 2. (*torcere*) to wring (*v. irr.*) out. ♦ spremersi *vr.* to rack oneself.

spremilimoni *sm.* lemon-squeezer.

spremitura *sf.* 1. squeezing 2. (*di panni bagnati*) wringing.

spremuta *sf.* squash.

spremuto *agg.* 1. squeezed 2. (*di panni*) wrung.

spretare *vt.* to unfrock. ♦ spretarsi *vr.* to renounce one's priesthood.

spretato *agg.* unfrocked. ♦ **spretato** *sm.* unfrocked priest.

sprezzante *agg.* scornful.

sprezzare *vt.* V. *disprezzare.*

sprezzo *sm.* scorn.

sprigionamento *sm.* 1. exhalation 2. (*violento*) bursting out.

sprigionare *vt.* to emit. ♦ **sprigionarsi** *vr.* 1. to be emitted 2. (*con violenza*) to burst (*v. irr.*) out.

sprimacciare *vt.* to shake (*v. irr.*) up.

sprizzare *vt. e vi.* to spurt: — *scintille,* to spit (*v. irr.*) sparks; — *gioia,* to burst (*v. irr.*) with joy.

sprizzo *sm.* spurt.

sprofondamento *sm.* 1. sinking 2. (*crollo*) collapse.

sprofondare *vt.* (*far cadere*) to cause to collapse. ♦ **sprofondare** *vi.* 1. to sink (*v. irr.*) 2. (*crollare*) to collapse 3. (*fig.*) to be absorbed. ♦ **sprofondarsi** *vr.* 1. to sink 2. (*crollare*) to collapse 3. (*fig.*) to be absorbed.

sproloquio *sm.* long rigmarole.

spronare *vt.* to spur.

spronata *sf.* spurring.

sprone *sm.* 1. spur 2. (*mar.*) ram || *a spron battuto,* at full speed.

sproporzionato *agg.* disproportionate, out of proportion (*pred.*).

sproporzione *sf.* disproportion.

spropositato *agg.* 1. full of blunders 2. (*fig.*) enormous.

sproposito *sm.* 1. blunder 2. (*eccesso*) excess || *a —,* off the point.

sprovveduto *agg.* 1. (*incauto*) unwary 2. (*sprovvisto*) devoid 3. (*impreparato*) unprepared.

sprovvisto *agg.* devoid || *alla sprovvista,* unawares.

spruzzare *vt.* 1. to spray 2. (*inzaccherare*) to splash.

spruzzata *sf.* spray.

spruzzatore *sm.* sprayer.

spruzzatura *sf.* spraying.

spruzzo *sm.* 1. spray 2. (*di liquido sporco*) splash.

spudoratezza *sf.* shamelessness.

spudorato *agg.* shameless.

spugna *sf.* 1. sponge 2. (*tessuto*) sponge-cloth || *cancellare con la —,* to sponge; *bere come una —,* to drink (*v. irr.*) like a fish.

spugnatura *sf.* sponge down.

spugnosità *sf.* sponginess.

spugnoso *agg.* spongy.

spulciare *vt.* 1. to look for fleas (on) 2. (*esaminare; fig.*) to peruse 3. (*raccogliere; fig.*) to gather here and there.

spuma *sf.* foam.

spumante *agg.* foaming. ♦ **spumante** *sm.* sparkling wine.

spumare *vi.* to foam.

spumeggiante *agg.* foaming.

spumeggiare *vi.* to foam.

spumoso *agg.* foamy.

spuntare¹ *vt.* 1. (*smussare*) to blunt 2. (*tagliare*) to trim 3. (*staccare*) to unpin || *spuntarla,* to succeed. ♦ **spuntarsi** *vr.* 1. (*smussarsi*) to get (*v. irr.*) blunt 2. (*staccarsi*) to become (*v. irr.*) unpinned.

spuntare² *vi.* 1. (*sorgere*) to rise (*v. irr.*) 2. (*germogliare*) to sprout 3. (*di capelli*) to begin (*v. irr.*) to grow 4. (*apparire*) to appear.

spuntato *agg.* pointless.

spuntatura *sf.* 1. (*lo smussare*) blunting 2. (*il tagliare*) trimming.

spuntino *sm.* snack.

spunto *sm.* 1. cue 2. (*punto di partenza*) starting point.

spuntone *sm.* spike.

spurgare *vt.* 1. to clean 2. (*med.*) to discharge. ♦ **spurgarsi** *vr.* (*espettorare*) to expectorate.

spurgo *sm.* 1. (*lo spurgare*) discharging 2. (*l'espettorare*) expectorating 3. (*ciò che viene espulso*) discharge.

spurio *agg.* spurious.

sputacchiare *vt.* V. *sputare.*

sputacchiera *sf.* spittoon.

sputacchio *sm.* spittle.

sputare *vt.* to spit (*v. irr.*).

sputasentenze *sm.* wiseacre.

sputo *sm.* spit.

squadra *sf.* 1. (*da disegno*) square 2. (*gruppo; sport*) team 3. (*di operai*) gang 4. (*mil.*) squad 5. (*mar.*) squadron || *— mobile,* flying squad.

squadrare *vt.* 1. to square 2. (*guardare*) to look (so.) up and down.

squadratura *sf.* squaring.

squadriglia *sf.* squadron.

squadro *sm.* squaring.

squadrone *sm.* squadron.

squagliamento *sm.* melting.

squagliare *vt.* to melt. ♦ **squagliarsi** *vr.* 1. to melt 2. (*andar via*) to steal (*v. irr.*) away.

squalifica *sf.* disqualification.

squalificare vt. to disqualify.

squàllido agg. dreary.

squallore sm. dreariness.

squalo sm. shark.

squama sf. scale.

squamare vt. to scale. ◆ **squamarsi** vr. to scale.

squamoso agg. scaly.

squarciagola (nella loc. avv.) a —, at the top of one's voice.

squarciamento sm. tearing.

squarciare vt. 1. to tear (v. irr.) 2. (fig.) to dispel. ◆ **squarciarsi** vr. to be torn.

squarcio sm. gash.

squartare vt. to mangle.

squartatore sm. mangler.

squassare vt. to jolt.

squasso sm. jolt.

squattrinato agg. penniless.

squilibrare vt. to unbalance. ◆ **squilibrarsi** vr. to lose (v. irr.) one's balance.

squilibrato agg. unbalanced. ◆ **squilibrato** sm. lunatic.

squilibrio sm. 1. lack of balance 2. (mentale) derangement.

squillante agg. 1. shrill 2. (di trombe) blaring 3. (di campane) pealing.

squillare vi. 1. to ring (v. irr.) 2. (di trombe) to blare.

squillo sm. 1. ring 2. (di tromba) blare.

squinternare vt. 1. to ruin 2. (fig.) to upset (v. irr.).

squisitezza sf. exquisiteness.

squisito agg. exquisite.

squittìo sm. squeak.

squittire vi. to squeak.

sradicare vt. to uproot.

sragionare vi. to talk nonsense.

sregolatezza sf. disorderliness.

sregolato agg. disorderly.

stabbio sm. 1. sty 2. (letame) manure.

stàbile sm. building. ◆ **stàbile** agg. 1. stable 2. (permanente) permanent: in pianta —, on the permanent staff.

stabilimento sm. 1. (fabbrica) factory 2. (edificio, lo stabilire) establishment.

stabilire vt. 1. to establish 2. (decidere) to decide. ◆ **stabilirsi** vr. to settle.

stabilità sf. stability.

stabilizzare vt. to stabilize.

stabilizzatore sm. stabilizer.

stabilizzazione sf. stabilization.

stabilmente avv. firmly.

stacanovismo sm. Stakhanovism.

staccàbile agg. detachable.

staccare vt. 1. to take (v. irr.) off 2. (tagliare) to cut (v. irr.) off 3. (separare) to separate 4. (slegare) to unfasten ‖ — un assegno, to issue a cheque. ◆ **staccarsi** vr. 1. to come (v. irr.) off 2. (sciogliersi) to break (v. irr.) loose 3. (scostarsi) to move away 4. (separarsi) to part 5. (distaccarsi) to pull ahead (of) 6. (esser diverso) to differ.

stacciare vt. to sieve.

staccio sm. sieve.

staccionata sf. fence.

stacco sm. detachment.

stadera sf. steelyard.

stadio sm. 1. stadium (pl. -ia), sports ground 2. (fase) stage.

staffa sf. stirrup ‖ perder le staffe (fig.), to lose (v. irr.) one's self-control.

staffetta sf. 1. courier 2. (sport) relay race.

staffilare vt. to lash.

staffilata sf. lash.

staffile sm. whip.

stafilococco sm. staphylococcus (pl. -ci).

staggio sm. 1. (di scala) shaft 2. (di sedia) back leg.

stagionale agg. seasonal.

stagionare vt. to season.

stagionato agg. 1. seasoned 2. (fig.) oldish.

stagionatura sf. seasoning.

stagione sf. season.

stagnaio sm. tinsmith.

stagnante agg. stagnant.

stagnare[1] vi. to stagnate.

stagnare[2] vt. 1. to tin 2. (saldare) to solder 3. (impermeabilizzare) to waterproof 4. (fermare) to staunch.

stagnatura sf. tinning.

stagnino sm. tinker.

stagno[1] sm. tin.

stagno[2] sm. (bacino d'acqua) pond.

stagno[3] agg. water-tight.

stagnola sf. tin-foil.

staio sm. bushel.

stalagmite sf. stalagmite.

stalattite sf. stalactite.

stalla sf. stable.

stalliere sm. stable-boy.

stallo sm. stall.

stallone sm. stallion.

stamattina *avv.* this morning.
stambecco *sm.* ibex.
stamberga *sf.* hovel.
stambugio *sm.* hole.
stame *sm.* (*bot.*) stamen.
stamigna *sf.* bunting.
stampa *sf.* 1. print 2. (*atto di stampare*) printing 3. (*periodici, giornali*) press 4. (*genere*) stamp || *agenzia di* —, news-agency; *errore di* —, misprint.
stampare *vt.* 1. to print 2. (*mecc.*) to press 3. (*coniare*) to coin. ♦ **stamparsi** *vr.* — *in mente*, to impress (sthg.) firmly on one's mind.
stampatello *sm.* block letters (*pl.*).
stampato *sm.* 1. printed matter 2. (*modulo*) form.
stampatore *sm.* printer.
stampatrice *sf.* printing-press.
stampella *sf.* crutch.
stamperìa *sf.* printing-office.
stampigliare *vt.* to stamp.
stampo *sm.* 1. die, mould 2. (*genere*) stamp.
stanare *vt.* to drive (*v. irr.*) out.
stancare *vt.* 1. to tire 2. (*infastidire*) to annoy. ♦ **stancarsi** *vr.* 1. to get (*v. irr.*) tired 2. (*annoiarsi*) to get bored.
stanchezza *sf.* tiredness.
stanco *agg.* tired.
standardizzare *vt.* to standardize.
stanga *sf.* 1. bar 2. (*di carro*) shaft 3. (*di passaggio a livello*) barrier.
stangare *vt.* 1. to bar 2. (*percuotere*) to thrash.
stanghetta *sf.* 1. (*degli occhiali*) bar 2. (*di serratura*) bolt.
stanotte *avv.* tonight.
stantìo *agg.* stale.
stantuffo *sm.* 1. piston 2. (*di pompa ecc.*) plunger.
stanza *sf.* 1. room 2. (*strofa*) stanza || *prendere, avere* —, to settle.
stanziamento *sm.* appropriation.
stanziare *vt.* to appropriate. ♦ **stanziarsi** *vr.* to settle.
stappare *vt.* to uncork.
stare *vi.* 1. to stay 2. (*abitare*) to live 3. (*di salute, essere*) to be 4. (*in piedi*) to stand (*v. irr.*) 5. (*dipendere*) to depend (on) 6. (*spettare*) to be up 7. (*andare*) to go (*v. irr.*) 8. (*di abito*) to suit || — *per*, to be going (to); *lasciar* —, to leave (*v. irr.*) alone; *sta' a sentire!*, listen!; *ben ti sta!*, it

serves you right!
starnazzare *vi.* to flutter.
starnutire *vi.* to sneeze.
starnuto *sm.* sneeze.
stasare *vt.* to unclog.
stasera *avv.* this evening.
stasi *sf.* 1. standstill 2. (*med.*) stasis (*pl.* -ses).
statale *agg.* State (*attr.*), of the State. ♦ **statale** *s.* State employee.
stàtica *sf.* statics.
stàtico *agg.* static.
statista *sm.* statesman (*pl.* -men).
statìstica *sf.* statistics.
statizzare *vt.* to nationalize.
statizzazione *sf.* nationalization.
stato *sm.* 1. state, condition (*anche posizione sociale*) 2. (*giur.*) status 3. (*pol.*) State || *ufficio di* — *civile*, registry office; *ufficiale di* — *civile*, registrar.
statua *sf.* statue.
statuaria *sf.* statuary.
statuario *agg.* statuesque.
statuire *vt.* to decree.
statunitense *agg.* United States (*attr.*). ♦ **statunitense** *sm.* United States citizen.
statura *sf.* stature.
statuto *sm.* statute.
stazionamento *sm.* standing.
stazionare *vi.* 1. to stay 2. (*di vetture*) to be parked.
stazionario *agg.* stationary.
stazione *sf.* station.
stazza *sf.* tonnage.
stazzare *vt.* to have the tonnage of.
stecca *sf.* 1. (*di ombrello, ventaglio*) rib 2. (*da biliardo*) cue 3. (*di persiana*) slat 4. (*di busto*) whalebone 5. (*stonatura*) false note.
steccare *vt.* 1. (*chiudere con steccato*) to fence in 2. (*mus.*) to fluff. ♦ **steccare** *vi.* 1. (*cantando*) to sing (*v. irr.*) a false note 2. (*suonando*) to play a false note.
steccato *sm.* fence.
stecchito *agg.* 1. (*secco*) dried up 2. (*magro*) skinny 3. (*morto*) stone dead.
stecco *sm.* 1. stick 2. (*persona magra*) bag of bones.
stecconata *sf.* paling.
stele *sf.* stele (*pl.* -lae).
stella *sf.* star: — *marina*, starfish; *a forma di* —, starlike.
stellare *agg.* 1. stellar 2. (*a forma di stella*) star-shaped.
stellato *agg.* starry.

stelletta *sf.* **1.** (*tip.*) asterisk **2.** (*mil.*) star.

stelloncino *sm.* short paragraph.

stelo *sm.* stem.

stemma *sm.* coat-of-arms.

stemperare *vt.* **1.** to mix **2.** (*diluire*) to spin out. ♦ **stemperarsi** *vr.* to dissolve.

stempiarsi *vr.* to go (*v. irr.*) bald.

stendardo *sm.* standard.

stèndere *vt.* **1.** to spread (*v. irr.*) **2.** (*allungare*) to stretch **3.** (*scrivere*) to draw (*v. irr.*) up **4.** (*rilassare*) to relax || — *il bucato*, to hang (*v. irr.*) out the washing. ♦ **stèndersi** *vr.* **1.** to stretch **2.** (*adagiarsi*) to lie (*v. irr.*) down.

stenodattilografìa *sf.* shorthand and typewriting.

stenografare *vt.* to write (*v. irr.*) down in shorthand.

stenografìa *sf.* shorthand.

stenògrafo *sm.* shorthand-writer.

stentare *vi.* **1.** to have difficulty (in) **2.** (*mancare del necessario*) to be in need.

stentato *agg.* **1.** hard **2.** (*cresciuto a stento*) stunted.

stento *sm.* privation: *a* —, hardly, with difficulty.

stentòreo *agg.* stentorian.

steppa *sf.* steppe.

sterco *sm.* dung.

stereofonìa *sf.* stereophony.

stereofònico *agg.* stereophonic.

stereografìa *sf.* stereography.

stereogràfico *agg.* stereographic(al).

stereoscopìa *sf.* stereoscopy.

stereoscopio *sm.* stereoscope.

stereotipato *agg.* stereotyped.

stereotipìa *sf.* stereotyping.

stèrile *agg.* barren.

sterilità *sf.* barrenness.

sterilizzare *vt.* to sterilize.

sterilizzatore *agg.* sterilizing. ♦ **sterilizzatore** *sm.* sterilizer.

sterilizzazione *sf.* sterilization.

sterlina *sf.* pound.

sterminare *vt.* to exterminate.

sterminatezza *sf.* immensity.

sterminato *agg.* (*smisurato*) immense.

sterminatore *sm.* exterminator.

sterminio *sm.* extermination.

sterno *sm.* breast-bone.

sterpaglia *sf.* brushwood.

sterpo *sm.* dry twig.

sterrare *vt.* to dig (*v. irr.*) up.

sterratore *sm.* navvy.

sterzare *vt.* to steer.

sterzata *sf.* sudden turn.

sterzo *sm.* (*auto*) steering-gear.

stesso *agg.* **1.** (*medesimo*) same **2.** (*intensivo*) *se* —, oneself; *io, me* —, myself; *tu, te* —, yourself; *egli, lui* —, himself; *ella, lei stessa*, herself; *esso* —, itself; *noi stessi*, ourselves; *voi stessi*, yourselves; *loro stessi*, themselves **3.** (*proprio*) very. ♦ **stesso** *sm.* same. ♦ **stesso** *avv.* all the same

stesura *sf.* **1.** (*redazione*) draft **2.** (*di contratto*) drawing up.

stetoscopio *sm.* stethoscope.

stigmate *sf. pl.* **1.** stigmata (*pl.*) **2.** (*marchio*) brand (*sing.*).

stigmatizzare *vt.* to stigmatize.

stilare *vt.* to draw (*v. irr.*) up.

stile *sm.* style: *aver* —, to be stylish; *con* —, stylishly.

stilettata *sf.* stab.

stilista *s.* stylist.

stilìstica *sf.* stylistics.

stilizzare *vt.* to stylize.

stilizzazione *sf.* stylization.

stilla *sf.* drop.

stillare *vi. e vt.* to ooze. ♦ **stillarsi** *vr.* — *il cervello*, to rack one's brain.

stiliicidio *sm.* dripping.

stilo *sm.* stylus.

stilogràfica *sf.* fountainpen.

stilogràfico *agg.* stylographic(al).

stima *sf.* **1.** (*valutazione*) estimate **2.** (*buona opinione*) esteem.

stimàbile *agg.* estimable.

stimare *vt.* **1.** (*valutare*) to estimate **2.** (*tenere in considerazione*) to esteem **3.** (*ritenere*) to consider.

stimatore *sm.* estimator.

stimolante *agg.* stimulating. ♦ **stimolante** *sm.* stimulant.

stimolare *vt.* to stimulate.

stimolo *sm.* **1.** stimulus (*pl.* -li) **2.** (*pungolo*) goad.

stinco *sm.* shin.

stìngere *vt.* to fade. ♦ **stìngersi** *vr.* to fade.

stinto *agg.* faded.

stipare *vt.* to cram.

stipato *agg.* crammed (with).

stipendiare *vt.* to pay (*v. irr.*) a salary (to so.).

stipendio *sm.* salary.

stìpite *sm.* jamb.

stipulante *agg.* stipulating. ♦ **stipulante** *s.* stipulator.

stipulare *vt.* to stipulate.

stipulazione *sf.* stipulation.
stiracchiare *vt.* 1. to stretch 2. (*distorcere*) to twist.
stiracchiato *agg.* (*fig.*) forced.
stiramento *sm.* 1. stretching 2. (*muscolare*) strain.
stirare *vt.* 1. to stretch 2. (*col ferro da stiro*) to iron.
stiratura *sf.* ironing.
stirerìa *sf.* (*e tintoria*) laundry shop.
stirpe *sf.* 1. stock 2. (*progenie*) issue.
stitichezza *sf.* constipation.
stìtico *agg.* constipated.
stiva *sf.* hold.
stivale *sm.* boot.
stivaletto *sm.* ankle-boot.
stizza *sf.* anger.
stizzire *vt.* to vex. ♦ **stizzirsi** *vr.* to get (*v. irr.*) cross.
stizzito *agg.* cross.
stizzoso *agg.* peevish.
stoccata *sf.* thrust: *lanciare una —* (*fig.*), to gibe (at).
stoffa *sf.* 1. cloth 2. (*fig.*) stuff.
stoicismo *sm.* stoicism.
stòico *agg.* e *sm.* stoic.
stoino *sm.* door-mat.
stola *sf.* stole.
stolidità *sf.* stolidity.
stòlido *agg.* stolid.
stoltezza *sf.* foolishness.
stolto *agg.* foolish. ♦ **stolto** *sm.* fool.
stomacare *vt.* to sicken. ♦ **stomacarsi** *vr.* to sicken.
stomachévole *agg.* sickening.
stòmaco *sm.* stomach: *dare di —*, to vomit; *restare sullo —*, to lie (*v. irr.*) on one's stomach.
stomatite *sf.* stomatitis.
stomatologìa *sf.* stomatology.
stonare *vi.* 1. to be out of tune 2. (*fig.*) to be out of place 3. (*di colori*) to clash. ♦ **stonare** *vt.* to upset (*v. irr.*).
stonato *agg.* 1. out of tune 2. (*fig.*) out of place 3. (*turbato*) upset 4. (*di nota*) false.
stonatura *sf.* false note.
stoppa *sf.* tow.
stoppaccio *sm.* wad.
stoppare *vt.* 1. to plug 2. (*sport*) to stop.
stoppia *sf.* stubble.
stoppino *sm.* wick.
stopposo *agg.* 1. towy 2. (*di carne*) stringy.

stòrcere *vt.* 1. to twist 2. (*un'articolazione*) to sprain || *— gli occhi*, to roll one's eyes. ♦ **stòrcersi** *vr.* 1. to twist 2. (*lussarsi, slogarsi*) to wrench.
stordimento *sm.* 1. dizziness 2. (*meraviglia*) bewilderment.
stordire *vt.* 1. to stun 2. (*di alcoolici*) to dull 3. (*assordare*) to deafen 4. (*innervosire*) to drive (*v. irr.*) crazy. ♦ **stordirsi** *vr.* to dull one's senses.
stordito *agg.* 1. (*sbalordito*) bewildered 2. (*sbadato*) heedless 3. (*sciocco*) foolish.
storia *sf.* 1. history 2. (*racconto*) story.
storicismo *sm.* historical method.
storicità *sf.* historicity.
stòrico *agg.* historical. ♦ **stòrico** *sm.* historian.
storiografìa *sf.* historiography.
storiògrafo *sm.* historiographer.
stormire *vi.* to rustle.
stormo *sm.* 1. flight 2. (*folla*) crowd || *suonare a —*, to ring (*v. irr.*) the tocsin.
stornare *vt.* to divert.
stornello[1] *sm.* ditty.
stornello[2] *sm.* (*zool.*) starling.
storno[1] *agg.* dapple-grey.
storno[2] *sm.* (*zool.*) starling.
storno[3] *sm.* (*comm.*) transfer.
storpiare *vt.* 1. to cripple 2. (*rovinare*) to mangle.
storpiatura *sf.* 1. crippling 2. (*fig.*) mangling 3. (*cosa malfatta*) botch.
storpio *sm.* cripple.
storta *sf.* 1. twist 2. (*in una articolazione*) sprain 3. (*chim.*) retort.
storto *agg.* 1. twisted 2. (*piegato*) crooked 3. (*di occhi*) squinting 4. (*sbagliato*) wrong.
stortura *sf.* 1. deformity 2. (*errore*) mistake.
stoviglie *sf. pl.* kitchenware (*sing.*).
stràbico *agg.* squinting. ♦ **stràbico** *sm.* squinter.
strabiliante *agg.* amazing.
strabiliare *vt.* to amaze (*anche far strabiliare*). ♦ **strabiliare** *vi.* to be amazed. ♦ **strabiliarsi** *vr.* to be amazed.
strabismo *sm.* squint.
straboccare *vi.* 1. to overflow 2. (*fig.*) to abound (in).
strabocchévole *agg.* overflowing.
strabuzzare *vt.* *— gli occhi*, to roll one's eyes.

stracàrico agg. overloaded (with).

stracciare vt. to tear (v. irr.). ♦ **stracciarsi** vr. to tear.

stracciato agg. 1. torn 2. (di persona) in rags.

straccio agg. torn, in rags || carta straccia, waste paper. ♦ **straccio** sm. rag: — per la polvere, duster.

straccione sm. ragamuffin.

straccivéndolo sm. rag-and-bone-man (pl. -men).

stracotto agg. overdone. ♦ **stracotto** sm. stew.

strada sf. 1. road 2. (di città) street 3. (percorso; fig.) way || — a senso unico, one-way street; — ferrata, railway; — maestra, main road.

stradale agg. road (attr.), of the road: fondo —, road-bed.

stradino sm. roadman (pl. -men).

strafalcione sm. blunder.

strafare vi. to overdo (v. irr.).

strafottente agg. 1. (noncurante) unconcerned 2. (arrogante) arrogant.

strage sf. 1. slaughter 2. (distruzione) destruction || fare una —, to slaughter.

stragrande agg. enormous.

stralciare vt. 1. (comm.) to remove 2. (fig.) to take (v. irr.) off.

stralcio sm. 1. removal 2. (estratto) extract.

strale sm. dart.

stralunare vt. — gli occhi, to roll one's eyes, to open one's eyes wide.

stralunato agg. 1. (di occhi) rolling, wild-eyed 2. (di persona) upset.

stramazzare vi. to fall (v. irr.) heavily.

stramberìa sf. oddity.

strambo agg. odd.

strame sm. litter.

strampalato agg. queer.

stranezza sf. oddity.

strangolamento sm. strangling.

strangolare vt. to strangle.

strangolatore sm. strangler.

straniero agg. foreign. ♦ **straniero** sm. foreigner.

strano agg. strange.

straordinario agg. extraordinary.

strapazzare vt. 1. to ill-use 2. (sgridare) to scold 3. (far lavorare troppo) to overwork 4. (di uova) to scramble. ♦ **strapazzarsi** vr. to overwork oneself.

strapazzata sf. 1. scolding 2. (fatica) overwork.

strapazzo sm. overwork: abiti da —, working-clothes; scrittore da —, hack.

strapieno agg. full up.

strapiombare vi. 1. to lean (v. irr.) 2. (scendere a precipizio) to fall (v. irr.) perpendicularly.

strapiombo sm. precipice: a —, sheer.

strapotente agg. very powerful.

strappare vt. 1. (lacerare) to tear (v. irr.) 2. (togliere) to snatch 3. (estirpare) to pull up 4. (un dente) to pull out 5. (estorcere) to wring (v. irr.). ♦ **strapparsi** vr. (lacerarsi) to tear.

strappo sm. 1. tear 2. (strappata) pull 3. (infrazione) breach || — muscolare, sprain.

strapuntino sm. folding seat.

straricco agg. immensely rich.

straripamento sm. overflowing.

straripare vi. to overflow.

strascicare vt. 1. to drag 2. (i piedi) to shuffle 3. (le parole) to drawl.

stràscico sm. 1. train 2. (residuo) after-effect 3. (rete) trawl.

strascinare vt. V. trascinare.

stratagemma sm. stratagem.

stratega sm. strategist.

strategìa sf. strategy.

stratègico agg. strategic(al).

stratificare vt. to stratify.

stratificazione sf. stratification.

strato sm. 1. layer 2. (di rivestimento) coat 3. (della società) class.

stratosfera sf. stratosphere.

stratosfèrico agg. stratospheric(al).

strattone sm. 1. pull 2. (sobbalzo) jerk || a strattoni, jerkily; (a intervalli) by fits and starts.

stravagante agg. odd, queer.

stravaganza sf. oddity.

stravecchio agg. very old.

stravedere vi. to see (v. irr.) badly: — per qu., to be crazy about so.

stravincere vt. to crush. ♦ **stravincere** vi. to win (v. irr.) all along the line.

stravizio sm. excess.

stravòlgere vt. 1. to twist 2. (gli occhi) to roll.

stravolto agg. 1. (turbato) upset 2. (di occhi) rolling.

straziante agg. tormenting, heart-rending (solo fig.).

straziare vt. to tear (v. irr.).
strazio sm. torment: far — di, to play havoc with.
strega sf. witch.
stregare vt. to bewitch.
stregone sm. wizard.
stregoneria sf. witchcraft.
stremare vt. to exhaust.
stremo sm. extreme.
strenna sf. gift.
strenuo agg. brave.
strepitare vi. to shout.
strèpito sm. din, uproar.
strepitoso agg. uproarious: successo —, striking success.
streptococco sm. streptococcus (pl. -ci).
streptomicina sf. streptomycin.
stretta sf. 1. grasp 2. (calca) press 3. (gola) gorge || — di mano, handshake; essere alle strette, to be in dire straits; mettere alle strette qu., to put (v. irr.) so. with his back against the wall.
strettezza sf. 1. narrowness 2. (povertà) financial difficulty.
stretto agg. 1. narrow 2. (serrato, piccolo) tight 3. (rigoroso) strict 4. (pigiato) packed. ♦ **stretto** sm. strait.
strettoia sf. narrow passage.
stria sf. streak.
striare vt. to streak.
stricnina sf. strychnine.
stridente agg. 1. shrill 2. (discordante) jarring.
stridere vi. 1. to creak 2. (di insetti) to chirp 3. (contrastare) to jar.
stridìo sm. 1. creaking 2. (di insetti) chirping.
strido sm. 1. scream 2. (di animale) screech.
stridulo agg. shrill.
striglia sf. curry-comb.
strigliare vt. 1. to curry 2. (fig.) to rebuke.
strillare vi. to scream.
strillo sm. scream.
strillone sm. newsboy.
striminzito agg. 1. stunted 2. (di persona) thin.
strimpellare vt. 1. (di violino) to scrape 2. (di pianoforte) to strum.
strinare vt. to singe.
stringa sf. lace.
stringare vt. 1. to lace tightly 2. (fig.) to condense.
stringato agg. 1. laced 2. (fig.) concise.

stringente agg. 1. (urgente) urgent 2. (convincente) persuasive.
stringere vt. 1. to press 2. (restringere, avvitare) to tighten 3. (abbracciare) to clasp 4. (impugnare) to grasp 5. (fare) to make (v. irr.) || — la mano a, to shake (v. irr.) hands with; — i pugni, to clench one's fists; stringi stringi, in conclusion. ♦ **stringere** vi. to be tight. ♦ **stringersi** vr. 1. to press (against) 2. (far spazio) to squeeze up || — nelle spalle, to shrug one's shoulders.
stringimento sm. 1. pressing 2. (restringimento, legamento, avvitamento) tightening 3. (l'impugnare) clasp 4. (fitta) pang.
striscia sf. 1. strip 2. (riga) stripe 3. (scia) trail || a strisce, striped.
strisciante agg. 1. creeping 2. (servile) fawning.
strisciare vi. 1. to creep (v. irr.) 2. (fig.) to grovel. ♦ **strisciare** vt. 1. to drag 2. (i piedi) to shuffle 3. (radere) to graze 4. (fig.) to fawn (on).
stritolamento sm. crushing.
stritolare vt. to crush.
strizzare vt. 1. to squeeze 2. (torcere) to wring (v. irr.) || — l'occhio, to wink (at so.).
strizzata sf. 1. squeeze 2. (il torcere) wring.
strofa sf. stanza.
strofinaccio sm. 1. duster 2. (per asciugare) towel.
strofinamento sm. rubbing.
strofinare vt. to rub.
strombatura sf. splay.
strombazzare vt. e vi. to trumpet.
strombettare vi. 1. to blow (v. irr.) a trumpet 2. (auto) to honk.
stroncare vt. 1. to break (v. irr.) off 2. (fig.) to demolish.
stroncatura sf. harsh criticism.
stronzio sm. strontium.
stropicciare vt. 1. to rub 2. (i piedi) to shuffle 3. (sgualcire) to crease. ♦ **stropicciarsi** vr. 1. (gli occhi) to rub oneself 2. (sgualcirsi) to crease.
stropiccìo sm. — di piedi, shuffling.
strozzare vt. 1. to strangle 2. (ostruire) to obstruct 3. (fig.) to choke.
strozzato agg. 1. strangled 2. (soffocato) choked 3. (con strozzature) with narrow passages 4. (med.)

strangulated **5.** (*ostruito*) obstructed.

strozzatura *sf.* **1.** strangling **2.** (*il soffocare*) choking **3.** (*ostruzione*) obstruction **4.** (*restringimento*) narrow passage **5.** (*med.*) strangulation.

strozzinaggio *sm.* usury.

strozzino *sm.* usurer.

struggente *agg.* pining.

strùggere *vt.* **1.** to melt **2.** (*fig.*) to wear (*v. irr.*) out. ♦ **strùggersi** *vr.* **1.** to melt **2.** (*affliggersi*) to be distressed **3.** (*languire*) to be consumed (with), to pine (for).

struggimento *sm.* longing.

strumentale *agg.* instrumental.

strumentalismo *sm.* instrumentalism.

strumentare *vt.* to instrument.

strumentazione *sf.* instrumentation.

strumento *sm.* instrument.

strusciare *vt.* **1.** to rub **2.** (*adulare*) to fawn (on). ♦ **strusciarsi** *vr.* to rub (oneself).

strutto *sm.* lard.

struttura *sf.* structure.

strutturale *agg.* structural.

strutturare *vt.* to structure.

strutturazione *sf.* structure.

struzzo *sm.* ostrich.

stuccare[1] *vt.* **1.** to stucco **2.** (*turare*) to fill.

stuccare[2] *vt.* **1.** (*nauseare*) to sicken **2.** (*annoiare*) to bore. ♦ **stuccarsi** *vr.* **1.** to get (*v. irr.*) sick **2.** (*annoiarsi*) to get bored.

stuccatura *sf.* **1.** plastering **2.** (*di dente*) filling.

stucchévole *agg.* **1.** filling **2.** (*nauseante*) sickening **3.** (*noioso*) boring.

stucco *sm.* **1.** stucco **2.** (*per vetri*) putty || *restare di —,* to be nonplussed.

studente *sm.* student.

studentesco *agg.* student (*attr.*).

studiacchiare *vt.* to study fitfully.

studiare *vt.* to study. ♦ **studiarsi** *vr.* to try.

studiato *agg.* (*affettato*) affected.

studio *sm.* **1.** study **2.** (*progetto*) plan **3.** (*cine*) studio || *programma di studi,* curriculum; *essere allo —,* to be under consideration.

studioso *agg.* studious. ♦ **studioso** *sm.* scholar.

stufa *sf.* stove.

stufare *vt.* **1.** to stew **2.** (*fig.*) to bore. ♦ **stufarsi** *vr.* to get (*v. irr.*) bored.

stufato *sm.* stew.

stufo *agg.* fed up (with).

stuoia *sf.* mat.

stuolo *sm.* crowd.

stupefacente *agg.* stupefying. ♦ **stupefacente** *sm.* drug.

stupefare *vt.* to stupefy. ♦ **stupefarsi** *vr.* to be stupefied.

stupefazione *sf.* stupefaction.

stupendamente *avv.* wonderfully.

stupendo *agg.* wonderful.

stupidàggine *sf.* stupidity.

stupidità *sf.* stupidity.

stùpido *agg. e sm.* stupid.

stupire *vt.* to astonish. ♦ **stupirsi** *vr.* to be astonished.

stupito *agg.* astonished.

stupore *sm.* astonishment.

stupro *sm.* rape.

sturare *vt.* **1.** to uncork **2.** (*botti*) to unbung.

stuzzicadenti *sm.* tooth-pick.

stuzzicare *vt.* **1.** to prod **2.** (*frugare*) to pick **3.** (*molestare*) to tease **4.** (*stimolare*) to whet.

su *prep.* **1.** on **2.** (*senza contatto; rivestimento*) over **3.** (*al di sopra di*) above **4.** (*circa*) about || *nove volte — dieci,* nine times out of ten. ♦ **su** *avv.* **1.** up **2.** (*al piano superiore*) upstairs **3.** (*indosso*) on || *— per giù,* more or less; *in — (in avanti),* onwards; *più —,* further up; *—, andiamo!,* come on!

sua *agg. e pron.* V. *suo.*

suadente *agg.* persuasive.

subàcqueo *agg.* underwater (*attr.*). ♦ **subàcqueo** *sm.* frogman (*pl. -men*).

subaffittare *vt.* to sublease.

subaffitto *sm.* sublease.

subalpino *agg.* subalpine.

subalterno *agg. e sm.* subaltern.

subbuglio *sm.* **1.** turmoil **2.** (*disordine*) mess.

subconscio *sm.* subconscious.

subcosciente *agg. e sm.* subconscious.

subdolamente *avv.* underhand.

sùbdolo *agg.* sly.

subentrare *vi.* to take (*v. irr.*) the place (of).

subire *vt.* to undergo (*v. irr.*).

subissare *vt.* **1.** (*sprofondare*) to sink (*v. irr.*) **2.** (*fig.*) to overwhelm.

subisso sm. (gran quantità) shower.
subitaneità sf. suddenness.
subitàneo agg. sudden.
sùbito avv. 1. at once 2. (presto) soon || — prima, just before; — dopo, just after.
sublimare vt. to sublimate.
sublimato sm. sublimate.
sublimazione sf. sublimation.
sublime agg. e sm. sublime.
sublimità sf. sublimity.
sublocazione sf. subletting.
sublunare agg. sublunar.
subodorare vt. to suspect.
subordinare vt. to subordinate.
subordinata sf. subordinate clause.
subordinato agg. e sm. subordinate.
subordinazione sf. subordination.
subornare vt. to suborn.
subornazione sf. subornation.
substrato sm. substratum (pl. -ta).
suburbano agg. suburban.
suburbio sm. suburb.
succèdere vi. 1. to succeed 2. (capitare) to happen. ♦ **succèdersi** vr. to follow one another.
successione sf. succession.
successivamente avv. afterwards.
successo sm. 1. success 2. (esito) outcome || aver —, to be successful.
successore sm. successor.
succhiare vt. to suck.
succhiata sf. suck.
succhiello sm. gimlet.
succinto agg. 1. (di abiti) scanty 2. (conciso) concise.
succo sm. 1. juice 2. (fig.) pith.
succosità sf. 1. juiciness 2. (fig.) pithiness.
succoso agg. 1. juicy 2. (fig.) pithy.
sùccubo agg. entirely dominated (by).
succulento agg. 1. juicy 2. (gustoso) rich.
succursale sf. branch.
sud sm. south: del —, southern, south (attr.); verso —, southwards.
sudare vi. to sweat: — sette camicie, to toil hard; — freddo, to be in a cold sweat.
sudario sm. shroud.
sudata sf. sweat.
sudaticcio agg. clammy.
sudato agg. 1. sweaty 2. (fig.) hard-earned.
suddetto agg. above-mentioned.

suddiàcono sm. subdeacon.
sudditanza sf. subjection.
sùddito sm. subject.
suddivìdere vt. to subdivide.
suddivisione sf. subdivision.
sùdicio agg. dirty.
sudicione sm. dirty fellow.
sudiciume sm. dirt.
sudore sm. 1. sweat 2. (fig.) toil.
sudorìfero agg. 1. (che secerne sudore) sudoriferous 2. (che produce sudore) sudorific.
sue agg. e pron. V. suo.
sufficiente agg. 1. sufficient 2. (altezzoso) conceited 2. (voto sufficiente) pass mark.
sufficienza sf. 1. sufficiency 2. (alterigia) conceit 3. (voto sufficiente) pass mark || aria di —, superior air; a —, enough.
suffisso sm. suffix.
suffragare vt. 1. to support 2. (eccl.) to pray for.
suffragio sm. 1. suffrage 2. (approvazione) approval.
suggellare vt. to seal.
suggello sm. seal.
suggerimento sm. 1. suggestion 2. (teat.) prompting.
suggerire vt. 1. to suggest 2. (dar l'imbeccata; teat.) to prompt.
suggeritore sm. prompter.
suggestionàbile agg. impressionable.
suggestionabilità sf. impressionability.
suggestionare vt. to influence. ♦ **suggestionarsi** vr. to will oneself (to do sthg.), to be influenced.
suggestione sf. suggestion.
suggestività sf. suggestiveness.
suggestivamente avv. evocatively.
suggestivo agg. evocative.
sùghero sm. 1. cork 2. (albero) cork-tree.
sugna sf. pork fat.
sugo sm. 1. juice 2. (di carne) gravy 3. (di pomodoro) sauce 4. (fig.) gist.
sugosità sf. V. succosità.
sugoso agg. V. succoso.
suicida agg. suicidal. ♦ **suicida** s. suicide.
suicidarsi vr. to commit suicide.
suicidio sm. suicide.
suino agg. swine (attr.) || carne suina, pork. ♦ **suino** sm. swine (pl. invariato).
sulfamìdico sm. sulphonamide.

sulfùreo *agg.* sulphureous.
sultanato *sm.* sultanate.
sultanina *sf.* sultana.
sultano *sm.* sultan.
summenzionato *agg.* aforesaid.
sunto *sm.* summary.
suo *agg.* **1.** (*di lui*) his **2.** (*di lei*) her **3.** (*di esso*) its **4.** (*formula di cortesia*) your. ♦ **suo** *pron.* **1.** (*di lui*) his **2.** (*di lei*) hers **3.** (*di esso*) its **4.** (*formula di cortesia*) yours || *i suoi* (*famigliari*), his, her family.
suòcera *sf.* mother-in-law.
suòcero *sm.* father-in-law.
suoi *agg.* e *pron.* V. *suo.*
suola *sf.* sole.
suolo *sm.* soil, ground.
suonare *vt.* V. *sonare.*
suono *sm.* sound.
suora *sf.* nun, sister.
superàbile *agg.* surmountable.
superaffollato *agg.* overcrowded.
superalimentare *vt.* **1.** to overrish **2.** (*mecc.*) to overcharge.
superalimentazione *sf.* **1.** overfeeding **2.** (*mecc.*) overcharging.
superamento *sm.* **1.** overcoming **2.** (*auto*) overtaking.
superare *vt.* **1.** (*oltrepassare*) to exceed **2.** (*auto*) to overtake (*v. irr.*) **3.** (*attraversare*) to cross **4.** (*vincere*) to overcome (*v. irr.*) **5.** (*una persona*) to surpass **6.** (*un esame, una prova*) to pass.
superbia *sf.* pride.
superbo *agg.* **1.** proud **2.** (*magnifico*) superb.
superdotato *agg.* highly gifted.
superficiale *agg.* superficial.
superficialità *sf.* superficiality.
superficie *sf.* **1.** surface **2.** (*area*) area.
superfluo *agg.* superfluous. ♦ **superfluo** *sm.* surplus.
superiora *sf.* Mother Superior.
superiore *agg.* **1.** superior **2.** (*sovrastante*) upper **3.** (*più avanzato*) advanced. ♦ **superiore** *sm.* superior.
superiorità *sf.* superiority.
superlativo *agg.* e *sm.* superlative.
supermercato *sm.* supermarket.
supernutrizione *sf.* overfeeding.
supersònico *agg.* supersonic.
supèrstite *agg.* surviving. ♦ **supèrstite** *s.* survivor.
superstizione *sf.* superstition.
superstizioso *agg.* superstitious.

superuomo *sm.* superman (*pl.* -men).
supervisione *sf.* supervision.
supervisore *sm.* supervisor.
supinamente *avv.* supinely.
supino *agg.* supine.
suppellèttile *sf.* furnishings (*pl.*).
supplementare *agg.* supplementary.
supplemento *sm.* **1.** supplement **2.** (*spesa supplementare*) additional charge **3.** (*di biglietto ferroviario*) excess fare.
supplente *agg.* temporary. ♦ **supplente** *s.* temporary teacher.
supplenza *sf.* temporary post.
suppletivo *agg.* supplementary.
sùpplica *sf.* **1.** entreaty **2.** (*petizione*) petition.
supplicante *agg.* e *s.* suppliant.
supplicare *vt.* to entreat.
supplichévole *agg.* entreating.
supplire *vi.* **1.** (*compensare*) to make (*v. irr.*) up (for) **2.** (*sostituire*) to substitute (for). ♦ **supplire** *vt.* to take (*v. irr.*) the place of.
supplizio *sm.* torment: *andare al* —, to go (*v. irr.*) to the scaffold.
supporre *vt.* to suppose.
supporto *sm.* support.
supposizione *sf.* supposition.
supposta *sf.* suppository.
supposto che *cong.* suppose (that).
suppurare *vi.* to suppurate.
suppurazione *sf.* suppuration.
supremazìa *sf.* supremacy.
supremo *agg.* supreme: *Comando* — (*mil.*), headquarters (*pl.*).
surclassare *vt.* to outclass.
surgelare *vt.* to deep-freeze (*v. irr.*).
surrealismo *sm.* surrealism.
surrealista *agg.* e *s.* surrealist.
surrealìstico *agg.* surrealistic.
surrenale *agg.* suprarenal.
surrettizio *agg.* surreptitious.
surriscaldamento *sm.* overheating.
surriscaldare *vt.* to overheat. ♦ **surriscaldarsi** *vr.* to get (*v. irr.*) overheated.
surrogàbile *agg.* replaceable.
surrogare *vt.* to replace.
surrogato *sm.* substitute.
surrogazione *sf.* (*giur.*) surrogation.
suscettìbile *agg.* **1.** susceptible **2.** (*permaloso*) touchy.
suscettibilità *sf.* **1.** susceptibility **2.** (*permalosità*) touchiness || *urtare la* — *di qu.*, to hurt (*v. irr.*) so.'s feelings.

suscitare vt. 1. to provoke 2. (eccitare) to stir up.
suscitatore sm. provoker.
susina sf. plum.
susino sm. plum-tree.
susseguente agg. following.
susseguire vi. to follow.
sussidiare vt. 1. to support 2. (di
governo) to subsidize.
sussidiario agg. subsidiary.
sussidio sm. subsidy.
sussiego sm. haughtiness.
sussistenza sf. 1. existence 2. (sostentamento) subsistence 3. (mil.)
Catering Corps.
sussistere vi. 1. to subsist 2. (reggere) to hold (v. irr.) water.
sussultare vi. 1. to start 2. (di cose) to shake (v. irr.).
sussulto sm. start.
sussurrare vt. e vi. 1. to whisper
2. (criticare) to murmur.
sussurro sm. whisper.
sutura sf. suture.
suturare vt. to suture.
svagare vt. 1. to divert 2. (divertire) to amuse. ♦ **svagarsi** vr. 1.
to divert one's mind 2. (divertirsi)
to amuse oneself.
svagatezza sf. absent-mindedness.
svagato agg. absent-minded.
svago sm. amusement.
svaligiamento sm. 1. robbery 2. (di
una casa) burglary.
svaligiare vt. 1. to rob 2. (una casa) to burgle.
svaligiatore sm. 1. robber 2. (di
case) burglar.
svalutare vt. 1. to devaluate 2. (sottovalutare) to undervalue.
svalutazione sf. devaluation.
svanire vi. 1. to disappear 2. (dileguarsi, di luce ecc.) to fade.
svanito agg. 1. (dileguato) vanished
2. (di mente) feeble-minded.
svantaggio sm. disadvantage.
svantaggioso agg. disadvantageous.
svaporamento sm. evaporation.
svaporare vi. to evaporate.
svariare vt. to vary.
svariato agg. various.
svarione sm. blunder.
svasare vt. (mecc.) to flare.
svasato agg. (di abito) bell-shaped.
svasatura sf. 1. (di abito) bell-
-shaping 2. (mecc.; lo svasare) flar-
ing 3. (apertura) countersink.
svàstica sf. swastika.
svecchiamento sm. renewal.

svecchiare vt. to renew.
svedese agg. Swedish. ♦ **svedese**
sm. Swede.
sveglia sf. 1. early call 2. (orologio)
alarm clock 3. (mil.) reveille.
svegliare vt. to wake (v. irr.) (up).
♦ **svegliarsi** vr. to wake (up).
sveglio agg. 1. awake (pred.) 2. (fig.)
quick-witted.
svelare vt. 1. to reveal, to disclose
2. (togliere il velo) to unveil.
svelenire vt. (fig.) to remove the
sting from.
svèllere vt. to extirpate.
sveltezza sf. quickness.
sveltire vt. 1. to quicken 2. (scal-
trire) to wake (v. irr.) up || — la
figura, to slim. ♦ **sveltirsi** vr.
1. to become (v. irr.) quick(er) 2.
(scaltrirsi) to wake up.
svelto agg. 1. quick 2. (slanciato)
slender 3. (intelligente) smart. ♦
svelto avv. fast || —!, hurry up!
svenare vt. to open so.'s veins. ♦
svenarsi vr. to cut (v. irr.) one's
veins.
svéndere vt. to undersell (v. irr.).
svéndita sf. (clearance) sale.
svenévole agg. maudlin.
svenimento sm. faint.
svenire vi. to faint.
sventagliare vt. to fan.
sventare vt. to baffle.
sventatezza sf. 1. thoughtlessness
2. (atto sventato) thoughtless action.
sventato agg. (sbadato) thoughtless.
♦ **sventato** sm. scatter-brain.
svèntola sf. (schiaffo) slap.
sventolare vt. e vi. to wave. ♦
sventolarsi vr. to fan oneself.
sventolìo sm. waving.
sventramento sm. 1. disembowelment 2. (demolizione) demolition.
sventrare vt. 1. to disembowel 2.
(demolire) to demolish.
sventura sf. misfortune: per —,
unluckily; per colmo di —, to
crown it all.
sventuratamente avv. unfortunately.
sventurato agg. unfortunate.
svenuto agg. unconscious.
svergognare vt. to shame.
svergognatamente avv. shamelessly.
svergognato agg. shameless.
svernamento sm. wintering.
svernare vi. to winter.

svestire *vt.* to undress. ♦ **svestirsi** *vr.* to undress.

svettare *vt.* to lop. ♦ **svettare** *vi.* to stand (*v. irr.*) out.

svezzamento *sm.* weaning.

svezzare *vt.* to wean.

sviamento *sm.* **1.** diversion **2.** (*il traviare*) leading astray **3.** (*il traviarsi*) going astray.

sviare *vt.* **1.** to divert **2.** (*traviare*) to lead (*v. irr.*) astray. ♦ **sviarsi** *vr.* **1.** to be diverted **2.** (*traviarsi*) to go (*v. irr.*) astray.

sviato *agg.* led astray (*pred.*).

svignàrsela *vr.* to slink (*v. irr.*) away.

svigorire *vt.* to weaken. ♦ **svigorirsi** *vr.* to grow (*v. irr.*) weak.

svilimento *sm.* depreciation.

svilire *vt.* to depreciate.

sviluppare *vt.* **1.** to develop **2.** (*sciogliere*) to loosen **3.** (*sprigionare*) to generate. ♦ **svilupparsi** *vr.* to develop.

sviluppatore *sm.* (*foto*) developer.

sviluppo *sm.* **1.** development **2.** (*sprigionamento*) generation.

svincolamento *sm.* **1.** release **2.** (*doganale*) clearance **3.** (*riscatto*) redemption.

svincolare *vt.* **1.** to release **2.** (*sdoganare*) to clear **3.** (*riscattare*) to redeem. ♦ **svincolarsi** *vr.* to get (*v. irr.*) free.

svisare *vt.* (*travisare*) to twist.

sviscerare *vt.* **1.** to disembowel **2.** (*fig.*) to dissect.

sviscerato *agg.* passionate.

svista *sf.* oversight.

svitare *vt.* to unscrew.

svìzzero *agg.* e *sm.* Swiss.

svogliatezza *sf.* **1.** unwillingness **2.** (*pigrizia*) laziness.

svogliato *agg.* **1.** unwilling **2.** (*pigro*) lazy. ♦ **svogliato** *sm.* lazy-bones.

svolazzare *vi.* to flutter.

svolazzo *sm.* **1.** fluttering **2.** (*tratto di penna*) flourish.

svòlgere *vt.* **1.** to unwind (*v. irr.*) **2.** (*trattare*) to develop **3.** (*mettere in opera*) to carry out. ♦ **svòlgersi** *vr.* **1.** to unwind **2.** (*svilupparsi*) to develop **3.** (*accadere*) to take (*v. irr.*) place.

svolgimento *sm.* **1.** unwinding **2.** (*trattazione*) treatment **3.** (*corso*) course **4.** (*sviluppo*) development.

svolta *sf.* **1.** turn **2.** (*fig.*) turning

point || *fare una* —, to turn.

svoltare *vi.* to turn.

svuotamento *sm.* emptying.

svuotare *vt.* **1.** to empty **2.** (*fig.*) to deprive.

T

tabaccaio *sm.* tobacconist.

tabaccare *vt.* to snuff.

tabaccherìa *sf.* tobacconist's.

tabacchiera *sf.* snuff-box.

tabacco *sm.* tobacco.

tabella *sf.* **1.** (*lista*) list **2.** (*quadro*) board.

tabellone *sm.* notice board.

tabernàcolo *sm.* tabernacle.

tabù *sm.* taboo.

tabulatore *sm.* tabulator.

tacca *sf.* **1.** notch **2.** (*fig.*) condition.

taccagnerìa *sf.* stinginess.

taccagno *agg.* stingy. ♦ **taccagno** *sm.* miser.

tacchino *sm.* turkey.

taccia *sf.* **1.** reputation **2.** (*accusa*) charge.

tacciare *vt.* to charge (with).

tacco *sm.* heel.

taccuino *sm.* note-book.

tacere *vi.* to be silent: *far* —, to silence.

tachicardìa *sf.* tachycardia.

tachìmetro *sm.* tachometer.

tacitare *vt.* **1.** to hush up **2.** (*un creditore*) to pay (*v. irr.*) off.

tàcito *agg.* **1.** silent **2.** (*non espresso*) tacit.

taciturno *agg.* silent.

tafano *sm.* gad-fly.

tafferuglio *sm.* brawl.

taglia *sf.* **1.** (*riscatto*) ransom **2.** (*ricompensa*) reward **3.** (*misura*) size.

tagliacarte *sm.* paper-knife (*pl.* -knives).

taglialegna *sm.* wood-cutter.

tagliando *sm.* coupon.

tagliapietre *sm.* stone-cutter.

tagliare *vt.* **1.** to cut (*v. irr.*) **2.** (*attraversare*) to cut across: — *via*, to cut off || — *a pezzi*, to cut into pieces; — *la corda* (*fig.*), to run (*v. irr.*) away; — *la strada a qu.*, to bar so.'s way. ♦ **tagliarsi** *vr.* to cut.

tagliatelle *sf. pl.* noodles.
tagliato *agg.* **1.** cut **2.** (*inclinato, disposto*) cut out, fit: *essere — fuori*, to be cut off.
tagliatore *sm.* cutter.
taglieggiare *vt.* to ransom.
tagliente *agg.* sharp.
tagliere *sm.* trencher.
taglio *sm.* **1.** cut **2.** (*il tagliare*) cutting **3.** (*parte tagliente, orlo*) edge **4.** (*dimensione*) size **5.** (*raccolto*) harvest.
tagliola *sf.* snare.
taglione *sm.* retaliation.
tagliuzzare *vt.* to mince.
talare *agg.* talaric: *veste —*, cassock.
talco *sm.* talc: *— borato*, talcum powder.
tale *agg.* **1.** such **2.** (*per tralasciare i dati determinati*) such and such: *il — giorno*, on such and such day **3.** (*suddetto*) above-mentioned || *— e quale*, exactly like, exactly as. ♦ **tale** *pron. indef.* someone.
talea *sf.* scion.
talento *sm.* talent.
talismano *sm.* talisman.
tallonare *vi.* to follow.
talloncino *sm.* slip.
tallone *sm.* heel.
talora *avv.* sometimes.
talpa *sf.* mole.
taluno *agg.* some. ♦ **taluno** *pron.* someone (*pl.* some people).
talvolta *avv.* V. *talora*.
tamarindo *sm.* tamarind.
tambureggiare *vi.* to drum.
tamburellare *vi.* to drum one's fingers on.
tamburino *sm.* drummer.
tamburo *sm.* **1.** drum **2.** (*mecc.*) cylinder.
tamponamento *sm.* **1.** plugging **2.** (*med.*) tamponage **3.** (*auto*) bumping.
tamponare *vt.* **1.** to plug **2.** (*med.*) to tampon **3.** (*auto*) to bump (against).
tampone *sm.* **1.** plug **2.** (*med.*) tampon **3.** (*di carta asciugante*) blotter.
tana *sf.* den.
tanfo *sm.* stench.
tangente *agg. e sf.* tangent.
tangenza *sf.* tangency: *punto di —*, tangential point.
tangenziale *agg.* tangential.
tànghero *sm.* boor.
tangìbile *agg.* tangible.
tangibilità *sf.* tangibility.

tànnico *agg.* (*chim.*) tannic.
tannino *sm.* tannin.
tanto *avv.* **i.** so **2.** (*coi verbi*) so much **3.** (*di tempo*) so long **4.** (*ad ogni modo*) anyhow || *— quanto*, as much as; *— ... quanto*, as... as (*sia... sia*) both ... and; *— meglio*, so much the better; *— per cambiare*, just for a change. ♦ **tanto** *agg.* so much (*pl.* so many): *— ... quanto*, as much... as (*pl.* as many... as). ♦ **tanto che** *cong.* so (that).
tapiro *sm.* tapir.
tappa *sf.* **1.** (*luogo*) halting-place **2.** (*parte di viaggio*) stage **3.** (*sport*) lap.
tappare *vt.* **1.** to stop **2.** (*con tappo*) to cork.
tapparella *sf.* rolling shutter.
tappeto *sm.* carpet.
tappezzare *vt.* **1.** (*con carta*) to paper **2.** (*coprire*) to cover **3.** (*foderare*) to upholster.
tappezzerìa *sf.* **1.** (*di carta*) paper **2.** (*di stoffa*) tapestry.
tappezziere *sm.* **1.** (*per pareti*) paper hanger **2.** (*per divani ecc.*) upholsterer.
tappo *sm.* **1.** plug **2.** (*per bottiglia*) cap.
tara *sf.* **1.** tare **2.** (*med.; difetto*) taint.
taràntola *sf.* tarantula.
tarare *vt.* **1.** (*mecc.*) to set (*v. irr.*) **2.** (*calibrare*) to calibrate **3.** (*comm.*) to tare.
tarato *agg.* **1.** (*comm.*) tared **2.** (*mecc.*) set **3.** (*med.*) with a taint **4.** (*fig.*) corrupted.
tarchiato *agg.* sturdy.
tardare *vi.* to be late. ♦ **tardare** *vt.* to delay.
tardi *avv.* late: *far —*, to be late.
tardivo *agg.* **1.** (*arretrato*) backward **2.** (*che viene tardi*) tardy.
tardo *agg.* **1.** tardy **2.** (*ottuso*) dull **3.** (*di tempo*) late || *a tarda notte*, late in the night; *tarda età*, old age.
targa *sf.* **1.** (*di metallo*) plate **2.** (*di marmo*) slab **3.** (*auto*) number-plate.
targare *vt.* (*auto*) to give (*v. irr.*) a number-plate (to a car).
tariffa *sf.* tariff.
tarlarsi *vr.* to get (*v. irr.*) worm-eaten.
tarlatura *sf.* worm-hole.

tarlo *sm.* **1.** woodworm **2.** (*fig.*) gnawings (*pl.*).

tarma *sf.* moth.

tarmarsi *vr.* to get (*v. irr.*) moth--eaten.

tarpare *vt.* to clip.

tartagliare *vi.* to stammer.

tartàrico *agg.* tartaric.

tàrtaro *sm.* tartar.

tartaruga *sf.* tortoise.

tartassare *vt.* to harass.

tartina *sf.* canapé.

tartufo *smf.* truffle.

tasca *sf.* pocket.

tascàbile *agg.* pocket (*attributivo*).

tassa *sf.* **1.** tax **2.** (*d'iscrizione*) fee.

tassàbile *agg.* taxable.

tassàmetro *sm.* taximeter: — *di parcheggio*, parking meter.

tassare *vt.* to tax.

tassativo *agg.* peremptory.

tassazione *sf.* taxation.

tassello *sm.* dowel.

tassì *sm.* taxi.

tassista *sm.* taxi-driver.

tasso[1] *sm.* (*comm.*) rate.

tasso[2] *sm.* (*bot.*) yew.

tasso[3] *sm.* (*zool.*) badger.

tastare *vt.* to feel (*v. irr.*): — *il terreno* (*fig.*), to feel one's way.

tastiera *sf.* keyboard.

tasto *sm.* **1.** key **2.** (*tatto*) feel **3.** (*argomento*) subject.

tastoni *avv.* *a* —, gropingly; *andare a* —, to grope.

tàttica *sf.* tactics.

tàttico *agg.* tactical. ◆ tàttico *sm.* tactician.

tàttile *agg.* tactile.

tatto *sm.* **1.** touch **2.** (*fig.*) tact. || *con* —, tactfully.

tatuaggio *sm.* tattoo.

tatuare *vt.* to tattoo.

taumatùrgico *agg.* thaumaturgic(al).

taumaturgo *sm.* thaumaturge.

taurino *agg.* bull-like (*attr.*): *dal collo* —, bull-necked.

tauromachìa *sf.* bullfight.

tautologìa *sf.* tautology.

taverna *sf.* tavern.

taverniere *sm.* tavern-keeper.

tàvola *sf.* **1.** table **2.** (*asse*) board **3.** (*di marmo*) slab **4.** (*illustrazione*) plate.

tavolaccio *sm.* plank-bed.

tavolata *sf.* table.

tavolato *sm.* **1.** (*di pavimento*) plank floor **2.** (*mar.*) planking **3.**

(*geogr.*) plateau.

tavolozza *sf.* palette.

tazza *sf.* cup: — *da tè*, tea-cup.

te *pron.* you.

tè *sm.* tea.

teatrale *agg.* theatrical.

teatro *sm.* theatre: — *di posa*, studio.

tècnica *sf.* technique.

tecnicismo *sm.* technicality.

tècnico *agg.* technical. ◆ tècnico *sm.* technician.

tecnologìa *sf.* technology.

tecnològico *agg.* technological.

tedesco *agg.* e *sm.* German.

tediare *vt.* to bore.

tedio *sm.* boredom.

tedioso *agg.* boring.

tegame *sm.* saucepan.

teglia *sf.* bakepan.

tégola *sf.* tile: *coprire di tegole*, to tile.

teiera *sf.* tea-pot.

teismo *sm.* theism.

tela *sf.* **1.** cloth **2.** (*teat.*) curtain **3.** (*dipinto*) painting **4.** (*per dipingere*) canvas || — *cerata*, oilcloth; — *di sacco*, sackcloth; — *di lino*, linen; — *di ragno*, cobweb.

telaio *sm.* **1.** loom **2.** (*ossatura, cornice*) frame.

telecàmera *sf.* camera.

telecomandare *vt.* to radiocontrol.

telecomunicazione *sf.* telecommunication.

telefèrica *sf.* cableway.

telefonare *vt.* to (tele)phone.

telefonata *sf.* (telephone) call.

telefonìa *sf.* telephony.

telefònico *agg.* telephone (*attr.*): *cabina telefonica*, telephone booth.

telefonista *sm.* (telephone) operator. ◆ telefonista *sf.* switchboard girl.

telèfono *sm.* (tele)phone: *dare un colpo di* —, to ring (*v. irr.*) up.

telefoto *sf.* telephotograph.

telegiornale *sm.* (television) news (-reel).

telegrafare *vt.* to telegraph.

telegrafìa *sf.* telegraphy.

telegràfico *agg.* telegraphic(al).

telegrafista *sm.* telegraphist.

telègrafo *sm.* **1.** telegraph **2.** (*ufficio*) telegraph-office.

telegramma *sm.* telegram, wire: *fare un* — *a qu.*, to wire so.

telèmetro *sm.* **1.** telemeter **2.** (*in arma da fuoco; foto*) rangefinder.

teleobbiettivo *sm.* telephoto lens.
teleologìa *sf.* teleology.
telepatìa *sf.* telepathy.
telerìe *sf. pl.* linen (*sing.*): *commerciante in* —, linen-draper.
teleschermo *sm.* television screen.
telescopio *sm.* telescope.
telescrivente *sf.* teletypewriter.
teleselezione *sf.* long distance dialing.
telespettatore *sm.* televiewer.
teletipìa *sf.* teletype.
teletrasméttere *vt.* to telecast (*v. irr.*).
televisione *sf.* television: *guardare la* —, to watch television; *alla* —, on television; *trasmettere per* —, to telecast.
televisivo *agg.* televisional, television (*attr.*): *trasmissione televisiva,* telecast.
televisore *sm.* television set.
tellùrico *agg.* telluric.
telo *sm.* sheet.
telone *sm.* **1.** (*teat.*) curtain **2.** (*cine*) screen.
tema[1] *sf.* (*paura*) fear: *per* — *che,* lest.
tema[2] *sm.* **1.** theme **2.** (*scolastico*) composition.
temàtica *sf.* themes (*pl.*).
temàtico *agg.* thematic(al).
temerarietà *sf.* rashness.
temerario *agg.* rash.
temere *vt. e vi.* **1.** to fear **2.** (*patire*) not to stand (*v. irr.*) || *temo di sì,* I fear so; *temo di no,* I fear not.
temìbile *agg.* dreadful.
tèmpera *sf.* **1.** (*metal.*) hardening **2.** (*pitt.*) distemper || *dipingere a* —, to distemper.
temperamatite *sm.* pencil-sharpener.
temperamento *sm.* **1.** temperament **2.** (*alleviamento*) mitigation.
temperante *agg.* temperate.
temperanza *sf.* temperance.
temperare *vt.* **1.** to temper **2.** (*matite*) to sharpen.
temperato *agg.* **1.** temperate **2.** (*di matita*) sharpened.
temperatura *sf.* temperature.
temperino *sm.* penknife (*pl.* -knives).
tempesta *sf.* tempest, storm.
tempestare *vt.* **1.** (*assalire*) to assail **2.** (*importunare*) to harass **3.** (*cospargere*) to strew (*v. irr.*) (*sthg.*

with). ◆ **tempestare** *vi.* **1.** to storm **2.** (*grandinare*) to hail.
tempestività *sf.* timeliness.
tempestivo *agg.* timely.
tempestoso *agg.* stormy.
tempia *sf.* temple.
tempio *sm.* temple.
tempo *sm.* **1.** time **2.** (*atmosferico*) weather **3.** (*gramm.*) tense **4.** (*fase*) stage **5.** (*cine*) part || *un* —, once; *col passare del* —, in the long run; *molto* — *prima, dopo,* long before, after; *a* — *perso,* in one's spare time; *per* —, early.
temporale[1] *agg.* temporal.
temporale[2] *agg.* (*anat.*) temporal.
temporale[3] *sm.* storm.
temporalesco *agg.* stormy.
temporaneità *sf.* temporariness.
temporàneo *agg.* temporary.
temporeggiare *vi.* to temporize.
tempra *sf.* **1.** temper **2.** (*metal.*) hardening **3.** (*fig.*) character.
temprare *vt.* **1.** to temper **2.** (*fig.*) to strengthen **3.** (*plasmare*) to form.
temprato *agg.* (*abituato*) inured.
tenace *agg.* tenacious.
tenacia *sf.* tenacity.
tenaglia *sf.* pincers (*pl.*).
tenda *sf.* **1.** curtain **2.** (*da campo*) tent.
tendaggio *sm.* curtain.
tendente *agg.* tending.
tendenza *sf.* **1.** tendency **2.** inclination.
tendenziale *agg.* tendential.
tendenziosità *sf.* tendentiousness.
tendenzioso *agg.* tendentious.
tèndere *vt.* **1.** (*protendere*) to stretch (out) **2.** (*mettere in tensione*) to tighten. ◆ **tèndere** *vi.* **1.** to tend **2.** (*mirare*) to aim (at).
tendina *sf.* curtain.
tèndine *sm.* tendon.
tenditore *sm.* turnbuckle.
tènebra *sf.* darkness.
tenebroso *agg.* **1.** dark **2.** (*sinistro*) sinister.
tenente *sm.* lieutenant.
tenere *vt.* **1.** to keep (*v. irr.*) **2.** (*sostenere, considerare, contenere*) to hold (*v. irr.*) || — *una lezione,* to give (*v. irr.*) a lesson. ◆ **tenersi** *vr.* (*seguire*) to follow: — *al corrente,* to keep tabs on.
tenerezza *sf.* tenderness.
tènero *agg.* tender. ◆ **tènero** *sm.* **1.** (*parte tenera*) tender part **2.** (*affetto*) sympathy.

tenia *sf.* tapeworm.
tennis *sm.* tennis.
tennista *s.* tennis-player.
tenore *sm.* tenor.
tenorile *agg.* tenor (*attr.*).
tensione *sf.* tension.
tentacolare *agg.* tentacular.
tentàcolo *sm.* tentacle.
tentare *vt.* 1. to tempt 2. (*provare*) to try.
tentativo *sm.* attempt.
tentatore *agg.* tempting. ♦ **tentatore** *sm.* tempter.
tentazione *sf.* temptation.
tentennamento *sm.* 1. shaking 2. (*traballamento*) tottering 3. (*esitazione*) hesitation.
tentennare *vt.* to shake (*v. irr.*). ♦ **tentennare** *vi.* 1. to totter 2. (*esitare*) to waver.
tentoni *agg.* gropingly.
tenue *agg.* 1. small 2. (*leggero*) soft.
tenuità *sf.* 1. smallness 2. (*levità*) slightness.
tenuta *sf.* 1. (*proprietà*) estate 2. (*capacità*) capacity 3. (*abiti*) clothes (*pl.*) 4. (*tec.*) seal || — *di strada*, roadability; *a — d'acqua*, watertight.
teocràtico *agg.* theocratic(al).
teocrazìa *sf.* theocracy.
teologale *agg.* theological.
teologìa *sf.* theology.
teològico *agg.* theologic(al).
teòlogo *sm.* theologian.
teorema *sm.* theorem.
teorìa *sf.* 1. theory 2. (*fila*) string.
teòrico *agg.* theoretic(al).
teorizzare *vi.* to theorize.
tepore *sm.* lukewarmness.
teppa *sf.* rabble.
teppista *sm.* teddy-boy.
terapèutico *agg.* therapeutic(al).
terapìa *sf.* therapy.
terebinto *sm.* terebinth.
tèrgere *vt.* to wipe (off).
tergicristallo *sm.* windscreen wiper.
tergiversare *vi.* to hesitate.
tergiversazione *sf.* hesitation.
tergo *sm.* back: *segue a —*, please turn over.
termale *agg.* thermal: *stazione —*, spa.
terme *sf. pl.* thermal springs.
tèrmico *agg.* thermic.
terminale *agg.* terminal.
terminare *vt.* e *vi.* to end.

tèrmine *sm.* 1. term 2. (*limite*) limit 3. (*fine*) end || *contratto a —*, time-contract; *portare a —*, to carry out.
terminologìa *sf.* terminology.
tèrmite *sf.* termite.
termocoperta *sf.* thermal blanket.
termodinàmica *sf.* thermodynamics.
termoelèttrico *agg.* thermoelectric(al).
termòforo *sm.* warming pad.
termògeno *agg.* thermogenetic.
termoiònico *agg.* thermionic.
termòmetro *sm.* thermometer: *il — segna...,* the thermometer stands at...
termonucleare *agg.* thermonuclear.
termos *sm.* vacuum bottle.
termosifone *sm.* (*radiatore*) radiator.
termòstato *sm.* thermostat.
ternario *agg.* ternary.
terno *sm.* tern. ♦ **terno** *agg.* triple.
terra *sf.* 1. (*globo terracqueo*) earth 2. (*paese; l'opposto del mare*) land 3. (*terreno*) ground || — —, earth bound; *raso —*, to the ground.
terracotta *sf.* terracotta: *vasellame di —*, earthenware.
terraferma *sf.* dry land.
terraglia *sf.* pottery.
terranova *sm.* (*cane*) Newfoundland dog.
terrapieno *sm.* 1. bank 2. (*di fiume*) embankment.
terràqueo *agg.* terraqueous.
terrazza *sf.* 1. terrace 2. (*balcone*) balcony.
terrazziere *sm.* digger.
terrazzo *sm.* V. *terrazza.*
terremoto *sm.* earthquake.
terreno[1] *agg.* earthly.
terreno[2] *sm.* ground.
tèrreo *agg.* 1. earthy 2. (*di colorito*) wan, sallow.
terrestre *agg.* terrestrial, earthly.
terrìbile *agg.* terrible.
terriccio *sm.* mould.
terriero *agg.* land (*attr.*).
terrificante *agg.* terrifying.
terrificare *vt.* to terrify.
terrina *sf.* tureen.
territoriale *agg.* territorial.
territorio *sm.* territory.
terrore *sm.* terror: *incutere — a qu.,* to strike (*v. irr.*) so. with terror.
terrorismo *sm.* terrorism.

terrorista *s.* terrorist.
terroristico *agg.* terroristic.
terrorizzare *vt.* to terrorize.
terroso *agg.* earthy.
terso *agg.* clear.
terza *sf.* **1.** (*di scuola, treno*) third class **2.** (*di auto*) third gear.
terzetto *sm.* trio.
terziario *agg.* e *sm.* tertiary.
terzina *sf.* tercet.
terzino *sm.* (*sport*) full back.
terzo *agg.* third. ♦ **terzo** *sm.* **1.** third **2.** (*terza persona*) third person || *terzi*, third party.
terzùltimo *agg.* e *sm.* last but two.
tesa *sf.* brim.
tesaurizzare *vt.* to treasure.
teschio *sm.* skull.
tesi *sf.* thesis (*pl.* -ses).
teso *agg.* taut.
tesorerìa *sf.* treasury.
tesoriere *sm.* treasurer.
tesoro *sm.* **1.** treasure **2.** (*pol.*) treasury.
tèssera *sf.* **1.** card **2.** (*di mosaico*) tessera (*pl.* -rae).
tesseramento *sm.* **1.** rationing **2.** (*reclutamento*) enrolment.
tesserare *vt.* **1.** to ration **2.** (*arruolare*) to enrol.
tèssere *vt.* to weave (*v. irr.*).
tèssile *agg.* textile. ♦ **tèssile** *sm.* weaver.
tessitore *sm.* weaver.
tessitura *sf.* **1.** weaving **2.** (*disposizione dei fili*) texture.
tessuto *sm.* **1.** fabric **2.** (*med.; fig.*) tissue || *negozio di tessuti*, draper's shop.
testa *sf.* head: *colpo di —*, rash act; *essere in — a tutti*, to be ahead of everybody.
testamentario *agg.* testamentary.
testamento *sm.* will.
testardàggine *sf.* stubbornness.
testardo *agg.* stubborn.
testata *sf.* **1.** head **2.** (*colpo*) butt **3.** (*di giornale*) heading.
teste *s.* witness: *— d'accusa, di difesa*, witness for the prosecution, the defence.
testìcolo *sm.* testicle.
testimonianza *sf.* **1.** witness **2.** (*prova*) evidence || *far —*, to bear (*v. irr.*) witness.
testimoniare *vt.* e *vi.* **1.** to witness **2.** (*attestare*) to testify.
testimonio *sm.* witness.
testo *sm.* text.

testuale *agg.* **1.** textual **2.** (*esatto*) exact.
tetànico *agg.* tetanic.
tètano *sm.* tetanus.
tetraedro *sm.* tetrahedron.
tetràggine *sf.* gloom.
tetràgono *agg.* (*fig.*) steadfast.
tetralogìa *sf.* tetralogy.
tetro *agg.* gloomy.
tettarella *sf.* dummy.
tetto *sm.* roof: *— a capanna*, saddle roof.
tettoia *sf.* shed.
tettònica *sf.* tectonics.
teutònico *agg.* Teutonic. ♦ **teutònico** *sm.* Teuton.
ti *pron.* **1.** you, to you **2.** (*r.*) yourself.
tiara *sf.* tiara.
tibia *sf.* tibia.
tic *sm.* tic.
ticchettare *vi.* to tick.
ticchettìo *sm.* ticking.
ticchio *sm.* fancy.
tièpido *agg.* tepid.
tifo *sm.* **1.** typhus **2.** (*fig.*) fanaticism.
tifone *sm.* typhoon.
tifoso *sm.* **1.** typhus patient **2.** (*fig.*) fan.
tiglio *sm.* lime.
tigna *sf.* ringworm.
tignola *sf.* moth.
tigrato *agg.* striped.
tigre *sf.* tiger.
timbrare *vt.* **1.** to stamp **2.** (*lettere*) to postmark || *— a secco*, to emboss.
timbratura *sf.* **1.** stamping **2.** (*postale*) postmarking.
timbro *sm.* **1.** stamp **2.** (*di suono*) timbre **3.** (*postale*) postmark || *— a secco*, embossed stamp.
timidezza *sf.* shyness.
tìmido *agg.* shy.
timo *sm.* thyme.
timone *sm.* helm.
timoniere *sm.* helmsman (*pl.* -men).
timorato *agg.* **1.** respectful **2.** (*scrupoloso*) scrupulous.
timore *sm.* fear: *aver —*, to fear, to be afraid.
timoroso *agg.* fearful.
tìmpano *sm.* **1.** eardrum **2.** (*mus.*) kettle-drum **3.** (*arch.*) gable.
tinca *sf.* tench.
tinello *sm.* living-room.
tingere *vt.* to dye (*v. irr.*). ♦ **tìngersi** *vr.* to dye oneself.

tino *sm.* vat.

tinozza *sf.* tub.

tinta *sf.* 1. (*colore*) hue 2. (*materia colorante*) dye 3. (*tingitura*) dyeing.

tinteggiare *vt.* to paint.

tintinnare *vi.* to tinkle.

tintinnìo *sm.* tinkling.

tintore *sm.* 1. dyer 2. (*anche per lavature a secco*) cleaner.

tintorìa *sf.* 1. dyeworks (*pl.*) 2. (*negozio anche per lavature a secco*) dry cleaners' shop.

tintura *sf.* V. *tinta*.

tìpico *agg.* typical.

tipo *sm.* 1. type 2. (*modello*) pattern 3. (*individuo*) fellow.

tipografìa *sf.* 1. typography 2. (*mecc.*) letterpress printing.

tipogràfico *agg.* typographic(al).

tipògrafo *sm.* typographer.

tiraggio *sm.* draught.

tiralìnee *sm.* drawing-pen.

tiranneggiare *vt.* to tyrannize.

tirannìa *sf.* tyranny.

tirànnico *agg.* tyrannical.

tirànnide *sf.* tyranny.

tiranno *sm.* tyrant.

tirante *sm.* 1. (*mecc.*) connecting rod 2. (*arch.*) tie-beam.

tirapiedi *sm.* drudge.

tirare *vt.* 1. to draw (*v. irr.*), to pull 2. (*scagliare*) to throw (*v. irr.*). ◆ **tirare** *vi.* 1. (*sparare*) to shoot (*v. irr.*) 2. (*di tiraggio*) to draw 3. (*di vestito*) to be tight. ◆ **tirarsi** *vr.* to draw.

tirata *sf.* 1. pull 2. (*invettiva*) tirade.

tiratore *sm.* shooter.

tiratura *sf.* 1. (*tip.*) printing 2. (*numero di copie stampate*) circulation.

tirchierìa *sf.* niggardliness.

tirchio *agg.* niggardly.

tiritera *sf.* rigmarole.

tiro *sm.* 1. (*trazione*) draught 2. (*lancio*) throw 3. (*sparo*) shot 4. (*scherzo*) trick.

tirocinio *sm.* apprenticeship.

tiròide *sf.* thyroid.

tisana *sf.* ptisan.

tisi *sf.* consumption.

tìsico *agg. e sm.* consumptive.

tisiologìa *sf.* phthisiology.

tisiòlogo *sm.* phthisiologist.

titànico *agg.* titanic.

titillare *vt.* to tickle.

titolare *agg.* 1. regular 2. (*nominale*) titular. ◆ **titolare** *s.* 1. regular holder 2. (*proprietario*) owner 3. (*capo*) principal.

titolato *agg.* titled.

tìtolo *sm.* 1. title 2. (*qualifica*) qualification 3. (*documento*) document 4. (*comm.*) security.

titubante *agg.* hesitating.

titubanza *sf.* hesitation.

titubare *vi.* to hesitate.

tizianesco *agg.* 1. Titianesque 2. (*di capelli*) titian.

tizio *sm.* fellow.

tizzone *sm.* brand.

toccare *vt.* to touch || — *un porto*, to call at. ◆ **toccare** *vi.* 1. (*capitare*) to happen 2. (*spettare*) to fall (*v. irr.*).

toccasana *sm.* cure-all.

tocco[1] *agg.* (*pazzoide*) touched.

tocco[2] *sm.* 1. touch 2. (*battito*) knock 3. (*rintocco*) toll || *al* —, at one o'clock.

tocco[3] *sm.* (*berretto*) toque.

toga *sf.* gown.

togato *agg.* gowned.

tògliere *vt.* 1. to take (*v. irr.*) 2. (*liberare*) to relieve. ◆ **tògliersi** *vr.* 1. to get (*v. irr.*) off 2. (*un indumento*) to take off || — *la vita*, to commit suicide.

toletta *sf.* toilet.

tolleràbile *agg.* tolerable.

tollerante *agg.* tolerant.

tolleranza *sf.* tolerance.

tollerare *vt.* 1. to tolerate 2. (*sopportare*) to bear (*v. irr.*).

tomaia *sf.* vamp.

tomba *sf.* grave.

tombale *agg.* grave (*attr.*).

tombino *sm.* manhole.

tòmbola *sf.* 1. (*gioco*) "tombola" 2. (*caduta*) tumble.

tombolare *vi.* to tumble down.

tomismo *sm.* Thomism.

tomista *agg. e sm.* Thomist.

tomo *sm.* 1. tome 2. (*persona*) chap.

tònaca *sf.* frock: *gettare la* —, to give (*v. irr.*) up the frock.

tonalità *sf.* tonality.

tonante *agg.* thundering.

tondeggiante *agg.* roundish.

tondeggiare *vi.* to be roundish.

tondello *sm.* round.

tondo *agg. e sm.* round || *chiaro e* —, clearly.

tonfo *sm.* splash.

tònico *agg. e sm.* tonic.

tonificare *vt.* to brace.

tonnellaggio *sm.* tonnage.

tonnellata *sf.* ton.

tonno *sm.* tunny.

tono *sm.* **1.** tone **2.** (*accordo*) tune **3.** (*mus.*) strain.
tonsilla *sf.* tonsil.
tonsillectomìa *sf.* tonsillectomy.
tonsillite *sf.* tonsillitis.
tonsura *sf.* tonsure.
tonsurare *vt.* to tonsure.
tonto *agg.* dull. ♦ tonto *sm.* dunce.
topaia *sf.* (*fig.*) hovel.
topazio *sm.* topaz.
tòpica *sf.* **1.** topic **2.** (*errore*) blunder.
tòpico *agg.* topical.
topo *sm.* mouse (*pl.* mice), rat ǁ — *di biblioteca* (*fig.*), bookworm; — *di albergo* (*fig.*), hotel thief.
topografìa *sf.* topography.
topogràfico *agg.* topographic(al).
topologìa *sf.* topology.
toponomàstica *sf.* toponymy.
toppa *sf.* **1.** (*pezza*) patch **2.** (*di serratura*) keyhole ǁ *mettere una* —, to patch up.
torace *sm.* thorax, chest.
torba *sf.* peat.
torbidezza *sf.* **1.** turbidity **2.** (*esser fosco*) gloominess.
tòrbido *agg.* **1.** turbid **2.** (*fosco*) gloomy **3.** (*inquieto*) troubled. ♦ tòrbido *sm.* (*disordine*) disorder: *pescare nel* —, to fish in troubled water.
torbiera *sf.* peat-bog.
tòrcere *vt.* **1.** to wring (*v. irr.*) **2.** (*attorcigliare*) to twist ǁ *dare del filo da* —, to give (*v. irr.*) a lot of trouble; — *il naso* (*fig.*), to turn up one's nose (at). ♦ tòrcersi *vr.* to twist.
torchiare *vt.* to press.
torchiatura *sf.* pressing.
torchio *sm.* press.
torcia *sf.* torch.
torcicollo *sm.* stiff-neck.
torcitore *sm.* twister.
torcitura *sf.* twist.
tordo *sm.* thrush.
torero *sm.* bullfighter.
torma *sf.* swarm.
tormalina *sf.* tourmaline.
tormenta *sf.* blizzard.
tormentare *vt.* to torment. ♦ tormentarsi *vr.* to worry.
tormentato *agg.* (*inquieto*) restless.
tormento *sm.* torment.
tormentoso *agg.* tormenting.
tornaconto *sm.* profit.
tornado *sm.* tornado.
tornante *sm.* bend.

tornare *vi.* **1.** to return **2.** (*di conti*) to be correct.
tornasole *sm.* litmus.
torneo *sm.* tournàment.
tornio *sm.* lathe.
tornire *vt.* **1.** (*mecc.*) to turn **2.** (*fig.*) to polish.
tornito *agg.* **1.** (*rotondo*) round **2.** (*ben fatto*) well-shaped.
tornitore *sm.* turner.
toro *sm.* bull.
torpediniera *sf.* torpedo-boat.
torpedo *sf.* torpedo.
torpedone *sm.* (motor-)coach.
tòrpido *agg.* torpid.
torpore *sm.* torpor.
torre *sf.* tower.
torrefare *vt.* **1.** to torrefy **2.** (*caffè*) to roast.
torrefazione *sf.* **1.** torrefaction **2.** (*di caffè*) roasting **3.** (*negozio*) coffee store.
torreggiare *vi.* to tower.
torrente *sm.* torrent.
torrentizio *agg.* torrent-like.
torrenziale *agg.* torrential.
torretta *sf.* (*mil.; mar.*) turret.
tòrrido *agg.* torrid.
torrione *sm.* donjon.
torrone *sm.* nougat.
torsione *sf.* torsion.
torso *sm.* **1.** trunk **2.** (*di statua*) torso.
tòrsolo *sm.* **1.** (*di verdura*) stump **2.** (*di frutta*) core.
torta *sf.* cake.
tortiera *sf.* bakepan.
torto *agg.* **1.** (*piegato*) bent **2.** (*contorto*) twisted.
torto *sm.* **1.** wrong **2.** (*colpa*) fault ǁ *aver* —, to be wrong; *far* — *a qu.*, to wrong so.; *a* —, wrongly.
tòrtora *sf.* turtle-dove.
tortuosità *sf.* tortuosity.
tortuoso *agg.* tortuous.
tortura *sf.* torture.
torturare *vt.* to torture. ♦ torturarsi *vr.* to worry.
torvo *agg.* grim.
tosare *vt.* to shear (*v. irr.*).
tosatrice *sf.* clippers (*pl.*).
tosatura *sf.* shearing.
toscano *agg. e sm.* Tuscan.
tosse *sf.* cough.
tossicchiare *vi.* to keep (*v. irr.*) on coughing.
tossicità *sf.* toxicity.
tòssico *agg.* toxic. ♦ tòssico *sm.* toxicant.

tossicologìa *sf.* toxicology.
tossicòlogo *sm.* toxicologist.
tossicomanìa *sf.* toxicomania.
tossina *sf.* toxin.
tossire *vi.* to cough.
tostapane *sm.* toaster.
tostare *vt.* **1.** to toast **2.** (*caffè*) to roast.
tosto[1] *avv.* at once.
tosto[2] *agg.* hard || *faccia tosta,* cheek.
tosto[3] *sm.* toast.
totale *agg.* e *sm.* total: *in —,* in all.
totalità *sf.* **1.** totality **2.** (*numero complessivo*) mass.
totalitario *agg.* totalitarian.
totalitarismo *sm.* totalitarianism.
totalizzare *vt.* **1.** to totalize **2.** (*sport*) to score.
totalizzatore *sm.* totalizer.
tovaglia *sf.* (table-)cloth.
tovagliolo *sm.* napkin.
tozzo[1] *agg.* squat, stocky.
tozzo[2] *sm.* piece· *un — di pane,* a crust of bread.
tra *prep.* **1.** (*fra due persone, cose, gruppi*) between **2.** (*fra più di due*) among **3.** (*nel mezzo di*) amid **4.** (*di tempo*) (with)in.
traballare *vi.* **1.** to· stagger **2.** (*di vettura*) to jolt || *entrare, uscire traballando,* to stagger in, out.
trabeazione *sf.* trabeation.
trabìccolo *sm.* ramsh4ckle vehicle.
traboccare *vi.* to overflow.
trabocchetto *sm.* trap.
tracagnotto *agg.* squat.
tracannare *vt.* to gulp down.
traccia *sf.* **1.** trace **2.** (*segno*) mark **3.** (*orme*) footsteps (*pl.*) **4.** (*schema*) outline.
tracciare *vt.* to trace (out): *— a grandi linee,* to outline.
tracciato *sm.* layout.
tracciatore *sm.* tracer.
trachea *sf.* windpipe.
tracheale *agg.* tracheal.
tracheite *sf.* tracheitis.
tracolla *sf.* baldric: *portare qc. a —,* to carry sthg. across one's back.
tracollare *vi.* **1.** to lose (*v. irr.*) one's balance **2.** (*cadere*) to collapse.
tracollo *sm.* collapse: *portare al —,* to bring (*v. irr.*) to ruin.
tracoma *sm.* trachoma.
tracotante *agg.* haughty.
tracotanza *sf.* haughtiness.

tradimento *sm.* **1.** treason **2.** (*infedeltà*) betrayal || *a —* (*agg.*), treacherous, (*avv.*) treacherously.
tradire *vt.* **1.** to betray **2.** (*di coniuge*) to be unfaithful (to).
traditore *agg.* treacherous. ◆ **traditore** *sm.* traitor.
tradizionale *agg.* traditional.
tradizionalismo *sm.* traditionalism.
tradizionalista *s.* traditionalist.
tradizione *sf.* tradition: *per —,* traditionally.
tradotta *sf.* troop-train.
traducìbile *agg.* translatable.
tradurre *vt.* to translate: *— in atto,* to carry out; *— in carcere,* to take (*v. irr.*) to prison.
traduttore *sm.* translator.
traduzione *sf.* translation.
traente *s.* (*comm.*) drawer.
trafelato *agg.* breathless.
trafficante *sm.* dealer.
trafficare *vi.* **1.** to deal (*v. irr.*) **2.** (*affaccendarsi*) to bustle about.
tràffico *sm.* **1.** traffic **2.** (*comm.*) trade.
trafiggere *vt.* to pierce (through).
trafila *sf.* **1.** procedure **2.** (*mecc.*) draw-plate.
trafilare *vt.* to draw (*v. irr.*).
trafiletto *sm.* paragraph.
traforare *vt.* **1.** to perforate **2.** (*ricamare*) to embroider with open--work.
traforato *agg.* **1.** perforated **2.** (*ricamato a traforo*) open-work (*attr.*).
traforatrice *sf.* fret-sawing machine.
traforo *sm.* **1.** perforation **2.** (*galleria*) tunnel **3.** (*falegnameria*) fret-work **4.** (*ricamo*) open-work.
trafugamento *sm.* stealing.
trafugare *vt.* to steal (*v. irr.*).
tragedia *sf.* tragedy.
tragediògrafo *sm.* tragedian.
traghettare *vt.* to ferry.
traghetto *sm.* ferry-boat.
tragicità *sf.* tragicalness.
tràgico *agg.* tragical. ◆ **tràgico** *sm.* tragedian.
tragicòmico *agg.* tragicomic(al).
tragicommedia *sf.* tragicomedy.
tragitto *sm.* **1.** way **2.** (*viaggio*) journey.
traguardo *sm.* goal.
traiettoria *sf.* trajectory.
trainare *vt.* to haul.
tràino *sm.* **1.** haulage **2.** (*carro*) truck.

tralasciare *vt.* to leave (*v. irr.*) out, to omit.

tralcio *sm.* shoot.

traliccio *sm.* 1. (*tela*) ticking 2. (*per costruzioni*) trellis || — *di ferro*, iron framework.

tralice (*nella loc. avv.*) *in* —, askance.

tralignamento *sm.* degeneration.

tralignare *vi.* to degenerate.

tralùcere *vi.* to shine (*v. irr.*) (through).

tram *sm.* tramcar.

trama *sf.* 1. weft 2. (*fig.*) plot.

tramaglio *sm.* trammel.

tramandare *vt.* to hand down.

tramare *vt.* 1. to weave (*v. irr.*) 2. (*fig.*) to plot.

trambusto *sm.* bustle.

tramenare *vt.* e *vi.* to move about.

tramenìo *sm.* bustle.

tramestare *vt.* to rummage.

tramestìo *sm.* 1. rummaging 2. (*trepestio*) stamping.

tramezzare *vt.* to partition.

tramezzino *sm.* sandwich.

tramezzo *sm.* partition.

tràmite *sm.* path: — *qu.*, through so.

tramoggia *sf.* hopper.

tramontana *sf.* 1. north 2. (*vento*) north wind || *perder la* —, to lose (*v. irr.*) one's head.

tramontare *vi.* 1. to set (*v. irr.*) 2. (*svanire*) to fade.

tramonto *sm.* 1. setting 2. (*del sole*) sunset 3. (*declino*) decline.

tramortimento *sm.* swoon.

tramortire *vt.* to stun.

trampoliere *sm.* wader.

trampolino *sm.* spring-board.

tràmpolo *sm.* stilt.

tramutare *vt.* to change. ♦ **tramutarsi** *vr.* to change.

trancia *sf.* 1. shears (*pl.*) 2. (*fetta*) slice.

tranciare *vt.* to shear.

tranello *sm.* snare.

trangugiare *vt.* to swallow.

tranne *prep.* but.

tranquillante *agg.* tranquillizing. ♦ **tranquillante** *sm.* tranquillizer.

tranquillità *sf.* calmness.

tranquillizzare *vt.* 1. to calm 2. (*rassicurare*) to reassure.

tranquillo *agg.* calm: *star* —, to keep (*v. irr.*) quiet; *sta'* —!, do not worry!

transalpino *agg.* transalpine.

transatlàntico *agg.* transatlantic. ♦ **transatlàntico** *sm.* liner.

transazione *sf.* 1. transaction 2. (*accomodamento*) arrangement 3. (*compromesso*) compromise.

transcontinentale *agg.* transcontinental.

transetto *sm.* transept.

trànsfuga *s.* runaway.

transigere *vt.* e *vi.* to compromise.

transistore *sm.* transistor.

transitàbile *agg.* practicable.

transitabilità *sf.* practicability.

transitare *vi.* to pass through.

transitivo *agg.* e *sm.* transitive.

trànsito *sm.* transit.

transitorio *agg.* transitory.

transizione *sf.* transition.

transoceànico *agg.* transoceanic.

transustanziazione *sf.* transubstantiation.

tranvìa *sf.* tramway.

tranviario *agg.* tramcar (*attr.*).

tranviere *sm.* 1. tram-driver 2. (*bigliettario*) tram-conductor.

trapanare *vt.* 1. to drill 2. (*med.*) to trepan.

trapanazione *sf.* 1. drilling 2. (*med.*) trepanation.

tràpano *sm.* 1. drill 2. (*med.*) trepan.

trapassare *vt.* to pierce through. ♦ **trapassare** *vi.* (*morire*) to die.

trapasso *sm.* 1. (*morte*) death 2. (*giur.; comm.*) transfer.

trapelare *vi.* to leak out.

trapezio *sm.* 1. trapezium 2. (*da ginnastica*) trapeze.

trapiantare *vt.* to transplant. ♦ **trapiantarsi** *vr.* (*stabilirsi*) to settle.

trapianto *sm.* 1. transplantation 2. (*tessuto trapiantato*) graft.

trappista *sm.* Trappist.

tràppola *sf.* trap: *prendere in* —, to trap.

trapunta *sf.* quilt.

trapuntare *vt.* 1. to quilt 2. (*ricamare*) to embroider.

trapunto *agg.* 1. quilted 2. (*ricamato*) embroidered || — *di stelle*, starry.

trarre *vt.* 1. to draw (*v. irr.*) 2. (*ottenere*) to get (*v. irr.*). ♦ **trarsi** *vr.* to draw.

trasalire *vi.* to startle: *far* —, to startle.

trasandato *agg.* shabby.

trasbordare vt. **1.** to transfer **2.** (traghettare) to ferry.

trasbordo sm. **1.** transfer **2.** (traghetto) ferrying across.

trascendentale agg. transcendental.

trascendentalismo sm. transcendentalism.

trascendente agg. transcendent.

trascendenza sf. transcendence.

trascéndere vt. to transcend. ♦ **trascéndere** vi. to let (v. irr.) oneself go.

trascinare vt. **1.** to drag **2.** (affascinare) to fascinate.

trascòrrere vt. (il tempo) to spend (v. irr.). ♦ **trascòrrere** vi. **1.** (di tempo) to pass **2.** (lasciar correre) to pass over.

trascorso agg. past. ♦ **trascorso** sm. (errore) slip.

trascrittore sm. transcriber.

trascrìvere vt. **1.** to transcribe **2.** (giur.) to register.

trascrizione sf. **1.** transcription **2.** (giur.) registration **3.** (trapasso) transfer.

trascuràbile agg. negligible.

trascurare vt. to neglect. ♦ **trascurarsi** vr. not to care of oneself.

trascuratezza sf. **1.** negligence **2.** (sciatteria) slovenliness.

trascurato agg. **1.** (negligente) careless **2.** (sciatto) sloven.

trasecolare vi. to be amazed.

trasecolato agg. amazed.

trasferìbile agg. transferable.

trasferimento sm. transfer.

trasferire vt. to transfer. ♦ **trasferirsi** vr. to (re)move.

trasferta sf. **1.** transfer **2.** (indennità) travelling allowance || in —, on transfer; partita in — (sport), out match.

trasfigurare vt. to transfigure. ♦ **trasfigurarsi** vr. to become (v. irr.) transfigured.

trasfigurazione sf. transfiguration.

trasfòndere vt. **1.** to transfuse **2.** (fig.) to instil.

trasformàbile agg. convertible.

trasformare vt. to change, to turn. ♦ **trasformarsi** vr. to change.

trasformatore sm. transformer.

trasformazione sf. transformation.

trasformismo sm. transformism.

trasfusione sf. transfusion.

trasgredire vt. e vi. to infringe.

trasgressione sf. infringement.

trasgressore sm. infringer.

traslazione sf. **1.** transfer **2.** (fis.; eccl.) translation.

traslocare vt. e vi. to move.

trasloco sm. removal.

traslùcido agg. translucent.

trasméttere vt. to transmit.

trasmettitore sm. transmitter.

trasmigrare vi. to transmigrate.

trasmigrazione sf. transmigration.

trasmissìbile agg. transmissible.

trasmissione sf. **1.** transmission **2.** (giur.) transfer **3.** (mecc.) drive || — radio, broadcast; — televisiva, telecast.

trasmittente agg. transmitting.

trasognato agg. dreamy.

trasparente agg. transparent.

trasparenza sf. transparence.

trasparire vi. **1.** to shine (v. irr.) through **2.** (esser trasparente) to be transparent || lasciar —, to betray.

traspirare vi. to transpire.

traspirazione sf. transpiration.

trasporre vt. to transpose.

trasportàbile agg. transportable.

trasportare vt. **1.** to carry **2.** (fig.) to carry away. ♦ **trasportarsi** vr. to go (v. irr.).

trasportatore sm. conveyer: — a nastro, belt-conveyer.

trasporto sm. transport: nave da —, cargo; spese di —, carriage.

trasposizione sf. transposition.

trastullare vt. to amuse. ♦ **trastullarsi** vr. **1.** (giocare) to play **2.** (scherzare) to trifle.

trastullo sm. **1.** plaything **2.** (divertimento) amusement.

trasudamento sm. sweating.

trasudare vt. e vi. to sweat.

trasversale agg. transversal, cross (attr.). ♦ **trasversale** sf. **1.** transversal **2.** (strada) cross-road.

trasvolare vt. to fly (v. irr.) across.

trasvolata sf. flight (across).

tratta sf. **1.** (traffico) trade **2.** (comm.) draft || — a vista, sight draft; spiccare una — su qu., to draw (v. irr.) upon so.

trattàbile agg. **1.** tractable **2.** (di argomento) that can be dealt with.

trattabilità sf. tractability.

trattamento sm. **1.** treatment **2.** (paga) salary.

trattare vt. **1.** to treat **2.** (maneggiare) to handle **3.** (commerciare) to deal (v. irr.) (in) **4.** (negoziare) to negotiate **5.** (un argomento) to deal (with). ♦ **trattarsi** v. imp. to be a question of, to be involved.

trattativa *sf.* negotiation.

trattato *sm.* 1. (*patto*) treaty 2. (*libro*) treatise.

trattazione *sf.* treatment.

tratteggiare *vt.* 1. to outline 2. (*ombreggiare*) to hatch.

tratteggio *sm.* 1. (*abbozzo*) outline 2. (*ombreggiatura*) hatching.

trattenere *vt.* 1. to keep (*v. irr.*) 2. (*dedurre*) to deduct 3. (*frenare*) to refrain || — *il respiro*, to hold (*v. irr.*) one's breath. ♦ **trattenersi** *vr.* (*fermarsi*) to stay || *non posso trattenermi dal fare*, I cannot help doing.

trattenimento *sm.* (*festa*) party.

trattenuta *sf.* deduction.

trattino *sm.* 1. dash 2. (*di unione*) hyphen.

tratto *sm.* 1. (*tirata*) pull 2. (*colpo*) stroke 3. (*linea*) line 4. (*brano*) passage 5. (*estensione di spazio*) way 6. (*lineamento*) feature 7. (*comportamento*) manners (*pl.*) || *d'un* —, suddenly; *di* — *in* —, now and then.

trattore[1] *sm.* (*mecc.*) tractor.

trattore[2] *sm.* (*oste*) inn-keeper.

trattoria *sf.* inn.

tratturo *sm.* cattle-track.

trauma *sm.* trauma.

traumàtico *agg.* traumatic.

traumatologìa *sf.* traumatology.

travagliare *vt.* V. *tormentare*.

travaglio *sm.* 1. (*fatica*) labour 2. (*cruccio*) trouble.

travasare *vt.* to pour off.

travaso *sm.* 1. pouring off 2. (*med.*) effusion.

travatura *sf.* truss.

trave *sf.* beam.

travéggole *sf. pl. avere le* —, to mistake (*v. irr.*) one thing for another.

traversa *sf.* 1. (*sbarra*) cross-bar 2. (*via*) side-road.

traversata *sf.* crossing.

traversìa *sf.* misfortune.

traversina *sf.* sleeper.

traverso *agg.* 1. transverse, cross (*attr.*) 2. (*obliquo*) slanting || *di* —, askance; *andare per* — (*fig.*), to go (*v. irr.*) wrong with.

travestimento *sm.* disguise.

travestire *vt.* to disguise (as).

traviamento *sm.* corruption.

traviare *vt.* to mislead (*v. irr.*). ♦ **traviarsi** *vr.* to go (*v. irr.*) astray.

travisamento *sm.* alteration.

travisare *vt.* to alter.

travolgente *agg.* sweeping.

travòlgere *vt.* 1. to sweep (*v. irr.*) away 2. (*investire*) to run (*v. irr.*) over.

trazione *sf.* traction.

tre *agg.* three.

trebbiare *vt.* to thrash.

trebbiatrice *sf.* thrasher.

trebbiatura *sf.* thrashing.

treccia *sf:* plait: *farsi le trecce*, to plait one's hair.

trecento *agg.* three hundred || *il* — (*secolo*), the fourteenth century.

tredicenne *agg.* thirteen years old, thirteen-year-old (*attr.*).

tredicèsimo *agg.* thirteenth.

trédici *agg.* thirteen.

tregua *sf.* 1. truce 2. (*riposo*) rest.

tremante *agg.* 1. trembling 2. (*di freddo*) shivering.

tremare *vi.* 1. to tremble 2. (*di freddo*) to shiver.

tremendo *agg.* awful.

trementina *sf.* turpentine.

tremila *agg.* three thousand.

trèmito *sm.* 1. tremble 2. (*di freddo*) shiver.

tremolante *agg.* 1. trembling 2. (*di luce*) flickering 3. (*di stelle*) twinkling.

tremolare *vi.* 1. to tremble 2. (*di luce*) to flicker 3. (*di stelle*) to twinkle.

tremolio *sm.* 1. tremble 2. (*di luce*) flickering 3. (*di stelle*) twinkle.

tremore *sm.* V. *trèmito*.

treno *sm.* 1. train: — *accelerato*, slow train; — *direttissimo*, fast train; — *rapido*, express train 2. (*tenore*) way of living, routine.

trenta *agg.* thirty.

trentenne *agg.* thirty years old, thirty-year-old (*attr.*).

trentennio *sm.* period of thirty years.

trentèsimo *agg.* thirtieth.

trentina *sf.* about thirty.

trepestìo *sm.* stamping.

trepidante *agg.* anxious.

trepidare *vi.* to be anxious.

trepidazione *sf.* anxiety.

treppiede *sm.* tripod.

tresca *sf.* intrigue.

tréspolo *sm.* trestle.

trìade *sf.* triad.

triangolare *agg.* triangular.

triangolazione *sf.* triangulation.

triàngolo *sm.* triangle.
tribale *agg.* tribal.
tribolare *vi.* **1.** to toil **2.** (*soffrire*) to suffer. ◆ **tribolare** *vt.* to vex.
tribolazione *sf.* suffering.
tribordo *sm.* starboard.
tribù *sf.* tribe.
tribuna *sf.* **1.** (*per oratori*) platform **2.** (*sport*) stand.
tribunale *sm.* court.
tribuno *sm.* tribune.
tributare *vt.* to bestow.
tributario *agg.* **1.** tributary **2.** (*fiscale*) fiscal. ◆ **tributario** *sm.* tributary.
tributo *sm.* tribute.
tricheco *sm.* walrus.
triciclo *sm.* tricycle.
triclinio *sm.* triclinium (*pl.* -nia).
tricolore *agg. e sm.* tricolour.
tricorno *sm.* tricorn.
tricromìa *sf.* **1.** trichromatism **2.** (*pezzo singolo*) trichromatic print.
tridente *sm.* **1.** trident **2.** (*per fieno*) hayfork.
tridimensionale *agg.* tridimensional.
triedro *sm.* trihedron.
triennale *agg. e sm.* triennial.
triennio *sm.* period of three years.
trifase *agg.* three-phase (*attr.*).
trifoglio *sm.* clover.
trigèmino *agg. e sm.* trigeminal: *parto* —, birth of triplets.
trigèsimo *agg.* thirtieth: *nel* — *della sua morte*, on the thirtieth day after his death.
trigonometrìa *sf.* trigonometry.
trilione *sm.* **1.** (*in sistema italiano, francese e americano* = 1000^4) billion; (*amer.*) trillion **2.** (*in sistema inglese e tedesco* = 1000^6) trillion; (*amer.*) quintillion.
trillare *vi.* **1.** to trill **2.** (*squillare*) to ring (*v. irr.*).
trillo *sm.* **1.** trill **2.** (*di sveglia, telefono*) ring.
trilogìa *sf.* trilogy.
trimestrale *agg.* quarterly.
trimestre *sm.* **1.** quarter **2.** (*scol.*) term **3.** (*paga trimestrale*) quarterage.
trimotore *agg.* three-engined aeroplane.
trina *sf.* lace.
trincare *vt.* to gulp. ◆ **trincare** *vi.* to drink (*v. irr.*).
trincea *sf.* trench.
trincerare *vt.* to entrench.

trincetto *sm.* shoemaker's knife (*pl.* knives).
trinchetto *sm. albero di* —, foremast; *vela di* —, foresail.
trinciante *agg.* sharp. ◆ **trinciante** *sm.* carver.
trinciare *vt.* **1.** to cut (*v. irr.*) (up) **2.** (*carne*) to carve || — *giudizi*, to judge rashly.
trinciato *sm.* cut-tobacco.
trinità *sf.* trinity.
trinomio *sm.* trinomial.
trionfante *agg.* triumphant.
trionfare *vt.* to triumph.
trionfatore *sm.* triumpher.
trionfo *sm.* triumph.
tripartito *agg.* tripartite.
tripartizione *sf.* tripartition.
triplicare *vt.* to treble.
triplo *agg.* triple. ◆ **triplo** *sm.* **1.** triple **2.** (*tre volte tanto*) three times as much.
trippa *sf.* (*cuc.*) tripe.
tripudiare *vi.* to exult.
tripudio *sm.* exultation.
trisàvolo *sm.* great-great-grandfather.
trisìllabo *agg.* trisyllabic. ◆ **trisìllabo** *sm.* trisyllable.
triste *agg.* sad.
tristezza *sf.* **1.** sadness **2.** (*dolore*) grief.
tristo *agg.* wicked.
tritacarne *sm.* mincer.
tritare *vt.* to mince.
tritatutto *sm.* mincer.
trito *agg.* (*fig.*) trite.
tritolo *sm.* trinitrotoluene.
trìttico *sm.* triptych.
trittongo *sm.* triphthong.
tritume *sm.* crumbs (*pl.*).
triturare *vt.* to triturate.
triumvirato *sm.* triumvirate.
triùmviro *sm.* triumvir.
trivalente *agg.* trivalent.
trivella *sf.* **1.** (*min.*) drill **2.** (*falegnameria*) auger.
trivellare *vt.* to drill.
trivellazione *sf.* drilling: *torre di* —, derrick.
triviale *agg.* coarse.
trivialità *sf.* **1.** coarseness **2.** (*detto triviale*) coarse expression.
trofeo *sm.* trophy.
troglodita *sm.* troglodyte.
troglodìtico *agg.* troglodytic(al).
trògolo *sm.* trough.
troia *sf.* (*zool.*) sow.
tromba *sf.* **1.** trumpet **2.** (*di scale*)

well || — *d'aria*, tornado; — *d'acqua*, water-spout.

trombettiere *sm.* trumpeter.

trombone *sm.* 1. (*mus.*) trombone 2. (*schioppo*) blunderbuss || *suonatore di* —, trombonist.

trombosi *sf.* thrombosis.

troncare *vt.* 1. to cut (*v. irr.*) off 2. (*fig.*) to break (*v. irr.*) off.

tronco[1] *agg.* 1. cut off 2. (*fig.*) broken.

tronco[2] *sm.* 1. trunk 2. (*d'albero abbattuto*) log 3. (*geom.*) frustum || — *ferroviario*, railway section; *licenziare in* —, to sack on the spot.

troncone *sm.* stump.

troneggiare *vi.* to dominate (sthg.).

tronfio *agg.* 1. conceited 2. (*di stile*) bombastic.

trono *sm.* throne.

tropicale *agg.* tropical.

tròpico *sm.* tropic.

tropismo *sm.* tropism.

troposfera *sf.* troposphere.

troppo *avv.* 1. (*con agg. e avv.*) too 2. (*con v.*) too much 3. (*di tempo*) too long. ♦ **troppo** *agg. e pron.* too much (*pl.* too many): *anche* —, only too; *essere di* —, to be unwelcome.

trota *sf.* trout (*pl. invariato*).

trottare *vi.* to trot: *far — qu.* (*fig.*) to make (*v. irr.*) so. run.

trottata *sf.* trot.

trottatore *sm.* trotter.

trotterellare *vi.* 1. to trot along 2. (*di bambini*) to toddle.

trotto *sm.* trot: *mettere un cavallo al* —, to trot a horse.

tròttola *sf.* top.

trovare *vt.* 1. to find (*v. irr.*) 2. (*far visita*) to see (*v. irr.*) 3. (*pensare*) to think (*v. irr.*). ♦ **trovarsi** *vr.* 1. (*essere*) to be 2. (*sentirsi*) to feel (*v. irr.*).

trovata *sf.* trick.

trovatello *sm.* foundling.

trovatore *sm.* troubadour.

truccare *vi.* 1. to make (*v. irr.*) up 2. (*sport*) to fix.

truccatore *sm.* maker-up.

truccatura *sf.* make-up.

trucco *sm.* 1. trick 2. (*cosmetici*) make-up 3. (*inganno*) deceit.

truce *agg.* grim.

trucidare *vt.* to slay (*v. irr.*).

trùciolo *sm.* shaving.

truculento *agg.* truculent.

truffa *sf.* cheat.

truffaldino *agg.* cheating.

truffare *vt.* to cheat.

truffatore *sm.* cheat.

truismo *sm.* truism.

truppa *sf.* troop.

tu *pron.* you.

tua *agg. e pron.* V. *tuo.*

tuba *sf.* 1. tuba 2. (*cappello*) top-hat.

tubare *vi.* to coo.

tubatura *sf.* piping.

tubercolare *agg.* tubercular.

tubercolina *sf.* tuberculin.

tubercolosario *sm.* sanatorium.

tubercolosi *sf.* tuberculosis: — *polmonare*, consumption.

tubercoloso *agg.* tuberculous. ♦ **tubercoloso** *sm.* consumptive.

tùbero *sm.* tuber.

tuberosa *sf.* tuberose.

tubino *sm.* bowler-hat.

tubo *sm.* 1. tube 2. (*di conduttura*) pipe 3. (*anat.*) canal.

tubolare *agg.* tubular.

tue *agg. e pron.* V. *tuo.*

tuffare *vt.* to plunge, to dip. ♦ **tuffarsi** *vr.* to plunge, to dive.

tuffatore *sm.* diver.

tuffo *sm.* plunge, dive.

tufo *sm.* tuff.

tugurio *sm.* hovel.

tulipano *sm.* tulip.

tumefare *vt.* to swell (*v. irr.*). ♦ **tumefarsi** *vr.* to swell.

tumefatto *agg.* swollen.

tumefazione *sf.* swelling.

tùmido *agg.* tumid: *labbra tumide*, thick lips.

tumore *sm.* tumour.

tumulare *vt.* to bury.

tumulazione *sf.* burial.

tùmulo *sm.* 1. tumulus (*pl.* -li) 2. (*tomba*) grave.

tumulto *sm.* tumult.

tumultuante *agg.* riotous.

tumultuare *vi.* to riot.

tumultuoso *agg.* tumultuous.

tundra *sf.* tundra.

tungsteno *sm.* tungsten.

tùnica *sf.* tunic.

tunnel *sm.* tunnel.

tuo *agg.* your. ♦ **tuo** *pron.* yours.

tuoi *agg. e pron.* V. *tuo* || *i* —, your family.

tuonare *vi.* to thunder.

tuono *sm.* thunder.

tuorlo *sm.* yolk.

turàcciolo *sm.* 1. stopper 2. (*di su-*

ghero) cork || *mettere il — a una bottiglia*, to cork a bottle.
turare *vt.* to stop, to fill up. ♦ **turarsi** *vr.* 1. to stop 2. (*chiudersi*) to shut oneself up.
turba¹ *sf.* crowd.
turba² *sf.* (*med.*) trouble.
turbamento *sm.* 1. perturbation 2. (*eccitazione*) .excitement 3. (*sconvolgimento*) upsetting.
turbante *sm.* turban.
turbare *vt.* 1. to upset (*v. irr.*) 2. (*agitare intorbidando*) to muddy. ♦ **turbarsi** *vr.* to get (*v. irr.*) upset.
turbina *sf.* turbine.
turbinare *vi.* to whirl.
tùrbine *sm.* 1. whirl 2. (*uragano*) hurricane.
turbinìo *sm.* whirling.
turbinoso *agg.* 1. whirling 2. (*tumultuoso*) tumultuous.
turbolento *agg.* boisterous.
turbolenza *sf.* boisterousness.
turbomotore *sm.* turbojet engine.
turbonave *sf.* turboship.
turboreattore *sm.* (*aer.*) turbojet.
turcasso *sm.* quiver.
turchese *sm.* turquoise.
turchino *agg.* deep blue.
turco *agg.* Turkish. ♦ **turco** *sm.* Turk.
turgidezza *sf.* turgidity.
tùrgido *agg.* turgid.
turìbolo *sm.* censer.
turismo *sm.* tourism.
turista *s.* tourist.
turìstico *agg.* tourist (*attr.*).
turlupinare *vt.* to swindle.
turlupinatura *sf.* swindle.
turno *sm.* 1. turn 2. (*servizio*) duty || *di —*, on duty; *a —*, on turn.
turpe *agg.* filthy.
turpiloquio *sm.* coarse language.
turpitùdine *sf.* baseness.
turrito *agg.* turreted.
tuta *sf.* overalls (*pl.*): *— spaziale*, spacesuit.
tutela *sf.* 1. guardianship 2. (*protezione*) protection.
tutelare *vt.* to guard.
tutelare *agg.* tutelary.
tutore *sm.* guardian.
tuttavìa *cong.* yet.
tutto *agg.* all, whole (*pl.* all); (*ogni*) every || *tutt'e due*, both; *tutt'al più*, at the most; *tutt'altro che*, anything but; *tutt'altro!*, on the contrary! ♦ **tutto** *pron.* all,

everything (*pl.* alìì); (*ognuno*) everybody. ♦ **tutto** *s.m.* whole: *del —*, quite.
tuttofare *agg.* *cameriera —*, maid-of-all-work.
tuttora *avv.* still.

U

ubbìa *sf.* whim.
ubbidiente *agg.* obedient.
ubbidienza *sf.* obedience.
ubbidire *vi.* to obey (so., sthg.).
ubicare *vt.* to locate.
ubicato *agg.* situated.
ubicazione *sf.* location.
ubiquità *sf.* ubiquity.
ubriacare *vt.* to make (*v. irr.*) drunk. ♦ **ubriacarsi** *vr.* to get (*v. irr.*) drunk.
ubriacatura *sf.* intoxication.
ubriachezza *sf.* drunkenness.
ubriaco *agg.* drunk. ♦ **ubriaco** *sm.* drunken man (*pl.* men).
ubriacone *sm.* drunkard.
uccellagione *sf.* feathered game.
uccellare *vi.* to fowl.
uccelliera *sf.* aviary.
uccello *sm.* bird.
uccìdere *vt.* 1. to kill 2. (*assassinare*) to murder 3. (*con pugnale*) to stab to death 4. (*con arma da fuoco*) to shoot (*v. irr.*). ♦ **uccìdersi** *vr.* 1. to get (*v. irr.*) killed 2. (*suicidarsi*) to commit suicide, to kill oneself.
uccisione *sf.* killing.
uccisore *sm.* killer.
udìbile *agg.* audible.
udienza *sf.* hearing.
udire *vt.* to hear (*v. irr.*).
uditivo *agg.* auditory.
udito *sm.* hearing.
uditore *sm.* 1. listener 2. (*nella scuola*) auditor.
uditorio *sm.* audience.
ufficiale *agg.* official. ♦ **ufficiale** *sm.* 1. officer 2. (*governativo, postale*) official.
ufficialità *sf.* official character.
ufficialmente *avv.* officially.
ufficiare *vi.* to officiate.
ufficio *sm.* office: *capo —*, head clerk; *d'—*, officially; *— informazioni*, information bureau.

ufficiosamente *avv.* unofficially.
ufficioso *agg.* unofficial.
ufo (*nella loc. avv.*) *a* —, without paying.
ugello *sm.* nozzle.
uggia *sf.* boredom: *questo libro mi è venuto in* —, I have grown tired of this book.
uggiolare *vi.* to whine.
uggioso *agg.* dull.
ùgola *sf.* 1. uvula 2. (*voce*) voice.
uguaglianza *sf.* equality.
uguagliare *vt.* 1. to be equal (to) 2. (*rendere uguale*) to make (*v. irr.*) equal.
uguale *agg.* 1. equal 2. (*simile*) like, alike (*pred.*) 3. (*stesso*) same.
ugualitario *agg.* equalitarian.
ugualmente *avv.* 1. equally 2. (*lo stesso*) all the same.
ùlcera *sf.* ulcer.
ulcerare *vt.* to ulcerate. ♦ **ulcerarsi** *vr.* to ulcerate.
ulcerato *agg.* ulcerated.
ulcerazione *sf.* ulceration.
ulceroso *agg.* ulcerous.
ulteriore *agg.* further.
ulteriormente *avv.* further on.
ultimamente *avv.* 1. recently 2. (*da ultimo*) finally.
ultimare *vt.* to finish.
ultimazione *sf.* conclusion.
ùltimo *agg.* 1. last 2. (*il più recente*) latest 3. (*estremo*) utmost.
ultramicroscòpico *agg.* ultramicroscopic(al).
ultramoderno *agg.* ultramodern.
ultrasensìbile *agg.* ultrasensitive.
ultrasònico *agg.* ultrasonic.
ultrasuono *sm.* ultrasound.
ultraterreno *agg.* supernatural.
ultravioletto *agg.* ultraviolet.
ululare *vi.* 1. to howl 2. (*di sirena*) to hoot.
ululato *sm.* 1. howl 2. (*di sirena*) hoot.
umanésimo *sm.* Humanism.
umanista *sm.* humanist.
umanìstico *agg.* humanistic.
umanità *sf.* humanity.
umanitario *agg.* humanitarian.
umanitarismo *sm.* humanitarianism.
umanizzare *vt.* to humanize.
umano *agg.* 1. human 2. (*comprensivo*) humane.
umerale *agg.* humeral.
umettare *vt.* to moisten.
umidità *sf.* humidity, dampness.

ùmido *agg.* damp.
ùmile *agg.* humble.
umiliante *agg.* humiliating.
umiliare *vt.* to humble.
umiliazione *sf.* humiliation.
umiltà *sf.* 1. humbleness 2. (*virtù dell'umile*) humility.
umore *sm.* humour: *essere di buon* —, to be in a good humour.
umorismo *sm.* humour.
umorista *s.* humorist.
umorìstico *agg.* humorous.
una *art.* e *agg.* V. *uno.*
unànime *agg.* unanimous.
unanimità *sf.* unanimity: *all'* —, unanimously.
uncinare *vt.* to hook.
uncinato *agg.* hooked ‖ *croce uncinata*, swastika.
uncinetto *sm.* crochet-hook: *lavorare all'* —, to crochet.
uncino *sm.* hook.
undicèsimo *agg.* eleventh.
ùndici *agg.* eleven.
ùngere *vt.* to grease.
unghia *sf.* 1. nail 2. (*di equino*) hoof 3. (*fig.*) clutch.
unghiata *sf.* scratch: *dare un'* —, to scratch.
unguento *sm.* ointment.
ungulato *agg.* hoofed.
unicamente *avv.* only.
unicellulare *agg.* unicellular.
unicità *sf.* uniqueness.
ùnico *agg.* 1. only 2. (*senza uguale*) unique.
unificare *vt.* 1. to unify 2. (*uniformare*) to standardize.
unificatore *agg.* unifying. ♦ **unificatore** *sm.* unifier.
unificazione *sf.* 1. unification 2. (*uniformazione*) standardization.
uniformare *vt.* 1. to conform 2. (*rendere conforme*) to standardize. ♦ **uniformarsi** *vr.* to conform (to).
uniforme[1] *agg.* uniform.
uniforme[2] *sf.* uniform.
uniformemente *avv.* uniformly.
uniformità *sf.* uniformity.
unigènito *sm.* only child.
unilaterale *agg.* unilateral.
unilateralmente *avv.* unilaterally.
uninominale *agg.* uninominal.
unione *sf.* union.
unionista *sm.* unionist.
unipolare *agg.* unipolar.
unire *vt.* to unite, to join. ♦ **unirsi** *vr.* to unite, to join.

unìsono *sm.* unison.

unità *sf.* 1. unity 2. (*fis.; mat.; mil.*) unit.

unitamente *avv.* unitedly: — *a*, together with.

unitario *agg.* unitary.

unito *agg.* 1. united 2. (*accluso*) enclosed.

universale *agg.* universal.

universalità *sf.* universality.

universalizzare *vt.* to universalize.

università *sf.* university.

universitario *agg.* university (*attr.*). ♦ universitario *sm.* university student.

universo *agg.* whole. ♦ universo *sm.* universe.

unìvoco *agg.* univocal.

uno, un, una *art.* a, an (*davanti a vocale e h muta*). ♦ uno, un, una *agg.* one. ♦ uno, una *pron.* 1. one 2. (*un tale*) a man; (*una tale*) a woman || — *a* —, one by one; *l'* — *e l'altro*, both; *l'* — *o l'altro*, either; *né l'* — *né l'altro*, neither; *l'* — *l'altro*, each other; *un po' per* —, a part each; *costano 5 sterline l'* —, they cost 5 pounds each.

unto *agg.* greasy.

untume *sm.* grease.

untuosamente *avv.* (*fig.*) unctuously.

untuosità *sf.* 1. greasiness 2. (*fig.*) unctuousness.

untuoso *agg.* 1. greasy 2. (*fig.*) unctuous.

unzione *sf.* unction.

uomo *sm.* man (*pl.* men): *un* — *da nulla*, a nobody.

uopo *sm.* esser *d'* —, to be necessary; *all'* —, if necessary.

uovo *sm.* egg: *rosso d'* —, yolk; *cercare il pelo nell'* —, to split (*v. irr.*) hairs.

uragano *sm.* hurricane.

uranìfero *agg.* uranic.

uranio *sm.* uranium.

uranite *sf.* uranite.

uranografìa *sf.* uranography.

urbanésimo *sm.* urbanization.

urbanista *s.* town planner.

urbanìstica *sf.* town-planning.

urbanìstico *agg.* town-planning.

urbanità *sf.* urbanity.

urbanizzare *vt.* to urbanize.

urbanizzazione *sf.* urbanization.

urbano *agg.* 1. urban 2. (*cortese*) urbane.

ùrea *sf.* urea.

uremìa *sf.* uraemia.

urèmico *agg.* uraemic.

uretra *sf.* urethra.

urgente *agg.* urgent.

urgentemente *avv.* urgently.

urgenza *sf.* urgency.

ùrgere *vt.* to urge. ♦ ùrgere *vi.* to be urgent.

uricemìa *sf.* uricaemia.

ùrico *agg.* uric.

urina *sf.* V. *orina.*

urinare *vi.* V. *orinare.*

urlare *vt. e vi.* 1. to shout, to scream 2. (*di vento, animale; per il dolore*) to howl.

urlatore *agg.* shouting. ♦ urlatore *sm.* shouter.

urlo *sm.* 1. shout 2. (*di vento, animale; per il dolore*) howl.

urna *sf.* 1. urn 2. (*per i voti*) ballot-box || *andare alle urne*, to go (*v. irr.*) to the polls.

urogallo *sm.* grouse.

urologìa *sf.* urology.

uròlogo *sm.* urologist.

urtante *agg.* irritating.

urtare *vt.* 1. to knock 2. (*infastidire*) to irritate 3. (*offendere*) to hurt (*v. irr.*). ♦ urtarsi *vr.* to get (*v. irr.*) cross. ♦ urtarsi *vr. rec.* to collide.

urticante *agg.* urticating.

urticaria *sf.* nettle rash.

urto *sm.* 1. push 2. (*scontro, contrasto*) collision || *essere in* —, to be at variance.

urtone *sm.* shove.

usanza *sf.* 1. custom 2. (*abitudine personale*) habit.

usare *vt.* to use: — *una cortesia*, to do (*v. irr.*) a favour. ♦ usare *vi.* 1. to be accustomed; (*solo al passato*) to use 2. (*essere di moda*) to be fashionable.

usato *agg.* 1. used 2. (*in uso*) in use 3. (*abituale*) usual 4. (*non nuovo*) second-hand.

uscente *agg.* 1. retiring 2. (*con espressioni di tempo*) closing.

usciere *sm.* 1. usher 2. (*ufficiale giudiziario*) bailiff.

uscio *sm.* door: *abitare* — *a* — (*con*), to live next door (to).

uscire *vi.* 1. to go (*v. irr.*) out, to come (*v. irr.*) out 2. (*sboccare*) to lead (*v. irr.*) 3. (*uscire di strada*) to go off || *uscirne bene, male*, to come off well, badly.

uscita *sf.* **1.** way out **2.** (*atto di uscire*) going out, coming out **3.** (*spese*) expense || *strada senza —*, blind-alley.

usignolo *sm.* nightingale.

uso[1] *agg.* accustomed.

uso[2] *sm.* use: *d'—*, usual; *all'— di*, after the fashion of.

ùssaro *sm.* hussar.

ustionare *vt.* to scald.

ustionato *agg.* scalded.

ustione *sf.* scald.

usuale *agg.* usual.

usufruire *vi.* to benefit (by).

usufrutto *sm.* usufruct.

usufruttuario *agg.* e *sm.* usufructuary.

usura *sf.* **1.** usury **2.** (*logorio*) wear and tear.

usuraio *sm.* usurer.

usurpare *vt.* to usurp.

usurpatore *agg.* usurping. ♦ **usurpatore** *sm.* usurper.

usurpazione *sf.* usurpation.

utènsile *sm.* utensil.

utente *s.* user.

uterino *agg.* uterine.

ùtero *sm.* uterus (*pl.* -ri).

ùtile *agg.* useful. ♦ **ùtile** *sm.* profit.

utilità *sf.* **1.** usefulness **2.** (*vantaggio*) profit || *non ne vedo l'—*, I do not see the use of it.

utilitaria *sf.* (*auto*) utility car.

utilitario *agg.* e *sm.* utilitarian.

utilitarismo *sm.* utilitarianism.

utilitarìstico *agg.* V. *utilitario*.

utilizzàbile *agg.* utilizable.

utilizzare *vt.* to utilize.

utilizzatore *agg.* utilizing. ♦ **utilizzatore** *sm.* utilizer.

utilizzazione *sf.* utilization.

utopìa *sf.* utopia.

utopista *s.* utopian.

utopìstico *agg.* utopian.

uva *sf.* grapes (*pl.*): — *passa*, raisin.

uxoricida *sm.* uxoricide.

uxoricidio *sm.* uxoricide.

V

vacante *agg.* vacant.

vacanza *sf.* **1.** holiday **2.** (*posto vacante*) vacancy.

vacca *sf.* cow.

vaccaro *sm.* cowherd.

vaccherìa *sf.* cowhouse.

vacchetta *sf.* cowhide.

vaccinàbile *agg.* that can be vaccinated.

vaccinare *vt.* to vaccinate.

vaccinazione *sf.* vaccination.

vaccino *sm.* vaccine.

vaccinògeno *agg.* vaccinogenous.

vaccinoterapìa *sf.* vaccinotherapy.

vacillamento *sm.* **1.** unsteadiness **2.** (*di luce*) flickering **3.** (*fig.*) wavering.

vacillante *agg.* **1.** unsteady **2.** (*di luce*) flickering **3.** (*fig.*) uncertain.

vacillare *vi.* **1.** to be unsteady **2.** (*di luce*) to flicker **3.** (*fig.*) to waver.

vacuità *sf.* vacuity.

vacuo *agg.* vacuous.

vademecum *sm.* vade-mecum.

vagabondaggio *sm.* vagrancy.

vagabondare *vi.* to wander.

vagabondo *agg.* vagabond. ♦ **vagabondo** *sm.* vagrant.

vagamente *avv.* vaguely.

vagante *agg.* wandering.

vagare *vi.* to wander.

vagheggiamento *sm.* longing (for).

vagheggiare *vt.* to long (for).

vagheggino *sm.* gallant.

vaghezza *sf.* **1.** charm **2.** (*indeterminatezza*) vagueness.

vagina *sf.* vagina (*pl.* -nae).

vagire *vi.* to wail.

vagito *sm.* wail.

vaglia[1] *sf.* (*valore*) worth.

vaglia[2] *sm.* money order: — *postale*, postal order.

vagliare *vt.* to sieve **2.** (*fig.*) to weigh.

vagliatura *sf.* screening.

vaglio *sm.* **1.** sieve **2.** (*fig.*) sifting.

vago *agg.* **1.** vague **2.** (*leggiadro*) pretty.

vagoncino *sm.* wag(g)on.

vagolare *vi.* to rove.

vagone *sm.* carriage, coach.

vaio[1] *agg.* dark grey.

vaio[2] *sm.* vair.

vaiolo *sm.* smallpox.

valanga *sf.* avalanche.

valchiria *sf.* Walkyrie.

valente *agg.* **1.** skilful **2.** (*valoroso*) brave.

valentemente *avv.* **1.** skilfully **2.** (*valorosamente*) bravely.

valentìa *sf.* **1.** skill **2.** (*valore*) worth.

valentuomo *sm.* worthy man.
valenza *sf.* valence.
valere *vi.* 1. to be worth: — *la pena*, to be worth while; *far* —: *i propri diritti*, to assert one's rights; *farsi* —, to make (*v. irr.*) oneself appreciated 2. (*contare*) to count 3. (*servire*) to be of use 4. (*essere valido*) to be valid. ♦ **valersi** *vr.* to avail oneself (of).
valeriana *sf.* valerian.
valévole *agg.* valid.
valicàbile *agg.* that can be crossed.
valicare *vt.* to cross.
vàlico *sm.* pass.
validamente *avv.* validly.
validità *sf.* validity.
vàlido *agg.* 1. valid 2. (*fondato*) well-grounded 3. (*forte*) strong.
valigeria *sf.* leatherware shop.
valigia *sf.* suit-case; *fare le valigie*, to pack up.
vallata *sf.* valley.
valle *sf.* valley.
valletto *sm.* valet.
vallo *sm.* rampart.
vallone *agg.* e *sm.* Walloon.
valore *sm.* 1. value 2. (*coraggio*) bravery.
valorizzare *vt.* 1. to turn to account 2. (*accentuare*) to emphasize.
valorizzazione *sf.* 1. turning to account 2. (*comm.*) valorization.
valorosamente *avv.* bravely.
valoroso *agg.* brave.
valsente *sm.* commercial value.
valuta *sf.* 1. value 2. (*moneta*) currency: — *estera*, foreign currency.
valutàbile *agg.* valuable.
valutare *vt.* 1. to value 2. (*considerare*) to consider.
valutazione *sf.* 1. evaluation 2. (*considerazione*) careful consideration.
valva *sf.* valve.
vàlvola *sf.* 1. valve 2. (*elettr.*) fuse 3. (*radio*) valve, tube.
valvolare *agg.* valvular.
valzer *sm.* waltz: *ballare il* —, to waltz.
vampa *sf.* 1. blaze 2. (*al viso*) flush.
vampata *sf.* 1. blaze 2. (*folata*) blast 3. (*al viso*) flush.
vampeggiante *agg.* blazing.
vampeggiare *vi.* to blaze.
vampiro *sm.* vampire.
vanagloria *sf.* vainglory.

vanagloriarsi *vr.* to boast.
vanaglorioso *agg.* boastful.
vanamente *avv.* vainly.
vandàlico *agg.* vandalic.
vandalismo *sm.* vandalism.
vàndalo *agg.* e *sm.* vandal.
vaneggiamento *sm.* raving.
vaneggiare *vi.* to rave.
vanesio *agg.* foppish. ♦ **vanesio** *sm.* fop.
vanga *sf.* spade.
vangare *vt.* to spade.
vangata *sf.* blow with a spade.
vangatore *sm.* spademan.
vangatura *sf.* spading.
vangelo *sm.* Gospel.
vaniglia *sf.* vanilla.
vanigliato *agg.* vanilla-flavoured.
vaniloquio *sm.* empty talk.
vanità *sf.* vanity.
vanitoso *agg.* conceited.
vano[1] *agg.* vain.
vano[2] *sm.* space, room.
vantaggio *sm.* 1. advantage 2. (*sport*) lead.
vantaggiosamente *avv.* advantageously.
vantaggioso *agg.* advantageous.
vantare *vt.* 1. to boast (of) 2. (*lodare*) to praise 3. (*millantare*) to brag. ♦ **vantarsi** *vr.* to boast (of).
vanteria *sf.* boast.
vanto *sm.* boast.
vànvera (*nella loc. avv.*) *a* —, at random.
vapore *sm.* 1. steam 2. (*mar.*) steamer.
vaporetto *sm.* steamboat.
vaporiera *sf.* steam-engine.
vaporizzare *vt.* to vaporize.
vaporizzatore *sm.* vaporizer.
vaporizzazione *sf.* vaporization.
vaporosità *sf.* 1. haziness 2. (*di abito*) gauziness.
vaporoso *agg.* 1. hazy 2. (*di abito*) gauzy.
varare *vt.* to launch (*anche fig.*).
varcare *vt.* to cross, to pass.
varco *sm.* passage, opening: *aprirsi un* — *fra la folla*, to force one's way through the crowd.
variàbile *agg.* variable, unsteady.
variabilità *sf.* variability, unsteadiness.
variante *sf.* variant.
variare *vt.* 1. to vary 2. (*di mercato*) to fluctuate.
variato *agg.* V. *vario*.
variazione *sf.* variation, change.

varice *sf.* varix (*pl.* varices).
varicella *sf.* chicken-pox.
varicoso *agg.* varicose.
variegato *agg.* variegated.
varietà *sf.* variety.
vario *agg.* 1. varied 2. (*differente*) various 3. (*parecchi*) several.
variopinto *agg.* many-coloured.
varo *sm.* launch.
vasaio *sm.* potter.
vasca *sf.* basin: — *da bagno*, bath (tub).
vascello *sm.* vessel.
vascolare *agg.* vascular.
vaselina *sf.* vaseline.
vasellame *sm.* 1. (*di terracotta*) earthenware 2. (*di porcellana*) china 3. (*d'argento, d'oro*) silver, gold plate.
vaso *sm.* 1. vase 2. (*rotondo*) pot 3. (*recipiente; anat.*) vessel.
vasocostrittore *agg. e sm.* vasoconstrictor.
vasodilatatore *agg. e sm.* vasodilator.
vasomotore *agg.* vasomotor.
vasomotorio *agg.* vasomotor.
vassallaggio *sm.* 1. (*stor.*) vassalage 2. subjection.
vassallo *agg. e sm.* 1. (*stor.*) vassal 2. subject.
vassoio *sm.* tray.
vastità *sf.* 1. vastness 2. (*estensione*) expanse.
vasto *agg.* wide, large.
vate *sm.* 1. prophet 2. (*poeta*) poet.
Vaticano *agg.* Vatican.
vaticinare *vt.* to prophesy.
vaticinio *sm.* prophecy.
vattelappesca *inter.* who knows!
ve *pron.* you: — *lo scrissi*, I wrote it to you. ♦ **ve** *avv.* there: — *ne sono due*, there are two.
ve' *inter.* look, see.
vecchiaia *sf.* old age.
vecchiezza *sf.* great age.
vecchio *agg.* 1. old 2. (*antico*) ancient 3. (*stantio*) stale. ♦ **vecchio** *sm.* old man.
veccia *sf.* vetch.
vece *sf.* stead, place.
vedere *vt.* to see (*v. irr.*): — *la luce* (*nascere*), to be born; *far —*, to show (*v. irr.*); *farsi —*, to show oneself; *non — l'ora di*, to look forward to (*con gerundio*). ♦ **vedersi** *vr.* 1. to see oneself 2. (*vedersela*) to deal (*v. irr.*) with.
vedetta *sf.* 1. (*sentinella*) watchman

(*pl.* -men) 2. (*posto di osservazione*) look-out.
védova *sf.* widow.
vedovanza *sf.* widowhood.
vedovile *agg.* 1. (*di vedova*) of a widow 2. (*di vedovo*) of a widower.
védovo *sm.* widower.
vedretta *sf.* small steep glacier.
veduta *sf.* 1. sight, view 2. (*opinione*) view, idea.
veemente *agg.* vehement.
veemenza *sf.* vehemence.
vegetale *agg. e sm.* vegetable.
vegetare *vi.* to vegetate.
vegetariano *agg. e sm.* vegetarian.
vegetativo *agg.* vegetative.
vegetazione *sf.* vegetation.
vègeto *agg.* 1. (*di pianta*) thriving 2. (*di persona*) vigorous, strong ‖ *vivo e —*, hale and hearty
veggente *sm.* seer.
veglia *sf.* 1. waking 2. (*il vegliare*) watch.
vegliardo *sm.* old man.
vegliare *vi.* 1. to be awake 2. (*far la veglia*) to watch.
veglione *sm.* masked ball.
veìcolo *sm.* vehicle.
vela *sf.* sail.
velame *sm.* 1. veil 2. (*mar.*) sails (*pl.*).
velare *vt.* to veil.
velario *sm.* curtain.
velatura *sf.* sails (*pl.*).
veleggiare *vi.* to sail.
veleno *sm.* poison.
velenoso *agg.* poisonous, venomous.
veletta *sf.* 1. (*mar.*) topsail 2. (*di cappello*) veil.
veliero *sm.* sailing-ship.
velina *sf.* tissue-paper.
velismo *sm.* sailing.
velìvolo *sm.* aeroplane.
velleità *sf.* foolish ambition, fancy.
vellicare *vt.* to tickle.
vello *sm.* fleece.
vellutato *agg.* velvety: *pelle vellutata*, downy skin.
velluto *sm.* velvet.
velo *sm.* veil.
veloce *agg.* fast, quick, swift.
velocìpede *sm.* velocipede.
velocità *sf.* speed, velocity: *a tutta —*, at full speed; *limite di —*, speed limit; *cambio di — (auto)*, gearbox; *indicatore di —*, speedometer.
velòdromo *sm.* cycle-racing track.

veltro *sm.* greyhound.
vena *sf.* vein.
venale *agg.* venal.
venalità *sf.* venality.
venare *vt.* 1. to vein 2. (*di legno*) to grain.
venato *agg.* 1. veined 2. (*di legno*) grained.
venatorio *agg.* venatorial.
venatura *sf.* 1. vein 2. (*di legno*) grain.
vendemmia *sf.* vintage.
vendemmiare *vi.* to gather grapes.
vendemmiatore *sm.* vintager.
véndere *vt.* to sell (*v. irr.*): — *a buι mercato*, to sell cheaply; — *a credito*, to sell on credit; — *all'ingrosso*, *al minuto*, to sell wholesale, by retail; — *a rate*, to sell by instalments.
vendetta *sf.* revenge.
vendìbile *agg.* salable.
vendicare *vt.* to revenge.
vendicativo *agg.* revengeful.
vendicatore *sm.* revenger.
véndita *sf.* sale: — *all'asta*, auction.
venditore *sm.* seller.
venduto *agg.* 1. sold 2. (*fig.*) corrupted.
veneficio *sm.* poisoning.
venèfico *agg.* poisonous.
veneràbile *agg.* venerable.
venerando *agg.* venerable.
venerare *vt.* to worship.
venerazione *sf.* worship.
venerdì *sm.* Friday: — *Santo*, Good Friday.
vènere *sf.* 1. Venus 2. (*fig.*) beauty.
venèreo *agg.* venereal.
veneziana *sf.* Venetian-blind.
veniale *agg.* venial.
venire *vi.* 1. to come (*v. irr.*): — *al sodo*, to come to the point; — *in mente*, to come into one's head; — *meno*, to faint; — *alla luce*, to come to light 2. (*riuscire*) to turn out 3. (*derivare*) to derive.
venoso *agg.* venous.
ventaglio *sm.* fan.
ventata *sf.* gust of wind.
ventèsimo *agg.* twentieth.
venti *agg.* twenty.
ventilare *vt.* to ventilate.
ventilato *agg.* airy, windy.
ventilatore *sm.* fan.
ventilazione *sf.* ventilation.
ventina *sf.* score: *essere sulla* — (*di anni*), to be about twenty.

vento *sm.* wind.
ventosa *sf.* sucker.
ventosità *sf.* flatulence.
ventoso *agg.* windy.
ventrale *agg.* ventral.
ventre *sm.* 1. abdomen 2. (*fam.*) tummy.
ventrìcolo *sm.* ventricle.
ventriera *sf.* body-belt.
ventriglio *sm.* gizzard.
ventriloquio *sm.* ventriloquism.
ventrìloquo *sm.* ventriloquist.
ventura *sf.* chance, fortune.
venturo *agg.* next, coming.
venustà *sf.* beauty.
venusto *agg.* beautiful.
venuta *sf.* coming, arrival.
vera *sf.* wedding-ring.
verace *agg.* true.
veracità *sf.* veracity, truth.
veramente *avv.* really, truly, indeed.
veranda *sf.* verandah.
verbale *agg.* verbal. ♦ **verbale** *sm.* minutes (*pl.*).
verbalizzare *vt.* to record.
verbo *sm.* 1. verb 2. (*parola*) word.
verbosità *sf.* verbosity.
verboso *agg.* verbose.
verdastro *agg.* greenish.
verde *agg.* green.
verdeggiante *agg.* verdant.
verdeggiare *vi.* to be verdant.
verdemare *sm.* sea-green.
verderame *sm.* verdigris.
verdetto *sm.* verdict.
verdògnolo *agg.* greenish.
verdura *sf.* vegetables (*pl.*).
verecondia *sf.* modesty.
verecondo *agg.* modest.
verga *sf.* 1. twig 2. (*bacchetta*) rod.
vergare *vt.* (*scrivere*) to write (*v. irr.*).
vergata *sf.* blow with a rod.
vergato *agg.* 1. striped 2. (*scritto*) written ‖ *carta vergata*, laid paper.
verginale *agg.* virginal.
vérgine *agg.* e *sf.* virgin.
vergineo *agg.* virginal.
verginità *sf.* virginity.
vergogna *sf.* shame: *aver* —, to be ashamed.
vergognarsi *vr.* to be, to feel (*v. irr.*) shamed.
vergognosamente *avv.* shamefully.
vergognoso *agg.* 1. shameful 2. (*timido*) shy.
veridicamente *avv.* veraciously.
veridicità *sf.* veracity.

verìdico *agg.* veracious.
verìfica *sf.* verification.
verificàbile *agg.* verifiable.
verificare *vt.* to verify, to check.
verificatore *sm.* verifier.
verificazione *sf.* V. *verifica.*
verismo *sm.* realism.
verista *sm.* realist.
verìstico *agg.* realistic.
verità *sf.* truth: *dire la* —, to tell (*v. irr.*) the truth.
veritiero *agg.* truthful.
verme *sm.* worm.
vermìfugo *agg.* e *sm.* vermifuge.
vermiglio *agg.* bright red.
verminoso *agg.* verminous.
vernàcolo *agg.* vernacular.
vernìce *sf.* 1. paint 2. (*apparenza*) varnish.
verniciare *vt.* to paint, to varnish.
verniciatura *sf.* painting, varnishing.
vero *agg.* true, real.
verosimigliante *agg.* likely.
verosimiglianza *sf.* iikelihood.
verosìmile *agg.* likely, probable.
verricello *sm.* windlass.
verro *sm.* boar.
verruca *sf.* wart.
versamento *sm.* 1. pouring 2. (*comm.*) payment, deposit.
versante *sm.* side, slope.
versare *vt.* 1. to pour 2. (*rovesciare*) to spill (*v. irr.*) 3. (*comm.*) to pay (*v. irr.*).
versàtile *agg.* versatile.
versatilità *sf.* versatility.
versato *agg.* 1. poured out 2. (*esperto*) versed.
verseggiare *vt.* to versify.
verseggiatore *sm.* versifier.
versetto *sm.* 1. short line 2. (*della Bibbia*) verse.
versificare *vt.* to versify.
versificatore *sm.* versifier.
versificazione *sf.* versification.
versione *sf.* version, translation.
verso[1] *sm.* 1. verse, line 2. (*suono*) sound 3. (*direzione*) way.
verso[2] *prep.* 1. towards, to 2. (*contro*) against 3. (*circa*) about.
vèrtebra *sf.* vertebra (*pl.* -rae).
vertebrale *agg.* vertebral.
vertebrato *agg.* e *sm.* vertebrate.
vertenza *sf.* 1. dispute 2. (*giur.*) litigation.
vèrtere *vi.* to be about, to concern.
verticale *agg.* vertical.
verticalità *sf.* verticality.

vèrtice *sm.* 1. vertex (*pl.* vertices) 2. (*fig.*) height, top.
vertìgine *sf.* dizziness (*solo sing.*).
vertiginoso *agg.* dizzy.
verza *sf.* cabbage.
vescica *sf.* bladder.
vescovado *sm.* bishop's residence.
vescovile *agg.* episcopal.
véscovo *sm.* bishop.
vespa *sf.* wasp.
vespaio *sm.* 1. wasps' nest 2. (*fig.*) hornets' nest.
vespro *sm.* 1. evening 2. (*relig.*) evensong.
vessare *vt.* to vex.
vessatorio *agg.* vexatious.
vessazione *sf.* vexation.
vessillo *sm.* flag.
vestaglia *sf.* dressing-gown.
vestale *sf.* vestal.
veste *sf.* 1. dress 2. (*eccl.*) vestment 3. (*qualità*) capacity.
vestiario *sm.* clothes (*pl.*).
vestìbolo *sm.* hall.
vestigio *sm.* vestige.
vestimento *sm.* V. *veste.*
vestire *vt.* 1. to dress 2. (*fig.*) to clothe 3. (*indossare*) to wear (*v. irr.*). ◆ **vestirsi** *vr.* to dress oneself.
vestito *sm.* 1. (*da uomo*) suit 2. (*da donna*) frock, dress.
vestizione *sf.* 1. (*eccl.*) ceremony of taking the habit 2. (*di monaca*) ceremony of taking the veil.
veterano *sm.* veteran.
veterinaria *sf.* veterinary science.
veterinario *sm.* veterinary.
veto *sm.* veto.
vetraio *sm.* glazier.
vetrame *sm.* glassware.
vetrata *sf.* glass partition: — *a colori*, stained glass window.
vetrato *agg.* glazed: *carta vetrata*, glass-paper.
vetrerìa *sf.* glass-work.
vetrificàbile *agg.* vitrifiable.
vetrificare *vt.* to vitrify.
vetrificazione *sf.* vitrification.
vetrina *sf.* shop-window.
vetrioleggiare *vt.* to vitriolize.
vetriolo *sm.* vitriol.
vetro *sm.* 1. glass 2. (*di finestra*) window-pane.
vetrocromìa *sf.* glass-painting.
vetroso *agg.* glassy.
vetta *sf.* top, summit.
vettore *sm.* vector.
vettoriale *agg.* vectorial.

vettovagliamento *sm.* provisi-n-ing.

vettovagliare *vt.* to provision.

vettura *sf.* 1. coach 2. (*automobile*) car || — *di piazza*, taxi-cab.

vetturino *sm.* cabman (*pl.* -men).

vetustà *sf.* antiquity.

vetusto *agg.* ancient.

vezzeggiare *vt.* to fondle.

vezzeggiativo *sm.* petname.

vezzo *sm.* 1. habit 2. (*collana*) necklace.

vezzosamente *avv.* charmingly.

vezzoso *agg.* charming.

vi[1] *pron.* you, to you.

vi[2] *avv.* 1. (*qui*) here 2. (*là*) there.

via[1] *sf.* 1. street 2. (*strada di comunicazione*) road 3. (*cammino*) way (*anche fig.*) 4. (*linea di condotta*) course. ♦ **via** *sm.* dare il —, to give (*v. irr.*) the starting.

via[2] *avv.* away: *andar* —, to go (*v. irr.*) away.

viabilità *sf.* state of a road.

viadotto *sm.* viaduct.

viaggiante *agg.* travelling.

viaggiare *vi.* to travel: — *in treno, automobile, aereo*, to travel by train, by car, by air.

viaggiatore *sm.* traveller: — *di commercio*, commercial traveller.

viaggio *sm.* 1. journey, trip 2. (*per mare*) voyage 3. (*in aereo*) flight.

viale *sm.* avenue; (*di giardino*) alley.

viandante *sm.* wayfarer.

viàtico *sm.* viaticum (*pl.* -ca).

viavai *sm.* coming-and-going.

vibrante *agg.* vibrating (with).

vibrare *vi.* 1. to vibrate 2. (*colpi*) to strike (*v. irr.*).

vibràtile *agg.* vibratile.

vibrato *agg.* energetic.

vibratore *sm.* vibrator.

vibrazione *sf.* vibration.

vicariato *sm.* vicariate.

vicario *sm.* vicar.

vicecònsole *sm.* vice-consul.

vicedirettore *sm.* assistant-director.

vicegovernatore *sm.* vice-governor.

vicenda *sf.* vicissitude 2. (*evento*) event 3. (*successione*) succession.

vicendévole *agg.* mutual.

vicendevolmente *avv.* mutually.

vicepresidente *sm.* vice-president.

viceré *sm.* viceroy.

vicesegretario *sm.* vice-secretary.

viceversa *avv.* vice versa. ♦ **viceversa** *cong.* whereas.

vicinale *sf.* local road.

vicinanza *sf.* 1. vicinity: *in — di*, close to 2. (*adiacenze*) neighbourhood: *nelle vicinanze*, in the neighbourhood.

vicinato *sm.* 1. neighbourhood 2. (*i vicini*) neighbours (*pl.*).

vicino[1] *agg.* near, close. ♦ **vicino** *sm.* neighbour.

vicino[2] *avv.* near, near by. ♦ **vicino** *prep.* near, close to.

vicissitùdine *sf.* vicissitude.

vìcolo *sm.* lane, alley.

vìdeo *sm.* video.

vidimare *vt.* 1. (*firmare*) to sign 2. (*autenticare*) to authenticate.

vidimazione *sf.* 1. (*firma*) signature 2. (*autenticazione*) authentication.

vietare *vt.* to forbid (*v. irr.*).

vietato *agg.* forbidden: — *fumare*, no smoking; — *entrare*, no admittance.

vieto *agg.* antiquated.

vigente *agg.* in force.

vìgere *vi.* to be in force.

vigilante *agg.* watchful.

vigilanza *sf.* watch.

vigilare *vt.* to watch over.

vigilato *agg.* watched.

vìgile *agg.* watchful. ♦ **vìgile** *sm.* policeman (*pl.* -men).

vigilia *sf.* 1. eve 2. (*relig.*) fast.

vigliaccamente *avv.* in a cowardly way.

vigliacchería *sf.* 1. cowardice 2. (*azione vigliacca*) cowardly action.

vigliacco *agg.* cowardly.

vigna *sf.* vineyard.

vigneto *sm.* vineyard.

vignetta *sf.* cartoon.

vigore *sm.* vigour: *in* —, in force.

vigoroso *agg.* vigorous.

vile *agg.* 1. cowardly 2. (*meschino*) mean 3. (*basso*) low.

vilipèndere *vt.* to despise.

vilipendio *sm.* contempt.

villa *sf.* villa.

villaggio *sm.* village.

villanìa *sf.* 1. rudeness 2. (*azione villana*) rude action.

villano *agg.* rude. ♦ **villano** *sm.* peasant, countryman (*pl.* -men).

villeggiante *s.* holiday-maker.

villeggiatura *sf.* holiday: *luogo di* —, (holiday) resort.

villino *sm.* cottage.

villoso *agg.* hairy.

viltà *sf.* 1. cowardice 2. (*azione vile*) cowardly action.

vilucchio *sm.* bearbind.
viluppo *sm.* tangle.
vimine *sm.* withe: *paniere di vimini*, wicker basket.
vinaccia *sf.* dregs of pressed grapes (*pl.*).
vinaio *sm.* wine-merchant.
vinario *agg.* wine (*attr.*).
vincente *agg.* winning. ◆ **vincente** *sm.* winner.
vincere *vt.* 1. to win (*v. irr.*) 2. (*battere*) to beat (*v. irr.*) 3. (*sopraffare*) to overcome (*v. irr.*) 4. (*superare*) to outdo (*v. irr.*).
vincibile *agg.* conquerable.
vincita *sf.* 1. win 2. (*denaro vinto*) winnings (*pl.*).
vincitore *agg.* winning. ◆ **vincitore** *sm.* winner.
vinco *sm.* withe.
vincolare *vt.* 1. to bind (*v. irr.*) 2. (*comm.*) to lock up.
vincolato *agg.* 1. bound 2. (*comm.*) locked up.
vincolo *sm.* tie, bond.
vinello *sm.* light wine.
vinicolo *agg.* wine (*attr.*).
vinificazione *sf.* wine-making.
vino *sm.* wine.
vinto *agg.* 1. that has been won 2. (*sconfitto*) beaten 3. (*sopraffatto*) overcome ‖ *darsi —*, to give (*v. irr.*) in. ◆ **vinto** *sm.* 1. (*al giuoco o in qualsiasi contesa*) loser 2. (*in battaglia*) vanquished man.
viola[1] *sf.* 1. violet: *— del pensiero*, pansy. ◆ **viola** *agg. e sm.* violet.
viola[2] *sf.* (*mus.*) viola.
violacee *sf. pl.* violaceae.
violaceo *agg.* violet.
violare *vt.* to violate.
violatore *sm.* violator.
violazione *sf.* violation: *— di domicilio*, house-breaking.
violentare *vt.* 1. to violate, to rape 2. (*fig.*) to do (*v. irr.*) violence to.
violento *agg.* violent.
violenza *sf.* violence, rape.
violetto *agg.* violet.
violinista *s.* violin-player.
violino *sm.* violin.
violoncellista *s.* violoncellist.
violoncello *sm.* violoncello.
viòttola *sf.* path, lane.
viòttolo *sm.* path, lane.
vipera *sf.* 1. adder 2. (*fig.*) viper.
viperino *agg.* viperous.
viraggio *sm.* (*foto*) toning.
virago *sf.* virago.

virare *vt. e vi.* 1. to veer: *— di bordo*, to veer round 2. (*fig.*) to turn about.
virata *sf.* veer.
virginale *agg.* virginal.
virginia *sm.* Virginia.
virgola *sf.* 1. (*gramm.*) comma 2. (*mat.*) point.
virgolette *sf. pl.* inverted commas: *tra —*, in inverted commas.
virgulto *sm.* shoot.
virile *agg.* manly.
virilità *sf.* 1. manliness 2. (*età virile*) manhood.
virilmente *avv.* manfully.
virologìa *sf.* virology.
virosi *sf.* virosis (*pl.* -ses).
virtù *sf.* virtue.
virtuale *agg.* virtual.
virtualità *sf.* virtuality.
virtuosismo *sm.* virtuosity.
virtuoso *agg.* virtuous.
virulento *agg.* virulent.
virulenza *sf.* virulence.
virus *sm.* virus.
viscerale *agg.* visceral.
viscere *sm.* 1. vital organ 2. (*f. pl.*) *le viscere*, viscera.
vischio *sm.* 1. mistletoe 2. (*pania*) bird-lime.
vischiosità *sf.* stickiness.
vischioso *agg.* sticky.
viscidità *sf.* viscidity.
viscido *agg.* 1. sticky 2. (*scivoloso*) slippery.
visciola *sf.* wild cherry.
visconte *sm.* viscount.
viscontessa *sf.* viscountess.
viscosità *sf.* viscosity.
viscoso *agg.* viscous.
visibile *agg.* visible, clear.
visibilio *sm.* great number: *andare in —*, to go (*v. irr.*) into raptures.
visibilità *sf.* visibility.
visiera *sf.* 1. (*di elmo*) visor 2. (*di berretto*) peak.
visionario *agg. e sm.* visionary.
visione *sf.* vision: *prendere — di*, to look over; *prima — (cine)*, first screening.
visita *sf.* 1. visit, call: *fare una —*, to pay (*v. irr.*) a visit 2. (*persona che visita*) visitor 3. (*med.*) examination.
visitare *vt.* to visit.
visitatore *sm.* visitor.
visivo *agg.* visual.
viso *sm.* face: *— a —*, face to face.
visone *sm.* mink.

vispo *agg.* lively, brisk.
vista *sf.* 1. sight 2. (*occhi*) eyes (*pl.*).
vistare *vt.* to visa.
visto[1] *sm.* visa.
visto[2] *agg.* seen ‖ — *che*, since as.
vistoso *agg.* 1. showy 2. (*fig.*) considerable.
visuale *agg.* visual. ♦ **visuale** *sf.* sight.
vita[1] *sf.* 1. life (*pl.* lives): *a* —, for life; *in* —, during one's life 2. (*necessario per vivere*) living: *costo della* —, cost of living.
vita[2] *sf.* (*anat.*) waist.
vitaiolo *sm.* bon viveur.
vitalba *sf.* clematis.
vitale *agg.* vital.
vitalità *sf.* vitality.
vitalizio *agg.* for life. ♦ **vitalizio** *sm.* annuity.
vitamina *sf.* vitamin.
vitaminico *agg.* vitaminic.
vite[1] *sf.* vine.
vite[2] *sf.* (*mecc.*) screw.
vitello *sm.* calf (*pl.* calves).
viticcio *sm.* vine-tendril.
viticolo *agg.* viticultural.
viticoltore *sm.* viticulturist.
viticoltura *sf.* grape-growing.
vitreo *agg.* vitreous.
vittima *sf.* victim.
vittimismo *sm.* victimization.
vitto *sm.* 1. food 2. (*pasti in pensione o albergo*) board: — *e alloggio*, board and lodging.
vittoria *sf.* victory.
vittorioso *agg.* victorious.
vituperare *vt.* to vituperate.
vituperio *sm.* insult.
viuzza *sf.* lane.
viva *inter.* hurrah!
vivacchiare *vi.* to live poorly.
vivace *agg.* 1. lively, sprightly 2. (*pronto, sveglio*) quick 3. (*di colori*) bright.
vivacemente *avv.* 1. lively 2. (*prontamente*) quickly 3. (*vivamente*) brightly.
vivacità *sf.* 1. liveliness 2. (*di colori*) brightness.
vivaio *sm.* 1. (*di pesci*) fish-pond 2. (*di piante*) nursery.
vivamente *avv.* deeply, keenly.
vivanda *sf.* food.
vivandiere *sm.* sutler.
vivente *agg.* alive (*pred.*), living. ♦ **vivente** *sm.* living being.
vivere *vt.* e *vi.* to live: *cessare di* —, to die; *insegnare a* — *a qu.*, to teach (*v. irr.*) so. good manners; — *alle spalle di qu.*, to sponge on so.
viveri *sm. pl.* victuals.
vivido *agg.* vivid.
vivificare *vt.* to enliven.
vivificatore *agg.* vivifying. ♦ **vivificatore** *sm.* vivifier.
viviparo *agg.* e *sm.* viviparous.
vivisezione *sf.* vivisection.
vivo *agg.* 1. living, alive (*pred.*) ‖ *a viva forza*, by main force; *argento* —, quicksilver; *calce viva*, quicklime; *farsi* —, to turn up 2. (*vivace*) lively 3. (*profondo, acuto*) deep, sharp 4. (*vivido*) vivid 5. (*di colori*) bright.
viziare *vt.* 1. to spoil (*v. irr.*) 2. (*guastare*) to vitiate.
viziato *agg.* 1. spoilt 2. (*guasto*) vitiated.
vizio *sm.* 1. vice 2. (*cattiva abitudine*) bad habit.
vizioso *agg.* vicious. ♦ **vizioso** *sm.* vicious man.
vocabolario *sm.* 1. vocabulary 2. (*dizionario*) dictionary.
vocabolo *sm.* word.
vocale[1] *agg.* vocal.
vocale[2] *sf.* vowel.
vocalizzare *vt.* e *vi.* to vocalize.
vocalizzo *sm.* vocalization.
vocativo *agg.* e *sm.* vocative.
vocazione *sf.* vocation, bent.
voce *sf.* 1. voice: *a* — *alta, bassa*, in a loud, low voice; *parlare sotto* —, to whisper 2. (*diceria*) rumour 3. (*articolo di elenco*) item.
vociare *vi.* to shout.
vociferare *vi.* 1. to shout 2. (*spargere una voce*) to rumour.
vocio *sm.* shouting.
voga[1] *sf.* (*mar.*) rowing.
voga[2] *sf.* 1. (*moda*) fashion 2. (*energia*) energy.
vogare *vi.* (*mar.*) to row.
vogata *sf.* row.
vogatore *sm.* rower.
voglia *sf.* 1. wish: *aver* —, to feel (*v. irr.*) like 2. (*volontà*) will.
voglioso *agg.* desirous, willing.
voi *pron.* you: — *stessi*, you yourselves.
volano *sm.* battledore and shuttlecock.
volante[1] *agg.* flying: *cervo* —, kite; *foglio* —, loose sheet. ♦ **volante** *sf.* (*di polizia*) flying squad.

volante² *sm.* steering-wheel.
volantino *sm.* leaflet.
volare *vi.* to fly (*v. irr.*): *far —*, to blow (*v. irr.*).
volata *sf.* **1.** flight **2.** (*corsa*) rush **3.** (*sport*) final sprint.
volàtile¹ *agg.* (*chim.*) volatile.
volàtile² *sm.* bird.
volatilizzare *vt.* to volatilize. ♦
  volatilizzarsi *vr.* to volatilize.
volente *agg.* — *o nolente*, willy-nilly.
volenterosamente *avv.* willingly.
volenteroso *agg.* V. *volonteroso*.
volentieri *avv.* willingly.
volere¹ *vt.* **1.** (*forte volontà*) (*pres. indicativo e congiuntivo*) will; (*passato indicativo e congiuntivo, condizionale*) would **2.** (*desiderio*) to want, to wish: *voglio che egli venga*, I want him to come **3.** (*gradire*) to like (*costr. pers.*): *vorrei, avrei voluto*, I should like, I should have liked **4.** (*desiderio intenso*) to wish: *vorrei essere ricco!*, I wish I were rich! **5.** (*aver bisogno di*) to need, to require **6.** (*con espressioni di tempo*) to take (*v. irr.*): *ci vogliono due ore per andare alla stazione*, it takes two hours to go to the station **7.** (*cercare*) to ask for: *c'è qualcuno che ti cerca*, there is somebody asking for you **8.** (*essere disposti*) to be willing || *che tu voglia o no*, whether you like it or not; *vuoi ... vuoi* (*sia ... sia*), both ... and; *Dio lo voglia, Dio non voglia!*, God grant it, God forbid!
volere² *sm.* will, wish.
volgare *agg.* vulgar, common.
volgarità *sf.* vulgarity.
vòlgarizzare *vt.* to divulge.
volgarizzatore *sm.* popularizer.
volgarizzazione *sf.* popularization.
volgarmente *avv.* vulgarly, commonly.
vòlgere *vt.* to turn.
vòlgere *sm.* course.
volgo *sm.* common people.
voliera *sf.* aviary.
volitivo *agg.* **1.** strong-willed **2.** (*gramm.*) volitive.
volo *sm.* flight: *prendere il —*, to run (*v. irr.*) away; *capire qc. al —*, to grasp sthg. immediately.
volontà *sf.* will: *di sua spontanea —*, of his own free-will.

volontariamente *avv.* voluntarily.
volontario *agg.* voluntary. ♦ **volontario** *sm.* volunteer.
volontarismo *sm.* voluntarism.
volonteroso *agg.* willing.
volontieri *avv.* V. *volentieri*.
volpe *sf.* fox.
volpino *agg.* foxy: *cane —*, Pomeranian.
volpone *sm.* old fox.
volta¹ *sf.* **1.** time: *una —*, once; *due, tre volte*, twice, three times; *ancora una —*, once again; *una — e mezzo*, half as much; *una — o l'altra*, sooner or later; *rare volte*, seldom; *una — tanto*, once in a while; *c'era una —*, once upon a time there was **2.** (*turno*) turn: *a mia —*, in my turn.
volta² *sf.* **1.** (*curva*) bend **2.** (*arch.*) vault.
voltafaccia *sm.* volte-face.
voltaggio *sm.* voltage.
voltàmetro *sm.* voltameter.
voltare *vt.* to turn.
voltastòmaco *sm.* sickness.
voltata *sf.* bend, turning, curve.
volteggiare *vi.* **1.** to whirl **2.** (*svolazzare*) to fly (*v. irr.*) about.
volteggio *sm.* vaulting.
volto¹ *sm.* **1.** face **2.** (*aspetto*) aspect.
volto² *agg.* **1.** turned **2.** (*rivolto*) directed.
volùbile *agg.* changeable.
volubilità *sf.* inconstancy.
volume *sm.* volume.
volumètrico *agg.* volumetric.
voluminoso *agg.* voluminous, bulky.
voluta *sf.* volute.
volutamente *avv.* intentionally.
voluttà *sf.* **1.** delight **2.** (*dei sensi*) voluptuousness.
voluttuario *agg.* voluptuary.
voluttuosamente *avv.* voluptuously.
voluttuoso *agg.* voluptuous.
vòmere *sm.* **1.** ploughshare **2.** (*anat.*) vomer.
vomitare *vt.* to vomit, to be sick.
vòmito *sm.* vomiting: *conato di —*, retch.
vòngola *sf.* mussel.
vorace *agg.* voracious, greedy.
voracità *sf.* voracity, greed.
voràgine *sf.* chasm.
vorticare *vi.* to whirl.
vòrtice *sm.* whirl: *— di vento*, whirlwind.

vorticosamente *avv.* in whirls.
vorticoso *agg.* whirling.
vostro *agg. poss.* your ‖ *in vece vostra*, instead of you. ♦ **vostro** *pron. poss.* yours ‖ *rispondiamo alla vostra del 3 giugno (comm.)*, in reply to your letter of June 3rd; *sono dalla vostra*, I am on your side.
votante *agg.* voting. ♦ **votante** *sm.* voter.
votare *vt.* to vote. ♦ **votarsi** *vr.* to devote oneself.
votato *agg.* 1. passed 2. *(dedicato)* devoted.
votazione *sf.* voting.
votivo *agg.* votive.
voto *sm.* 1. *(promessa solenne)* vow 2. *(augurio)* wish 3. *(per elezioni)* vote 4. *(scolastico)* mark: *prendere un bel, brutto —*, to get (*v. irr.*) a good, bad mark.
vulcànico *agg.* volcanic.
vulcanismo *sm.* vulcanism.
vulcanizzare *vt.* to vulcanize.
vulcanizzato *agg.* vulcanized.
vulcanizzazione *sf.* vulcanization.
vulcano *sm.* volcano.
vulneràbile *agg.* vulnerable.
vulnerabilità *sf.* vulnerability.
vuotare *vt.* to empty: *— il sacco*, to speak (*v. irr.*) out one's mind.
vuoto *agg.* 1. empty 2. *(sprovvisto)* devoid. ♦ **vuoto** *sm.* 1. empty space 2. *(recipiente vuoto)* empty 3. *(vacuità)* emptiness.

X

xenofobìa *sf.* xenophobia.
xenòfobo *sm.* xenophobe.
xilòfono *sm.* xylophone.
xilografìa *sf.* 1. *(incisione)* xylograph 2. *(arte)* xylography.

Z

zaffata *sf.* whiff.
zafferano *sm.* saffron.
zaffiro *sm.* sapphire.
zàino *sm.* knapsack.
zampa *sf.* 1. paw 2. *(con zoccolo)*

hoof 3. *(di uccello)* claw 4. *(di insetto)* leg ‖ *zampe di gallina (scrittura)*, scrawl; *(rughe)* crow's feet.
zampata *sf.* blow with a paw.
zampettare *vt.* to toddle.
zampillante *agg.* gushing.
zampillare *vi.* to gush.
zampillo *sm.* gush.
zampino *sm.* little paw ‖ *mettere lo — in una faccenda*, to have a hand in the matter.
zampogna *sf.* 1. reed-pipe 2. *(cornamusa)* bag-pipe.
zampognaro *sm.* piper.
zanna *sf.* 1. fang 2. *(di elefante)* tusk.
zanzara *sf.* mosquito.
zanzariera *sf.* mosquito-net.
zappa *sf.* hoe.
zappare *vt.* to hoe.
zappata *sf.* blow with a hoe.
zappatore *sm.* 1. hoer 2. *(mil.)* pioneer.
zappatura *sf.* hoeing.
zar *sm.* czar.
zarina *sf.* czarina.
zarista *s.* czarist.
zàttera *sf.* raft.
zavorra *sf.* 1. ballast 2. *(fig.)* rubbish.
zavorrare *vt.* to ballast.
zàzzera *sf.* mane.
zazzeruto *agg.* shockheaded.
zebra *sf.* zebra.
zebrato *agg.* striped.
zebratura *sf.* stripes *(pl.)*.
zebù *sm.* zebu.
zecca[1] *sf.* mint: *nuovo di —*, brand-new.
zecca[2] *sf.* *(zool.)* tick.
zecchino *sm.* sequin: *oro —*, first-quality-gold.
zèfiro *sm.* zephyr.
zelante *agg.* zealous.
zelantemente *avv.* zealously.
zelo *sm.* zeal.
zenit *sm.* zenith.
zénzero *sm.* ginger.
zeppo *agg.* crammed (with).
zerbino *sm.* door-mat.
zerbinotto *sm.* dandy.
zero *sm.* 1. nought 2. *(in gradazioni)* zero 3. *(tel.)* 0 ‖ *ridursi a —*, to come (*v. irr.*) to nought.
zia *sf.* aunt.
zibaldone *sm.* miscellany.
zibellino *sm.* sable.
zigano *agg. e sm.* tzigane.
zìgomo *sm.* cheek-bone.

zigrinare *vt.* to knurl.
zigrinato *agg.* knurled.
zig-zag (*nella loc. avv.*) *a* —, zigzag.
zigzagare *vi.* to zigzag.
zimbello *sm.* **1.** decoy **2.** (*fig.*) laughing-stock.
zincare *vt.* to zinc.
zincatura *sf.* zinc-plating.
zinco *sm.* zinc.
zincografia *sf.* zincography.
zingaresco *agg.* gipsy (*attr.*).
zingaro *sm.* gipsy.
zio *sm.* uncle.
zircone *sm.* zircon.
zirconio *sm.* zirconium.
zitella *sf.* spinster.
zittire *vt.* to hiss.
zitto *agg.* silent: *star* —, to be silent.
zizzania *sf.* **1.** darnel **2.** (*fig.*) discord.
zoccolaio *sm.* clog-maker.
zoccolare *vi.* to clatter about with one's clogs.
zoccolo *sm.* **1.** clog **2.** (*di animale*) hoof **3.** (*piedistallo*) base.
zodiacale *agg.* zodiacal.
zodiaco *sm.* zodiac.
zolfanello *sm.* match.
zolfatara *sf.* V. *solfatara.*
zolfatura *sf.* sulfurization.
zolfo *sm.* sulphur
zolla *sf.* clod.
zolletta *sf.* lump.
zona *sf.* zone, area.
zonzo (*nella loc. avv.*) *andare a* —, to loaf.
zoo *sm.* zoo.
zoofilia *sf.* zoophilia.
zoofilo *agg.* zoophilous. ♦ **zoofilo** *sm.* animal-lover.

zoofobia *sf.* zoophobia.
zoologia *sf.* zoology.
zoologico *agg.* zoological.
zoologo *sm.* zoologist.
zootecnia *sf.* zootechny.
zootecnico *agg.* zootechnic: *patrimonio* —, live-stock. ♦ **zootecnico** *sm.* animal expert.
zoppicamento *sm.* limping.
zoppicante *agg.* lame.
zoppicare *vi.* **1.** to limp **2.** (*di mobile*) to be shaky.
zoppo *agg.* **1.** lame **2.** (*di mobile*) shaky. ♦ **zoppo** *sm.* lame person.
zoticaggine *sf.* boorishness.
zotico *agg.* boorish. ♦ **zotico** *sm.* boor.
zuavo *sm.* zouave || *calzoni alla zuava*, knickerbockers.
zucca *sf.* **1.** pumpkin **2.** (*testa*) pate.
zuccherare *vt.* to sugar.
zuccherato *agg.* sugared.
zuccheriera *sf.* sugar-basin.
zuccherificio *sm.* sugar-refinery.
zuccherino *sm.* **1.** sweet **2.** (*fig.*) sugar-plum.
zucchero *sm.* sugar.
zucchina *sf.* vegetable marrow.
zucconàggine *sf.* **1.** (*ottusità*) dullness **2.** (*ostinatezza*) stubbornness.
zuccone *sm.* **1.** (*ottuso*) blockhead **2.** (*testardo*) donkey.
zuffa *sf.* brawl.
zufolare *vt.* e *vi.* to whistle.
zufolio *sm.* whistle.
zufolo *sm.* **1.** whistle **2.** (*mus.*) pipe.
zuppa *sf.* soup.
zuppiera *sf.* tureen.
zuppo *agg.* soaked.
zuzzurellone *sm.* skittish boy.

NOMI PROPRI, STORICI E GEOGRAFICI

Abele Abel.
Abissinia Abyssinia.
Abramo Abraham.
Achille Achilles.
Ada Ada.
Adamo Adam.
Adolfo Adolph.
Adone Adonis.
Adriano Hadrian.
Adriatico (Mar) Adriatic Sea.
Afganistan Afghanistan.
Africa Africa.
Afrodite Aphrodite.
Agamennone Agamemnon
Agata Agatha.
Agnese Agnes.
Agostino Augustin.
Aia (L') The Hague.
Aiace Ajax.
Albania Albania.
Alberto Albert.
Aldo Aldous.
Alessandra Alexandra.
Alessandro Alexander.
Alessio Alexis.
Alfredo Alfred.
Algeri Algiers.
Algeria Algeria.
Alice Alice.
Alpi Alps pl.
Alsazia Alsace.
Amazzoni (Rio delle) Amazon.
Ambrogio Ambrose.
Amburgo Hamburg.
Amelia Amelia.
America America.
Amleto Hamlet.
Andalusia Andalusia.
Ande Andes pl.
Andrea Andrew.
Angelo Angel.
Anna Ann(e).
Annibale Hannibal.
Antartide Antarctica.
Antonino Antoninus.
Antonio Ant(h)ony.
Apollo Apollo.
Appennini Apennines pl.
Arabia Arabia.
Aragona Aragon.
Arcadia Arcadia.
Archimede Archimedes.

Argentina Argentina.
Arianna Ariadne.
Aristofane Aristophanes.
Aristotele Aristotle.
Armando Armand.
Arnaldo Arnold.
Aroldo Harold.
Arrigo Henry.
Arturo Arthur.
Asia Asia.
Atene Athens.
Atlantico Atlantic.
Augusta Augusta.
Augusto Augustus.
Australia Australia.
Austria Austria.
Azzorre Azores pl.

Babele Babel.
Babilonia Babylon.
Bacco Bacchus.
Balcani Balkans pl.
Baldassarre Balthazar.
Baleari Balearic Islands pl.
Baltico (Mar) Baltic Sea.
Baltimora Baltimore.
Barbara Barbara.
Barcellona Barcelona.
Barnaba Barnaby, Barnabas.
Bartolomeo Bartholomew.
Basilea Basel.
Basilio Basil.
Battista Baptist.
Beatrice Beatrix.
Belgio Belgium.
Belgrado Belgrade.
Benedetto Benedict.
Bengala Bengal.
Beniamino Benjamin.
Berenice Berenice.
Berlino Berlin.
Bermude Bermudas pl.
Bernardo Bernard.
Berta Bertha.
Betlemme Bethlehem.
Bianca Blanche.
Birmania Burma.
Boemia Bohemia.
Bolivia Bolivia.
Bonifacio Boniface.
Bosforo Bosporus.

Brandeburgo Brandenburg.
Brasile Brazil.
Bretagna Brittany.
Bruto Brutus.
Bulgaria Bulgaria.

Cadice Cadiz.
Caino Cain.
Caio Caius.
Cairo Cairo.
California California.
Calvino Calvin.
Cambogia Cambodia.
Campidoglio Capitol.
Canadà Canada.
Caraibi (Mar dei) Caribbean Sea.
Carlo Charles.
Carlomagno Charlemagne.
Carlotta Charlotte.
Carolina Caroline.
Carpazi Carpathian Mountains *pl.*
Cartagine Carthage.
Cascemir Cashmere, Kashmir.
Caspio (Mar) Caspian Sea.
Cassio Cassius.
Cassiopea Cassiopeia.
Castiglia Castile.
Caterina Catherine.
Catone Cato.
Caucaso Caucasus.
Cecilia Cecily.
Cecilio Cecil.
Cecoslovacchia Czechoslovakia.
Cenerentola Cinderella.
Cesare Caesar.
Chiara Clara.
Cicerone Cicero.
Cile Chile.
Cina China.
Cinzia Cynthia.
Cipro Cyprus.
Cirillo Cyril.
Ciro Cyrus.
Clara Clara.
Claudio Claudius, Claude.
Clemente Clement.
Clementina Clementine.
Cleopatra Cleopatra.
Clitennestra Clytemnestra.
Colombia Colombia.
Colonia Cologne.
Congo Congo.
Corea Korea.
Corfù Corfu.
Corinto Corinth.
Cornelio Cornelius.
Cornovaglia Cornwall.
Corrado Conrad.

Corsica Corsica.
Costantino Constantine.
Costantinopoli Constantinople.
Costanza Constance.
Creta Crete.
Crimea Crimea.
Cristina Christine.
Cristo Christ.
Cristoforo Christopher.
Cuba Cuba.

Dafne Daphne.
Damasco Damascus.
Damocle Damocles.
Daniele Daniel.
Danimarca Denmark.
Danubio Danube.
Danzica Danzig.
Dardanelli Dardanelles *pl.*
Dario Darius.
Davide David.
Debora Deborah.
Delfo Delphi.
Democrito Democritus.
Demostene Demosthenes.
Desdemona Desdemona.
Diana Diana.
Didone Dido.
Diocleziano Diocletian.
Diogene Diogenes.
Dionigi, Dionisio Dionysius.
Domenico Dominic.
Domiziano Domitian.
Dorotea Dorothy.
Dublino Dublin.

Ebridi Hebrides *pl.*
Edgardo Edgar.
Edimburgo Edinburgh.
Edipo Oedipus.
Edmondo Edmund.
Edoardo Edward.
Egeo (Mar) Aegean Sea.
Egitto Egypt.
Elena Helen.
Eleonora Eleanor.
Elettra Electra.
Elia Elias, Elijah.
Elisa Eliza.
Elisabetta Elizabeth.
Ellade Hellas.
Emanuele Emanuel.
Emilia Emily.
Enea Aeneas.
Enrichetta Henrietta, Harriet.
Enrico Henry, Harry.
Epaminonda Epaminondas.

Epicuro Epicurus.
Eraclito Heraclitus.
Erasmo Erasmus.
Erberto Herbert.
Ercole Hercules.
Eritrea Eritrea.
Ermete Hermes.
Ernesto Ernest.
Erode Herod.
Erodoto Herodotus.
Esaù Esau.
Eschilo Aeschylus.
Esiodo Hesiod.
Esopo Aesop.
Ester Esther.
Etiopia Ethiopia.
Ettore Hector.
Euclide Euclid.
Eufrate Euphrates.
Eugenio Eugene.
Euripide Euripides
Europa Europe.
Eva Eve.
Evelina Evelyn.
Ezechiele Ezekiel.

Farsalo Pharsalus.
Fausto Faust(us).
Federico Frederic.
Fedra Phaedra.
Felice Felix.
Ferdinando Ferdinand.
Filadelfia Philadelphia.
Filippi Philippi.
Filippine Philippines *pl.*
Filippo Philip.
Finlandia Finland.
Firenze Florence.
Formosa Formosa.
Francesca Frances.
Francesco Francis.
Francia France.
Franco Frank.
Francoforte Frankfurt.

Gabriele Gabriel.
Galilea Galilee.
Galles Wales.
Gallia Gaule.
Genova Genoa.
Geova Jehovah.
Gerardo Gerard.
Geremia Jeremiah.
Gerico Jericho.
Germania Germany.
Gerolamo Jerome.
Gerusalemme Jerusalem.

Gesù Jesus.
Giacobbe Jacob.
Giacomo James.
Giamaica Jamaica.
Giappone Japan.
Giasone Jason.
Giava Java.
Gibilterra Gibraltar.
Gilberto Gilbert.
Ginevra Geneva.
Giobbe Job.
Giona Jonah, Jonas.
Gionata Jonathan.
Giordano Jordan.
Giorgio George.
Giosuè Joshua.
Giovanna Jane, Jean, Joan.
Giovanni John.
Giove Jove, Jupiter.
Giovenale Juvenal.
Giuda Judas, Jude.
Giudea Judea.
Giuditta Judith.
Giulia Julia, Julie.
Giuliana Juliana.
Giuliano Julian.
Giulietta Juliet.
Giulio Julius.
Giunone Juno.
Giuseppe Joseph.
Giuseppina Josephine.
Goffredo Geoffrey, Jeffrey.
Golgota Golgotha.
Golia Goliath.
Gran Bretagna Great Britain.
Grazia Grace.
Grecia Greece.
Gregorio Gregory.
Groenlandia Greenland.
Guaiana Guiana.
Gualtiero Walter.
Guascogna Gascony.
Guglielmo William.
Guido Guy.
Guinea Guinea.
Gustavo Gustavus.

Iacopo James.
Iberia Iberia.
Icaro Icarus.
Ignazio Ignatius.
Ilario Hilary.
Imalaia Himalaya.
India Indiá.
Indostan Hindustan.
Inghilterra England.
Innocenzo Innocent.
Ionio (Mar) Ionian Sea.

Ippolito Hippolytus.
Irene Irene.
Iride Iris.
Irlanda Ireland.
Irlanda (Stato Libero di) Eire.
Isabella Isabel.
Isacco Isaac.
Isaia Isaiah.
Iside Isis.
Islanda Iceland.
Ismaele Ishmael.
Israele Israel.
Italia Italy.
Iugoslavia Yugoslavia.

Lamberto Lambert.
Lancillotto Launcelot.
Laocoonte Laocoon.
Lapponia Lapland.
Laura Laura.
Lazio Latium.
Lazzaro Lazarus.
Leandro Leander.
Leonardo Leonard.
Leone Leo(n).
Leonida Leonidas.
Leopoldo Leopold.
Lete Lethe.
Letizia Letitia.
Libano Lebanon.
Libia Libya.
Licurgo Lycurgus
Lidia Lydia.
Liegi Liege.
Lione Lyons.
Lisbona Lisbon.
Livio Livy.
Livorno Leghorn.
Lodovico Ludwig.
Lombardia Lombardy.
Londra London.
Lorena Lorraine.
Lorenzo Lawrence.
Losanna Lausanne.
Lotario Lothar.
Lovanio Louvain.
Luca Luke.
Lucerna Lucerne.
Lucia Lucy.
Luciano Lucian.
Lucifero Lucifer.
Lucio Lucius.
Lucrezio Lucretius.
Luigi Louis, Lewis.
Luigia, Luisa Louise.
Lussemburgo Luxemburg.
Lutero Luther.

Maddalena Magdalene.
Maiorca Majorca.
Malesia Malaya.
Malta Malta.
Manciuria Manchuria.
Manfredi Manfred.
Manica (La) The Channel.
Mantova Mantua.
Maometto Mohammed.
Maratona Marathon.
Marcello Marcellus.
Marco Mark.
Margherita Margaret.
Maria Mary.
Marianna Marianne.
Mario Marius.
Marocco Morocco.
Marta Martha.
Marte Mars.
Martino Martin.
Marziale Martial.
Massimiliano Maximilian.
Matilde Matilda.
Matteo Matthew.
Matusalemme Methuselah.
Maurizio Maurice.
Mecca, La Mecca.
Mecenate Maecenas.
Mediterraneo Mediterranean.
Medusa Medusa.
Mefistofele Mephistopheles.
Melanesia Melanesia.
Menelao Menelaus.
Mercurio Mercury.
Merlino Merlin.
Mesopotamia Mesopotamia.
Messalina Messalina.
Messico Mexico.
Micene Mycenae.
Michele Michael.
Mida Midas.
Milano Milan.
Minerva Minerva.
Minosse Minos.
Minotauro Minotaur.
Mitridate Mithridates.
Molucche Moluccas pl.
Monaco (Principato di) Monaco.
Monaco di Baviera Munich.
Mongolia Mongolia.
Mosa Meuse.
Mosca Moscow.
Mosè Moses.
Mozambico Mozambique.

Napoleone Napoleon.
Napoli Naples.
Narciso Narcissus.

Nerone Nero.
Nettuno Neptune.
Nicola, Niccolò Nicholas.
Nilo Nile.
Nizza Nice.
Noè Noah.
Normandia Normandy.
Norvegia Norway.
Nuova Zelanda New Zealand.

Oceania Oceania.
Ofelia Ophelia.
Olanda Holland.
Olimpo Olympus.
Oliviero Oliver.
Omero Homer.
Orazio Horace, Horatio.
Orcadi Orkneys *pl.*
Oreste Orestes.
Orfeo Orpheus.
Orione Orion.
Orlando Roland.
Orsola Ursula.
Osiride Osiris.
Osvaldo Oswald.
Otello Othello.
Ovidio Ovid.

Pacifico Pacific.
Padova Padua.
Paesi Bassi Netherlands *p.*.
Palestina Palestine.
Pancrazio Pancras.
Paola Paula.
Paolina Pauline.
Paolo Paul.
Papuasia Papua.
Paride Paris.
Parigi Paris.
Parnaso Parnassus.
Partenone Parthenon.
Patagonia Patagonia.
Patrizia Patricia.
Patrizio Patrick.
Pechino Peking.
Peloponneso Peloponnesus.
Penelope Penelope.
Pensilvania Pennsylvania.
Pericle Pericles.
Perseo Perseus.
Persia Persia.
Perù Peru.
Piemonte Piedmont.
Pietro, Piero Peter.
Pigmalione Pigmalion.
Pindaro Pindar.
Pio Pius.

Pirenei Pyrenees *pl.*
Pireo Piraeus.
Pitagora Pythagoras.
Platone Plato.
Plinio Pliny.
Plutarco Plutarch.
Polinesia Polynesia.
Polonia Poland.
Pompeo Pompey.
Portogallo Portugal.
Praga Prague.
Prometeo Prometheus.
Prussia Prussia.
Puglia Apulia.

Quintino Quentin.

Rachele Rachel.
Raffaele, Raffaello Raphael.
Raimondo Raymond.
Ramsete Ramses.
Rebecca Rebecca.
Remo Remus.
Reno Rhine.
Riccardo Richard.
Roberto Robert.
Rodano Rhone.
Rodi Rhodes.
Rodolfo Rudolph.
Rodrigo Roderick.
Rolando Roland.
Roma Rome.
Romania Ro(u)mania.
Romeo Romeo.
Romolo Romulus.
Rosa Rose.
Rosalia Rosalie.
Rosalinda Rosalind.
Rossana Roxana.
Rubicone Rubicon.
Ruggero Roger.
Russia Russia.

Saffo Sappho.
Salomone Solomon.
Samuele Samuel.
Sansone Samson.
Sara Sarah.
Sardegna Sardinia.
Sassonia Saxony.
Satana Satan.
Saturno Saturn.
Saul Saul.
Savoia Savoy.
Scandinavia Scandinavia.
Scipione Scipion.

Scozia Scotland.
Sebastiano Sebastian.
Sempione Simplon.
Serse Xerxes.
Siam Siam.
Siberia Siberia.
Sibilla Sibyl.
Sicilia Sicily.
Silla Sulla.
Silvestro Silvester.
Silvia Sylvia.
Simeone Simeon.
Simone Simon.
Siracusa Syracuse.
Siria Syria.
Smirne Smyrna.
Socrate Socrates.
Sodoma Sodom.
Sofia Sophia.
Sofocle Sophocles.
Somalia Somaliland.
Spagna Spain.
Sparta Sparta.
Stati Uniti United States (of America - U.S.A.).
Stefano Stephen.
Stoccolma Stockholm.
Strasburgo Strasbourg.
Sudan S(o)udan.
Susanna Susan(nah).
Svezia Sweden.
Svizzera Switzerland.

Tacito Tacitus.
Tailandia Thailand.
Tamigi Thames.
Tangeri Tangier(s).
Tasmania Tasmania.
Tebe Thebes.
Telemaco Telemachus.
Temistocle Themistocles.
Teodorico Theodoric.
Terenzio Terence.
Teresa Theresa.
Termopili Thermopylae *pl.*
Terranova Newfoundland.
Teseo Theseus.
Tevere Tiber.
Tiberio Tiberius.
Tirolo Tirol, Tyrol.

Tirreno (Mar) Tyrrhenian Sea.
Tito Titus.
Tiziano Titian.
Tobia Tobias.
Tolomeo Ptolemy.
Tommaso Thomas.
Tonchino Tonkin, Tongking.
Torino Turin.
Toscana Tuscany.
Traiano Trajan.
Tristano Tristan, Tristram.
Troia Troy.
Tullio Tully.
Tunisi Tunis.
Tunisia Tunisia.
Turchia Turkey.

Uberto Hubert.
Ucraina Ukraine.
Ugo Hugh.
Ulisse Ulysses.
Umberto Humbert.
Ungheria Hungary.
Urbano Urban.
URSS USSR (Union of Socialist Soviet Republics).

Valentino Valentine.
Valeria Valeria.
Valerio Valerius.
Varsavia Warsaw.
Vaticano Vatican.
Venere Venus.
Veneto Venetia.
Venezia Venice.
Vesuvio Vesuvius.
Vienna Vienna.
Vincenzo Vincent.
Virgilio Virgil.
Virginia Virginia.
Vittoria Victoria.
Vittorio Victor.
Viviana, Viviano Vivian.
Vulcano Vulcan.

Zaccaria Zachary.
Zurigo Zurich.

SIGLE E ABBREVIAZIONI USATE IN ITALIA

A., *alto*: H., high.

A.C., *Automobile Club*: A.A., Automobile Association.

a.C., *avanti Cristo*: B.C. Before Christ.

A.D., *Anno Domini, nell'anno del Signore*: A.D., Anno Domini, (After Christ).

ago., *Agosto*: Aug., August.

A.M., *Aeronautica Militare*: A.F., Air Force.

am., amer., *americano*: Am., American.

anon., *anonimo*: anon., anonymous.

app., *appendice*: app., appendix.

appross., *approssimativo*: approx., approximate.

apr., *aprile*: Apr., April.

A.R., *altezza reale*: R.H., Royal Highness.

ar., *arrivo*: arr., arrival.

ass., *associazione*: ass., association.

b.f., *bassa frequenza*: L.F., low frequency.

boll., *bollettino*: bull., bulletin.

brev., *brevetto*: pat., patent.

C., *centigradi*: cent., centigrade.

c., **1.** *conto*: acc., account **2.** *cubico*: cu., cubic.

ca., **1.** *circa*: a., about **2.** *corrente alternata*: a.c., alternating current.

cad., *cadauno*: ea., each.

Cap., *capitano*: Capt., captain.

cap., *capitolo*: c., chapter.

capit., *capitolo*: c., chapter.

Capp., *capitoli*: cc., chapters.

Card., *Cardinale*: Card., cardinal.

C/c, *conto corrente*: c/a, current account.

cc., *corrente continua*: dc., direct current.

C.D., *Corpo Diplomatico*: C.D., Corps Diplomatique.

C.E.E.A., *Comunità europea per l'energia atomica*: A.E.C., Atomic Energy Commission.

cent., centg., *centigrado*: cent., centigrade.

Cf., *confronta*: cp., compare.

cm., *centimetro*: cent., centimetre.

c.m., *corrente mese*: inst., instant.

cm.c., *centimetro cubo*: c.c., cubic centimetre.

Col., *colonnello*: col., colonel.

coll., *collegio*: coll., college.

coop., *cooperativa*: coop., co-operative.

C.P., *Casella Postale*: P.O.B., Post Office Box.

C.S., *Corte Suprema*: Sup. Ct., Supreme Court.

D., *dottore*: dr., doctor.

d.C., *dopo Cristo*: A.D., Anno Domini.

dic., *dicembre*: Dec., December.

Dirett., *direttore*: dir., director.

dom., *domenica*: Sun., Sunday.

dott., *dottore*: dr., doctor.

dozz., *dozzina*: doz., dozen.

E, *est*: E, East.

ecc., *eccetera*: etc., and so on.

ed., **1.** *edito*: ed., edited **2.** *edizione*: ed., edition.

Egr., *egregio*: Esq., Esquire.

es., *esempio*: ex., example.

feb., *febbraio*: Feb., February.

fed., *federazione*: fed., federation.

F.lli, *fratelli*: br., bros., brothers.

g., *grammo*: g., gram.

Gen., *generale*: Gen., General.

gen., **1.** *generale*: gen., general **2.** *gennaio*: Jan., January.

giov., *giovedì*: Thur., Thursday.

h., *ora*: h., hour.

H.P., *cavallo vapore*: H.P., horse power.

ibid., *ibidem, nello stesso luogo*: ibid., in the same place.

id., *idem, come sopra*: id., the same.

iun., *iunior, giovane*: jr., junior.

kg., *chilogrammo*: kg., kilogram.
km., *chilometro*: km., kilometre.
kw., *chilowatt*: kw., kilowatt.

l., 1. *latino*: Lat., Latin **2.** *litro*: l., litre.
lat., *latitudine*: lat., latitude.
lib., *libro*: b., book.
long., *longitudine*: long., longitude.
L.st., *Lira sterlina*: L., pound.
lun., *lunedì*: Mon., Monday.

M., *monte*: Mt., mount.
m., 1. *morto*: d., dead **2.** *mese*: m., month **3.** *metro*: m., metre **4.** *minuto*: m., minute.
M.AA.EE., *Ministero degli Affari Esteri*: F.O., Foreign Office.
Magg., *Maggiore*: Maj., Major.
mar., *marzo*: Mar., March.
mart., *martedì*: Tues., Tuesday.
mass., *massimo*: max., maximum.
m.c.d., *minimo comun denominatore*: L.C.D., Lowest Common Denominator.
m.c.m., *minimo comune multiplo*: L.C.M., Least Common Multiple.
M.E.C., *Mercato Comune Europeo*: E.C.M., European Common Market.
mer(c)., *mercoledì*: Wed., Wednesday.
mg., *milligrammo*: mg., milligram.
mm., *millimetro*: mm., millimetre.
M/n., *motonave*: Ms., motorship.
ms., *manoscritto*: ms., manuscript.
mss., *manoscritti*: mss., manuscripts.
Mus., *museo*: mus., museum.

N., 1. *nato*: b., born **2.** *Nord*: N., North **3.** *numero*: N., Number.
nov., *novembre*: Nov., November.
N.U., *Nazioni Unite*: U.N., United Nations.

O., *ovest*: W., West.
on., *onorevole*: hon., honourable.
O.N.U., *Organizzazione Nazioni Unite*: U.N.O., United Nations Organization.
ott., *ottobre*: Oct., October.

P., *padre*: fr., father.
p., *pagina*: p., page.
P.A., *Patto Atlantico*: N.A.T.O., North Atlantic Treaty Organization.
paragr., *paragrafo*: par., paragraph.
p.at., *peso atomico*: a.w., atomic weight.
P.C., *Partito Comunista*: C.P., Communist Party.
p.e., *per esempio*: e.g., for example (exempli gratia).
pres., *presidente*: pres., president.
proc., *procuratore*: att., attorney.
prof., *professore*: prof., professor.
P.S., *poscritto*: P.S., postscript.
p.za, *piazza*: sq., square.

Q.G., *Quartier Generale*: G.H., General Headquarters.

ref., *referenze*: ref., reference.
reg., *registro*: reg., register.
Rev., *Reverendo*: rev., Reverend.
R.M., *ricchezza mobile*: PAYE, Pay As You Earn.
R.U., *Regno Unito*: U.K., United Kingdom.

S., 1. *Santo*: St., Saint **2.** *secolo*: cen., century **3.** *società*: co., Company **4.** *Sud*: S., South.
sab., *sabato*: Sat., Saturday.
S.A.R., *Sua Altezza Reale*: H.R.H., His (Her) Royal Highness.
Sc., *scuola*: sch., school.
S.E., *Sua Eccellenza*: H.E., His Excellency.
segg., *seguenti*: fol., following.
segr., *segretario*: sec., secretary.
serg., *sergente*: sergt., sergeant.
sett., *settembre*: Sept., September.
sig., *signore*: Mr., Mister.
sig.na, *signorina*: Miss.
sig.ra, *signora*: Mrs., Mistress.
S.M.B., *Sua Maestà Britannica*: H.B.M., His (Her) Britannic Majesty.
S.O., *Sud Ovest*: S.W., South West.
s.p.a., *società per azioni*: inc., incorporated.
spec., 1. *speciale*: spec., special **2.** *specialmente*: spec., specially.
s.r.l., *società a responsabilità limitata*: ltd., limited (in inglese); corp., corporation (in americano).
S.S., *Sua Santità*: H.H., His Holiness.
S.U., *Stati Uniti*: U.S., United States.

S.U.A., *Stati Uniti d'America*: U.S.A., United States of America.

T., *tonnellata*: t., ton.
T.B.C., *tubercolosi*: T.B., Tuberculosis.
tel., *telefono*: tel. telephone.

U., *unione*: U., Union.
U.P., *Unione postale*: P.U., Postal Union.
U.R.S.S., *Unione Repubbliche Socialiste Sovietiche*: U.S.S.R., Union of Socialist Soviet Republics.

V., **1.** *vaglia*: P.O., Postal Order **2.** *volume*: vol., volume.
v., *verso*: v., verse.
Ven., *Venerabile*: Ven., Venerable.
ven., *venerdì*: Fr., Friday.
vesc., *vescovo*: Bp., Bishop.
v.le, *viale*: Ave., Avenue.
vol., *volume*: vol., volume.
voll., *volumi*: voll., volumes.
vv., *versi*: vv., verses.